FOURTH EDITION

BUSINESS COMMUNICATION

Polishing Your Professional Presence

FOURTH EDITION

BUSINESS COMMUNICATION
Polishing Your Professional Presence

BARBARA SHWOM
Northwestern University

LISA GUELDENZOPH SNYDER
North Carolina A&T State University

New York, NY

Vice President, Business, Economics, and UK Courseware: Donna Battista
Director of Portfolio Management: Stephanie Wall
Editorial Assistant: Linda Siebert Albelli
Vice President, Product Marketing: Roxanne McCarley
Product Marketer: Kaylee Carlson
Product Marketing Assistant: Marianela Silvestri
Manager of Field Marketing, Business Publishing: Adam Goldstein
Field Marketing Manager: Nicole Price
Vice President, Production and Digital Studio, Arts and Business: Etain O'Dea
Director of Production, Business: Jeff Holcomb
Managing Producer, Business: Melissa Feimer
Content Producer: Yasmita Hota

Operations Specialist: Carol Melville
Design Lead: Kathryn Foot
Manager, Learning Tools: Brian Surette
Content Developer, Learning Tools: Lindsey Sloan
Managing Producer, Digital Studio and GLP, Media Production and Development: Ashley Santora
Managing Producer, Digital Studio: Diane Lombardo
Digital Studio Producer: Monique Lawrence
Digital Studio Producer: Alana Coles
Project Manager: Heidi Allgair, Cenveo® Publisher Services
Interior Design: Cenveo® Publisher Services
Cover Design: Cenveo® Publisher Services
Cover Art: Life On White/DigitalVision/Getty Images
Printer/Binder: LSC Communications, Inc.
Cover Printer: Phoenix Color/Hagerstown

ISBN 10: 0-13-474022-X
ISBN 13: 978-0-13-474022-5

Dedication

We dedicate this book:

To our students at Northwestern and North Carolina A&T for challenging us to learn more every day, to stretch our perspectives, and to be better teachers.

To our colleagues in our universities, in the Association for Business Communication, and in business for providing valuable feedback and insight about best practices in polishing professional presence.

To you, who are learning and teaching from this book. We thank you for giving us the opportunity to contribute to your success.

—Barbara and Lisa

About the Authors

Barbara Shwom

Barbara Shwom, PhD, is Professor of Instruction in Writing at Northwestern University, where she teaches in the Weinberg College of Arts and Sciences, Kellogg School of Management, and McCormick School of Engineering and Applied Science. For more than 30 years, she has designed and taught communication courses that have influenced this textbook, including *Writing in Organizations, Communicating Complex Data, Engineering Design and Communication,* and *How to Become an Expert in Roughly 10 Weeks.* Professor Shwom's teaching at Northwestern has been recognized by both an outstanding teacher award and an appointment as a fellow of Northwestern's Searle Center for Advancing Teaching and Learning. Professor Shwom has gained industry experience as the managing principal of Communication Partners, a consulting practice that works with clients from a range of industries, including biotechnology, high tech research and development, pharmaceuticals, management consulting, market research, financial services, engineering, and consumer products. Professor Shwom's research interests include evolving genres of business communication, visual communication of data, and methods of persuasion. In addition to many articles, she is also the coauthor of a textbook on graphics and visual communication for managers. She currently sits on the Board of Directors of the Association for Business Communication and the editorial review board of *Business and Professional Communication Quarterly* and has served as president for both the Association for Business Communication and the Association of Professional Communication Consultants.

Lisa Gueldenzoph Snyder

Lisa Gueldenzoph Snyder, PhD, is a Professor and the Chairperson of the Department of Business Education in the College of Business and Economics at North Carolina Agricultural and Technical State University in Greensboro. She earned a doctorate in Higher Education Administration from Bowling Green State University in Ohio, where she also received a master's degree in Business Education. Her Bachelor's in Business Education is from Northern Michigan University.

Dr. Snyder is widely published in journals such as the *Business Communication Quarterly, Journal of Business Communication, Business Education Digest, The Delta Pi Epsilon Journal,* and *NABTE Review.* She regularly presents sessions on business communication and instructional practices at local, regional, and national professional development events, workshops, and conferences. Dr. Snyder received the Meada Gibbs Outstanding Teacher Award from the Association for Business Communication, and the Distinguished Alumni Award from the Business Education program at Bowling Green State University. She also has received the Innovative Instructional Practices Award from Delta Pi Epsilon, the Distinguished Service Award from the Ohio Business Teachers Association, and the Collegiate Teacher of the Year Award from both the North Carolina Business Education Association and the Southern Business Education Association.

Dr. Snyder is the 2018 President of the Association for Business Communication and has served as the National President of the Association for Research in Business Education, the Research Coordinator for the National Association for Business Teacher Education, and the Past-Chair of the Policies Commission for Business and Economic Education. She is also actively involved with the National Business Education Association.

Brief Contents

Contents

3   Managing the Communication Process: Analyzing, Composing, Evaluating 78

6   Communicating Bad News 192

7   Using Social Media in Business 230

PART 3 Researching, Proposing, Reporting, and Presenting

 8 Finding and Evaluating Business Information 272

9 Preparing Persuasive Business Proposals 312

10 Preparing Business Reports 346

11 Preparing and Delivering Business Presentations 412

PART 4   Persuading an Employer to Hire You

12 Communicating Your Professional Brand: Social Media, Résumés, Cover Letters, and Interviews 468

NEW TO THIS EDITION

Every chapter contains new material designed to help you become a more powerful communicator.

- **New collaboration features:** Each chapter includes a new collaboration feature, helping you apply the chapter concepts when you work in teams—both local and virtual.
- **New end of chapter exercises:** New exercises are integrated with old favorites to provide a range of opportunities to practice the concepts you learn.
- **New videos:** On MyLab Business Communication, you'll find two engaging videos for each chapter. One video offers insight from the authors and the other video is a "how to" animation that brings abstract concepts to life.
- **New @work features:** Nine new end-of-chapter company profiles showcase how businesses are addressing the challenges of business communication. Seven new "new hires" tell us how they put their communication skills to work.
- **New figures and new models:** New models include a new formal report that both illustrates concepts and addresses an authentic business challenge—developing an organic restaurant. You will also find new PowerPoint models and a new graphical white paper from Welch's Global Ingredients.
- **Updated appendix on documentation and reference styles:** The new appendix includes guidance for the MLA 8th edition.

SOLVING TEACHING AND LEARNING CHALLENGES

A memorable model

At the heart of the book is a flexible communication process called ACE—Analyzing, Composing, and Evaluating—that applies to any situation, from simple email messages to formal business presentations. As you go through the book, you continue to acquire knowledge about how to apply this framework and why it is important. There are many practice opportunities both in the book and in MyLab Business Communication.

> *"I anticipate using the ACE communication process beyond this course when I write emails, prepare papers, and apply for internships and jobs because the first impression of writing is very important."*
> —Andronico P., Student at the University of California–Santa Barbara

Analyze your purpose, audience, and content before you begin writing.

Compose by organizing the content, creating a first draft, and designing a professional format.

Evaluate by revising, editing, proofreading, and—when possible—incorporating feedback.

A perforated pull-out reference card on how to write business email is provided that you can use throughout the course and after the course ends.

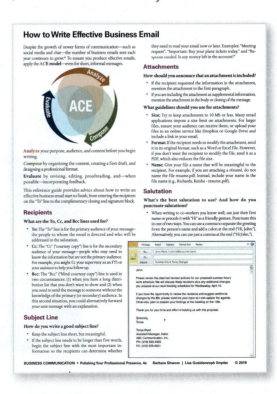

Practical advice

The chapters are full of annotated examples that show you how to apply concepts to your own work.

"I like all the examples of the various communications, such as emails, memos, thank-you notes, etc. I use them as a guide when I am writing."
—Kenneth P., Student at Middle Tennessee State University

Business focus

An "@ WORK" section in each chapter highlights contemporary businesses and professionals who are implementing the core concepts of each chapter.

The New Hires @ Work feature helps you imagine yourself as part of a larger business communication community. At the beginning of each chapter, and on select pages within each chapter, a recent graduate describes communication challenges on the job and how communication skills help meet those challenges.

New Hires @ Work

Shannon Rocheleau
Western Michigan University
Business Services Credit Specialist @ Consumers Credit Union

When I worked as a member services representative in the Credit Union call center, I learned how to listen carefully and match my communication style with the person to whom I was talking. If callers get to the point immediately, I provided information promptly. If they began by chatting, I chatted, too. And if callers seemed to need a lot of support, I knew not to apply pressure. Instead, I gave them time to decide and then provided reassurance when they made a decision. Great member service involves understanding your audience.

Examples of authentic business documents and presentations help you see the principles of the book at work.

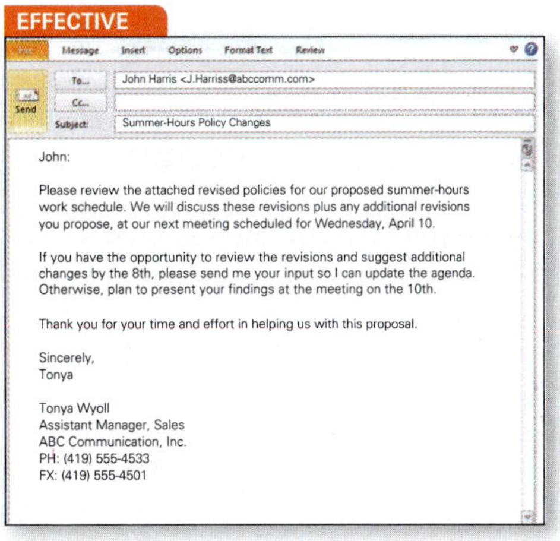
EFFECTIVE

To... John Harris <J.Harriss@abccomm.com>

Cc...

Subject: Summer-Hours Policy Changes

John:

Please review the attached revised policies for our proposed summer-hours work schedule. We will discuss these revisions plus any additional revisions you propose, at our next meeting scheduled for Wednesday, April 10.

If you have the opportunity to review the revisions and suggest additional changes by the 8th, please send me your input so I can update the agenda. Otherwise, plan to present your findings at the meeting on the 10th.

Thank you for your time and effort in helping us with this proposal.

Sincerely,
Tonya

Tonya Wyoll
Assistant Manager, Sales
ABC Communication, Inc.
PH: (419) 555-4533
FX: (419) 555-4501

Integrated knowledge

Business communication involves more than just writing and speaking well. A competent business communicator must also be ethical, collaborative, and open to new technologies and new cultures. Every chapter of this book includes an in-depth focus on ethics, technology, culture, and collaboration. To build your skills in these areas, you will see end-of-chapter exercises linked to each feature that challenge you to think critically about these topics and provide you with hands-on practice. You can complete many of these exercises at MyLab and receive instant feedback.

ETHICS
REPRESENTING DATA ETHICALLY

Businesses rely on data to make informed decisions. To support those decisions, graphs must display data ethically and not mislead the audience. Graphs can mislead in many ways. For example, they can manipulate the scale, distort perspective, and show data out of context. Even if graph designers do not intend to be dishonest, they may make design choices that result in bad graphs. As Naomi Robbins, an expert in data visualization, says, "The designers of many of the graphs we see daily pay more attention to grabbing the audience's attention than to communicating clearly and accurately. They choose design options that they think look better but are actually graphical mistakes, since they mislead or confuse their readers."[21]

Because ethical representation of data is so important, many organizations have developed guides to data ethics.[22] The following guidelines are among the most important to follow in business communication. The graphs on the left are potentially misleading. The versions on the right correct the errors.

For an ETHICS exercise, go to Exercise 21 on page 406.

TECHNOLOGY
HOW TO USE SOFTWARE FEATURES TO HELP FORMAT FORMAL REPORTS

Microsoft Word and other word processing programs offer powerful features that help you format formal reports. The following features will save you time and improve the professional look of your work. To learn about other features, use your program's help files.

- **Automated styles.** Word has a number of different text styles that control fonts, sizes, colors, and placement on the page. You can use one style for normal paragraphs, another for headings, a third for quotations, and a fourth for captions. Using styles rather than manually formatting paragraphs offers an important advantage: If you mark text as a specific style and then decide to change that style, the change occurs to all the marked text throughout the document.
- **Automated headings.** Word offers a set of styles called *Heading 1*, *Heading 2*, and *Heading 3*. You can customize those styles with any font and size. If you use these heading styles in your report, you can take advantage of Word's automated table of contents feature.
- ...**tents.** Many word processing ...process for designing and insert- ...en you select "Insert Table of ...ogram finds all of the headings that
- **Automated page numbering, using both Roman and Arabic numerals.** You can control the placement of page numbers in your document by inserting headers or footers. You can further control page numbers by using Word's "Insert Section Break" feature and formatting the page numbers differently for each section. For example, you can create a title page with no page number. Then insert a section break and use small Roman numerals (i, ii, iii, and so on) for the page numbering on the table of contents page and executive summary. Insert another section break and begin the numbering again with Arabic numerals (1, 2, 3, and so on), with the introduction counting as page 1, even though sequentially it is not the first page of the file.
- **Automated footnotes, endnotes, citations, bibliographies.** Most word processing applications allow you to insert and number footnotes, endnotes, and citations automatically. As you add, remove, or cut and paste text in your draft, your note numbers automatically change to reflect their new position. Note, however, that some citation formats assign one style for the first use of a citation and a different style for all subsequent occurrences. So if you move text around, make sure to double-check your footnote styles in the final

CULTURE
MAKING REPORTS READER-FRIENDLY FOR INTERNATIONAL AUDIENCES

Reports often have larger audiences than typical correspondence, such as emails. A useful report may be distributed broadly throughout an organization and to colleagues or clients around the world. If the report is not confidential, it may even be shared with the general public.

If you work in an international organization or an organization that disseminates information globally, you need to think about how to make your reports accessible to international audiences—even those who speak English. The number of English speakers is growing worldwide, as English is taught to more people and at an earlier age in both Europe and Asia.[2] As a result, English has become the international *lingua franca* of business—the common language used by native speakers of different languages.[3]

However, not all these English speakers are fluent in the language. Although almost 2 billion people speak English worldwide, only 25 percent of those people speak English as a first language.[4] If any members of your audience are in the remaining 75 percent, will they understand long sentences and eloquent word choices? How can you make your reports as easy as possible for everyone in your audience to read?

Professionals in the field of international technical communication have developed a number of guidelines to use when preparing English documents for readers who are not native English speakers. Even if your communication is not technical, use the following guidelines adapted from the *Global English Style Guide*:[5]

- **Use simple English.** English arguably has more words than any other language. Studies published by *Science*[6] and the *Global Language Monitor*[7] estimate the current number of words at more than a million. Although this breadth of word choice makes English a very precise language ... will not be familiar with all the vocal... avoid slang and clichés, and check th... text when you evaluate your writing... "Local regulations prohibit installati... permit." Instead, say "Acme must get...
- **Do not vary terms needlessly.** U... and phrases. For example, if you ar... biles, consistently call them "autom... than occasionally calling them "veh... portation." This repetition minimiz... reader will need to remember.
- **Eliminate the "fat" from conten...** by providing only the information ... eliminating extra details and words ... pose. An international audience ma... this wordy sentence: "It is respectfu... committee be formed by A. G. Will... tigation into potential wrongdoing... tive board." They could more easily... version: "We recommend that A. G... executive board's recent actions."

For CULTURE exercises, go to Critical ... page 401 and Exercise 7 on page 402.

COLLABORATION
WRITING A REPORT AS A TEAM

In the course of your career, you might be tasked to write a report as part of a team, especially for long and comprehensive reports. There are many ways to write collaboratively, and what your team chooses to do will depend on factors such as the date the report is due, the size of the team, the location of team members, and the specific expertise of team members. Here are some things to keep in mind when approaching collaborative report writing at work. These same considerations can help you plan a better collaborative process in school also.

- **Team structure.** Before starting the writing process, it is helpful to establish the team's structure and assign members different responsibilities, according to their skills and expertise. Sometimes this might be decided for you from the outset; for instance, your manager might be part of your team and automatically take on the role of final reviewer before the report is submitted. Or some members may be on the team because they are subject matter experts who will provide data but do less actual writing. But in teams where hierarchy and job scope are less clear, it might take a preliminary discussion to go over everyone's skill sets and see how they can best serve the team.[15] At work, you do not need to assume that the team writing means that everyone should play an equal role on the team, which is what typically happens in school. Remember that in school, the goal is that all students learn from the report-writing process. At work, the goal is to ensure that the process leads to an excellent report.
- **Writing procedure.** Research in collaborative writing shows that writing teams approach their tasks in many different ways.[16] Sometimes they work in parallel, with the entire team planning the document and dividing the work into subtasks
- **Communication protocol.** Writing can be a very solitary exercise, especially for writers who are not used to working on extensive projects in groups. But in group projects, it is unwise for writers to work without consulting each other. So, at the start of a project, it is important to discuss how team members will check in and communicate with each other, and what kind of discussion is appropriate for what stage of the writing process. For instance, a team on a months-long project might decide to meet in person or via conference call every two weeks to assess its progress and email each other between meetings. A small team on a tight deadline might prefer to meet every other day and use text messaging in addition to email. You might even consider discussing limits on informal communication to avoid disrupting each other's writing process.[17]
- **Feedback and editing.** In the process of collaborative report writing, you will likely receive feedback on your work or have your work edited by someone else in your team. You might also be expected to provide feedback on a team member's writing. Today, this back-and-forth is easier than ever before using groupware or platforms with commenting and change-tracking functions (for example, Microsoft Word and Google Docs). However, as information science professors Birnholtz and Ibara point out, these digital platforms are often "impoverished environments" for communication where "people [may] overinterpret certain cues," possibly leading to "exaggerated interpretations or impressions" and affecting "how credit and blame are attributed."[18] For instance, heavily editing someone else's work directly when that person expected a say in the changes could be construed

Hands-on practice

Exercises for all key concepts

The book's main headings are structured as numbered study questions. These questions are answered in subheadings throughout the section. The end-of-chapter summary and "Key Concept Exercises" are also grouped by both the study question and the subheadings. This structure helps you focus on the key points of the chapter, assess what you know, and complete exercises that help you polish your skills.

Case scenarios in every chapter

Each chapter concludes with a realistic case scenario that relates to the content of the chapter. This feature is an excellent tool for reviewing the chapter content to ensure that you have learned it and can apply it.

CASE SCENARIO

Culinary Adventure Tour Presentation

This case scenario will help you review the chapter material by applying it to a specific situation.

Planning a Presentation

Stephanie Lo graduated from college with a major in French and a minor in communication. She was very happy to get a job with JourneyFree, LLC, a company that specializes in organizing educational tours for students, professionals, and other groups. Ultimately, Stephanie would like to become a tour leader, but for now she is the assistant to the vice president of Tour Operations, Rachel Jones. Stephanie's role is to work on marketing communications.

Stephanie's first project required that she use all her strengths—developing communications to market JourneyFree's newest product, a culinary tour of France, specifically designed for culinary arts and nutrition teachers in high schools and trade schools. In addition to advertising online and sending brochures to high schools, Stephanie's supervisor, Rachel, plans to visit school districts in major cities and present the program to superintendents, principals, department chairs, and teachers. She will give a brief and colorful slide presentation and offer samplings of the French food that culinary arts teachers will experience on the tour.

Thirty culinary arts teachers have invited Rachel to give a presentation next week, so she needs a slide presentation fast. She asks Stephanie to design and develop a draft of the presentation. Together they work out the following outline:

- The Educational Experience
- Trip Overview
- Trip Logistics and Costs
- About JourneyFree, LLC
- Q&A

Rachel and Stephanie also discuss the audience and key selling points to make in the presentation. The next day, Stephanie puts together a draft of presentation slides. She is planning to meet Rachel to review the slides and to discuss the talking points that will go with the slides.

Stephanie would like your help in analyzing the audience, evaluating the presentation, and composing the content for the presentation. After the slides, you will find questions designed to help you think systematically about the presentation, using the ACE approach. Answer the questions to review the key concepts in the chapter.

France: A Seven-Day Culinary Adventure Tour

RACHEL JONES
VP, TOUR OPERATIONS
JOURNEYFREE, LLC

Why this tour will help culinary teachers

- Explore range of French culinary arts over a fun-filled seven-day journey through France
- Diversify and expand knowledge of culinary teachers in your vocational high schools
- Foster a stronger connection between teachers and French gastronomic culture

---

SPELLING ALERT! MISUSE OF APOSTROPHE

Do not confuse *their/they're*, *your/you're*, or *its/it's*. Possessive pronouns are never formed with an apostrophe, but contractions ending in *-s* always are.

They're the lawyers who handle corporate mergers in *their* law firm. (contraction of *they are*; possessive pronoun)

Your application is due if *you're* interested in being considered for the job. (possessive pronoun; contraction of *you are*)

You can't tell a book by *its* cover, although *it's* tempting to try. (possessive pronoun; contraction of *it is*)

1.1.2. Action and Being Words: Verbs

Verbs	express action, occurrence, or state of being.
Action	Stock prices *rose* in late December.
Occurrence	That often *happens* at the end of the year.
State of Being	The phenomenon *is known* as the "year-end bump."

a. **Verb forms.** Verbs change form to show **time (tense)**, **person**, **number**, **voice**, and **mood**, as illustrated in **Table C.6**.
b. **Expletives** are introductory words such as *there* or *it* followed by a linking verb (*is*, *are*, *was*, *were*).

It is probable that Jean won't attend.

There were six people on the conference call.

Expletives function more as signal expressions used for emphasis than as true conveyers of content. For example, *There were six people on the conference call* could as easily be expressed as *Six people were on the conference call*. Examine your writing to eliminate expletives, when possible. Although they can be used effectively to manage the pace and emphasis in a sentence, expletives can also add words that may not be necessary.

GRAMMAR ALERT! SUBJECT–VERB AGREEMENT ERROR

Verbs must agree with their subjects in person and number. The subject cannot be in a prepositional phrase. Find the true subject and make the verb agree.

Incorrect	The members of the Federal Reserve Board *sets* interest rates. (Verb *sets* is incorrect because subject *members* is plural.)
Correct	The *members* of the Federal Reserve Board *set* interest rates.

Contractions should be separated and matched with the correct person.

Incorrect	He *don't* want to be late, and I don't either. (Verb form *don't* or *do not* disagrees with third-person singular subject *he*.)
Correct	He *doesn't* want to be late, and I don't either. OR He *does not* want to be late, and I *do not* either.

Also see "Subject–Verb Agreement" in *Common Sentence Errors*.

Wordy	It is probable that Jean won't attend.
Revised	Jean probably won't attend.

GRAMMAR ALERT! AGREEMENT ERROR WITH *THERE*

When a sentence begins with the expletive *there*, the verb is singular or plural depending on the number of the noun or pronoun that follows it. In other words, the verb must agree with the true grammatical subject of the sentence; *there* and *here* are adverbial modifiers and cannot be grammatical subjects.

Incorrect	There was two possible solutions.
Correct	There *were* two possible *solutions*.

To check for correct agreement between subject and verb, try putting the sentence in subject–verb word order: Two possible *solutions were* there.

TABLE C.6 Features of Verbs

FEATURE	VARIATIONS	EXAMPLE
Time (tense)	present, past, future	The stock market *rose* 58 points. Prices *will increase*.
Person	first, second, third	*You* and *I* think it is a bull market. *He* thinks it is a bear market.
Number	singular, plural	A rising *tide raises* all boats, but ill financial *winds raise* many fears.
Voice	Active voice: Subject performs action of verb. Passive voice: Subject receives action of verb.	Corporate losses *caused* a market decline. The market decline *was caused* by corporate losses.
Mood	Indicates whether action expresses a fact or question (indicative), gives a command (imperative), or expresses a condition contrary to fact (subjunctive).	Indicative: She *saves* part of every paycheck. *Does she save* part of every paycheck? Imperative: *Save* part of every paycheck. Subjunctive: If she *were saving* part of every paycheck, she would be financially secure. [But the fact is she is not saving, so she is not secure.]

Grammar exercises test your knowledge

Appendix C includes a complete grammar text that you can use for reference or for independent review. You can test your knowledge with exercises at the end of each chapter. Answers are in Appendix D.

DEVELOPING EMPLOYABILITY SKILLS

Communication skills top the list of what employers want, and working through this course gives you opportunity to practice your communication abilities, receive feedback, and polish your professional presence. However, the skills you will gain do not stop there. This course will also help you develop these other skills that employers value.

What	Why	How
Critical thinking	Critical thinking is foundational to problem solving.	Every chapter includes a set of questions that focus on critical thinking, and most of the end-of-chapter exercises are designed to engage your critical thinking abilities.
Collaboration	Today's workplace is team oriented, and collaboration is a core ability for team success.	Every chapter includes a collaboration feature and a set of collaborative exercises to practice your teamwork skills.
Ethical reasoning	Poor ethical decisions put the entire company at risk.	Every chapter includes an ethics feature and end-of-chapter questions that explicitly address ethical reasoning.
Ability to apply knowledge in new situations	Employers hire new employees expecting that those employees can translate the knowledge they have gained in school to the practical requirements of the job.	At the end of every chapter, a case scenario challenges you to apply the chapter concepts and skills to a new situation. Many of the end-of-chapter exercises provide similar opportunities.
Ability to use technology effectively	Communication technology is evolving quickly, and employers require that you adapt quickly to use new technology effectively.	Every chapter includes a technology feature and at least one end-of-chapter exercise for more practice with technology.
Data literacy	For data to be useful in making business decisions, employees must know how to analyze the data and communicate it effectively to a variety of audiences.	Exercises throughout the book give you the opportunity to communicate insights from data, use data to support arguments, and communicate data effectively in tables, graphs, and text.

MYLAB BUSINESS COMMUNICATION

Reach every student with MyLab

MyLab is the teaching and learning platform that empowers you to reach *every* student. By combining trusted author content with digital tools and a flexible platform, MyLab personalizes the learning experience and improves results for each student. Learn more at MyLab Business Communication.

Deliver trusted content

You deserve teaching materials that meet your own high standards for your course. That's why we partner with highly respected authors to develop interactive content and course-specific resources that you can trust — and that keep your students engaged.

MyLab Business Communication offers a variety of grammar exercises, flashcards, and audio lessons to test your learning and skills and get instant feedback.

Empower each learner

Each student learns at a different pace. Personalized learning pinpoints the precise areas where each student needs practice, giving all students the support they need — when and where they need it — to be successful.

Teach your course your way

Your course is unique. So whether you'd like to build your own assignments, teach multiple sections, or set prerequisites, MyLab gives you the flexibility to easily create *your* course to fit *your* needs.

Improve student results

When you teach with MyLab, student performance improves. That's why instructors have chosen MyLab for over 15 years, touching the lives of over 50 million students.

INSTRUCTOR TEACHING RESOURCES

This program comes with the following teaching resources.

Supplements available to instructors @ www.pearsonhighered.com	Features of the Supplement
Instructor's Manual	• Chapter-by-chapter summaries • Examples and activities not in the main book • Teaching outlines • Teaching tips • Solutions to all questions and problems in the book
Test Bank	More than 1,500 multiple-choice, true/false, short- answer, and graphing questions with these annotations: • Difficulty level (1 for straight recall, 2 for some analysis, 3 for complex analysis) • Type (multiple-choice, true/false, short-answer, essay) • Question category (the type of knowledge required to solve the question) • AACSB learning standard (Written and Oral Communication; Ethical Understanding and Reasoning; Analytical Thinking; Information Technology; Interpersonal Relations and Teamwork; Diverse and Multicultural Work; Reflective Thinking; Application of Knowledge)
Computerized TestGen	TestGen allows instructors to: • Customize, save, and generate classroom tests • Edit, add, or delete questions from the Test Item Files • Analyze test results • Organize a database of tests and student results.
PowerPoints	Slides include Key images and tables in the textbook. PowerPoints meet accessibility standards for students with disabilities. Features include, but not limited to: • Keyboard and Screen Reader access • Alternative text for images • High color contrast between background and foreground colors

Acknowledgments

A Word of Thanks

Writing a textbook requires a high-performing team to complement what we, as authors, can do. We have been fortunate to work with such a team of talented and dedicated people at Pearson.

The following publishing professionals have guided our experience. Some have been with us since the first edition; others have joined the team for this fourth edition. We are grateful to all of them for their dedication and commitment.

Heidi Allgair
Yasmita Hota
Judy Leale
Jackie Martin
Bincy Menon
Ginny Munroe
Lenny Ann Raper
Nicole Sam
Janet Slowik
Daniel Tylman
Stephanie Wall
Denise Weiss

The feedback and guidance of many business communication instructors and their students helped shape the content and features of this book. We greatly appreciate their assistance and commitment to the craft of preparing students to communicate effectively in business.

Class Testers

We are grateful to both the instructors who class tested manuscript versions of each chapter and to the more than 1,000 students who provided recommendations on how to make the chapters the best they could be.

Carolyn Ashe, University of Houston–Downtown
Sherry Baker, Rich Mountain Community College
Mary Barton, University of California–Chico
Kathleen Blackwell, University of South Florida
Deborah Bowen, University of South Florida
Cherilyn Boyer, University of Arizona
Alma G. Bryant, University of South Florida

Kelly Paschal Carr, Arizona State University
John Catalini, University of California–Santa Barbara
Sandra Chrystal, University of Southern California
Janice Cools, University of South Florida
Anthony Corte, University of Illinois–Chicago
Auli Ek, University of California–Santa Barbara
Betty Foust Chapman, North Carolina A&T State University
Gina L. Genova, University of California–Santa Barbara
Claudia Hart, Northern Michigan University
K. Virginia Hemby, Middle Tennessee State University
Kristie Loescher, University of Texas–Austin
Joyce Lopez, Missouri State University
Renee McConnell, University of Arizona, retired
Elizabeth Metzger, University of South Florida
Lisa Murray, University of Tennessee–Knoxville
Nancy Nygaard, University of Wisconsin–Milwaukee
Deborah Richey, Owens Community College
Sandra S. Rothschild, University of Arizona, retired
Stacey Short, Northern Illinois University
Sally Stanton, University of Milwaukee
Jan Starnes, University of Texas–Austin

Reviewers

Over the course of four editions, the following instructors have contributed to the review process. Some have reviewed key sections of one edition; others have reviewed multiple editions. We are grateful to everyone for their input and advice to ensure the content is both relevant and realistic.

Mary Albrecht, Maryville University
Melody Alexander, Ball State University
Carolyn Ashe Butler, University of Houston Downtown
Sara Baker, University of Nebraska–Lincoln
Sherry Baker, Rich Mountain Community College
Fiona Barnes, University of Florida
Barclay Barrios, Florida Atlantic University
Mary Barton, University of California–Chico
Julie Basler, Platt College

Tatiana Batova, University of Wisconsin–Milwaukee
Rhonda Baughman, Brown Mackie College–North Canton
Reginald Bell, Prairie View A&M University
Shavawn Berry, Arizona State University
Kara Fahey Blackburn, Massachusetts Institute of Technology
Kathleen Blackwell, University of South Florida
Kay Blasingame-Boike, Middle Tennessee State University
Cherilyn Boyer, University of Arizona
Charlotte Brammer, Samford University
Ellen B. Bremen, Highline Community College
Alma G. Bryant, University of South Florida
Scott Buechler, Elon University
Jean Bush-Bacelis, Eastern Michigan University
Stephen M. Byars, University of Southern California
Sharon Cannon, Washington University in St. Louis
Donna Carlon, University of Central Oklahoma
Kay C. Carnes, Gonzaga University
Lana W. Carnes, Eastern Kentucky University
Brennan Carr, Long Beach City College
Kelly Paschal Carr, Arizona State University
Rodney Carveth, Morgan State University
Sandra Chrystal, University of Southern California
Jennifer Chunn, Harrisburg Area Community College
Paige Clark, Indiana University
Dorinda Clippinger, University of South Carolina
Anthony Corte, University of Illinois–Chicago
Jan R. Costello, Georgia State University
Valerie Creelman, Saint Mary's University
Mercidee Curry, Jackson State University
Dale Cyphert, University of Northern Iowa
Babara D'Angelo, Arizona State University
Barbara Davis, University of Memphis
David Dewberry, Rider University
Lise Diez-Arguelles, Florida State University
Dianne Donnelly, University of South Florida
Michael J. Doolin, Monroe Community College
Cynthia Drexel, Western State College of Colorado
Auli Ek, University of California–Santa Barbara
Marcella Enos, Idaho State University
Donna R. Everett, Morehead State University

Stevina Evuleocha, CSU East Bay

Joyce Ezrow, Anne Arundel Community College

Kathy Fletcher, Indiana University

Janis Forman, University of California

Serena D. Frost, Virginia Polytechnic Institute and State University

Gail Garton, Ozark Technical Community College

Jorge Gaytan, North Carolina A&T State University

Gina L. Genova, University of California–Santa Barbara

Vanessa Germeroth, Ozarks Technical Community College

Robert J. Goldberg, Prince George's Community College

Mark Grass, UW–Milwaukee

Bob Gregory, Bellevue University

Frances K. Griffin, Oklahoma State University

Anne Bradstreet Grinols, Baylor University

Alice Griswold, Clarke University

Michelle Hagan-Short, Ivy Tech Community College

Roxanne Hamilton, Landmark College

Claudia Hart, Northern Michigan University

Lynn Hanson, Francis Marion University

William Hargrave, University of Georgia

Rachel Harlow, University of Texas of the Permian Basin

Patricia L. Harms, University of North Carolina–Chapel Hill

Kathleen Haspel, Fairleigh Dickinson University

Carolyn Hawley, Georgia State University

Susan Heller, Reading Area Community College

K. Virginia Hemby, Middle Tennessee State University

Ronda Henderson, Middle Tennessee State University

Pat Herb, North Central State College

Kathy Hill, Sam Houston State University

Sheila Hostetler, Orange Coast College

Chie Ishihara, Riverside Community College

Elizabeth Jackson, Lone Star College–CyFair

Kathy Jesiolowski, Milwaukee Area Technical College

Roger Johansen, Coastal Carolina University

Carol Johnson-Gerendas, Texas Wesleyan University

Marguerite P. Joyce, Sam Houston State University

Kayla Kelly, Tarleton State University

Susan Kendall Sonia Khatchadourian, University of Wisconsin–Milwaukee

Thomas Kiddie, West Virginia State University

Margaret Kilcoyne, Northwestern State University of Louisiana

Renee King, Eastern Illinois University

Lorraine Krajewski, Louisiana State University–Shreveport

Tim Krause, University of Wisconsin

Gary Lacefield, University of Texas @ Arlington

Helene Lamarre, DeVry University

Christine Laursen, Red Rocks Community College

Sally Lederer, University of Minnesota Carlson School of Management

Daisy Lee, San Jose State University

Gloria Lessmann, Bellevue University

Sue Lewis, Tarleton State University

Holly Littlefield, University of Minnesota

Kristie Loescher, The University of Texas at Austin, McCombs School of Business

Joyce Lopez, Missouri State University

Anna Maheshwari, Schoolcraft College

Joan Mansfield, University of Central Missouri

Jeanette S. Martin, University of Mississippi

Gary May, Clayton State University

Dorothy McCawley, University of Florida

Renee McConnell, University of Arizona, retired

Lisa McCormick, Community College of Allegheny County

Patricia McLaughlin, St. Ambrose University

Jane McPhail, College of William & Mary

Lisa Meloncon, University of Cincinnati

Elizabeth Metzger, University of South Florida

Annie Laurie I. Meyers, Northampton Community College

Gregory H. Morin, University of Nebraska, Omaha

Charles Moses, Clark Atlanta University

Lisa Murray, University of Tennessee–Knoxville

Pam Needham, Northeast Mississippi Community College

Dawn New, Indiana University

Jim Nugent, Oakland University Department of Writing and Rhetoric

Nancy Nygaard, University of Wisconsin–Milwaukee

Ephraim Okoro, Howard University

Kathryn ONeill, Sam Houston State University

Lorelei Ortiz, St. Edward's University

Karen Otto, Florida State University at Jacksonville

Marvin Parker, Fort Valley State University

Pamela Passen, School of Business—Office Administration

Lisa Pawlik, University of Michigan

Susan A. Peterson, Scottsdale Community College

Melinda Phillabaum, Indiana University

Mya Poe, Northeastern University (previously Penn State)

Cornelia Pokrzywa, Oakland University

Deborah Richey, Owens Community College

Joy Roach-Duncan, Murray State University

Kathleen Robinson, University of South Florida

Marcel Marie Robles, Eastern Kentucky University

Deborah Britt Roebuck, Kennesaw State University

Kimberly Rosenfeld, Cerritos College

Karen J. Roush, Independence Community College

Chip Rouse, Stevenson University

Sandra S. Rothschild, University of Arizona, retired

Michael J. Salvo, Purdue University

Kathryn Schifferle, California State University–Chico

Carolyn Seefer, Diablo Valley College

Glenda Seiter, Northeastern State University

Teresa Sekine, Purdue University

Mageya Sharp, Cerritos College

Stacey Short, Northern Illinois University

Allen Shubb, Northeastern Illinois University

Michael Shuman, University of South Florida

Sandra Smith, University of Minnesota, Carlson School of Management

Rachel Smydra, Oakland University, Department of English

Karen Sneary, Northwestern Oklahoma State University

Jason Snyder, Central Connecticut State University

Harvey Solganick, LeTourneau University

Randye Spina, Norwalk Community College

Valarie Spiser-Albert, University of Texas at San Antonio

Dianna Stair, Business School

Sally Stanton, University of Wisconsin–Milwaukee

Jan Starnes, University of Texas–Austin

Kyle Stedman, University of South Florida

Natalie Stillman-Webb, University of Utah

Robert Stowers, College of William & Mary

Cheryl L. Sypniewski, Macomb Community College

JoAnn Syverson, University of Minnesota

Linda Szul, Indiana University of Pennsylvania

Lee Tesdell, Minnesota State University, Mankato

Ann Tippett, Monroe Community College

Pamela Todoroff, Oakland University Department of Writing & Rhetoric

Allen Truell, Ball State University

Beverly Turner, Tarleton State University

Pam Uhlenkamp, Iowa Central Community College

Jennifer Veltsos, Minnesota State University, Mankato

Mary Wallace, University of Tennessee at Martin

John L. Waltman, Eastern Michigan University

Josephine Walwema, Oakland University

Susan Hall Webb, University of West Georgia

Debra Westerfelt, Ashland University
Carol S. White, Georgia State University
Julianne White, Arizona State University
Beth Williams, Stark State College
Lucinda Willis, Indiana University of
    Pennsylvania
Bennie J. Wilson III, University of Texas–San
    Antonio
Maryann Wysor, Georgia State University
Robert Yamaguchi, Fullerton College
Judith Young, Norwalk Community College
Louise Zamparutti, University of
    Wisconsin-Milwaukee
Jensen Zhao, Ball State University
Michael Zirulnick, Fairleigh Dickinson
    University
Gail Zwart, Norco College–Riverside
    Community College District

Accuracy Checkers

Carolyn Ashe, University of Houston–
    Downtown
Cherilyn Boyer, University of Arizona
Cole Holmes, University of Texas–Austin
Nancy Nygaard, University of Wisconsin–
    Milwaukee

Contributors to the Instructor's Resources

John Anderson, Northwestern University
Jan R. Costello, Georgia State University
Barbara D'Angelo, Arizona State University
Leslie Fischer, Northwestern University
Joyce Lopez, Missouri State University
Deborah Richey, Owens Community
    College
Susan Schanne, Eastern Michigan University
Julie Boyles, Portland State University

Graduate Assistants

Jennifer Callaghan, Northwestern
    University
Jessica Hinds-Bond, Northwestern
    University
Alexandra Lindgren-Gibson, Northwestern
    University

Undergraduate Assistant

Karen Gwee, Northwestern University

MyLab Contributors

Jan R. Costello, Georgia State University
Heidi Fuller, American River College
Gina L. Genova, University of California,
    Santa Barbara
Nancy Nygaard, University of Wisconsin–
    Milwaukee
Storm Russo, Valencia College

1 Developing Your Professional Presence

Sergey Nivens/Fotolia

STUDY QUESTIONS

(SQ1) Why is it challenging to communicate well? pages 4–6

Communication is a complex process
Communication is affected by context
Communication is more than transmission of messages

(SQ2) What are the benefits of being a good communicator? pages 6–9

Effective business communicators have a competitive edge in the job market
Communication skills will contribute to your company's and your own success

(SQ3) What characteristics will help you communicate effectively? pages 9–21

Being strategic
Being professional
Being adaptable

(SQ4) What other important career skills will this textbook help you develop? pages 21–23

MyLab Business Communication
⭐Improve Your Grade!

If your instructor is using MyLab Business Communication, visit **www.pearson.com/mylab/business-communication** for videos, simulations, and writing exercises.

New Hires @ Work

Ryan Croy
University of Tennessee
Content Writer @ Asurion

I've built credibility in two ways: intelligent communication and dependability. The way you ask for something is just as important as what you're asking for. When I request a favor, I offer something in return. Even if there isn't much I can do for that person, he will remember (and appreciate!) the gesture. It's also important to be reliable. If somebody asks you to do something, do it—and get it back to her before the deadline. You earn more responsibility as you build a dependable reputation.

Chapter 1 | Introduction

What do employers look for in people they hire to be future leaders? Clearly, employers are looking for *competence*—your ability or potential to do the job you are hired to do. They are also looking for **credibility**. In other words, they want employees who have good character and real substance, who are trustworthy, and who will represent the organization well. Just as importantly, they are looking for *confidence*. That doesn't mean that they admire arrogance. Instead, it means they want employees and leaders who believe in themselves and have an attitude and style of communication that inspires confidence in others.

These three elements—competence, credibility, and confidence—form the core of **professional presence**.[1] Some people equate presence with the "wow" factor that allows you to make a great first impression, similar to the peacock that is the emblem of this book.[2] While that wow factor is certainly impressive, presence goes deeper than that. Presence emanates from within, reflecting your comfort with yourself and the rapport you develop with people around you. As social psychologist Amy Cuddy defines it, "presence is the state of being attuned to and able to comfortably express our true thoughts, feedings, values, and potential."[3] Presence manifests itself primarily through your ability to communicate—verbally and nonverbally—so that others recognize your competence, are eager to listen to what you have to say, trust you, and have confidence in you.

How do you develop professional presence? While you are in school, you undoubtedly have been developing your *competence* as you take courses in your major and other fields. Ideally, you have also been learning how to learn so that you can continue to increase your competence on the job. Your *credibility* is based in part on your character, which you have been developing since you were a child. You also earn credibility by doing good work, being trustworthy, and empathizing with others, which shows that you understand their needs and point of view. You develop *confidence* by believing in yourself and by learning communication skills that allow you to project that belief as you communicate your ideas. Confidence also comes from the knowledge that you can use your **critical thinking**, abilities to adapt what you have learned as new situations arise.

This book and this course are designed to help you polish your professional presence by developing the communication competencies that will set you apart from others, no matter what career you pursue. Communication is what makes presence possible. Think of this first chapter as a preview of the book. It will help you understand why communication is challenging, how you will benefit from learning to communicate well, what characteristics you will be able to demonstrate when you successfully complete this course, and how this course will help you develop other skills—beyond communication—that employers value.

 Why is it challenging to communicate well?

Professional presence depends on communicating well, and that is not an easy task. Even in its most basic form, **communication** is a complex process of encoding and decoding messages (information, ideas, and feelings). However, as communication theory has developed, our understanding of communication has evolved. Communication is more than just the exchange of messages. It is the process by which people co-create and share meaning. Success in communication is affected by an array of factors that go beyond the language you use, including the physical, social, and cultural context in which you communicate; your relationship with your audience; and the audience's knowledge and expectations. The following sections provide more insight into why communication is so challenging.

Communication is a complex process

Communication experts have been developing models of the communication process for decades, and each new model provides additional insights into the complexities of communication. One of the earliest models, the *transmission model*, is illustrated in **Figure 1.1**. This model focused on a single communication exchange and portrayed communication as the linear transmission of a message from a sender to a receiver.[4] A sender has an intention; selects a **medium** of communication; **encodes** that intention into words, images, or actions; and sends the message through that medium. The receiver gets that message and **decodes** it to understand its meaning, unless the message is blocked by some kind of noise or barrier.

FIGURE 1.1 An Early Model of the Communication Process: The Transmission Model

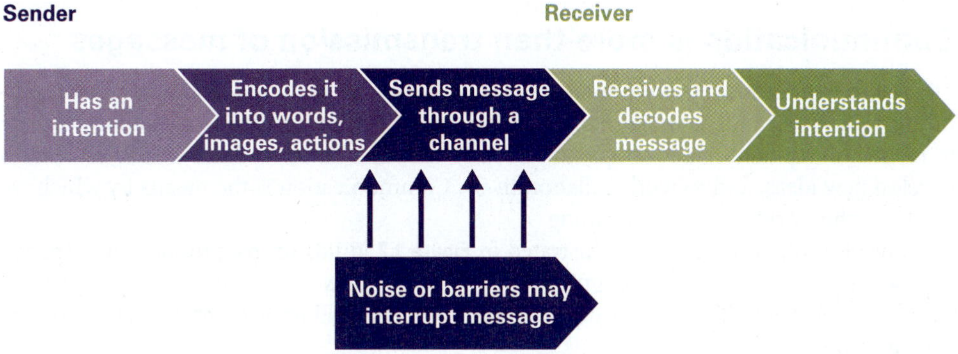

The concept of **barriers** helps explain why communication often fails. Barriers come in many forms. They may be *physiological*. For example, if you are speaking to someone who has a hearing loss or a migraine headache, he may not be able to listen effectively or interpret what you are saying. Barriers may be *psychological*. If you compliment someone who does not trust you, she may interpret that compliment as a subtle criticism. *Semantic barriers* occur when language is ambiguous or difficult to understand. If a colleague rushes into a meeting late and says to you, "I was held up at the train station," you might ask if the robber had a gun, when your colleague simply meant that the train was delayed. *Language barriers* arise when senders and receivers do not have a shared language. Sometimes the problem is obvious: The sender speaks only Spanish and the receiver speaks only English. Other times the problem is less obvious. For example, employees who are new to a company or an industry may not yet understand the jargon people use.

Communication is affected by context

Despite its contributions to communication theory, the transmission model does not provide a full understanding of what happens when we communicate. For example, it does not take into account the iterative back-and-forth process that good communicators use to ensure understanding. Receivers become senders as they provide verbal and nonverbal **feedback**. The transmission model also does not account for the various contexts that affect a sender's encoding choices and a receiver's decoding process.

More recent models of communication address the complexities of feedback and context. For example, the *interaction model* of communication portrays communication as a dynamic process.[5] Messages and meanings evolve as senders and receivers communicate

credibility An audience's belief that you have expertise and are trustworthy based on your knowledge, character, reputation, and behavior.

professional presence Your ability to project competence, credibility, and confidence in your communication.

critical thinking A disciplined approach to analyzing, synthesizing, and evaluating information to guide actions and decisions.

communication The process by which participants not only exchange messages (information, ideas, and feelings) but also co-create and share meaning.

medium The method you use to deliver a message (for example, telephone, face-to-face meeting, email, text message, or website).

encode To translate the meaning of a message into words, images, or actions.

decode To interpret the words, images, and actions of a message and attach meaning to them.

barrier An obstacle that gets in the way of effective communication.

feedback Any form of verbal or nonverbal response to a message.

context The external circumstances and forces that influence communication.

back and forth, giving each other feedback. The interaction model also introduced the concept of **context**—the external circumstances and forces that influence communication. This model considers the *physical context* in which communication takes place, including the physical distance between communicators as well as what's going on around them. For example, shouting across a noisy room is different from whispering in someone's ear. The model also considers *psychological context*: what's going on in the communicators' minds. Someone who fears losing a job may interpret a boss's comment differently than someone who feels secure.

The *transactional model* of communication expands on the concept of context and recognizes that communication is influenced by a broader set of external forces: social, relational, and cultural.[6] *Social context* refers to the set of learned behaviors and norms that guide communication choices. In some social contexts (such as a classroom), you may wait to be acknowledged before speaking. In other social contexts, you will talk more freely and may even interrupt someone else. *Relational context* arises from past history and current relationships with your audience. For example, if you have had a difficult relationship with someone, you may choose to email that person rather than talk face to face. *Cultural context* refers to the role that culture plays in influencing expectations about communication. For example, if you come from a culture that is comfortable being direct and straightforward, you may have difficulty communicating in a culture where people imply negative messages rather than communicate them directly.

Communication is more than transmission of messages

The transactional model of communication also offers a different view of *why* people communicate. Communication is more than an exchange of information. People also communicate to form and maintain relationships, to persuade others, to learn, to increase self-esteem, to develop new ideas, and to work collaboratively. Communication is the means by which we influence the world and create meaning.

The communication model illustrated in **Figure 1.2** builds on past models, incorporating the range of complexities recognized today. In a business communication class, you will learn to account for all of these complexities as you make and implement your communication decisions.

FIGURE 1.2 Updated Model of the Communication Process

 What are the benefits of being a good communicator?

As the previous section described, being an effective communicator is challenging. Not everyone is good at it. However, if you take advantage of this course to become a better communicator, you will benefit in several ways. In addition to enhancing your professional presence, you will also develop skills that will give you a competitive edge in the job market, contribute to your company's success, and contribute to your personal success.

Effective business communicators have a competitive edge in the job market

Despite predictions that technology will make many professional jobs obsolete,[7] research shows that certain categories of jobs have experienced significant job growth over the past several decades. The jobs growing most quickly are the kinds of jobs that you are training for by attending college—those that require a combination of cognitive skills and social skills, such as teamwork and communication.[8] And the people most successful in these jobs are those who have developed strong social and communication skills.

Surveys and interviews of corporate recruiters make very clear that employers want to hire good communicators. The National Association of Colleges and Employers (NACE) routinely surveys employers to determine the skills and qualities that they most value in employees. In a recent survey, employers rated the following communication-related skills in the top 10 skills that employers are looking for:

- Ability to work in a team structure
- Ability to verbally communicate with people both inside and outside the organization
- Ability to obtain and process information
- Ability to create and/or edit written reports

In fact, employers rated the first three of these skills as more important than technical knowledge.[9]

Communication also tops the list of the essential workplace skills identified by MBA alumni and recruiters surveyed by the Graduate Management Admission Council. In fact, 94% of alumni ranked communication as the most important skill—and identified communication as equally important at all levels of the organization. Job recruiters make a similar point, identifying oral communication, listening skills, written communication, and presentation skills in the top five desired skills.[10] Echoing this point, a member of the Goldman Sachs recruiting team said that one trait she always looks for in every candidate is "strong communication skills."[11] Other recruiters interviewed at a job fair similarly indicated that they wanted to recruit people with "communication and writing skills" as well as "more polish, confidence, and passion," which are elements of nonverbal communication and professional presence.[12]

Ironically, although these communication skills are widely considered important, few people in the workplace have mastered them well enough to meet employers' needs. A report produced collaboratively by American Express and Millennial Branding found that "managers have an overall negative view of young workers, and point to their lack of soft skills regarding communication and interpersonal interactions, time management abilities and willingness to work as a team."[13] Another industry report pinpointed critical thinking, writing, and public speaking as skills that managers want but find lacking in recent college grads.[14] Similarly, corporate recruiters say that people with strong communication skills are very difficult to find.[15]

Why is it that well-educated students leave college without the communication skills that employers need? Research suggests that young workers do not sufficiently prepare themselves before entering the workforce because they do not recognize their deficits in these areas. A study conducted by Hart Research for the Association of American Colleges & Universities (AACU) finds a large gap between college students' perception of their abilities and employers' perceptions. In fact, students are more than twice as likely as an employer to think that they are well prepared to think critically, communicate orally and in writing, and work well in teams—skills that employers believe are crucial for job success. **Figure 1.3** on page 8 graphs the surprising results of the AACU survey.[16]

When employees come to the job with insufficient communication skills, employers need to provide on-the-job training—and that costs time and money. A study conducted by the American Management Association found that of the 721 senior-level professionals interviewed, 66 percent said they invested company resources in training their employees in communication skills—more than any other kind of professional activity.[17]

This bad news for the workforce may be good news for you. It means you have an opportunity to stand out in the crowd. If you are able to apply the range of skills you learn in this course, you will be a valuable asset to your business, which will increase your professional

FIGURE 1.3 How Employers' Perceptions of Student Preparedness Differ from Students' Perceptions

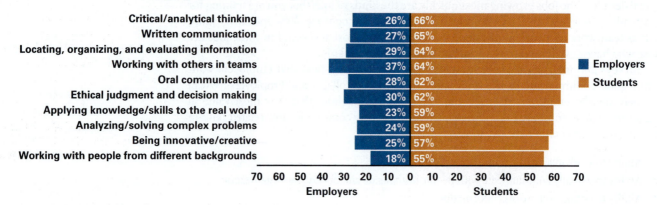

Adapted from Hart Research Associates (2015), p. 12.

success and perhaps even your income. You will also be able to use these skills to be more effective in your personal life.

Communication skills will contribute to your company's and your own success

Because communication is a valued commodity in the workplace, it can enhance your professional and personal success in a variety of ways.

Communication skills will make you a more valuable employee

Companies want good communicators because good communication is profitable: It *saves* money, and it *makes* money. Consider the following ways in which better communication skills can increase your value to a company:

- **Writing.** Clear, effective writing can save organizations hundreds of thousands of dollars, while ineffective communication can cost time and money. Although there are few documented studies of cost savings from improved writing, the findings that do exist are impressive. For example, Federal Express improved the readability of a ground-operations manual, making it so much easier for employees to read that the company saved an estimated $400,000 in the first year due to increased efficiency.[18]

  In the public sector, the state of Washington found it was losing tax revenue because businesses did not clearly understand an important letter explaining the requirements about a specific type of tax. After the state simplified the letter, the improved communication led to an additional $800,000 of tax revenue being collected.[19] When the Veterans Administration revised just one of its form letters, asking veterans to update their insurance beneficiary forms, the improved response rate was so significant that the organization estimated it saved more than $4,000,000 because employees had to spend less time identifying and locating beneficiaries.[20]

  Even one good email can contribute to business success. Venture capitalist Varun Jain tells the story of writing an email to the CEO of a company in which he was interested in investing. Although he did not know the CEO and the company was not seeking early stage investments, the email was so effective that he got this response: "Well, Varun, I have to say, that was one of the best blind intro emails I've ever received from a VC. Well played." The CEO proposed a meeting date, the investment deal was ultimately finalized, and less than six months later, the company was acquired by General Motors for more than $1 billion. Without that email, Jain's company would not have participated in the venture.[21]

  If you are a good strategic writer, you can contribute to these kinds of financial benefits and impress your employer.

- **Listening and speaking.** Writing is not the only communication skill that makes you a more valuable employee. As a salesperson, you can bring in more sales if you know how to listen effectively to customers' needs, demonstrate how a product or service meets those needs, and close the sale at the end of a conversation. As a customer service representative, you can retain customers and attract new ones by answering their questions efficiently and communicating solutions to their problems. As a team member who collaborates well with other team members to solve problems, you may be able to bring a product to market earlier, increasing the opportunity to sell the product.

- **Developing communication strategy.** If you work at a managerial or executive level, you may have the opportunity to influence how your organization communicates with employees, investors, and the general public. That communication can directly impact the organization's success. Research by a global consulting firm found that companies that are highly effective at communicating also experience greater employee satisfaction, greater productivity, and greater investor confidence. As a result, these companies are three-and-a-half times more likely to financially outperform their peers than companies that communicate less effectively.[22]

- **Implementing social media.** Your expertise with **social media** also can benefit your company. Effective communication through social media—such as blogs, Facebook, Twitter, and Instagram—improves employee satisfaction and builds brand awareness to reach more customers.[23] In addition, if you run your own small business as an entrepreneur, your communication abilities will be especially critical because you will be responsible for most, if not all, of your company's social media communication.[24]

social media Web-based applications, such as blogs, Facebook, and Twitter, designed to promote social interaction.

Communication skills may improve your salary

A growing body of research shows that jobs requiring both social and cognitive skills are the only ones with consistent wage growth and that good communicators earn more money than comparable employees with less developed social skills.[25] Employers who recognize the value of communication skills are willing to pay a premium to get employees with those skills. For example, Kip Tindell, the CEO of The Container Store, explains that communication is at the heart of his company's success, and he is willing to pay double the industry average for a great employee who has the right skills. Tindell said, "One great person could easily be as productive as three good people," so paying twice as much is a bargain.[26]

Good communication skills can improve your personal life

Good business communication skills—such as speaking and writing clearly, being aware of who will receive your message, listening to others, and persuading others—are beneficial in your personal life, too. For example, you may be able to use your communication skills to persuade your cell phone provider to lower your monthly bill or convince a dealer to give you a better price for a car. Or you might use your listening skills to negotiate, or even prevent, an argument with a friend or family member. Studying business communication and practicing your skills will generate a positive return on your investment of time and energy, both for your professional career and your personal life.

New Hires @ Work

Shruti Shah
University of Florida

**Operations Analyst
Development Program Intern @
JPMorgan Chase**

I was surprised how broad but significant being a good communicator is. It does not just involve giving powerful presentations; it also involves asking the right questions, carrying conversations with coworkers and managers, and contributing during meetings.

Photo courtesy of Shruti Shah

(SQ3) What characteristics will help you communicate effectively?

As you begin to polish your professional presence, consider your current skills and abilities. Think about your core abilities: writing, speaking, listening, and interpersonal communication. The best business communicators—those who have real presence, are able to connect with other people, and successfully deal with communication challenges—share the specific characteristics illustrated in **Figure 1.4** on page 10. These are the characteristics that make writing, speaking, and other interactions effective. The remainder of this chapter previews these characteristics, which you will continue to develop throughout the course and throughout your career. As you read about each one, determine your current strengths and identify the gaps you need to fill to become a more effective communicator.

FIGURE 1.4 Characteristics of Effective Business Communicators

STRATEGIC	PROFESSIONAL	ADAPTABLE
✓ Purposeful	✓ Appropriate to the situation	✓ Current with technology and social media
✓ Audience-oriented	✓ Clear and concise	✓ Able to work with diverse cultures and ages
✓ Persuasive	✓ Ethical	✓ Collaborative

Being strategic

The best communicators always have a **communication strategy**—a plan for what and how to communicate to ensure that their message achieves its **purpose**. Strategic communicators are always making decisions, asking themselves these questions:

- What do I want to accomplish with this communication? What is my goal?
- Who is my audience? With whom should I communicate to accomplish my goal?
- What content will my audience need?
- What medium will work best: a face-to-face meeting, a teleconference, an email, a presentation, a report, or a combination of medium options?
- How can I frame and organize the message to state the main point and effectively support it?

As these questions suggest, to be a strategic communicator, you must be purposeful, audience-oriented, and—in many cases—persuasive.

Purposeful

Business communication involves more than self-expression. It needs to be purposeful and constructed to achieve an intended **outcome**. You can judge the effectiveness of your communication by whether it accomplishes its purpose. For example, when you write a cover letter for a job, the letter is effective if you get an interview. Other features of effective communication—such as grammatical correctness, clarity, and conciseness—will also help you achieve your purpose.

Consider the two versions of the email message in **Figure 1.5** by Zack Kramer, a business major and a member of his university's chapter of Students for a Cleaner Environment. The two emails appear to have similar purposes: to get information from a civil engineering professor for one of the club's projects. However, only one of them is likely to get Zack what he wants.

Audience-oriented

Good business communicators understand that their messages must reach and influence their **audience**—the intended recipients of your communication. Being able to influence an audience requires two complementary sets of skills. First, you must be a good reader and listener so that you can understand audience concerns. Second, you must be able to compose messages that address those concerns and are also easy to understand.

Reading and listening provide you with insights into what is important to the audience. For example, when a good communicator receives an email asking a question, she replies only after reading it carefully to identify why the writer is asking the question and what kind of answer he needs.

Being a good listener is arguably even more important than being a good reader. Research suggests that people in school and in the workplace spend much more of their communication time listening than they do speaking, reading, or writing.[27] Too often people assume that they are good listeners simply because they *hear* things every day. However, hearing is not the

You will learn more about being strategic in Chapter 3: Managing the Communication Process.

communication strategy A plan for what and how you are going to communicate to ensure that your message achieves your purpose.

purpose The reason you are communicating.

outcome The result of your communication; what you want the recipients of your message to know, do, or feel about the subject of your message.

audience The intended recipients of your communication.

New Hires @ Work

Bailey Anderson

University of Northern Iowa

UX Designer @ Principal Financial Group

The most surprising aspect of being a good communicator in my work has been asking lots of questions. Questions show you care about the work you are doing. You might even ask a question that your boss hasn't thought of, which brings a new perspective to the table.

Photo courtesy of Bailey Anderson

FIGURE 1.5 How to Write a Purposeful Email

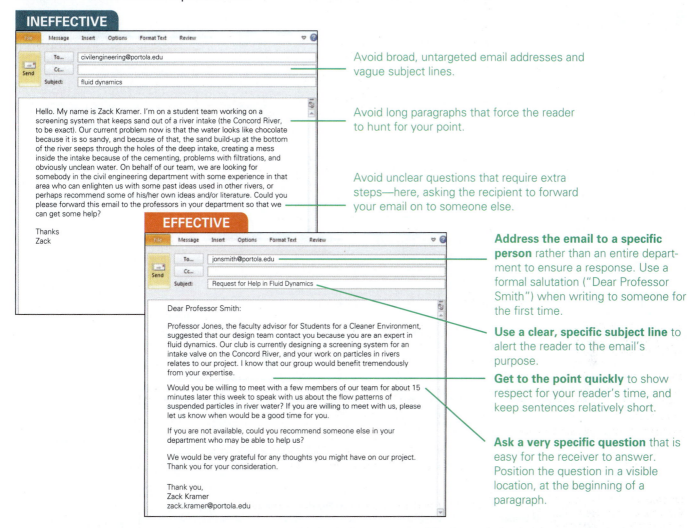

Avoid broad, untargeted email addresses and vague subject lines.

Avoid long paragraphs that force the reader to hunt for your point.

Avoid unclear questions that require extra steps—here, asking the recipient to forward your email on to someone else.

Address the email to a specific person rather than an entire department to ensure a response. Use a formal salutation ("Dear Professor Smith") when writing to someone for the first time.

Use a clear, specific subject line to alert the reader to the email's purpose.

Get to the point quickly to show respect for your reader's time, and keep sentences relatively short.

Ask a very specific question that is easy for the receiver to answer. Position the question in a visible location, at the beginning of a paragraph.

same as listening, which is a learned skill. **Active listening** involves focusing on the speaker, working to understand both what the speaker is saying and why he or she is saying it, and providing feedback to ensure that you understand it correctly.

An active listener will go beyond listening to words and will also perceive emotional cues and body language—and even think about what is not being said. For example, if a person's voice sounds strained, he may be nervous or concerned about the information he is communicating. Or if a person is using defensive body language, such as crossing her arms, she may feel skeptical or upset, although her words do not convey that same meaning. Most importantly, good listeners do not remain silent. They engage in a dialogue with the speaker and ask questions that prompt the speaker to think harder and gain new insights and perspectives.[28] If you develop good listening skills, your coworkers and customers will communicate with you more frequently and more fully. As a result, you will learn more and be able to do your job more effectively. You will also better understand your audience and be able to plan communications that meet their needs.

When you understand your audience, think about meeting their needs in two ways:

1. **Making the message easy for your audience to understand.** If you organize a message for easy comprehension, you will increase the chances that people will accurately read or listen to the message.
2. **Providing the content that the audience needs or wants.** If you address the questions on the audience's minds and anticipate their possible objections, you increase the chances that you will get the response you want.

Figure 1.6 on page 12 illustrates two versions of a business recommendation. To evaluate whether these documents are audience-oriented, try reading them in two steps. First, skim each version for about 10 seconds to see what stands out and to determine which one is easier to read. Then, read each version more carefully to identify which one more clearly provides reasons and explanations that will be compelling to the audience.

active listening A learned skill that requires you to attentively focus on the speaker's communication, interpret the meaning of the content, and respond with feedback to ensure understanding.

You will learn more about active listening in Chapter 2: Working with Others.

FIGURE 1.6 How to Compose an Audience-Oriented Business Recommendation

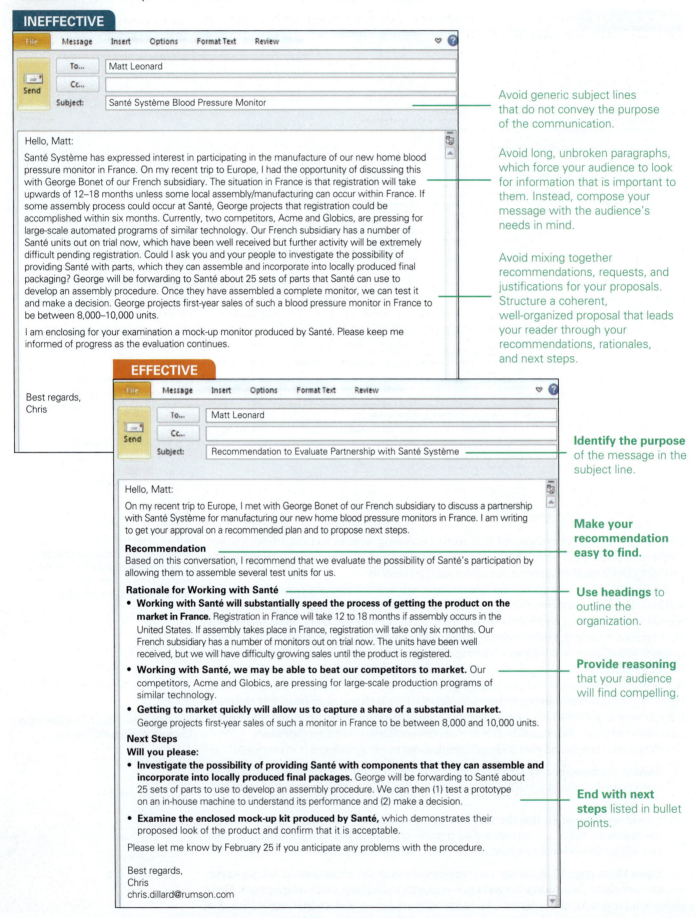

INEFFECTIVE

To... Matt Leonard
Cc...
Subject: Santé Système Blood Pressure Monitor

Hello, Matt:

Santé Système has expressed interest in participating in the manufacture of our new home blood pressure monitor in France. On my recent trip to Europe, I had the opportunity of discussing this with George Bonet of our French subsidiary. The situation in France is that registration will take upwards of 12–18 months unless some local assembly/manufacturing can occur within France. If some assembly process could occur at Santé, George projects that registration could be accomplished within six months. Currently, two competitors, Acme and Globics, are pressing for large-scale automated programs of similar technology. Our French subsidiary has a number of Santé units out on trial now, which have been well received but further activity will be extremely difficult pending registration. Could I ask you and your people to investigate the possibility of providing Santé with parts, which they can assemble and incorporate into locally produced final packaging? George will be forwarding to Santé about 25 sets of parts that Santé can use to develop an assembly procedure. Once they have assembled a complete monitor, we can test it and make a decision. George projects first-year sales of such a blood pressure monitor in France to be between 8,000–10,000 units.

I am enclosing for your examination a mock-up monitor produced by Santé. Please keep me informed of progress as the evaluation continues.

Best regards,
Chris

Avoid generic subject lines that do not convey the purpose of the communication.

Avoid long, unbroken paragraphs, which force your audience to look for information that is important to them. Instead, compose your message with the audience's needs in mind.

Avoid mixing together recommendations, requests, and justifications for your proposals. Structure a coherent, well-organized proposal that leads your reader through your recommendations, rationales, and next steps.

EFFECTIVE

To... Matt Leonard
Cc...
Subject: Recommendation to Evaluate Partnership with Santé Système

Hello, Matt:

On my recent trip to Europe, I met with George Bonet of our French subsidiary to discuss a partnership with Santé Système for manufacturing our new home blood pressure monitors in France. I am writing to get your approval on a recommended plan and to propose next steps.

Recommendation
Based on this conversation, I recommend that we evaluate the possibility of Santé's participation by allowing them to assemble several test units for us.

Rationale for Working with Santé
- **Working with Santé will substantially speed the process of getting the product on the market in France.** Registration in France will take 12 to 18 months if assembly occurs in the United States. If assembly takes place in France, registration will take only six months. Our French subsidiary has a number of monitors out on trial now. The units have been well received, but we will have difficulty growing sales until the product is registered.

- **Working with Santé, we may be able to beat our competitors to market.** Our competitors, Acme and Globics, are pressing for large-scale production programs of similar technology.

- **Getting to market quickly will allow us to capture a share of a substantial market.** George projects first-year sales of such a monitor in France to be between 8,000 and 10,000 units.

Next Steps
Will you please:
- **Investigate the possibility of providing Santé with components that they can assemble and incorporate into locally produced final packages.** George will be forwarding to Santé about 25 sets of parts to use to develop an assembly procedure. We can then (1) test a prototype on an in-house machine to understand its performance and (2) make a decision.

- **Examine the enclosed mock-up kit produced by Santé,** which demonstrates their proposed look of the product and confirm that it is acceptable.

Please let me know by February 25 if you anticipate any problems with the procedure.

Best regards,
Chris
chris.dillard@rumson.com

Identify the purpose of the message in the subject line.

Make your recommendation easy to find.

Use headings to outline the organization.

Provide reasoning that your audience will find compelling.

End with next steps listed in bullet points.

Persuasive

When you want to influence people's thoughts or actions, your message needs to be persuasive. **Persuasion** is the process of influencing your audience to agree with your point of view, recommendation, or request. In your daily life, you often need to communicate persuasively. You may be persuading people to accept a proposal or recommendation, give you a refund, agree with your argument, donate money to a charity, become a customer, or remain a customer—the list goes on and on. The more persuasive you are, the more effective your communication will be.

Being persuasive requires thinking about the topic from your audience's point of view. What benefits do you offer? What audience objections do you need to address? What reasons and factual evidence support your claim? In **Figure 1.7** on page 14, Fran Patera of MaxiWeb Web Hosting wants to persuade a potential customer to switch to MaxiWeb as its Internet provider. As you read Fran's message, notice how she stresses benefits, addresses actual and potential objections, and provides support for her claims.

You will learn more about persuasion in Chapter 5: Communicating Persuasive Messages.

persuasion The process of influencing an audience to agree with your point of view, accept your recommendation, grant your request, or change their beliefs or actions in a way that facilitates a desired outcome.

Being professional

A survey by York College of Pennsylvania's Center for Professional Excellence found that professionalism is a key issue for students entering the workforce: "Almost 40% of faculty responded that less than half of students demonstrate professionalism."[29] **Professionalism** refers to the qualities that make you appear businesslike in the workplace. Professionalism is expressed by your actions, your attire, your wording in an email, your body language during a meeting, your tone of voice on the telephone, and your attention to correct grammar and proofreading. However, professionalism goes beyond projecting a professional image. It also involves living up to the standards of your profession, including ethical standards. An effective professional communicator is appropriate to the situation, clear and concise, and ethical.

professionalism The qualities that make you appear businesslike in the workplace.

Appropriate to the situation

Different situations require different behaviors. For example, if you have lunch with friends, you may not think to stand up when a new person joins you at the table or to introduce that person formally to the others. In addition, you may assume it is okay to tell your friends funny stories about another student. However, during a business lunch, professionalism requires that you observe etiquette and actively participate in conversations without disrespecting others. Etiquette errors become barriers that negatively impact other people's perceptions of you.

Professionalism is as important in writing as it is in speaking. For example, assume that you just found out you have to cancel your evening plans because your marketing team needs to finish a new client proposal before an 8 am meeting. You may want to email this message to your team: *"hey guys, i hope you didn't get too wasted last night, cuz we gotta pull an all-nighter tonite to get that project done by 8 AM or we'll be in deep trouble! i'll order pizza—what should I get?"*

The informal style and wording may be appropriate for your friends. However, informality in the workplace can be a problem because your email could be forwarded to others at the company. The challenge is to be professional in your work email without being overly formal. A more professional message would use standard English and eliminate references to personal life as well as negative references to the project and supervisor: *"Hi John, Deepa, and Elaine: It looks as if we will have to work late tonight to meet the 8 AM deadline. I'll order a pizza for us—any requests?"* Consider the two emails in **Figure 1.8** on page 15 and assess the level of professionalism in each one.

Clear and concise

In school, you might have developed a wordy writing style to fulfill word-count requirements in assignments such as a 500-word essay. You may also have developed the habit of writing complicated sentences in an attempt to sound sophisticated and well educated. If you have developed these bad habits, you will need to change them to sound professional

FIGURE 1.7 How to Compose a Persuasive Letter

letter

MaxiWEB

2929 Avenue of the West, Houston, TX 77002

June 25, 20XX

Mr. Will Johnson
SaveOnCrafts
1349 Lothrop Street
Topeka, KS 66605

Dear Mr. Johnson:

Thank you for meeting with me last week to discuss changing your web hosting company from your current provider to MaxiWeb. We believe that MaxiWeb will offer you two important benefits.
> **Begin with a clear purpose.**

The first benefit is reliability. With our integrated backup systems, we average only five minutes of outage time per month. According to an independent survey published in *E-Commerce Today*, your current provider loses connectivity at least once per day. I have enclosed an article from *E-Commerce Today* that provides a method for estimating what this amount of down time may be costing your company in lost sales.

The second benefit is responsiveness and customer service. MaxiWeb has the highest customer service rating in the industry. Unlike many other providers, we offer 24-hour telephone support from our home office in Houston. Our average time for resolving problems is less than 30 minutes.
> **Focus on benefits.** Present them in separate, clear paragraphs to make them easier to see and provide support for claims.

At the meeting, you expressed concern that MaxiWeb may cost more per month than your current service. As an attachment to this letter, I've included a detailed comparison between MaxiWeb's flat fee, which includes all services, and Interflex's fee structure, which requires you to pay for each service separately. By the time you add up all the extra services you need, I think you will find that Interflex's yearly cost is 10 percent more than our flat fee.
> **Respond to objections** your audience has previously raised.

Only a few days are necessary to set up and test your site. We will be glad to coordinate that work with your IT department. In more than 95 percent of cases, the actual transfer is so quick and seamless that you will not lose even one sale from your site.
> **Anticipate and respond to potential objections** your audience may raise.

I will call you next week to see if you have any additional questions. We are ready to begin the transfer process as soon as you authorize it.
> **Use the closing to emphasize next steps** and to make it easy for your reader to implement the change you are proposing.

Sincerely,

Fran Patera

Fran Patera
Director of Sales

Enclosures

in the workplace. In business, people value clarity and conciseness. **Clarity** is the quality of being unambiguous and easy to understand. Clear communication has only one possible meaning. In addition, it uses simple words in well-constructed sentences and well-organized paragraphs. **Conciseness** means that a message uses no more words than are necessary to accomplish its purpose. Clarity and conciseness are valued in business because time is a scarce resource. Your audience will understand a clear and concise message more quickly than a wordy and complicated one.

clarity The quality of being unambiguous and easy to understand.

conciseness Using no more words than necessary for a message to accomplish its purpose.

FIGURE 1.8 How to Convey Professionalism in an Email

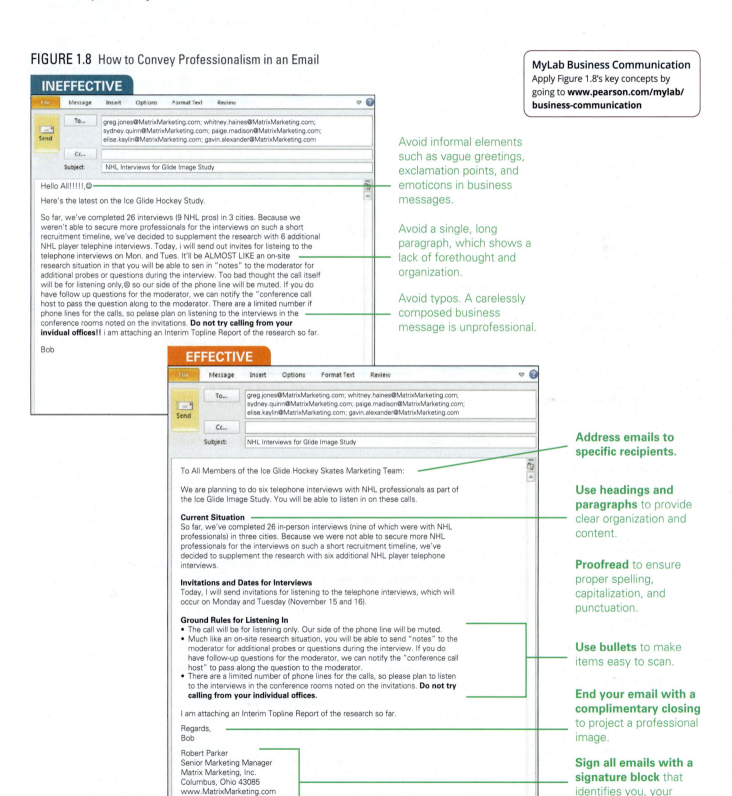

MyLab Business Communication
Apply Figure 1.8's key concepts by going to **www.pearson.com/mylab/business-communication**

Avoid informal elements such as vague greetings, exclamation points, and emoticons in business messages.

Avoid a single, long paragraph, which shows a lack of forethought and organization.

Avoid typos. A carelessly composed business message is unprofessional.

Address emails to specific recipients.

Use headings and paragraphs to provide clear organization and content.

Proofread to ensure proper spelling, capitalization, and punctuation.

Use bullets to make items easy to scan.

End your email with a complimentary closing to project a professional image.

Sign all emails with a signature block that identifies you, your position, and your contact information.

Consider the two versions of a voice mail message in **Figure 1.9**. The ineffective message is long and unorganized. The effective message is short and to the point.

FIGURE 1.9 How to Compose a Voice Message That Is Clear and Concise

INEFFECTIVE	EFFECTIVE
Hi, Ahmad. This is Don. The meeting yesterday went on for two hours after you left and there was a lot of discussion about the new pricing system and how it will affect our sales and marketing campaign. No one could really agree about what the impact will be, which isn't surprising since we didn't have your charts to review, and we never agree about anything right away, so we decided to hold another meeting on Friday, which you are welcome to come to but you don't really have to. But what we do need from you are the sales projections for the four regions, which you never got a chance to present yesterday. Can you get those to Mary by Friday morning? Also, if you don't plan to come and there's anything else you want us to discuss, let me know.	Hi, Ahmad. This is Don. I'm sorry we didn't have a chance to discuss your sales projections at the meeting yesterday. We've scheduled a new meeting to discuss them at 2 pm on Friday. Could you let me know if you are available to attend? If not, please get the sales projections to Mary by noon on Friday so she can distribute them at the meeting. Thanks.

You will learn more about ethics and communication throughout the book. Each chapter includes an ethics feature that focuses on an aspect of ethics relevant to the chapter topic. Look for the ethics icon.

ethics The principles used to guide decision making and lead a person to do the right thing.

Ethical

As a professional, you are likely to face a number of ethical dilemmas that are difficult to resolve—and as the AACU survey indicates, employers believe that recent graduates are not well prepared to resolve them.[30] **Ethics** are the principles you use to guide decision making, leading you to do the right thing. However, the right thing is not always immediately obvious, and making a decision that violates ethical standards may put your career, your colleagues, your customers, or your company at risk. Being ethical means telling the truth, taking responsibility for your actions, and imagining the impact of your actions on others:

- **Telling the truth.** Assume that your supervisor asks your team to prepare a persuasive presentation to support her recommendation that your company move some of its manufacturing facilities to Mexico. Most of your research supports the move because it will save the company money without decreasing product quality. However, you are not certain you have done enough research into the labor situation in Mexico. You have heard rumors that the move may expose the company to risks resulting from excessive employee absenteeism and turnover. You don't have time to do more research because your supervisor is presenting the information tomorrow. Here is your ethical dilemma: Should you mention the potential risk, which will weaken your argument? Or should you ignore this potential risk and present the strongest case you can to support the move to Mexico? After all, your supervisor has asked you put together a strong argument because management really wants to move several facilities to Mexico. In addition, you have no actual evidence that there will be a labor problem.

  This scenario places you in an ethical dilemma in which you must choose between two competing responsibilities. The first is your responsibility to tell the truth. If your presentation gives the impression that no problems exist in moving facilities to Mexico, you would not be living up to that responsibility. The second is your responsibility to your supervisor and your organization. If your supervisor wants a change that you believe may be risky to the organization, you face a difficult decision. You might think, *"I'll just give my supervisor the strong argument she asked for, and she can do with it what she likes."* However, if you feel tempted to respond in this way, you might want to impose the *headline test* on your actions. How would you feel if the company had problems in Mexico, and the media coverage started with this headline: *"Business analyst failed to inform company of potential labor risks"?* If the headline makes you feel uncomfortable or guilty, then you have probably acted against your own ethical principles. In general, it is better to tell your supervisor the entire truth: There are unconfirmed rumors of labor unrest in Mexico that should be investigated before reaching a final decision. This allows everyone to make the best and most informed decision.

- **Taking responsibility for your actions.** If you read or watch the news, you will routinely see reports of companies that endanger the safety of customers, bribe officials, cheat customers, provide incorrect information to the government or shareholders, or in other ways do not live up to their promises. In some cases the actions appear to have been deliberate—such as Volkswagen's manipulation of software to make it appear that its diesel engines were meeting emission standards.[31] In other cases, the crisis surprised the company as much as the public—such as the contaminated ingredients at Chipotle that endangered the lives of nearly 200 customers in nine states.[32] Finally, in some cases, it is unclear whether the problem was deliberate or accidental—such as when Whole Foods systematically overcharged customers for fruits and vegetables in at least two states.[33]

  Whoever is at fault, the public and stockholders clearly expect the company to be honest, take responsibility, apologize, and make a plan to provide restitution and prevent reoccurrence. However, not all companies do so effectively. In the case of Volkswagen, the CEO made a statement but never actually admitted fault. Whole Foods responded to accusations of overcharging first by denying the claim and refusing to take responsibility. When Whole Foods finally acknowledged the problem and apologized,, the company shifted the blame to the workers. Even though Whole Foods outlined a clear and compelling plan to solve the overcharging problem, the press and social media reactions were not good.[34] By contrast, Chipotle took immediate responsibility for endangering the safety of customers, apologized, and took action by developing a plan to prevent future occurrences and win back customers' trust.[35]

  Just as businesses need to take responsibility for their actions, so do individual employees. Those who deny responsibility or shift blame to others quickly lose their colleagues' respect and trust. As a business communicator, you may not always easily identify the best and most ethical course of action to take. However, a good communicator recognizes the responsibility to try.

- **Imagining the impact of your actions on others.** As you prepare for your professional career, think carefully about the distinction between the behaviors you currently consider personally acceptable and those considered acceptable in business. For example, people who actively participate in social networking are so comfortable with openness and sharing that they may not always maintain the boundary between content that a business owns and content that an individual employee may keep and share. In fact, a national business ethics survey conducted by the Ethics Resource Center found that active social networkers were more likely than others in the workplace to believe it is acceptable to keep copies of confidential company documents in case they need them in the next job with a different employer or to take copies of work software home to use on personal computers.[36]

  In most businesses, this behavior would be considered ethically questionable. Imagine the potential impact of these actions on others. For example, if you take electronic copies of confidential documents when you leave a job and if your computer gets lost or stolen, you are not likely to report the incident to your previous employer. If the documents contain trade secrets or other proprietary information, you put the company at risk.

Being adaptable

The business world evolves continually, requiring you to adapt both as an employee and as a communicator. Think of all the changes that occur during a typical person's 40-year business career. For example, a new college graduate who began working for IBM in the mid-1980s joined a company whose key business was building and selling stand-alone mainframe computers for large corporate clients. IBM basically had one product to make and one product to sell to one kind of customer. Communication with those clients—and with colleagues—took place by phone calls, letters, memos, and face-to-face meetings.

However, in a few short years, the world changed dramatically. IBM employees saw the company's one product being overshadowed by the personal computer and networks. The Internet was rapidly growing as both a means of communication and a business platform. Clients began looking for software solutions, not hardware products. So IBM changed its focus from being a product provider to being a service provider.

During this change, an employee who wanted to remain at IBM had to learn to adapt—no longer focusing on communicating the benefits of one product but listening to client needs and providing solutions to those needs. Employees also had to adapt to other cultures because IBM's customer base outside the United States was growing. In addition, employees needed to become more collaborative as IBM created more global teams to serve its customers around the world. New communication media—email, video conferencing, online meetings—replaced the old ones.[37]

These kinds of significant transformations continue today. Before 2003, Facebook and social networking between businesses and customers did not exist, and before YouTube launched in 2005, there was no easy way to post videos on the web. Now Facebook and YouTube are both standard tools of business communication.

It is impossible to predict how business will change in the future and how communication will change as a result. Only one thing is certain: More change will come, and as a business communicator, you must learn to adapt—to new technologies, diverse colleagues and customers, and new ways of working with others.

Current with technology and social media

You will learn more about business uses of social media in Chapter 7: Using Social Media in Business. In addition, each chapter includes a technology feature that focuses on an aspect of communication technology relevant to the chapter topic. Look for the technology icon.

Being an effective business communicator requires that you take advantage of new communication technologies such as smartphones and tablets as well as new communication media such as Web 2.0 applications and social media. Technology changes so quickly that the hardware and software applications you use now will likely be outdated by the time you reach the workplace. New options—and new challenges—will arise to make your business communication both more efficient and more prone to error. You will need to adapt to these changes as well as to the ways businesses use familiar platforms. To take the best advantage of technology, communicators continually need to address three questions: What is the best technology for the task? How can I avoid the technology traps that hinder effective communication? And how can I adapt familiar technology to business use?

Choosing the best technology for the task. Imagine that you are working for a company in Palo Alto, California. You are collaborating on a project with a team in your company's Tokyo office, where the time zone is 16 hours ahead. At the end of your workday at 5 PM, it is 9 AM the next day in Tokyo. You need to update your Tokyo colleagues about your progress on the project for the day so they can continue the work. What technologies can you use to do this? As the following analysis shows, no technology is perfect, and you will need to make thoughtful decisions:

- **Should you call your colleagues to let them know the status of the project?** The advantage of a phone call is that your colleagues can ask questions. The disadvantage is that there is no written documentation of your update. If someone in Tokyo misses your phone call, he won't have access to the information.
- **Should you email your colleagues?** Email is very efficient, and it allows you to communicate with many people at once. But sending an email does not guarantee that your colleagues will read it, especially if they receive many emails in a day. In addition, email is not always reliable because there may be network delays, or someone's spam filter may block your message.
- **Should you upload your documents to the company intranet or a collaborative worksite?** Uploading to an intranet or a collaborative worksite offers the advantage of having all the documents in a central location that employees with the password can access. In addition, collaborative web applications such as Google Drive and Box allow multiple people to work on material at the same time. The disadvantage, though, is that your colleagues in Tokyo will need to remember to go to the site to download documents. The documents aren't delivered to their mailboxes.

Avoiding technology traps. Technological competence goes beyond selecting a communication technology. It also requires knowing how to avoid traps. Have you experienced any situations similar to these?

- You receive a text message from your boss asking "Do you have the project update ready?" You intend to text back "No I don't. I'll have it tomorrow." However, your smartphone "autocorrects" your message to read "No idiot. I'll have it tomorrow." It is hard to recover from that kind of mistake. (To prevent this problem, always proofread your texts carefully before sending them.)

- You send an email with a large attachment to someone outside your organization. You assume that the recipient got the file because you do not receive a message saying your email failed. However, two days later, you get an email asking when you intend to send the file. (To prevent this problem, avoid emailing large files. Instead upload them to a collaboration site such as Dropbox or Google Drive and email your recipient a link.)

- You've created a PowerPoint presentation that includes specialized fonts, which you have downloaded to your computer. However, when you give the presentation using someone else's computer, your fonts don't work. Instead, the presentation computer has substituted alternative fonts that not only look unprofessional but also change your line spacing. (To prevent this problem, learn how to "embed" fonts within a PowerPoint or Word document.)

- You have written a long and complex email that carefully and thoroughly analyzes a problem, but when your recipients read it on a mobile device, as is increasingly common in business,[38] they see big blocks of text and have to scroll a long way to find your main point. Many of them choose not to read your entire email and, as a result, never get to your main point. (You can prevent this problem by writing all emails with the mobile reader in mind: Keep the email short, summarize the main ideas at the beginning, and provide headings and other visual cues that keep mobile readers on track.)

- You are starting a Facebook page for your new business, and a fan of your company tags you in an offensive post, which then appears on your own wall. (This problem is solved by paying attention to privacy and access settings on your page, which will allow you to control who can tag you in their posts as well as enable you to review any posts before they reach the public.)

As a good communicator, you don't need to know all technologies, but you do need to think about the implications of technology choices and use your options wisely.

Adapting familiar technology to business use. You will also need to adapt to the business uses of familiar social media platforms such as Facebook, Twitter, YouTube, and Instagram as well as social media platforms that are used primarily for business, such as LinkedIn and SlideShare. You may already be using social media to connect with friends, to broadcast your current activities, to share pictures, and even to play games. However, businesses use social media strategically to accomplish a number of different goals:

- **Reach customers.** Think of all the ways that companies use social media to reach customers, promote their products and services, enhance brand awareness, and build a community of followers.[39] Examples include YouTube videos of new products, community discussion boards on corporate websites, coupons and discounts distributed through Facebook pages, and social media promotions designed to generate customer interest. As new social media technologies gain popularity, businesses find creative ways to use and benefit from them.

   IKEA Norway offers a good example of creativity. The company wanted people to engage with and talk about its products on social media. To accomplish that goal, IKEA offered customers an opportunity to win their favorite item from the catalog (which is mailed to every residence in Norway) by taking a photo of the page containing the item and posting the picture on Instagram with the hashtag #ikeakatalogen. Within four weeks, every page of the catalog had been uploaded to Instagram. IKEA had its first "social catalog" at very little cost, and IKEA's Instagram account had 12,000 new followers.[40]

- **Provide customer support and education.** For example, Salesforce, the enterprise cloud-computing company, uses YouTube to host training videos and best-practice webinars about its software. Potential customers also have access to the videos and comments from current customers. This education and validation builds consumer confidence.

- **Find new employees through social recruiting.** Social media outlets such as LinkedIn and Facebook are excellent places to publicize jobs and search for new employees, and organizations are continually finding new ways to use both social media and messaging apps to attract job candidates. For example, the company HireVue not only sells a digital recruiting platform but also uses Snapchat and Periscope to communicate with candidates and help them visualize what it's like to work at the company.[41]

LinkedIn, the world's largest professional social networking site, grew from half a million members in 2004 to more than 400 million members in 2016.

- **Engage existing employees and improve productivity.** Companies use social media in various ways to engage employees. Many companies create internal social media sites, such as the computer manufacturer Lenovo's internal network Lenovo Social Champions. The site encourages employees to learn from each other, share stories, and create buzz about events.[42]

  Even more companies encourage their employees to be brand ambassadors, writing and talking about the company on external social media. That kind of employee presence on social media builds both brand awareness and **goodwill**—that is, a positive relationship between the company and the audience. The software company Adobe is a leader in empowering employees to communicate broadly about the brand through social media. Adobe provides employees training in how to responsibly talk about Adobe in their personal social media accounts, and for those who want to go further, Adobe provides additional training and branded social media accounts. Adobe has found that social media is responsible for 20 percent of subscriptions to Adobe Creative Cloud and that in some months brand ambassadors are responsible for more revenue than Adobe's official social media accounts.[43] The benefit of employee social media goes beyond increased sales and customer goodwill. Research shows that employees who engage in work-related social media are more productive than those who do not.[44]

As the previous examples suggest, by being adaptable to changes in technology, businesses create communication opportunities and strengthen their connections with employees, customers, and the general public. Businesses rely on their employees—especially younger employees—to find new ways to use technology effectively.

Able to work with diverse cultures and ages

Workplaces are becoming increasingly diverse, bringing together people from different countries, cultures, backgrounds, and generations. Although these differences create a collective wealth of knowledge and breadth of perspectives, the differences also can make communication challenging. Bridging these differences requires self-awareness, respect, and patience. Consider some of the challenges of communicating with people who come from an older generation. To Baby Boomers (born 1946–1964) telephone and email are comfortable forms of communication. To Millennials (born 1981–2000), texting seems much more convenient. By contrast, the digital natives of Generation Z (born 2000–2015) prefer talking face-to-face, in person.[45] When working in a multigenerational workplace, your chances of being heard may depend on choosing the medium that works best for your audience.

Also consider the challenges of communicating with people from other cultures. If they are not native English speakers, language choices can be challenging. To keep your writing and speaking easy to understand by a diverse audience, use short sentences and avoid **idioms**—expressions that mean something different from the literal meaning of their words, such as "we are on the same page." Idioms may confuse people who are unfamiliar with them.

Even people who are adept at English may come from *cultures* that approach business and communication differently than you do. **Culture** refers to the learned and shared patterns in a society. People demonstrate their culture through values, ideas, and attitudes—and their approach to communication. Some cultures, such as the Chinese, are more formal than others. Chinese businesspeople follow a prescribed set of rules about how to show respect to managers and other senior colleagues. As another example, some cultures, such as the Germans, are more concerned with punctuality than others. German businesspeople may be offended if someone arrives at a meeting 10 minutes late.

Cultural differences can lead to communication challenges. Consider the following scenario involving two companies doing business together—one from China and the other from Britain.[46] Communication challenges arise from a key difference between Chinese and British business cultures: Chinese businesses are hierarchical, and British businesses are more democratic or egalitarian. This means that in China, senior members of the company are accorded special respect and treated differently than their employees, while in Britain everyone is accorded equal respect.

The British company hired a Chinese firm to act as the sales representative for its products in China. The British regional manager in charge of Asia Pacific sales created an email distribution list to communicate efficiently with the entire group in China. The head of sales in China was insulted at being included in the list with junior colleagues. This method of communication does

---

goodwill   A positive relationship between you (or your company) and the audience.

You will learn more about working with other cultures in Chapter 2: Working with Others. In addition, each chapter includes a culture feature that focuses on an aspect of culture relevant to the chapter topic. Look for the culture icon.

idiom   An expression that means something other than the literal meaning of its words.

culture   The learned and shared attitudes, values, and behaviors that characterize a group of people.

not show him enough respect. If the British manager had learned more about Chinese corporate culture, he probably would have sent the communication only to the Chinese director, who could have then decided how to communicate the information to his employees.

As you can see from this scenario, basic communication decisions that seem normal in your own cultural context may offend colleagues from another culture. By increasing your awareness of cultural differences and keeping an open dialogue with your colleagues, you can adapt your behavior as needed.

Cultural sensitivity does not apply only to international communication. Even within the same country, younger people are likely to be less hierarchical and formal than their older counterparts. While the older head of sales from the Chinese firm may have been insulted at receiving information at the same time as his junior colleagues, the junior members may have responded differently. Like their younger British counterparts, they may have felt that respect is earned rather than owed based on hierarchy.[47]

Even if you conduct comprehensive research on a culture, you will not be able to predict every intercultural problem. However, your attempts to accommodate cultural differences will communicate professionalism and respect.

Collaborative

In school, you complete much of your work on your own. Even when you work on a group project with other students, the grade you earn at the end of the class is usually an individual one. In business, although you will routinely have to communicate as an individual, many of your projects will be team-based because they are too big to be completed by just one person. As a result, **collaboration**—working with others to achieve a common goal—is crucial in the workplace.

Being collaborative requires that you adapt to the working styles of many different people. In addition, it requires that you coordinate, compromise, negotiate, and manage conflict. For example, assume that you work for an airline and have been assigned to a cross-disciplinary team that is researching various ways to decrease costs. Your team has 30 days to complete its research and present findings and recommendations to management. Think about all the decisions you need to make to coordinate your work:

- How to identify talents of team members and divide the research
- How and when to share information with each other
- What criteria to use to evaluate the options
- Which options to present to management
- How to organize your presentation
- How to divide the task of writing the presentation
- How to organize and deliver your recommendations to management

In the process of working together and making these decisions, you and your teammates are likely to experience disagreements and conflicts. Perhaps one teammate, based on his research, firmly believes that the best option for decreasing costs is to eliminate the lowest-volume routes that the airline flies, while another teammate argues that her research shows this option has hidden public relations costs. As this scenario suggests, effective communicators need to know more than just how to research, write, and present. They also need to know how to coordinate work, manage conflicts, and negotiate agreements.

collaboration The process of working with others to achieve a common goal.

 You will learn more about communicating effectively in groups in Chapter 2: Working with Others. In addition, each chapter includes a collaboration feature that focuses on an aspect of collaboration that is relevant to the chapter topic. Look for the collaboration icon.

(SQ4) What other important career skills will this textbook help you develop?

As you have learned in this chapter, communication is central to your success no matter what career you plan to pursue. Communication skills top the list of what employers want, and working through this course gives you opportunity to practice your communication abilities, receive feedback, and polish your professional presence.

However, the skills you will gain do not stop there. By paying attention to the boxed features in the text and working through the case scenarios and exercises, you will enhance

data literacy The ability to access, assess, interpret, manipulate, summarize, and communicate data.

a wide range of other skills that are vital for success in the 21st-century workplace: critical thinking, collaboration, ethical reasoning, the ability to apply knowledge in new situations, the ability to use technology effectively, and **data literacy**. **Figure 1.10** explains why employers value these skills and how you can practice them.

FIGURE 1.10 How This Textbook Will Help You Develop Additional Employability Skills

SKILL	WHY EMPLOYERS VALUE IT	HOW YOU CAN PRACTICE IT
Critical thinking: A disciplined approach to analyzing, synthesizing, and evaluating information to guide actions and decisions	Critical thinking is foundational to problem solving. Employers value employees whose education has gone beyond memorization and who can use what they have learned to solve problems.	Each chapter in this text includes a set of questions that focus specifically on critical thinking. In addition, most of the end-of-chapter exercises are designed to engage your critical thinking abilities. You will also see many scenarios in the book in which people are exercising critical thinking to solve problems. Use these examples as models to practice your own critical thinking skills.
Collaboration: The ability to work with others to achieve a common goal	In the workplace, many tasks require multiple perspectives; other tasks require more work than one person can accomplish on his or her own. Today's workplace is team oriented, and collaboration is a core ability for team success.	Each chapter includes a collaboration feature that focuses on an aspect of collaboration relevant to the chapter topic. In addition, each chapter includes a set of collaborative exercises that challenge you to work effectively with others.
Ethical reasoning: Using a set of principles to guide thinking and lead a person to do the right thing	Employers rely on employees to distinguish between right and wrong and to make well-thought-out decisions that consider the interests of all stakeholders. Poor ethical decisions put the entire company at risk.	Each chapter includes an ethics feature that focuses on an aspect of ethics that is relevant to the chapter topic. In addition, each chapter includes critical thinking questions or exercises that explicitly address ethical reasoning.
Ability to apply knowledge in new situations: The ability to learn a concept and then appropriately apply that knowledge in another setting	Employers hire new employees expecting that those employees can translate the knowledge they have gained in school to the practical requirements of the job. If you cannot apply your education in flexible ways, you will be a less valuable employee.	At the end of every chapter, a case scenario challenges you to apply the chapter concepts and skills to a new situation. Many of the end-of-chapter exercises provide similar opportunities.
Ability to use technology effectively: The ability to select and use appropriate technology to accomplish a given task	Every job requires the ability to select and use the appropriate technology. Communication technology is evolving quickly, and employers require that you adapt quickly to use new technology effectively.	Every chapter of the text includes a technology feature that focuses on effectively using a technology that is relevant to the chapter. Each feature references at least one end-of-chapter exercise for more practice.
Data literacy: The ability to access, assess, interpret, manipulate, summarize, and communicate data	Technology has made it possible for businesses to generate and access increasing amounts of data. For this data to be useful in making business decisions, employees must know how to analyze the data and communicate it effectively to a variety of audiences.	While you may learn techniques for analyzing and evaluating data in other courses, this course gives you the opportunity to practice the complementary skills of data literacy: communicating insights from data, using data to support arguments, and communicating data effectively in tables, graphs, and text.

As you work through this course, reflect on how you are using and developing these skills and how they will apply to the work you will do in your career. If you do, then when you are ready to write your résumé and prepare for job interviews, you will be better able to showcase what you have learned.

■ **In summary,** employers want to hire people who are effective communicators and project a strong professional presence. However, becoming a successful communicator is not as simple as you may first believe. In addition to developing effective writing, speaking, listening, and interpersonal skills, a good communicator needs to be strategic, professional, and adaptable. Because communication is so critical to your success, working on communication skills will also give you the opportunity to enhance other skills that are vital for employment, including critical thinking, collaboration, ethical reasoning, and data literacy. This course will give you ample opportunity to practice all these skills and develop a competitive edge at work and in other facets of your life.

SUCCESSFUL COMMUNICATION @ WORK Patrick Engineering, Inc.

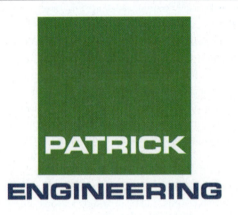

Patrick Engineering is a national engineering and construction company that plans, designs, and builds infrastructure projects, such as bridges, dams, mass transit systems, railways, water systems, power delivery systems, and communications systems. With 12 offices across the United States, the company works with the state and federal agencies and industrial clients that own these systems, and it often partners with peer companies on specialized aspects of these projects.

According to Dan Dietzler, CEO of Patrick Engineering, being successful in this business requires a culture of communication. Clear technical communication utilizing drawings, maps, tables, graphs, reports, and technical specifications is vital to the company's work. Equally important is clear, concise, and persuasive business communication. Employees routinely communicate with team members, project owners, inspectors, vendors, craftspeople, and even project neighbors—both orally and in writing. Letters, proposals, interviews, and presentations at meetings are all vital elements of their work. In all this communication, professionalism is as important as content.

To build this culture of communication, the company looks for employees with three fundamental characteristics that are foundational to communication success and that reflect professional presence:

1. **Intellectual and emotional intelligence:** "In this business, employees need to be smart," says Dietzler, "but not just book smart. They need to get along with other people." In other words, they also need *emotional intelligence*: the ability to listen to others, understand their points of view, and use that understanding to guide behavior.

2. **Teamwork:** Projects—whether large or small—depend on teamwork. People need to work together toward a common goal and to communicate with each other in professional and respectful ways that encourage collaboration. According to Dietzler, there is no room for people who need to get their own way all the time. That's why the company looks for employees who have team experience, whether it's on a soccer team, or as part of a band, or in the military. People with good team experience know how to pass the ball to others, to keep in tune with others, and to trust others to do good work. A key question to ask yourself, Dietzler says, is "Do you want to be right, or do you want to be successful?"

3. **Passion:** Finally, success requires passion. Employees must care about the job, the company's values and culture, and their contribution to the larger goals. Without passion for the job, people are likely to refuse to be team players or to communicate as frequently and effectively as is required. "You can't build a company around people who treat the job as a placeholder in their careers."

Source: Based on an interview with Dan Dietzler, 2016.

End of Chapter

Study Questions in Review

 SQ1 Why is it challenging to communicate well? *(pages 4–6)*

Professional presence—your ability to project competence, credibility, and confidence—depends on communicating well, and that is not an easy task. Communicating well requires understanding some foundational principles.

- **Communication is a complex process.** Communicating even a single message involves many steps: having an intention, encoding that intention into a message, selecting an appropriate medium, decoding the message, and providing effective feedback. Barriers often block successful communication. Successful communication requires overcoming physiological, psychological, semantic, and linguistic barriers. These complexities are magnified when you consider that communication rarely involves a single exchange but instead an interaction in which messages and meanings evolve.
- **Communication is affected by context.** Within a communication interaction, a range of contexts may affect someone's ability to understand your communication: that person's *physical* or *psychological* state, the specific *social* situation that dictates expectations, your *relational* history with that person, and the broader *cultural* context of learned behaviors and norms.
- **Communication is more than just transmission of messages.** Adding to the complexity is the fact that people communicate not just to transmit messages but for an array of other reasons: to form and maintain relationships, to persuade others, to learn, to increase self-esteem, to work collaboratively and develop new ideas, and to get work done. Communication is the means by which we create meaning and influence the world.

 SQ2 What are the benefits of being a good communicator? *(pages 6–9)*

Being a good communicator will benefit you and any organization you work for.

- **Effective business communicators have a competitive edge in the job market.** Research continually shows that employers want to hire good communicators. Yet employers find too few people who communicate well.
- **Communication skills will contribute to your company's and your own success.** Your ability to write well, listen and speak effectively, develop communication strategies, and even implement social media will increase your value as an employee. In addition, the skills you use on the job will help you in your personal life to improve relationships, negotiate better deals, and persuade others.

 SQ3 What characteristics will help you communicate effectively? *(pages 9–21)*

Your writing, speaking, and interpersonal communication skills are clearly important. But the best business communicators—those who have real presence—share a number of specific characteristics that make their writing, speaking, and other communication effective.

- **Being strategic.** Effective communicators are purposeful and design their communication to achieve a specific outcome. They are also audience-oriented, considering what content the audience requires and also what organization, format, and language will make the content easy to understand. Finally, when their communication purpose requires persuading others to agree and/or to act, effective communicators know how to be persuasive and influence the audience's thoughts and actions. Three useful techniques for persuasion are (1) identifying benefits, (2) anticipating audience objections, and (3) providing reasons and evidence to support claims.
- **Being professional.** Professionalism refers to the qualities that make you appear businesslike. Business communicators appear professional when they act in a manner appropriate to the situation, are clear and concise, and live up to the ethical standards of their profession.
- **Being adaptable.** Effective communicators are adaptable. Being adaptable means being willing and able to change to meet new business needs. In business, communicators must adapt to remain current with technology, including social media, which changes very quickly. In addition, because business is increasingly global and values diversity, communicators must adapt to work well with other cultures and generations. Finally, because many business projects require teamwork and coordination with others, communicators must adapt their work styles to collaborate well with others.

 SQ4 What other important career skills will this textbook help you develop? *(pages 21–23)*

Although communication is the single most important asset you can polish as you launch and manage your career, a range of other skills are vital to job success in the 21st century. These include critical thinking, collaboration, ethical reasoning, the ability to apply knowledge in new situations, the ability to use technology effectively, and data literacy. Each of these skills is integrally connected to communication, and by completing this course, you will have the opportunity to work on all of them.

Visual Summary

STRATEGIC

Purposeful

Anna Osborn

University of Tennessee

Business Analyst - Audit Liaison @ Georgia-Pacific, LLC

In communicating via email, I try to use an informative subject that will be useful in future searches for the email. I begin with a personal introduction and then think about what I want to convey and communicate it clearly. After completing the e-mail, I proofread and then send.

Photo courtesy of Anna Osborn

Audience-Oriented

Christian Tucker

Georgia Southern University

Intern @ Bank of America

When we develop internal apps for BOA employees, our proposals focus on what the users can and can't do with the new app, demonstrate how it's going to make their work better, and show them what's in it for them. It's all about focusing on the end-user.

Photo courtesy of Christian Tucker

Persuasive

Bianca Wallace

Eastern Kentucky University

Human Resources Representative @ Hendrickson Trailer Commercial Vehicle Systems

In manufacturing, the most important thing is production and numbers. But in HR, it's our job to persuade decision makers to take people into account, also. Without the people to produce the product, we have no product.

Photo courtesy of Bianca Wallace

PROFESSIONAL

Appropriate to the Situation

Suzie Loveday

Eastern Kentucky University

Grants Management Officer @ Frontier Nursing University

Writing professionally is extremely important, especially in my position as a grant writer. If I do not show professionalism in my writing and communication, people will not take me seriously. This, in turn, could negatively impact funding opportunities for my employer.

Photo courtesy of Suzie Loveday

Clear and Concise

Chris Harlow

Northwestern University

Consultant @ Capgemini Consulting

My first interaction with new colleagues and clients is often through email and meeting requests. Clean and clear writing creates an impression from the beginning of being professional and composed.

Photo courtesy of Chris Harlow

Ethical

Megan Sugrue

Northwestern University

Senior Manager, Social Media Strategy @ Viacom International Media Networks

When developing our social media strategy, it's important for us to be transparent and authentic. If we need to say "sorry, we messed up," we will.

Photo courtesy of Megan Sugrue

ADAPTABLE

Current with Technology and Social Media

Ray Holloman

Belmont University

Business Continuity Administrator @ HCA Healthcare

I use WebEx because I communicate with employees in twenty states. With WebEx, I can share my screen with them and record the meetings if necessary. WebEx also allows me know who is on the call without having to stop and ask each time someone joins.

Photo courtesy of Ray Holloman

Able to Work with Many Cultures

Amber Osborn

University of Northern Iowa

Quality Control Analyst @ Principal Financial Group

My job requires me to communicate with different cultures in different countries. There are always cultural communication barriers, and these increase when communicating from a distance. After 3 years of daily calls, it has become much easier for me to communicate across cultures.

Photo courtesy of Amber Osborn

Collaborative

Byron Smith

North Carolina A&T State University

Business Sales Manager @ AT&T Mobility

I don't know of any job that doesn't require collaboration of some kind. Whether you are a new hire, an experienced manager, or the CEO, you have to be able to work well with others to get things done. I've learned that you don't have to be best friends with someone to collaborate. You can ignore the things other people do that bug you, work through conflict when needed, sometimes agree to disagree, and still be a team.

Photo courtesy of Byron Smith

Key Terms

Active listening p. 11
Audience p. 10
Barrier p. 5
Clarity p. 15
Collaboration p. 21
Communication p. 4
Communication strategy p. 10

Conciseness p. 15
Context p. 6
Credibility p.4
Culture p. 20
Critical thinking p. 4
Data literacy p. 22

Decode p. 5
Encode p. 5
Ethics p. 16
Feedback p. 5
Goodwill p. 20
Idiom p. 20

Medium p. 5
Outcome p. 10
Persuasion p. 13
Professional presence p. 4
Professionalism p. 13
Purpose p. 10
Social media p. 9

MyLab Business Communication

If your instructor is using MyLab Business Communication, go to **www.pearson.com/mylab/business-communication** to complete the problems marked with this icon ⭐.

Review Questions

1 What is professional presence?

2 What does it mean to encode and decode a message?

3 Identify three barriers to communication.

4 Identify three types of contexts that can influence communication.

5 In what ways can communication skills save money or make money for a business?

6 Define active listening.

7 Define culture. How does it influence communication?

8 How does being concise differ from simply reducing the length of your communication?

9 How does business use of social media differ from personal use?

10 Why are collaborative skills necessary in the workplace?

Critical Thinking Questions

1 The chapter recommends that communicators address potential audience objections. Describe a communication scenario—either from your personal experience or a hypothetical business example—where you expect that the audience might have objections. What would the objections be, and how would you address them?

2 Imagine that you are trying to persuade a teammate to agree with an idea for a presentation, and the teammate accuses you of being manipulative—trying to influence someone for your own advantage. What is the difference between being persuasive and being manipulative?

3 Assume that your supervisor asked you to lie to a customer in an email about why a shipment is delayed. Would it be unethical for you to write the email if you believe it is wrong to lie? Conversely, would it be unethical for you to refuse to write the email if you believe you have a responsibility to your employer? How would you resolve this issue?

4 Imagine that you have been asked to collaborate on a project with a colleague whose work style is very different from yours. For example, you like to plan carefully and follow a schedule, whereas your colleague is spontaneous. You like to write thorough drafts that require only minimal revision, whereas your colleague likes to write incomplete drafts and revise heavily later. Based on these differences, you think it would be more efficient and cost-effective for the company to have you work on this project by yourself. Should you make that argument to your supervisor? What might be the benefits of collaborating? What are the drawbacks?

5 Although it is important to consider your audience's potential questions and objections when you communicate, you may not always know a lot about the people in your audience in advance. Imagine, for example, that you are sending a business proposal to a new client you have never met before. How can you learn more about your audience before writing the proposal?

⭐ **6** Cross-cultural communication requires you to use clear language. What are some of the other challenges of communicating across cultures?

⭐ **7** Students who are not used to writing professional emails sometimes make the mistake of composing them as if they were text messages. What are some key elements of text messages that you should avoid in professional emails?

8 Businesses use different social media tools and mobile apps for different purposes. Based on your knowledge of Facebook, LinkedIn, YouTube, and Instagram, how do you expect businesses would use each of these tools?

⭐ **9** Readers often judge a person's professionalism based on whether a document is spell-checked and free of grammatical errors. Do you believe this is a fair basis for making a judgment?

10 Some people argue that using emoticons in business emails is unprofessional. Others say that emoticons are useful because they help the audience interpret the writer's intention more effectively. Would you choose to use emoticons in your business email? Explain why or why not. Provide evidence or reasoning to support your decision.

Key Concept Exercises

 Why is it challenging to communicate well?
(pages 4–6)

1 Communication is a complex process

Think of a personal or business experience when someone "decoded" your message incorrectly and misinterpreted your meaning. Write a brief paragraph explaining the situation and the result.

2 Communication is affected by context

Think of a personal or business situation when you tried to persuade someone with whom you have a personal or business relationship. In that situation, how did the relational context affect your credibility? In other words, was the person more or less likely to believe you based on his or her personal history with you? Write a brief paragraph explaining the situation and the result.

3 Communication is more than transmission of messages

Think of a personal or business situation when you had a conversation with someone that resulted in a new and shared understanding, different from what you originally intended to communicate. Write a brief paragraph explaining the situation and the result.

 What are the benefits of being a good communicator? *(pages 6–9)*

4 Effective business communicators have a competitive edge in the job market

Use an online job bank, such as Monster, to search for job advertisements related to your career goals. How many of them include communication skills in their descriptions or requirements? Summarize your findings in a paragraph that outlines your career goals, two or three jobs you found, and the communication skills they require.

5 Communication skills will contribute to your company's and your own success

Typically when people think about business success, they think of financial success. In addition to making and saving money, what other business benefits can result from employees' effective communication? Write a paragraph identifying and explaining at least two additional benefits.

 What characteristics will help you communicate effectively? *(pages 9–21)*

6 Being strategic—purposeful

Read the memo at the top of the next column and identify its main purpose. Rewrite the subject line and the first sentence of the memo to make them clearer.

7 Being strategic—audience-oriented

When the U.S. government's General Services Administration (GSA) learned that a historic building site was contaminated with pigeon droppings, a staff member drafted the following announcement to warn construction workers in historic buildings about the dangers of working near this potential biological hazard.

Imagine that you are asked to offer advice about revising the message and choosing a medium to inform workers of the hazard. After

---

memo

TO: Gloria Paradi
FROM: Josh Benson
DATE: March 23, 20XX
SUBJECT: Staffing

This office has not had the benefit of full staffing at any time in the past year. There is no relief from continual pressure due to a limitation of staff. An analysis of overtime during the November/December time period provides a clear indication of the inability of the office to enjoy full coverage of all the required work within regular work hours. Additional help can be usefully provided in purchasing, design, fabrication, assembly, and shipping since we are understaffed in all areas. As we can set aside no time for training right now, it is required that all new employees be experienced.

Accompanies Exercise 6

Bulletin: Potential Biological Hazard

Background: During evaluations in a historic building that GSA proposes to restore, a large accumulation of pigeon droppings was discovered, which had collected through long habitation of the birds. Samples of the droppings were collected and analyzed by the Centers for Disease Control in Atlanta, Georgia.

Discussion: The CDC identified the droppings as containing a fungus capable of causing very serious infection in humans. This fungus is called "Cryptococcus Neoformans." It attacks the lungs, central nervous system, skin, eyes, liver, and joints and has a marked target of the brain and meninges. It is contained in the accumulation of excretion of birds and pigeons in old nesting areas and in soil contaminated with bird and pigeon droppings.

Workers who work around or demolish bird and especially pigeon habitations should use extreme caution due to the potential risk of illness involved when disturbing accumulation prior to decontamination. Infection is primarily due to inhalation. Prevention is possible by wearing appropriate facemasks and personal protective clothing.

Recommendation: If such an area is identified, do not disturb it. Leave the area and report the finding immediately to your supervisor. Supervisors will coordinate with Regional Accident and Fire Prevention Branches for evaluation, preventive measures, and decontamination action.

Further information: Avoid a suspected area until it has been determined not hazardous.

Accompanies Exercise 7

reading the message, write a memo to your instructor recommending (1) three changes to make it easier for the audience to find the most important ideas, (2) any additional information that the message

(continued)

should include to address audience concerns, and (3) the medium (or combination of media options) that you think will work best to reach the audience: a face-to-face meeting, a teleconference, an email, a presentation, an announcement posted on the wall of buildings, or something else. Be sure to justify your recommendations.

8 Being strategic—persuasive

You are the manager of a large supermarket that borders a residential neighborhood. A customer who lives nearby comes into the store and says, "I am completely out of patience with the trucks that make deliveries to your store. Deliveries start at 7 AM and end at 9 PM. Early in the morning and into the evening, trucks are banging their trailers into the loading docks. And the engines! The drivers keep the trucks running while they're making deliveries. I can't talk with friends in my yard because of all the noise of the trucks. And it's not just the noise. The trucks also block the alley so I sometimes can't get out of my garage to get to work in the morning."

To respond, you could just choose to explain the situation. Clear reasons exist for each of the behaviors that the neighbor is complaining about:

- Local laws have set truck delivery hours from 7 AM to 9 PM. To accommodate all the deliveries, management needs to spread them throughout the day.

- The engines are on in refrigerator trucks because they run the generators that keep food from spoiling.

- The trucks block the alley for only a short time while they are waiting for other trucks to leave. Drivers politely move if they are asked.

However, suppose your main goal is to retain this "neighbor" as a customer and increase goodwill. In that case, you may choose to respond in a way that is more persuasive. Brainstorm content to include in your response. As you brainstorm, consider these persuasive techniques:

- Show that you understand your audience's concern.

- Address the objections.

- Show the benefits to the audience.

As part of your brainstorming, think of possible solutions to the problem. If you mention possible solutions, your response may be even more persuasive. Be prepared to discuss in class or submit your responses, according to your instructor's directions.

9 Being professional—appropriate

You work for HungerFighters United, a not-for-profit organization dedicated to eradicating hunger in the United States. One of your colleagues, Sheryl Greene, drafts a letter to a potential donor who has also expressed an interest in volunteering for your organization. Sheryl gives you a copy of the letter to review before sending it. You think it sounds friendly, but you wonder if Sheryl is projecting a sufficiently professional image of herself and HungerFighters. Identify at least five changes you would suggest that Sheryl make.

letter

December 14, 20XX

Ms. Anita Lawrence
4949 Daily Drive
Cleveland, OH 44101

Dear Anita:
As mentioned in my voice mail to you today, I am enclosing my card and other information that you might be interested in.

I have been with HungerFighters United in the Detroit Office since 1997 and have just moved to Development Director of the Midwest region . . . long title but the work is pretty much the same except I've expanded from Detroit to 11 states and am encouraged by the wonderful reception I've received and especially by the powerful resources Midwesterners are sharing with the families we serve.

Steve Cannon mentioned that you might consider reaching out to others in your circle of friends. If you would like to host a gathering in or around your area, that would be an idea. We have wonderful stories to tell, literature to share, and handouts people can take home. Or, a small group in a restaurant or your home is also effective. At any rate, this serves as an introduction to our efforts and ideas on expanding the help we need to end hunger.

I wish you and yours a wonderful holiday season and look forward to talking to you in the New Year.

Gratefully,

Sheryl Greene
Director of Development

Accompanies Exercise 9

10 Being professional—clear and concise

Select a message you received, such as a letter from a company or an email from a colleague. Identify specific content that can be revised to be clearer and more concise. Offer specific revisions based on the content presented in the chapter. Prepare to present your suggestions in class or submit it according to your instructor's directions.

11 Being professional—ethical

Your supervisor is preparing a speech for the company's chief executive officer to distribute to shareholders. He asks you to read the speech and provide feedback on how effective you think it will be. As you read the speech, you think you recognize some of the points—and the wording—from a speech by a financial analyst you heard a few weeks ago on C-SPAN. You fear that parts of your supervisor's speech are plagiarized. You wonder if you should tell him that you recognize some of that speech from another source, but you decide not to for two reasons. First, if you tell your supervisor the speech sounds familiar, he may get angry or insulted. Second, the speech was televised very late at night, so it's unlikely that many people watched it. Evaluate the pros and cons of that choice. Is your choice ethical? Be prepared to discuss your decision in class or submit it according to your instructor's directions.

12 Being adaptable—current with technology

You are planning to hold a conference call with three other people. You are in the United States, and the other participants are from Mexico, Canada, and Ireland. You are looking for a technology that balances expense and convenience. Three kinds of conference call services are available to you:

- **Option 1.** Everyone calls in to an international toll-free number. Your credit card will be charged 4 cents per minute for each person on the call. If people need to join the call late, they can do so without inconveniencing the rest of the participants.

- **Option 2.** Everyone calls in to a U.S. number. Each person pays whatever he or she would normally pay for a call to the United States. For you and the participant from Canada, the call will be free because your telephone services offer free calls within the United States and Canada. The remaining two people will each pay 7 cents per minute. They will each need to be reimbursed. This option offers the same call-in convenience as Option 1.

- **Option 3.** You initiate a web-based conference call using Skype. This call will be free for everyone. However, all participants need to be available at the moment you call them. Otherwise, you will need to repeatedly redial their numbers until they are available. If, for some reason, any calls are dropped, participants will have no easy way to rejoin the conference call.

The technology choice must balance costs and convenience. Which option would you choose, and why? Be prepared to discuss your choice in class or submit it according to your instructor's directions.

13 Being adaptable—current with social media

Choose a company that interests you, and search for it on Facebook, LinkedIn, YouTube, and Twitter. Based on what you find, write a message to your instructor explaining how the company uses each social media tool, whether you believe the company uses each tool effectively, and why or why not.

14 Being adaptable—collaborative

You are working with a team of five colleagues to research and write a report recommending a new sales strategy for your client. Because you are a very good writer, you are designated the lead writer on the project. Everyone else is writing drafts—except for one colleague, Emma Yamaguchi. Emma has recently transferred to the United States from the Tokyo office, and her English writing is weak. Your team thinks Emma is contributing quite a lot to the project with her quantitative analysis, which is strong. Everyone is happy with the distribution of labor—except Emma. She transferred to the United States to improve her written English, and now she finds she isn't being given the opportunity. Fortunately, she confides in you and tells you that she'd like to help with

writing the report. How can Emma contribute in ways that will help improve her English writing but will not compromise the quality of the final product? Think of two or three ideas you can suggest to the team and to Emma. Be prepared to discuss your ideas in class or submit them according to your instructor's directions.

15 Being adaptable—able to work with diverse cultures and ages

Reread Exercise 14. Assume that you suggested to Emma that she write one short section of the report, which another teammate can then edit. Emma writes her part, and you volunteer to edit that section. Emma gasps when she sees all your edits. She looks down and tells you she is ashamed to have submitted such poor-quality work.

You are shocked by her response because you thought you were helping her learn to write better English. As you read more about Japanese culture, you think that your response has made Emma "lose face"—that is, feel embarrassed. How could you handle the situation differently in the future? What approach can you take that will make Emma feel comfortable rather than ashamed? Be prepared to discuss your suggestion in class or submit it according to your instructor's directions.

 What other important career skills will this textbook help you develop? *(pages 21–23)*

16 Analyzing skills required for jobs

Go to the Bureau of Labor Statistics *Occupational Outlook Handbook* at https://www.bls.gov/ooh/. On that site, select an occupation group and then a specific occupation that interests you or that you would like to explore. For example, under the Business and Financial occupation group, you might select Market Research Analyst. Read the description of what a person in your selected occupation does, and then imagine how the following career skills will be useful in that job:

- Communication
- Collaboration
- Critical thinking
- Ethical reasoning
- Ability to apply knowledge in new situations
- Ability to use technology effectively
- Data literacy

From the list above, select three skills that you believe will be particularly important. Write a memo to your instructor that briefly summarizes what the job entails and explains how the three skills you chose will help you be successful in that job.

Writing Exercises

17 Analyzing your own experience

Think about the writing you have done in the past year, whether for school, work, or personal business. Write a list of the most significant writing experiences you have completed during that time. Select two or three experiences to develop in more detail and write what you remember about each one. Why was the outcome important to you? What was new, interesting, or difficult about the experience? What did you learn from it? What steps did you take to complete it?

Write an email to your instructor in which you briefly summarize the two or three experiences and answer the following questions:

- **a.** How similar or different are these experiences from the writing you expect to do in you professional career?
- **b.** If some aspect of writing was difficult in the past, how could you address that aspect in the projects you expect to work on in the future?
- **c.** What lessons learned from past experiences do you want to apply to upcoming writing projects?

18 Analyzing communication effectiveness

In the "Your Money" column that he writes for the The *New York Times*, Ron Lieber shared what he calls "the single best tool I've ever found for getting my money back or getting my money's worth."[48] When he has exhausted all other avenues of complaint (for example, talking to customer service representatives and their supervisors), he writes an Executive Email Carpet Bomb—that is, a polite but specific email that he sends to as many company executives as he can identify. The email itself contains a number of features that contribute to its success. Lieber says it has never failed him. Below is a copy of one email he sent that received good results.[49] The names of people and the store have been replaced with XXX. Write a one or two paragraph email to your instructor, providing your analysis of the features that make this such an effective message.

---

email

Subject: Dangerous conditions and your unwillingness to fix them

Gentlemen—

I'm writing on behalf of my mother, who lives at XXX and whose townhouse backyard backs up directly against the rear wall of the XXX Supermarket. You can view the precise geography via Google Maps; my mom is in the last row of townhouses.

For years now, there have been a variety of infestations—rats, bees, etc.—related to the fact that XXX Supermarket simply will not cut down the thick tangle of vines that grow all over the rear of the store building. This year, the problem is a plague of wasps, and we have had enough of it. My mother, who is retired and on a fixed income, just spent her hard-earned retirement money on a new grill, but she cannot use it thanks to the swarm of insects out back.

Every year, she or someone from her condo association has gone to the local store management and tried to get them to cut down the vines and do something to keep them from coming back. And each year they're met with little in the way of help. If it's not affecting XXX Supermarket's customers, who never see the back of the building, why should they care? That seems to be the prevailing attitude.

Someone is going to get hurt—badly—as a result of the danger that your company has created and that you have so far refused to fix. So here is what we are asking you to do:

1) Respond via email within 24 hours to both me and my mother, who is cced, and explain what you are going to do and who the point person will be on fixing this. We'd like their cell phone number, their email address, and a promise that they will not blow off our messages.

2) Agree to send someone out to assess the situation visually within 7 days and send a crew to cut the vines once and for all within 14 days. It will take many people many days to do this, but it's long overdue. Moreover, we want a commitment that if the vines come back, you will be out before Memorial Day each year to cut them down again.

[Name of CEO], with one pointed phone call to the right person, you especially could make this problem go away very quickly. Please imagine that this was your own mother when you consider how best to handle this.

Thanks to all of you for your prompt consideration of this matter.

Yours,

Ron Lieber

Accompanies Exercise 18

Collaboration Exercises

19 Planning a virtual team meeting

Imagine that you are working on a team with members in the United States, Singapore, and the Netherlands. You need to check in with each other at least once a week to address issues and plan for the upcoming week. This requires that you decide on a technology for your weekly discussions. You are considering the following options:

- Email
- Wiki

- Internet chat
- Teleconferences (for example, using Skype)
- Videoconferences (for example, using WebEx)

Use your favorite search engine to learn more about these technologies. If you have five members in your team, assign one technology to each team member. Then collaborate to create a chart that analyzes the pros and cons of each option. As a team, determine which technology (or technologies) you would choose and explain why. Be prepared to discuss your chart in class or submit it according to your instructor's directions.

20 Increasing cultural sensitivity

Divide into teams of three to five students—or work as a whole class. Select at least three cultures not represented by anyone on your team. When you identify cultures, do not limit yourself to thinking about different countries of origin. Also consider the following variables:

- Region of the country (for example, the South or the Northeast in the United States)
- Ethnicity
- Age (for example, people in their teens, 20s, 30s, 40s, and so on)

- Gender
- Disability

For each of the cultures you have identified, list two or three "communication characteristics"—things to keep in mind when communicating with people of that culture. Illustrate each with a concrete example.

Prepare a class presentation of your findings. If the findings of different teams conflict, have a class discussion about why the teams drew different conclusions about a particular culture.

21 Analyzing online privacy policies

Work with two to four other students to obtain online privacy policies from three organizations—businesses, government agencies, not-for-profit organizations. Working individually, read the policies carefully, paying special attention to the parts of each policy that discuss how the end user's personal information will or will not be used. Select two or three sentences from each policy that you think are not clear. Working as a team, compare and contrast the individual examples. Identify what the examples have in common and discuss as a group how they could mislead readers. Summarize your findings for your instructor in a collaboratively drafted email.

Social Media Exercises

22 Analyzing business Facebook pages

Imagine that you work for a local restaurant in a small city. The owner of the restaurant would like to begin using social media—especially a Facebook page—to publicize the restaurant and attract customers. She has asked you to find two restaurant Facebook pages that you believe are effective and to summarize the key features you believe make the pages effective. Depending on your instructor's preferences, write a brief report or prepare a brief presentation analyzing the two pages.

23 Identifying how for-profit and not-for-profit organizations use Twitter

Go to Twitter.com and search for one for-profit company you like and one not-for-profit organization whose cause you support. Both must have Twitter accounts. Select at least three tweets produced by each organization. Identify the purpose of each tweet and then write a brief summary (fewer than 100 words) analyzing how each organization uses Twitter to communicate.

Speaking Exercises

24 Informal impromptu presentations

a. Describe a time when you were very successful at achieving a specific communication goal, such as persuading someone to do something. Identify at least one reason for your success.

b. Describe a time when you wanted to achieve a specific goal with communication but were unsuccessful. Identify at least one reason why you were not successful.

c. Based on your experience, give your classmates one or two tips about collaborating successfully with a teammate.

d. Do you think you are better at writing or at speaking? Provide examples to support your answer.

e. Think of a time when you have communicated with people from a different culture. What was your biggest challenge?

25 Executive briefings

a. **Are they thinking like business communicators?** Find an "official email" that you have received from an organization you

do business with—for example, from a retail store or your school, employer, bank, or insurance company. Analyze the message to determine whether the writers were thinking like effective business communicators, as described in this chapter. Identify two features of the email that you can discuss; both features can be effective, both can be ineffective, or you can discuss one example of each.

b. **Analyzing cultures.** Select a country that you have visited or would like to visit in the future and conduct a web or library search about communication in that country. (Be sure your sources are authoritative. Do not use Wikipedia.) Make two or three recommendations about communication for colleagues who will be traveling to that country.

c. **Analyzing professionalism.** Imagine that you are a small business owner and need to purchase a product or service (for example, executive coaching). Find two competitive websites that offer what you've chosen. Imagine that you were going to choose a vendor based on the professionalism of the website. Prepare a brief presentation about which site inspires more confidence and explain why.

CHAPTER 1

Grammar Exercises

26 Nouns and pronouns (see Appendix C—Section 1.1.1)

Type the following two paragraphs, correcting the errors in use or formation of nouns and pronouns. Underline all your corrections.

Whomever answers the phone may be the only contact a caller has with a business. Everyone has their own personal preferences. However, find out how your employer wants the telephone answered, what your expected to say. When you pick up the phone, it's important to speak politely and provide identifying information. Clearly state the company's name and you're name. Should you identify the Department, too?

These are the kinds of question's to settle before the phone rings. If the caller asks for you by name, say, "This is me." Don't leave the caller wondering who he or she has reached. Remember that when on the telephone at work, you are the Company.

MyLab Business Communication

Go to **www.pearson.com/mylab/business-communication** for Auto-graded writing questions as well as the following Assisted-graded writing questions:

1. What benefits do companies receive from communicating using social media?

2. In audience-oriented writing, you can make key ideas easy to find by using headings. How can you make important ideas stand out in a voice mail message?

References

1. Bixler, S., & Duggan, L. S. (2001). *5 steps to professional presence: How to project competence, confidence, and credibility at work.* Avon, MA: Adams Media Corporation.

2. Goudreau, J. (2012, October 29). Do you have "executive presence"? *Forbes.* Retrieved from http://www.forbes.com/sites/jennagoudreau/2012/10/29/do-you-have-executive-presence/

3. Cuddy, A. (2015). *Presence* (p. 24). New York, NY: Little, Brown and Company.

4. Shannon, C., & Weaver, W. (1949). *The mathematical theory of communication.* Urbana, IL: University of Illinois Press.

5. Schramm, W. (1997). *The beginnings of communication study in America.* Thousand Oaks, CA: Sage Publishing.

6. Barnlund, D. (1970). A transactional model of communication. In K. K. Sereno & C. D. Mortensen (Eds.), *Foundations of communication theory* (pp. 83–102). New York, NY: Harper & Row.

7. Frey, C. B., & Osborne, M. A. (2013). The future of employment: How susceptible are jobs to computerization? [Working paper]. Retrieved from http://www.oxfordmartin.ox.ac.uk/downloads/academic/future-of-employment.pdf

8. Deming, D. J. (2015, August).The growing importance of social skills in the labor market. [Working paper]. Retrieved from http://www.nber.org/papers/w21473

9. National Association of Colleges and Employers. (2015). Job outlook 2016. Retrieved from http://www.naceweb.org/surveys/job-outlook.aspx

10. Graduate Management Admissions Council. (2017). Corporate recruiters survey report 2017. Retrieved from http://www.gmac.com/market-intelligence-and-research/research-library/employment-outlook/2017-corporate-recruiters-survey-report.aspx. Also Graduate Management Admissions Council. (2016). 2016 alumni perspectives survey report. Retrieved from http://www.gmac.com/~/media/Files/gmac/Research/Measuring-Program-ROI/2016-alumni-perspectives-web.pdf

11. Smith, J. (2016, April 29). I interviewed over 100 people at Goldman Sachs, and this was the one trait I looked for in every job candidate. *Business Insider.* Retrieved from http://www.businessinsider.com/ex-goldman-sachs-interviewer-one-trait-she-looked-for-in-every-job-candidate-2016-4

12. Hurlbert, M. (2014, April 11). Voices across the skills gap: Recruiters and students at a college career fair. Retrieved from http://www.skilledup.com/blog/voices-across-skills-gap-recruiters-and-students-at-career-fair/

13. Vasel, K. B. (2014, January 30). The skills employers wish college grads had. Retrieved from http://www.foxbusiness.com/personal-finance/2014/01/30/skills-employers-wish-college-grads-had/

14. Payscale Human Capital. (2016, May). 2016 workforce skills preparedness report. Retrieved from http://www.payscale.com/data-packages/job-skills

15. Levy, F., & Cannon, C. (2016, February 9). The Bloomberg job skills report 2016: What recruiters want. Retrieved from http://www.bloomberg.com/graphics/2016-job-skills-report/

16. Hart Research Associates. (2015). Falling short? College learning and career success. Retrieved from https://aacu.org/leap/public-opinion-research/2015-survey-results

17. Business and Legal Resources. (2014). Communication skills rank tops in developing individual contributors says new survey. Retrieved from http://hr.blr.com/HR-news/HR-Administration/Communication/Communication-skills-rank-tops-in-developing-indiv#

18. Hackos, J., & Winstead, J. (1995). Finding out what users need and giving it to them: A case study at Federal Express. *Technical Communication, 42*(2), 322–327.

19. Washington sees results from plain talk initiative. (2006, December 10). *USA Today.* Retrieved from http://www.usatoday.com/news/nation/2006-12-10-washington-plain-talk_x.htm

20. Kimble, J. (2014). *Writing for dollars, writing to please: The case for plain language in business, government, and law*. Durham, NC: Carolina Academic Press.

21. Jain, V. (2016, March 17). Cruise: From a cold email to a $1B+ exit. Retrieved from http://www.linkedin.com/pulse/cruise-from-cold-email-1b-exit-varun-jain?trk=v-feed

22. Towers Watson. (2013). *How the fundamentals have evolved and the best adapt: 2013/2014 Change and Communication ROI Study report*. Summary retrieved from http://www.towerswatson.com/en-US/Insights/IC-Types/Survey-Research-Results/2013/12/2013-2014-change-and-communication-roi-study

23. Marketing Profs Research. (2009). *The state of social media marketing*. Los Angeles: Marketing Profs LLC. Cited in Harte, B. (2009, December 10). Introducing "The State of Social Media Marketing" report. [Web log message]. Retrieved from http://www.mpdailyfix.com/introducing-the-state-of-social-media-marketing-report/

24. Mitchelmore, S., & Rowley, J. (2010). Entrepreneurial competencies: A literature review and development agenda. *International Journal of Entrepreneurial Behavior & Research, 16*(2), 92.

25. Deming, D. J. (2015, August).The growing importance of social skills in the labor market. [Working paper]. Retrieved from http://www.nber.org/papers/w21473

26. Bryant, A. (2010, March 12). Three good hires? He'll pay more for one who's great. The *New York Times*. Retrieved from http://www.nytimes.com/2010/03/14/business/14corners.html?scp=1&sq=tindell&st=cse

27. See Janusik, L. A., & Wolvin, A. D. (2009). 24 hours in a day: A listening update to the time studies. *International Journal of Listening, 23*(2), 104–120. See also Flynn, J., Valikoski, T., & Grau, J. (2008). Listening in the business context: Reviewing the state of research. *International Journal of Listening, 22*(2), 141–151.

28. Zenger, J., & Folker, J. (2016, July 14). What great listeners actually do. *Harvard Business Review*. Retrieved from https://hbr.org/2016/07/what-great-listeners-actually-do?

29. Vasel, K. B. (2014, January 30). The skills employers wish college grads had. Retrieved from http://www.foxbusiness.com/personal-finance/2014/01/30/skills-employers-wish-college-grads-had/

30. Hart Research Associates. (2015). Falling short? College learning and career success. Retrieved from https://aacu.org/leap/public-opinion-research/2015-survey-results

31. Wattles, J. (2015, September 20). Volkswagen CEO sorry for "broken trust." *CNN*. Retrieved from http://money.cnn.com/2015/09/20/autos/volkswagen-ceo-apology/

32. Lorenzetti, L. (2015, December 16). Chipotle's founder just issued another very public apology. *Fortune*. Retrieved from http://fortune.com/2015/12/16/chipotle-ad-apology-safety/

33. Smith, A. (2015, July 2). Whole Foods CEOs admit to overcharging, apologize. *CNN*. Retrieved from http://money.cnn.com/2015/07/02/news/companies/whole-foods-overcharge-apology/

34. Greenberg, W. (2015, July 2). Whole Foods admits overcharging, blames employees and apologizes. *The Washington Post*. Retrieved from https://www.washingtonpost.com/news/morning-mix/wp/2015/07/02/whole-foods-admits-over-charging-blames-employees-and-apologizes/

35. Gregorcyk, J. (2015, Dec 21). Chipotle's response to *E.coli* woes. Retrieved from https://www.hahnpublic.com/blog/chipotles-response-to-e-coli-woes/

36. Ethics Resource Center. (2012). 2011 national business ethics survey. Retrieved from http://www.ethics.org/files/u5/Final-NBES-web.pdf

37. Gerstner, L. (2002). *Who says elephants can't dance? Leading a great enterprise through dramatic change*. New York: HarperCollins Publishers, Inc.

38. van Rijn, J. (2016). The ultimate mobile email stats overview. Retrieved from http://www.emailmonday.com/mobile-email-usage-statistics

39. Stelzner, M. (2016). 2016 social media marketing industry report. *Social Media Examiner*. Retrieved from http://www.socialmediaexaminer.com/social-media-marketing-industry-report-2016/

40. Akhtar, O. (2014, January 9). How IKEA got customers in Norway to recreate its entire print catalog on Instagram. *The Hub*. Retrieved from http://www.thehubcomms.com/news/how-ikea-got-customers-in-norway-to-recreate-its-entire-print-catalog-on-instagram/article/328963/

41. White, S. K. (2016, May 23). Recruiters increasingly rely on social media to find talent. *CIO*. Retrieved from http://www.cio.com/article/3073589/hiring/recruiters-increasingly-rely-on-social-media-to-find-talent.html

42. Shareen, P. (2015, July 28). Lenovo created an internal social network to improve employee engagement. Retrieved from http://digiday.com/brands/lenovo-created-internal-social-network-improve-employee-engagement/

43. Julig, L. (2014, October 21). Four ways to turn your employees into brand ambassadors. *Social Media Examiner*. Retrieved from http://www.socialmediaexaminer.com/turn-employees-brand-ambassadors/

44. Meister, J. (2013, April 18). Want to be a more productive employee? Get on social networks. *Forbes*. Retrieved from http://www.forbes.com/sites/jeannemeister/2013/04/18/want-to-be-a-more-productive-employee-get-on-social-networks/

45. Schwabel, D. (2014, September 2). Gen Y and Gen Z global workplace expectations study. Retrieved from http://millennialbranding.com/2014/geny-genz-global-workplace-expectations-study/

46. Spencer-Oatley, H. (2007). Rapport in an international business meeting: A case study. [Online forum comment]. Retrieved from http://dialogin.com/index.php?id=58&tx_mmforum_pi1[action]=list_post&tx_mmforum_pi1[tid]=54&tx_mmforum_pi1[page]=1&tx_mmforum_pi1[sword]=international%20business%20meetings#pid275

47. For insight into China's younger workforce, see Lynton, N., & Thøgersen, K. H. (2010, January 25). Reckoning with Chinese Gen Y. *Bloomberg Businessweek*. Retrieved from www.businessweek.com/print/globalbiz/content/jan2010/gb20100125_065225.htm. See also Lynton, N., & Thøgersen, K. H. (2010, February 16). Working with China's Generation Y. *Bloomberg Businessweek*. Retrieved from www.businessweek.com/print/globalbiz/content/feb2010/gb20100216_566561.htm

48. Lieber, R. (2017, May 5). The best consumer self-advocacy tool you've never used. *The New York Times*. Retrieved from https://www.nytimes.com/2017/05/05/your-money/the-best-consumer-self-advocacy-tool-youve-never-used.html

49. Lieber, R. (2016, July 26). Dangerous conditions and your unwillingness to fix them. [Published email]. Retrieved from https://assets.documentcloud.org/documents/3700320/LieberGmail.pdf

2

Working with Others

Interpersonal, Intercultural, and Team Communication

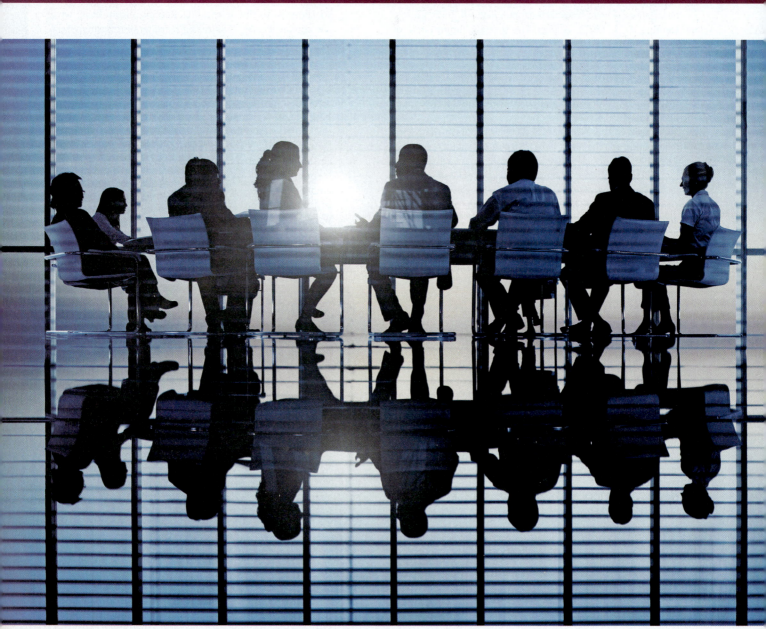

Rawpixel/Shutterstock

STUDY QUESTIONS

SQ1 **What listening skills will help you communicate better with others?**
pages 36–42

Hearing accurately
Comprehending and interpreting
Evaluating
Responding

SQ2 **How can you help others be good listeners when you speak?** pages 42–45

Focus on your audience
Share the conversation
Use clear, concrete, unambiguous language
Support your message with good nonverbal communication
Avoid language that triggers a negative response
Frame negative comments positively

SQ3 **How can you manage interpersonal conflict?** pages 45–52

Identify the cause of the conflict
Select an appropriate management technique

SQ4 **How can you improve your communication with people from different cultures?** pages 52–56

Understand how cultures differ
Develop strategies that help you communicate with diverse groups

SQ5 **How can you work effectively as part of a team?** pages 56–63

Assemble an effective team
Agree on team goals and standards
Pay attention to team development and dynamics
Develop good leadership practices
Plan for effective meetings
Be a good team member

New Hires @ Work

Shannon Rocheleau
Western Michigan University

Business Services Credit Specialist @ Consumers Credit Union

When I worked as a member services representative in the Credit Union call center, I learned how to listen carefully and match my communication style with the person to whom I was talking. If callers get to the point immediately, I provided information promptly. If they began by chatting, I chatted, too. And if callers seemed to need a lot of support, I knew not to apply pressure. Instead, I gave them time to decide and then provided reassurance when they made a decision. Great member service involves understanding your audience.

Photo courtesy of Shannon Rocheleau

Chapter 2 | Introduction

Unless you work completely by yourself, your success on the job depends on working well—and communicating well—with others. These people can include coworkers and teammates, supervisors and managers, vendors and service providers, and customers and clients. This ongoing process of interacting with others, exchanging information and meaning, and achieving understanding is called **interpersonal communication**. People who are good at it typically have what experts call **emotional intelligence**—the ability to perceive and understand emotions and to use that knowledge to guide their own behavior and respond to others.[1] Research by experts such as psychologist Daniel Goleman has shown that emotional intelligence is as necessary to good leadership and effective teamwork as are more traditionally valued skills and capacities.[2]

Many businesses are concerned that as the world becomes more digital, people spend less time developing their emotional intelligence and interpersonal communication abilities and, as a result, feel more comfortable emailing and texting than talking with others in "real-time" conversations and discussions.[3] While no one disputes the value of digital communication, it cannot replace conversations that encourage people to understand each other's point of view more deeply. In a face-to-face conversation, you have the opportunity to listen actively and pay attention to tone, facial expression, and body language—all of which are critical aspects of emotional intelligence. Research shows that this kind of **synchronous communication**—where all the communicators are present at the same time—will help you build trust and forge the positive and productive working relationships that are critical to business.[4]

This chapter will help you strengthen your interpersonal communication skills, develop your emotional intelligence, and improve your ability to work well with others. First, the chapter addresses how to be an effective listener and speaker. Then, it helps you apply your listening and speaking skills in three challenging contexts that arise when you work with others: managing conflict, communicating with people from diverse cultures and generations, and communicating in teams.

What listening skills will help you communicate better with others?

interpersonal communication The ongoing process of interacting with others and exchanging information and meaning to achieve understanding.

emotional intelligence The ability to perceive and understand emotions and to use that knowledge to guide your own behavior and respond to others.

synchronous communication Communication in which all communicators are present at the same time; face-to-face conversations, telephone conversations, and meetings are examples of synchronous communication.

Every day, without thinking about it, you engage in an important communication skill—listening. In fact, research shows that college students spend more than half their communication time listening.[5,6] In the workplace, listening is widely considered to be one of the most important communication skills,[7] and it is easy to understand why. When you are listening—unlike when you are speaking—you are learning, and the more you learn, the better able you will be to do your job. In addition, listening is a key element of emotional intelligence. Only when you listen deeply to others (rather than interrupting or thinking about what you're going to say next) can you accurately assess the emotional significance of a message. This understanding will help you respond in a way that shows others that you understand and care.

Most people assume that they are good listeners because they have listened throughout their entire lives. Yet decades of research show that listening is a complex process. Without good listening skills, people often mishear, misinterpret, misunderstand, and misremember.[8] One common problem is **passive listening**—hearing what someone says without actively paying attention to ensure understanding. In business, passive listening leads to costly mistakes, unhappy employees, and customer complaints. Here are a few examples:

passive listening Hearing what someone says without actively paying attention to ensure understanding.

- An employee does not pay close attention to a customer providing a mailing address and then sends a shipment of 1,000 computers to Springfield, Massachusetts, rather than Springfield, Illinois. The shipping and return charges are extremely high, and the customer is angry because the computers arrive late.
- A manager does not listen carefully—or ask good follow-up questions—when an employee says she is sick and needs to go home. The manager insists that the employee stay, which exposes the entire office to a contagious flu.
- The social media team does not pay attention to customer complaints on Twitter and product review sites, and negative product reviews spread throughout the social network.

People rarely become better listeners on their own. However, with study and training, you can become an active listener and significantly improve your communication skills. This section will help you master each of the steps necessary for **active listening**,[9] which are illustrated in **Figure 2.1**. The process begins with hearing accurately by focusing attentively on what a speaker says. Additional steps include actively working to interpret and evaluate the content, and then responding to acknowledge understanding.

active listening A learned skill that requires you to attentively focus on the speaker's communication, interpret the meaning of the content, and respond with feedback to ensure understanding.

FIGURE 2.1 The Active Listening Process

Hearing accurately

Listening typically starts with hearing: perceiving sounds and focusing on them. Because sounds are all around us, listening requires that you first distinguish the sounds you need and want to listen to and then concentrate on fully hearing those sounds.

Some barriers to hearing are physical. For example, the environment may distract you. Think about the last time you tried to have a conversation in a noisy restaurant or talk on your cell phone while standing at a busy intersection. You probably found it difficult to concentrate on what the other person was saying. At work, you may be distracted by ringing telephones, people passing by your desk, or noise from the next office.

Other barriers to hearing are physiological. For example, you might have a temporary hearing problem, such as blocked ears due to a head cold. One significant physiological barrier to hearing is the speed at which your brain can process what you hear. Most people can process information twice as fast as the average person speaks. While you are waiting to process more information, your brain is not fully engaged, and you may begin to think of other things rather than actively listen and focus on the words you hear. Similarly, if you choose to multitask while listening, your brain becomes engaged in a different task, and you don't accurately hear what the speaker says. Research shows that true *multitasking* is almost impossible. What actually happens is task-switching, and as your brain quickly switches from task to task, your cognitive functions slow down, and you perform poorly on both tasks.[10] Research also shows that the people who believe they are the best multitaskers are often the worst.[11]

The key to hearing accurately is focus. Eliminate as many distractions as possible. Look at the speaker and concentrate on what he or she says. Ask the speaker to repeat if you think you have missed something important. Make a comment or ask a question to keep yourself engaged. A benefit of this approach is that you earn the respect of the speaker by being attentive.

Comprehending and interpreting

comprehension How well you understand what you hear or read.

You might very clearly hear someone speaking in Portuguese, Dutch, or Arabic, but you probably can't comprehend all those languages. Listening **comprehension** refers to how well you understand what you hear. In culturally diverse workplaces, language differences—including accents—can become significant barriers, but they are not the only obstacles to comprehension. You may have difficulty comprehending vocabulary or **jargon** that is unfamiliar to you. For example, imagine that you accompany a sick friend to a medical appointment. You hear the physician tell an assistant: *"The patient presented with acute febrile illness."* Unless you have medical training, you probably won't comprehend that this means your friend suddenly got a high fever. You may also have difficulty comprehending something that is explained badly, is confusing, or is contradictory.

jargon The specialized language of a specific field.

interpretation Analyzing the meaning of what you hear, read, or see to determine its intention.

Interpretation is different from comprehension. **Interpretation** involves analyzing the meaning of what you hear, read, or see in order to determine its intention. You might misunderstand a comment because you interpret it from a different frame of reference. For example, imagine you work in your company's Los Angeles office and your colleague is meeting with clients in Boston. Late in the evening, you receive an email from your colleague, saying he needs information for a client meeting, and he'd like you to email it to him first thing in the morning. You could interpret that statement in two different ways. Does he want the information by 9 AM in Boston (Eastern time) or by 9 AM in Los Angeles (Pacific time)? If you interpret the statement from your frame of reference—Pacific time—you may be sending the summary too late (noon Eastern time).

Understanding what someone really means also requires being empathetic and paying attention to feelings. Being an empathetic listener does not come naturally to everyone. Both research and experience show that there is a wide range of individual differences.[12,13] Some people tend to pay attention to the literal content of communication. Others are skilled at focusing on the emotional content. Consider this scenario: Ron rushes late into a meeting with Dan and Erica. Dan asks Ron if everything is okay. Ron looks distracted and tense but says, "I'm okay." After Ron leaves the meeting room, Erica comments that Ron seemed very upset when he arrived. Dan responds, "There's no problem. He said he's okay." Dan focused on the content of the words, and Erica focused on the emotions that accompanied the words.

Even if you are not naturally empathetic, you can train yourself to comprehend and interpret more effectively in three ways:[14]

- "Listen" to nonverbal communication
- Ask questions and paraphrase to ensure understanding
- Be aware of gender-specific communication styles

"Listen" to nonverbal communication

nonverbal communication Messages conveyed through means other than words, such as tone of voice, facial expressions, gestures, and body language.

Nonverbal communication refers to messages that are conveyed through something other than words—for example, tone of voice, facial expression, gestures, body language, or other behavior. These forms of nonverbal communication can help you better understand the nuances of a message and its emotional content:

- **Emphasis and tone of voice.** Words carry different meanings depending on how they are said. Imagine someone speaking the simple phrase "I called him." Say that phrase three times, each time emphasizing a different word: "*I* called him"—"I *called* him"—"I called *him*." What three different meanings do those three statements convey? Now imagine saying those three words in an angry tone of voice and a happy tone of voice. Each time, you will be conveying a different meaning. As a good listener, you will benefit from paying close attention to tone of voice and letting it influence your interpretation of what you hear.

- **Facial expression.** If someone says "hello" with a smile, you will interpret a very different meaning than if someone says "hello" with lowered eyebrows and a clenched jaw. While experts may disagree about whether facial expression is an unconscious reflection of emotion or a conscious technique that people use to convey meaning, most people agree that facial expression is an important element of communication. Beware, though, of assuming that all people interpret facial expressions in the same way. As you will read in the Culture feature (page 40), biologists have determined that facial expressions are not universal across all cultures.[15]

- **Body language, posture, and gestures.** You can uncover clues about a person's attitude toward what he or she is saying by observing body language. Is that person ashamed, proud, or uncertain? The speaker's posture—and even eye contact or lack of it—can help you interpret that attitude. In fact, you can often interpret attitude from body language without listening to any words.

  Remember, though, that body language and gestures may be ambiguous. As **Figure 2.2** illustrates, gestures can mean different things in different contexts. Accurate interpretation requires analyzing gestures and facial expressions together.

  In addition, gestures must be interpreted within the context of culture. In Japan, it is a sign of respect to avoid eye contact and look down when an older or more powerful person is talking to you. In the United States, looking away when someone is talking is often interpreted as a sign of disrespect or guilt. Before reaching a conclusion about what nonverbal communication means, consider alternative meanings.

- **Behavior.** Observing behavior can also help you interpret meaning, especially if the behavior is inconsistent with a spoken statement. For example, imagine that you work in a clothing store. A customer complains that the zipper on a jacket is broken and asks you to find a duplicate with a functioning zipper. As you observe the customer struggle with the zipper, you realize that this particular zipper is not broken but instead requires more fine motor control than the customer has. Rather than search for a duplicate item, you might respond, "Some people have a hard time with this zipper because it is so small and hard to grip. Can I help you find a jacket with a larger zipper?" In this case, observing behavior provides more information than listening to language.

FIGURE 2.2 How to Interpret Nonverbal Signals in Context

Image A

Image B

NONVERBAL SIGNAL	MEANING COMMUNICATED IN IMAGE A	MEANING COMMUNICATED IN IMAGE B
Leaning forward	Openness	Hostility
Eye contact	Friendliness	Anger
Extended hands	Welcome	Accusation, frustration
Chin forward	Greeting, openness	Irritation

CULTURE
FACIAL EXPRESSIONS ARE NOT UNIVERSAL

Not all cultures around the world interpret facial expressions the same way.[16] In fact, research suggests that people from East Asia (for example, China, Japan, and Korea) focus mainly on the eyes when they are reading facial expressions. By contrast, people from the West (for example, the United States, Germany, and Mexico) focus on the entire face, including both the eyes and the mouth.[17]

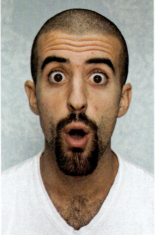

William Perugini/Shutterstock

As a result of this difference in perception, people from East Asia sometimes confuse surprise, shock, fear, and anger because these emotions are difficult to extract from the eyes alone. As the figure to the left illustrates, key differences in these emotions are reflected by the mouth.

The East Asian focus on the eyes is also reflected in their *emoticons*—the series of characters used to represent facial expressions in emails and texts. As the following table illustrates, in American emoticons, the face is represented on its side, and differences of emotion are represented by the mouth. In East Asian emoticons, the face is right-side up, and differences in emotion are expressed by the eyes.[18]

How Emoticons Differ Between Eastern and Western Cultures

EMOTION	WEST	EAST
Surprise	:-0	o.o
Sad	:-(	(;_;)

For a CULTURE exercise, go to Exercise 30 on page 74.

Ask questions and paraphrase to ensure understanding

In addition to "listening" to nonverbal behavior, you can improve comprehension and understanding by asking questions and by paraphrasing. Questions are straightforward. You can ask someone to repeat what he or she is saying, or you can offer two alternative meanings and ask which is correct. For example, you can ask your colleague, "By 'first thing in the morning,' do you mean 9 AM Boston time or when I get in to work in the morning in Los Angeles?"

paraphrasing Restating someone's point in different words to ensure that you completely understand.

Paraphrasing is a little more complicated than asking for clarification. Paraphrasing involves restating what you hear in different words to ensure that you completely understand. Because meaning has multiple dimensions, you might paraphrase in multiple ways to capture those dimensions. As **Figure 2.3** illustrates, you can paraphrase to ensure that you understand the literal content, the ultimate intention, and the emotional content—or feeling—behind the speaker's statement.

FIGURE 2.3 How to Paraphrase for Content, Intent, and Feeling

Comment from the supervisor:
"I'd like all employees to take at least half of their vacation days by November 1."

CONTENT	INTENT	FEELING
Restate the message in different words to ensure you understand it.	Dig beneath the content to understand the reason for the statement.	Confirm your understanding of the speaker's emotions.
"So you are saying that you want us to use our vacation days before the end of the year."	"Are you concerned that too many people will want to take vacations in December?" "Are you concerned that people are working too hard and need a break?"	"You sound frustrated that people seem to be saving their vacation time and burning out on the job."

Be aware of gender-specific communication styles

Men and women are often socialized to behave differently from each other and may develop different gender-related styles of communication.[19] Neither style is better than the other. However, communication can break down if people are intolerant of other speaking styles or draw incorrect judgments about a speaker based on his or her style.

As sociolinguist Deborah Tannen points out, men are often socialized to value autonomy and independence and therefore learn to communicate in ways that assert independence, power, and their place in the social hierarchy.[20] For example, in conversations, men tend to interrupt more than women do. In contrast to men, women are often socialized to value connections with other people and to communicate in ways that preserve equity and relationships.[21] Therefore, women tend to wait their turn to speak as an act of respect to the speaker. In addition, women more often minimize the assertiveness of what they say by using what linguists call *hedges*, *hesitations*, and *tag questions*:[22]

Hedge	I don't know if this is a good idea, but we could get an editor for our presentation slides.
Hesitation	Um, well, we could, uh, we could get an editor for our presentation slides.
Tag question	We can get an editor, can't we?

Gender-specific characteristics may have negative results in conversation. Interruptions can easily lead to communication breakdowns, especially when men interrupt women. Males are often very comfortable with both interrupting others and being interrupted, whereas women are more likely to get angry or feel silenced. Tag questions, hesitations, and hedges also cause problems. They lead some listeners to conclude that the speaker lacks confidence and does not deserve to be taken seriously.[23] However, by recognizing gendered characteristics of your own and others' language, you can avoid drawing incorrect conclusions about others and instead pay more attention to their ideas.

Evaluating

Once you fully understand what someone says, you can evaluate. **Evaluating** is the practice of critically reviewing and judging what you hear. Is it accurate, well supported, and convincing? As a listener, you may find it difficult to reach a fair evaluation. Think of all the things that can block your ability to evaluate fairly. First, you may prejudge a speaker, especially if you find that speaker to be annoying or distracting. Second, you may prejudge an idea, especially if it is an idea you have already considered and dismissed. If you don't listen carefully to the speaker's rationale or explanation, you lose the opportunity to reconsider your previous evaluation. Third, you may jump to conclusions based on the beginning of a message and interrupt the speaker or tune out while you wait your turn to speak.

Making good business decisions depends on your ability to evaluate as you listen. For example, imagine that you own a children's clothing store. In a meeting with your employees, the assistant manager suggests that you open another store in an up-and-coming neighborhood on the west side of the city. For support, she points to the growing population in the neighborhood and the fact that the three new stores that opened in that neighborhood are doing very well.

Evaluating that proposal fairly requires that you remain open-minded. Even if you live far away from the west side of the city and would prefer a closer location, you need to consider the business arguments. Evaluating fairly also requires that you critically analyze what you hear. Does the success of other new stores necessarily mean that a children's clothing store will succeed? To evaluate that opinion, you would need to know how many children live in the area and what competition exists.

Finally, evaluating fairly requires that you separate emotions from logic. Your assistant manager may try to convince you that a store in that neighborhood will be a path to wealth

evaluating The process of critically reviewing your communication to ensure that it is complete, clear, concise, easy to understand, and error free.

and prestige because the neighborhood is so desirable. These emotional appeals may be strong enough to make you want a store in that neighborhood, even if the rent is extremely expensive and the children's clothing market in the neighborhood is not big enough to ensure a profit.

Responding

Responding has two roles in the listening process: It lets the speaker know that you understand the point, and it initiates the next step in the conversation. Some responses quickly stop any further exchange; others move the discussion forward. For example, a response such as "That's a ridiculous idea" may discourage someone's further input. By contrast, a more tactful response would encourage the speaker: "That's interesting. How would that work?"

Responses can be verbal and nonverbal. On some occasions, the nonverbal messages communicate more information than the verbal ones. Imagine that a coworker says, "I need some advice about how to describe our new product." You verbally respond, "Okay." But what is your nonverbal message? Did you make eye contact with your colleague and smile as you said "Okay"? Did you gesture for her to take a seat? Or did you keep your eyes on your computer, sigh deeply, and tense your body? Whichever approach you take, your colleague will interpret your response based on your nonverbal message. In other words, *how* you say something is often taken more seriously than *what* you say.

To become a more effective responder, pay attention to the type of response you offer. As **Figure 2.4** illustrates, you can respond to a speaker in many different ways. For example, you can ask a question, give your opinion or advice, disagree, or express empathy.

FIGURE 2.4 How to Respond in Different Ways

SPEAKER: *"The auditors are coming tomorrow to look at our books. We're not ready. I don't know what to do."*

YOUR RESPONSE OPTIONS	
Ask a Question	What do we need to do to get ready? How long do you think it will take?
Give an Opinion	I think if you have most of the documents they will need tomorrow, they can get a good start.
Give Advice	Let's try to reschedule the audit until next week.
Argue/Disagree	Actually, I think we are ready. We have completed everything on the checklist.
Express Empathy	It's nerve-wracking to get everything ready for a major audit. You're doing fine, and I'll be glad to help.

This set of active listening skills—hearing, comprehending and interpreting, evaluating, and responding—will help you put your emotional intelligence to work and thereby increase opportunities for successful collaboration. As one organizational leader explains, "If people feel they were listened to, that their views were taken into account, that they had a chance to show you the world from their point of view, they're going to be much more likely to go along with a decision."[24] In addition, active listening can be self-directed. Remember that emotional intelligence includes recognizing your own emotions. Listening deeply to yourself and your own nonverbal signals (such as a knot in your stomach or a crack in your voice) can help you identify your emotional responses to workplace situations. Equipping yourself with knowledge of your own feelings is key to identifying what makes you most productive and engaged at work and to facilitating a work environment where others can also thrive.

How can you help others be good listeners when you speak?

Engaging your emotional intelligence is just as important in speaking as it is in listening. Think of listeners and speakers as partners in the communication process. Just as listeners need to work hard to understand meaning, speakers need to work hard to engage listeners and make meaning clear. This section provides six general speaking strategies that help listeners pay attention and interpret your meaning effectively:

- Focus on your audience.
- Share the conversation.
- Use clear, concrete, unambiguous language.
- Support your message with good nonverbal communication.
- Avoid language that triggers a negative response.
- Frame negative comments positively.

Focus on your audience

Many speakers fail to connect with the audience's interests or knowledge about a topic and, as a result, the audience tunes out. To avoid that problem, follow this advice:

DON'T . . .	DO . . .
Stay trapped in your own perspective and fail to connect with your audience's interests and knowledge.	Take time to analyze the following questions about your audience: • Why will they be interested in what you are saying? • What barriers will prevent them from listening carefully? • What questions or objections might they have? • What is the best way to connect with them?
For example . . . If you want a busy colleague to help you with a project, don't begin with details about the project and state the request at the end.	**For example . . .** To obtain your colleague's help, begin by explaining how your message relates to him or her. "I could really use your help on my current project. It requires the kind of database programming that you learned on your last project."

Share the conversation

Have you ever noticed how some speakers, once they have "the floor," continue talking for a long time and resist all attempts of other people to share the conversation? To encourage your audience to listen to your point, follow this advice:

DON'T . . .	DO . . .
Monopolize the conversation or talk for a long time without letting other participants speak.	Make your point concisely and invite your audience to respond.
For example . . . Don't say "Please let me finish" or "Don't interrupt me" when someone interrupts you before you finish. Doing that might give you more time to talk, but your audience won't be listening anymore.	**For example . . .** Finish by asking questions to move the conversation forward: "What do you think?" or "Has anyone else tried this approach in the past?"

Use clear, concrete, unambiguous language

When language can be interpreted multiple ways, your audience may arrive at a different meaning than you intended. To help your audience interpret correctly, follow this advice:

DON'T . . .	DO . . .
Use ambiguous language—that is, phrasing that may mean different things to different people. Pay particular attention to pronouns.	Make sure your language is specific and can be interpreted in only one way.
For example . . . The pronoun "they" is ambiguous in this statement: "I called the purchasing managers about the new vendors we want to use. **They** are too busy to meet with us for a few weeks." Does "they" refer to the purchasing managers or the vendors?	**For example . . .** Replace ambiguous pronouns with nouns: "I called the purchasing managers about the new vendors we want to use. **The managers** are too busy to meet with us for a few weeks."

Support your message with good nonverbal communication

Many studies on the role of nonverbal communication have found that a speaker's body language, facial expressions, gestures, and tone of voice carry more significance than the speaker's words.[25] To ensure that your nonverbal communication supports your message, follow this advice:

DON'T . . .	DO . . .
Turn your back to your audience or tense your face and body. Using a hesitant tone of voice or body language that conflicts with your message can also undermine your persuasiveness.	Face your audience and maintain eye contact. Keep your face and body language open and energetic, and speak in an enthusiastic tone of voice to help prime your audience to be receptive to your ideas.[26] Use nonverbal signals to reinforce your ideas and help listeners remember longer.[27] Mirroring the body language of your audience may also lead to a more positive response.[28]
For example . . . If you say you are confident, but you fidget or frown while you speak, your audience will not have confidence in your words.	**For example . . .** If you smile and maintain eye contact while you say you are confident, your audience will more likely believe you.

Avoid language that triggers a negative response

Just as your choice of language can encourage listeners to pay careful attention, it can also evoke negative emotional responses. If you make your audience defensive or angry, they may refuse to pay attention to your ideas.

DON'T . . .	DO . . .
• **Use biased language,** which suggests prejudice, prejudgment, or disrespect. For example, "Kevin, as our resident geek, tell us your opinion on whether we should upgrade our computer operating system."	• **Use neutral language** that is more respectful. For example, "Kevin, you're familiar with the pros and cons of the new operating system upgrade. Do you think we should implement it now or wait?"
• **Ask provocative questions,** which are designed to annoy and inflame. For example, "We have three days of bad data now. Why didn't you find the solution earlier?"	• **Ask authentic questions,** which are genuine requests for information and opinions. For example, "How did you figure out the problem?"

(continued)

DON'T . . .	DO . . .
• **Use accusatory language,** which focuses negatively on the person rather than the issue. Examples: 　▪ "Your instructions are confusing." 　▪ "This is the third time this month that you have been late."	• **Use positive language, or "I" language,** which focuses on your perception or response and does not assign blame. Examples: 　▪ "I got lost on step three of the instructions. Could you please explain further?" 　▪ "I am uncomfortable making excuses when people call for you. That's why I hope you can arrive on time." However, if you begin every sentence with "I," your audience will think you are egotistical.
• **Use trigger words and phrases** that make people feel dismissed, such as "That doesn't concern you." Other triggers include absolutes and exaggerations such as "always" and "never."[29] For example, "You never get to work on time."	• **Respect others' feelings.** Pay attention to people's emotional responses to identify trigger words so that you can find alternatives. For example, "I feel frustrated that we have started our morning meetings late for the past few days."

Frame negative comments positively

You may find that you need to offer constructive criticism to a coworker or an employee. If you phrase that criticism simply as a negative statement, your listener may become defensive or tune out. David C. Novak, president, chairman, and CEO of Yum! Brands—whose chains include KFC, Pizza Hut, Taco Bell, and Long John Silver's—offers two pieces of advice for giving feedback: Start out positively and avoid the word *but.*

> The best way to give feedback is to start out with, "This is what I appreciate about you." They might have great strategy, good vision, they're good at execution, or whatever you think they're really doing well. When you start out by talking to people about what they're doing well, that makes them very receptive for feedback because at least you're giving them credit for what they've done.
> Then I say, "And you can be even more effective if you do this." I think that really works.[30]

Novak recommends introducing constructive criticism with the word *and,* instead of *but,* to avoid undermining the good feelings generated by the opening statement.

(SQ3) How can you manage interpersonal conflict?

Even if you follow all of this chapter's advice about listening and speaking, conflict will inevitably arise when you work with others. Conflict can include differences in opinion, disagreements about how to handle issues, complaints about performance or fairness, criticism about the behavior of others, and personality conflicts between people who just do not get along.

Conflict is one of the most significant and costly problems in a workplace. A study by CPP, Inc., a company that specializes in conflict management, found that U.S. companies spend more than 2.8 hours per week addressing workplace conflict, which adds up to approximately \$359 billion in paid hours per year.[31] When companies do not effectively address conflict and workplace incivility, the negative emotions result in wasted time, loss of productivity, poor work performance, and decreased work effort, which are also costly to an organization.[32] They may also lead to people leaving their jobs. In fact, a study of exit interviews from people who voluntarily left jobs found that more than 50 percent of all resignations resulted from unresolved interpersonal conflict.[33] For every employee who leaves, a business needs to hire and train a new employee, which costs at least 1.5 times that employee's salary.[34]

Of course, not all workplace conflict is bad—in fact, conflict is often productive. Conflict can be divided into two broad categories: **cognitive conflict,** which results from differences in understanding content or tasks, and **affective conflict,** which results from differences in

cognitive conflict A conflict that results from differences in understanding content or tasks. Working through a cognitive conflict often leads to better decisions and work products.

affective conflict A conflict that results from differences in personalities and relationships. If affective conflicts remain unstated and unaddressed, they can lead to tension, stress, and dysfunctional work processes.

personalities and relationships. All high-performing work teams experience disagreements (cognitive conflict) while collaborating. Working through these disagreements can have positive results on the quality of team decisions and the final work product.[35] As teamwork expert Paul Glover points out, "If a team always agreed on everything, they'd be satisfied with the *first* answer to the problem instead of working, arguing, and debating to figure out the *best* answer."[36]

In fact, some organizations encourage active disagreement and clashes of opinion. For example, Southwest Airlines teaches managers how to spark conflict and debate among their staff in order to reach better decisions faster.[37] Similarly, at Bridgewater Associates, one of the world's biggest hedge funds, founder Ray Dalio encourages his employees to challenge one another's views. Dalio says, "I believe that the biggest problem humanity faces is ego sensitivity to finding out whether one is right or wrong and identifying what one's strengths and weaknesses are."[38] In an atmosphere where people know how to challenge others' ideas respectfully, people's sensitivity about their ego decreases, and their productivity increases.

However, problems arise if teams allow these cognitive conflicts to become affective conflicts. For example, two people working on a marketing plan may disagree about the best way to reach the company's target market. If they work through the cognitive conflict, listen carefully to each other's concerns, and achieve consensus, the result may be better than if they pursued only one idea without challenging it. But if the two people cannot reach agreement and leave the meeting in anger, this emotional conflict may damage the working relationship. Problems also arise if conflicts remain unstated and unaddressed, leading to tension, stress, and dysfunctional work processes.

Although people often use the term *conflict resolution* to discuss handling conflict, *conflict management* is a more helpful term. "Conflict resolution" implies that the conflict will go away. By contrast, "conflict management" recognizes that some conflicts cannot be resolved. The next section of the chapter offers a two-step process for managing conflict: First identify the cause of the conflict and then decide how to respond.

Identify the cause of the conflict

As **Figure 2.5** illustrates, cognitive and affective conflicts generally occur for a few well-defined reasons. Note in Figure 2.5 that the line between cognitive and affective conflicts is not definitive. In fact, it is sometimes difficult to know whether a conflict is cognitive or affective—for example, whether you truly object to that person's idea (cognitive) or you simply do not like that person (affective). However, analyzing the cause of a conflict is useful because different causes call for different conflict management strategies.

Competing goals

People who collaborate may not always be motivated to achieve the same goals. In fact, for a business to succeed, it must work toward a number of goals that are sometimes in competition with each other. A business strives to make a profit while planning for future growth, keeping employees and customers satisfied, and meeting governmental requirements for employee and consumer safety. Employees have their own goals, such as increasing their income, enhancing their reputation, gaining new customers, getting a promotion, or spending more quality time with family and friends.

FIGURE 2.5 Causes of Conflict

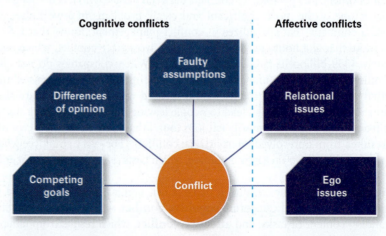

Conflicts routinely arise because people work with different goals in mind. Consider this scenario:

EXAMPLE	ANALYSIS
Marcus and Allison of Green Earth Landscapes are barely speaking to each other. This morning, Marcus promised one of the company's best customers, a large museum, that Green Earth could complete a major landscape installation by the end of October. Marcus's supervisor had told him that keeping this customer happy was a high priority because the museum was responsible for 30 percent of Green Earth's revenue last year. When Marcus approached Allison, who does the scheduling, Allison exploded: "We are 100 percent booked through the end of the year! We cannot take on any new projects, no matter who the client is. I received explicit instructions from the head of project management that we need to keep costs down. I'm not going to schedule any overtime. We'd lose money rather than make it. Why didn't you talk to me before you made a promise?"	**Marcus's goal:** To keep the customer happy. **Allison's goal:** To keep costs in line by eliminating overtime. **Conflict:** Allison thinks Marcus does what he wants without concern for the consequences. Marcus thinks Allison always argues with him and that she doesn't understand the big picture of how the company works. This example illustrates how easily competing goals—a cognitive conflict—can disintegrate into an affective conflict.

RESOLUTION

By recognizing that they each are trying to achieve different goals, they can discuss the issue with their supervisors to determine which goal has priority. At that point, they can agree to satisfy the most important goal or collaborate to find a solution that addresses both goals.

Differences of opinion

Even if people agree on a goal, they may have differences of opinion about how to achieve it. Consider this scenario:

EXAMPLE	ANALYSIS
Rotel Plumbing Supplies wants to become the premier plumbing distributor in the Southwest. What is the best way to accomplish this goal? Valerie argues that investing in marketing and customer relations is the key because Rotel needs more and bigger customers. Corrine argues that investing in distribution is the key. To be the premier distributor, Rotel needs to guarantee next-day delivery, which will require creating more distribution centers.	**Valerie's opinion:** Rotel should invest in marketing and customer relations. **Corrine's opinion:** Rotel should invest in distribution. **Conflict:** Even though Valerie and Corrine both want the same thing, they have different opinions about the right strategy. Differences of opinion also can easily lead to affective conflicts, especially if the differences result in a contest of wills.

RESOLUTION

By using a rational decision-making process, which involves evaluating the pros and cons of each strategy and may require some compromise for both parties, Valerie and Corrine can avoid escalating into an affective conflict.

Faulty assumptions

People often draw conclusions or make decisions based on faulty assumptions. They do not have all the information they need, and they jump to conclusions. Consider this scenario:

EXAMPLE	ANALYSIS
Janelle gave her sales team a schedule of dates to submit quarterly sales data. She told them she expected them to meet these dates. On the due date for the fourth-quarter data, Shawn realized that he could include a very large sale worth hundreds of thousands of dollars if he waited just a few days to submit his figures. He knew that Janelle, his supervisor, was interested in increased sales figures, so he decided to wait and surprise her with unexpectedly positive results. The next morning, Shawn arrived to work at 9 AM to find an angry email from Janelle: "Where are your sales figures? I was up all night preparing a presentation for management at 8 AM and didn't realize until 4 AM that you hadn't submitted your numbers. You knew they were due yesterday. I looked like a fool at the meeting."	**Shawn's assumption:** That Janelle cares more about an increase in reported sales than about his punctuality. **Janelle's assumptions:** That Shawn understands the importance of sending his reports on time this quarter. **Conflict:** Janelle did not consider that her staff might need to know she had scheduled an 8 AM presentation that required up-to-date data. From her perspective, she had already told them she expected them to deliver the figures on time. She assumed that they would follow instructions, and no further information was necessary. Shawn did not consider telling Janelle in advance the reason why he wanted to submit his sales numbers later. He assumed that a few days would not make a major difference.

RESOLUTION
By sharing more information with each other, Janelle and Shawn can avoid such conflicts. When Janelle sends the schedule of dates to her sales team, she can explain why she needs the sales figures by the specific date. More importantly, Shawn can ask Janelle for an extension on deadlines so he can include the increased sales numbers.

Relational issues

Sometimes people just don't get along well, and they don't work to overcome their differences. You may have heard the old adage "We like those most who are most like us." In a workplace context, this means that most of us prefer to work with people whose styles resemble our own. For example, if you are detail oriented, you most likely feel comfortable working with other detail-oriented people. If you like to make quick decisions, you enjoy working with other decisive people. You also might feel more comfortable working with people of your own generation, as they often have similar assumptions about how best to communicate and collaborate. Styles that differ from our own often create tension—they violate our comfort zones—and we may place a negative label on that behavior. We may also begin to treat the other person badly, which leads to conflict. A more productive perspective is to realize that different styles may complement each other and help a team achieve balance.

The following example illustrates how relational conflicts can stand in the way of productive discussions about content and substance:

EXAMPLE	ANALYSIS
At first, Derek was excited to work on a new project with his consulting company's biggest client because it would give him a chance to learn new skills and gain valuable exposure. However, from the first day of the project, he has been in conflict with his new teammate Ed. Ed interrupts him, argues against his ideas, and then tries to take credit for his ideas when they work. Sometimes Ed has a good idea of his own, but Derek has difficulty acknowledging it because he is so angry at Ed most of the time. Derek often finds himself arguing against an idea just because Ed brought it up.	**Derek's style:** Collaborative, prioritizing reflective and respectful discussion **Ed's style:** Antagonistic, prioritizing fast-paced disputes and debates **Conflict:** Different work styles and lack of understanding of each other's approaches. Personality conflicts such as this are costly to a business. A survey conducted by researchers at the University of North Carolina found that: • 53 percent of workers said they lost time at work because they worried about confrontations with coworkers.

(continued)

- 37 percent said that arguments with colleagues caused them to reduce their commitment to the job.
- 22 percent said that they put less effort into their work because of conflicts with colleagues.[39]

RESOLUTION

Derek and Ed's relational conflict will not simply go away if they ignore it. When you have a personality clash with someone, explore ways to resolve it. Pick your battles and argue only about things that make a real difference. Rather than ignore Ed, Derek might ask for a meeting to discuss the cause of the conflict. In that meeting, Derek would benefit by using neutral rather than accusatory language. He might say, "We seem to have different decision-making styles in our meetings. I like to discuss, and you like to debate. These differences sometimes get us off-track. How do you think we can resolve this conflict?" If that approach does not work, then Derek may next ask for help from managers, if needed. Mediation from supervisors may be helpful.

Ego issues

Ego conflicts threaten someone's sense of professional identity or self-image. In professional contexts, people typically see themselves as honest, reasonable, intelligent, and committed to the well-being of the organization. When someone accuses you of something negative or challenges your sense of identity, you may find it difficult to work productively with that person. Consider the following scenario:

EXAMPLE	ANALYSIS
Nadia is the youngest customer relationship manager in the company, and she is proud of her quick rise through the ranks. In three years, she has progressed faster than any other employee, and she is responsible for 35 percent of the company's sales. Yet whenever she meets with Brian, the head of engineering, to discuss her customers' needs, she feels personally insulted. If Brian does not like what she proposes for a project, he often says, "We can't do that. You're not an engineer. You don't know what you're talking about." Or he might say, "How old are you? You've only been here for three years. I've been doing this kind of work for 20 years, and I know the best way to get it done." Things are so strained between Brian and Nadia that they avoid face-to-face encounters, resorting to email to discuss projects.	**Nadia's perception:** Brian won't take her seriously, despite her rapid advancement. **Brian's perception:** Nadia doesn't appropriately value his age and experience, despite his many years on the job. **Conflict:** A business disagreement has become personal, producing an affective conflict. Both Brian and Nadia feel that the other person doesn't adequately value his or her skills.

RESOLUTION

One wise approach is to shift the focus back to business. Nadia might say, "I know you have 20 years of experience. That's why I'm sure you can help me meet this customer's needs." This approach not only shifts the focus of the conversation but also offers Brian a subtle compliment and may make him more willing to take Nadia seriously. For his part, Brian might say, "I respect your skill at securing sales, but sometimes we cannot do exactly what the customer wants because, from an engineering perspective, it's not feasible."

Select an appropriate management technique

As the scenarios in the previous section suggest, not all conflicts are best managed the same way. If you are involved in affective conflict—one that focuses on relationships or ego—you will need to address the emotional issues before you can productively discuss the content of your work. If you are involved in a cognitive conflict, however, consider the five different techniques illustrated in **Figure 2.6**—avoid confrontation, accommodate or give in, compete to win, compromise, or collaborate.[40] This figure provides guidance for choosing a strategy based on the situation.

FIGURE 2.6 How to Select an Appropriate Management Technique

TECHNIQUE	USE THIS TECHNIQUE WHEN...	AVOID THIS TECHNIQUE WHEN...	EXAMPLE
Avoid confrontation Deny the problem exists, change the topic, screen your telephone calls, or avoid the person completely.	you believe you have no chance of resolving the conflict and the conflict does not interfere with productivity.	you have any other alternative. Problems that are not addressed tend to get worse.	Nadia and Brian (introduced on page 49) used this technique, and it was not effective. Because of an ego conflict, they avoided personal interaction. If they continue to avoid each other and communicate only by email, they will have no opportunity to develop shared goals; ultimately, the customers will suffer.
Accommodate or give in Allow the other person to have his or her own way.	• you decide that your position was wrong. • the conflict is trivial. • you are negotiating; sacrifice something less important to gain something you want more. • maintaining a harmonious relationship is more important than the outcome of the issue.	accommodation means sacrificing your principles and beliefs. Such accommodation can lead to loss of self-esteem or **groupthink**. Groupthink is a practice of achieving unanimity by eliminating all critical thinking that threatens consensus. A groupthink approach to eliminating conflict can lead a group to ignore differing opinions that may be valuable.	Imagine you are on a marketing team with people of diverse backgrounds. Your team's goal is to generate cutting-edge marketing ideas for a new product. During the first brainstorming session, many ideas come up. But as soon as the marketing manager endorses one idea, everyone agrees with him. You think a different idea might work better, but don't want to be the only dissenting voice. To show that you "fit with the company," you "go along to get along." This is an example of groupthink that may cause the team to settle on a solution that is wrong, or may sacrifice creativity and innovation.[41]
Compete to win Turn the conflict into a contest with a winner and loser, often determined by a third party. Use competitive tactics to win the advantage: find fault, assign blame, or reject others' point of view.	• a quick resolution is needed or demanded and compromise isn't possible. • a third-party, such as a supervisor, CEO, or board of directors—is available to decide the issue.	a more collaborative strategy or compromise is possible, since competition can lead to relational conflicts.	Marcus and Allison of Green Earth (introduced on page 47) bring their conflict to the president of the company to decide which goal to prioritize: keeping customers happy or keeping costs down. The president decides to accommodate current customers. This decision gives Marcus and Allison a clear direction, but they still need to work out the personal anger that has developed between them.
Compromise Approach the problem cooperatively so that all the parties involved get something they want or can accept, but everyone also sacrifices.	• a quick resolution is needed or demanded. • people have differences of opinion or competing goals, and a compromise allows each to be partially satisfied.	the outcome will fail to adequately resolve the conflict or achieve the ultimate goal.	Valerie and Corrine of Rotel Plumbing (introduced on page 47) need to present a budget to the board of directors the next day, even though they continue to have differences of opinion: Should they invest in marketing or distribution? They reach a compromise and create budgets for two smaller projects—one on marketing and another on distribution. Neither gets everything she wants, but this solution offers several benefits: Each gets part of what she wants, they are able to project a united front at the board of directors meeting, and they will gather data from the two projects that may help them resolve their difference of opinion.

(continued)

FIGURE 2.6 *(continued)*

TECHNIQUE	USE THIS TECHNIQUE WHEN...	AVOID THIS TECHNIQUE WHEN...	EXAMPLE
Collaborate Work with all parties to determine the best possible solution.	collaboration is possible. This is the best approach for managing complex conflicts in the absence of pressing deadlines. Collaboration has the benefit not only of providing a solution but also ensuring buy-in from all parties and strengthening the relationships among people.	an immediate resolution is needed, because collaboration is a time-consuming process.	Marcus and Allison of Green Earth realize they will not be able to easily resolve their conflict because their supervisors gave them conflicting requirements. Although they could individually talk to their supervisors, they decide to work together to find a solution in the best interest of the company. Perhaps the company could charge more for rush jobs, give clients the option of paying a retainer to leave space on the Green Earth schedule, or develop a new procedure for calculating revenues versus overtime costs. Marcus and Allison then present these collaborative solutions in a meeting with their two supervisors.

If you choose to address the conflict (rather than avoid it or give in), the following advice can help achieve an effective result:

- **Act promptly.** The longer a conflict goes unresolved, the more likely it is that misunderstandings will accumulate, which will escalate the issue. When you experience affective conflict, take the time needed for strong emotions to subside; however, do not to let the conflict last so long that feelings are suppressed or people are no longer willing to communicate.[42]
- **Meet in person at a neutral location.** Participants can take nonverbal cues into account when they meet, and neither party has the advantage of meeting in a space in which they feel at home.
- **Formalize the solution.** Outline the agreements and course of action on paper so both parties are clear about the understanding. Documentation can also minimize future disagreement on the solution.
- **Set a date for follow-up.** Follow-up encourages accountability and, in the case of affective conflict, decreases the potential for enduring resentment.

TECHNOLOGY
INTERGENERATIONAL CONFLICTS OVER TECHNOLOGY

Intergenerational communication can sometimes be a source of conflict in the workplace, and one of the biggest work-related differences between generations is their relative familiarity with technology. Millennials (people born after 1980) are considered "digital natives" and easily adopt and learn new technology. By contrast, many older workers have developed a diverse set of technological skills, but may be more cautious about adopting new technology.

The differences can be seen in the different rates at which generations adopt social media platforms. The Pew Research Center found that only 50% of Baby Boomers (born between 1946 and 1964) use social media of any kind, compared to 73% of Generation X (born between 1965 and 1980) and 89% of Millennials. The generational differences become more pronounced when it comes to specific platforms; while 50% of Boomers use Facebook, only 8% use Instagram, compared to 24% of

Generation X and 47% of Millennials.[43] These differences can have implications in the workplace as companies try to decide on the most effective means of disseminating information to the public.

Conflicts result when members of different generations have different ideas about when technology use is appropriate and which technologies are most effective. A Millennial worker might consider sending a work text on her phone during a meeting as an efficient and responsible use of time, while an older worker might perceive the same action as disrespectful. A Millennial might see Slack as an efficient platform to get a question answered, while an older worker might value face-to-face communication.[44,45]

The following example illustrates a typical workplace technology conflict and how to resolve it.

(continued)

TECHNOLOGY
INTERGENERATIONAL CONFLICTS OVER TECHNOLOGY *(Continued)*

EXAMPLE	ANALYSIS
Madison, who has recently graduated from college, and Karen, who has been working in HR for over 20 years, are heading a team that is developing new employee evaluation criteria for their company. They want to use a file-sharing system to collaborate on the document. Madison writes a first draft, uploads it to Google Docs, and invites Karen to edit the draft. Instead of comments on the draft and praise for taking initiative, Madison gets an email from Karen reprimanding her for setting up the Google Doc without approval and requesting she immediately remove it and use Box instead. Madison is confused; she always used Google Docs to collaborate on group projects in college and thought it would be an easy solution.	**Madison's perception:** Karen doesn't respect her work and wants to assert her authority by having the team use her file-sharing technology instead of Madison's. **Karen's perception:** Madison was unprofessional and did not use a secure file-sharing system. As a result, she has put company information at risk. **Conflict:** Both Karen and Madison assume that the technologies they are familiar with are the best. Karen did not consider that Madison needs mentoring about company technology expectations. She expects that security concerns are self-evident. Madison did not consider that businesses have concerns that differ from student concerns in college.

RESOLUTION
Madison and Karen need to communicate more effectively about what they expect from the technology they use as well as from their collaboration. Madison could propose a technology before using it. And Karen could explain to Madison the importance of security and privacy when working with company materials.

For TECHNOLOGY exercises, go to Exercises 25, 26, and 27 on pages 73–74.

(SQ4) How can you improve your communication with people from different cultures?

culture The learned and shared attitudes, values, and behaviors that characterize a group of people.

You may have heard the saying "We cannot escape our culture." **Culture** describes the learned and shared patterns in a society. Differences in culture exist among countries, such as the United States and China, as well as subsets of a population, such as urban and rural. People are shaped by the cultures they come from, and they develop a set of assumptions about how to act based on these cultures. For example, for most Americans, the following statements are noncontroversial truths:

- If you have a 10 AM appointment, you should arrive a little before 10 AM to be on time.
- If someone makes a mistake, it's best to be honest (though polite) and point it out so that he or she has an opportunity to correct the mistake.
- To be efficient, it is important to get right to business quickly at a meeting.
- If you are a man, as a sign of politeness, you should allow a woman to enter a doorway before you or exit an elevator before you.

However, not every culture subscribes to these codes of behavior. For example, in a Latin American culture—that is, in the cultures of North or South American countries where Spanish or Portuguese are spoken—you would be rude to jump immediately to business at the beginning of a meeting, especially a first meeting. Latin American cultures value getting to know the other person and building a relationship of trust. In Korea, a young woman would be rude to exit an elevator before an elderly man because respecting elders is highly valued in the Korean culture. Although it would be unrealistic to try to learn about every culture all at once, you can prepare yourself to communicate with people from other cultures by taking two important steps. First, understand some of the key ways that cultures differ, and second, develop communication strategies that help you communicate with diverse groups.

Understand how cultures differ

Because workplaces are increasingly multicultural and businesses are increasingly global, learning about other cultures is required, not optional. Cultural understanding will help you avoid misinterpreting the verbal and nonverbal communication of colleagues and customers

New Hires @ Work

George Gwee
National University of Singapore
Accountant @ Walsh Pte. Ltd.

Making small talk with people from different cultures is not always easy. We had office bonding sessions, we went out to dinner together, we chatted, etc. Over time the "ice thawed," and it was easier to get along, both as people and as colleagues.

Photo courtesy of George Gwee

who do not share your culture. It will also help you to avoid displaying **ethnocentrism**—an inappropriate belief that your own culture is superior to all others. People who are ethnocentric are often trapped by cultural **stereotypes**—oversimplified images or generalizations of a group. Although stereotypes may describe a generally observed cultural norm, if you assume everyone from that culture follows that norm, you ignore the fact that individuals are, in fact, individual. People are influenced by many different factors in their lives, including education, travel, family values, friendships, and job requirements. Just as it is wrong to assume that all Americans are loud (a common stereotype), it would be equally wrong to assume that all French people are rude.

Although it is important to avoid cultural stereotypes, it is equally important to recognize that cultures do differ. Over the years, anthropologists, sociologists, and intercultural experts have identified many dimensions of those differences. This section covers five of those dimensions, all of which have implications for business communication.

ethnocentrism An inappropriate belief that your own culture is superior to all others.

stereotypes Oversimplified images or generalizations of a group.

High context versus low context

Anthropologist Edward T. Hall first used the term **context** to describe how people deliver, receive, and interpret messages.[46] Hall proposed that cultures exist on a continuum from high context to low context, as illustrated in **Figure 2.7**. In a *high-context* culture, such as in China or Japan, communicators intend to convey meaning not just through words but also through the context surrounding the words: how something is said, the nonverbal behavior of the communicator and audience, the history of the relationship between the two communicators, and even the silences in the conversation. In a *low-context* culture, such as in the United States or Canada, communicators rely less on context and more on explicit language to communicate a message as clearly and unambiguously as possible.

Reflecting this difference, people in the United States typically value direct conversations that immediately get to the point, in contrast to people from Japan, who rely on more subtle

context (relating to culture) A term that describes how people in a culture deliver, receive, and interpret messages. Low-context cultures rely on explicit language to communicate. High-context cultures derive meaning not just from words but from everything surrounding the words.

FIGURE 2.7 Continuum of Low- to High-Context Cultures

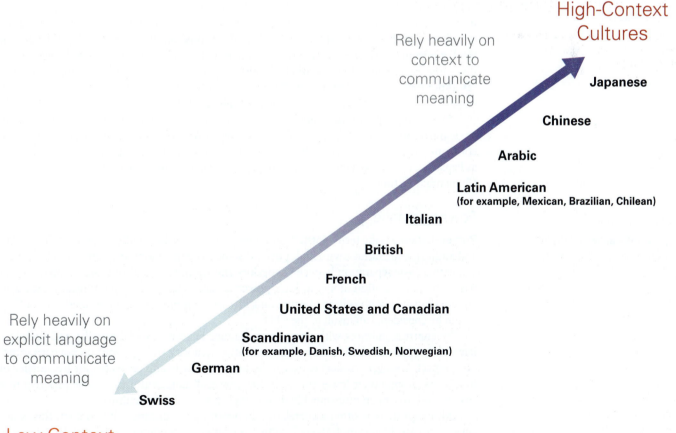

cues. If a Japanese businessperson wants to say "no," she may not actually use that word but instead may respond with silence or with a reserved reply such as, "That is very interesting." She will rely on you to interpret the message correctly, based on the context of the communication. By contrast, if an Iranian businessperson wants to say "yes"—for example, if a store owner wants to be paid for a product or service—he will first refuse to accept the payment, out of politeness. This custom of politely refusing something you really want is called *taroffing*. According to custom, someone being offered payment or even a cup of tea will refuse twice before graciously agreeing when asked for the third time.[47] This ritual can be confusing to a low-context Westerner, who believes that "no means no," and it would be impolite to keep asking.

Individualism versus collectivism

individualistic culture A culture that values an individual's achievements, satisfaction, and independent thinking.

collectivist culture A culture that puts the good of the group or organization before people's individual interests.

Individualism versus collectivism is one of the key dimensions of culture identified by Dutch intercultural expert Geert Hofstede.[48] In an **individualistic culture**, people value an individual's achievements, satisfaction, and independent thinking. By contrast, in **collectivist cultures**, people put the good of the group or organization before their own individual interests. Obligation and loyalty to the group are more important than one's own achievement. Harmony is important.

Individualistic and collectivist values influence communication and business in a number of ways. In the individualistic United States, many companies reward individual leaders—for example, CEOs and other executives—with multimillion-dollar bonuses for the companies' successes. By contrast, in more collectivist China, PepsiCo learned during its early years in that country that rewarding an individual leader was not an effective incentive. When one highly regarded manager chose to divide his bonus equally among his employees, PepsiCo changed its practice to reward an entire group when goals are met.[49] Similarly, in collectivist cultures, employees may be embarrassed—or even ashamed—if they are singled out and praised for accomplishments, whereas in individualistic cultures, employees expect to be acknowledged for individual achievements.

face In Chinese, Indian, and other collectivist cultures, the position or standing that a person has in the eyes of others.

In collectivist cultures, where harmony is important, people are equally embarrassed and ashamed if they are publicly disrespected, making them lose **face**. The concept of face in traditional Chinese and Indian cultures refers to the respect and prestige a person enjoys. In the individualistic United States, we typically tell someone explicitly what they have done wrong so that they can improve. We also might dismiss an idea at a meeting if we do not think it is valuable. However, in a more collectivist culture that is concerned with face-saving, that same form of directness would be humiliating. It is wiser to find something positive to say about that idea to help the contributor save face. It is also extremely important to show respect to one's boss because that is a means of giving face.[50]

Although people in the United States tend to think of individualism as the norm, there are significantly more collectivist cultures in the world than individualistic cultures.[51] U.S. companies that respect these collectivist values and build business practices around them, as Pepsi did, can be extremely successful. Pepsi has been named one of the best employers in China multiple times.[52]

Power distance

power distance A characteristic of cultures that describes how the culture perceives inequality and authority.

Power distance is the term Hofstede developed to describe how cultures perceive inequality and authority. In cultures with high power distance, organizations are formal and hierarchical, with a clear separation between superiors and subordinates. People are granted respect based on their position alone. In high-power-distance cultures, people typically expect to conduct business with others of equal rank. To send a junior executive to meet with a CEO would be considered an insult to the CEO.

By contrast, cultures with low power distance believe in social equality and therefore have a more relaxed attitude about title and status. Seniority and age alone do not earn someone respect. Younger workers expect to be taken seriously and respected for the quality of their work despite their lower status. In low-power-distance cultures, people progress to a first-name basis much more quickly than in high-power-distance cultures.

Although there is often a correlation between power distance and context, this is not always the case. For example, French culture is relatively low context and direct. However, the French have more respect for formality and authority than do people from other low-context cultures, such as Canadians.

Uncertainty avoidance

Uncertainty avoidance relates to how comfortable a culture is with ambiguity, risk, and change. Cultures that are uncomfortable with uncertainty tend to rely on rituals, rules, and codes of conduct that help make the future more predictable. For example, employees in these cultures tend to like clear guidelines that lead to a predictable result. These employees value learning by observation so that results are repeatable. By contrast, cultures that are more comfortable with uncertainty and ambiguity tend to like more flexible work environments that allow risk-taking and entrepreneurial behavior. These employees value learning by doing, even though the result may be less predictable.

Attitudes toward uncertainty and ambiguity affect communication on many levels. Cultures that avoid uncertainty are often collectivist and tend to be cautious about integrating new people into a group. They also value harmony and consensus. Cultures that tolerate uncertainty are open to new people, new ideas, and risks.

> **uncertainty avoidance** A measure of how comfortable a culture is with ambiguity, risk, and change.

Time orientation

In addition to cultural context, anthropologist Edward T. Hall introduced the terms *monochronic* and *polychronic* to describe two very different cultural orientations toward time. **Monochronic cultures**, such as the United States and Northern European countries, value punctuality and efficiency. Meetings begin on time and are expected to follow a set agenda. Deadlines are usually strict. Although most monochronic cultures are also individualistic, some collectivist cultures, such as Japan, also value punctuality and efficiency. In their view, keeping to an agreed schedule shows respect for the entire group. **Polychronic cultures** are more relaxed about time and punctuality. Polychronic cultures typically put people and relationships before schedules. In a meeting, participants may easily change the order of items on the agenda. While it is important for work to be completed, people may choose to spend time building a relationship over completing a task. In polychronic cultures, deadlines can often be adjusted.

> **monochronic culture** A culture that values punctuality and efficiency.

> **polychronic culture** A culture that has a relaxed attitude toward time and punctuality.

Understanding the various approaches to time is crucial to maintaining smooth relationships. An American who lived for many years in both Denmark and Latin America said, "When you are invited to dinner at 7 PM in Denmark, this means you'll be sitting at the table at 7 PM. When you are invited to dinner at 7 PM in Argentina, this means you'll be expected to arrive at around 8 PM. The only thing they have in common is this: For both cultures, to arrive at 7 PM would be rude."

Develop strategies that help you communicate with diverse groups

You may not know the cultural backgrounds of the people you work with. **Figure 2.8** on page 56 presents both verbal and nonverbal strategies to help you communicate and work well with people, regardless of their backgrounds.

> **guanxi** In China, a network of long-term mutually beneficial relationships built on trust.

ETHICS
THE ETHICS OF GUANXI

Traditionally, much of Chinese business has depended on **guanxi** (pronounced "gwan-shee"), a network of long-term, mutually beneficial relationships.[53] When looking to make a business deal, Chinese executives traditionally look to work with someone they can trust from within their guanxi network. The concept of guanxi makes sense in China because "commercial law has historically been underdeveloped."[54] Without a robust system of laws to regulate business transactions, business people relied upon relationships and trust to get business done.

However, Westerners often question the ethics of guanxi because it gives people with close social relationships an insider business advantage that is not available to outsiders.[55] In addition, guanxi may lead to corruption as officials have been known to accept bribes to use their guanxi to facilitate business transactions.[56] For an outsider coming in to China, developing guanxi can be challenging, which is why many advisors suggest that Americans hire Chinese employees and executives to represent them in China.[57]

Some experts predict that as Chinese business becomes more global, guanxi will become less prominent.[58] Internet-based businesses, for example, do not rely on personal relationships for customers. They simply rely on providing a product and service that the market wants.

> For an ETHICS exercise, go to Exercise 17 on page 72.

FIGURE 2.8 How to Communicate with Diverse Groups

CATEGORY	DO	DON'T
Nonverbal Communication	**Pay attention to the other person's nonverbal communication and, when appropriate, mirror it.** If you are doing business with someone from another culture, pay attention to how that person acts. For example, in the United States, a comfortable conversational distance ranges from 2 to 4 feet; in the Middle East, the distance may be less than 1 foot.[59] By observing and learning, you can avoid cultural mistakes.	• Ignore or discount how people from other cultures maintain eye contact, shake hands, or stand when talking.
	Smile. Look like you are friendly, open, and willing to communicate.	• Presume that an unsmiling countenance will be taken more seriously.
Verbal Communication	**Be clear and concise.** Remember to talk relatively slowly and pronounce words clearly. To ensure your meaning is understood, also be very specific with your choice of words.	• Use **idioms**, expressions that mean something other than the literal meaning of their words. For example, *"drive me up the wall"* and *"pass with flying colors"* are culture-specific and as a result may confuse people from other cultures • Use jargon, specialized language of a specific field. Even business jargon like *"in the red"* or *"headcount"* may be unfamiliar to people from other cultures.
	Listen carefully. Listen to more than the words to ensure you understand the intended meaning. Listen for tone and emphasis.[60]	• Get distracted by differences in accent and dialect.
	Request feedback to ensure understanding. Ask friendly questions that encourage people to give you verbal feedback so you can ensure mutual understanding.	• Assume that smiles and head nodding mean that people from other cultures understand what you are saying. These nonverbal responses mean different things in different countries.
Both	**Exhibit formality and respect.** Americans are often less formal than people from European and Eastern cultures. When in doubt, be polite, courteous, and respectful. For example, address people by their last names (*"Hello, Ms. Tsai"*) until they ask you to call them by their first names (*"Hi, Fu-Nien"*).	• Assume that people from other cultures are impersonal and distant, as they may be behaving with decorum appropriate to their culture. • Attempt humor, since humor often doesn't translate across cultures.
	Apologize sincerely if your inadvertently offend or confuse your audience. Occasional misunderstanding is inevitable in cross-cultural communication. Taking responsibility for miscommunication helps your audience save face. If you do offend or confuse your audience, explain and be open to learning to avoid future missteps.	• Pretend that nothing happened or blame your audience for being overly sensitive.

 How can you work effectively as part of a team?

idiom An expression that means something other than the literal meaning of its words.

team Two or more people who recognize and share a commitment to a specific, common goal and who collaborate in their efforts to achieve that goal.

This chapter focuses on developing communication skills to help you work effectively with others. In workplace environments, your work with others will often be accomplished in teams. A team is more than a group of people working together. An effective **team** involves two or more people who recognize and share a commitment to a specific, common goal and who collaborate in their efforts to achieve that goal.

Teams are integral to an organization's success largely because one individual does not have all the skills needed to compete in today's business world. In addition, if a company needs to bring a product to market before a competitor does, it cannot wait for one or two people to do all the work involved. Instead, the company must rely on a well-coordinated team, with each person doing his or her part to achieve the common goal. Individuals benefit from teamwork, too. By working on a team, you will improve your interpersonal skills, expand your personal network, and use your best individual strengths while learning new skills from others. This section suggests six ways you and your teammates can improve team performance and make teamwork an enjoyable and productive experience.

Assemble an effective team

If you have the opportunity to assemble a team for a project, choose team members carefully. Friends are not always the best choices for teammates. The most effective team will be one composed of individuals with the right skills and attitudes to get the job done well. To select strong team members, consider the following questions and strategies:

QUESTIONS	STRATEGIES
1. How big should my team be?	• **Create teams of three to five people,** which are typically more productive than larger ones. Research in teamwork has shown that as teams grow larger, individuals contribute less effort.[61] • **Appoint an odd number of people** to eliminate the possibility of a 50/50 split if the team votes on a decision.[62] • **Break into subteams** to complete different parts of the project if you need more people on a team to complete a more complex project.
2. What are the skills needed to complete this team project effectively?	**Identify the work that needs to be done and the skills necessary for doing it.** For example, if your project involves market research, identify who has experience conducting surveys. Aim for a mix of different skills and perspectives in order to foster creative and innovative thinking.[63]
3. Who has the time and resources to contribute effectively to the team project?	**Ask colleagues with area expertise to join the team or to recommend a substitute.** You may have someone in mind, but if that person is too busy to do a good job on your team, get a personal recommendation for an alternative.
4. Who may be most interested in this topic (and therefore motivated to participate)?	**Consider prior experience and professional development.** You may know someone who has worked on the topic before, or you might consider a new employee who you know is eager to learn about the topic.
5. Who knows how to collaborate well?	**Consider interpersonal skills and previous collaboration experience as well as project-specific skills.** To do their project well, team members need more than just skills and knowledge. They also need to know how to work with others and be able to identify, confront, and resolve issues as they arise. If people do not have past collaboration experience, they will require some training.

Agree on team goals and standards

For a team to be successful, all team members need to agree on key elements at the beginning of the project:[64]

- **Goals.** Good teams are goal oriented. All members understand their purpose as a team, share a concrete goal and vision for success, and believe that what they are doing is worthwhile. They know their work will make a significant contribution to their organization, their client, the community, or something they care about. In addition, each individual member must be willing to do whatever it takes to make the team successful, including helping each other if the need arises. To promote commitment, teams should make sure that all members get a chance to participate in decisions and feel they are being heard.

- **Expected results.** Good teams are also results oriented. In other words, the team's success is measured by results, not effort, and the team is organized to achieve those results. Specifically:
  - All team members have a clear role and are held accountable for their contributions.
  - Workload is divided equitably. Some tasks may require more effort than others, so it is important to discuss the work to ensure that the team is aware of each member's responsibilities and no one is overburdened with too much work.
  - The team has an effective communication system to keep all team members informed in a timely way.
  - Team members give each other prompt and helpful feedback on their performance so each person can do his or her best work.

- **Team standards.** Finally, good teams have standards and hold each team member accountable for them. You may develop standards about any or all of the following topics: conducting meetings, communicating between meetings, keeping records, making decisions, and managing conflict. Working together to create team standards helps a team get off to a strong start. If conflict begins to arise during a project, the team standards can help a team resolve the conflict.

Pay attention to team development and dynamics

There is more than one way to approach team dynamics. Different approaches will work better in different contexts.

For teams that aim to work together for the long term, it can be productive to give team members time to develop their collaborative working relationship. **Figure 2.9** illustrates a model for understanding team development first proposed by Bruce W. Tuckman. He identified four stages of development in teams that had no formal team training: **forming**, **storming**, **norming**, and **performing**.[65]

FIGURE 2.9 Stages of Team Development: What Team Members Do at Each Stage

FORMING	STORMING	NORMING	PERFORMING
Exchange vital information	Experience conflict and tension	Discuss and resolve problems	Work collaboratively
Learn about each other	Feel disillusioned and discouraged	Create standards for communicating	Use individual differences as a source of strength
Have high expectations for success		Plan regular meetings	Put project above individual goals
Act politely and considerately	Identify reasons for conflict	Hold members accountable	Achieve high level of productivity

Here is what happens in each stage:

- **Forming.** When a team first begins to form, everyone is usually polite and considerate. You exchange information about your schedules, when and where you can meet, and how you can contact each other. Usually, expectations for the team and its success are high, and conflicts are not evident.

forming A stage of team development in which members get to know each other.

- **Storming.** The team eventually begins to encounter problems that aren't easily resolved. Members begin to feel tense and anxious about the success of the project. Some team members may begin to feel disillusioned and discouraged. As you experience conflict, try to identify the reasons for the conflict to help the group move to the next stage of development.

- **Norming.** Norming begins when team members start to manage conflict and establish consensus about how to work together efficiently. This is the stage at which many teams decide to create standards about communication and accountability.

- **Performing.** At the performing stage of team development, team members have learned how to work collaboratively and are able to use their differences as a source of strength, not weakness. Although problems will continue to arise, a performing team feels comfortable confronting and resolving the problems that might jeopardize the success of the project. Members begin to enjoy working together and are glad they don't have to complete the project alone. They often get so involved and excited about what they are doing that they lose track of time, and the success of the project becomes more important than individual goals.

One reason to study teamwork in a business communication course is so that you can move more quickly to the performing stage. A performing team may also evolve into a *high-performing team:* a team whose members are deeply committed to each other's growth and success.[66]

Harvard Business School professor Amy Edmondson provides an alternative model for achieving high performance in short-term teams that don't have time to progress through Tuckman's four stages. Because teams often come together and dissolve so quickly, she argues that the concept of a stable "team" should be replaced by that of a fluid process: **teaming**. "Teaming is a verb," she maintains. "It is a dynamic activity, not a bounded, static entity."[67] This shift reflects the needs of a complex contemporary work environment, where businesses must be flexible enough to change gears quickly and effectively. Because people are often grouped together only temporarily for specific projects, they often don't have the opportunity to "gel" over time and develop stable structures and relationships. Working in these dynamic conditions requires team members to communicate frequently in order to learn collectively, fix issues quickly as they arise, and ensure that the best ideas are put into action. To achieve these goals, Edmondson recommends that participants do the following:

- Ask for help and clarification early and often
- Share information quickly and broadly
- Discuss mistakes
- Try out new strategies and ideas
- Continuously seek out feedback to improve ideas and processes[68]

Develop good leadership practices

While different team development strategies fit different needs, both Tuckman and Edmondson emphasize that successful teamwork depends on the vision and guidance that can be provided only by effective *leadership*. A team leader may not be the team member who has the most creative ideas. An effective leader is the person who has the skills to motivate people, manage work processes, and help the team succeed.

A team can establish leadership in a number of ways. One person can serve as leader, leadership can rotate during phases of the project, or different leaders can take responsibility for different aspects of the project. It is not crucial for the team to have one single leader. However, it is crucial for the team to have capable leadership that keeps the good of the team in mind. Remember that if you volunteer to be a team leader, that role does not put you in charge of the team. Instead, it puts you in service of the team.

Here is a partial list of ways that a leader can serve the team and help it succeed:

- **Establish and maintain a vision of the future.** One of the most valuable roles for any leader is to keep the team focused on the ultimate goal and remind the team why that goal is valuable. Teams can easily get bogged down in the details of the work and forget why the project is worthwhile. A good leader reenergizes team members, refocuses them on the goal, and makes the team believe in itself.

- **Create a supportive climate.** Teams work best when team members feel that they can take risks and that they will be listened to and respected. Google's research on team effectiveness concluded that psychological safety is one of the most important factors leading to team success.[69] A team leader can set the tone for the team by encouraging contributions from everyone and by being respectful to everyone.

---

storming A stage of team development in which teams experience conflict and begin to confront differences.

norming A stage of team development in which team members learn how to manage conflict and work with each other effectively.

performing A stage of team development in which team members work collaboratively and achieve a high level of productivity.

teaming The process of bringing people together for a short period of time to solve a specific problem or complete a specific project.

- **Delegate responsibility and assign tasks equitably.** Delegating responsibility and assigning tasks is a balancing act. On the one hand, the team needs to take full advantage of its human resources and assign people tasks that call on their strengths. On the other hand, teams need to provide members with opportunities to learn, stretch, and develop new skills. A good leader can help maintain this balance by considering each individual's talents and goals. In addition, a good team leader can help ensure that workloads are shared equitably. As a project progresses, work assignments may need to shift: Some tasks may prove to be bigger than anticipated, some may be smaller, and new tasks may arise.
- **Establish a timeline.** Once the team collaboratively determines a plan for the project, a team leader can oversee the creation of a timeline to help the team progress and ensure deadlines are met. Then, throughout the process, a leader can help the team reevaluate and reassess the plan. One project scheduling tool that teams often use to establish a timeline and track the project is a *Gantt chart* (named after its inventor, Henry Gantt). As **Figure 2.10** shows, one advantage of a Gantt chart is that it helps manage time by identifying tasks that can take place simultaneously versus those that need to be completed sequentially.

FIGURE 2.10 Gantt Chart

Gantt Chart

Assignment Key

Team	Alma	Fiona	John	Michael

Project: Client Website Development

Current Week ↓ (at 4/20 to 4/27)

Tasks	3/2 to 3/9	3/9 to 3/16	3/16 to 3/30	3/30 to 4/6	4/6 to 4/13	4/13 to 4/20	4/20 to 4/27	4/27 to 5/4	5/4 to 5/11	5/11 to 5/19	5/19 to 5/25	5/25 to 6/1
Document Client Requirements	* (Team)	* (Team)										
Acquire Client Approval - Requirements		▮ (Michael)										
Create Code			▮ (John)	▮ (John)								
Create Artwork Alternatives			▮ (Fiona)									
Present Artwork Alternative				▮ (Team)								
Acquire Client Approval - Artwork					▮ (Michael)							
Integrate Artwork and Code						▮ (John)	▮ (John)	▮ (John)				
						▮ (Fiona)	▮ (Fiona)	▮ (Fiona)				
User Testing									** (Team)	** (Team)		
Fix Bugs and User Interface Issues									▮ (John)	▮ (John)		
Present Final Site to Client											▮ (Team)	
Acquire Client Approval - Final Site											▮ (Michael)	
Launch Site												▮ (Team)

* Michael is lead   ** Alma manages multiple testers from outside of team

- **Keep the project on track.** Although individual members of the team may work on separate tasks, a good leader brings the team together throughout the project to discuss progress, encourage group feedback, and share ideas. Scheduling regular meetings keeps the project on track to meet established deadlines while also allowing for changes in the plan based on continual input and feedback.
- **Manage meetings effectively and encourage positive collaboration.** A good leader uses effective listening, questioning, and restating techniques to ensure that all members of the team participate in meetings and provide input. Leaders also encourage positive collaboration among team members and referee any unconstructive feedback or personality conflicts.
- **Ensure effective decision making.** Although teams can take many approaches to decision making, important decisions should never be made by giving in to the team member who is the loudest and most assertive. A team leader can ensure that the team makes fact-based judgments and is able to support all its decisions with sound evidence and reasoning. Although a good leader will help a team work toward consensus, the leader must also protect the team against engaging in **groupthink**, the practice of achieving unanimity by eliminating all critical thinking that threatens consensus.

groupthink A process by which a group reaches a decision by eliminating all critical thinking that threatens consensus.

- **Resolve differences.** When team members have differences of opinion and need an impartial point of view, a team leader can take responsibility for listening carefully and offering a resolution.

Plan for effective meetings

Team meetings are crucial for determining tasks, sharing ideas, and making decisions. To avoid falling into the trap of holding too many meetings where not enough gets done, plan your meetings in advance following these guidelines:

- **Create an agenda.** Base the **agenda**—a detailed plan or outline for the meeting—on input from each team member. **Figure 2.11** shows an agenda for a team that is developing an online handbook for summer interns. Notice that the agenda provides the list of topics to be discussed, the name of the individual responsible for each item, and the amount of time to spend discussing each item.

- **Distribute the agenda sufficiently in advance.** Distributing the agenda before the meeting ensures that all the team members know what is expected, who is responsible, and what their roles will be during the meeting.

- **Assign someone to serve as a timekeeper during the meeting.** The timekeeper can keep track of how well the meeting follows the agenda. If the meeting becomes sidetracked on unrelated matters or if participants get stuck on unproductive tangents, the timekeeper can bring the conversation back to the necessary topic.

> **agenda** A detailed plan or outline of the items to be discussed at a meeting.

FIGURE 2.11 How to Create a Meeting Agenda

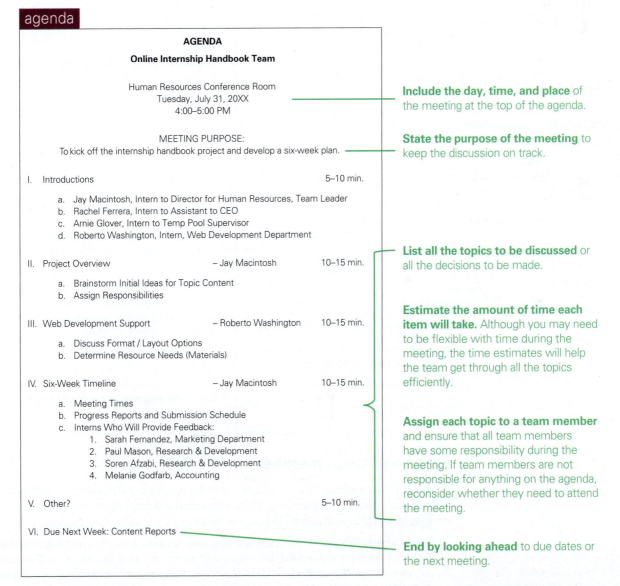

agenda

AGENDA

Online Internship Handbook Team

Human Resources Conference Room
Tuesday, July 31, 20XX
4:00–5:00 PM

MEETING PURPOSE:
To kick off the internship handbook project and develop a six-week plan.

I. Introductions		5–10 min.

    a. Jay Macintosh, Intern to Director for Human Resources, Team Leader
    b. Rachel Ferrera, Intern to Assistant to CEO
    c. Arnie Glover, Intern to Temp Pool Supervisor
    d. Roberto Washington, Intern, Web Development Department

II. Project Overview   – Jay Macintosh   10–15 min.

    a. Brainstorm Initial Ideas for Topic Content
    b. Assign Responsibilities

III. Web Development Support   – Roberto Washington   10–15 min.

    a. Discuss Format / Layout Options
    b. Determine Resource Needs (Materials)

IV. Six-Week Timeline   – Jay Macintosh   10–15 min.

    a. Meeting Times
    b. Progress Reports and Submission Schedule
    c. Interns Who Will Provide Feedback:
        1. Sarah Fernandez, Marketing Department
        2. Paul Mason, Research & Development
        3. Soren Afzabi, Research & Development
        4. Melanie Godfarb, Accounting

V. Other?   5–10 min.

VI. Due Next Week: Content Reports

Include the day, time, and place of the meeting at the top of the agenda.

State the purpose of the meeting to keep the discussion on track.

List all the topics to be discussed or all the decisions to be made.

Estimate the amount of time each item will take. Although you may need to be flexible with time during the meeting, the time estimates will help the team get through all the topics efficiently.

Assign each topic to a team member and ensure that all team members have some responsibility during the meeting. If team members are not responsible for anything on the agenda, reconsider whether they need to attend the meeting.

End by looking ahead to due dates or the next meeting.

meeting minutes Notes that describe what was discussed at a meeting, what was decided, and what actions will follow.

- **Assign someone to serve as a note taker during the meeting.** The note taker produces **meeting minutes**, a written description of what was discussed, what was decided, and what actions will follow. **Figure 2.12** shows the minutes of the online handbook team's meeting.
- **Plan for follow-up.** Include a wrap-up as the last item on your agenda. This reminds you to end the meeting by reviewing the actions and deadlines that everyone agreed upon and scheduling the next meeting's time and place.

FIGURE 2.12 How to Create Meeting Minutes

minutes

MINUTES

Online Internship Handbook Team

Human Resources Conference Room
July 31, 20XX

Include the day, time, and place of the meeting at the top of the agenda.

Present: Jay Macintosh, Intern to Director for Human Resources, Team Leader
Rachel Ferrera, Intern to Assistant to CEO
Arnie Glover, Intern for Temp Pool Supervisor
Roberto Washington, Intern, Web Development Department

Include a list of who attended.

I.   **Introductions:** Jay Macintosh called the meeting to order, introduced himself, and asked the others to state their department, experience, and skills.

II. **Project Overview:** Jay Macintosh explained the project goals. The team brainstormed ideas for topics and assigned content as follows:

   a. Welcome to the Company   - Rachel Ferrera
      1. History of the Organization
      2. Mission / Vision Statements
      3. Organizational Chart
      4. Your Role as an Intern

   b. Policies and Procedures   - Arnie Glover
      1. Maintaining Work Hours and Reporting Absences
      2. Sending and Responding to Email
      3. Logging Telephone Calls
      4. Using the Internet
      5. Using Social Media
      6. Submitting Reimbursement Requests

   c. Human Resources   - Jay Macintosh
      1. Salary and Payroll Procedures
      2. Health Benefits
      3. Educational Resources
      4. Applying for Permanent Employment

Organize content by categories. If possible, match the agenda.

III. **Web Development Support:** Roberto Washington explained company policies about website format, layout, and design options. The team discussed where on the current company website the internship handbook should be located. Decision: Roberto will check with his supervisor about content and resource needs and report to the team by email before the end of the week.

Focus on what the team decided and do not repeat everything that was said.

IV. **Six-Week Timeline: Decisions:**
      1. We will meet on Tuesdays from 3–5 PM. Between meetings we will update each other by email.
      2. Jay will send our weekly meeting minutes to his supervisor as our progress reports.
      3. We will send the completed version of our first draft to the other interns who volunteered for this project to get their feedback by Week 3.
      4. We will submit a draft to the Director of Human Resources by Week 4.
      5. Roberto will begin putting the material on the web in Week 5.

Include assignments (who agreed to do what) and deadlines (when you agreed to submit deliverables).

V.   **Next Meeting:** The team will meet on August 7 to discuss the content reports.

End with decisions about the next meeting.

Be a good team member

Although a team works together to achieve a common goal, it is still made up of individuals. Each individual needs to take responsibility for his or her own tasks and also contribute to a productive working relationship with others. To be a good team member, follow these guidelines:

- **Make a commitment to the team and its goals.** At times, it may be tempting to do minimal work for the team and assume that others will take up the slack. But a team will succeed only if everyone shares a similar level of commitment. Every member must be reliable and pull his

COLLABORATION
EXTROVERTS AND INTROVERTS: MAKING THE MOST OF YOUR DIFFERENCES

Are you an extrovert or an introvert? Extroverts become energized when connecting with people. They love thinking out loud and sharing in the process of developing ideas and collaborating on projects. By contrast, introverts often prefer to work on their own in quiet spaces and develop their ideas thoroughly before sharing them. Because extroverts and introverts have opposite tendencies, they sometimes have difficulty understanding each other and working together.

The problem is particularly acute for introverts because American workplaces have developed into environments that prize extroverted models of communication and leadership. Open-plan offices assume that creativity comes from people constantly exchanging ideas, though many introverts find that environment to be over-stimulating and not conducive to creativity. Extroverts are more outgoing performers in a meeting and are identified early as potential leaders, while introverts may go unrecognized.[70]

The tendency to privilege extroverts is unfortunate. Research by Adam Grant at The Wharton School at the University of Pennsylvania has shown that in some instances, introverts are better leaders than extroverts.[71] While extroverts are particularly good at motivating people who are passive and need a lot of direction, extroverts are less successful with teams that are already motivated and proactive. The extrovert wants to be center stage and can inhibit others from speaking up. By contrast, an introvert is more open to accepting suggestions and making contributors feel valued. The research also shows that teams are most cohesive and effective when they have a balance of extroverted and introverted members.[72]

How do you get that balance to work effectively? Much has been written about how introverts can better navigate an extrovert's world—pushing beyond your comfort zone, acting like an extrovert, and thus desensitizing yourself—but Jennifer Kahnweiler, author of *The Genius of Opposites*, *Quiet Influence*, and *The Introverted Leader*, suggests an ABCDE model that both extroverts and introverts can follow for smoother collaboration:[73]

- **Accept the alien:** Don't try to change the other person; just try to understand him or her.
- **Bring on the battles:** Embrace the inevitable disagreements, and recognize that they will help you develop a better idea than you could on your own.
- **Cast the character:** Think of your opposite as playing a character in a scenario, and cast that character to bring out his or her best in the role.
- **Destroy the dislike:** Learn to respect, like, and enjoy each other.
- **Each can't offer everything:** Accept that you and your organization will be better off if you consider a full diversity of options, and that one person, alone, cannot generate sufficient diversity.

Kahnweiler argues that when opposites learn to work well together, they can develop mutually complementary roles, leading to successful outcomes.

For a **COLLABORATION** exercise, go to Exercise 24 on page 73.

---

or her own weight. In addition, every team member must be willing to do whatever it takes to make the team successful, including helping each other if the need arises.

- **Create a collaborative working climate.** To work well together, team members need to trust each other and believe that everyone is working in the team's best interests. This means that, as a good team member, you need to be worthy of that trust. Listen to your teammates without criticism or judgment and give everyone a chance to participate in decision making. Respond constructively to feedback from others, and address conflicts when they arise rather than letting them grow silently and weaken team cohesion.

- **Support and encourage your teammates.** Individuals appreciate recognition, even when they are working as a team. A good team member shows gratitude for the efforts of others and identifies how individual contributions support the larger team effort. This technique can also help ensure that good ideas are recognized. In the early years of the Obama presidency, female staff members on the leadership team developed a technique they called "amplification." When a woman made an important point, other women on the team would repeat it and give credit to its author to ensure that everyone in the room heard the idea and knew where it came from.[74]

- **Support team decisions.** Even if the team has made a decision that differs from what you wanted, once the decision is made, support that decision and work toward implementing it. If you have concern about the decision or believe it may cause problems, voice your concerns to the team. Do not try to undermine the decision.

- **Focus on continuous quality improvement.** No matter how well your team is performing, individual team members may see ways that the team can do better. By making productive suggestions, you can help improve the team and its results.

■ In summary, the interpersonal skills you learned in this chapter are wide-ranging—spanning from basic listening and speaking skills to the more complex skills of emotional intelligence, managing conflict, working with people from other cultures, and working well in teams. As you move forward through the course, you will find many opportunities to apply these skills both in the classroom and within team projects.

Many organizations have national headquarters, with employees and teams located around the country and even the world. Communicating with all those teams—and helping them work to their highest capacity—can be both challenging and rewarding.

Design for America (DFA) is an organization that has eagerly taken that challenge and is reaping the rewards. DFA is a national network of campus design studios committed to shaping "the next generation of social innovators."[75] Each studio comprises multiple student design teams working with community partners or corporate sponsors to tackle projects that will have a positive social impact. For example, DFA teams have designed a toy to educate children with diabetes about their disease,[76] a device to help disaster victims signal their location when all communication systems are down,[77] and a sensor that reduces hospital-acquired infections by improving the hand hygiene of medical professionals.[78]

In 2017, DFA supported more than 160 student teams from 36 studios in schools as dispersed and diverse as University of California at Davis, Vanderbilt, University of Oregon, Virginia Tech, and Yale.

How does the national office of DFA, located at Northwestern University, communicate with these teams to help them stay on track and learn the design methodology that will contribute to their success? According to Stacy Klingbeil, former program manager for DFA's national office, the strategy for communicating with teams is multifaceted and has evolved over the years, with each communication touchpoint having a specific goal.

- **Annual Leadership Studio:** Each summer, DFA kicks off the new academic year with face-to-face communication, bringing together representatives from all the studios for a week long design experience. Michelle Baverman and Deniz Alpay, DFA fellows who helped facilitate the 2016 Leadership Studio, explain that it is important to have people from every studio together in the same room to experience the fun and hard work of design. The energy of Leadership Studio generates excitement that is "the fuel that drives the studios to do all the awesome projects they do for the rest of the year." As Rob Calvey, DFA instructional coordinator notes, bringing people together in one place also allows DFA to teach core design concepts and to model what a studio can do so that participants can recreate the design ecosystem back home.

Courtesy: Sally Ryan Photography

- **Monthly video calls:** Each month, DFA National sponsors several virtual group meetings attended by leaders from various studios. Each meeting focuses on a specific stage in the design process, and a studio typically

chooses to attend the meeting most relevant to its current stage in the design process. One goal of these meetings is to ensure that the studios are engaged and on track. As Klingbeil notes, DFA decided to disseminate design advice in these group calls rather than individual calls because "we realized that people liked connecting with each other, sharing best practices, and discussing the challenges they were facing." To make these meetings most effective, DFA asks participants to select the specific topic of the meeting and to indicate in advance who will be attending, making the studios more accountable. Social media plays a role in these meetings, too. Alpay explains that "At the end of each meeting we have three take-aways that we tweet out to everyone. And we take screenshots of everyone smiling and share those images on social media." This communication helps everyone in the organization benefit from each meeting.

- **Bi-weekly emails:** DFA supplements the face-to-face and video communication with email communication that is designed to provide just-in-time information to studios as they need it. Every two weeks, studios submit update forms that communicate to DFA National where they are in the design process, what they have accomplished in the previous two weeks, what challenges they are facing, and what their goals are for the next two weeks. Based on a studio's goals, DFA responds with an automated email that provides resources appropriate for that stage of the design process. Klingbeil explains that "the real value of the emails may not be the content but just that they are hearing from DFA National every other week. We are pushing them and reminding them they are part of a larger organization and not alone."

- **One-on-one calls:** Although most DFA communication is group communication, one-on-one phone calls allow DFA National to help studios that are struggling or who have missed group calls.

- **Facebook group:** DFA uses Facebook to post job opportunities and "cool things" about design.

- **Slack:** DFA uses the social collaboration tool Slack for some of the more administrative communication tasks. For example, the organization has a created a Slack channel to communicate with project leads and other channels that teams can use for specific communication tasks such as suggesting meeting topics, submitting slides before a video call, or submitting reimbursement requests.

Managing communication with 36 teams dispersed throughout the country is a real challenge. One of the lessons learned, according to Calvey, is that first impressions are important. For DFA's communication strategy to be successful, every studio's first experience with a communication touchpoint must be a good experience. "If a studio gets nothing out of the first group call they are on, then they are less likely to come to the second one. So we try very hard to make sure that every studio's first experience with each touchpoint is high quality."

Source: Interview with Deniz Alpay, Michelle Baverman, Rob Calvey, and Stacy Klingbeil

Working as a Cross-Cultural Team

This case scenario will help you review the chapter material by applying it to a specific situation.

The first three weeks of your internship at Baer, Kramer, & Dreslin Market Research in Nashville were great. You enjoyed brainstorming marketing ideas with your manager and designing a survey for an important client. However, the past week has been pure misery. Your supervisor assigned you to join three other interns on a team to create a comprehensive online handbook for interns. Each summer, the company hires seven interns at your location in Nashville and seven more in the company's data processing department in New Delhi, India. You will work on your project with one other intern from the Nashville office and two interns from New Delhi.

Planning the first meeting was difficult. You lost two days of work trying to set a meeting time because there is a 10½-hour time difference between Nashville and New Delhi; at 9 AM Central Daylight Time in Nashville, it is 7:30 PM in New Delhi. You suggested a 7 AM teleconference, but your Nashville teammate, Roberto, said he could not arrive in the office early for a meeting. You suggest an 8:30 AM teleconference, which would be 7 PM in New Delhi, but both your New Delhi teammates, Maansi and Anant, are vague about whether they could stay late. You beg Roberto to arrange to get to work early just one day so that your team can hold a kick-off meeting. Roberto admits that he could easily get to the office early but prefers to sleep later. "And anyway," he admits, "I didn't sign up for human resources work when I accepted an internship in consumer research. How will this help me get a job?"

Finally, you are able to convince Roberto to accommodate Maansi and Anant. The first meeting is scheduled for 7:30 AM Central Daylight Time. The meeting seems to begin well enough. Everyone arrives on time, the teleconferencing system works, and the meeting starts with friendly introductions. Within five minutes, though, you know you are in trouble. When Anant introduces himself, he speaks so quickly that you miss everything he says. You would be too embarrassed to ask him to repeat it, so you remain quiet and pretend to understand. After the introductions, things get worse. No one has thought to make an agenda, so no one knows what the team is trying to accomplish. After a few moments of painful silence, you say, "Well maybe we should just start sharing ideas about coming up with a plan for the online handbook."

Anant jumps right in. You don't understand much of what he says, but you do hear the words "user interface," "programming," "database," and "search functions." You and Roberto look at each other in amazement. Why is Anant talking about computer programming? And why is he continuing to talk without stopping for five minutes? Is it rude to interrupt? Finally, Roberto says, "Anant, it sounds like you may have some good ideas, but we don't understand. We thought our job was to plan an online handbook." Anant replied, "That's what I'm talking about." Throughout all of this, Maansi remains silent. After the first meeting, you feel that it is going to be a long five weeks until the end of your summer internship.

Question 1: What interpersonal, intercultural, and teamwork communication issues are emerging in this scenario?

Listening for Understanding

After your first team meeting, Roberto says, "It doesn't sound like Maansi and Anant will be too helpful on this project. Maybe we should do it on our own. We can come up with a plan for a handbook in a week and then coast through the rest of the summer." You think Roberto has a good point. The project would be easier to complete without participating in a cross-cultural team. And you ask yourself "Why *are* Maansi and Anant on this team? Why am *I* on this team? What are we supposed to be doing?"

You decide that this confusion stems from a communication problem—not with Maansi and Anant but with your supervisor. You thought you were listening intently when she asked you to "come up with a plan for an online handbook." But did you really understand what she meant? You were too intimidated to ask any clarifying questions:

- What does "plan" mean? What is the goal of the team?
- Is there some reason you and Roberto were put on the team? Is there some specific reason Maansi and Anant are on the team?
- What should be the final deliverable this summer?

With these questions in mind, you propose this plan to Roberto: "Let's try to arrange a meeting with our supervisor this afternoon. Rather than just sitting there and listening, let's ask lots of questions to be sure we understand. At the end of the meeting, we can summarize what we learned and email it to Maansi and Anant. We need to be sure we all have the same idea of what we are supposed to do."

Question 2: Listening involves a number of specific skills: hearing, comprehending and interpreting, evaluating, and responding. Which of these areas contributed to the communication problem in this scenario? Identify specific examples.

Framing Negative Criticism Positively

Fortunately, the meeting with your supervisor is helpful. Through much questioning and paraphrasing, you and Roberto identify four tasks for the summer: evaluate the material in the current paper handbook, gather information from current interns in both locations, put together a content outline for the website, and develop an easy-to-use structure for the website.

Although the meeting is successful, you are angry at Roberto because he simply cannot hide his contempt for this project. Before the meeting, he whispers to you, "Let's just get this meeting over with. No one needs a handbook. This project is just more busywork for interns." You find it difficult to begin focusing on content in the meeting because you are fuming about Roberto's attitude. Originally, you were looking forward to working with Roberto because he is smart and creative, but now you are afraid that his attitude may stand in the way of completing the project.

You prepare two different ways to talk with Roberto about this:

- **Option 1.** "Roberto, you are so negative all the time. I know you really don't want to do this project, but that's our job. We both need good evaluations from this internship. If you don't change your mindset, you'll cause us both to fail."

- **Option 2.** "Roberto, I'm really looking forward to working with you. You always have such great ideas. But I'm worried that you don't think this project is important and won't give it your best effort. I want to get a strong evaluation from this internship. I know if we work together we can plan a great handbook—and I think we can have a good time working together."

Question 3: How would you describe the difference between the two approaches? Which approach would help Roberto accept the criticism?

Understanding Conflict

By the second week of the project, the team is working efficiently, with all team members doing their tasks. Yet there is tension at every team meeting. Roberto appears to be looking for the fastest way through the project, and he gets frustrated with your attention to detail. You also are losing patience with Roberto. He is capable of great work, but it is never quite finished. Meanwhile, Maansi and Anant continue to focus just on the programming aspects of the online handbook and aren't interested in talking about content. When you ask Maansi to help you gather information about content needs from New Delhi interns, she says, "I won't have time to do that. We can take content from the current handbook. To have an excellent handbook, what's really important is developing an interactive website." You find this insulting because you have been working hard to develop content.

Before bad feelings take over, you decide to schedule a meeting with your supervisor to talk about these conflicts and see if she has any ideas about how to handle them. She asks, "What kind of conflicts are these? Are these personality conflicts? Or do the conflicts stem from differences of opinion about how to get the best handbook? Or do team members have competing goals?" As you think about the problems, you realize these conflicts go beyond simple personality clashes.

The conflict with Roberto seems to be one of competing goals. Your goal is to create a great handbook. Roberto's goal from the start has been to work on a project that will look good on his résumé. Perhaps you and Roberto can talk and find common ground between these two goals.

The conflict with Maansi and Anant is different. They seem to want an excellent handbook. However, they have a very different opinion about what is required to achieve that goal. They believe that programming is the key. Existing content can simply be imported into the new site. As a result, they are not interested in interviewing their fellow interns to gather information. The New Delhi interns may need different information from the handbook, but you have no way to find out. Perhaps the best way to address this conflict is simply to accommodate Maansi and Anant and let them focus solely on programming. You and Roberto can determine a different way to gather information from New Delhi interns.

Question 4: Besides accommodating, what specific actions could you take to manage the conflict with Maansi and Anant if you decided to avoid, compete, compromise, or collaborate? Which approach do you believe would lead to the best outcome?

Managing Cultural Diversity

To streamline communication while working with Anant and Maansi, you set weekly meeting times on Tuesdays and Thursdays at 8 AM Central Daylight Time, which fortunately works well for both the U.S. and India team members. Every meeting has an agenda, and teams exchange important information in writing before and after the meeting, which eases the problem of understanding foreign accents. (You were surprised that Anant had as much difficulty understanding your southern American accent as you had understanding his Indian accent. But he had learned British English.)

Nonetheless, your team has had some real difficulties working together. Anant and Maansi always seem busy with several projects, not just the internship project, and do not treat this one with any urgency. They are indirect in presenting what they have accomplished, and you are never confident about how far along they are. At one meeting, when you ask Maansi to see their prototype website so that you can figure out how to structure your content, she becomes silent. You hadn't meant the question as a criticism, but perhaps she understood it that way. Anant, by contrast, is never silent and is always trying to engage in an intellectual debate about various programming techniques. Trying to figure out how to communicate with people from other cultures without knowing them or their culture has proved challenging.

Question 5: What factors may explain the cultural differences between the U.S. and Indian team members?

Reaping the Benefits of Teamwork

At the end of the summer internship, despite the conflicts and your communication challenges, you are surprised at all your team accomplished. Working as a team, you:

- Interviewed all the current interns and compiled the results into a report identifying the most important content for the handbook
- Developed a site map for the handbook
- Wrote content for two sections of the handbook
- Gathered inspirational quotations from senior management
- Programmed a prototype site
- Conducted a round of user testing
- Developed a list of necessary revisions

You think about two of Roberto's comments from earlier in the summer. At one point he complained, "You know, it doesn't sound like Maansi and Anant will be too helpful on this project. Maybe we should do it on our own." It would have been easier to create the content with just you and Roberto, but consider how much less work would have been done: no site mapping, no programming, and no user testing. You needed people with programming expertise on your team to get that done. At another point, Roberto asked, "How will this help me get a job?" The answer to that question is now obvious: You learned to work collaboratively with others, manage conflict, and complete a complicated project. Compared to other interns who learned only technical skills in market research, you have developed a transferrable set of skills that will be crucial on the job no matter what field you enter.

Question 6: Study Question 5 (pages 56–63) describes some of the characteristics that successful teams share. This team ultimately was successful. How did it demonstrate these characteristics?

Study Questions in Review

 What listening skills will help you communicate better with others?

(pages 36–42)

Use active listening techniques to ensure understanding:

- **Hearing accurately** depends on eliminating distractions and focusing on the speaker.
- **Comprehending and interpreting** what is being said involves observing people's behavior, listening to their non-verbal communication, being aware of tone of voice and emphasis, asking questions and paraphrasing, and being aware of gender-specific communication styles.
- **Objectively evaluating** what you hear requires you to remain open-minded, focus on ideas instead of prejudgments about the speaker, and use sound reasoning.
- **Responding** lets the speaker know you understand and initiates the next step in the conversation.

 How can you help others be good listeners when you speak? *(pages 42–45)*

Engage listeners and make meaning clear by doing the following:

- **Focus on your audience** to analyze the audience's interests.
- **Share the conversation** by inviting others to speak.
- **Use clear, concrete, unambiguous language** to avoid misinterpretation.
- **Support your message with good nonverbal communication** that reinforces your spoken message.
- **Avoid language that triggers a negative response.**
- **Frame negative comments positively.**

 How can you manage interpersonal conflict? *(pages 45–52)*

Although cognitive conflict can be productive in improving team outcomes, affective conflict focusing on personalities does not enhance team performance. To manage conflict:

- **Identify the cause of the conflict,** which can include competing goals, differences of opinion, lack of information, relational issues, and ego issues.
- **Select an appropriate management technique.** You might avoid confrontation, accommodate or give in, compete to win, compromise, or collaborate to find the best solution.

 How can you improve your communication with people from different cultures? *(pages 52–56)*

Cultural differences affect communication style. To prepare yourself to communicate with people from other cultures, do the following:

- **Understand how cultures differ.** Low-context cultures value explicit communication, whereas high-context cultures rely more on subtle cues. Individualistic cultures value an individual's achievements. By contrast, collectivist cultures put the good of the group first. Cultures with high-power distance are very hierarchical. Low-power-distance cultures are less formal. Cultures also differ in their tolerance for uncertainty (including ambiguity, risk, and change) and their orientation toward time.
- **Develop strategies that help you communicate with diverse groups.** Be relatively formal, mirror the other person's behavior, be clear and concise, talk slowly, request feedback to ensure understanding, and smile to express friendliness and willingness to communicate.

 How can you work effectively as part of a team? *(pages 56–63)*

To improve team performance and make teamwork an enjoyable and productive experience, do the following:

- **Assemble an effective team.** A group of people with the correct skills, resources, and attitude is needed to succeed.
- **Agree on team goals and standards.** Do not expect the team to perform at a high level immediately.
- **Pay attention to team development and dynamics.** For long-term teams, let teams gel through states of forming, storming, norming, and performing. For short-term teams, take advantage of "teaming" strategies to learn collectively and fix issues quickly.
- **Develop good leadership practices.**
- **Plan for effective meetings.**
- **Be a good team member** by doing your job and supporting other team members.

Visual Summary

SQ1

LISTENING

- Hear accurately to comprehend and interpret meaning.
- "Listen" to nonverbal communication.
- Ask questions and paraphrase to ensure understanding.
- Evaluate information: is it accurate, well-supported, and convincing?
- Respond to provide feedback.

SQ2

SPEAKING

- Focus on your audience.
- Share the conversation.
- Use clear, concrete, unambiguous language.
- Support your message with good eye contact, strong and positive tone, and complementary gestures and facial expressions.
- Avoid biased, provocative, or accusatory language.

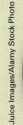

SQ3

MANAGING CONFLICT

- Identify conflict as affective or cognitive.
- Identify the reason for the conflict.
- Shift focus away from ego and back to business.
- Decide how to manage conflict: avoid confrontation, accommodate, give in, compete to win, compromise, or collaborate to find the best solution.

COMMUNICATING ACROSS CULTURES

- Understand how cultures differ.
- Identify dimensions of the specific culture: high or low context? individualistic or collectivistic? high or low power distance? comfortable or uncomfortable with uncertainty? monochronic or polychronic?
- Develop strategies to communicate with diverse groups: use formality and respect, pay attention to nonverbal cues, be clear and concise, talk slowly, and request feedback to ensure understanding.

SQ4

SQ5

WORKING IN TEAMS

- Assemble effective teams by identifying skills, resources, and interests.
- Determine goals and standards.
- Plan time to form, storm, norm, and perform.
- Develop good leadership by focusing on the purpose, encouraging participation, creating timelines, assigning tasks, keeping the project on track, and resolving differences.
- Plan effective meetings supported by agendas and minutes.
- Be a good team member through commitment, collaboration, and continuous quality improvement.

Key Terms

MyLab Business Communication

If your instructor is using MyLab Business Communication, go to **www.pearson.com/mylab/business-communication** to complete the problems marked with this icon ⭐.

Review Questions

1 Name two barriers that interfere with hearing.

⭐ **2** How does comprehension differ from interpretation?

3 What are three types of paraphrasing?

4 Describe how a person "listens" to nonverbal communication.

⭐ **5** What is the difference between a provocative question and an authentic question?

⭐ **6** Under what circumstances is it a good idea to accommodate (or give in) during a conflict?

7 What is ethnocentrism?

8 Name one way that an individualistic culture differs from a collectivist culture.

9 What are the four stages of team formation?

10 Describe two ways that file-sharing tools such as Google Docs help teams collaborate.

Critical Thinking Questions

1 Some research suggests that emotional intelligence is a stronger predictor of job success than traditional intelligence—how smart you are.[79] Why do you think emotional intelligence is so important for many jobs?

⭐ **2** Explain a situation—either at home, school, or work—in which you listened passively and neglected to hear important information. Describe the negative result and identify how you could have used active listening strategies to improve your communication process.

3 Designers of consumer products argue that to understand what customers really need, you have to do more than listen to what they say. You have to observe what they do. Why do you think there is often a gap between what people say and what they do?

4 Review the speaking strategies listed at the beginning of SQ2 on page 43. Divide them into two lists: strategies that you currently try to use when you speak and strategies that you typically do not think about. Of the strategies that you typically do not think about, identify one that you'd like to begin using immediately and explain why.

5 What words or phrases trigger a negative emotional response from you? If someone repeatedly uses one of your "trigger words," what are your options for responding? Which option would you choose?

⭐ **6** Some organizations provide the services of mediators to help resolve workplace conflicts. What are the advantages of having a disinterested party resolve a conflict? What are the advantages of having people involved in the conflict work it out on their own?

7 Imagine you have been hired by a global company that is holding a two-week orientation for all new employees at the head office in San Francisco. You will be staying in a hotel for two weeks, and you have been assigned to share a room with a new employee from Zurich, Switzerland. What can you do to find out in advance a little bit about the culture in Zurich? Once you have identified some characteristics of that culture, what can you do to ensure that you do not stereotype your roommate?

8 Explain a team situation in which you experienced conflict. What was the purpose of the team? Why did the affective and/or cognitive conflict occur? How did the team resolve the conflict? What was the impact on the final product?

9 Imagine you have a teammate who wants to do all the project work himself because he does not trust anyone else on the team to produce high-quality results. How would you respond to that teammate?

10 *Social loafing* refers to the tendency of certain people to do less work when they are part of a team than they would when working independently. What strategies can a team use to minimize social loafing of team members?

Key Concept Exercises

 What listening skills will help you communicate better with others? *(pages 36–42)*

1 Hearing accurately

In each of the following situations, identify what you can do to improve the ability of listeners to hear accurately.

a. One member of your team has a hearing impairment and often misses key things that are said at meetings. Suggest at least four things that you and the rest of the team can do to make it easier for your teammate to hear well. Suggest at least four things your hearing-impaired teammate can do to hear you better.

b. At departmental meetings, your mind wanders when your boss is speaking because he has a monotonous tone of voice and rarely gets to the point. As a result, during the last two meetings you have missed important information. What can you do to improve your ability to hear what your boss says?

2 Comprehending and interpreting: Listening to tone of voice

A speaker's tone of voice and emphasis provide clues about his or her attitudes and feelings. Imagine at least two different ways that you can say each of the following four statements. What are the different meanings conveyed by the different sets of nonverbal cues?

a. I didn't do anything wrong.

b. We need to talk now.

c. I'll give you my phone number after the meeting.

d. When did you come up with that idea?

3 Comprehending and interpreting: Paraphrasing to ensure understanding

Learning how to paraphrase in multiple ways is challenging. Note the two conversational exchanges that follow, with paraphrases in *italics*. Identify which *italicized* statements are paraphrases of content, intent, and feeling. Remember, when you paraphrase for content, you state your understanding of the explicit message. When you paraphrase for intent, you try to uncover why someone made that statement. When you paraphrase for feelings, you try to uncover the emotions in the statement.

a. Accounts payable: We keep getting invoices for partial shipments, and I can't figure out when a purchase order is completely filled. I can't pay an invoice for a partial shipment. The purchase order has to be closed out before we pay the invoice.

Purchasing: *So you are saying that our computer system will not allow you to pay a partial invoice?*

Accounts payable: I don't know. The computer system might allow it.

Purchasing: *So, it's company policy not to pay partial invoices?*

Accounts payable: Well, it's not really a company policy. It's just so confusing to match these partial invoices with purchase orders. I'm never sure I get it right, so I don't think it's a good idea for us to do this.

Purchasing: *You sound like you might want some help with the invoices since you're spending so much time matching the invoices with the purchase order. Would you like me to match them for you? Because I wrote the purchase orders, I can do it more easily.*

Accounts payable: That sounds like a good idea.

b. Interviewer: What gets you excited about public relations?

Interviewee: I've been thinking about public relations for a long time.

Interviewer: *Your goal has always been to go into public relations?*

Interviewee: Well, no. My original goal was to be a lawyer, and I worked as a paralegal for a few years, but there was really no career path, so I decided to do something else.

Interviewer: *So, you were frustrated and that led to a career change?*

Interviewee: Yes, exactly. I want to do something that allows me to be more creative and contribute more to an organization.

Interviewer: *You believe that public relations will make better use of your talents.*

4 Comprehending and interpreting: Being aware of gender-specific communication styles

Although there is no absolute "female" communication style or "male" communication style, researchers in sociolinguistics have identified a number of widespread differences between the way men and women typically communicate. In business, people need to accommodate different styles in order to work well together. In small groups (or as a whole class), discuss the following three scenarios. In your past experience, have you noticed these types of differences? What would you recommend the participants do to bridge the differences?

a. Ella and Michael are assigned to work on a project together. Ella goes to her supervisor to ask for clarification of details and to ensure she understands what the project requires. By contrast, Michael jumps right in and begins to work. He says he'll figure it out along the way. Michael tells Ella she's wasting time. Ella believes Michael hates to ask for help or directions, even if he needs them.

b. In meetings, Richard illustrates his points with metaphors about war and sports: "I think we'll score a touchdown with this new product. But if we don't get it to market soon, the competition will outflank us." By contrast, Alice uses anecdotes and metaphors about relationships and home: "Our products are always the bridesmaids. This one will be the bride." Richard and Alice understand the other person's metaphors, but they are not comfortable with them.

c. At the monthly department meeting, Denise and James's manager asked for suggestions about how to research a client problem. Denise spoke immediately and began to make a suggestion. Before she had time to finish, James interrupted and said, "That gives me another idea," and he began presenting his thoughts. The conversation in the meeting then focused on James's idea. Denise waited for a break in the conversation to return to her point. She quietly tried to interrupt, but could not break the momentum of the conversation. She left the meeting feeling angry with James.

5 Evaluating

Your coworker Bob is always complaining about something and makes only negative comments at meetings. He came into your office this morning to share a proposal he plans to make in a manager's meeting tomorrow. He proposes that the department change the hiring requirements so that all new hires have three years of experience in addition to a bachelor's degree. He claims that "A college education is not sufficient for the job." He supports his claim with this evidence: "The two newest employees, fresh out of college, have been making mistakes and cannot seem to learn the details of the job. We have no time to train them. We need to hire people who are already trained." He asks if you will support his idea at the meeting.

Your immediate reaction is "I don't know." You have made friends with one of the new hires, and you know from your own experience it takes time to learn a job. You were hired right out of college too. You will need to evaluate this proposal critically before you take a stance. What steps would you take to evaluate what you heard?

6 Responding

Imagine that you are working on a project with three other people. One of your teammates provides great ideas during team meetings but consistently misses deadlines and provides only partial work. Her lack of follow-through has significantly slowed the project, and you are now concerned that your team will not complete the project on time. Your teammate says she will meet the next deadline. How could you effectively respond to her statement? Practice six different kinds of responses: (1) ask a question, (2) make a judgment, (3) contribute an opinion, (4) give advice, (5) argue or disagree, and (6) express empathy.

Identify the one response you think is best and be prepared to discuss your answer in class.

 How can you help others be good listeners when you speak? *(pages 42–45)*

7 Focus on your audience

Imagine that you receive a phone call from an actual friend or relative who asks you "How is school going?" or "How is your job?" Write a two-paragraph email to your instructor, identifying how you will respond to this specific audience:

- In the first paragraph, identify the friend or relative you have in mind and explain what you think that person really wants to know in asking that question.
- In the second paragraph, explain how you will respond. What will you tell your friend or relative and why? What won't you tell him or her and why?

8 Share the conversation

Observe a conversation at a meeting or between two or three people at lunch or dinner. Does any one person monopolize the conversation? If so, does that have any negative results? If the conversation is shared fairly, how long is each person's typical turn? How do people signal that they want to speak?

9 Use clear, concrete, unambiguous language

Each of the following sentences contains at least one ambiguous phrase. Identify the possible ambiguity and rephrase the statement so that it has one clear, concrete meaning. Feel free to make up details if necessary.

- **a.** You did a great job on that report.
- **b.** Mary's job performance hasn't been satisfactory this year.
- **c.** Our presentation needs to be perfect.
- **d.** There are just a few small problems to clear up before signing the contract.
- **e.** Clean up the conference room before the end of the day.
- **f.** Let's talk after the project is finished.

10 Support your message with good nonverbal communication

Ask someone you do not know for directions to a nearby location, and pay attention to that person's verbal and nonverbal communication.

- What is that person's verbal message; in other words, does the person provide directions or decline to help, or say something else?
- What nonverbal elements support that message?
- Are there any nonverbal elements that conflict with that message?

11 Avoid language that triggers a negative response

Read the following scenario and identify alternatives for the biased language.

Your first job after graduating is as an internal consultant with a small, local company. On your first day of work, the vice president who hired you asked you to come to a meeting where he will introduce you to the head of every department in the company. As you stand up at the front of the conference room, the vice president says, "I'd like to introduce the _____ who has been hired to help us." Imagine that the blank was filled in with each of the following terms (consider only the gender terms appropriate for you):

- Young lady/Young man
- Consultant
- Woman/Man
- Genius
- Gal/Guy
- College girl/College boy
- Expert

Which term(s) would you prefer the vice president use to introduce you? What are the problems with each of the remaining terms? What kinds of bias, if any, do they represent?

12 Frame negative comments positively

Although most people do not enjoy providing negative feedback, it is necessary in most work environments. People respond better to negative feedback if it is framed in a positive way and if the criticism is not preceded by "but." For each of the following scenarios, provide criticism, starting out with a positive comment and avoiding "but."

- **a.** You asked your assistant, Paolo, to make 50 photocopies of 15 individual handout sheets that you will use during the training session you are conducting tomorrow. Paolo decided that it would be easier for you to distribute the handouts as one set, so he collated and stapled the photocopies. However, your plan was to distribute each handout separately at specific points throughout the training session. How do you respond to Paolo?

- **b.** Your supervisor, Jean, asks you to suggest how the department can improve employee morale, which has been low since she took over six months ago. The former supervisor often told people they were doing a good job, but Jean has not mentioned anything to anyone—positive or negative. You are sure that employee morale would improve dramatically if she would share encouraging feedback once in a while. How do you tell her this?

- **c.** You and Sheena met during your company orientation two years ago and were placed in similar positions in two different departments. Since then, you have met for lunch once a week. Sheena is known for gossiping about coworkers, and even though you know it's not appropriate, you often look forward to her tantalizing tales. You don't share the gossip with others, but you know Sheena does, and you believe this may be why you have been promoted twice while she has remained in the same position. After the standard gossip-fest at lunch today, Sheena mentions that she was passed over yet again for a promotion. She asks you why you think she can't seem to get ahead in the company. You do not want to hurt her feelings, but you do want to see her succeed. How do you respond?

How can you manage interpersonal conflict? *(pages 45–52)*

13 Identify the cause of the conflict

Identifying the cause of conflict is not always easy. Review the five different causes of conflict you learned in this chapter: competing goals, differences of opinion, faulty assumptions, relational issues, and ego issues. For each of the following scenarios, identify the cause—or causes—of the conflict and explain your reasoning.

- **a.** Your company is planning to install a new air-conditioning system for the administrative offices. The vice president of operations has asked you and a coworker to research air-conditioning systems and recommend one. You and your coworker have narrowed your search to two systems, but you've reached an impasse. Your coworker argues that you should propose the AirCo system because it is the most cost-efficient to install. You, by contrast, want to propose Cool-Rite because it has the best long-term reliability record.

b. You and two classmates have decided to start a small business to help fund your college education. As part of your planning, you have asked an art student friend to design a logo for you. You have all decided that, above all else, the logo must look professional. Your friend gives you four options to choose from, but you and your business partners cannot agree on an option.

c. It's 9 AM Tuesday morning, and it doesn't look as if your team paper will be finished and edited to hand in by the 10 AM deadline. When you received the parts from everyone on Monday at 8 PM, you saw many grammatical and formatting errors that you needed to fix. You've been working on the paper all night. Your teammates say, "Just print it out and hand it in. It's good enough—and it's important that the paper be in on time." You say, "We'll get points off for grammar errors—and the paper will only be an hour or so late." Your teammates are getting angry and feel as though you are holding them hostage because the edited version of the paper is on your computer. One of your teammates says, "You are such a nit-picky perfectionist. That's what we get for having an English major on our team!"

14 Select an appropriate management technique

You and a teammate are working on a presentation that will be given at a budget meeting on Monday. On Thursday night, you think the project is far from complete. You'd like the presentation to be as polished as possible, so you suggest to your teammate that you get together over the weekend to finish it. He says that he wants to finish the presentation by Friday because he wants to relax over the weekend. You begin to argue. You know you won't be able to complete the presentation in one day. What is the cause of this conflict and how would you respond?

In a memo to your instructor, explain how you could use each of the following conflict management techniques:

- **Avoid.** How could you avoid dealing with the conflict?
- **Accommodate.** What would you do to accommodate your teammate?
- **Compete.** What would a competitive approach look like?
- **Compromise.** What would a compromise look like?
- **Collaborate.** What would you do to try to collaborate?

Identify the approach you would recommend and explain your selection.

 ### SQ4 How can you improve your communication with people from different cultures? *(pages 52–56)*

15 Understand how cultures differ

Nonverbal communication differs among cultures. For example, eye contact is important to establish credibility in the United States. However, people in Japan and other Asian cultures often show respect by avoiding direct eye contact. Using an Internet search engine or sources recommended by your instructor, research nonverbal communication in a country or culture other than the United States. (Tip: Use the search terms *nonverbal communication* and the name of the country of your choice.) Be prepared to share your findings with the class.

16 Develop strategies that help you communicate with diverse groups

Imagine that you are talking to a group of international businesspeople and in conversation you use one of the following idiomatic phrases (or another one of your choice):

- Drive me up the wall
- Threw me for a loop
- Out of sync
- That's cool
- Out of the box

Your international visitors ask you to explain. How would you explain that phrase? What could you have said instead of that phrase in the first place to be more easily understood?

17 Intercultural issues [Related to the Ethics feature on page 55]

As you learned in this chapter, different cultures often have different perceptions about ethical issues, which can affect international business interactions. Using your library's online index of business-related publications, find at least two recent articles about instances of bribery between the United States and foreign countries. What companies were involved? How large were the bribes? What did the countries offer in exchange for the bribes? Were either of the companies charged under the Foreign Corrupt Practices Act? Summarize your findings in a paragraph or two. Then use your favorite web-searching tool—such as Google or Bing—to find one of the online "Bribe Payers' Indexes." How do the countries in your articles rank on the list? Add this documentation to your summary and be prepared to share your findings in class.

 ### SQ5 How can you work effectively as part of a team? *(pages 56–63)*

18 Assemble an effective team

Assume that you are the president of your school's student investment club. The provost emailed you to let you know that your group is eligible to apply for a $5,000 grant to support students' travel expenses to attend professional development opportunities, such as conferences and symposiums. You need to submit a three- to five-page proposal that justifies your group's financial need, outlines the potential use of the funds, and demonstrates how your group will benefit. The grant is competitive, and proposals are due in two weeks. You have eight people on your executive board but know that's too many people to collaborate on this project. Select three or four of the following people to help you write the proposal. Justify your selections both in terms of how they would benefit the project as well as how the remaining people would not.

- **Jill Hawthorne, Vice President.** Jill is a junior and has been a member of the group since her freshman year. She will run for president next year. She admits her writing skills are not good, but she is creative and never misses a meeting.
- **Amber Robinson, Treasurer.** Amber is a senior accounting major. She has been the treasurer for the last two years. She will graduate this semester and has missed the last several meetings because she has been out of town on job interviews.
- **Pilar Seehorn, Secretary.** Pilar is a sophomore. She never says anything during meetings but takes excellent minutes. She writes well and regularly sends emails to the executive board and membership about upcoming events and activities.
- **Michael Anderson, Professional Development.** Michael is a senior but needs another year to graduate. He arranges all the group's educational activities. He's a self-proclaimed extrovert and is very outgoing but he struggles with written assignments.
- **David Miller, Membership.** David is a junior marketing major. He is very creative and outgoing. He managed to increase your group's membership by 50 percent in the past two semesters. He writes well and helped write a similar proposal for a different group last year.
- **Manuel Hernandez, Publicity.** Manuel is a sophomore accounting major. He is new on the executive board, but he attends every meeting, writes well, and is very eager to help the group. He is interested in taking over as treasurer next semester, after Amber graduates.
- **Jon Sawyer, Fundraising.** Jon is a junior finance major. With Michael's help, he raised over $1,000 last semester for the group's professional development fund. Jon is very task-oriented, works hard, and writes well. He has already asked if he could help you with the proposal.

- **Sabrina Trotter, Service Learning.** Sabrina is a junior management major. She organizes the club's volunteer activities. With David's help, she has managed to double the level of charitable involvement. She has also asked if she could help you with the proposal.

19 Agree on team goals and standards

Search the web for "team contract" and find three examples that outline goals and standards for productive working teams. What content do the examples share? What differences exist? Consider a recent team experience that could have benefited from a team contract. What elements from the sample contracts would you recommend? Create an outline of the topics you would include in a team contract for a similar group experience.

20 Pay attention to team development and dynamics

Some teams do not advance through all stages of the forming, storming, norming, and performing process. Some teams get stuck in the storming stage and never reach norming, which is the stage where team members work effectively with each other. Other teams work through their conflicts but run out of time before they can effectively perform. Summarize one of your recent team experiences, using some (but not necessarily all) of the following questions to help you describe the development of your team:

- What was the goal or purpose of the team?
- How was the team formed (for example, assigned or selected)?
- What happened during the forming stage?
- Did the team experience any storming? If so, describe what happened.
- Did your team develop an approach to working together well? If so, what was it? If not, why not?
- Did the team end up accomplishing its goal?
- Would you want to work with that team again?

21 Develop good leadership practices

Some people are born leaders. Other people have to work hard to develop good leadership skills. Researchers have investigated leadership styles for decades. As early as 1939, Kurt Lewin identified three major leadership styles—authoritarian (autocratic), participative (democratic), and delegative (laissez-faire).[80] Search the web to learn more about leadership styles and identify one that best represents a leadership style with which you would be comfortable. Document your source, describe the leadership style, and explain how it best fits your personality. Summarize your findings in a few paragraphs.

22 Plan for effective meetings

Meetings are common—often daily—events for most businesspeople. You may be asked to take minutes at a meeting, either as one of your team assignments or for someone who is not able to attend the meeting. To practice your note-taking skills, watch a half-hour news broadcast, either by a local news station or a national network; or attend a seminar or workshop offered by your school. Record the important information you hear, and organize the content for easy reference. Because you won't have an agenda, you will need to listen (and watch) carefully for major ideas. Create a professional-looking document similar to the sample provided in the chapter. Proofread carefully before submitting your minutes to your instructor.

23 Be a good team member

For each of the following scenarios, identify the conflict and describe how you would respond. Explain your reasoning.

a. You and four other students have just been assigned to work together on a presentation that will be delivered in three weeks. You are appointed as the team leader. After class, you meet briefly with your team to determine when you can schedule time in the next few days to meet in the library to plan your project. However, a single day and time does not seem to work well for the entire group. Joe, who is already late for his next class, gets impatient and says to go ahead and meet without him. He'll go along with whatever the group decides and walks away. When asked for his contact information, he says, "Don't bother. I'll catch up with you next class."

b. Your group meets later that evening without Joe and assigns tasks to all team members. At the next class session, you tell Joe that the rest of the team members will research the content and that he has been assigned to put the content together in a PowerPoint file and present the summary slide. Joe says, "That's nuts! I'd have to wait to work on the file until the rest of you guys have finished your work, which will probably be the night before the presentation. No way! That's not fair!" You disagree.

c. You agree to swap assignments with Joe, but he does not send his part of the content to you by the deadline. You call him to ask if you can help, and he says, "Don't worry. I'm working on it now, and I'll bring it to the presentation tomorrow." You tell him that you can't create a summary slide if you don't have his information. He says, "You can work it in tomorrow before class and fake your way through a summary. No problem." You disagree.

d. During your presentation, Joe's part takes less than one minute, which means you have to fill the extra time during the summary to ensure that your team meets the 10-minute requirement. Although you manage to fake your way through the presentation, you do not feel that you did as well as you could have if Joe had provided his information on time. Back at your seats, Joe says to you, "Great job! We pulled it together. I think we had the best presentation in the class." You disagree.

e. At the next class session, your instructor asks your team to write a one-paragraph assessment of its effectiveness, both in terms of the team's collaborative process and the quality of the presentation. Each team member must sign the assessment. Joe thinks everything was great. You disagree.

Writing Exercises

24 Analyzing collaboration: Extroverts and introverts [Related to the Collaboration feature on page 63]

Select a recent team experience in which you participated, whether for a sport, an organization, or a class project. In a few paragraphs, describe the team, identify the goal for the activity, and describe the various team members. Then identify which team members (including yourself) seem to you to be extroverts and which seem to be introverts. Finally, in a few paragraphs, explain how you think the combination of styles helped and/or hurt the team.

25 Selecting social collaboration tools [Related to the Technology feature on pages 51–52]

Assume your company is looking to invest in collaboration tools to support teamwork. Currently, teams in your company share files via email or by uploading them to a server. You brainstorm on flip charts and then type up your brainstorming lists. Your supervisor, Maury Phillips, specifically thinks that web-based collaboration tools will help teams be more productive. Research at least three of these tools and write a brief memo (no more than one page) identifying all three tools and then persuasively recommending one. Be sure to identify key features of the tool and why those features will help teams.

26 Using Google Docs for collaboration [Related to the Technology feature on pages 51–52]

Go to Google Drive, at www.drive.google.com, and create a Google account if you do not already have one. If you are not familiar with the applications, learn about them by reading the support files on the Google Drive site. Once you are familiar with the applications, create a few sample files—a document, spreadsheet, and presentation—to become familiar with the file-creation process. Practice sharing files with others and publishing them as web pages. Depending on your instructor's preference, provide your instructor a link to the sample documents or email them, to document your Google Docs experience.

27 Using GroupMe for collaboration [Related to the Technology feature on pages 51–52]

GroupMe is a group messaging app that is popular with students for group work in and out of class. Install the app on your phone and create an account if you do not already have one. Familiarize yourself with its features and send practice messages to friends or classmates. Imagine that you must collaborate on an intergenerational team with members who have not used GroupMe or any other group messaging application. Draft a brief email (one or two paragraphs) explaining the benefits of GroupMe for project work—and persuading them to try GroupMe. Your email can also include images if you think that is useful.

Collaboration Exercises

28 Improving active listening skills

In groups of four, assign one of these roles to each group member: Speaker, Listener 1, Listener 2, and Observer. Complete the following exercise:

- **Speaker:** Talk for two to three minutes about a problem you faced in a past job search or a concern you have about a future job search.
- **Listeners:** Use clarifying questions and paraphrases to understand the speaker's content, intent, and feelings. Consider nonverbal messages as you paraphrase.
- **Speaker:** After the conversation ends, describe the degree to which you feel satisfied that the paraphrasing represented meaning accurately.
- **Observer:** Point out specific examples of effective and ineffective techniques the listeners used.
- **Listeners:** Discuss how the paraphrasing and questioning felt. Was it difficult? Awkward? Useful in uncovering additional meaning? How did you pick up on nonverbal cues?
- **Each Individual:** Based on what you learned from this exercise, write an email to your instructor explaining the challenges and benefits of active listening. Use examples from the exercise to support your analysis.

29 Analyzing trigger words

Work with a group of three or four classmates to analyze trigger words. Each person should identify at least two words or phrases that he or she reacts to negatively. Tell your team how you react when you hear the words you suggest. Also try to identify the source of this reaction. Does it result from your upbringing, your past experiences, or an association with a particular person? Summarize your team's discussion and prepare to report to the rest of the class the most interesting insights.

30 Comparing cultural differences [Related to the Culture feature on page 40]

Have each person in your team select a different country. Be sure the countries represent a range of geographical regions. Research your selected country to determine the cultural differences, such as customs and body language, that could affect your ability to communicate effectively with people from this country. (Tip: Begin your search on the web, using the search terms "doing business in *Country*" or "business etiquette in *Country*," inserting the name of the country you are researching.) Then compare your findings with your teammates. If you were hosting a business meeting with representatives from each country, what factors would you have to consider? As a team, write a memo to your instructor that summarizes your findings.

31 Comparing models of team formation

In a small group of three to five people, compare and contrast Tuckman's model of team formation (forming, storming, norming, and performing, pages 58–59 and Figure 2.9) with Edmondson's concept of teaming (page 59). Based on your past team experiences, which model more accurately describes the way teams form and function? Which is more realistic, given the time frame in which the teams with which you are most familiar must operate? Which model are you interested in investigating further, and why? Work together to summarize the results of your discussion in a short post (two to four paragraphs) to a group discussion board or other online learning management system tool.

Social Media Exercises

32 Social media and interpersonal communication

Some people argue that reliance on social media prevents a person from developing good interpersonal communication skills. Other people take the opposite point of view, arguing that use of social media may help a person improve interpersonal communication skills. Take a position on this issue and write a one-page paper arguing your position. Be sure to provide clear reasons and supporting evidence.

33 Social media conversations and customer support

Research shows that customers appreciate being able to receive customer support through social media—for example, through chats, tweets, or Facebook. Employees who provide this customer support will be more effective if they have good interpersonal communication skills. Review this chapter, and identify three specific interpersonal communication skills that you believe are important in communicating with customers through social media. Provide explanations and examples for your three choices.

Speaking Exercises

34 Making informal impromptu presentations

For each of the following topics, prepare a five-minute presentation.

a. Identify your collaborative strengths and weaknesses and describe one way you could improve your communication skills to become a better team member.

b. Describe a recent team experience in which your group suffered from an affective conflict. How was the conflict resolved? If it wasn't, how could it have been resolved?

c. Describe a team situation in which your group experienced groupthink. How could it have been avoided?

d. Have you used an electronic collaboration tool that you have found effective? Describe the tool, how you have used it, and why you like it.

35 Presenting executive briefings

As a team, prepare a five-minute presentation on one of the following topics. Include at least one visual aid.

a. You work for a company in Detroit, Michigan, and the vice president of purchasing is planning a series of teleconferences with business suppliers in various parts of the world: China, Saudi Arabia, Israel, India, and Costa Rica. Each country is in a different time zone. The vice president has asked you to help schedule these meetings. He would like each meeting to take place during the standard workweek for the country and he wants to avoid offending any participants by suggesting a meeting time that conflicts with any weekly or daily religious observations for the dominant religions in these countries: Buddhism, Islam, Judaism, Hinduism, and Christianity. Research the time zones, standard workweek, and days of religious observation in the various countries. Prepare a five-minute briefing for the vice president, proposing a series of meeting times and supporting your proposal with your research. Include at least one visual aid.

b. Your company is considering installing video conferencing equipment to support meetings between employees in distant locations. However, your manager is concerned that the challenges of video conferencing will outweigh the benefits. Your manager has asked you to prepare a five-minute presentation outlining some challenges and benefits of video conferencing, which you will present at the beginning of an executive committee meeting. Prepare that presentation, including at least one visual aid. You can find information about video conferencing by conducting a web search using combinations of the terms *video conferencing benefits challenges*. Also try *virtual collaboration* and *telepresence*.

c. Your company is considering offering a seminar or workshop in conflict management. You have been asked to research possible courses. Conduct a web search to identify three training seminars in conflict management. Prepare a five-minute executive briefing providing details about the three courses; comparing them in terms of length, content, and cost; and recommending one of them. Include at least one visual aid.

Grammar Exercises

36 Verbs (See Appendix C: Grammar, Punctuation, Mechanics, and Conventions—Section 1.1.2)

Type the following paragraph, correcting the errors in use or formation of verbs. Underline all your corrections.

If my first boss had ran his businesses the way he answered the phone, he would have went broke long ago. Usually he grabbed the receiver and growls, "Barker." The person at the other end probably thought, "That don't sound like a human, more like a rottweiler." If George Barker was a dog, he would probably be more courteous on the phone. No doubt there was lots of offended customers. The other day he asked my coworker, Jess, and me to stop by his office. He still answered the phone the same way. George's phone offenses amounts to quite a long list. Instead of "barking," there is several other things he could say. "Hello, Barker Contracting" or "This is George Barker" make a better impression.

MyLab Business Communication

Go to **www.pearson.com/mylab/business-communication** for Auto-graded writing questions as well as the following Assisted-graded writing questions:

1. As described in this chapter, people from the United States are typically both individualistic and monochronic. How do these characteristics complement each other? How might they contradict each other? Explain your reasoning.

2. Groupthink occurs when people convince each other to agree. What are the problems with groupthink, and what can you do to avoid the groupthink syndrome?

References

1. Bradberry, T., Greaves, J., & Lencioni, P. (2009). *Emotional intelligence 2.0*. San Diego, CA: TalentSmart. For the original definition of Emotional Intelligence, see Mayer, J., & Salovey, P. (1990). Emotional intelligence. *Imagination, Cognition, and Personality, 9*, 185–211.

2. Goleman, D. (2004, January). What makes a leader? *Harvard Business Review*. Retrieved from http://hbr.org/2004/01/what-makes-a-leader/ar/1

3. Turkle, S. (2012, April 22). The flight from conversation. *The New York Times*. Retrieved from http://www.nytimes.com/2012/04/22/opinion/sunday/the-flight-from-conversation.html?_r=1

4. Vanderkam, L. (2015, September 30). The science of when you need in-person communication. *Fast Company*. Retrieved from http://www.fastcompany.com/3051518/the-future-of-work/the-science-of-when-you-need-in-person-communication. For the original research cited in the article, see Schroeder, J., Risen, J., Gino, F. & Norton, M. I. (2014, May 29). Handshaking promotes cooperative dealmaking. Retrieved from http://ssrn.com/abstract=2443551 or http://dx.doi.org/10.2139/ssrn.2443551

5. Janusik, L., & Wolvin, A. (2009). 24 hours in a day. *International Journal of Listening, 23*(2), 104–120.

6. Emanuel, R., Adams, J., Baker, K., Daufin, E., Ellington, C., Fitts, E., & Okeowo, D. (2008). How college students spend their time communicating. *International Journal of Listening, 22*(1), 13–28.

7. Flynn, J., Valikoski, T., & Grau, J. (2008). Listening in the business context: Reviewing the state of research. *International Journal of Listening, 22*(2), 141–151.

8. Wolvin, A. D. (Ed.). (2010). *Listening and human communication in the 21st century.* Chichester, U.K.: Wiley-Blackwell.

9. For more detail on the HURIER model of listening, which this discussion adapts, see Brownell, J. (2010). The skills of listening-centered communication. In A. D. Wolvin (Ed.), *Listening and human communication in the 21st century* (pp. 141–157). Chichester, U.K.: Wiley-Blackwell.

10. Gupta, S. (2016, August 1). Your brain on multitasking. *CNN.* Retrieved from http://www.cnn.com/2015/04/09/health/your-brain-multitasking/

11. Sanbonmatsu, D. M., Strayer, D. L., Medeiros-Ward, N., & Watson, J. M. (2013). Who multi-tasks and why? Multi-tasking ability, perceived multi-tasking ability, impulsivity, and sensation seeking. *PLOS ONE, 8*(1), e54402.

12. Bodie, G. D., Gearhart, C. C., Denham, J. P., & Vickery, A. J. (2013). The temporal stability and situational contingency of active-empathic listening. *Western Journal of Communication, 77*(2), 113–138.

13. Spahn, J., & Purses, J. (2012, March/April). 3 steps to empathic active listening. Practice Management Center. [Blog post]. Retrieved from http://www.fpanet.org/professionals/Practice-Management/PracticeSolutionsMagazine/MarchApril2012/3StepstoEmpathicActiveListening/

14. Riordan, C. M. (2014, January 16). Three ways leaders can listen with more empathy. *Harvard Business Review.* Retrieved from https://hbr.org/2014/01/three-ways-leaders-can-listen-with-more-empathy

15. Gendron, M., Roberson, D., van der Vyver, J. M., & Barrett, L. F (2014). Perceptions of emotion from facial expressions are not culturally universal: Evidence from a remote culture. *Emotion, 14*(2), 251–262.

16. Gendron, M., Roberson, D., van der Vyver, J. M., & Barrett, L. F. (2014). Perceptions of emotion from facial expressions are not culturally universal: Evidence from a remote culture. *Emotion, 14*(2), 251–262.

17. Jack, R. E., Blais, C., Scheepers, C., Schyns, P., & Caldera, R. (2009). Cultural confusions show that facial expressions are not universal. *Current Biology, 19,* 1543–1548. See also Yuki, M., Maddux, W. W., & Masuda, T. (2007). Are the windows to the soul the same in the East and West? Cultural differences in using the eyes and mouth as cues to recognize emotions in Japan and the United States. *Journal of Experimental Social Psychology, 43*(2), 303–311.

18. Park, J., Barash, V., Fink, C., & Cha, M. (2013). Emoticon style: Interpreting differences in emoticons across cultures. *Proceedings of the Seventh International AAAI Conference on Weblogs and Social Media,* 466–475. Retrieved from https://www.aaai.org/ocs/index.php/ICWSM/ICWSM13/paper/view/6132

19. McHugh, M., & Hambaugh, J. (2010). She said, he said: Gender, language and power. In J. Chrisler & D. McCreary (Eds.), *Handbook of gender research in psychology* (Vol. 1, pp. 379–410). New York: Springer.

20. Tannen, D. (1991). *You just don't understand: Women and men in conversation.* London: Virago.

21. Wood, J. (2013). *Gendered lives: Communication, gender, & culture* (10th ed.). Boston, MA: Wadsworth.

22. Leaper, C., & Robnett, R. D. (2011). Women are more likely than men to use tentative language, aren't they? A meta-analysis testing for gender differences and moderators. *Psychology of Women Quarterly, 35*(1), 129–142.

23. Craig, T., Blankenship, K., & Lewis, A. (2015). Leveraging processing to understand linguistic cues, power and persuasion. In R. Schulze, & H. Pishwa (Eds.), *The exercise of power in communication* (pp. 199–220). London, U.K.: Palgrave Macmillan.

24. Faust, D. G. (2009, October 31). Leadership without a secret code. Interview conducted by Adam Bryant. *The New York Times.* Retrieved from http://www.nytimes.com/2009/11/01/business/01corner.html

25. Hargie, O. (2011). Communicating without words: Skilled nonverbal behavior. In O. Hargie, *Skilled interpersonal communication: Research, theory and practice* (5th ed., pp. 43–82). New York, NY: Routledge.

26. Hargie, O. (2011). Communicating without words: Skilled nonverbal behavior. In O. Hargie, *Skilled interpersonal communication: Research, theory and practice* (5th ed., pp. 43–82). New York: Routledge.

27. Knapp, M., & Hall, J. (2009). *Nonverbal communication in human interaction* (7th ed.). Belmont, CA: Wadsworth Publishing.

28. Goman, C. K. (2011, June 25). The art and science of mirroring. Retrieved from http://www.forbes.com/sites/carolkinseygoman/2011/05/31/the-art-and-science-of-mirroring/

29. Schroth, H. A., Bain-Chekal, J., & Caldwell, D. F. (2005). Sticks and stones may break bones and words can hurt me: Words and phrases that trigger emotions in negotiations and their effects [Electronic version]. *The International Journal of Conflict Management, 16*(2), 102–127.

30. Novak, D. (2009, July 11). At Yum Brands, rewards for good work. Interview conducted by Adam Bryant. *The New York Times.* Retrieved from http://www.nytimes.com/2009/07/12/business/12corner.html

31. Lawler, J. (2010, June 21). The real cost of workplace conflict. *Entrepreneur.* Retrieved from http://www.entrepreneur.com/article/207196. For the original research report, see CPP, Inc. (2008, July). *Workplace conflict and how businesses can harness it to thrive.* Retrieved from http://img.en25.com/Web/CPP/Conflict_report.pdf

32. Porath, C., & Pearson, C. (2009, April). How toxic colleagues corrode performance. *Harvard Business Review.* Retrieved from http://hbr.org/2009/04/how-toxic-colleagues-corrodeperformance/ar/1

33. Bobinski, D. (2006). The hidden costs of conflict. Retrieved from http://www.management-issues.com/opinion/3291/the-hidden-costs-of-conflict/

34. Bliss, W. G. (2012, January 14). Cost of employee turnover. Retrieved from http://www.isquare.com/turnover.cfm

35. CPP, Inc. (2008, July). Workplace conflict and how businesses can harness it to thrive. Retrieved from http://img.en25.com/Web/CPP/Conflict_report.pdf

36. Glover, P. (2012, March 12). Team conflict: Why it's a good thing. *Fast Company.* [Blog post]. Retrieved from http://www.fastcompany.com/1824515/team-conflict-why-its-a-good-thing

37. Lublin, J. (2014, February 14). The high cost of avoiding conflict at work. *The Wall Street Journal.* Retrieved from http://online.wsj.com/news/articles/SB10001424052702304315004579382780060647804

38. Cassidy, J. (2011, July 25). Mastering the machine: How Ray Diallo built the world's richest and strangest hedge fund. *The New Yorker,* 56–65.

39. Zupeck, R. (2008, January 2). Six tips to managing workplace conflict. Retrieved from http://www.cnn.com/2008/LIVING/worklife/01/02/cb.work.conflict/index.html

40. Kilmann, R. H. (2011, April). Celebrating 40 years with the TKI assessment. CPP Author Insights. Retrieved from https://www.cpp.com/PDFs/Author_Insights_April_2011.pdf

41. Rabe, C. B. (2006). *The innovation killers: How what we know limit what we can imagine—and what smart companies are doing about it.* New York, NY: AMACOM.

42. Gerzon, M. (2014, June 26). To resolve a conflict, first decide: Is it hot or cold? *Harvard Business Review.* Retrieved from https://hbr.org/2014/06/to-resolve-a-conflict-first-decide-is-it-hot-or-cold

43. Rainie, L., & Perrin, A. (2016, March). Technology adoption by Baby Boomers (and everybody else). Retrieved from http://www.pewinternet.org/2016/03/22/technology-adoption-by-baby-boomers-and-everybody-else/

44. Zelavansky, N. (2014, December 1). Bridging the gap at work: Improving intergenerational communication. Retrieved from http://www.coca-colacompany.com/stories/bridging-the-gap-at-work-improving-intergenerational-communication

45. The Slack generation: How workplace messaging could replace other missives. (2016, May 14). *The Economist*. Retrieved from http://www.economist.com/news/business/21698659-how-workplace-messaging-could-replace-other-missives-slack-generation

46. Spencer-Oatey, H., & Franklin, P. (2009). *Intercultural interaction: A multidisciplinary approach to intercultural communication* (pp. 22–24). London: Palgrave Macmillan. For Hall's original analysis, see Hall, E. T. (1977). *Beyond culture*. New York: Anchor Books.

47. Valle, J. (2016, November14). The Persian art of etiquette. *BBC News*. Retrieved from http://www.bbc.com/travel/story/20161104-the-persian-art-of-etiquette

48. Hofstede, G., Hofstede, G. J., & Minkow, M. (2010). *Cultures and organizations: Software of the mind* (3rd ed.). New York: McGraw-Hill.

49. Formula for success. (1992, December). *Financial World*, 161(24), 40.

50. Teon, A. (2017, February 25). The concept of face in Chinese culture and the difference between *mianzi* and *lian*. *The Greater China Journal*. Retrieved from https://china-journal.org/2017/02/25/the-concept-of-face-in-chinese-culture-and-the-difference-between-mianzi-and-lian/

51. ITIM International. (2009). Geert Hofstede cultural dimensions. Retrieved from http://www.geert-hofstede.com/-hofstede_united_states.shtml

52. PepsiCo Greater China Region receives international renowned certification of "Top Employers China" for the 8th time. (2016, December 7). Retrieved from http://www.globaltimes.cn/content/1022361.shtml

53. Goh, A., & Sullivan, M. (2011, February 4). The most misunderstood business concept in China. *Business Insider*. Retrieved from http://www.businessinsider.com/the-most-misunderstood-business-concept-in-china-2011-2

54. Pearce, J. A., & Robinson, R. B. (2000, January/February). Cultivating *guanxi* as a foreign investor strategy. *Business Horizons*, 31–38.

55. Chang, R. Y. K., Cheng, L. T. W., & Szeto, R. W. F. (2002). The dynamics of *guanxi* and ethics for Chinese executives. *Journal of Business Ethics*, 41, 327–336.

56. Hwang, D. B., Golemon, P. L., Chen, Y., Wang, T., & Hung, W. (2009) Guanxi and business ethics in Confucian society today: An empirical case study in Taiwan. *Journal of Business Ethics*, 89, 235–250.

57. Goh, A., & Sullivan, M. (2011, February 4). The most misunderstood business concept in China. *Business Insider*. Retrieved from http://www.businessinsider.com/the-most-misunderstood-business-concept-in-china-2011-2

58. Hope, K. (2014, October 8). Doing business the Chinese way. Retrieved from http://www.bbc.com/news/business-29524701

59. Craver, C. B. (2011, May). The impact of culture on transnational interactions. *The Negotiator Magazine*. Retrieved from http://negotiatormagazine.com/articles/AR201105101.php

60. Beall, M. L. (2010). Perspectives on intercultural listening. In A. D. Wolvin (Ed.), *Listening and human communication in the 21st century* (pp. 141–157). Chichester, U.K.: Wiley-Blackwell.

61. Mueller, J. S. (2012). Why individuals in larger teams perform worse. *Organizational Behavior and Human Decision Processes*, 117(1), 111–124.

62. Harrison, K. (2013). What's the ideal number of people in a work team or committee? Retrieved from http://www.cuttingedgepr.com/articles/ideal-number-people-in-team.asp

63. Love, J. (2013, Nov. 4). A "virtuous mix" allows innovation to thrive. *Kellogg Insight*. Retrieved from https://insight.kellogg.northwestern.edu/article/a_virtuous_mix_allows_innovation_to_thrive

64. Shapiro, M. (2015, September 8). Help your team agree on how they'll collaborate. *Harvard Business Review*. Retrieved from https://hbr.org/2015/09/help-your-team-agree-on-how-theyll-collaborate

65. Harris, T. E., & Sherblom, J. C. (2011). *Small group and team communication* (Chapter 4). Upper Saddle River, NJ: Pearson. For Bruce Tuckman's original research, see Tuckman, B. W. (1965). Developmental sequence in small groups. *Psychological Bulletin*, 63, 384–399.

66. Thompson, L. L. (2011). *Making the team: A guide for good managers* (4th ed.). Upper Saddle River, NJ: Pearson. For the classic discussion on high-performance teams, see Katzenbach, J., & Smith, D. (1993). *The wisdom of teams: Creating the high performance organization*. Boston: Harvard Business School Press.

67. Edmondson, A. (2012, April 25). The importance of teaming. Retrieved from http://hbswk.hbs.edu/item/6997.html

68. Edmondson, A. (2012). *Teaming: How organizations learn, innovate, and compete in the knowledge economy*. San Francisco, CA: Jossey-Bass.

69. Duhigg, C. (2016, February 25). What Google learned from its quest to build the perfect team. *The New York Times*. Retrieved from https://www.nytimes.com/2016/02/28/magazine/what-google-learned-from-its-quest-to-build-the-perfect-team.html?_r=0

70. Cunningham, L. (2013, September 24). The science of introverts and the workplace. *The Washington Post*. Retrieved from https://www.washingtonpost.com/news/on-leadership/wp/2013/09/24/the-science-of-introverts-and-the-workplace/?utm_term=.724ed0489647

71. Brancaccio, D. (2017, February 27). Why it might be a good thing if your boss is an introvert. Retrieved from https://www.marketplace.org/2017/02/22/life/introverts-leadership

72. Gino, F. (2015, March 16). Introverts, extroverts, and the complexity of team dynamics. *Harvard Business Review*. Retrieved from https://hbr.org/2015/03/introverts-extroverts-and-the-complexities-of-team-dynamics

73. Caprino, K. (2015, September 7). Can introverts and extroverts ever work well together? How opposites can collaborate brilliantly. *Forbes*. Retrieved from https://www.forbes.com/sites/kathycaprino/2015/09/07/can-introverts-and-extroverts-ever-work-well-together-how-opposites-can-collaborate-brilliantly

74. Landsbaum, C. (2016, September 13). Obama's female staffers came up with a genius strategy to make sure their voices were heard. *New York Magazine*. Retrieved from http://nymag.com/thecut/2016/09/heres-how-obamas-female-staffers-made-their-voices-heard.html

75. Design for America (2017). Retrieved from http://designforamerica.com/about

76. Sproutel (2017). Case study: Jerry the Bear. Retrieved from https://www.sproutel.com/#work

77. Illumiloon (2017). Empowering the community. Retrieved from http://www.illumiloon.com

78. Swipesense (2017). Hand hygiene redefined. Retrieved from http://www.swipesense

79. O'Boyle, E. H., Humphrey, R. H., Pollack, J. M., Hawver, T. H., & Story, P. A. (2011). The relation between emotional intelligence and job performance: A meta-analysis. *Journal of Organizational Behavior*, 32, 788–818.

80. For the original research article by Lewin et al., see Lewin, K., Llippit, R., & White, R. K. (1939). Patterns of aggressive behavior in experimentally created social climates. *Journal of Social Psychology*, 10, 271–301.

CHAPTER 2

Managing the Communication Process

Analyzing, Composing, Evaluating

Vladgrin/Shutterstock

STUDY QUESTIONS

MyLab Business Communication

⭐**Improve Your Grade!**

If your instructor is using MyLab Business Communication, visit **www.pearson.com/ mylab/business-communication** for videos, simulations, and writing exercises.

New Hires @ Work

George Gwee

National University of Singapore

Accountant @ Walsh Pte. Ltd.

I have found that grasping different people's communication styles is often the most difficult part of communicating at work. Communication style is linked deeply to how people see the world. Some people are very numbers-driven, some people are very detailed-oriented, and others can be very strategic; they take a broad view of things. You need to adapt your style to theirs to ensure effective communication.

79

Chapter 3 | Introduction

Imagine that you want to apply for a job at a company that is not advertising any open positions. How do you decide the best way to contact this company, and what you should say? Or imagine that you want to convince your boss to support a new summer-hours work schedule. Will your boss be open to this idea? Should you talk about it in person or send an email first? What information will you need to provide, and how should you organize it? What persuasive techniques should you use? This chapter explains a flexible communication process called ACE—*Analyzing, Composing, and Evaluating*—that will help you answer all those questions and communicate successfully in any situation. As **Figure 3.1** explains, ACE is a circular process. Each ACE step plays a unique role in effectively communicating a message.

At first, you may be concerned that following the ACE process will be too time-consuming. However, with practice these steps will become a familiar part of your normal communication routine—even for informal conversations and email messages. The more you use the ACE process, the more successful your communication will be. This chapter will guide you through the ACE process by providing strategies for each step.

FIGURE 3.1 The ACE Communication Process

Analyzing "sets the stage" for your business message and helps you make good decisions. Before you begin to compose, analyze four important elements:

- **Purpose and outcome**—the reason why you are communicating and what you want to achieve.
- **Audience**—the person or people for whom your message is intended. Who are they? What are their concerns and interests?
- **Content**—the specific information to include in your message. If you do not have all the content you need, determine where to find it.
- **Medium**—how you will deliver your message. Should you communicate by telephone, face-to-face, email, text message, Twitter, or some other choice?

Taking the time to analyze the purpose, audience, content, and medium will prepare you for the second ACE step: composing.

Evaluating is the process of reviewing your message by asking yourself questions such as these:

- Have you included all the necessary content to achieve your purpose?
- Is the message organized well?
- Is it worded effectively?
- Is it formatted professionally?

As part of the evaluation process, share your draft or plan with others to get feedback.

Reviewing your message and considering feedback may lead you to return to the first step of the process—analyzing—to reconsider the decisions you made about purpose, audience, content, and medium.

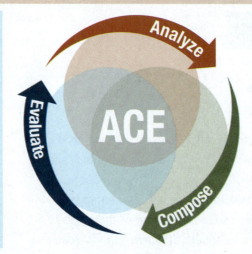

Composing involves more than putting words on the page or speaking them aloud. Use your analysis of the purpose, audience, content, and medium to make decisions about how you will compose the message, such as:

- Will you state the main idea first, or after explaining the details?
- How much detail do you need to provide?
- How will you organize the details?
- Do you need to be persuasive?
- How should you format the message?

Once you have a plan in place, draft your message.

SQ1 What are the benefits of analyzing?

When people don't communicate effectively, it's often because they skip the analyzing phase and jump ahead to composing the message. **Analyzing** is the process of planning your message by thinking critically about four elements: *purpose and outcome, audience, content,* and *medium.* Analyzing each of these elements offers distinct benefits.

Analyze

Analyzing the purpose focuses the message

Before thinking about *what* you are communicating, analyze *why* you are communicating. Think about *why* from two points of view: (1) what is the purpose of the communication, and (2) what outcome would you like to achieve?

Business communication always has a **purpose,** or reason why you are communicating. Typically you will phrase the purpose as what you want to do. For example, you may want to:

- *Inform* a client about a problem
- *Persuade* a supervisor to implement a new program
- *Request* permission to extend a deadline
- *Report* financial information to a client
- *Propose* a solution to a problem

By contrast, your desired **outcome** is what you want your **audience**—the intended recipients of your communication—to know or do as a result of the communication. Typically, you will phrase the outcome as how you want your audience to respond. Notice the difference between general purpose statements and outcome statements in **Figure 3.2.**

analyzing The process of looking critically at four elements of your message: purpose and outcome, audience, content, and medium.

purpose The reason you are communicating.

outcome The result of your communication; what you want the recipients of your message to know, do, or feel about the subject of your message.

audience The intended recipients of your communication.

FIGURE 3.2 Examples of Purpose and Outcome Statements

MY PURPOSE IS . . .	AND	MY DESIRED OUTCOME IS THAT . . .
To inform my client that I cannot take on a new project right now.	→	My client will postpone the project rather than hire someone else to do it.
To persuade my supervisor to approve a summer-hours work schedule.	→	My supervisor will present the plan to upper management.
To ask my supervisor for an extension on a project deadline.	→	My supervisor will let me submit the project next Friday so I can finish it during the week.

Keeping both your overall purpose and your desired outcome in mind as you compose your message helps you evaluate whether your content supports your goal. For example, consider how you would address the first item in Figure 3.2. If you think only about your general purpose—to inform your client that you cannot take on the project—you might draft a message that thanks the client for his interest, explains that you cannot take on the project right now because you are fully booked, and concludes with a forward-looking **goodwill** statement intended to reinforce a positive relationship between you (or your company) and the audience.

However, if you think about the outcome you would like to achieve, you may decide that you want the client to give you the opportunity to do this project at a later date, if possible. You do not want the client to look for another vendor. How can you word your reply to achieve that outcome? Compare the two versions of the message in **Figure 3.3** on page 82. The draft message considers only the purpose—to delay the project. The revised message is designed to achieve a better outcome—to ensure that the client will still want you to complete the project, even though it's delayed.

Analyzing both your purpose and desired outcome also helps you determine how persuasive you need to be. **Persuasion** is the ability to influence an audience to agree with your point of view, accept your recommendation, or grant your request. If your communication

goodwill The positive relationship between you (or your company) and your audience.

persuasion The process of influencing your audience to agree with your point of view, accept your recommendation, grant your request, or change their beliefs or actions in a way that facilitates a desired outcome.

FIGURE 3.3 Achieving a Desired Outcome

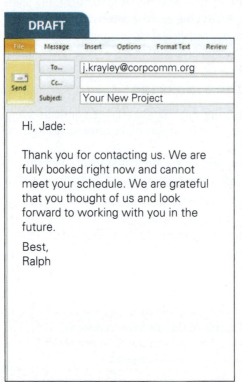

PURPOSE: *To inform my client that I cannot take on a new project right now.*

DRAFT

To... j.krayley@corpcomm.org
Cc...
Subject: Your New Project

Hi, Jade:

Thank you for contacting us. We are fully booked right now and cannot meet your schedule. We are grateful that you thought of us and look forward to working with you in the future.

Best,
Ralph

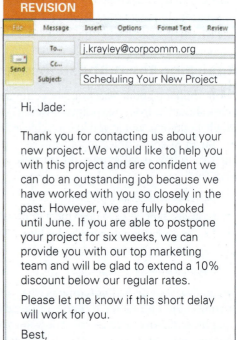

DESIRED OUTCOME: *My client will postpone the project rather than hire someone else to do it.*

REVISION

To... j.krayley@corpcomm.org
Cc...
Subject: Scheduling Your New Project

Hi, Jade:

Thank you for contacting us about your new project. We would like to help you with this project and are confident we can do an outstanding job because we have worked with you so closely in the past. However, we are fully booked until June. If you are able to postpone your project for six weeks, we can provide you with our top marketing team and will be glad to extend a 10% discount below our regular rates.

Please let me know if this short delay will work for you.

Best,
Ralph

FIGURE 3.4 Informational Message—No Persuasion Needed

L_arnica/Fotolia

is purely informative, no persuasion is necessary. For example, an email to all department employees about a room change for a meeting simply needs to provide clear and complete information, as shown in **Figure 3.4**.

However, many business messages require a persuasive strategy. They need to influence the audience either to agree with an idea or to take action. For example, say that you want to convince your supervisor, Cherilyn Martins, to implement a summer-hours work schedule for your department. Your standard workday hours begin at 9 AM and end at 5 PM. A flexible summer-hours schedule would allow employees to begin and end an hour earlier so that they can take advantage of the increased daylight and warmer weather during the summer. You propose that your department's workday hours begin at 8 AM between June 1 and August 31. Because you want to motivate action, this message clearly needs to be persuasive. **Figure 3.5** shows your purpose statement and desired outcome statement. With this desired outcome in mind, you can analyze your audience to get a better idea of how you can persuade her to support your proposal.

FIGURE 3.5 Sample Purpose and Outcome Statements

PURPOSE	DESIRED OUTCOME
To persuade my supervisor to approve a summer-hours work schedule.	My supervisor will support the proposal and believe it is in the best interest of the department to adopt the plan. She will forward the proposal to upper management and request a meeting to discuss it, with the goal of having the proposal accepted in time to implement it for the summer.

Analyzing the audience helps you meet their needs

When analyzing your **audience** consider both primary and secondary audiences:

- The **primary audience** is the direct recipient of your message—the person or people to whom your message is addressed.
- The **secondary audience** is anyone else who may receive a copy of your message (or hear about it), either from you or from the primary audience.

For example, if you email your supervisor about incorporating a flexible summer-hours schedule and she likes the idea, she may forward your message to the vice president of operations. Although you planned your message for your supervisor—the primary audience—the vice president becomes a secondary audience.

Once you have identified your audience, consider the questions listed in **Figure 3.6** to determine what content to include as well as how and when to deliver the message. Figure 3.6 also illustrates how you might answer these questions for the summer-hours work schedule scenario.

Notice that question 5 in Figure 3.6 asks you to analyze **audience benefits**—advantages the recipient or the organization gains from agreeing with or acting on your message. People are more likely to agree with what you propose if they understand the advantages they—or their business—will gain from granting your request.

primary audience The person or people to whom your message is addressed.

secondary audience People other than the primary audience who may read or hear your message.

audience benefits The positive outcomes your audience will experience by agreeing with or acting on your message.

FIGURE 3.6 Audience Analysis Questions

1. What does the primary and secondary audience already know?

My supervisor and upper management already know about the structure of our current workday, so I do not need to explain that.

2. What information does the audience need to know—and why?

Both audiences need to know what I mean by "summer hours," how summer hours will work in our department, and how the change will affect the productivity of the department during the summer months.

3. When does the audience need this information?

My supervisor needs the information soon so we can gain support from upper management in time to implement the change for this summer.

4. How will the audience react to this information?

I don't know how my supervisor or upper management will react, so I will try to anticipate potential problems and provide solutions.

If the purpose is primarily persuasive, also consider these questions:

5. How will my audience benefit from my idea or proposal?

- Providing flexible summer hours may improve employee morale, which may lead to the following additional benefits:
  a. reduced employee turnover rates
  b. increased employee productivity
  c. increased quarterly sales figures
- Providing flexible summer hours may improve employees' perceptions of my supervisor.

6. What questions or objections will my audience have?

My audience may ask these questions:

- How will we ensure that someone is available to answer phone calls after 4 PM if all employees ask to start and end their day earlier?
- When workdays begin and end earlier, will we have to rearrange lunch hours and breaks? If so, how will we determine those changes?
- Will there be additional costs?
- Will any employees think this schedule is unfair?
- Will any customers be negatively affected by the change?
- Has this plan worked well in other departments or companies?
- Is there any evidence to support the benefits?

New Hires @ Work

Ray Holloman
Belmont University

Business Continuity Administrator @ HCA Healthcare

Your communications precede you, and you never know if something you write will be forwarded on to others. Make sure all of your messages represent you well.

Photo courtesy of Ray Holloman

Unfortunately, when trying to persuade others, people often make the mistake of emphasizing their own benefits. Focusing on the benefits to you is easy. For example, by implementing a summer-hours schedule, you get to leave work an hour earlier each day. You have more time to enjoy outdoor activities, family, and friends during the warmer summer months. Further, if you have the option to choose between summer hours or regular hours each day, you can take advantage of the flexibility to schedule your work hours to meet your own needs. These outcomes are good for you, but they do not suggest any benefits for your supervisor or company. Therefore, those benefits are not likely to persuade your audience.

The challenge is to identify audience-focused benefits, such as those listed in item 5 of Figure 3.6, and then select the ones that will be most effective. You would certainly want to stress that a flexible summer schedule may improve morale, reduce turnover rates, and increase productivity. However, you may choose to omit the other potential benefits. It will be difficult to prove that quarterly sales figures will increase, and it would be unwise to suggest that summer hours will improve employees' perceptions of your supervisor. Although your supervisor may consider this a valid reason to change the work schedule, your secondary audience—the vice president—may not.

Analyzing the content ensures a complete message

content The substance of your message.

In addition to analyzing your purpose and audience, you should also analyze what **content** you need to include. What is the substance of your message? Do you have enough information about the topic or situation to compose your message? Do you have enough data to support your main ideas? Or do you need to do additional research?

For example, assume that you have identified the list of potential benefits for a summer-hours plan illustrated in Figure 3.6 as well as the list of questions your supervisor may ask. Before composing the message, you will need to gather the required information. You may be able to get it from *internal sources* such as company reports, databases, and experts. Or you may have to consult *external sources* such as industry journals, web-based search tools, or experts outside your company. The following research would provide you with effective content:

- **Investigate existing company information.** To learn whether other departments in the company have implemented summer hours, you will need to consult internal sources. You could call or email other managers, contact your human resources office, or research the company's employee handbook.

- **Survey people's opinions or perceptions.** To learn whether employees will support the summer schedule or think it is unfair, you may need to survey the people in your department.

primary research The process of collecting your own data from original sources.

- **Research external sources of information.** To learn if other companies have found a summer-hours schedule to provide tangible benefits, such as increased productivity, you will need to search external sources. You can conduct **primary research**, which involves collecting your own original data. For example, you might call the human resources departments of other local companies. A more efficient method might be to look in libraries or online sources for **secondary research**, which is information other people have collected. For example, the U.S. Department of Labor provides several articles about flexible schedules.[1]

secondary research The process of searching published reports, articles, and books for information other people have collected.

You may decide to postpone some of this time-consuming research until you learn whether your supervisor is receptive to the idea of summer work hours. However, your initial communication with your supervisor will be stronger if you can communicate that you have done at least a little research and have objective support for your proposal. More detailed information about finding and evaluating sources is available in Chapter 8: Finding and Evaluating Business Information.

Analyzing the medium helps you choose the best delivery option

medium The method you use to deliver a message (for example, telephone, face-to-face meeting, email, text message, or website).

For a message to be effective, it also has to be delivered through the right **medium**. **Figure 3.7** lists many common methods of communication and identifies the advantages and disadvantages of each. Making a good choice about the best medium to use is challenging. For example, if you need to send financial data to your supervisor, you might choose to present that information in a spreadsheet and attach it to an email that summarizes the data. However, if the spreadsheet requires a more detailed explanation, a face-to-face meeting will be more effective.

FIGURE 3.7 Selecting the Best Medium to Communicate Your Message

MEDIUM	ADVANTAGES	DISADVANTAGES
Face to Face *(one-to-one conversation)*	• Allows personal explanation targeted to an individual • Provides for immediate feedback	• Is not efficient for disseminating information to many people • Is not usually permanently documented (recorded)
Meeting *(several people)*	• Disseminates information to many people • Provides for immediate feedback • Is documented by minutes	• Can be difficult to schedule • Is time-consuming—takes employees away from other duties
Telephone	• Allows personal explanation targeted to an individual • Allows short messages to be delivered via voice mail if individuals are not at their desks • Provides immediate feedback if the person answers the phone	• Is time-consuming if individual calls need to be made to several people • Is not usually permanently documented (recorded)
Text Message, Instant Message	• Allows quick communication • Creates a permanent record if saved	• Is not efficient if message is long, complex, or sensitive • Does not ensure immediate feedback
Email	• Allows quick communication • Disseminates information to one or many people • Creates a permanent record if saved or printed	• May not be a private and secure medium for sending sensitive content • Does not ensure immediate feedback because not everyone checks email regularly
Memo *(printed hardcopy to audiences within the organization)*	• Can accompany original documents or forms that need signatures • Can be used for employees who have no access to email • Creates a permanent record	Unless emailed as an attachment: • Incurs costs to copy to many people • Is delivered more slowly than email • Does not provide for immediate feedback
Letter *(formatted on letterhead and either mailed or emailed to audiences outside the organization)*	• Projects a more "official" or formal image than email • Can accompany original documents, such as forms with signatures • Can be emailed as an attachment for fast delivery • Creates a permanent record	Unless emailed as an attachment: • Incurs cost of letterhead and postage • Takes at least a day to deliver • Does not provide for immediate feedback
Newsletter *(printed hardcopy, HTML-designed email, or file attachment)*	• Disseminates a lot of information to many people simultaneously • Creates a permanent record	Unless emailed as an attachment: • Incurs cost to copy and distribute by mail • Does not provide for immediate feedback
Website	• Makes information available to anyone with access • Can be password protected to limit access • Enables combinations of text, video, and audio through podcasts, MP3 files, webcasts, webinars, and web conferencing tools • Is easy to keep up to date • May provide for feedback (by linking to feedback forms)	• Is not effective with audiences who have limited Internet access • Requires the audience to access the site • May not reach the audience • May reach unintended audiences • Does not provide for immediate feedback • May not provide a permanent record, unless web files are archived
Social Media: Networking Websites *(for example, Facebook, Instagram, LinkedIn)* and **Wikis, Blogs, and Microblogs** *(for example, Twitter)*	• Disseminates information simultaneously to a community of people who have linked with you and expressed an interest • Enables combinations of text, images, and video • Allows interactive communication • Encourages discussion • Is easy to keep up to date • Provides a complete record	• Requires the audience to access the social media application • Is not effective with audiences who have limited Internet access • May not reach the audience • May reach unintended audiences

ETHICS
HOW TO HANDLE INFORMATION THAT CONFLICTS WITH YOUR POSITION

Inexperienced communicators often make the mistake of looking for content that supports their own point of view rather than looking for content that provides a complete picture of the issue. As an ethical business communicator, you have the responsibility to provide information that allows your audience to make good business decisions—even if that information conflicts with your own ideas.

For example, assume that you find positive information about flexible work hours from a not-for-profit workforce newsletter and two independent news agencies. You select information from each source to prepare a short email report intended to persuade your supervisor to adopt flexible summer hours. However, suppose you also find a source suggesting that some employees abuse the flexibility by arriving to work late and leaving early. Should you ignore this source because it will weaken your point? No! If you fail to analyze and address relevant information that

contradicts your point of view, you are committing an ethical error of omission.

Decide how to deal with that information. Is it strong enough to make you modify your point of view? Is it weak enough that you can argue against it? Does it bring up a problem that you can solve? To be ethical, report the information, cite the source, and then argue against it or provide a solution to the problem the source raises. For example, you could suggest that the company implement a reporting process that documents employees' actual work hours. By addressing potentially negative information, you demonstrate your integrity as a business communicator as well as your ability to think critically and solve problems.

For an ETHICS exercise, go to Critical Thinking Question 3 on page 111.

In choosing a medium from the list, you may find two decision-making frameworks helpful. The first framework is the medium richness model introduced by Daft and Lengel, who categorize medium options according to the level of richness in the information they provide.[2] They rank medium options in the following order, from richest to leanest: face-to-face communication, video-based communication, audio-only communication, and text (such as emails or letters). Face-to-face communication is the richest medium because it uses a rich variety of means to convey information: words, oral cues, and visual cues. In addition, it allows personalization of information and immediate feedback. By contrast, email is typically a lean communication medium because it conveys information with words only. It is a good medium for getting answers to clear questions but is less effective for discussing complex problems.

The second framework is one used by the Project Management Institute, which categorizes communication as interactive, push, or pull.[3] Each category of communication is best matched with specific medium options. **Interactive communication**, as its name implies, is a multi-directional exchange of information; it is an efficient approach when you need an immediate answer or a discussion. Good medium options for interactive communication include meetings, phone calls, instant messaging, and video conferencing. Email can also be effective, although response is not always immediate. **Push communication** is typically one-way communication, often "pushed out" to multiple people. Effective medium options for push communication include letters, memos, reports, blogs, newsletters, and email. By contrast, **pull communication** is stored in a convenient location so that recipients can access, or "pull," it when needed. Effective medium options for pull communication include websites, intranet sites, and other forms of knowledge repositories. If you believe that multiple people will need to access information at various times, then communicating by a pull medium is a good choice.

Social media is expanding the number of medium options available, and companies are finding creative ways to use social media to communicate both externally with customers and internally with employees. Externally, social media such as Facebook, Twitter, and Instagram are good choices when companies want to maintain positive interaction with current customers and engage potential customers. Internally, many companies choose to create company-wide social networks to encourage interactive communication with and among employees. Gatehouse, a European-based internal communication agency, conducted a study of more than 300 organizations in 70 countries and found that 64 percent of them had implemented internal social channels, and most of the remaining companies were planning to launch them in the near future.[4] The benefits of internal social media include enhancing employees' sense of belonging to the organization and increasing interaction among employees—especially in large organizations with people in many time zones.[5] Employees use these channels to network, share progress on company-wide goals, and celebrate each other's successes. Employers use them to create a sense of transparency and openness, get feedback on new initiatives, and respond quickly to ideas and issues that employees raise.[6] For example, the technology company Red Hat supports

interactive communication Multi-directional exchange of information.

push communication One-way communication, often "pushed out" to multiple people.

pull communication Information stored in a convenient location so that recipients can access, or "pull," it when needed.

its commitment to open communication through an internal discussion forum called Memo List. CEO Jim Whitehurst uses this medium when he needs to make a major company decision. It allows him to achieve his desired outcome: He gains good ideas from employee input, and employees gain a deeper understanding of the issues involved.[7,8]

You might use social media in a similar way and begin a departmental blog about summer hours to give your coworkers an opportunity to express their points of view and contribute critical information to the decision-making process. Or if your organization's employees are active on social media, you could conduct a poll with Twitter.

Compose

SQ2 What is involved in composing?

Composing involves more than just putting your thoughts into words. **Composing** includes organizing the content so that it is understandable from the audience's perspective, putting that content into logical paragraphs and coherent sentences, and then designing a format that makes the communication easy to follow in the medium you have chosen.

composing The multistep process of producing content, organizing it so that it is understandable from the audience's perspective, putting it into coherent sentences and logical paragraphs, and designing a format or delivery approach that is professional and makes the communication easy to follow.

COLLABORATION
HOW TO MANAGE COLLABORATIVE WRITING

How often have you participated in a group project that resulted in a disjointed document with no real beginning, middle, and end? Or maybe the document had too many beginnings and endings, making it obvious that each section was written by a different person? While it is a good idea to divide the work of composing among team members, successful collaboration requires that team members work together in the analyzing and evaluating phases of the ACE process. Here are some tips that will help you use the ACE process to manage collaborative projects and create an effective end result.

ANALYZING: MAKE JOINT DECISIONS

*   **Agree on the purpose and outcome of the document or project.** Ensure that everyone on the team is working toward the same goal. Start each team meeting or group email thread with your purpose and outcome statements to your keep ongoing efforts on target.
*   **Spend time collectively defining the audience and their needs.** If your project needs to be persuasive, discuss a strategy. Outline the content the audience needs to know—and what they do not need to know.
*   **Identify team members' skills and roles in the collaboration.** Capitalize on people's strengths and be honest about your own weaknesses.
*   **Determine the best medium to share drafts and support frequent feedback throughout the collaboration.** If your team isn't able to meet in person, agree on how and when to share. Establishing a good communication system is necessary to support effective collaboration.
*   **Agree on important elements of writing style that lead to a consistent voice.** For example, how formal will the tone be? Will you refer to your team as "we" or "the team"? Will you all aim to avoid passive voice whenever possible? Will you use a paragraph style that begins with key points in topic sentences rather than a narrative style that builds up to the main point?

COMPOSING: COORDINATE THE WRITING RESPONSIBILITIES

*   **Draft an outline together.** Drafting becomes more efficient when the entire team agrees on the organization of the

content. Then, when individuals write sections, they know where their section fits and how it contributes to the whole.
*   **Assign each person a section of the outline or supporting duties.** For example, someone might be responsible for researching content, and another might be tasked with developing the format or design. Clearly define who is doing what, how much, and when work is due.
*   **Maintain consistent communication.** Communicating throughout the composing phase is important, even if just to touch base with the team about deadlines and to share questions or concerns.
*   **Share drafts frequently.** Provide clear feedback and be open to constructive criticism. Focus on the writing, not the writer. If you identify a problem, compose a specific solution.

EVALUATING: PLAN AN EFFECTIVE REVIEW AND REVISION PROCESS

*   **Create a consistent voice.** One way to create a consistent voice is to assign a team member with strong writing skills to combine all the contributions and revise the document using a consistent style and tone. The audience should not be able to tell that different sections were written by different people.
*   **Create a consistent flow throughout the document.** Add transitions between sections, use uniform heading formats, and ensure consistent citation styles.
*   **Involve each team member in the evaluation process.** Involving everyone in the process results in a more a comprehensive review. Different people will see different problems.
*   **Determine an effective process for sharing feedback.** If input from many people is provided simultaneously, assign one person to "own" the original working draft, collect the feedback, edit the document, and share updated drafts with the team.

Collaborative projects can be challenging, but they can also be also very rewarding if planned well. Welcome differences of opinion, acknowledge that misunderstandings likely will occur, and agree that conflicts will be negotiated and resolved.

For a COLLABORATION exercise, go to Exercise 26 on page 118.

New Hires @ Work

Shruti Shah

University of Florida

Operations Analyst Development Program Intern @ JPMorgan Chase

In composing, I first think about my audience and tailor my salutation, message, and closing accordingly. I use active verbs and clear, succinct sentences that get the message across quickly and accurately. If the message is long, I break it into separate sections with headers and bullets. The overall purpose is to be clear and concise, but thorough.

Photo courtesy of Shruti Shah

Composing is much easier if you have effectively analyzed your communication situation first. However, even a simple and well-planned message benefits from at least two drafts. The first draft allows you to get your thoughts on paper. The second draft allows you to refine your thoughts and pay attention to evaluating the language and grammar. More complex messages may require more than two drafts to make the message complete, clear, and persuasive. This section helps you think through some key elements of the composing process: deciding when and where to compose, organizing the message, drafting the message, and designing a professional format and delivery.

Deciding when and where to compose

When you write a short email or plan a brief telephone call, you may not need to analyze how you will manage your time or control your environment. However, when you are preparing a complex report or presentation, you'll benefit from making good decisions about the following factors:

- **Time management.** How much time will you need for composing? If you're working on a lengthy document or presentation, spread the time across a few days to balance your workload. Giving yourself "downtime" between drafts helps you review the content more objectively.
- **Environment.** Are you able to concentrate on your writing in a quiet location with no distractions? Or are you more effective in an energetic atmosphere with sounds and movement, such as a crowded coffee shop? Select an environment that helps you focus.
- **Interruptions.** If the phone rings or someone stops by your office, will you stop composing to chat? If your mind wanders while writing, will you be tempted to check your email? If you are easily distracted, control your environment by closing your door, turning off your email, and eliminating other distractions that prevent you from focusing on your task.

A more effective composing process will result in a more effective message.

Organizing the message

Whether you compose a short email or create a detailed presentation, every message you prepare needs an organization that is logical and easy for your audience to follow. Outlining is an all-purpose tool that can help you plan this organization. An **outline** allows you to break a topic into major ideas and supporting details and then list that content in the order in which you will present it. **Figure 3.8** is an example of a traditional outline with several sections, each with a few items. **Figure 3.9** provides two short outlines, one for an email message and the other for a meeting discussion. Finally, **Figure 3.10** illustrates a tree chart outline that provides a visual representation of how the information is connected.

After you plan the overall organization of your communication, consider where you want to place the main idea. In most business situations, stating the main point directly at the beginning of the message is better than placing it after the details. Audiences will become impatient if they don't know why you are communicating with them and how the details support your message. In addition, research in cognitive science has shown that readers better understand and remember details when you provide them with an **advance organizer** before the details.[9] The main point serves as an advance organizer because it provides a framework for understanding the details. **Figure 3.11A** on page 90 illustrates a **direct organization**.

However, in some circumstances, it may be more effective to lead up to the main point, using an **indirect organization**, as illustrated in **Figure 3.11B** on page 90—for example, when you communicate unexpected negative news, when you anticipate that your audience will be resistant to your message, or when you need to provide explanation before your main point makes sense. In the figures, note the difference in the **subject line**—the line in the header of the email that communicates what the message is about and influences whether the audience will read the message. In the direct approach, the subject line previews the main message of the email. In the indirect approach, the subject line previews only the topic.

outline An organizational plan that identifies key topics in the order they will be presented.

advance organizer Information that precedes details and provides a framework for understanding details.

direct organization The method of arranging content in a message to present the main idea of the message before the supporting details.

indirect organization The method of arranging content in a message to present the supporting details before the main idea.

subject line The line in the header of an email that communicates what the message is about and influences whether the audience will read the message.

FIGURE 3.8 Traditional Outline

outline for a proposal

Proposal for Summer-Hours Work Schedule

PURPOSE: To propose that ABC Communication's Sales Department adopt a summer-hours work schedule between June 1 and August 31.

Introduction
- Statement of problem
- Proposed solution

Detailed Description of Proposed Summer-Hours Work Schedule
- Flextime options emphasizing core workday hours
- Suggested policies to ensure balanced staffing

Benefits (documented by primary and secondary research)
- Increased employee morale
- Reduced employee turnover rates
- Increased employee productivity

Implementation Plan
- Survey employees to assess flextime preferences
- Develop policies and procedures
- Create an assessment plan

This traditional outline format summarizes information gathered for a report about a summer-hours schedule. Long documents, such as reports or proposals, may require several heading levels with multiple points under each topic.

FIGURE 3.9 Short Outlines

NOTES FOR PLANNING AN EMAIL

Notes for Email to Cherilyn
SUBJECT: Update on Summer-Hours Schedule Proposal
- Ask for feedback on attached rough draft
- Briefly explain research gathered to date
- Outline information to be included
- Thank her for taking time to provide input

Not every outline needs to be elaborate.

The notes to the left illustrate an outline for a short, informative email message. Each bullet point will become a short paragraph in the email message.

The list of questions to the right outlines the content for a short discussion during a meeting.

OUTLINE FOR DISCUSSION AT A MEETING

Overview of Summer-Hours Schedule Proposal

1. What is a flexible summer-hours schedule?
2. How will the company benefit from the schedule?
3. How will we avoid/overcome potential problems?
4. When/how will we implement the schedule?
5. How will we assess the schedule's effectiveness?

FIGURE 3.10 Tree Chart Outline

If you are a visual thinker, you might organize your communication using a *tree chart*, which lets you see the hierarchical structure and connections between your ideas.

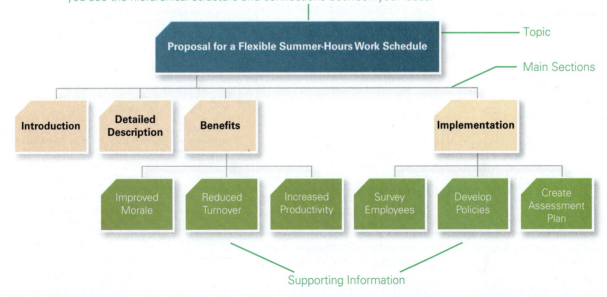

Proposal for a Flexible Summer-Hours Work Schedule — Topic

Main Sections

Introduction | Detailed Description | Benefits | Implementation

Improved Morale | Reduced Turnover | Increased Productivity | Survey Employees | Develop Policies | Create Assessment Plan

Supporting Information

FIGURE 3.11 Direct and Indirect Messages

A **Use a DIRECT organization to emphasize the main idea if the audience will have a positive or neutral reaction.**

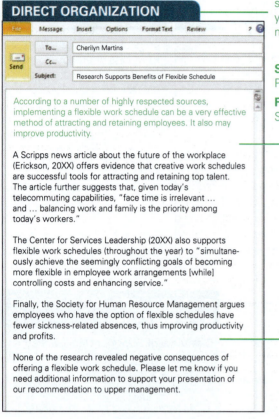

Imagine that you presented the summer-hours proposal to your supervisor in a meeting, and she requested that you email her some follow-up research to provide an industry perspective of the advantages and disadvantages of summer hours. If your supervisor liked your proposal, you would organize your email directly. Note that in a direct email, the subject line previews the main message of the email.

SUBJECT LINE:
Preview main message

FIRST PARAGRAPH:
State main idea

MIDDLE PARAGRAPHS:
Provide support

LAST PARAGRAPH:
Conclude with any or all of the following:
• Restate main point
• Add a call to action
• Provide deadlines and contact information

B **Use an INDIRECT organization to explain the reasons before the main idea if the audience will be resistant to your idea.**

If your supervisor was skeptical about your proposal, you would organize your email indirectly with the main idea after the supporting details. Note that in the indirect approach, the subject line is more neutral and indicates only the purpose and topic.

SUBJECT LINE:
Introduce the topic

FIRST PARAGRAPH:
State the purpose

MIDDLE PARAGRAPHS:
Provide details

LAST PARAGRAPH:
Conclude by stating the main idea and any or all of the following:
• Restate the main point
• Add a call to action
• Provide deadlines and contact information

MyLab Business Communication
Apply Figure 3.11's key concepts by going to **www.pearson.com/mylab/business-communication**

INDIRECT ORGANIZATION

| File | Message | Insert | Options | Format Text | Review | ? |

To... Cherilyn Martins
Cc...
Subject: Industry Perspective on Flexible Schedules

As you requested, I researched several external resources about industry's perspectives of flexible work hours.

A Scripps news article about the future of the workplace (Erickson, 20XX) offers evidence that creative work schedules are successful tools for attracting and retaining top talent. The article further suggests that, given today's telecommuting capabilities, "face time is irrelevant … and … balancing work and family is the priority among today's workers."

The Center for Services Leadership (20XX) also supports flexible work schedules (throughout the year) to "simultaneously achieve the seemingly conflicting goals of becoming more flexible in employee work arrangements [while] controlling costs and enhancing service."

Finally, the Society for Human Resource Management argues employees who have the option of flexible schedules have fewer sickness-related absences, thus improving productivity and profits.

All this research suggests that implementing a flexible work schedule offers substantial benefits at very low or no additional cost. None of the research revealed negative consequences of offering a flexible work schedule. Please let me know if you need additional information to support your presentation of our recommendation to upper management.

Drafting the content

If you are speaking, drafting means saying your message aloud or in your head so that you can hear it and evaluate it. If you are writing, **drafting** involves getting the information on paper (or the computer screen). Drafting is a creative process. Using your outline as a guide, you can begin to draft freely, knowing that your first draft will not be your final product.

During the drafting stage, writers often experience problems that block their progress. If you feel each sentence has to be perfect before you begin the next one, you suffer from *perfectionist syndrome*. To solve this problem, ignore the editor in your brain while you write and focus on getting words on the page without revising them. Switching between drafting and revising is inefficient because the two activities require very different mental processes. In contrast to the creative process of drafting, **revising** is a logical process that involves evaluating the effectiveness of your message in relation to your audience and purpose and then making changes in content, organization, or wording, as necessary. Assuming that you have given yourself sufficient time to draft and revise, separating the activities allows you to be more creative in your drafting and more logical in your revising.

A second problem you may experience when drafting is **writer's block**: an inability to start to write or continue writing. The concept was first introduced in the 1940s by psychiatrist Edmund Bergler, who proposed that it is a psychological block requiring therapy. Fortunately, subsequent researchers proposed different theories of writer's block and identified other kinds of psychological techniques to help reduce writer's block, such as becoming more flexible about the rules for writing,[10] using mental imagery, or doing other types of creative work to stimulate creative thinking.[11] Here are other ways to unblock your thoughts:

- **Think aloud.** Rather than writing, you may find it more helpful to get your ideas out by speaking anything that comes to mind. Some writers find it useful to record their thoughts, play back the recording, and then type the most important points they hear.
- **Write the easiest parts first.** You don't have to begin your draft with the first sentence or even the first paragraph. Begin at any point in the document that is easiest, and then cut and paste or insert text throughout the writing and evaluating process.
- **Free write.** Write down anything that comes to mind, regardless of whether it is appropriate or even meaningful. Even if you won't use all of it, you might create some content that is usable. See **Figure 3.12** for an example of *free writing*.
- **Take a break.** Changing your focus can give you a different perspective on the same writing task. Take a break to enjoy a physical activity, listen to music, or even take a nap. In fact, research suggests that brain activity is at its highest while and immediately after we're asleep.[12]

Whether you are thinking aloud, writing the easiest parts first, freewriting, or coming back to writing after a break, you may find that once you have some words on the page, the rest of the content more easily falls into place. However, don't try to write before you spend time thinking about your purpose, audience, and content. Research suggests that writers can be blocked by starting their writing projects in ineffective ways, such as failing to plan—in other words, composing before analyzing.[13] Following the steps of the ACE process will help reduce your chances of suffering from writer's block.

drafting A creative process that involves getting information on the paper or computer screen before revising and editing it.

revising A logical process that involves evaluating the effectiveness of a message in relation to your audience and purpose and then making changes in content, organization, or wording, as necessary.

writer's block An inability to begin or continue writing.

FIGURE 3.12 Example of Free Writing

free writing

Okay ... I need to start the introduction of this report with a statement of the problem and the purpose of the report. There really wasn't a serious problem, but the summer-hours plan sounded like a good idea to me. A friend told me about it at his company, I mentioned it to some colleagues here, and they thought I should recommend it. So what's the problem? Well, low morale could be contributing to our typical third-quarter sales slump. The summer numbers are always the lowest each year. I can document this with the data I collected from the last 10 years. But since I found that data after I started the research, it shouldn't really be the problem we're trying to solve, just a possible benefit of the schedule. So the summer flex hours could be a solution that boosts morale and productivity thereby potentially increasing third-quarter sales. If I start with that in the introduction and then support the idea with findings from sources in the middle, I could close with a recommendation to try summer hours and assess its effect on both morale and sales.

Designing a professional format and delivery

After you have composed a message, arrange it into a professional format that is easy to read and understand. A document's format plays a role similar to your dress and behavior in face-to-face communication. A format that looks professional communicates to an audience that you are professional. A format that is difficult to read or confusing undermines your credibility.

Although the specific techniques you use for designing a message will depend on the medium you choose, some design principles apply to all medium options. For example, good business communicators do the following:

- Start with an easily identifiable introduction.
- Break messages into short chunks (paragraphs).
- Begin each paragraph with a strong **topic sentence** that identifies the main point or overall idea of the paragraph.
- Indicate shifts in content by using headings or transitional terms such as *first* and *second* or *as a result*.
- Use bulleted or numbered lists for easy comprehension and skimming.
- End with a specific conclusion or recommendation.

topic sentence A sentence that identifies the main point or overall idea of the paragraph. Most frequently, it is the first sentence in a paragraph.

The following sections provide examples of professional formats for email messages, memos, letters, voice mail messages, and social media postings. Other chapters discuss methods of creating professional formats for longer and more complex documents, such as formal proposals, reports, and presentations. For a comprehensive formatting guide, see Appendix A: Formats for Business Documents.

Email messages

Business email messages should focus on only one topic, which is clearly identified in the subject line. However, one topic does not mean the message should contain only one paragraph. Consider the two versions of the email message in **Figure 3.13**. Both messages contain the same information; the subject line and all the sentences are identical. However, the design is very different. Examine the layout. Which one looks more readable? Which one looks better organized? Which one looks more professional?

FIGURE 3.13 Poorly Designed Versus Professionally Designed Email Messages

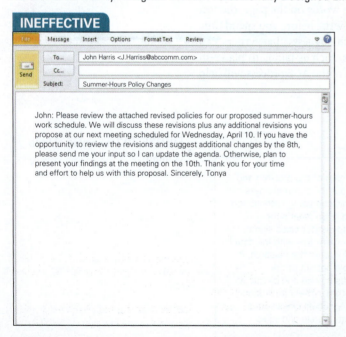

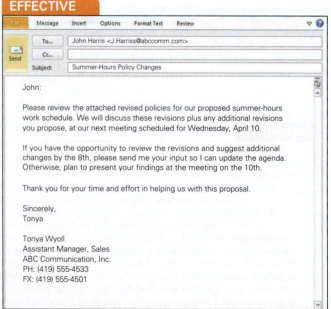

When you write longer emails, you can enhance the organization and design even further by using five important techniques:

- Clearly identify the topic and purpose in the subject line.
- Begin with a focused first paragraph.
- Use **topic-specific headings**.
- Format important lists as **bullet point lists**.
- End with a signature block.

The email in **Figure 3.14** illustrates all these techniques.

topic-specific headings Section or paragraph titles that are short but include key ideas. They are often in the form of a short sentence and include a verb.

bullet point lists Vertically formatted lists, with each item preceded by a dot or another simple shape.

MyLab Business Communication
Apply Figure 3.14's key concepts by going to **www.pearson.com/mylab/business-communication**

FIGURE 3.14 How to Format and Design an Email

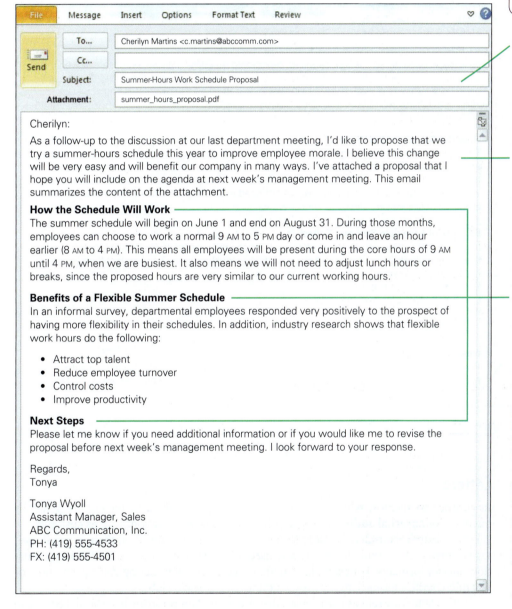

Clearly identify the topic and purpose in the subject line.

Begin with a focused first paragraph that identifies your purpose and previews your content. Strong first paragraphs are increasingly important as more people read emails on mobile devices with small screens. No one wants to scroll to find the main idea of the message.

Use topic-specific headings or paragraph titles that are short but include a key idea. For example, instead of using a generic heading such as "Benefits," compose a topic-specific heading such as "Benefits of a Flexible Summer Schedule" to help the audience immediately grasp the content of the paragraph.

Format important lists as bullet point lists to make the information easy to skim. The listed items should be parallel —each using the same grammatical structure. In this list, each item begins with a verb.

End emails with a complimentary closing, your name, and a signature block. The signature block helps readers quickly find your contact information.

Memos

Memos are hardcopy documents typically sent to **internal audiences**—people within your organization. Before email existed, organizations relied on memos for most internal communication. Today, memos are sent much less frequently, primarily in situations when email is not feasible. For example, you may see memos accompanying documents that cannot be sent

memos Hardcopy documents that follow a set format and are typically sent to internal audiences.

internal audiences People with whom you communicate inside your organization.

electronically, such as booklets, pamphlets, or contracts and legal documents that require signatures. You may also see people producing memo reports if they have important information that is too long for a typical email message but too short for a formal report with a title page and table of contents.

Figure 3.15 provides a memo version of the email message in Figure 3.14. As the annotations explain, memos have a lot in common with emails. For more detailed advice on formatting memos, see Appendix A: Formats for Business Documents.

FIGURE 3.15 How to Format a Memo

Write a header block similar to that of an email, with the lines in this order: To, From, Date, Subject. Follow each of these headings with a colon and then tab to add content. The words following the colon are left-aligned.

Do not include a salutation. This is a difference between emails and memos.

As in emails, **use short paragraphs** and, if applicable, headings to make the content easier to skim.

Do not include a complimentary closing or signature block.

If any additional documents accompany the memo, **include the word "Attachment"** at the end of the memo.

---

memo

TO: Ms. Cherilyn Martins, Vice President, Sales
FROM: Ms. Tonya Wyoll, Assistant Manager, Sales
DATE: February 12, 20XX
SUBJECT: Summer-Hours Work Schedule Proposal

As a follow-up to the discussion at our last department meeting, I'd like to propose that we try a summer-hours schedule this year to improve employee morale. I believe this change will be very easy and will benefit our company in many ways. I've attached a proposal that I hope you will include on the agenda at next week's management meeting. This memo summarizes the content of the attachment.

How the Schedule Will Work
The summer schedule will begin on June 1 and end on August 31. During that period, employees can choose to work a normal 9 AM to 5 PM day or come in and leave an hour earlier (8 AM to 4 PM). This means all employees will be present during the core hours of 9 AM until 4 PM, when we are busiest. It also means we will not need to adjust lunch hours or breaks, since the proposed hours are very similar to our current working hours.

Benefits of a Flexible Summer Schedule
In an informal survey, departmental employees responded very positively to the prospect of having more flexibility in their schedules. In addition, industry research shows that flexible work hours do the following:

- Attract top talent
- Reduce employee turnover
- Control costs
- Improve productivity

Next Steps
Please let me know if you need additional information, or if you would like me to revise the proposal before next week's management meeting. I look forward to your response.

Attachment

Letters

letters Formal correspondence, generally intended for external audiences. Letters can be sent through postal mail or by email attachment for quicker delivery.

external audiences People with whom you communicate outside your organization.

In contrast to memos, which are intended for internal audiences, **letters** are generally intended for **external audiences**—people outside your organization, such as customers or clients. A letter is considered a more formal method of communication than an email message or memo. As a result, letters are also used for internal communication when the situation calls for formality. For example, you might receive a letter offering you a promotion, or you might write a formal letter of resignation when you leave a job.

When letters are sent as hard copies, they are printed on company letterhead. Letters can also be sent electronically as email attachments. In fact, many companies often use electronic letterhead templates so that letters attached to emails will look the same as printed letters. An attached letter maintains the formality of the message, while the email transmission takes advantage of quick delivery and electronic documentation.

Several letter formats exist, such as block style, modified block, and simplified. However, block style, as shown in **Figure 3.16** and throughout this text, is the most efficient letter style and the one most commonly used in business. Block-style letters use no indentions or centering. Instead, all elements begin at the left margin. Paragraphs are separated with a blank line.

FIGURE 3.16 How to Format a Letter

ACME PROMOTIONS, INCORPORATED
1206 Presque Isle Avenue, Marquette, MI 49855
906-555-2600 | FAX 906-555-2601 | www.acmepromotions.com

March 6, 20XX

Ms. Patricia Douglas
Dickinson Memorial Hospital
1721 S. Stephenson Avenue
Iron Mountain, MI 49801

Dear Ms. Douglas:

Thank you for your interest in Acme Promotions. I enjoyed talking with you about our mobile cell phone chargers as give-aways at your hospital's next in-service retreat. As you requested, enclosed is a charger with the DMH logo. This unit is yours to keep, regardless of whether you place an order with us.

As we discussed on the phone, we are certain that our products and service will meet your needs. Our chargers have a one-year warranty. Special orders can be processed within one week, depending on the size of your order. Additionally, we offer discounts for large orders. Complete pricing information is available at our website at www.acmegadgets.com, and I have enclosed a quote specific to the quantities you and I discussed.

I look forward to hearing from you soon. Please contact me at chris.grant@acmepromotions.com or on my direct line (906-555-2691) to schedule your order.

Sincerely,

CGrant

Christopher A. Grant
Vice President of Sales

Enclosures

Use letterhead stationery for formal letters.

Center the content vertically between the letterhead and the bottom of the page.

Date the letter by writing out the month and separating the day from the year with a comma. Three blank lines separate the date from the inside address.

Address the letter to the recipient by including the person's name and address—called the *inside address*. Leave one blank line to separate the inside address from the salutation.

Include a salutation. End the salutation with a colon, not a comma, and leave one blank line before the first paragraph.

Format all paragraphs at the left margin with no indentation. Leave one blank line between paragraphs. Depending on the content and audience, you might choose to include topic-specific headings, paragraph titles, and bullet point lists.

End with a complimentary closing such as "Sincerely," followed by three blank lines to leave room for your signature before the signature block.

Use a professional signature block that includes your full name and the title of your position.

Include an "Enclosure" notation only if you are sending an additional item (document, product sample, etc.) with the letter.

For guidelines for formatting letters and examples of modified block style, see Appendix A: Formats for Business Documents.

Voice mail messages

You may think it is odd to consider the design of oral communication because design is typically considered a visual concept. However, voice mail messages will be easier to understand if you follow the same principles used in designing emails: Focus on one topic, keep the message short, make the main point easy to find, and provide contact information. Take a few minutes to plan your message before calling. **Figure 3.17** on page 96 illustrates two voice mail messages. Although the version on the left is more formal than the version on the right, both include the relevant elements described in the annotations.

FIGURE 3.17 How to Compose a Voice Mail Message

FORMAL VOICE MAIL MESSAGE		INFORMAL VOICE MAIL MESSAGE
Hello, Ms. Douglas.	**Greet the recipient** by name to personalize the message.	Hi, Pat.
This is Chris Grant from Acme Promotions. My phone number is 906-555-2691.	**Identify yourself** and include your affiliation or position if the audience is not familiar with you. Leave a callback number if you want a return call.	This is Chris from Acme Promotions. Number is 906-555-2691.
I am calling about the cell phone charger sample we mailed you last week and am curious about two things. First, did you receive the package? Our tracking information indicates that someone else signed for it. Second, assuming you have had a chance to use the charger, I wanted to follow up to discuss any issues to ensure we meet your needs so we can move forward with your order.	**State your purpose and main point.** Let your audience know why you are calling. **Include necessary details but keep the message short.** If you mention at the beginning that you have more than one point, signal each with words such as "first" and "second." **Identify actions.** Do you want your audience to return your call, send you something, or do something else? If you are requesting an action, be both polite and specific.	Two things about that cell phone charger we mailed last week … First, did you receive it? Our tracking info says someone else signed for it. Second, have you had a chance to use it yet? Let's discuss any issues to ensure we're meeting your needs. I'm eager to move forward with your order.
Again, this is Chris Grant. Please call me at your earliest convenience at 906-555-2691. That's 906-555-2691. I look forward to talking with you soon.	**Provide contact information.** Even if you state your contact information at the beginning, repeat it at the end of your message. Speak slowly when leaving your telephone number or repeat it so the recipient doesn't have to listen to your message again to be able to write down the complete number to return your call.	Hope to hear from you soon, Pat. My number again is 906-555-2691. That's 906-555-2691.
Thank you. Goodbye.	**Sign off** with an appropriate closing.	Thanks. Bye.

Evaluate

(SQ3) How does evaluating improve your communication?

The final step in the ACE process is to evaluate your communication to ensure that it is complete, clear, concise, professional sounding, and correct. Evaluation may occur at different points for written and oral communication. When you write, you are able to evaluate these elements *before* delivering your message. Take the time to reread, revise, and edit your written drafts several times before sending them. If you skip the evaluating stage of writing, even for short messages, your content could include incomplete thoughts, awkward sentences, and grammatical errors that computer editing tools such as spelling and grammar checkers may miss. In addition, by the time you get to the end of your first draft, you may discover new ideas about what to say and how to say it. The **evaluating** phase gives you the opportunity to make those changes before you send the message.

By contrast, oral communication allows you to evaluate *while* you are delivering the message based on immediate feedback you receive. Imagine that you are making a point in a meeting. As you look around the room, you can gauge your audience's reaction and begin to adjust or revise your explanation on the spot. Written communication does not provide this type of immediate feedback or the opportunity to revise your message as you are communicating it.

This section describes several ways to evaluate your communication: evaluating content, evaluating for style, evaluating for tone, proofreading, and using feedback to improve your future communication.

Evaluating content helps you achieve your purpose and outcome

As a first step in the evaluating process, reread the entire document from the audience's perspective. Think about the analysis stage of the ACE process and the purpose and outcome you identified for the communication. Ask yourself these questions to determine whether the document has the right content and the right approach to achieve your goal:

- **Are your purpose and your main point clear?** Underline your purpose and main point. If you cannot find explicit statements to underline, you need to revise your draft.

- **Have you provided all the information you need to support your purpose?** Consider all the pieces of information you believe your audience will need to know and mark each of them in your draft. If any information is missing, revise. If you cannot imagine what your audience will need to know, ask friends or colleagues to provide feedback.
- **Will the organization of that information make sense to the audience?** Read the topic sentence of each paragraph. Does each topic sentence identify the main idea of the paragraph? Do the details of the paragraph relate to the topic sentence? Does the progression from one topic sentence to the next seem logical?
- **Is the message persuasive enough to be successful?** If your message is intended to be persuasive, identify key objections your audience may have. Also identify audience benefits. Additional persuasive techniques are addressed in Chapter 5: Communicating Persuasive Messages.

evaluating The process of critically reviewing a communication to ensure that it is complete, clear, concise, easy to understand, and error free.

TECHNOLOGY
HOW TO COMPOSE EMAILS FOR MOBILE DEVICES

While you may write your emails on a computer, most email messages are opened and read on mobile devices, such as tablets, smartphones, smartwatches, and other wearable technologies.[14] Because of the smaller viewing screens on these devices, you need to think about the physical space of your message, including images and font sizes.[15,16] Use the following advice to make all your email messages mobile friendly.

First Screen of Mobile Email

Preview Text in Inbox

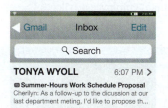

ANALYZING
- Identify the main purpose of the email and stress it in the subject line and first paragraph.
- Identify what you need your audience to do and make sure it appears within the first screen of the email.

COMPOSING
- Use short and meaningful subject lines.
- Make the first 75 characters of the message meaningful. That content will be displayed in the inbox as preview text and can persuade your audience to open the email.
- Organize the content directly, placing the most important and persuasive information first to engage the audience and convince them to scroll if your message requires more than one screen.
- Keep paragraphs short. One-sentence paragraphs aren't often used in formal documents, but they look good on small screens and can actually draw attention to questions and calls to action.
- If you include an attachment, summarize it briefly in the email. Attachments can be hard to read on a mobile device.
- Make it easy to reply. When people read an email requiring a complex reply on a mobile device, they are likely to put it aside—and then forget to respond.[17]

EVALUATING
Send an important email to yourself first, before sending to your audience, to see how it looks on a small screen. Ask yourself these questions as you review your email:
- Is the subject line specific to the meaning of the message?
- Will the first few lines be effective as preview text?
- Does the first paragraph include the main point or purpose of the message—and at least hint at what you want the audience to do?
- Have you revised for conciseness and eliminated unnecessary information?

For a TECHNOLOGY exercise, see Exercise 24 on page 117.

Evaluating for style improves readability and comprehension

style How you express yourself as distinct from what you express.

Style refers to how you express yourself rather than what you say. Even if you include all the appropriate content, when you do not express that content clearly, concisely, and coherently, your audience will be confused. Libraries contain shelf after shelf of style manuals, full of advice about how to write well. Classic manuals, such as the 1959 *Elements of Style* by Strunk and White, remain popular today.[18] However, the rules in *Elements of Style* are limited and more targeted to narrative and essay writing than to business communication. Contemporary manuals are more helpful, especially those that draw on research in cognitive science and neuroscience. Books such as *Style* by Williams,[19] *The Sense of Style* by Pinker,[20] and *The Reader's Brain* by Douglas[21] all help explain why certain word choices and sentence structures are easier to understand than others. Effective sentences and paragraphs share a number of characteristics, including *clarity, conciseness, cohesion,* and *coherence.*

Clarity

clarity The quality of being unambiguous and easy to understand.

Achieving **clarity** means your audience can easily understand your intended meaning. The process of reading involves recognizing words, understanding them in context, and if the sentence doesn't make sense, drawing inferences about what they mean. When language is unclear and sentence structures are difficult to process, the audience may need to read the text multiple times and may still misinterpret it. When language is clear, audiences are more likely to understand and to remember. The best business writing communicates its meaning as quickly and as simply as possible.

To evaluate your writing for clarity, review and edit it to ensure that it complies with the following advice:

- **Use natural-sounding language rather than big words intended to impress.** One of the first mistakes many new employees make is trying to impress their audience by using big words in long sentences. People are rarely impressed by writing that is long and difficult to understand, such as the poorly worded sentences in **Figure 3.18**. The clearly worded sentences in that figure have the same meaning but use natural-sounding language that the audience can easily grasp.

abstract language Language that refers to broad concepts that an audience can interpret in multiple ways.

- **Use concrete language rather than abstract language. Abstract language** refers to broad concepts that an audience can interpret in multiple ways. Consider the sentence "We need to solve the transportation problem ASAP." In this sentence, the terms "transportation" and "ASAP" (as soon as possible) are abstract. What do they mean? A dictionary defines *transportation* as conveyance (carrying, moving, shipping, or hauling), but does everyone think of the same kind of transportation when they visualize the word? Probably not. Does "ASAP" mean by today, or by the end of the week, or whenever you have the time to do it? **Concrete language** is specific. The more concrete your language, the more likely it is that you and your audience will interpret the same message in the same way. Here is a better way to word the original sentence: "By tomorrow morning, we need to determine why trucking shipments are leaving the warehouse one to two days late."

concrete language Language that is specific, making it likely that everyone will interpret it the same way.

If you have trouble looking for the right word to express your meaning, you can use your word processing software's thesaurus to identify options. A *thesaurus* is a reference tool that provides synonyms and antonyms. *Synonyms* are words that have the same or similar meaning, such as "quickly" and "rapidly." *Antonyms* are words that have opposite meanings, such as "clear" and "confusing." However, choose carefully among the words that you see in the thesaurus, and look up unfamiliar words in the dictionary before using them. Even when a thesaurus lists two words as synonyms, they may not have the same meaning. For example, a thesaurus usually lists the word "privileges" as a synonym for "benefits."[22] However, if you were writing about "employee benefits," you could not simply swap the word "privileges" for "benefits." "Employee benefits" has a different meaning than "employee privileges."

FIGURE 3.18 Using Natural Language

POORLY WORDED	CLEARLY WORDED
Please apprise me of what transpired during my absence.	Please tell me what happened while I was gone.
I sincerely appreciate your exertion on this critically important endeavor.	Thank you for your work on this important project.

- **Avoid slang and clichés.** To communicate effectively in business, you need to use words that your audience will understand. **Slang** is nonstandard, informal language that may work well within a certain group but often excludes people of different generations and from different countries, cultures, and social groups. Examples of slang include "cool," "my bad," "off the chain," "plugged in," "TBH," and "go missing." **Clichés** are commonplace and often overused phrases that have lost their force and meaning. Like slang, clichés are also specific to cultures and languages, and they may exclude international audiences. Would a businessperson who learned English in India or China understand the clichés in **Figure 3.19**?

CLICHÉ		MEANING
His proposal is all over the map.	➡	His proposal is disorganized.
The bottom fell out of that investment.	➡	The investment lost money.
Hiring him was a bad call.	➡	Hiring him was a bad decision.

slang Nonstandard, informal language that may communicate well within a certain group but often excludes people from different countries, cultures, and social groups.

clichés Commonplace and often overused phrases that have lost their force and meaning.

FIGURE 3.19 Eliminating Clichés

- **Use active voice and passive voice effectively.** *Voice* refers to the relationship between the subject and verb in a sentence. In **active voice** sentences, the subject is the actor, performing the action of the verb.

$$\underbrace{\text{subject}}_{\text{(actor)}} \quad \underbrace{\text{verb}}_{} \quad \underbrace{\text{object}}_{}$$

ACTIVE VOICE: The employees completed the project early.

active voice A sentence structure in which the subject performs the action of the verb.

In **passive voice** sentences, the subject does not act. Instead, the subject receives the action expressed by the verb.

$$\underbrace{\text{subject}}_{\text{(acted on)}} \quad \underbrace{\text{verb}}_{}$$

PASSIVE VOICE: The project was completed early by the employees.

passive voice A sentence structure in which the subject is passive and receives the action expressed by the verb.

Good business communication relies on active voice because active voice represents the natural language order, with the actor coming before the action. As a result, people understand active voice sentences more quickly. Understanding passive voice requires mentally reassembling the pieces of the sentence.

However, passive voice is in the language for a reason, and as a good communicator, you may deliberately choose passive voice in a few specific circumstances:

- **You do not want to assign blame.** For example, instead of "Camilla misfiled the contract" (active voice), you can say "The contract was misfiled" (passive voice).
- **You want to emphasize that something was done, not who did it.** For example, instead of "Roger scheduled the meeting for Friday at 2 PM" (active voice), you can focus on the outcome by saying "The meeting is scheduled for Friday at 2 PM" (passive voice).
- **You need a specific word at the beginning of a sentence, to improve the flow of a paragraph.** For example, in the following pair of sentences, the beginning of the second sentence does not clearly relate to the first sentence. "The new contract will be ready tomorrow. All the parties involved must sign it." That problem can be solved by beginning the second sentence by referring to the contract, which results in passive voice. "The new contract will be ready tomorrow. It must be signed by all parties involved."

- **Avoid nominalizations. Phrase your actions as verbs, not nouns.** A **nominalization** is a noun formed from a verb (or an adjective). For example, "decision" is a nominalization created from the verb "decide," and "announcement" is a nominalization created from the verb "announce." Nominalizations increase wordiness and often lead to passive voice. If you find nominalizations when you evaluate your writing, ask yourself "Who is doing what?" Use the answer to transform the nominalizations into verbs and make your sentences clearer and shorter.
  - **Nominalizations:** An *evaluation* of the proposals will take place next week, and an *announcement* of the winner will occur the week after. (21 words)
  - **Actions phrased as verbs:** We will *evaluate* the proposals next week and *announce* the winner the week after. (14 words)

nominalization A noun formed from a verb or an adjective.

- **Put subjects and verbs close together, toward the beginning of the sentence.** Readers and listeners do not know what a sentence is about until they reach the subject and verb. When subjects and verbs are separated by long interrupters, the audience can lose the connection between them. Similarly, when verbs come at the end of a sentence, readers have difficulty remembering the details that came before. As you evaluate your writing, check the position of subjects and verbs and move them toward the beginning of the sentence.

- **Verb comes late:** Making connections, learning of job opportunities, expanding your knowledge, increasing your confidence, and raising your profile are five benefits of networking.
- **Subject and verb come early:** Networking offers five benefits: making connections, learning of job opportunities, expanding your knowledge, increasing your confidence, and raising your profile.

- **Use parallel phrasing for all lists, including bulleted and numbered lists.** *Vertical lists* are a key feature of much business writing. For these items to communicate clearly, a reader must be able to see what is being listed and how the items differ from each other. The best way to accomplish that goal is to introduce the list with a full or partial sentence that identifies what is being listed and then to use **parallel phrasing**—that is, the same grammatical form—for each item in the list. In the list below, the introductory sentence identifies that this will be a list of benefits. The bulleted benefits are all phrased with the same grammatical form: verbs ending in "ing."

> **parallel phrasing** Using the same grammatical form for each item in a list.

Parallel phrasing: Networking offers five benefits:

- making connections
- learning of job opportunities
- expanding your knowledge
- increasing your confidence
- raising your profile

Conciseness

> **conciseness** Using no more words than necessary for a message to accomplish its purpose.

Conciseness is as important as clarity. Concise communication is short and to the point, expressing ideas clearly in the fewest possible words. In business communication, shorter is usually better. Guy Kawasaki, managing director of Garage Technology Ventures, argues that, schools "should teach students how to communicate in five-sentence emails and with 10-slide PowerPoint presentations. If they just taught every student that, American business would be much better off." He goes on to say, "No one wants to read 'War and Peace' emails. Who has the time? Ditto with 60 PowerPoint slides for a one-hour meeting."[23] The following advice will help you reduce wordiness in your writing and speaking:

- **Edit wordy phrases.** When possible, replace multiple words with a single word. **Figure 3.20** provides examples of how you can edit wordy phrases to be more clear and concise.
- **Eliminate obvious fillers and any information that is not necessary or helpful to achieve your purpose.** When you include extra words and unnecessary information, you waste your time as you compose the message as well as the audience's time as they read or listen to it. Consider the examples in **Figure 3.21**.

FIGURE 3.20 Using Concise Wording

WORDY	CONCISE
This email is in reference to our approval of your prior request . . .	We approve your request . . .
Enclosed in this mailing you will find three photocopies . . .	Enclosed are three copies . . .
If you have any questions, please do not hesitate to contact me at . . .	Please contact me if you have any questions . . .

FIGURE 3.21 Eliminating Unnecessary Words

WORDY	CONCISE
As you know, we met yesterday to discuss next year's budget. Based on the auditor's review, I recommend that we . . .	Based on the auditor's review of our budget, I recommend that we . . .
As your assistant manager, I am suggesting that we review our departmental procedures.	I suggest we review our departmental procedures.
There are three people who will attend the meeting.	Three people will attend the meeting.

- **Eliminate redundancies, unnecessary repetitions of an idea.** Consider the examples of redundancies in **Figure 3.22**.

redundancy Unnecessary repetition of an idea.

REDUNDANT	CONCISE
Please refer back to the minutes from your last department meeting.	Please refer to the minutes from our last department meeting.
Advance planning on your project will allow our departments to combine together our resources and divide up the work to be done.	Good project planning will allow our departments to combine resources and divide the work.
The first issue we need to address is travel reimbursement. Travel reimbursement is an important issue to address because nearly 70% of our employees have expense accounts.	First, we need to address travel reimbursement because nearly 70% of our employees have expense accounts.

FIGURE 3.22 Avoiding Redundancies

Cohesion

Cohesion is the connection of ideas at the sentence level. Writing is cohesive when readers see how sentences link together. While composing, you may not pay much attention to cohesion because you already know how the ideas connect. However, your reader needs connectors to understand the relationship you intend to convey. When you evaluate your writing, check the beginnings of sentences and paragraphs to make sure they do one of the following to connect with previous sentences:

cohesion The connection of ideas at the sentence level.

- **Use transitional words and phrases. Transitions** are words and phrases that signal the relationship between sentences and paragraphs. Transitions such "moreover," "in addition," and "also" indicate that the next sentence adds on to the previous one. The transitions "however," "but," and "by contrast" indicate that the next sentence will differ from what came before.

transition Words and phrases that signal the relationship between sentences and paragraphs.

- **Begin with ideas you have already been discussing and introduce new ideas at the end of the sentence.** The order of information in a sentence makes a difference. Beginning a sentence with familiar information provides context for understanding new information. Compare these two versions of a short paragraph:

    Second sentence begins with new ideas (in italics): "Although the Miramont Hotel is offering an affordable price for our meeting venue, I recommend that we reject the offer. *Distance from the city center, lack of onsite restaurants, and aging facilities* explain the low price."

    Second sentence begins with an idea already introduced (in italics): "Although the Miramont Hotel is offering an affordable price for our meeting venue, I recommend that we reject the offer. The *price* is low because the hotel is far from the city center, has no onsite restaurants, and suffers from aging facilities."

    The second version is easier to understand, because the reader can quickly see how the ideas in the paragraph connect.

Coherence

Coherence is the connection of ideas throughout the entire document. Text is coherent when it is unified and makes sense as a whole. Coherence allows readers to skim quickly to get an overall sense of the meaning and then read in depth to understand the details. As you evaluate your writing, check its coherence by ensuring that you have followed these guidelines:

coherence The connection of ideas at the level of the entire text.

- Begin with a paragraph that identifies the main point or purpose of the text.
- Begin each paragraph with a topic sentence that relates to the main point or purpose of the piece as a whole—and that sets clear expectations for the rest of the paragraph.
- Develop paragraphs with material that focuses only on the topic of the paragraph. If the topic changes, begin a new paragraph. Readers easily become confused when paragraphs shift topics or change their focus, and comprehension suffers.

One test for coherence is to read just the topic sentences of each paragraph throughout your document. Those sentences *alone* should explain the meaning of your message.

New Hires @ Work

Megan Sugrue
Northwestern University

University Senior Manager,
Social Media Strategy @ Viacom
International Media Networks

For social media, the language
you use depends on the
audience you're addressing.
For example, MTV's target
audience is young
people ages 14 to 24.
The language we use
is *their* language—we
aim to sound like a
friend, not a business.

Photo courtesy of Megan Sugrue

tone The attitude your language conveys
toward your topic and your audience.

Evaluating for tone helps you project a professional image

Tone refers to the attitude your language conveys toward your topic and your audience. Tone in writing is similar to your tone of voice when you speak. Your tone can be friendly or angry, positive or negative, formal or casual, humorous or serious, objective or passionate, courteous or rude. Achieving an appropriate tone is challenging. It requires you to determine what attitude will best help you accomplish your goals and ensure that your audience will interpret your tone as you intended. In fact, tone is so challenging that the U.S. Department of Education reviews its tweets about its Free Application for Student Federal Aid (FAFSA) three times before releasing them to ensure that the tone is right.[24]

Here are some guidelines to help you achieve a tone that is appropriate for most business communication:

- **Use positive wording.** Whenever possible, effective business writers choose positive wording to communicate their messages, even in negative situations. *Positive wording* creates an optimistic, encouraging, and often more informative message. For example, consider the sentences in **Figure 3.23**. The sentences on the left focus on the negative meaning of the messages. Note how in each example subtle changes in wording on the right focus on the positive meaning.

- **Sound conversational.** Business communication should sound *conversational* rather than academic. Academic writing and speaking often sound too formal for everyday communication. Instead, use relatively short sentences and familiar words. When read aloud, the text should sound as if the writer is talking with the audience. A conversational tone is especially important in social media messages, where the goal is to create interaction and build a positive image about your corporate brand.

To test the power of reading aloud to achieve a conversational tone, see the examples in **Figure 3.24**. Read the sentences on the left aloud. Would you speak this way to someone? Probably not. The sentences on the right convey the same meaning but with a better conversational tone.

FIGURE 3.23 Using Positive Wording

NEGATIVE	POSITIVE
We will not be able to approve a new budget until the analysis is complete.	We will be able to approve a new budget when the analysis is complete.
The board has not yet voted on the salary increases.	The board will vote on the salary increases at the next meeting.
If you do not sign the form before 5 PM, we will not be able to fund your travel request.	If you sign the form before 5 PM, we will be able to fund your travel request.

FIGURE 3.24 Using Conversational Tone

TOO FORMAL	CONVERSATIONAL
Henceforth all documentation is to be completed within two business days.	Please complete all forms within two business days.
As per your instructions, I have initiated discussions with the previously identified employees.	I began talking with the employees you mentioned last week.
This new policy will facilitate the implementation of more beneficial scheduling decisions.	This new policy will let us schedule shipments more efficiently.

- **Match your tone to your purpose.** For example, in a thank-you message, aim to sound appreciative. In a report, have an objective tone. In an apology, sound conciliatory. In a persuasive proposal, take a confident tone. In an email outlining a problem, you might adopt a worried tone. While many tone choices are available, avoid the following tones, which are rarely effective in business communication: angry, arrogant, condescending, defensive, egotistical, flippant, resentful, self-righteous, or sarcastic.

- **Use humor appropriately.** Humor is rarely appropriate in a formal report or an email conveying bad news. However, in presentations, conversations, and social media posts, a humorous tone can be very effective in capturing attention and helping you connect with people.[25] For example, to encourage students to apply for federal aid, the Department of Education uses humorous tweets, such as this one, accompanied by a picture of a kitten: "You haven't filled out your FAFSA yet? Are you kitten me? #Caturday."[26] By contrast, when tweeting words of wisdom to students, the Department of Education adopts a very different tone: "Getting a student loan is a big decision—remember, borrow only what you need and know what you owe. #WednesdayWisdom."[27]

Evaluating for correctness increases your credibility

You can spend hours writing a report, but if it is full of errors, your audience may focus more on your mistakes than on your message. Even an email with typographical errors can give your audience the impression that you lack attention to detail. A quick scan of a document is not sufficient to catch problems. Instead, **proofread** by checking your documents carefully and systematically for all types of errors and take advantage of technology tools, such as spelling and grammar checkers.

proofread A systematic process of reviewing writing for errors.

Familiarize yourself with five types of errors

Most writing errors fall into one of five categories: *content errors, spelling and typographical errors, usage errors, grammatical errors,* or *format errors*:

- **Content errors** are mistakes in the substance of a message, such as incorrect or missing information. To avoid content errors, make a mental list of all things that need to be included and correct in your document and review to check them—for example, prices, dates and days of the week, locations and times of meetings, and deadlines. Ask a colleague to help you proofread to provide a more objective perspective.

- **Spelling and typographical errors** result from lack of knowledge about how to spell words and from typing too quickly, transposing letters, and duplicating letters. Don't assume that automated spelling checkers will catch all your errors. Instead, look up spellings of unfamiliar words and proofread carefully just for spelling errors and typos. Also double-check addresses, telephone numbers, and spellings of names.

- **Usage errors** are errors in the way language is used, such as using "imply" instead of "infer" or "economical" instead of "economic." It is difficult to catch these errors on your own; ask a colleague to help you find them.

- **Grammatical errors** are violations of grammar rules, such as sentence fragments, run-on sentences, and incorrect subject–verb agreement (just to name a few). Although automated grammar checkers can help you identify these problems, the tools will sometimes miss errors and suggest inappropriate changes. You need to check suggested changes and review for additional grammar errors on your own. To refresh your memory, review the grammar rules in Appendix C: Grammar, Punctuation, Mechanics, and Conventions and complete the grammar exercises at the end of each chapter of this text.

- **Format errors** are inconsistencies in design techniques within a document, such as including both indented and block-style paragraphs, bullets that do not align correctly, and differences in font sizes or styles. To avoid formatting errors, reformat text copied and pasted from other documents or paste it as unformatted text. Also, use tabs instead of spaces to align text. Finally, take advantage of automatic formatting features, such as heading styles and hanging indents.

Proofread systematically to check for errors

Proofreading has long been a best practice. To check systematically for all these types of errors, take full advantage of technology tools and follow these guidelines:

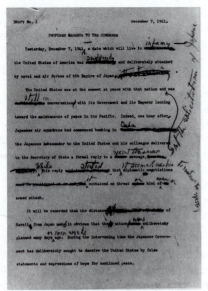

President Franklin D. Roosevelt edited his famous "Day of Infamy" speech for content and style before delivering it.
Source: National Archives.

- **Read your work multiple times.** If you proofread just once for all errors, you most likely will not find them all. However, if you narrow each proofreading pass to scan for a particular problem, you will be more successful in finding your mistakes.
- **Pay special attention to headers, footers, headings, and titles.** People often skip these elements when proofreading.
- **Look for your own common errors.** Most writers repeat the same kinds of errors based on their individual writing style. Identify your common errors by reviewing your graded writing assignments or asking your instructor for assistance. Make a list of these errors and look for them in your drafts.
- **Read your work later.** If possible, put some time between your composing and evaluating stages. Too often, writers quickly compose a first draft and immediately try to proofread their work. Taking even a five-minute break can clear your thoughts and let you proofread with a more objective and fresh perspective. Read each word and proofread the message slowly.
- **Read from the bottom up.** Start with the last sentence and read up the page sentence by sentence. This backward approach slows your reading pace and lets you examine the information out of context to help you find typos and missing words.
- **Read your draft aloud.** Generally, people speak more slowly than they read. Therefore, reading your draft aloud slows your reading pace and helps you focus on the text and find more errors. Also, when you hear what you have written, you are more likely to identify a missing word or notice awkward phrasing.
- **Have the computer read your draft aloud to you.** You can use an app such as Narrator, which you can turned on through the accessibility settings in Microsoft Word.
- **Ask a colleague for help.** For a more objective perspective, ask a colleague to proofread your draft. An objective reader can often find errors that you have overlooked. If you routinely proofread the work of others, you may want to familiarize yourself with the standard symbols that professional proofreaders use to mark errors. (To learn proofreading marks, see Appendix E: Proofreading Marks.)
- **Use a spellchecker after you have finished proofreading.** Your review process may introduce new errors for you to catch.

Reviewing feedback helps you become a better communicator

Whether you ask for it or not, you often get feedback that indicates how effectively you have communicated. This feedback may take the form of a smile, a puzzled look, a phone call asking for clarification, or compliance with your request. Even lack of response is a type of feedback. One of the key advantages of social media communication is that it allows a company to get continuous feedback on its communication and to adapt its message based on the audience's response. Tweets, Facebook postings, and social networking polls all allow companies to evaluate their communication as well as their business strategy and brands.[28]

To take full advantage of feedback, don't wait for it. Instead, ask for it early in the communication process and use it to evaluate and revise your communication strategy. For example, when you share your summer-hours proposal with your supervisor, she may suggest that you reorganize your content, include additional possible disadvantages, or develop an assessment plan as part of the proposal. This feedback will require you to spend more time analyzing, composing, and evaluating, which may be disappointing if you thought you were done with the writing process. However, the additional work will lead to a more successful proposal.

Also, pay attention to more subtle feedback that you may receive without asking. For example, if you email someone but do not receive a response, what does that mean? Did the audience not receive the message? Or did they choose not to read it because the subject line didn't capture their attention? If you send driving directions to a friend and he gets lost, did he read the directions incorrectly, or were the directions ambiguous? Reviewing the feedback you receive will help you make better decisions the next time you communicate.

How to Write Effective Business Email

Despite the growth of newer forms of communication—such as social media and chat—the number of business emails sent each year continues to grow.* To ensure you produce effective emails, apply the **ACE model**—even for short, informal messages.

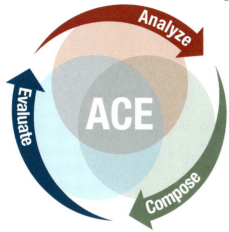

Analyze your purpose, audience, and content before you begin writing.

Compose by organizing the content, creating a first draft, and designing a professional format.

Evaluate by revising, editing, proofreading, and—when possible—incorporating feedback.

This reference guide provides advice about how to write an effective business email start to finish, from entering the recipients on the "To" line to ending with a complimentary closing and signature block.

Recipients

What are the To, Cc, and Bcc lines used for?

- **To:** The "To" line is for the primary audience of your message—the people to whom the email is directed and who will be addressed in the salutation.
- **Cc:** The "Cc" ("courtesy copy") line is for the secondary audience of your message—people who may need to know the information but are not the primary audience. For example, you might Cc your supervisor as an FYI or your assistant to help you follow up.
- **Bcc:** The "Bcc" ("blind courtesy copy") line is used in two circumstances: (1) when you have a long distribution list that you don't want to show and (2) when you need to send the message to someone without the knowledge of the primary (or secondary) audience. In this second situation, you could alternatively forward your sent message with an explanation.

Subject Line

How do you write a good subject line?

- Keep the subject line short, but meaningful.
- If the subject line needs to be longer than five words, begin the subject line with the most important information so the recipients can determine whether they need to read your email now or later. Examples: "Meeting request," "Important: Buy your plane tickets today," and "Response needed: Is any money left in the account?"

Attachments

How should you announce that an attachment is included?

- If the recipient requested the information in the attachment, mention the attachment in the first paragraph.
- If you are including the attachment as supplemental information, mention the attachment in the body or closing of the message.

What guidelines should you use for attachments?

- **Size:** Try to keep attachments to 10 Mb or less. Many email applications impose a size limit on attachments. For larger files, ensure your audience can receive them, or upload your files to an online service like DropBox or Google Drive and include a link in your email.
- **Format:** If the recipient needs to modify the attachment, send it in its original format, such as a Word or Excel file. However, if you don't want the recipient to modify the file, send it as a PDF, which also reduces the file size.
- **Name:** Give your file a name that will be meaningful to the recipient. For example, if you are attaching a résumé, do not name the file *resume.pdf*. Instead, include your name in the file name (e.g., *Richards, Keisha - resume.pdf*).

Salutation

What's the best salutation to use? And how do you punctuate salutations?

- When writing to co-workers you know well, use just their first name or precede it with "Hi" as a friendly gesture. Punctuate this in one of two ways. You can use a comma to separate the greeting from the person's name and add a colon at the end ("Hi, John:"). Alternatively, you can use just a comma at the end ("Hi John,").

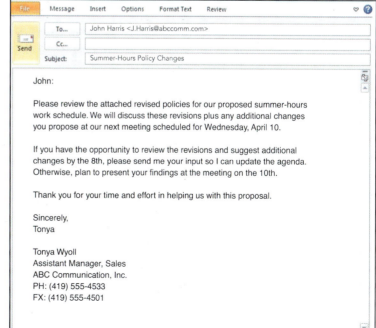

How to Write Effective Business Email (continued)

- When writing to superiors, colleagues you don't know well, or people outside your organization, use good judgment based on how you would address the recipient in person. In formal situations, last names may be appropriate ("Dear Mr. Smith:" or "Hello, Mr. Smith:"). Note that no comma separates "Dear" from the name. End with a colon or comma, depending on the level of formality.

Body of the Message

How long can an email message be?

- **Be concise.** Keep email messages relatively short, preferably without requiring the reader to scroll to read the entire message. Exceptions include email reports, which can be much longer than typical email messages.
- **Use attachments.** If a routine email has to be long, summarize the entire message in a paragraph and attach the lengthy content as a separate document.

How do you format an email for easy reading?

- **Put your main point in the first paragraph.** If you believe your audience needs background information before the main point, begin by stating your purpose before providing background. Example: "I am writing for your advice about how to handle a sensitive situation."
- **Use paragraph headings.** If the message includes several topics, use informative headings that help the audience quickly find the information they need.
- **Use bulleted or numbered lists.** Use bullets or numbers to outline lists of information to help the audience see the elements or understand the sequence of information.

What's the best writing style and tone to use?

- Ensure that all business emails sound professional, no matter who your audience. Remember that your recipient may forward your email to others in the company.
- Choose a level of formality based on how well you know the audience and on the content of the message. A routine message to a colleague confirming tomorrow's meeting location would be less formal than an email to a potential client finalizing a meeting to negotiate a contract.

How much of the prior conversation needs to be included in an email thread?

- **When responding,** maintain the entire thread to help participants track the conversation.
- **When forwarding email to others,** consider how much of the thread is necessary. Before forwarding, read through the thread to eliminate comments that weren't intended for others to see.
- **When changing topics,** change the subject line or start a new thread.

How do you make an email message easy to read on a smart phone?

- Make the main idea easy to find by getting directly to the point in the first paragraph.
- Keep the message short and avoid larger-than-normal fonts.

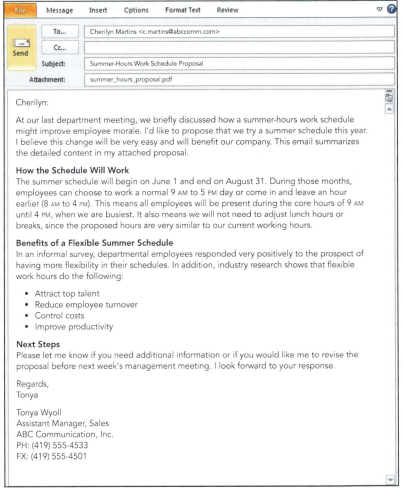

Closing

How should an email message end?

- End the message with a friendly sentence to promote goodwill. Include a call for action and any dates or deadlines, when appropriate.
- Sign off with a complimentary closing and your name. Match the formality of the closing with the salutation. "Thanks" or "Best" are less formal than "Sincerely" or "Best regards." End the complimentary closing with a comma, and place your name on the next line.

Signature Block

What should be included in a signature block? Are signature blocks necessary for all emails?

- At a minimum, include your first and last names, position title, company name, and phone number. If you believe the additional information is useful, also include your mailing address, fax number, and email address. If an email conversation continues with several replies, you do not need to include your signature block throughout the thread.

Endnote

*The Radicati Group, Inc. (2017). Email statistics report 2017–2021. Retrieved from http://www.radicati.com/wp/wp-content/uploads/2017/01/Email-Statistics-Report-2017-2021-Executive-Summary.pdf

CULTURE
TRANSLATION, LOCALIZATION, AND GLOBALIZATION

Imagine that you work for a global organization and are preparing a document that will be read by people of many cultures in many countries and translated into many languages. You may be writing an advertisement, a product brochure, a website, or product documentation.

What should you do to prepare the document for international audiences? If you answer "translate it," you are only one-third correct. In addition to translation, you need to be familiar with two other processes: *localization* and *globalization* (sometimes called *internationalization*).[29]

Localization, which occurs during the composing stage, is the process of adapting text to local languages, cultures, and countries. Of course, this process requires professional translation, but it also involves other types of adaptation:

- Changing the formats of dates, times, and telephone numbers
- Changing the units for currency, temperature, and measurements
- Changing colors and symbols to be meaningful to another culture
- Ensuring that the translation adopts the local voice and regional variations of vocabulary
- Ensuring that text and graphics will not be misinterpreted or seen as insensitive
- Addressing local regulations and laws

Consider the changes that would be required to localize a U.S. automobile manual for the United Kingdom, even though both countries speak English. Engine temperatures would be changed to degrees Celsius, fuel capacity would be changed from gallons of gasoline to litres of petrol, trunk space becomes boot space, the hood becomes the bonnet, and tires become tyres.

Localization for culture is just as important as for language, as not all cultures have the same values or expectations. For example, the California Milk Processor Board found that the familiar "Got Milk?" ads offended Hispanic consumers. Instead of seeing the ads as comical, Hispanics found the idea of a Latina mother running out of milk to be insulting because it implied that she was not taking good care of her family. The Milk Processor Board localized its advertising campaign to be more effective, with the slogan "Family, Love, and Milk."[30]

Globalization (or **internationalization**) comes before localization, in the analyzing phase. It is the process of preparing a document to be localized. Among other things, it involves eliminating unnecessary cultural references that cannot be translated easily as well as designing the document to accommodate languages that use more words than English and languages written in a different direction, such as Arabic and Hebrew. If you do not consider these things in the analyzing phase of ACE, you may not be prepared to localize the text later—and you may make unfortunate mistakes. For example, a U.S. pharmaceutical company did not sufficiently internationalize an advertisement for one of its products. When it translated the ad into Arabic, which is read from left to right, the company only translated the language. It did not swap the positions of "before and after" pictures. In the Arabic version, for people reading left to right, the ad implied that if you were healthy before taking the medicine, then taking it would make you ill.[31]

For a CULTURE exercise, go to Exercise 28 on page 119.

■ # In summary, the ACE process will help you communicate more effectively by ensuring that you analyze, compose, and evaluate in a systematic way. In the following chapters, you have an opportunity to apply this process to a range of business communication, from short routine messages through complex reports and presentations. Short email messages may take only a few minutes to analyze, compose, and evaluate; more complex messages will require more time. However, as you become an experienced communicator, you will increasingly be able to go through each step of the process more quickly and effectively, regardless of the length or purpose of your communication. If you follow the process well, your messages will more likely achieve your purpose, attain your desired outcome, build goodwill with your audience, and project your polished professional presence.

localization The process of adapting text to local languages, cultures, and countries.

globalization (or **internationalization**) The process of preparing a document to be localized.

MedImmune

Courtesy of MedImmune

Throughout this chapter, we have focused on how the ACE process can help an *individual* communicate more effectively. But many organizations adopt a similar process—on a larger scale—for writing important organizational documents.

MedImmune is the biologics division of AstraZeneca, a global pharmaceutical company in Maryland that researches and develops biological-based drugs to address a range of diseases, including cancer, respiratory diseases, and cardiovascular diseases. To obtain approval to test and market these drugs in the United States, MedImmune must submit a series of documents to the Food and Drug Administration (FDA), including:

- Investigational New Drug (IND) applications, which allow the company to ship the products across state lines for clinical trials
- Briefing documents for meetings with global regulatory agencies
- Biologic License Applications (BLAs), which are submitted to obtain licenses to market biological-based drugs

These submissions can be hundreds, even thousands, of pages long. How does MedImmune organize the process of writing and reviewing the documents—a process that involves large teams of scientists, writers, and regulatory affairs professionals?

According to Orit Scharf, MedImmune's director of Research and Development Science Submission Management, the process for writing one of these documents incorporates all the ACE elements:

- **Analyzing.** The process begins with a kickoff meeting to help all contributors begin with the same set of assumptions. For more detailed and complicated documents, like BLAs, the teams also hold initial strategy meetings to ensure that everyone is in agreement on key elements: what the key message of the document will be, what information to include, in what sections to place that information, how MedImmune will explain its statistical approach, etc. If the team were to skip this step, differences would surface at the end of the writing process, when it is too late to address them.

- **Composing.** Following the kickoff, authors have several weeks to draft their material. The more complex the document, the longer it may take. Writers in the science submission group work with subject matter experts in the various functions to collect and compile clear and complete content, and they work to ensure that the document has a single voice.

- **Evaluating.** The document undergoes a rigorous review and revision process. Designated reviewers read the document and provide review comments that authors and the submission team must address. Frequently, the stakeholders will hold comment resolution meetings and do live editing together. This process of evaluating and revising may go on for several iterations before the document is submitted.

To make this process more efficient, MedImmune routinely analyzes what it learns through writing, reviewing, and submitting an application—and uses this information to develop "guides" that serve as a starting point for future documents. As Scharf explains, developing the Clinical Trial Application guide began by analyzing a successful IND. Then the writers stripped out of the Word file any information specific to that product; retained any text that should be included in all applications and any text that could serve as useful examples to writers; and added guidance from the FDA about what needs to be included in each section. Using this guide as a template for writing INDs saves the writers a lot of time and worry about what to include.

Scharf explains that although the first draft of the guide was useful, it did not remain static. Over time, it developed and improved: "Every time we get comments from our reviewers or requests from the regulators that will apply to future projects—for example, a request from the FDA to add a new test—we not only make the change in our current document but also add it to our guide so that when the next team comes along, that new content is already in there." In addition, she says, the organization periodically evaluates the guides to determine whether they need to be revised for clarity or for content and, if so, she says, "we work with stakeholders to make sure we have buy-in."

With so many people involved in writing documents that are critical to MedImmune's business success, the company needs a writing process that is efficient and effective. MedImmune's application of the ACE process serves that purpose and contributes to their success.

Source: Based on an interview with Orit Scharf.

Using ACE to Improve Communication Results

This case scenario will help you review the chapter material by applying it to a specific situation.

Suppose your employer asks you to inform everyone in the Customer Relations department about an upcoming workshop on communication skills. You quickly create the following flyer and post copies on the break room bulletin board and in the cafeteria.

Communication Skills

Workshop

Wednesday, November 2 @ 2:30 PM

Training Room A

Although your department includes 60 people, when you arrive for the workshop, only 4 people are there. What went wrong? How could using ACE help improve the communication results?

What Is the Desired Outcome?

Your supervisor may have simply instructed you to tell the employees about the workshop, but what is the desired outcome? Your supervisor wants most of the department's 60 employees to attend. Simply telling employees that the workshop exists will not achieve that outcome. You need to persuade them.

What Content Does the Audience Need?

What will the audience need to hear to persuade them to attend? To answer this question, you need to analyze the audience and anticipate their questions and objections.

The 60 employees from the Customer Relations department are usually busy. They also may believe they are already good communicators—after all, they are in Customer Relations. They will attend a workshop only if they are required to do so, if they believe they will benefit, or if they believe they will enjoy the workshop. Here are some questions that will be on their minds when they hear about the workshop and some possible objections they may have to attending.

Possible Questions:

- Is this workshop required?
- Is the presenter good?
- How long will the workshop last?
- Will it be worthwhile?

- How will I benefit from attending?
- Will my manager be upset if I don't attend?

Possible Objections:

- I have too much work to do.
- I studied communication in school.
- Somebody needs to answer the phones.
- I'm not interested.
- A workshop won't help me get promoted.

Question 1: What other questions and objections can you anticipate? If you revised the message, which questions and objections would you want to address? Are there any you would choose not to address? If so, why?

Which Medium Is Best?

You realize now that posting a flyer was not the most effective way to communicate about the workshop because some people simply walk past flyers without reading them. Perhaps other options would be better.

Question 2: What are the advantages and disadvantages of the following other options: making an announcement on the company's internal website, sending a memo to each employee, sending an email to each employee, and calling each employee?

How Can I Structure My Content?

Assume that you decide to send an email and now have the challenge of structuring the content. The next page shows a draft.

Question 3: Review how the ACE process led to the improved message on page 108 by answering the questions that follow.

Analyzing

1. What information in the revised version addresses the need for persuasion?
2. How does the email message emphasize reader benefits?
3. What content appears in the email that was not included in the original flyer? Why is that content useful?

Composing

4. Is the information in the email organized effectively? Explain.
5. What determines which information goes in which paragraph?
6. How would you decide whether to organize the content directly or indirectly?

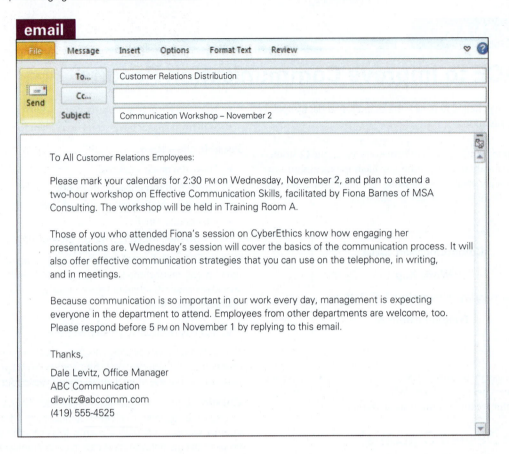

To: Customer Relations Distribution
Cc:
Subject: Communication Workshop – November 2

To All Customer Relations Employees:

Please mark your calendars for 2:30 PM on Wednesday, November 2, and plan to attend a two-hour workshop on Effective Communication Skills, facilitated by Fiona Barnes of MSA Consulting. The workshop will be held in Training Room A.

Those of you who attended Fiona's session on CyberEthics know how engaging her presentations are. Wednesday's session will cover the basics of the communication process. It will also offer effective communication strategies that you can use on the telephone, in writing, and in meetings.

Because communication is so important in our work every day, management is expecting everyone in the department to attend. Employees from other departments are welcome, too. Please respond before 5 PM on November 1 by replying to this email.

Thanks,

Dale Levitz, Office Manager
ABC Communication
dlevitz@abccomm.com
(419) 555-4525

Evaluating

7. In evaluating content, are there additional persuasive points you could add?

8. Does this email message use clear and concise wording as well as professional tone and style?

9. Which elements promote a conversational style?

10. When proofreading this email, which content elements would you proofread for accuracy?

11. Is the message designed well? Explain.

12. Would you keep the current subject line, or would you revise it? Explain.

Study Questions in Review

 ## What are the benefits of analyzing?
(pages 81–87)

Analyzing puts you in a position to compose a message that achieves your goals.

- **Analyzing the purpose focuses the message.** Develop an outcome-oriented purpose statement, consider how you will maintain goodwill, and determine whether your message will need to be persuasive.
- **Analyzing the audience helps you meet their needs.** Think about what the audience needs to know, how they will benefit from your message, and what objections they may raise. Consider both the primary audience and possible secondary audiences.
- **Analyzing the content ensures a complete message.** It helps you determine whether you have enough information or need to conduct additional primary or secondary research.
- **Analyzing the medium helps you choose the best delivery option** —such as an email, a memo, or social media—to ensure that your message reaches your audience effectively.

 ## What is involved in composing?
(pages 87–96)

Composing is an interactive process that involves the following steps:

- **Deciding when and where to compose** begins by considering how to manage your time, choose the best composing environment, and minimize distractions.
- **Organizing the message** requires that you determine the overall structure of the communication. Long documents may benefit from using a multilevel outline. To organize short documents, you can use a more informal outline. When organizing, also decide where to state the main point. Messages can be organized either directly (main idea first) or indirectly (supporting details before main idea).
- **Drafting the content** is a creative process. Save revising (a logical process) until later. Use strategies such as free writing and thinking aloud to avoid writer's block.
- **Designing a professional format and delivery** requires that you consider specific formatting techniques for emails, memos (for internal audiences), letters (for external audiences), voice mail messages, and social media postings. When appropriate, use topic-specific headings to signal the structure and meaning of the document. Design emails so that they will be easy to read on the small screen of a mobile device.

How does evaluating improve your communication? *(pages 96–105)*

When you evaluate, you assess whether your communication will be effective and then make changes to improve it.

- **Evaluating content helps you achieve your purpose and outcome.** Check to ensure that your main point is clear, you have included all the information you need, the organization will make sense to the audience, and the message is persuasive enough to be successful.
- **Evaluating for style improves comprehension.** Style refers to how you express your ideas. Audiences more quickly and easily understand language that is clear, concise, cohesive, and coherent. To achieve clarity, use natural, conversational language. Eliminate abstract wording, slang and clichés, unnecessary passive voice, and nominalizations. Use strong verbs and place them early in the sentence. To achieve conciseness, eliminate wordy phrases, fillers, and redundancies. To achieve cohesion, connect sentences with transitions, and begin sentences with familiar information. Finally, to achieve coherence, include purpose statements and main points in the beginning of a document and ensure that all paragraph topic sentences point back to that purpose or main point.
- **Evaluating for tone helps you project a professional image.** Use positive wording. Do not be overly casual but keep a conversational style. Match your tone to your purpose, and if you use humor, use it appropriately.
- **Evaluating for correctness increases your credibility.** To improve your proofreading skills, familiarize yourself with the five different kinds of errors: content, spelling and typographical, usage, grammatical, and format. Systematically check for these errors, and take advantage of technology tools.
- **Reviewing feedback helps you become a better communicator** because it helps you identify places to improve your communication.

Visual Summary

Managing the Communication Process

The ACE process will improve your communication whether you are texting your assistant with an urgent request, emailing your boss with a status update on a project, or presenting a report to an important client. Take the time to effectively analyze, compose, and evaluate every message.

ANALYZE

- What is the purpose of the message?
- What do I want the outcome to be?
- Who is the audience?
- What does the audience need to know?
- What content should I include?
- Do I need more information?
- If so, where do I get it?
- What medium is best for this audience and content?

COMPOSE

- What's the best way to organize the content?
- Should I be direct? Or indirect?
- Are headings needed?
- If so, how can I make them topic specific
- How should the message be formatted?

EVALUATE

- Is the message complete, concise, clear, and correct?
- Does it address the audience's questions and concerns?
- Is the style readable? Is the message easy to skim?
- Is the tone appropriate?
- Does the message look professional?
- Are all errors corrected?

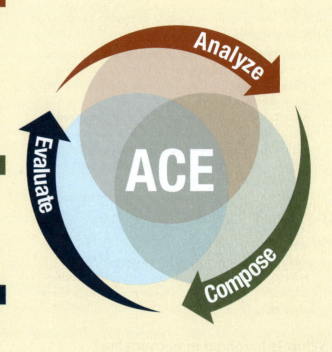

FIRST DRAFT

| File | Message | Insert | Options | Format Text | Review |

To... budget-comm@abccomm.com
Cc...
Subject: Meeting

To all: We need to reschedule our meeting for next week. Sorry for the inconvenience.

thnx, dale

The first draft was written with only the sender in mind.

The revised draft considers the audience's needs and uses ACE to achieve a more effective message by...

Including a specific subject line

Clearly stating the message

Providing details

Requesting a specific response

Closing the message professionally

Providing contact information

REVISED DRAFT

| File | Message | Insert | Options | Format Text | Review |

To... budget-comm@abccomm.com
Cc...
Subject: Reschedule Meeting to Sept. 13?

To All Budget Committee Members:

We need to reschedule our budget meeting. Are you available on Thursday, September 13, at 2 PM?

Jim's team is backlogged and won't have the projections we need until Wednesday.

Please reply or call me before you leave today so I can finalize things. I'll email you tomorrow morning to confirm.

Thank you,
Dale

Dale Levitz, Office Manager
ABC Communication
dlevitz@abccomm.com
(419) 555-4525

Key Terms

Abstract language p. 98	Content p. 84	Letters p. 94	Purpose p. 81
Active voice p. 99	Direct organization p. 88	Localization p. 105	Push communication p. 86
Analyzing p. 81	Drafting p. 91	Medium p. 84	Redundancy p. 101
Advance organizer p. 88	Evaluating p. 96	Memos p. 93	Revising p. 91
Audience p. 81	External audiences p. 94	Nominalization p. 99	Secondary audience p. 83
Audience benefits p. 83	Globalization (or	Outcome p. 81	Secondary research p. 84
Bullet point lists p. 93	internationalization) p. 105	Outline p. 88	Slang p. 99
Clarity p. 98	Goodwill p. 81	Parallel phrasing p. 100	Style p. 98
Clichés p. 99	Indirect organization p. 88	Passive voice p. 99	Subject line p. 88
Composing p. 87	Interactive communication	Persuasion p. 81	Tone p. 102
Conciseness p. 100	p. 86	Primary audience p. 83	Topic sentence p. 92
Coherence p. 101	Internal audiences p. 93	Primary research p. 84	Topic-specific headings p. 93
Cohesion p. 101	Internationalization (or	Proofread p. 103	Transition p. 101
Concrete language p. 98	globalization) p. 105	Pull communication p. 86	Writer's block p. 91

MyLab Business Communication

If your instructor is using MyLab Business Communication, go to **www.pearson.com/mylab/business-communication** to complete the problems marked with this icon ⭐.

Review Questions

⭐ 1 Why is analyzing your purpose important to composing an effective message?

⭐ 2 Explain the difference between the primary audience and the secondary audience.

⭐ 3 What is the difference between primary research and secondary research? Describe a business communication situation in which you would want to use both types of research to support a message.

⭐ 4 Why is it important to consider your audience when analyzing your medium options?

⭐ 5 Why is direct organization usually the better choice for business communication?

6 Explain the difference between the following elements of style: clarity, concision, cohesion, and coherence.

7 Compose a sentence that uses passive voice. Revise the sentence to use active voice.

8 How do the following types of errors differ: content errors, spelling errors, typographical errors, usage errors, grammatical errors, and format errors?

9 Explain how reviewing feedback helps you improve your communication strategy.

10 Why should you leave some time between the composing and evaluating stages?

Critical Thinking Questions

1 Think about the last paper, report, or business email you wrote. What percentage of your writing time did you spend on each element of the ACE process (analyzing, composing, and evaluating)? Will you change your approach in the future? Explain why or why not.

⭐ 2 Analyzing your audience helps you compose effective messages. However, sometimes you may need to communicate with people you do not know. What methods can you suggest to learn about and analyze an unfamiliar audience?

3 Assume that you work for a company that designs and manufactures uniforms and protective equipment. Your company would like to expand its offerings and is considering manufacturing firefighter uniforms. As part of the research necessary to make this decision, your supervisor asked you to gather information about the market for these uniforms. How big is it? Is it growing or shrinking? In your research, you found this

statement on the Education-Portal.com website: "According to the Bureau of Labor Statistics, www.bls.gov, the occupation of firefighter is projected to grow faster than the average for all occupations." However, you also found several newspaper sources on the web that cite shrinking budgets and personnel cutbacks in fire departments. How would you present this conflicting information in your report? Would you need to do any additional research on the topic before composing? If so, what questions would you research? [**Related to the Ethics feature on page 86**]

4 Assume that you work at a bookstore near campus and would like to propose to your supervisor that the bookstore stay open two hours later each evening during the week. You need to choose whether to write your proposal in an email or to request a face-to-face meeting. Your supervisor has no preference about how you communicate. Which medium would you choose, and why?

5 Refer to question 4 and assume that when you either write or speak to your supervisor proposing expanded evening hours, you decide to organize your message indirectly, building up to the main point. Because you are using an indirect organization, what content can you include in the introduction of the email or opening of the conversation that will help your audience follow your logic and understand where you are going? Provide an example.

6 Assume that you work for a supervisor who generally prefers to receive email messages rather than have face-to-face meetings. Identify at least two circumstances in which you believe it would be better to request a meeting to discuss an issue rather than send an email. Explain your rationale.

7 Assume that you work in an academic department at your school as a work study student, and your department chairperson wants to enhance communication with all students through social media. Currently email blasts are sent to all students to inform them of department events and deadlines. However, the chairperson knows that students don't read their email as often as they check social media. Consider which social media options would be most effective in sharing department information with students. Explain your rationale.

8 Retrieve a recent email message that you wrote to someone other than a family member or friend. Do you believe that the email portrays a professional image? If so, what elements of the email create that image? If not, what elements undermine that image?

9 Retrieve and read three email messages (or a class paper) you recently wrote and begin to create your personal list of common errors. To help you identify them, ask a colleague to help you assess your messages or seek assistance from your school's writing center. What kinds of errors do you frequently make? How can you ensure that you do not continue to make these errors in the future?

10 Much of the advice about evaluating in this chapter refers to written communication. What are some ways that you can evaluate your oral communication—for example, when you speak at a meeting or interview, leave a voice message, or give an oral presentation? Consider things that you can do before delivering the oral message, things that you can do while you are delivering the message, and things you can do afterward that will help you improve your communication in the future.

Key Concept Exercises

SQ1 **What are the benefits of analyzing?** *(pages 81–87)*

1 Analyzing the purpose focuses the message

For each of the following business communication situations, (1) identify a desired outcome, (2) identify whether achieving that outcome will require persuasion, and (3) explain your reasoning. For situations that require persuasion, list at least two audience benefits that would make your message more persuasive.

a. Informing department employees of a new form to use when requesting expense reimbursement

b. Convincing your supervisor to create a new staff position in your department

c. Informing a subordinate of his frequent tardiness and poor performance and encouraging improvement

d. Documenting a subordinate's tardiness and poor performance and recommending the employee's termination in a memo report to your supervisor

e. Informing department employees of a mandatory change in vacation policy: If vacation days are not used by the end of the year, they will be lost

2 Analyzing the audience helps you meet their needs

Currently your company does not provide company cell phones for members of the sales force who travel as part of their regular job responsibilities. Instead, salespeople are required to submit monthly reimbursement requests for business-related calls made on personal cell phones. This process is time-consuming for salespeople. You would like to propose that the sales department purchase cell phones for all salespeople to use for business calls only and then simply pay the monthly bill. What questions and objections do you think the department head will have about this proposal? How will you address the objections?

3 Analyzing the content ensures a complete message

Your supervisor asks you to give a brief presentation at your company's annual sales meeting that analyzes sales trends for each of the company's three regions over four years. You collect the data about gross sales and then create the following exhibit.

As you look at the graph, you realize it will raise questions during the presentation and that you should prepare answers. What questions and observations about sales do you think your graph will raise? What additional research would you do to answer those questions?

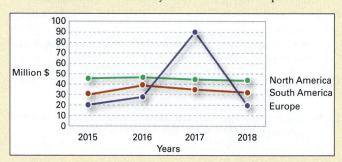

Accompanies Exercise 3

4 Analyzing the medium helps you choose the best delivery option

For each of the following scenarios, identify which medium would be the best choice to communicate your message. Select your choice from the list of medium options in Figure 3.7 on page 85 or other options you deem appropriate. Explain your reasoning.

a. Your employer leaves a voice mail message for you, asking you to work overtime this weekend, but you plan to attend your cousin's out-of-town wedding. What medium would you use to explain why you can't work overtime?

b. You are developing a new procedure manual for the sales associates in your department and need input on several issues from your department manager and training staff. What medium would you use to gather the input you need?

c. Your supervisor approves your request to schedule a one-hour yoga class each Wednesday after work. This class is ongoing. How do you (1) inform all the employees of this new program and (2) keep publicizing the program throughout the year?

d. You ordered 14 boxes of 8½″ × 11″ copy paper from a local office supply store, but you received 11 boxes of 8½″ × 14″ legal paper. After you talk with Paul, an associate manager of the store, he personally delivers the 14 boxes of standard copy paper to your office, carries the boxes into your supply room, and retrieves the boxes of legal paper—all within an hour of your initial contact. You are so impressed with Paul's personal attention and quick service that you want to inform his supervisor. How do you contact Paul's supervisor to recognize his efforts?

e. The weekly Wednesday yoga classes have been so popular that your supervisor suggests expanding the program to include weekly healthy living tips, fitness information, and healthy recipe ideas. How do you deliver this information to your employees each week? Explain how your choice of medium would change if the size of your audience changed: 50 employees, 500 employees, and 5,000 employees.

(SQ2) What is involved in composing? *(pages 87–96)*

5 Deciding when and where to compose

Assume that you are interning part-time for a marketing company this semester while taking classes. Your supervisor's project team is working on an ad campaign for a new client that produces big and tall men's apparel. In preparation for the team's initial brainstorming session next week, you've been asked to gather preliminary information about the client's leading competitors. You've researched the three companies that currently dominate the market and have gathered sample TV ads, website screen shots, and print media sources. You need to create a five-page report that summarizes your research. The report is due in seven days. How much time do you estimate you will need to compose and evaluate this report? How would you spread that work over the seven days?

6 Organizing the message—using outlines

Select a current writing project from one of your other courses. Following the guidelines illustrated in Figures 3.8 and 3.10 (see page 89), prepare both a traditional outline and a tree chart outline. Submit them to your instructor, along with answers to the following questions:

a. Which outline are you more satisfied with, and why?

b. Which method(s) have you used before? Explain the writing project, how the outline method helped, and whether a different format would have been better.

c. Which method do you prefer, in general, and why?

d. After completing this exercise, will you be more likely to use outlines for future writing projects? Explain why or why not.

7 Organizing the message—direct versus indirect

Compare the email messages below, and answer the questions about them on page 114. Email A is organized directly, and Email B is organized indirectly. Note that the only difference between these two messages is the placement of the main idea: "My analysis determined that Adaptive Solutions' website is more effective based on its ease of use, comprehensive content, and general appearance."

EMAIL A - DIRECT

To... s.mcewen@fieldspatterson.com
Cc...
Subject: Competitors' Website Comparison

Susan:

As you requested, I compared the websites of our two main competitors: Creative Communications (CC) and Adaptive Solutions (AS). My analysis determined that Adaptive Solutions' website is more effective based on its ease of use, comprehensive content, and general appearance.

The AS website uses a consistent navigation format throughout. By contrast, the CC menus differ on several pages, which make finding specific information very difficult. Additionally, the AS website describes workshop topics, provides sample PowerPoint demonstrations, and links their handout examples. The CC site lists their workshop topics with a brief description of each, but does not provide additional materials. Finally, the overall appearance of the AS website is more professional. The content is well organized and the text is easy to read. I found it difficult to find information at the CC site and had a hard time reading the 10-point text.

Let me know if you need a more detailed analysis of these two sites. I look forward to working on our own company's web design team.

Best,
Nichole

Nichole Perkins, Consultant
The Fields-Patterson Group
2376 Madison Avenue
Atlanta, GA 30345
www.fieldspatterson.com
PH: 404-555-2646
FX: 404-555-2601

EMAIL B - INDIRECT

To... s.mcewen@fieldspatterson.com
Cc...
Subject: Competitors' Website Comparison

Susan:

As you requested, I compared the websites of our two main competitors: Creative Communications (CC) and Adaptive Solutions (AS).

The AS website uses a consistent navigation format throughout its site. The CC menus differ on several pages, which make finding specific information very difficult. Additionally, the AS website describes workshop topics, provides sample PowerPoint demonstrations, and links their handout examples. The CC site lists their workshop topics with a brief description of each, but does not provide additional materials. Finally, the overall appearance of the AS website is more professional. The content is well organized and the text is easy to read. I found it difficult to find information at the CC site and had a hard time reading the 10-point text.

My analysis determined that AdaptiveSolutions' website is more effective based on its ease of use, comprehensive content, and general appearance. Let me know if you need a more detailed analysis of these two sites. I look forward to working on our own company's web design team.

Best,
Nichole

Nichole Perkins, Consultant
The Fields-Patterson Group
2376 Madison Avenue
Atlanta, GA 30345
www.fieldspatterson.com
PH: 404-555-2646
FX: 404-555-2601

Accompanies Exercise 7

CHAPTER 3

CHAPTER 3

a. Under what circumstances would Nichole choose to write a direct message to Susan? Explain at least two circumstances.

b. Under what circumstances would Nichole write this same message indirectly? Explain at least two circumstances.

c. Would you choose to be direct or indirect? Explain why.

d. How would you revise this message (regardless of whether it was direct or indirect) to emphasize audience benefits?

8 Drafting the content

Select a topic you're researching for a class or group project—or a topic assigned by your instructor. Use free writing to fill at least a half page (typed and single-spaced). Print the page and review your free writing. Then, in a separate paragraph, identify how you might use this free-written material in your project.

9 Designing a professional format and delivery

Use the formatting techniques outlined in the chapter to improve the draft letter from Kirchen Art Museum below. Determine the best place for paragraph breaks. Add headings if you believe they are useful. Break up paragraphs into bullet points if you find lists.

---

letter

KIRCHEN ART MUSEUM
2815 CLAIRMONT AVE.
BIRMINGHAM, ALABAMA 35222

Dear Past Member:

Think spring. Think Impressionists. Our blockbuster exhibition—*The Influence of Impressionism*—promises to be the finest exhibition on Impressionism ever assembled by any museum in the past 40 years. So why not get ahead of the crowds? We want to make sure you have exclusive access to this extraordinary show opening in March. In fact, for immediate access to *The Influence of Impressionism* bring the enclosed reply to the museum on March 18 or 19 to join and attend the Member Previews before the exhibition opens to the public. As a member, you'll also receive a members-only behind-the-scenes experience by attending one of our exhibition lectures given by the curator and private viewings of the exhibition the first hour of every day—and every Thursday evening for members only. *The Influence of Impressionism* will surely be the highlight of our year—and yours. This landmark exhibition will showcase nearly 250 pivotal paintings, sculptures, drawings, and prints. The exhibit will include some of the most famous works of artists like Matisse, Monet, and Degas. Remember, membership benefits extend beyond special exhibitions. There are more than 260,000 works of art in our collection for you to enjoy. Be part of it all and experience the benefits of membership. These include free admission every day to the entire museum, dining in our world class roof top restaurant, member discounts at all of our fabulous museum stores, and access to our Members Lounge. Renew your membership today, and mark your calendar for your exclusive member-only hours to visit *The Influence of Impressionism*.

Sincerely,

Kara Waltman

Kara Waltman
Director of Annual Giving

Accompanies Exercise 9

SQ3 **How does evaluating improve your communication?** *(pages 96–105)*

10 Evaluating content helps you achieve your purpose and outcome

Refer to the Kirchen Art Museum letter in Exercise 9 and evaluate it for content, writing answers to the following questions.

a. Are the purpose and main point clear? Underline the statement of purpose.

b. Does it provide the information needed to support the purpose? What information does it include? Is anything missing?

c. How is it organized? Does the organization make sense to the audience? What would make the organization clearer?

d. Is the message persuasive enough to be successful? Does it stress audience benefits? Does it answer key objections the audience may have?

11 Evaluating for style improves readability and comprehension—eliminating slang and clichés

Edit the following sentences by removing the slang and clichés (in italics) to clarify the meaning. If you are unfamiliar with a cliché, look it up online before editing.

a. Everyone in the department knows that the *buck stops here.*

b. His manager thinks she needs to *dangle a carrot* in front of him to get anything done.

c. Personally, I think this proposal will go *gangbusters* with upper management.

d. She has really been *a good soldier* about the change in leadership.

e. The union representative said we need to *sweeten the pot* if we want to end the labor strike.

f. He will be *swimming with the sharks* if he tries to present that proposal to the management team.

g. If this stock offer is not accepted, we may *take a bath.*

h. To be successful in business, you really need to *think outside the box.*

12 Evaluating for style improves readability and comprehension—active voice

Edit the following sentences to change passive voice to active voice. (Note: In some sentences, you will need to supply subjects for the active verbs.)

a. The proposal was written by the marketing team based on in-depth research.

b. The decision was made to extend overtime allowances by 10 percent.

c. Because two proposals were submitted, a meeting was scheduled to discuss the differences.

d. The survey instrument was created to gather information about the employees' perspectives.

e. The report will be delivered tomorrow so a decision can be made before the end of the week.

f. The problem can be solved only after the data have been analyzed.

g. His marketing plan was presented with very convincing supporting documentation.

h. Positive feedback about the presentation was received from the clients.

i. The salary increase will be seen in your next pay check.

j. The retirement party for Ira will be held at the College Club next week.

13 Evaluating for style improves readability and comprehension—strengthening verbs

Edit the following sentences to eliminate nominalizations and put active verbs toward the beginning of the sentence. (Hint: Focus on who is doing what to whom.)

a. Determination of employee skill level will occur during orientation.

b. The elimination of all personal debt, resulting from student loans, credit cards, and automobile loans, is my goal this year.

c. Attempts were made on the part of the information technology staff in regard to discovery of the source of the data breach.

d. The appearance of the defendant in court was on August 8.

e. There are expectations by management that the report submission will meet the deadline.

f. An accurate assessment of our budget deficit was made by independent auditors.

g. An appeal by the president of the company for conservation of electricity in an attempt to reduce costs was made.

h. The status of our loan application can be checked through a login on the bank's web site using the application number and password.

14 Evaluating for style improves readability and comprehension—conciseness

Edit the following sentences to make them more concise.

a. The emergence of the Information Age and its corresponding technology has forever modified our societal norms and the methodologies of conducting business in today's world of corporate America.

b. Computer technology and its associated software applications in conjunction with the widespread usage of the World Wide Web have had the most profound and visible effects of any invention in modern history.

c. Technologies have dramatically impacted and modified our complex communication systems, exchanges of information, and our commercial endeavors.

d. As technology permeates nearly every facet of business entities, the question is whether today's college students receive adequate information and assistance as they prepare for the high-tech world of business.

e. A multitude of employers are now testing prospective employees prior to employment to determine if their information technology knowledge and skill levels will meet or exceed their technology expectations in terms of meeting their workplace needs.

f. For people in the workforce who lack the absolutely essential knowledge and skills to succeed in today's highly competitive world of work, many institutions of higher learning are now beginning to offer distance-learning courses at an astronomical rate.

g. Of the thousands of public universities that offer distance learning and online educational courses at the collegiate level, many are of the opinion that they are meeting the needs of tomorrow's workforce when in fact they are providing good content, but not the interpersonal skills students need to be successful in workplace situations.

h. At the same time that the greater society in general and the world of academia in particular race to stay abreast of the wealth of new technologies and the newest software and hardware available, they appear to be unable to stem the tide of the growing and dangerously pervasive problem of unethical computer use that permeates society.

i. It is incredible to believe that for some people the ethical problems of piracy, identity theft, and computer fraud were unexpected surprises.

j. Our morals and values can become subjective considering that what one believes is morally incorrect may not be conceived as such by someone else.

15 Evaluating for style improves comprehension and readability—cohesion

In the pairs of sentences below, edit the beginning of the second sentence to begin either with an effective transition phrase or with ideas already introduced.

a. I have no experience communicating in a business environment. I do have some background in communicating in an organizational setting as a result of my experience in student government.

b. With increasing competition and decreasing margins, airlines are becoming more innovative. Southwest Airlines recently created a family section on its airplanes.

c. The financial services sector evolved to offer limited microfinance products, but a gap remained—no access to credit. A regulated micro-lending sector emerged to fill the gap.

d. In Brazil's sugar industry, roughly one-third of sugarcane stalk is transformed into sugar or ethanol, one-third is burned to run refining mills, and the final one-third is left in the field. The development of an enzyme that can break down organic material more effectively can lead to higher utilization of the sugarcane stalk, thereby decreasing the unused portion of the plant.

16 Evaluating for style improves comprehension and readability—coherence

Add a topic sentence to the beginning of this paragraph, expressing an idea that unifies the paragraph.

> Uptown is an excellent location for our new store, especially if we want to take advantage of property tax incentives. On the other hand, if we want to be close to our largest group of customers, Easttown is an ideal location because of the growing population of millennials. Or, if we want a location where no competition currently exists, then Westtown is a good choice.

17 Evaluating for tone helps you project a professional image—positive wording

Edit the following negatively worded sentences to sound more positive.

a. He will not do well on the employment exam if he does not review the company's procedures.

b. The committee will not make their decision until next week.

c. The workers will receive no bonus if they do not submit their performance evaluations on time.

d. If you do not present your corporate ID card at the new cafeteria, you will not receive the 10 percent discount.

e. The project is not yet complete.

f. The reception will not be scheduled if the clients do not sign the contract.

g. I cannot attend the meeting if this report is not finished on time.

h. Because the construction plans were not delivered, we could not determine a timeline for completion.

i. Please do not schedule meetings on Fridays because the sales associates can't attend.

j. You do not have access to those documents because you neglected to complete the registration form.

18 Evaluating for tone helps you project a professional image—conversational tone

Edit the following sentences to make the tone more conversational.

a. We do not concur that an equally advantageous investment opportunity will manifest itself again in the future.

b. Scheduling of the meeting is contingent upon affirmative responses from all constituents.

c. Kindly refrain from all interruptions for the duration of the presentation.

d. Our clients' allegiance rests upon our satisfactory achievement of performance criteria.

e. Utilize the most recently approved form to make your request to receive reimbursement for your travel expenses.

f. Apprise the departmental workers under your supervision that their efforts have been recognized and duly noted with appreciation.

g. We are satisfied with our pre-identified levels for end-of-year sales requirements.

h. I am curious as to your thought processes concerning the amendments to the proposal.

i. My opinion is that his work is not of the caliber to warrant promotion to division manager.

j. I would appreciate your perspectives on this issue in support of my decision-making process.

19 Evaluating for tone helps you project a professional image—sounding conversational

Identify a paragraph that you find complicated and difficult to read from any of these sources: a paper you have written for class, a document you have written for work, an email you recently received, a textbook, a flyer, a magazine, or a brochure. If you do not already have an electronic copy of the paragraph, key it into your word processing software.

Then make a copy of the paragraph and rewrite it in a conversational style using simple words in short sentences. In a three- to five-minute presentation to the class, display both the original and revised versions and describe how you revised the paragraph to be more readable. Identify which version you believe is most effective and explain why.

20 Evaluating for correctness increases your credibility — proofreading systematically to check for errors

Type the following paragraph in a word processing software application of your choice. Enter the words and punctuation exactly as shown. Proofread the paragraph and highlight any errors that you see. Then run the application's spelling and grammar tools. Make a list of any (a) spelling errors that the spelling checker did *not* find and (b) changes the grammar checker suggested that would create an error. Do the results of this exercise change the methods you will use for proofreading in the future? Summarize your findings in an email message or memo to your instructor.

> Do to recent security events, are technology upgrades our scheduled to be implemented at the beginning of next months. This change requires you to ask yourself what applications you current use and predicted those you may knee during the next fiscal year. How will you now what you what you might need in the future? That is a difficult question to answers. However, you're in put is necessary to assure that hour resources our used correct. Thank in advance for you're effort too improve this process.

Accompanies Exercise 20

21 Reviewing feedback helps you become a better communicator

Assume that you are a manager at a bank in Chicago and want to market new savings products to a growing Hispanic population. You are looking forward to Carlos Sanchez joining your marketing team because he has experience working with this population. At the first team meeting, you make several enthusiastic suggestions about ways to market these products, and you expect Carlos and other teammates to debate with you, point out weaknesses in your ideas, and make alternative suggestions. However, Carlos remains quiet. He simply nods and says, "That sounds like a good idea." You can't understand why he has so little to offer. After the meeting, you mention your concern to another colleague who suggests that Carlos is reluctant to disagree with you. Since Carlos grew up in a Latin American culture, he may see himself as below you in the hierarchy of the team and feel that contradicting you may be disrespectful.

You want to use this feedback to help revise your communication strategy for the next meeting so that Carlos feels more comfortable contributing. Use your favorite web search engine to research sources that provide information about working effectively with people from Latin American cultures. Identify some different ways you might begin the meeting so that Carlos can offer his perspective and suggestions without worrying about disrespecting you. Summarize your findings in an email message to your instructor.

Writing Exercises

22 Using ACE to inform

Select a recent technical issue you have encountered. Examples include almost any hardware, software, or networking problem: a malfunctioning piece of office equipment, such as a projector, copier, or printer; a recurring computer operating system error message; a web application that produces unexpected or misleading results, etc. Write a short report documenting the issue that can be submitted via email. Assume that your report will be read by the support staff who will attempt to replicate the problem you describe as well as try to solve it. Use the ACE process (see the Visual Summary on page 110) to ensure that the report is effectively organized and contains sufficient detail.

After completely evaluating your final draft, print your message and submit it to your instructor. On a separate sheet, also submit a paragraph explaining how you implemented the ACE process and how it helped you prepare this communication.

23 Using ACE to inform and persuade

Assume that your student group has successfully organized a business-dress fashion show, which will be presented on February 3 at 7 PM. The show will feature 12 business-ready outfits, which are available at a local store. In addition, a representative from the store will be available to explain the appropriate fit of clothing, such as the right length of a tie and the position of a cuff for men, and the height of a heel, length of a skirt, and appropriate jewelry for women You now need to compose an email that will invite business majors to attend the show, free of charge. Use the list of ACE questions in the Visual Summary on page 110 to work through the ACE communication process and determine the information you will include in the email to interest your audience and persuade them to attend. Also consider the tone that you think will be most effective. Compose a draft of the email and ask at least two students who are not in your class to read the draft and provide feedback. Do they find it clear and persuasive? Revise your draft based on their feedback, evaluate it thoroughly, and submit both your first draft and your revised draft to your instructor. On a separate sheet, submit a paragraph explaining how you changed your draft based on feedback.

24 Revising and designing an email message for a mobile device [Related to the Technology feature on page 97]

Craig and Darryl work for a product design firm in New York. This morning, Craig received a call from a client in Chicago, asking if he and Darryl could fly to Chicago to consult on a new project. Craig and Darryl agreed, checked their calendars, and chose a 2 PM flight from JFK Airport the next day. However, when Craig called American Airlines to book two seats for the flight, he learned that no seats were available. He did a little research and decided that, of the options available, he would prefer to take a later flight leaving from Newark Liberty International Airport. See the draft on page 118 of Craig's email to Darryl. Using the ACE guidelines in the Technology Box on page 97, revise and redesign this this email to communicate effectively on a mobile device.

CHAPTER 3

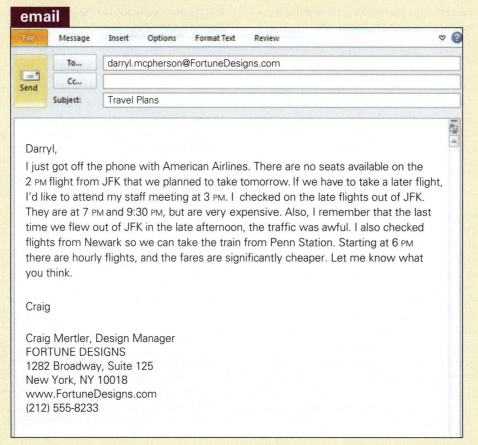

email

File	Message	Insert	Options	Format Text	Review

To... darryl.mcpherson@FortuneDesigns.com

Cc...

Subject: Travel Plans

Darryl,

I just got off the phone with American Airlines. There are no seats available on the 2 PM flight from JFK that we planned to take tomorrow. If we have to take a later flight, I'd like to attend my staff meeting at 3 PM. I checked on the late flights out of JFK. They are at 7 PM and 9:30 PM, but are very expensive. Also, I remember that the last time we flew out of JFK in the late afternoon, the traffic was awful. I also checked flights from Newark so we can take the train from Penn Station. Starting at 6 PM there are hourly flights, and the fares are significantly cheaper. Let me know what you think.

Craig

Craig Mertler, Design Manager
FORTUNE DESIGNS
1282 Broadway, Suite 125
New York, NY 10018
www.FortuneDesigns.com
(212) 555-8233

Accompanies Exercise 24

25 Revising and designing a voice mail message

Alex and Marika are planning to attend an 8 AM meeting with their boss to discuss a report they completed the night before. On the way to work, Alex gets into a car accident. The paragraph on the right is the voice message Alex leaves Marika to tell her that he will not be able to get to work in time for the meeting. He also needs to tell Marika where to find the photocopies of the report he made last night. Before Alex gets to the end of his message, the electronic "operator" interrupts and says: "If you are satisfied with this message, press 1. If you would like to record the message again, press 2." Alex realizes he should revise the message, and he presses 2. Revise this message for Alex.

voice mail

Marika, this is Alex. You won't believe what happened on the way to work today. I was driving down Sherman Avenue when a car ran a red light and hit me. I'm okay, but I'm at least 30 minutes from work and my car is undrivable. I can't leave anyway because the police officer is writing up the report really slowly, and I need to wait to get my license back and to make sure the tow truck comes for my car. Then I'll need to get a taxi. I'm really glad I have my cell phone with me. Otherwise, I'd be in big trouble. I don't know when I'll get to work, so can you present our report at the meeting this morning? The photocopies are on Lucy's desk because . . ."

Accompanies Exercise 25

Collaboration Exercises

26 Preparing to write collaboratively [Related to the Collaboration feature on page 87]

Form teams of three or four students. Have each student in the team independently write a draft of the same email. You may use the email in Exercise 24 or an email with a different purpose, for example, an invitation to a local business person whom you'd like to come speak to your class.

In class, compare the emails from all members of your team and identify key differences and similarities. Are they organized differently? Do they have different tones? Do they use different writing styles? Based on your understanding of each other's writing styles,

determine what agreements you would make if you were working as a team on a larger collaborative project. Use the questions in the collaboration feature on page 87 as a guide. Summarize your decisions in an email to your professor and include everyone's original emails as an attachment.

27 Providing and receiving feedback

Feedback is a valuable element of the evaluation process, but many writers find it challenging both to provide effective feedback and to use the feedback they receive. This collaborative activity is designed to give you practice in giving and receiving feedback.

Identify an administrative office at your school that you believe could be more helpful or could make a change that will benefit students. Examples of administrative offices include admissions, financial aid, student housing, technology support, and athletics, among others. Alternatively, you can select a student club, a local store, or a local restaurant. Before coming to class, write a message to the person in charge of that organization, offering your proposed change and providing reasons. Be sure to analyze your purpose, audience, and content before you write. In class, in groups of three or four, read each other's draft letters and, through discussion, provide feedback to each writer. First discuss the elements of the message you believe are effective, and then discuss recommended changes. In your evaluation, use the questions in the evaluation checklist in the Visual Summary on page 110.

Based on the feedback you receive, revise your message and then evaluate it. Submit both your first draft and revision to your instructor.

28 Exploring cultural communication errors [Related to the Culture feature on page 105]

Assume that your team of three or four students works for a company that is about to launch its products worldwide. In preparing to globalize its advertisements and website, your company wants to understand cultural communication mistakes that other organizations have made. As a team, research cultural communication errors or mistakes and identify two that you would like to analyze. Be sure to try several variations of search terms as you look for examples. Write a brief report to your supervisor (your instructor) explaining the mistake and identifying whether it is a problem with language, culture, or document design. Provide suggestions for what the organization could have done to prevent that problem.

Speaking Exercises

29 Impromptu presentations

Select one of the following topics and plan a brief one- to two-minute presentation that you organize directly. Begin with the main idea followed by supporting information and conclude with a short summary or wrap-up. Then select a second topic and plan a brief presentation that you organize indirectly. For this presentation, begin with supporting information, followed by the main point with a brief summary or wrap-up at the end.

a. Describe your last vacation.

b. Explain why you chose your major.

c. Describe your dream job.

d. Explain why you selected this university/college.

e. Where do you see yourself in five years?

30 Executive briefings

Prepare presentations for the following exercises.

a. **Analyzing websites.** Visit the website of a successful, well-known company and print the home page. Based on your analysis, what is the purpose of the page? Who is the primary audience? Who might be the secondary audience? Is the page persuasive? Identify the content of the page and explain how it supports the purpose of the page.

Prepare a three- to five-minute presentation that conveys this information to the class. Display the website if possible.

b. **The art of persuasion.** Most business communication uses some level of persuasion. Presenting audience benefits is just one of many strategies writers use to persuade an audience. Search the web for other methods of persuasion that are applicable to business communication and prepare a three- to five-minute presentation that outlines this information for the class.

c. **A method to the medium.** Selecting the best medium for your communication is often difficult. Assume that you need to communicate with your professor. Create a realistic scenario or perhaps share a personal experience. In a three- to five-minute presentation to the class, describe the situation you need to communicate and outline the pros and cons of using a face-to-face conversation, telephone call, or email message.

d. **Designing effective documents.** Select a business message that you have received, such as a sales letter, an email or a mailing from a bank or insurance company, a promotional offer from a credit card company, or a solicitation for donations from a charity. Identify features of the message that you believe are effective, making the message professional-looking and easy to read. Also identify features that you find ineffective. In a three- to five-minute presentation, present your analysis. Either display or distribute a copy of the message.

Social Media Exercises

31 Analyzing a company's social media presence

Select a company that you have "liked" on Facebook, linked to on LinkedIn, or followed on Twitter. Analyze the collective social media presence of that company. Describe how, what, and with whom the company communicates through social media. Explain the interaction the company supports among its fans or followers, and describe how the company reacts to negative posts/comments. Describe the tone of one or more posts, and explain how that tone does or does not support the purpose of the post. Summarize your findings in a one- or two-page memo report or prepare to present your findings in class using screen shots of the social media sites.

32 Composing internal messages with social media

Consider the scenario about the flexible summer-hours schedule described in the chapter. How could you use social media to gather employees' input about the flex-time proposal? Provide at least two or three examples. What are the pros and cons of using social media versus other medium options? Explain your answers in an email message to your professor.

Grammar Exercises

33 Adjectives and adverbs (see Appendix C: Grammar, Punctuation, Mechanics, and Conventions—Section 1.1.3)

Type the following paragraphs, correcting the errors in use or formation of adjectives and adverbs. Underline all your corrections.

Does your telephone etiquette speak good of you? Because most people answer their own phones at work, poor phone manners make both you and your company look badly. Which greeting will make the best impression: "How may I help you?" or "What do you want?" It is important to sound cheerfully on the phone.

Even if you don't feel well, try to respond positively. A more simple way to sound positive is to smile when speaking. Smiling actually does make a person seem more friendlier over the phone. Some people like to have the most unique telephone greeting in the office: "Yo, super service representative Skip speaking!" A greeting like that just makes "Skip" seem real unprofessional. Instead of being named "Best Employee of the Month," he is likely to be awarded "Worse Phone Manners of the Year."

MyLab Business Communication

Go to **www.pearson.com/mylab/business-communication** for Auto-graded writing questions as well as the following Assisted-graded writing questions:

1. Explain why your first draft should not be your last draft—even for short messages.

2. Explain a situation in which you have experienced writer's block. What were you writing about? How much time did you have to complete the project? Which of the suggestions to overcome writer's block from the chapter might have helped you? Which ones will you use in the future?

References

1. U.S. Department of Labor. (n.d.). Work hours: Flexible schedules. Retrieved from http://www.dol.gov/dol/topic/work-hours/flexibleschedules.htm
2. Lengel, R. H., & Daft, R. L. (1989). The selection of communication media as an executive skill. *The Academy of Management Executive (1987–1989)*, 225–232.
3. Project Management Institute. (2013). A guide to the project management body of knowledge. (5th ed.). Newtown Square, PA: Project Management Institute.
4. Gatehouse. (2016). State of the sector: Internal communication & employee engagement. Volume 8. Retrieved from http://www.gatehouse.co.uk/knowledge_bank_resources/SOTS/SOTS_2016_FULL.pdf
5. Musso, A. (2016, March 3). Why internal communicators need enterprise social networks. Retrieved from http://bananatag.com/hub/internal-comms/why-internal-communicatiors-need-enterprise-social-networks/
6. Dagliano, A. (2016, January 20). The pros and cons of social media in the workplace. Retrieved from http://www.egroupengage.com/blog/the-pros-and-cons-of-social-media-in-the-workplace
7. Bryant, A. (2012, March 10). The memo list: Where everyone has an opinion. *The New York Times*. Retrieved from http://www.nytimes.com/2012/03/11/business/jim-whitehurst-of-red-hat-on-merits-of-an-open-culture.html?pagewanted=allm
8. Craig, V. (2014, June 12). Red Hat CEO: Tech nerd to tech pro. Retrieved from http://www.foxbusiness.com/features/2014/06/12/red-hat-ceo-tech-nerd-to-tech-pro.html
9. Marsh, E.J., & Butler, A.C. (2014). Memory in educational settings. In D. Reisberg (Ed.), *The Oxford handbook of cognitive psychology* (pp. 299–317). Oxford, U.K.: Oxford University Press.
10. Rose, M. (1980). Rigid rules, inflexible plans, and the stifling of language: A cognitivist analysis of writer's block. *College Composition and Communication*, 31(4), 389–401.
11. Konnikova, M. (2016, Mach 11). How to beat writer's block. *The New Yorker*. Retrieved from http://www.newyorker.com/science/maria-konnikova/how-to-beat-writers-block
12. Bane, R. (2012). *Around the writer's block: Using brain science to solve writer's resistance*. New York, NY: Tarcher/Penguin.
13. Rose, M. (1984). *Writer's block: The cognitive dimension*. Carbondale, IL: Southern Illinois University Press.
14. Kewkowicz, K. (2016, June 9). May email market share: Mobile drops for the first time since January to 54%. Retrieved from https://litmus.com/blog/mobile-market-share-drops-for-the-first-time-since-january-to-54
15. Patel, N. (2015, April 15). How to write content that engages mobile readers. Retrieved from http://contentmarketinginstitute.com/2015/04/content-engages-mobile-readers/
16. Gerhardt, D. (2015, September 14). 5 simple tips for mobile-friendly emails. [Blog post]. Retrieved from http://blogs.constantcontact.com/mobile-friendly-emails/
17. Eurich, T. (2015, April 7). The hidden cost of ignoring email. *Entrepreneur*. Retrieved from www.entrepreneur.com/article/244751
18. Strunk, W., & White, E. B. (1999). *The elements of style* (4th ed.). Hoboken, NJ: Pearson.
19. Williams, J., & Bizup, J. (2013). *Style: Lessons in clarity and grace*. (11th ed.). Hoboken, NJ: Pearson.
20. Pinker, S. (2014). *The sense of style*. New York, N.Y.: Viking.
21. Douglas, Y. (2015). *The reader's brain: How neuroscience can make you a better writer*. Cambridge, UK: Cambridge University Press.
22. Benefit. (n.d.). In The Princeton Language Institute (Ed.), *Roget's 21st century thesaurus* (3rd ed.). Retrieved from http://thesaurus.reference.com/search?r=20&q=benefit
23. Kawasaki, G. (2010, March 20). Just give him 5 sentences, not "War and Peace." Interview by Adam Bryant. *The New York Times*. Retrieved from http://www.nytimes.com/2010/03/21/business/21corner.html

24. Viswanatha, A., & Andrews, N. (2016, December 29). Tweeting in government is hard, if you're not Donald Trump. *The Wall Street Journal*. A8.

25. Goudreau, J. (2012, February 21). Are funny people more successful in business? *Forbes*. Retrieved from http://www.forbes.com/sites/jennagoudreau/2012/02/21/funny-people-more-successful-in-business-humor-workplace

26. Federal Student Aid [FAFSA]. (2016, December, 17). Do it right meow. (Yeah we went there). Retrieved from https://twitter.com/FAFSA

27. Federal Student Aid [FAFSA]. (2016, December, 24). Getting a student loan is a big decision—Remember, borrow only what you need and know what you owe. Retrieved from https://twitter.com/FAFSA

28. March, J. (2012, February 27). How to turn social feedback into valuable business data. Retrieved from http://mashable.com/2012/02/27/social-data-insights/

29. Globalization and Localization Association. (2017). Introduction to the language industry. Retrieved from https://www.gala-global.org/industry/introduction-language-industry

30. Raine, G. (2001, August 25). Lost in translation. Milk Board does without its famous slogan when it woos a Latino audience. *San Francisco Chronicle*. Retrieved from http://www.sfgate.com/business/article/Lost-in-the-translation-Milk-board-does-without-2884230.php

31. Trusted Translations. (2014, May 16). The importance of localization in advertising campaigns. [Blog post]. Retrieved from http://translation-blog.trustedtranslations.com/the-importance-of-localization-in-advertising-campaigns-2014-05-16.html

4 Communicating Routine Messages and Building Goodwill

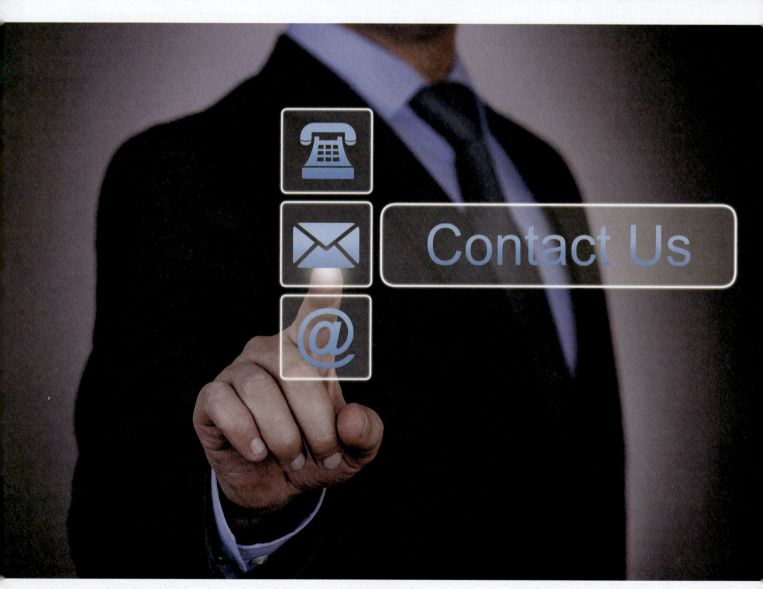

Turgaygundogdu/Fotolia

STUDY QUESTIONS

SQ1 — How do you compose messages containing questions and requests?
pages 124–129

Decide between a direct or an indirect message

Provide reasons for the request

Adopt a "you" perspective and include audience benefits

Conclude with gratitude and a call for action

SQ2 — How do you compose informational messages? pages 129–136

Reply to questions with a direct answer

Respond to customer requests and comments by creating goodwill

Highlight key points in confirmation messages

Organize routine announcements so they are easy to skim

Format instructions so readers can easily follow the steps

Keep text and IM messages short and focused

SQ3 — What kinds of messages build goodwill in business relationships?
pages 136–141

Thank-you messages

Congratulatory messages

Sympathy messages

"For-your-information" messages

New Hires @ Work

Hayeon Kim

Northwestern University

Intern in Legal Operations, Trademark Division @ Google

In email, be courteous, but not so much that you're adding unnecessary content to your messages. Keep in mind that people are busy—often really busy!—and are taking the time to read what you're writing. Sometimes new employees start an email saying "Hi, how are you? I hope you're having a great day, it's been so long!" They take up five sentences when you're thinking "Just ask your question!" Be courteous, but get to the point. It's a delicate balance.

Photo courtesy of Hayeon Kim

123

Every day, businesses produce millions of messages as a routine part of getting work done. As a result, you will have daily opportunities to exercise your communication skills delivering **routine business messages**—the short, nonsensitive, straightforward, day-to-day communication that asks or answers questions, provides information, or confirms agreements.

Routine messages take advantage of every medium available, especially *lean media* such as texting and email. Although email is currently the most frequently used medium for routine communication,[1,2,3] email overload has become such a significant problem that many companies are now relying on other options for routine internal communication, including internal social media. In fact, an information technology services company, Atos Origin, has gone as far as banning the use of email for any routine internal communication in order to increase productivity. Instead, the company uses a social networking platform, and employees communicate

through threaded conversations that they can access when their schedules allow.[4]

No matter what medium you use—email, texting, telephone calls, face-to-face conversations, or social media—if you take routine communication for granted, you may make careless mistakes that undermine your professional presence. Wording errors and typos, sloppy formatting, missing information, and poor organization are just a few of the common mistakes that occur when you compose your message too quickly and don't take the time to analyze and evaluate.

This chapter offers guidelines to help you effectively communicate specific types of routine messages, including questions and requests, informational messages, and **goodwill messages**—messages that give you the opportunity to establish and sustain a positive relationship with your audience. Throughout the chapter, you will see the ACE logo where the discussion offers new insight on how to use ACE to prepare routine and goodwill messages.

Analyze **Compose** **Evaluate**

(SQ1) How do you compose messages containing questions and requests?

Compose

Most day-to-day requests require very little strategizing. When you ask people to do things that are easy for them to do or that are clearly part of their job responsibilities, you do not need to be persuasive. You just need to be clear and polite. However, in some cases, you will be asking people to do you a favor, something that they have no obligation to do. This second kind of request often requires more explanation and persuasion. In both cases, you want to ensure that your audience responds well. The guidelines in this section will help you achieve that goal.

Decide between a direct or an indirect message

Use a direct organization for most routine requests. In other words, begin with your question or request, often as early as the first sentence. Then support that request with the necessary explanation or details. With so many messages to navigate throughout a day, your audience will appreciate routine messages that are organized directly. **Figure 4.1** illustrates the advantages of organizing a request directly compared to an indirect organization or **implicit request** that only hints at what you want.

In some circumstances, you may find it's better to organize your request indirectly, with the request at the end. An indirect organization is a better choice if your audience will not understand your question or request without knowing the context. **Figure 4.2** on page 126 illustrates a message that is better organized indirectly.

routine business message A short, nonsensitive, straightforward communication that asks questions, answers questions, provides information, or confirms agreements.

goodwill message Any message that gives you the opportunity to establish and sustain a positive relationship with your audience.

implicit request A request that hints at what you want rather than stating it directly.

DIRECT REQUEST	
Example of a direct request . . . **Please send me the latest draft of the third-quarter sales figures.** I know your report is not yet complete, but we are discussing the data in tomorrow's budget meeting at 4 PM, and the latest version I have of the third-quarter sales figures is dated three weeks ago. Thanks!	The direct organization places the request at the beginning of the message and is often the better choice because it: • states the request first, before the details. • lets the audience immediately know why they are reading the message. • is usually easier to understand.
INDIRECT REQUEST	
Example of an indirect request . . . The latest version I have of the third-quarter sales figures is dated three weeks ago. I know your report is not yet complete, but we are discussing the data in tomorrow's budget meeting at 4 PM. **Can you please send me the most up-to-date figures?** Thanks!	The indirect organization moves the main idea after the details and is often not as **effective** because the audience may miss the request at the end if they quickly skim the message. In addition, the audience may need to reread the details after reading the request.
IMPLICIT REQUEST	
Example of an implicit request . . . The latest version I have of the third-quarter sales figures is dated three weeks ago. I know your report is not yet complete, but we are discussing the data in tomorrow's budget meeting at 4 PM. I will not be able to prepare for the meeting if I don't have the latest draft.	In all cases, avoid simply implying your request, which requires your audience to figure out what you want. Are you implying that you have decided not to prepare for the meeting? Or are you asking for an updated draft so that you can prepare? To eliminate that ambiguity, state your request explicitly.

FIGURE 4.1 Advantages of Organizing a Request Directly

Provide reasons for the request

As you analyze the content to include in the message, consider how much detail the audience needs to know. If the reason for your request is not obvious, you will need to explain it, as Figure 4.2 on page 126 illustrates. If the audience expects requests like yours, much less detail is required. For example, most customer requests for refunds or merchandise exchanges—sometimes called *claim requests*—require little explanation.

Figure 4.3 on page 127 provides an example of a request a customer submitted to a company that shipped the wrong order. Many companies provide online customer service support, and this message was entered on the company's website. Although it may seem abrupt to begin the message by stating what you want, your audience will appreciate the direct approach. Companies deal with many claim messages each day, and readers need to find the

New Hires @ Work

Byron Smith
North Carolina A&T State University

Business Sales Manager @ AT&T Mobility

Explain "what's in it for me" (WIIFM), but from the other person's perspective. Think about what the receiver wants to hear or will find interesting. That perspective makes all the difference when building relationships with co-workers and clients. It's all about them, not me.

Photo courtesy of Byron Smith

FIGURE 4.2 A Request Requiring an Indirect Organization

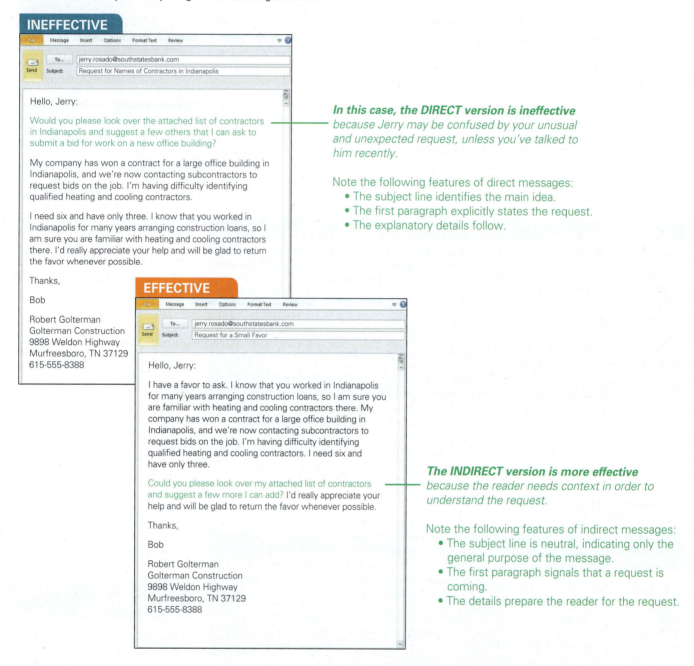

In this case, the DIRECT version is ineffective because Jerry may be confused by your unusual and unexpected request, unless you've talked to him recently.

Note the following features of direct messages:
- The subject line identifies the main idea.
- The first paragraph explicitly states the request.
- The explanatory details follow.

The INDIRECT version is more effective because the reader needs context in order to understand the request.

Note the following features of indirect messages:
- The subject line is neutral, indicating only the general purpose of the message.
- The first paragraph signals that a request is coming.
- The details prepare the reader for the request.

main point quickly, followed by a short explanation of the reason. If a claim request requires more explanation or evidence, you would write a persuasive claim, which is described in Chapter 5: Communicating Persuasive Messages.

Adopt a "you" perspective and include audience benefits

"you" perspective An approach to communication that presents the information from the audience's point of view. The "you" perspective focuses on what the audience needs and wants. It also considers how the audience benefits from the message.

Your audience will be more receptive to your request if you compose the message from their perspective, not your own. In fact, this is true for all communication. Too often, writers and speakers focus on what they want or what is important to them, often organizing the communication to reflect their own thought process and needs. This "I" perspective is likely to confuse or bore the audience. By contrast, using a **"you" perspective**

FIGURE 4.3 How to Make a Claim Request

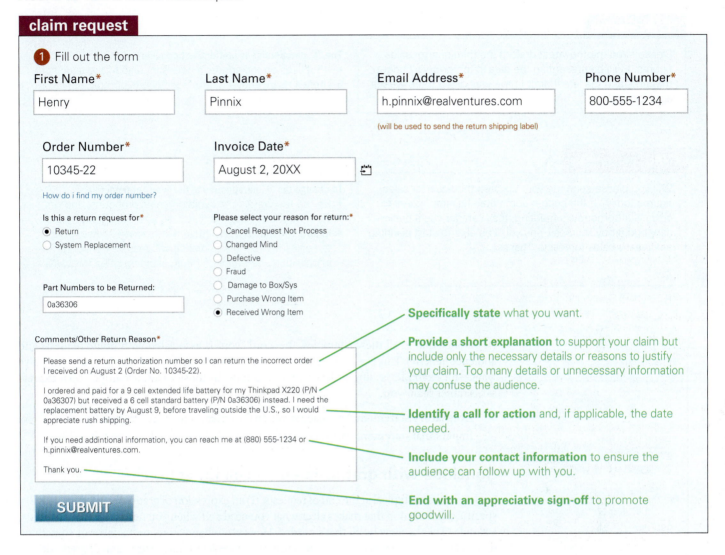

claim request

1 Fill out the form

First Name* — Henry
Last Name* — Pinnix
Email Address* — h.pinnix@realventures.com
(will be used to send the return shipping label)
Phone Number* — 800-555-1234

Order Number* — 10345-22
How do i find my order number?
Invoice Date* — August 2, 20XX

Is this a return request for*
◉ Return
○ System Replacement

Please select your reason for return:*
○ Cancel Request Not Process
○ Changed Mind
○ Defective
○ Fraud
○ Damage to Box/Sys
○ Purchase Wrong Item
◉ Received Wrong Item

Part Numbers to be Returned:
0a36306

Comments/Other Return Reason*

Please send a return authorization number so I can return the incorrect order I received on August 2 (Order No. 10345-22).

I ordered and paid for a 9 cell extended life battery for my Thinkpad X220 (P/N 0a36307) but received a 6 cell standard battery (P/N 0a36306) instead. I need the replacement battery by August 9, before traveling outside the U.S., so I would appreciate rush shipping.

If you need addinitial information, you can reach me at (880) 555-1234 or h.pinnix@realventures.com.

Thank you.

SUBMIT

Specifically state what you want.

Provide a short explanation to support your claim but include only the necessary details or reasons to justify your claim. Too many details or unnecessary information may confuse the audience.

Identify a call for action and, if applicable, the date needed.

Include your contact information to ensure the audience can follow up with you.

End with an appreciative sign-off to promote goodwill.

helps you think primarily about what your audience needs to know, the questions they may have about your request, and how they will benefit from your message. Taking a "you" perspective motivates your audience to respond positively to your request. **Figure 4.4** on page 128 illustrates how to transform an "I" perspective message to focus on the "you" perspective.

Making a request from the "you" perspective requires focusing on **audience benefits**— the positive outcomes your audience will experience by agreeing with or acting on your message. Creating a "you" perspective can be challenging because it requires you to consider other people's viewpoints. Although you can never be certain what someone else will perceive as a benefit, brainstorming ideas can help. As you brainstorm, analyze two different categories of benefits. **Internal benefits** are advantages that your audience directly receives from complying with your request. For example, *"By volunteering for this project, you will be eligible for a bonus of 5 percent of your salary."* **External benefits** are advantages that someone else—a third party—gains. For example, *"By volunteering your time during Help Our Community Day, you will not only help our department achieve its community service goals, but you'll also be helping our local schools."* For best results, the third party should be one that your audience cares about.

audience benefits The positive outcomes your audience will experience by agreeing with or acting on your message.
internal benefits Advantages that your audience will directly receive from complying with your request. Examples include a reduced workload, increased professional recognition, and financial gains.

external benefits Advantages that someone else—a third party that your audience cares about—gains when your audience complies with a request.

FIGURE 4.4 How to Change the "I" Perspective to the "You" Perspective

"I" perspective

Please send me the latest draft of the third-quarter sales figures. I will be presenting the data in tomorrow's budget meeting, and the latest draft I have was dated three weeks ago. Thanks!

The "I" perspective is ineffective because:
- It focuses on the sender's needs instead of the audience's.
- There's no incentive for the audience to comply.

"YOU" perspective

Will you please send me your updated third-quarter sales figures today? If the budget committee has the figures to discuss at tomorrow's meeting, they can get you a preliminary budget by Thursday, and you'll be able to start planning next year's sales forecasts. Thanks!

To change the "I" perspective to the "you" perspective:
- Revise the wording to avoid personal pronouns, such as "I," "me," and "my," and instead use "you" and "your."
- Include audience benefits. In this example, by sending the sales figures, the audience will receive the budget information she needs to begin planning sales forecasts.

Notice that in all these examples, the word "you" is associated with polite requests and audience benefits. This is a positive use of "you." To be effective, avoid using "you" in negative ways—for example, issuing orders and accusations. In those cases, use impersonal expressions rather than "you."

Accusatory statement: You made errors on the forms. You must correct and resubmit them.
Impersonal statement: Please correct the highlighted errors and resubmit the forms.

Conclude with gratitude and a call for action

Two elements are typical at the end of requests: (1) an expression of gratitude or thanks and (2) a specific call for action that makes clear what you need and when you need it. In short requests, a simple "Thanks" may be all that's needed. However, when you request a favor or something that will be an inconvenience, your audience will appreciate a fuller expression of gratitude.

Figure 4.5 illustrates a short request that is spoken but could also be emailed. In this case, Stan's manager is asking him to give a presentation at a meeting on short notice. The manager chose a face-to-face conversation because doing so might encourage Stan to respond more positively. Stan would most likely find it more difficult to refuse the request in a face-to-face conversation, or over the phone, than if he had received the same message by email. Figure 4.6 illustrates a more complex request that requires a detailed call for action as well as expressions of gratitude.

Analyze

FIGURE 4.5 How to Request a Favor

simple request

Stan, can you cover for me at the 2 PM division meeting today?

I have a client lunch that I'm sure will run long, and you know all the data we need to report—you researched everything and put it together. I'd appreciate your help, and this might be a great opportunity for you to impress the VP.

Sound okay?

When asking for a favor, follow this advice:
- Begin by stating the request directly. An introduction or explanation is not needed unless the favor won't make sense without the context.
- Provide a concise explanation or rationale for the favor.
- If applicable, explain why your audience is the best person to do this favor.
- Express gratitude and offer possible audience benefits.
- Conclude with a call for action. If a deadline is important, identify when you need the favor.

FIGURE 4.6 How to Compose a Written Request for Information

complex request

Reed Hall, Box 1054
Lineville, VA 28615
January 14, 20XX

Ms. Paulina Rashid, Advisor
Students in Free Enterprise
Atlantic University
410 Bedden Hall
Patterson, VA 28664

Dear Ms. Rashid:

My cousin, Marlina Robertson, is a member of the Students in Free Enterprise (SiFE) chapter you advise at Atlantic University. She gave me your name and address. We are hoping to start our own SiFE club here at Tabor College and would greatly appreciate your answers to a few questions that I did not find answered on the SiFE website (www.sife.org).

1. How many student members are required for a club to be recognized by the governing international organization?

2. Does the governing organization provide any financial assistance for newly developed clubs to support on-campus promotions for membership drives, such as t-shirts and brochures?

3. Do you develop relationships with other SiFE clubs to collaborate on projects? Or are the projects competitive?

Since our first membership drive is scheduled in March, could you get back to us before January 31? If you prefer to discuss my questions by phone, please call me at your convenience at (409) 555-1234.

If SiFE projects can be collaborative, rather than competitive, we would enjoy developing a collaborative relationship with your SiFE club to design a joint project that would benefit both our campuses and communities. I look forward to talking with you about that once our club is under way.

Thank you for sharing your knowledge with us.

Sincerely,

Dominique Robertson

Dominique Robertson
Tabor College

When requests need to be put in context to be clearly understood, begin with an introduction. A sentence may be all that is needed to explain why you're writing.

End the first paragraph with the request, phrased politely.

Explain preliminary work you have done, if applicable, to document that you are not wasting the audience's time.

If you have many questions, number them to help the audience respond to each item when they reply.

Indicate when a response is needed, and provide contact information if your audience will need it. Consider giving your audience options for replying.

Include potential audience benefits, if applicable, to persuade the audience to respond favorably to your request.

End with an expression of gratitude for responding to your request. Although it may seem presumptuous to thank the audience for something they have not yet done, you can usually assume that routine requests for information will be accepted positively, especially if you have followed these guidelines.

(SQ2) How do you compose informational messages?

Some business messages simply convey information rather than make requests or ask questions. For example, you may reply to requests, respond to claims, confirm information, make announcements, or provide instructions. You can consider these messages routine if the information will not surprise, disappoint, or anger the audience. The following sections explain how to address each kind of informational message.

Compose

Reply to questions with a direct answer

When someone asks you a question in a face-to-face or telephone conversation, you can organize your message exactly as you would when writing a response. If your response is not controversial or likely to disappoint, begin with a direct answer and then include the details. If you do not have the answer immediately available, then say that right away. **Figure 4.7** is a response to the letter in Figure 4.6.

Even though you are direct, be careful not to be too abrupt, especially in email messages. If someone writes you an email asking a question, respond with more than "yes" or "no." A one-word reply may seem dismissive.[5] Instead, provide a response that indicates you actually read the message—for example: *"Yes. That sounds like a good plan. Let me know if you need any help."*

Respond to customer requests and comments by creating goodwill

When a customer requests a refund, an exchange, or a repair, a business has an opportunity to create goodwill. Assuming that the company decides to satisfy the customer's claim, a well-written response can strengthen the company's relationship with the customer. However, if you fail to build goodwill when responding to a customer, you may lose more than

FIGURE 4.7 How to Reply to a Request for Information

letter

ATLANTIC UNIVERSITY

Patterson, VA 28664

January 18, 20XX

Ms. Dominique Robertson
Tabor College
Reed Hall, Box 1054
Lineville, VA 28615

Dear Ms. Robertson:

Congratulations on your goal to begin a SiFE club at Tabor College. Below are the answers to your questions.

1. Your campus club can be as small or large as you like. SiFE does not require a specific number of student members to recognize a campus club. However, based on our experience, you should have at least 15 active members (including your executive officers) to ensure your club's success. Of course, the more members you have the better.

2. Although SiFE does not provide financial assistance to help you promote your club, I am enclosing several sample documents that we have successfully used here. Your cousin, Marlina, has helped us design many of these materials. Her desktop publishing skills are exceptional. Perhaps she can share these files with you.

3. We look forward to developing a collaborative relationship with your SiFE club. Our current president is Colin Withers. His email address is cwithers@atlantic.edu. Please contact him to discuss this possibility.

If you have any other questions, please feel free to call me at (409) 555-9874. I would be happy to serve as a mentor until you establish your own faculty advisor.

Best regards,

Paulina Rashid

Paulina Rashid, M.Ed.
SiFE Faculty Advisor

Enclosures

When replying to requests, determine the best medium to respond. Typically, audiences respond with the same medium that was used to make the request. In addition, choosing to reply to a letter with a letter, in this case, allows the writer to include hard copy enclosures.

Begin with a direct response if the audience will respond favorably to your message.

Then provide explanatory details. Follow the organization of the original message by answering each question in sequence.

End with a friendly closing to promote goodwill.

that customer's business. Disgruntled customers often use social media outlets, such as Yelp, to share their bad experiences with others, which can reach thousands of people. In fact, research indicates that customers are "more likely to share bad customer service experiences than good ones no matter what communication channel they used."[6] However, if you are strategic in your response to a negative comment, you may be able to win back that customer as well as gain the confidence of new customers. Research also indicates that "customers with issues that are resolved quickly can often turn into loyal customers and even brand advocates."[7] To achieve a positive result, craft a response that shows understanding for the customer's complaint, apologizes when appropriate, and identifies a solution.

Figure 4.8 illustrates a positive response to the claim in Figure 4.3 on page 127. Notice that although the sales representative does not apologize, he does include a goodwill strategy: the offer of free shipping for the returned item.

The three-part formula—understanding, apology, and solution—works equally well when responding to complaints received through Twitter, Facebook, or other social media outlets. **Figure 4.9** is a Twitter exchange between a customer and Uber, a company that has

FIGURE 4.8 How to Respond Positively to a Claim Request

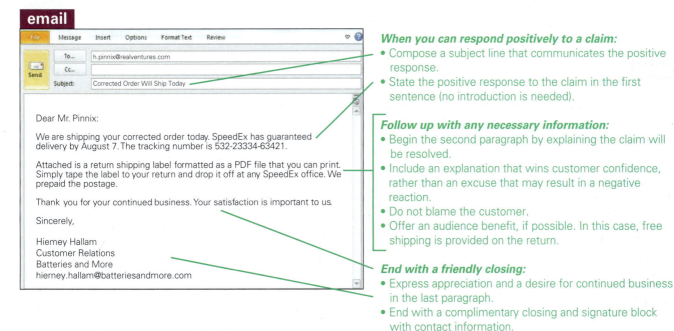

FIGURE 4.9 Example of a Twitter Exchange Responding to a Customer Complaint

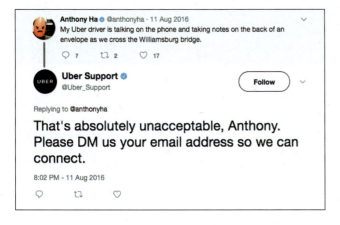

developed a positive reputation for responding quickly to tweets.[8] In this exchange, a customer in New York complained that his Uber driver was driving unsafely. The Uber support team responded within a few minutes, indicating genuine concern. The tweet from Uber expressed understanding and implied an apology and a solution—in fewer than 140 characters.[9]

Highlight key points in confirmation messages

confirmation message An acknowledgment that you have received information or understood a message correctly.

A **confirmation message** acknowledges that you have received information or that you have understood it correctly. When you make oral agreements with someone, it is a good practice to confirm those agreements in writing afterward. For example, assume that you see a colleague at lunch and informally chat about next week's budget meeting. You discuss possible days to reschedule the meeting and make notes on a napkin. However, you inadvertently throw away the napkin before returning to your office and need to follow up to ensure that you remember the dates correctly. Compare the two versions of the confirmation email drafts in **Figure 4.10**. The revised version is not only clearer; it is also more professional.

FIGURE 4.10 How to Confirm Information

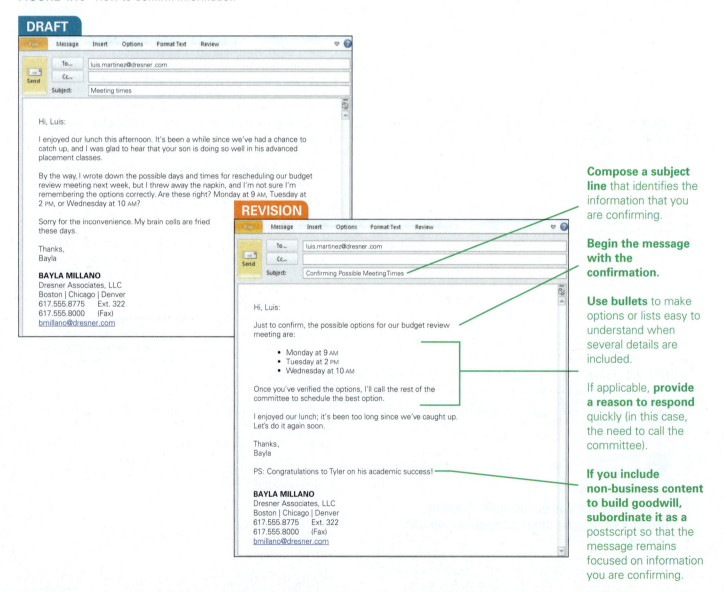

DRAFT

To... luis.martinez@dresner.com
Cc...
Subject: Meeting times

Hi, Luis:

I enjoyed our lunch this afternoon. It's been a while since we've had a chance to catch up, and I was glad to hear that your son is doing so well in his advanced placement classes.

By the way, I wrote down the possible days and times for rescheduling our budget review meeting next week, but I threw away the napkin, and I'm not sure I'm remembering the options correctly. Are these right? Monday at 9 AM, Tuesday at 2 PM, or Wednesday at 10 AM?

Sorry for the inconvenience. My brain cells are fried these days.

Thanks,
Bayla

BAYLA MILLANO
Dresner Associates, LLC
Boston | Chicago | Denver
617.555.8775   Ext. 322
617.555.8000   (Fax)
bmillano@dresner.com

REVISION

To... luis.martinez@dresner.com
Cc...
Subject: Confirming Possible Meeting Times

Hi, Luis:

Just to confirm, the possible options for our budget review meeting are:

- Monday at 9 AM
- Tuesday at 2 PM
- Wednesday at 10 AM

Once you've verified the options, I'll call the rest of the committee to schedule the best option.

I enjoyed our lunch; it's been too long since we've caught up. Let's do it again soon.

Thanks,
Bayla

PS: Congratulations to Tyler on his academic success!

BAYLA MILLANO
Dresner Associates, LLC
Boston | Chicago | Denver
617.555.8775   Ext. 322
617.555.8000   (Fax)
bmillano@dresner.com

Compose a subject line that identifies the information that you are confirming.

Begin the message with the confirmation.

Use bullets to make options or lists easy to understand when several details are included.

If applicable, **provide a reason to respond quickly** (in this case, the need to call the committee).

If you include non-business content to build goodwill, subordinate it as a postscript so that the message remains focused on information you are confirming.

TECHNOLOGY
USING TECHNOLOGY TO SIMPLIFY ROUTINE COMMUNICATION: SCHEDULING A MEETING

Scheduling a meeting with a few coworkers may seem like an easy task. However, the logistics of coordinating schedules can be a time-consuming activity, especially if you rely on email to determine the best day and time. You may end up with a long thread of replies over several days before you agree on the best option. And what if you need to coordinate a meeting with 25 people or make a presentation to 50 people? Without using online scheduling tools, you would have to set an arbitrary date and hope that most people can attend.

Feng Yu/Alamy Stock Photo

Fortunately, technology gives you several options for scheduling meetings. Your company may use specific software designed to coordinate events, such as Microsoft Outlook's calendar feature, which is part of the Office suite of applications. If you are meeting with people within the company, you may be able to check their calendars to find a mutually convenient meeting time.

If you don't share calendars, or if you are coordinating a meeting with people outside your organization, online tools—such as Doodle, Calendly, and NeedToMeet[10]—can help you quickly identify scheduling options through "polls." To set up a poll, enter options for meeting times. The application creates a link that you then share with participants, who will enter their names and select the times when they are available. As the poll administrator, you can view the poll at any time and identify the best option to schedule.

JANUARY 20XX Mon 9		Wed 11		Tue 17	Thu 19
4 participants	9:00 AM - 12:00 PM	1:00 PM - 4:00 PM	10:00 AM - 11:00 AM	2:30 PM - 3:30 PM	5:00 PM - 8:00 PM	8:00 AM - 9:00 AM
Tammy Smith		✓		✓		✓
John Doe		✓	✓	✓	✓	
Sarah Long	✓	✓	✓	✓		
Kregg Smith				✓	✓	✓
Your name	☐	☐	☐	☐	☐	☐
	1	3	2	4	2	2

Save

Once you have determined a time, you can use your calendar software to communicate that time to participants. Before you do so, familiarize yourself with the basic etiquette of email invitations to create a functional and informative meeting invitation:

1. **Use a descriptive invitation title.** If you are meeting with Rebecca, do not title your meeting invitation "Meeting with Rebecca." That will not be helpful to her when she receives the invitation. Instead, title it "Meeting in 7th floor conference room to discuss budget: Rebecca and Taylor." When Rebecca gets the email with the invitation, she will know exactly who is meeting, where, and why.

2. **When possible, add all the attendees to the same invitation.** That way, everyone will know who has been invited.

3. **Include a brief but meaningful message to put the meeting in context.** Some people skip writing a message and assume that the invitation title is enough. However, including a message will help your audience prepare for the meeting. Remind them about any action items from past meetings, if applicable, and list the agenda items for this meeting. If they need to bring reports or other information with them, include those details as well. Keep the message short by including only the information they need to know before you meet.

4. **Attach files you want your meeting participants to read.** Refer to the attachments in the message, and explain what participants need to read or do ahead of time to prepare for the meeting.

5. **Schedule automatic meeting reminders.** If you set up reminders as part of your meeting invitation options, your participants will receive the reminders a day before the meeting and an hour before the meeting.

When you receive a meeting invitation from someone else, etiquette requires that you respond to it just as you would respond to an email. Accept or decline the invitation. If your plans change, inform the organizer.

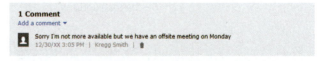

1 Comment
Add a comment ▾
Sorry I'm not more available but we have an offsite meeting on Monday
12/30/XX 3:05 PM | Kregg Smith

For TECHNOLOGY exercises, go to Exercise 20 on page 151 and Exercise 31b on page 152.

Organize routine announcements so they are easy to skim

announcement A message that publicly notifies people of information they need or want to know.

Announcements are messages that publicly notify people of information they need or want to know. For example, you might notify customers about a sale or a change in policy, employees about a new CEO or promotions within the organization, or the public about job opportunities in your company. Announcements are communicated both externally (social media, company websites, customer email) and internally (company emails, meetings, flyers). **Figure 4.11** illustrates a routine announcement to bank customers. The bank is changing some of its policies and is required by law to notify customers.

FIGURE 4.11 How to Compose Routine Informational Announcements

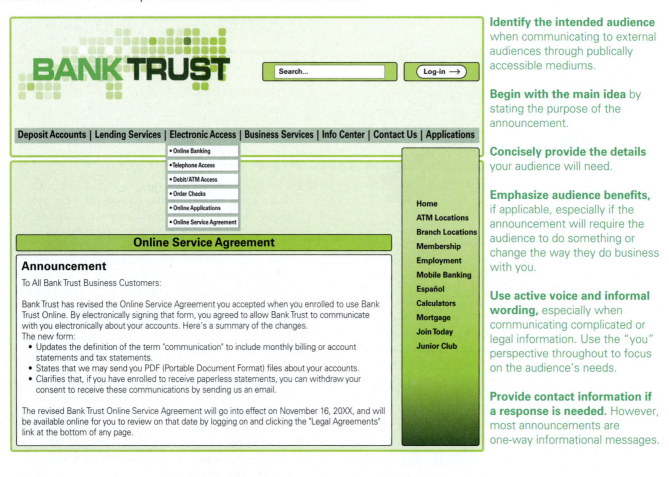

Format instructions so readers can easily follow the steps

In addition to requests, replies, and announcements, a fourth category of routine business messages is instructions. Examples include instructions for how to complete a new travel authorization form, process budget requests, and submit reimbursement documentation. Good instructions use writing techniques such as **parallel phrasing** that allow the audience to understand the task and complete it accurately. To make it easy for the audience to follow the instructions, use the guidelines illustrated in **Figure 4.12**.

parallel phrasing Using the same grammatical form for each item in a list.

Keep text and IM messages short and focused

As an article on the *Inc.* website proclaimed, "texting is the new email" in business.[11] In a survey of 500 business professionals, 67 percent said that they use texting for business, with almost half of those indicating that if they need to leave a message, they would use

FIGURE 4.12 How to Write Instructions

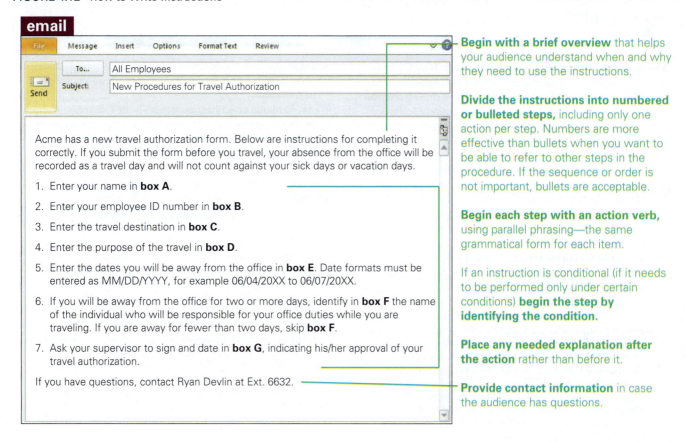

email

| File | Message | Insert | Options | Format Text | Review |

To... All Employees
Subject: New Procedures for Travel Authorization

Send

Acme has a new travel authorization form. Below are instructions for completing it correctly. If you submit the form before you travel, your absence from the office will be recorded as a travel day and will not count against your sick days or vacation days.

1. Enter your name in **box A**.
2. Enter your employee ID number in **box B**.
3. Enter the travel destination in **box C**.
4. Enter the purpose of the travel in **box D**.
5. Enter the dates you will be away from the office in **box E**. Date formats must be entered as MM/DD/YYYY, for example 06/04/20XX to 06/07/20XX.
6. If you will be away from the office for two or more days, identify in **box F** the name of the individual who will be responsible for your office duties while you are traveling. If you are away for fewer than two days, skip **box F**.
7. Ask your supervisor to sign and date in **box G**, indicating his/her approval of your travel authorization.

If you have questions, contact Ryan Devlin at Ext. 6632.

Begin with a brief overview that helps your audience understand when and why they need to use the instructions.

Divide the instructions into numbered or bulleted steps, including only one action per step. Numbers are more effective than bullets when you want to be able to refer to other steps in the procedure. If the sequence or order is not important, bullets are acceptable.

Begin each step with an action verb, using parallel phrasing—the same grammatical form for each item.

If an instruction is conditional (if it needs to be performed only under certain conditions) **begin the step by identifying the condition.**

Place any needed explanation after the action rather than before it.

Provide contact information in case the audience has questions.

texting rather than voice mail.[12] The advantage of texting or *instant messaging* is that your audience can access the texts more quickly and discretely than a voice message. Texting provides many other benefits over calling; for example, texting can be done more privately than a telephone call, it offers a written record of the conversation, and it is less distracting to the receiver.[13] Texting is an ideal medium for short routine messages—as long as the messages can be easily answered by text.

However, in many organizations, you will be discouraged from using your personal texting app for business. Companies in the financial services industry, which has widely adopted mobile messaging, use secure programs that encrypt and archive messages.[14] Other organizations rely on computer-based enterprise messaging systems for internal communication, which are accessed on a computer and are also archived.[15] For external communication—to customers and clients—you may be using an enterprise messaging program on your computer, sending the message to the customer's phone. Or you may be using a platform such as Slack, that allows users to subscribe to message channels to facilitate messaging work groups and organizing messages.[16]

Whichever tools you use for sending short messages, follow these guidelines for evaluating your text messages and instant messages in business contexts:

1. Keep the message short and to the point. There is no need to add a salutation ("Hello, Jane") to the beginning of a text.
2. Do not text messages that require a long or complicated response. Your audience will not be able to text back easily.
3. Do not expect a quick response. Although industry research shows that 97 percent of texts are read within three minutes of being sent[17] and that response time for personal texts is typically 90 seconds,[18] your business audience may be too busy to reply immediately.
4. When texting a client or business acquaintance you do not know well, avoid abbreviations, be explicitly polite, and use complete sentences so that you do not sound too harsh or flippant.
5. Double-check to ensure that autocorrect has not changed your intended message.

Evaluate

ETHICS
TO BCC OR NOT TO BCC?

Most email systems support three recipient lines: TO, CC (courtesy copy), and BCC (blind courtesy copy). The TO line is mandatory; you can't CC or BCC anyone without also including an email address on the TO line. Both CC and BCC are optional features that send copies of your message to other people. When you use the CC feature, all the TO recipients and the CC recipients will see each other's names listed in the header of the email message. When you use the BCC feature, neither the TO nor the CC recipients will see anyone who is BCC'd. Those names remain private. The BCC recipients will see everyone else.

The BCC feature has many benefits, but depending on how you use it, it can be unethical as well.[19,20] So the question is . . . to BCC or not to BCC?[21]

It's okay to BCC routine messages when you want to:

- **Eliminate long recipient lists and reduce unwanted reply-all messages.** If you are sending the same informational message to many people, listing those people on the BCC line eliminates the recipients' need to scroll through the long list to get to the message. One way to signal to the audience that you are using the BCC feature is to use your own name on the TO line. If you also use a salutation that identifies the group (such as, To All Managers:), everyone who receives the message will know the intended audience. Putting your own address on the TO line also reduces the possibility that an individual's reply will be sent to all recipients. Even if a recipient accidentally hits Reply All, the message will go only to you.
- **Protect the privacy of your recipients' email addresses.** In situations when your recipients do not know each other, you could use the BCC feature to protect the privacy of their

email addresses. Examples include emailing information about a new service to several clients or sending a newsletter to volunteers.
- **Avoid blame or embarrassment.** The BCC feature can also be useful in situations when you need to email several people about a negative topic, such a missed deadline. Everyone who missed the deadline gets the information, but no one knows who else missed it.

However, in all other situations, avoid the BCC feature, especially if you are using it to do the following:

- **Share negative information covertly with a third party.** When you send an email to someone about a sensitive or confidential matter, that person is likely to assume that the only people who receive the email are those listed on the TO and CC line. If you covertly BCC someone else on that email, you are being deceptive and thus unethical. If a third party needs to be informed of this sensitive or negative information, it is better to explicitly include that person on the CC line—or send a separate email addressing your concern.
- **Gain a personal or business advantage.** Imagine that you are trying to get a good deal on a product or service and are negotiating with two different vendors. If you BCC one vendor on an email about a quote to the other vendor, you are putting the first vendor at an advantage over the other. Even if you BCC both vendors surreptitiously on each other's messages, the fact that you are being covert is an ethical breach.

For ETHICS exercises, go to Critical Thinking Question 3 on page 147 and Exercise 31a on page 152.

(SQ3) ## What kinds of messages build goodwill in business relationships?

New Hires @ Work

Erica Masters
University of West Georgia

Advanced Staff Auditor @ Georgia Department of Audits and Accounts

Despite advances in technology, communication in the workplace still benefits from face-to-face interaction. You need to think about which medium option is most appropriate for each situation.

Photo courtesy of Erica Masters

thank-you message An expression of appreciation when someone has done something for you.

Goodwill is a term used to describe the attitude of friendliness and caring that is central to creating, solidifying, and maintaining relationships. Building and sustaining positive working relationships through goodwill is critical to your productivity and career success.[22] As the Better Business Bureau explains to its members, "Your most important asset [in business] is the relationships you build along the way. Whether those be with customers, suppliers or others in your supply chain, these are more important than bricks and mortar. If you want to put it into business terms, it's called social capital."[23]

Because relationships are so important, take advantage of opportunities to express appreciation and thoughtfulness. Throughout this chapter, you have seen examples of goodwill techniques in routine messages: expressing appreciation, offering help, using a "you" perspective, and highlighting audience benefits. In addition to emphasizing goodwill in your routine messages, you can maintain goodwill and keep the channels of communication open by sending special messages designed specifically for that purpose. These include thank-you messages, congratulations, expressions of sympathy, and for-your-information messages.

Thank-you messages

Thank-you messages offer the opportunity to express appreciation and make recipients feel good about something they have done for you. They also offer you the opportunity to express and display your professionalism. For example, a well-written thank-you note following a job interview communicates to an employer that you are motivated, thoughtful, and articulate. The main challenge in writing a good thank-you note is to include specific content that relates to the reason you are thanking someone.

CULTURE
DIFFERENCES IN SAYING THANK YOU

A thank-you note or email is more than just a polite gesture. It is a way to show genuine appreciation for the effort someone has made and to make that person feel good about the effort. However, different cultures have different ways of expressing thanks and perhaps different expectations about the length of the thank-you note and the amount of detail it includes. The following two messages are real thank-you notes business students wrote to thank their supervisors for summer internships. Letter 1 is written by a U.S. student who interned in a U.S. company. Letter 2 is written by a Korean student who interned in a Singapore company. Both letters are very polite and were well received by their audiences. What differences do you notice about the two letters?

Letter 1, the American thank-you letter, follows the advice in this chapter. The letter is:

- Personalized and sincerely expresses thanks.
- Short and to the point, an appropriate approach in a low-context culture.
- Informal, which signals the close working relationship between the student and mentor. This approach is appropriate in cultures with low power distance.

- Detailed, which signals that the writer has spent much time thinking about what to say to someone he respects. This approach is appropriate in cultures with high power distance.

letter

Letter 2: Asian Thank You

Dear Mr. Jeehun:

Please accept my apology for not writing this letter earlier. After returning to the United States, I was busy with the details of moving.

Now that I reflect on my summer internship at Capital Investors, I see that I was able to complete it successfully primarily thanks to your consideration and support. I especially appreciate that you taught me the values that are necessary to be a successful investment banker.

First, I learned a professional attitude from you. Every kind manner you showed—such as thorough service for clients, a fine sense of being a salesperson, and a charismatic but warm-hearted leadership style—fascinated me.

Second, you showed me devotion to a job. Whenever I watched you absorbed in work, I felt your passion as an investment banker and the dignity of the vocation.

Last but not least, I learned it is possible to be a professional and also enjoy life by seeing you achieve a balance between work and family. It was impressive that you tried hard to invest your time and energy in playing with your children every weekend.

To sum up, having you as a boss during this summer internship was a great professional and personal experience for me. I have decided to look to you as my role model, and I will try to follow you in my career path.

I look forward to seeing you as soon as possible.

Sincerely,

Dong Gyu Lee

letter

Letter 1: North American Thank You

Dear David:

Thank you for providing me with an internship that exceeded my expectations. I have never had a manager who spent so much time developing my skills. I have learned so much—not only about marketing and strategy but also about how to be a good manager.

I really enjoyed working with you and the rest of the team. I would love to join the group again next summer and would be pleased to hear from you.

Thanks again for everything,

Leslie

Letter 2 is written with the Asian culture in mind. The letter is:

- Longer and more formal.
- Focused on the relationship between the writer and audience, which is appropriate in high-context cultures.

For CULTURE exercises, go to Critical Thinking Question 10 on page 147 and Exercise 25 on page 151.

The form your thank-you message takes will depend on the situation. However, your audience may perceive a handwritten note to be a particularly meaningful expression of gratitude because "a handwritten note can actually help you stand out in this era of overflowing electronic inboxes."[24] **Figure 4.13** on page 138 illustrates a handwritten thank-you note and two versions of a thank-you letter: one that is too generic to be effective and one that is more personalized.

FIGURE 4.13 How to Write a Personalized Thank-You Note

For all thank-you notes:

- **Begin by expressing gratitude.** Identify the specific reason you are thanking the recipient.
- **Avoid generic statements** that sound as if they could refer to anyone. A thank-you message should sound as if it was written specifically for that person.
- **Mention specific details and related information** that reflect the value of what the recipient did to receive your thanks (such as why the attendees appreciated the speech).
- **Reiterate your appreciation** near the end of the message.
- **Conclude with a forward-looking statement,** if applicable.

Note how the effective thank-you letter below follows this advice.

INEFFECTIVE THANK-YOU LETTER

Prairie State
ENTREPENEURS
7212 MAIN STREET SPRINGFIELD, IL 62701

September 30, 20XX

Mr. Robert Goldberg
Goldberg, Richey, and Short, LLC
9882 West Jefferson
Springfield, IL 62704

Dear Mr. Goldberg:

Thank you for speaking at the monthly meeting of Prairie State Entrepreneurs on September 29. The information in your speech and additional reference material you provided were both fascinating and timely.

We hope you enjoyed meeting the members of our organization and that you will consider returning in the future to continue the discussion.

Thank you again for taking the time to speak at our meeting.

Sincerely,

Charlotte Waltman

Charlotte Waltman
President

EFFECTIVE THANK-YOU LETTER

Prairie State
ENTREPENEURS
7212 MAIN STREET SPRINGFIELD, IL 62701

September 30, 20XX

Mr. Robert Goldberg
Goldberg, Richey, and Short, LLC
9882 West Jefferson
Springfield, IL 62704

Dear Mr. Goldberg:

Thank you for speaking at the monthly meeting of Prairie State Entrepreneurs on September 29. Our members enjoyed your presentation on protecting intellectual property rights.

We were particularly interested in the case studies showing how inventors lost the ability to patent their work by publicly disclosing their inventions too early, such as at meetings like ours. Our Board of Directors immediately voted to require all attendees to sign confidentiality agreements at any meeting when a new invention is presented.

Thank you again for taking the time to speak at our meeting and for providing us such valuable information. We hope that you will consider returning in the future. We would be very interested in your advice about how to work effectively with a patent attorney.

Sincerely,

Charlotte Waltman

Charlotte Waltman
President

If you hand write a thank-you note:

- Use quality stationery, a good pen, and legible penmanship.
- Consider drafting the message in a word processing application before writing it to ensure that you are using good grammar, spelling, and punctuation.

EFFECTIVE THANK-YOU NOTE

Hi, Tom:

Thank you for inviting me to your club while I was in Santa Barbara last week. I really enjoyed the spa, and the workout equipment was spectacular. If I had access to that kind of facility around here, I would be in great shape.

I look forward to seeing you again next month for our regional conference in Phoenix.

Regards,
Holt

Congratulatory messages

Congratulatory messages build goodwill by recognizing someone's achievements or important events, which could be professional or personal. For example, you can write a congratulatory message when your supervisor is promoted, your colleague has a baby, or your customer wins her city's entrepreneur-of-the-year award. Consider the differences between the two email messages in **Figure 4.14**.

congratulatory message Communication sent to recognize someone's achievements or important events.

FIGURE 4.14   How to Compose a Personalized Congratulations Message

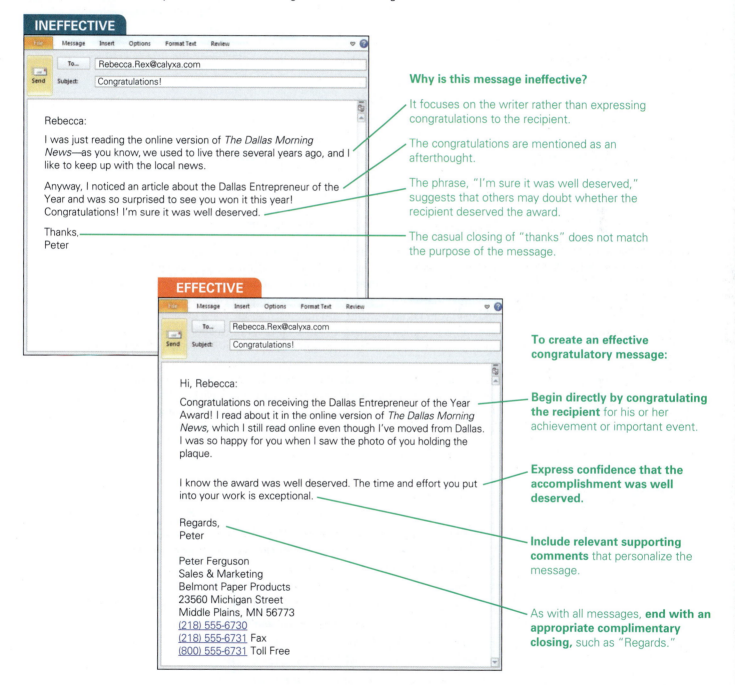

INEFFECTIVE

File   Message   Insert   Options   Format Text   Review

To...   Rebecca.Rex@calyxa.com
Subject: Congratulations!

Rebecca:

I was just reading the online version of *The Dallas Morning News*—as you know, we used to live there several years ago, and I like to keep up with the local news.

Anyway, I noticed an article about the Dallas Entrepreneur of the Year and was so surprised to see you won it this year! Congratulations! I'm sure it was well deserved.

Thanks,
Peter

Why is this message ineffective?

It focuses on the writer rather than expressing congratulations to the recipient.

The congratulations are mentioned as an afterthought.

The phrase, "I'm sure it was well deserved," suggests that others may doubt whether the recipient deserved the award.

The casual closing of "thanks" does not match the purpose of the message.

EFFECTIVE

File   Message   Insert   Options   Format Text   Review

To...   Rebecca.Rex@calyxa.com
Subject: Congratulations!

Hi, Rebecca:

Congratulations on receiving the Dallas Entrepreneur of the Year Award! I read about it in the online version of *The Dallas Morning News*, which I still read online even though I've moved from Dallas. I was so happy for you when I saw the photo of you holding the plaque.

I know the award was well deserved. The time and effort you put into your work is exceptional.

Regards,
Peter

Peter Ferguson
Sales & Marketing
Belmont Paper Products
23560 Michigan Street
Middle Plains, MN 56773
(218) 555-6730
(218) 555-6731 Fax
(800) 555-6731 Toll Free

To create an effective congratulatory message:

Begin directly by congratulating the recipient for his or her achievement or important event.

Express confidence that the accomplishment was well deserved.

Include relevant supporting comments that personalize the message.

As with all messages, **end with an appropriate complimentary closing,** such as "Regards."

Sympathy messages

Even if you do not have a close personal relationship with coworkers or business acquaintances, they will appreciate your expressions of sympathy when they have experienced a loss. Just like thank-you notes, **sympathy messages** (also called *condolences*) are more meaningful when handwritten and sent shortly after you hear about the situation. If you

sympathy message A message that expresses compassion and understanding when someone experiences a loss.

take advantage of get-well cards and preprinted sympathy notes to deliver your messages, also include a few lines that show your compassion and understanding. Read the example in **Figure 4.15**.

FIGURE 4.15 How to Compose a Sympathy Message

> Dear George:
>
> I was sorry to hear about the passing of your mother last week. I can only imagine how great your loss must be at this difficult time. Please know that you have many friends here at work who are keeping you in their thoughts. If I can do anything to help you or your family, please do not hesitate to call me.
>
> With sympathy,
> Camilla

When possible, **send a handwritten note or card rather** than an email message.

Begin with a direct expression of sympathy.

Personalize the message by mentioning something specific about the recipient or the deceased.

Close on a friendly note, such as offering to provide assistance.

Write legibly and use a good pen.

"For-your-information" messages

for-your-information (FYI) message
A message written as an act of kindness to pass along information you think someone might appreciate knowing.

Although they have no formal name, **for-your-information (or "FYI") messages** are sent to share information or communicate something you believe your audience will appreciate. For example, when reading an article on the web about a new restaurant in New Orleans, you may remember that a customer is planning a vacation in New Orleans the next month. Or while talking to your tax accountant, you may learn about a new tax rule that you think a colleague may appreciate knowing. Rather than keep that information to yourself, you can share it by email, social media connections, or simply stopping by someone's office for a friendly chat.

Taking the opportunity to pass along this information leads to several benefits. First, you keep channels of communication open, which is an important part of networking. Second, friendly messages solidify relationships because they have benefits for both parties. You will get personal satisfaction from writing these messages, and your audience will be pleased to hear from you. Finally, these messages may start a dialogue that can lead to possible business benefits. See the example in **Figure 4.16**.

FIGURE 4.16 How to Compose an "FYI" Message

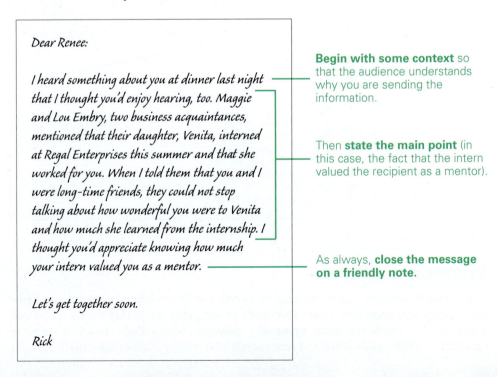

> Dear Renee:
>
> I heard something about you at dinner last night that I thought you'd enjoy hearing, too. Maggie and Lou Embry, two business acquaintances, mentioned that their daughter, Venita, interned at Regal Enterprises this summer and that she worked for you. When I told them that you and I were long-time friends, they could not stop talking about how wonderful you were to Venita and how much she learned from the internship. I thought you'd appreciate knowing how much your intern valued you as a mentor.
>
> Let's get together soon.
>
> Rick

Begin with some context so that the audience understands why you are sending the information.

Then **state the main point** (in this case, the fact that the intern valued the recipient as a mentor).

As always, **close the message on a friendly note.**

COLLABORATION
GET BY WITH A LITTLE HELP FROM YOUR FRIENDS

In addition to the big-project collaborations that require effective teamwork skills, some of your routine communication tasks may benefit from informal collaboration as well. For example, if you are writing an informational message to all the employees in your organization, getting input from your colleagues on a draft will help you evaluate the effectiveness of the message and save you time later. A good message can prevent dozens of follow-up phone calls from confused readers. Similarly, if you are making a time-critical request and need a quick answer, showing the message to a colleague can help you determine if the request is sufficiently clear.

Here are some questions to ask about your routine messages to get a little help from your (workplace) friends.

- How would you describe—in your own words—my main point in this message?
- Is my message organized appropriately for this audience?
- If I am making a request, did I sufficiently explain the reason for the request? Is there too much extraneous information getting in the way?
- If I am replying to a question, did I reply with a direct answer?
- Have I highlighted key points and/or confirmed important information?

- If I am writing an announcement, is it easy to skim?
- If I am writing instructions, are they easy to follow?
- At the end of any message, do I express sufficient gratitude? Are the next steps obvious?
- Does my message create goodwill?

Remember, though, not to overburden your colleagues with too many requests for help. Businesses are becoming increasingly more global, mobile, and connected. This new business model requires employees to be more collaborative, which can lead to "collaborative overload."[25] Before asking for help on a routine message, be sure the message is sufficiently important and that you use the questions listed here to review the message yourself. By reviewing your own draft before asking for feedback, you will give your colleagues a better draft to review and save them time. And you may find that you answer your own questions and won't need any help at all.

For COLLABORATION exercises, go to Exercise 22 on page 151.

■ **In summary,** routine and goodwill messages like those explained in this chapter are fundamental elements of business communication. They are the day-to-day messages you produce to get work done and to build and maintain healthy working relationships. To accomplish your goals with these messages, use the ACE process—analyzing, composing, and evaluating. The ACE process will help ensure that you target the message to your purpose and audience, make it easy to understand, and avoid errors that will undermine your professionalism.

PAPERLESS OFFICES @ WORK   Trend Hunter

Routine communication can lead to a lot of paper! Although smartphones, tablet PCs, cloud computing, social media, and mobile devices create the foundation for paperless communication, the number of paper documents is increasing by 22 percent each year, accounting for approximately 660 billion pieces of paper.[26]

Insadco Photography/Bilderbox/Alamy Stock Photo

Why is the number of paper documents going up rather than going down? There are many reasons. Electronic access to information paradoxically creates incentives to produce paper documents: When people find information on the web, they often print a copy so they do not have to search for it again—and so they will have a copy if the web link disappears. In addition, although email messages have replaced letters and memos, and although documents are typically transmitted electronically rather than on paper, the ability to print and copy these documents is so easy that people choose to print and read offline. As much research has shown, people often prefer to read on paper because it is more comfortable and more effective.[27,28] The result is more paper, not less. In fact, according to Trend Hunter—a "trend community" that features innovative ideas, viral news, and pop culture—the average U.S. office worker prints 10,000 pages per year.[29]

Bucking the trend of increased paper usage, Trend Hunter itself has committed to being a truly paperless office. The company's president, Shelby Walsh, suggests that it's easier to organize information digitally than in paper form: "In this day and age, not only is digital communication a more environmentally-friendly option, but it's also more convenient. Trend Hunter uses as little paper as possible, sending off Trend Reports to our Fortune 500 clients via PowerPoint files, communicating virtually inside of the office, and making use of tools on the cloud to stay organized and keep the company as a whole informed."

Courtesy of Trend Hunter, Inc.

So what technology does Trend Hunter use to communicate routine information? Walsh says,

Everyone in the office is expected to sign into Skype from 9:00 AM to 5:00 PM so that anyone can ping them with urgent questions or requests. In terms of collaboration on projects and sharing of data, we use Google Drive for everything from tracking payments to storing training documents and collaborating in real-time on large-scale ongoing projects. Storing our work in the cloud means the entire team can access files from all of their devices as long as they have Internet access. One piece of communication technology I use quite frequently is Rapportive. It is a plug-in for your email inbox that shows you everything about your contacts within your email. You see an image of the person as well as where they're located and links to their social network profiles. This has helped me greatly in terms of staying connected with business partners, clients, and media and has enhanced my online social networks as well as my rapport with these people.

Trend Hunter's paperless efforts also demonstrate the company's concern about the environment. Walsh notes, "[W]e have an Eco category on the site that has driven millions of views to sustainable and eco-friendly innovations, and we've posted over 15,000 trends about this topic. For those in the office, it's great to have the ability to say we truly practice what we preach. Also, it's great not to have the extra clutter of papers and folders lingering around the office!"

Source: Interview with Shelby Walsh, President of Trend Hunter.

A Day's Worth of Routine Messages

This case scenario will help you review the chapter material by applying it to a specific situation.

For the past year, Miguel Ramirez has worked for his father's insurance agency, Ramirez & Associates Insurance. The small company has only five employees: Miguel and his father, Carlos; Melinda and Reggie, both senior associates; and Theresa, the office manager.

On a Friday morning, Miguel opens the office and checks the company's voice mail. The first message is from his father, saying he won't be in today because he decided to leave for vacation one day early. The second message is from Reggie, reminding everyone that he will be out calling on clients. The third message, from Melinda, says that the insurance supplier she planned to visit next week requested that she come today instead, so she will be out of the office all day. The last message is from Theresa, the office manager, who says she has the flu and will not be in today. This leaves Miguel in charge.

Miguel sits down at Theresa's computer and opens the central email for the office. He also glances at the stack of regular mail on Theresa's desk. Here is a summary of the 11 messages he finds.

In the Email

1. A notice from one of the insurance companies whose products Ramirez & Associates sells. The company has adjusted auto insurance rates and coverage for all customers in the state based on claims and costs from the previous year. These changes will affect almost all customers.

2. A notice from another company that it will not renew the insurance for a customer who filed three claims during the past year.

3. Two requests for insurance quotes from new customers.

4. A request from a summer intern for a job recommendation.

5. A request from a corporate client asking that Ramirez & Associates confirm the details of an insurance policy covering its fleet of 1,000 cars.

6. A notice that a customer's claim for wind damage to her garage will be completely covered by the insuring company, minus the $250 deductible.

7. An email from Melinda asking someone in the office to place an order of office supplies with Office-To-Go. She left the list of supplies on her desk, and she needs them by Monday.

In the Regular Mail

8. Three insurance policies that need to be mailed to customers. These policies are complex, and the customers will not understand the details without a clear summary.

9. An invitation addressed to Miguel's father, Carlos, asking him to speak at a college career night next month. The school requests a reply within 10 days, and Miguel's father is not going to be back in the office for two weeks.

10. A letter from the National Association of Insurance and Financial Advisors, indicating that Carlos Ramirez has been nominated for the prestigious John Newton Russell Memorial Award, the industry's highest honor.

11. A news release from Office-To-Go, one of the major office equipment suppliers in the area. The company has been purchased by a larger corporation, which may affect pricing and delivery policies. The news release offers no details but raises many questions about whether Office-To-Go will remain competitive with other suppliers.

Analyzing Tasks and Choosing the Best Medium

Because Miguel is alone, he decides to spend the day following up on business leads, answering the phone, and responding to emails and letters. As a first step, Miguel uses the first phase of the ACE process to analyze his communication tasks using three criteria: Do others need the information quickly? Will the task be easy for me to do, or should someone else handle it later? Is it in the business's best interest for me to answer quickly?

TASK 1: Review the 11 messages and prioritize each item by putting a 1 next to those that must be handled today, a 2 next to items that should be handled today if there is time, and a 3 next to items that can wait. Then, for each item, do a quick analysis. Identify the purpose of Miguel's communication, the audience, and the best medium option: letter, memo, email, IM, telephone, meeting, and so forth. Be prepared to explain your choices.

Composing Good News in Response to a Claim

Miguel has good news to deliver to his client, Kristina Ivanska. He received an email from her insurer, indicating that the company will pay 100 percent of the replacement/repair cost for her roof, which was severely damaged in a wind storm, minus the $250 deductible.

Ms. Ivanska will get her payment in two installments. She will immediately receive a check for $7,242, which is the value of her seven-year-old roof. Then when she has the roof repaired, the company will pay the difference between what it has already paid and the actual repair cost minus the $250 insurance deductible. She doesn't need to rush to have the roof repaired because she has up to 180 days to submit the bill for the repairs.

Miguel is eager to communicate this news to Ms. Ivanska, so he decides to call her. He begins the conversation with good news: *"Ms. Ivanska, I wanted to let you know that Bill Baker, the insurance adjuster, will be stopping by your house next week with a check for $7,242 to cover your roof damage."* Much to Miguel's surprise, Ms. Ivanska was very upset. She said: *"But I just got an estimate from the roofing company for $9,850 to replace the roof. I thought my insurance covered 'replacement value.' There's a $2,500 difference! How can I pay for that?"*

Miguel immediately realizes that he had organized his message the wrong way. He tries to calm Ms. Ivanska: *"Don't worry. The insurance will cover the full cost except for your $250 deductible. I'm just explaining it wrong. Let me write you a letter, and I'll drop it by your house on my way home. It will make everything clear."*

TASK 2: Write the good-news letter for Miguel. Be sure that it accomplishes the following goals:

- Delivers the good news in a way that Ms. Ivanska will understand and that calms her concerns

- Explains what the insurance company will do and what she needs to do

- Reestablishes her confidence in Ramirez & Associates as an insurance broker

Evaluating a Routine Message

After he handles the priority messages, Miguel turns his attention to the Office-To-Go announcement. Although it looks like a routine message, it is bad news to Miguel because he spent the past two months researching new office furniture and computer equipment from Office-To-Go. He made his choices and was about to prepare a proposal for his father. Now it is unclear whether the new vendor will carry the same brands, charge the same prices, or have the same service agreements.

Miguel decides to compose an email to the Office-To-Go manager to request information that will help him decide whether to find a new vendor. Miguel quickly composes the letter below and hopes to revise it by the end of the day.

TASK 3: Evaluate this letter and suggest revisions and corrections Miguel should make before sending it.

Spending a Few Moments to Create Goodwill

It is 4:45 PM, and Miguel has barely left his desk. He has been talking on the telephone, composing messages, and placing orders. As Miguel sits back in his chair, he recalls his father saying, *"Miguel, every day before I leave work, I make sure I've given someone a 'gift'—a thank you, a word of congratulations, or even just a smile. Remember, the time you invest making someone else feel good will help you build goodwill."*

Miguel has been so intent on his work today that he hasn't spent one moment thinking about how to give someone a "gift." He glances down at his list of messages, looking for an opportunity to build goodwill for Ramirez & Associates—or for himself.

TASK 4: Review the 11 messages at the beginning of this case scenario to identify ways to build goodwill. This is a good opportunity to think creatively. Summarize your ideas in a message to your instructor.

---

letter

Ramirez & Associates Insurance

8713 Hillview | Quincy, MA 02170 | 800-555-9000 | fax: 617-555-0000

November 18, 20XX

Sales Manager
Office-To-Go
7633 Raintree Drive
Weymouth, MA 02188

Subject: Your Recent Announcement

I have been planning a large order of furniture and computer equipment with Office-To-Go and was very upset to receive the announcement that your company has merged with another and may not be carrying the same items. Ramirez & Associates has been a loyal customer of Office-To-Go for the past five years, and this change will greatly inconvenience us.

I need to determine whether to continue my plans to order from your company or to switch to another office equipment supplier in the South Shore area. To make a decision, I need to know whether you will be honoring the prices in your current furniture and equipment catalog and what discounts you will offer for bulk purchases. That assumes, of course, that you will be carrying the same items as in your current catalog. Will you?

I also need to know what freight company you will be using and how insurance will be handled. Will OTG technicians set up the furniture and equipment delivered? What's the turnaround time from order to delivery? Since I'm also deciding on whether to use OTG for other things, I'd also like to know whether OTG will be able to personalize stationery on site, or will it have to be outsourced?

Please respond by November 30 so that I may place an order by the end of the year. You can contact me at the phone number provided above or by email (mramirez@ramirezinsurance.com).

Sincerely,

Miguel Ramirez

Study Questions in Review

 How do you compose messages containing questions and requests? *(pages 124–129)*

Most workplace communication involves routine business messages that are short and to the point. Use the ACE process to make good decisions when analyzing, composing, and evaluating your messages.

- **Decide between a direct or an indirect message** when composing routine messages that ask questions or make requests. In most cases, state your request directly. However, if the audience needs information to understand or be convinced about your request, use an indirect message.
- **Provide reasons for the request** when necessary.
- **Adopt a "you" perspective and include audience benefits** in all messages that ask questions or make requests. Internal benefits are advantages that your audience directly receives, and external benefits are advantages that someone else gains.
- **Conclude with gratitude and a call for action.**

 How do you compose informational messages? *(pages 129–136)*

The best informational messages are direct and easy to read. They also take advantage of opportunities to build goodwill.

- **Reply to questions with a direct answer.** Begin with a positive response, follow the organization of the original message—using corresponding numbers when appropriate—and end with a friendly closing.
- **Respond to customer requests and comments by creating goodwill.** This is especially important when customers are requesting refunds, exchanges, or repairs.
- **Highlight key points in confirmation messages.** A confirmation is a message acknowledging that you have received information or checking that you have understood information correctly.
- **Organize routine announcements so they are easy to skim.** Announcements are messages that publicly notify people of information they need or want to know.
- **Format instructions so readers can easily follow the steps.** Begin with an overview, divide instructions into numbered or bulleted lists, and begin each step with an action verb (or a conditional phrase, if the step is necessary only under certain conditions). Use parallel phrasing to ensure the same grammatical form for each item. Position any needed explanation after the action rather than before it.
- **Keep text and IM messages short and focused.** Do not include extraneous information or start conversations that will be hard to continue as texts.

 What kinds of messages build goodwill in business relationships? *(pages 136–141)*

Goodwill is a term used to describe the attitude of friendliness and caring that is central to creating, solidifying, and maintaining relationships.

- **Thank-you messages** offer you the opportunity to express appreciation and make your recipients feel good about something they have done for you. They also offer you the opportunity to express and display your professionalism. Thank-you messages range from formal letters to informal emails, handwritten notes, and telephone calls. The main challenge in writing a good thank-you note is to include specific content that relates to the act for which you are thanking someone. A generic note loses much of its effectiveness.
- **Congratulatory messages** build goodwill by recognizing someone else's achievements or important events. These events could be professional or personal.
- **Sympathy messages** are written to colleagues and business acquaintances to show your compassion and understanding. Although you can take advantage of preprinted sympathy cards to deliver your messages, also include a few handwritten lines to personalize the message and promote goodwill.
- **"For-your-information" messages** are sent to pass along information or communicate something you believe your audience will appreciate. These friendly messages keep channels of communication open, solidify relationships, and initiate dialogues that may lead to business benefits.

Visual Summary

Medium
Routine messages are the day-to-day communications that take advantage of every medium avilable.

Requests
Requests should be DIRECT when your audience will easily understand your question and why you are asking it.

Goodwill Messages
Create goodwill and maintain relationships by sending messages that offer thanks, congratulations, sympathy, and information (FYI).

Be INDIRECT only when your audience needs to know the context of the situation to understand your request.

Avoid IMPLICIT requests that leave your audience searching for the meaning of your message.

ACE — Analyze, Compose, Evaluate

Depending on the context, goodwill messages...
- express professionalism,
- include specific content,
- recognize achievements,
- show compassion and understanding, and
- personalize the message.

Informational Messages

For informational messages, start with the main idea, highlight any benefits, follow up with details, and end with a friendly closing.

Key Terms

Announcement p. 134
Audience benefits p. 127
Confirmation message p. 132
Congratulatory message p. 139
External benefits p. 127

For-your-information (FYI)
    message p. 140
Goodwill message p. 124
Implicit request p. 125
Internal benefits p. 127

Parallel phrasing p. 134
Routine business message
    p. 124
Sympathy message (also
    called condolences) p. 139

Thank-you message p. 136
"You" perspective p. 126

MyLab Business Communication

If your instructor is using MyLab Business Communication, go to **www.pearson.com/
mylab/business-communication** to complete the problems marked with this icon ⭐.

Review Questions

1 Under what circumstances would you choose to use an indirect routine message rather than a direct one?

⭐ **2** Why is the "you" perspective important for routine requests?

⭐ **3** Why is goodwill so important to business communication, especially when responding to customer requests?

4 What goodwill techniques can you use in routine messages?

5 How can you organize a routine announcement to make it easy to skim?

6 Explain three formatting techniques that make instructions easy for readers to follow.

⭐ **7** What pitfalls should you watch out for in sending business text messages?

8 Why should you personalize a thank-you message?

⭐ **9** Describe three benefits of sharing FYI messages with colleagues.

10 What are two communication tools (other than email and telephone) that facilitate paperless communication of routine messages?

Critical Thinking Questions

1 Many of the routine messages in this chapter are just a few sentences long. Explain why using each phase of the ACE communication process—analyzing, composing, and evaluating—is helpful even for short, routine messages.

2 Explain the possible negative outcomes of sending routine messages that do not include audience benefits or wording that promotes goodwill.

3 As this chapter explains, in some instances it may be unethical to include a bcc in an email. Explain a situation, other than those described in the chapter, in which forwarding an email might be considered unethical. **[Related to the Ethics feature on page 136]**

4 Writing a message to request a refund, a repair, or an exchange provides one advantage over a telephone call: You have written documentation of your request, and you will receive a written response. However, sometimes you may prefer to call a customer service representative because an oral conversation allows better feedback and a quicker resolution. If you choose to communicate your claim request by telephone, what details about the conversation should you document? What method of documentation would you choose?

5 This chapter explains one reason you might choose to make a request in person rather than by email: It may be more difficult for your audience to refuse the request. What are other reasons you may choose to make a request in person?

6 If you were granting a customer a refund for a faulty product, why might you also include a discount for a future purchase? The customer is getting what she asked for, so why do more?

7 Assume that you need to communicate to all employees a new policy about business use of texting. Explain the factors that would affect your choice of medium to share this information.

⭐ **8** Explain why you should send a thank-you note after all your employment interviews, even with companies you are no longer interested in pursuing.

9 American business culture is competitive. People compete for jobs, promotions, and raises. In this competitive culture, why would you concern yourself with building goodwill with colleagues?

⭐ **10** If you were writing a goodwill message to someone from another culture, would you choose to follow your own cultural standards or those of your audience? Why? How could you find out what those cultural standards are? **[Related to the Culture feature on page 137]**

Key Concept Exercises

 SQ1 **How do you compose messages containing questions and requests?** *(pages 124–129)*

1 Decide between a direct or an indirect message

Most routine messages should be organized directly, with the main point positioned at the beginning of the message. Rewrite the following messages to use a direct approach and revise the wording to create a more effective message based on clarity, conciseness, style, and tone. Compare your direct revision to the indirect original. Which version would you choose to send? Explain why.

a. **Email** to Professor Fisher: My sister is getting married this weekend, and I am in the wedding party. It's a five-hour drive, so in order to get to the wedding rehearsal Friday afternoon, I have to leave before noon on Friday, which means I won't be able to attend our 2 pm class. I know that missing your lecture will put me at a disadvantage for next week's exam, but you said you would take our term papers early if we got them done, which I did, so it's attached. Please confirm that you received the attachment. I'd be happy to bring by a hard copy if you would prefer. Thanks, [Your Name]

b. **Voice mail message** to a customer service department: Hi. This is Kent from Simi Valley Automotive. Last week, we placed an order from your recent promotional catalog. We ordered 24 sets of your model #42 windshield wipers. We received the shipment today, but found 42 sets of your model #24 windshield wipers. Although we stock both models, our supply of model #42 is very low, and we now have twice as many model #24 sets. What can you do to help? Please call me at 555-1234. Thanks!

c. **Letter** to a prospective tenant: Dear Mr. Abrams: Thank you for your recent request for additional information about our summer rental facilities. I agree that we have several interesting options to choose from, and without specific pricing details, it is difficult to make an informed decision. If you reserve your rental from the attached pricing list before April 1, I can offer you a 10 percent discount. Enclosed is the price list you requested. Thanks, [Your Name]

d. **Memo** to department managers: As you know, recycling is a very important goal for our company. Our efforts to make the planet clean and green extend beyond our corporate walls. We encourage every employee to recycle at home as well as work. The original blue recycling containers that were placed in each break room and reception area several years ago will be replaced with larger green containers that have separate receptacles for paper, plastic, glass, and metals. Please remind the employees in your department to recycle as much as possible. Thanks, [Your Name]

e. **Face-to-face conversation:** Hi, Hiro. You know that memo about the new travel forms we're supposed to use? Well, I'm going to a conference next week in Las Vegas—nice, huh?—although I've already asked Thad to cover for me while I'm gone, after reading the memo, I wasn't sure if we had to ask someone who is actually in our department to cover for us. I was hired to replace Thad when he moved up to management, so he knows my job better than anyone else—not that I think there will be much for him to do while I'm gone—but I didn't want my travel request to get hung up in the process if I had to ask someone else. Do you know?

2 Provide reasons for the request

Your first job after college requires you to move to a new city, Louisville, Kentucky, where you don't know anyone. You want to get involved with activities outside of work where you can meet people, so you attend a meeting of the Young Professionals Association of Louisville. Because you enjoyed the meeting, you sign up to join and provide your credit card number for the membership fee. Two weeks later, as you review your online credit card statement information, you notice that your annual dues were charged at the $100 premium member fee rather than the $50 new-member fee that was advertised during the meeting. To get your $50 back, you email the organization. You do not know the name of the president or the treasurer. However, you do have a general email address: YPAL@louisville.net. Draft your email requesting a refund.

3 Adopt a "you" perspective and include audience benefits

For each of the following claim responses, revise the message to use the "you" perspective and include audience benefits.

a. Thank you for contacting us about the Internet outage in your area. We restored the connection.

b. We are sorry that one of the pizzas delivered to your office last week was cold. Enclosed is a refund.

c. We regret that one of the eight office chairs you ordered was damaged during delivery. We are shipping a replacement today.

d. You're right. You were charged incorrectly. We will credit your account today.

e. The headset you returned could not be repaired. We're enclosing a new one for your convenience.

4 Conclude with gratitude and a call for action

The following email exchange consists of five separate short messages. Revise the messages to conclude with an appropriate call for action. Where appropriate, include other techniques such as an expression of gratitude, a "you" perspective, and audience benefits.

a. Hi, Peter: Will you be able to take on the new Meggison marketing project? I'm simply overwhelmed with the Pagel campaign and don't know how I would handle both projects simultaneously. Thanks, Larry

b. Hi, Larry: Sure, I can work on the Meggison project.—Peter

c. Peter: I am so glad you accepted my offer to lead the new Meggison marketing project. I have so much on my plate right now, you just can't imagine! I expect you will call me with any questions you have. I need your proposal as soon as possible.—Larry

d. Larry: Attached is my rough draft for the Meggison proposal.—Peter

e. Peter: Attached are my suggested revisions for the Meggison proposal.—Larry

 SQ2 **How do you compose informational messages?** *(pages 129–136)*

5 Reply to questions with a direct answer

As the director of human resources at UrbanLife, you receive several requests each week from students for information about internship opportunities at your company. Although you respond to each request individually, you often reply with the same information. Rather than typing the same information each time, you decide to create a template of responses that you can cut, paste, and modify as necessary to personalize each message. The requests often include the following questions:

a. Do you provide internships? *Answer:* Yes.

b. If so, in what areas? *Answer:* All departments.

c. What is the timeline for reviewing applications? *Answer:* Usually a four- to six-week response.

d. When during the academic year do you hire interns? *Answer:* Accepted throughout the year.

Draft a sample email response that you could use to respond to any request for internship information. Include the suggested elements: Begin with the positive response, include all requested information, and end with a friendly closing. Remember the importance of creating goodwill with your response by striking an appropriate tone.

6 Respond to customer requests and comments by creating goodwill

Callan Reis wrote to her company's employee benefits director to appeal the director's decision not to reimburse certain health care expenses. The benefits director drafted the following message, responding positively to Callan's appeal. However, in evaluating this message before sending, the writer determined the message did not do a good job of promoting goodwill. What changes would you recommend to the writer?

Accompanies Exercise 6

7 Highlight key points in confirmation messages

As a new intern at a large marketing company, you provide assistance to a wide variety of project managers and their staff. The diverse experience is valuable but requires significant attention to detail to ensure you remember what you're supposed to do for whom and by when. You have been keeping detailed notes; however, sometimes in the course of running an errand someone will ask you to do something when you don't have your notes with you. This happened today. As you were copying documents and collating materials into presentation packets for a client meeting, Lydia Homer, the team leader for the project presentation, looked in the copy room and said, *"Don't forget to include the original RFP in the packets. When you're done with all that, take the packets to Brian for labeling. Use the 5164 size. Sally has the list of names. Thanks."* Before you could respond, Lydia hurried down the hall to another meeting. You realize you don't know what an RFP is, you don't know Brian or Sally, and now you can't remember whether she said 5164 or 5614. Because your copy machine has another 500 pages

to print, you decide to email Lydia to confirm the information and ask for clarification. Draft the message.

8 Organize routine announcements so they are easy to skim

You manage *City Kids*, a large daycare facility in the downtown area. You want to announce your expanded hours to your current clientele as well as employees of local businesses (potential customers) near your facility. Your old hours were 7:30 AM to 6:30 PM. Beginning the first of next month, you will be open from 7:00 AM until 7:00 PM. The daycare facility has a comprehensive website and an active listserv that includes each parent's email address. Create additional information to draft an announcement, and identify the medium options you could use to distribute this message. How would the draft change based on the medium?

9 Format instructions so readers can easily follow the steps

Your company is planning to recruit new employees at several college-sponsored job fairs and has decided to staff the booths with current employees from throughout the company. You have a full schedule of volunteers for the fairs. You wrote the short set of instructions in the following paragraph, which you plan to distribute at an orientation session for volunteers. Before the session, though, you decide to revise the instructions to make them easier to follow. Reformat (and revise, if necessary) the following text to create a one-page instruction sheet for volunteers. As you revise, consider which steps are separate and which can be grouped together.

instructions

Protocol for Job Fair Booth Volunteers

Greet the student (that is, prospective employee). Shake hands and introduce yourself. Ask the student's name. Give the student the company brochure. Outline the nature of the jobs you are recruiting for, without going into too much detail. Focus on the benefits of working for our company. Ask if the student has any questions. Answer any questions you can and take notes about any question that you cannot answer. Thank the student for his or her interest in our company and wish the student good luck in his or her job search.

Accompanies Exercise 9

10 Keep text and IM messages short and focused

You have been assigned to pick up office supplies for a project team retreat. When you get to the store, you cannot remember whether your team's leader said that she already had sticky notes of the specific size and color the team needs. (a) Draft a text message asking for clarification. (b) Next, assume that the store will close in ten minutes, and the meeting starts first thing tomorrow. Your text has not been answered. List your options and give your reasons for selecting one. (c) Write a second text to the team leader to explain what you did.

 What kinds of messages build goodwill in business relationships? *(pages 136–141)*

11 Thank-you messages

You work for a large tax accounting firm, and one of your satisfied customers, Andrea Stockton, wrote a very complimentary email about you to the senior vice president. Based on your work, the customer also referred a colleague (Evan Russert) to your company. The senior vice president forwarded you a copy of this email. Send your customer a thank-you message.

12 Congratulatory messages

This is your fifth year as the head of new client development for a small consulting company. Your assistant, Madeline, has been extremely helpful since your first day. After 30 years of service to the company, Madeline is retiring. You have organized her retirement party and selected a beautifully inscribed silver plaque. However, you're not sure what to write in her farewell card. Although you will miss her knowledge and talents, you know she is looking forward to retirement and plans to begin with a two-week Caribbean cruise. Draft a congratulatory message to Madeline.

13 Sympathy messages

You are a sales consultant for a regional distribution company. Your biggest client, Jana, has also become a good friend. Last year, Jana's son, Brian, was diagnosed with leukemia. Your client meetings have been less frequent lately, since Jana has been working from home, but you've managed to stay in contact by email. This morning, the first email you open is from Jana. It's a message sent to dozens of people to inform them that Brian died peacefully in his sleep a week ago. Jana's message thanks the group for their continued support during the past year and indicates that donations can be made in Brian's name to the Children's Leukemia Center. Although your instinct is to reply by email, you know a handwritten sympathy note is more appropriate. Draft your message.

14 "For-your-information" messages

Jim O'Callahan is your company's vice president of marketing. Last week you sat next to Jim at a business dinner. In conversation, Jim mentioned how much he admired Abraham Lincoln as a leader. The next day, as you were browsing through your local bookstore, you saw a book by Eric Foner, *The Fiery Trial: Abraham Lincoln and American Slavery*. This made you think of Jim's comments, and you bought the book. You've read only three chapters, but you are really enjoying it. You wonder if Jim has read it. Write a message to Jim that lets him know about this new book.

Writing Exercises

15 Revising a routine message

Refer to a routine informational message that you received recently—perhaps an email from your school or a letter from your insurance agent or utility company. Explain how the message adheres to or deviates from the suggestions outlined in this chapter. Summarize your findings in an email message to your instructor. Use headings to target each key concept outlined in the chapter.

16 Writing routine messages

Each of the following messages has a problem. It may be too short, too wordy, or have the wrong tone. For each of the scenarios represented by the message, compose a new message that you believe is well organized, includes enough information to be effective, and builds goodwill. Create any additional information that you need.

   a. **Email.** Hi, Jane: Attached are the files you requested. Regards, Jill.

   b. **Voice mail message.** This is Maria Martinez from Accounting. I need more information than you provided on your recent travel expense report. Please call me at Ext. 1440 as soon as possible. Thanks.

   c. **Memo.** To All Employees: Please stop throwing away your plastic water bottles. We have recycling bins in several convenient locations. Thanks!

   d. **Flyer posted in break room.** Volunteers Needed for Blood Drive—Call Ext. 550 for Info!

   e. **Comment made during a meeting.** As the chair of the social committee, I think it's important that we do a better job of recognizing birthdays in our department. I'll take the responsibility of buying and routing cards for signatures prior to each person's birthday, but you all need to chip in. Five dollars per person will cover the cost of the card and muffin from the coffee shop. Sound okay?

17 Requesting a favor

You own a consulting business that provides communication training. This morning, Tim Merrick of LabCorp left a voice mail message on your office phone to request that you present a one-hour email etiquette workshop for his staff of 25 people next week during their professional development retreat. You have presented several workshops for Tim's company in the past and look forward to continuing your business relationship with him, but you will be out of town next week on another consulting job and won't be available. Rather than reply to Tim with bad news, you would prefer to find a replacement and decide to ask one of your associates, Kathryn, to conduct the email etiquette workshop. Although Kathryn has not presented this topic before, she is an excellent presenter. You have an email etiquette PowerPoint presentation, handout materials, and group activities you have used successfully in the past. Kathryn just needs to get familiar with the content to prepare for the workshop. Because you need a response quickly, you decide to send an email to Kathryn, asking her to conduct the workshop. Use the ACE process to analyze the situation, compose the email, and evaluate it. Submit your final draft email to your instructor.

18 Requesting information

In your role as a human resources specialist, you help new employees determine which retirement benefit packages best fit their personal needs. After spending the entire morning meeting separately with three people about the same issues, you realize that you typically ask each person the same questions. Rather than continue to take the time to collect this information in person, you decide it would be more efficient to have employees prepare this information ahead of time. Your questions involve their current age and planned retirement age, minimum level of annual income needed in retirement for recurring expenses, anticipated special circumstances in retirement (such as children's college tuition or weddings), desired lifestyle during retirement, and current rate of savings. You also need to know whether they prefer low-risk investments that are more stable but may provide less return on investment or high-risk investments that are less stable but may provide a high return on investment. Compose a memo to new employees that will be included with their orientation materials. Your memo should indicate that as a human resources specialist, you are available to schedule individual appointments to discuss retirement benefit packages. You would like the new employees to bring typed responses to these questions to their scheduled appointments.

19 Respond to claim requests by creating goodwill

Assume that you are a private attorney running your practice out of your home. A friend suggests that creating a website for your business might enhance your client base and recommends a college student, Kent Miller. You contact Kent, discuss content and images, and agree to his hourly fees. A week later, Kent sends you a draft of your website and an invoice for $300. The site looks great, so you send him a check and thank him for his work. A few days later, Kent emails you to indicate that although he looks forward to continuing to work on your website project, he is concerned that the check you sent was for $200, which was $100 less than the invoiced amount. You refer to your checking account register and realize you made a mistake. Respond to Kent's email.

20 Scheduling a meeting [Related to the Technology feature on page 133]

Assume that you need to determine the best day and time to schedule a team meeting with eight colleagues to discuss the agenda for an upcoming staff retreat. Create an online poll to determine when everyone can meet. Identify five different options. Then compose an email message that explains the meeting and includes directions about how to use the poll. (Assume that your colleagues have not used this poll feature before.)

21 Responding with both congratulations and sympathy

You are a regional supervising manager for a large retail chain and have 36 store managers who report to you. One of them, Paulina, asked you to write a recommendation letter to support her application to be a supervising manager in another region, which you happily provided. You knew that several well-qualified people were applying for the job as well and that it would be a significant accomplishment if Paulina got the promotion. This morning, Paulina emailed you to let you know that she was offered the position but couldn't accept it. After she applied, her parents—who live nearby—were in a car accident and suffered serious injuries. They both required surgery and will need Paulina's help during the next several months as they recover. This is not a good time for her to move to another state. Draft a reply that sympathizes with Paulina's situation and ensures your support as she juggles her job with her care-giving responsibilities but also congratulates her for earning the promotion and assures her that she will have similar opportunities in the future.

Collaboration Exercises

22 Improving routine messages with informal collaboration [Related to the Collaboration feature on page 141]

Figure 4.12 on page 135 is an email message from Ryan Devlin that explains how to complete a new travel authorization form. Assume that you are Ryan and are about to send the message to all the employees at your company—all 728 people! You want to make *very sure* that the message is as perfect as possible, so you forward it to a coworker, Marilyn, and ask her to help you review it. Compose a message to Marilyn to ask for her input. Use the questions in the Collaboration feature as a guide but do not copy the questions verbatim. Make them specific to this situation.

23 Analyzing goodwill messages: Dr. Martin Luther King Jr.

As a minister, manager, and leader of an organization, Martin Luther King Jr. was a prolific communicator. Beyond the speeches for which he is famous, he wrote many letters and telegrams, including goodwill messages. You can find many of these messages at http://kingencyclopedia.stanford.edu/encyclopedia/documents_contents.html, including:

- Congratulations telegram to Thurgood Marshall on being appointed to the Supreme Court
- Sympathy telegram to Mrs. Malcolm X on the death of her husband
- Telegram to Cesar Chavez

As a team, select two messages and analyze how they reflect the guidelines for goodwill messages in the textbook—and teach you additional things about achieving goodwill, beyond the textbook. What do you notice about King's writing style? How would you describe the tone of these messages? If you believe King achieves a sense of authenticity in his messages, what leads to that authenticity? Write a short email to your professor that summarizes the results of your discussion.

24 Identifying audience benefits

As a team, assume that you are the human resources staff for a small regional hospital with a workforce of approximately 500 (physicians, nurses, administrators, support staff, and volunteers). Your department routinely sends messages to all employees. For each of the following "To All" scenarios, brainstorm audience benefits that you can incorporate into the message. Revise each message to include at least one audience benefit and build goodwill.

a. To All: The employee parking area will be repaved next week. The crew will pave the north half of the lot on Monday and the south half on Tuesday. Although half of the employee lot will be available at all times, arrangements have been made with the volunteer transportation services unit to run shuttles every 10 minutes from the overflow parking area to the main hospital entrance. Thank you for your cooperation.—HR Dept.

b. To All: Next Friday between 10 AM and 2 PM, the Volunteers' Association will be hosting a bake sale in the lobby area outside the cafeteria. All proceeds from the sale will support the new free clinic. Donations are also accepted. Thank you for supporting this worthy cause!—HR Dept.

c. To All: Our new insurance forms are now available. Please stop by the HR Dept. to register for the new coverage options. If you don't update your records by the end of the month, you will not be able to select plan options until the next quarter.—HR Dept.

d. To All: The gift shop in the lobby will be renovated next month. To help reduce the inventory before the renovations begin, all items have been reduced 25 percent. As usual, your hospital ID badge gives you an extra 10 percent discount. Thanks for helping us clear the shelves before we tear them down!—HR Dept.

e. To All: Although our hospital campus has been tobacco-free for several years, we've recently received several complaints from the custodian services supervisor that cigarette butts have been found in the garbage cans of several employee bathrooms throughout the building. Please refrain from using any tobacco products in the hospital or on the grounds. Thank you for your cooperation.—HR Dept.

25 Exploring cultural expectations [Related to the Culture feature on page 137]

As a team, select a country and research its customs and expectations for showing gratitude, saying thank you, and building goodwill. For example, what are the customs and expectations about gift giving? Is it expected, discouraged, or optional? Is a written thank-you note more appropriate than a spoken one? Or is an oral thank you more expected? Each team member should look at different sources and discuss similarities and differences among the findings. Potential resources include the eDiplomat and CyborLink websites. Use your favorite search engines to find others. Prepare a two-minute presentation for your class about saying thank you and building goodwill in that country. Be sure to include a list of your sources and be prepared to identify which one was most helpful and why.

Social Media Exercises

26 Analyzing routine "visual" messages in companies' nonverbal posts

Find a company's posts on Pinterest, Instagram, Snapchat, or another social media application that uses images more than words to share information. Copy three or more posts and explain what each one communicates. Who is the intended audience? What is the purpose of each message? Do they build goodwill? Summarize your findings in a short report to your instructor.

27 Analyzing goodwill in companies' Facebook announcements

Find announcements from three different companies' Facebook sites that communicate routine information, such as a new product offering, an upgrade, or new version of a software application. Identify the elements of the messages that communicate goodwill with the audience. For messages that do not include any content designed to build goodwill, identify how they could be revised to do so. For messages that do, compare how they create goodwill with the audience. Summarize your findings in a one- to two-paragraph email to your instructor.

28 Analyzing responses to social media complaints

Use a public social review site—such as Yelp, Amazon, or TripAdvisor—to find an example of a complaint or negative post about a company's product or service. Identify how the company responds to the post to rebuild goodwill and to give potential customers confidence in the company. Summarize your findings in a one- to two-paragraph email to your instructor.

Speaking Exercises

29 Impromptu speaking: Business role-plays

Refer to Exercise 7 on page 149. Assume the same scenario, except that Lydia gives you an opportunity to respond before she hurries down the hall to another meeting. Instead of "thanks," she ends her request with "Got that?" What do you say? Role-play this conversation with another student in class or record your response as a short video clip.

30 Making informal/impromptu presentations

a. Identify a routine message you recently wrote and explain the purpose, audience, content, and medium of the message. Was the message successful in achieving its purpose? How do you know? Share your information with your class in a short, informal oral presentation.

b. Identify one situation in which a business sent you a goodwill message or added goodwill content to a routine message. In a short, informal presentation, explain what the business communicated to you and whether the goodwill message made you feel positively about the business. Explain why or why not.

c. Explain how you have built and maintained goodwill with your friends. Provide at least three examples.

31 Presenting executive briefings

a. Imagine that your business wants to create a policy about when and how to use the blind carbon copy (bcc) feature in emails. Your team has been assigned to draft that policy. As a team, brainstorm situations when using bcc is effective and acceptable as well as some situations when it is not. Develop a short set of guidelines and share them with the class in a three- to five-minute presentation that includes a few slides. [**Related to the Ethics feature on page 136**]

b. Assume that you work for a small consulting company that provides training workshops and seminars to other companies, primarily in three states that cover two time zones. Scheduling these events for your clients involves coordinating schedules among many people, usually 25 to 40 people. You prefer to use Doodle, but your boss has heard that other free online scheduling tools may provide more features. Review at least three similar scheduling tools and compare the features they support. Set up polls with each one, research any articles or product reviews you can find, and summarize your findings in a three- to five-minute presentation. Support your presentation with slides that include screen shots of each scheduling tool as well as a recommendation slide that outlines why one of the tools is better than the others. [**Related to the Technology feature on page 133**]

Grammar Exercise

32 Prepositions and conjunctions (see Appendix C: Grammar, Punctuation, Mechanics, and Conventions—Section 1.1.4)

In the following paragraph, identify the prepositions (P), coordinating conjunctions (CC), correlative conjunctions (CorC), subordinating conjunctions (SC), and conjunctive adverbs (CA). There are a total of 10 prepositions and conjunctions. Count correlative conjunction pairs as one.

The way you begin a business call is very important; however, the conclusion is equally important. Have you ever been caught in an awkward spot, wondering who should end the call? If you initiated the call, the convention is for you to conclude it. After you have obtained the information you need, thank the person you called and then say good-bye. The person at the other end either can just say good-bye or can end with a pleasantry: for example, *"I'm glad I could help."*

MyLab Business Communication

Go to **www.pearson.com/mylab/business-communication** for Auto-graded writing questions as well as the following Assisted-graded writing questions:

1. Explain the possible negative outcomes of sending routine messages that do not include audience benefits or wording that promotes goodwill.

2. Why would customers feel better about a response to a complaint if the response is personally signed and if the responder says he will forward the complaint to someone who can solve the problem?

References

1. Chudnova, N. (2014, April 25). Business communications still defined by email according to results of new DeskAlerts survey. Retrieved from http://www.prweb.com/releases/2014/04/prweb11789898.htm

2. The Radicati Group. (2015). Email statistics report 2015–2019. Retrieved from http://www.radicati.com/wp/wp-content/uploads/2015/02/Email-Statistics-Report-2015-2019-Executive-Summary.pdf

3. Naragon, K. (2016, October 3). Email—Still the alpha channel. *Adobe Conversations*. Retrieved from https://blogs.adobe.com/conversations/2016/10/email-still-the-alpha-channel.html

4. Burkus, D. (2016, July 12). Why Atos Origin is striving to be a zero-email company. *Forbes*. Retrieved from http://www.forbes.com/sites/davidburkus/2016/07/12/why-atos-origin-is-striving-to-be-a-zero-email-company/

5. Shellenbarger, S. (2014, March 12). Email enigma: When the boss's reply seems cryptic. *The Wall Street Journal*. Retrieved from http://online.wsj.com/news/articles/SB10001424052702304704504579433233994478174

6. On the web, customer service stories move fast. (2013, April 23). Retrieved from http://www.emarketer.com/Article/On-Web-Customer-Service-Stories-Move-Fast/1009834

7. MacDonald, S. (2013, May 23). Why customer complaints are good for your business. Retrieved from http://www.superoffice.com/blog/customer-complaints-good-for-business/

8. McCann, D. (2016, July 24). Uber versus Lyft. The battle of ride-sharing customer service on Twitter. Retrieved from https://medium.com/help-handles-insight-series/uber-versus-lyft-the-battle-of-ride-sharing-customer-service-on-twitter-8bff5cfc7a3f#.iqrix02vk

9. Uber Support [Uber_Support]. (2016, August 11). That's absolutely unacceptable, Anthony. Please DM us your email address so we can connect. [Tweet]. Retrieved from https://twitter.com/Uber_Support/status/763933551817400327

10. Cook, K. (2016, October 17). 9 meeting scheduler tools to make your day more productive. [Blog post]. Retrieved from https://blog.hubspot.com/marketing/meeting-scheduler-tools-more-productive#sm.0000c0iew8z3mdkgrwb1aiu9h38mf

11. James, G. (2013, March 13). 16 rules for business texting. *Inc.* Retrieved from http://www.inc.com/geoffrey-james/16-rules-for-business-texting.html

12. HeyWire Business. (2014, January 29). HeyWire Business text messaging survey shows 67 percent of professionals are texting for business. Retrieved from http://heywire.com/in-the-news/heywire-business-text-messaging-survey-shows-67-percent-of-professionals-are-texting-for-business-2/

13. Burke, K. (2016, April 5). The 6 P's of texting in business. Retrieved from http://www.textrequest.com/blog/6-ps-texting-business/

14. DeFranco, M. (2015, August 26). Messaging and mobile in financial services. *Forbes*. Retrieved from http://www.forbes.com/sites/michaeldefranco/2015/08/26/messaging-and-mobile-in-financial-services/#1ddf409c2c48

15. Carr, D. (2016, August 15). Why messaging has the momentum in business collaboration. *Forbes*. Retrieved from http://www.forbes.com/sites/davidcarr/2015/08/18/why-messaging-has-the-momentum-in-business-collaboration/

16. The Slack generation: How workplace messaging could replace other missives. (2016, May 14). *The Economist*. Retrieved from http://www.economist.com/news/business/21698659-how-workplace-messaging-could-replace-other-missives-slack-generation

17. Mobile Marketing Association. (2012). Mobile wake up call: State of mobile today. Retrieved from http://www.slideshare.net/gregstuart/state-of-mobile-mma-simmons-final

18. Kindzierski, L. (2016, August 6). 8 great questions answered on providing text message customer service. Retrieved from http://www.execsintheknow.com/8-great-questions-answered-on-providing-text-message-customer-service/.

19. Tschabitscher, H. (2016, November 20). Sending an email to multiple recipients—cc: and bcc:. Retrieved from http://www.lifewire.com/sending-an-email-to-multiple-recipients-cc-and-bcc-1171178

20. Thompson, V. (2016). Is it ethical to include blind carbon copies in business e-mails? *Small Business Chronicle*. Retrieved from http://smallbusiness.chron.com/ethical-include-blind-carbon-copies-business-emails-81260.html

21. Atlas Updates. (2016, September 15). To BCC or not to BCC: Blind carbon copy etiquette. Retrieved from https://updates.atlas.co/to-bcc-or-not-to-bcc-blind-carbon-copy-etiquette

22. Garfinkle, J. (2014). Building positive relationships at work. Retrieved from http://garfinkleexecutivecoaching.com/articles/build-positive-work-relationships/building-positive-relationships-at-work

23. Better Business Bureau. (2016, February 23). The importance of relationships in business. Retrieved from http://www.bbb.org/mbc/news-centre/bbb-mbc-blog/2016/02/the-importance-of-relationships-in-business/.

24. Lewis, R. (2014, March 22). Quick tips: Handwritten notes making a comeback. *USA Today*. Retrieved from http://www.usatoday.com/story/money/personalfinance/2014/03/22/money-quick-tips-handwritten-note/6710895/

25. Cross, R., Rebele, R., & Grant, A. (2016 Jan–Feb). Collaborative overload. *Harvard Business Review*. Retrieved from https://hbr.org/2016/01/collaborative-overload

26. Milliken, G. (2014, January 6). The paperless office: 30-year old pipe dream? *Wired*. Retrieved from http://www.wired.com/2014/01/paperless-office-30-year-old-pipe-dream/

27. Mims, C. (2016, September 18). Why the paperless office is finally on its way. *The Wall Street Journal*. Retrieved from http://www.wsj.com/articles/why-the-paperless-office-is-finally-on-its-way-1474221512

28. Jabr, F. (2013). Why the brain prefers paper. *Scientific American*, *309*(5), 48–53.

29. Trend Hunter. (2014). Paper preservation: Innovations that promote paperless living. Retrieved from http://www.trendhunter.com/protrends/paper-preservation (see also http://www.gopaperless.com/Green-Commitment.aspx)

5 Communicating Persuasive Messages

STUDY QUESTIONS

(SQ1) How can the ACE process help you persuade your audience? pages 156–161

Analyzing helps you plan your message
Composing implements the persuasive plan
Evaluating helps you review the draft for effectiveness

(SQ2) What are the basic elements of persuasion? pages 161–170

Building credibility
Constructing a logical argument
Appealing to your audience's emotions

(SQ3) What types of business messages typically require persuasion? pages 170–178

Recommendations for action
Requests for favors
Persuasive customer claims
Sales messages

MyLab Business Communication

⭐Improve Your Grade!

If your instructor is using MyLab Business Communication, visit **www.pearson.com/mylab/business-communication** for videos, simulations, and writing exercises.

New Hires @ Work

Byron Smith
North Carolina A&T State University

Business Sales Manager @ AT&T Mobility

Persuasion is a skill you need to practice. The key is to figure out what people need to know to agree with your point of view. If you provide too much information, your point might get lost, and if you don't tell your audience enough about how your perspective benefits them, it will be easy for them to disagree with you. When I write a persuasive email, I go through several drafts and consider all the angles. In-person conversations are often a better option—it can be more difficult for someone to say no to your face.

Chapter 5 | Introduction

Your ability to engage and persuade an audience is a key element of your professional presence—and perhaps the most important ability you can develop as a business communicator. However, don't fall into the trap of thinking that being persuasive means winning arguments. Being argumentative is rarely a good persuasive strategy. Instead, think of **persuasion** as the process of influencing your audience to change their beliefs or actions in a way that leads to a desired outcome. In other words, persuasion is about creating change.

This chapter offers guidelines for applying the ACE process—analyzing, composing, and evaluating—to many types of persuasive situations. Being persuasive requires that you analyze your audience to understand what will motivate them and why they may resist your ideas. It also requires composing with persuasive techniques that will help you overcome resistance. Finally, it requires evaluating your communication objectively to ensure that you are providing the persuasive content that will, in fact, influence your audience.

(SQ1) How can the ACE process help you persuade your audience?

persuasion The process of influencing an audience to agree with your point of view, accept your recommendation, grant your request, or change their beliefs or actions in a way that facilitates a desired outcome.

To be persuasive, a message must do more than just state your point of view. It must also motivate your audience to agree with you. Using the ACE process will help you develop a message that accomplishes this goal.

Let's consider an example. Imagine that you are Pedro Baca, a customer service manager for an e-commerce company that has an annual goal to increase profits by improving customer service and cutting costs. To improve customer service, the company installed new computer software that tracks orders and allows employees to provide customers with immediate, accurate information. To cut costs, the company eliminated the training budget. Now you have a dilemma. Your employees received only a brief orientation and don't know how to use all the features of the new software. Customer complaints have increased, and you fear the company may alienate customers because of poor service. To solve this problem, you want to persuade your supervisor, Maria, to authorize money for training.

Your first thought is to write a quick email to Maria to request the funds. You sit down at the computer and write the following message:

> Maria: I am requesting funding to support a computer training workshop to ensure my department's employees will be more productive and customer complaints will decrease. I will call your assistant to schedule an appointment to discuss this soon. Thanks, Pedro.

This message simply asks for what you want. As you review this message, you wonder how Maria will react. Instead of sending the message, you rethink what you will say and how you will say it, using the ACE process.

Analyzing helps you plan your message

When persuading, you will increase your chances of getting a positive response by spending extra time on the analyzing phase of the ACE process. Recall that analyzing involves thinking strategically about these elements:

- Purpose, desired outcome, and desired business results of your message
- Audiences' and stakeholders' needs
- Content needs
- Medium choices

Analyze your purpose, desired outcome, and business result

Before focusing on what you will say in your message, think about your goal. What is the *purpose* of the message and what *outcome* would you like to achieve? In other words, why are you communicating and how would you like your audience to respond? If your audience agrees to your request or recommendation, what will the *business result* be? Understanding how your request will affect others and your business helps you anticipate how the audience might respond.

For example, your message to persuade Maria has the following purpose, outcome, and business result:

- The *purpose* is to request funding to support a training workshop.
- The *outcome* is that your audience (your supervisor) will provide the requested funds.
- The *business result* is that the employees will be more productive and provide improved customer service.

Analyze your audiences' and stakeholders' needs

Next, consider how to persuade your audience by analyzing them. Audience analysis involves imagining yourself in your audience's position and interpreting your message from your audience's perspective. Because persuasion involves influencing your audience's thinking and behavior, the more you know about your audience, the more persuasive you can be.

Consider both the **primary audience**, the direct recipients of the message, as well as the **secondary audience**, other people who may read or hear your message. The secondary audience may receive a copy of your message either from you or from your primary audience. You may even want to consider **stakeholders** who may be affected by the message. In the computer training workshop example, your supervisor (Maria) is your primary audience. The secondary audience may include the vice president of finance if Maria forwards your request to approve additional funds. Additional stakeholders include employees in the department and customers. Although employees and customers will not see your message, they will certainly be affected by the outcome.

To create a persuasive message for your audience, focus on analyzing what your audience needs to know, what might motivate or benefit them, and what might cause them to resist your proposal. Then design your message to address those needs and issues. **Figure 5.1** on page 158 presents Pedro's analysis and illustrates both how to analyze the audience and how to use the results to shape the content of your message.

Note in Figure 5.1 that you may respond to potential objections in two different ways: **refutation** or **concession**. You refute points by arguing that they are wrong. Alternatively, you concede points by admitting that they have merit or are partially correct but do not invalidate your argument. Think of refutation as saying, "*No, that is wrong, and here's why,*" and concession as saying, "*Yes, that may be true, but. . . .*" Whichever approach you use, be sure to state the opposing argument fairly, thoroughly, and in a way that lets the audience know that you understand their concerns.

Note, too, that you will be more effective if you avoid articulating objections, especially when your audience has not explicitly stated them: "*You may believe that training is too costly. However, customer service problems caused by insufficient training will cost more.*" Rather than putting words into your audience's mouth, simply build your argument so that it accounts for potential objections. Here's a better way to word the same information: "*Although training is costly, customer service problems caused by insufficient training will cost even more.*" Remember, the more objections you anticipate and address, the more persuasive you will be.

Analyze medium choices

Selecting the best medium for your persuasive message depends on many variables:

- The number of people in your audience and your ability to reach them all in a timely way
- The complexity of your content
- The amount of resistance you expect
- Your audience's communication preferences

Figure 5.2 on page 159 shows how to choose among various medium options when you need to persuade an audience.

primary audience The person or people to whom your message is addressed.

secondary audience People other than the primary audience who may read or hear your message.

stakeholders People who will be affected by the outcome of your message.

refutation A response intended to prove that an objection is wrong.

concession An admission that the opposing point of view has merit but does not invalidate your argument.

FIGURE 5.1 Example: How to Use Audience Analysis to Identify Content Needs

CATEGORY	QUESTIONS	PEDRO'S ANALYSIS OF PRIMARY AUDIENCE (MARIA) AND SECONDARY AUDIENCE (VP)	CONTENT TO PROVIDE
Information needs	What does your audience know about the situation? What do you need to tell your audience?	Maria knows that budget cuts have eliminated all professional development activities throughout the organization. She also knows that the company is committed to improving customer service. Maria does not yet know that productivity and customer service have suffered in your department because employees have not been trained to use the new computer systems.	Inform Maria that a costly problem exists and that the problem is related to insufficient training. You may have to research the actual costs associated with this problem.
Motivations and benefits	What will motivate your audience to accept your idea or comply with your request? How will your audience benefit from your proposed idea?	Maria probably will be motivated to solve the problem once she is aware that it exists. The VP of finance may be motivated to solve the problem if he understands that his investment in the new computer system is not yielding the expected benefit. Maria, the VP, and the company will benefit from improved productivity and customer satisfaction, as long as it does not cost too much.	Stress cost savings, improved productivity, and customer retention in order to highlight benefits for Maria. Stress an additional benefit for the VP: The training will increase the value of the investment he has already made in purchasing customer service software. The company will not see benefits from the software until the representatives are adequately trained.
Potential resistance	What concerns and objections will the audience have?	Maria may argue that: (1) training is the wrong solution because employees received some training when the system was installed and (2) the department simply cannot afford the training. She may be hesitant to bring a request for funds to the VP of finance because the company is committed to cutting costs. The VP will be opposed to spending more money unless he can see a clear financial benefit.	Address each potential argument with refutation or concession. **Possible objection:** *Employees already received sufficient training.* **Refutation:** *The training didn't teach employees many of the software functions necessary to deal effectively with customers' needs.* **Possible objection:** *Training is costly, and one of our corporate goals is to cut costs.* **Concession:** *Although training is costly, customer service problems caused by insufficient training will cost even more.*

Because persuasion is a process, it often requires multiple communications, with each message contributing to your persuasive goal. For example, if you know that Maria does not like surprise requests, you might consider sending an email message to mention your training idea and then scheduling an appointment to discuss the issue in more detail. The email must be persuasive to ensure that Maria will meet with you and be interested in what you have to say.

ACE

Compose

Composing implements the persuasive plan

After you analyze the content to make a persuasive plan, the composing stage helps you put the plan into action and draft the message. As **Figure 5.3** on page 160 illustrates, a well-planned message will be much more persuasive than a message composed without planning.

FIGURE 5.2 How to Select the Best Medium for Persuasive Messages

Choose a medium based on the criteria below. Do you want to:	One-to-One	Group Meeting	Telephone	Text/IM	Email	Memo	Letter	Newsletter	Website	Social Networking	Wikis, Blogs
Audience-Related Criteria											
Communicate a personal appeal to an individual?	■		■	■	■		■				
Communicate with large audiences?		■		■	■	■		■	■	■	■
Communicate with people already interested in your topic?	■	■	■	■	■	■	■	■	■	■	■
Communicate with potential audiences you cannot yet identify?									■	■	■
Content- and Response-Related Criteria											
Communicate a complex message?	■	■	■		■	■	■	■	■		
Include additional documents or supporting material (images, charts, video, etc.) that may help persuade your audience?	■	■			■	■	■	■	■	■	■
Receive immediate feedback so you can alter your appeal "on the fly" if necessary?	■	■	■								
Take time to think about any objections in the audience's reply, collect evidence if necessary, and compose a response?				■	■	■	■				
Give the audience time to consider your appeal carefully before responding?				■	■	■	■	■	■	■	■
Make it more uncomfortable for the audience to respond negatively (given the interpersonal interaction)?	■	■	■								

FIGURE 5.3 How to Compose a Persuasive Message

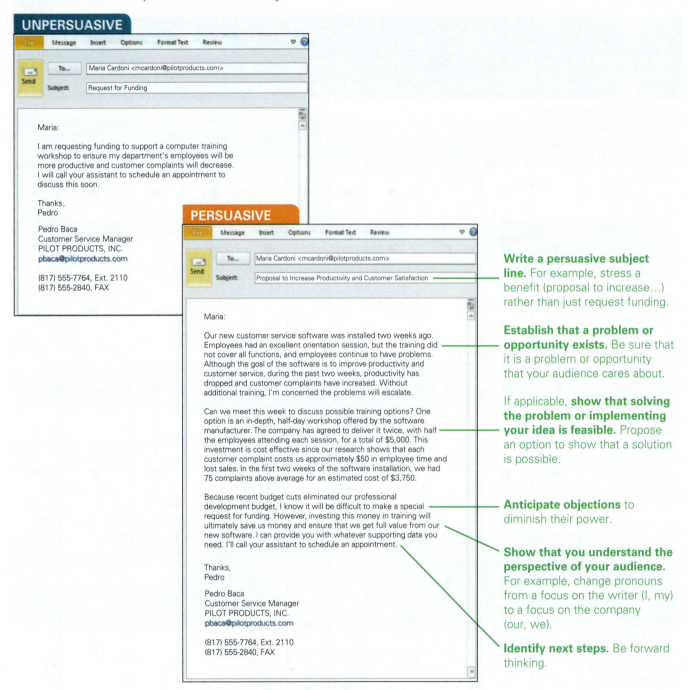

Write a persuasive subject line. For example, stress a benefit (proposal to increase…) rather than just request funding.

Establish that a problem or opportunity exists. Be sure that it is a problem or opportunity that your audience cares about.

If applicable, **show that solving the problem or implementing your idea is feasible.** Propose an option to show that a solution is possible.

Anticipate objections to diminish their power.

Show that you understand the perspective of your audience. For example, change pronouns from a focus on the writer (I, my) to a focus on the company (our, we).

Identify next steps. Be forward thinking.

Evaluating helps you review the draft for effectiveness

Even when you have thoroughly analyzed all the elements that contribute to a message and carefully composed the content, you should take additional time to evaluate the message before delivering it. Ask yourself several questions to ensure that you have implemented an effective persuasive strategy. **Figure 5.4** enumerates these key questions and provides examples of how you might respond to them as you evaluate the email to Maria. Although the final email to Maria is much longer than the original draft, the revised message takes advantage of the ACE process and has a greater chance of helping Pedro gain funding because its content and structure are persuasive.

FIGURE 5.4 Checklist for Evaluating a Persuasive Message

	EVALUATION QUESTIONS	EVALUATION OF PEDRO'S EMAIL TO MARIA
✓	**Have you convincingly shown that a problem or opportunity exists?**	**Yes.** The email shows that productivity is dropping and customer complaints are rising. The email also shows that customer complaints are costly.
✓	**Is the proposed solution or plan a good one?**	**Yes.** The email presents the training option as a realistic solution that is also cost effective.
✓	**Is the evidence and reasoning sound?**	**Yes.** The email shows documented evidence that each complaint costs $50. It provides sound reasoning that the cost of training is less than the cost of the problem.
✓	**Have you addressed all of the objections that you can anticipate?**	**Yes.** It addresses all the identified objections: Initial training should have been sufficient, the company has no money, and it's difficult to secure special funding.
✓	**Have you stressed benefits?**	**Yes, although the benefits are just implied.** If this solution solves the problems, it will increase productivity, reduce complaints, and retain more customers. The last paragraph of the message addresses one additional benefit: getting full value from the customer service software.
✓	**Is the message easy to read?**	**Yes.** The order of the content is logical (introduce problem, request meeting to discuss possible solutions, show that solutions are feasible, address objections, and identify next steps). In addition, the email uses effective paragraphing techniques.
✓	**Is the information complete, concise, clear, and correct?**	**Yes.** The message includes only the necessary information. The wording is clear, and the language and content are correct.
✓	**Do you need to change anything to get the result you want from your audience?**	**It looks good.** The desired result is a meeting. Evaluate the message from Maria's perspective. Will she believe a problem exists and the solution is reasonable? Will she believe she will benefit from a meeting? If so, then the message is ready to send. If not, then revise the message to get the desired result.

(SQ2) What are the basic elements of persuasion?

To develop the most effective content for your persuasive messages, you will need to understand the basics of persuasion. What kind of content will motivate your audience to trust you, believe your points, agree with your position, and do what you request? You learned about three elements of persuasion earlier in this chapter when Pedro prepared his email to Maria. His persuasive strategy included the following elements:

- Establishing a problem or need
- Focusing on benefits
- Anticipating potential resistance and objections

This section addresses three additional elements that have been recognized to be important since Aristotle identified them as the core of effective persuasion:[1,2]

- Building credibility (*ethos*)
- Constructing a logical argument (*logos*)
- Appealing to your audience's emotions (*pathos*)

Most persuasive business arguments combine all these elements, but you may decide to emphasize one element more than another.[3]

New Hires @ Work

Darrell Coleman
Georgia Southern University

Data Analyst @ George Southern
Career Services

You build credibility
by creating a sense
of responsibility
and trust. Once
that foundation is
created, people
will be more
willing to listen
and follow you.

Photo courtesy of Darrell Coleman

credibility An audience's belief that you
have expertise and are trustworthy based on
your knowledge, character, reputation, and
behavior.

Building credibility

Many experts suggest that the most critical element in persuasion is **credibility**.[4] If your audience believes you have expertise and are trustworthy based on your knowledge, character, reputation, and behavior, then they will be predisposed to accept your ideas.[5,6] You may already have credibility with your audience if they know and respect you, if you are an acknowledged expert, or if your beliefs and attitudes align with theirs.[7] However, if your audience is not predisposed to believe you, you will need to establish credibility. Even if your audience does know you, it's important to maintain credibility. Spelling your audience's name wrong and failing to proofread—among other things—will undermine your credibility and eliminate any advantage you may gain from using other persuasive techniques.

Use one or more of the following techniques to establish and maintain credibility:

- **Get to know your audience.** Have you ever noticed that skilled salespeople often spend a few minutes chatting with potential customers before trying to make a sale?[8] Talking with your audience before trying to persuade them allows you to build rapport and trust. It is easier to persuade an audience who likes you and believes that you understand their worries and goals.[9] Getting to know your audience has the added benefit of helping you identify their needs and concerns so that you can make sure to address them directly in your communication.

- **Establish your credentials.** You can build credibility with your audience by providing key credentials, including education, experience, awards, and expertise. You can also mention your relationship with someone the audience knows, respects, and believes to be credible. This *affinity*, or connection with a credible source, will help convince the audience that you are trustworthy.

- **Present your ideas effectively.** The quality of your communication also builds credibility. Audiences are more likely to believe you if you present an unbiased point of view, organize your ideas logically, and support those ideas with good research and sound reasoning. Even if you are not an expert yourself, you can add weight to your ideas by citing authorities and experts.

- **Tell the truth.** Billionaire investor Warren Buffett reportedly warns that, "It takes 20 years to build a reputation and five minutes to ruin it."[10] A person or company with a reputation for honesty or excellence can quickly lose credibility by making statements that prove to be untrue or by making promises that are not fulfilled. In the past few years, the Internet and social media have vastly increased the speed with which statements circulate and the scope of the audience who will be made aware of a company's mistakes or missteps.[11]

  Efforts to tap into the credibility-generating power of social media can also backfire. For example, many companies pay *social influencers* to promote products through social media. This persuasive tactic increases the company's credibility with people who follow the influencer's social media. However, when the company does not disclose that it is paying for the social media promotion, then it is both breaking the law and damaging its reputation. That is what happened to retailer Lord & Taylor when customers purchased outfits that fashion bloggers claimed to love, only to discover later that the retailer had paid the bloggers to promote the merchandise. The company was charged with a violation by the Federal Trade Commission for this error of omission and was forced to issue an apology.[12]

- **Take responsibility for mistakes.** One of the best ways to maintain and regain credibility is to admit personal responsibility.[13] Several years ago, when Toyota recalled 3.8 million vehicles for "unintended acceleration," Toyota Group Vice President Bob Carter stated that Toyotas had no additional problems and accused critics of engaging in "unwarranted speculation." Soon after, however, additional issues, including braking problems, came to light. Carter admitted that he had "shot some of [his] personal credibility" with his earlier comments.[14] These issues, and Toyota's unprecedented recall of millions of vehicles following Carter's acknowledgment, were associated with a significant drop in consumer confidence. But through accepting responsibility and avoiding further problems, Toyota has gradually been building back credibility and consumer trust.[15]

  Years later, Volkswagen faced similar issues. When the U.S. Environmental Protection Agency uncovered that Volkswagen had been lying about emissions results and had installed software in cars that resulted in cars falsely passing emissions tests, the company agreed to cooperate with authorities, and the CEO resigned. But neither the old nor the new CEO accepted personal responsibility. In fact, in an interview with National Public Radio, the new CEO claimed, "It was a technical problem. We had not the right interpretation of the American law . . . . We didn't lie. We didn't understand the question first."[16] Volkswagen's actions and attitudes undermined the company's credibility among consumers. In the year following the scandal, U.S. sales of Volkswagens significantly dropped.[17] It will take many years for Volkswagen to regain its credibility.

Because credibility is so critical for capturing an audience's attention and persuading them to listen, small companies often devote substantial space on their websites to building credibility. **Figure 5.5** illustrates how one small company presents itself online to instill confidence in potential clients.

FIGURE 5.5 How to Build a Small Business Website That Establishes Credibility

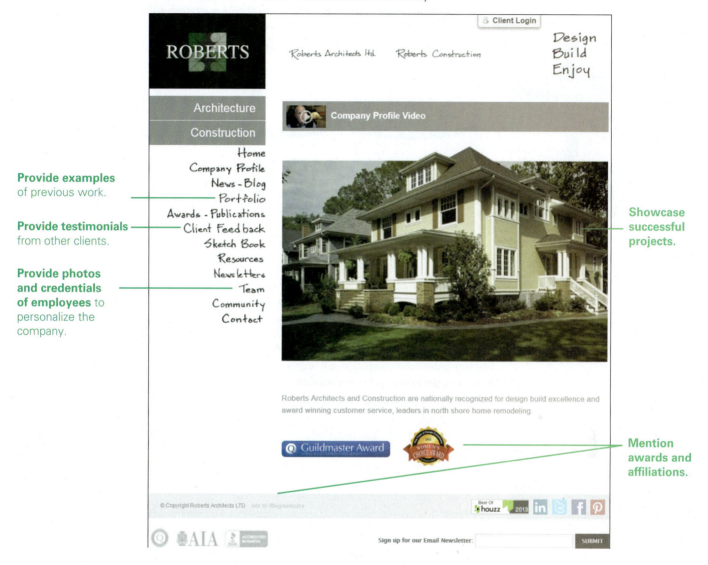

Constructing a logical argument

Developing credibility is a first and critical step in the process, but successfully persuading an audience also requires additional persuasive techniques, including building a logical argument.

Argumentation means taking a position and supporting the position with reasons further supported by evidence. Logical arguments provide the foundation for most persuasive business messages.

Earlier in this chapter, you considered how Pedro could persuade his supervisor, Maria, to support his request for funds to provide computer training to the customer service department. Pedro emailed Maria a short version of his argument (see Figure 5.3 on page 160) to persuade her to meet with him. Assume that Maria responded to Pedro with the following email message:

> *Pedro, your recommendation makes sense, and your timing is good. I am scheduled to meet with the vice president of finance tomorrow morning and would like to present your recommendation so that we can schedule the training as soon as possible. Please write a one-page document outlining the reasons and evidence that I can bring to the meeting. Thanks, Maria.*

argumentation A persuasive appeal that supports a position with reasons and evidence.

Figure 5.6 shows a way to structure that argument logically by defining the position, identifying reasons, and outlining evidence.

FIGURE 5.6 How to Structure a Logical Argument

In a logical argument like the one shown in Figure 5.6, the quality of your evidence is important. You can collect evidence by conducting your own original research (*primary research*) or by reading research that others have conducted (*secondary research*). Your evidence may take different forms, depending on the argument you are trying to support and the needs of your audience. Try to diversify your evidence. Like a stool that rests on three legs instead of one, arguments that combine a number of different types of evidence tend to be stronger and better balanced than ones that rely solely on a single kind. Consider the types of evidence that Pedro can use to support his argument:

- **Numerical data.** Many business arguments are based on numbers. Some arguments require data about costs, time, or revenue. Other arguments require data about customer preferences or business trends. You may find some of the numbers you need in published sources. Others will come from company records or from surveys and questionnaires. You can present the data in tables, graphs, or paragraphs. It's always important to provide context, such as comparisons or analogies, in order to emphasize the significance of the numbers—and therefore make them more persuasive.

- **Facts.** A fact is information documented either by your own research or by an external source—either way, it must be verifiable. If the fact is not already well known to the audience, you should cite the source. The more credible the source, the more persuasive the fact will be. A complete citation will include enough information that your audience can find the source on their own. For more information about how to cite effectively, see Appendix B: Documentation and Reference Styles.

- **Expert authority.** For additional support, you may cite the opinions of people with acknowledged expertise.

- **Personal experience.** Your experiences and observations may provide compelling support for a claim, but they are rarely conclusive on their own.

- **Examples.** Although examples are not conclusive evidence, they can clarify your point and help your audience understand.

Figure 5.7 illustrates how Pedro uses all of these types of evidence in his memo to Maria and the vice president of finance. As you read the memo, notice that it also follows the logical structure outlined in Figure 5.6.

Appealing to your audience's emotions

Although logic is critical for business decisions, logic alone may not always be enough to persuade an audience. Psychologists and other researchers argue that persuasion is more emotional than rational,[18,19] and they have identified several techniques for engaging your audience on an emotional level.

FIGURE 5.7 How to Compose a Persuasive Message Using Logical Arguments

> Pedro Bacca's memo uses several types of evidence to persuade his supervisor, Maria, to solve a customer service problem by implementing training. This memo follows the logical structure illustrated in Figure 5.6.

memo

TO: Maria Cardoni
FROM: Pedro Baca
DATE: June 11, 20XX
SUBJECT: Proposed Solution for Costly Customer Service Problems

Problem

Two weeks ago, the customer service department installed new software designed to improve productivity and customer service. Employees received the standard three-hour orientation that comes with the software package. However, the training did not cover the customized functions necessary to process returns, exchanges, and refunds.

In the two weeks that employees have been using the software, we have logged 75 complaints more than average. Customers have complained about dropped calls, exchanged orders being lost, and refunds not being credited. In addition, because representatives are addressing so many time-consuming complaints, they are handling fewer calls, and their productivity has decreased by 15 percent. Although we cannot prove that lack of training on the new software caused the customer service problems, the coincidence is too great to be ignored.

These problems are costly to our company. Last year, we researched the cost of customer complaints and determined that each complaint costs us approximately $50 in employee time and lost sales. This means that in the past two weeks, handling the 75 additional complaints has cost us $3,750. If these problems continue, costs will conservatively exceed $10,000 in two months.

We also need to consider the long-term costs of unhappy customers. According to sales expert Jonathan Farrington, "the cost of an unhappy customer is much greater than the cost of any individual lost sale."[1] It includes the loss of that person's future business and the potential lost sales from people who have talked to the unhappy customer. A survey conducted by American Express found that, on average, an unhappy customer is likely to tell 21 people about a bad customer service experience.[2]

Proposed Solution

I have discussed this problem with the software developer, Mark Richey from Viking Systems, and he has agreed to provide an additional three-hour training session for all employees addressing the important customized functions in our system. To ensure that all employees are trained, he has also agreed to deliver the session twice, with half of the representatives attending each session.

The cost for this customized training will be $5,000, the exact amount it would have cost us to add the training to our original purchase. Although the amount may seem expensive, it is actually cost effective, considering the losses we project if the customer service problems persist. I do not believe employees will be able to master the system without training. I've spent 10 hours trying to learn all the functions of the new system on my own, and I still cannot figure out how to issue a refund.

Mark is prepared to deliver the session next week if we can approve the funding. The more quickly we provide the training, the more quickly we can realize the customer service benefits from the company's investment in the new system.

[1] Farrington, J. (2008). Customer complaints: The income multiplier effect. Retrieved from http://www.crm-daily.com

[2] American Express. (2014). 2014 global service barometer. Retrieved from http://about.americanexpress.com/news/docs/2014x/2014-Global-Customer-Service-Barometer-US.pdf

Main idea: Training customer service reps to use the new system will improve service and productivity and will reduce costs.

Supporting reason 1: Since installation, customer service and productivity have suffered.
Evidence:
- *Numerical data* about increase in customer complaints and decrease in number of customers served.
- *Examples* of customer complaints.

Supporting reason 2: The problem is costly.
Evidence:
- *Numerical data* from primary research calculating the cost of customer complaints.
- *Expert authority* opinion about the cost of unhappy customers.

Supporting reason 3: Training is an effective and efficient solution.
Evidence:
- *Numerical evidence* that training will cost less than the cost of complaints.
- *Personal experience* showing that Pedro could not learn the software without additional training.
- *Facts* showing that training can be offered within a week.

ETHICS
AVOIDING LOGICAL FALLACIES

When constructing an argument, you may be tempted to strengthen a weak position by overstating your case, diverting attention from problems with your position, or even attacking an opponent. These violations of logical reasoning that lead to a flawed argument are called **fallacies**, and intentionally using them is both dishonest and misleading.

Pedro might have used some of the following fallacies in his argument to Maria and the vice president of finance. Fortunately,

he did not. As you read each fallacy, identify what is misleading about the statement. Avoid fallacies in your own communication, and recognize fallacies when others use them so that you are not persuaded by unsound ideas.

For ETHICS exercises, go to Critical Thinking Question 8 on page 184 and Exercise 6 on page 186.

TYPE OF FALLACY	DESCRIPTION	EXAMPLE FALLACY FROM PEDRO TO MARIA
Appeal to popular opinion	Offering as evidence statements such as "everybody knows"	*Everybody knows that without training, new computer systems lead to productivity losses. It's obvious.*
Hasty generalization	Drawing a conclusion from a sample that is either too small or does not represent the larger population	*Two of our most experienced sales reps say that they are having difficulty with the computer system. If they are having trouble, it's likely everyone is.*
Ignoring the burden of proof	Stating a claim but providing no evidence to support it	*Providing computer training will immediately reverse our losses.*
False cause	Assuming that there is a cause and effect between two things without proving the relationship	*As soon as we got new computers, customer complaints increased. The new system is clearly the cause.*
False analogy	Supporting an idea by comparing it to something that is not comparable	*We require everyone to receive sufficient instruction before operating a car. Similarly, we should require all customer service reps to get sufficient training before operating the new computer system.*
False dilemma	Asserting that only two choices exist, while ignoring other options	*Either we provide more training or we will continue to see losses in productivity.*
Red herring	Focusing on an irrelevant issue to draw attention away from a central issue	*If management wants to cut budgets, then it would be much better to eliminate executive bonuses. The company spends millions on bonuses, and what benefit do we see from that?*
Ad hominem attack	Attacking a person who disagrees with you rather than addressing the issues	*The managers who instituted the budget cuts are just a bunch of corporate pencil pushers who don't have any idea what employees really need to do their jobs well.*

fallacy A violation of logical reasoning that leads to a flawed argument.

Appeal to your audience's emotional and psychological needs

You may wonder how you can address your audience's psychological needs, especially when communicating with an audience you do not know. However, psychologist Abraham Maslow argued that all people—even people of different cultures and different generations—share a common set of needs.[20] At the basic level are the physiological needs for food, clothing, and shelter. Once those needs are met, people seek to meet increasingly higher levels of need. Advertisers routinely appeal to these needs as part of their persuasive strategy:

- **Safety.** Home security companies appeal to the audience's desire for safety. Banks and investment companies appeal to the audience's desire for financial security.
- **Love and belonging.** Hair products and cosmetics companies appeal to the audience's desire to be attractive and admired. Manufacturers of convenience foods appeal to the audience's desire for dinners that bring the family closer, even when you have no time to cook.
- **Self-esteem.** Charities often appeal to the increase in self-esteem that donors feel when contributing to an organization's good works: *Your donation of a dollar a day will prevent a child from starving.* Educational institutions focus on the respect you earn—and the self-respect you feel—from completing your education.

- **Self-actualization.** Two of the U. S. Army's long-lived advertising slogans, "Be all that you can be" and "Army Strong," appeal to people's desire to make the most of their abilities. Advertisements for luxury travel experiences often appeal to travelers who want to "find themselves" in exotic places.

Although anthropological research suggests that some needs and perspectives may be culture specific, Maslow's advice remains relevant in persuading Western cultures.[21]

Make appeals based on widely studied psychological principles

Social science researchers such as Robert Cialdini have identified a number of psychological principles that help explain why certain types of persuasive appeals are particularly effective.[22] These principles include:

- **Consistency.** People like to act consistently and to make decisions similar to the ones they made in the past. Persuasive appeals often remind the audience of past decisions.
- **Social proof.** People follow the lead of others they respect. Persuasive appeals often include names of respected figures and testimonials from past clients.
- **Liking.** People respond more positively to those whom they like and who like them. Persuasive appeals often express liking and appreciation for the audience.
- **Reciprocity.** People typically want to reciprocate if they receive a gift. The gift can be as small as a compliment or a recommendation of a book to read. Persuasive appeals often include a free gift.
- **Scarcity.** People want things more if those things are scarce. Persuasive appeals often highlight the exclusivity of their offer. For example, the beauty retailer Sephora persuades customers to sign up for its subscription box PLAY! by stressing that the opportunity is limited: "PLAY! by SEPHORA is in very high demand, and we are adding new subscriptions every month as we grow. Click the link below to see if a spot is currently available for you to subscribe."[23]

Figure 5.8 on page 168 illustrates how one charitable organization combined emotional and psychological appeals to encourage continued support from a donor who has supported the organization in the past.

Pre-suade your audience before delivering your message

Cialdini also introduced the term **pre-suasion** based on his research which shows that "the effectiveness of persuasive messages will be drastically affected by the type of opener experienced immediately in advance."[24] In other words, your audience's state of mind will affect their response to your message. To be more effective, aim to influence that state of mind *before* delivering your persuasive message. For example, if you want your supervisor to respond positively to a proposal, preface your discussion of the proposal by asking your supervisor for advice, not approval. Asking for advice is likely to put your audience in a cooperative state of mind rather than a critical one.[25] In addition, people are more likely to support an idea that they participate in creating.[26]

As another example, if you want to persuade a busy teammate to help conduct time-consuming interviews, you might begin a meeting by asking everyone on the team whether they think the project is worth some personal sacrifice to achieve a high quality. If your teammate agrees to this idea, then—later in the meeting—she is more likely to agree to conduct interviews, even though that task will involve spending more time than she would like.

pre-suasion The process of influencing an audience's state of mind before delivering a persuasive message.

Show your own emotional commitment

If you want your audience to commit to an idea, they need to know that you are committed to it, too. In other words, you will be more persuasive if you speak—or write—from the heart.[27] One reason that Rio de Janeiro won the bid for the 2016 Olympics may have been that Brazilian President Luiz Inacio Lula da Silva demonstrated extraordinary emotional commitment to hosting the Olympics. Not only did he spend two years personally lobbying the Olympic Committee and other heads of state, he also spent the week before the final vote visiting with members of the International Olympic Committee to make his case. The day before the vote, he gave a heartfelt speech explaining what it would mean to

FIGURE 5.8 How to Use Emotional Appeals to Compose a Persuasive Message

letter

2025 Chatham Drive • Burlingame, CA 94010 • P: 808.555.1477 • F: 808.555.1478

> This fund-raising letter from The Greenwald Center uses several forms of emotional appeal to persuade a past donor to contribute again. The letter also uses quantitative data to illustrate that the donor's support makes a difference.

November 18, 20XX

Ms. Julie Benjamin
106 W. Third Avenue
San Mateo, CA 94401

Dear Ms. Benjamin:

Thank you for your past support of The Greenwald Center. Your generosity has helped create opportunities and successes for people in our community who live with disabilities. As you make your year-ending giving decisions, please consider renewing your support with a gift of $100.

Appeal to **consistency** *(by praising past action).*

Each year at The Greenwald Center, 5,000 people with disabilities strive to increase their independence step by step—finding accessible housing or steady employment, learning to read or cook, or managing household finances. The Greenwald Center supports these efforts one person at a time, helping people achieve their individual goals. As our four-star rating from Charity Navigator indicates, every dollar that you contribute goes directly toward helping people.

Appeal to **social proof** *(by citing a "four-star rating").*

Here are some of the successes your contribution supported this past year:

Appeal to **self-esteem** *("Here are some of the successes your contribution supported").*

- 350 people found jobs ranging from car porter to sales representative
- 93 people learned to read bus signs, make medical appointments, and conduct personal banking on their own
- 100 percent of families surveyed have learned ways to assist their children's development at home

In an era of shrinking government support, we increasingly rely on sustainable funding from friends like you, extraordinary people who see ability in everyone. Your gift can help train a literacy volunteer, facilitate a "mock" interview session, hire a guest cooking instructor, or in other ways support the success of people living with disabilities.

Appeal to **liking** *and* **love and belonging** *(by referring to "friends like you").*

Appeal to **self-actualization** *(by describing contributors as "extraordinary people who see ability in everyone").*

Please use the enclosed self-addressed stamped envelope to return your pledge today or contribute on our website at www.greenwaldcenter.org.

Thank you for generously continuing to support The Greenwald Center.

Sincerely,

Allan I. Bergman

Allan I. Bergman
President/CEO

P.S. As a token of our appreciation, we have enclosed a DVD, *Introduction to The Greenwald Center*, so that you can see the good work you are supporting. We also have a limited number of tickets available for a December 15 holiday concert at City Orchestra. The tickets sell for $75 each, but we will give them free of charge to donors who request them, on a first-come first-served basis.

Appeal to **reciprocity** *(by providing a DVD).*

Appeal to **scarcity** *(by stressing the limited number of tickets).*

South America to host the Olympic Games for the first time in the competition's history. He described how athletes throughout South America would be affected by being part of this experience—and how the world would take notice if the International Olympic Committee awarded this honor to a continent that it had previously ignored. After the speech, Lula said, "It was extraordinary the emotion we put into our presentation . . . I almost cried two times during my speech."[28] One delegate of the International Olympic Committee commented, "I told the president (Lula), whom I know very well for a long time, that his speech went under my skin."[29]

TECHNOLOGY
PERSUASIVE VIDEOS: LEARNING BY WATCHING

TED (short for Technology, Entertainment, and Design) Talks are popular short-format talks aimed at bringing innovative ideas to the widest audiences possible. Filmed in front of live audiences and uploaded to the TED website daily, TED Talks have received more than 1 billion views.[30] TED limits the length of the talks to 18 minutes or less, forcing speakers to use elements of persuasion to engage audiences of diverse backgrounds and create convincing presentations. Watching these presentations can teach you a lot about being persuasive.

For example, Amy Cuddy's TED Talk about power stances and projecting confidence has had nearly 35.5 million views.[31] Cuddy argues that the way we position our bodies, whether closed off in a low-power stance, or opened and confident in a high-power stance, influences not only how other people perceive us but how we perceive ourselves.

A major reason the talk is popular is that Cuddy is effective at constructing a logical argument. Cuddy draws on secondary research to argue that body language matters—and she engages her audience in that argument by providing examples of powerful, or "alpha," body language on display by both world leaders and primates. She then moves on to her own primary research and presents numerical data showing that when people take a high-power stance for two minutes before doing a challenging task, such as a job interview, they are perceived as more authoritative and are more likely to be hired. People who take a low-power stance for two minutes before a job interview are less likely to be hired. Cuddy concludes that using "alpha" body language can make you act more powerfully.

A and N photography/Shutterstock

Hikdaigaku86/Fotolia

Cuddy could have stopped there, as she had already proven her point by *constructing a logical argument*. But to drive the argument home, she also made an *emotional appeal*. Cuddy explained how a car accident when she was in college left her with temporarily diminished cognitive function. Although she ultimately graduated from college and began graduate school, she recalled feeling like an impostor in her academic career. The night before a particularly important presentation during her first year in graduate school, her advisor told her to "fake it until you make it," advice that took her through a PhD and to a faculty position at a top business school. Cuddy became visibly emotional as she recalled giving the same advice to one of her own struggling students and seeing her student put it into action—making tiny tweaks in self-perception that led to confidence.

Drawing on personal experience and an emotional presentation, Cuddy appealed to her audience's desire for *belonging*, *self-esteem*, and *self-actualization*. Although more recent research suggests that PowerPosing may not be as conclusive as Cuddy argues,[32] her presentation is so persuasive (as is her rebuttal to the arguments) that her TED Talk continues to attract and compel a large audience.

For TECHNOLOGY exercises, go to Exercise 8 on page 186 and Exercise 25 on page 189.

Use storytelling and powerful language to make evidence compelling

Although presenting evidence is a key part of any persuasive strategy, storytelling is one of the most powerful tools you have for shaping your evidence persuasively and engaging your audience at the same time.[33] For example, in 2007, Steve Jobs introduced Apple's newest product, the iPhone, during his keynote speech at Macworld, a yearly trade show and developer conference. He aimed to generate excitement about the device amongst users and investors—and to prove that Apple continued its cutting-edge product development. In order to outshine competitors in the smartphone market, Jobs listed the features and functions that were unique to Apple's device. But equally as powerfully, Jobs raised audience expectations by locating the new product within Apple's history of innovation. He began,

> *Every once in a while, a revolutionary product comes along that changes everything. [You are] very fortunate if you get to work on just one of these in your career. Apple's been very fortunate. It's been able to introduce a few of these into the world. In 1984, we introduced the Macintosh. It didn't just change Apple, it changed the whole computer industry. In 2001, we introduced the first iPod, and it didn't just change the way we all listen to music, it changed the entire music industry. . . . Today, today Apple is going to reinvent the phone, and here it is.*[34]

In telling this story, Jobs transformed a faceless company, Apple, into a thinking and feeling protagonist that, against all odds, "changed everything." He framed Apple's previous successes as both evidence of the company's capability to make "revolutionary products" and as a prelude to the unveiling of the iPhone, implying that the iPhone will be even more revolutionary than what came before. This strategy made his claim about the "reinvention" of the phone more emotionally dramatic and more logically persuasive, showing how the best persuasive strategies employ logic and emotion together. Jobs also used classic persuasive speaking techniques, such as parallel sentence structure ("It didn't just change X, it changed Y") and repetition ("Today, today") to clarify his message and make it more vivid and memorable. The iPhone went on to become the fastest-growing smartphone in 2008, and Job's 2007 keynote is widely considered to be one of the most memorable corporate speeches.[35,36,37] Storytelling is persuasive because stories stick in the memory and they attach emotions to facts and figures.[38]

What types of business messages typically require persuasion?

In addition to fundraising messages and motivational speeches, other types of communication that require persuasion include recommendations for action, requests for favors, persuasive customer claims, and sales messages. This section discusses some special challenges for each type.

Recommendations for action

recommendation A business message that suggests a solution to a business problem.

When you make a **recommendation**, you establish that a problem or a need exists, and then you show how your solution is effective. The content of your recommendation can include a range of persuasive elements: focusing on benefits, anticipating objections, building credibility, constructing a logical argument, and appealing to the audience's emotion.

Pedro's memo to Maria and the vice president of finance in Figure 5.7 is a recommendation for action. One challenge for this type of persuasive document is to determine the order for this content. Should your recommendation be direct, starting with the main point? Or should it be indirect, building up to the main point? **Figure 5.9** shows how to choose between direct and indirect recommendations and then organize your message accordingly. The two most important variables in making that decision are (1) whether the audience expects the recommendation and (2) whether the recommendation will negatively affect stakeholders.

In Figure 5.7, Pedro chose to organize his memo indirectly. Even though Maria knows that a problem exists and requested that he write the recommendation, the vice

FIGURE 5.9 How to Decide on an Organization for Recommendations

Use **DIRECT ORGANIZATION** if …	**DIRECT ORGANIZATION** follows this pattern …
your audience • requests the recommendation, prefers directness, or is likely to react positively, **and the recommendation will not** • negatively affect stakeholders or require additional effort from stakeholders.	**BEGIN WITH MAIN POINT** Propose a specific recommendation. **PROVIDE CONTEXT** • Identify the issue, problem, or opportunity. • Provide evidence that the problem or opportunity is significant. **SUPPORT YOUR PROPOSAL** For example: • Justify recommendations with persuasive rationale. • Describe alternative solutions and negative implications. • Address potential objections. • Stress benefits. **MOTIVATE ACTION** Conclude with a call to action.

Use **INDIRECT ORGANIZATION** if …	**INDIRECT ORGANIZATION** follows this pattern …
your audience • is not expecting the recommendation, • prefers indirectness, or • is likely to react negatively, **and the recommendation will** • negatively affect stakeholders, or • require additional effort from stakeholders.	**BEGIN WITH CONTEXT** • Identify the issue, problem, or opportunity. • Provide evidence that the problem or opportunity is significant. **OPTIONAL: ELIMINATE OTHER ALTERNATIVES** • Describe alternative solutions and negative implications. **STATE MAIN POINT** • Propose a specific recommendation. **SUPPORT YOUR PROPOSAL** For example: • Justify recommendations with persuasive rationale. • Address potential objections. • Stress benefits. **MOTIVATE ACTION** Conclude with a call to action.

persuasive request A request that persuades the audience to do you a favor by making the audience feel good about doing the favor and, if possible, by stressing audience benefits.

president of finance, who will ultimately receive this recommendation, is not aware of the problem. Pedro needs to establish the importance of the problem before recommending a solution.

Requests for favors

When you ask people to do something that is easy for them to accomplish or that they will be happy to do, little persuasion is required. By contrast, more persuasion is required if you ask people to do something that involves effort, requires them to choose between alternatives, or differs from their plans. In those cases, you will need to make a **persuasive request** that helps the audience feel good about doing the favor. If possible, the request will also show how the audience will benefit from helping you.

For example, assume that as a member of your state's bar association, you volunteered to help organize a local awards luncheon for the 450 association members in your area. This morning—less than a week before the event—you receive a phone call from the keynote speaker, the mayor, indicating that she is no longer able to speak at the luncheon due to a death in the family. You have just a few days to find a replacement. Fortunately, you know the perfect person to contact. Dr. Gunther Maher was your business law professor in college. He retired last year and has many anecdotes he can share during a keynote presentation. Your concern is whether he is available and, more important, whether he would be willing to make the presentation with less than a week to prepare. To plan your persuasive request, use the ACE process.

Analyze

Analyze

Remember to analyze the elements that were outlined at the beginning of this chapter, including your purpose, your audience and content needs, and your medium choices:

- **Purpose: What are your purpose, desired outcome, and business result?** You want Dr. Maher to agree to deliver the bar association keynote presentation next week. If he agrees, the result will be that the attendees will not mind that the original presenter canceled.

- **Information needs: What does Dr. Maher need to know (what does he already know)?** Dr. Maher may not remember who you are, so you will need to reintroduce yourself. He then needs to know the date and time of the bar association awards luncheon, the length of his presentation, why you are asking him to speak at the last minute, and what you would like him to speak about.

- **Motivation and benefits: What will motivate Dr. Maher to comply with your request? How will he benefit?** You can appeal to Dr. Maher's self-esteem. Dr. Maher may be persuaded if he believes that he can influence the careers of hundreds of lawyers. He might have chosen to become a professor to help mold the minds of future professionals. This keynote gives him the opportunity to further influence many of today's lawyers. This is a benefit to him because it helps him achieve his personal goals.

- **Potential resistance: What concerns and objections will he have?** He may be concerned that he has to prepare carefully for the presentation and he does not have time.

- **Medium: What is the best medium for this message based on the purpose, audience, and content?** You need to know quickly if Dr. Maher can fulfill your request, so a telephone conversation is the best medium. In a telephone call, you can also answer any questions he has.

Compose

Compose

Consider the order and organization of the message:

- **Should the message be direct—with the main point at the beginning—or indirect?** You decide that you need to begin the conversation by reintroducing yourself and building your credibility as a business professional and active member of the bar association. Your request will be indirect, coming after you have reestablished this relationship.

- **How can you best organize the message? Figure 5.10** illustrates how to organize a message that makes a persuasive request. Figure 5.10 assumes that you are leaving a voice message, but the same organization will work for an actual conversation.

Evaluate

Evaluate

Remember to evaluate before finalizing the voice mail message. Consider it from Dr. Maher's perspective. How do you imagine he will react when he receives this message? Is the message persuasive enough to justify a positive response? You can use the evaluation checklist from Figure 5.4 to review and adjust your message.

Persuasive customer claims

You have probably read store policies with the phrases "no returns," "all sales are final," or "limited warranty." In those situations, if you want to request a full or partial refund, you need to submit a **customer claim** message that persuades the seller that the policy should not apply in your situation or that it is in the seller's best interest to fulfill your request.

For example, assume that you are starting a home-based business and need a an all-in-one printer that also copies and scans. You purchase a refurbished printer from a discount electronics store, E-Tronics, which clearly posts its no-return policy in the store and on every

customer claim A request from a customer to a store or vendor to accept a return, exchange an item, refund money, or perform a repair.

FIGURE 5.10 How to Make a Persuasive Request for a Favor

voice mail message

Hello, Dr. Maher. This is Alexa Hampton. I was in your business law class several years ago and found it very useful. I now work as an associate lawyer at Betts, Miller, and Russo here in town, and I'm calling to ask you a favor.

> **Introduce yourself** as a former student to establish credibility. Mention how much you like the course to **appeal to self-esteem and liking.** Preface the request by indicating that you're calling to ask for a favor.

I'm on the planning committee for the local bar association, and our awards luncheon is next Monday. The mayor was our original keynote speaker, but a sudden death in the family prevents her from attending. I immediately thought of you as a replacement. Would you be able to deliver a one-hour speech based on anecdotes and lessons you learned during your career?

> **Provide context** for the request.

> **Make a direct request.**

> **Address a potential objection:** He will not have time to research material for a speech.

Your years of experience and wealth of knowledge could make a significant difference in the professional lives of the 450 lawyers who will attend the luncheon. In a one-hour speech, you will address more people than you were able to teach in an entire academic year as a business law professor. I know you are the perfect keynote replacement for the mayor.

> **Motivate with self-esteem** by praising his experience and knowledge.

> **Include audience benefits** that appeal to self-actualization: He will continue to make a difference in the lives of others.

Please call me at 555-1887 as soon as you get this message so we can discuss the details. I look forward to talking with you soon. Again, Alexa Hampton, 555-1887.

Thank you.

> **Conclude with a call for action:** Request a reply and provide a phone number.

receipt. Although the sales associate who helped you with the purchase assured you that the printer would work with your specific laptop model, you cannot get the any of the functions to work. You decide to bring both your laptop and the printer to E-Tronics so the "Tech Team" can fix your problem. However, after seeing your laptop, they explain that the printer model was discontinued before your computer's operating system was created. Therefore, the driver that you need to enable the laptop to communicate with the printer does not exist. They would be happy to sell you a printer that would work with your laptop, but they cannot exchange it for your current printer or refund your money. After explaining to the store's manager that a sales associate assured you the printer and laptop were compatible, the manager provides you with the URL for the E-Tronics customer service website so you can explain the problem and request a refund or exchange. You return home to draft your persuasive claim message. Where do you begin? The ACE process can help.

Analyze

As you analyze, answer the following questions:

- **Purpose, desired outcome, and business result: What do you want the audience to do after receiving this message?** You want the store to exchange the printer for the one that works with your laptop.
- **Information needs: What does the audience need to know?** The audience needs to know what happened and why you are requesting an exchange. The audience also needs to know why you believe their policy should not apply in this instance.
- **Motivation and benefits: What will motivate the audience to accept your idea? How will the audience benefit?** The audience will be motivated by appeals to fairness and integrity: You purchased the printer because the sales associate assured you that it would work with your specific laptop model. The benefit is that you will continue to be a customer.
- **Potential resistance: What concerns and objections will the audience have?** The audience may resist because the store's stated policy allows no exceptions. Therefore, it is

important to stress that you are requesting an exchange because of a mistake the store made, not a mistake that you made. You can also overcome resistance by showing you are willing to purchase a more expensive item if necessary.

- **Medium: What is the best medium for this message based on the purpose, audience, and content?** By following the store's policies, you start with a message posted to the company's customer service website to begin the claim process and receive a claim number. Then you plan to call to speak directly with a customer service representative.

Compose

As you compose, ask the following questions:

- **Should the message be direct—with the main point at the beginning—or indirect?** Because you're writing to a customer service department that knows most messages are based on problems, they will not be surprised to receive your message. You decide to state the main point directly.
- **How can you best organize the message?** Divide the message into clear paragraphs: (1) state the request; (2) explain the problem; (3) demonstrate goodwill and understanding, and explain why the policy should not apply; and (4) conclude by providing contact information and expressing continued confidence in the store. Avoid emotions.
- **How should you format this message to be professional and support your purpose?** Compose the message in a word processing application, keeping in mind that any formatting will not apply when you cut and paste the message to the company's website.

Based on these decisions, you draft the message illustrated in **Figure 5.11**.

FIGURE 5.11 How to Make a Persuasive Claim

online submission

Directly state the reason for the claim. — My local E-Tronics store in Eagle Heights, Ohio, sold me a refurbished all-in-one printer that does not work with my computer's operating system. I would like to exchange it for one that does work with my computer.

Clearly explain the problem and the technical details. — On October 10, 20XX, I purchased a refurbished HP printer, Model #5770, because a sales associate at the store mistakenly assured me that this HP printer would work with my Toshiba Tecra C40-D1412 laptop, which is running Windows 10. It was only when I got home that I discovered that a driver does not exist for Windows 10, only for Windows 7 and 8.

Demonstrate understanding and goodwill. Explain why the policy should be waived in this case (to counter potential objections).

Appeal to fairness. — Any sales associate can make an honest mistake, and I am very willing to return this printer and purchase one, even a more expensive one, that works with my computer. However, my local store will not exchange the printer because of your no returns / no exchange policy. Although I understand that such a policy may be necessary to keep prices low, in this instance, I believe that my request to exchange this printer for one that will work with my laptop is reasonable given that I received incorrect sales advice.

Close positively with a forward-looking statement that emphasizes a continued business relationship (audience benefit). — Please call me at (419) 555-8623 to discuss how we can resolve this matter. I look forward to hearing from you and continuing to purchase electronics from your stores.

Sincerely,

Elaine Mackiewetz

Elaine Mackiewetz

Evaluate

After drafting the message but before submitting it online, evaluate it using the checklist in Figure 5.4 on page 161. Plan to follow up with a telephone call, if necessary.

Sales messages

Persuasion is also an important element in most sales messages, where your goal is to motivate someone to buy a product or service. Sales and marketing people often use the acronym **AIDA**—for *attention, interest, desire,* and *action*—to create persuasive sales messages, brochures, advertisements, and websites. **Figure 5.12** summarizes the four AIDA components.

AIDA An acronym used in marketing to suggest the organization of sales communication: attention, interest, desire, action.

FIGURE 5.12 AIDA Model for Organizing Persuasive Sales Messages

Attention: **Grab your audience's attention so they want to know more.**

Interest: **Build their interest by meeting their needs and emphasizing benefits.**

Desire: **Create desire through authority, social proof, or perceived scarcity.**

Action: **Make it easy for the audience to act and respond.**

Rather than using AIDA as a formula, imagine it as a guided process in which you lead your audience from attention to action, using the basic components of persuasion that you learned earlier in the chapter:

- **Attention.** The first part of a sales message should grab the audience's attention. Your wording should make the audience want to read or hear more about your product or service by focusing their awareness. In business communication, you can grab the audience's attention in a professional way by sharing a startling fact, thought-provoking story, or motivating question. Consider these examples:

Startling fact:	Did you know that 50 percent of all small businesses fail within the first five years?
Thought-provoking story:	Imagine yourself running your own business with no one to answer to except yourself! You're the boss. Your ideas are taken seriously, and everyone looks to you for guidance. Sound too good to be true? For most people it is, but entrepreneurs who use our CustomerBase software suite have a good chance of achieving this dream.
Motivating question:	Would you like to achieve your full financial potential rather than limiting your income to a monthly salary? Of course! Make your dream job come true with the CustomerBase software suite designed to build your business and increase your financial success.

- **Interest.** After gaining the audience's attention, you need to build their interest in the product or service by describing how you can meet their needs and provide benefits. The better your audience analysis, the more likely you are to understand—and potentially meet—their needs.
- **Desire.** Creating a sense of desire involves reducing the audience's resistance to the sales message, which is especially important when you create **unsolicited sales communication**, or *cold-call sales messages*—messages you send to audiences who did not request the information. However, reducing resistance is also important in **solicited sales communication**—messages you send to audiences who did request the information. Although customers who request information want the product or service, you may have to reduce their resistance if the price is more than they predicted or if the item does not fulfill all their needs. To create a sense of desire, consider using one of the techniques of emotional appeal discussed in SQ2 on pages 164–169. Appealing to social proof and scarcity can be particularly effective.

unsolicited sales communication Sales messages you send to audiences who did not request the information, also called "cold-call sales messages."

solicited sales communication A response to a request for sales information.

- **Action.** The final step of the AIDA persuasive strategy is to motivate your customer to act and purchase the product or service. Motivating action requires a professional approach. You do not want to assume the customer will purchase the product, but you don't want to be vague, either. Motivate action by making the response easy and providing specific direction. If you want to motivate the customer to download your software package, the message should take the form of an email that includes a link to easily download the product. If your sales message is a phone call, you should be able to process the customer's order over the telephone. If you are mailing a letter or sales brochure, enclose a postage-paid return envelope in which the customer can easily place an order.

Figure 5.13 illustrates how to use the AIDA strategy to compose a persuasive unsolicited sales message. Although AIDA is usually associated with sales messages to a general audience, you can use the AIDA approach even more effectively in situations when you know the audience. For those messages, you can apply your knowledge of audience needs to determine what specific information will effectively grab their attention, build interest, create desire, and motivate action.

FIGURE 5.13 How to Use AIDA to Compose an Unsolicited Sales Message

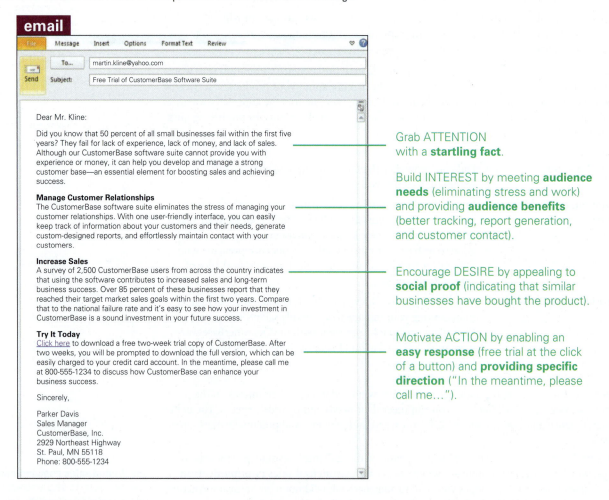

COLLABORATION
USING PERSUASION TO IMPROVE TEAMWORK AND COLLABORATION

You may not think of persuasion as a skill that is useful in teamwork and collaboration. However, persuasion is just as important in a teamwork context as it is in communication with managers, customers, suppliers, and potential business partners. When working with people on a team, your persuasive skills can be useful in two distinctly different ways: They can help you motivate others to perform to the best of their ability and also help you collaborate with teammates to make effective decisions.

USE PERSUASION TO MOTIVATE OTHERS

Have you ever been part of a work team with members who had other priorities or did minimal work? Even if you are not designated as a team leader, you can adopt a leadership role and use your persuasive skills to help the team—and individual team members—get back on track. In this context, persuasion means influencing your team members' attitudes to bring about a change in behavior.

I want you to know how much I appreciate the time and effort you've put into this project. It's turning out better than any of us expected.

Icons vector/Shutterstock

Effective team leaders use the following techniques to influence attitudes and motivate people to make a commitment to a team:

- **Remind the team why the work is important.** As you learned in Chapter 2: Working with Others, the best teams share a concrete goal and vision for success. Depending on the project, success may mean that the company will launch a new product or save time and money—or that each team member will receive a bonus. If team members lose sight of the goal, remind them of their vision for success and why it is important.
- **Help others feel pride in their work.** People lose motivation when they feel unappreciated. By showing appreciation and acknowledging team members' contributions, you can persuade team members to continue working at a high level.
- **Understand and acknowledge the emotions of team members.** Emotions can stand in the way of a team's success. If a team member feels angry, frustrated, or excluded from decision making, productivity will decline. Rather than try to convince someone to feel differently, actively listen, try to understand the feelings, and acknowledge their validity. With that kind of support, many team members persuade themselves to make changes and work harder.[41]
- **Make it possible for a team member to succeed.** Sometimes, external factors stand in the way of team success. For example, team members may have competing responsibilities

at home and may not be able to commit to the team as fully as necessary. If you help people resolve these conflicts, you may be able to persuade them to work harder on your project. Can you reschedule a meeting? Allow them to work from home? Redistribute tasks? Helping others makes it more possible for them to participate in the team and, following Cialdini's principle of reciprocity, may also lead them to reciprocate and do more for your project.[42]

INCORPORATE PERSUASION INTO THE TEAM DECISION-MAKING PROCESS

In the context of decision making, you might think that persuasion means convincing others that you are right so that they make the decision you prefer. However, when you work in a team, persuading others to agree with you can be counterproductive, leading to the type of groupthink described in Chapter 2: Working with Others. The goal of team decision making is to generate the best possible solution based on everyone's input.

One approach to achieve this goal is to ask team members to make a strong persuasive case for a specific decision and allow other team members to challenge the selection. If you hear the strongest arguments for each position, the team can evaluate each position objectively. This process of persuasion requires all team members to listen carefully and be willing to change their minds; however, it often produces a better plan of action than any one individual could devise.

Here's why I support hiring a full-time employee...

Icons vector/Shutterstock

But an intern would be less expensive and give us more flexibility. Here's why...

Icons vector/Shutterstock

For COLLABORATION exercises, go to Exercises 20 and 21 on pages 188–189.

CULTURE
ADAPTING PERSUASIVE APPEALS

Although many people believe that the key to persuasion is providing a strong, logical argument, you've learned in this chapter that persuasion depends on many additional factors: strengthening your credibility, engaging your audience's emotions, and adapting to their preferences.

Adapting is particularly important when you want to persuade people from different cultures. You may need to adapt in these ways:

- Using a different medium for persuasion
- Emphasizing different persuasive content
- Accommodating a different decision-making process

The following two scenarios involve cross-cultural persuasion. If you were involved in these scenarios, what would you do? After deciding, compare your answers with those provided (upside down).

1. You are working on a project with a team of people from Mexico and the United States, communicating primarily by email. One of your Mexican teammates often takes three to four days to respond to messages that you have marked urgent. So far, this has not been a problem. However, now you need a quick response from him. Your team is running late on a project deadline, and your ability to meet this deadline will impact on your performance review. How would you persuade your Mexican teammate to respond to you quickly and to help meet the deadline?

   a. Write an email message politely explaining exactly what you need and by when. Apologize for the short notice, and explain that you will both share the success for meeting the deadline or the blame for missing it.

   b. Write an email message explaining the urgency of the situation, providing detailed instructions, and showing appreciation for his extraordinary efforts to help you. Follow the email with a telephone call to ensure he understands.

   c. Call to explain the situation and ask for help. Ask about his workload to see if your request is realistic. Invite him to call you to ask for help in meeting the deadline, and end the conversation by saying you hope to meet in the future.

2. You are part of a team that is presenting a proposal to a client in the Netherlands. Your client has sent you a list of people who will be attending the meeting, along with background information on each. You notice that they represent a wide range of functions in the company. You also notice that no senior decision maker will be attending the meeting. Typically, when your company presents a persuasive proposal, you target the senior decision maker and aim primarily to persuade that person. This approach has been successful and led to quick sales. In this case, what should your team do?

   a. Call your main contact and persuade him or her to include a senior decision maker in the meeting, rearranging the time of the meeting if necessary.

   b. Structure your presentation to provide specific information on the benefits of your product for the representatives of each of the functional areas attending the meeting.

   c. Structure your presentation in the same way you would if a senior decision maker attended, leave a handout, and encourage your main contact to pass this information along to the senior decision maker.

For a **CULTURE** exercise, go to Exercise 9 on page 186.

Answers

1. C is the best choice. In Mexico, it is important to develop working relationships. A phone call signals that you are making an effort to build a relationship. In addition, by asking about your colleague's workload, you are showing that you recognize the value of his work and that you are not egotistical. This will provide you with credibility and your credibility, you increase the chances that your colleague will make an extra effort to help you.[39]

2. B is the best choice. Although the Netherlands is a highly individualistic culture, important business decisions are made slowly and by consensus, using what is called the "polder model."[40] This means that you will achieve more success if you persuade each person in the meeting that his or her specific functional area will benefit from your product.

■ **In summary,** being a persuasive business communicator requires that you adopt a "you" perspective and understand what will motivate your audience as well as what will prevent them from agreeing with you. The techniques you learned in this chapter are tools that you can use to address your audience's needs and concerns—and help your audience agree with and accept your ideas. If your content is sufficiently targeted to your audience, you may find that they will persuade themselves to agree with you.

PERSUASION @ WORK   The Ebisch Law Firm

Photo courtesy of Jane Ebisch

Jane Ebisch

When we think of persuasion and the law, what first comes to mind is probably the image of a trial lawyer persuading a jury to convict or acquit a defendant. This is the image we see most frequently in the media. But the media gives us only a limited picture of persuasion and the law.

Jane Ebisch, an attorney with the Ebisch Law Firm in Lakewood, Colorado, says that in her civil law practice, only 10 percent of the cases ever get to court. Much more often, she is called on to make a persuasive case in writing. In some instances, she might draft a motion to dismiss a case, which makes an argument to the judge that the case can be dismissed as a matter of law. Or, following a deposition in which she has questioned the opposing side, she may write a motion for a summary judgment. This type of document aims to persuade the judge that none of the facts in the case are in dispute and therefore the case does not require a trial; the judge can decide the case based on interpretation of law. Both these types of documents need to make very specific arguments, and the judge will agree only if the lawyer effectively proves that there is not a set of facts that could possibly result in a judgment against her client.

However, one of Ebisch's favorite types of persuasive documents to write is a demand letter—a letter demanding payment or some other form of restitution from another party on behalf of her client. For example, if a client believes he was fired unfairly, Ebisch may write a demand letter to his employer, seeking reinstatement and/or financial compensation. While we don't usually associate the term "demand" with persuasion, the goal of a demand letter is not actually to demand but instead to persuade the audience to agree with the story she is telling and the outcome she proposes (or demands).

Ebisch finds writing a demand letter to be both interesting and challenging. It requires first understanding what happened and what the client wants so that she can determine whether the client has a legitimate claim. It then requires melding together the relevant facts of the case and the law in order to tell a compelling story that leads the audience to believe the demand is reasonable. If the audience does not agree, they may come back with a counteroffer or the case may go to trial. Or Ebisch may aim to persuade her client that it is not worth his time and money to pursue the case.

Although legal writing seems very specialized, Ebisch finds that the persuasive skills honed by practicing law have many uses in everyday life and business. As a lawyer, she has learned to shape facts into a story that shows how her client deserves a specific outcome. The same skills can help a person argue for a product refund, a policy exception, or even a raise at work.

Source: Based on an interview with Jane Ebisch

Starting a New Business

This case scenario will help you review the chapter material by applying it to a specific situation.

Kelly Lee and Noah Walker meet in a marketing class and recognize that they have two things in common. First, they enjoy working with animals. Kelly's family breeds Irish setters, and Noah works part time in a veterinary office. Second, they both want to be entrepreneurs. After some initial market analysis, they decide to collaborate on creating a pet daycare center, Pet Haven, that will offer daily workouts for the animals, hourly playtime and petting with individual handlers, and clean and roomy cages or containment areas.

To get Pet Haven up and running, Kelly and Noah realize they must persuade either a bank or other investors to give them a small business loan. Then they must persuade potential customers to use their service.

Persuading Lenders to Fund a Loan

When Kelly and Noah go to the bank to discuss a loan for Pet Haven, the banker is interested in the idea but tells them their interest rate will be very high because they have an insufficient credit history and no collateral for the loan. To secure a more reasonable rate, he suggests they ask relatives to co-sign the loan application. In other words, their parents would have to agree to repay the loan if Kelly and Noah could not.

Kelly and Noah decide they need to convince their parents that Pet Haven is a sound financial idea. To prepare for these meetings, they brainstorm a list of questions their parents might ask:

- Are you ready to run a business?
- What services will you provide? How do you know these are the right services? What will you need in order to deliver these services?
- Who is your customer base? Are there enough customers to support your business?
- What is the competition in your city? What will you offer to make your business stand out?
- Have these kinds of pet daycare businesses been successful in other towns?
- How will you market your services to your customers? How will you communicate and what will you communicate?
- What kind of licensing and credentials do you need?
- Do you have a location yet? What kind of space do you need? What kinds of equipment do you need?
- What will the start-up costs be for leases, employees, licenses, advertising, and equipment?
- What size loan do you need? How will you repay this loan from cash flow?
- Why don't you get a job first and get some experience? You can open a business later.

Question 1: How can Kelly and Noah prepare for a successfully persuasive conversation with their parents?

a. What questions require a logical argument, using claims, reasons, and evidence?

b. How should Kelly and Noah gather information to support these arguments?

c. How can Kelly and Noah establish credibility about their ability to run a business and repay a loan?

d. What kinds of emotional appeals might be effective to motivate their parents?

Identifying Benefits and Objections

Based on Kelly's and Noah's persuasive business plans, their parents agree to cosign the loan. However, they insist that Kelly and Noah begin to market their business before graduation. As a next step, Kelly and Noah decide to learn more about their potential customers:

- What do they know about pet daycare services?
- What benefits will they perceive from the service?
- What objections and concerns may prevent them from using the service?

Question 2: How can Noah and Kelly learn this information? What would you do?

a. Alone or with a small group search the web for animal or pet daycare centers. Select at least two companies and read their websites thoroughly. List the customer benefits that each company stresses. Which benefits seem most compelling? What benefits would you recommend Noah and Kelly stress? Can you think of other potential benefits that you did not read about in competitors' websites?

b. In small groups or as a class, brainstorm objections that pet owners may raise about the pet daycare concept. What may prevent pet owners from using Pet Haven's services? What will convince them to send their pets? Prepare for this brainstorm by talking to friends and relatives outside of class and getting their opinions. For each objection or question, give Kelly and Noah ideas about how to anticipate those issues in their marketing materials. What objections should they refute and how? What objections might they concede and how?

Building Credibility Through a Website

Noah and Kelly know that small businesses need to have a presence on the web to attract customers. However, they are not sure how best to use a website to increase their credibility with potential customers, especially because they are new to the business and do not have much experience.

Question 3: Working by yourself or with a small group of classmates, identify at least two ways that Noah and Kelly can use their website to increase their credibility as part of their persuasive strategy.

Writing a Persuasive Sales Message

As a next step, Kelly and Noah compose two sales letters for Pet Haven. One is targeted to pet owners in the area. The other is more personalized, targeted to pet owners Kelly and Noah know.

Question 4: Noah and Kelly have brainstormed some claims that they would like to include in the sales letters. Evaluate each claim to determine if it can be supported or if it represents a logical fallacy. If it can be supported, what kinds of evidence would be effective for each claim? Where can Kelly and Noah find this evidence?

a. If you have a pet and work all day, you can either allow your pet to remain lonely or take advantage of high-quality daycare services.

b. Pets that are stimulated during the day are happier and healthier than pets left alone.

c. If you are willing to bring a child to day care, then you should certainly be willing to do the same for your pet.

d. Day care is as good as medicine for a pet's health. For example, Mrs. Jones's dog was sickly before becoming a daycare client. Now the dog is healthy and energetic.

e. Daycare clients receive a discount on routine grooming.

Question 5: Noah and Kelly have decided to use the AIDA form for both letters. Alone or working with a small group of classmates, draft either of the sales letters. Use your imagination to develop specific details for the pet owners Kelly and Noah know. End each letter by asking the audience to go to the Pet Haven website for more information.

In class, compare and evaluate the various letters to see different implementations of AIDA.

Study Questions in Review

 How can the ACE process help you persuade your audience? *(pages 156–161)*

Each step of the ACE process plays a role in persuasion.

- **Analyzing helps you plan your message** by focusing on your purpose, desired outcome, and business result. Analyzing your primary and secondary audiences' (and stakeholders') needs helps you determine the content of the message. If you anticipate specific objections, you can use refutation or concession to address them. Analyzing also helps you select the best medium based on audience-, content-, and response-related criteria.
- **Composing implements the persuasive plan** by putting your plan into words.
- **Evaluating helps you review the draft for effectiveness** by considering whether the message is convincing, proposes a good solution, includes sound reasoning, anticipates possible objections, and stresses audience benefits. Evaluating also ensures a complete, concise, clear, and correct message.

 What are the basic elements of persuasion? *(pages 161–170)*

Effective persuasion combines three elements: credibility, logic, and emotion. Depending on the situation, you may need to emphasize one element over the others.

- **Building credibility** enhances the audience's perception that you have expertise and are trustworthy. You can build credibility by getting to know the audience, introducing yourself effectively, and presenting your ideas persuasively.
- **Constructing a logical argument** involves making a claim that is supported by reasons and evidence, which can be in the form of numerical data, facts, expert opinion, personal experience, or examples. When constructing arguments, avoid fallacies, which are violations of logic. They are dishonest and misleading.

- **Appealing to your audience's emotions** helps you sell your persuasive idea by appealing to your audience's emotional or psychological needs, such as safety, love and belonging, self-esteem, and self-actualization. Other psychological principles include consistency, social proof, liking, reciprocity, and scarcity. You can show your own emotional commitment by using compelling evidence and powerful language.

 What types of business messages typically require persuasion? *(pages 170–178)*

Although much business communication benefits from persuasion, four types of messages always require persuasion: recommendations for action, requests for favors, customer claims, and sales messages.

- **Recommendations for action** require that you convince someone that a problem or opportunity exists and that your idea is a good way to address the opportunity or problem.
- **Requests for favors** involve asking people to do something that takes effort, requires them to make choices, or differs from what they had planned to do. For persuasive requests, you can motivate your audience to comply by making them feel good about their actions or showing them how they will benefit.
- **Persuasive customer claims** are used when a seller is not obligated to approve a refund, exchange, or repair. Therefore, you need to persuade the seller that its policy should not apply in your situation or that it is in the seller's best interest to grant your request.
- **Sales messages** often incorporate the components of AIDA—an acronym used to suggest the organization of sales communication: attention, interest, desire, and action. These components are useful in both solicited and unsolicited sales communication.

Visual Summary

SQ1 **How can the ACE process help you persuade your audience?**

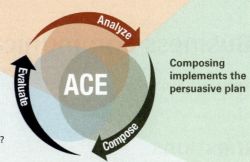

Analyzing helps you plan your message
- Purpose, desired outcome, and business result
- Audience's and stakeholders' needs
- Content needs
- Medium choices

Composing implements the persuasive plan

Evaluating helps you review the draft for effectiveness
- Have you convincingly shown that a problem or opportunity exists?
- Is the proposed solution or plan a good one?
- Is the evidence and reasoning sound?
- Have you addressed objections and stressed benefits?
- Is the information complete, concise, clear, and correct?

Analyze · **Compose** · **Evaluate** · **ACE**

SQ2 **What are the basic elements of persuasion?**

Building credibility

Provide examples of previous work.

Provide testimonials from other clients.

Provide photos and credentials of employees to personalize the company.

Showcase successful projects.

Mention awards and affiliations.

Constructing a logical argument

STEP 1 What is your position?

STEP 2 What reasons support your position?

STEP 3 What evidence supports your reasons?

Training customer service reps to use the new system will improve service and productivity and will also reduce costs.

Since installation, customer service and productivity have suffered. · The problem is costly. · Training is a cost-effective and efficient solution.

- Customer complaints have increased 50 percent.
- Number of customers served daily has decreased 15 percent.
- Increased complaints cost us $1,800 per week.
- Complaints may also cause us to lose customers.
- Targeted training will cost less than the cost of complaints.
- Manufacturer has agreed to provide the training within one week.

Appealing to your audience's emotions
- Rely on proven principles:
   Maslow: safety, love, belonging, self-esteem, self-actualization
   Cialdini: consistency, social proof, liking, reciprocity, scarcity
- Show emotional commitment
- Use storytelling and powerful language

SQ3 **What types of business messages typically require persuasion?**

online submission

Persuasive claims

My local E-Tronics store in Eagle Heights, Ohio, sold me a refurbished all-in-one printer that does not work with my computer's operating system. I would like to exchange it for one that does work with my computer.

On October 10, 20XX, I purchased a refurbished HP associate at the store mistakenly assured me that t Tecra C40-D1412 laptop, which is running Window discovered that a driver does not exist for Windows

Any sales associate can make an honest mistake, purchase one, even a more expensive one, that w store will not exchange the printer because of you I understand that such a policy may be necessary that my request to exchange this printer for one th given that I received incorrect sales advice.

Please call me at (419) 555-8623 to discuss how v hearing from you and continuing to purchase elect

Sincerely,

Elaine Mackiewetz

Elaine Mackiewetz

voice mail message

Requests for favors

Hello, Dr. Maher. This is Alexa Hampton. I was in your business law class several years ago and found it very useful. I now work as an associate lawyer at Betts, Miller, and Russo n, and I'm calling to ask you a favor.

I'm on the planning committee for the local awards luncheon is next Monday. The may keynote speaker, but a sudden death in the attending. I immediately thought of you as you be able to deliver a one-hour speech ba lessons you learned during your career?

Your years of experience and wealth of kn significant difference in the professional live who will attend the luncheon. In a one-hour more people than you were able to teach in as a business law professor. I know you are replacement for the mayor.

Please call me at 555-1887 as soon as you can discuss the details. I look forward to ta Again, Alexa Hampton, 555-1887.

Thank you.

memo

Recommendations for action

TO: Maria Cardoni
FROM: Pedro Baca
DATE: June 11, 20XX
SUBJECT: Proposed Solution for Costly Customer Service Problems

Problem
Two weeks ago, the customer service department installed new software designed to improve productivity and customer service. Employees received the standard three-hour orientation that comes with the softwa ver, the training did not cover the customized functions necessary to exchanges, and refunds.

In the two weeks that employees have been u 75 complaints more than average. Customers exchanged orders being lost, and refunds not t representatives are addressing so many time-c fewer calls, and their productivity has decrease prove that lack of training on the new software the coincidence is too great to be ignored.

These problems are costly to our company. La customer complaints and determined that each $50 in employee time and lost sales. This mea the 75 additional complaints has cost us $3,75 conservatively exceed $10,000 in two months.

We also need to consider the long-term costs sales expert Jonathan Farrington, "the cost of than the cost of any individual lost sale."* It in business and the potential lost sales from peo customer.

Proposed Solution
I have discussed this problem with the softwa Systems, and he has agreed to provide an add employees addressing the important customizi that all employees are trained, he has also agr half of the representatives attending each sess

The cost for this customized training will be $5 cost us to add the training to our original purch expensive, it is actually cost effective, conside customer service problems persist. I do not be the system without training. I've spent 10 hou new system on my own, and I still cannot figu

Mark is prepared to deliver the session next w more quickly we provide the training, the more service benefits from the company's investme

* Farrington, J. (2008). Customer complaints: T CRM-Daily.com. Retrieved from http://www.c

email

Sales messages

martin.kline@yahoo.com

Free Trial of CustomerBase Software Suite

Dear Mr. Kline:

Did you know that 50 percent of all small businesses fail within the first five years? They fail for lack of experience, lack of money, and lack of sales. Although our CustomerBase software suite cannot provide you with experience or money, it can help you develop and manage a strong customer base—an essential element for boosting sales and achieving success.

Manage Customer Relationships and Increase Sales
The CustomerBase software suite eliminates the stress of managing your customer relationships. With one user-friendly interface, you can easily keep track of information about your customers and their needs, generate custom-designed reports, and effortlessly maintain contact with your customers.

A survey of 2,500 CustomerBase users from across the country indicates that using the software contributes to increased sales and long-term business success. Over 85 percent of these businesses report that they reached their target market sales goals within the first two years. Compare that to the national failure rate and it's easy to see how your investment in CustomerBase is a sound investment in your future success.

Try It Today
Click here to download a free two-week trial copy of CustomerBase. After two weeks, you will be prompted to download the full version, which can be easily charged to your credit card account. In the meantime, please call me at 800-555-1234 to discuss how CustomerBase can enhance your business success.

Sincerely,

Parker Davis
Sales Manager
CustomerBase, Inc.
2929 Northeast Highway
St. Paul, MN 55118
Phone: 800-555-1234

Key Terms

AIDA p. 175
Argumentation p. 163
Concession p. 157
Credibility p. 162
Customer claim p. 172

Fallacy p. 166
Persuasion p. 156
Persuasive request p. 171
Pre-suasion p. 167

Primary audience p. 157
Recommendation p. 170
Refutation p. 157
Secondary audience p. 157

Solicited sales
    communication p. 175
Stakeholders p. 157
Unsolicited sales
    communication p. 175

MyLab Business Communication

If your instructor is using MyLab Business Communication, go to **www.pearson.com/ mylab/business-communication** to complete the problems marked with this icon ⭐.

Review Questions

1 What elements do you need to analyze to plan your message?

2 What is the difference between your primary audience and your secondary audience?

3 How is refutation different from concession? Describe the circumstances in which you would use one over the other.

4 What are the eight questions you should ask yourself when evaluating your persuasive messages?

5 What techniques can businesses use to build credibility through a website?

6 What are five types of evidence you can use in a logical argument?

7 What are four types of business messages that typically require persuasion?

8 What does AIDA stand for?

9 Explain the difference between social proof and scarcity.

10 How does persuasion help team decision making?

Critical Thinking Questions

⭐ 1 This chapter defines *persuasion* as "the process of influencing your audience to change their beliefs or actions in a way that facilitates a desired outcome." In what way is persuasion a process?

2 When you identify potential audience objections to your ideas—as part of planning a persuasive conversation or written message—should you address those objections directly as part of your persuasive strategy? Or should you ignore them? Describe a situation in which it might be better to address possible objections. Then identify another situation where it might be better to ignore potential objections until your audience actually objects.

3 Motivating your audience is particularly important when you are asking them to do something that is difficult or that they are resistant to doing. Imagine that you are writing a persuasive email, requesting a colleague to organize a holiday fundraising drive. Assume that the recipient would be initially resistant because of the responsibility and effort required. What content could you include to motivate that person to agree to the job?

4 Suppose you are making a presentation to your boss that recommends a change that will eliminate budget overruns. Is it important to present details about the budget overruns, or is it better just to focus on your solution to this problem? How would you decide the best approach?

⭐ 5 A study conducted on a college campus found that students soliciting donations from other students were twice as effective when they began their request by saying "I am a student here, too."[43] How would you explain this success? Why did this statement make the students more persuasive to their audience?

⭐ 6 In what key ways is a persuasive customer claim different from other kinds of requests, such as requests for information, a favor, or a donation? Why are different persuasive techniques necessary?

7 AIDA—attention, interest, desire, and action—is a long-established and widely used pattern for persuasive sales messages. Why do you think AIDA works so well?

8 In this chapter, you learned that fallacious reasoning can be unethical if you intentionally use it to mislead your audience. What else could you do in an attempt to persuade that could be considered unethical? **[Related to the Ethics feature on page 166]**

9 To be persuasive, business websites must present a company as credible. Assume you are starting a new business and you do not have any customer testimonials or past projects to present on your website. How else can you communicate credibility?

10 Imagine you are starting a new business and you are developing a persuasive presentation to give to potential investors. What questions do you imagine investors would need answered in order to be persuaded to invest?

Key Concept Exercises

 SQ1 **How can the ACE process help you persuade your audience?** *(pages 156–161)*

1 Analyzing helps you plan your message

Assume that you have an opportunity to travel to China during the summer as part of a Global Business Initiative project at your school. The goal of the trip is to visit businesses in that country, learn more about the differences between American and Chinese businesses, and make some international contacts. The school will provide the funding for your trip. Each student, however, is asked to request donations from local companies to support the project. You decide to approach Keith Dinsmore, the president of a shoe manufacturing company in your community, to request a donation. You selected this person because he graduated from your university and because many of his company's products are manufactured in China. Analyze the communication situation to plan your communication:

a. What should be the specific purpose of your communication? What specific outcome do you want? Will you ask for a specific amount of money, or will you have some other message?

b. What information will Mr. Dinsmore need?

c. What reasons or benefits can you offer Mr. Dinsmore to support why he should donate?

d. What objections do you anticipate? Prepare possible responses for each objection.

e. What medium should you use to communicate with Mr. Dinsmore? Should you make your request by email? By phone? Or should you ask to meet in person? What are the advantages and disadvantages of each option?

2 Composing implements the persuasive plan

Refer to Exercise 1. Assume that you chose to write a persuasive email to Mr. Dinsmore. Based on your analysis from that exercise, compose a first draft of the message.

3 Evaluating helps you review the draft for effectiveness

Refer to Exercises 1 and 2. Evaluate your first draft and explain how it meets the following criteria. If it doesn't, explain how you could modify the message.

a. Have you convincingly shown that a problem or an opportunity exists?

b. Is the proposed solution or plan a good one?

c. Is the evidence and reasoning sound?

d. Have you addressed potential objections and stressed benefits?

e. Is the message easy to read?

f. Is the information complete, concise, clear, and correct?

g. Do you need to change anything to get your desired result?

SQ2 **What are the basic elements of persuasion?** *(pages 161–170)*

4 Building credibility

a. In your entrepreneurship class, you and three classmates developed an idea that you would like to turn into a business: a tutoring service for high school and middle school students in your community. Tutors would be students at your college or university who are majoring in the subject that they are tutoring and who have prior experience tutoring in the subject. The tutoring services would be advertised online. Prices would be $40/hour if the clients come to campus and $50/hour if tutors go to the clients' homes or other locations. For the business to succeed, you know that you will need to build credibility with the local school administration and with local families. Review the approaches to building credibility on page 162. How would you build credibility for yourself and your new company?

b. You are a sales associate in the fine china and glassware department of an exclusive department store. Every few months, your department runs a big sale, and your manager requires all associates to call customers to persuade them to come to the store and shop during the sale. You feel that you have very little credibility in these phone calls. The customers believe you are just interested in increasing your sales commission. Brainstorm ways that you can build your credibility in these calls so that more people will be persuaded to shop during the sale.

c. You are a project manager for a software company. One of your developers, a recent hire, is having difficulty fitting in with her team. Her skills are excellent, and you would like to promote her to a leadership position, but her coworkers do not seem to value her expertise and perspectives as highly as you do. Her previous experience is in research and higher education rather than business, and she has a PhD in mathematics. In contrast, most of the other developers have worked at software companies for most of their careers and do not have advanced degrees. You have heard several members of the team dismiss her ideas (which are frequently good and often excellent, in your view) because they are "impractical" or even "naive." The other developers tend to emphasize their own practical experience of "shipping code" when they argue with her, to criticize her lack of "real-world experience." What suggestions would you give your new hire for building her credibility with coworkers who do not share her background? What reasons would you give the other members of the team to accept her as an expert despite the fact that her career has been different from theirs?

5 Constructing a logical argument

You work for a development and construction company that specializes in commercial real estate. You need to make a persuasive presentation to your town council, requesting that the town rezone a parcel of land—Parcel 5812—from residential to commercial in a fast-growing area so you can build a retail shopping area anchored by a grocery store. Based on your research, you are going to provide three reasons the town should rezone the land for a new shopping area:

1. The residential population in the area is growing, while nearby shopping options are not.

2. The nearest grocery store, which is 4 miles away and in a different town, is accessible only by a two-lane highway, suggesting that without a nearby store, traffic congestion may increase.

3. The retail space will stimulate growth and help increase the town's tax base.

What kind of evidence would you include to support each of these three reasons? For example, what kind of evidence would help you prove that the residential population is growing?

6 Avoiding logical fallacies [Related to the Ethics feature on page 166]

The following list includes examples of weak and illogical arguments. Explain the problem with each. Why should you disagree with each statement?

a. Of the three ad campaigns presented by the marketing department, I think we should go with the second one because it's the best.

b. The media is biased against our products. For the past two days, the *City Journal* has featured stories about our competitors but hasn't mentioned us.

c. Our current travel authorization forms are not efficient. We should either not require authorization or decline all travel requests.

d. I'm not surprised sales have dropped. The sales reps are completely incompetent.

e. If democracy is the best way to run a government, then it must be the best way to run a company also.

f. Sales in our international branches nearly doubled after the CEO hired a new assistant. We should promote the assistant to vice president of sales.

7 Appealing to your audience's emotions

You are a real estate agent who has just shown a home to Tom and Serena Phillips, a young professional couple who seemed very interested in the property. They are looking to start a family in the next few years and like the large backyard. They also like the neighborhood and reputation of the local schools. Most important, the house is in their price range. They are hesitant to make an offer on the house, however, because it's a large investment and because the house needs new carpeting.

You know this house will not stay on the market long. In fact, you have two other buyers who have shown an interest. However, you think this is a perfect house for Tom and Serena, and you'd like to persuade them to make an offer. They have the facts, so you decide to compose a message that emphasizes emotional appeals. Review all the techniques for motivating an audience with emotional appeals on pages 164–170. Using at least three of the techniques, develop content that you could use in your message.

8 Analyzing persuasion in presentations [Related to the Technology feature on pages 169]

Visit the TED website (www.ted.com) and choose a presentation on a subject that interests you. Take a look at both the video and transcript of the presentation. Write one or two paragraphs, describing how the speaker uses the elements of persuasion—building credibility, constructing a logical argument, and appealing to the audience's emotions—to make his or her point. Submit your description along with a link to the TED talk. Be prepared to show a portion of the talk and present your analysis in class.

9 Persuading in different cultures [Related to the Culture feature on page 178]

If you attend a school with people from other cultures, interview two or three people from these cultures to gather information about how they would approach the same persuasive task in their home cultures—for example, asking a professor to speak at an event, asking a supervisor to be assigned to a specific project, asking an acquaintance for a ride to the airport. Compare results relating to different cultures and write a brief message to your instructor describing your findings. Be sure to support each finding with evidence.

 What types of business messages typically require persuasion? *(pages 170–178)*

10 Recommendations for action

You are the director of volunteer services for a regional hospital. Most of your volunteers are retirees who work four-hour shifts one or two days a week, providing various services such as transporting patients to X-ray, delivering lab results to doctors' offices, and greeting visitors in reception areas. During the summers, many of your volunteers go on vacation, which leaves you with a lot of empty shifts to fill. During a directors' meeting, you suggest that the hospital create a summer student volunteer program to recruit high school and college students. The job would provide valuable experience to students interested in pursuing a medical career. However, several of the department heads expressed concern about whether the student volunteers would be mature enough or responsible enough to commit to unpaid summer work. You believe that requiring high GPAs, letters of recommendations, and interviews will help the hospital select mature and responsible students. The committee asks you to write a recommendation report outlining the idea in more detail. Write a persuasive recommendation using the following outline:

- Propose a specific recommendation.
- Identify the problem that needs solving.
- Provide evidence that the problem is important.
- Propose a solution and support it with persuasive reasoning, stressing benefits and providing evidence to support your claims.
- Address potential objections.
- Conclude by requesting action.

11 Requests for favors

Assume that you are a sales representative for Acme Widget Company. Acme has just developed a new and improved widget, which you are planning to present to your biggest account, Southline Manufacturing, in two days. You are proofreading your sales presentation when your mother calls to share the sad news that your favorite uncle passed away this morning and your aunt has asked you to deliver the eulogy. Your uncle had been ill for some time, so the news was not a shock. However, the fact that the funeral conflicts with your presentation Monday morning does cause concern. You know you have to attend the funeral. Your choice is to ask the client to reschedule the meeting or ask a colleague to make your presentation for you. Because Southline wants to make an immediate purchasing decision, you decide to ask another sales representative, Jamal Harrison, to fill in for you. Jamal does not know anything about the customer, but he is familiar with the new widget and he has exceptional presentation skills. Consider audience benefits and persuasive techniques to convince Jamal to fill in for you. Draft the message, using whichever medium you think is most appropriate, to request that Jamal do you this favor.

12 Persuasive customer claims

Assume that you are the purchasing agent for Henderson Market Research. You process orders for office supplies, equipment, and furniture. The chairs in the executive conference room are 20 years old and show signs of wear and tear. The CFO approved the funds to purchase new chairs, and the CEO's administrative assistant, Ronda, selected the style and color to coordinate with the room. You process the order with the same local office furniture company you've always used and were pleased to receive a substantial discount because the chairs Ronda selected are being discontinued and the store is selling its remaining stock. All sales of discontinued merchandise are final. Three weeks later when the chairs arrive, Ronda calls you to complain that the chairs are the wrong color. She wanted black chairs, but received brown. Ronda complains that the brown chairs simply will not work with the color scheme in the conference room. You quickly retrieve your order and realize that you entered the wrong SKU number. You tell Ronda you will try to take care of it as quickly as possible. Compose a message to the office furniture company—Winchester Furniture—explaining the problem and requesting that it replace the chairs. Your contact person at the furniture company is Danielle Connors.

Use the ACE process. Identify the purpose and outcome of your message. Analyze your audience to determine what questions and objections they may have. Identify how you will build credibility, construct a logical argument, and motivate action.

13 Sales messages: AIDA

You are the assistant sales director for a company that is a market leader in the hand sanitizer industry. You have a new product—the SaniPlus—that you plan to target to existing business customers through unsolicited sales messages. The product is a portable, touch-free dispenser of hand sanitizer. The dispenser stands on the floor, can be positioned in strategic locations, and can be moved to other locations. The director of sales asks you to draft a message that incorporates the AIDA elements to persuade existing customers to purchase your new product. Create information about the product to support your persuasive message.

14 Sales messages: Credibility, logic, and emotion

Evaluate the persuasive strategy in the letter from real estate agent Scott Navas, reproduced below. How effective is it at building credibility, presenting an evidence-based argument, and engaging emotion? What revisions would you suggest? Summarize your analysis in a brief memo to your instructor.

letter

ReNew Properties

| 555 Red Lion Road | Westlake, TN 38590 | 555-555-4673 |

ReNew Properties
555 Red Lion Road
Westlake, TN 38590

Dear Neighbor:

I am writing to introduce myself. My name is Scott Navas, a real estate broker and your neighbor with ReNew Properties at 1804 Westlake Avenue. While my clients' needs take me all over the metro area, my passion is working with buyers and sellers in Westlake.

When it comes to buying or selling a home, differentiation is one of the keys to success. Westlake Properties and I have created differentiation in a number of ways to give my clients an advantage in today's competitive marketplace.

- Cutting–edge technology like the ReNew agent app leverages ReNew's "market within a market"
- Custom brochures, high–res photos, and floorplans
- Custom signage with property–specific URLs
- Weekly report that provides a data snapshot of your home, comparable properties, and your local market
- Enhanced listings on the most active online listing sites

To learn more about how ReNew Properties and I set clients apart from the crowd through innovative marketing and technology, contact me today at 555-555-4673 or ScottNavas@ReNewproperties.com.

Scott Navas

Scott Navas | Broker

ScottNavas@ReNewproperties.com
www.ScottNavas.com

Accompanies Exercise 14

Writing Exercises

15 Writing a persuasive request: Intern needed

You are the head of the accounting department for a large company that hires student interns each summer. You have always requested two or three interns, depending on the needs of your staff. In years past, the human resources (HR) department not only fulfilled your intern requests but was also able to send you students who were accounting majors. This year, however, HR announced that due to budget cuts, the internship pool would be reduced by half. You can request an intern—only one—but HR will assign interns only to selected departments, and HR cannot guarantee that your intern, if assigned, will actually be an accounting major. HR will determine the intern assignments based on justified requests from each department head. During a department meeting with your staff, you explain the situation and ask for their input. The group offers the following justification:

- The accounting department employs 15 full-time staff members. Your department is one of the smallest in the company, yet is responsible for critical operational and budgetary functions upon which all other departments depend.

- The company's fiscal year ends June 30, which means significant work is required in the summer months to generate year-end reports in addition to regular accounting operations.

- Coincidentally, two employees in the accounting department will be out on maternity leave, one during May and June, and the other during June and July. These absences will further limit the department's ability to fulfill its end-of-year responsibilities.

Use the ACE process to write a message to the HR department requesting an intern (an accounting major, if possible) for your department. Do not simply repeat the points just outlined. Develop credibility, put the arguments in an effective order, supply evidence to support your arguments, and use techniques to motivate action.

16 Writing a persuasive recommendation: University tablet computers

A friend attends Northern State University (NSU), where each student receives a tablet computer as part of his or her tuition. Many of the classes at NSU use e-books, which significantly reduce textbook costs. You believe the students at your campus would benefit from the savings as well as the technology. You want to persuade your school's administration to become a "tablet campus." However, you predict many objections. The costs to purchase and maintain the tablets are an obvious concern. Other potential problems include theft and misuse. In addition, some faculty may not want students to be distracted by web browsing and social networking during class.

To prepare a persuasive communication, first identify possible concessions or refutations for these and other objections. Then focus on audience benefits and other persuasive strategies you learned in this chapter. Compose a message requesting a meeting to discuss the program in more detail, and then draft a presentation to use during the meeting.

17 Writing a persuasive recommendation: Afterschool program

You are an employee of a midsized company. You estimate that 40 percent of the employees have school-aged children. You want to persuade the company to create an afterschool program in the empty warehouse space adjacent to the office building. Obvious objections include the expenses for personnel, decorating and furnishing the space, toys, and additional liability insurance. Brainstorm other possible obstacles, determine audience benefits (for all stakeholders), and use effective persuasive techniques to sell your idea. Write a short recommendation to the company president.

18 Writing a persuasive recommendation: Using Facebook to attract customers

Your school recently opened a new food-court-style dining facility in the student union. Although the union is more convenient for most students, several fast-food restaurants across the street offer value meals and special deals that are more cost-effective for students. To encourage students to eat at the new food court, you suggest to the facilities director that the union update its Facebook strategy to motivate students to come to the food court. The director is intrigued by this idea, but she needs more information. Do some research about how restaurants use Facebook to attract customers, and compose a persuasive recommendation to the facilities director.

Collaboration Exercises

19 Analyzing persuasion in websites

As a team, find a website that effectively uses the techniques and principles described in this chapter to persuade its audience, and analyze the persuasive techniques the website uses. Develop a short slide presentation that identifies three ways in which the website is persuasive. Organize your slides this way:

Slide 1. Your title slide. Include the name of the website, a screen shot of the home page, and information that identifies your team and assignment.

Slide 2. Identify the purpose and audience of the website.

Slide 3. Identify and illustrate the first way in which the site is persuasive.

Slide 4. Identify and illustrate the second way in which the site is persuasive.

Slide 5. Identify and illustrate the third way in which the site is persuasive.

For slides 2–5, use a short sentence headline that briefly states the main point of the slide. Then, on the body of the slide, present evidence to support the headline. Evidence may include screen shots, excerpts of text, and graphics from the website.

20 Making a team-based decision: Recommending a guest speaker [Related to the Collaboration feature on page 177]

Assume that you and two or three other students in your class have been appointed as a committee to propose a guest speaker

to talk to your business communication class. The speaker can be from the business community, the not-for-profit world, your school, or some other context. The only requirements are that the speaker lives or works within 100 miles of your location and that the speaker can address a topic that is, in some way, relevant to the material of the course. As a team, recommend one speaker by following this process:

- Identify several possible candidates.

- Develop criteria for making a decision.

- Discuss and evaluate all the candidates. Assign team members to make a persuasive case for each candidate.

- Collaboratively select one candidate.

- Write a persuasive message to your instructor recommending the speaker you have chosen and providing reasons to support your recommendation.

21 Making a team-based decision: Proposing a solution to a problem [Related to the Collaboration feature on page 177]

As a team, identify an issue in your school or community that you believe should be addressed. Pick an issue that is important to everyone in your team. For example, you may believe the school should offer more career assistance, better dining options, or better on-campus transportation. Then, as a team, follow this process:

1. Identify several possible solutions.

2. Develop and challenge strong arguments for each solution.

3. Collaboratively determine a team recommendation.

4. Write a message to your instructor identifying the issue, your team's proposed solution, and the reasons to support it.

22 Gathering information and evidence

Referring to Exercise 21, gather additional information and evidence to support your team's proposed solution. Each person on your team should ask 10 other students whether they support your proposal and why. Your goal is to collect persuasive evidence from students to justify your recommendation. Spend a day or two gathering the feedback and then compare your findings with your team. Identify commonalities among the responses and make a list of persuasive reasons to support your recommendation. Based on your findings, draft a persuasive message to the person or committee in a position to implement your recommendation.

Social Media Exercises

23 Using emotional appeals in social media

Consider how you have been persuaded by emotional appeals or motivational strategies through a business's social media sites. Have you purchased products or services you would not have known about without these appeals? Or have you received discounts or deals for being part of the company's social media community? Describe one company's social media appeals and how they have (or have not) successfully persuaded you to purchase products or services you may not have otherwise considered. You may be asked to summarize your experiences in writing, discuss them in small groups, or present them in class.

24 Offering third-party deals through social media

Companies like Living Social, Groupon, FatWallet, and Ebates are the "middle men" that offer deals to potential consumers from the companies that provide the actual products and services. In small groups, discuss why companies use these middle men rather than offering the deals through their own social media communities. What are the advantages and disadvantages of paying another company to offer reduced prices on your products and services? Summarize your discussion and conclusions in writing and be prepared to present them to the class.

Speaking Exercises

25 Giving a TED-style talk [Related to the Technology feature on page 169]

Write and deliver a five- to six-minute TED-style talk to persuade your college to implement a new policy you care about. Highlight the places in your transcript where you use the elements of persuasion to convince your audience, and submit the transcript to your instructor.

26 Impromptu presentations

Make a one- to two-minute presentation designed to persuade your classmates to do one of the following things:

a. Change their major to yours

b. Join a new student organization that has an expensive membership fee

c. Attend graduate school full time immediately after graduation and defer full-time work, OR attend graduate school part time while working full time, OR defer graduate school for a few years to work full time

d. Spend a year doing public service before entering the workforce

e. Begin contributing to individual retirement accounts as soon as they can

In your presentation, include at least one statement designed to establish credibility, one logical argument with reasons and evidence, and one benefit designed to motivate.

27 Impromptu speaking: Business role-plays

In a one- to two-minute presentation, explain how you would persuade your audience in each of the following business situations:

a. Assume that you are the new director of fundraising for a not-for-profit organization. In the past, your organization has created targeted fundraising events, such as galas and pledge drives, to increase donations and contributions. You think a monthly e-newsletter to regular donors could keep them informed of how their money is put to use and promote the events now promoted only through fundraising letters and web advertising. Although collecting email addresses and developing an email database would be time consuming, you believe the benefits would certainly outweigh the effort.

The board of directors supports your idea, but the membership director—who would be responsible for collecting the email addresses and distributing the monthly e-newsletter—is resistant because she is very busy and does not have the time. You see her at lunch and decide to discuss the matter with her individually. In one to two minutes, persuade her to agree to this idea.

b. You are on a sales team that is planning an important presentation for a prospective client. During the meeting, the team leader discusses the content to present and the kind of visual aids and handouts to create. During the discussion, you are surprised that no one mentions analyzing the audience. You believe that audience analysis is necessary to create a presentation that meets the client's need. In one to two minutes, persuade your team to analyze the audience.

c. You coordinate the purchase of office supplies and equipment for your company. Since the company began 22 years ago, it has used Office Rx as its supply and equipment vendor. You call or email Office Rx with your order, and the order is personally delivered to your office within a few business days. As a small local company, Office Rx does not support online ordering. However, it does not charge delivery fees. Although the ordering process is tedious, you prefer this company over the larger online vendors because of its low prices and friendly customer service. In fact, you usually speak with the same person, Annette. During a telephone conversation with Annette to place a new order, you decide to ask her about the possibility of online ordering. She indicates that the company had never considered online ordering because of its small size and local clientele. In one to two minutes, persuade Annette to develop an online ordering system. Address possible objections and include benefits for both Annette's company and yours.

28 Executive briefings

Conduct research to prepare for a three- to five-minute persuasive presentation on one of the following topics. Prepare a slides or some other visual support for your presentation.

a. Conduct a web search on "motivating millennials." Skim business articles, and gather suggestions for understanding, inspiring, and managing millennial workers. Select three specific suggestions and then persuade an executive to adopt these suggestions.

b. Assume you work for a company that is reevaluating which schools it will visit to recruit new employees. The company has decided not to recruit at your school because it is too far away. Identify at least three benefits of recruiting at your school and prepare a presentation to persuade the company to add your school to its recruitment list. Be sure to both emphasize benefits and address objections.

c. Your company has five minivans in the motor pool that it purchased 10 years ago and that need to be replaced. The most important criteria are that the minivans have at least six-person capacity and that they be fuel efficient. Research current purchasing options and create a visual that compares your three top choices. Then provide a persuasive presentation recommending one of the options.

d. Each year your company identifies at least one local nonprofit organization to which it will give a large donation. Typically the company supports organizations focusing on the arts, education, or community building. Research two local nonprofit organizations, and make a persuasive recommendation to support one of them based on your findings.

e. Your employer would like to contract with a university to offer an online MBA program to support employees' continuing education. Research the current opportunities available online and prepare a persuasive presentation recommending one of the options.

Grammar Exercises

29 Phrases and clauses (see Appendix C: Grammar, Punctuation, Mechanics, and Conventions— Section 1.2.2)

It is easier to write grammatical sentences when you understand the difference between phrases and clauses. In the following paragraph, circle or highlight each phrase. Underline each dependent clause once and each independent clause twice. There are a total of 10 dependent and independent clauses and a total of 15 phrases.

In the list of tech-etiquette offenders, the "misguided multitasker" may be the worst, although the "broadcaster" is a close second. Holding their iPhones under the table, multitaskers send email or text messages during meetings. The nonverbal message that they are sending to everyone else is that the meeting is not important to them. Broadcasters use their cell phones anytime, anywhere, and they apparently don't mind being overheard by others. On a crowded elevator, they will discuss the intimate details of a medical procedure or they will talk loudly about confidential business matters.

MyLab Business Communication

Go to **www.pearson.com/mylab/business-communication** for Auto-graded writing questions as well as the following Assisted-graded writing questions:

1. If you are persuading someone to make a business decision, why is it important to include a strong logical argument rather than just appeal to that person's emotions?

2. If the goal of persuasion is to influence people to agree with your point of view, why is listening an important skill in persuasion?

References

1. Aristotle. (trans. 2006). *On rhetoric: A theory of civic discourse* (G. A. Kennedy, Trans.) (2nd ed.). New York: Oxford University Press.

2. Dlugan, A. (2010, January 24). Ethos, pathos, logos: 3 pillars of public speaking. *Six Minutes: Speaking and Presentation Skills.* Retrieved from http://sixminutes.dlugan.com/ethos-pathos-logos/

3. As examples of combining elements of persuasion, see the essays in Kenrick, D. T., Goldstein, N. J., & Braver, S. L. (Eds.). (2012). *Six degrees of social influence: Science, application, and the psychology of Robert Cialdini.* New York: Oxford University Press; Conger, J. (1998, May–June). The necessary art of persuasion. *Harvard Business Review,* 84–95; and Cialdini, R. (2001, October). Harnessing the science of persuasion. *Harvard Business Review,* 72–79.

4. Heinrichs, J. (2013). *Thank you for arguing, revised and updated edition: What Aristotle, Lincoln, and Homer Simpson can teach us about the art of persuasion.* New York: Three Rivers Press.

5. Stiff, J. B., & Mongeau, P. A. (2016). *Persuasive communication* (3rd ed.). New York: The Guilford Press.

6. Wallace, E. (2009, May–June). *Business relationships that last.* Austin, TX: Greenleaf Book Group Press. Also, Conger, J. (1998, May–June). The necessary art of persuasion. *Harvard Business Review,* 84–95.

7. Zhu, L. L., Aquino, K., & Vadera, A. K. (2016). What makes professors appear credible: The effect of demographic characteristics and ideological beliefs. *Journal of Applied Psychology,* 101(6), 862–880.

8. Cialdini, R. (2009). *Influence: Science and practice* (5th ed., pp. 142–152). Boston, MA: Pearson/Allyn & Bacon.

9. Many social scientists have done research to confirm what is called the "liking heuristic." For a brief literature review, see Metzger, M., & Flannigan, J. (2013). Credibility and trust of information in online environments: The use of cognitive heuristics. *Journal of Pragmatics, 59*, Part B, 210–220.

10. Lipschultz, J. H. (2013, September 4). Social media trust, credibility, and reputation management. *The Huffington Post.* Retrieved from http://www.huffingtonpost.com/jeremy-harris-lipschultz/social-media-trust-credib_b_3858017.html

11. Aula, P., & Heinonen, J. (2016). *The reputable firm: How digitalization of communication is revolutionizing reputation management.* Cham, Switzerland: Springer International Publishing.

12. Beck, M. (2015, April 3). Did Lord & Taylor's Instagram influencer campaign cross the line? Retrieved from http://marketingland.com/did-lord-taylors-instagram-influencer-campaign-cross-the-line-123961

13. Kouzes, J. M., & Posner B. Z. (2011). *Credibility: How leaders gain and lose it, why people demand it* (rev. ed.). San Francisco: John Wiley & Sons.

14. Eisenstein, P. A. (2010, February 17). Toyota official says credibility is damaged. Retrieved from http://www.msnbc.msn.com/id/35369379/ns/business-autos/

15. Kelly, A. M. (2012, March 5). Has Toyota's image recovered from the brand's recall crisis? *Forbes.* Retrieved from http://www.forbes.com/sites/annemariekelly/2012/03/05/has-toyotas-image-recovered-from-the-brands-recall-crisis/

16. Smith, G., & Parloff, R. (2016, March 7). Hoaxwagen: How the massive diesel fraud incinerated VW's reputation—And will hobble the company for years to come. *Fortune.* Retrieved from http://fortune.com/inside-volkswagen-emissions-scandal/

17. Mittleman, M. (2016, April 1). Volkswagen brand's U.S. sales decline 10% in fifth straight drop. Retrieved from https://www.bloomberg.com/news/articles/2016-04-01/volkswagen-brand-s-u-s-sales-decline-10-in-fifth-straight-drop

18. Chamorro-Premuzic, T. (2015, June 2). Persuasion depends mostly on the audience. *Harvard Business Review.* Retrieved from https://hbr.org/2015/06/persuasion-depends-mostly-on-the-audience

19. Heinrichs, J. (2013). *Thank you for arguing: What Aristotle, Lincoln, and Homer Simpson can teach us about the art of persuasion* (rev. ed.). New York, NY: Three Rivers Press.

20. Maslow, A. (1998). *Toward a psychology of being* (3rd ed.). Hoboken, NJ: Wiley. (Original work published in 1962)

21. Henrich, J. (2015). Culture and social behaviour. *Current Opinion in Behavioral Science, 31*, 84–89.

22. Cialdini, R. (2009). *Influence: Science and practice* (5th ed.). Upper Saddle River, NJ: Pearson Education.

23. PLAY! by SEPHORA. (2017). Retrieved from http://www.sephora.com/play

24. Cialdini, R. (2016). *Pre-Suasion.* New York: Simon & Schuster, p. 75.

25. Schwabel, D. (2016, September 6). Robert Cialdini: How to master the art of "pre-suasion." *Forbes.* Retrieved from http://www.forbes.com/sites/danschawbel/2016/09/06/robert-cialdini-how-to-master-the-art-of-pre-suasion

26. Cialdini, R. (2016). *Pre-Suasion* (pp. 202–207.). New York, NY: Simon & Schuster.

27. Gordon, J. (2006, May–June). *Presentations that change minds* (pp. 69–98). New York, NY: McGraw-Hill.

28. Brazil's weeping President Luiz Inacio Lula da Silva revels in 2016 Olympics vote. (2009, October 3). *The Telegraph.* Retrieved from http://www.telegraph.co.uk/sport/othersports/olympics/news/6257463/Brazils-weeping-President-Luiz--Inacio-Lula-da-Silva-revels-in-2016-Olympics-vote.html

29. Grohmann, K. (2009, October 2). Olympics-FIFA's Blatter moved by Lula's Rio 2016 bid speech. Retrieved from http://www.reuters.com/article/olympicsNews/idUSL257623920091002

30. TED. (n.d.). History of TED. Retrieved from http://www.ted.com/about/our-organization/history-of-ted

31. Cuddy, A. (2012). *Your body language shapes who you are* [Video]. Retrieved from http://www.ted.com/talks/amy_cuddy_your_body_language_shapes_who_you_are?language=en

32. Singal, J., & Dahl, M. (2016, September 30). Here is Amy Cuddy's response to critiques of her power-posing research. Retrieved from http://nymag.com/scienceofus/2016/09/read-amy-cuddys-response-to-power-posing-critiques.html

33. O'Hara, C. (2014, July 30). How to tell a great story. *Harvard Business Review.* Retrieved from https://hbr.org/2014/07/how-to-tell-a-great-story

34. Steve Jobs 2007 Macworld Keynote. Posted by Michael Noriega, iPhone Keynote 2007 Complete. *YouTube.com.* Retrieved from https://www.youtube.com/watch?v=t4OEsI0Sc_s&feature=kp

35. Elmer-DeWitt, P. (2009, March 12). iPhone sales grew 245% in 2008—Gartner. Retrieved from http://tech.fortune.cnn.com/2009/03/12/iphone-sales-grew-245-in-2008- gartner/

36. Vogelstein, F. (2013, October 4). And then Steve said, "Let there be an iPhone." *The New York Times.* Retrieved from http://www.nytimes.com/2013/10/06/magazine/and-then-steve-said-let-there-be-an-iphone.html

37. Rosen, R. J. (2013, September 10). The original iPhone keynote is still amazing to watch. *The Atlantic.* Retrieved from http://www.theatlantic.com/technology/archive/2013/09/the-original-iphone-keynote-is-still-amazing-to-watch/279518/

38. Morgan, N. (2014). *Power cues.* Cambridge, MA: Harvard Business Review Press.

39. Burnes, S. (2016, April 28). Seven cultural aspects to know before doing business in Mexico. Retrieved from http://www.susanburnsllc.com/cultural-differences-to-do-business-in-mexico

40. Passport to Trade 2.0. (2014). Business communication in the Netherlands. Retrieved from http://businessculture.org/western-europe/business-culture-in-netherlands/business-communication-in-netherlands/ www.invest.uktradeinvest.gov.uk/download/107212_100410/Doing%20Business%20in%20Netherlands.html

41. Making room for emotions at work. (2005). Retrieved from http://www.managingpeopleatwork.com/Article.php?art_num=3902

42. Cialdini, R. (2009). *Influence: Science and practice* (p. 49). Boston, MA: Pearson/Allyn & Bacon.

43. Aune, K., & Basil, M. (1994). A relational obligations approach to the foot-in-the-mouth effect. *Journal of Applied Social Psychology, 24*, 546–556.

6 Communicating Bad News

STUDY QUESTIONS

MyLab Business Communication
★ Improve Your Grade!

If your instructor is using MyLab Business Communication, visit **www.pearson.com/ mylab/business-communication** for videos, simulations, and writing exercises.

New Hires @ Work

Kishwar Mehmood
City University of Hong Kong

Personal Assistant to Directors @ Prism Group

When a potential client declines our proposal, it's my job to report the bad news to my superiors. I explain the reasons why they declined and use their feedback to identify whether we might be able to resubmit the proposal at some point in the future. I assure my superiors that I will be following up with the prospective client from time to time. In this way, my goal is to turn the bad news into a future opportunity.

Photo courtesy of Kishwar Mehmood

Chapter 6 | Introduction

Have you ever received a job rejection letter? Or been told that your idea for a group project wouldn't be used? Bad news is hard to get—and for that reason it is also challenging to give. Communicating bad news tactfully and achieving a good outcome is a difficult combination that requires preparation and practice. You need to accomplish a number of goals that may seem incompatible at first:

- How can you state the bad news clearly and at the same time project a positive image of yourself and your organization?
- How can you convince the audience to accept the news without protest or further discussion?
- And how can you do all this without making your audience feel as if they have been treated unfairly or even have grounds for a lawsuit?[1]

Organizations that routinely communicate bad-news messages develop standard **templates** to accomplish these goals. This explains why so many job rejection letters sound similar. In most instances, you cannot rely on a template to communicate bad news effectively. However, you *can* use the ACE process to think critically about your "bad-news" situation and compose a message that will achieve good results. You may even be able to use the bad-news situation as an opportunity to create **goodwill**—a positive relationship between you and your audience. **Figure 6.1** provides a helpful set of questions for adapting ACE to bad-news messages.

The next three sections of this chapter address each stage of the ACE process separately and cover each question posed in Figure 6.1. How can you analyze and plan a bad-news message? What strategies are useful for composing the content? What special challenges occur when evaluating bad-news messages?

template A model or file that contains key features of a document and serves as a starting point for creating a new document.

goodwill A positive relationship between you (or your company) and your audience.

Analyze
- What is the bad news?
- What business result do you want to achieve?
- How will the audience react to this news?
- What justification and explanation should you include?
- Is there anything you can say to soften the bad news?
- Should you include an apology?
- Can you do anything else to project a positive image and maintain goodwill?
- What is the best medium for this message?

Evaluate
- Is the bad news stated clearly yet sensitively?
- Will the message convince the audience to accept the bad news?
- Does the message project a good image of you and maintain goodwill with the audience?
- Will the message achieve a good business result?
- Have you avoided legal complications?

Compose
- Should you begin with the bad news or build up to it?
- How can you clearly phrase the bad news?
- What content and techniques should you use to soften the impact of the message?
- How can you close the message appropriately?

FIGURE 6.1 Using ACE for Bad-News Messages

SQ1 How should you analyze and plan a bad-news message?

Before composing a bad-news message, analyze the situation by asking yourself several questions that help you develop content. The answers will also help you choose the best medium. The following sections describe this process in the context of a specific scenario: delivering bad news to a client.

Analyze

Ask questions that help you develop content

Imagine that you run a one-person web development business. Yesterday, you made a proposal to a new client, Great Expectations Books, a small local business, to add an e-commerce function to its website. After meeting with the manager, you proposed installing an inventory database and online ordering function within a month. However, today you receive a request from a long-time client, South Shore Community Television (SSCT), which needs your immediate help with a critical repair to its website. This client is one week away from a major fund-raising pledge drive and needs the online pledge function repaired.

You feel obligated to help SSCT for two reasons: (1) You originally programmed the SSCT website and may be the only person who can fix it quickly, and (2) SSCT is a long-time client that gives you a lot of business each year. Although you made a commitment to Great Expectations and do not want to disappoint this new client, you decide to inform the manager at Great Expectations that you cannot meet the original deadline and need a two-week extension. How will you deliver this bad news? Analyzing is crucial to developing a message that supports your business goals and positively affects audience reaction. Consider the analyzing questions outlined in Figure 6.1:

- **What is the bad news?** The bad news is that you cannot meet the original deadline, but you can get the job done with an additional two weeks.

- **What business result do you want to achieve?** You would like Great Expectations to grant you an extension rather than withdraw its agreement and hire a new web developer.

- **How will the audience react to this news?** Although you cannot exactly predict the audience's reaction, you can think about the situation from the perspective of Great Expectations. It currently does not use an e-commerce function and has an informational website that works. You also know it plans to launch an "order online" advertising campaign at the end of the month. You think Great Expectations will be disappointed with the extended deadline but won't be upset enough to find a different website developer. You would like the company to accept your request and postpone its ad campaign for two weeks.

- **What justification and explanation should you include?** To be effective, a bad-news message should explain the reasons behind the bad news. Of all the features in your message, this explanation has the most power to influence the audience to accept your bad news.[2,3] Consider the questions the audience may have: *"Why can't you deliver your services in the agreed-upon time? Why do you need an additional two weeks?"* If you want a continued relationship with Great Expectations, you will need to provide a reason for the delay. You can explain, for example, that another client has had an emergency that only you can handle. You do not need to name the client or explain the nature of the emergency.

- **Is there anything you can say to soften the bad news?** For example, is there any good news to include? Will the audience benefit in any way? Does this cloud have a silver lining? To soften the bad news, you can communicate to Great Expectations that you value its business. You can also let the company know why the other client's request took priority, without making Great Expectations feel less important. If you are not able to think of any direct audience benefits in this situation, you can subtly suggest that this situation demonstrates that your commitment to customers extends beyond the website development process. You are available for updates and revisions, especially in critical circumstances when time is an issue. Finally, you might find a *silver lining*, or a hidden benefit, in this delay. For example, with more time before programming the e-commerce site, Great Expectations can survey customers to learn more about how they would like the site organized.

- **Should you include an apology?** Because you were responsible for not meeting the agreed-upon deadline—and perhaps delaying Great Expectations' advertising campaign—you decide that you owe this new client a sincere apology that acknowledges that you understand the implications of this delay.

- **Can you do anything else to project a positive image and maintain goodwill?** Your professionalism and apology will project a positive image. In addition, you can offer your client an alternative, rather than simply agreeing to your request. For example, Great Expectations might allow you to complete the most critical parts of the project by the original deadline, with the rest coming later. By giving the company options, you can manage the relationship.

Select the best medium to achieve your goal

The final analyzing question in Figure 6.1 focuses on choosing a medium. When you communicate bad news, select a medium that best fits the purpose of the message, the audience, and the situation. **Figure 6.2** suggests medium options to use when you want to accomplish specific goals with a bad-news message.

FIGURE 6.2 Selecting the Best Medium to Communicate Bad News

Choose a medium based on the criteria below. Do you want to:	One-to-One	Group Meeting	Telephone	Text/IM	Email	Memo	Letter	Newsletter	Website	Social Networking	Wikis, Blogs
Audience-Related Criteria											
Share bad news with a single person?	■		■	■	■	■	■				
Communicate to many employees and shareholders simultaneously?		■		■	■	■	■	■	■	■	
Provide instantaneous news to people at geographically diverse locations?				■	■				■	■	■
Share bad news with the public?								■	■	■	■
Content- and Response-Related Criteria											
Share insignificant bad news quickly, such as letting your lunch appointment know you're running a few minutes late?			■	■	■						
Share important bad news in a way that does not seem impersonal or evasive?	■	■	■		■	■	■				
Hear your audience's one of voice and silences, which convey meaning and feedback?	■	■	■								
See facial expressions and body language, and hear tone of voice, which convey meaning and feedback?	■	■									
Encourage immediate discussion of the news	■	■	■	■						■	■
Prevent immediate discussion or give the audience (and you) time to carefully consider a response?					■	■	■	■	■	■	■
Ensure that you have written documentation of the communication?					■	■	■	■	■	■	■

TECHNOLOGY
CAN YOU EMAIL, TEXT, OR TWEET BAD NEWS?

You might be tempted to send bad news by text or email so you don't have to deal with the audience's negative reaction in person. However, most experts agree that, when possible, a face-to-face conversation is usually the best choice, especially when the bad news is serious.[4,5] When companies choose email or texts to deliver bad news, they often suffer serious public relations consequences.

For example, when a Chicago sandwich shop abruptly fired 20 employees in an email sent just a few days before Christmas, the story appeared in local and national newspapers, and local blogs printed the text of the offending email.[6,7] Similarly, when *Men's Wearhouse* fired its chairman and advertising spokesperson, George Zimmer, the public's negative response reverberated in news stories, blogs, and tweets.[8]

Even worse is the practice of firing someone by text message, which some offenders justify by saying it is their primary mode for all communicating with employees.[9] They may also argue that texting communicates the message quickly and helps avoid confrontation.[10] However, these are not good excuses for the disrespect communicated by this use of texting. The repercussions of firing someone by text go beyond hurt feelings. Angry employees may post negative comments on social media sites, talk to the media, or even seek legal counsel. A face-to-face conversation may be more uncomfortable but will be more effective.

In perhaps the most controversial use of texting to communicate bad news, Malaysia Airlines texted the families of Flight 370, which disappeared in March 2014. The text read: "*Malaysia Airlines deeply regrets that we have to assume beyond any reasonable doubt that MH370 has been lost and that none of those on board survived. As you will hear in the next hour from Malaysia's Prime Minister, we must now accept that all evidence suggests the plane went down in the Southern Indian Ocean.*" In justifying its decision to send a text message, the airline explained that families were contacted by telephone calls and that the text was used only as an additional means of communication.[11] However, some families did first learn the news by text, leading to outrage as well as grief.

Is email, text, or social media *ever* a good choice for communicating bad news? It may be in the following circumstances:

- **If you want to give your audience time to think carefully before having to reply.** In the Great Expectations scenario, you may choose to communicate the bad news by email to give your audience time to think about the implications of the news and to consider the best way to respond to your request.

- **If it is crucial that you avoid miscommunication and misinformation.** Some research suggests that people who are uncomfortable communicating bad news face to face are more likely to sugarcoat the bad news when talking in person to reduce their own and their audience's discomfort. This distortion can lead to misunderstandings. By contrast, communicators are more likely to be accurate, complete, and honest in email because they do not worry about being confronted by an angry audience.[12]

- **If you need to get the word out quickly.** Bad news travels fast, whether through the grapevine or the media. Carol Leaman, CEO of Axonify, notes that "no matter how big or small the event, in my experience, if it's negative, people are awfully good at making stuff up in the absence of information." Leman suggests that the best way to deliver bad news is to swiftly address challenges in an open and honest way and to quickly deliver a clear, consistent message. "Explain to everyone what happened, why it happened, and how you plan to move forward."[13]

- **If you need to communicate bad news to many people in different locations at exactly the same time.** When it is critical to communicate bad news to a broad audience, companies sometimes use multiple media to ensure the audience receives the message. For example, when Chipotle stores were tied to a serious outbreak of food-bourne illness, the company apologized about its food safety issues and shared information about the problem through videos and posts in Facebook and Twitter, in full-page newspaper ads including *The New York Times* and *The Wall Street Journal*, and on TV talk shows such as *The Today Show*. While this approach was effective at getting message out, financial analysts and communication experts criticized Chipotle for not doing more to personally apologize to the people who got sick. The message of these analysts was clear: an apology on social media may supplement a personal apology, but it cannot replace one.[14]

Most experts agree that when it comes to communicating bad news through social media, the best advice is "Just to be careful."[15] The news media is often more likely to report bad-news tweets than positive ones. And if you decide to use social media to apologize, be concise but genuine.[16]

For TECHNOLOGY exercises, go to Critical Thinking Question 10 on page 221 and Exercise 2 on page 222.

What medium should you use to communicate the bad news to your client, Great Expectations? Only three options in Figure 6.2 are good choices: a face-to-face meeting, a telephone conversation, or an email message. The remaining options will not be effective: Letters take too long to arrive, memos are for internal communication, text messages are too informal, and the other choices—newsletters, websites, social media, wikis, and blogs—are clearly not good choices for communicating with an individual.

Of the three acceptable choices, which is best? A face-to-face meeting would be appropriate but may take some time to arrange. Both email and telephone have advantages and disadvantages. A telephone call allows you to make a personal contact and to hear your audience's tone of voice. You will be able to gauge whether the manager at Great Expectations is upset, and you can adjust what you say accordingly. However, the manager may not answer the phone immediately, and you will not want to leave the bad news in a voice mail. If you ask for a return call, you may play telephone tag all day. If the manager does answer the telephone, your call may be putting him on the spot, suggesting that he needs to answer you immediately. An email may make your audience feel less pressured, allowing more time to review the original contract and to think about whether this delay will have serious impacts.

In this case, no one best medium choice exists. You will need to weigh the pros and cons, thinking about how your audience will react to a surprising telephone call versus an email. You will need to adjust the wording of your message based on your medium.

What are effective strategies for composing bad-news messages?

Compose

The analyzing questions in Figure 6.1 will help you develop *what to say* in a bad-news message. The composing questions in this section will help you focus on *how to say it*. Should you begin with the bad news or build up to it? How should you phrase the bad news? What is the best way to soften its impact? And how can you close the message on a positive note to maintain goodwill?

Decide where to state the bad news

Although most routine messages benefit from a *direct organization*, the decision of where to introduce unwelcome news is more complex and depends on both your audience and the context.[17,18] The direct approach may be a good idea if your audience is expecting to hear from you and the news will not come as a big surprise.[19] For example, if your manager asks you to provide updated sales figures because she is concerned about the impact of an economic slump, the news of sales decline will not be a shock. You can lead with that news because she will want to hear it immediately. In other bad-news situations, you can help your audience better understand and accept the news by using an *indirect organization*, providing explanation before the main idea. For example, if the economy is good and your manager has no reason to believe sales are declining, you may want to provide some explanation about the problems leading to decreased sales before you share the exact numbers. An indirect organization allows you to prepare the audience before delivering the bad news.

Figure 6.3 outlines the differences between the direct and indirect approaches for communicating bad news and identifies the situations in which each is likely to be more effective. Note that the only difference between the two organizations is the relative order of the bad news and the explanation. Either organization may make use of a **buffer**—an introductory sentence or paragraph that softens the bad news.

buffer An introductory sentence or paragraph that leads up to and softens a bad-news message.

FIGURE 6.3 Selecting the Best Organization to Communicate Bad News

Use **DIRECT ORGANIZATION** if ...	**DIRECT ORGANIZATION** follows this pattern ...
your audience • is unlikely to be upset or angry, or • expects the news and will not be surprised, **and the news** • is easy to explain and understand, • is important for the audience to see immediately, or • is relevant to health and safety.	1. Optional: Begin with a buffer. 2. **STATE THE BAD NEWS DIRECTLY.** (main idea) 3. **Provide supporting explanation.** 4. **Conclude with goodwill.**

Use **INDIRECT ORGANIZATION** if ...	**INDIRECT ORGANIZATION** follows this pattern ...
your audience • is likely to be upset or angry, or • does not expect the news and will be surprised, **or the news** • is difficult to understand without introductory explanation.	1. Optional: Begin with a buffer. 2. **Provide supporting explanation.** 3. **SUBORDINATE THE BAD NEWS.** (main idea) 4. **Conclude with goodwill.**

Figure 6.4 illustrates why a direct organization is best for an announcement warning customers about a health and safety problem. If the problem is buried, as it is in the indirect version in Figure 6.4, the audience may mistake the message for a routine communication and decide not to read beyond the first paragraph. The more effective direct version solves that problem by stating the main idea in the first sentence.

By contrast, **Figure 6.5** on page 200 illustrates a bad-news message that needs to be organized indirectly. The email is from a software company responding to a customer's

FIGURE 6.4 Example of a Bad-News Message Requiring a Direct Organization

INEFFECTIVE (INDIRECT)

Dear Richards Electronics Customer:

Thank you for your recent purchase of our LS520 microwave oven.

Although all of our products are rigorously tested before they are put on the market, we have found some minor abnormalities with the model LS520 under certain conditions. Recent customer experience revealed risk of overheating and fire when the microwave operates at the highest level for more than one hour. Therefore, we are recalling the LS520 and will either refund your full purchase price or exchange your microwave for another product.

Please contact the retail store where you purchased your LS520 microwave to arrange to return it, or call our toll-free number to request free express shipping pickup. We regret the inconvenience this recall will cause you but assure you that your health and safety are our primary concern.

Regards,

WHAT'S WRONG WITH THE INEFFECTIVE VERSION?

The ineffective version is misleading. It begins by thanking customers for their purchase. Although this is a neutral buffer, the audience may assume this message is a routine thank-you letter and not read the rest of the message, putting them at risk for a kitchen fire.

No important ideas stand out. Someone reading quickly may miss the main point.

EFFECTIVE (DIRECT)

IMPORTANT PRODUCT SAFETY RECALL NOTICE
RICHARDS LS520 MICROWAVE OVEN FIRE HAZARD

Dear Richards Electronics Customer:

Richards Electronics is voluntarily recalling the LS520 microwave oven because we have received 11 reports worldwide of overheating and fires when the oven operates for longer than one hour at full power.

Our records indicate you have purchased this model. To protect your health and safety, Richards advises you to take the following steps:

- Stop using the microwave oven immediately.
- Return the product to the retail store where you purchased it, or call us toll free at 888-555-4567 to request free express shipping pickup. You can either receive a full refund or exchange your microwave for another model.

We apologize for the inconvenience this recall will cause you. We are modifying our research protocols to ensure future products exceed all industry specifications. Your safety and satisfaction with our products are our primary goals.

Regards,

WHY IS THE EFFECTIVE VERSION BETTER?

The effective version **gets to the point directly** by announcing the product recall in a headline and then repeating the main idea—the bad news—in the first sentence. Although the audience will be surprised and potentially upset with this information, their health is too important not to grab their attention.

The bulleted content **highlights the necessary actions** so they stand out.

The message **concludes with goodwill** by assuring readers that the company is taking action to prevent similar problems in the future.

complaint. After investigating the cause of the problem, you need to explain that the client was in fact responsible for the problem based on a complex set of circumstances. This message is not only likely to upset the audience, but it also will be difficult to understand without introductory explanation. As a result, the indirect version of the email illustrated in Figure 6.5 will be more effective than the direct version.

FIGURE 6.5 Example of a Bad-News Message Requiring an Indirect Organization

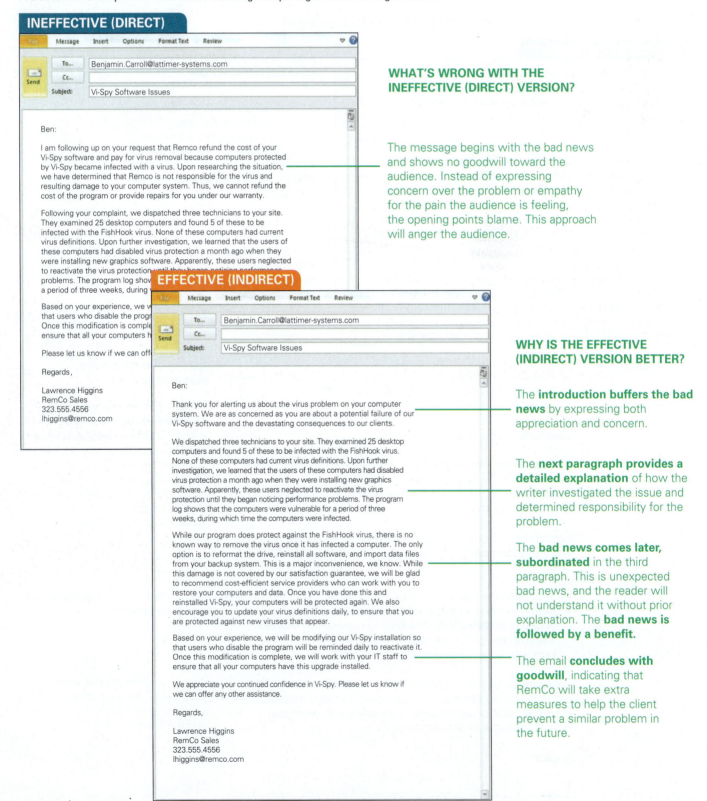

INEFFECTIVE (DIRECT)

To... Benjamin.Carroll@lattimer-systems.com
Cc...
Subject: Vi-Spy Software Issues

Ben:

I am following up on your request that Remco refund the cost of your Vi-Spy software and pay for virus removal because computers protected by Vi-Spy became infected with a virus. Upon researching the situation, we have determined that Remco is not responsible for the virus and resulting damage to your computer system. Thus, we cannot refund the cost of the program or provide repairs for you under our warranty.

Following your complaint, we dispatched three technicians to your site. They examined 25 desktop computers and found 5 of these to be infected with the FishHook virus. None of these computers had current virus definitions. Upon further investigation, we learned that the users of these computers had disabled virus protection a month ago when they were installing new graphics software. Apparently, these users neglected to reactivate the virus protection until they began noticing performance problems. The program log show a period of three weeks, during

Based on your experience, we that users who disable the prog Once this modification is comple ensure that all your computers h

Please let us know if we can offe

Regards,

Lawrence Higgins
RemCo Sales
323.555.4556
lhiggins@remco.com

WHAT'S WRONG WITH THE INEFFECTIVE (DIRECT) VERSION?

The message begins with the bad news and shows no goodwill toward the audience. Instead of expressing concern over the problem or empathy for the pain the audience is feeling, the opening points blame. This approach will anger the audience.

EFFECTIVE (INDIRECT)

To... Benjamin.Carroll@lattimer-systems.com
Cc...
Subject: Vi-Spy Software Issues

Ben:

Thank you for alerting us about the virus problem on your computer system. We are as concerned as you are about a potential failure of our Vi-Spy software and the devastating consequences to our clients.

We dispatched three technicians to your site. They examined 25 desktop computers and found 5 of these to be infected with the FishHook virus. None of these computers had current virus definitions. Upon further investigation, we learned that the users of these computers had disabled virus protection a month ago when they were installing new graphics software. Apparently, these users neglected to reactivate the virus protection until they began noticing performance problems. The program log shows that the computers were vulnerable for a period of three weeks, during which time the computers were infected.

While our program does protect against the FishHook virus, there is no known way to remove the virus once it has infected a computer. The only option is to reformat the drive, reinstall all software, and import data files from your backup system. This is a major inconvenience, we know. While this damage is not covered by our satisfaction guarantee, we will be glad to recommend cost-efficient service providers who can work with you to restore your computers and data. Once you have done this and reinstalled Vi-Spy, your computers will be protected again. We also encourage you to update your virus definitions daily, to ensure that you are protected against new viruses that appear.

Based on your experience, we will be modifying our Vi-Spy installation so that users who disable the program will be reminded daily to reactivate it. Once this modification is complete, we will work with your IT staff to ensure that all your computers have this upgrade installed.

We appreciate your continued confidence in Vi-Spy. Please let us know if we can offer any other assistance.

Regards,

Lawrence Higgins
RemCo Sales
323.555.4556
lhiggins@remco.com

WHY IS THE EFFECTIVE (INDIRECT) VERSION BETTER?

The **introduction buffers the bad news** by expressing both appreciation and concern.

The **next paragraph provides a detailed explanation** of how the writer investigated the issue and determined responsibility for the problem.

The **bad news comes later, subordinated** in the third paragraph. This is unexpected bad news, and the reader will not understand it without prior explanation. The **bad news is followed by a benefit.**

The email **concludes with goodwill**, indicating that RemCo will take extra measures to help the client prevent a similar problem in the future.

Phrase the bad news clearly

As career coach Hallie Crawford phrases it, "Give it to them straight."[20] The best way to ensure that an audience understands bad news is to state it clearly. If you convey bad news in vague terms or only imply the answer, the audience may misunderstand. For example, imagine that you work for a company that sells MP3 players. You receive an emailed request from a customer to replace the broken screen of his recently purchased player because it is still under warranty. **Figure 6.6** provides two versions of a reply. The ineffective version might lead to confusion.

FIGURE 6.6 How to Phrase Bad News Clearly

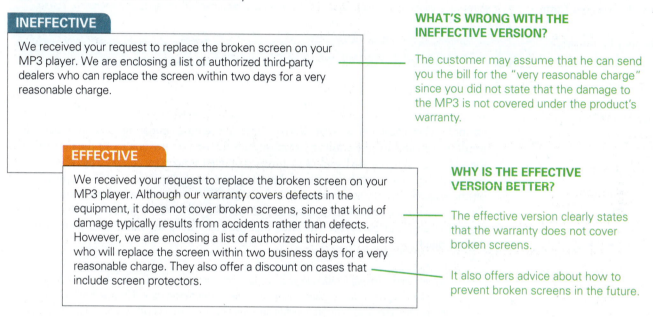

INEFFECTIVE

We received your request to replace the broken screen on your MP3 player. We are enclosing a list of authorized third-party dealers who can replace the screen within two days for a very reasonable charge.

EFFECTIVE

We received your request to replace the broken screen on your MP3 player. Although our warranty covers defects in the equipment, it does not cover broken screens, since that kind of damage typically results from accidents rather than defects. However, we are enclosing a list of authorized third-party dealers who will replace the screen within two business days for a very reasonable charge. They also offer a discount on cases that include screen protectors.

WHAT'S WRONG WITH THE INEFFECTIVE VERSION?

The customer may assume that he can send you the bill for the "very reasonable charge" since you did not state that the damage to the MP3 is not covered under the product's warranty.

WHY IS THE EFFECTIVE VERSION BETTER?

The effective version clearly states that the warranty does not cover broken screens.

It also offers advice about how to prevent broken screens in the future.

Soften the bad news

Regardless of whether you present bad news directly or indirectly, you want to "soften the blow" of the bad news, even if it is expected. You can do this by using one of the following techniques: developing an effective buffer, stating the good news before the bad news, subordinating the bad news, and using positive or neutral language.

Develop an effective buffer

Buffers are introductory statements that lead up to bad news and soften its impact. Buffers may provide a context for the message or provide positive information that builds goodwill. They can also "hook" the audience and get them interested in your message. For example, imagine that you have scheduled a meeting with 30 employees to discuss the problem of having to either reduce everyone's hours by 10 percent or lay off three people. **Figure 6.7** on page 202 suggests several buffer statements you can use at the beginning of the meeting to encourage your audience to listen to the rest of your message with a positive attitude. Notice that all the buffer statements in Figure 6.7 indicate that bad news may be coming later in the message. A buffer statement that does not provide this signal may mislead—and ultimately anger—the audience.

Position good news ahead of bad news

"Do you want the good news first or the bad news first?" Research suggests that most people receiving bad news want it first. You know it's coming, after all. Why wait? That same research suggests that communicators often prefer to put the good news first primarily to alleviate their own discomfort.[21]

However, there may be times when it's a good idea to put the good news first. Good news can put bad news in context or at least makes it seem reasonable by comparison. For

FIGURE 6.7 Types of Buffer Statements

TYPE OF BUFFER	EXAMPLE
Background Information	*"Over the past six months, the economy has slowed, and our sales have dropped significantly."*
Facts That Signal a Problem	*"In order to stay in business, our store needs to meet its payroll obligations."*
Good News	*"Despite the soft economy and slowing sales, we have identified a way to keep the store open and meet our payroll obligations."*
Thanks or Compliments	*"Thank you for your efforts this past year to improve sales at our store. Your knowledge of the merchandise and concern for customers have resulted in our highest-ever customer satisfaction rating, even in these difficult economic times."*
Generally Accepted Truths	*"In these lean times, we need to watch our budget and eliminate all unnecessary spending. These cuts will require sacrifices from us all."*
Empathy with Audience	*"I know how hard you have worked to keep costs down, so I understand that you might think we're unfair coming back to you this year with yet another request."*

example, when the wireless carrier Verizon announced it was updating customers' data plans to add more capacity, the company's website ads focused on the quality of the network and the additional benefits, such as data carryover, included at no extra charge. That was the good news. The bad news—that the cost of the data plans would increase as well—appeared later on the page.[22] Verizon took a similar "good news first" approach in a letter sent to heavy data users who had unlimited data plans. The letter began with the good news about providing more value and only then explained that the customer's unlimited data plan would be discontinued.

> *Dear _____:*
> *We are always looking for ways to give our customers more value, and earlier this month we revamped our plans to give customers more control over their mobile experience. The new Verizon Plan allows you to carry over data to the next month and includes talk, text, and data use to and from Mexico and Canada. Because our network is a shared resource and we need to ensure all customers have a great mobile experience with Verizon, we will no longer offer your current unlimited data plan after August 31, 2016. If you do not sign up for a new plan before that date, your service will be disconnected....*[23]

Subordinate the bad news

Although you need to state bad news clearly, you can ease its impact by using subtle subordinating techniques, such as *passive voice* or a *subordinate clause*. The term *voice* refers to the relationship between the subject and verb in a sentence. In *active-voice* sentences, the subject performs the action of the verb. In *passive-voice* sentences, the subject does not perform the action of the verb. In the following examples, the passive version avoids placing blame on the audience.

subject verb   verb
ACTIVE: You damaged your MP3 player and invalidated the warranty.

subject   verb
PASSIVE: Your MP3 player was damaged by an accident or misuse, invalidating the warranty.

Putting the bad news in a subordinate clause means preceding the bad news with a word like *although*, which will soften the impact. The following example shows a comparison of bad news in the main clause and in a subordinate clause. The bad news is italicized.

Main clause: *The repairs on your MP3 player are not covered by the warranty.* However, we have enclosed a list of third-party vendors that can replace the screen within two days for a very reasonable charge.

Subordinate clause: *Although the repairs on your MP3 player are not covered by the warranty,* we have enclosed a list of third-party vendors who can replace the screen within two days for a very reasonable charge.

Notice that when you place the bad news in a subordinate clause (*"Although the repairs on your MP3 player are not covered by the warranty"*), you can emphasize the good news in the main clause (*"we have enclosed a list of third-party vendors"*). Another way to de-emphasize the bad news while remaining clear is to put the bad news in a main clause surrounded by two subordinate clauses.

> **Main clauses surrounded by subordinate clauses:** Although our warranty covers defects in the equipment, *it does not cover broken screens* because that kind of damage typically results from accidents rather than defects.

Use positive or neutral language

The language you use in bad-news messages influences the audience's response as much as the organization of the message itself. The tone and style of the message should help the audience feel good about you, the situation, and themselves. The following guidelines will help you use effective language when composing your message.

- **Avoid blaming your audience.** Your audience will be more open to accepting the bad news if you treat them politely and respectfully. Show that you understand their needs and concerns. Avoid using language that is accusatory or blaming. For example, if you use the word *you* too much in a bad-news message, the audience might feel blamed rather than respected.

   Accusatory: Your warranty does not cover breakages that you caused.

   More neutral: The warranty does not cover accidental breakage.

- **Avoid excessive negatives.** As you compose your message, you may be tempted to use words like *unfortunately* to convey the bad news. As much as possible, avoid negative words and expressions like these: *unfortunately, we cannot, your fault, unable, unwilling, misunderstand, regret, violate, refuse, reject, deny, I regret to inform you.*

   Negative: Unfortunately, we cannot repair your MP3 player free of charge.

   More positive: Your warranty includes repair only for manufacturer's defects, not for accidental breakage.

Remember, though, that you must remain clear, which will often require using some negative words.

Close the message positively

Several strategies help create a sense of goodwill when communicating bad-news messages, including using a positive opening, explaining audience benefits, and subordinating the bad news. The conclusion provides an additional opportunity to stress the positive, instill confidence, and promote goodwill. A positive closing does not mention the negative news or apologize for it. The closing should be forward-looking and optimistic. Depending on the situation, any of the following approaches may be appropriate:

- **Propose a solution.** If your bad news focuses on a problem, you may want to conclude by proposing a solution: *"To increase your investment return next year, I suggest we rebalance your portfolio to include less risky investments."*

- **Propose an alternative.** If you are refusing a request, consider whether you can grant a portion of the request or offer an alternative: *"We encourage you to contact our affiliates to see if they have any internship openings for the coming summer. Enclosed is a brochure listing all our affiliates and their locations."*

- **Create options for future business.** If you are turning down a vendor's proposal because it does not meet technical requirements, you could close your response by inviting the vendor to submit a proposal for a different project. *"Our next round of requests for proposals will begin in six months. We hope you will consider submitting a proposal that meets the enclosed technical requirements."*

- **Focus on a benefit.** When communicating negative situations, try to focus on the "silver lining," if one exists. For example, assume you learn that a new product designed by your company has flaws. When communicating this bad news to management, conclude by stressing good news: *"Fortunately, the flaw appeared before the design went into production."*

The letter from Verizon to its unlimited data users ends on a positive note because the company wants to keep the customers despite cutting their data usage:

> *We are committed to making this a smooth transition for you. We value you as a customer and look forward to continuing to bring you the best in wireless for years to come.*[24]

CULTURE
IS THE BAD NEWS LOST IN TRANSLATION?

In the United States and many other Western business cultures, people tend to communicate bad news explicitly. They may soften the bad news by using a buffer or by subordinating it, but at some point in the message, they will state the bad news. By contrast, in many Eastern cultures, including India, people are much more uncomfortable saying "no" and rely on the audience to infer the bad news.

The table below illustrates the difference between how someone from the U.S. and someone from India might deliver bad news in answer to the question "Have you finished analyzing the data for the meeting?" The sample responses from India are from intercultural expert Craig Storti's book *Speaking of India—Bridging the Communication Gap When Working with Indians*.[27]

When you communicate with people from different cultures, listen carefully to be sure you hear the bad news and do not assume a positive answer just because your audience avoids saying "no." Similarly, you may need to change the way you deliver bad news—and even good news. Storti also suggests that people from Western cultures be more explicit when giving a positive response to people from Eastern cultures. For example, if a Westerner said *"the analysis will probably be ready,"* an Easterner may assume that the answer is "no." Any kind of qualification or hesitation is perceived as a negative reply. The best way to respond positively in an Eastern culture is to say "yes" and to clearly state what you mean: *"Yes, we will be ready tomorrow."*

QUESTION: Are you finished analyzing the data for the meeting?	
Typical Answers from Western Cultures: • *Although the analysis isn't complete, we have enough for the meeting.* • *The analysis was more difficult than I anticipated, so I am not quite ready yet.* • *If we can move the meeting to Friday, I'll be able to complete the analysis.*	**Explanation:** U.S. and other Western cultures tend to communicate bad news explicitly. They may soften the bad news with a buffer, but at some point, they state the bad news. Sometimes the bad news is implied, but even then the message is obvious.
Typical Answers from Eastern Cultures: • *Who exactly is going to be at the meeting?* • *Do you mean all the data?* • *Is tomorrow good for you?* • *Let me ask my team.* • *We'll try our best.* • *We have been working late every night.*	**Explanation:** By contrast, many Eastern cultures say "no" in a very different way. They may ignore the question, change the subject, respond with another question, or make a statement from which you will infer the negative news. In Eastern cultures, these kinds of answers are not considered evasive—they equally mean that the analysis is not ready and the speaker is uncomfortable saying "no."

For CULTURE exercises, go to Critical Thinking Question 4 on page 221 and Exercise 24 on page 226.

Although it is valuable to end on a positive note, it is important not to give your audience false hope.[25] For example, if you reject a proposal and do not intend to reconsider it in the future, do not say you will. Instead, simply thank the proposer for taking the effort to submit a well-thought-out proposal. It is also important not to be so positive that you undermine your goal. Research suggests that if the goal of your bad-news message is to motivate change—as in a negative performance review—ending too positively may convince your audience that change is not essential.[26]

How should you evaluate bad-news messages?

All communication requires evaluation to ensure that the message is effective. For sensitive communication like bad-news messages, evaluation is particularly important because the message can have significant negative business results. As you evaluate your message, look at it objectively and consider whether it is clear, easy to understand, and honest. Also consider whether you are communicating a sense of goodwill toward your audience. Then, step back and put yourself in your audience's position to evaluate how they are likely to respond and whether the message will achieve the business result that you intend.

Evaluate the message's clarity, honesty, and sense of goodwill

Evaluate

Consider the scenario that began on page 195 of this chapter. You want to give your new client, Great Expectations Books, the bad news that you cannot complete its project as quickly as you initially promised. You determined that both telephone and email were appropriate medium choices. In this situation, however, you decide to convey the bad news in a telephone call rather than by email, for a more personal touch.

Before you make the phone call, you decide to plan what you will say. Evaluate the first draft in **Figure 6.8**. It is certainly concise, clear, and easy to understand. However, is it honest? You say circumstances are beyond your control, but that is not true. You *could* choose to prioritize Great Expectations over your other client. The choice is within your control. Also consider how effective this message will be for maintaining the client relationship. It does not communicate a sense of goodwill or make the client feel valued. It does not express appreciation or apologize. It offers no good news or any alternatives. It does not give the client any reason to work with you rather than hire someone else to do the job. This message clearly needs revising.

FIGURE 6.8 How to Evaluate Drafts of a Bad-News Message

TELEPHONE CALL	
FIRST DRAFT Hello, Bill. I have some bad news. Due to circumstances beyond my control, I cannot begin working on your website for two weeks. As a result, it will take me an additional two weeks to complete the project. I hope that you will understand and be willing to reschedule your promotional campaign accordingly.	**PROS** • Clearly states the bad news **CONS** • Is not honest • Is not sensitive to the audience's needs • May not convince the audience to accept the bad news • Does not project a good image of you or maintain goodwill with the audience • Will not likely achieve a good business result
SECOND DRAFT Hello, Bill. I'd like to talk with you about the completion date I promised for your project. One of my other clients has a time-sensitive web emergency that has to be addressed by next week. Because that organization's website is uniquely programmed, I am the only person who can solve this problem. As a result, I will not be able to begin your project for two weeks. I appreciate your understanding and your willingness to reschedule your promotional campaign.	**PROS** • Clearly states the bad news • Is honest • Is more sensitive by buffering the bad news **CONS** • May not convince the audience to accept the bad news • May not project a good image of you because you are prioritizing another client over the audience • Does not offer an alternative to maintain good will • Will not likely achieve a good business result
FINAL DRAFT Hello, Bill. I have a favor to ask. Would it be possible to extend the due date for your project for two weeks? As I mentioned yesterday, I'm committed to doing the best possible job for all my clients, and I plan to do an outstanding job for you. However, one of my other clients—a not-for-profit agency—has an emergency and requires a last-minute reprogramming of its website so that the site will work with a new server. The work must be done before the launch of the agency's annual pledge drive next week. Because I did the original programming, I'm the only person who can reprogram the system quickly. I realize that I made a commitment to you, and I apologize for any inconvenience a delay will cause. I would very much appreciate your extending the deadline. If that is not possible, could we identify the most crucial elements of the project that need to be done by the original deadline, with the remainder coming later?	**PROS** • Clearly states the bad news • Is sensitive by asking for an extension rather than assuming • Provides an explanation that will likely convince the audience to accept the bad news • Projects a good image of your professionalism and dedication to your clients • Maintains goodwill by apologizing for the inconvenience and providing alternatives to meet the audience's needs • Is more likely to achieve a good business result—a continued relationship with the client

For your second draft, you make a few changes. You use an indirect organization to build up to the bad news, eliminate dishonesty, provide some reasons for the news, and express appreciation. Is the second draft better? It softens the unexpected bad news by moving it later in the message. In addition, this version provides an honest explanation without giving too much information about the other client, and it does express some appreciation. However, it still doesn't apologize, offer alternatives, communicate goodwill, or indicate that Great Expectations is a valuable customer. It is even a little presumptuous, assuming that Bill will accept the bad news graciously and reschedule his promotional campaign.

Evaluate

Evaluate the business result

Review the second draft in Figure 6.8 from your audience's point of view and think carefully about the business result you want to achieve. Your goal is to get your client to extend the deadline. However, the first two drafts of the message gave your client no reason to comply with your request. If you want this new client to accept your news, you may need to take a different approach. Therefore, you try a third version—one that offers alternatives and provides a better possible business result. You also rethink the purpose of this message. Do you want to impose bad news on your new client? Or would it be better to make a request and allow your client to determine if he can afford to wait for you?

The evaluation process led to a very different message than the first draft. The most important change is that you are giving your client the opportunity to do you a favor or to say *"No, you may not extend the deadline"* and to negotiate a mutually acceptable solution. This message is much more likely to achieve a good business result than the two previous versions.

(SQ4) What types of bad-news messages are common in business?

This section provides examples of common types of bad-news messages in business: denying requests or turning down invitations, denying consumer claims, rejecting recommendations or proposals, identifying issues or problems, and communicating negative change.

Denying requests or turning down invitations

When you cannot—or are not willing to—grant a request or accept an invitation, you need to find a tactful, professional way to say "no" and, at the same time, not make your audience feel guilty for asking. For example, the voice message in **Figure 6.9** uses a direct approach to deny a request. Although the recipient may be disappointed, she will not be offended or hurt by the direct approach, given the explanation.

FIGURE 6.9 How to Compose a Direct Message Denying a Request

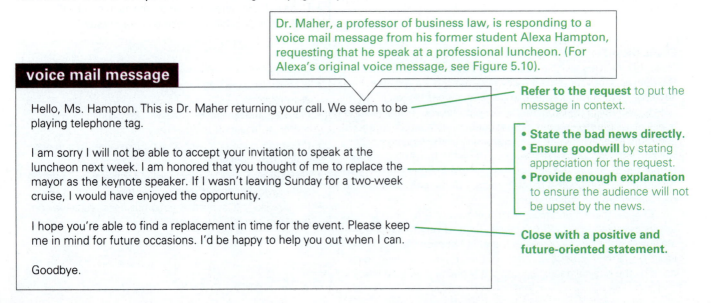

Dr. Maher, a professor of business law, is responding to a voice mail message from his former student Alexa Hampton, requesting that he speak at a professional luncheon. (For Alexa's original voice message, see Figure 5.10).

voice mail message

Hello, Ms. Hampton. This is Dr. Maher returning your call. We seem to be playing telephone tag.

I am sorry I will not be able to accept your invitation to speak at the luncheon next week. I am honored that you thought of me to replace the mayor as the keynote speaker. If I wasn't leaving Sunday for a two-week cruise, I would have enjoyed the opportunity.

I hope you're able to find a replacement in time for the event. Please keep me in mind for future occasions. I'd be happy to help you out when I can.

Goodbye.

Refer to the request to put the message in context.

- **State the bad news directly.**
- **Ensure goodwill** by stating appreciation for the request.
- **Provide enough explanation** to ensure the audience will not be upset by the news.

Close with a positive and future-oriented statement.

Denying customer claims

A **customer claim** is a request for a replacement item, a refund, or other compensation. When you are denying customer claim requests, maintaining goodwill is important because you want to retain your customers' future business as well as win the business of their colleagues and acquaintances. Bad news about customer service travels fast and far. Research shows that customers tell nearly twice as many people about their bad experiences than they tell about their good experiences.[28]

What communication techniques help customers feel good about continuing their relationship with a company? When you have to communicate bad news, customers need to know that you value them and have acceptable reasons for denying their request. Most importantly, customers need to know the company has corrected all errors and is willing to apologize if it is at fault. If customers believe that you are listening to them and that they received a fair resolution, they are likely to remain customers.[29,30,31]

Figure 6.10 offers an example of a denial message that follows these guidelines. Notice that the email leads with good news and that the tone of the email is both factual and polite. It is designed to convince the customer that the company values him.

If you have no good news to offer in response to a customer claim, you still need to be polite, demonstrate understanding, and offer clear reasons and alternatives. In cases when the customer is at fault, it may be tempting simply to say, "*Company policy does not allow refunds*

customer claim A request from a customer to a store or vendor to accept a return, exchange an item, refund money, or perform a repair.

FIGURE 6.10 How to Deny Part of a Claim Request

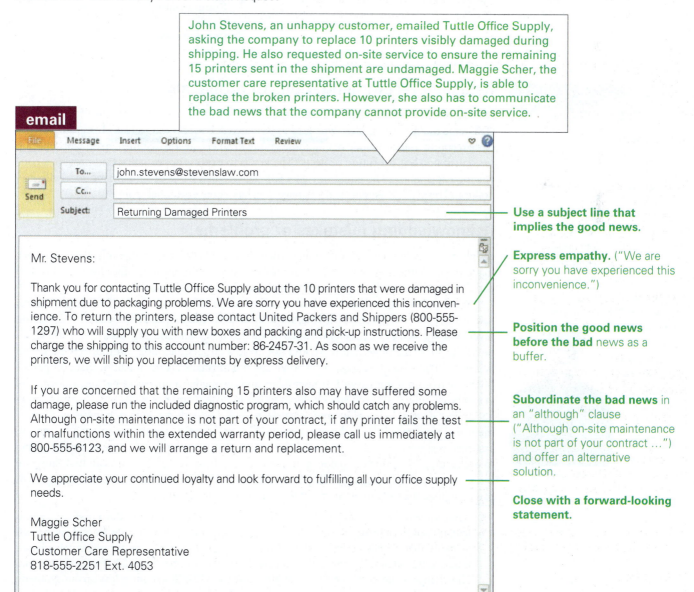

John Stevens, an unhappy customer, emailed Tuttle Office Supply, asking the company to replace 10 printers visibly damaged during shipping. He also requested on-site service to ensure the remaining 15 printers sent in the shipment are undamaged. Maggie Scher, the customer care representative at Tuttle Office Supply, is able to replace the broken printers. However, she also has to communicate the bad news that the company cannot provide on-site service.

email

To... john.stevens@stevenslaw.com
Cc...
Subject: Returning Damaged Printers

Mr. Stevens:

Thank you for contacting Tuttle Office Supply about the 10 printers that were damaged in shipment due to packaging problems. We are sorry you have experienced this inconvenience. To return the printers, please contact United Packers and Shippers (800-555-1297) who will supply you with new boxes and packing and pick-up instructions. Please charge the shipping to this account number: 86-2457-31. As soon as we receive the printers, we will ship you replacements by express delivery.

If you are concerned that the remaining 15 printers also may have suffered some damage, please run the included diagnostic program, which should catch any problems. Although on-site maintenance is not part of your contract, if any printer fails the test or malfunctions within the extended warranty period, please call us immediately at 800-555-6123, and we will arrange a return and replacement.

We appreciate your continued loyalty and look forward to fulfilling all your office supply needs.

Maggie Scher
Tuttle Office Supply
Customer Care Representative
818-555-2251 Ext. 4053

Use a subject line that implies the good news.

Express empathy. ("We are sorry you have experienced this inconvenience.")

Position the good news before the bad news as a buffer.

Subordinate the bad news in an "although" clause ("Although on-site maintenance is not part of your contract ...") and offer an alternative solution.

Close with a forward-looking statement.

for nonrefundable rates." However, this approach will not win customer loyalty. Instead of referring to the policy, explain the reasoning behind the policy and the refusal. **Figure 6.11** illustrates one way to deliver the bad news.

FIGURE 6.11 How to Deny a Claim Request

telephone conversation

> Imagine you work in the reservations office for Greenways Hotel. You receive a telephone call from a guest who is cancelling a prepaid reservation for a one-night stay and requesting a refund. The guest had reserved the room at a deeply discounted nonrefundable rate, and company policy prevents you from refunding reservations made at this discounted rate. How will you deny that request and still maintain positive customer relations and goodwill?

Mr. Franks, thank you for letting us know in advance about the cancellation. We are sorry you won't be able to stay with us.

I see you booked the room at our nonrefundable weekend getaway rate. We offer this rate at a 50 percent discount as a benefit to people who are able to plan their travel early. Our ability to offer these discounts depends on being able to count on the income from these rooms. Although your deposit cannot be refunded with this discounted rate, we would like you to stay here the next time you are in Memphis, so we'll be glad to offer you an upgrade voucher for your next stay.

Begin with a buffer. In this case, thank the audience for calling about the cancelation.

Express empathy. ("We are sorry you won't be able to stay with us.")

Explain the rationale for the policy.

Subordinate the bad news.

Conclude with goodwill. In this case, a discount is offered for future use.

New Hires @ Work

Ben Lahue
University of Northern Iowa

Experienced Associate @ PricewaterhouseCoopers Pvt Ltd.

When someone suggests an idea that isn't feasible, it's important to try to understand the concept. Rather than dismissing the idea right away, take time to explore alternatives. People are generally more receptive if you considered the options and explained why their idea is not necessarily the best.

Photo courtesy of Ben Lahue

Rejecting recommendations or proposals

In today's team-based businesses, collaboration increases the number of ideas that are generated—and many of those ideas will need to be rejected. How do you tactfully turn down someone's recommendation while maintaining goodwill and ensuring that the person will continue to contribute ideas for future projects? The key is to express appreciation and provide a convincing explanation. The email in **Figure 6.12** delivers bad news but maintains goodwill. It is polite and respectful, uses neutral language, and has a conversational tone.

Acknowledging mistakes or problems

People are usually very uncomfortable when they need to acknowledge mistakes they have made or problems they have caused. Yet in business, taking responsibility for mistakes and bad decisions is critical for maintaining both credibility and goodwill.

When J. P. Morgan Chase lost billions of dollars in risky stock trades, CEO Jamie Dimon had to share the news with employees, stockholders, customers, and the media.[32,33] Given the severity of the situation, the significance of the bad news, and the large audience with which he had to share the news, Dimon could not avoid a large-scale public announcement of the bad news. Therefore, he chose to acknowledge the mistakes via the medium that companies often use to communicate with stockholders and the media: a *stockholder meeting conference call* via webcast, which allowed stockholders to log in, listen, and ask questions.[34] Dimon, who has a reputation as being blunt and outspoken, took a very direct approach in his announcement. He announced the bad news, provided an explanation, put it in context to soften it, assumed responsibility, and explained the bank's plan to recover and prevent similar events in the future. The following paragraphs are excerpts from the conference call that illustrate these elements.[35] Although you may be unfamiliar with some of the technical language, you can recognize the various elements of the bad-news announcement:

- **Announce the bad news.** "I would like to thank you all for joining on short notice. I want to update you on a few items that we have in our just-filed 10-Q. Specifically, we had given prior guidance that . . . net income in the Corporate segment . . . would be approximately plus or minus $200 million. We currently estimate this number to be minus $800 million after-tax. This change is due to two items, . . . slightly more than $2 billion trading loss on our synthetic credit positions and $1 billion of securities gain, largely on the sale of credit exposures."

FIGURE 6.12 How to Reject a Recommendation

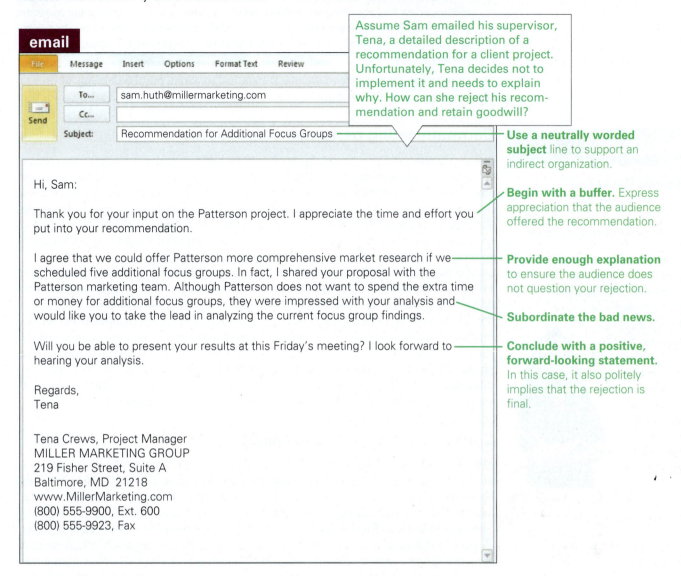

Assume Sam emailed his supervisor, Tena, a detailed description of a recommendation for a client project. Unfortunately, Tena decides not to implement it and needs to explain why. How can she reject his recommendation and retain goodwill?

Use a neutrally worded subject line to support an indirect organization.

Begin with a buffer. Express appreciation that the audience offered the recommendation.

Provide enough explanation to ensure the audience does not question your rejection.

Subordinate the bad news.

Conclude with a positive, forward-looking statement. In this case, it also politely implies that the rejection is final.

- **Provide an explanation.** "Regarding what happened, the synthetic credit portfolio was a strategy to hedge the Firm's overall credit exposure, which is our largest risk overall in its trust credit environment. We're reducing that hedge. But in hindsight, the new strategy was flawed, complex, poorly reviewed, poorly executed and poorly monitored. The portfolio has proven to be riskier, more volatile and less effective an economic hedge than we thought."

- **Put it in context to soften it.** "However unfortunate this event is, I do want to put this in perspective. One of the reasons we keep a fortress balance sheet is to handle surprises . . . if you did adjust current analyst estimates for the loss, we still earned approximately $4 billion after-tax this quarter give or take."

- **Assume responsibility.** "Neither of these things absolves us from blame. So speaking for the Senior Management team and myself, while we can't assure you we won't make mistakes, we will—we can assure you we are going to try not to. These were grievous mistakes, they were self-inflicted, we were accountable and we happened to violate our own standards and principles by how we want to operate the company. This is not how we want to run a business."

- **Announce next steps to fix the problem and prevent reoccurrence.** "What have we done? We've had teams from audit, legal, risk and various control functions all from corporate involved in an extensive review of what happened. We have more work to do, but it's obvious at this point that there are many errors, sloppiness, and bad judgment. I do remind you that none of this has anything to do with clients.

> We've had many lessons learned and we've already changed some policies and procedures, as we've gone along. In addition, you should know that all appropriate corrective actions will be taken, as necessary, in the future. Most important, some of our best talent from across the company, particularly traders and risk managers, are fully engaged in helping to manage the portfolio."

Not all mistakes are as severe as the one Dimon had to admit, but the elements of his bad-news message provide a useful guide.

Communicating performance problems

Just as you may need to acknowledge your own mistakes in business, you may also need to communicate about problems or mistakes that others have made—and hold them accountable. For example, you may need to tell employees that their performance is poor or tell vendors their service is unacceptable. Although you might think that being sensitive to a vendor about bad news is not important, in most cases you will want to fix the problem and continue a positive business relationship. In addition, a disgruntled vendor can easily damage your reputation by complaining to your customers and competitors.

Consider the example of Esther Davies, the vice president of corporate communications at Central Auto Fabricators. Esther has to communicate bad news to a vendor, Morrell Public Relations, because the vendor has failed to deliver agreed-upon services. If Morrell cannot deliver on its agreements, then Esther will need to cancel the service agreement. The best medium would be a face-to-face meeting or a telephone conversation because these options allow for discussion. However, because Esther has not been able to contact Morrell by telephone, she decides to write the letter in **Figure 6.13**. One advantage of any written message is that it documents the communication. Like other bad-news messages, this letter needs to balance a clear statement of the bad news with positive statements of goodwill.

Communicating negative change

There's a saying that "nothing is constant in business except change." To remain competitive, businesses need to change their procedures and policies in response to the state of the economy, customer needs, and new opportunities that arise. Change is so pervasive in business and industry that "change management" has emerged as a discipline to help organizations and individuals implement and adapt to change. Communication is typically a key element in change management plans, especially when change negatively affects an audience, as is the case with layoffs and reductions in benefits. How effectively you communicate negative change will have a direct impact on your company's goodwill, not only with your employees, but with the community as well. The key to success is to communicate the bad news in an emotionally intelligent way, being transparent and respectful, and not taking a defensive stance.[36] The message in **Figure 6.14** on page 212, which communicates a plant closing, illustrates one way to communicate negative change and still maintain the goodwill of the audience.

As Sally Blount and Shana Carroll from the Kellogg School of Management point out, communicating effectively with people who resist change requires listening, keeping an open mind, and having multiple conversations. Communicating effectively is not always efficient.[37]

FIGURE 6.13 How to Communicate Performance Problems

Esther Davies, the vice president of corporate communications at Central Auto Fabricators, has to communicate bad news to a vendor that has failed to deliver agreed-upon services. How can Esther be clear about the performance problem and expected resolution—and still maintain goodwill?

letter

CENTRAL
AUTO FABRICATORS, Inc.

22 Denwood Avenue,   Chicago, IL 60601 | 312.555.8447

April 2, 20XX

Ms. Cara Denholm
Morrell Public Relations
7943 Callaway Drive
Barrington, IL 60010

Dear Cara:

I am concerned that Morrell is not delivering the publicity our company needs. Since I have not been able to reach you by telephone, I am writing this letter to be sure that we have a mutual understanding.

When we hired your firm six months ago, our goal was to increase our company's exposure among automobile manufacturers and others in the auto industry. To help us achieve this goal, Morrell agreed to two major accomplishments:

- A feature story about our business in a top auto industry publication.
- An invitation for our CEO to give a speech at one of three trade organizations.

So far, no one in the company has been interviewed for a feature story, and our CEO has received no invitations for speaking engagements.

We cannot afford to wait much longer. If your agency is not able to deliver on these promises within 90 days, we will be forced to cancel our agreement according to the provisions of the contract we signed.

We've admired the work Morrell has done for other companies like ours and hope you can deliver the same level of results for us. I'd like to schedule a phone conversation next week to discuss how we can work together to achieve these goals.

Sincerely,

Esther Davies

Esther Davies, Vice President
Corporate Communications

Directly state the problem in general terms to communicate the purpose of the message.

Soften the impact of the bad news by using "we," "our," and "us" rather than "you."

Explain the necessary details. In this case, the audience's commitments are spelled out to put the problem in context.

Highlight information by using bullets. This formatting technique is effective when itemizing several points, either issues to resolve or actions to take.

Clearly present the bad news and, if applicable, specifically outline expectations.

Build goodwill by being positive and forward-looking in the closing.

FIGURE 6.14 How to Communicate Negative Change

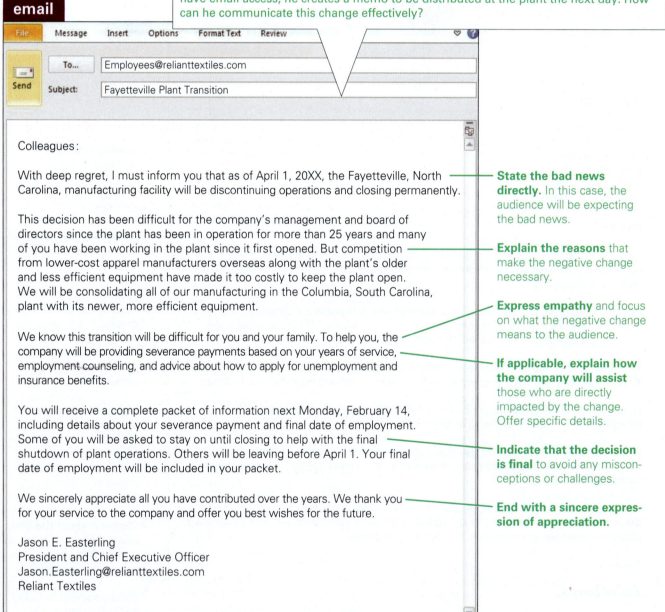

Jason Easterling, CEO of Reliant Textiles must communicate to all employees in the Fayetteville, North Carolina, plant that the plant will be closing and all operations will be moving to the Columbia, South Carolina, facility. Only half the employees will be offered transfers. Although this is a final decision, he needs to help employees accept the decision and to secure their assistance with the plant closing.

Because he wants all plant employees to learn this news at the same time, he holds a meeting. However, because some employees work a night shift and cannot attend the meeting, he decides to send an email immediately after the meeting so that he can communicate simultaneously with everyone in the facility. For workers who do not have email access, he creates a memo to be distributed at the plant the next day. How can he communicate this change effectively?

email

File Message Insert Options Format Text Review

Send

To... Employees@relianttextiles.com

Subject: Fayetteville Plant Transition

Colleagues:

With deep regret, I must inform you that as of April 1, 20XX, the Fayetteville, North Carolina, manufacturing facility will be discontinuing operations and closing permanently.

This decision has been difficult for the company's management and board of directors since the plant has been in operation for more than 25 years and many of you have been working in the plant since it first opened. But competition from lower-cost apparel manufacturers overseas along with the plant's older and less efficient equipment have made it too costly to keep the plant open. We will be consolidating all of our manufacturing in the Columbia, South Carolina, plant with its newer, more efficient equipment.

We know this transition will be difficult for you and your family. To help you, the company will be providing severance payments based on your years of service, employment counseling, and advice about how to apply for unemployment and insurance benefits.

You will receive a complete packet of information next Monday, February 14, including details about your severance payment and final date of employment. Some of you will be asked to stay on until closing to help with the final shutdown of plant operations. Others will be leaving before April 1. Your final date of employment will be included in your packet.

We sincerely appreciate all you have contributed over the years. We thank you for your service to the company and offer you best wishes for the future.

Jason E. Easterling
President and Chief Executive Officer
Jason.Easterling@relianttextiles.com
Reliant Textiles

State the bad news directly. In this case, the audience will be expecting the bad news.

Explain the reasons that make the negative change necessary.

Express empathy and focus on what the negative change means to the audience.

If applicable, explain how the company will assist those who are directly impacted by the change. Offer specific details.

Indicate that the decision is final to avoid any misconceptions or challenges.

End with a sincere expression of appreciation.

COLLABORATION
HOW TO GIVE (AND TAKE) CONSTRUCTIVE CRITICISM AND MAINTAIN COLLABORATIVE WORKING RELATIONSHIPS

Unless you are an entrepreneur with no employees, much of the work you will do in your career will be collaborative—meetings, team reports, group presentations, etc. Even when working on individual projects, you will likely depend on other people to provide you with the information you need to complete your work. In these situations, you may find it necessary to give a colleague constructive criticism—negative feedback on someone's work that is given with the intent to improve their performance.

Use the following advice when giving constructive criticism:

- **Buffer the negative feedback** by saying something positive first. Focus on what the person is doing well before pivoting to the issues of concern.[38]

- **Ask questions** to determine what is causing the poor performance so you can suggest the best advice to improve. Listen first—without judging—to try to define the problem.[39,40]

- **Explain how to improve** by recommending specific corrective measures. Discuss options and agree on a solution.[41]

- **Describe the impact.** Focus on the positive results that will occur from the improvement, and when those results occur, follow up to let the person know you noticed and appreciate the change.[42]

The BET/BEAR framework illustrated below can help you deliver constructive criticism effectively. BET—behavior, effect, thanks—is for positive feedback, while BEAR—behavior, effect, alternative, result—provides a constructive spin on negative feedback.[43]

It is as important to learn how to receive criticism as it is to give it. When receiving constructive criticism:[44]

- **Be receptive** by focusing on the constructive criticism as a way to improve yourself and how others perceive your work.

- **Get a second opinion.** Ask other colleagues for their input and advice.

- **If you agree with the criticism, be grateful for the advice** and ask for follow-up feedback to ensure your corrective measures fix the problem.

- **If you disagree with the criticism, start a dialog to negotiate** the situation so it does not become a continual problem in your working relationship.

Whether giving or receiving constructive criticism, you can maintain goodwill and prioritize your ongoing working relationship with your colleagues by demonstrating respect, being honest, focusing on the positives, and building trust.[45]

BET/BEAR Framework for Constructive Criticism

"Your work on our project has been very good. Your research provided most of the evidence we need to support our recommendations. Thanks for helping us create a better report.

B	**Behavior:**	The behavior you want to compliment
E	**Effect:**	The positive effect the behavior has on the team's success
T	**Thanks:**	Expression of appreciation

However, you have arrived late to five our last six team meetings. Our meetings are running longer than anticipated, which negatively impacts everyone else's schedule.

B	**Behavior:**	The behavior that is causing the problem
E	**Effect:**	The negative effect the behavior has on the team's success

Would moving our meetings back a half hour enable you to arrive on time?

A	**Alternative:**	Your recommendation to solve the problem

If so, we will be more productive, and the rest of the team will be able to schedule their time more effectively."

R	**Result:**	The positive outcome from solving the problem

Based on Teaching the Art and Craft of Giving and Receiving Feedback by Patricia L. Harms, Deborah Britt Roebuck. Published by Sage, 2010.

For a COLLABORATION exercise about constructive criticism, go to Exercise 13 on page 224.

ETHICS
REBUILDING TRUST AFTER A CORPORATE SCANDAL

Many of the circumstances that lead to bad-news messages can't be avoided. Regardless of what job you hold or what business you work for, at some point you will likely have to deny requests, turn down invitations, and acknowledge mistakes or problems. These are routine experiences in business communication. However, the unethical actions that create corporate scandals are different. They *can* be avoided, which makes it more challenging to effectively communicate the solution to stakeholders in the wake of the bad news.

Although many corporate scandals occur directly from unethical decisions made by top-level executives, that was not the case with the Wells Fargo's fake bank account fiasco. Thousands of local branch-level employees were involved in creating millions of dollars' worth of new bank accounts for customers who did not request them, often resulting in charges and fees. Analysts believe that this widespread unethical behavior resulted from employees feeling pressured to meet overly aggressive performance goals coupled with "moral muteness"—a reluctance to report unethical behaviors.[46]

In its statement to customers,[47] Wells Fargo did not apologize for a mistake. Instead the message focused on taking responsibility for correcting the issues that led to their employees' unethical behavior and outlining specific measures to ensure similar ethical breaches would not happen again. Note how the Wells Fargo statement that follows incorporates most of the expert advice to:

- Communicate the issue quickly[48]
- Take responsibility for the problem[49,50]
- Show genuine concern for the well-being of the people directly affected[51]
- Outline solutions and remedial measures[52]
- Be honest and direct in your tone[53]

Wells Fargo letter

Dear Customer,

Over the past several weeks, you may have heard about the settlements we've made involving some of our customers receiving products or services that they did not want or request. We are deeply committed to serving you and your financial needs, and in those instances, we did not live up to our commitment. This is inconsistent with our values and with the culture we work hard to maintain. It's not who we are as a company.

It's important for you to know that making things right and restoring the faith you have in us is the very top priority for our entire Wells Fargo leadership team. There is nothing more important than for you to experience the very best from us. Here's what we're doing:

- **Putting your interests first:** We have eliminated product sales goals for our Retail Banking team members who serve customers in our bank branches and call centers.
- **Proactively communicating with you:** We send a confirmation after you open a new consumer or small business checking, savings, or credit card account so that you know what is happening and can tell us if anything we've confirmed is different than what you expected.

- **Full transparency:** You can always see your eligible accounts any time when enrolled in Wells Fargo Online®.

- **Fixing what went wrong:** We have provided full refunds to customers we have already identified and we're broadening our scope of work to find customers we may have missed. If we have any doubt about whether one of your accounts was authorized, and any fees were incurred on that account, we will contact you and refund fees.

If you have any concerns about your accounts or any aspect of your relationship with Wells Fargo, please come to a branch and speak with our team in person, or call us on our dedicated hotline. We will continue to update wellsfargo.com/commitment to keep you informed.

The trust you place in us means everything and we will work hard every day to earn your trust back.

For an ETHICS exercise, go to Exercise 29 on page 227.

■ **In summary,** although bad news may disappoint your audience, you still want them to understand your rationale, to believe you are reasonable, and to feel good about you and about themselves. This chapter provides techniques that will help you state bad news clearly and also soften its negative effect. Using these techniques will help you achieve your overall business goal: to project a positive image of your business and maintain goodwill.

GIVING BAD NEWS TO CLIENTS @ WORK   Communication Partners

Communication Partners, a small communication consulting company, provides customized communication training, communication coaching, writing services, and consulting services to clients in several industries. The company has a reputation for being very responsive to client needs. Even so, clients sometimes make requests that Communication Partners cannot immediately agree to. For example, a client might ask:

- Can you provide communication training at all of our European locations, over the course of two consecutive weeks in June?
- Can you create web-based communication training that will be ready to deliver in the second quarter of the year?
- Can you deliver a customized writing training course at our company offsite conference? The training must be delivered between 9 and 2 PM on March 24.
- Can you train our executives to present more powerfully in a two-hour workshop?

Communication Partners cannot agree to these requests if it has already committed the time to another client or if the request is unrealistic. So, how does Communication Partners handle these requests and still maintain good relationships with the client?

According to Karl Keller, a principal at Communication Partners, "Even if we cannot do what the client is asking, we never start by saying no. Instead, we probe to learn more." He explains that clients often frame requirements in terms of their position—the "what"—instead of their interests—the "why." Understanding their interests can lead to a positive solution. "For example, if the client wants two consecutive weeks of training in Europe—and we do not have two consecutive weeks available—we need to know why the client is making that request: Is he primarily interested in ensuring that everyone is trained at the same time or is he interested in reducing travel expenses? If it's a cost issue, we can find other ways to reduce costs."

Then, says Keller, we offer alternatives. "We might offer to provide the training at a different time but soon enough to meet their needs. Or we could modify how we deliver the training, to lower costs. Or we might combine trips from two different clients, to lower travel expenses for each."

What if the client is asking for an unrealistic result— for example, training executives to be better presenters in just a two-hour workshop? The trick there, says Keller, is to tell clients what we recommend, not why they are unrealistic. "For example, we might say 'In our experience, people need to practice multiple times and get feedback in order to improve as presenters. We'd urge you to consider starting with a two-hour workshop but go beyond that and provide video-recorded practice sessions for each presenter, along with feedback from the instructors. This approach will get a better outcome than just a two-hour workshop.'"

Finally, what if the client is adamant and insists, for example, that the training must be delivered on March 24, from 9 to 2 PM—and Communication Partners does not have that time available? "Then," Keller explains, "if we have to say no, we will recommend someone else to do the job—and even work with that person to ensure he or she can do the job well. The advantage of this approach is that we build goodwill with our client and with the colleagues that we recommend. Recommending talented colleagues is a good way to build partnerships and ensure business success."

Source: Based on an interview with Karl Keller, 2017.

Making the Best of Bad News

This case scenario will help you review the chapter material by applying it to a specific situation.

Henry Lai is having a bad week. On Monday, Henry got into a minor car accident on his way to his business communication class. It was his third accident of the year, and he was late for class. Today, he is almost late again. As Henry left his apartment, his neighbor stopped him in the hallway to ask if he read the landlord's email announcing an increase in rent. Henry does not know how he'll handle these extra expenses. On top of a rent increase, he may need to pay for a repair to his broken computer printer, which may not be covered by a manufacturer warranty. And he also needs to help pay for the anniversary party he and his brothers are throwing for their parents in May.

Henry slips into class just in time to get Professor Anderson's assignment sheet. As Henry reads it, he begins to smile. This is an assignment he can definitely handle. Professor Anderson is requiring students to pick one or two types of writing—routine, persuasive, good news, or bad news—and over the next five weeks collect samples to analyze. The goal is to evaluate these pieces according to the guidelines in the textbook and suggest revisions. A lot is going on in Henry's life, and many people are communicating with him. In fact, he could begin the assignment right after class by reading his landlord's email about the rent increase.

Softening the Impact of Bad News

After class, Henry opens up his laptop to check his email. Would his landlord raise the rent to more than he could afford? He is not looking forward to reading the bad news. See the landlord's email message to the right.

As Henry finishes reading, he thinks, *"I'd like to stay. This must be a pretty good email."* Would you agree?

Question 1: Evaluate the landlord's email. Would you recommend any revisions?

Bad News in the Mail

When Henry returns home from class, he finds a letter in his mailbox from his auto insurance company. He opens it, looks at it quickly, and then puts it aside. At first glance, the letter appears to be announcing a raise in premiums. He doesn't have time to read it carefully. Later that evening, though, he decides to pick it up again to read more carefully. See the letter on page 217.

Henry has to read the letter twice to understand what it means, and when he finally understands, he is shocked. This isn't what he expected at all! His family has had City Mutual Insurance since before he was born. How could the company drop him?

Question 2: A reader should be able to understand a bad-news message quickly—and not feel insulted or abandoned. How would you advise City Mutual to revise its letter?

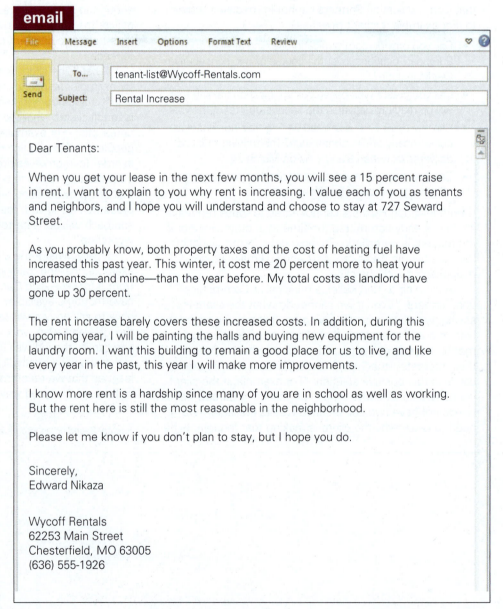

email

File   Message   Insert   Options   Format Text   Review

To...   tenant-list@Wycoff-Rentals.com

Subject: Rental Increase

Dear Tenants:

When you get your lease in the next few months, you will see a 15 percent raise in rent. I want to explain to you why rent is increasing. I value each of you as tenants and neighbors, and I hope you will understand and choose to stay at 727 Seward Street.

As you probably know, both property taxes and the cost of heating fuel have increased this past year. This winter, it cost me 20 percent more to heat your apartments—and mine—than the year before. My total costs as landlord have gone up 30 percent.

The rent increase barely covers these increased costs. In addition, during this upcoming year, I will be painting the halls and buying new equipment for the laundry room. I want this building to remain a good place for us to live, and like every year in the past, this year I will make more improvements.

I know more rent is a hardship since many of you are in school as well as working. But the rent here is still the most reasonable in the neighborhood.

Please let me know if you don't plan to stay, but I hope you do.

Sincerely,
Edward Nikaza

Wycoff Rentals
62253 Main Street
Chesterfield, MO 63005
(636) 555-1926

Accompanies Case Scenario Question 1

City Mutual Insurance

8851 Lincoln Way, St. Louis, MO 63114

March 15, 20XX

Mr. Henry Lai
727 Seward Street
Chesterfield, MO 63005

Dear Mr. Lai:

At City Mutual Insurance, our ability to provide cost-effective insurance to all our customers depends on our periodically assessing and reevaluating risk. Our internal guidelines and policies are carefully constructed to ensure that we remain a financially secure company. It is in this way that we can provide financial security to our customers in their times of need. Our guidelines take into account a number of risk factors, including a customer's driving record.

When a customer account falls out of the accepted parameters, we have the legal option to cancel or refuse to renew automobile insurance at the next renewal date. Based on your recent record of chargeable automobile accidents, our guidelines require that your automobile insurance be cancelled 30 days from the date of this letter. You will receive a pro-rated reimbursement check within 60 days, as required by law.

We encourage you to act quickly to secure new insurance since it is required for all registered automobiles in your state to have insurance.

Adjustment Department
City Mutual Insurance

Accompanies Case Scenario Question 2

Bad News from the Professor

After arriving late to his business communication class a third time, Henry is not surprised to see an email from Professor Anderson in his inbox. Professor Anderson has a strict attendance policy for his course, which Henry is finding difficult to follow. If this is a bad-news email, Henry hopes it is well written. He does not want to be in the position of critiquing his teacher in his final project.

Henry reads the email reproduced below and wonders: *"If I can't pass the course, maybe I should drop it. Is that really the goal of this email?"*

Question 3: Is this an effective bad-news email? Would you recommend that Professor Anderson make any revisions?

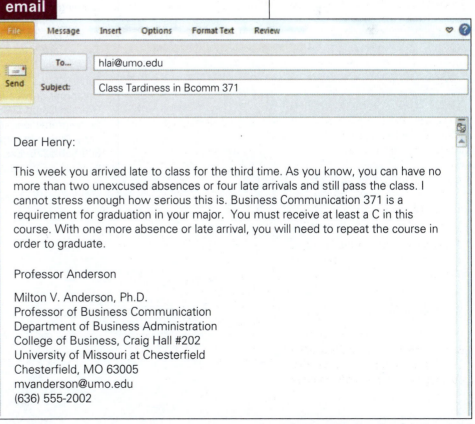

email

| File | Message | Insert | Options | Format Text | Review |

To... hlai@umo.edu

Subject: Class Tardiness in Bcomm 371

Dear Henry:

This week you arrived late to class for the third time. As you know, you can have no more than two unexcused absences or four late arrivals and still pass the class. I cannot stress enough how serious this is. Business Communication 371 is a requirement for graduation in your major. You must receive at least a C in this course. With one more absence or late arrival, you will need to repeat the course in order to graduate.

Professor Anderson

Milton V. Anderson, Ph.D.
Professor of Business Communication
Department of Business Administration
College of Business, Craig Hall #202
University of Missouri at Chesterfield
Chesterfield, MO 63005
mvanderson@umo.edu
(636) 555-2002

Accompanies Case Scenario Question 3

As a Customer, How Do You Feel?

As Henry prepares to write his final business communication report analyzing messages he has received during the term, he thinks about how important it is for a business to communicate effectively with its customers. Henry asks himself, *"As a customer, how do I feel about the people who have been communicating with me? How do I feel about my landlord, City Mutual Insurance, and Professor Anderson? Would I choose to have a continuing relationship with them or do business with them again? Will I speak positively about them when talking to others?"* These questions remain on Henry's mind as he analyzes his last set of business messages: an email from the manufacturer of his broken computer printer and a voice mail from the River Inn where he planned his parents' anniversary party. Would he choose to do business with these organizations again?

Question 4: Based on these bad-news communications, would you like to do business with these organizations?

voice mail message

Mr. Lai. This is Darryl at the River Inn. We need to make some changes in the arrangements for your party in May. The room you reserved is undergoing extensive repairs for water damage caused by the storm and will not be ready by the 15th of next month. All of our other rooms are taken for that evening. Is it possible for you to change the date of your event to Sunday the 29th? If not, we will be glad to completely refund your deposit. Please return my call at your earliest convenience. I'm at 678-555-1344.

Accompanies Case Scenario Question 4

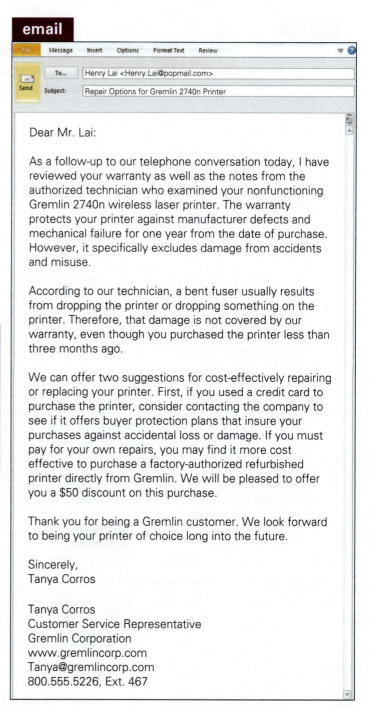

email

To... Henry Lai <Henry.Lai@popmail.com>

Subject: Repair Options for Gremlin 2740n Printer

Dear Mr. Lai:

As a follow-up to our telephone conversation today, I have reviewed your warranty as well as the notes from the authorized technician who examined your nonfunctioning Gremlin 2740n wireless laser printer. The warranty protects your printer against manufacturer defects and mechanical failure for one year from the date of purchase. However, it specifically excludes damage from accidents and misuse.

According to our technician, a bent fuser usually results from dropping the printer or dropping something on the printer. Therefore, that damage is not covered by our warranty, even though you purchased the printer less than three months ago.

We can offer two suggestions for cost-effectively repairing or replacing your printer. First, if you used a credit card to purchase the printer, consider contacting the company to see if it offers buyer protection plans that insure your purchases against accidental loss or damage. If you must pay for your own repairs, you may find it more cost effective to purchase a factory-authorized refurbished printer directly from Gremlin. We will be pleased to offer you a $50 discount on this purchase.

Thank you for being a Gremlin customer. We look forward to being your printer of choice long into the future.

Sincerely,
Tanya Corros

Tanya Corros
Customer Service Representative
Gremlin Corporation
www.gremlincorp.com
Tanya@gremlincorp.com
800.555.5226, Ext. 467

Accompanies Case Scenario Question 4

Study Questions in Review

(SQ1) How should you analyze and plan a bad-news message? *(pages 195–198)*

- **Ask questions that help you develop content.** Bad-news messages require planning to achieve a good business goal without alienating your audience. To begin planning, ask questions such as these:
  - What is the bad news? What business result would you like to achieve in communicating the news?
  - How will the audience react to this news?
  - What justification and explanation should you include?
  - Is there anything you can say to soften the bad news? For example, is there any good news to include? Will the audience benefit in any way? Does this cloud have a silver lining?
  - Should you include an apology?
  - Can you do anything else to project a positive image and maintain goodwill?
- **Select the best medium to achieve your goal.** Consider audience-related criteria, such as whether you need to share the bad news with one or many people. Also consider content- and response-related criteria, such as whether you want to see or hear the audience's reaction, receive their immediate feedback, or give the audience time to consider a response carefully.

(SQ2) What are effective strategies for composing bad-news messages?

(pages 198–204)

- **Decide where to state the bad news.** State it at the beginning (direct organization) when the bad news is expected, easy to understand, unlikely to upset the audience, or relevant to health and safety. In other situations, use an indirect organization, stating the bad news after an explanation.
- **Phrase the bad news clearly.** If you are ambiguous, your audience may not recognize you are delivering bad news.
- **Soften the bad news** with a buffer, subordination, and positive or neutral language. When possible, position good news ahead of bad news. You may also use passive voice, rather than active voice, to subordinate the bad news.
- **Close the message positively** to promote goodwill.

(SQ3) How should you evaluate bad-news messages? *(pages 204–206)*

- **Evaluate the message's clarity, honesty, and sense of goodwill.** Look at your message objectively and consider whether it is clear, easy to understand, and honest. Also consider whether the message will maintain a positive relationship with your audience.
- **Evaluate the business result.** Review the message from your audience's point of view and consider how the audience is likely to respond. Will the message achieve your intended outcome? Will it hurt or help your business?

(SQ4) What types of bad-news messages are common in business? *(pages 206–215)*

In business, you may face certain recurring situations that require you to deliver bad news:

- **Denying requests or turning down invitations**
- **Denying customer claims**
- **Rejecting recommendations or proposals**
- **Acknowledging mistakes or problems**
- **Communicating performance problems**
- **Communicating negative change**

In each situation, follow the basic guidelines for bad-news messages and adapt the message to your specific content.

Visual Summary

Dear Customer Service:
Help! Of the 25 printers I received today, 10 are damaged and do not work. Please send your onsite maintenance team as soon as possible!
Thanks,
John Stevens

Monkey Business/Fotolia

Analyze

- What is the bad news?
- What business result do you want to achieve?
- How will the audience react to this news?
- What justification and explanation should you include?
- Is there anything you can say to soften the bad news?
- Should you include an apology?
- Can you do anything else to project a positive image and maintain goodwill?
- What is the best medium for this message?

Monkey Business/Fotolia

Evaluate

- Is the bad news stated clearly yet sensitively?
- Will the message convince the audience to accept the bad news?
- Does the message project a good image of you and maintain goodwill with the audience?
- Will the message achieve a good business result?
- Have you avoided legal complications?

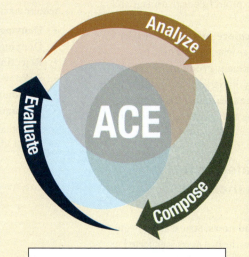

ACE
Analyze
Compose
Evaluate

Compose

- Should you begin with the bad news or build up to it?
- How can you clearly phrase the bad news?
- What content and techniques should you use to soften the impact of the message?
- How can you close the message appropriately?

Monkey Business/Fotolia

Mr. Stevens:

Thank you for contacting us about your shipment. We are sorry that 10 of your 25 printers were damaged during delivery. To return the printers at no charge, use the attached shipping instructions. As soon as we receive the printers, we will ship you replacements by express delivery.

If you are concerned that your remaining 15 printers may have suffered some damage as well, please run the included diagnostic program, which should catch any problems. Although onsite maintenance is not part of your contract, if any printer fails the test or malfunctions within the extended warranty period, please call us immediately so we can arrange a return and replacement.

We appreciate your continued loyalty and look forward to fulfilling all your office supply needs.

Sincerely,

TO SOFTEN THE BAD NEWS:

Develop an effective buffer.

Position the good news ahead of the bad news.

Subordinate the bad news.

Use positive or neutral language.

Close the message positively.

Key Terms

Buffer p. 198   Customer claim p. 207   Goodwill p. 194   Template p. 194

MyLab Business Communication

If your instructor is using MyLab Business Communication, go to **www.pearson.com/ mylab/business-communication** to complete the problems marked with this icon ⭐.

Review Questions

1 Name two goals that bad-news messages must simultaneously accomplish.

2 Name one technique an organization might use if it routinely communicates similar bad-news messages.

3 What questions should you ask yourself to help you develop content for bad-news messages?

4 What factors should you consider when selecting a medium to communicate bad news?

⭐ 5 Under what circumstances should you state the bad news directly?

⭐ 6 What techniques can you use to soften the bad news in an indirect message?

⭐ 7 What are some options for closing a bad-news message on a positive note?

⭐ 8 Explain what you should look for when evaluating a bad-news message.

⭐ 9 How can you evaluate the business result of your bad-news message?

⭐10 Identify the best strategies for communicating change.

Critical Thinking Questions

⭐ 1 Identify a situation that required you to share bad news in the past. Were you successful in accomplishing potentially incompatible goals such as being clear and maintaining goodwill? If so, how did you accomplish that? If not, how could you have accomplished those goals, based on reading this chapter?

2 Think of a realistic bad-news message that a business would have to communicate. Describe a positive outcome that could result from communicating it. Be specific about the context, the bad news, the audience, the message, the medium you would recommend, and the desired business result.

3 Sincere apologies can be effective tools for communicating bad news. By contrast, insincere apologies can alienate your audience. Think of a situation in which you might want to offer someone an apology. Phrase that apology in an insincere way, as if you don't really mean to apologize. Then change it to sound sincere. Describe some at least three features that distinguish the two kinds of apologies.

4 Before communicating bad news in cross-cultural situations, you should research the cultures' expectations about the organization of bad-news messages. Some cultures prefer directness, and others value indirectness. Assume that you are presenting bad news in a face-to-face meeting with stakeholders who represent several different cultures, including high-context cultures (Arabic and Latin American) as well as low-context cultures (German and Scandinavian). How do you balance their differing perspectives about how bad news should be presented? [**Related to the Culture feature on page 204**]

5 When possible, face-to-face meetings are usually the best medium for sharing bad news, even if they need to be supplemented with an email or memo for documentation. If you are apprehensive about communicating bad news in person, what can you do to prepare yourself for a face-to-face meeting?

6 Assume you are on the executive board of a student organization at your school, and one of your friends is the chair of the organization's fund-raising committee. Your friend has been doing a bad job, and the board has asked you to replace him with someone else. How would you communicate this bad news to your friend?

7 *"Do you want the good news first or the bad news?"* This question is a common method of beginning a face-to-face conversation when you have both good and bad news to share with an audience. The response usually is based on the situation. As suggested in this chapter, you should often position the good news ahead of bad news in business communication. However, describe a specific situation in which you might decide to share the bad news before the good news. Create a scenario that is not already presented in the chapter.

8 The chapter suggests that you do not justify refusing a customer claim by saying *"It's company policy."* Instead, explain the rationale for the policy, without mentioning policy. What if you do not understand the rationale behind a policy? What can you do?

⭐ 9 The goal of some bad-news messages, such as job rejection letters, is to convince the audience to accept the bad news as final. Explain a situation in which you might not want to convince the audience that the news is final.

⭐10 The Japanese company Line[54] designed a popular messaging app that allows people to message with "stickers": cartoons of cute animals (and people) accompanied by captions like "thank you," "of course," and "let's go shopping." They offer many stickers to communicate bad news, for example, "sorry," "I'm too busy with work," and "I'm broke."[55] What are the pros and cons of communicating bad news with stickers like these? [**Related to the Technology feature on page 197**]

Key Concept Exercises

 How should you analyze and plan a bad-news message? *(pages 195–198)*

1 Ask questions that help you develop content

Imagine that you manage a video processing lab where customers bring in old home movies and have them transferred to DVDs. Yesterday, a long-time client brought in a video of her daughter's wedding. She plans to pick up the DVD in two weeks after she returns from vacation. Today, one of your employees accidentally damaged the videotape and all your efforts to retrieve the data have failed. Answer these questions:

  a. What is the bad news?

  b. What business result do you want to achieve in communicating it?

  c. How will the audience react to this information?

  d. How do you want the audience to respond?

  e. What justification and explanation should you include?

  f. Is there anything you can say to soften the bad news? For example, is there any good news to include (audience benefits)?

  g. Should you include an apology?

Be sure to explain and justify your answers.

2 Select the best medium to achieve your goal [Related to the Technology feature on page 197]

Assume that you manage a local clothing store. One of your part-time employees who frequently misses work or arrives late emails to ask you to recommend her for a supervisory position. How will you communicate the bad news that you do not feel comfortable recommending her for a promotion? What is the best medium for communication: Would you write an email or choose face-to-face communication? Would you state the bad news directly or indirectly? Explain your reasoning.

 What are effective strategies for composing bad-news messages? *(pages 198–204)*

3 Decide where to state the bad news

For each of the following scenarios, explain whether you would organize the content directly or indirectly when communicating the bad news, and justify your decision:

  a. You are a marketing representative for a textbook publishing company. You told a customer that a new edition of a book would be available by July 1, in plenty of time to prepare for use in the fall semester. Today you learn that the book's publication has been delayed and that it won't be available until August 15, just days before the semester begins. How would you organize the message communicating this information to the customer: directly or indirectly? Compose a brief outline of the content.

  b. You are a customer service agent for a company that sells gifts, cards, and seasonal items such as holiday ornaments through catalog and online sales. Through your website, a customer orders personalized holiday cards, approves the personalization information when finalizing the order, and receives a confirmation email with a sample of the personalized card. Two weeks later when the customer receives the order, she calls you to complain about a misspelling on the cards. Because she approved the personalization when ordering the cards and did not reply to the email confirming the order, you cannot refund her purchase (obviously, the cards cannot be resold). How would you organize the message communicating this information to the customer: directly or indirectly? Compose a brief outline of the content.

  c. You are the Director of Housekeeping at a full service hotel. Due to the recent economic downturn in your industry, the CEO asks you to reduce your budget by 20 percent and strongly recommends cutting staff, which is the largest individual line item in your budget. Rather than lay off 20 percent of your employees, you suggest the department adopt a furlough program that reduces the workweek from five to four days. The department will rotate days off among staff to ensure adequate coverage every day. The CEO approves your plan and asks you to send a memo to employees explaining the furlough program. Explain whether you would organize the message directly or indirectly, and compose a brief outline of the content.

4 Phrase the bad news clearly

The following badly written messages are partial responses to the scenarios outlined in Exercise 3. Revise the wording to state the bad news more clearly. For each response, identify (1) what phrase is ambiguous, (2) how the audience might misinterpret it, and (3) what you could say instead.

  a. (See Exercise 3a): Thank you for ordering the new marketing textbook, *Marketing Concepts, Third Edition,* by Allen and Tate. We are sure you and your students will be pleased with this new edition. The revised shipping date is August 10, and the book should be in your mailbox and at your campus bookstore no later than August 15.

  b. (See Exercise 3b): We can replace personalized items only when we are responsible for an error.

  c. (See Exercise 3c): To help the company stay in business during these tough economic times, changes will be made to our staffing procedures to reduce the budget by 20 percent. Check with your supervisor to determine how these changes will affect you.

5 Soften the bad news

Rewrite each of the following badly written messages to soften the impact of the bad news.

  a. Thank you for your recent order. I'm sorry you think your shipment was not complete. According to our records, all the items you ordered were delivered. Please refer to the attached copies of your order form and packing slip to confirm your complete shipment.

  b. Although I hate to do it, we cannot offer bonuses this year due to declining sales. I'm sorry to disappoint you, especially during the holiday season. Better luck next year!

  c. As we indicated last month, travel budgets have been frozen until next quarter. Why did you submit a request when you knew I'd have to deny it?

  d. Thank you for your email indicating concern about the monthly premiums for family health insurance coverage. I agree that the difference between employee-only coverage ($10) and family coverage ($345) is unreasonable. Your proposal to split the difference makes sense. I wish I could support it, but the premiums are set by the insurance company.

  e. Sorry to hear your coffee maker broke after only a week. We sell them, but we don't fix them. You'll have to contact the manufacturer, who offered the warranty.

6 Close the message positively

For each of the badly written messages outlined in Exercise 5, create a concluding statement or paragraph that closes the message positively. Use one or more of the following techniques: propose a solution, propose an alternative, create options for future business, and focus on a benefit.

 How should you evaluate bad-news messages? *(pages 204–206)*

7 Evaluate the message's clarity, honesty, and sense of goodwill

Two months ago, Marla requested a week of vacation in early June to participate in her children's end-of-year school activities. However, yesterday she found out her husband's family reunion would be held over the July 4 holiday. She decides to email her supervisor, Paul, to see if she can request a change in her vacation schedule. Unfortunately, Paul is not able to grant her request. Evaluate Paul's email message to the right. Is it clear and easy to understand? Is it honest? Does it project a sense of goodwill with the audience? What changes would you recommend?

8 Evaluate the business result

You are an event planning consultant at Renew Retreat Center. Several months ago, Rena Murphy at Smith-Morrison and Associates (SMA) called you to coordinate the company's annual volunteer training seminar to be held at the retreat center May 1–2. Rena booked the center from 1 PM on Friday, May 1, through 6 PM on Saturday, May 2. Today is April 1, and Rena emails you to begin working on the logistics of the seminar. As you retrieve the reservation from the system, you realize you accidentally mixed up the reservation. You have SMA coming in at 6 PM on Friday and leaving by 1 PM on Saturday. Other events have already been booked before and after these times, and it would be difficult to make changes. Saturday afternoon's event is a wedding, and you're quite sure the invitations have already been sent. How do you communicate this bad news to Rena without losing the event? Evaluate the email message to Rena, located above. Assume you would like to retain this customer's business. Do you think that message will help you achieve the result? If so, why? If not, how would you recommend changing it?

Accompanies Exercise 7

Accompanies Exercise 8

 What types of bad-news messages are common in business? *(pages 206–215)*

9 Denying requests or turning down invitations

Assume that you are a business professional who hires management majors for internship positions from the regional university located in your city. Paolo Miguel, one of your current interns, emailed you

to request that you serve as the advisor next year for the university's chapter of Future Business Leaders of America. In his request, Paolo emphasized how much the students can learn from you and how your management skills can help ensure the organization's future success. Given your workload and other community service commitments, you don't think you'll have enough time to devote to this student organization. How will you effectively decline Paolo's request? Compose an email response.

10 Denying customer claims

You are the shipping manager for a toy company that does most of its sales through catalog and online ordering. However, you also sell products to select retail stores across the country, including Toys R Us. Martha Hagler of Delaware, Ohio, ordered a train set for her grandson's fifth birthday. The large set came in a unique tin container, which was damaged during shipping. Martha emailed your company to complain about the damage and request that a replacement be shipped to her overnight. Her grandson's birthday is in three days, and she wants another train set before the party. However, because the tin containers are made by another manufacturer and you are currently out of stock, you cannot replace her order before the party. Reply to Ms. Hagler with the bad news and an alternative solution.

11 Rejecting recommendations or proposals

You are the assistant principal at a large metropolitan high school. The head of the business education department, Jacqueline DeMarta, has complained for years that the computer labs need to be updated. This morning, she emailed a proposal to purchase 30 new laptop computers that convert into tablets and could be used in several classrooms to support teaching and learning. The convertible laptops she wants are $1,000 each. You do not have the funds in the budget to cover her request, and you are concerned that the laptops would be easier to steal than standard desktop computers. Your school has experienced several break-ins in the last year, and you do not want to provide additional targets for future robberies. Rather than completely deny her request, email Ms. DeMarta with an alternative solution. Research desktop computers priced at $750 or less that would be applicable for a high school computer lab. Using what you have learned, compose a response to Ms. DeMarta.

12 Acknowledging mistakes or problems

Use a review site, such as TripAdvisor, Yelp, or OpenTable, to find a negative customer review that includes a response from the business.

Identify how the response uses the advice in this chapter, or how it could be revised to provide a more effective response. If it could be improved, provide a revised response. Copy both the review and the response, and submit them with your evaluation of the response, and your revised response, if applicable.

13 Communicating performance problems [Related to the Collaboration feature on page 213]

Part of your job as the assistant manager of a large department store is to evaluate trainees as they transition from probationary status to regular full-time employees. Most of the time, you are able to begin your face-to-face conversations with positive feedback before subordinating any constructive criticism. However, today you have to tell Phillip that if he wants to continue to work for the store, he will remain on probationary status for two more weeks. He has not yet demonstrated that he can process returns on his own, and he struggles with the computer when processing any transaction. In fact, none of his supervisors could provide any positive feedback. How would you begin your face-to-face conversation with Phillip? Refer to the Collaboration feature on page 213 and use the BEAR technique—behavior, effect, alternative, results—to draft what you would say. Start by identifying the behavior and explaining the negative effect the behavior creates. Then outline our recommendation to solve the problem and the positive outcome that will result if Phillip improves.

14 Communicating negative change

You work for Plimpton Financial Services, a company that offers an extremely generous tuition plan for employees. The company pays 100 percent of college tuition for the children of all employees who have worked at the company for more than five years. This benefit can be worth hundreds of thousands of dollars for employees with multiple children. The CEO of Plimpton explains why the company has been so generous: *"If we can take away the worry of paying for college, employees will concentrate more and be more productive. We value our employees, and this is a great way to keep them."*

Because of difficulties in the financial market, Plimpton has decided to phase out this benefit over a period of five years. This news will disappoint and anger many people who have been staying at the company in order to receive the benefit.

Your job is to plan the announcement. Use the ACE process to analyze the audience and compose a message. Because you do not have an actual audience available, imagine yourself as an employee of Plimpton, who has three children to put through college.

Writing Exercises

15 Apologizing for a mistake

Assume that you own Sherwood Florist, a local flower shop that specializes in customized arrangements. Last Saturday, you had floral orders for two large events: a fund-raising dinner at Beaumont Community College's alumni center, and a wedding and reception at a nearby church and banquet hall. The college ordered 20 centerpieces to match the school's colors (purple and yellow) and integrate their mascot (the pirates). The wedding order also includes 20 purple and yellow centerpieces but without the pirate theme. During delivery, the centerpieces for each event are mistakenly reversed. The college doesn't notice the missing pirates from its purple-and-yellow arrangements, but the bride's mother, Clarice Branson, is very upset. No one associated with the wedding noticed the pirates in the centerpieces until after the guests had arrived at the reception. The next day, Clarice Branson calls you to complain about the mix-up and indicates that she

will quickly spread the word about Sherwood Florist's ineptness. You apologize for the error and significantly discount the order. Compose an apology letter to accompany the revised bill that you will mail to Mrs. Branson. Submit the letter to your instructor for evaluation.

16 Cancelling a keynote speaker

Your company has invited one of its biggest clients, Vince Embry, to be a keynote speaker at a company retreat. Vince has cancelled other engagements and arranged his calendar to accommodate your schedule. Vince also purchased an airline ticket at his own expense and has begun writing his speech. However, you've just learned that the company must cancel the retreat due to budget cuts. Create a message to Vince that communicates the bad news that the retreat is cancelled so he will not have the opportunity to speak. Consider what you can offer that will make up for his inconvenience and expense.

17 Responding to a customer's complaint

You are a manager at Home Goods, which sells a wide variety of bath, kitchen, and other household items. Several months ago, you offered a special sale on a specific FreshAir humidifier, Model 2850. A customer who purchased one of these humidifiers returned to your store last week to purchase more filters for the humidifier. However, your store no longer carries the FreshAir brand. Although the store offers several replacement filters for other brands, you do not carry the specific model the customer requires. He wrote a letter to "The Manager" complaining about the problem and indicating that he plans to tell everyone he knows not to bother buying products from your store because you don't stock the items needed to maintain them. Although you don't have the filters in your store, you can special order them. How do you respond to the letter? What medium would you use? Draft a message.

18 Responding to a customer request

Imagine that you manage a catering business. Two weeks ago, you met with Ellyn Jones to discuss the details of catering a reception for her parents' 50th wedding anniversary. The party is in another week. She indicated that her maximum catering budget for the party is $2,500, and she signed a contract that outlined a price of $25 per person for up to 100 guests. The contract provided for several "finger-food" stations, including a sushi bar, crudités, hot hors d'oeuvres, and a large cake in addition to punch, tea, and coffee. You special order the sushi from an out-of-town supplier to be shipped fresh just in time for the event. The rest of the items are available locally and can be prepared a day in advance. Today, Ellyn emails you with some bad news. Her mother decided most of the relatives won't like sushi and would like to replace that station with a chocolate fountain. In addition, she would like to increase the head count to 120. Your heart sinks when you read the message. With these changes, you will no longer be able to keep the price within Ellyn's budget. Not only will you have to pay a $200 cancellation fee if you cancel the sushi order, but renting the chocolate fountain and buying the chocolate, dipping foods, and skewers will cost $300 more than the sushi it is replacing. In addition, accommodating 20 additional guests will cost $500. These changes bring the cost of catering to $1,000 over Ellyn's budget. How do you respond? Decide what your message will be, which medium you will use, and how you will organize the message. Compose a draft.

19 Giving bad news to your team

You are the project manager for a client project at a small consulting firm. Your final presentation to the client is in two weeks and you are just beginning to put together very rough drafts of your presentation slides. Your company typically outsources the creation of the final slides to a graphic design firm in India that it has been working with for several years. You are shocked when your boss tells you that the senior managers of the firm have fired the graphic design firm and have decided that, for financial reasons, all teams must produce their own slides until further notice. You must now communicate this decision to the team, knowing that they were really counting on having external help on the slides. You will meet with the team tomorrow. Write a draft of what you plan to say to them.

20 Giving bad news to your manager

You are a part-time accountant for a small, local retail company. You provide Patricia Zho, the owner of the company, with quarterly reports summarizing her income and expenses. Together you determine a budget and compare it to actual data to help make important decisions such as ordering merchandise and providing raises.

After two years of continual losses in sales, you believe Patricia must reduce her payroll. She has consistently refused to consider this suggestion in the past, stating that her employees are like family, and she cannot reduce their wages or fire anyone. She'd rather go out of business. At this point, the data are telling you that she will have to close her doors if she does not reduce payroll. Five people are on the payroll, averaging $35,000 a year each. Sales continue to decline, as described in the accompanying table. Inventory costs her 40 percent of the sales price. To help her understand the situation, write a message giving her the bad news. If possible, support it with a graph that visually represents the data below.

Quarter	Sales
20XX–Q1	$510,000
20XX–Q2	$480,000
20XX–Q3	$452,000
20XX–Q4	$412,000
20XY–Q1	$389,000
20XY–Q2	$381,000
20XY–Q3	$325,000
20XY–Q4	$315,000

Accompanies Exercise 20

21 Giving bad news to a job applicant

You are the hiring manager for a mid-sized company. You have narrowed the applicants for a managerial position to two: (1) a 22-year-old college graduate who interned at a different division of your company two summers ago but has no additional industry experience and (2) a 48-year-old MBA with over 20 years of experience related to your industry. Although the older candidate is better qualified, your budget restrictions will not allow you to meet the older candidate's salary requirements. Whom do you hire? Indicate the medium you would choose and draft a bad-news message to one of the applicants.

22 Communicating about product recalls

Go to the Consumer Product Safety Commission's website (www.cpsc.gov) and search for recent product recalls. Select five to seven examples of products that have been recalled because of a serious safety issue. Save a copy of the text of each product recall announcement. For each example, go to the website of the manufacturer of the recalled product and search for information about the recall. Answer the following questions for each example:

a. Does information about the recall appear on the company's website?

b. If the information is on the website, how easy is it to find that information? For example: is it linked, is it listed in a specific section on safety or customer support, can it be searched for on the site itself, can it be found by aiming a Google search at the site's domain, etc.

c. How complete is the information presented? How well organized is it? How clear are the specific statements?

d. How does the language used by the company to explain the problem or defect compare to the language used by the CPSC?

Write a short report in which you summarize the results of your inquiry. How well do the companies you selected communicate the information about the recalled products: why the product was recalled, what the risks are to their customers, and what the customers

should do? Include examples of specific communication strategies used by the companies in presenting this information online that you think are especially effective or ineffective. Pay special attention to ethical concerns. In your opinion, is the response of each company adequate? Why or why not?

23 Projecting a positive image and maintaining goodwill

Although Samsung is a diverse brand with more than 78 different companies and affiliates in a wide range of technology-related fields, when it comes to bad news, they are most well known for their exploding Galaxy Note7 that became headline news less than a month after it was released.[56] Reports of exploding batteries led the U.S. Department of Transportation to ban the Note7 on airplanes, and Samsung immediately announced replacement

devices as part of its voluntary recall. At that time, Samsung reported that 90 percent of their customers opted to receive a replacement Note7 rather than change to a different model.[57] This level of customer loyalty and trust documented Samsung's positive brand. However, when the replacement phones continued to be fire hazards, the U.S. Consumer Product Safety Commission issued a mandatory recall of all the phones, including the replacements. A few days later, Samsung announced that it was discontinuing the model.

Research Samsung's press releases, website content, and social media posts about the Note7 between the first recall and the final decision to discontinue the model. In a short report to your instructor, describe the strategies Samsung used to project a positive image and maintain goodwill.

Collaboration Exercises

24 Preparing to communicate bad news in other countries [Related to the Culture feature on page 204]

Your team is organizing a training seminar for new managers who will be working closely with clients in the four largest markets in your industry: Brazil, Russia, India, and China. You know that businesspeople in these countries have differing expectations about how bad news should be communicated. Some online research might help. You may want to start with websites like www.cyborlink.com and www.executiveplanet.com. Assign one country to each of the four members in your team. Each team member should write a paragraph summarizing best practices for communicating bad news. Then collaborate on a one-page message that provides information new managers would find useful when communicating bad news to clients from each of these countries. Be sure your message includes an introduction and conclusion.

25 Preparing to communicate change

Assume that the dean of academic affairs at your school is considering adding a one-credit senior seminar as a requirement for graduation. Although the seminar will provide soon-to-be graduates with beneficial information, such as interviewing skills and résumé writing, most students perceive the additional requirement as bad news. To help the dean "sell" the bad news to the student body, your group has been asked to collect student responses that the administration can address. Each member of your group is assigned to collect input from 10 students across campus (be sure to tell them this is a hypothetical scenario). Do they think the senior seminar requirement is a good idea? If not, why not? Meet as a group to combine all members' data and summarize your findings to provide the dean with an audience analysis. Provide suggestions about how the dean can best create a message that addresses the concerns of those students who will consider the change to be bad news.

Social Media Exercises

26 Using social media to communicate change

Refer to Exercise 25. Assume that the dean of academic affairs has asked you to help disseminate the information about the new senior seminar requirement. Although the news will be emailed to the campus community, the dean knows that some students do not read university emails, especially lengthy emails that explain new policies. To help promote a positive perspective, you have been asked to identify social media options for explaining the seminar, including Twitter, Instagram, and blog posts that come out before the announcement. Outline your strategy to use social media to effectively communicate the senior seminar requirement to the student body, including sample content.

27 Apologies in social media

Find an example of a company that posted an apology about a problem on its website as well as on at least one social media outlet, such as Twitter, Facebook, or YouTube. Compare the apologies in these different social media outlets. Identify the timing of the problem and when the apology was posted to each medium. For each message, determine how (or if) the company acknowledged the mistake, expressed sympathy and concern, explained how the mistake occurred, and showed how it will prevent the problem from reoccurring. If the company did not do these things, suggest how the company could have improved its communication. Summarize your findings in a one-page message to your instructor, or be prepared to present your findings in class.

Speaking Exercises

28 Making informal/impromptu presentations

Plan a brief (less than one minute) response for the following scenarios:

a. Your brother gave you two tickets to the final game of the basketball championship series because he will be out of town and cannot use his tickets. You plan to go to the game, and you offer

the extra ticket to a friend—a real basketball fan who has done a number of favors for you. The day before the game, your brother calls, says his travel plans have changed, and he wants to go to the game with you. How will you tell your friend you can no longer take him to the game?

b. You have promised to send 10 bound copies of a document to your client by overnight express delivery. He needs to distribute these documents to his board of directors at a meeting the next afternoon. You package the reports, bring them to the express delivery company, fill out the address form, and pay for early morning delivery. Later that night, however, you realize that you made a mistake when filling out the address form. You included the wrong zip code, so the package is on its way to Iowa instead of Michigan. How will you tell your client that the package will not be delivered on time?

29 Presenting executive briefings [Related to the Ethics feature on page 214]

Use your favorite web search tool to research a corporate scandal that occurred in the past 12 months. Read news stories about the scandal so you understand the ethical breach, whose actions created problem, and the stakeholders involved. Find the company's public statement or message to their customers apologizing for or explaining the issue. Did the company follow the advice in this chapter? If so, how? If not, what could they have done to improve their message? Prepare a five-minute presentation with at least one visual aid that answers these questions.

Grammar Exercises

30 Common sentence errors: Run-on (fused) sentences and comma splices (see Appendix C: Grammar, Punctuation, Mechanics, and Conventions—Section 1.3.2)

Type the following paragraph, correcting the 10 run-on or fused sentences and comma splices (see Section 1.3.2). Underline all your corrections.

One business etiquette consultant believes that good telephone manners begin in childhood, children should be taught how to answer the phone courteously and take messages. Diane Eaves says, "I work with a lot of people who are technically ready for work however, they apparently missed a lot of the teaching of manners." For instance, asking who is calling can be taught in childhood then it will be a habit. Parents know how annoying it is to have a child report that "somebody called and wants you to call back" Sonny doesn't remember who it was and didn't write down the number. Thank goodness for caller ID it can be a big help, nevertheless, children should be taught to ask for and write down names and numbers. It's surprising how many people don't identify themselves when they make business calls, they expect listeners to recognize their voice. That may be OK if you speak frequently with the caller on the other hand it's mystifying when a voice you don't recognize launches right into a subject. It is the caller's responsibility to identify himself or herself, if he or she doesn't you can politely say, "Excuse me, I didn't catch your name."

MyLab Business Communication

If your instructor is using MyLab Business Communication, go to **www.pearson.com/mylab/business-communication** for Auto-graded writing questions as well as the following Assisted-graded writing questions:

1. Why are face-to-face conversations usually the best medium choice for communicating bad news?

2. Some people might consider positive language as "sugar coating" bad news and being insincere. What are the benefits of using positive language when communicating bad-news messages?

References

1. DeKay, S. H. (2012). Where is the research on negative messages? *Business Communication Quarterly, 75*(2), 173–175.
2. Creelman, V. (2012). The case for "living" models. *Business Communication Quarterly, 75*(2), 176–191.
3. Jansen, F., & Janssen, D. (2010). Effects of positive politeness strategies in business letters. *Journal of Pragmatics, 42*(9), 2531–2548.
4. Bies, R. J. (2014, March 20). 10 tips for delivering bad news. Retrieved from http://www.cnbc.com/id/101512079
5. Donnelly, T. (2011, January 14). How to deliver bad news to employees. *Inc.* Retrieved from http://www.inc.com/guides/201101/how-to-deliver-bad-news-to-employees.html
6. Bellware, K. (2014, February 4). Sub shop workers offered jobs back after being fired via email. *The Huffington Post.* Retrieved from http://www.huffingtonpost.com/2014/02/04/snarfs-settlement_n_4719806.html
7. Hickman, B. (2013, December 23). Snarf's closes; Fires employees via e-mail. Retrieved from https://chicago.eater.com/2013/12/23/6308235/snarfs-closes-fires-employees-via-e-mail
8. McNary, R. (2013, December). 7 reasons why firing someone by email will never make you look good, I guarantee it. Retrieved from http://rickmcnary.me/7-reasons-why-firing-someone-by-email-will-never-make-you-look-good-i-guarantee-it
9. Weber, L. (2013, July 18). Text from the boss: U R fired. *The Wall Street Journal.* Retrieved from http://blogs.wsj.com/atwork/2013/07/18/text-from-the-boss-u-r-fired/
10. Parris, J. (2016, November 18). Getting fired by text message. Retrieved from http://www.flexjobs.com/blog/post/getting-fired-by-text-message/

11. Engel, P. (2014, March 24). Here's the text message Malaysia Airlines sent to the families of the lost passengers. Retrieved from http://www.businessinsider.com/malaysia-airlines-text-message-to-families-2014-3

12. Sussman, S., & Sproull, L. (1999). Straight talk: Delivering bad news through electronic communication. *Information Systems Research*, 10(2), 150–166.

13. Leaman, C. (2016, January 6). Here's what happens when you don't deliver bad news quickly. *Fortune*. Retrieved from http://fortune.com/2016/01/06/deliver-bad-news-quickly/

14. Kowitt, B. (2016, December 14). Chipotle's crisis of communication leaves analysts unimpressed. *Fortune*. Retrieved from http://fortune.com/2016/12/14/chipotles-crisis-communication-steve-ells-monty-moran/

15. When companies tweet, investors listen. (2017, January 5). Retrieved from https://insight.kellogg.northwestern.edu/article/when-companies-tweet-investors-listen

16. Moore, D. (2015, January 16). Now trending: Social media apologies. Retrieved from http://www.newsgeneration.com/2015/01/16/social-media-apologies/

17. Creelman, V. (2012). The case for "living" models. *Business Communication Quarterly*, 75(2), 176–191.

18. Legg, A. M., & Sweeny, K. (20013, October). Do you want the good news or the bad news first? The nature and consequences of new order preferences. *Personality and Social Psychology Bulletin*, 40(3), 279–288.

19. Halperin, J. (2012, February 13). Presentation tip: Communicating bad news. *Forbes*. Retrieved from http://www.forbes.com/sites/propointgraphics/2012/02/13/presentation-tip-communicating-bad-news/

20. Crawford, H. (2016, April 20). 6 tips to successfully deliver bad news in the workplace. *U.S. News and World Report*. Retrieved from http://money.usnews.com/money/blogs/outside-voices-careers/articles/2016-04-20/6-tips-to-successfully-deliver-bad-news-in-the-workplace

21. Legg, A. M., & Sweeny, K. (2013, October 31). Do you want the good news or the bad news first? The nature and consequences of news order preferences. *Personality and Social Psychology Bulletin*, 40(3), 279–288.

22. Verizon Wireless. Unlimited plans. Retrieved from https://www.verizonwireless.com/plans/

23. Northrup, L. (2016, July 28). Here's a letter Verizon Wireless sent to a user of "extraordinary amounts" of data. Retrieved from https://consumerist.com/2016/07/27/heres-a-letter-sent-to-a-verizon-wireless-customer-using-extraordinary-amounts-of-data/

24. Northrup, L. (2016, July 28). Here's a letter Verizon Wireless sent to a user of "extraordinary amounts" of data. Retrieved from https://consumerist.com/2016/07/27/heres-a-letter-sent-to-a-verizon-wireless-customer-using-extraordinary-amounts-of-data/

25. Carmichael, S. G. (2016, October 3). Writing a rejection letter (with samples). *Harvard Business Review*. Retrieved from https://hbr.org/2016/10/writing-a-rejection-letter-with-samples

26. Legg, A. M., & Sweeny, K. (20013, October). Do you want the good news or the bad news first? The nature and consequences of new order preferences. *Personality and Social Psychology Bulletin*, 40(3), 279–288.

27. Storti, C. (2015). *Speaking of India: Bridging the communication gap when working with Indians*. Boston, MA: Intercultural Press.

28. Buttle, F. A. (2011). Word of mouth: Understanding and managing referral marketing. *Journal of Strategic Marketing*, 6(3), 241–254.

29. Hocutt, M. A., Bowers, M. R., & Donavan, D. T. (2006). The art of service recovery: Fact or fiction? *Journal of Services Marketing*, 20(3), 199–207.

30. Yahalom, T. (2010, April 28). How to handle customer complaints. *Inc*. Retrieved from http://www.inc.com/guides/2010/04/handling-customer-complaints.html

31. Beard, R. (2014, May 5). 9 customer retention strategies for companies. Retrieved from http://blog.clientheartbeat.com/customer-retention-strategies/

32. Langley, M. (2012, May 18). Inside J. P. Morgan's blunder. *The Wall Street Journal*. Retrieved from http://online.wsj.com/article/SB10001424052702303448404577410341236847980.html

33. Clarke, D., & Henry, D. (2012, June 10). Mr. Dimon goes to Washington. Retrieved from http://www.reuters.com/article/2012/06/10/us-jpmorgan-loss-senate-idUS-BRE85908J20120610

34. J. P. Morgan Chase & Co. (2012, May 10). Investor presentations. Retrieved from http://investor.shareholder.com/jpmorganchase/presentations.cfm

35. J. P. Morgan Chase & Co. (2012, May 10). Business update. Retrieved from http://i.mktw.net/_newsimages/pdf/jpm-conference-call.pdf

36. Economy, P. (2016, September 27). How to deliver bad news in an emotionally intelligent way. Retrieved from http://www.businessinsider.com/how-to-deliver-bad-news-in-an-emotionally-intelligent-way-2016-9

37. Blount, S., & Carroll, S. (2017, May 16). Overcome resistance to change with two conversations. *Harvard Business Review*. Retrieved from https://hbr.org/2017/05/overcome-resistance-to-change-with-two-conversations

38. The art of giving constructive criticism. (2016, January 19). Retrieved from http://www.utahbusinessinfo.org/2016/01/the-art-of-giving-constructive-criticism/

39. Nair, R. (2016, December 17). Mastering the art of constructive employee feedback. Retrieved from http://www.kipsen.com/2016/12/mastering-the-art-of-constructive-employee-feedback/

40. Fisher, A. (2016, September 2). How to give difficult employees constructive criticism that gets results. *Fortune*. Retrieved from http://fortune.com/2016/09/02/constructive-criticism-results/

41. Frangos, C. (2016, February 9). 3 tips for delivering bad news to employees. *Fortune*. Retrieved from http://fortune.com/2016/02/09/tips-bad-news-employees/

42. Anderson, E., Buchko, A. A., & Buchko, K. J. (2016). Giving negative feedback to millennials: How can managers criticize the "most praised" generation? *Management Research Review*, 39(6), 692–705.

43. Harms, P. L., & Roebuck, D. B. (2010). Teaching the art and craft of giving and receiving feedback. *Business Communication Quarterly*, 73(4), 413–431.

44. Weisinger, H. (2017, January 7). Criticism: Can you take it? *The Huffington Post*. Retrieved from http://www.huffingtonpost.com/hendrie-weisinger/criticism-can-you-take-it_b_8940138.html

45. Ryan, L. (2016, December 19). The ugly truth about constructive criticism. *Forbes*. Retrieved from http://www.forbes.com/sites/lizryan/2016/12/19/the-ugly-truth-about-constructive-feedback/#3d8138ca5e60

46. Kouchaki, M. (2016, September 15). How Wells Fargo's fake accounts scandal got so bad. *Fortune*. Retrieved from http://fortune.com/2016/09/15/wells-fargo-scandal/

47. Couret, J. (2016, October 22). Wells Fargo sends customers statement about unauthorized account opening scandal. *Atlanta Business Chronicle*. Retrieved from http://www.bizjournals.com/atlanta/news/2016/10/22/wells-fargo-sends-customers-statement-about.html

48. Thomas, D. (2015, October 15). How to handle a corporate crisis. Retrieved from http://www.bbc.com/news/business-34504868

49. Almendrala, A. (2016, April 13). The 6 essential elements of an effective apology. *The Huffington Post*. Retrieved from http://www.huffingtonpost.com/entry/how-to-apologize-effective-apology_us_570d928ee4b03d8b7b9ec65c

50. Yuan, D., Cui, G., & Lai, L. (2016). Sorry seems to be the hardest word: Consumer reactions to self-attributions by firms apologizing for a brand crisis. *Journal of Consumer Marketing, 33*(4), 281–291.

51. Grenny, J. (2016, October 21). What a real apology requires. *Harvard Business Review*. Retrieved from https://hbr.org/2016/10/what-a-real-apology-requires

52. Lewicki, R. J., Polin, B., & Lount, Jr., R. B. (2016, April 6). An exploration of the structure of effective apologies. *Negotiation and Conflict Management Research, 9*(2), 177–196.

53. Rigby, R. (2016, February 17). The delicate art of the workplace apology. *Financial Times*. Retrieved from http://www.ft.com/content/f5726166-d004-11e5-831d-09f7778e7377

54. Line Corporation. (n.d.). Free calls & messages. Retrieved from https://line.me/en-US/

55. Tabushi, H. (2014, May 25). No time to text? Say it with stickers. *The New York Times*. Retrieved from http://www.nytimes.com/2014/05/26/technology/no-time-to-text-apps-turn-to-stickers.html?_r=0

56. Brown, B. (2017, October 11). Samsung Note7: A phenomenal phablet flame-out timeline. Retrieved from http://www.networkworld.com/article/3130214/android/samsung-note7-a-phenomenal-phablet-flame-out-timeline.html

57. Ribeiro, J. (2016, September 22). Majority of U.S. users opt to stay with Galaxy Note7 after recall. Retrieved from http://www.networkworld.com/article/3123433/majority-of-us-users-opt-to-stay-with-galaxy-note7-after-recall.html

7

Using Social Media in Business

STUDY QUESTIONS

MyLab Business Communication
⭐**Improve Your Grade!**

If your instructor is using MyLab Business
Communication, visit **www.pearson.com/
mylab/business-communication** for videos,
simulations, and writing exercises.

New Hires @ Work

Megan Sugrue

Northwestern University

University Senior Manager, Social Media Strategy @
Viacom International Media Networks

A business shouldn't try to get "likes" on Facebook for the sole
purpose of getting "likes." Companies should know how and why
using social media can support the organization's or project's overall
objectives. When we develop social strategies for our brands, such
as MTV, Comedy Central, and Nickelodeon, it's important to identify
our objectives, whether they are to drive TV ratings, social buzz, fan
engagement, or website views. One of the benefits of social media
is that it allows you to test your messages, analyze results, and
improve your messaging based on the insights you receive.

Photo courtesy of Megan Sugrue

Chapter 7 | Introduction

In the past, a business would typically advertise on television or in newspapers and magazines to let consumers know about a new product, service, or sale. Today, social media platforms such as Facebook, Twitter, Pinterest, Instagram, and blogs create new opportunities for businesses to engage existing and potential customers. For customers, social media has also created new opportunities to endorse a business—or criticize it.

Businesses use social media more strategically than most individuals do and have invested significant resources in researching how to use social media to communicate effectively with customers. Do not assume that your personal experience with Facebook or Instagram has taught you all you need to know to contribute to your company's social media efforts. To use social media effectively in business, you will need to be strategic about how, what, and when you communicate.

Being strategic means making a plan: identifying what you want your social media presence to accomplish, which types of social media are best suited for those goals, and how to get the most value from the platforms you choose. As a report by the *Harvard Business Review* indicates, the most effective social media strategies thoughtfully match tools with goals. For example, the report describes how a large U.S.-based construction company uses a four-tiered social media strategy to communicate messages with different goals: (1) Twitter to communicate news to the media, (2) LinkedIn to share content that customers will value, (3) Facebook to publicize social responsibility efforts, and (4) a blog to hold conversations with customers.[1] The most successful strategies also incorporate regular evaluation, using feedback to identify what works (and what doesn't) so costs can be justified and improvements can be made.

Being strategic also means using social media to achieve common business communication objectives, including building goodwill, persuading customers, and controlling bad news. This chapter provides guidelines about how to develop a strategy and use different social media tools effectively to help your business keep pace with a rapidly evolving marketplace.

(SQ1) How can businesses plan, implement, and evaluate a social media strategy?

Social media offers a suite of powerful tools for helping you engage new customers and both maintain and strengthen your connections with existing ones. But it's important to use these tools strategically. Communicating through social media requires investments of money and resources, and businesses want to ensure that they get a return on their investment. This section provides a framework based on the ACE model for planning, implementing, and evaluating a social media strategy for business. That framework is illustrated in **Figure 7.1**.

Analyze goals, audience, and social media options to develop a social media strategy

According to the *eBizMBA Rankings*, the top five social media sites are Facebook, YouTube, Twitter, LinkedIn, and Pinterest.[2] However, no business should automatically create accounts

FIGURE 7.1 Using ACE for Social Media

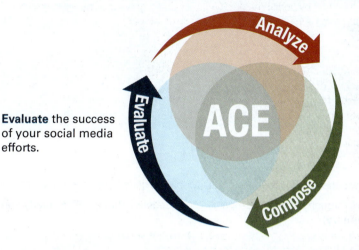

Analyze goals, audience, and social media options to develop a social media strategy.

Evaluate the success of your social media efforts.

Compose effective social media content to implement the strategy.

on all these sites and simply start communicating. To be effective, you need to know what platforms your target audience uses and what those audiences are looking for on social media. **Figure 7.2** on page 234 outlines a set of questions that will help you and your organization develop a social media strategy.

Compose effective social media content for each platform

Different types of social media have different capacities, and the most effective messages take advantage of those differences. For example, **Figure 7.3** on page 235 shows the different ways that the American Red Cross communicates across three different types of social media: a Twitter feed, a Facebook page, and a blog.

No matter what social media platform you use, you have the opportunity to go beyond the printed word and use interactive, dynamic features that engage the audience. These features include links to other sources for additional information, short videos, and photos.

Once you've chosen your platforms and your messaging strategy, develop a weekly schedule for social media updates. **Figure 7.4** on page 236 illustrates the schedule developed by a small independent bookstore.

Evaluate the success of your social media efforts

Developing and implementing a social media strategy requires a business to invest a significant amount of time and resources. How will you measure the success of your investment in social media? The more quantifiable your metrics are, the more easily you will be able to determine whether your communication is a success and how to continuously improve it.

As you plan a method for evaluating your social media efforts, refer to the goals you set in your analysis. Use **Figure 7.5** on page 236 to evaluate your social media strategy based on your specific goals.[3,4]

How can you gather the information outlined in Figure 7.5? Social media and web-hosting companies offer analytic tools that not only measure numbers, such as clicks and "likes," but also help you perform qualitative analyses such as "customer sentiment analysis."[5] Qualitative analysis helps you gauge whether, where, and to what extent people are talking positively or negatively about your business or product online. To gather more information, you can supplement this data with customer surveys. Experts recommend conducting regular evaluations to monitor and adjust your strategy.[6]

FIGURE 7.2 How to Create a Social Media Strategy

ELEMENTS	STRATEGY QUESTIONS
Goals	Why is your company communicating by social media? Which of these goals are you aiming to achieve? (You may want to achieve more than one.) • Assert brand leadership? • Attract new customers? • Motivate people to talk about your business? • Persuade people to view your website? • Create interest in and demand for your products? • Build a sense of community around your business so that people return to your site for more information?
Audience (followers)	Who are you trying to reach? Why will they want to interact online with your business? Where and how do they access the web? Through laptops? Mobile devices? Their computers at work? How do they access content? Through following companies on Facebook? Through **RSS (really simple syndication** or **rich site summary)**?
Social media platforms	What social media platforms should you use to reach these audiences? What goals do you intend to accomplish through each platform? Which audience do you intend to reach with each platform? How can you make your social media content easy for your audience to find? How can you create connections among your social media platforms? For example, will your tweets link to blogs and websites?
Timeline for content	How often should you post on social media? On what days of the week and at what times of the day should you post new content?
Content	What kind of content best supports your goals? What kind of content will your audience consider valuable?
Contributors	Who will be responsible for creating and posting content? Will all the content be "corporate," or will employees have access to participate in the company's posts? If employees post, should the company have guidelines about the differences between personal and professional communication? How much will your customers be allowed to contribute, whether via Facebook wall posts, Twitter replies and retweets, comments on blog posts, or other forms of interactivity?
Monitoring, reporting, and responding	Who will be responsible for reading comments and posts and replying on behalf of your company? Who will track and report the amount of social media interaction?

RSS (really simple syndication or rich site summary) A format for delivering frequently changing web content to subscribers; referred to as an RSS feed or news aggregator.

FIGURE 7.3 How to Compose Messages for Different Platforms

Use Twitter to get interesting information and news to your followers. Compose tweets that are no more than 100 characters to leave room for your followers to reply and quote you while remaining within the 140 character limit. As part of those 140 characters, include links to more specific information.

Use Facebook for longer messages, but keep posts relatively short (100–250 characters) to increase engagement.

Use blogs for ideas that require more development, and pay careful attention to design. To make posts and other web texts visually appealing and easy to read, use images, short paragraphs, blank space, informative headings and subheadings, lists, and bold text.

FIGURE 7.4 Example of a Social Media Schedule

	TWITTER	FACEBOOK	BLOG
3/11 **Monday**	**10:00 AM** Announce a new book **12:00 PM** Tweet a link to a book trailer video **5:00 PM** Announce a special one-night only sale	**12:00 PM** Post a short article with interesting information about an author **5:00 PM** Spotlight 1–2 new books	**MyLab Business Communication** Apply Figure 7.4's key concepts by going to **www.pearson.com/mylab/business-communication**.
3/12 **Tuesday**	**10:00 AM** Tweet a tip from a new "how-to" book **1:00 PM** Link to blog post **5:00 PM** Announce a book signing	**12:00 PM** Link to the guest blog **5:00 PM** Post a picture of a book an employee recommends, with a brief description	**11:00 AM** Post guest blog with book review from a customer
3/13 **Wednesday**	**10:00 AM** Retweet a book-related tweet **12:00 PM** Link to a published book review **5:00 PM** Link to a coupon for free coffee	**12:00 PM** Post a picture of readers in the store **5:00 PM** Ask fans to vote for their favorite book in a popular book series	
3/14 **Thursday**	**11:00 AM** Link to today's blog **1:00 PM** Announce Saturday children's story hour **5:00 PM** Tweet link to a YouTube video of a favorite author	**12:00 PM** Link to today's blog **5:00 PM** Post article about books that will be read during children's story hour	**12:00 PM** Post blog by owner of bookstore recommending his favorite book of the year

FIGURE 7.5 How to Evaluate Your Social Media Strategy

GOAL	EVALUATION QUESTIONS
Increase conversation about your business or product	a. How many followers do you have on Facebook, Twitter, and Instagram? How many people subscribe to your blog? b. At what rate are you adding (or losing) new followers or subscribers? c. How many other websites link to your blogs? d. How many other bloggers mention your blog? e. On which platforms are your key customers talking most about your business or product? f. What percentage of your content do your followers share with others? g. What subjects or keywords have been most successful in generating online conversation?
Attract new customers	a. What percentage or amount of new traffic has your social media presence driven to your website? b. What percentage or number of followers have become customers? c. How many people have visited your physical or online stores based on social media reviews or promotions?
Build community and manage your business's reputation	a. How many positive comments or recommendations have customers made about your business online? b. How many complaints have been made online, what percentage was addressed, and how quickly were they addressed? c. What types of messages have been most successful in encouraging engagement, measured in "likes," "retweets," or time spent on a blog page?

CULTURE
THE EFFECT OF CULTURE ON SOCIAL MEDIA AND E-COMMERCE

Most businesses use social media to attract customers, maintain customer relationships, and build trust for their brand. They also use social media as a starting place for e-commerce. However, global culture and politics impact how social media serves business purposes. Consider these examples from around the world:

- **Europe.** In Europe, familiarity with language is one of the key factors in trust of an Internet site.[7] A survey from the European Commission found that "Only 18% of EU Internet users buy online in another language frequently or all the time, and 42% said they never buy online in a language other than their own."[8] This finding suggests that U.S. businesses that want to attract European customers would benefit from providing sites in multiple languages.
- **South America and Africa.** Research suggests that individualistic cultures (which are prevalent in developed economies such as the United States) are more likely to trust e-commerce because purchases are backed by guarantees.[9] By contrast, these legal guarantees are less relevant in collectivist cultures such as those in South America and Africa, which rely more on a sense of community and social position for trust.[10] This finding suggests that U.S. businesses that want to attract customers from Africa may want to

partner with opinion leaders with high social standing to support their products.

- **Asia.** Although China does not allow Facebook, Twitter, or YouTube, China has the most active social media environment in the world, and social media channels such as Weitao and WeChat play a significant role in consumers' purchasing decisions. For example, marketing experts have found that purchasers rely on recommendations from opinion leaders in their social networks.[11] Purchasers in Asia are also influenced by social media that is entertaining. The cosmetics company Clinique achieved great success by producing a 40-episode social media drama series called *Sufei's Diary* that displayed Clinique products but that viewers perceived as entertainment. Clinique's brand awareness rose dramatically.[12]
- **Hispanic communities in the United States.** According to a survey commissioned by Facebook, U.S. Hispanics prefer to read online content in Spanish, and they are more likely to purchase items that are advertised in Spanish. They also require the language to be well translated and culturally appropriate.[13]

For a CULTURE exercise, go to Critical Thinking Question 5 on page 263.

SQ2 What are good practices for composing and publishing social media content?

Social media content refers to any text, image, audio, or video published through a social media platform, such as Facebook, Twitter, Pinterest, Instagram, or a blog.

In business, social media content is most effective when it engages your audience, gives them something of value, makes them trust your company, persuades them to share information with others, and motivates them to return to your site. When social media content is used for marketing, its main goal is to inspire browsers to become customers.

Compose

What makes social media content effective? How do you get people to want to read what you have to say? Social media experts have identified five key characteristics that all effective social media content shares: it is casual and conversational, valuable, original, passionate, and interactive. They also provide advice about how to implement these characteristics on specific social media platforms.

Social media content is most effective when it is:

- **Casual and conversational.** Social media content is often less formal than a typical business message. In fact, tweets, Facebook posts, and Instagram posts work best when they are casual and conversational. Before posting content, read it aloud to be sure it does not sound too formal or stilted. As the American Library Association suggests for library social media, "type like you would talk."[14]
- **Valuable.** Focus on topics that are related to your business—and that your audience will find interesting and useful. Avoid blatant self-promotion or content that is designed only to sell your company's products and services. For example, the online clothing company ModCloth, which specializes in vintage-inspired women's wear, provides extra value to its target customers by peppering its blog with recipes, hair and makeup tutorials, and crafting tips.[15] Whole Foods Market, the upscale grocery chain, offers lifestyle tips on such topics as environmental stewardship and parenting in addition to regular food-themed posts with recipes, cooking techniques, and nutritional guidelines.[16]

- **Original.** Audiences appreciate a new point of view, new insights on a topic, or new information they can use. They do not want to read content they already know.

- **Passionate.** Before you can motivate your audience to care about your topic, you need to care about it yourself. Consider the "social glue: the one thing you, your business, and your customers have in common," and generate posts and tweets based on that concept.[17] Show why you are passionate about your topic, and invite others with similar passion to contribute to the conversation.

- **Interactive.** Give your audience something to do or a reason to respond. Ask a question, provide an offer, or encourage readers to share their stories, ideas, and content.[18]

When composing social media content, your goal is to create a valuable and engaging social experience that persuades people to return. The following sections outline strategies for creating conversational, valuable, original, passionate, and interactive content for five of the most common social media outlets used to communicate to customers and potential customers—Facebook, Twitter, Pinterest, Instagram, and blogs.

Facebook: Post strategically

Tanuha2001/Shutterstock

Surprisingly, very few "fans" actually see the Facebook posts of the businesses they follow. In fact, one study indicates that an average post reaches 10.71 percent of the total audience of that page. If you do not pay for Facebook advertising, the number is even lower.[19] Why is that?

One reason may be that your fans have not been visiting your Facebook page. Most fans read the posts that appear in their own Facebook newsfeeds. If your posts do not appear near the top of their newsfeeds, fans may never see them. Facebook uses a complex algorithm to determine where posts will be positioned on newsfeeds. Although numerous factors determine whether your post appears on someone's page, one key element is interactivity: The more a visitor interacts with your Facebook page, the more noticeable your posted material will be in that fan's newsfeed.[20]

In other words, interactivity is the key to being seen on Facebook. The following advice will help you compose posts that encourage audience interaction and responses—and lead to wider visibility. As you implement these ideas, be sure to check to see if Facebook has updated any of its features. New features will offer you new opportunities. Also, be sure to stay current with Facebook's privacy and sharing settings, to ensure that your posts are distributed as widely as possible.

- **Post regularly and take the size of your Facebook following into account when determining a schedule.** Traditionally, marketers have advised companies of a "two posts a day" rule for Facebook in order to achieve maximum clicks per post.[21] Current benchmarks, however, suggest that this rule only applies to companies with more than 10,000 Facebook followers. Research shows that companies below this threshold achieve better results by posting much less frequently—no more than five times a month.[22]

- **Take advantage of social media prime time.** Many market research organizations suggest that the best time to post to Facebook is toward the end of the week. The time of day is also a factor. Hootsuite found that Facebook posts published between 12 PM and 3 PM on Mondays, Wednesdays, Thursdays, and Fridays as well as between 12 PM and 1 PM on Saturdays and Sundays receive the most likes, comments, and shares.[23] Three other studies narrow the optimal windows to between 1 PM and 3 PM on Thursdays and Fridays.[24,25,26]

- **Diversify content to keep things lively.** Variety is the spice of life: Status messages, videos, photos, breaking news, links, events, and responses to visitor posts are all effective in generating interaction.

- **Be brief, but target character counts to the needs of the post.** One of the Facebook stats most frequently quoted is that posts consisting of fewer than 40 characters receive the most responses. However, as Kurt Gessler of the *Chicago Tribune* argues, this recommendation may no longer be accurate. In a study of the *Tribune*'s Facebook posts, Gessler found that those "in the range of 160 to 175 characters" received the most reader engagement. He suggests that you should evaluate the needs of the individual post, and if nuance or length is needed, "then ignore ridiculous social media recommendations of 40-character max posts. Just write it 'til it's done."[27]

- **Be visual.** Visual content receives more attention than text. BuzzSumo found that posts with images had 2.3 times the level of engagement as posts without them.[28] Conversely, links draw the least amount of interaction.[29]

- **Add a video to your post.** The use of video on Facebook has grown dramatically, and marketing experts project that its popularity and value will continue to grow. One study suggests that as many as 61 percent of companies now use video as a marketing tool because video is informative, it appeals even to lazy buyers who may not feel inclined to read an article, and its entertainment value increases the number of social shares.[30] When adding videos to Facebook posts, keep these two things in mind: Consumers are most likely to view to completion videos between 30 and 60 seconds long,[31] and the vast majority of videos are viewed with sound off, meaning that subtitles are necessary.[32]

- **Focus the audience's attention.** Facebook advises that businesses put the most important information within the first 90 characters of a post.[33] As with most other communication, the direct organizational plan is effective.

- **Reward your audience.** Offer access to limited opportunities and exclusive deals, such as sales or coupon codes that are available only online, and make sure to promote these offers so that your audience sees them. Motivate users to interact with your business by asking them to weigh in on these special offers in advance, asking them which offers they would be most interested in receiving.[34]

- **Value your audience: Solicit, listen, and respond.** Create posts that ask your audience questions and/or seek feedback. Posts asking questions are likely to receive twice as many comments as posts that do not request a response, and perhaps even more if you integrate your question into an eye-catching image.[35,36] By asking questions and responding to them in a timely fashion, you also show users that you value their input, making them feel like respected contributors rather than faceless fans.

- **Manage important posts to keep them in front of your audience.** You can use several Facebook tools to manage posts. First, you can "pin" highly significant posts to ensure that they stay near the top of your page for one week.[37] You can also "hide" outdated posts that are no longer relevant. Finally, you can pay to "boost" a post, which allows you to extend the post's reach. All these techniques make it more likely that your audience will see your page.[38]

Twitter: Be short and focused

In contrast to Facebook, which is a network of socially connected users, Twitter generates a "selective feed" of content for interested users, giving you many quick opportunities to provide valuable information and insights.[39] Tweets are most effective when they are easy for your audience to find and share. The following advice will help you write tweets that your audience will want to read and *retweet*—or forward to their followers.

- **Help your audience find your business by choosing keywords strategically.** Potential followers may look for your business on Twitter using keyword searches, so incorporate keywords and phrases in your Twitter bio and tweets.[40] Consider the number of keywords and phrases incorporated in the Boston Harbor Cruises Twitter bio: *"Whale watches. Thrill rides. Historic tours. Sunset, lunch and brunch cruises. Provincetown Fast Ferry. Whatever your interest, set sail with us."*[41] Another good example of utilizing key search terms is the company Adaptly, whose Twitter bio reads: *"Adaptly enables the world's biggest advertisers to scale campaigns across Twitter, Facebook, Instagram, Snapchat, and Pinterest through technology and services."*[42]

- **Be a tweeter who is worth following.** You must have "followers" for your tweets to be seen. However, Twitter advises against asking people to follow you, as this practice rarely works. It also advises against paying third-party services that promise to attract many followers to your account, as this practice violates Twitter's terms of service. A better strategy is to write posts worth reading: "Engage with people, follow others whose Tweets are interesting or meaningful to you, and be an active part of the Twitter community by reading and posting high-quality information."[43] When you engage with others, make it "about *them*, not you," by tweeting, retweeting, and responding to their questions.[44] Other ways to gain more followers include interviewing someone who has a large social media following and writing a guest post on an influential blog. When the influencer or the blogger tweets about these articles, the tweet will include your Twitter handle and increase your exposure.[45]

- **Keep it short to ensure the greatest exposure.** Each tweet is limited to a maximum of 140 characters, with the exception of leading "@" replies and attachment URLs.[46] However, experts recommend making tweets even shorter: 85 to 100 characters.[47] The fewer characters you use, the easier it is for your followers to retweet the message, especially if they prefer to use the classic method of retweeting, which is to add "RT" and "@senders-username" to the beginning of a retweeted message. If you leave sufficient space, followers using this method may even add their own blurb or endorsement to your tweet when they retweet it to their followers.[48] Note the examples in **Figure 7.6**. Short tweets also leave you room to include a link to a blog or website. Twitter will automatically change all links to a length of 23 characters, even if the original link is shorter.[49]

FIGURE 7.6 Examples of Retweeted Content

TYPE OF TWEET	LENGTH OF TWEET	EXAMPLE
Original message	64 characters	SandwichKing: FREE COOKIE with the next 12 sandwich orders! Call 312-555-2345.
Retweet	83 characters	CookieLover: RT @ SandwichKing: FREE COOKIE with the next 12 sandwich orders! Call 312-555-2345.
Retweet with added endorsement	122 characters	CookieLover: Get the best cookie in town for free. RT @ Sandwich King: FREE COOKIE with the next 12 sandwich orders! Call 312-555-2345.

- **Put the key idea first.** Provide the most compelling information in the first 85 to 100 characters. Then link to the rest of the full story or to a relevant visual picture on a blog or website.[50]
- **Keep the message simple.** Keep one tweet to one topic and make it easy to read by being clear and concise.
- **Use "hashtags."** You can help potential followers find you through Twitter's internal search engine by adding a hashtag (#) before keywords and phrases. A hashtag-word combination becomes a clickable link that leads to other tweets on that topic.[51] Combine multiple-word key terms into one word (such as "*#harborcruise*" instead of "*#harbor cruise*"). Be careful not to overdo it, though. Experts argue that best practice is to use one or two short hashtags per tweet.[52]
- **Follow up.** Typing "@" in front of a username on Twitter allows you to aim your tweet at a particular person or groups. You can use this technique to respond to a compliment, a complaint, or a question. The comment is posted on your Twitter stream and shows up in the "mentions" section of the user's Twitter account. Following up demonstrates responsiveness and caring, but it is important to use this technique sparingly, as comments directed to only one person can exclude the rest of your followers.[53]
- **Retweet with comments.** Twitter's "retweet with comment" feature allows you to add a 116-character comment to a tweet, no matter what the length of the original tweet. This extra space allows you to explain why you are retweeting.

Pinterest: Engage with visual content

Pinterest is a "visual social network."[54] It uses the metaphor of a "pinboard" on which you can pin visual images, videos, or documents. Before committing time and resources to building your business's presence on Pinterest, make sure that your business has valuable visual content to share. The content may include pictures of your brands or visual stories of people using your products or services. The following guidelines will help you use Pinterest to communicate visually.

- **Divide your page into several pinboards to capture browsers' interest.** Give each board its own topic and its own collection of images or videos. That breadth gives the audience a sense of the company's products and personality, while making it simple for the audience to browse content.[55] For example, the furniture store West Elm has created more than 75 pinboards with titles such as "Gifts for Fancypants Mixologists," "Houseplants," "Urban Back-yards + Outdoor Spaces," and "Patterns," all dedicated to specialized topics in decorating and all designed to inspire the store's followers.[56]

- **Generate original content.** Start by building a repertoire of original images because those tend to be the most popular on Pinterest.[57] Instead of pinning only images of your products, consider the lifestyle that your audience enjoys or to which they aspire. What images would be compelling for them to see? Pin these to your boards as well.[58] For example, the Greek yogurt producer Chobani includes not only pinboards with product recipes on its Pinterest site but also pinboards focusing on health and fitness that are designed to motivate followers to exercise and adopt a healthy lifestyle.[59]

- **Link your images.** The intent of Pinterest is to have users click on images they like, which draws users to your business's website and blog—or to the websites of other companies whose content you have pinned.[60] For example, the Chobani "Fit With It" pinboard pins images from other fitness sites, including those of fitness trainers. All pins include links to the original sources.[61]

- **Be conspicuous but concise.** Use keywords and phrases in your pin descriptions to lead current and potential followers to your Pinterest boards.[62] Like Twitter, Pinterest supports hashtags to categorize content. However, keep the descriptions concise. You don't need to use all 500 available characters to describe an image. The image should speak for itself and link to the original source.

- **Optimize photos to encourage repinning.** The more compelling your pinned images are, the more likely that they will draw the audience's attention and interest, leading your audience to "repin" them to their own boards. Pictures are most effective if they are in full color rather than black and white, and if they are not too dark or too muted. Pictures without faces are repinned more often than pictures with faces. Also make sure that your images look good on tablets and phones, as mobile devices are responsible for 75 percent of Pinterest usage. For example, avoid pictures that include text that will be too small to read on a phone screen.[63]

- **Create special offers to increase interest in your page.** Pin a compelling image to accompany an exclusive promotion, and possibly create a board dedicated to deals available solely to your followers on Pinterest.[64] Consider hosting a contest that invites participants to share an original image on their Pinterest boards.[65] For example, to celebrate Valentine's Day, the T-shirt company Threadless challenged followers to create a special pinboard for the person they loved and include 10 images of great gifts for that person. At least five of the gifts had to be Threadless products. The creator of the winning board received $100 in Threadless credits and a $100 Amazon gift certificate.[66]

- **Use Facebook to grow your business's Pinterest presence.** If your business has a following on Facebook, it is possible to use Facebook as a tool to guide fans to your Pinterest account. Consider the following options:[67]

  - Install a Pinterest tab on your Facebook page.
  - Post specials or contests on both Pinterest and Facebook.[68]
  - Post a Facebook status update telling fans why they should also follow you on Pinterest.
  - Create a Facebook post that references and includes a link to one of your Pinterest boards or to a particular pinned image.

Instagram: Build a visual brand

Instagram is a social media platform that, like Pinterest, is "all about the visuals."[69] Created in 2010 and purchased by Facebook in 2012, Instagram is considered the "single most important social network" by American teens,[70] and it is skyrocketing in popularity among companies, primarily because it has brand engagement 10 times higher than on Facebook and more than 50 times higher than on Pinterest or Twitter.[71] Here are some guidelines to help you effectively utilize Instagram for your business.

- **Choose a filter for your brand.** Instagram offers more than 40 "filters," which are preset groupings of photo effects. For example, Clarendon "intensifies shadows and brightens highlights," while Lark "brightens your images and intensifies all your colors, with the exception of red."[72] Experts advise choosing just one or two filters that you will use for most of your photos. This consistency of filter application establishes a visual style that followers will immediately recognize and associate with your business.[73]

- **Post images for a small screen.** Instagram was originally designed as a mobile app, and up to 98 percent of traffic on the service comes through mobile devices.[74] Make sure to choose high-quality images that will appear well on a small screen.

- **Don't neglect the caption.** Hootsuite advises that a great caption should "add context, show off your brand's personality, entertain the audience, and prompt your followers to take action."[75] See **Figure 7.7** for an example of a short, engaging caption by DivinityLA, a small business that makes beaded bracelets. Yet, don't be afraid to write long captions that tell a story or appeal to your audience's emotions, such as the caption in **Figure 7.8**. Finfolk Productions—a small business that designs and manufactures silicon "mermaid tails"—received its highest number of responses from this photo and long caption.

- **Make use of hashtags, both popular and branded.** Like Twitter and Pinterest, Instagram allows you to add hashtags to your posts. These searchable tags allow you to reach audiences beyond those who already follow your posts. For example, #TBT (Throwback Thursday) is a hugely popular hashtag that accompanies old images like baby photos and other nostalgic images. Integrating #TBT into your marketing strategy can be a great way to build your brand's popularity.[76]

- **Leverage user-generated content to build your brand.** One of the best ways to engage with your followers on Instagram is to encourage users to post content using your brand hashtag. You can then comment on these images and—with permission—repost them to your Instagram account to share them with your followers. REI, a member-owned outdoor recreation company, has been particularly successful with this strategy. REI launched the #rei1440project in 2012, encouraging users to post photos in "celebration of every single minute spent outside."[77] Over the next four years, the project reached over 250,000 photos, all of them contributed by the REI Instagram community.[78]

FIGURE 7.7 Example of an Instagram Photo with an Engaging Short Caption (Mobile View)

divinityla

3,909 likes

divinityla Comment 🐢 if you want a turtle friend in your life!

View all 72 comments

Abby Roberts/Finfolk Productions

FIGURE 7.8 Example of an Instagram Photo with an Engaging Long Caption (Desktop View)

- **Consider using Instagram as a sales channel.** Although Instagram was not designed as a sales channel, many entrepreneurs have found great potential to expand their businesses in this direction. The art gallery Unit London, for example, attributes roughly half of its sales to its Instagram account. As one of its founders explained, "I don't think there is any other app that could be as powerful as Instagram for what we do. It's so good exactly because it's not all focused on art; people stumble across the art."[79] And in an article on the explosive popularity of homemade slime among adolescent girls, *The Wall Street Journal* reported that Instagram was the preferred sales avenue, as Instagram videos serve to alert customers (classmates) to new batches of slime.[80]

Blogs: Offer insights, advice, and information

Many social media experts recommend using a blog as the "hub" of your social media content.[81] Facebook and Instagram posts, tweets, and pins can all link to your blog. Unlike other social media platforms, blogs offer expansive space where you can communicate original ideas and become a thought leader in your industry. The following tips provide a good start:

- **Find a focus.** What is the theme of your blog? What does your audience need or want to know? What topics will attract your audience to your business?
- **Plan how to offer value to your audience.** You can offer insight and advice, provide information that is difficult to find elsewhere, or subtly promote your business by using these strategies:
  - Writing a tutorial about your product
  - Interviewing experts in your field
  - Sharing stories of positive customer interactions
- **Do not tout your business's success.** Focus on your audience, not on your business. You may mention key milestones in your business, such as "we just reached our 10,000th customer," but business-focused posts should be used sparingly and only to convey the stability and solidity of your business.
- **Avoid controversial or divisive topics.** Unless your blog's focus is about politics, law, government, or religion, don't address controversial or potentially divisive issues on your business blog.[82] You will likely offend some members of your audience.
- **Pay special attention to the headline.** Make the title of your blog posts exciting, and incorporate keywords or questions that may lead search engines directly to your post. If these cannot be included in a title, weave them into the body of the post.[83] For example, consider these intriguing blog titles:
  - *7 Subtle Fashion Mistakes You're Making Every Day*[84]
  - *The One Thing You Need to Succeed*[85]
  - *23 Secrets to Booking Cheap Flights*[86]

Syda Productions/Shutterstock

- **Add an image to your blog post to increase appeal, and connect the image to Pinterest.** By pinning a striking image from your blog on Pinterest, you provide the option for other Pinterest users to pin your image to their own Pinterest boards. Then, Pinterest users who click on this image in Pinterest will be led to your original blog post. You can also create a Pinterest button or widget for your blog that will allow your blog readers to easily pin images and blog posts to their own Pinterest boards, expanding your reach.[87]

- **Format so that readers can navigate easily.** Use lists and bullets, bold or italicize key points, and organize with subheadings. These techniques help readers skim your blog for relevant information.[88]

- **Make it conversational.** You have to work hard to make blog posts conversational enough to invite interaction. Imagine that you are addressing your post to an individual reader, your biggest fan, rather than an anonymous mass of people. Let your personality and your voice shine through. Experts suggest avoiding complicated words and using short sentences, asking questions to promote a sense of dialogue, splitting up paragraphs for better flow, and proofreading aloud to hear how the words sound.[89]

- **Encourage comments, subscriptions, and sharing.** To increase the number of readers of your blog, encourage participation through comments and make it easy for readers to "subscribe" to your blog and share comments through social media. Here are a few techniques you can use:[90,91]

  - Implement a mobile-friendly design for your blog so that people can read and respond to blog posts from their phones.

  - Add an RSS (really simple syndication or rich site summary) button to your blog as well as text that explains that RSS is a method to have blog posts delivered to a newsreader.

  - Offer email subscriptions to the blog, and create a dedicated subscription page where readers can sign up.

  - Add a sentence of encouragement to the bottom of the blog template that will invite people to subscribe if they enjoyed the post they read.

  - Offer free downloads only to subscribers.

- **Set a schedule for publishing.** To gain steady followers, publish posts on a regular schedule. Although some business bloggers post daily, others find that twice a week is ideal to keep visitors engaged. One study based on blogging data from HubSpot found that small businesses publishing at least 11 posts per month—averaging 3 posts per week—generated much more traffic to their websites and more sales leads than companies publishing less.[92]

- **Use a template to write your posts.** Using a consistent pattern for blog posts can help you write more quickly. Michael Hyatt, who writes a leadership blog at **michaelhyatt.com**, uses the following organizational pattern:[93]
  - Compelling title
  - Lead paragraph
  - Relevant image
  - Personal experience
  - Main body
  - Discussion question

By ending his blog posts with a question, Hyatt invites discussion, and many of his posts get 80 to 100 comments.[94]

Other bloggers have developed different templates to organize their posts.[95] John Bonini, who blogs for Impact Branding and Design, offers a simple template for a 350- to 500-word blog post that is similar to that for a five-paragraph essay—plus a bonus:[96]

- An attention-getting title or headline

- An introduction that engages the audience, introduces the topic, and provides definitions the audience needs

- Three clear and highly informative body paragraphs that use plenty of keywords that search engines can find

- A conclusion that relates the topic—and everything you've discussed—back to the audience

- The bonus: a final section that lists the three most important "takeaways" of the article

TECHNOLOGY
MAKING SOCIAL MEDIA MORE EFFICIENT

A company that fully embraces social media communication may find itself investing a large amount of time managing its social media platforms. To make the job more efficient, companies take advantage of tools that speed the process of creating and posting content as well as monitoring their brand's social media presence. The following examples describe popular tools. You can find many more tools through a simple web search.

CREATING VISUAL CONTENT

Visual content captures attention on social media, but creating meaningful visual content other than photos is time-consuming. These two applications allow you to create infographics and animated videos quickly and inexpensively:

Creating infographics
Piktochart is an application that allows you to create graphics—including infographics—even if you have no graphic design skills.

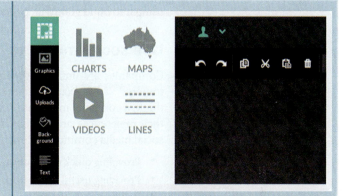

Creating animated videos
Wideo's intuitive user interface allows you to animate visual elements and produce a high-quality video in just a few hours, without any previous editing experience.

AUTOMATING, ANALYZING, AND MONITORING DATA

It can be challenging to manage varying publication schedules and monitor customer interaction across multiple social media platforms. It is equally challenging to track mentions of your brand across the web. Many tools can help, such as the following examples:

Managing your social media platforms
Buffer service allows you to schedule posts of new and curated content across multiple social media platforms. It also offers analytics that measure audience clicks, reach, and engagement.

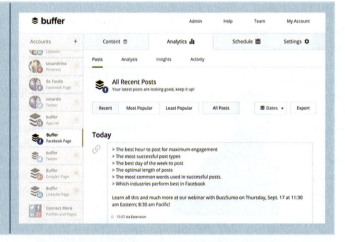

For a TECHNOLOGY exercise, go to Exercise 15 on page 265.

(SQ3) How can businesses use social media to accomplish specific communication goals?

Although much discussion of social media in business focuses on marketing and building a customer base, social media has broader uses and poses some significant risks. On the plus side, social media offers excellent opportunities to build goodwill with existing and potential customers. Social media also offers opportunities to interact with targeted users and persuade them to buy your product or service. However, social media can also amplify the effect of any business mistake or misstep, and dissatisfied customers have many public ways to broadcast their unhappiness.

This section focuses on how businesses can get the most benefit from social media by using it to build goodwill, persuade, and control the spread of bad news.

Use social media to build goodwill

Companies are increasingly using social media to manage relationships with their customers.[97,98] For example, rather than hire a market research firm to learn what customers think, a company might use social networking sites to interact with customers, learn about their preferences, and increase their loyalty. Companies also generate goodwill through their social media communication by using the following strategies:

- Providing quick responses to questions and concerns
- Providing useful information that audiences want and need
- Building a positive, online community

Provide quick responses to questions and concerns

Social media networks give businesses more opportunities to receive customer suggestions and complaints—and respond to them quickly to satisfy customers and maintain goodwill. To do this, some companies hire social media specialists or create social media listening platforms to monitor reviews, blogs, or posts shared through various social media applications. Unfortunately, these services are often not successful at converting quantitative data into actionable, qualitative data, and therefore their usefulness is limited.[99] If you work as a social media specialist, you will need to spend time and effort to inspect social media for customer questions and concerns. If you are able to respond quickly, you can significantly improve your customer service and increase sales.

Consider this complaint tweeted to a European airline that charges for baggage according to weight:

> *Paid for 25KG but baggage scale at Schilpol allowed only 23. Had to rearrange luggage. Help! Booking# 2HBA3S*

Within 24 hours, a customer service representative responded:

> *I sincerely apologize. I have authorized a refund of the bag fee charged 25.00 Euros plus the excess fee of 10.00 Euros.*

This response helped the company regain credibility with a customer and win loyalty in fewer than 140 characters.

The following techniques can help businesses respond effectively to customers' questions or concerns communicated through social media:

- **Monitor online chatter.** In addition to "listening" to your own social media sites, set up Google Alerts and subscribe to RSS feeds that push specific keywords to you. These tools allow you to see what people are saying about your company on other social media sites. If a site that you want to monitor does not include RSS feeds, you can use tools such as Feed43 to create RSS feeds for those sites.

  In addition, you can monitor social media mentions of your company and products through services such as Google Alerts and TweetDeck that collect data from different sources and allow you to view them on a single-screen display, called a **dashboard**.[100] You can also purchase data mining reports and analytical metrics from companies such as Sysmosos that gather consumer perceptions based on social media posts.[101]

dashboard A single-screen display of data aggregated from different sources.

- **Respond quickly, even if you cannot resolve the issue immediately.** Unfortunately, 70 percent of companies ignore Twitter complaints.[102] However, research suggests that responding through social media can improve customers' goodwill 83 percent of the time.[103] When you read a request or negative comment, respond as quickly as possible. Jim Belosic, CEO of Shortstack, a cross-platform application that helps businesses maximize their social media presence, suggests that "if you take more than a day to respond to a post, you may have just lost a customer."[104] If you can't resolve an issue right away, reply to let the customer know you are working on it or, if the matter is sensitive, ask the customer to contact you privately to work out the details.[105]
- **Use a personal response, not a corporate reply.** Let customers know there is a personal presence behind the computer screen. Rather than quote policy, "speak like a human," using a friendly tone, showing empathy, and using your real name.[106]

Provide useful information that audiences want and need

In addition to *reacting* to customers, you can build goodwill by *proactively* enhancing customer relationships through social media. Psychologists from Rutgers University categorize Twitter users into two groups: *informers*, who provide useful information to their followers, and *meformers*, who Tweet primarily about themselves.[107] The informers have more social followers. Businesses can earn audience goodwill by becoming informers, providing their audiences with interesting and useful information about products and services. For example, Doughnut Vault, a Chicago-based doughnut company with two storefronts and a traveling van, tweets the van's location so customers know where to find it. It also tweets when each location sells out of doughnuts.[108] JetBlue tweets information about flight delays and flash sales on plane tickets.[109]

Businesses can also provide educational content that customers and potential customers will value. For example, Rubbermaid tweets about organizational and cleaning tips that are useful with or without its products.[110] Social strategist Lisa Barone suggests that businesses increase their presence in the marketplace by becoming an educational hub and a resource that consumers rely on for information.[111] Barone and other experts outline the following suggestions for providing useful information through social media:

- **Identify your social media goals.** What do you want to be an *informer* about? Consider what kind of information you can provide that will best *inform* your audience about your products or services. Also consider what kinds of information you can provide to educate your audience.
- **Broadcast through multiple mediums.** You can generate awareness of your company's products and services by using social media to share information previously shared only by email. For example, continue to send your newsletters through marketing tools such as Constant Contact and Fishbowl, but also post them on Facebook and Twitter in order to expand your audience.[112]
- **Integrate information feeds.** If your company supports multiple social media platforms and website content, combine the sources for a one-stop information shop. For example, **Figure 7.9** on page 248 illustrates how to integrate information from different platforms into a blog, like that of online retailer Zappos, to share more information with a wider social network.

Build a positive online community

You can also use your company's social media tools to build a positive online community, which will enhance communication, solidify the company's reputation, and ultimately build business.[113] One research study by a major consulting firm found that "nearly one in three U.S. consumers are influenced by social media in their purchases," including 47 percent of millennials. Further, it noted that "consumers who use social media during their shopping process are four times more likely to spend more on purchases than those who do not."[114]

Chicago Strength and Conditioning (CS&C), a gym that specializes in strength training exemplifies a company that builds community through social media. CS&C sponsors a Facebook page (**Figure 7.10** on page 248) that serves as a community forum for members and potential members. Members post photos of their successes that provide inspiration to others, post messages to hold each other accountable for maintaining their workout schedule,

FIGURE 7.9 How to Integrate Information Feeds into a Corporate Blog

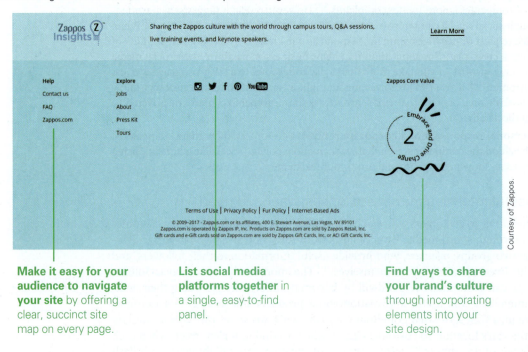

Make it easy for your audience to navigate your site by offering a clear, succinct site map on every page.

List social media platforms together in a single, easy-to-find panel.

Find ways to share your brand's culture through incorporating elements into your site design.

and post short articles to offer each other advice. Because the Facebook page helps members feel they belong to a community, the members are more likely to stay motivated. Equally important, when potential members search the Internet to find a gym for strength training, the community spirit on that page becomes a powerful selling tool.

Here are some strategies for building a positive social media community by engaging and interacting with existing and potential customers:

- **Create meaningful customer relationships** rather than merely asking your audience to "like us" on Facebook or "follow us" on Twitter. For example, Best Buy's dedicated Twitter account called Best Buy Support is monitored by Best Buy agents who respond immediately to customer questions about products and address customer service issues.[115]

FIGURE 7.10 Using Social Media to Build an Online Community

Courtesy of Chicago Strength & Conditioning

- **Encourage input through surveys.** Use social media surveys to engage consumers in your company's decision making about its products and services. You can elicit consumers' input about ideas for new products, preferences for service options, or locations for new stores. For example, the Container Store asked its Facebook fans where they would like to see a new store located.[116] Dell Computer asks customers to visit its Idea Storm page to suggest and vote on new product ideas.[117]

- **Offer social media followers exclusive perks,** such as coupons or discounts.[118] As **Figure 7.11** illustrates, large companies such as the restaurant chain P.F. Chang's create mobile applications to interact with customers through games and rewards programs. However, even small companies can publish offers through Facebook[119] and other social media sites.

- **Provide a space for customers to interact with each other.** When customers interact with each other in a forum that is "sponsored" by the company, the communication becomes a cultural transaction rather than an economic transaction, and the customers' emotional connection with the company increases.

FIGURE 7.11 How to Use a Mobile App to Engage Customers

Create incentive programs, such as Warrior Rewards, to entice consumers to frequently return.

Design interactive games and tools, like "Dish of Destiny," to personalize products and enhance consumers' knowledge about products (such as menu items) and services.

Include creative features, such as the MadLib-style "Fortune Cookie," to encourage consumers to share their interactive experience with friends through social media connections.

Use social media to persuade

In addition to creating goodwill, social media communication can be ideal for persuading people, especially consumers who have indicated some interest in your products and services by becoming part of your social media community. This section describes how to communicate persuasively with your social media audience and motivate them to purchase your company's products or services.

Build credibility by providing valuable content

Surprisingly, one of the best ways of being persuasive in social media is by trying not to be persuasive. Businesses are increasingly recognizing the value of **content marketing**— providing information that audiences value. The Content Marketing Institute explains the concept this way: "Basically, content marketing is the art of communicating with your customers and prospects without selling. It is non-interruption marketing. Instead of pitching your products or services, you are delivering information that makes your buyer more

content marketing A technique for persuading customers by providing them valuable information without trying to sell them anything.

intelligent. The essence of this content strategy is the belief that if we, as businesses, deliver consistent, ongoing valuable information to buyers, they ultimately reward us with their business and loyalty."[120]

The following examples illustrate how businesses are using content marketing as a persuasive tool to build their credibility and to strengthen their brand.

- **Blogs.** Blogs are an effective tool for delivering content to customers and potential customers—and for establishing an organization as a thought leader in a field. One company that uses its blog very effectively is Adaptly, a young and quickly growing business that simplifies social media advertising by offering customers the ability to schedule advertising campaigns across multiple social media networks at once. Adaptly's blog (illustrated in **Figure 7.12**) provides customers with insights and tips about social media advertising. Customers can also rely on Adaptly's blog to update them about any changes in the social media platforms that will affect their advertising. The friendly voice and useful content in the blog reinforce customers' perceptions that Adaptly is a trusted partner committed to its customers' success.

FIGURE 7.12 How to Use a Blog for Content Marketing

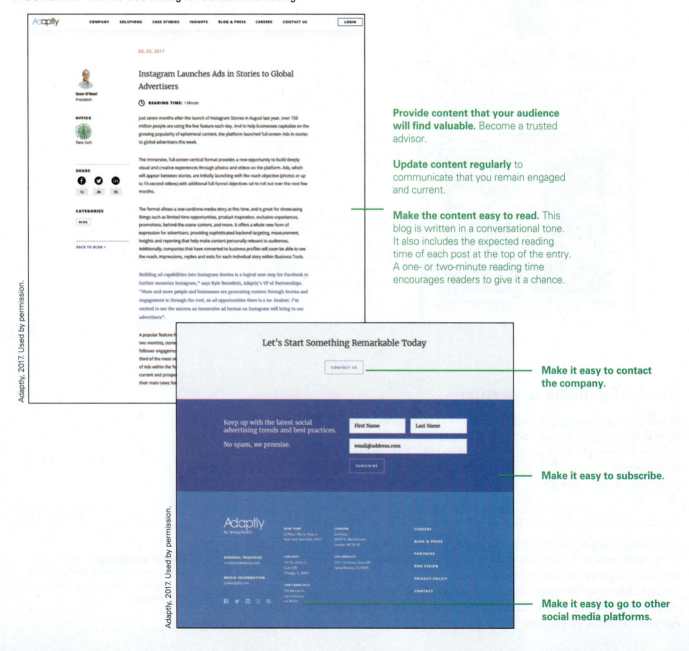

- **Twitter.** Family travel expert Eileen Ogintz uses Twitter to communicate vacation ideas, travel tips and news, and personal travel stories to the families who subscribe to her TakingtheKids Twitter feed (see **Figure 7.13**). The short tweets always include links to news stories or to the TakingtheKids blog. Ogintz's goal is to be the trusted advisor for families planning vacations.

- **Custom content marketing sites.** Other businesses are creating custom content marketing sites that do not simply advertise their products but instead aim to create a sense of community for their customers. For example, food company General Mills launched the "Hello, Cereal Lovers" campaign designed to "remind people how awesome [cereal] is and how much they love it, and get it out of the pantry and into breakfast bowls."[121] One of the centerpieces of the initiative is a cross-platform initiative aimed at inspiring consumers and re-engaging them with cereal, regardless of brand.[122] On the "Hello, Cereal Lovers" Facebook page, audiences can share and engage with cereal-related recipes, crafts, and games. The page also links to other social media platforms, such as Instagram; the campaign gained over 600,000 followers on Facebook.[123] By embracing content that isn't strictly branded and encouraging users to develop and share their own content, companies create engaged and loyal consumers.

FIGURE 7.13 How to Use Twitter to Become a Trusted Advisor

Cross-link to leverage your network and advertise the various places where you have a web presence.

Provide followers with recommendations, including photos and videos.

Provide content from other sources that followers will value and use.

Develop a strategy to move your audience to act

Beyond providing valuable content, you can also use social media as a persuasive sales tool to motivate action. B. J. Fogg from the Stanford Persuasion Lab created a behavior model to explain the complexities of motivating action. Fogg's Behavior Model suggests that you can influence people's behavior through a social media strategy that combines three elements: *motivation, triggers,* and *ability*.[124] The subscription beauty box service Ipsy uses all three elements to persuade its customers to subscribe and buy beauty products.

Ipsy was created by beauty **vlogger** (video blogger) Michelle Phan, who got her start making hugely popular YouTube makeup tutorials, and she continues to use tutorials to fund and grow her business. Ipsy works like a typical subscription box service, but the company uses social media in an innovative way to persuade its audience to act. Customers can sign up for a beauty box subscription and receive a monthly "GlamBag" filled with sample-sized makeup, skincare, and hair care products. Ipsy promotes these products through its group of beauty vloggers—called stylists—who record their makeup tutorials in Ipsy's studio space at Ipsy Open Studio, exclusively using the products Ipsy sells. Ipsy uses its vloggers to both

vlogger Video blogger, a blogger who provides content primarily through video rather than text or images.

motivate and *trigger* customers to make individual purchases and to sign up for their monthly beauty boxes—and it gives customers the *ability* to make purchases easily. Here is how Ipsy uses motivation, triggers, and ability to fuel its growth to 1.5 million:[125]

- **Motivation.** The first step in influencing behavior is to motivate your audience. One way to motivate customers further is to create an engaging experience that invites them to think more deeply about the products being offered and to comment on them. Experts agree that initiatives to encourage customer participation can be motivational. Jay Baer, a social media consultant with Convince & Convert, LLC, emphasizes that the goal of social media is not to collect friends like baseball cards but to "activate" them.[126] Ipsy encourages its customers to make their own vlogs using Ipsy products, inviting very popular vloggers to be sponsored stylists and film with the company in their media development studio. The company refers to its customers as "ipsters," suggests hashtags, and includes easily accessible buttons allowing users to post about their purchases or makeup techniques on social media.

- **Triggers.** Triggers are cues or prompts that call your audience to action. Social media provides businesses with a unique opportunity to put triggers in the paths of motivated people. Ipsy uses a point system to get "ipsters" to connect on social media and market Ipsy's products. Users get points for following stylists, sharing purchased on social media, and referring friends. They can use these points to earn extra items in their monthly GlamBags. Ipsy also offers giveaways and special promotions to trigger potential customers to subscribe or make an additional purchase. The offer of products at a significant discount might trigger a beauty vlog viewer who was on the fence about joining Ipsy to finally decide to both subscribe to the GlamBag and make a separate purchase.

- **Ability.** Once you have motivated your audience and provided an effective trigger, the last step in Fogg's Behavior Model is to simplify the audience's ability to respond. Abandoned shopping carts—online orders left right before the point of purchase—are a major problem for online retailers. Up to $4 trillion is lost annually in abandoned online purchases.[127] If the process is difficult to navigate or requires more information (or clicks) than customers are willing to provide, they will likely terminate the transaction.[128] Instead, create an easy "yes" response to your persuasive appeal.

    Ipsy gets around the problem of abandoned shopping carts by operating primarily on an automatically renewing subscription basis. The only point at which the customer needs to follow through on a purchase by entering payment information is at the moment of initial subscription. Subscriptions renew automatically, so a subscriber needs to take no additional action. And if a subscriber is viewing a beauty vlog and wants to purchase a featured product, all she has to do is click on the link below the video to be taken to the product page to click "purchase." Payment information is already in her account, giving her the ability to make a purchase easily without the additional clicks that have the potential to lose business.

Use persuasive techniques to appeal to emotion

Although the Fogg Behavior Model will help you develop an effective social media strategy for persuading customers to act, you will still need to determine what persuasive content or messages to deliver to your audience. In Chapter 5: Communicating Persuasive Messages, you learned about Cialdini's techniques for appealing to emotion—scarcity, social proof, liking, reciprocity, consistency, and authority. You can use these persuasive techniques in your social media communication.[129] The following discussion illustrates how Ipsy uses several of them:

- **Scarcity.** The more exclusive the offer, the more valuable your audience may perceive it to be. Ipsy promotes a sense of scarcity around its products by producing only a limited number of GlamBags per month. New subscribers may be placed on the waiting list, increasing their eagerness to receive products.

- **Social proof.** Ipsy's YouTube beauty tutorial videos display the number of viewers who have already watched the video. This known as "informational social influence,"[130] and it increases the value of your product by showing that others value it. You can do this by indicating the number of people following your company's tweets, the number of people that "like" your Facebook page, the number of reviews (and stars) your business has on a TripAdvisor site, and the number of shares or RSS subscriptions for your website.

- **Liking.** The more your audience likes you and your company, the more persuasive you can be with them. Use your social media communication to be "likable." Ipsy talks about itself as a community rather than a company, and founder Michelle Phan is a frequent and popular presence in its social media. The stylists display distinct and relatable personalities, encouraging customers to follow the advice and purchase products from stylists they identify with or emulate.

- **Reciprocity.** Ipsy offers points that customers can exchange for additional beauty products if they refer friends who sign up within 24 hours. The technique also relies on the principle of "liking." Your friends are more likely to purchase the subscription if they hear about it from you; people trust reviews from family, friends, and colleagues.[131]
- **Consistency.** Subscription boxes work because they create commitment and consistency in their customers. Ipsy can rely on its customers because they have purchased a monthly subscription. As a result, Ipsy can provide samples and products at a reduced cost. The subscription box model forces customers to make a commitment to purchase and use the company's products. Ipsy counts on subscribers to remain subscribed and to continue to purchase the sample products in full sizes, ensuring good relationships with suppliers.

COLLABORATION
USING SOCIAL COLLABORATION TO INCREASE PRODUCTIVITY

Social media is a key tool for helping you build your brand and communicate with your audience. More than that, however, social media is changing the way that business is done today by facilitating new methods of internal collaboration. Social collaboration platforms such as *Basecamp* and *Slack* offer team messaging, file sharing, tool integration, and multi-device connectivity. As one expert explains, while such platforms do offer employees a social networking outlet—a place for chatting, gif-sharing, and more— "social networking was never supposed to be the ultimate point of adopting social software. The big picture, strategic goal has always been to boost the agility, adaptability, resiliency, and cohesion of organizations, with social networking as a means to an end."[132]

Although Slack—one of the most popular social media collaboration platforms—employs no sales or marketing team, its client list has grown exponentially since it launched in 2013.[133] Clients include Nordstrom, BuzzFeed, PayPal, eBay, and *Slate*. According to a *Slate* article, Slate staffers exchanged more than 1 million messages through Slack in the company's first year using the social platform.[134] Part of Slack's appeal is that it is built for mobile and fun to use. Slack's founder Stewart Butterfield has deep experience in game development that has influenced Slack's design: "Slack can become such a lively platform for developing an office bond that it almost feels like the app itself has a pulse."[135]

Basecamp works on different model. Going beyond a group chat function, Basecamp "provides small businesses with a centralized system that brings together internal communications, projects and client work in one location."[136]

Social media collaboration platforms encourage conversation and team building, but they also run the risk of lowering productivity. It is not simply a matter of employees losing themselves in non-work chatter, although such a danger exists. Rather, as many experts have lamented, the "always on" nature of these platforms can cause information—and collaboration—overload, stifling action in the midst of constant discussion, turning "workdays into one long Franken-meeting."[137] Yet, when used smartly, the benefits can outweigh the dangers, fostering a positive company culture, facilitating deeper engagement of workers in their jobs, and leading to increased innovation.[138] In fact, one study found that "the potential for value creation when social technologies are used to improve collaboration and communication within and across enterprises is *twice* as big as the value that can be created through all other uses across the value chain."[139]

For a COLLABORATION exercise, go to Exercise 16 and Exercise 17 on page 266.

Courtesy of Basecamp

Basecamp increases productivity by integrating group chat, a message board, a to do list, a project calendar, and a project document list all on one screen.

Control the spread of bad news through social media

While social media provides businesses with an opportunity to reach customers, it also provides customers with an opportunity to complain publicly when they are dissatisfied. These negative posts have serious consequences. Research suggests that consumers trust online commentary almost as much as they trust recommendations from friends.[140] One study found that 60 percent of consumers questioned the quality of a local business if they read negative reviews, and one in three of these consumers would actually choose not to use a local business if they read negative reviews.[141]

The bad news may originate as critical reviews on the company's e-commerce website, negative comments on reservation sites such as TripAdvisor or OpenTable, damaging posts on social media sites such as Facebook, complaints on blogs and microblogs such as Twitter, and videos of product disasters on YouTube. No matter where the bad news originates, it travels fast on social media. News can be reposted and shared worldwide. When bad news goes viral, it escalates what could have been a minor problem into a widespread public relations crisis.

Research by Altimeter Group, a technology advisory firm, suggests that 76 percent of social media crises could have been avoided if the company had been prepared to respond by having a social media crisis management plan in place.[142] This plan includes assessing your business's risk, strengthening relationships with fans and customers, and understanding how to prevent minor problems from escalating.[143] The guidelines below are ones that any business can follow.

Have a plan in place

Do not wait for negative comments and then plan how to respond. Instead, be proactive.

First, assess your risk for negative comments and think about who might post them: Unhappy customers? Competitors? Activists and special interest groups? The Dutch grocery chain Albert Heijn planned the launch of its Facebook page for months, but it did not plan well enough. During the first several days after the debut, conversations on the store's Facebook wall were dominated by an activist group that protested the store's sale of chicken grown quickly with hormones.[144] Similarly, the Italian clothing giant Dolce & Gabbana was barraged by Facebook postings from the Clean Clothes Campaign, an activist group demanding that the company stop sandblasting jeans to give them a worn look, claiming that the production method is dangerous to workers.[145]

Then, ensure that you catch problems quickly by monitoring all mentions of your brand and company on all social media platforms, even on the weekends.[146] You cannot respond if you don't know what is being said. Finally, ensure that employees who monitor social media are empowered to respond. The bad news may go viral if employees need to wait for official permission before responding.

Respond quickly

Don't ignore bad news. If you use social media to respond quickly, most of your audience will read your explanation before they see the original bad-news message. In addition, by anticipating the audience's questions and concerns and incorporating them into your response, you can create a positive impression that enhances your business's image.[147]

Begin by responding in the social medium channel where the bad news originates. Consider the video of a FedEx driver throwing a computer monitor delivery over a security gate. The delivery was recorded by a customer's security camera, and the customer posted the video to YouTube. Within five days, the video had over 5 million views.[148] Just a few days later, FedEx responded with a video apology that was posted both to YouTube and FedEx's corporate blog. Customers and employees commented, most with positive responses about the company.

If you are replying to an individual's complaint, publicly commit to follow up privately with the person who originally posted the complaint. When an employee of a Papa John's pizza restaurant included a racial slur on a customer's receipt, the customer posted the receipt on Twitter with the comment "*@PapaJohns just FYI my name isn't 'lady chinky eyes.'*"[149] The next day, Papa John's posted its own tweet, telling the public that the company had apologized to the customer and fired the employee.[150] Although tweets are limited in length, they provide enough space for a genuine response.

After the initial response, continue to comment on all your social media platforms to ensure that your response reaches as large an audience as possible. Link your tweets to your company's Facebook page, and post more detailed information to your company website and blog. For example, to further quell the backlash from the negative Twitter post, Papa John's posted this statement to its Facebook page: *"This act goes against our company values, and we've confirmed with the franchisee that this matter was addressed immediately and that the employee is being terminated. We are truly sorry for this customer's experience."*[151] Such a response allows you to begin a more positive conversation with customers and supporters.

Respond genuinely

Do not use a template or a generic message to respond to negative posts or even complaint emails. Research shows that social media audiences respond much better to personal-sounding responses than to impersonal ones.[152] Frederic Gonzalo, the vice president of marketing for Le Massif, a ski resort in Canada, regrets his use of a generic message in the midst of a social media crisis.[153] During a poor skiing season, the staff at Le Massif were delighted that a snowstorm was predicted for the Saturday of a late winter weekend and took the opportunity to generate excitement by posting about it on the company's Facebook wall. By Sunday morning, however, all the chairlifts were frozen, and Le Massif needed to turn away hundreds of disappointed customers, many of whom posted negative messages on the resort's Facebook wall. Gonzalo exacerbated the problem by posting this message (translated from French): *"Thank you for your comments. Can you please send directly to our customer service at sac@lemassif.com. We thank you for your understanding in advance, the Management Team."* This response only made customers angrier. Gonzalo did not realize until Monday that he needed to post a genuine apology and explanation. The response he eventually posted received very positive and understanding replies.

In contrast to the generic message, note in **Figure 7.14** how the owner of a popular restaurant in Amsterdam responded to a negative review a customer posted to TripAdvisor. The owner responded quickly, politely, and personally.[154]

This kind of personal response signals to the dissatisfied customer and to others reading restaurant reviews that the restaurant is concerned about patrons and responsive to complaints. The bad news provides an occasion for communicating a positive image of the business.

FIGURE 7.14 How to Respond to a Negative Review

"A Little Disappointed"

3 of 5 stars Reviewed 6 June

We found this restaurant around the corner from our B&B and managed to get a table one evening, it is very popular. It has a couple of fixed price 2 or 3 course menus, very good value. Food was acceptable but not exceptional, lamb was very tough, plenty of it though. Service was ever so slow, I know they say Dutch service can be a little off hand, but this was poor. We were offered the desserts from two other tables before we received our main course! and our main course arrived 45 minutes after we had finished our starter.

Owner at Seasons Restaurant responded to this review, 7 June

Dear Allan,

In regards to your comment above, we apologize for the service and experience that you received.

I believe you were with us this past weekend, when we were extremely busy as you pointed out. Surprised to hear about the lamb, but will review this and see what went wrong. We have addressed the slowness that caused the delay with your main course and this was due to a large table in the restaurant. This is no excuse, just an explanation. We have reviewed our reservations for large tables during peak times, so this does not happen.

As for getting dessert from another table before your main (twice) there is no excuse and we will discuss this with our staff.

Thanks for your comments and we hope you can come by again to see that we can do better.

Kind regards,

Side annotations:

Refer to the customer by name or handle in order to personalize the response.

Acknowledge the reviewer's comment and apologize for a bad experience.

Indicate specifically how and when you will address and/or remedy the negative product or service.

Include details to show that you have carefully read the complaint.

ETHICS
CAN YOU TRUST CONSUMER REVIEWS IN SOCIAL MEDIA?

According to Bazaarvoice—a network in which shoppers share opinions, questions, and experiences about products—84 percent of Millennials say their purchasing decisions are influenced by consumer-written content on the web,[155] which often takes the form of product reviews. But is this content trustworthy?

Fraudulent reviews are widespread online, often posted by businesses themselves. For example, an unethical business may write (or hire someone else to write) negative false statements about competitors on review sites such as Yelp and TripAdvisor—sites where virtually anyone can post anonymously. An unethical business may also post flatteringly positive reviews about itself—a practice that is just as fraudulent as falsely maligning the competition.[156]

A study by Michael Luca of the Harvard Business School and Georgios Zervios of Boston University found that "roughly 16 percent of restaurant reviews on Yelp are identified as fraudulent, and tend to be more extreme (favorable or unfavorable) than other reviews."[157] These reviews have a major impact on business. In an earlier study, Luca found that for a restaurant, a one-star increase in a Yelp rating leads to a 5 to 9 percent increase in revenue[158]—creating a huge incentive to publish fraudulent positive reviews.

Not only is such social media behavior unethical, it may also be illegal. A U.S. federal law, the Lanham Act, prohibits false advertising—advertising that is deceptive and as a result injures

the target of the advertising. In 2009, the Federal Trade Commission (FTC) extended its definition of advertising to include social media. The FTC began to monitor social media communicators "masquerading as independent third parties" who "might be taking advantage of the millions of consumers whose buying decisions are increasingly shaped by social media."[159]

And it is not just businesses that engage in unethical social media behavior; consumers sometimes do it as well. TripAdvisor says it occasionally hears from a hotel owner about a guest who threatens to write a bad review "unless a demand for a refund, upgrade, or other request is met."[160]

Social media has, on balance, been highly beneficial for consumers and businesses, giving consumers detailed information about products and providing businesses with an efficient way to reach buyers quickly and inexpensively. But social media also offers opportunities for unethical and illegal communication. Ethics and the law clearly converge on a clear set of principles: Online reviews and social media statements must be transparent and honest and must never deceive.

> For an ETHICS exercise, go to Critical Thinking Question 10 on page 263.

SQ4 How can you, as an employee, use social media responsibly?

In the early days of social media, employers were concerned that access to social media sites at work might interfere with employees' concentration. As a result, many companies blocked social media—and some still do. However, many businesses have come to realize that employees can be effective *brand evangelists* in their use of social media—if the company provides guidelines for employees to follow and if employees are trained to communicate effectively within those guidelines. Organizations as different as the Coca-Cola Company[161] and the International Olympic Committee[162] have produced social media guidelines for their employees.

Follow guidelines to avoid damage to your and your company's reputations

Unfortunately, not all companies have social media guidelines. In fact, multiple surveys have found that only around 25 to 30 percent of companies have guidelines in place and instruct employees how to use them.[163] If the company you work for has no guidelines, the following suggestions provide a good starting point for professional social media behavior. They are adapted from the guidelines Monster.com produced for its own employees.[164]

- **If it's personal, keep it personal.** For topics not related to business, use your personal social media and email accounts, and don't mention your employer.
- **Identify your connection.** If you use social media as part of your job, identify the company you work for. Keep to topics related to your area of expertise, and let people know that your views are yours, not the company's.
- **Be honest and professional.** Communicate as you would in face-to-face conversations. Avoid discriminatory content. Avoid arguments. Identify who you are; "anonymous" is not professional.
- **Respect and protect what's confidential.** Never reveal financial, legal, copyrighted, proprietary, or personal information about the customers, employees, or the company.

New Hires @ Work

Shruti Shah
University of Florida

Operations Analyst Development Program Intern @ JPMorgan Chase

I worked at a large bank, which has a strong policy against using social media to disseminate company-related information. They warned us to err on the side of caution whenever sharing anything about our jobs on social media because we work with confidential information.

Photo courtesy of Shruti Shah

- **Add value.** Share interesting, helpful information and ideas. Link to relevant content on your company's website.
- **Present recommendations as personal.** When you recommend or endorse colleagues on LinkedIn and other social networking sites, be clear that your recommendation is based on your personal experience and is not an official recommendation of your company.
- **Know the risks.** Ignoring these rules could lead to your company firing you. The media routinely reports on employees who are fired for posting offensive comments, revealing confidential information, posting information that reflects badly on employers, and using public social media for job searches.[165]

■ **In summary,** social media gives employees greater opportunities to communicate on behalf of a business, to build that business's reputation, and to increase the number of people who interact with the company. If you, as an employee, take advantage of this opportunity, it is more important than ever before that you "polish your professional presence" so that you help rather than harm the business.

BLOGGING @ WORK APA Style Blog

Most discussions of social media for businesses and professional organizations focus on marketing. How can the organization use social media to increase its presence and reputation? How can it use social media to entice customers? But many organizations use social media in a very interactive way to build community and, in fact, *deliver* their services. One such organization is the American Psychological Association (APA).

If you have written research papers in college, you may be familiar with APA's writing style, which many business disciplines use for formatting reference lists and citations. The APA publishes a manual that provides an extensive set of guidelines for using APA Style. Yet it is very difficult for a book to answer all possible questions that users have about APA Style. In addition, books are not published frequently enough to address new documentation challenges as they arise.

To fill in the gaps, APA publishes the APA Style Blog, which is the "official companion of the *Publication Manual of the American Psychological Association, Sixth Edition.*" In the blog, APA Style experts "explore what APA Style is and how it works in a variety of areas, including reference citations of every sort, grammar and usage, the publication process, and social media."[166] Equally important, they answer questions about APA Style that the manual does not explicitly address---for example:

- How do you alphabetize a reference list entry that begins with a number?

[*Answer from April 12, 2017, blog post:* Alphabetize the first word as if it were spelled out. For example, the entry for the article "50 Ways to Improve Your Life With Cats," which has no author, would begin with the digits "50" and would be alphabetized as if it were "Fifty."]

- How do you cite people with only one name?

[*Answer from May 24, 2017, blog post:* Use the one name, and spell it out completely: "Madonna." If the author is well known by one name but publishes under his or her full name, use the last name and first initial—not "Oprah" but "Winfrey, O."]

- How do you cite a reference for a work published with a typo in the title?

[*Answer from June 15, 2017, blog post:* Include a footnote in the reference list entry that indicates the title has a typo.]

Anne Woodworth, senior editor for APA Style, and Timothy McAdoo, product development manager for APA Style, explain that APA created the blog because "we wanted to have a way to build a community, reach out to the existing community, and address things as they change over time." APA also wanted a way to "make the material come alive." That is why the blog posts are written in a friendly voice that makes the material interesting and approachable.

How do the writers and editors determine topics for the blog? Sometimes the writers use blog entries to alert users to changes that occurred after the publication of the manual. For example, after the sixth edition of the manual was published, the organization that assigns digital object indicators (DOIs) to articles changed the DOI display guidelines. McAdoo wrote a blog post with the new guidelines.[167] Other blog posts respond to community questions: "We get questions on the blog, by email, and by Twitter, Facebook, and Google+. With all of that, we sometime see trends. We have regular meetings where everyone who writes on the blog discusses what questions have come in and brainstorms what would be useful to write about."

The blog posts not only help the community, but they also help APA. Each blog post contributes to the library of material that the editors and writers have available to answer questions. So when a student poses a question on the blog or on Twitter or Facebook, the writers can often point the student to an existing post. These questions also inform the APA Style team's work when developing new APA Style products (such as APA Style CENTRAL®, a cloud-based writing solution) and when considering updates for later editions of the *Publication Manual* and related APA Style publications.

Source: Interview with Anne Woodworth and Timothy McAdoo

Developing a Social Media Program

This case scenario will help you review the chapter material by applying it to a specific situation.

The EdgeGlen Theatre is an independent movie house located in a densely populated urban neighborhood in a historic landmark building near Glenwood University. The EdgeGlen showcases new and classic movies that are designed to appeal to both the university community and local residents, many of whom are young professionals.

While the EdgeGlen has had a website for five years, the theatre does not have a social media presence or social media strategy. That is why the theatre's owner, Bob Sackett, hired Harris Brown, a recent college graduate who managed social media outreach during two internships, one for a comedy club and the other for a music club in the city.

Developing a Social Media Strategy

During Harris's first week of work, Bob gave him a straightforward assignment: Develop a social media strategy for the EdgeGlen. After reviewing the social media presence of competitive theatres in the city, Harris proposed that the EdgeGlen Theater's social media strategy prioritize the following three goals:

a. Make the theatre the preferred movie destination for Glenwood University students.

b. Increase awareness and engagement within the local community.

c. Make the theatre and its social media sites a hub for movie-related discussions.

To achieve these goals, Harris recommended three specific social media platforms—a Facebook page, a Twitter feed, and a blog. Finally, to increase customer engagement, he recommended that all content serve one or more of these three purposes:

- *Entertain* people with interactive content.
- *Educate* people about movie-related content.
- *Entice* people to come to the theatre.

Question 1: Evaluate Harris's proposed strategy.

a. Are there other goals the theatre might accomplish through social media?

b. In what ways might the EdgeGlen use other social media platforms (for example, YouTube, Pinterest, and Instagram) to achieve its goals?

c. Are there other themes that the posts might convey?

d. Propose some content ideas for Facebook posts, tweets, and blog posts that will convey one or more of the three themes.

Composing Social Media Content That Engages the Audience

It's a Monday morning in mid-December, and Harris is pleased to show Bob that the theatre's Facebook page, Twitter feed, and blog are up and running. And Bob has good news for Harris, too: The EdgeGlen has received the rights to show a recent Cannes Film Festival award-winning movie, *The Dim Lights of the Winter Solstice*. EdgeGlen will be the only theatre in the entire city showing the movie. Bob wants to start showing the film this upcoming weekend. However, because

the theatre's schedule is planned six weeks in advance, the EdgeGlen will be able to show the film only at 11 PM Friday and Saturday nights. Moreover, Bob won't be able to place advertisements in the student or local papers until Friday. So it's up to Harris to get the word out on social media. He has five days to persuade both the university community and the local residents to buy tickets in advance to attend the late night showing of this movie. At the same time, he knows that the theatre's social media messages must also publicize the other movies that are showing throughout the week.

With those thoughts in mind, Harris starts to revise his social media schedule and content, and he begins writing.

Question 2: Assume that the EdgeGlen's social media schedule typically includes three tweets a day, two Facebook posts a day, and two blog posts per week. Help Harris plan a five-day social media schedule and write posts:

a. Create a five-day social media schedule for Harris, following the model in Figure 7.4. Consider how many of his posts should focus on the special showing of *The Dim Lights of the Winter Solstice* and how many should support his other goals and other films being shown that week. Be sure to include topics for the tweets, Facebook posts, and blog.

b. What persuasive techniques can Harris use on the three social media platforms to entice people to buy tickets in advance to see the new film? Consider the Fogg Behavior Model of persuasion: motivation, triggers, and ability. Also consider Cialdini's concepts of scarcity, social proof, liking, reciprocity, and consistency.

c. What Twitter hashtag should he use?

d. What images or pictures could Harris use on Facebook, a blog, or Twitter?

e. What web-based content could he link to?

f. What interactive questions or activities could he include to increase audience engagement?

g. Write at least one tweet that Harris could use.

Using Social Media to Control the Spread of Bad News

Harris's social media campaign is a success. By Thursday at noon, more than 100 advance tickets had been sold for each of the 11 PM showings of *The Dim Lights of the Winter Solstice*. With that many tickets sold, the theatre was sure to be at least half full on Friday and Saturday nights. Satisfied with this success, Bob gave Harris a half-day off, and Harris left work happy.

Harris's happiness did not last long. At 5 PM, he received a call at home from Bob with bad news. Friday's performances—including *The Dim Lights of the Winter Solstice*—may have to be canceled.

That afternoon, city inspectors had discovered electrical problems at the theatre that need to be fixed before the theatre can reopen. Bob will have electricians working at the theatre Thursday night and into Friday. The work will certainly be completed in time for the show on Saturday, but it may not be completed in time for any shows on Friday. Bob asks Harris to get the word out on social media.

Harris sits down at his computer to write a Facebook post. He wants to be sure that people do not come to the theatre at 11 PM on a cold winter night only to find that the theatre is closed. He can only imagine the complaints that will reverberate on Facebook.

Here is his first draft.

The EdgeGlen Theatre is currently undergoing electrical work. City inspectors recently inspected the theatre and found some issues. Electricians are in the theatre now doing the necessary work. With luck, Friday's screening of *The Dim Lights of the Winter Solstice* will go on as scheduled.

However, we may have to cancel the screening. We do not have answers yet, but as soon as we do we will let you know. Tickets bought in advance will be refunded.

Watch our Facebook page and Twitter feed for details.

Not completely happy with this draft, Harris decides to write a second version. Here it is:

Friday night's screening of *The Dim Lights of the Winter Solstice* may be cancelled due to electrical problems. We are working as hard as we can to resolve the problems, and we are confident that Saturday's screenings will definitely happen. If we do cancel Friday's screening, ticket holders can apply for a refund, use the tickets at the Saturday night showing, or use the tickets for a future movie. We apologize for the possible inconvenience.

Watch our Facebook page and Twitter feed for details. We will have hourly updates throughout Friday. Stay tuned!

Question 3: Evaluate these drafts of a Facebook post.

a. What should be the goal of the post?

b. Compare the two drafts. What are the strengths and weaknesses of each?

c. Which one would you choose? Why? What changes would you suggest for the post you chose?

d. Is a Facebook post sufficient? What other communication media should Harris use?

Study Questions in Review

 How can businesses plan, implement, and evaluate a social media strategy?
(pages 232–237)

- **Analyze goals, audience, and social media options to develop a social media strategy.** Make decisions about your social media goals and the audience you want to reach. Then choose the social media platforms and publishing strategies that will help you achieve your goals.
- **Compose effective social media content for each platform.** Some criteria, such as being conversational, valuable, original, passionate, and interactive, will help your content stand out on any social media platform. However, optimizing your use of different tools, such as Facebook, Twitter, Pinterest, and blogs, requires tailoring your content for each one.
- **Evaluate the success of your social media efforts.** Return to your original goals to determine the best way to track your progress. A range of measures, such as number of Facebook or Twitter followers, or percentage of positive online comments, will help you determine how you are doing and what you need to tweak or expand.

 What are good practices for composing and publishing social media content?
(pages 237–245)

- **Facebook: Post strategically.** Post frequently and diversify content. Be brief and be visual to focus and capture your audience's attention. Reward your audience with offers, and value them by soliciting their opinion and responding. Manage important posts to keep them in front of your audience.
- **Twitter: Be short and focused.** Choose keywords strategically so that your potential audience can find you and follow you. Write posts worth reading: Be useful, consistent, polite, positive, and interesting. Put the key idea first, and keep the message simple. Extend your reach by using hashtags effectively and by writing posts short enough that they are easy to retweet.
- **Pinterest: Engage with visual content.** Generate original content, and link your images back to your business's website and blog. Organize your content into thematic pinboards and invite participation from your audience by encouraging them to pin images to their own boards or by creating special offers. Use your Facebook site to grow your Pinterest presence.
- **Instagram: Build a visual brand.** Instagram is extremely popular with younger consumers, and its success depends on visuals. To use Instagram successfully, choose a visual look, or filter, and use it consistently. Be sure that your images appear well in mobile applications. Take advantage of captions to tell the story. Take advantage of hashtags to help users find you. Take advantage of user-generated content to engage users

with your brand. And, if you are a small business or entrepreneur, consider using Instagram as a sales channel.

- **Blogs: Offer insights, advice, and information.** Blogs provide you with an opportunity to be more expansive. Use that opportunity wisely. Provide your audience with content they will value: advice, insights, and information that is difficult to find elsewhere. Avoid focusing solely on your business's success or products. Also avoid controversial topics. Increase appeal and readability by using a great headline, adding images, formatting so that the reader can navigate easily, and being conversational. To be most effective, set a schedule for publishing, and use a template to write your posts.

 How can businesses use social media to accomplish specific communication goals? *(pages 246–256)*

- **Use social media to build goodwill.** Create positive customer relationships by providing quick responses to questions and concerns, providing useful information that the audience wants and needs, and building a positive social media community that encourages consumers to connect with each other.
- **Use social media to persuade.** Build credibility by providing valuable content. Motivate action by creating an engaging experience, providing a trigger that prompts people to act, and making it easy for them to respond or "buy now!" Use persuasive techniques to appeal to emotion. Be likable by using a conversational tone and humor when appropriate. Provide social proof that others have bought your product or used your services. Promote a sense of scarcity by creating an exclusive or limited time offer. Help your audience reciprocate: Give them benefits before they buy. Help your audience be consistent: Remind them of past purchases and past actions.
- **Control the spread of bad news through social media.** Have a plan in place. Assess your risk for negative comments, and think about who might post them. Catch problems quickly by monitoring social media platforms, even on weekends. Ensure employees who monitor social media are empowered to respond. Then respond quickly and genuinely. Do not provide a generic response for all comments. Tailor the response to the specific comment, and use language that sounds natural rather than overly formal.

 How can you, as an employee, use social media responsibly? *(pages 256–257)*

- **Follow guidelines to avoid damage to your and your company's reputations.** Separate your work and personal use of social media. Make sure that you identify messages as your own, rather than the company's. Be professional. And protect company confidentiality. Ignoring these rules could result in your termination.

Visual Summary

Courtesy of Chicago Strength & Conditioning

Facebook: Post strategically. Create community. Be brief and visual to capture interest.

Abby Roberts/Finfolk Productions

Instagram and Pinterest: Engage with visual content and build a visual brand.

Twitter: Be short, focused, and timely.

Blog: Offer insights, advice, and information.

Key Terms

Content marketing p. 249   Dashboard p. 246   RSS (really simple syndication or rich site summary) p. 231   Vlogger p. 251

MyLab Business Communication

If your instructor is using MyLab Business Communication, go to **www.pearson.com/ mylab/business-communication** to complete the problems marked with this icon ⭐.

Review Questions

1 What are the most popular social media platforms in business?

2 Name three elements that are part of a social media strategy.

3 How can social media affect customer relationships?

4 Provide at least three examples of how a company can engage a social media audience in the decision-making process.

5 What are the three elements of B. J. Fogg's Behavior Model?

⭐ 6 How do subscriptions services such as Ipsy use the persuasive principle of social proof?

⭐ 7 What are three ways that companies can use social media to create goodwill?

8 Identify two guidelines for using social media responsibly as an employee.

9 What features of a Facebook post can increase audience response and interaction?

10 Name two measurements a company can use to evaluate the success of its social media efforts.

Critical Thinking Questions

1 Some analysts argue that the prevalence of social networking and social media excludes older workers and older customers who are not comfortable with digital communication. If this is true, what can businesses do to address this problem?

⭐ 2 Identify how any three of Cialdini's techniques for appealing to emotion can be used by businesses in social media communication.

3 Experts say that a business's Facebook post should include a call to action within the first 90 characters. Why is it important to include a call to action early in the post?

4 Virgin America Airlines says on its Twitter site: "Welcome to our mood-lit Twitter feed. Check out our app vgn.am/appydance. For official complaints please visit us at vgn.am/GstHlp. Cheers!" Why do you think Virgin America does not want to use Twitter for guest service issues?

5 Hypothesize about the role that social media and social networking might play in cultures where people are skeptical of formal institutions and authority. **[Related to the Culture feature on page 237]**

6 According to the market research organization Bazaarvoice, 71 percent of consumers who read a company's response to an online review change their opinion of the company.[168] Explain why a company's response to a review is often more influential than the review itself.

7 If a company's response to a social media review is so influential, why do experts recommend that companies receiving complaints by tweet communicate with the customer privately, not in public where others can see the conversation?

8 While many businesses direct their social media communication to consumers, some businesses direct their social media primarily to other businesses or professionals. What social media platforms do you expect to be most popular with businesses that want to communicate with business professionals? Which ones will be least popular? Explain why.

9 Imagine that you work for an electrician in your community. Recommend some ways that an electrician might use social media to engage customers or enhance the reputation of the business.

10 After receiving an extremely negative review on TripAdvisor, a popular restaurant in a resort area posted this response: "La Brochette Restaurant's personnel is positive that this review is suspicious and written by the next door competition because we recognized the reviewer's email address. We will appreciate if this malicious and false review could be removed. La Brochette Restaurant gives top priority to the quality of its food and service every day."[169] TripAdvisor posted the response but left the negative review on the site. Do you think this is an appropriate and ethical way for TripAdvisor to handle this situation, or would you recommend a different approach? **[Related to the Ethics feature on page 256]**

Key Concept Exercises

 SQ1 **How can businesses plan, implement, and evaluate a social media strategy?** *(pages 232–237)*

1 Analyze goals, audience, and social media options to develop a social media strategy

Imagine you just got a summer job as a social media intern for a fitness club in your community. The club would like to expand its membership, particularly among retirees in the community, who are likely to have time to visit the club during the day when the club is currently underused. Using the strategy plan in Figure 7.2, create a social media strategy for the fitness club.

2 Compose effective social media content for each platform

Refer to Exercise 1. Imagine the fitness club decides to experiment with four different social media platforms to see which is most effective at reaching its target audience. Your supervisor asks you to plan four social media messages for this experiment:

a. A tweet aimed to persuade the target audience to take a tour of the club

b. A short Facebook post, including a picture, designed to achieve the same goal: persuade the audience to tour the club

c. A blog post that will appeal to the target audience

d. A Pinterest board that will appeal to the target audience

Write the tweet and the Facebook post. Write a brief description of the blog post and the Pinterest board. As you plan these efforts, remember that interactive posts receive the most attention. Present all four ideas to your manager in a short memo.

3 Evaluate the success of your social media efforts

Refer to Exercises 1 and 2. Imagine that the fitness club has started a blog, Facebook page, Twitter feed, and Pinterest site aimed at attracting more retired members of the community to join the club. Identify at least two strategies to use to evaluate the success of these social media efforts.

SQ2 **What are good practices for composing and publishing social media content?** *(pages 237–245)*

4 Facebook: Post strategically

A popular independent restaurant posted these the three Facebook entries in 4a, 4b, and 4c. Evaluate the strategy of each entry. Identify if the entry is designed to build goodwill, build credibility, entice the audience to come to the restaurant, link to useful information, or achieve some other purpose. If you would recommend any revisions, explain them.

a. A link to an article that says a major magazine named one of the restaurant's dishes the "best vegetarian sandwich in America"

Accompanies Exercise 4a

b. A "shout out" to a new restaurant in the neighborhood

Accompanies Exercise 4b

c. A highlight of a new dish on the menu

Accompanies Exercise 4c

5 Twitter: Be short and focused

Select a local company and imagine that its owner wants your help to begin using Twitter to engage with potential customers. Analyze the company's potential audience, and create a plan for using Twitter persuasively. Then compose five tweets that the company could post during one week. In a one-page message to your instructor, summarize your analysis and explain how your tweets will persuade the audience.

6 Pinterest: Engage with visual content

Find a Pinterest page for a business with which you are familiar. Potential examples include:

- www.pinterest.com/toysRus
- www.pinterest.com/Macys
- www.pinterest.com/Starbucks
- www.pinterest.com/SherwinWilliams

Write a one- to two-paragraph memo analyzing the strategy of that page and address the following content:

a. Who do you believe is the audience for that page? What is the evidence for your answer?

b. Pick two pinboards on the site and calculate how much of the content is original and how much is repinned from other sites.

c. Pick two different pinboards on the site and calculate how many pins focus on the company's products (including creative ideas for using the company's products) and how many focus on related topics that are likely to interest the specific audience.

d. Would you consider the site to be successful? If so, why? If not, why not?

7 Instagram: Build a visual brand

Find a business that has both a Pinterest account and an Instagram account. Examples include ToysRUs, Macy's, Starbucks, Home Depot, and ESPN. Write a one- to two-paragraph memo comparing how the organization uses the two social media channels by answering the following questions:

a. How would you describe the way the organization uses each channel?

b. How many followers does the organization have on each channel?

c. Which channel generates more user-interaction for the organization?

d. Would you consider the Pinterest and Instagram sites to be successful? If so, why? If not, why not?

8 Blog: Offer insights, advice, and information

Experts recommend that businesses gain a social media following by providing information that an audience finds valuable rather than by focusing on the company's products. The content may be insights, advice, information that is difficult to find elsewhere, or answers to frequently asked questions. For the following types of businesses, identify two blog topics that the audience may find valuable:

a. An auto insurance company

b. An ice cream shop

c. A yarn store

d. A photo studio

e. A restaurant

SQ3 **How can businesses use social media to accomplish specific communication goals?** *(pages 246–256)*

9 Use social media to build goodwill

Select a company that you frequently purchase products or services from and that has established a social media presence. Analyze its social media interactions with customers. Provide examples of how it responds to consumer questions and concerns. Explain how the company builds goodwill in its responses or, if it does not, how its communication could be improved to support consumer goodwill. Summarize the information in a one-page memo or email to your instructor. Be prepared to share your summary in class, either in small groups to identify commonalities in your research or in a more formal presentation to your classmates.

10 Use social media to persuade

Review Cialdini's persuasive techniques—consistency, social proof, likability, reciprocity, and scarcity. In small groups, discuss a company that promotes its products or services using these techniques. If possible, find a company that demonstrates *all* five elements in its social media communication. Provide specific examples of each technique. You may be asked to summarize your findings in writing or to present them using screen grabs on presentation slides.

11 Control the spread of bad news through social media

Imagine two small businesses in your community—a bakery and a bank. Assume that these businesses want to plan for negative comments on social media.

a. Who might post negative comments, and what might they comment about?

b. Provide one or two ideas for each business about how they might minimize the chance of negative comments.

Now imagine a company that manufactures a baby seat that the Consumer Product Safety Commission has judged unsafe. The company has voluntarily recalled the seat. Assume this company wants to plan for negative comments on social media.

c. What types of negative postings should the company anticipate? Where would people post these messages?

d. What can the company do to minimize the chance of negative messages?

SQ4 **How can you, as an employee, use social media responsibly?** *(pages 256–257)*

12 Follow guidelines to avoid damage to your and your company's reputations

Do a web search using the search terms *employee fired social media*. Select one example of an employee who was fired for a specific use of social media. Analyze the situation by answering the following questions in the format that your instructor requests:

a. What did the employee do?

b. How did that action damage the employee's or company's reputation?

c. Do you believe the firing was justified?

d. What guidelines from Section SQ4, if any, did the employee violate?

e. If the employee's actions were not covered by any of the guidelines, recommend a new guideline to cover that situation.

Writing Exercises

13 Composing a blog entry

Assume that you are employed part time as an assistant manager for a local sporting goods store (or another type of merchant of your choice). In a conversation with the owner about what you're learning in your college classes, you mention that content marketing can be a useful technique to persuade potential customers. The owner asks you to compose a sample blog entry that could provide useful information about the store's products or services to a target audience. Compose the blog entry and, in a separate paragraph, identify the business and explain how the entry provides useful information and will persuade potential customers.

14 Composing a Facebook entry

Refer to Exercise 13. Compose a Facebook entry that links to the blog entry you wrote for the sporting goods store. In addition to a link to the blog entry, include either a visual element or a question designed to encourage participation, or both.

15 Composing an infographic or video [Related to the Technology feature on page 245]

Imagine that you are writing a blog entry on some aspect of business communication, and you would like to include an infographic or an animated video. Use one of the tools described in the Technology feature or find a different tool on the web and create the infographic or video. If you choose an infographic, be sure to research the data and cite the sources for your information.

Collaboration Exercises

16 Developing a social media strategy [Related to the Collaboration feature on page 253]

Identify a real business in your community and imagine that the owner has asked your team to develop a social media strategy. To develop the strategy, work collaboratively to answer the questions in Figure 7.2, using a social collaboration app such as Slack. Be prepared to present that strategy in class or to write a short strategy memo. Be sure that you can justify all of your answers, either with your knowledge of that company or information you learn from analyzing the social media of similar businesses.

17 Developing a social media schedule [Related to the Collaboration feature on page 253]

Identify a real business in your community, and imagine that the owner asked your team to develop a social media publishing schedule for one week. Follow the model in Figure 7.4. Using a social collaboration app such as Slack, work collaboratively to plan a one-week (seven-day) schedule that includes three tweets a day, two Facebook posts a day, and two blog entries for the week. You may be asked to prepare a short document that presents the schedule and the rationale for the choices you made. Or you may be asked to present your schedule to the class.

Social Media Exercises

18 Avoiding social media controversies

Search the web for *business social media controversy* or *social media crisis*. Select three to five recent examples of news stories or blog posts about social media campaigns that had negative unintended consequences. For each example, write a short evaluation of both the campaign itself (its intended goal, its consequences for the company, and how these consequences could have been avoided) and the source reporting it (its factual accuracy, fairness, significance, and clarity). Sum up what you think these examples demonstrate about the potential pitfalls of social media for businesses.

19 Building a positive online community

Select a company that has established a positive social media community and perhaps uses social media to engage consumers in the decision-making process about products and/or services. Analyze how it engages the audience on different social media platforms. If possible, determine how it uses audience input. For example, does it report survey results or identify consumers' preferences when the company posts its final decisions? Summarize the information in a one-page memo or email to your instructor. Be prepared to share your summary in class, either in small groups to identify commonalities in your research or in a more formal presentation to your classmates.

Speaking Exercises

20 Impromptu presentations

Prepare a two- to three-minute informal presentation for one of the following scenarios.

a. Identify a business that you follow on Facebook or Instagram. Explain why you follow that business and how that business's posts persuade, entertain, or inform you.

b. If you want to lodge a complaint with a business, would you prefer to communicate that complaint by email, Facebook post, or tweet? Explain why.

c. Many companies have both websites and Facebook pages. Select a company that interests you. Explain what you would be looking for on that company's website versus what you would be looking for on its Facebook page.

d. As a consumer, would you choose to subscribe to any company's Twitter feed? If so, what company and why? If not, why not?

21 Executive briefing

Prepare formal presentations for one of the following scenarios:

a. You are the assistant sales director for a company that is a market leader in the hand sanitizer industry. You have a new product—the SaniPlus—that you plan to target to existing business customers through unsolicited sales messages. The product is a portable, touch-free dispenser of hand sanitizer. The dispenser stands on the floor, can be positioned in strategic locations, and can be moved to other locations. The director of sales asks you to identify ways that the company can persuasively communicate to its social media audience about the new product. Use Fogg's Behavior Model to determine how you will motivate interest, provide a trigger, and ensure the audience is easily able to purchase the product. Discuss your ideas in small groups. Then prepare a five-minute executive briefing to present your plan to the director of sales.

b. The owner of local handmade jewelry shop would like your advice. She plans to launch either a Pinterest site or an Instagram site but can't decide between the two. Research the key differences between these two social media platforms and, in a five-minute presentation, compare the advantages of Pinterest versus the advantages of Instagram for the shop. End the briefing with a recommendation.

c. The management of your company, a funeral home, has issued a ban on social media. You think that their fear of bad publicity is exaggerated and that your company is missing an opportunity by not connecting with potential customers on Facebook and Twitter. You are invited to present your views to the board. To prepare, research the Facebook pages and Twitter streams from other funeral services to identify potential benefits you can present.

d. The new public relations director for your company, a manufacturer of industrial coffee grinders and other food processing equipment, wants to make the company appear more modern and attractive by launching a campaign on Twitter and Instagram. You think the campaign badly misunderstands your company's mission, focus, and customers: your company's clients are other large companies, most of which do not review vendors' social media sites. Present your reasons why the campaign should be cancelled. To prepare, research business-to-business (B2B) social media to identify the types of companies that use social media most successfully.

Grammar Exercises

22 Common sentence errors: Subject–verb agreement (see Appendix C: Grammar, Punctuation, Mechanics, and Conventions—Section 1.3.3)

Type the following paragraph and edit it, correcting the 10 errors in subject–verb agreement. Underline all your corrections.

When making a business call, being put on hold for countless minutes fray even patient people's nerves. Having to wait, as well as not knowing for how long, are upsetting. Each of us have our own way of coping with this irritant. *The Sounds of Silence* apply not only to the Simon and Garfunkel song but also to endless minutes on hold. Three minutes feel like forever to the person waiting. If you must put someone on hold, there is several things you should do. First, ask, "May I put you on hold?" and then give the caller an estimate of the probable waiting time. The person on the other end might be one of those callers who really need to know how long the wait might be. The unknown number of minutes are what drive people crazy. Data collected by Hold On America, Inc., shows that callers become frustrated after 20 seconds. After 90 seconds, 50 percent of callers hangs up.

23 Common sentence errors: Pronoun–antecedent agreement (see Appendix C: Grammar, Punctuation, Mechanics, and Conventions—Section 1.3.4)

Type the following paragraph and edit it, correcting the 10 errors in pronoun–antecedent agreement. Underline all your corrections.

Everybody has preferences about their communication tools. A person may prefer email rather than telephone, so they might respond to a voice mail message by sending an email instead of returning the call. If you ask either of my managers, Jenny or Kurt, they will tell you that I would rather email them. Business professionals will often choose the one with which he or she is most at ease. Considering its total number of calls versus emails per month, the sales team obviously would rather talk than write. Each of these communication media has their advantages and disadvantages. Text messages and email may be best because it will be delivered whether the recipient is there or not. On the other hand, someone who leaves a voice mail message probably assumes you will call them back, not send a text. Otherwise, they would have texted you instead of calling.

MyLab Business Communication

Go to **www.pearson.com/mylab/business-communication** for Auto-graded writing questions as well as the following Assisted-graded writing questions:

1. Experts recommend making a blog the central element of a business's social media strategy. In other words, tweets and Facebook posts should link to a blog. Explain the benefits of this approach.

2. Identify two types of businesses that might benefit from a Pinterest site and two types of businesses that are not well suited for Pinterest.

References

1. The new conversation: Taking social media from talk to action. (2010). *A Harvard Business Review Analytic Services Report*, p. 12. Retrieved from http://www.sas.com/resources/whitepaper/wp_23348.pdf

2. eBiz. (2017, January). Top 15 most popular social networking sites. Retrieved from http://www.ebizmba.com/articles/social-networking-websites

3. Handley, A. (2014). *Everybody writes: Your go-to guide to creating ridiculously good content.* Hoboken, NJ: John Wiley & Sons.

4. Kabani, S. (2012, August 2). 5 ways to measure your success in social media. Retrieved from https://www.bizjournals.com/bizjournals/blog/socialmadness/2012/07/5-ways-to-measure-your-success-in.html

5. The new conversation: Taking social media from talk to action. (2010). *A Harvard Business Review Analytic Services Report*, p. 16. Retrieved from http://www.sas.com/resources/whitepaper/wp_23348.pdf

6. Agius, A. (2016, November 8). 10 metrics to track for social media success. Retrieved from http://www.socialmediaexaminer.com/10-metrics-to-track-for-social-media-success/

7. OECD. (2014). Measuring the digital economy: A new perspective. Retrieved from http://dx.doi.org/10.1787/9789264221796-en

8. Europa.eu. (2011, May 11). Digital agenda: More than half EU Internet surfers use foreign language when online. Retrieved from http://europa.eu/rapid/press-release_IP-11-556_en.htm

9. Kang, K., & Sohaib, O. (2016). Individualists vs. collectivists in B2C e-business purchase intention. *Journal of Internet and e-Business Studies.* Retrieved from http://ibimapublishing.com/articles/JIEBS/2016/948644/948644-1.pdf

10. Isherwood, D., Coetzee, M., & Eloff, J. H. P. (2012). Towards trust and reputation for e-commerce in collectivist rural Africa. In N. L. Clarke & S. M. Furnell (Eds.), *Proceedings of the Sixth International Symposium on Human Aspects of Information Security & Assurance* (pp. 198-118). Plymouth, U.K.: Plymouth University.

11. Lamb, B. (2016). 5 key features of Chinese social media. Retrieved from http://www.jeffbullas.com/5-key-features-chinese-social-media/

12. Chiu, C., Ip, C., & Silverman, A. (2012, April). Understanding social media in China. *McKinsey Quarterly.* Retrieved from http://www.mckinsey.com/insights/marketing_sales/understanding_social_media_in_china

13. Facebook. (2016, October 4). Gains in translation: What your language choices say to U.S. Hispanics. Retrieved from https://www.facebook.com/iq/articles/gains-in-translation-what-your-language-choices-say-to-us-hispanics

14. King, D. L. (2015). Managing your library's social media channels. *Library Technology Reports, 53*(1). Retrieved from http://dx.doi.org/10.5860/ltr.51n1

15. ModCloth. (2017). ModCloth blog. Retrieved from https://blog.modcloth.com

16. Whole Foods Market. (2017). Whole story: The official Whole Foods Market blog. Retrieved from http://www.wholefoods-market.com/blog/whole-story

17. McDonald, J. (2017). Social media marketing workbook 2017: Social media for business. San Jose, CA: JM Internet Group and Excerpt Communications, Inc.

18. Vahl, A. (2015, April 20). 11 ways to boost Facebook engagement for small businesses. *Social Media Examiner*. Retrieved from http://www.socialmediaexaminer.com/boost-facebook-engagement-for-small-businesses/

19. Pestov, I. (2017, February 6). 34 stats to help you plan your social media strategy on Facebook, Twitter, Instagram & more. Retrieved from https://blog.hubspot.com/marketing/plan-social-media-strategy-stats

20. Walters, K. (2016, September 12). The Facebook algorithm: What you need to know to boost organic reach. Retrieved from https://blog.hootsuite.com/facebook-algorithm/

21. Patel, N. (2016, September 12). How frequently you should post on social media according to the pros. Retrieved from https://www.forbes.com/sites/neilpatel/2016/09/12/how-frequently-you-should-post-on-social-media-according-to-the-pros

22. Kolowich, L. (2015, April 20). How often should you post on Facebook? [New benchmark data]. Retrieved from https://blog.hubspot.com/marketing/facebook-post-frequency-benchmarks

23. Fontein, D. (2016, November 21). The best time to post on Facebook, Twitter, and Instagram. Retrieved from https://blog.hootsuite.com/best-time-to-post-on-facebook-twitter-instagram/

24. Kolowich, L. (2016, January 6). The best times to post on Facebook, Twitter, LinkedIn & other social media sites [infographic]. Retrieved from https://blog.hubspot.com/marketing/best-times-post-pin-tweet-social-media-infographic

25. Benna, S. (2015, July 29). The best times to post on Facebook, Instagram, and Twitter. Retrieved from http://www.businessinsider.com/best-times-to-post-on-facebook-instagram-twitter-2015-7

26. Bennett, S. (2015, January 6). What are the best times to post on #Facebook, #Twitter and #Instagram? Retrieved from http://www.adweek.com/digital/best-time-to-post-social-media/

27. Gessler, K. (2016, October 13). Stop mindlessly following character count recommendations on Facebook posts. Retrieved from https://medium.com/@kurtgessler/stop-mindlessly-following-character-count-recommendations-on-facebook-posts-e01103b4d349

28. Pinantoan, A. (2015, May 20). How to massively boost your blog traffic with these 5 awesome image stats. Retrieved from http://buzzsumo.com/blog/how-to-massively-boost-your-blog-traffic-with-these-5-awesome-image-stats/

29. Concoran, L. (2016, May). Links aren't getting as much engagement as they used to on Facebook. Retrieved from https://www.newswhip.com/2016/05/facebook-engagement-restructure/

30. Hainla, L. (2017, July 31). 8 powerful reasons you need to use video marketing. Retrieved from https://www.dreamgrow.com/8-reasons-why-your-business-should-use-video-marketing/

31. What video ad length is best on Facebook? (2016, September 6). Retrieved from https://www.emarketer.com/Article/What-Video-Ad-Length-Best-on-Facebook/1014438

32. Dringoli, L. (2016, June 16). How to boost Facebook engagement using video subtitles. Retrieved from http://mediacause.org/create-add-facebook-video-subtitles/

33. Facebook. (2017). 8 advertising best practices for local businesses. Retrieved from https://www.facebook.com/business/a/ads-best-practice

34. Brennan, J. (2015, March 19). How to reward your fans with Facebook offers. Retrieved from http://www.socialmediaexaminer.com/reward-your-fans-with-facebook-offers/

35. Cooper, B. (2013, July 23). 7 powerful Facebook statistics you should know for a more engaging Facebook page. Retrieved from https://www.fastcompany.com/3022301/7-powerful-facebook-statistics-you-should-know-about

36. Biswas, P. (2015, April 8). Five creative ways to engage with your Facebook fans and start conversations. *Social Media with Priyanka*. Retrieved from https://socialmediawithpb.com/5-creative-ways-to-engage-with-your-facebook-fans-and-start-conversations/

37. Zantal-Wiener, A. (2017, September 10). 14 essential tips for an engaging Facebook business page. Retrieved from https://blog.hubspot.com/marketing/how-to-create-facebook-business-page-ht

38. Facebook. (2017). Create and boost Facebook posts. Retrieved from https://www.facebook.com/business/learn/facebook-page-create-posts

39. Smith, D. (2011, November 11). Facebook vs. Twitter: How to write effective posts. Retrieved from http://www.ibtimes.com/facebook-vs-twitter-how-write-effective-posts-368764

40. Dugan, L. (2011, November 28). 3 tips for writing a killer Twitter bio to get targeted followers. Retrieved from http://www.adweek.com/digital/3-tips-for-writing-a-killer-twitter-bio-to-get-targeted-followers/

41. BostonHarborCruises. (2017). Retrieved from https://twitter.com/cruiseBHC

42. Adaptly. (2017). Retrieved from https://twitter.com/adaptly

43. Twitter. (2017) FAQs about following. Retrieved from https://support.twitter.com/articles/14019#

44. Petersel, B., & Schindler, E. (2012). *The complete idiot's guide to Twitter marketing*. New York, NY: Alpha Books.

45. Quinn, S. (2015, August 12). 8 easy ways to build more Twitter followers. Retrieved from http://www.socialmediatoday.com/social-networks/wyzowl/2015-08-11/8-easy-ways-build-more-twitter-followers

46. Heath, A. (2016, September 19). Twitter just changed how tweets work. Retrieved from http://www.businessinsider.com/twitter-140-character-limit-no-longer-includes-media-replies-2016-9

47. Handley, A., & Chapman, C. C. (2012). *Content rules*. Hoboken, NJ: John Wiley & Sons.

48. Fitton, L. (2015, April 15). How to retweet the right way (with a comment) on Twitter. Retrieved from https://blog.hubspot.com/blog/tabid/6307/bid/27675/How-to-Retweet-the-Right-Way-in-4-Easy-Steps.aspx

49. Twitter. (2017). Posting links in a Tweet. Retrieved from https://support.twitter.com/articles/78124#

50. Handley, A., & Chapman, C. C. (2012). *Content rules*. Hoboken, NJ: John Wiley & Sons.

51. Petersel, B., & Schindler, E. (2012). *The complete idiot's guide to Twitter marketing*. New York, NY: Alpha Books.

52. LePage, E. (2014, August 27). The do's and don'ts of how to use hashtags. Retrieved from https://blog.hootsuite.com/how-to-use-hashtags/

53. O'Leary, S., Sheehan, K., & Lentz, S. (2011). *Small business smarts: Building buzz with social media*. Santa Barbara, CA: Praeger.

54. Li, Y. (2012, March 26). Pinterest basics for bloggers. Retrieved from http://www.problogger.net/archives/2012/03/26/pinterest-basics-for-bloggers/

55. Walter, E. (2014, April 21). 6 ways to use Pinterest to promote your brand. Retrieved from http://www.socialmediaexaminer.com/how-to-promote-with-pinterest/

56. West Elm. (2017). West Elm. Retrieved from http://pinterest.com/westelm/

57. Ray, M. (2012, May 14). 6 tips for using Pinterest for business. Retrieved from http://www.socialmediaexaminer.com/using-pinterest-for-business/

58. Schiff, J. L. (2012, March 21). 14 tips for how to use Pinterest for business. Retrieved from http://www.cio .com/article/702539/14_Tips_for_How_to_Use_Pinterest_ for_Business.html

59. Chobani. (2017). Fit with it. Retrieved from http://pinterest .com/chobani/fit-with-it/

60. Rosales, L. (2012, February 22). Pinterest imposes character limits on captions. Retrieved from https://theamericangenius .com/social-media/pinterest-imposes-character-limits-on-captions/

61. Chobani. (2017). Fit with it. Retrieved from https://www .pinterest.com/chobani/fit-with-it/

62. Andrews, A. L. (2017, January 20). 35+ Pinterest tips from basics to beyond. Retrieved from https://amylynnandrews .com/pinterest-tips/

63. Jeske, S. (2016, April 26). How to get more repins on Pinterest. Retrieved from https://viralwoot.com/blog/get-repins-pinterest/

64. Duncan, M. (2012, August 7). 5 ways to build a Pinterest following with Facebook. Retrieved from http://www.socialmediaexaminer.com/build-a-pinterest-followingwith-facebook/

65. Ray, M. (2012, May 14). 6 tips for using Pinterest for business. Retrieved from http://www.socialmediaexaminer.com/using-pinterest-for-business/

66. Sharma, P. (2012, August 20). 9 businesses using Pinterest contests to drive traffic and exposure. Retrieved from http:// www.socialmediaexaminer.com/pinterest-contest/

67. Duncan, M. (2012, August 7). 5 ways to build a Pinterest following with Facebook. Retrieved from http://www.socialmediaexaminer.com/build-a-pinterest-followingwith-facebook/

68. Duncan, M. (2012, August 7). 5 ways to build a Pinterest following with Facebook. Retrieved from http://www.socialmediaexaminer.com/build-a-pinterest-followingwith-facebook/

69. LePage, E. (2015, June 17). How to use Instagram for business: A beginner's guide. Retrieved from https://www.linkedin.com/ pulse/how-use-instagram-business-beginners-guide-joseph-duda/

70. Hootsuite. (2015, May 27). 9 slides from the 2015 Meeker Report social media marketers need to see. Retrieved from https://blog.hootsuite.com/9-slides-from-the-2015-meeker-report-social-media-marketers-need-to-see/

71. Smith, K. (2016, May 6). 37 Instagram statistics for 2016. Retrieved from https://www.brandwatch.com/blog/37-instagram-stats-2016/

72. Messieh, N. (2015, December 10). How Instagram filters work, and can you tell the difference? Retrieved from http://www. makeuseof.com/tag/instagram-filters-work-can-tell-difference/

73. LePage, E. (2015, June 17). How to use Instagram for business: A beginner's guide. Retrieved from https://www.linkedin.com/ pulse/how-use-instagram-business-beginners-guide-joseph-duda/

74. Lella, A. (2014, April 7). Users engage with major social networks predominantly via mobile. Retrieved from http:// www.comscore.com/Insights/Data-Mine/Users-Engage-with-Major-Social-Networks-Predominantly-via-Mobile?cs_edg-escape_cc=US

75. Aynsley, M. (2016, September 19). How to write great Instagram captions that drive engagement. Retrieved from https:// rainmakermediany.com/write-great-instagram-captions-drive-engagement-2/.

76. Walters, K. (2016, January 21). The power of nostalgia: How to use #TBT for marketing. Retrieved from https://blog .hootsuite.com/how-to-use-tbt-for-marketing/

77. REI STAFF. (2017, January 13). A tribute to the REI 1440 Project. Retrieved from http://blog.rei.com/news/rei-1440-project/

78. REI STAFF. (n.d.). The 1440 Project reaches the quarter-million milestone on Instagram. Retrieved from http://blog.rei.com/ camp/the-1440-project-reaches-the-quarter-million-milestone-on-instagram/

79. Heilpern, W. (2016, January 17). Meet the 26-year-old entrepreneurs using Instagram to build an art empire from scratch. *Business Insider.* Retrieved from http://www.businessinsider .com/instagram-gallery-unit-london-1-2015/

80. Byron, E. (2017, February 20). Knead slime? These business girls can fix you up. *The Wall Street Journal.* Retrieved from https://www.wsj.com/articles/knead-slime-these-business-girls-can-fix-you-up-1487611563

81. Handley, A., & Chapman, C. C. (2012). *Content rules.* Hoboken, NJ: John Wiley & Sons.

82. Patel, N. (2014, June 18). Should you write controversial blog posts? A data driven answer. Retrieved from https://www .quicksprout.com/2014/06/18/should-you-write-controversial-blog-posts-a-data-driven-answer/

83. Wainwright, C. (2016, February 23). How to write catchy headlines and blog titles your readers can't resist. Retrieved from https://www.hubspot.com/how-to-write-catchy-headlines-and-blog-titles-your-readers-cant-resist

84. Blalock, M. (2014, August 28). 7 subtle fashion mistakes you're making every day. Retrieved from http://www.whowhatwear .com/fashion-mistakes

85. Altman, I. (2012, June 25). The one thing you need to succeed [Blog post]. Retrieved from http://www.bizjournals.com/ washington/blog/2012/06/the-one-thing-you-need-to-succeed .html

86. Krasny, J. (2012, July 24). 23 secrets to booking cheap flights [Blog post]. Retrieved from http://www.businessinsider .com/23-secrets-to-booking-cheap-flights-2012-7?op=1

87. Fontein, D. (2016, November 8). Pinterest for business: The definitive marketing guide. Retrieved from https://blog .hootsuite.com/how-to-use-pinterest-for-business/

88. Henry, J. (2016, August 23). 10 killer tips: How to format a perfect blog post. Retrieved from http://writtent.com/blog/ format-perfect-blog-post-10-tips/

89. Duistermaat, H. (2016, February 2). How to write conversationally: 7 tips to engage and delight your audience. Retrieved from http://www.copyblogger.com/how-to-write-conversationally/

90. Dowdle, E. (2016, December 2). 8 things every blogger should do right now to increase their email subscribers. Retrieved from http://optinmonster.com/8-things-every-blogger-should-do-right-now-to-increase-their-email-subscribers/

91. Boswell, W. (2017, March 1). RSS 101 for beginners. Retrieved from https://www.lifewire.com/rss-101-3482781

92. Kolowich, L. (2015, April 9). How often should companies blog? [New benchmark data]. Retrieved from https://blog .hubspot.com/marketing/blogging-frequency-benchmarks

93. Hyatt, M. (2011, January 31). Anatomy of an effective blog post. Retrieved from https://michaelhyatt.com/anatomy-of-an-effective-blog-post.html

94. See, for example, Hyatt, M. (2014, June 3). Why people who sleep longer achieve more. Retrieved from http://michaelhyatt .com/sleep-longer-to-achieve-more.html

95. Blogelina. (2015). Top 7 blog post templates that work! Retrieved from https://blogelina.com/the-top-7-blog-post-templates-that-work/

96. Bonini, J. (2012, March 14). How to write a blog post in five easy steps. Retrieved from http://www.impactbnd.com/ write-blog-post-easy-steps/

97. Morgan, J. (2010, November 3). What is social CRM? Retrieved from http://www.socialmediaexaminer.com/what-is-social-crm/

98. Anthony, C. (2017, Feb. 22.) On the horizon: The social CRM market is expanding—Are you on board? Retrieved from https://www.business.com/articles/on-the-horizon-the-social-crm-market-is-expanding-are-you-onboard/

99. Kaneshige, T. (2015, January 27). Why social listening platforms are failing. Retrieved from http://www.cio.com/article/2876295/social-media/why-social-listening-platforms-are-failing.html

100. Lacy, K. (2012, February 17). 5 problems generated by customer's social media complaints and the solutions. *Business 2 Community*. Retrieved from http://www.business2community.com/social-media/5-problems-generated-by-customers-social-media-complaints-and-the-solutions-0134876

101. Mills, S. (2014, May 28). 6 tools for gathering insight from digital customer interactions. Retrieved from http://streetfightmag.com/2014/05/28/6-tools-for-gathering-insight-from-digital-customer-interactions/

102. Baer, J. (2011, October 12). 70% of companies ignore customer complaints on Twitter. Convince & Convert. Retrieved from http://www.convinceandconvert.com/social-media-strategy/70-of-companies-ignore-customer-complaints-on-twitter/

103. evolve24. (2011, September). Maritz Research and evolve24—Twitter study. Retrieved from http://www.maritzresearch.com/~/media/Files/MaritzResearch/e24/ExecutiveSummaryTwitterPoll.ashx

104. Belosic, J. (2012, May 9). Providing exceptional customer service through social media. Retrieved from http://www.cmswire.com/cms/customer-experience/providing-exceptional-customer-service-through-social-media-015425.php

105. Shukle, R. (2015, December 29). How to handle customer complaints via social media. Retrieved from http://www.socialmediaexaminer.com/how-to-handle-customer-complaints-via-social-media/

106. Sernovitz, A. (2012, February 22). 10 ways to deal with upset customers using social media. Retrieved from http://www.socialmediaexaminer.com/10-ways-to-deal-with-upset-customers-using-social-media/

107. Naaman, M., Boase, J., & Lai, C-H. (2010). Is it really about me? Message content in social awareness streams. CSCW 2010, February 6–10, 2010, Savannah, GA. Retrieved from http://infolab.stanford.edu/~mor/research/naamanCSCW10.pdf

108. Doughnut Vault. (2017). Retrieved from https://twitter.com/@doughnutvault

109. JetBlue Airways. (2017). Retrieved from https://twitter.com/JetBlue

110. Rubbermaid. (2017). Retrieved from https://twitter.com/rubbermaid

111. Barone, L. (2012, June 13). 7 ways to make your small business stand out online. Retrieved from http://smallbiztrends.com/2012/06/7-ways-make-your-small-business-stand-out-online.html

112. Collier, A. (2016, August 2). 10 ways social media marketing can help grow your business. Retrieved from https://blogs.constantcontact.com/why-social-media-marketing/

113. Business strategy for social media and customer relationship management: Q&A with Brent Leary from CRM Essentials (2012, February 2). Retrieved from http://bizblog.blackberry.com/2012/02/business-strategy-for-social-media-and-customer-relationship-management-qa-with-brent-leary-from-crm-essentials/

114. Roesler, P. (2015, May 29). How social media influences consumer buying decisions. Retrieved from http://www.bizjournals.com/bizjournals/how-to/marketing/2015/05/how-social-media-influences-consumer-buying.html

115. Best Buy Support. (2017). Retrieved from https://twitter.com/BestBuySupport

116. The Container Store. (2012). Retrieved from http://www.facebook.com/containerstore

117. Dell Computer. (2017). Retrieved from http://www.ideastorm.com

118. Kelly, N. (2012, May 10). 5 ways social media can increase your revenue from existing customers. Retrieved from http://www.socialmediaexaminer.com/turn-customers-into-increased-revenue/

119. Black, T. (2016, October 19). What you need to know about Facebook offers. Retrieved from https://www.lifewire.com/facebook-offers-information-1240619

120. McPhillips, C. (2016, January 13). What is content marketing? Retrieved from http://www.contentmarketingworld.com/what-is-content-marketing/

121. Lukovitz, K. (2013, October 10). General Mills launches national cereal lovers week. Retrieved from http://www.mediapost.com/publications/article/211055/general-mills-launches-national-cereal-lovers-week.html

122. Gioglio, J. (2013, August 8). General Mills embraces collaborative storytelling with "Hello, Cereal Lovers" social media community. Retrieved from http://www.convinceandconvert.com/social-media-case-studies/general-mills-embraces-collaborative-storytelling-with-hello-cereal-lovers-social-media-community/

123. Social Bakers. (2017). Hello, Cereal Lovers. Facebook page statistics. Retrieved from http://www.socialbakers.com/facebook-pages/364278496996893-hello-cereal-lovers

124. Fogg, B. J. (2016). BJ Fogg's Behavior Model. Retrieved from http://behaviormodel.org/index.html

125. Laporte, N. (2016, January 11). How Ipsy founder Michelle Phan is using influencers to reinvent the cosmetics industry. Retrieved from https://www.fastcompany.com/3054926/behind-the-brand/how-Ipsy-founder-michelle-phan-is-using-influencers-to-reinvent-the-cosmeti

126. Baer, J. (2017). Friend or faux – Six ways to activate customers. Retrieved from http://www.convinceandconvert.com/social-media-strategy/friend-or-faux/

127. Smith, C. (2015, March 4). Shopping cart abandonment: Online retailers' biggest headache is actually a huge opportunity. *Business Insider*. Retrieved from http://www.businessinsider.com/heres-how-retailers-can-reduce-shopping-cart-abandonment-and-recoup-billions-of-dollars-in-lost-sales-2014-4

128. Cooke, G. (2012, May 23). Why your online checkout system hurts your sales. Retrieved from http://mashable.com/2012/05/23/online-checkout-problems/

129. Patel, N. (2011, November 16). 6 ways to be more persuasive with social media. Retrieved from http://mashable.com/2011/11/16/social-media-persuasive/

130. Vaughan, P. (2012, April 17). 10 ways to instantly amplify the social proof of your marketing. [Blog post] Retrieved from http://blog.hubspot.com/blog/tabid/6307/bid/32418/10-Ways-to-Instantly-Amplify-the-Social-Proof-of-Your-Marketing.aspx

131. Levin, L. (2012, April 10). 6 tips for becoming more persuasive on social media. Retrieved from http://www.business2community.com/social-media/6-tips-for-becoming-more-persuasive-on-social-media-0160951

132. Carr, D. F. (2015, April 27). How social should social collaboration be? Retrieved from https://www.forbes.com/sites/davidcarr/2015/04/27/how-social-should-social-collaboration-be/

133. Zax, D. (2014, August 13). Slack wins over another doubter, scoring a sandwich video in the deal. Retrieved from https://www.fastcompany.com/3034277/most-creative-people/slack-wins-over-another-doubter-scoring-a-sandwich-video-in-the-deal

134. Hess, A. (2015, April 19). Slack off: How workplace chat is changing office culture. Retrieved from http://www

.slate.com/articles/technology/users/2015/04/slack_and_the_office_chat_several_people_are_typing_who_s_working.html

135. Hess, A. (2015, April 19). Slack off: How workplace chat is changing office culture. Retrieved from http://www.slate.com/articles/technology/users/2015/04/slack_and_the_office_chat_several_people_are_typing_who_s_working.html

136. Burlingham, B. (2017, May 9). Forbes small giants 2017: America's best small companies. *Forbes*. Retrieved from https://www.forbes.com/sites/boburlingham/2017/05/09/forbes-small-giants-2017-americas-best-small-companies

137. Hulick, S. (2016, February 29). Slack, I'm breaking up with you. Retrieved from https://ux.useronboard.com/slack-i-m-breaking-up-with-you-54600ace03ea

138. Wolf, D. (2015, July 26). 5 benefits of social media for teamwork. Retrieved from https://www.govloop.com/community/blog/5-benefits-social-media-teamwork/

139. Manyika, J., Chui, M., & Sarrazin, H. (2012, August 21). Social media's productivity payoff. Retrieved from https://hbr.org/2012/08/social-medias-productivity-pay

140. Nielsen. (2012, April 10). Global consumers' trust in "earned" advertising grows in importance. Retrieved from http://www.nielsen.com/us/en/press-room/2012/nielsen-global-consumers-trust-in-earned-advertising-grows.html

141. BrightLocal. (2016). Local consumer review survey. Retrieved from https://www.brightlocal.com/learn/local-consumer-review-survey/

142. Owyang, J. (2011). Social Readiness: How advanced companies prepare internally. Retrieved from https://www.slideshare.net/jeremiah_owyang/social-readiness-how-advanced-companies-prepare

143. Agnes, M. (2012, May 10). 4 steps to preventing a social media crisis. Social Media Crisis Management. Retrieved from http://www.melissaagnes.com/4-steps-to-preventing-a-social-media-crisis/

144. Kerkhof, P. (2012, June 2). Talking to customers: Characteristics of effective social media conversations. Conference presentation at the 11th European Conference of the Association for Business Communication, Nijmegen, Netherlands.

145. Barrie, L. (2011, August 10). ITALY: Dolce & Gabbana deletes Facebook protests. Retrieved from https://www.just-style.com/news/dolce-gabbana-deletes-facebook-protests_id111852.aspx

146. Collier, M. (2011). Social media crisis management: A no nonsense guide. MackCollior.com. Retrieved from http://www.mackcollier.com/social-media-crisis-management/

147. Kerpen, D. (2011). *Likeable social media*. New York: McGraw-Hill, pp. 75–84.

148. Dietrich, G. (2012, January 13). FedEx customer video turned good PR. Social Media Today. Retrieved from http://www.socialmediatoday.com/content/fedex-customer-video-turned-good-pr

149. Duke, A. (2012, January 8). Papa John's apologizes for receipt's racial slur. Retrieved from http://www.cnn.com/2012/01/08/us/new-york-papa-johns-receipt/

150. Papa John's Pizza. (2012, January 7). Twitter/PapaJohns. Retrieved from https://twitter.com/PapaJohns/status/155823644143124480

151. Duke, A. (2012, January 8). Papa John's apologizes for receipt's racial slur. Retrieved from http://www.cnn.com/2012/01/08/us/new-york-papa-johns-receipt/

152. Kerkhof, P., Schultz, F., & Utz, S. (2011, May). How to choose the right weapon. Social media represent both a catalyst for and weapon against brand crises. *Communication Director*, 76–79.

153. Agnes, M. (2012). Lessons shared from a real live social media crisis. Retrieved from http://www.MelissaAgnes.com

154. TripAdvisor. (2012). Seasons restaurant. Retrieved from https://www.tripadvisor.co.uk/Restaurant_Review-g188590d697013-Reviews-Seasons_Restaurant-Amsterdam_Noord_Holland.html

155. Bazaarvoice. (2013, July). Social trends report 2013. Retrieved from http://resources.bazaarvoice.com/rs/bazaarvoice/images/Bazaarvoice_Social-Trends-Report-2013.pdf

156. Lappas, T., Sabnis, G., & Valkanas, G. (2016). The impact of fake reviews on online visibility: A vulnerability assessment of the hotel industry. *Information Systems Research, 27*(4), 940–961. http://dx.doi.org/10.1287/isre.2016.0674

157. Luca, M., & Zervios, G. (2013). Fake it till you make it: Reputation, competition, and Yelp review fraud (Harvard Business School NOM Unit Working Paper No. 14-000). Retrieved from SSRN: http://ssrn.com/abstract=2293164

158. Luca, M. (2011). Reviews, reputation, and revenue: The case of Yelp.com (Harvard Business School Working Paper 12-016). Retrieved from http://www.hbs.edu/faculty/Pages/item.aspx?num=41233

159. Lawrence, D. (2009) Social media and the FTC: What businesses need to know. Retrieved from http://mashable.com/2009/12/16/ftc-social-media/

160. TripAdvisor for Business. (2013, July 29). Reporting potential blackmail to TripAdvisor: Report threats immediately. Retrieved from https://www.tripadvisor.com/TripAdvisorInsights/n694/reporting-potential-blackmail-tripadvisor-report-threats-immediately

161. The Coca-Cola Company. (2013, August). Social media principles. Retrieved from http://assets.coca-colacompany.com/3f/33/9099818649d09dd1c638643c394b/social-media-principles-english.pdf

162. International Olympic Committee. (2011, August). IOC social media, blogging and Internet guidelines for participants and other accredited persons at the London 2012 Olympic Games. Retrieved from https://stillmed.olympic.org/Documents/Games_London_2012/IOC_Social_Media_Blogging_and_Internet_Guidelines-London.pdf

163. Barnes, N., & Lescault, A. (2013). LinkedIn rules but sales potential may lie with Twitter: The 2013 Inc. 500 and social media. *UMass Dartmouth Center for Marketing Research.* Retrieved from http://www.umassd.edu/cmr/socialmediaresearch/2013inc500/. See also Dougherty, J. (2013). Study: 73% of companies don't tell employees how to use social media. *Leaders West Digital Marketing Journal.* Retrieved from http://leaderswest.com/2013/04/09/study-68-of-companies-dont-share-the-purpose-of-social-media-with-employees/

164. Monster. (n.d.). Monster social media: Employee social media guidelines. Retrieved from https://www.about-monster.com/sites/default/files/Monster_Social_Media_Guidelines.pdf

165. Elliott, M. (2016, December 3). 7 social media mistakes that can get you fired from your job. *Money and Career Cheatsheet.* Retrieved from https://www.cheatsheet.com/money-career/7-social-media-mistakes-that-can-get-you-fired-from-your-job.html/?a=viewall

166. American Psychological Association. (2009, June 30). APA Style experts. Retrieved from http://blog.apastyle.org/apastyle/apa-style-experts.html

167. McAdoo, T. (2017, March 1). DOI display guidelines update (March 2017) [Blog post]. Retrieved from http://blog.apastyle.org/apastyle/2017/03/doi-display-guidelines-update-march-2017.html

168. Bazaarvoice. (2014). Social commerce statistics. Retrieved from https://www.bazaarvoice.com/research-and-insight/social-commerce-statistics/

169. La Brochette. (2014). Retrieved from https://www.tripadvisor.com/Restaurant_Review-g644388-d6029255-Reviews-La_Brochette-Humacao_Puerto_Rico.html

8

Finding and Evaluating Business Information

Duncanandison/Fotolia

STUDY QUESTIONS

MyLab Business Communication

⭐**Improve Your Grade!**

If your instructor is using MyLab Business Communication, visit **www.pearson.com/mylab/business-communication** for videos, simulations, and writing exercises.

New Hires @ Work

Rashida Gatewood
North Carolina A&T State University

IT Engineer @ Cisco Systems, Inc.

Part of my job requires me to search the company's knowledge base to find technical solutions for the case projects I manage. Our company maintains internal blogs, project posts, and news archives on all the tools we support. However, in some cases, the information I find is out of date. When I need help, I try to find the person who submitted the last post to the knowledge base to get more details and updated information.

Photo courtesy of Rashida Gatewood

Chapter 8 | Introduction

If you are like most other students, you frequently use the web to find information. But, as the novelist Dan Brown reminds us, "Google is not a synonym for research."[1] The information you need is not always on the web. For example, you may have to:

- Investigate why product sales declined
- Determine which product features are most important to your customers
- Compare benefits packages offered by your company and its competitors
- Analyze how new state tax laws will affect your company
- Decide where to open a new store

You cannot find this information with a simple Google search. Some of these tasks require interviewing experts or surveying customers. Others require synthesizing information from multiple sources. Still others require figuring out what specific information you need before you can begin to search for it. When you are given a complex research assignment, employers will not expect you to have the information in your head, but they *will* expect you to have the skills to find the information you need to complete the task.

This chapter provides a process for finding and evaluating the business information necessary to prepare well-researched and well-documented business proposals, reports, and presentations. Throughout this process, you will use elements of ACE. You will learn how to analyze your research needs and develop a research plan, search print and online sources, conduct your own original research, and organize and evaluate the results. Chapters 9, 10, and 11 build on this chapter and help you incorporate research into proposals, reports, and presentations.

SQ1 How do you determine what information you need?

Workplace research typically starts with a specific question or problem. The goal of the research is to find, organize, and analyze information that will help you answer the question or solve the problem. The best way to achieve that goal is to follow a structured process that helps you identify exactly what you are looking for and where to look for it.

As you read this chapter, keep the following research scenario in mind: Assume that you are Alan Cotton, learning and development manager for Ipswich Brands, a large consumer product company with offices around the globe. You report to Mitchell Harris, chief learning officer. Your department is responsible for orienting new employees and providing training and professional development opportunities for employees in all of the company's offices. Specific tasks include designing instructional materials, organizing training sessions, training new trainers, maintaining employee training records, and providing data for supervisors to use during performance reviews.

Currently, the company's system for managing these tasks is expensive and inefficient. All training is conducted face to face, with trainers traveling to specific offices or employees traveling to a central location. In addition, all training schedules and records exist only on one central computer at the company's headquarters. To reduce costs and improve efficiency, you suggest that the company invest in a learning management system (LMS) that will allow the company to provide some training online as well as manage all the content and record keeping for the system. Mitchell thinks it's a great idea and asks you to research and recommend an LMS. He gives you four weeks to complete this project.

Here are some of the specific questions you will need to answer before you can determine which system to recommend:

- What are the major differences between the types of learning management systems: products primarily used in academia (such as Blackboard, Canvas, or Brightspace), products specifically designed for business use (such as Adobe Captivate and NetDimensions), and open-source products that can be customized (such as Moodle and Opigno)?
- What criteria should you use to evaluate LMS packages?
- What are the experiences of other companies with specific LMS packages?
- What are the costs of different options?

As you research, you will think of other questions. Where do you find the data you need to answer all these questions? And once you find the data, how do you evaluate whether the information is useful?

Analyze the research question and topic

Analyze

Be sure you have a good understanding of your major research question or problem as well as the assumptions it is based upon. You may need to broaden the question to find the information you need. For example, in the Ipswich Brands scenario, Mitchell Harris asked you to research which LMS is best for the company. This question assumes that an LMS in general is the best solution to the problem of excess training expense and inefficient content management and record keeping. Perhaps a different kind of solution may be better. Based on this analysis, you might broaden your research questions to include those illustrated in **Figure 8.1**. Notice that each research question also includes subquestions that you will need to explore to answer your main question.

Before doing in-depth research to explore these specific questions, you need to understand your general topic by conducting background research. **Figure 8.2** on page 276 illustrates a set of background questions focusing on the topic's history, context, structure and categories.[2] The figure then adapts those questions to apply to learning management systems. For your specific topic, you will need to decide which questions listed in Figure 8.2 are most important.

Research Question 1:	Would a learning management system (LMS) be an effective tool for our company? • What specific training and content management needs does our company have? • What current problems are we facing? • What are options for solving these problems? • Is an LMS the best option?
Research Question 2:	If an LMS would be effective, which one is the best option to meet our specific training needs? • What are the various options for LMS programs? • What criteria will we use to judge the options? • Which option best meets the criteria?
Research Question 3:	What will be the costs of the recommended option in money and time? • What is the initial purchase and installation cost? • What are the ongoing costs, such as customer support? • How much time will it take to get the new system up and ready to use?

FIGURE 8.1 Questions to Guide LMS Research

FIGURE 8.2 Background Research Questions

CATEGORY	GENERIC QUESTION	SAMPLE QUESTIONS FOR THE LMS RESEARCH PROJECT
History	When and why did X first develop?	When and why did learning management systems first develop?
	How has X developed over time?	How have learning management systems changed and why? What have been the biggest influences on these systems?
Context and structure	How does X function as part of a larger context or system?	How does a learning management system fit into the larger system of workplace training and development? What role does it play in relationship to the other elements in the system?
	What else exists that serves similar purposes?	Instead of a learning management system, what else could help solve our problem?
	What are the parts of X and how do the parts fit and work together?	What are the various elements of a learning management system? How do all the parts work together?
Categories	What types or categories of X exist?	What kinds of learning management systems are there? How are they grouped, and why are they grouped that way?
	How do different types of X compare and contrast with each other?	How do typical academic learning management systems, such as Blackboard, Canvas, and Brightspace, compare and contrast with those primarily used in the workplace, such as Captivate and NetDimensions?

You may not directly include the results of this background research in your final presentation or report. However, gaining a broader understanding of your topic can help you structure your research. For example, doing background research on the parts and functions of an LMS may help you identify which functions are most important to your company.

Identify audience concerns and needs

Analyzing the audience and other stakeholders enables you to consider the problem from their point of view and identify concerns that you will need to address. To analyze the audience and stakeholders, answer these questions:

- **Who is the primary audience?** For example, in the LMS research, your primary audience is your supervisor, Mitchell Harris, who asked you to research LMS training options.
- **Who is the secondary audience?** In this case, it is the company's senior-level decision makers who will finance an LMS.
- **Who else may be affected by this problem or decision?** Additional stakeholders include the employees who will be affected by the integration of an LMS or other changes to the current training practices.
- **What does the audience already know? What do they need to know?** Your decision makers know that the company needs a new approach for training and they know that adopting a new system will be a major investment. To make a decision, they need to know the pros, cons, and costs of the different options available.
- **What questions will your audience expect you to answer when you present the research?** They will expect you to answer at least three core questions: Will an LMS be an effective training tool for the company? If so, which tool best meets the company's needs? What is the cost?
- **What sources will your audience expect you to consult?** This final question is important for your credibility. If you perform a quick Google search or rely on a general and nonvalidated source such as Wikipedia, even for background information, your audience

may not respect your findings. The acceptability of sources and research methods vary greatly from field to field. For example, search engine optimization (SEO) firms rely on Google searches as part of their routine research practice.[3] By contrast, consumer product firms are less likely to value the results of a Google search on the psychology of consumer behavior.[4] A professional audience is more likely to value your information if you use professional and highly credible sources. These sources include journals and websites published by professional associations in the industry, research published in academic journals, books by reputable authors and publishers, and newspapers. For example, in researching options for learning management systems, your audience may expect you to consult:

- *TD*, a magazine published by the Association for Talent Development (ATD)
- *Training Magazine* and *Training Journal*, two additional highly respected publications in the training industry
- The *Learning Technologies* blog hosted by ATD
- Books such as *E-Learning and the Science of Instruction: Proven Guidelines for Consumers and Designers of Multimedia Learning* by Clark and Mayer
- The websites and marketing departments of each LMS you are considering

Your audience may even expect you to conduct your own original research, such as interviewing people who have experience with your topic or surveying potential stakeholders.

Establish the scope of the research

The **scope** of a research study refers to the breadth and depth of the research. Establishing the scope is like looking through binoculars. You can choose to view the landscape of a large area (broad scope) or to focus on the details of a small object (narrow scope). In your LMS research, you may look broadly at the information about many LMS packages to determine if online content management and training would be an effective format for your company. However, to determine which system is the best option, you might have to narrow your focus to collect a lot of information about two or three packages.

Establishing the scope of your research also allows you to define the limitations of your research. **Limitations** are the characteristics of the research that prevent you from generalizing your findings more broadly. For example, if you choose to narrow the scope of your research to established LMS packages that have been widely used and reviewed rather than investigating new options, then you cannot generalize and suggest you have selected the best of all possible learning management systems—just the best widely reviewed system.

How do you decide on the scope of the research? The answer depends on the needs of the project, the amount of time available, and what you learn in your initial research. For example, if you have only a week to research LMS options, you may limit your research to include only material that is available from companies and product reviews in professional journals. With more time available, you may choose to interview people who use the programs. If you learn in your initial background research that only two programs seem appropriate for your company, you may decide to narrow your research to focus deeply on those two programs.

Define research activities

Research activities are the steps you take to answer the research questions. For example, how will you research the currently available LMS options? How will you determine the most relevant criteria for judging those options? For each question, list possible steps you might take to find the necessary information, as illustrated in **Figure 8.3** on page 278.

The list of research activities helps you identify sources for the information. Typically, sources fall into one of three categories: primary, secondary, and tertiary sources.

- **Primary sources** provide raw data. You can collect primary data by surveying, interviewing, or observing people. Another form of primary research involves reading primary texts, such as websites and marketing materials. Primary research falls into two categories:

scope The range of your research; a broad scope includes a wide range of content, whereas a narrow scope focuses on specific aspects of the topic.

limitations The characteristics of your specific research that prevent you from generalizing your findings more broadly.

primary sources Sources from which you collect your own raw data.

FIGURE 8.3 Examples of Research Activities to Answer Research Questions

Research Question 1: Would an LMS be an effective training tool for the company?

SPECIFIC QUESTION	RESEARCH ACTIVITY
What specific training and content management needs does our company have?	Interview department heads in the company.
What current problems are we facing?	Interview the chief learning officer and department heads.
What are alternatives/options for solving these problems?	Survey other companies and research training and education journals, books, and websites.
Is an LMS the best option?	Compare options against the company's training needs.

Research Question 2: If an LMS would be effective, which one is the best option to meet the company's specific training needs?

SPECIFIC QUESTION	RESEARCH ACTIVITY
What are the various options for LMS programs?	Review training and education journals, books, and websites. Do a web search for LMS programs. Speak to other companies in the industry.
What criteria will we use to judge the options?	Interview chief learning officers and department heads.
Which option best meets the criteria?	Conduct a comparative analysis of alternatives against selected criteria.

Research Question 3: What will be the cost of the selected option?

SPECIFIC QUESTION	RESEARCH ACTIVITY
What is the initial purchase and installation cost?	Speak to the sales department of the selected company.
What are the ongoing costs, such as customer support?	Speak to the sales department of the selected company. Interview other companies using the system.

quantitative research Research that relies on numerical data, such as that gathered from structured survey responses to which you can assign numbers.

qualitative research Research that provides insight into the attitudes, values, and concerns of research subjects through interviews and observation.

secondary sources The results of other people's research that you consult as part of your research.

tertiary sources Books and articles that synthesize material from secondary sources.

- **Quantitative research** gathers numerical data, such as structured survey responses to which you can assign numbers. Quantitative research allows you to classify, count, and compare data in order to measure results and to identify patterns.
- **Qualitative research** uses open-ended questions and observations to gather data that provide insights into the attitudes, values, and concerns of the research subjects.
- **Secondary sources** are the results of other people's research, published in articles, books, or research reports and usually written by the researchers themselves.
- **Tertiary sources** are books and articles that synthesize material from secondary sources, framing them for general readers. Tertiary sources include encyclopedias, textbooks, online tools such as Wikipedia, and the results of most standard web searches. Tertiary sources are often very good for background research. However, they may oversimplify the research they present. You will have more credibility if you try to find the original material that these sources summarize.

For the Ipswich Brands LMS project, you will need to do primary research: reading the marketing materials and specifications of several learning management systems, speaking to salespeople, interviewing users of these systems, and interviewing people within your organization to identify criteria for judging the options. Finding good secondary sources will also make your job easier. You can save time by reading reviews of learning management systems, articles comparing different systems, or case studies describing how companies have used learning management systems. Although you should not rely on the material from a tertiary source—such as a Wikipedia article on learning management systems—quickly reading that article or a summary article on the ATD website may be a good place to get background information or a list of other resources to consult.

Develop a work plan

The last step before beginning your research is to develop a work plan like the one illustrated in **Figure 8.4** to help you track your progress over time and ensure you meet deadlines. Although you may need to modify your work plan as you discover new information, an initial plan helps you focus on the project. The work plan in Figure 8.4 spreads the research over three weeks, leaving you one week to prepare your presentation.

FIGURE 8.4 How to Develop a Work Plan

RESEARCH QUESTIONS	RESEARCH ACTIVITIES	TARGET DATE
Background Research • What are the various types of learning management and course management systems? • How do the types compare? • What are the various elements of a system and how do they work?	Research training and education journals, books, and websites. Find and interview an LMS expert.	Weeks 1–2 Week 1
1. *Would an LMS be an effective training tool for our company?* • What specific training and content management needs does our company have? • What current problems are we facing? • What are alternatives/options for solving these problems? • Is an LMS the best option?	Interview the company's chief learning officer and department heads. Survey or interview other companies. Research training and education journals, books, and websites. Compare options against company's training needs.	Week 2 Week 2 Weeks 1–2 Week 2
2. *If an LMS would be effective, which one is the best option to meet our specific training needs?* • What are the various options for LMS programs? • What criteria will we use to judge the options? • Which option best meets the criteria?	Review training and education journals, books, and websites. Conduct a web search for LMS programs. Speak to other companies in the industry. Interview the chief learning officer and department heads. Conduct a detailed comparative analysis. Compare alternatives against selection criteria.	Week 1 Week 1 Week 2 Week 1 Week 3 Week 3
3. *What is the cost of the selected option?* • What are the initial purchase and installation costs? • What are the ongoing costs, such as customer support?	Speak to the sales department of the selected company. Interview other companies using the system.	Week 3 Week 3

To develop a work plan:

• **Create a table.**
• **List your research questions** in the left column.
• **List associated research activities** in the next column.
• **Assign each activity a target date.**

Note that the target dates are not always sequential. You may conduct several research tasks concurrently, during the same week. In addition, if you are already interviewing people in other companies to find out how they handle training and record keeping (Research Question 1), you may also want to find out what specific LMS they use (Research Question 2).

COLLABORATION
CONDUCTING RESEARCH AS A TEAM

When you are in school, the goal of research is often to enhance your individual learning and understanding of the content. As a result, research projects are often individual efforts. However, to prepare you for research in the world of work, some schools provide more opportunities for students to research, write, and present as teams. In business and science, research is routinely conducted by collaborative teams for a variety of reasons:

- **Efficiency.** Research often needs to be done under tight time constraints. Completing the job in reasonable amount of time requires multiple people. Consider the work plan in Figure 8.3 of this chapter. This amount of work would be difficult for one person to accomplish under short time constraints.
- **Diversity of skills and knowledge.** Projects often require a range of knowledge and research skills—beyond the scope of any one person. Team-based research takes advantage of cross-disciplinary knowledge and blends complementary strengths to address more complex problems.
- **Diversity of thinking.** Even beyond diversity of knowledge, teams with diverse membership benefit from diverse thinking, as members challenge each other and checking

each other's biases. Research shows that diverse teams are, in fact, smarter and achieve better results than individuals or homogenous teams.[5]

Despite the power of and reliance on teams, collaborations do not always work well. People may not be motivated to work on a team, and differences in point of view can lead to dysfunction.[6] When planning collaborative research, here are some key points to keep in mind:

- Have conversations at the beginning of the project to be sure that everyone has a shared understanding of the goals of the project, the constraints, the requirements, and the research questions.
- Use a work plan to keep everyone on track.
- Create shared collaboration space online so that everyone has up-to-date access to all research materials.
- Respect each other's work but be willing to challenge it.
- When it comes time to present the research, acknowledge it as a shared work product. Avoid taking "ownership" of your own contributions to the research.

For a **COLLABORATION** exercise, go to Exercise 31 on pages 308–309.

(SQ2) How do you conduct research in print and online sources?

New Hires @ Work

Christian Tucker
Georgia Southern University

Database Engineer
@ General Motors

Much of the information I need to access is in internal documents, in SharePoint, which I never used before my internship. Fortunately, we have an in-house online learning environment with tutorials that are very helpful.

Photo courtesy of Christian Tucker

desktop search tool A search engine designed to search for files on your computer or file server that contain specific words or that were produced within a specific time period.

You may be able to gather most of the material you need from print or online sources. The challenge is to find those sources and to evaluate them to ensure that they are credible. **Figure 8.5** summarizes a range of tools and identifies what you can find with each.

This section presents techniques to help you use these tools effectively to do the following:

- Gather relevant print and electronic files
- Search the web strategically
- Use an online index or database to find articles from print publications
- Use a library or bookseller to find relevant books
- Follow leads in good sources
- Evaluate your sources for credibility

Gather relevant print and electronic files

If you already have files on your computer or your company's network and/or relevant hard-copy materials, organize them in one central location. For paper documents, you can use file folders or a three-ring notebook with tabbed dividers to organize your information by topic. Or you can scan the material to create electronic files. Be sure to record the information required for citations and reference list entries if you photocopy or scan articles from books, journals, or magazines.

For electronic files, consider using a **desktop search tool**, which is a search engine designed to search for files on your computer or file server that contain specific words or that were produced within a specific time period. **Figure 8.6** illustrates the results of a desktop search for files containing the term *learning management*. Many search tools are available for download or purchase. However, before investing in new software, try the search functions built into your computer's operating system.

FIGURE 8.5 Tools for Finding Research Sources

TOOL	EXAMPLES	WHAT THE EXAMPLE SEARCHES	WHAT IT FINDS
General search engine	Google, Yahoo!, Bing	Web	Publicly available content
Deep web search engine	Science.gov, Biznar.com	Web	Specialized content often not accessible through a general search engine
Regional open data portal	OpenDataPhilly Denver Open Data Catalog City of Chicago Data Portal	Official data and statistics about cities, counties and states	Spreadsheets of regional data on the economy, environment, crime, transportation, etc.
Desktop search tool	Windows Search, OS Finder, OS Spotlight, Copernic, HoudahSpot	Your computer or your organization's server	Company or personal unpublished content
Online publication index	*New York Times* Index	One publication, such as *The New York Times*	Articles in that publication
Online article database	Ebsco Business Source Premier Lexis/Nexis Sociological Abstracts	Abstracts and full texts of thousands of publications, gathered together in the database	Articles originally published in print journals, magazines, and newspapers
Online business research tool	Thomson ONE Banker IBIS World Hoover's Standard and Poor's Yahoo! Finance	Corporate and industry research reports from various sources	Company, industry, and market data
Library online catalog	Northwestern University NUsearch University of Michigan Mirlyn University of Wisconsin MadCat	The library's paper and electronic holdings	Material in the library's collection, typically including books, journals, journal and newspaper articles, videos, sound recordings, and digital images
Online bookstore	Amazon.com Barnesandnoble.com	Books available through that online bookstore and other used booksellers	Books and ebooks available for sale

FIGURE 8.6 Results of a Desktop Search for *Learning Management*

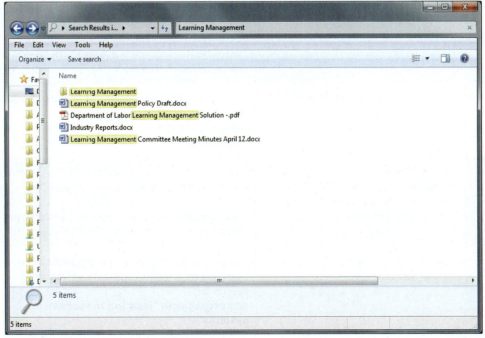

Use a desktop search tool to find electronic files such as meeting minutes, budgets, proposals, or previous research.

Use web search engines strategically

Basic search engines, such as Google, Bing, Yahoo!, and Ask, index sites throughout the web. When you enter keywords, the search engine provides links to sites that use those terms. The sites that appear at the top or near the side of the list are usually those whose organizations have paid a fee to be featured in the search results. The main body of the results page begins with sites that are frequently accessed or that most closely match your search terms. As you scroll through the list or click on subsequent pages, the results are likely to be less relevant.

Although searching the web seems easy, finding useful information is challenging. A Google search for the words *learning management system* returns almost 89 million results. Which ones will be relevant to you? Use the search tips in **Figure 8.7** to narrow your search.

FIGURE 8.7 How to Conduct a Smarter Web Search

TECHNIQUE	PURPOSE	EXAMPLE
Use quotation marks around your search terms	To find sites that include the exact phrase rather than sites that include each of the words somewhere on the page	**"learning management system"**
Add relevant words to the search. Think of words that must be included on a website that is relevant to your research, and add that word to your search terms.	To get more relevant results	If you would like only corporate systems that offer assessment features, use **"learning management system" corporate assessment**
Use the minus symbol (–) before a search term	To exclude pages that mention a term	If you want to find information about learning management systems that do not use open-source software, use **"learning management system" –"open source"**
Use an asterisk (*) as a wild-card within a search phrase	To find a phrase that includes an un-known or variable word	If you want to find websites about companies that have selected one specific LMS—for example, Plateau—use an asterisk to represent the name of any company: **"* selects Plateau"** or **"* chooses Plateau"**
Use Boolean operators: AND, OR, or NOT	To expand or reduce your search results	If you want to expand results by finding sites that use either the term *learning management system* or *learning management software*, use **"learning management system" OR "learning management software"**
Use synonyms or alternative wording	To search for sites using different terms to discuss your subject	If you notice that discussions of learning management systems often use the term *e-learning*, search for **"e-learning"**
Use file types	To search for files, such as PDF files, PowerPoint files, or .doc files	If you want to find additional articles, documents, or case studies that are downloadable files, search for **"learning management systems" filetype: pdf** or **"learning management systems" filetype: doc**
Search a specific website	To search within a specific website	If you want to conduct a search specifically within pcmag.com, a technology reviews website, search for **site:pcmag.com "learning management systems"**

CULTURE
RESEARCHING COUNTRIES AND CULTURES ONLINE

Currently, more than 195 countries and independent territories exist in the world.[7] Among these countries, people belong to hundreds of different cultures and speak more than 7,000 languages and dialects.[8] With all of this diversity, preparing yourself to work internationally or in a multicultural workforce is a huge task.

You cannot anticipate all the countries and cultures you may need to know about during your career. Fortunately, the web will make this information easy to find, if you know how to look for it. Specific websites will change over the years. However, as this chapter discusses, you can find the information you need by using effective search terms.

The following table provides three sets of search terms and examples of resources that resulted from a web search using these terms. These sites and others like them can help you begin your research on doing business and communicating with people around the world. By using these and similar sets of search terms, you will be able to find additional resources on your own.

For CULTURE exercises, go to Exercise 30 on page 308 and Exercise 35d on page 309.

SEARCH TERMS: "CULTURAL DIFFERENCES IN BUSINESS"

RESOURCE	CREATED BY	WHAT YOU WILL FIND
BusinessCulture.org	Passport to Trade 2.0, a project funded with support from the European Union	A business culture guide for online, face-to-face, and social media communication for 31 European countries
WorldBusinessCulture.com	Global Business Culture, a training and development company that helps organizations make international business more efficient and profitable	Comprehensive description of business culture, including communication, in 39 countries

SEARCH TERMS: "INTERNATIONAL BUSINESS DATA"

RESOURCE	CREATED BY	WHAT YOU WILL FIND
GlobalEDGE™	International Business Center at Michigan State University and partly funded by the U.S. Department of Education	A knowledge web portal that connects international business professionals worldwide to a wealth of information, insights, and learning resources on global business activities
Doing Business	International Finance organization and the World Bank	Reports on business regulations in countries throughout the world

SEARCH TERMS: "INTERNATIONAL BUSINESS ETIQUETTE"

RESOURCE	CREATED BY	WHAT YOU WILL FIND
International Business Etiquette and Manners	Global Leadership MBA Graduates from University of Texas—Dallas	Analysis of business etiquette in more than 30 countries around the world
Executive Planet	International Business Center, a not-for-profit organization	A wiki where experts in specific cultures provide advice about communicating and conducting business in those cultures

Use deep web portals

Experts estimate that only a tiny portion of the material available on the web—as little as 4 percent—is located on the surface of the web and indexed by major search engines.[9] The rest of the content is available below the surface, in the dark web or the deep web. The dark web is not appropriate for business research, as it is always encrypted, and the information is often illegal. However, the deep web contains a wealth of material that businesses find useful, including material from private research organizations, government sources, corporations, and professional associations. To take greater advantage of the deep web in the course of your research, familiarize yourself with deep web portals.[10] These portals perform *federated searches*, which means they select several useful databases and subscription services that are available on the web and simultaneously search through all of them, returning results that do not appear in a Google search. For business research, you will find two deep web portals particularly useful:

- **Biznar.com.** This site is designed for professional business researchers. Although it includes information from sources such as Wikipedia and blogs, it also searches databases of professional industry reports, academic articles, and business news.
- **Science.gov.** This database provides access to federally sponsored research on almost any topic. It also provides access to articles in the medical database PubMed and the educational database ERIC. A search for "learning management systems" in this deep web portal will reveal much of the research done on learning management systems in the medical and educational fields.

Remember that even when using material found through these reliable portals, you need to verify the credibility and objectivity of the source.

Use an online index or database to find articles and business data

Many useful articles are not available through a Google search because their publications require a paid subscription. Almost every academic and public library purchases subscriptions to specific publications such as *The Wall Street Journal* and the *Journal of International Business Studies*. They also purchase subscriptions to online databases, such as *LexisNexis*, that collect articles from thousands of publications, including newspapers such as *The New York Times*, magazines such as *Businessweek*, professional publications (also called trade journals) such as *Financial News*, and academic journals such as *Research in Learning Technology*. Articles from these publications are regarded as more reliable than content from websites because editors carefully review them. Articles in academic journals offer another advantage: They are written and peer reviewed by professionals in their respective fields to ensure that the content of the articles is accurate and honest.

You can check with your university or public library to learn what online databases are available. Searching for articles in these databases is much like searching the web. You must use good search terms to get relevant results. **Figure 8.8** illustrates search results from one widely available database, *Business Source Premier*.

You can also use online databases and other research tools to find business data and analyses. For example, research organizations, such as Standard & Poor's, Hoover's, and Thomson, publish in-depth financial data about companies, markets, and industries. You can access some of this data on the web through publicly available tools, including Yahoo! Finance. Other data is available only through a library subscription.

Use a library or bookseller to find relevant books

Because the web contains so much information, students often neglect to search for books. However, books—like print articles—can be more valuable than online resources because books are often professionally reviewed, edited, and produced by reputable authors and publishing companies with established credibility. By contrast, anyone can post resources online about nearly anything. The drawback with books is that they may become outdated more quickly than online content, which can be updated regularly.

To find books that remain relevant and timely, your first stop may be your library's online catalog. The catalog will probably allow you to do a keyword search using many of the same techniques you use for a web search. If you find one book that seems relevant to your research, check the online record to see what broader subject categories are associated with that book and then search for other books in the same category. You may find it equally useful to browse through the library bookshelves. If you find one book that looks useful, go to its location in the library and look at other books in the same section.

The advantage of looking at books in a school library is that the librarians and faculty have determined those books are worthy of being in the library's collection. The disadvantage is that libraries rarely have the newest books since it often takes a long time for a library to acquire a book. For more recent books, try searching the websites of online booksellers such as amazon.com or barnesandnoble.com. If your library does not own the book—and you cannot buy it—you may be able to ask your library to borrow it from another library.

FIGURE 8.8 How to Search an Online Database

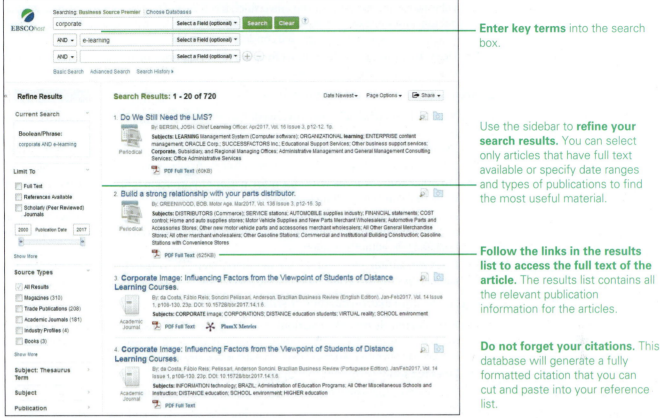

Enter key terms into the search box.

Use the sidebar to **refine your search results.** You can select only articles that have full text available or specify date ranges and types of publications to find the most useful material.

Follow the links in the results list to access the full text of the article. The results list contains all the relevant publication information for the articles.

Do not forget your citations. This database will generate a fully formatted citation that you can cut and paste into your reference list.

Follow leads in good sources

If you find a good book or article on your subject, check the bibliography or reference list to find additional resources for your research. For example, if you read an interesting article in the magazine *Chief Learning Officer* about transitioning an organization from traditional to online learning, look at the article's references. If the article is valuable to your research, then the references used to write the article might also be useful. As you browse through the library, check the bibliographies of the books you find. You may see references to other books and articles you should read. Footnotes, endnotes, and in-text citations might also contain useful references.

Evaluate your sources for credibility

Even after narrowing your search results, you are often left with thousands of options. How do you decide which resources to use? No matter what kind of source you find—print or electronic—you must evaluate it for credibility. To determine the reliability and relevance of a source, use the "three *As*"—authorship, accuracy, and age:

Evaluate

Authorship: Can you trust the author and publisher?

- **Does the source identify the author?** Most reliable websites and print publications identify the author of the material. Although corporate websites typically do not identify an author for individual webpages or articles, the corporation itself serves as a corporate author (and should be listed as such in a reference list). By contrast, news and opinion sites that publish anonymous articles are often unreliable and may be guilty of publishing "fake news" or "fake research."

- **Is the author qualified or an expert in this content?** Check the author's biography or research the author on the web. If the author is a blogger, do not immediately assume that the material lacks credibility. Though bloggers are not always qualified commentators, some experts disseminate ideas through blogs as well as published works. To verify credibility, determine where the author works and what other books or articles the author has published.

- **Is the source published by a reputable press, or is the website sponsored by a reputable organization?** On the web, you can generally feel confident about information that is published by the government and universities. If you are unfamiliar with an organization that publishes information you would like to use, read more about that organization to determine whether it is respected by others and considered reputable.
- **Does the author provide support for claims?** Unsupported opinions are less credible than arguments supported by evidence.

Accuracy: Can you trust the information?

- **Was the book or article peer reviewed?** If a text has been reviewed by other experts before publication, the result is likely to be more accurate.
- **Do others frequently cite the source?** You can find out by using a citation index such as Social Science Citation Index, ISI Science Citation, or Google Scholar (www.scholar.google.com).
- **Do other sources agree with this information?** Information is likely to be more accurate if you find it in multiple, unrelated sources.
- **Does the author acknowledge and respond to opposing points of view?** When an author addresses other points of view instead of evading them, you have a broader context for evaluating the author's position.
- **Does the author cite sources for numbers, facts, or research findings?** Or does the author expect you to assume the data is correct?

Age: Is the information current or still relevant?

- **How current is this information?** If you're researching a technology topic, the material needs to be very current. By contrast, if you're researching an issue in business ethics, the source may offer useful perspectives even if it is decades old.
- **Does the source provide a last-updated date or copyright?**
- **Are any web links broken?** This often indicates an outdated page.

Evaluating sources using these criteria—authorship, accuracy, and age—helps you decide whether a source is useful and what to use it for. **Figure 8.9** illustrates an evaluation of three articles on learning management systems.

How do you conduct primary research?

Some research questions or problems require that you conduct your own original, or primary, research. Imagine that you want to know which learning management systems are used most widely in your industry. If no one else has already done this research, you could use any of the following primary research techniques:

survey A predetermined list of questions used to collect a structured set of information from a selected audience.

interview A research method involving a structured discussion between two or more people, usually in a question-and-answer format.

observational research A research method that involves watching people perform relevant activities and recording details about what you observe.

- Compose a **survey**—or standardized questionnaire—to distribute to the head of training of each company in your industry.
- Conduct an **interview** with content experts to get their in-depth thoughts about available systems.
- Conduct **observational research** to determine how difficult it will be for new managers to learn how to use a system. You could get a trial version of the software, input trial data, ask specific managers to do a task with the data, and observe them as they do this task, noting any problems that need to be addressed.

Each of the three types of research—survey, interview, and observation—is widely used in business. The sections that follow introduce you to all three methods. However, if you are working on an extensive project that requires you to become very skilled at any of these approaches, you may need to take a course or read a text in research methods.

Conduct survey research to gather quantifiable information about opinions and attitudes

Survey research uses a predetermined list of questions, also known as a *survey instrument*, to collect a structured set of information from a selected audience. Surveys allow you to quantify the results and compare the number of participants who respond in specific ways.

FIGURE 8.9 Example of How to Evaluate Research Sources

SOURCE	EVALUATION	DECISION
Article 1: White Paper Element K. (2003). *Learning management systems in the work environment: Practical considerations for the selection and implementation of an e-learning platform.* [White paper]. Rochester, NY: Element K.	**AUTHORSHIP** Element K—a training and development organization that implements learning solutions for its clients **ACCURACY** • Includes citations • Is cited in several peer-reviewed articles • May be biased because Element K sells learning management systems **AGE** Not a recent source	**Decision:** Use only for background information. **Reason:** This article is too old to cite as factual on this topic. In addition, as a white paper, it is probably biased toward certain LMS systems. However, it may provide useful background information.
Article 2: Article published on an industry online newsletter Radhakrishnan. M. (2012, May 21). LMS reporting that works. *Association for Talent Development.* Retrieved from http://www.td.org/Publications/Newsletters/Learning-Circuits/Learning-Circuits-Archives/2012/05/LMS-Reporting-That-Works	**AUTHORSHIP** The Association for Talent Development is a well-respected organization that specializes in corporate learning. The author of the article, Mohana Radhakrishnan, is a learning solutions strategist who has been recognized by Training-Industry.com as one of the most influential training professionals in the country. **ACCURACY** • Was reviewed by ATD editors, who are experts in the field • Cites various other experts and points of view. **AGE** Published more recently than Article 1 but still old. May refer to outdated technology.	**Decision:** Use as an expert opinion to understand the flaws of current LMS reporting systems. Because Radhakrishnan is an expert in the field, her opinions of the strengths and limitations of LMS reporting systems are worth including. However, it is important to acknowledge that they are just her opinions.
Article 3: Research Report Forrester. (2016, September 15). *Vendor Landscape: Standalone learning management system vendors.* [Research Report]. Cambridge, MA: Forrester Research, Inc.	**AUTHORSHIP** Forrester is a highly respected, independent consumer research organization. Forrester sells this report for more than $2,000. **ACCURACY** • Includes primary research • Includes citations • Has a reputation for unbiased research **AGE** Published most recently	**Decision:** If available or affordable, use to understand the criteria for comparing and selecting systems. However, this is an expensive report, and the information may be available elsewhere.

To analyze whether survey research will be useful, you first need to determine what data you need to gather and from whom. As you'll recall from Figure 8.1, these are the three main research questions about learning management systems:

Analyze

Research Question 1: Would an LMS be an effective tool for our company?

Research Question 2: If an LMS would be effective, which one is the best option to meet our specific training needs?

Research Question 3: What will be the costs of the recommended option in money and time?

A survey asking employees and managers for their opinions about Questions 1 and 2 will not be useful. Their answers would simply give you a set of vague and general opinions about LMS systems without any detailed explanation to help you analyze those systems. However, as you consider how to answer Question 2, you may decide to survey employees to learn about their prior work experiences with specific learning management systems. Such a survey can provide information about what systems are used in other companies, how they are used, and how employees respond to the systems.

To administer a survey like this, you will need to decide which people to survey, how to word the questions, how to administer the survey, and how to analyze the results.

Choose which people to survey

survey population   The audience from whom you want to collect survey responses.

sample   A representative portion of your survey population.

convenience sample   A survey population selected because you have easy access to that group.

targeted sample   A population sample that consists of only specific people from the group you are studying.

random sample   A population sample selected broadly from all available members of the population you want to study.

The audience from which you want to collect survey responses is your **survey population**. The size of that population is referred to as "N," standing for the total number. You can rarely survey the entire population because there are simply too many people to contact. In these cases, you can identify a **sample**, or a representative portion of your population. Different kinds of samples can be used for different purposes:

- A **convenience sample** is a sample selected because you have easy access to that population. For example, you might determine that it would be easier or that you would get a better response rate by surveying the employees in your building rather than all the branches across the country. The fact that they know you might motivate them to respond.
- A **targeted sample** is restricted to specific people within the group you are studying. For example, if you do most of your training with new hires, you might survey employees who were hired within the last year.
- A **random sample** is a sample selected broadly from all available members of the population you want to study. This is the best alternative if you want to generalize your findings to everyone you are studying. A sample is random when every member of the population has an equal chance of being selected. For example, if you want to survey all 500 employees in a company, you could generate an alphabetical list and distribute a survey to every second person on the list. A random sample increases the likelihood that the responses will be statistically valid and accurately represent the larger population.

Decide on a survey medium

To select a medium for delivering your survey questions to your participants, consider the advantages and disadvantages of the various options. Face-to-face and telephone surveys allow you to ask clarifying and follow-up questions, leading to more in-depth information. However, these in-person surveys are time-consuming and they require you to manually enter data into a spreadsheet or tabulate data manually. Mailed surveys also require manual entry of data, and responses may come in slowly. Online surveys address all those problems and offer additional advantages: They are inexpensive, fast to distribute, and easy for the audience to complete. However, research shows that response rates are often lower for online surveys than for mailed surveys. To increase the response rate, experts suggest notifying participants in advance that they will get a link by email.[11]

Compose effective survey questions

Compose

To determine the content of your survey questions, use your broader research questions as a guide. For example, if you want to determine which LMS would be most effective, you might ask your survey population how satisfied they were with systems they used in the past. Once you know what you want to ask, the next step is to determine how to write questions so that you get the information you need. Avoid ambiguous questions that can be interpreted in multiple ways. For instance, don't ask, *"How would you rate the learning management system?"* because you will have no way of knowing what criteria the respondent is using for the rating. To fix this problem, identify the criteria for their response such as, *"How would you rate the effectiveness of the online training you have taken compared to traditional face-to-face training?"* To ensure your survey questions are effective, you can pilot test them with a focus group before distributing the survey.

median   The number that represents the middle number in a distribution or the most central number.

mode   The number that most frequently appears in a distribution.

Figure 8.10 shows examples of several survey question formats. Examples include questions that require respondents to select a specific response (yes or no), rate or rank the listed options, or assign a value to a statement. Your survey may include a variety of question formats, or you might find that one format, such as multiple choice, works well to gather data that answer your research questions.

FIGURE 8.10 Five Types of Survey Questions

YES/NO

Have you used a learning management system (LMS) for training in any of your prior work experiences?

○ Yes ○ No

MULTIPLE CHOICE

If yes, how would you rate your satisfaction with the effectiveness of the online training you have taken compared to traditional face-to-face training?

○ = More satisfied with LMS for ALL learning experiences

○ = More satisfied with LMS for MOST learning experiences

○ = Neither more satisfied nor more dissatisfied with LMS

○ = Less satisfied with LMS for MOST learning experiences

○ = Less satisfied with LMS for ALL learning experiences

LIKERT (AGREEMENT) SCALE

For each statement, indicate to what extent you agree with the statement.

IF THE COMPANY ADOPTS AN ONLINE LMS OPTION . . .	STRONGLY DISAGREE	DISAGREE	NEUTRAL	AGREE	STRONGLY AGREE
it would improve our company's overall training experience.	○	○	○	○	○
I might sign up for more elective training sessions.	○	○	○	○	○
I would miss the social interaction of meeting employees from other offices.	○	○	○	○	○

RATING SCALE

If you have experience with any of the following LMS systems, please rate how strongly you recommend that Ipswich Brands adopt it, on a scale of 1 to 10. A score of 1 indicates you do not recommend the product, and a score of 10 indicates that you strongly recommend the product.

SYSTEM	DO NOT RECOMMEND				NEUTRAL				STRONGLY RECOMMEND	
A2Z	1	2	3	4	5	6	7	8	9	10
Eclipse	1	2	3	4	5	6	7	8	9	10
Teach2Me	1	2	3	4	5	6	7	8	9	10

OPEN ENDED

If you recommend an LMS based on your experience, please provide the name of the LMS and explain why you recommend it.

Many surveys also request demographic information that allows you to categorize respondents' answers in relevant ways. For example, in some surveys, you may find it important to ask participants about their age or where they live. For this LMS survey, however, age and location are not relevant. Instead, you might ask a question about when the participants joined the company and how many training courses they have taken.

Analyze

Analyze, interpret, and evaluate results

After the survey is completed, you need to count, summarize, and analyze the responses. For each question, you will need to decide which measures to use to report responses: percentage, **range**, **mean**, **median**, **mode**, or the total count, represented as "n" for number of responses.

range The span between the highest and lowest values.

mean The average derived by adding all responses and dividing the sum by the number of responses.

TECHNOLOGY
CHOOSING AN ONLINE SURVEY PLATFORM

If you choose to conduct research through an online survey, you will have to decide what survey software or website to use. There are numerous options available; some of them are more familiar than others. Examples include SurveyMonkey, Google Forms, and Qualtrics. Here are some things to consider when choosing a platform for your survey[12]:

- **Cost.** Although many survey platforms are free to use, some have paid plans or versions that give you more functions and greater freedom to customize your survey. Weigh your options and needs when determining the advantages of free versions over paid plans.

- **Types of questions offered.** Be sure to check if a survey platform provides the types of questions you need for your survey—for example, multiple-choice questions, free-response questions, and sliding scales. You might also want a survey platform that lets you make use of skip logic or branch logic, which sets up questions that lead respondents to different topics, depending on how they answer.[13] For example, the yes/no question "Have you used a learning management system (LMS) for training in any of your prior work experiences?" might branch into two paths. Respondents who answer "yes" can be directed to questions that evaluate the systems they have used. And respondents who answer "no" can be directed to questions about traditional face-to-face training.

- **Media.** Some surveys may benefit from having embedded images or video—for example, surveys testing response to different advertisements. You might want to consider embedding images or videos in your survey. Research shows

that videos help improve the respondents' recall and recognition, making the respondents more likely to give a useful response.[14] However, research also shows that if respondents are unable to view the videos, they may not complete the survey, leading to *selection bias* in the study sample—that is, a study sample that is unrepresentative because it includes only people with the ability to view the video content.[15]

- **Mobile compatibility.** Given how frequently people use their mobile devices to browse content, you might want to ensure that your survey platform is easy to view and use on a smartphone, especially for a short survey that requires a large number of respondents. According to a blog post posted by popular survey platform SurveyMonkey, 20 percent of the millions of respondents answering SurveyMonkey surveys were doing so on mobile devices.[16]

- **Ability to offer incentives.** Some platforms allow you to increase the reach of your survey and the diversity of participants by offering incentives.[17,18] For example, you can disseminate your survey and pay respondents directly through Amazon's service Mechanical Turk.[19] SurveyMonkey offers a different type of incentive through its Contribute program: It recruits a large panel of respondents, who then choose to take surveys in exchange for donations to a charity and a chance to win a sweepstakes prize. You pay SurveyMonkey for this service.[20]

For TECHNOLOGY exercises, go to Critical Thinking Question 6 on page 304 and Exercise 13 on page 306.

For some questions, percentage and total count are the most logical data to report. For example, consider the first question in Figure 8.10 :

> *"Have you used a learning management system (LMS) for training in any of your prior work experiences?*   ○ *Yes* ○ *No"*

Determining the percentage of people who have used a system in the past lets you know whether most people or very few people in the population have LMS experience. In addition, you need to know exactly how many people this percentage represents. If only 20 percent of the 130 people surveyed have LMS experience, you will have data from only 26 people. You will need this total count information to analyze the results of the second question in Figure 8.10 that asks,

> *"If yes, how would you rate your satisfaction with the effectiveness of the online training you have taken compared to traditional face-to-face training?"*

When you analyze the answers to this question, you will need to take into account that only 26 people are qualified to answer it. If you report the multiple-choice results of this question as percentages, you must acknowledge that these are percentages of 26, a very small number.

Other questions require data relating to averages: range, mean, medium, and mode. For example, consider the rating scale question in Figure 8.10 :

> *"If you have experience with any of the following LMS systems, please rate how strongly you recommend that Ipswich Brands adopt it, on a scale of 1 to 10. A score of 1 indicates you do not recommend the product, and a score of 10 indicates that you strongly recommend the product."*

Assume that you receive responses from 26 employees, summarized in **Figure 8.11**. The figure shows how the different measures provide different information about the data.

In addition to analyzing the survey results, you also need to evaluate them to determine how you can best represent them. You may not feel confident about using your survey results if you did not get enough responses or responses from the right people. Even if you feel confident about your responses, you need to evaluate what you can say about them. Assume that your company has 130 employees and you received 80 responses, with 26 responses from employees who indicated experience with the three learning management systems you are considering. It is less accurate to say 20 percent of *all employees* (26 out of 130) have experience with one of the three systems than it is to say 33 percent of *the employees who responded* (26 out of 80) have experience with one of the three systems.

Another way to ensure that your survey is representative is to weight your data. If you find that some groups responding to the survey are overrepresented compared to the population and some groups are underrepresented, you can assign an adjustment weight to each respondent. For example, if a disproportionately large number of managers and a disproportionately small number of engineers responded to your survey, you would assign the managers a weight smaller than 1 and the engineers a weight larger than 1. People in overrepresented groups get a weight lower than 1, and people in underrepresented groups get a weight greater than 1. Weighting the responses calibrates the survey according to the makeup of the population and produces findings that are more realistically representative of the larger population.[21]

Evaluate

FIGURE 8.11 Responses to Rating Scale Question in Figure 8.10

Question: If you have experience with any of the following LMS systems, please rate how strongly you recommend that Ipswich Brands adopt it on a scale of 1 to 10. A score of 1 indicates you do not recommend the product, and a score of 10 indicates that you strongly recommend the product.

	A2Z SYSTEMS	ECLIPSE SOFTWARE	TEACH2ME
Employee Ratings	1, 1, 1, 3, 6, 6, 7, 7, 8, 8, 9	5, 5, 5, 6, 6, 6, 7, 7, 7, 7	8, 9, 9, 9, 10
Number of Responses*	n = 11 (42%)	n = 10 (38%)	n = 5 (19%)
Range	1–9	5–7	8–10
Mean	5	6	9
Median	6	6	9
Mode	1	7	9

*Total does not add to 100% because of rounding.

This figure compiles the responses of 26 employees about their experiences with various learning management systems. Looking at the range, mean, median, and mode can tell us different things about these responses.

- The **range**—the span between the highest and lowest values—demonstrates that their responses varied greatly. Some people ranked A2Z poorly, but other people ranked it fairly well. The ranges for the other two products indicate a narrow distribution, indicating more consistent perceptions among the employees.
- The **mean** is the average and is determined by adding all the responses and dividing the sum by the number of responses. Although Teach2Me has the highest mean, only five people (19 percent) had experience with that system. The high mean would inspire more confidence if it represented the opinion of more people.

- The **median** is the number that represents the middle of the responses or the most central number. Although the median and mean are the same for two of the products, for A2Z Systems the median is slightly higher than the mean, which indicates that more people responded above the average than below.
- The **mode**—the number that most frequently appears in the distribution—can help you differentiate between items that have similar means or similar medians. For example, here the median rating for both A2Z and Eclipse is 6. However, the two programs have very different modes. For A2Z, the mode is 1, meaning that the program received more 1s or "do not recommend" than any other rating. By contrast, the mode for Eclipse is much higher, 7, reflecting a stronger recommendation for the product.

Conduct interview research to gather qualitative information

An interview is a discussion between two or more people, usually in a question-and-answer format. The interviewer asks questions and records the interviewee's responses. You can also conduct an interview by email, especially if you have only a few questions to ask. If you secure an interview with someone, you will have only one chance to ask all the questions you need. Therefore, you need to plan carefully. Use the checklist in **Figure 8.12** to plan the interview, conduct the interview, and evaluate the results.

Interviews have at least one significant benefit compared to surveys. Although survey research gives you numbers to analyze, it does not give you the opportunity to delve deeply into

FIGURE 8.12 Checklist for Planning, Conducting, and Evaluating an Interview

Planning an interview

✓ **Generate a list of questions.** Brainstorm as many questions as possible, then evaluate your list to eliminate redundant or extraneous questions.

✓ **Organize related questions into categories.** For the LMS research, these categories may include questions about how the company selected its LMS, how the system is used at that company, how the employees perceive the system, and where additional sources of information can be found.

✓ **Identify sources to answer questions.** You may need to consult a variety of sources or people to answer your questions. Identify the sources for each question and create a second list of the same questions organized by source.

✓ **Determine how you will record responses.** Even if you tape record the interview, take notes in case a mechanical problem occurs with your recording. Also, be sure to get the interviewee's permission to make a recording.

✓ **Write an interview guide.** An interview guide is a plan of action for the interview that outlines the questions you will ask and ensures that you do not forget something important. You may want to leave room for taking notes. You may also want to provide the interviewees with the list of questions before the interview. Doing so allows them to organize their thoughts and possibly collect examples or additional information that they would not otherwise have readily available.

Conducting an interview

✓ **Arrive early.** You may need to set up recording equipment or review your notes to prepare.

✓ **Provide a foundation.** Introduce yourself, describe your research, state your purpose, and confirm the length of the interview. Even if you mentioned these things in your initial email or telephone conversation, providing this information again will set the context for the discussion and clarify expectations. Before proceeding, encourage the interviewee to clarify any concerns or ask any questions they may have.

✓ **Be professional.** Speak clearly and be sure the interviewee understands your questions.

✓ **Listen carefully.** If you do not understand an answer, do not be afraid to ask for clarification. You may have to ask questions like "Why is that?" or "Can you explain that again?" to get the information you need.

✓ **Keep returning to the interview guide.** Responses to questions can lead to tangents that can provide useful information, but also distract you from your plan. Watch the clock to ensure you do not run out of time before you have asked all the questions on your list. If the answers start to wander, bring the conversation back to its purpose.

✓ **Be flexible.** If an answer triggers a question not on the guide, ask it. For example, if the people you're interviewing comment about slow response from the technical support department of the software developer, ask if that was a pattern and how the slow response time affected the company.

✓ **Don't argue.** Your interviewees may make incorrect statements or state opinions as facts. Instead of correcting them or arguing their point, probe more deeply to understand why they hold their opinion. Putting them on the defensive may make them less willing to share their knowledge with you. For example, if an interviewee says her company decided against a specific LMS because it was too expensive, don't argue that the LMS actually costs less than comparable products. Instead, you could ask if there were any other reasons why the company rejected that program or why it believed the program it chose was a better value.

✓ **Follow up with a thank-you.** Expressing appreciation at the end of an interview is important. In addition, following up with a phone call or an email is good professional practice. Follow-up gives you the opportunity to ask your interviewee clarification questions and may even prompt the person to provide additional feedback.

Evaluating interview results

✓ **Draft a concise, well-organized summary of the conversation.** In some situations, you may decide to share your summary with your interviewee to confirm the information that you gathered is correct.

✓ **Organize your findings so that related information is grouped together.** Despite having an organized list of interview questions, you may find that the interviewee's responses included tangents that were informative, but not systematically organized. That means you should not type your notes in the order in which you recorded them. Instead, you will need to organize your notes into logical categories. These categories may be different from the ones you used to organize your questions in the interview guide.

✓ **Determine what additional information you now need and how to get it.** The interviewee might not have been able to answer all your questions, may have suggested new questions, or may have been able to give only part of an answer.

the answers. By contrast, interview research allows you to get richer, more detailed information because interviewees are not limited to predefined responses. In fact, your preplanned questions are often just a starting point that can lead to discussions you might not predict. However, interviews are more time-consuming than surveys; it would take you much longer to interview each of the 80 people who responded to the LMS survey than simply distributing the survey questions.

Depending on the research questions you need to answer, consider interviewing *subject matter experts*, employees, customers, or product users. Experts can include authors of the books or articles you read, columnists who publish related blogs, and people who post comments to community message boards. You may choose to conduct your interview by email, posing specific questions. However, a conversation typically allows more in-depth discussion and may lead to valuable information that you had not originally planned to discuss.

For the learning management systems research, interviews are a key element of the work plan illustrated in Figure 8.4. The plan calls for you to find appropriate people in other companies and interview them about their experiences with learning management systems. You will notice that the checklist in Figure 8.12 recommends creating an interview guide to ensure that you remember to ask important questions. Although your interview questions will depend on the nature of your problem or decision, the sample interview guide in **Figure 8.13** provides some categories of questions you can adapt to meet the needs of your research.

FIGURE 8.13 Sample Interview Guide

interview guide

1. **Introduce yourself and the purpose of the interview.** Thank the interviewee for spending time with you.

2. **Questions about the interviewee:**
   a. What does your organization do?
   b. Who does your organization serve?
   c. What is your position in the organization?

3. **Questions about the problem:**
   a. How many LMS options did you consider before selecting one?
   b. What criteria did you use to select your learning management system?

4. **Questions about users and stakeholders:**
   a. What do your employees think about your learning management system?
   b. How often do your employees use your learning management system?
   c. How do you update your training modules?

5. **Questions about features:**
   a. What are the strengths of your learning management system?
   b. What are the weaknesses of your learning management system?

6. **Questions about the research:**
   a. Can you suggest experts or other people and put me in contact with them, if possible?
   b. Can you suggest relevant secondary sources (books, articles, websites)?
   c. What advice can you give me as we determine the best learning management system for our company?

7. **End the interview on a positive note** by thanking the interviewee again.

Conduct observational research to understand how people act

For many topics, observation is an important supplement to survey and interview research. Observational research involves watching people perform relevant activities and recording details about what you have observed. For example, when gathering information about learning management systems, you could ask an LMS provider if you can observe—and even participate in—an online training session it is conducting for another customer.

Observation offers advantages over self-reported data from surveys and interviews. When people describe and evaluate a past experience in a survey or an interview, they may not completely remember what happened, or they may want to give you the answer they

---

 ## ETHICS
HOW TO BE AN ETHICAL RESEARCHER

When you present research in a business report or proposal, your audience has the right to expect that the information is reliable, accurate, and complete. To meet those expectations, as a researcher you have ethical responsibilities. The following six guidelines address both how to gather information and how to report it.

1. **Use reputable sources.** If you use secondary sources, take responsibility to ensure that those sources are credible using the criteria authorship, accuracy, and age. Also, ensure that you can verify the information by cross-referencing it with other sources. Although Wikipedia may be a useful first stop for a research project to gain understanding about the topic, it is not widely considered a credible source. If you originally found useful information in Wikipedia, look at the reference list at the end of the article and see if you can verify the information in a more credible source that you can cite.

2. **Cite all sources.** In business research, just as in academic research, you are responsible for citing sources for all ideas and opinions that are not your own by giving credit to the original writers. In addition, you are responsible for citing facts that are not general knowledge. Source citations for statistics and other facts help your audience evaluate the accuracy of the information. Imagine, for example, that you want to report the unemployment rate in the United States. The credibility of that "fact" may differ depending on whether you got the information from a blog on the web or from the Bureau of Labor Statistics. Practices for citing sources differ depending on your field and documentation style your field prefers. For more information about citing sources, see Appendix B: Documentation and Reference Styles.

3. **Ensure that all interview and survey sources provide informed consent.**[22] When you interview or survey people—especially when the survey is not anonymous—let those people know how you plan to use the information and whether they may experience any negative consequences from the way you use the data. For example, imagine that you are interviewing residents of a town to identify opinions for and against building a new shopping mall. In conducting this research, you need to ensure that people know you will be quoting them in a report to the city council. They also need to know that the city council will use the results to help decide whether to provide a zoning variance for a shopping mall. Once your interview subjects have this information, you need to be sure that they consent to their responses being used this way.

4. **Report research accurately.** Be sure that you understand the intention of a source before reporting it. Do not take quotations out of context, report data in a misleading way, or make claims that your research cannot support. For example, if your research consisted of interviewing 10 customers about to enter a coffee shop, you cannot say "According to our interviews, consumers prefer coffee over tea." You have data from only 10 people. You do not have enough data to support the larger conclusion. In addition, your sample may be biased as you are interviewing people who are likely to be coffee drinkers. Similarly, if your data about economic growth came from a reputable source published in 2002, you cannot say, "According to the *International Economics Statistics Database*, Equatorial Guinea has the fastest-growing economy in the world." That was true in 2002, but is it true now? It would be more accurate and ethical to say, "In 2002, Equatorial Guinea had the fastest-growing economy in the world."

5. **Include all relevant information.** You may find it tempting to report only research that supports the position you want to argue. However, if you find information that contradicts your position, you have an ethical responsibility to address it in your report. If strong counterarguments exist, neglecting to address them will undermine the legitimacy of your work. For example, suppose you plan to argue that your company should not advertise through direct mail but instead use email advertising. You'd like to be able to show that direct mail is not environmentally friendly because it contributes significantly to the municipal solid waste stream. In researching, however, you find data from the U.S. Environmental Protection Agency showing that paper products, which include direct bulk mailing, are the third-most-recycled category of waste product and the most-recycled consumable product.[23] Instead of ignoring this fact and maintaining your original position, choose one of these other options:

   - **Concede the fact and explain why it does not undermine your position.** "Although direct mail advertising often ends up recycled, every bit of extra solid waste costs money for disposal and takes up valuable space in landfills."
   - **Eliminate this environmental argument** from your report and stress other arguments against direct mail advertising.
   - **Modify your position.** You may not expect to find information that convinces you to change your point of view, but this routinely happens when people conduct thorough research.

6. **Respect intellectual property and "fair use" of other people's material.** Under U.S. copyright law and the doctrine of fair use, you may include brief quotations from others' work in your reports and presentations. However, you cannot quote substantial portions of another work in your own, even if you cite that work, because you are benefitting from that person's intellectual property.[24] If you plan to draw heavily from someone else's text, it is safest to receive written permission from the copyright owner.

For ETHICS exercises, go to Exercises 28 and 29 on page 308.

believe you want to hear. Direct observation of actual behavior can give you much more accurate results.

When you observe, do not trust your memory. Carefully record important information about what you saw and heard as the observation proceeds, and take time immediately after you conclude the observation to make additional notes.

Follow these guidelines to get the most information from your observational research:

- **Decide what kinds of observations will be most helpful.** In other words, don't observe for the sake of observing. Ideally, observe people performing the actual activities with the actual products in the actual settings where they are normally used.
- **Plan time to set up and follow up.** You may need time beforehand to set up recording equipment, as well as time afterward to make notes or follow up with participants.
- **Write an observation plan.** The plan includes the day, time, and length of the observation, as well as questions about features or actions and other issues relevant to your research.
- **Summarize the results in writing after the observation.**

(SQ4) How can you use social media in your research?

Social media sources can extend your reach in gathering information. Consider the following possible ways that blogs, tweets, online videos, and slide-sharing sites can contribute to your research:

- They can help you find experts and other useful sources not published through books or articles.
- You can request information through surveys and question–answer sites.
- They give you a platform for conducting primary research by collecting **anecdotal evidence**— evidence from people's experiences—which may not be scientifically valid or representative but may still provide insight into your topic.

This section discusses strategies for taking advantage of social media in your research process. Remember that when you conduct research through social media, you are responsible for documenting your sources just as you are when using more traditional media.

anecdotal evidence Information you can get from a subjective report that may not be scientifically valid or representative but that may provide insight on your topic.

Search for experts

Many experts write and publish blogs on their topics of expertise. Reading those blogs is similar to interviewing experts. In addition, many companies sponsor blogs to promote discussions about their products or industry. To find relevant blogs, search for the name of your subject plus the word *blog*. Be sure to evaluate the blog for authorship, accuracy, and age. Many blogs provide biographical profiles outlining the authors' professional credentials and expertise. Because experts often post comments on other people's blogs—as well as their own—you may identify experts by reading through comments.

Post questions to your network and beyond

Because social media encourages two-way communication, it offers many opportunities to find experts, ask questions, and get quick responses. For example, if you have a LinkedIn account, you can type in a search term in the search box and see if any people in your network include that term in their profile. That may help you find a knowledgeable person who can answer your questions. You can also use the social media site Quora to post questions to people outside your network, and you can search Quora to see if others have posed questions and answers relevant to your research. A search for "learning management systems" on Quora revealed expert discussions about current trends in learning management systems, the top systems used by corporations, and gamification in LMS systems.

Posting a question on a social media site benefits both you and the person who answers. You get expert consulting for no cost, and the expert gets professional exposure. Questions and answers are archived on the site, and responses will benefit others who are looking for expert points of view.

New Hires @ Work

Ryan Croy
University of Tennessee
Content Writer @ Asurion

I write about consumer electronics, and I have to understand common problems with them to write about them. Examples of resources I find useful include owner's manuals, YouTube tutorials, and Amazon product reviews.

Photo courtesy of Ryan Croy

Social media also allows you to reach out to customers to get feedback about innovations or plans. This kind of informal research helps an organization gauge its effectiveness quickly and inexpensively. For example, the day after Christmas 2016, Brian Chesky, the CEO of Airbnb, asked his Twitter followers this question: "If @Airbnb could launch anything in 2017, what would it be?"[25] What followed was a day-long discussion between Chesky and Airbnb's loyal fans, with Chesky responding to every suggestion that people made, often asking them to elaborate. This informal research cost Airbnb nothing—and won the company dozens of new ideas to explore as well as goodwill with its customers.

Gather anecdotal evidence

Anecdotal evidence comes from subjective reports or stories that people tell. It is not scientific or verifiable evidence, but you may find accounts of other people's experiences useful in your research. In social media sources, *social reviews*, such as consumer-generated product reviews on sites such as Amazon, provide a wealth of anecdotal information about products you may be researching. In fact, research by The Nielsen Company shows that approximately 25 to 30 percent of social media users actively review products and services online.[26] You can also find anecdotal evidence on blogs, microblogs, and videos, all of which can be excellent sources of testimonials or complaints about a product.[27] One good way to locate this anecdotal evidence is to use the social search engines *socialmention.com* and *social-searcher.com*, which search multiple social media platforms for sources mentioning the topic you are researching. In addition to providing search results, these social search engines also provide analysis, such as the ratio of positive versus negative mentions and a list of keywords associated with your search topic.

 # How can you effectively organize the results of your research?

If your research is successful, you may be overwhelmed with sources by the time you finish. Use the following steps to ensure that your information will be easy to access as you begin to prepare your report or presentation.

Build your reference list as you research

As you collect sources, record all the information you need to prepare a reference list, such as authors' names, date of publication, the publication's name, the complete web address if online, volume and issue numbers, and all page numbers (not just the starting page). This information will save you time as you prepare your final report and presentation. It will also ensure that you can find the information again when you need it. If you are concerned that web sources may disappear, save them as PDF files or use a web clipping application such as Evernote or Clipix to save a copy.

Several *citation management programs* are available to organize citations and sources, such as EndNote, RefWorks, and EasyBib. Some versions of Microsoft Word will do this also. These programs prompt you for information and then format your references in any one of several citation styles, including American Psychological Association (APA) Style, Modern Language Association (MLA) style, and Chicago style, based on the *Chicago Manual of Style*. If you use the same sources for multiple research projects or courses, you can save the sources in a master list and reformat the references in any of the output formats.

The citation style you use will depend on the industry in which you work, the organization that is publishing your work, or your instructors' preferences. Both APA Style and Chicago style are widely used in business. Although businesses rarely use MLA style, it may be required by your instructor. **Figure 8.14** illustrates how a citation from the same source would be formatted in APA, Chicago, and MLA style. Appendix B: Documentation and Reference Styles includes additional information about documentation in APA and MLA styles.

FIGURE 8.14 Examples of Reference Citation Styles

APA STYLE (6TH ed.)	CHICAGO STYLE (16TH ed.)	MLA STYLE (8TH ed.)
In-text citation: . . . Moodle was used in a landmark case study analysis to demonstrate how course management systems can generate effective results (Romero, Ventura, & Garcia, 2008). This study effectively . . . **Reference page citation:** Romero, C., Ventura, S., & Garcia, E. (2008). Data mining in course management systems: Moodle case study and tutorial. *Computers & Education, 51*(1), 368–384.	**In-text citation:** . . . Moodle was used in a landmark case study analysis to demonstrate how course management systems can generate effective results (Romero, Ventura, and Garcia 2008, 368). This study effectively . . . **Reference page citation:** Romero, Cristobal, Sebastian Ventura, and Enrique Garcia. 2008. Data Mining in Course Management Systems: Moodle Case Study and Tutorial. *Computers & Education 51* (1): 368–384.	**In-text citation:** . . . Moodle was used in a landmark case study analysis to demonstrate how course management systems can generate effective results (Romero, Ventura, and Garcia 368). This study effectively . . . **Works Cited page citation:** Romero, Cristobal, Sebastian Ventura, and Enrique Garcia. "Data Mining in Course Management Systems: Moodle Case Study and Tutorial." *Computers & Education*, vol. 51, no. 1, 2008, pp. 368–384.

Organize documents and notes on your computer and "in the cloud"

As you research, you can organize your files on your computer, or you can take advantage of **cloud computing** to store your files remotely so that they are available through the web to share with collaborators and to use on all your devices, including computers, tablets, and smartphones.

To organize your research on your computer, use a logical filing system that helps you find and retrieve documents when you need them. Also be sure to back up your files so you don't lose valuable resources. The following guidelines will help you organize your information for easy reference:

- **Create identifiable filenames.** When you download a file from the web, such as a PDF, the filename may not adequately identify the file's contents. For example, if a file is labeled "DEC1417.pdf," you would have to open it to determine its contents. Rename the file so that you will be able to quickly identify it when you skim your file list later. You may decide to save the DEC1417.pdf file with the article's title, "Overview of Open Source Learning Management Systems," or by topic and publisher, "Open Source LMS–EDUCAUSE."

- **Group similar content for easy synthesis.** On your computer, create a folder for each research project. Within that folder, create subfolders that allow you to organize the information. You can organize folders by topic or by type of information (for example, survey results and software reviews) or by the research questions from your work plan.

To organize your research to share with others, consider using applications such as Google Drive, Dropbox, or Box. For more complex research projects, an application such as Mendeley allows you to create a personal digital library on your computer (see **Figure 8.15** on page 298). In that library, you can organize and annotate documents and create reference lists that you can import into Microsoft Word. The app also creates a web-based version of your library (see **Figure 8.16** on page 298) that is synchronized with the library on your computer and that supports file sharing with colleagues.

Cloud computing is highly convenient but can also pose security risks. Although reputable cloud services take measures to ensure that files are secure, if you are working with material or data that is sensitive or confidential, it might be safer to store them off the cloud, or only on a secure file-sharing service unique to your company. Whenever using cloud services, make sure you manage sharing permissions carefully and take advantage of built-in security measures like passwords and encryption. Your company might have cloud usage policies that you should adhere to.[28]

cloud computing Software applications that either run on the Internet and are accessed through the web or that allow you to store files remotely to access through the web.

FIGURE 8.15 Desktop
Version of Mendeley

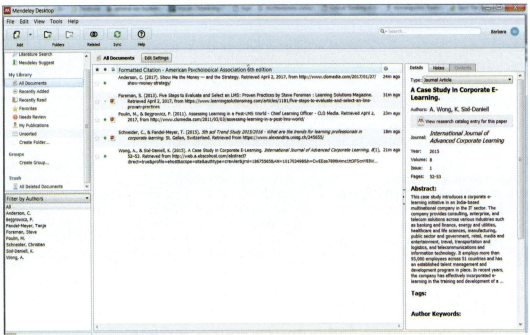

FIGURE 8.16 Web
Version of Mendeley

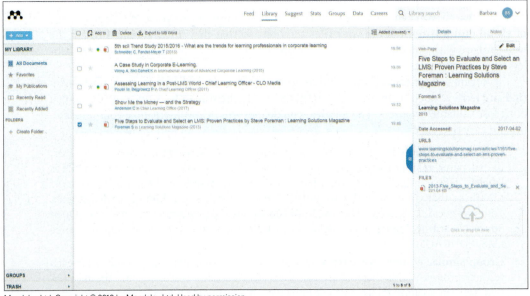

Organize your findings by research questions

In addition to organizing your documents throughout your research process, you also need to organize what you extract from the documents and the rest of your notes. Inexperienced researchers often make the mistake of organizing their research by the source of information. Although you might first record information in that way, you will find it more useful to *synthesize*, or combine, information from various sources as you work through the research process.

You can use an expanded version of the work plan outlined in Figure 8.4 on page 279 to organize your findings within the original research questions. You may need to expand the format of the table to fit your data. **Figure 8.17** provides an example of findings organized for the first LMS research question: "Would a learning management system (LMS) be an effective training tool for our company?" Note that the information in the figure is not organized by source. Instead, the information is integrated into the work plan by research activity. If you listed the information about A2Z Systems separately, you would find it difficult to compare it to the other options. By organizing the information by question, you will be able to make good comparisons more easily.

FIGURE 8.17 How to Add Findings to the Work Plan

RESEARCH QUESTIONS	RESEARCH ACTIVITIES	TARGET DATE	KEY FINDINGS	IMPLICATIONS/ CONCLUSIONS	RECOMMENDA-TIONS
1. Would an LMS be an effective training tool for our company?					

RESEARCH ACTIVITIES	TARGET DATE	KEY FINDINGS — LMS OPTIONS		
		A2Z SYSTEMS (A2Z.COM)	ECLIPSE SOFTWARE (ECLIPSE.COM)	TEACH2ME (TEACH2ME.COM)
Research training and education journals, books, and websites.	Weeks 1–2	• Supports multiple platforms • Online demo only; no onsite rep support	• Requires a single platform • Online demo and onsite rep support	• Supports multiple platforms • Online demo and onsite rep support
Compare options against company's training needs.	Week 2	• Customizable modules may provide flexible training; no online support provided • Supports both stand-alone and instructor-led training	• All modules are completely customizable; online support provided • All support included	• Customizable modules must be purchased separately • Online support billed separately
Survey or interview people in other companies.	Week 2	Agrulo Interview: • Initial learning curve was difficult; required extensive start-up training • Lack of online support frustrating • Phone support not enough • Bottom line: It's better than nothing	Millersby Interview: • Learning curve difficult, but manageable • Online support helpful • Bottom line: It's okay; we're still learning	Takata Interview: • Easy setup; user-friendly interface • No need yet for online support • Bottom line: We love it!

As you continue your research, you can use the same work plan to organize your conclusions and recommendations. Simply add extra columns to the right.

■ **In summary,** the process of doing research and organizing your findings begins during the analyzing phase of the ACE process and may continue until your document or project is completed. At any stage in the process, you may develop new questions that uncover new research needs. Your ability to research efficiently and effectively depends on your having a clear research plan—knowing what you want to learn and what sources and research activities will provide the information. Organizing your research materials and findings puts you in a good position to use your research to write proposals, reports, and presentations.

CONDUCTING RESEARCH @ WORK   HealthScape Advisors

HealthScape Advisors is a management consulting firm that serves clients in the healthcare industry. Like most other management consulting firms, HealthScape Advisors works with its clients to improve business performance, address business challenges, and anticipate changes in the business environment. Doing this work requires a great deal of research.

Managing Partner Arjun Aggarwal identifies three levels of research that successful consultants must master:

- **Answering simple questions.** The ability to find facts, data, or articles with a quick Google search is important.
- **Gathering deep knowledge.** The process of becoming a market expert requires continuous research: reading news clippings, magazine articles, and industry analysis to develop a deep but general understanding of the business, not specific to a particular client project.
- **Building on that deep knowledge to conduct specific client research.** A consultant's deep knowledge allows him or her to build a framework for conducting targeted research to address specific client issues.

Aggarwal suggests that young staff people may rely too much on that first level of research: jumping on the web and finding articles. He offers this advice to beginning consultants—or to anyone who wants to become a better and more efficient researcher in business:

- **Understand the purpose of the research.** Before assigning research, Aggarwal briefs the team on the purpose of the research, the types of outcomes that are required, and the framework he is using in his analysis. To conduct good research, it is critical to "understand what you are looking for and why."
- **Have a "short list" of relevant and trusted sources.** So much information is available that it is difficult to know where to begin. Aggarwal recommends developing a short list of relevant sources to begin the research and then branching from those sources. This helps ensure credible, accurate, and meaningful information.
- **Align the information with the original objective of the assignment.** As you find information, keep referring to the original research objective to ensure that the information is relevant.
- **Communicate early and often with your supervisor.** Do not wait until the end of the research process to communicate your findings. Early communication is important for two reasons: First, "sometimes we have a hypothesis, and the data shows something different. We need to be able to make corrections early." Second, "sometimes you find something that will suggest a shortcut in the research process." Your supervisor may help you take advantage of that.

Aggarwal adds a final note about the importance of research in business: "When industry is going through major changes, as the healthcare industry is, no one knows what success will look like in the new world. The only way to succeed and to be on top is to be up on your research."

Source: Based on an interview with Arjun Aggarwal.

Logo courtesy of Healthscape Advisors.

Researching to Answer Business Questions

This case scenario will help you review the chapter material by applying it to a specific situation.

Receiving a Research Assignment

Shuang Yu is a recent graduate of Milford University. She has started working in new business development at Affordable World Energy (AWE), a company that designs affordable products that generate electricity. The primary market for these products is countries with large rural populations that do not have access to electricity. As its next project, AWE is designing small-scale wind turbines to generate power for individual homes. The company needs to decide on the first market for this product and has narrowed the scope of its search to three countries that all have large populations without electricity: India, Kenya, and Panama. Shuang's assignment is to research which country has the best consumer base, the most suitable wind conditions, and the best manufacturing infrastructure to manufacture the wind turbines locally.

Question 1: Shuang will be presenting her findings to the company president and board of directors in a month. She needs to start structuring this research project immediately. If you were in Shuang's position, how would you proceed? Where would you look for information, what would you look for, and how would you organize this information?

Developing a Work Plan

As a first step in planning her research, Shuang develops a purpose statement:

> **Purpose:** To determine whether India, Kenya, or Panama is the best country in which to produce and sell small-scale wind turbines to provide power to rural homes.

She also begins to develop a set of research questions:

1. What criteria should I use to evaluate these countries? How should I weight the criteria?
2. Which country has the best market for small wind turbines?
3. What are the necessary wind conditions for wind turbines?
4. Which countries have the necessary wind conditions?
5. What government regulations may affect the production and sale of wind turbines?
6. How much can the rural population afford to spend on a wind turbine?

Question 2: Are there additional questions that Shuang should add to her work plan? For all the questions, what research activities would you plan to answer the questions?

Researching Online Sources

Shuang begins her research by trying to identify which country has the best market for small-scale wind turbines. She hopes to find this information on the web. But what should she search for?

- **Search 1:** For her first Google search, she uses the terms *"small wind turbine market."* This search yields some interesting results, including a market study by the American Wind Energy Association titled "2015 Distributed Wind Market Report."[29] Although the research report focuses primarily on the U.S. market, it does include a small section on global markets and, more important, a discussion of the types of regulations that prevent countries from adopting wind power. This helps answer one of her research questions.

- **Search 2:** Shuang then decides to try a second set of terms to approach the search from a different angle. She decides that one way to identify the biggest market is to identify what country has the largest population without electricity. So she uses *people "without electricity."* Much to her surprise, she finds a spreadsheet published by the International Energy Agency that lists the number of people (in millions) without electricity for countries around the world.[30] Shuang finds that Panama has fewer than half a million people without electricity. By contrast, Kenya has about 36 million, and India has about 244 million. By reading the source citations in an older report by the International Energy Agency,[31] Shuang also learns about several other agencies that study global energy needs and methods for financing energy development, including the Alliance for Rural Electrification, the International Finance Corporation, and the World Bank. She also identified a book to read: *The Hidden Energy Crisis: How Policies Are Failing the World's Poor* by Sanchez.

Question 3: Identify another research question that Shuang needs to answer and develop some alternative search terms to research this question using a general search engine, a deep web search engine, or an online article database. Which search terms offer the most useful results?

Conducting Primary Research

Shuang has already identified at least one primary source she needs for research: her boss, the head of marketing at Affordable World Energy. As part of her research, Shuang needs to understand what criteria she should be using to evaluate the market opportunity in the three selected countries and how she should rank those criteria. Is it more important that the market is big? Or is it more important that the country has an industry that can manufacture the wind turbines? Her boss will know what criteria the company believes is most important.

She wonders, though, if she should be talking with anyone else or conducting any surveys. She has only a few weeks left to complete her research.

Question 4: Is there any information that Shuang could get more easily by interview than by researching secondary sources? If so, what is this information, and who would you recommend that she contact?

Organizing Research Results

Because Shuang's research project is such a major undertaking, she needs to develop a systematic plan to keep track of her sources and her results. Here is what she does:

1. She starts a Word file titled "Reference list," and she includes an entry for each item she reads. She formats these according to APA Style and keeps the list in alphabetical order. She keeps a separate list of everyone she talks to, with the person's name, title, contact information, and date of interview.
2. She either prints or downloads a PDF of her web-based sources. This ensures that the material will remain available to her even if the website changes. She saves the files in folders organized by research question.
3. She creates a Word file for each of her research questions and types notes from her research right in those files, being sure to provide citations to all her sources.

Question 5: Do you have any additional tips and tricks that you use to organize research results? If so, explain how they would be useful for this project.

End of Chapter

Study Questions in Review

SQ1 How do you determine what information you need? *(pages 274–280)*

- **Analyze the research question and topic** to understand the information you need to gather. You may find it useful to divide your research question into several subquestions. In addition, conduct background research to understand your topic's history, context and structure, and categories.
- **Identify audience concerns and needs** by determining what the primary and secondary audiences already know and need to know.
- **Establish the scope of the research** (how broad or specific your focus will be) by considering the needs of the project and the time available to do the work.
- **Define research activities** to gather information from primary, secondary, or tertiary sources.
- **Develop a work plan** that organizes your research process and ensures that you gather information to answer all your research questions.

SQ2 How do you conduct research in print and online sources? *(pages 280–286)*

- **Gather relevant print and electronic files,** and organize them for easy reference.
- **Use web search engines strategically** by using quotation marks, wildcards, and alternative wordings. You can also search for specific file types.
- **Use deep web portals** to find high-quality knowledge designed for professionals. These portals provide access to professional literature that is often not indexed by major search engines.
- **Use an online index or database to find articles and business data** such as newspapers, magazines, trade journals, and academic journals. Peer-reviewed articles have more credibility than nonvalidated web articles.
- **Use a library or bookseller to find relevant books.** Much excellent information is published only in books. However, in some fields, books can quickly become outdated.
- **Follow leads in good sources** to identify additional good sources.
- **Evaluate your sources for credibility** using the three As: authorship, accuracy, and age.

SQ3 How do you conduct primary research? *(pages 286–295)*

- **Conduct survey research to gather quantifiable information about opinions and attitudes** that can be reported as counts, percentages, ranges, means, medians,

and modes. Before conducting survey research, choose which people to survey by identifying the population and determining what kind of sample you will use (convenience, targeted, or random). Write effective survey questions, and decide on a survey medium. Following the survey, analyze, interpret, and evaluate the data.
- **Conduct interview research to gather qualitative information.** Effective researchers know how to plan the interview, what to do during the interview, and how to evaluate the interview results.
- **Conduct observational research to understand how people act.** A person's actions are often more revealing than his or her words.

SQ4 How can you use social media in your research? *(pages 295–296)*

- **Search for experts.** Experts often write blogs as well as published books and articles. In addition, companies often sponsor blogs about their products and their industries.
- **Post questions to your network and beyond.** Social media platforms are perfect for posting research questions to people in your network as well as people outside your network, through sites such as Quora. They also allow you to pose questions to customers who are following your social media accounts.
- **Gather anecdotal evidence.** Although anecdotal evidence may not be scientific, it can be useful in making business decisions. You can find anecdotal evidence in blogs, on Facebook, and in customer-generated product reviews.

SQ5 How can you effectively organize the results of your research? *(pages 296–299)*

- **Build your reference list as you research** to save time as you prepare your final report and presentation and to ensure you can find the information again.
- **Organize documents and notes on your computer and "in the cloud."** On your computer, create identifiable filenames and a useful filing system. Also organize your files online in the cloud with programs such as Dropbox or Mendeley so that you can access your files from any computer and also share them with collaborators.
- **Organize your findings by research questions.** This will help you synthesize the material when it is time to compose.

Visual Summary

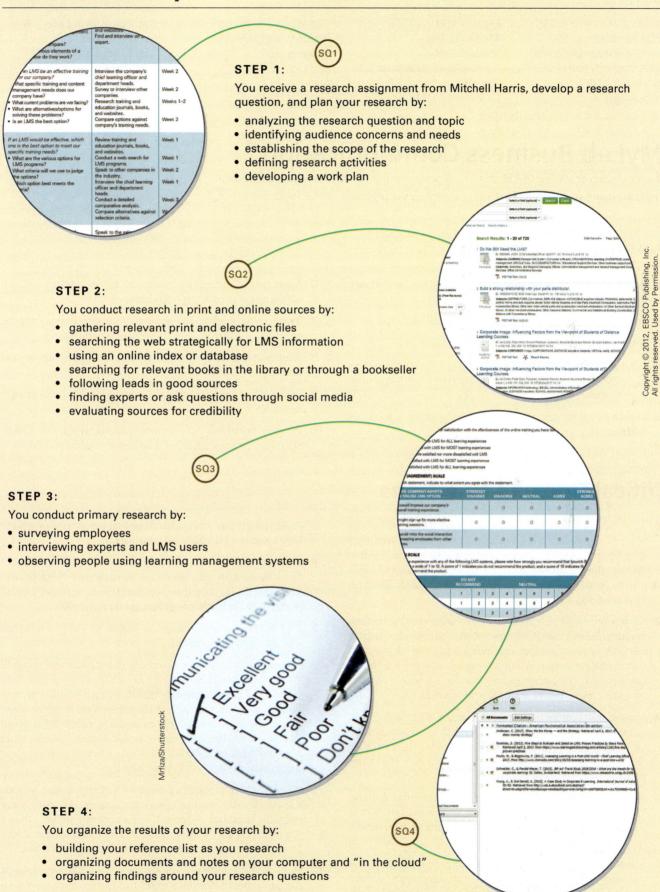

SQ1

STEP 1:

You receive a research assignment from Mitchell Harris, develop a research question, and plan your research by:

- analyzing the research question and topic
- identifying audience concerns and needs
- establishing the scope of the research
- defining research activities
- developing a work plan

SQ2

STEP 2:

You conduct research in print and online sources by:

- gathering relevant print and electronic files
- searching the web strategically for LMS information
- using an online index or database
- searching for relevant books in the library or through a bookseller
- following leads in good sources
- finding experts or ask questions through social media
- evaluating sources for credibility

SQ3

STEP 3:

You conduct primary research by:

- surveying employees
- interviewing experts and LMS users
- observing people using learning management systems

Mfriza/Shutterstock

SQ4

STEP 4:

You organize the results of your research by:

- building your reference list as you research
- organizing documents and notes on your computer and "in the cloud"
- organizing findings around your research questions

CHAPTER 8

Key Terms

Anecdotal evidence p. 295	Mean p. 289	Quantitative research p. 278	Secondary sources p. 278
Cloud computing p. 297	Median p. 289	Random sample p. 288	Survey p. 286
Convenience sample p. 288	Mode p. 289	Range p. 289	Survey population p. 288
Desktop search tool p. 280	Observational research p. 286	Sample p. 288	Targeted sample p. 288
Interview p. 286	Primary sources p. 277	Scope p. 277	Tertiary sources p. 278
Limitations p. 277	Qualitative research p. 278		

MyLab Business Communication

If your instructor is using MyLab Business Communication, go to **www.pearson.com/mylab/business-communication** to complete the problems marked with this icon ⭐.

Review Questions

1 What is the difference between primary, secondary, and tertiary sources? Give an example of each.

2 What are the key elements of a research work plan?

3 What is a desktop search tool and how can it help you?

4 What is the effect of using quotation marks around search terms in web or database searches? What happens if you do not use quotation marks?

5 Explain the three criteria for evaluating whether a source is credible.

6 Name two advantages of conducting survey research and two advantages of conducting interview research.

7 Range, mean, median, and mode are four ways of reporting the quantitative data from a survey. Explain how they differ.

8 Identify at least two ways to find experts you can interview on a topic.

⭐ 9 What is anecdotal evidence and how may it be useful in your research?

10 What are two benefits of organizing and storing research materials online, in the cloud, rather than just on your computer?

Critical Thinking Questions

⭐ 1 As a researcher, how will you benefit from taking the time to analyze the research problem, analyze the audience, determine the purpose, establish the scope, and develop a work plan before finding information? Wouldn't it be easier to find a lot of information about a topic and then organize the content based on what you find?

⭐ 2 Some people argue that libraries are becoming obsolete because so much research material is now available on the web. Compare the kinds of resources that are freely available on the web versus the kinds of resources that you can access only via a library. Based on that comparison, what value do you believe libraries offer? As a researcher, what would you use a library for?

3 Assume that you are interested in getting a master's degree in accounting in your state or a nearby state. Design a search string for Google that will help you identify available programs. How would using quotation marks and minus signs help you in this research?

4 An Amazon.com book search reveals a book titled *Learning Management Systems Market Trends* dated September 2001. Would you include this book in your research on learning management systems? Why or why not?

5 Assume that you have distributed a survey to determine what frustrates employees most about the company's current approach to training, and you received only 25 responses from a population of 200 employees. How would you proceed? How

could you use the information from your survey in your report? How could you get additional information?

6 Some researchers are concerned that offering survey respondents an incentive may invalidate the responses. What do you imagine is the basis for their concern? Do you agree with them? **[Related to the Technology feature on page 290]**

⭐ 7 If an interviewee's responses can lead to meaningful tangents, why is an interview guide useful?

8 Assume that you work for a company that manufactures luggage. The company would like to design a new line of luggage that meets the needs of business travelers who fly frequently. You have been assigned to conduct research to identify business travelers' needs. Where could you conduct observational research? What would you be able to learn from observational research that you could not learn from survey research or interviews? Is there any way social media can help you in your research?

9 When you cite a published book or article you find in your research, it's important to include the date the information was originally published. When you cite a company website, should you try to find out the original date that the information was published or is the current date more useful? Explain your answer.

10 HealthScape Advisor's Arjun Aggarwal (page 300) recommends that professionals develop a "short list" of trusted sources where you can go to begin your research. What are some strategies you can use to develop that list?

Key Concept Exercises

 How do you determine what information you need? *(pages 274–280)*

1 Analyze the research question and topic

a. Identify a problem at your school—for example, a problem concerning parking, meal plans, class registration, or credit for community service—and imagine that you are beginning a research project to identify a solution to the problem. Develop a set of research questions to guide your research.

b. What background research will help you understand your topic? Use the table in Figure 8.2 on page 276 to list a set of relevant background research questions.

2 Identify audience concerns and needs

In Exercise 1, you identified a campus problem and a set of research questions. Assume you plan to conduct the research and propose a solution to the appropriate audience(s) on your campus. Answer the following questions related to this problem:

a. Who is the primary audience?

b. Who is the secondary audience?

c. Who else may be affected by this problem or decision?

d. What does the audience already know? What do they need to know?

e. What questions will your audience expect you to answer when you present the research?

f. What sources will your audience expect you to consult?

3 Establish the scope of the research

Use the problem identified in Exercise 1 and the audience analysis outlined in Exercise 2 to determine a purpose statement (or statements) and research questions. Refer to the examples in Figure 8.1 and Figure 8.2 on pages 275 and 276.

4 Define research activities

Use the problem identified in Exercise 1, the audience analysis outlined in Exercise 2, and the scope determined in Exercise 3 to define at least two research activities for each research question. Create a table similar to that in Figure 8.3 on page 278.

5 Develop a work plan

How would you sequence the research activities identified in Exercise 4? Create a work plan like that in Figure 8.4 on page 279 and justify the order of events.

 How do you conduct research in print and online sources? *(pages 280–286)*

6 Gather relevant print and electronic files

Use your computer's file search feature to search for all files on your computer containing a key phrase such as the name of your school, the name of your city, or another phrase you believe you'd find on your computer. Try searching for the phrase within quotation marks and without quotation marks. Is there a difference in the files you find?

7 Use web search engines strategically

Conduct a Google search for PDF documents using the search string *"campus parking problem" filetype:pdf*. Conduct a second search, this time for PowerPoint documents, using the search string *"campus parking problem" filetype:ppt*. From each of these searches, identify at least one document you might use in researching a proposal to improve parking on your campus. (If you use a different search engine, use the advanced search feature to narrow your search to .pdf or .ppt files.)

8 Use deep web portals

Use the same keywords to search a topic of your choice using two different online search engines, including one deep web search engine such as Biznar or Science.gov. Compare the first page of each list of results. Do differences exist between the two lists? Summarize the differences and similarities between the two lists and explain why the results were not identical.

9 Use an online index or database to find articles and business data

a. Use an online database available through your school's library to find at least three articles or books related to the research topic you chose in Exercise 8 or a different topic of your choice. Of the three sources, find at least one article from a magazine or trade journal, and find at least one article from an academic journal. Compare the information in the three sources. How does the information differ? How is it similar? If you found a book also, compare the information in the articles to that in the book. What are some key differences?

b. Use the online index for your school newspaper, a local newspaper (for example, *St. Louis Post Dispatch, Chicago Tribune, Los Angeles Times, The Boston Globe*), or a national newspaper (*The New York Times, The Wall Street Journal*) to search for at least one newspaper article related to the topic you chose in Exercise 8. Identify all the search terms you tried. If your search was successful, summarize the information you found in the article. If your search was unsuccessful, explain why you believe you could find no newspaper articles on your topic.

c. Use two online business research tools, such as Yahoo! Finance, Hoover's, or Standard & Poor's, to search for financial data on a single company that interests you. Compare the results from the two searches. Does one provide more information than the other? Is one easier to use or read than the other? Which tool would you choose to use the next time you need to research financial data about a company? Be prepared to discuss your answer in class.

10 Use a library or bookseller to find relevant books

You would like to propose that your university adopt or expand its service learning opportunities. You plan a research project to propose a new service learning model. One of your research questions is this: "How have other colleges and universities implemented service learning?" Using your college or community library's online catalog, find two books that you think would be relevant. Then complete the following steps:

a. Read through all the information in the online catalog entry. Identify any information that helps you decide whether this book will be useful to your research.

b. Go to the Amazon.com website and search for the books you found in the library. If Amazon has listings for the books, read through the product descriptions and reviews to learn more about the books.

c. Using the information you found in your library catalog and on Amazon, explain whether each book would be helpful to your research and, if it would be helpful, how. Be sure to provide a reference list using the documentation style that your instructor prefers.

d. Assume that you would like to expand your search for information about service learning to identify good books on the subject that your library does not own. Go to Amazon's website and search for "service learning" in the books department. Identify any books that you believe would be useful but are not in your library. Be sure to provide a reference list using the documentation style that your instructor prefers.

11   Follow leads in good sources

a. Assume that in your research on learning management systems, you found the following reference in one of the articles you read: Perry, B. (2009). Customized content at your fingertips. *T+D, 63*(6), 29–31. How would you go about finding that source?

b. Assume that in your research on learning management systems, you read a white paper by the consulting company Element K, titled *Learning Management Systems in the Work Environment*. This document cites a report by the Hudson Institute stating that "By 2020, 60 percent of jobs will require skills that only 20 percent of the workforce now possesses." Unfortunately, the white paper does not provide complete documentation for the Hudson Institute report. How would you go about finding that report?

12   Evaluate your sources for credibility

a. Find one or both of the sources identified in Exercise 11 and evaluate it for credibility based on the three *A*s: authorship, accuracy, and age. Would you use this source in your research?

b. Assume that you have just started a new job. Before you get your first paycheck, you would like to research how to minimize the amount of income tax you will have to pay. Conduct a web search for sources relating to minimizing or decreasing income taxes. Find at least one source that you believe is credible based on the three *A*s. Find at least one source that you believe is not credible based on the same criteria. Write a brief comparison of the two sources, explaining which you would use and why.

c. Conduct a web search to find at least one blog on taxes and economics and write a brief explanation of whether you consider this source to be credible.

(SQ3)   How do you conduct primary research?
(pages 286–295)

13   Conduct survey research to gather quantifiable information about opinions and attitudes [Related to the Technology feature on page 290]

a. You and a few classmates would like to launch your own entrepreneurial business. You want to provide a product or service that will meet a need in your community. As part of your initial research, you would like to conduct a survey to get ideas about products or services people in the community need. Write five survey questions that you believe will give you useful information. Be prepared to explain why you think these are good questions. Also, select what you believe to be the best medium for this survey. Be prepared to explain why you think this is the best medium. If you select an online medium, pick one survey platform and explain why you chose it.

b. How would you select a sample of the population for your survey in Exercise 13a? Would you choose a convenience, targeted, or random sample? Explain why.

c. Calculate the mean, median, and mode for the following data and report your answers on a table adapted from the one in Figure 8.11 on page 291. Below your table, write a brief summary that highlights the differences among the three results.

1. Have you used a learning management system for training purposes in any of your prior work experiences?

Yes = 25 responses

No = 32 responses

2. If yes, how would you rate the use of a learning management system (LMS) compared to traditional face-to-face training?

Rating	Meaning	Number of Responses
5	More satisfied with LMS for all learning experiences	8
4	More satisfied with LMS for most learning experiences	6
3	Neither more nor less satisfied with LMS	9
2	Less satisfied with LMS for most learning experiences	1
1	Less satisfied with LMS for all learning experiences	1

14   Conduct interview research to gather qualitative information

As part of your research for launching an entrepreneurial business (see Exercise 13a), you would like to interview successful small business owners in your community to get their advice about how to be successful and avoid mistakes. Identify at least one person to interview and write an interview guide you can use.

15   Conduct observational research to understand how people act

A large consumer products company is interested in understanding how consumers make choices about which breakfast cereal to buy. In addition to surveying and interviewing consumers, the company would like to observe people's purchasing behavior. Plan an observation session in a local supermarket. Assume that you will be standing near the cereal aisle for approximately 30 minutes, watching people make cereal decisions. What specific types of behavior will you be looking for, and why do you think that information will be useful? (For example, you might gather information about how many different cereal boxes a consumer looks at before selecting one.)

(SQ4)   How can you use social media in your research? *(pages 295–296)*

16   Search for experts

Refer to Exercise 10. Assume that you would like to propose that your university adopt or expand its service learning opportunities. You want to identify some experts on service learning to interview. Conduct a web search for blogs about service learning. Start by using the term *service learning blog*. To find additional resources, search for *service learning* at www.blogsearchengine.org or www.searchblogspot.com. Read at least three of the blog entries that appear in the search results. Write a brief message to your instructor evaluating the three blog entries using the three *A*s approach.

17 Post questions to your network and beyond

Referring to Exercises 10 and 16, assume that for your proposal on service learning, you would like to identify people in your network who have had experience with service learning or who know others with experience. What approach would you take to identify these individuals? Be prepared to discuss your plan in class.

18 Gather anecdotal evidence

Referring to Exercises 10, 16, and 17, assume that for your proposal on service learning, you would like to include evidence of students' positive experience with service learning. You'd like to use social media to gather this information. Experiment with approaches to finding anecdotes and stories about service learning on the web. Can you find stories in blogs, on Facebook, or in YouTube videos? Be prepared to present in class at least two items of anecdotal evidence you find in your search.

 How can you effectively organize the results of your research? *(pages 296–299)*

19 Build your reference list as you research

a. In the case scenario on page 301, Shuang found a number of sources that she will cite in her research to identify an initial market for Affordable World Energy's small-scale wind turbines. Build a reference list for these sources, using the documentation style that your instructor prefers. You can find information for building reference lists in Appendix B: Documentation and Reference Styles.

b. Assume that Shuang also conducted telephone interviews with two or three experts whom she will cite in her paper. What is the correct method for documenting these sources in the documentation style you are using (APA, MLA, or Chicago)?

20 Organize documents and notes on your computer and "in the cloud"

You are an assistant to Madelyn Dupré, the director of training at a large company. She has been asked to make an hour-long presentation to new account representatives about business etiquette issues in the four countries where your company does most of its international business: Brazil, Russia, China, and India. Madelyn asks you to help find information by gathering relevant sources. Use the search tools outlined in the chapter to find at least 10 electronic sources. Ensure the files include complete citation information, save the sources with filenames that are easily identifiable, and group them in a logical manner on a flash drive or CD to submit to your instructor. Alternatively, if your instructor requests, upload copies of the sources to an online tool such as Box, Dropbox, or Mendeley, and share the files with your instructor.

21 Organize your findings by research questions

Assume that you are researching how to minimize your income tax, as described in Exercise 12b. Brainstorm some research questions or categories you can use to organize your findings. For example, one category might be findings relating to tax credits. What other categories may be useful to your research?

Writing Exercises

22 Finding advertising information

Your neighbor, Mrs. James, recently retired after 30 years as an elementary school teacher and wants to open a knitting shop in your community. She's been finding information about available storefronts, small business loan opportunities, and suppliers, but doesn't know where to begin to advertise her business. Yesterday, she asked if you could help her gather some information about advertising opportunities and costs. Find local information about how to use the following advertising outlets, including costs for small ads:

a. Radio

b. Newspaper

c. Direct mail

d. Coupons

Write a one-page summary of your findings that you will share with Mrs. James. Be sure to include necessary citations and a reference list so that Mrs. James can follow up on your research.

23 Finding information to address sales issues

You work part time at a local bookstore, The Book Nook, which has suffered declining sales over the past six months. Because no new bookstores or mega discount stores have opened recently to draw away customers, the owner, Inez Higgins, assumes more people are buying their books online rather than in her store. However, that's just a guess. She has asked you to help her find useful information on ways to increase in-store book sales. Determine what kinds of books, changes in hours, added services, and other factors might increase sales.

a. Using the search term "increasing bookstore sales," conduct a web search and identify at least five sources you recommend Ms. Higgins read.

b. Using the search term "book buying behavior," conduct a web search and identify at least two additional sources.

c. Experiment with different strings of search terms, conduct a web search, and identify at least two additional sources.

d. Identify at least two primary research activities you recommend that Ms. Higgins do.

Write a message to Ms. Higgins listing the research sources and primary research activities you recommend she pursue. For each research source, provide the name, the URL, and a brief sentence describing why the source will be valuable. Give her advice for finding additional sources.

24 Finding information to make a persuasive appeal

You are interning in the city commissioners' office this semester. The city council has developed a plan for a new bypass around the city limits to decrease the flow of traffic on local streets, especially during morning and evening rush hours. However, the bypass is dependent on the passing of a new tax. Your manager asks you to find information that would help "sell" the bypass idea (and therefore the tax) to the electorate. Where would you find the information you need to persuade people in your community? Brainstorm sources of information for your city and write a one-page summary of your ideas for collecting information that you will submit to the city commissioners.

25 Finding information about corporate policies

You are interning this semester for McConnell Consulting, a newly established consulting company in your area. The company's CEO has been so busy managing the start-up of the organization and developing a client network that he has not had time to create personnel policies. Mr. McConnell has asked you to find information about the kind of content to include, paying close attention to harassment policies that protect both employees and clients. Using the web, online databases, and a library book catalog, find at least five credible sources that relate to creating personnel policies, and outline your sources with citations in a one-page report to Mr. McConnell.

26 Finding information about building modifications

You are the assistant manager for a large art gallery in a metropolitan area. The gallery has grown significantly in the last few years and has finally outgrown the building it has rented for nearly 25 years. Recognizing your need for additional space, a generous benefactor recently donated a large historical building downtown. The location is excellent and the building has a lot of open spaces for showings and exhibits, as well as storage areas and office space. However, it is not handicap accessible. Because the building is listed in the city's historical register, you're not sure if you can make noticeable renovations to the exterior, such as a wheelchair ramp at the entrance. Determine where you could find information about historical renovations, especially handicap-access renovations. Outline your sources with citations in a one-page report.

27 Recommending a citation management software program

A friend asks you to recommend a citation management software program that stores and formats references. Compare the features of two programs and summarize your findings in a persuasive message to your friend, recommending one program.

28 Evaluating conflicting information [Related to the Ethics feature on page 294]

Assume that, during your search for information about learning management systems, you find a lot of support for Teach2Me software. Although only five of your employees indicated prior experience with this product, all of their responses were very positive. The cost of the product, including initial start-up costs and ongoing maintenance and technical support, is less than your current travel budget for training. Your interviews with other companies who use Teach2Me have been positive. The online demo you went through impressed you more than the other two options. Therefore, you decide that in your report to your supervisor, you will recommend that your company choose Teach2Me as its LMS.

However, as you review the information you gathered, you find a product review in a trade journal that suggests Teach2Me is not as robust as either A2Z Systems or Eclipse Software. The review indicates that Teach2Me does not offer as many features, the interface is more complicated to learn, and the tech support, though affordable, often requires long wait times.

Because this article is the only negative information you can find about Teach2Me, you consider not including it in your report to your supervisor. You are concerned that because the information does not support your recommendation, your supervisor will question your

decision. However, you know that would not be ethical. Write a message to your instructor explaining how you would include the information while supporting your recommendation for Teach2Me.

29 Making an ethical choice [Related to the Ethics feature on page 294]

Suppose you are searching for secondary information to support a paper for your economics class. You find an article in a trade journal that nearly matches your assignment requirements. The headings are similar to the outline you have prepared for your paper, and you have found and evaluated many of the cited sources listed at the end of the article. Because your economics professor has listed this trade journal (although not this article) as a resource on the class website, you are concerned that she may assume you plagiarized the article. Even if you do not use any of the same wording as the article, the similarities to the outline of your paper may be interpreted as copying the author's content. How do you proceed?

a. Do you ignore the source, hoping not to draw your professor's attention to the article in case she is not familiar with it? If your wording is different enough from the article, you assume you can claim you never read the article.

b. Do you write the paper as you planned and simply cite the source?

c. Do you try to explain the problem to your professor and ask for guidance? If so, how can you document that you did not read the article prior to developing your outline?

d. Is there another step you could take?

Write a message to your instructor explaining what you would do, and outline the specific pros, cons, and ethical issues related to your decision.

30 Finding secondary information sources [Related to the Culture feature on page 283]

Your consulting company provides public relations services to a wide variety of manufacturing companies. Your headquarters are in Palo Alto, California, but branch offices are located throughout the country. Your CEO is considering opening a new office in Guangdong Province, China, where many U.S.-based firms have outsourced their manufacturing contracts. Your manager asks you to provide information about the logistics of opening a branch in the province. He also wants to know how doing business in China may differ from doing business in the United States. Where would you find this information?

Outline a purpose statement and research questions. Then determine where you could find sources of secondary information. Create a work plan similar to the ones presented in the chapter that outlines your sources. List the possible sources for each research activity using the documentation style requested by your instructor. You do not need to summarize the findings of the sources.

Collaboration Exercises

31 Conducting team-based research [Related to the Collaboration Feature on page 280]

Assume that your team has been asked by your school's admissions office to evaluate the accessibility of your campus for prospective students who use wheelchairs. They are especially interested in better serving off-campus students who use transport vans to commute to campus and powered chairs to navigate campus during the school day. As a team, conduct develop a work plan and conduct primary and secondary research to evaluate both obstacles and resources:

a. Conduct a literature search to find relevant background information about issues facing higher education students with physical disabilities.

b. List the campus offices that provide resources for students with disabilities, and interview a contact person in each office to learn what would be most important to a student with a disability when considering your school.

c. Find out which office on campus is responsible for ensuring that university buildings comply with local, state, and federal laws concerning accessibility.

d. Investigate resources for wheelchair users provided by the city or town where your school is located, including public transportation.

e. Identify the most likely parking lots and paths between buildings that these students would use. Photograph obstacles that would impede a wheelchair and organize them by type and severity (e.g., potholes, damaged sidewalks, construction sites, curbs, and other barriers, etc.).

f. Plot the obstacles on a campus map to give a geographic overview of the problems facing students in wheelchairs.

Based on your research, write a report addressed to the admissions office highlighting information they may wish to provide to prospective students with disabilities and their families.

32 Finding and comparing information

A manager at your company asks your team to find information about local car dealerships that lease corporate vehicles. Use one or two search engines to assign a different dealer to each member of your team. Have the team members find information about their assigned dealer from the dealers' websites as well as external reviews by third parties. Each team member is to create a one-page document identifying the main features of his or her assigned dealer and summarizing the reviews, which should be appropriately cited.

Share your individual documents during a team meeting—either in person or electronically. Analyze the similarities and differences among the dealer options. Determine which dealer provides the most flexible leasing options and/or which one has the best reviews. Write a one-page report to your instructor identifying all the dealers considered and supporting your team's recommendation of a specific dealer. Attach the individual reports as documentation.

33 Writing survey questions/comparing analyses

Your school would like to assess students' perspectives of its current course management system. Your instructor has assigned your business communication class to survey students about their likes and dislikes, as well as recommend possible changes to the system. In small teams, create a survey questionnaire that includes a variety of question types, including at least one qualitative (open-ended) question. Before creating a final draft and collecting data, test your survey with other members of your class to ensure the questions are worded effectively.

Each member of your team should collect at least 10 survey responses from students around campus. Be sure not to survey students enrolled in your business communication class or students who have answered a similar questionnaire from other business communication students. Have each team member analyze the data he or she received and report the range, median, mean, and mode for quantitative responses. Summarize the qualitative responses, indicating any commonalities among responses.

In a team meeting, compare your individual findings. Discuss how the qualitative responses were analyzed. Then combine the data from all team members and summarize your findings in a report to your school administration.

Social Media Exercises

34 The role of social media in research

Many researchers are finding blog posts and tweets to be effective tools for both gathering information and sharing their research with a broader audience. Conduct your own research to learn what experts are saying about the role of social media in research and, depending on your instructors' preferences, prepare a two-page report or a three-minute presentation about your findings.

Speaking Exercises

35 Presenting information

Conduct research to prepare for a three- to five-minute presentation on one of the following topics. Prepare a visual aid to support your presentation. The visual should cite your source(s) using a complete reference citation. (See Appendix B: Documentation and Reference Styles for examples.)

a. Find two websites that provide information about a topic of your choice. One website should be a credible site based on the three As—authorship, accuracy, and age. The second website's credibility should be questionable based on the same criteria. Present the two sources to the class, and identify how you used the three As to assess their credibility. Explain why the questionable source lacks credibility.

b. Create a five-question survey on a topic of your choice. Use a variety of question types. Create one version of the survey that includes weak or vague wording that could possibly be misinterpreted. Create a second version of the survey that ensures measurable responses and elicits the information needed. Present the two versions of the survey to the class, explaining why the second set of questions will achieve better results.

c. Identify a specific research question you would like to answer. Search for sources using a general search engine, a deep web search engine, and an online database. Prepare a brief presentation comparing the results using the three different search tools. Identify which source gave you the most valuable results for your research, and explain why.

d. Assume that you work for Affordable World Energy (see the Case Scenario on page 301), and your managers have decided that India is a good market for the company's new wind turbine. Now, they are interested in understanding some of the cultural elements that may affect doing business in India. The managers ask you to do some research and prepare a five-minute presentation. Research Indian culture, using some of the sources identified in the Culture feature on page 283—or other sources that you find. Prepare a five-minute presentation that highlights your most important findings. **[Related to the Culture feature on page 283]**

e. Wikipedia is a convenient source for research. However, many people argue it is not a credible source and should not be cited in high-quality research reports. Find and read at least two articles in the academic or popular press about Wikipedia, and develop a five-minute presentation supporting an opinion about whether a researcher should or should not avoid citing Wikipedia. Be sure to cite your sources in your presentation. For advice about how to cite sources in a presentation, see Appendix B: Documentation and Reference Styles.

f. Refer to Exercise 31. Prepare a five-minute presentation identifying existing obstacles on campus for students in wheelchairs, using the photographs you took as part of your primary research. Explain the type of obstacle illustrated by each example and assess its seriousness.

Grammar Exercises

36 Commas: Clauses and phrases (see Appendix C: Grammar, Punctuation, Mechanics, and Conventions—Section 2.2)

Type the following paragraph, correcting the 10 errors in the use of commas with independent clauses, dependent clauses, and phrases (see Section 2.2.1). Underline all of your corrections.

Although most final job interviews are face to face telephone interviews have become common for screening interviews. Employers find that phone interviews are not only economical but they are also an effective way to determine which candidates merit a closer look. While you are on the job market a potential employer or networking contact might call, and ask, "Do you have a few minutes to talk?" Being interviewed over the phone isn't easy so you need to be prepared. What initially seems like an informal conversation about a job might actually be the first round of screening, or the first test of your communication skills. After the initial introductions and pleasantries let the caller take the lead, and guide the conversation. When you answer questions keep your responses short and to the point. The caller will ask follow-up questions if necessary, and will bring the interview to a close.

37 Commas: Coordinates, cumulatives, and series (see Appendix C: Grammar, Punctuation, Mechanics, and Conventions—Section 2.2)

Type the following paragraph, correcting the 10 errors in the use of commas with coordinate and cumulative adjectives and with serial words, phrases, and clauses. Each missing or unnecessary comma counts as one error (see Sections 2.2.2 and 2.2.3). Underline all of your corrections.

After you have sent out résumés and applied for jobs, be ready willing and able to handle a telephone interview. Keep your resume a pad and pen and a bottle of water near the phone. You will need your résumé for reference the pad and pen to take notes and the water in case your throat gets dry. Is your cell phone, service, provider reliable, or do you have to worry about dropped calls? If so, consider using a landline. Send roommates, friends, spouses, children and pets from the room when a potential employer calls. You want to be completely calmly focused and undistracted during a telephone interview.

38 Commas: Restrictive elements (see Appendix C: Grammar, Punctuation, Mechanics, and Conventions—Section 2.2)

Type the following paragraph, correcting the 13 errors in the use of commas with restrictive, nonrestrictive, or parenthetical words, phrases, or clauses. Each missing or unnecessary comma counts as one error. There are also two mistakes in the use of *that*, *which*, or *who* (see Sections 2.2.2 and 2.2.3). Underline all of your corrections.

Anyone, who has been through an employment interview, knows it is nerve-wracking. A telephone interview which provides none of the nonverbal cues available in a face-to-face situation can be even trickier. The interviewer's word choice, tone of voice, and level of enthusiasm may therefore be important indicators. The interviewee the person that is being interviewed must listen carefully. The advice, "sit up and pay attention," certainly applies in this situation. Companies, who use telephone interviews for employment screening, have heard it all everything from bad grammar to burping.

MyLab Business Communication

Go to **www.pearson.com/mylab/business-communication** for Auto-graded writing questions as well as the following Assisted-graded writing questions:

1. Wikipedia can be a useful tool in your research. Why do researchers not consider Wikipedia a credible source for information to cite? What should you do if you find information in Wikipedia that you would like to include in your report or presentation?

2. Surveys are typically used to collect quantitative information. Explain how a researcher could use a survey to collect qualitative information also.

References

1. Brown, D. (2009). *The lost symbol*. New York, NY: Doubleday, p. 98.

2. Booth, W. C., Colomb, G. G., Williams, J. M., Bizup, J., & Fitzgerald, W. T. (2016). *The craft of research* (4th ed.). Chicago, IL: University of Chicago Press, 39-40.

3. Steimle, J. (2014, May 14). What does an SEO firm do? *Forbes*. Retrieved from https://www.forbes.com/sites/joshsteimle/2014/05/02/what-does-an-seo-firm-do/#72f3a546742d

4. American Psychological Association. (n.d.). How to be a wise consumer of psychological research. Retrieved from http://www.apa.org/research/action/mer.aspx

5. Rock, D., & Grant, H. (2016, November 4). Why diverse teams are smarter. *Harvard Business Review*. Retrieved from https://hbr.org/2016/11/why-diverse-teams-are-smarter

6. Coutu, D. (2009, May). Why teams don't work. *Harvard Business Review*. Retrieved from https://hbr.org/2009/05/why-teams-dont-work

7. U.S. Department of State. (2017). Independent states in the world. Retrieved from http://www.state.gov/s/inr/rls/4250.htm

8. Simons, G. F., & Fennig, C. D. (Eds.). (2017). *Ethnologue: Languages of the world* (20th ed.). Dallas, Texas: SIL International. Retrieved from http://www.ethnologue.com

9. Yale, B. (2014, October 21). How the Internet works: The deep web. [Blog post] Retrieved from http://www.informit.com/blogs/blog.aspx?uk=How-the-Internet-Works-The-Deep-Web

10. Zillman, M. P. (2017). Deep web research and discovery resources 2017. Retrieved from http://www.deepweb.us; and O'Leary, M. (2008, April). New portals enrich STM menu. *Information Today*. Retrieved from http://www.deepwebtech.com/talks/InfoTodayReprint.pdf

11. Tourangeau, R., Conrad, F., & Couper, M. (2013). *The science of web surveys*. Oxford, England: Oxford University Press, pp. 40–43.

12. For more potential factors to consider, see Masnick, M. (2013). Survey software rating criteria: 2013-03-22. Retrieved from http://masnick.github.io/survey-review/2013-03-22-criteria_export.html

13. For more tips on how to use skip logic, see Constant Contact. (2017, January 9). When to use skip logic in a survey. Retrieved from https://knowledgebase.constantcontact.com/articles/KnowledgeBase/6145-when-to-use-skip-logic-in-a-survey

14. Mendelson, J., Gibson, J. L., & Romano-Bergstrom, J. (2016, August 18). Displaying videos in web surveys: Implications for complete viewing and survey responses. *Social Science Computer Review*. Advance online publication. Retrieved from http://journals.sagepub.com/doi/abs/10.1177/0894439316662439

15. Shapiro-Luft, D., & Cappella, J. (2013). Video content in web surveys: Effects on selection bias and validity. *Public Opinion Quarterly, 77*(4), 936–961.

16. Cho, S. (2014, February 13). Five tips on optimizing your surveys for smartphones. *SurveyMonkey Blog*. Retrieved from https://www.surveymonkey.com/blog/2014/02/13/five-tips-surveys-smartphones/

17. Marder, J., & Fritz, M. (2015, February 11). The Internet's hidden science factory. *PBS Newshour*. Retrieved from http://www.pbs.org/newshour/updates/inside-amazons-hidden-science-factory/

18. Singer, E., & Ye, C. (2013, January). The use and effects of incentives in surveys. *Annals of the American Academy of Political and Social Science, 645,* 112–141. Retrieved from http://www.jstor.org/stable/23479084

19. Dupuis, M., Endicott-Popovsky, B., & Crossler, R. (2013). An analysis of the use of Amazon's Mechanical Turk for survey research in the cloud. *ICCSM 2013—Proceedings of the International Conference on Cloud Security Management* (pp. 10–18). Retrieved from http://faculty.washington.edu/marcjd/research/index.html

20. Buying responses with SurveyMonkey Audience. (n.d.). Retrieved from https://help.surveymonkey.com/articles/en_US/kb/SurveyMonkey-Audience

21. Bethlehem, J. (n.d.). Weighting adjustment. Retrieved from http://www.applied-survey-methods.com/weight.html

22. Merriam, S. B., & Tisdell, E. J. (2015). *Qualitative research: A guide to design and implementation* (4th ed.). San Francisco, CA: Jossey-Bass.

23. United States Environmental Protection Agency. (2014). Advancing sustainable materials management: 2014 fact sheet. Retrieved from https://www.epa.gov/sites/production/files/2016-11/documents/2014_smmfactsheet_508.pdf

24. U.S. Copyright Office. (2017, January). More information on fair use. Retrieved from https://www.copyright.gov/fair-use/more-info.html

25. Chesky, B. [@bchesky]. (2016, December 26). If @Airbnb could launch anything in 2017, what would it be? [Tweet]. Retrieved from https://twitter.com/bchesky/status/813219932087390208

26. The Nielsen Company. (2017). 2016 Nielsen social media report. Retrieved from http://www.nielsen.com/us/en/insights/reports/2017/2016-nielsen-social-media-report.html

27. For an example of a testimonial video on a learning management system, see CorpUtv. (2008, July 3). Aaron's—Selecting an LMS vendor. [YouTube video]. Retrieved from http://www.youtube.com/watch?v=n_Cx7qZjSdQ

28. Bradshaw, K. (2016, March 23). Business to cloud: Protecting your company's information when it leaves your network. Retrieved from http://www.dobson.net/business-to-cloud-protecting-your-companys-information-when-it-leaves-your-network/

29. Orrell, A. C., & Foster, N. F. (2015). 2015 distributed wind market report. Retrieved from the U.S. Department of Energy website: https://energy.gov/sites/prod/files/2016/08/f33/2015-Distributed-Wind-Market-Report-08162016_0.pdf

30. International Energy Agency. (2016). WEO 2016 electricity access database. Retrieved from http://www.worldenergyoutlook.org/resources/energydevelopment/energyaccessdatabase/

31. International Energy Agency. (2011). Energy for all—Financing access for the poor. Retrieved from http://www.worldenergyoutlook.org/media/weowebsite/2011/weo2011_energy_for_all.pdf

Preparing Persuasive Business Proposals

Pathdoc/Shutterstock

STUDY QUESTIONS

New Hires @ Work

Megan Conrad

University of Illinois at Urbana-Champaign

Supply Chain Analyst @ Intel Corporation

When trying to persuade people with a proposal, speak to what is important to them. For example, if I propose a new investment to a logistics organization, which is a very cost-driven business, I have to provide a strong business case for how that investment will drive better efficiencies and lower costs. By contrast, if I am proposing that a sales person change a process or consider a new business or fulfillment model, I need to make a strong case for how that change will increase revenue and drive the bottom line. It's all about what's in it for them—WIIFM!

Photo courtesy of Megan Conrad

Chapter 9 | Introduction

A **proposal** is a document designed to convince a specific person or organization to take a specific action—for example, to hire your organization for a job, to fund a project, to buy new equipment, or to adopt a new policy, procedure, requirement, or program.

Proposals are common in all forms of business. If you work for a small bookstore, you might send your manager an informal email to propose a new story hour for children. If you manage a chain restaurant and want to change the menu, you might make a proposal presentation to an executive committee. If you are a consultant, you might respond to a *request for proposal* (RFP) from a potential client by submitting a formal document complete with a title page, table of contents, and charts and tables. Whatever form it takes, a good proposal will provide your audience with all the information they need to make an informed decision, and it will motivate your audience to act.

Because so many business activities depend on proposals, having good proposal-writing skills will make you a valuable employee or effective entrepreneur.[1] This chapter explains how to use ACE to manage the proposal process and provides examples of three common types of persuasive business proposals:

- Internal proposals for action or change
- External sales proposals to sell products or services
- Funding or grant proposals

Finally, the chapter provides guidelines for formatting formal proposals, including responses to RFPs and for using online proposal software to increase your efficiency.

(SQ1) How do you use ACE to prepare an effective proposal?

Preparing a proposal is complicated. It requires that you propose an idea that meets your audience's needs, develop a persuasive appeal, provide details about how to implement the proposal, and explain costs. **Figure 9.1** illustrates how the ACE process can help you ask good questions when preparing a proposal.

To apply these questions to a specific situation, imagine that you work for Northways Press, a small publishing company. One of your employees, Marina Jacobs, recently retired. To help reduce expenses, your supervisor, Doug Seaver, wants to wait six months to hire a full-time replacement. You and Doug have taken on additional work to compensate for the reduced staff. After a few weeks, you believe the additional workload is affecting the quality of your work and is distracting Doug from his main responsibilities—acquiring new books to publish and developing online publications. To solve these problems, you want to propose that the company hire a part-time replacement. You know the university in town offers an internship program. After learning more about the program, you decide to suggest that Doug hire an intern. How will you analyze, compose, and evaluate your proposal?

proposal A communication designed to persuade a business decision maker to adopt a plan, approve a project, choose a product or service, or supply funding.

Analyze: Understand the purpose, context, and content

Analyze

Like any other persuasive communication, a proposal requires in-depth analysis. You will be able to persuade your audience only if you understand these elements:

- **Purpose:** The need your proposal meets
- **Context:** The circumstances that influence your proposal
- **Content:** The arguments and information that will motivate your audience

FIGURE 9.1 Using ACE for Persuasive Proposals

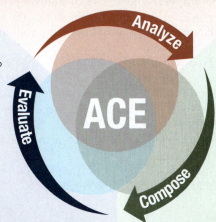

- What are you proposing and why?
- What is the context of your proposal? Is it external or internal? Is it solicited or unsolicited? Is it competitive or noncompetitive?
- Will your audience already be interested, or will you need to grab their attention?
- What requirements, if any, must this proposal meet?
- How will the audience benefit from the proposal?
- What objections should you anticipate?
- Should you do any initial research before writing the proposal? What do you need to learn?

Analyze

- Will the audience be convinced that the proposal addresses a real need?
- Have you stated what you are proposing?
- Have you shown that your proposal meets the need?
- Have you stressed audience benefits?
- Have you shown you are qualified?
- Have you explained the details: deliverables, costs, schedule?
- Have you asked for agreement?
- Have you used good headings and highlighted main points?
- Have you edited for style and tone?
- Have you proofread for errors?

Evaluate

ACE

- How formal or informal should this proposal be?
- What is the best medium for the proposal?
- How can you establish credibility?
- What content must you include?
- How should you organize the content?
- How can you use a "you" perspective?

Compose

Purpose

The first step in preparing a proposal is to develop a clear idea of your purpose: What need are you addressing, and how do you propose to meet that need? In proposing that your company hire an intern, you are addressing the need to ensure quality work until a full-time replacement is hired. For the proposal to be successful, your supervisor must feel confident that your proposal will solve the problem without costing more than he is willing to spend.

Context

By considering the context, you can identify the level of persuasion necessary as well as the appropriate form for the proposal. Ask yourself three questions:

1. **Is the proposal external or internal?** An **external proposal** is addressed to people outside your organization, such as a potential client or an agency that will provide funding. An external proposal usually takes the form of a letter, a report-style document, or a presentation. An **internal proposal** is addressed to people within your organization. An internal proposal may be less formal than an external one and may be written as a memo or, in some cases, just an email.

    For the internship, you will be writing an internal proposal to your supervisor, Doug. It may require only a few paragraphs, so an email message would be appropriate.

2. **Is the proposal solicited or unsolicited?** A **solicited proposal** is one your audience has asked you to submit. By contrast, an **unsolicited proposal** is one that you initiate. The distinction is important.

    If a proposal is solicited, your audience has already identified a problem or need and has requested a solution. An organization might solicit proposals by contacting you directly or by distributing a **request for proposal (RFP)** in order to get multiple competitive responses. Solicited proposals typically use a direct organization because your audience is expecting to hear your main idea.

external proposal A proposal addressed to people outside your organization.

internal proposal A proposal addressed to people within your organization.

solicited proposal A proposal that your audience has requested.

unsolicited proposal A proposal that your audience did not request.

request for proposal (RFP) An invitation for suppliers to competitively submit proposals to provide a product or service.

If the proposal is unsolicited, your audience has not asked for the proposal and may not even be aware that a problem or an opportunity exists. As a result, an unsolicited proposal needs to do more than just convince your audience that you have a good idea or product. You first need to grab your audience's attention by convincing them that they have an unmet need or can benefit from a new opportunity. If your audience doesn't know you, you will also need to build your credibility by explaining your experience and qualifications within the proposal. Unsolicited proposals are often organized indirectly because you first need to prepare your audience for your idea.

In the internship scenario, the proposal is unsolicited, so you will need to persuade your audience that the problem is significant enough to warrant the cost of the part-time intern. You also need to convince Doug that the intern will be able to reduce the workload for both you and Doug.

competitive proposal A proposal that will compete with other proposals for the same sale, funding, or opportunity.

noncompetitive proposal A proposal that has no competition because your audience will not be considering any offers other than yours.

3. **Is the proposal competitive or noncompetitive?** In a **competitive proposal** situation, others will be competing with you for the sale, the funding, or the opportunity. In a **noncompetitive proposal** situation, your audience will not be considering any offers other than yours.

Proposals that respond to RFPs are always competitive. The RFP will outline the important criteria on which you will compete. In some situations, price will be the most important criterion. In other situations, your ability to deliver your product or service quickly or your ability to meet specific requirements may be most important. When submitting a competitive proposal, think carefully about what your audience expects and what criteria your audience will use to evaluate your proposal compared to competitors' proposals.

In the internship scenario, the proposal is noncompetitive, so you do not need to prove that your idea is better than a competitor's.

Content

Analyze content needs by considering requirements, benefits, and potential objections.

- **Requirements.** Every proposal must address audience requirements. When a proposal is solicited, the audience will tell you their requirements. For an unsolicited proposal, you will need to put yourself in the audience's position and brainstorm those requirements on your own. As you analyze, create a checklist of requirements that your proposal must meet. For example, in the internship proposal, you will need to determine the qualifications Doug will require an intern to have. If Doug has taken responsibility for all marketing after Marina's retirement, he may require that an intern be experienced in marketing (rather than accounting or editing).

- **Benefits.** A good proposal also describes how your audience or organization will benefit from your proposal. Does the proposal save time or money? Does it help produce a better product? Does it help meet regulatory requirements? Does it help advance the company's mission? If your proposal is competitive, also consider the benefits you provide compared to your competition. In the internship proposal, you might mention the positive public relations your company will gain from hiring a student intern. You might also suggest that hiring a qualified intern will allow Doug to groom a future full-time employee.

- **Potential objections.** To complement your list of benefits, also consider the objections your audience may raise and brainstorm ways to respond to those objections. Will your audience believe your proposed plan costs too much or that it will not solve their problems? For example, if you think that hiring an intern will cost more than Doug is willing to spend, you can stress that a part-time intern will certainly cost less than a full-time employee. You can also suggest that hiring a marketing intern will give Doug more time to develop online publications and acquire new books to publish.

As you analyze content needs, consider whether you need to conduct research to strengthen your argument. Do you need to learn more about your client's industry or about competitors who may be submitting proposals? Do you need to learn more about alternatives or solutions you can offer? Do you need to find evidence that your solution has been successful in other organizations? Do you need to learn more about costs in order to put together a budget? For the internship proposal, you may need to do additional research to learn how the internship program at the university works and how a company advertises for an intern.

Compose: Develop persuasive content

Compose

Although proposals can be delivered in any form, they most frequently are delivered in writing rather than in presentations. Proposal expert Tom Sant argues that written proposals offer a number of advantages. For example, they clarify complex information, help the audience compare offers, and make the decision process more objective.[2]

As you compose your proposal, develop content that will support the audience's decision-making process and motivate the audience to act. Proposals typically do the following, though not necessarily in a specific order:

- Articulate the problem, need, or opportunity
- Present a compelling recommendation with supporting details
- Identify the outcomes and benefits
- Establish feasibility and credibility
- Request action

Articulate the problem, need, or opportunity

At the beginning of the proposal, explain the current business problem, need, or opportunity. This explanation serves three persuasive purposes:

- *In a solicited proposal,* the summary gives the audience confidence that you have listened to them carefully, truly understand what they are trying to accomplish, and are able to present an appropriate solution. The summary builds your credibility.
- *In an unsolicited proposal,* summarizing the problem, need, or opportunity helps convince the audience that they will benefit from continuing to read so they can learn about your proposed solution or idea.
- *In any proposal,* the initial summary is the "setup" for the final recommendation. If you articulate the problem, need, or opportunity at the beginning of the proposal, you will be able to show at the end of the proposal how your recommendation solves the problem, addresses the need, or takes advantage of the opportunity.

Present a compelling recommendation with supporting details

Once you have identified the problem or opportunity, present your proposed solution or approach, and demonstrate how it meets the audience's needs and requirements. Refer to the checklist of requirements you created during the analyzing stage, and show how you meet every requirement. Be sure to provide enough detail about cost and implementation that your audience can make an informed decision.

Identify the outcomes and benefits

When you discuss how you will solve the audience's problem or meet their need, you are identifying the audience's *pain.* However, it is equally important in a proposal to identify their *gain*—in other words, how they will benefit. Consider the audience's benefit from two perspectives:

- **How will solving this problem benefit the audience?** Many proposals—especially those that are unsolicited—are unsuccessful not because the audience accepts a different proposal but because the audience decides to do nothing at all. Help the audience understand why this problem deserves attention and how the benefits of fixing it will outweigh the proposed cost.
- **How will your specific proposal benefit the audience?** Most problems have several possible solutions. Why is your proposed solution particularly good? What are the benefits of your approach? What unique value does your plan offer?

Be sure to highlight the key reasons for accepting your proposal. You can mention these at the beginning and again at the end of the proposal. You can also integrate the discussion of benefits with the detailed discussion of your plan.

Establish feasibility and credibility

No matter what other persuasive content you include, the details of a proposal must always prove two things: that the plan is *feasible* and that you are *credible*.

Proving feasibility means showing that the plan is achievable and based on good analysis, research, and evidence. In the internship scenario, if you were to propose that Northways Press hire an intern who receives academic credit from the university, your proposal is feasible only if the university offers this option to its students. You need to show that you have done your research. You also have to show that your implementation plans are feasible. What is the timeline for the project? When and how will the work be completed? What are the **deliverables** (the items or services you agree to provide)? What are the costs? What gives you confidence that the plan will succeed? Where relevant, cite information from your research to demonstrate that your estimates are reasonable.

Establishing credibility means showing that you have the ability to deliver what you propose. Whether you are writing a sales proposal or a proposal for funding, your audience will need to have confidence that you can deliver your promises. That is why your proposal should show that you have the qualifications, facilities, time, staff, and expertise to complete the project. You can demonstrate this by including testimonials, describing similar projects you have completed, identifying resources available to you, and providing brief biographical sketches of the staff.

Request action

A persuasive proposal will look forward to next steps and request a response. Otherwise, it may be easy for your audience to forget or ignore your proposal. Solicited sales proposals often include an acceptance or authorization sheet that your audience can sign. For unsolicited proposals, however, you may want to suggest a meeting or telephone call as the next step.

Figure 9.2 is the proposal written to Doug Seaver of Northways Press. It illustrates one approach to organize this information. You will see examples of other organizational strategies throughout this chapter. Notice that the organization of this email is a hybrid between direct and indirect. Although the subject line is direct, the body of the proposal presents the detailed solution in a more indirect manner, after persuading Doug that a problem needs to be solved.

Evaluate: Assess the effectiveness of the proposal

The more important a proposal is to your business, the more important it is to take extra time to evaluate it. In competitive proposals, omissions and mistakes can exclude you from consideration. In addition, once your audience accepts your proposal, you will be obligated to provide what you propose, so you need to evaluate your promises carefully. Use the checklist in **Figure 9.3** on page 320 to evaluate your proposal. If you are writing a sales proposal that is complicated and critical to your business's success, consider using a more collaborative review process, such as the one described in the collaboration feature on page 333.

What should you do if you send a solicited proposal to someone who has requested it, and you get no response, even after several weeks? Unfortunately, this scenario is common and very frustrating when you have invested a good deal of time and resources into producing a proposal. When you receive no feedback, you do not know whether the client did not receive your proposal, accepted a different proposal, is waiting for management approval, or abandoned the project altogether. Telephone calls and email follow-ups within a week are appropriate. If those get no response, then consider writing an email like the "magic email" created by sales trainer Blair Enns:[3]

> **Subject: Closing the Loop**
> Hi [FirstName]:
> I haven't heard back from you on [project/opportunity] so I'm going to assume you've gone in a different direction or your priorities have changed.
> Let me know if we can be of assistance in the future.
> Regards,
> [You]

Evaluate

FIGURE 9.2   How to Write an Informal Persuasive Proposal

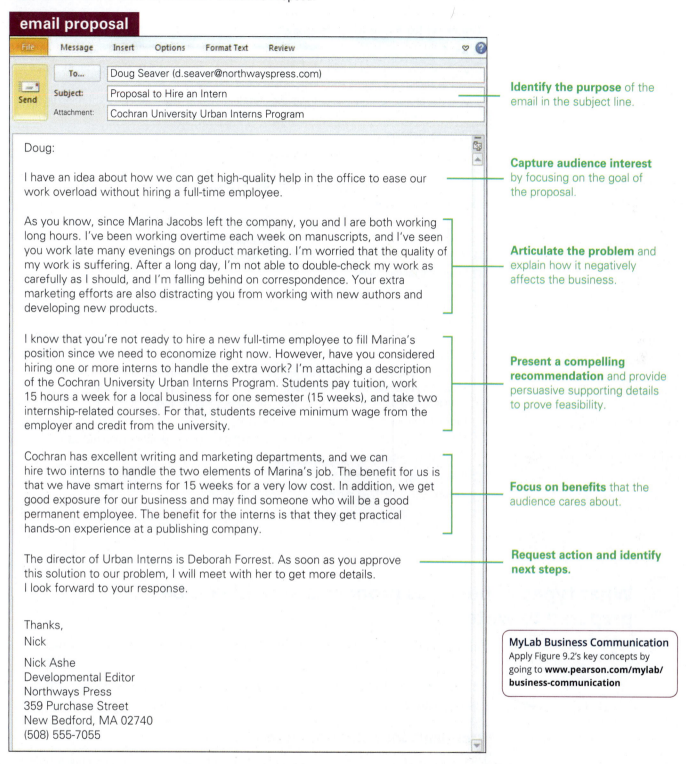

email proposal

| File | Message | Insert | Options | Format Text | Review |

To...	Doug Seaver (d.seaver@northwayspress.com)
Subject:	Proposal to Hire an Intern
Attachment:	Cochran University Urban Interns Program

Doug:

I have an idea about how we can get high-quality help in the office to ease our work overload without hiring a full-time employee.

As you know, since Marina Jacobs left the company, you and I are both working long hours. I've been working overtime each week on manuscripts, and I've seen you work late many evenings on product marketing. I'm worried that the quality of my work is suffering. After a long day, I'm not able to double-check my work as carefully as I should, and I'm falling behind on correspondence. Your extra marketing efforts are also distracting you from working with new authors and developing new products.

I know that you're not ready to hire a new full-time employee to fill Marina's position since we need to economize right now. However, have you considered hiring one or more interns to handle the extra work? I'm attaching a description of the Cochran University Urban Interns Program. Students pay tuition, work 15 hours a week for a local business for one semester (15 weeks), and take two internship-related courses. For that, students receive minimum wage from the employer and credit from the university.

Cochran has excellent writing and marketing departments, and we can hire two interns to handle the two elements of Marina's job. The benefit for us is that we have smart interns for 15 weeks for a very low cost. In addition, we get good exposure for our business and may find someone who will be a good permanent employee. The benefit for the interns is that they get practical hands-on experience at a publishing company.

The director of Urban Interns is Deborah Forrest. As soon as you approve this solution to our problem, I will meet with her to get more details. I look forward to your response.

Thanks,
Nick

Nick Ashe
Developmental Editor
Northways Press
359 Purchase Street
New Bedford, MA 02740
(508) 555-7055

Identify the purpose of the email in the subject line.

Capture audience interest by focusing on the goal of the proposal.

Articulate the problem and explain how it negatively affects the business.

Present a compelling recommendation and provide persuasive supporting details to prove feasibility.

Focus on benefits that the audience cares about.

Request action and identify next steps.

MyLab Business Communication
Apply Figure 9.2's key concepts by going to **www.pearson.com/mylab/ business-communication**

This short, practical email offers two benefits. First, it is likely to get you a response. If the potential client has already decided not to hire you, you have made it easy to respond without having to write a bad news message. Instead, the client can write a goodwill message saying "thank you and we will be in touch if we have future needs." If the potential client is still interested, this message will prompt a response because the client will want to stop you from walking away. The second benefit is that this email allows you to move on. Even if you do not get a response, you will know for certain that the client is not interested, and you can invest your time on other projects.

FIGURE 9.3 Checklist for Evaluating Proposals

Checklist for Evaluating Proposals

☐ **Need**

✓ If the proposal is solicited, does the introduction clearly indicate that you understand the audience's needs and clearly state what you are proposing?

✓ If the proposal is unsolicited, will the introduction grab the audience's attention and convince them that your proposal is addressing a real need?

☐ **Proposal/Solution**

✓ Have you stated your proposal clearly and shown convincingly that your proposal is a good way to meet the audience's needs?

✓ Have you specified sufficient details: deliverables, costs (if any), and a schedule?

☐ **Requirements/Benefits**

✓ Have you explained clearly how the proposal addresses the audience's requirements and priorities?

✓ Have you focused on how the proposal will benefit the audience?

☐ **Feasibility/Qualifications**

✓ Will the audience be convinced that the proposed idea is feasible and can be implemented effectively? If you are proposing work that you or your company will perform, will the audience be convinced that you have the qualifications to perform the proposed work—or deliver the proposed services? Have you provided enough evidence?

☐ **Call to Action**

✓ Have you specifically asked for agreement? Have you provided contact information so the audience can tell you whether to move forward with the proposal? Have you indicated a date by which you need a response, if applicable?

☐ **Format/Language**

✓ Is the proposal easy to read with good headings and key points that stand out?

✓ Is the language clear, concise, and professional?

☐ **Proofreading**

✓ Have you proofread the document to eliminate errors?

What types of business proposals should you be prepared to write?

This section provides examples of the three most common types of business proposals:

- Proposals for action or change
- Sales proposals (either solicited or unsolicited) to provide products or services
- Proposals for grants or other funding

Proposals for action or change

If you have an idea at work that you would like to implement or a project that needs funding, a proposal may win you the support you need. In business, proposals for action are strongest when they make a **business case**—that is, when they argue that a specific course of action is good for an organization and makes business sense. When writing a business case, you need to discuss benefits, costs, risks, and implementation plans.[4]

business case A justification for a proposal showing that the recommended course of action is good for an organization and makes business sense.

The internship proposal in Figure 9.2 is an informal email proposal for action or change. **Figure 9.4** offers advice for structuring a more formal internal proposal that makes a business case. It incorporates many of the same steps from the informal proposal, such as explaining the need addressed by your proposal and how it will benefit the organization, providing detailed information about your implementation plan,

FIGURE 9.4 How to Write a Proposal for Action or Change

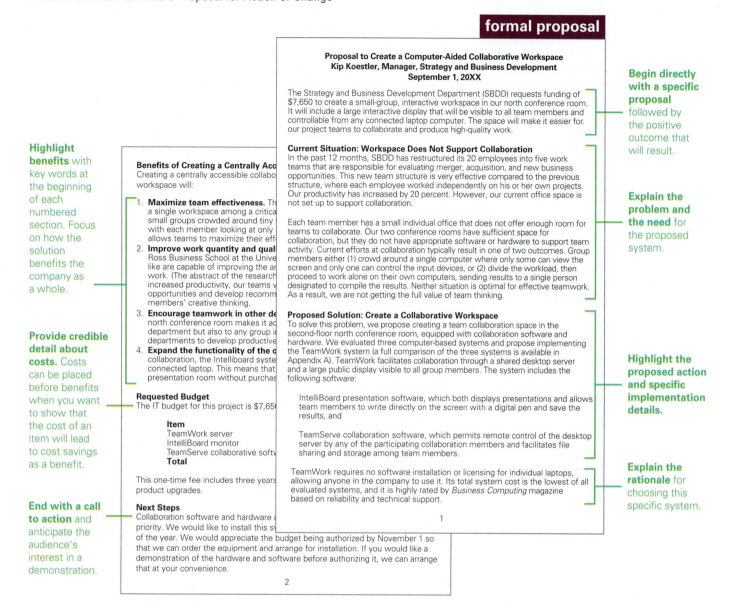

Begin directly with a specific proposal followed by the positive outcome that will result.

Explain the problem and the need for the proposed system.

Highlight the proposed action and specific implementation details.

Explain the rationale for choosing this specific system.

Highlight benefits with key words at the beginning of each numbered section. Focus on how the solution benefits the company as a whole.

Provide credible detail about costs. Costs can be placed before benefits when you want to show that the cost of an item will lead to cost savings as a benefit.

End with a call to action and anticipate the audience's interest in a demonstration.

and offering a clear next step. It also includes helpful organizational prompts, such as headings and highlighting in order to help the audience see the structure of the document at a glance and find important points. You can send this report-style proposal in hard copy or electronically as an email attachment. One advantage of sending it by email is that you can summarize the proposal in the email and request action—for example, a meeting to discuss the proposal.

Solicited sales proposals

If you work in an organization that sells products or services, you may have to prepare *sales proposals* for your customers and clients. Like an action proposal, a strong sales proposal makes a persuasive case that the audience will benefit from what you propose. In addition to serving as a persuasive tool, a sales proposal often serves as a sales contract. It identifies exactly what you will deliver, at what cost, in what time frame, and under what circumstances. When your client signs the proposal, both parties have made a commitment. If a solicited sales proposal is noncompetitive, it may contain only the contractual information. This type of proposal is referred to as a **statement of work (SOW)**.

statement of work (SOW) A proposal or section of a proposal that identifies exactly what you will deliver, at what cost, in what time frame, and under what circumstances.

CULTURE
WRITING PROPOSALS FOR DIFFERENT CULTURES

The advice in this chapter is particularly relevant for business proposals intended for audiences within the United States. But what if you need to make a proposal to a business associate or potential business partner from another country? Is it realistic to believe that you can simply write a proposal—including both persuasive elements and the terms of the agreement—and expect your audience to sign that document and abide by the agreement?

Here are some differences between the U.S. approach to business proposals and the approaches in three other countries—China, Brazil, and Italy:

- **Differences in the proposal process.** According to China Trade.com, "Chinese business people will seldom make a snap decision and prefer to give a business proposal careful and measured consideration."[5] As intercultural communication expert Linda Beamer explains, the Chinese "generally consider the effect of a solution on the people and relationships involved before they take action. . . . A stress on context and relationships could explain why Chinese often want to discuss alternative procedures and plans long after their foreign counterparts have finished."[6] Because relationships are so important to Chinese businesspeople, the process of negotiating an agreement can take a long time. To propose and negotiate an agreement in China, begin with conversations and discussions that allow the people involved to socialize and learn more about each other's values and needs.[7] You may even be invited to help your potential customer define their needs.[8] Plan to meet face-to-face to and involve several members of your team at different hierarchical levels. Negotiate your proposal verbally, and then finalize it with a written contract.[9]

- **Differences in persuasive content.** In the United States, businesspeople are conditioned to think that profit and financial advantage are the biggest benefits to emphasize in a business proposal. In some countries, however, other benefits are more important. For example, in Brazil, many businesspeople consider gains in status and power to be more important than gains in profit.[10] Therefore, in a proposal to a Brazilian company, you should identify the social and status benefits as well as the financial benefits.

- **Differences in attitude toward signed agreements.** For most Americans, a signed proposal or contract represents a final agreement that must be honored. However, in other cultures, a signed contract signals only an interest in doing business rather than a commitment. For example, in China, contracts are always open to renegotiation. This is the accepted business norm.[11] Similarly, in India, contracts are treated as fluid documents without a clear expectation that the terms of the contract will be honored.[12]

- **Differences in attitude toward oral agreements.** For most Americans, an agreement is not finalized until it is put in writing. In other cultures—for example, Italy—it is expected that oral commitments will be honored. Signing a contract is a mere formality, reflecting the commitment between business partners.[13]

If you are proposing a business arrangement to someone from a different country or culture—even if you are both in the United States—take the time to research the person's cultural norms and expectations. A good starting place is the book *Negotiating International Business—The Negotiator's Reference Guide to 50 Countries Around the World* by Lothar Katz, the president of the cross-cultural consultancy Leadership Crossroads. Portions of the book are available online.

For CULTURE exercises, go to Critical Thinking Question 8 on page 339 and Exercise 11 on page 341.

Figure 9.5 illustrates good practices in solicited sales proposals. It demonstrates how to begin by identifying the purpose of the proposal, stressing your company's qualifications, and previewing the organization of the document. Like the proposal in Figure 9.4, a sales proposal requires headings and numbered points for easy reading. This example also shows how to indicate what you will need from the client in order to move forward—in this case, a signed agreement.

FIGURE 9.5 How to Write a Solicited Sales Proposal

letter

This letter is a sales proposal from Cronin Environmental Services (CES) to a new client, Davis College. Because this is an external sales proposal to a new client, the tone is formal.

CRONIN
Environmental Services, Inc.

1442 Industrial Parkway West
Rollins, MN 55555

612.555.5555
Fax: 612.555.6666
www.cronin.com

Choose the best medium. If a sales proposal is short, if often takes the form of a letter. If the proposal exceeds three pages, a report format may be better.

October 24, 20XX

Mr. Paul Phillips
Director of Physical Plant
Davis College
285 S. Kings Way
Rollins, MN 55555

Use a subject line that identifies the subject of the proposal.

Subject: Proposal to Update Davis College's Waste Reduction Plan

Dear Mr. Phillips:

Begin the proposal by:
(1) identifying the purpose of the proposal,
(2) stressing your company's qualifications, and (3) previewing the organization of the proposal.

Cronin Environmental Services, Inc., (CES) is pleased to submit this proposal to assist Davis College (DC) in preparing an updated Waste Reduction Plan as required by the Minnesota Department of Community Affairs (MDCA). CES has extensive experience producing MDCA waste reduction plans. Based on that experience, this letter identifies CES's recommended scope of work, time frame, and budget. It also provides background about CES's expertise.

SCOPE OF WORK

Identify exactly what you will do or provide.

To evaluate the waste composition at Davis College and prepare the required analyses and report, CES proposes to do the following:

- Review waste hauling and recycling records for the past 12 months.

- Coordinate with the Facilities Management staff to schedule a representative sampling of the waste generated at the DC main campus. CES will work with the Facilities Management staff to identify a location for sorting to minimize inconvenience and, if needed, for temporarily storing the material being sorted (for less than one day).

- Conduct a sort-and-weigh audit using one-day's worth of waste from the campus. The sort will address all the waste components required by MDCA, including glass, aluminum containers, plastic (high-density and low-density polyethylene, and polyethylene terepthalate), and landscape waste. In addition, the sort will identify weight components of newsprint, cardboard, white and computer paper, magazines, and a mixed paper category.

Use headings and bullets that make the proposal easy to skim.

- Conduct a walkthrough of the college's buildings to evaluate the recycling and waste reduction activities throughout the campus.

- Meet with Facilities Management staff as necessary to discuss questions pertinent to the report.

- Prepare a draft report for DC to review and approve.

- Prepare four copies of the Waste Reduction Plan Update, which DC can submit to MDCA, and two copies for the college's records.

(continued)

FIGURE 9.5 *(Continued)*

The scope of work assumes that DC will provide the following information necessary to prepare the report:

- Data on procurement of recycled materials, such as paper
- Waste hauling and recycling records
- Data on numbers of students and employees

CES will supply the required forms to obtain this information.

Identify what your client must provide if your work depends on information or timely responses.

PROPOSED TIME SCHEDULE

CES is able to begin the fieldwork within two weeks of the notification to proceed. The fieldwork will take three days. We can have the analysis complete within four weeks from the completion of the fieldwork, depending on how quickly DC provides the other required data for the report.

Identify the amount of time the project will take and when the project can begin.

BUDGET

CES proposes a not-to-exceed budget of $9,200 to complete this scope of work. The budget is based on the time estimated to complete the work. DC will be billed for only the actual time and expenses related to the project. If our time and expenses are lower, the fee will be lower.

State the price of the project and whether this price is a flat fee or is conditional on the time and materials actually required.

CES EXPERIENCE

CES is an engineering consulting firm with offices throughout the state, including one in St. Paul (located three blocks from the MDCA building). CES offers your organization the following benefits:

- **Extensive experience** conducting waste audits, performing analyses of recycling programs, and developing waste reduction plans for a diverse range of facilities, including commercial offices, elementary schools and colleges, hospitals, and other institutions. CES was recently selected by Winona County to provide waste reduction services for businesses and multifamily complexes throughout the county.
- **A track record of success.** In the past year, CES has produced waste reduction plans for 11 organizations. All of the plans were approved by the MDCA. In addition, CES has been extremely successful in helping its clients secure more than $2 million in grant funds.

Add credibility by outlining your experience. You can also provide testimonials and publications to support your claims.

An extensive client list is enclosed with this proposal. I have also enclosed a short article on CES, published in the *Engineering News Record*.

CONTRACT

Enclosed are two copies of our Standard Agreement for Professional Services. If you agree to this proposal, please sign both agreements, return one, and keep one for your records.

Attach an agreement sheet to make it easy for your client to accept your proposal.

Mr. Phillips, we look forward to working on your project. With our experience in producing MDCA reports, we are confident we can produce the documentation you need with minimal disruption to campus life. If you have any questions before signing the contract, please contact me at 612-555-5555 or kim.colgate@cronin.com.

Sincerely,

Kim Colgate

Kim Colgate
Project Manager

Enclosures

TECHNOLOGY
USING PROPOSAL-WRITING SOFTWARE TO INCREASE EFFICIENCY

Businesses that routinely write sales proposals often invest in *proposal-writing software* that makes the writing process more efficient. This software allows a business to:

- create a customized template for a proposal (including all the sections that are important to the business),
- write multiple versions of text for each section,
- store the text along with pricing information in an online online content library,
- select text from the library for each proposal, and
- deliver the completed proposal as a web document.

Software companies typically sell proposal-writing software as a service. In the **Software as a Service (SaaS)** model, the application is not saved on your computer but is hosted by the software company and is available through the web, often for a monthly fee. One advantage of the SaaS model is that all your content is online and available to use from multiple computers and mobile devices.

Many different proposal applications are available. Your organization may already have a preferred software, or you may have the opportunity to choose one. Each program will have particular features.

The figure below illustrates some of the features of one popular proposal program, Proposify. Writing proposals with customized software such as Proposify offers many benefits:

- **Saves time.** The software stores your templates as well as the text and pricing information that you have prepared. You simply need to select content from the content library, insert it into the template, and then customize it using a text editor that is similar to Microsoft Word. By **repurposing content**—reusing content you have already created—you save a good deal of time.

- **Distributes assignments among team members and tracks progress.** The software helps manage collaborative work by allowing you to assign sections to particular individuals. The software also grants different types of access to team members according to their responsibilities.

- **Delivers the proposal electronically as a web document or as a PDF.** When your proposal is a web-based document, it can include links to websites and to multimedia, such as videos, that may include additional persuasive content.

- **Helps you track and analyze proposals.** Because the web-based proposal remains on the server, you can track whether—and how many times—someone has opened the document to read it. You can also receive data about how much time people spend viewing each section. These *data analytics* or *metrics* help you understand what most interests your audience so you can create targeted proposals in the future. If you find that a particular persuasive appeal captures audience interest in one proposal, you can add that to your library and use it for future proposals. Proposify even lets you check on the status of proposals from your smartphone.

- **Supports online signing for faster agreements.** Clients can read, review, and sign proposals online. If clients request changes, you can make the modifications instantly.

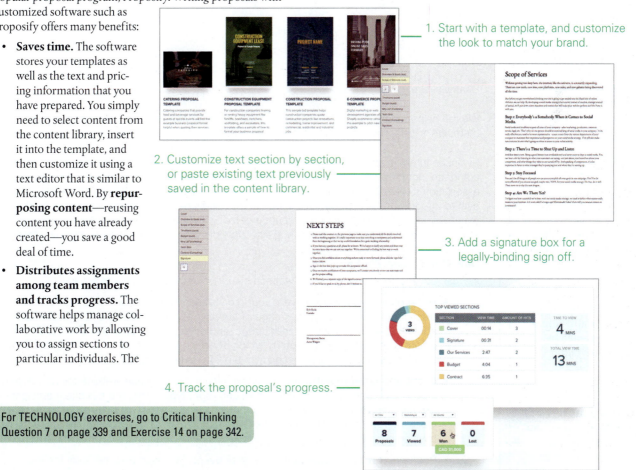

1. Start with a template, and customize the look to match your brand.

2. Customize text section by section, or paste existing text previously saved in the content library.

3. Add a signature box for a legally-binding sign off.

4. Track the proposal's progress.

For TECHNOLOGY exercises, go to Critical Thinking Question 7 on page 339 and Exercise 14 on page 342.

Software as a Service (SaaS)
Software that is hosted by the software provider and available through the web.

repurposing content Reusing content you have already created.

Unsolicited sales proposals

An unsolicited sales proposal is essentially a targeted marketing letter directed to someone you believe may benefit from your products or services. Your goal is to generate interest in your business proposal and to encourage further discussions. **Figure 9.6** illustrates good practices in writing an unsolicited sales proposal. The letter was sent by an event planning company to the Association of Investment Professionals, a group that holds several events throughout the year. It illustrates how to entice a potential client to read further by demonstrating your familiarity with their needs and your ability to meet those needs. It also illustrates how to provide an easy way for the reader to move forward with your proposal.

FIGURE 9.6 How to Write an Unsolicited Sales Proposal

letter

SWANSON

I N T E R N A T I O N A L

5250 W. 6th Street, Reston, VA 20191
800.555.1780 | Fax: 800.555.1781 | www.swanson.com

May 11, 20XX

Address an unsolicited sales proposal to an individual in the organization.

Ms. Eva Greenwald
Executive Director
Association of Investment Professionals
931 East 59th Street
New York, NY 11234

Dear Ms. Greenwald:

Begin the proposal with an attention-getting sentence that identifies audience benefits.

We can help your organization reduce your costs, increase your revenue, and enhance your members' satisfaction with your professional events.

Personalize the proposal and show that you have researched your audience's business and their needs.

Persuade the audience that there is a problem or opportunity to address.

Swanson International is an event registration and housing service that provides support for corporate, not-for-profit, and athletic events throughout North America. After reviewing your association's website, I noticed that AIP sponsors two annual conventions and several training events throughout the country. I also noticed that all event and housing registration for these events is done manually, through telephone or mail. I believe our services at Swanson can streamline your registration process and also increase your revenue and member satisfaction.

How Our System Works

Use section headings and paragraph topics to help the audience skim the content quickly.

AIP can benefit from working with Swanson by out-sourcing the following activities:

- **Hotel planning:** For each event your organization sponsors, Swanson negotiates discounted room rates with a range of hotels in the area. Your members receive an attractive set of choices to meet budget and other needs. Swanson also builds in a rebate with each of these hotels, which Swanson then shares with AIP. This will pay for all of Swanson's services and also provide revenue for AIP.

- **Event and hotel registration:** Swanson also builds a unique website for your event, including property pictures, directions, and room types. Through this site, participants can register for an event, register for housing, and purchase event-related merchandise (such as T-shirts and pins). For those members not willing or able to use the web, we have an in-house call center to process registration requests.

Describe your services or product, addressing the key features you believe your audience will value.

- **Post-event rebate collection:** After your event, Swanson bills the hotel for any rebates you have been promised, using our automated invoicing system.

(continued)

FIGURE 9.6 *(Continued)*

Ms. Eva Greenwald
May 11, 20XX
Page 2

Benefits to Your Association

Our list of satisfied clients is growing because we provide value to our clients in three areas:

- **Reduced administrative costs:** Our online registration services eliminate many time-consuming tasks facing event organizers, thus reducing administrative costs and hassle.

- **Increased revenue:** Our event registration tool will increase your hotel-related revenue because the web-based system drives participants to your hotels through the registration process.

- **Increased member satisfaction:** Participants can register for the event and accommodations in one easy step. In addition, the selection of hotels is designed to satisfy a range of budgets.

The most attractive benefit is that there are no out-of-pocket costs to AIP.

Next Steps

Please consider using our services for the next event you plan.

I will be in New York on business the week of June 15. May we set up a meeting to discuss how Swanson can help AIP? I would like to learn more about how many people typically attend AIP events and the kinds of hotels your members prefer. With this information, I will be able to estimate the revenue you can expect with our services.

I will call you next week to see if you are available to meet or talk by phone. Or you can reach me at (800) 555-1780 or k.nylund@swanson.com. I look forward to talking with you.

Regards,

Kathryn Nylund

Kathryn Nylund
Sales Manager
Swanson International

Do not discuss contractual agreements in unsolicited proposals.

Highlight the benefits you offer your audience.

Emphasize the most important benefit that you believe will. persuade the audience.

End with a call to action. For an unsolicited proposal, one appropriate call for action is to request a meeting. If the meeting is successful, the audience may solicit a more formal proposal.

Grant proposals and other proposals for funding

If you work for a nonprofit organization, you may need to request funding from an external source to support one of your organization's projects. For example, a homeless shelter may need to request funding from the city to replace its roof. An arts organization may request funding from the local arts council to support an after-school arts program. An academic organization may request funding from a foundation to support a business plan competition. Receiving that funding will be essential for the project's success. Depending on the requirements of the agency, these proposals for funding, also called **grant proposals**, may be prepared as formal reports, letters, or online submissions.

The following guidelines will help you plan, organize, and submit an effective grant proposal:

1. **Identify a funding agency that is a good match with the project you are trying to fund.** For example, imagine that you are the business manager of a hospital's physical therapy clinic in central Oklahoma. You realize that many low-income people in rural Oklahoma

grant proposal A proposal requesting funding, typically from government agencies or charitable foundations.

are not getting the medical help they need because their communities do not have physical therapists. In addition, it is too expensive for those people to travel to your center. You would like to write a grant proposal to receive funding to subsidize the travel expenses for low-income patients within 200 miles of your center. Where can you apply for that funding?

A web search reveals that the Walmart Foundation may be a good source. The tagline of the Walmart Foundation is "Giving people access to a better life. One community at a time."[14] One way the Foundation does this is by providing grants to organizations that share its mission.

On the application form for its State Giving grant, Walmart identifies "medical transportation" as one of the program categories it supports. In addition, Walmart is committed to giving back to the communities in which it does business:[15,16]

> *Walmart awards grants to local organizations making a difference on key issues in communities where Walmart Stores, clubs, and distribution center associates live and work. [Last year], over 46,000 grants equaling more than $47 million were provided to organizations, including law enforcement agencies, fire departments, schools, recreation centers and more.*

Your project meets Walmart's criteria in two ways. First, it is a medical transportation project. And second, your organization is in a community that Walmart serves: Walmart has more than 50 stores in Oklahoma. These matching criteria will be important facts to mention in the grant proposal.

2. **Identify a contact person at the funding organization and arrange a personal meeting.** You have two goals for this meeting: (1) to communicate your passion for the project and (2) to ask the granting agency if it will accept a proposal from you for the specific amount of money that you are requesting. This information ensures that you send the proposal to an appropriate agency and do not waste your time.
3. **Draft a proposal that addresses each topic area. Figure 9.7** illustrates a possible table of contents for the Walmart funding proposal. Notice the section called "Evaluation." This section helps the audience measure the success of the program. Directions for formatting the major sections of the proposal are provided later in this section.
4. **Draft a cover message for proposals submitted by mail or email.** When funding agencies review multiple proposals, they expect the cover letter to help them quickly understand who you are, what you are requesting, why the request is important, how it addresses the agency's mission, and why you believe your project is feasible. As you plan a letter using the ACE process, develop answers to these questions. Then when you compose, organize and format the letter to make these answers easy to find. **Figure 9.8** illustrates a cover letter for the Walmart Foundation proposal that answers all these questions.
5. **Submit the proposal online for funders who require it.** Sometimes you may need to submit a proposal through someone else's software. For example, the Walmart Foundation's community grant program requires you to use their online application. If you need to submit a proposal online, analyze the application in advance to get an idea of what it requires. Consider printing the online application for a reference as you gather data. Compose detailed content offline using a word processing program so you can monitor your word or character counts, and use the ACE process to make sure you are writing a proposal that will persuade your audience.

FIGURE 9.7 Table of Contents for a Funding Proposal

Table of Contents

Executive Summary	Page i
Introduction	Page 1
Statement of Need	Page 2
Goals and Objectives	Page 4
Implementation	Page 6
Benefits	Page 8
Evaluation	Page 9
Budget	Page 11
Appendix A: Past Projects	Page 12
Appendix B: List of Participating Hotels and Transportation Companies	Page 15

New Hires @ Work

Suzie Loveday
Eastern Kentucky University

Grants Management Officer @ Frontier Nursing University

Grant writing is all about building credibility and writing persuasively. People aren't just going to hand over their money to you. You have to convince a potential funder that you are really good at what you do and that you are already doing what the grant program is asking for.

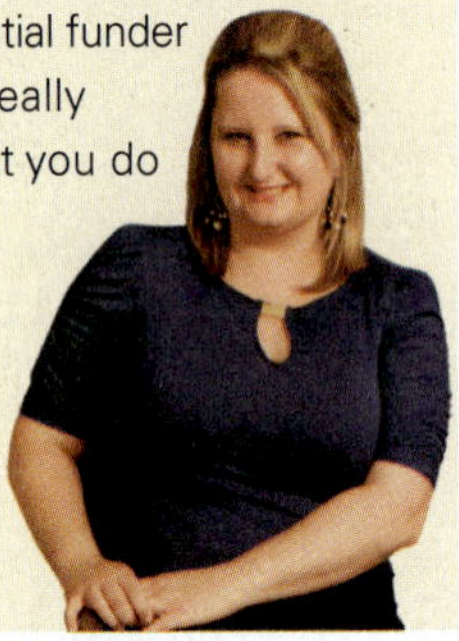

Photo Courtesy of Suzie Loveday

FIGURE 9.8 How to Write a Cover Letter for a Funding Proposal

> This proposal cover message from Central Oklahoma Regional Hospital to the Walmart Foundation is in itself a persuasive document. It is written to a specific person at the funding agency and is designed to convince the audience to read the proposal carefully and positively.

letter

CENTRAL OKLAHOMA
Regional Hospital

1795 NW Highway
Edmond, OK 73003

June 15, 20XX

Ms. Earlyn Felix
Grant Administrator
The Walmart Foundation
501 SW 19th Street
Moore, OK 73852

Dear Ms. Felix:

Thank you for the opportunity to meet with you Thursday and for your interest in the project, *Providing Access to Physical Therapy for Low-Income Patients in Central Oklahoma.* We believe this project will help us meet the Walmart Foundation goal of improving the health and wellness of underserved populations in communities in the state. In addition, this project can be replicated in other states where Walmart serves its customers.

We ask you to invest $10,000 to provide transportation and lodging to low-income patients who do not have the means to travel to our hospital for physical therapy services. Your investment will provide travel funds for up to 100 patients who live more than 100 miles from Central Oklahoma Regional Hospital. We have agreements from two bus companies and a local hotel to provide services at half price for this program.

As we discussed in our meeting, our preliminary research shows that each year physicians in the Central Oklahoma area prescribe physical therapy for more than 3,000 patients. However, many communities in Central Oklahoma do not have physical therapists nearby. The nearest comprehensive physical therapy center is in our hospital in Edmond. While the cost of the therapy is often covered by Medicare or Medicaid, the cost of transportation and lodging is not. As a result, many patients do not see a physical therapist and thus experience a lower quality of life.

Our project goal over the next 12 months is to establish a program that will allow physicians to apply for travel grants on behalf of their patients. We ask for your help in funding these grants.

I will contact you next Tuesday after you've had an opportunity to review this proposal. In the meantime, if you have any questions, please contact me at Sean.Wittwer@CORH.com or 800-555-5555.

Best regards,

Sean Wittwer

Sean Wittwer
Grant Coordinator

Try talking to someone at the funding agency before you write the cover letter, and refer to that conversation at the beginning of the letter.

Stress how your proposed plan will **meet at least one of the funding agency's goals.**

Identify the specific amount of money you are requesting and how that money will be spent.

Show that the plan is feasible and has community support.

Persuade your audience that you are meeting a real need.

Conclude by focusing on goals and next steps.

ETHICS
DOES YOUR PROPOSAL DEMONSTRATE INTEGRITY?

Companies that request proposals and those that provide proposals each have ethical obligations. A company that requests a proposal has an obligation to read it carefully and evaluate it according to the stated requirements. In the worst-case scenario, a company may request competitive proposals but give "inside information" to a preferred competitor, allowing that person to produce a more persuasive proposal. It is unethical to ask someone to spend time and energy to produce a proposal if you know in advance that you will be awarding the contract to someone else. It is equally unethical to use the proposal process to fish for free ideas.[17]

A company that submits a proposal has an ethical obligation to provide content that is honest and accurate. It is not only unethical to bend the truth to make the sale; it is also bad business. As proposal expert Harold Lewis observes, "Once clients come to believe that they cannot rely on you to deliver what you promise, you will have your work cut out to regain their confidence."[18]

As a writer, avoid these common traps that undermine the integrity of your proposal:[19]

- Do not knowingly exaggerate the benefits of your proposal or hide the costs in order to meet your audience's requirements or expectations.
- Do not overpromise what you can deliver.
- Do not ignore technical difficulties.
- Do not dismiss or suppress other viable options that your audience should consider.
- Do not make negative statements about your competitors' products and services. If you must compare, make sure your comparisons are factual and not biased.[20]

Consider the following example of how to revise an overblown phrase to make it more accurate:

Inaccurate original: "Our wireless router is the most powerful on the market and can be self-installed by following the instructions in the accompanying installation manual."

Problem: The writers are leaving out the fact that the installation manual is 35 pages long and extremely technical. It is written primarily for people with significant hardware installation experience. They are making the router seem easier to install than it actually is. The writers are also making an unsubstantiated and overblown claim about the power of the router. More powerful routers exist, but they are aimed at large businesses, and this is aimed at small businesses.

More ethical revision: "Our wireless router has been rated by *PC World* as the most powerful small-business router on the market. It can also be installed easily either by your internal information technology group using the included installation manual or by our technical support staff at a nominal fee."

The revised version is more ethical because it is more accurate. Although the claims are more limited, they still stress benefits. Your audience will appreciate your honesty, and the credibility you earn may lead to a stronger long-term relationship.

> For ETHICS exercises, go to Exercise 5 on page 340 and Exercise 9 on page 341.

(SQ3) How do you structure and format a formal proposal?

If your proposal responds to an RFP—a request for proposal—it will likely be longer than three or four pages and will require a good structure so that readers can navigate the document and easily find the information they are looking for. This section provides guidelines for structuring formal proposals, including responses to RFPs.

Read RFPs carefully to identify content requirements

Requests for proposal typically include a very specific set of requirements that the proposer must meet. In some industries, RFPs can generate proposals that are more than 100 pages long. In most cases, though, proposals are much shorter.

The key to writing an effective proposal in response to an RFP is to create a checklist of requirements and to ensure that your proposal addresses all these requirements. **Figure 9.9** is the cover letter that accompanies a 15-page RFP sent to Revson Communication Group. When Revson received this RFP, a manager read through the entire document and made notes about the proposal's requirements. Figure 9.9 shows the Revson Communication Group's annotations on the cover letter.

The formal RFP introduced in the Figure 9.9 cover letter requires Revson to prepare a formal response that includes elements of both information and persuasion. To be successful, the proposal must do the following:

- Provide a quick overview at the beginning, either in an executive summary (a condensed version of the document that summarizes key ideas) or an introduction
- Make the information easy to find, using a table of contents or other contents list
- Show an understanding of the client's needs
- Propose a solution that meets the needs as listed in the RFP
- Provide confidence that the course designers and instructors are qualified
- Propose a competitive fee
- Provide the required documentation

FIGURE 9.9 How to Annotate an RFP with Notes to Help Prepare a Response

> The key to writing an effective proposal in response to an RFP is to create a checklist of requirements and to ensure that your proposal addresses all these requirements. Making notes on the RFP, like the notes on the cover letter below, helps ensure that the proposal contains the right content.

letter

Linus Industries

1000 Brandywine Blvd., Wilmington, DE 19800

November 7, 20XX

Revson Communication Group
5500 Kirkwood Highway
Wilmington, DE 19808

Subject: RFP for Strategic Communications Course

Linus Industries (Linus) is requesting a proposal to design and deliver a one-day Strategic Communications course for senior-level managers who communicate with all levels of the organization.

Key Requirements:

Must be a one-day course.

Context

Linus is a broad-based health care company that discovers, develops, manufactures, and markets products and services that span the continuum of care—from prevention and diagnosis to treatment and cure. The Strategic Communications course will be one of the final pieces in a 16-course, in-depth communications cluster as part of our Business Skills curriculum. This advanced course will help Linus do a better job of communicating strategic messages with employees and leaders within the company as well as communicating externally. An initial description of the course is included on page 3 of the enclosed RFP.

Must focus on communicating strategic messages internally and externally.

Project Purpose

This project is to establish an instructor-led course that will help senior managers create appropriate strategic messages and communicate effectively with peers and employees. We have three broad areas of interest:

- Communicating strategic messages downward within the organization
- Creating an environment where dialogue is encouraged, both one-on-one and within a larger group setting
- Creating strategic communication plans for major initiatives such as organizational changes

Must address three key areas:
- *Communicating downward*
- *Creating an environment that encourages dialogue*
- *Creating strategic communication plans*

Scope

You may propose an entirely new course created to meet our needs or a revised version of a course that you currently offer. Linus does not have a method of forecasting how many people might take this course during a year. However, 50 to 100 participants per year is a reasonable estimate.

(continued)

FIGURE 9.9 *(Continued)*

Revson Communication Group
November 7, 20XX
Page 2

Please include the cost of developing materials, the proposed audience size per session and the total costs of facilitating the course for a given session (excluding travel costs, which are reimbursed afterwards—see Travel & Living Expenses in the attached RFP. Linus must approve the primary instructor, but such approval is not part of this RFP. Please include information about the instructors who will facilitate the course.

Proposal must include:
- *Costs of developing materials*
- *Proposed class size*
- *Costs for facilitating the course*
- *Information about instructors*

Critical Success Factors

The course must meet the following objectives:

- Emphasize skill-building, rather than merely "learning about" the topic of strategic communication
- Offer opportunities for practice
- Be appropriate for senior-level managers who expect a high-level course and have little tolerance for basic information
- Be appropriate for international audiences
- Account for cross-cultural nuances regarding both the speaker and audience
- Be able to be customized to fit Linus branding standards

Description of the course must emphasize:
- *Skill building*
- *Opportunities for practice*
- *High-level content*
- *Cross-cultural elements*
- *Method of customizing to branding standards*

Material Included in the RFP

The enclosed RFP includes the following information:

1. Project Charter
2. Project Milestones
3. Response Terms and Conditions
4. Response Content and Evaluation
5. Proposal Submission Guidelines
6. Supplier Evaluation Criteria
7. Confidentiality Agreement

Check proposal submission guidelines and evaluation criteria.

Linus expects the utmost in professional associations with its suppliers. We strive to work together in a harmonious relationship that is beneficial for both Linus and our chosen supplier(s). This RFP is an instrument designed to enable Linus to make the best possible decision in creating a mutually beneficial business relationship.

For more information, please contact me at 800.555.3978 or r.sklar@linusind.com. I look forward to receiving your proposal.

Sincerely,

Richard Sklar

Richard Sklar, Manager
Professional Development

Enclosure

Structure a formal proposal like a formal report

A formal proposal is similar to a formal report. In addition to the body of the proposal itself, formal proposals include a title page, an **executive summary**, a table of contents, references or works cited, and appendices, if needed.

The executive summary in a formal proposal, as in a report, is a separate, stand-alone mini-document included at the beginning of the proposal that summarizes the document's

executive summary A separate, stand-alone mini-document, included at the beginning of a longer document, that summarizes the document's main ideas.

main ideas. However, in a proposal, the executive summary also has a persuasive purpose and is designed to sell your solution.[21] To be persuasive, include the following elements:

- An opener that generates attention and interest in your proposal
- A compelling description of the client's need
- The solution you are proposing
- A brief description of your qualifications, focusing on evidence that you can be successful
- A call to action

Formal proposals are often also accompanied by some form of **cover message** (letter, memo, or email). Figure 9.8 on page 329 is an example of a cover message.

Figure 9.10 on page 334 shows a thumbnail view of Revson Communication Group's response to the Linus RFP. Notice how the proposal includes all the formal elements. Also notice how the section headings are designed to respond specifically to the content in the RFP.

cover message   A letter, a memo, or an email accompanying a formal report or proposal, designed to explain the document and persuade the audience to read it.

COLLABORATION
REVIEWING A PROPOSAL WITH COLOR TEAMS

When large organizations prepare proposals that are critical for their business, they often invest months of many people's time in the process. To get the most benefit from that investment and to increase the chances of their proposal succeeding, those organizations adopt a formal, multiphase review process, with each stage of the review focusing on a different goal.

One review technique widely used by organizations bidding for large government contracts is the *color team review.*[22,23] As the graphic below illustrates, each review is performed by a designated team whose role is defined by its color name. The roles of each team are well-established in the methodology. The blue team begins its work even before the organization commits to doing the proposal. This team assesses whether the organization is well suited for the job and helps determine the proposal strategy. The pink team reviews the proposal in the planning stage; reviewing outlines and storyboards ensures that the proposal is not missing key requirements of the RFP, one of the major mistakes proposers make.[24] The red team reviews the entire document after it is drafted to ensure it is comprehensive and persuasive. Finally,

a gold team provides an editing and proofreading review. Some organizations also conduct green reviews, which focus on pricing. Each of the teams comprises people who are familiar with the proposal as well as those who have not been involved with the prior steps and may therefore be more objective.

While this process is too elaborate for small proposals, it does suggest some good practices for reviewing all proposals:

- Evaluate the proposal at several stages of the development process. If reviews happen only at the end, it will be too late to take advantage of good suggestions for improvement.
- Ensure that each review has a specific focus. For example, do not worry about editing in an early review. If you do, you may be spending time fine-tuning text that ultimately will be deleted.
- Assign multiple people to review the proposal at each phase and ensure that some of those people are able to provide "fresh eyes" on the work.

For a COLLABORATION exercise, go to Exercise 23 on page 343.

Blue Team Review

When: When the RFP is received

Why: Determine solution and strategy

Outcome: Decision to submit or not to submit

Who: Managers, subject matter experts, contractors

Pink Team Review

When: When the outline and storyboards are final

Why: Confirm it complies with RFP requirements and messaging is clear

Outcome: Revised outline and storyboard

Who: Blue team members and experts on reviewing RFPs

Red Team Review

When: When the document is 90% completed

Why: Ensure the proposal complies with RFP requirements, is comprehensive, and is persuasive

Outcome: Revised draft

Who: Pink team members and subject matter experts

Gold Team Review

When: When document is final

Why: Determine that document is accurate, editorially consistent, and well-edited

Outcome: Final draft to submit

Who: Select color team members and proposal manager

Vitalii Krasnoselskyi/123RF

FIGURE 9.10 How to Structure a Formal Proposal Responding to an RFP

Key Elements of a Formal Proposal

Title page: Include the following content on the title page:

- Title of the proposal
- Name of the recipient of the proposal–company or individual
- Name of the writer of the proposal–company, author, or authors submitting the proposal
- Date the proposal was submitted

Executive summary: Include an executive summary that briefly summarizes the most important information for key decision makers. An executive summary for a proposal also has a persuasive purpose. Think of it as a short version of your proposal, designed to sell your solution. It typically includes the following:

- An opener that generates attention and interest in your proposal
- A compelling description of the client's need
- The solution you are proposing
- A brief description of your qualifications, focusing on evidence that you can be successful
- A call to action

Table of contents: To help readers find the material that interests them, provide a table of contents that includes a complete and accurate listing of the headings covered in the proposal. The complexity of the proposal will determine how many levels of headings you include.

References or works cited: If you refer to other sources in your proposal, list all those sources on a reference page. These sources might include articles, books, reports, websites, interviews, and brochures. References add to your credibility and help your audience easily find any information they want to explore further.

Appendices: Use appendices for additional information that may interest the reader but is too detailed to include in the body of the proposal. Typical proposal appendices include examples of previous work you have done, biographies, testimonials, survey results, product descriptions and technical specifications, complicated work schedules, or long tables that will not fit on one page. To ensure that you include only relevant appendices, refer to each appendix at least once in the body of the proposal. For example:

For the biographies of the consultants who will manage your project, see Appendix A.

We have many satisfied clients, as illustrated by the testimonials in Appendix B.

Appendix C includes a complete list of our products.

Label and arrange the appendices in the order you refer to them in the text.

■ **In summary,** proposals may be as informal as an email to your supervisor or as formal as a report written in response to an RFP. No matter what their form, all proposals are persuasive documents that share four common elements. They all do the following:

- Demonstrate an understanding of a problem, need, or opportunity
- Propose a solution that solves the problem, meets the need, or takes advantage of the opportunity
- Instill confidence that the idea is feasible and, if applicable, you are qualified to implement the idea
- Help the audience see meaningful benefits from implementing the proposal

With new proposal-writing software to make the process more efficient, businesses are able to produce more proposals more quickly, leading to increased business.

GRANT PROPOSALS @ WORK: Curt's Café

Photo courtesy of Curt's Cafe

People looking at Curt's Café from the outside may simply see it as a warm and inviting place to stop for a nice lunch or a great cup of coffee and a pastry. But the community of people who support Curt's Café knows that it is something more: a lifeline for underserved young men and women aged 15–24. Curt's serves youths who have had more than their share of challenges. Some have been involved with the criminal justice system; they might have been brought up in homes with domestic violence; they might have been involved with gangs; they might live in poverty and are housing insecure and food insecure; or they might have failed at school and at work. Regardless of their situation, they can see no path forward.

The other thing they have in common is that they are hungry to get on their feet and support themselves. Curt's turns away no one who asks for help. The mission of Curt's Café is to offer its clients the training in the job skills and life skills they need to stabilize their lives, get a job, and keep a job—and the café pays them a stipend while they learn.

Providing this service is expensive, and only 50 percent of the costs are covered by sales. Approximately 20 percent comes from individual donations. For the remaining 30 percent, the café relies on grants from funding agencies.

Laurie Kaplan, the director of development at Curt's Café, explains some of the challenges of writing

successful grant proposals. One challenge is to explain how Curt's Café works. Funders will not be interested if they think of Curt's as a café that simply hires and trains youths in need of short-term, easily accessible jobs. Instead, Kaplan and her colleagues need to reframe funders' thinking so that they understand Curt's as a not-for-profit job training center for underserved youths that both operates a café as a job training site and provides young people with social service support to help ensure their forward momentum in life.

A second challenge in writing grant proposals is the time it takes to prepare a proposal. According to Kaplan, the easiest proposals take 5 to 10 hours to write. Government proposals take up to a week. Often it is difficult to get information in advance about what the agencies want to fund; for example, they might have a specific focus one year that differs from their focus the previous year. As a result, it's challenging to know whether to invest time in writing a subsequent proposal. That's why Kaplan appreciates the growing trend among funders to ask for letters of intent before proposals. The funders review shorter letters of intent and then invite organizations to submit proposals, which saves time for people on both the writing and reviewing sides of the process.

According to Kaplan, the biggest challenge is ensuring that a proposal aligns what the café needs with what the funders want to support. Kaplan points out that "Many foundations, upwards of 80 percent, are program and project based." That means they do not provide funds for operating cash flow. To get funding, Curt's must design projects that help accomplish its mission and at the same time meet funders' objectives. For a funder interested in supporting Curt's training mission, Kaplan and her team wrote a successful grant proposal for an out-of-house experiential training curriculum for its employees. The curriculum included field trips to hear speakers or visit museums—designed to broaden perspectives—combined with visits to other food service organizations as part of job skills training. For a different funder—a private corporation interested in funding workplace improvements, including equipment—Curt's crafted a proposal that resulted in a $15,000 refrigeration unit and an $8,000 stand mixer for the café.

(continued)

GRANT PROPOSALS @ WORK: Curt's Café (*Continued*)

Kaplan also emphasizes how important follow-up communication is—regardless of whether a grant proposal is successful. When a funder has supported a successful program, Kaplan makes sure to communicate that success. For example, she sent video clips to the organization that funded the experiential training curriculum so the funder could see how much the students benefitted from the program. Kaplan explains that it is equally important to follow up when grant proposal is not funded: "Particularly on the ones we lose,

I always go back and request information from the program officer. That gives me insight for future grants with that agency and others, too. What did we say? What were they not comfortable with? What were they looking for that we didn't include? Sometimes it's nothing that we said or did. You don't always know the drivers for decisions. This is the part of the process that is more art than science."

Source: Based on an interview with Laurie Kaplan

CASE SCENARIO

Proposing a Corporate Volunteer Program

This case scenario will help you review the chapter material by applying it to a specific situation.

Craig Allen enjoys his job at Kramer Electronics. Just three years out of college, Craig received a promotion and has new responsibilities. Craig's one regret is that he doesn't have as much time to devote to community service as he did in college. During college, Craig volunteered at a local children's hospital and worked as a baseball and soccer coach at a children's camp.

One day last week, Craig saw a newspaper article about corporate volunteer programs. He read that a growing number of companies are allowing employees to take one or two paid days off work each year to volunteer their time for special community projects. A committee within the company selects the projects based on applications from not-for-profit organizations and schools in the community.

Craig researched corporate volunteer programs and found that benefits of the programs include increased employee satisfaction and decreased employee turnover rates, as well as good public relations for the company. He became convinced that a corporate volunteer program would help both the community and Kramer Electronics. Craig decided to do some additional research and then propose to Tom Kramer, the CEO of the company, that Kramer Electronics adopt a corporate volunteer program.

Analyzing the Context

Craig first analyzes purpose, context, and content needs using the following list of questions. Put yourself in Craig's place.

Question 1: How would you answer these questions? Brainstorm some possible answers.

a. What am I proposing, and why?

b. What is the context of my proposal? Is it external or internal? Is it solicited or unsolicited? Is it competitive or noncompetitive?

c. Will my audience already be interested, or will I need to grab their attention?

d. What requirements, if any, must this proposal meet?

e. How will the audience benefit from the proposal?

f. What objections should I anticipate?

g. Should I do any initial research before writing the proposal? What do I need to learn?

Brainstorming Content for a Proposal

As the next step in preparing his proposal, Craig creates a draft outline using the following headings. He begins by brainstorming

content for each section. His goal is both to compose the most persuasive content possible and to answer the questions he anticipates Tom will ask.

a. Problem or opportunity

b. Proposed solution

c. Requirements

d. Benefits to Kramer Electronics and to employees

e. Implementation details

f. Feasibility

g. Costs

h. Next steps

Question 2: If you were brainstorming with Craig, what content would you consider for each of these section headings? To help you develop ideas, do a web or database search for corporate volunteer programs to see how other companies have structured their programs and what benefits they have enjoyed.

Identifying What to Include and What to Leave Out

As Craig researches companies that offer volunteer programs, he discovers at least one company that abandoned its program because the company found that employees abused it. Instead of doing volunteer work, some employees took a day off. This problem is a risk of corporate volunteer programs. Craig wonders, "What should I do with this information? Should I mention it, or should I ignore it?"

Question 3: If you were Craig, what would you do, and why?

Deciding on a Goal and Choosing the Best Format

As Craig sits down to draft his proposal, it occurs to him that he is not sure about the form of the proposal—or even its real goal. Should he write a formal proposal with a title page, executive summary, and appendices documenting his research? Is he ready to propose a detailed plan for implementing a volunteer program? Or should he write a more informal proposal to get Tom interested in the idea and then present additional research in a meeting?

Question 4: If you were Craig, what choice would you make, and why?

Study Questions in Review

SQ1 How do you use ACE to prepare an effective proposal? *(pages 314–320)*

- **Analyze: Understand the purpose, context, and content.** To analyze purpose, focus on the audience's needs and how you are proposing to address those needs. To analyze context, ask three questions: (1) Is your proposal external or internal? (2) Is it a solicited proposal or an unsolicited proposal? (3) Is it a competitive or noncompetitive proposal? Analyze the content by considering the requirements, benefits, and potential objections.
- **Compose: Develop persuasive content.** Use your analysis to develop content. A proposal typically accomplishes the following goals:
    - **Articulates the problem, need, or opportunity.**
    - **Presents a compelling recommendation, with supporting details.** Be sure to address the problem or opportunity and show how your proposal meets the requirements. Provide sufficient detail so that the audience can make an informed decision.
    - **Identifies the outcomes and benefits** of addressing the problem or opportunity.
    - **Establishes feasibility and credibility.** Show that the plan is achievable and that you are qualified to do the work.
    - **Requests action.**
- **Evaluate: Assess the effectiveness of the proposal.** Use a checklist that prompts you to think about key ideas: Have you convinced the audience that there is a problem? Is your solution a good one? Have you stressed benefits? Did you include enough information about implementation? If your proposal receives no response, follow up with an email that makes it easy for your audience to respond.

SQ2 What types of business proposals should you be prepared to write? *(pages 320–330)*

Three kinds of proposals are common in business. All three can be solicited or unsolicited, competitive or noncompetitive, and internal or external.

- **Proposals for action or change** are strongest when they make a business case.
- **Solicited sales proposals** and **unsolicited sales proposals** make a persuasive case that the audience will benefit from what you are proposing to sell.
- **Grant proposals and other proposals for funding** are targeted to specific funding agencies that are a good match with the project you are trying to fund. Identify a contact person at the funding organization, and arrange a personal meeting. Then draft a proposal identifying how you meet the agency's criteria and a cover letter summarizing the main points of your proposal.

SQ3 How do you structure and format a formal proposal? *(pages 330–335)*

- **Read RFPs carefully to identify content requirements.** To help readers find information they are looking for, write headings that relate to the RFP requirements. Place required documentation in appendices.
- **Structure a formal proposal like a formal report,** with a cover message, title page, executive summary, table of contents, references or works cited list, and appendices (if applicable). Ensure that your executive summary is not just informative; it must be designed to persuade.

Visual Summary

- What are you proposing and why?
- What is the context of your proposal? Is it external or internal? Is it solicited or unsolicited? Is it competitive or noncompetitive?
- Will your audience already be interested, or will you need to grab their attention?
- What requirements, if any, must this proposal meet?
- How will the audience benefit from the proposal?
- What objections should you anticipate?
- Should you do any initial research before writing the proposal? What do you need to learn?

Analyze

- Will the audience be convinced that the proposal addresses a real need?
- Have you stated what you are proposing?
- Have you shown that your proposal meets the need?
- Have you stressed audience benefits?
- Have you shown you are qualified?
- Have you explained the details: deliverables, costs, schedule?
- Have you asked for agreement?
- Have you used good headings and highlighted main points?
- Have you edited for style and tone?
- Have you proofread for errors?

Evaluate

ACE

Compose

- How formal or informal should this proposal be?
- What is the best medium for the proposal?
- How can you establish credibility?
- What content must you include?
- How should you organize the content?
- How can you use a "you" perspective?

Make the proposal persuasive by:

- Articulating the problem, need, or opportunity
- Identifying the outcomes and benefits
- Presenting a compelling recommendation
- Providing persuasive supporting details
- Requesting action

Use the same structure for formal proposals that you would use for formal reports:

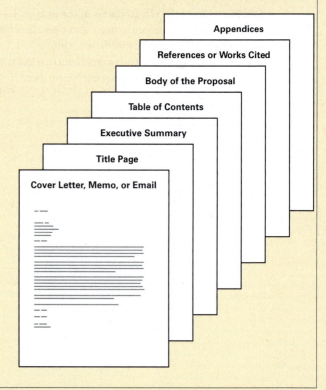

- Appendices
- References or Works Cited
- Body of the Proposal
- Table of Contents
- Executive Summary
- Title Page
- Cover Letter, Memo, or Email

Key Terms

Business case p. 320
Competitive proposal p. 316
Cover message p. 333
Deliverables p. 318
Executive summary p. 332
External proposal p. 315

Grant proposal p. 327
Internal
  proposal p. 315
Noncompetitive
  proposal p. 316
Proposal p. 314

Repurposing
  content p. 325
Request for proposal (RFP)
  p. 315
Software as a Service
  (SaaS) p. 325

Solicited
  proposal p. 315
Statement of work (SOW)
  p. 321
Unsolicited
  proposal p. 315

MyLab Business Communication

If your instructor is using MyLab Business Communication, go to **www.pearson.com/
mylab/business-communication** to complete the problems marked with this icon ⭐.

Review Questions

1 What is the difference between an internal proposal and an external proposal? Which is more likely to be formal, and which is more likely to be informal?

2 What is a solicited proposal? What is an unsolicited proposal? Identify a situation not already mentioned in the chapter in which you might send an unsolicited proposal.

3 What are the key persuasive elements that all proposals contain?

⭐ **4** If a client has already identified a need, why is it important to summarize that need in a solicited proposal?

⭐ **5** Why is it important to demonstrate feasibility and credibility in a proposal?

6 What are two ways that a proposal may be unethical?

⭐ **7** When you write a grant proposal, why is it important to find an appropriate funding agency?

8 When you respond to an RFP, why is it important to read the document carefully and take notes?

⭐ **9** Why is an executive summary important in a longer proposal?

10 How can proposal-writing software save you time and potentially improve a proposal?

Critical Thinking Questions

⭐ **1** You work for a restaurant, and you want to propose to the chef/owner that he update the menu to include more low-fat options. What research would you do in the analyzing phase of ACE to support your proposal? Where would you find that information?

⭐ **2** If you were going to propose an innovation or change in your college or university, what would you propose? Identify at least two benefits you could include in your proposal.

3 You work for a painting company, and you received an RFP from the city that asks you to submit a competitive proposal to paint the interior of the City Hall. What research should you do before writing the proposal? Where would you find that information?

4 Assume that you are writing the proposal to paint City Hall and want to include a section about your company's qualifications. How would you decide what details to include?

5 The sales proposal in Figure 9.5 on pages 323–324 lists both what the proposer (CES) agrees to do and what the client (Davis College) must do. Why is it important in this proposal to identify specific things that the client is required to do?

6 You work for a restaurant that is just beginning to offer catering services. You receive an RFP from a nearby company that requests a proposal for catering a large corporate event for 200 people. The RFP specifies that you must supply a list of other corporate events you have catered. Because you have never offered catering services before, you cannot meet that RFP requirement. Should you decide not to submit a proposal? If you do submit a proposal, what can you say to respond to that requirement?

7 Some proposal-writing software allows you to prepare a proposal as a web-based document that can include links to websites and to multimedia, such as videos. Imagine that Cronin Environmental Services (CES) decided to use proposal-writing software to prepare the proposal illustrated in Figure 9.5 on pages 323–324. What links or electronic attachments could CES include in the proposal to make the proposal more persuasive or easier for the client to use? **[Related to the Technology feature on page 325]**

8 As you learned in the Culture feature, in China, proposals initiate negotiations. In Italy, proposals finalize negotiations. What are the implications of these differences for how you would approach the proposal process in these two countries? **[Related to the Culture feature on page 321]**

Key Concept Exercises

 SQ1 **How do you use ACE to prepare an effective proposal?** *(pages 314–320)*

1 Analyze: Understand the purpose, context, and content

a. You work in the business office of Hotel Oldham, and you received an RFP from the National Sports Collectors Association (NSCA), which would like to hold its annual convention and memorabilia sale in your hotel. The planners anticipate that more than 1,000 people will attend. It's your job to write a proposal to the NSCA. How would you describe that proposal? Solicited or unsolicited? Competitive or noncompetitive? Internal or external? Identify at least one requirement that you will need to meet in your proposal. Identify one potential benefit you may want to include. Identify at least one potential objection you may have to address. What medium would you use to compose and deliver that proposal?

b. You work for SurveyKing, a company that designs customer satisfaction surveys. One of your long-time customers, a regional airline, has requested that you submit a proposal to design a customer survey to assess satisfaction with a new service. Would you consider this proposal to be solicited or unsolicited? Competitive or noncompetitive? Internal or external? Review Study Question 9.2 of this chapter, which lists typical content for a proposal. In this situation, what content do you think will be most important for getting the sale? What content will be less important? What medium would you choose to compose and deliver the proposal?

2 Compose: Develop persuasive content—Articulate the problem, need, or opportunity

You work for Natural Organix, a company that makes organic personal care products such as soaps, shampoos, lotions, and deodorants. Currently, the company advertises its products in traditional ways: through magazine and newspaper advertising, on television, and through in-store displays. You want to propose that the company use social media—such as Facebook, Instagram, Twitter, and YouTube—to gain greater visibility among its target customers—women and men aged 16 to 30.

Conduct web-based research on social media marketing. Based on that research and what you know from your own experience, draft a paragraph that articulates the problem or opportunity that the company can address by having a presence on social media. You may choose to focus on one particular social media tool rather than all of them.

3 Compose: Develop persuasive content—Present a compelling recommendation with supporting details

Refer to Exercise 2. Write a paragraph articulating a specific recommendation or proposal that you will make to your company management. What specifically will you propose that they do? Decide whether you want to propose that the company invest heavily in social media marketing or implement a pilot project. Provide compelling reasons for your recommendation.

4 Compose: Develop persuasive content—Identify the outcomes and benefits

Refer to Exercises 2 and 3. Write a list of benefits that social media marketing will provide for Natural Organix. Be sure to provide reasoning and, if possible, evidence to support those benefits.

5 Compose: Develop persuasive content—Establish feasibility and credibility [Related to the Ethics feature on page 330]

You and one of your classmates plan to launch a new business after graduation—running a delivery service for dry cleaners in your town. Twice a week, you will pick up dry cleaning from customers to drop off at the dry cleaner, and twice a week you will deliver cleaned clothes back to the customers. Your partner, an information technology major, has developed an app that allows customers to schedule this service and pay in advance. The two of you plan to make an unsolicited sales proposal to all the dry cleaners in your town. You are concerned, however, about what to say about your qualifications. You and your classmate have no previous business experience, and you cannot truthfully say that you have delivery experience, customer service experience, or experience running an e-commerce website.

Brainstorm some ideas that you might include in your proposal to persuade your audience that you are capable of doing the job and providing the company with a real benefit. For this exercise, assume that each idea is true and could be included ethically.

6 Compose: Develop persuasive content—Request action

Refer to Exercise 5. Assume that you write an unsolicited sales proposal in the form of a letter to the dry cleaners in town. How will you end that letter? What action will you request?

7 Evaluate: Assess the effectiveness of the proposal

You manage the ticket sales department of a new women's professional soccer franchise in your city. You asked each of the three associates in your department to propose one possible community outreach program that will help the soccer club promote ticket sales. After doing initial research, each associate wrote an introduction to a proposal with a brief problem statement and solution. Evaluate each of the following problem statements. Will the audience be convinced that the proposal is addressing a real need? Will the audience be convinced that the proposal is a good way to meet the need? Explain your answers.

a. Because our soccer club is new, we do not yet have a fan base and sufficient ticket sales. I propose that we increase ticket sales by placing posters throughout the community and advertising on local television stations. These marketing strategies will raise awareness about our team. The cost will be minimal, but the publicity will provide our team exposure to potential fans.

b. I think the real reason we are not selling tickets is that our community has never had a women's sports team. I propose that we hold a "Dollar Day," charging only a dollar per ticket to encourage people to attend the women's soccer games and help them see how exciting women's sports can be. The cost will be minimal, since we are practically giving away seats that will otherwise be empty, but the $1 tickets will provide our team positive publicity and exposure to potential fans.

c. Interviews with general managers of five women's professional basketball teams revealed that these teams have modestly increased ticket sales each year by developing two fan bases: (1) women who are interested in fitness and participate in recreational sports and (2) young female athletes and their families. I propose that we reach out to these two audiences by sponsoring free soccer clinics for area fitness clubs and for youth soccer teams throughout the city. The cost will be minimal—only our players' time—but the clinics will provide our team positive publicity and exposure to potential fans.

What types of business proposals should you be prepared to write? *(pages 320–330)*

8 Proposals for action or change

You work at a bank that recently reduced its workforce to save money. Tellers are handling more transactions per hour to get through the workload, and many are not as friendly to customers as they used to be. You notice that customer complaints have increased. You would like to make a proposal to management to address customer complaints. You are considering two alternatives: (1) hiring an additional teller to reduce the workload and (2) investing in customer service training for all tellers. You know that you will need to make a business case for any solution you propose. What will you need to research to make a business case? Create a list of questions you want to answer before making your proposal.

9 Does your proposal demonstrate integrity? [Related to the Ethics feature on page 330]

Refer to Exercise 8. Assume that you spoke with the teller supervisor, Anna, who agreed that both of your suggestions should be forwarded to the bank's manager. She encourages you to draft a proposal and offers the following "evidence" to include in your proposal:

- Customer complaints will continue to increase if a solution is not found quickly.
- Hiring a teller will reduce overall complaints, which will increase our customer base.
- The investment in customer service training will ensure all customers are happy and satisfied with the bank's services.
- This two-pronged approach to solving the problem is the only way to ensure the bank's success.

Although you appreciate Anna's support, you do not believe that including these statements would be ethical because they are not based on real evidence. How could you modify these statements to be more accurate?

10 Solicited sales proposals

Refer to Exercises 5 and 6. Assume that you and your classmate have graduated, and your delivery service for dry cleaners is now well established. You have been working with six local dry cleaners, and you have even been able to hire two employees to help with the deliveries so you can keep up with the bookkeeping, invoicing, and marketing needs of your company. Today, you receive a call from Pam McNeely of Hoff Industries, one of the largest employers in town. Pam often uses your services for her personal needs, but today she is calling to see if you would be interested in providing corporate delivery service for employees of Hoff Industries. Of its 500 employees, 150 have indicated interest in regular dry cleaning delivery service to/from their offices so they don't have to drive to the cleaners before or after work. Pam would like you to send her a sales proposal so that she can submit it to her supervisor. You are very interested in this possibility because you would nearly double your current client base. In addition, being able to pick up and drop off orders at one location will reduce your travel costs per run. However, you need to hire at least one more driver and perhaps even purchase a van to accommodate the volume of clothing. You tell Pam you are very interested and will work on a proposal with your business partner. What headings would you include in the proposal? Identify several bullet points for each heading as a working outline of your proposal.

11 Writing proposals for different cultures [Related to the Culture feature on page 322]

As a fashion industry major, you were very happy to get a job as business manager for an independent clothing designer whose clothing is sold in boutiques in Los Angeles, New York, Chicago, and Atlanta. The designer, your boss, would like to expand her distribution into international markets, starting with Japan. A trendy boutique, Parco, has expressed interest in being the exclusive outlet for her designs in Japan. Your boss is planning a trip to Japan to begin discussions with Parco. She hopes the discussions will culminate in a proposal and agreement. However, she has never done business in Japan before. She asks you to do some initial research to help her prepare to write a proposal.

As part of your research, you look at cultural anthropologist Geert Hofstede's theory of cultural dimensions and learn that Japan rates high on the "uncertainty avoidance index."[25] According to Hofstede:

> The uncertainty avoidance dimension expresses the degree to which the members of a society feel uncomfortable with uncertainty and ambiguity. The fundamental issue here is how a society deals with the fact that the future can never be known: should we try to control the future or just let it happen?[26]

Based on this research, you hypothesize that anyone writing a proposal for a Japanese audience should try to minimize uncertainty. But what does that mean? Here are some questions to discuss with your boss. What are your answers, and why?

a. When should you write the proposal—before meeting with the potential business partner to discuss at the meeting or later?

b. Should the proposal contain very general and flexible agreements or very detailed and specific agreements?

c. You imagine that your Japanese business partners will want to be very certain of the quality of your products before signing an agreement. What can you say in a proposal that will help your audience feel confident about product quality?

d. If you present a proposal either before or after your visit, should you expect the Japanese to sign it quickly to get the project started, or to study it and perhaps request clarification?

12 Unsolicited sales proposals

You work for a web design company that is looking for new clients. In addition to advertising and sending direct mail, your company would like to send unsolicited sales proposals to small businesses with websites that need to be updated. Your boss has asked you to search the web to find one or two sites that would benefit from your design expertise and then develop a sales proposal to send to those businesses.

Find a small business website that you believe can be improved. Write the first one or two paragraphs of a proposal (in letter form) to that company. In this introductory material, be sure to introduce yourself and your design company, explain what you are proposing, and offer a statement persuading your audience that you can help the company solve a problem or take advantage of an opportunity. Also, be sure not to offend your potential client by saying that its current website is not effective.

13 Grant proposals and other proposals for funding

The Highwood Police Department plans to apply for a Community Development Grant (CDG) from the City of Highwood. Each year, the city funds more than $200,000 in grants. The city's website describes the goals of these grants in this way: Highwood uses its CDG funds to further its community development objectives by focusing on low- and moderate-income individuals, families, and neighborhoods to:

- Provide decent housing
- Provide a suitable living environment
- Expand economic opportunities

The Highwood Police Department would like to fund a workout room in the police station. Read the introduction to the following grant proposal. Evaluate whether you think this proposal will persuade the grant committee that the proposed project meets the funding goals of the grant. Would you recommend any revisions?

> Police officers in the Highwood Police Department experience a high rate of cardiovascular and musculoskeletal problems. With more officers becoming sick and injured, fewer are available to protect public safety. To keep the officers fit for duty, the Highwood Police Department requests that the City Council authorize a Community Development Grant to pay for a fitness center for Highwood police officers. According to research by the American Fitness Council, regular exercise will help keep law enforcement officers healthy. Project objectives include reducing by 20 percent the use of sick leave due to these problems.
>
> Specifically, we request $32,000 to renovate the loft of the police garage as a workout room, buy exercise equipment, and train all participants. Future maintenance of the project will be possible through volunteer fundraising efforts carried out by the Highwood Police Department Benevolent Association.

14 Using proposal-writing software [Related to the Technology feature on page 325]

You work for a catering company that writes proposals to event companies and individuals planning private events. Use your favorite web search tool, such as Google or Bing, to find three proposal-writing software programs that allow you to create a template for catering company sales. Analyze the proposal options from each program and compare the differences. Write a one-page summary that outlines the similarities and differences among these programs and the specific opportunities for a catering company that uses proposal-writing software.

 How do you structure and format a formal proposal? *(pages 330–335)*

15 Read RFPs carefully to identify content requirements

You work for a clothing manufacturer that specializes in law enforcement and military uniforms. You are responding to an RFP to provide uniforms for the Washtenaw County Sheriff's Department in Ann Arbor, Michigan. The RFP outlines very specific requirements for the uniforms. You can meet all the requirements except one: "The front and rear creases in the trouser legs must incorporate a permanent modified silicone crease produced by the Lintrak™ System." Your company does not use this system but instead a competitive system called SIROSET, developed in China. You believe the SIROSET system is equally good. How will you address this issue in your proposal?

16 Structure a formal proposal like a formal report

Refer to the informal proposal to hire an intern in Figure 9.2 on page 319. Assume that the recipient, Doug Seaver, agrees with your proposal and asks you to write a formal proposal that he can share with the company executive committee for a formal vote. Describe the formal structure you would use to assemble your proposal, and explain the content you would include in each section. Identify supporting evidence you might include in appendices.

Writing Exercises

17 Writing a cover message

The proposal in Figure 9.4 on page 321 is a short formal proposal. Assume that Kip Koestler is sending this proposal as an email attachment to Leann Towner, the director of information technology at his company, United Consolidated, Inc. Write a persuasive cover email for the proposal.

18 Writing a proposal to cut costs

Your university just announced that it is increasing tuition for next year to cover increased costs. Yet everywhere you look—in the cafeteria, in the dormitories, in the athletic facilities—you see areas where the university could cut costs. Write a letter to your university administration that proposes one specific cost-cutting initiative. Do some research that will help you estimate current costs and potential savings by implementing your initiative. If your initiative will result in benefits beyond cost savings, be sure to stress those also. Use the ACE process to analyze, compose, and evaluate your letter.

19 Proposing renovations

You are a manager at a small independent restaurant. The building, while quaint and charming, has restrooms that are small, badly located, and awkwardly arranged, with plumbing and electrical fixtures that are showing their age. Lately you have been having difficulty keeping the restrooms tidy and managing the flow of customers in and out of the restrooms. These are some of the specific problems:

- The door to the men's restroom opens outward into a narrow hallway. If the person exiting the restroom opens the door too quickly, he may hit someone who is walking past.

- Customers frequently turn off the lights when they leave either restroom, making it difficult for the next people entering to find their way. Occasionally, the switch in the women's restroom will cause a short circuit, leaving the restroom and the hallway dark.

- The old toilets in both restrooms clog immediately if anything heavier than special fast-dissolving toilet paper is used. Customers sometimes discard ordinary paper tissues or even paper towels in the toilets, causing expensive plumbing mishaps. You have been told by the owners that plans to renovate the building are in development, but there is "no money available" to buy new fixtures or make repairs or modifications to the restrooms now. They suggest posting better signs to remind customers to open the door carefully, not turn out the lights, and not throw away paper towels in the toilets. However, you are convinced that better signs will not produce any significant improvements, while also annoying the customers and embarrassing the staff.

The restaurant's busiest season is about to begin, and you are confident that if you work with a local contractor, you can get the door rehung, the wiring fixed, and the toilets replaced before the business accelerates. Use the ACE process to write a letter to the owners in which you propose to renovate the bathrooms. Remember to highlight the benefits of your plan, and address their potential objections.

20 Writing a letter of inquiry for a funding proposal

You work as an administrator in an elementary school in a low-income neighborhood. The school district has recently cut the school's budget for the arts, but your school would like to offer an after-school arts enrichment program for its students. Look online for an appropriate agency or foundation interested in funding education programs. Write a letter of inquiry to this agency or foundation, explaining the details of a program—for example, your school's need for $25,000 for teachers and equipment, the community the program would serve, the number of students who will use the program, and the ultimate objective of the program. To develop the details for your proposal, you can either research existing after-school art programs or use your imagination to create realistic details.

Collaboration Exercises

21 Analyzing requests for proposals

As a team with a few other students, review at least three websites that publish requests for proposals. The following websites may be helpful. You can find these sites with a web browser by typing in the name and the letters "RFP." You may also find RFPs in other places by searching for "RFP" on the web.

- **FedBizOpps.** The single government point-of-entry (GPE) for federal government procurement opportunities.
- **BizWiz.** A website for general business opportunities, listed under the link "RFP-Direct."
- **Network Computing.** A site requesting proposals for LANs, WANs, web management, network security, and more.
- **Pollution Prevention Request for Proposal Clearinghouse.** Provides information on current and pending RFPs related to pollution prevention.
- **City of Los Angeles.** Lists bids, RFPs, and grants for construction, auditing, supplies and equipment, and telecommunications.
- **City of Houston.** Provides downloadable bids for various services.
- **City of Boston.** Lists bids and RFPs.

  In a brief report to your instructor or a presentation to the class, discuss the following questions.

  a. What are some of the industries that are requesting proposals, and what types of products or services are these industries interested in?

  b. What kind of information do these RFPs provide?

  c. What kind of information do the RFPs request?

22 Proposing a change at your school

As a team with a few other students, identify a change that would benefit your school, a department within your school, or a specific course. Write a formal proposal to the decision maker, offering a recommendation for change. Your proposal may include the following sections or different sections if they are more useful for your topic. If you use these sections, modify the headings to be content specific.

- Problem
- Proposed Solution
- Rationale and Benefits
- Implementation Suggestions
- Cost

  Structure the team activity in this way, following the ACE process:

  Analyze: As a team, identify the change and conduct research to learn more about the problem and to develop a feasible and effective solution. Together outline the content and develop notes for each section.

  Compose: Have half the team members work as a subteam to make key composing decisions and draft the proposal.

  Evaluate: Have the remaining half of the team evaluate and revise the proposal, following the evaluation checklist in Figure 9.3 on page 320.

  Submit your notes, first draft, and revised draft to your instructor.

23 Reviewing proposals with color teams [Related to the Collaboration feature on page 333]

Refer to Exercise 22. Do the same assignment but pair with another team in the class and structure the ACE process in the following way:

  Analyze: As a team, identify the change and conduct research to learn more about the problem and to develop a feasible and effective solution. Together outline the content and develop notes for each section.

  Evaluate (pink team): Work with your paired team to provide each other pink reviews of each other's outline and notes to help ensure that document will meet the requirements and has clear messaging. Provide your feedback in writing.

  Compose: Based on the review, make key composing decisions and draft the proposal.

  Evaluate (red team): Work with your paired team to provide each other red reviews of the completed draft. Focus on whether the document is clear, complete, and persuasive. Provide your feedback in writing.

Revise your team's draft. Then submit to your instructor your notes, first draft, and revised draft, and the reviews you received.

Social Media Exercises

24 Proposal to use social media

Refer to Exercises 2, 3, and 4 on page 340. Conduct the research and analysis required in those exercises and write a one- to two-page memo proposing that your company use social media as a marketing tool. Your proposal may focus on using a specific social media program, a specific type of marketing program using social media, or both.

25 Evaluating proposals on Kickstarter

Go to Kickstarter (www.kickstarter.com), a social crowdfunding platform, and familiarize yourself with the process and the rules for creating projects. Identify eight to ten projects of interest to you, and quickly skim the projects to reduce the number to a short list of three projects. Use the checklist for evaluating proposals (Figure 9.3) to evaluate the pitch for each project on your short list. Rank the projects according to how well you think their pitches address the questions on the checklist. Then select one of the following options:

  a. Summarize the results of your selection and evaluation process in a short memo to your instructor. Explain your criteria for selection at each step: How did you select the first set of eight to ten projects, why did you include or reject each project when composing the short list of three to five projects, and how did you assign your rankings?

b. Prepare a short slide presentation (stand-alone slide deck) explaining how Kickstarter pitches for funding differ from other proposals to an audience of potential executives. Use examples from the best and worst projects from the set you examined to illustrate your points.

c. Draft an extended comment to the creator(s) of one of the Kickstarter projects you examined. Highlight the most and least effective parts of the proposal and offer suggestions for making the proposal more persuasive.

Speaking Exercises

26 Making informal/impromptu presentations

a. Identify a change in graduation requirements that you would recommend for your school or major. In a two–minute presentation, identify the problem, your proposed solution, and one benefit to the school or the major.

b. An anonymous benefactor has given your business communication class $100 to donate to one charity. In a two–minute presentation to the class, propose a charity. Provide at least two reasons the class should select this charity.

27 Executive briefings

a. You work for an organization that prepares many proposals during the year. Your supervisor asks you to evaluate software designed to help write or generate proposals. Search the web to find two programs and prepare a five-minute executive briefing that answers three questions: (1) In what ways can proposal-writing software help an organization? (2) What are the limitations of this kind of software? (3) What specific software program would you recommend and why? Be sure to cite specific details to support your points.

b. Select a sample proposal from either Figure 9.2, Figure 9.4, Figure 9.5, or Figure 9.6. Imagine that you want to present this proposal orally to a decision maker in a five-minute presentation. Prepare that presentation and deliver it to your class.

Grammar Exercises

28 Semicolons and colons (see Appendix C: Grammar, Punctuation, Mechanics, and Conventions—Sections 2.3 and 2.4)

Type the following paragraph, correcting the 10 errors or omissions in the use of semicolons and colons (see Sections 2.3 and 2.4). Underline all your corrections.

In the online article "How to Give a Professional Voicemail Greeting The Business Etiquette of Voicemail Greetings," author James Bucki asks, "What would I want to know from the voicemail greeting?" The greeting may be perfectly clear to you however, the caller may be mystified. His advice create the greeting as if you were the listener at the other end. As a general rule, the length of a voicemail greeting should be: no longer than 20–25 seconds. Some of the most annoying greetings are: long introductions, greetings that are too casual or personal, and background music of any kind (especially music that drowns out the message). Avoid endings that are not business related (such as "have a blessed day"); because they may strike customers and clients as presumptuous. Here is an example of a bad voicemail greeting; "Hi. This is Accounting. Leave me a message." Callers have no idea whether they have reached the right person; nor do they know if they even have the right company. Too little information is bad, conversely, so is too much information.

Business callers don't want personal details, including: the fun spot where you are vacationing; or that you are out sick with the flu.

29 Quotation marks and italics (see Appendix C: Grammar, Punctuation, Mechanics, and Conventions—Section 2.5)

Type the following paragraph, correcting the 10 errors or omissions in the use of quotation marks and italics. Count each pair of quotation marks as one (see Sections 2.5.1 and 2.5.2). Underline all your corrections.

It's a *good* idea to review the voicemail greeting on your personal phone, especially if potential employers might call. As part of his greeting, my friend Joe recorded John Cleese speaking lines from the *Dead Parrot Sketch* from the British television comedy "Monty Python's Flying Circus." His friends all thought it was really funny, using the words hilarious and clever to describe the greeting. One afternoon he retrieved a phone message that said, You really should use a more professional greeting. The voice continued, I called to offer you a job interview, but I've changed my mind. Joe thought, 'I wouldn't want to work for someone who didn't understand the humor in the "Dead Parrot Sketch," anyway. Sounds like this guy just doesn't get it.' Maybe not, but Joe's chances with that company are kaput.

MyLab Business Communication

Go to **www.pearson.com/mylab/business-communication** for Auto-graded writing questions as well as the following Assisted-graded writing questions:

1. In Chapter 5: Communicating Persuasive Messages, you learned about persuasive sales letters. In what ways might an unsolicited sales proposal be different from a persuasive sales letter?

2. Many funding agencies request that you send them a letter or schedule a meeting to express interest before submitting a full grant proposal. Why do you imagine these agencies require this initial communication? How does it benefit both the funding agency and the proposer?

References

1. Landes, T. (2013). Proposal writing: Choose your battles. *Canadian Consulting Engineer, 54*(2), 34–37. Retrieved from http://www.canadianconsultingengineer.com/features/proposal-writing-choose-your-battles/

2. Sant, T. (2012). *Persuasive business proposals: Writing to win more customers, clients and contracts.* New York. AMACOM Books.

3. Enns, B. (n.d.). The magic email. Retrieved from http://www.winwithoutpitching.com/magic-email/

4. Gambles, I. (2009). *Making the business case: Proposals that succeed for projects that work.* Farnham, UK: Gower Publishing, Ltd.

5. Business meeting etiquette. (2008). Chinatrade.com. Retrieved from http://www.chinatrade.com/blog/business-meeting-etiquette

6. Beamer, L. (1998). Bridging business cultures. *China Business Review, 25*(3), 54–58.

7. Gong, K. (2011). Cultural difference effects on business: Holding up Sino-U.S. business negotiation as a model. *Cross-Cultural Communication, 7*(2), 101–104.

8. Harrison, M., & Hedley, M. (n.d.). Marketing and selling to Chinese business. Retrieved from https://www.b2binternational.com/publications/chinese-marketing-selling/

9. Schuster, C. (2004, November 1). How to manage a contract in China. *Agency Sales Magazine.* Retrieved from http://business.highbeam.com/19/article-1G1-125067432/manage-contract-china

10. Katz, L. (2014). *Negotiating international business: Brazil.* [E-book]. Amazon Digital Services.

11. Hupert, A. (2017, August 7). The international negotiator: Apple in China (from flashmba.com). Retrieved from http://chinasolved.com/2017/08/international-negotiator-apple-china-from-flashmba-com/

12. Kumar, R., & Sethi, A. (2016). Negotiating and resolving conflicts in India (pp. 130–139). *Doing business in India: A guide for Western managers.* New York. NY: Palgrave Macmillan.

13. Katz, L. (2014). *Negotiating international business: Italy.* [E-book]. Amazon Digital Services.

14. The Walmart Foundation. (2017). Our focus. Retrieved from http://giving.walmart.com/our-focus

15. The Walmart Foundation. (2017). State giving program. Retrieved from http://corporate.walmart.com/_foundation_/apply-for-grants/state-giving-program

16. The Walmart Foundation. (2017). Community. Retrieved from http://giving.walmart.com/walmart-foundation/community

17. Anne Bergeron & Co. Consulting. (2015, May 27). The winning bid: Do's and don'ts for RPFs. [Blog post.] Retrieved from http://www.bergeronconsult.com/blog/2015/5/27/the-winning-bid-dos-and-donts-for-rfps

18. Lewis, H. (2012). *Bids, tenders and proposals: Winning business through best practice.* London, UK: Kogan.

19. Gambles, I. (2009). *Making the business case: Proposals that succeed for projects that work.* Farnham, UK: Gower Publishing, Ltd.

20. Murray, J. W. (2008). Ethical considerations: What not to write. In J. W. Murray, *The complete guide to writing effective and award winning business proposals* (pp. 41–50). Ocala, FL: Atlantic Publishing Co.

21. Faulkner, J. (2015 September 15). How to write an executive summary for your proposal. [Blog post]. Retrieved from https://www.proposify.biz/blog/executive-summary

22. XPRT. (2015, February 15). Secrets of successful color team reviews. Retrieved from https://www.xprts.co/blog/secrets-of-successful-color-team-reviews

23. Brisson, D. (2013, December 12). A guide to proposal color reviews & ratings. [Blog post]. Retrieved from https://www.aockeysolutions.com/blog/articles/gold-at-the-end-of-the-rainbow-proposal-color-reviews-ratings/

24. Lieberman, R. D. (2007, January). 10 big mistakes in government contract bidding. *Contract Management, 47*(1), 30–38.

25. The Hoftstede Centre. (2017). What about Japan? Retrieved from http://geert-hofstede.com/japan.html

26. The Hofstede Centre. (2017). National culture. Retrieved from https://geert-hofstede.com/national-culture.html

Preparing
Business Reports

Aila Images/Shutterstock; ESB Professional/Shutterstock; Hans Kim/Shutterstock

STUDY QUESTIONS

MyLab Business Communication

⭐Improve Your Grade!

If your instructor is using MyLab Business Communication, visit **www.pearson.com/mylab/business-communication** for videos, simulations, and writing exercises.

New Hires @ Work

Darrell Coleman
Georgia Southern University

Data Analyst @ Georgia Southern Career Services

At Georgia Southern, all departments need to justify their budget requests. As a data analyst for Career Services, I generate reports to support my department's requests. I report on how many students use our services, how many attend specific events, how many employers recruit on campus, and what those employers are looking for. My tables and graphs have to be clear and easy to read so that my supervisor can use them to persuade the vice president of student affairs that we need a specific pool of funding for the next year.

Photo courtesy of Darrell Coleman

347

Chapter 10 | Introduction

As a student, you probably have experience writing reports—or papers—for your classes, so you may assume that you are well prepared to write business reports. Maybe not! Most student reports are assigned to further your education. They prove to your instructors that you have learned material relevant to the course. By contrast, *business reports* are "assigned" to share information and analysis with people who need to manage projects, make decisions, and solve problems. The end result can make or break the business's bottom line. This chapter introduces you to a variety of report types and formats, along with some key writing techniques that will help you produce reports that are useful, clear, concise, readable, and accurate—no matter what the purpose or format of the report.

(SQ1) How can ACE help you write a business report?

All business reports have one thing in common: They answer business questions. When you write a report, your job is to provide the information and analysis that answers those questions in a document that is easy for your audience to read and use. The ACE communication process can guide you through the steps of analyzing, composing, and evaluating to create a report that meets this goal.

Analyze to understand purpose and report type

Analyze

informational report A report that provides readers with facts that they can easily understand and refer to when necessary. Meeting minutes, trip reports, and progress reports are types of informational reports.

analytical report A report that analyzes information to solve a problem or support a business decision.

Typically, a report is either informational or analytical, depending on its purpose and the key question it answers. For example, reports summarizing business trips or decisions made at meetings would be **informational reports**. Their main goal is to provide facts that readers can easily understand and refer to when necessary. By contrast, **analytical reports** help readers draw conclusions to solve problems or support business decisions. For example, a report that analyzes what you learned on a business trip and then makes a recommendation would be an analytical report. The first step in writing a report is to identify the question you are answering and the type of report you are writing. **Figure 10.1** lists common business questions and the types of reports that answer them.

FIGURE 10.1 How to Determine What Type of Report to Write

QUESTION	INFORMATIONAL REPORTS	ANALYTICAL REPORTS
What have you accomplished so far?	Progress Report	
What were the key results of the meeting?	Meeting Minutes	
What happened on the trip?	Trip Report	
What did your investigation reveal?	Investigation Report	
Are we complying with policies and regulations?	Compliance Report	
Is this plan feasible?		Feasibility Report
What is the better choice? Have our actions been successful?		Evaluation Report
What should we do?		Recommendation Report

Analyze to understand audience needs

When the process of researching a report is long and involved, you cannot include all the information you find. If you do, your report will be overly long and unfocused. Instead, analyze your audience to determine what information they need. **Figure 10.2** lists questions that will help you determine what information to include.

To analyze your audience, answer these questions:

1. **Who are the primary and secondary audiences?**
   - Why will they be using and reading this report?
   - Will they be motivated to read it, or will you need to provide motivation?

2. **What does the audience already know about the situation or topic?**
   - How much context or background do they need?

3. **What does the audience need to know?**
   - What are their key questions and concerns?
   - What information is important to include?

4. **What is the audience's expectation?**
   - Does the audience expect just information?
   - Or do they expect analysis and recommendations?

5. **How much credibility do you have with your audience?**
   - How can you increase your credibility in the report to ensure the audience has confidence in the information and analysis you provide?

FIGURE 10.2 Audience Analysis Questions

Analyze to choose the best medium

Reports may be prepared in many different forms: email, memo, formal manuscript, online report, or **report deck**—a report written in PowerPoint or other presentation software. When choosing the best medium for your report, consider the length, audience, and formality. In addition, consider the way you will deliver the report and how others will use it. **Figure 10.3** on page 350 presents the most common options.

report deck A report document written in PowerPoint or other presentation software.

Compose your report to meet audience expectations

When audiences read reports, they expect to find key elements of the report to be located in specific places, depending on the report format. These elements include identifying information, preview, detailed discussion, and (optionally) additional documentation:

- **Identifying information.** Business reports clearly identify the author, the date, and the topic or title. Some reports also identify the intended audience.

- **Preview.** Almost all business reports use a direct organization, beginning with one or more preview elements that provide readers with a quick understanding of the purpose, structure, content, and main ideas of the report. In reports written as emails, letters, or memos, the first paragraph provides the preview. Longer formal reports include a combination of preview elements, including a table of contents, an introduction, and either an abstract or an executive summary. Informational reports may begin with an **abstract**—one or two paragraphs that summarize the purpose and main points. By contrast, analytical reports often begin with an **executive summary**: a separate, stand-alone mini-report that completely summarizes the report's main ideas and recommendations. An executive summary is designed for decision makers who may not have time to read the detailed discussion.

- **Detailed discussion.** Following the introduction, the body of the report provides the detailed discussion. The discussion is typically divided into sections that are signaled by headings. The best headings are not generic but are content-focused and specific to that report. For example, "Analysis" is vague, but "Risks and Benefits of Using Groupon as a Marketing Tool" identifies the specific content of the section.

abstract One or two paragraphs—often included at the beginning of a formal informational report—that either (a) describe the content of the report so that a reader can decide whether to read the report or (b) briefly summarize the report, including the main points, conclusions, and recommendations.

executive summary A separate, stand-alone mini-document, included at the beginning of a longer document that completely summarizes the document's main ideas.

FIGURE 10.3 Selecting the Best Medium for Reports

MEDIUM/FEATURES	ADVANTAGES	DISADVANTAGES
MEMO REPORT—See Figure 10.6, page 355		
What it is best used for: short internal reports **What it looks like:** • Uses standard memo headings (To, From, Date, and Subject—and often Copies) • Identifies the topic in the subject line • Uses content headings to signal how information is organized	• Is short and easy to read • Can include physical attachments such as DVDs or brochures, when produced in hard copy • Can be delivered securely—even hand delivered—to the audience • Can be filed in hard copy or electronically for future reference	• Is appropriate only for internal audiences • Incurs costs to print or copy if it is not sent as an email attachment
EMAIL REPORT—See Figure 10.8, page 357		
What it is best used for: short internal or external reports **What it looks like:** • Uses standard email headings • Identifies the topic in the subject line • Uses content headings to signal how information is organized	• Is short and easy to read • Can be distributed and received quickly, even to large audiences • Can be filed in hard copy or electronically for future reference	• May not be a private or secure medium for reporting sensitive content • Cannot easily support tables and graphs • Cannot include attachments that exist only in hard copy unless they are scanned
LETTER REPORT—See Figure 10.9, pages 358–359		
What it is best used for: relatively short reports (less than 10 pages) for external audiences **What it looks like:** • Is formatted on company letterhead • Uses traditional letter elements (date, inside address, salutation, complimentary close, signature block) • Includes a subject line to indicate the letter contains a report • Uses content headings to signal how information is organized	• Projects a more "official" or formal image than email • Can include physical attachments such as DVDs or brochures • Can be delivered securely to the audience • Can require the recipient's signature to ensure report was received • Can be produced as a PDF file to distribute and file electronically	• Is appropriate only for external audiences • Incurs costs of letterhead, printing, and postage if sent through postal mail • Takes at least a day to deliver if not emailed as an attachment
FORMAL REPORT (manuscript style)—See Figure 10.10, pages 361–372		
What it is best used for: reporting the results of significant research or a project **What it looks like:** • Includes title page, table of contents, executive summary, references, and appendices (if necessary) • Is prepared on plain paper (not letterhead) • Always includes headings to signal key sections	• Can be distributed internally or externally • Projects a formal image • Can be used for very long reports • Can easily include tables, graphs, and other graphics • Provides table of contents to help the audience find information • Can include supporting information as appendices • Can be produced as a PDF file to distribute and file electronically	• Incurs costs to print and deliver if sent through postal mail • Can be time-consuming to organize and format effectively
ONLINE REPORT—See Figure 10.14, page 379		
What it is best used for: • Reports that benefit from interactivity, including navigation by hyperlinks • Reports generated from online forms that pull data from a database • Reports that are "living documents" that continue to develop and be updated over time **What it looks like:** • Can be in the form of a web page, a wiki, or a blog	• Makes the report accessible to broad audiences • Allows data from several people to be combined into a master report • Can be easily updated to provide the audience with real-time information	• May not be a private and secure medium for sending sensitive content • Does not ensure immediate receipt because the audience must check the website

FIGURE 10.3 *(Continued)*

MEDIUM/FEATURES	ADVANTAGES	DISADVANTAGES
PRESENTATION REPORT DECK—See Figure 10.17, pages 383–384		
What it is best used for: • Reports that need to be presented orally as well as read **What it looks like:** • Is created with presentation software, such as PowerPoint • Includes much less text than traditional reports but more than traditional slide presentations • Is written to be understandable without a presenter • Conveys much of its information through graphs, diagrams, and other visual elements	• May serve double-duty as both a presentation file and a report • Can easily include tables, graphs, and images • Can be delivered securely to a targeted audience when it accompanies a presentation	• Can be time consuming to organize and format effectively • Does not provide as much detail as a formal report • Can be difficult to understand without a presenter, if not well written

• **Supporting information.** At the end of the report, you have the opportunity to add extra documentation to support your main points. In memo, email, and letter reports, additional documentation takes the form of an **attachment** or *enclosure*—a supplemental document that is included with the report. Attachments might provide details that not all readers would need and that would clutter the report if included. In more formal reports and in report decks, this additional information is included in an **appendix** or in multiple appendices. Research reports that include information from secondary sources also include a **reference list** or *bibliography*.

attachment A document that is included with a memo, an email, or a letter report to provide supplementary information.

appendix A section (or multiple sections, called appendices) included at the end of a formal report or proposal that provides supplementary information.

reference list A list of secondary research sources used in a research report.

Figure 10.4 summarizes where these elements appear in the various report formats. It also explains how to handle page numbering in formal manuscript reports. As you read through

FIGURE 10.4 How Elements of a Report Appear in Various Report Forms

	LETTER REPORT	MEMO OR EMAIL REPORT	FORMAL REPORT MANUSCRIPT *Elements*	*Page Numbering*
	At the beginning: letterhead or return address, inside address, date, subject line At the end: signature, distribution list	To:, From:, Date:, Subject:, Distribution:, cc:/xc:	Title Page	No number on the title page
PREVIEW	Introductory paragraph: purpose, overview of the report, summary of key points	Introductory paragraph: purpose, overview of the report, summary of key points	Table of Contents List of Figures and Tables	Small Roman numeral page numbers (i, ii, iii, etc.) for all pages between the title page and the introduction
			Abstract or Executive Summary	
			Introduction	Arabic page numbers (1, 2, 3 etc.) begin with the introduction, on page 1
DETAILED DISCUSSION	Paragraphs or sections that develop and support the main idea/conclusions	Paragraphs or sections that develop and support the main idea/conclusions	Sections of the report that develop and support the main idea/conclusions	Page numbers continue from the introduction
SUPPORTING INFORMATION	Attachments	Attachments	References Lettered appendices (Appendix A, Appendix B)	Page numbers continue from the detailed discussion

the chapter, notice how the sample reports in the figures follow these guidelines. In addition, be sure to look at other reports generated by your organization to see if there are any organizational norms for handling these report elements. Following organizational models can help you meet audience expectations.

Compose

Compose using an objective and easy-to-read style

The writing style of a report lends credibility to your results. To adopt an effective report-writing style, follow this advice:

- **Avoid narrative.** Do not waste your reader's time by including a detailed account of what you did to collect the information. Instead, focus on the significance of the findings, conclusions, and recommendations that resulted from your research. Include information about your research process only if it will help your audience understand your conclusions and/or lend your findings credibility. Even in a progress report, focus on accomplishments rather than activities.
- **Be objective.** For every claim you make, provide reasoning and supporting evidence. Also, be fair. Include information from all sides of an issue and demonstrate that you have evaluated the issue using reasonable and objective criteria.
- **Use an appropriate tone.** Although some internal reports may use informal wording (including contractions such as *isn't*, *won't*, or *we'll*), reports for external audiences are typically formal.
- **Make the report easy to skim and the information easy to find.** Use headings that flow logically, and outline how the report is organized. In addition, begin each paragraph with a topic sentence that summarizes the main point of the paragraph so the audience can easily find the main ideas.
- **Use a straightforward sentence style.** All reports benefit from a writing style that uses concise sentences and active voice. This style makes the report easier to read and easier to translate for international audiences. For more details about sentence style, see Chapter 3, pp. 98–101.

New Hires @ Work

Erica Masters
University of West Georgia

Advanced Staff Auditor @ Georgia Department of Audits and Accounts

In our internal and external audit reports, it can be challenging to be clear and concise when dealing with complex information, so we involve the entire team in report writing.

Photo courtesy of Erica Masters

Evaluate

Evaluate by reviewing on your own and getting feedback from others

Evaluating involves both reviewing your own work and also responding to feedback from others. As you evaluate your report, answer the questions in **Figure 10.5** and use your answers as a guide for revising.

When a report is particularly important, be sure to have multiple people read it and provide feedback before you finalize the content. In fact, experienced writers ask for feedback continually, throughout the writing process, instead of waiting until a draft is complete.[1] In that way, writers improve the effectiveness of important reports by ensuring that the reports meet audience and stakeholder needs. If you do not have access to multiple readers or the time to gather feedback, evaluate your own work by reading it out loud. Reading aloud helps you catch errors more easily and assess of the flow of your writing. For more details about how to evaluate your writing, see Chapter 3.

The evaluating process does not end when you have submitted the report. Your audience's response provides valuable feedback that can help you make better decisions the next time you write. If your report achieves your intended results, review it carefully to identify its strengths. If it does not achieve the results you wanted—for example, if your analysis confused the audience or your recommendation was not approved—try to determine the cause of the problem. Did you confuse the reader by providing too much detail or too little organization? Did you fail to persuade the reader because you did not include enough support for your recommendations? Or did you fail to achieve results because of an external factor you could not control, such as budget cuts? Whatever you learn from this evaluation will improve your future writing.

FIGURE 10.5 Report Evaluation Questions

To evaluate your report, answer these questions:

1. **Is the report's purpose clear?**
   - What question is the report answering?
   - Is the answer to the question easy to find?
   - Is the title (or subject line) of the report focused and informative?

2. **Is the report well organized?**
   - Does it provide a preview in the introduction?
   - Where appropriate, does it include a table of contents, executive summary, or abstract?
   - Does the body of the report provide all the information and analysis the audience needs?
   - Are the headings logical? Will someone who reads all the headings sequentially understand how the report is organized?
   - Is the main point of each section easy to find?
   - Are tables, graphs, and other visuals effective? Are they labeled and introduced within the document?
   - Are the appendices relevant and useful to the audience?

3. **Is the report well written?**
   - Are the paragraphs relatively short (four to eight sentences)? Does each paragraph begin with a strong topic sentence that states the main point of the paragraph?
   - Are the sentences relatively short and, when possible, written in the active voice?
   - Has the report been proofread carefully?

CULTURE
MAKING REPORTS READER-FRIENDLY FOR INTERNATIONAL AUDIENCES

Reports often have larger audiences than typical correspondence, such as emails. A useful report may be distributed broadly throughout an organization and to colleagues or clients around the world. If the report is not confidential, it may even be shared with the general public.

If you work in an international organization or an organization that disseminates information globally, you need to think about how to make your reports accessible to international audiences—even those who speak English. The number of English speakers is growing worldwide, as English is taught to more people and at an earlier age in both Europe and Asia.[2] As a result, English has become the international *lingua franca* of business—the common language used by native speakers of different languages.[3]

However, not all these English speakers are fluent in the language. Although almost 2 billion people speak English worldwide, only 25 percent of those people speak English as a first language.[4] If any members of your audience are in the remaining 75 percent, will they understand long sentences and eloquent word choices? How can you make your reports as easy as possible for everyone in your audience to read?

Professionals in the field of international technical communication have developed a number of guidelines to use when preparing English documents for readers who are not native English speakers. Even if your communication is not technical, use the following guidelines adapted from the *Global English Style Guide*:[5]

- **Use simple English.** English arguably has more words than any other language. Studies published by *Science*[6] and the *Global Language Monitor*[7] estimate the current number of words at more than a million. Although this breadth of word choice makes English a very precise language, many of your readers will not be familiar with all the vocabulary. Use concrete words, avoid slang and clichés, and check the reading level of your text when you evaluate your writing. Avoid sentences like this: "Local regulations prohibit installation of signage without a permit." Instead, say "Acme must get a permit to put up a sign."

- **Do not vary terms needlessly.** Use consistent terminology and phrases. For example, if you are writing about automobiles, consistently call them "automobiles" or "autos" rather than occasionally calling them "vehicles" or "means of transportation." This repetition minimizes the number of terms a reader will need to remember.

- **Eliminate the "fat" from content.** Keep your writing lean by providing only the information that people need and by eliminating extra details and words that serve no clear purpose. An international audience may find it difficult to read this wordy sentence: "It is respectfully recommended that a committee be formed by A. G. Williams to conduct an investigation into potential wrongdoing by members of the executive board." They could more easily understand this leaner version: "We recommend that A. G. Williams investigate the executive board's recent actions."

For CULTURE exercises, go to Critical Thinking Question 1 on page 401 and Exercise 7 on page 402.

What types of short, routine reports are typical in business?

progress report A report that updates supervisors or clients on the status of a long-term project.

minutes A written report of a meeting that identifies who was present, summarizes the discussion, and records specific decisions and action items.

trip report A report that documents activities on a business trip and presents accomplishments and issues.

feasibility report A report that analyzes whether a plan can be implemented as proposed. It may also consider how to change the plan to make it feasible.

Most day-to-day business reports are short—less than five pages—and written in memo, email, or letter format. This section provides guidelines for three types of informational reports that are usually short: progress reports, meeting minutes, and trip reports. These reports are designed to inform your audience quickly about the work you have done and to provide documentation for future use. The section also provides guidelines for a short analytical report—in this case, a feasibility report.

Progress reports

If you are working on a long-term project, your supervisor or client may ask for a **progress report** that updates others on your status and indicates any potential problems or issues. **Figure 10.6** illustrates a progress report written by a team of product designers who work for Adaptive Living, a company that designs and sells products to help people with disabilities function independently. The team has been working on a special project for several months and needs to answer two questions: How is the project progressing, and when will a tested prototype be complete? The figure's annotations provide advice about how to organize a progress report.

Meeting minutes

Minutes are written reports of meetings. The type of minutes you write will depend on the type of meeting you are summarizing and the purpose of the minutes. If you are documenting a formal group meeting, then the minutes will summarize all the discussions. Organize the minutes using the categories outlined in the meeting's agenda, such as announcements, old business, and new business. Reports, votes, and decisions will be included with the relevant category. More often, your minutes will record the more informal meetings of small committees or work teams. Those minutes are action oriented, focusing more on outcomes and decisions. **Figure 10.7** on page 356 illustrates the minutes for a short committee teleconference.

Trip reports

When you return from a business trip, your supervisor or manager may ask you to write a **trip report** to document your activities and to share what you accomplished or learned. The biggest mistake writers make in preparing trip reports is to organize them chronologically in a narrative style. Instead, identify the most useful way to categorize the information from the audience's perspective—for example, by the results you achieved, what you learned, or the customers you visited. In **Figure 10.8** on page 357, Warren Abbott reports on his trip to Washington, D.C., to meet with current and potential clients. See the annotations for advice about how to write a report in email form and how to organize a trip report.

Feasibility reports

Short analytical reports, such as a feasibility report, can also be written in email, memo, or letter form. A **feasibility report** analyzes whether a plan can be implemented as proposed. It may also consider how to change the plan to make it feasible. A feasibility report will always include the criteria that decision makers can use to judge the proposal. The criteria may include cost, technical functionality, or potential for employees or the public to accept the proposal. Then the report will evaluate the proposal based on those criteria.

See **Figure 10.9** on pages 358–359, for advice about how to write a feasibility report.

FIGURE 10.6 How to Write a Memo-Style Progress Report

progress report

> This **progress report** is written in a memo format because it is a short report intended for an internal audience.

MEMORANDUM

TO: Rudy Glenn, VP of Fashion Products
Janice Kerwin, Production Manager
FROM: Eve Ireland, Lead Designer
Niki Jantzen, Design Associate
DATE: November 22, 20XX
SUBJECT: Progress on SleekLine Adaptive Swimsuit Design

IDENTIFYING INFORMATION

Identify the names and titles of the recipients and the senders in the header.

PREVIEW

Provide a subject line that serves as the title of the report.

Project Summary

We are on schedule with the design and prototyping of the SleekLine adaptive swimsuit. The product fills an unmet market need: a swimsuit that women with rheumatoid arthritis can independently put on and take off despite their limited flexibility and range of motion. Over the past month, we have created three mockups that we have tested with potential users in a focus group. Based on the information gathered, we have narrowed our design to a tankini-style swimsuit with a top that opens in the front so that it can slip on like a shirt or jacket. The swimsuit top is secured with magnetic snaps that hold tightly but do not require finger flexibility to open or close. We are currently in the process of testing and prototyping the design.

Begin by identifying the purpose of the project and briefly summarizing the progress made.

DETAILED DISCUSSION

Work Completed Since Last Report

From October 30 until now, we have accomplished the following activities:

- Met with the occupational therapists at Central Rehabilitation Hospital to identify the specific requirements for our design
- Developed three alternative designs using three different closure systems: magnets, Velcro, and zippers
- Produced mock-ups of five designs
- Conducted two focus groups and user-tested our mock-ups with 30 women, aged 30 to 60, who have rheumatoid arthritis

Use specific and meaningful headings for your content to organize your discussion.

Provide detail about the work completed.

Preliminary Findings (See Figure 1)

1. Women testing the swimsuits overwhelmingly (28 out of 30) preferred the closure to be in the front of the swimsuit.
2. The majority (19 out of 30) found magnetic closures to be easiest to use.

Include preliminary findings or results, if you have any.

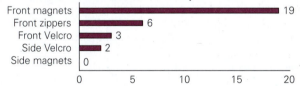

Figure 1: Number of Users Who Preferred Specific Swimsuit Closure Styles

Front magnets: 19
Front zippers: 6
Front Velcro: 3
Side Velcro: 2
Side magnets: 0

> **MyLab Business Communication**
> Apply Figure 10.6's key concepts by going to **www.pearson.com/mylab/ business-communication**

Work Planned for Next Two Weeks

During the next two weeks, we plan to conduct rigorous functional testing of fabric and magnets, simulating the conditions of swimming and water aerobics. Our goal is to determine the optimal strength, spacing, and polarity of magnets.

We will incorporate the results of the testing into prototypes and conduct a second round of swim tests. We will have a tested prototype by December 15.

Discuss work planned.

Anticipated Problems

While users overwhelmingly like the magnets, users lack confidence that the magnets will hold safely and securely during water activities. Our marketing department will need to address these issues in product labeling and advertising.

Identify any anticipated problems to alert the reader to potential issues and allow others to start planning solutions.

Other important features to note in this report:

- The project summary begins with the most important idea, answering the key question of the report: How is the project progressing?
- Bullet points in the "Work Completed" section are grammatically parallel.
- A graph helps readers compare numbers.

FIGURE 10.7 How to Write Meeting Minutes

These **meeting minutes** from a short teleconference are written as a stand-alone document that can be attached to an email, printed, and filed for future reference.

meeting minutes

Western Association of Accounting Professionals Communications Committee

Meeting Minutes

Date:	April 17, 20XX
Purpose:	To address website problems and discuss methods of disseminating the new logo to the membership.
Present:	Nick Lawrence (presiding), Fiona Cray, Larry Evans, Carol Gielgud, Karla Jensen (recording), Lyle Lerner, Elaine Sears
Absent:	Susan Edwards, Vic Matthews
Location:	Teleconference
Convened:	7:30 PM CST
Adjourned:	8:15 PM CST

Discussion of Website Problems

Lyle Lerner reported that updating the website is cumbersome and time-consuming. To help solve this problem, Vic Matthews will update the website to a new version of Joomla, but many problems need to be identified and fixed. We discussed the best way to fix these problems and agreed to develop a requirements document and to hire a professional web developer. Nick Lawrence will ask Paul Walters about his ability to do what we need, his availability, and his fees. Carol Gielgud will also talk to Adam Earle to find out the same from him. Nick and Carol will present their findings at our June meeting.

> **Decision:** Because of problems with Joomla, we will allocate up to $2,000 to pay a professional to fix the problems with the site, earmarking $1,000 to fix the items that Lyle, Vic, and Nick identify as critical.
> **Vote:** Fiona Cray moved, Larry Evans seconded, and the motion passed unanimously.

Discussion of Logo

Everyone is pleased with the new, more contemporary logo. Larry Lerner will get all the associated electronic files from the designer and upload them to the intranet site. Elaine Sears will upload a simple version of the logo to the website for members to download and will send a message to the membership on the listserv informing them of this by April 25, 20XX.

Action Items

Action	Person	Goal Date	Completed Date	Follow up
Upload simple logo to website and communicate its availability to membership by email.	Sears	April 25, 20XX		
Upload all logo design files to Association intranet site for board members to use.	Lerner	April 25, 20XX		
Identify what needs to be done to make Joomla easy to work with and write up a requirements document.	Lawrence, Lerner, and Matthews	May 18, 20XX		
Contact Paul Walters to request a bid for web development.	Lawrence	May 31, 20XX		
Contact Adam Earle to request a bid for web development.	Gielgud	May 31, 20XX		
Update to current version of Joomla.	Matthews	August 15, 20XX		

IDENTIFYING INFORMATION and PREVIEW

Create a heading that includes the purpose of the meeting, who attended, and the place and time.

Write the purpose statement so that it previews the content of the minutes.

DETAILED DISCUSSION

Divide the discussion into distinct topics with meaningful headings.

Summarize the discussion rather than record all the details.

Highlight key items such as decisions and votes.

Highlight action items using either a bulleted list or a table that summarizes the actions and serves as both a checklist and follow-up tool to use at the next meeting.

FIGURE 10.8 How to Write an Email-Style Trip Report

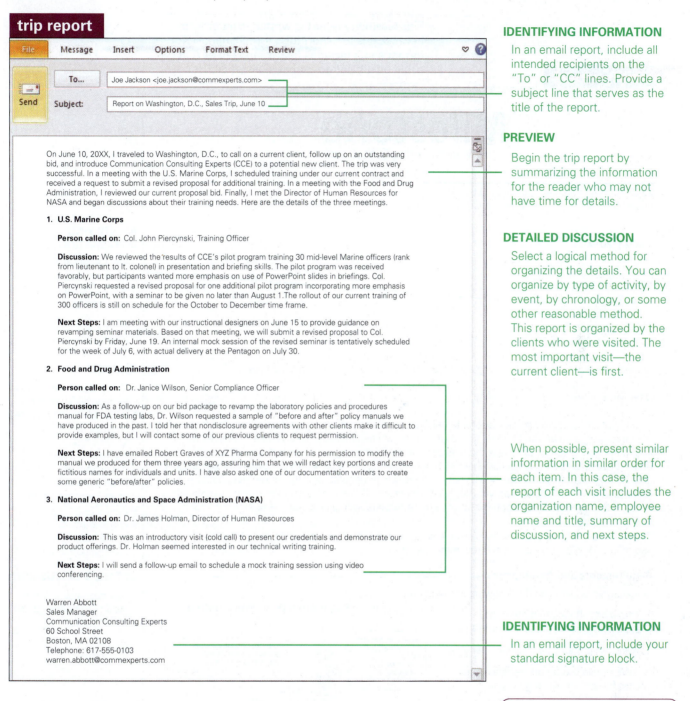

IDENTIFYING INFORMATION

In an email report, include all intended recipients on the "To" or "CC" lines. Provide a subject line that serves as the title of the report.

PREVIEW

Begin the trip report by summarizing the information for the reader who may not have time for details.

DETAILED DISCUSSION

Select a logical method for organizing the details. You can organize by type of activity, by event, by chronology, or some other reasonable method. This report is organized by the clients who were visited. The most important visit—the current client—is first.

When possible, present similar information in similar order for each item. In this case, the report of each visit includes the organization name, employee name and title, summary of discussion, and next steps.

IDENTIFYING INFORMATION

In an email report, include your standard signature block.

MyLab Business Communication
Apply Figure 10.8's key concepts by going to **www.pearson.com/mylab/business-communication**

FIGURE 10.9 How to Write a Letter-Style Feasibility Report

> This **feasibility report** is written in letter form because it is too short for a formal manuscript format and it includes figures and tables that could be difficult to format in an email.

feasibility report

Milestone
Manufacturing Consultants

2245 Sherwin Parkway, Golden, CO 80401
800.555.6642 | www.milestone-consultants.com

July 23, 20XX

Mr. James Burgess
VP of Product Development
Affordable World Energy
130 West Union Street
Pasadena, CA 91103

Subject: Feasibility of Manufacturing a $100 Wind Turbine for Developing Countries

Dear Mr. Burgess:

Thank you for hiring Milestone Manufacturing Consultants to perform a feasibility analysis for manufacturing a small wind turbine to provide household electricity for rural families in developing countries. You asked us to assess the feasibility of manufacturing a turbine that can be sold for under $100. Based on our discussions with manufacturers, we believe this price goal will be feasible only if Affordable World Energy (AWE) can contract with a manufacturer to custom manufacture a motor that meets the specifications. The least expensive off-the-shelf motor that meets the specifications is $133 per unit. Based on this price, a more feasible selling price for the turbine is $175.

The remainder of this report outlines requirements and assumptions, presents our cost analysis, and offers specific conclusions and recommendations.

Requirements and Assumptions

Our analysis is based on the following assumptions:

1. The wind turbine must meet the specifications illustrated in Figure 1.

2. AWE will produce 50,000 units per year.

3. AWE would like to recover the capital cost for tooling within one year.

4. To keep the sales cost under $100, the total materials cost can be no more than $82 per unit, based on the assumption that nonmaterials costs (labor, assembly, marketing) will average $10 per unit and AWE's profit margin will be 8 percent, or $8 per unit.

Figure 1: Requirements for Wind Turbine

Rotor: 1.5m diameter
- 3 injection-molded blades
- Glass-filled polypropylene
- NACA 4412 airfoil

Generator: DC brushless motor
- 30W rated power at 250RPM
- Outputs 14.2V starting at minimal RPM

Overspeed Protection: Tail-fin furling
- 1.35m and 1.8kg tail fin rotates around a hinge angled 38° from vertical
- Tail vane surface area of 0.39m²

IDENTIFYING INFORMATION

Identify the recipient of the letter report in the inside address, below the dateline.

Include a subject line that functions as a report title.

PREVIEW

Use a direct organization for feasibility reports. Begin by identifying the purpose of the report. Identify the criteria you will use to determine if the project is feasible. Then summarize the main point about feasibility.

End the introduction by previewing the organization of the report.

DETAILED DISCUSSION

Use headings in letter reports to help organize the content.

Use figures when they help you communicate more concisely and effectively.

FIGURE 10.9 *(Continued)*

Mr. James Burgess
Page 2
July 23, 20XX

Cost Analysis

Injection-Molded Blades

We received three cost quotes for injection-molding the blades, summarized in Table 1. Detailed price quotations for each are available in Attachment 1.

Table 1: Cost quotations for tooling a mold and producing blades

Quote	Annual Volume	Material	Tooling Cost	Unit Cost	Mfg. Location
A	150,000	Polypropylene (quoted based on range of additives)	$74,250	$3.99 to $5.99	United States
B	150,000	Glass-filled Polypropylene	$27,360	$4.82	Shenzhen, China
C	50,000	Glass-filled Polypropylene	$31,750	$4.65	Bombay, India
	100,000			$4.30	
	150,000			$3.94	

The most cost-effective pricing is from the manufacturer in Bombay, where the total cost per turbine will be $12.45, as shown in Table 2.

Table 2: Per-turbine cost for blades

Item	Calculation		Per Turbine Cost
Tooling	$ 31,750.00	per 50,000 turbines	0.63
Blades	$ 11.82	per turbine	11.82
Total			**$12.45**

Motor

We priced motors from seven manufacturers in India and China. The details are in Attachment 2. Only one motor met the specifications required for this turbine. Its price is **$133 per unit** for 50,000 units.

Additional Costs

Because AWE does not yet have detailed design specifications for the tail fin or turbine housing, we were not able to price those. On comparable wind turbines, the cost of these items is approximately 7 percent of the total unit cost. We recommend that AWE budget **$7 per unit**.

Conclusions and Recommendations

Based solely on the cost of blades and motors, we believe it will be difficult to sell the wind turbines for less than $100. One option will be to increase your price target to $175. A second option will be to negotiate with motor manufacturers for a lower-cost custom motor. Attachment 2 contains contact information for all the motor manufacturers we interviewed. To achieve the $100 price point for the turbine, AWE will need to source a motor that costs $62 per unit or less.

We will be glad to discuss our findings with you or provide additional details.

Best regards,

Austin Nichols

Austin Nichols
Senior Consultant

Attachment 1: Blade manufacturers: detailed price quotations and contact information

Attachment 2: Motor manufacturers: detailed specifications, price quotations, and contact information

SQ3 How should you structure longer, formal reports for print and online distribution?

recommendation report A report that analyzes options and recommends a course of action.

evaluation report A report that assesses the success of a project.

When you report on a major project or substantial research, you will most likely need to create a formal report. Formal reports may be primarily informative, organizing the results of a project or information from research. However, long business reports are often analytical—for example, **recommendation reports** that analyze options and recommend a course of action or **evaluation reports** that assess the success of a project or a decision. A formal report may be as short as 8 to 10 pages or as long as several hundred pages. As outlined in Figure 10.4 on page 351, a formal report includes a number of elements that organize the complex material and help the reader find information easily. This section provides guidelines for how to implement those elements and create a report that is both readable and useful. It discusses how to organize the report into sections and design it to meet the audience's needs. It also discusses how to choose the best format if you plan to distribute your report online.

Organize the report into useful sections

To help your reader understand the organization of your report, separate the content into distinct sections. Most formal reports include a title page, preliminary sections, a detailed body with subheadings, and a conclusion. Some reports also include supplementary sections with supporting information.

Figure 10.10 on pages 361–372 illustrates how to construct the sections of a formal report to make it both readable and useful, using the following guidelines:

title page The first page of a formal report, which includes identifying information, such as the report's title; the name of the person or organization for whom the report was written; the author's name, position, and organization; and the date of submission.

- **Create a title page for identifying information** (title page of Figure 10.10). A **title page** includes identifying information, such as the report's title; the name of the person or organization for whom the report was written; the author's name, position, and organization; and the date of submission.

- **Preview the report with preliminary sections** (pages ii, iii, and 1). A formal report should include several ways to preview the report contents, including a table of contents, a list of figures and tables (if applicable), an executive summary, and an introduction.

- **Develop the details within sections** (pages 2–8). The detailed discussion (sometimes called the *body*) of a formal report is typically organized with content-specific headings. For example, if you are writing a recommendation report, then each major heading may be one key recommendation. Provide citations for all material derived from interviews and secondary sources.

- **Conclude the report with supporting information** (pages 9 and 10). Formal reports may conclude with two types of supporting information: reference lists and appendices.

Design the report for your audience and purpose

Reports may be designed differently depending on whether they are intended for internal or external audiences.

Internal reports

The report illustrated in Figure 10.10 is formatted in a traditional *manuscript style*. Although it incorporates some design features, such as headings and bullet points, it does not use more elaborate elements such as borders, multiple columns, callout boxes, or contrasting fonts. Manuscript-style reports are common in conservative fields, such as banking and accounting. You will also see manuscript style used for internal company reports (such as the one in Figure 10.10). Although internal reports must be easy to read, with effective headings and paragraphing, they do not have to be eye-catching. The audience of internal reports typically needs the content and is motivated to read the information.

FIGURE 10.10 How to Write a Formal Report

Rosehip Restaurant Group operates four traditional sit-down restaurants in Denver. The group is considering expanding by opening a different type of restaurant: a sustainable fast-casual cafe featuring local, GMO-free organic food. Rosehip is new to the fast-casual format and to sustainable dining. Before making a decision about whether to invest time in a financial analysis and business plan, Rosehip wants to learn more about the market for organic fast-casual foods in Denver, the competition in the area, and the costs and sourcing issues associated with sustainable dining. Rosehip assigned a summer intern, Kandace Nichols, to conduct preliminary research and prepare an evaluation report providing information that can inform a decision.

**Evaluating the Opportunity for Opening a
Sustainable Fast-Casual Restaurant in Denver**

Prepared for
Rosehip Restaurant Group

Prepared by
Kandace Nichols, Marketing Intern

August 1, 20XX

Create a title page for identifying information.
Include the following content:
- Title of the report
- Name of the person or organization for whom the report was written
- Name and position of the author(s), the name of the author's organization
- Date of submission

(continued)

FIGURE 10.10 *(Continued)*

Contents

ii

Preview the report with preliminary sections:
- Table of Contents
- List of Figures and List of Tables
- Executive Summary
- Introduction

The table of contents serves two functions: It gives readers a quick overview of the content and structure, and it also helps readers find specific sections of the report.

In the table of contents:
- **Include all headings** in the report and their page numbers. Number all pages before the Introduction with lowercase Roman numerals. The title page counts as page number i, even though it is not numbered.
- **Use dot leaders** to connect the headings and page numbers. To ensure proper alignment, do not create the leaders by inserting periods. Instead, create a right-aligned tab for placement of page numbers, and format that tab to insert dot leaders automatically.

This report does not need a list of figures and tables because the report is not heavily illustrated. It includes only one figure and one table.

FIGURE 10.10 *(Continued)*

Executive Summary

Rosehip Restaurant Group is considering expanding in Denver by opening a sustainable fast-casual café featuring local, GMO-free organic food. Industry and media research suggests that such a restaurant can be successful for Rosehip for several reasons:

- Fast casual has been the fastest and most consistently growing dining category over the past five years. Denver was an early adopter of fast casual dining, making the area highly receptive to a new fast casual restaurant concept from Rosehip.

- Interest in local and organic foods is growing, especially in urban areas and in the western United States where Denver is located.

- Organic/GMO-free food appeals to younger, more affluent diners, which could increase the number of new customers with ample disposable income.

However, to be successful, Rosehip must address four challenges:

- **Competition:** Because Denver has twice as many fast-casual restaurants per 100,000 people as the national average, Rosehip will face substantial competition. However, no competitors have settled into the sustainable fast casual niche, so Rosehip can distinguish itself from others. In addition, Rosehip restaurants have an excellent reputation and loyal following in Denver, giving this new restaurant an initial base of customers.

- **Sourcing:** Finding a consistent and reliable source of local, organic foods can be challenging. Rosehip can source this food through food hubs or directly from farmers. Sourcing directly from farmers offers several benefits: it allows Rosehip to foster good relationships with farmers, request that the farmers plant the food that Rosehip wants to serve, and get information from farmers that will help the restaurant plan menus. Fortunately, the Denver area has many organic farms.

- **Cost:** The cost of organic food is higher than conventional food. To make prices affordable, Rosehip can follow best practices in sustainability that have been developed by other restaurants.

- **Seasonality:** Maintaining a supply of local, organic food during the Colorado winter is difficult, but not impossible. Restaurants committed to local foods have developed a number of successful strategies, including using root cellars, preserving food during the growing season, and growing some foods indoors.

In the executive summary, provide a condensed version of the entire report:
- Include all important findings, conclusions, and recommendations
- Use highlighting techniques such as bullets, boldface, and headings to guide the reader

iii

(continued)

FIGURE 10.10 *(Continued)*

Introduction

Rosehip Restaurant Group operates four traditional sit-down restaurants in Denver: a fine dining restaurant, a tapas restaurant, a brew pub, and a contemporary French bistro. The group is considering expanding by opening a sustainable fast-casual café featuring local, GMO-free organic food. Rosehip is new to the fast-casual format and to sustainable dining. Before deciding whether to invest in a financial analysis and business plan, Rosehip wants to learn more about the market for organic fast-casual foods in Denver, the competition in the area, and the costs and sourcing issues associated with sustainable dining. Rosehip requested this preliminary study to evaluate whether opening a new fast-casual café that supports organic and locally sourced food has the potential to be successful in the Denver area.

Based on media and industry research, this study found that both the fast casual and the organic GMO-free segments of the market are growing (Bryant, 2016; Maze, 2015; O'Connor, 2013). Because the fast casual market is so crowded in Denver, this research suggests that the best way for Rosehip to distinguish itself from competitors is to be local, organic, and GMO-free. Taking this approach requires that Rosehip address two challenges: finding reliable and cost-effective suppliers and remaining seasonal and local in the winter. Fortunately, the Denver area has many organic growers, and the culinary community in Colorado has developed strategies for serving local food throughout the year.

This report addresses the following topics:

- Why a fast casual restaurant will appeal to the Denver market
- Why a local, organic, GMO-free restaurant will appeal to the Denver market
- How Rosehip can meet the challenges of implementing this restaurant concept

Why a Fast Casual Restaurant Will Appeal to the Denver Market

Fast-casual restaurants are the fastest-growing category of restaurants in the U.S. (Specter, 2015). Customers are increasingly looking for quick, high-quality food in well-designed environments. Fast-casual restaurants appeal in particular to younger diners who have disposable income and who have grown up in foodie cultures that prize ingredients and variety over value and predictability (Barron, 2015; Hennessy, 2015).

As the birthplace of Chipotle, the restaurant chain credited for starting the fast-casual trend, Denver has long been an incubator of fast-casual dining, with more restaurants opening each year ("Fast-Casual Dining in Denver," n.d.; O'Connor, 2015). Although the market is crowded, there is no sign that it is saturated. In fact, some restaurant experts suggest that having multiple restaurants of similar styles in one area actually improves business for all those restaurants. Once diners adopt a new restaurant style—like fast casual—they are eager to visit similar establishments (Fields, 2007).

1

In the introduction, provide a complete preview of the report.

Give context for the report.

Describe the reason for the research and the question(s) the report is addressing.

Summarize the report's most important findings and recommendations.

Preview the organization of the content.

Divide the detailed discussion into sections, beginning each section with a heading. Depending on you're the design of your report, either center main headings or left-align them.

Include all cited sources in the reference list.

FIGURE 10.10 *(Continued)*

Why an Organic GMO-free Restaurant Will Appeal to the Denver Market

Widespread skepticism exists about the safety of genetically modified food and food grown with pesticides. Of the adults surveyed by Pew Research, 57% think that genetically modified food is unsafe, and 67% doubt that scientists fully understand how genetically modified food affects the human body (Funk & Rainie, 2015). Likewise, Americans overwhelmingly believe that foods grown with pesticides are unsafe to eat. Of those surveyed by Pew, 69% think pesticides are unsafe, with the majority of Americans agreeing across racial, economic, political, gender, and educational demographics (Funk & Rainie, 2015).

This skepticism about food safety is accompanied by an increasing interest in organic foods. According to a 2014 Gallup poll, 45% of Americans are interested in including organic food in their diet (Riffkin, 2014). As Figure 1 shows, this interest is even higher in urban areas and in the western United States, suggesting that residents of Denver are particularly interested in organic food.

Location and Eating Organic Foods

Thinking about the food you eat, for each of following please say if it is something you actively try to include in your diet, something you actively try to avoid, or something you dont't think about either way. How about organic foods?

	%Actively try to include	%Actively try to avoid	%Don't think about either way
East	39	18	41
Midwest	47	17	34
South	43	13	41
West	54	12	34
Big/Small city	50	16	32
Suburb	46	8	44
Town/Rural	37	19	41

July 7-10, 2014

Fig. 1 Results of Gallup poll comparing interest in organic food, by location. Source: Riffkin, 2014.

The research also suggests that restaurants can benefit from offering healthy, organic foods. In a survey of fast casual restaurant visitors, 38% said they were "motivated to visit more often" by higher quality, fresh ingredients; 36% found healthier options attractive, and 20% wanted more organic ingredients (Bryant, 2016).

This interest in local, organic fast food is supported by an analysis of Yelp searches in Denver, which shows persistent occurrence of the search terms "organic," "local," and "fast" (see Figure 2).

2

(continued)

Maintain a consistent heading style. In this report, all major headings take the same grammatical form: a relative clause

Introduce all figures and tables, and direct the reader to look for specific information in the figure or table.

Add captions to figures and tables to explain the data and to cite sources

Cite tables and graphs correctly. If you copy a table or graph from a source, use the label "source" in your caption. If you create an original table or graph yourself, using data you found in a source, use the label "data source." If you modify a table or graph that you have copied, use the label "adapted from" in your caption. If you display data you generated through primary research, no source citation is needed.

FIGURE 10.10 *(Continued)*

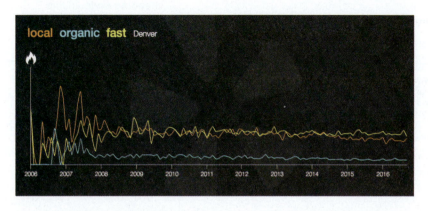

Fig. 2: Longitudinal comparison of search terms "local," "organic," and "fast" in Denver-area Yelp searches from 2007 to 2016. "Local" rendered in orange, "organic" rendered in blue, and "fast" rendered in yellow. Source: Yelp Trends, 2017.

How Rosehip Can Meet the Challenges of Implementing This Restaurant Concept

Although the Denver market is strong for a sustainable fast-casual restaurant, Rosehip will need to overcome several challenges. The discussion below identifies the challenges and offers some suggestions for addressing them.

Competition

The Denver market is already crowded with fast casual restaurants. In 2013, the metro area boasted 12.76 fast casual restaurant locations per 100,000 people, over twice the national average (Maze, 2013). Rosehip already has one advantage in this competitive landscape: an excellent reputation and a loyal following among its four other Denver restaurants. However, to succeed in the fast-casual market, Rosehip must distinguish itself from other competitors.

Marketing this new restaurant as organic and GMO-free will give Rosehip a way to set itself apart from the competition. As the evaluation discussion in Appendix A shows, none of the competitors have settled into the sustainable fast-casual niche. If Rosehip can work with local farmers, then the locally sourced food will solve potential supply chain issues and be an additional selling point for consumers.

Sourcing

To meet customer expectations, Rosehip must be able to consistently and reliably source local organic food. Broadly speaking, restaurants have two choices for sourcing local foods.

- **Food hubs:** They can source local food from regional food hubs, which sell food from a variety of local sellers. As defined by the U.S. Department of Agriculture, a regional food

3

Add captions to figures and tables to explain the data and to cite sources.

Include sources for figures and tables in the referene list.

Divide your sections into subsections, when useful. Start subsection headings at the left margin.

Design subsection headings to look different from main headings, by differentiating placement, font size, or both.

FIGURE 10.10 *(Continued)*

hub is "business or organization that actively manages the aggregation, distribution, and marketing of source-identified food products primarily from local and regional producers to strengthen their ability to satisfy wholesale, retail, and institutional demand" (Barham et al., p. 4).

- **Farmers:** Alternatively, restaurants can work with farmers directly—a trend that has been called the Farm-to-Table movement (Benjamin & Virkler, 2016). Food hubs may offer lower prices, but working with a farmer directly provides the opportunity to negotiate good prices in exchange of guaranteed business. Working with local sellers also allows information sharing: restaurants let farmers know what food is in high demand and famers can plan their planting accordingly (Avant, 2013). Fostering close relationships with growers also gives restaurants fast access to information on peak-eason produce and fluctuations in supply, allowing them ample time to adjust their menus for seasonal produce.

The only way to ensure that food is GMO-free is to source food that is certified as organic. The Colorado Farm Fresh Directory lists dozens of certified organic farms in Colorado (Colorado Department of Agriculture, 2016). Appendix B includes the names and products of the farms located in the Metro Denver area. Another strategy for identifying sources is to scout for growers at farmers' markets in the Denver area ("6 Strategies to Integrate," n.d.).

Costs

Organic, GMO-free products can be expensive. Even Chipotle, which can use economies of scale to take advantage of a massive supply chain, spends more on food than on staffing (Yohn, 2014). However, researchers, restaurants, and other food service providers have developed a set of best practices to make local, organic, and GMO-free food affordable. These include reducing food waste, rethinking portion size, using the whole animal, and marketing effectively to draw in new customers (Flaccavento & Harvey, 2014).

The fast casual chain Sweetgreen, for example, features a popular "wastED" salad made of typically discarded food, such as carrot tops and broccoli stems (Specter, 2015). And SCALE, an advocacy group promoting sustainable food, finds that reducing portion sizes by small amounts can make a big impact on costs. SCALE reports that this practice

> most commonly relates to meat items, where portions of locally sourced items might be reduced by 1 – 2 oz., depending upon the dish and the cost. Because portion sizes have grown so much in recent years, this "reduction" in portion size is in most respects a return to the more reasonable size portions that were once the norm. According to the chefs and dining service leaders surveyed, most patrons did not notice these reductions, and in some cases were pleased not to have to waste excess food. (Flaccavento & Harvey, 2014, p. 7)

By developing good supplier relationships and thinking creatively about how to eliminate waste, Rosehip can effectively manage costs.

4

Use bullets for elements of your discussion that are organized as a list.

Highlight the topic or main point of bulleted content bolded words, phrases, or sentences that guide the reader.

Refer at least once in the report to each appendix.

In APA Style, **format quotations of 40 words or more as block quotations,** with no quotation marks. Start block quotations on a new line and indent approximately ½ inch. Place the source citation, with page or paragraph number, after the final punctuation mark.

(continued)

FIGURE 10.10 *(Continued)*

Seasonality

Sourcing local foods in Colorado during the winter can be challenging because the growing season ends in November. However, restaurants can take advantage of year-round farmers' markets, such as the Four Seasons Farmers and Artisans Market in Wheat Ridge, that sell local cheese, meat, and grain products.

In addition, chefs in the Denver and Boulder area recommend the following strategies for remaining local and seasonal in the winter (Silver, 2014):

- Develop seasonal menus and a repertoire of seasonal foods.
- Create a root cellar to store root vegetables—or ask the local farmers that you buy from to store the vegetables in their root cellars.
- Preserve food during the growing season. Methods include curing, pickling, freezing, canning, dehydrating, and fermenting.
- Grow your own sprouted beans, lentils, and grains indoors to add fresh tastes to meals.

Finally, when a restaurant does need to use foods that are not local, organic, or GMO-free, the restaurant must be honest with customers and explain clearly what foods do not meet those standards—and why the restaurant is using them. This strategy will help manage customer expectations.

Use bullets for elements of the discussion that are organized as a list.

Use parallel construction for bulleted lists. In this case, each bulleted item begins with a verb.

A short report may not require a conclusion. If your report is long, a conclusion brings your audience's attention back to the key ideas they read in the executive summary and introduction.

5

FIGURE 10.10 *(Continued)*

References

Avant, M. (2013, May). Can quick serves save the world? *QSR*. Retrieved from
https://www.qsrmagazine.com/ingredients-dayparts/can-quick-serves-save-world

Barham, J., Tropp, D., Enterline, K., Farbman, J., Fisk, J., & Kiraly, S. (2012, April). Regional food
hub resource guide. Washington, D.C.: U.S. Dept. of Agriculture, Agricultural Marketing
Service. Retrieved from http://www.ngfn.org/resources/ngfn-database/knowledge/
FoodHubResourceGuide.pdf

Barron, P. (2015). *The Chipotle effect: The changing landscape of the American food consumer
and how fast casual is impacting the future of restaurants.* [Kindle Edition]. New York
City, NY: Transmedia. Retrieved from https://www.amazon.com

Benjamin, D., & Virkler, L. (2016). *Farm to table: The essential guide to sustainable food systems
for students, professionals, and consumers.* White River Junction, CT: Chelsea Green
Publishing.

Bryant, C. (2016). Fast casual restaurants - US - February 2016. Mintel. [White paper]. Retrieved
from http://store.mintel.com/fast-casual-restaurants-us-february-2016

Colorado Department of Agriculture. (2016). 2016 Colorado farm fresh. Retrieved from
https://www.colorado.gov/pacific/sites/default/files/Colorado%20Farm%20Fresh%20Di
rectory_1.pdf

Fast-casual dining in Denver (n.d.). Retrieved from http://www.denver.org/restaurants/denver-
dining/fast-casual/

Fields, R. (2007). *Restaurant success by the numbers.* Berkeley, CA: Ten Speed Press.

Flaccavento, A., & Harvey, L. (2014, August 10). Putting local on the menu: Tools and strategies
for increasing the utilization of locally raised food in restaurants and food service.
[White paper]. *Sequestering Carbon, Accelerating Local Economies.* Retrieved from
http://www.ruralscale.com/resources/downloads/PuttingLocalOnTheMenu.pdf

Funk, C., & Rainie, L. (2015, July 1). Public opinion about food. *Pew Research Center: Internet,
Science & Tech.* Retrieved from http://www.pewinternet.org/2015/07/01/chapter-6-
public-opinion-about-food/

Hennessy, M. (2016, 22 July). Fine dining restaurants turning fast casual: Food trends in Chicago,
IL. [Blog post]. Retrieved from https://www.thrillist.com/eat/chicago/fine-
dining-restaurants-turning-fast-casual-food-trends-in-chicago-il

Maze, J. (2013, August). Colorado: World's fast casual capital: Restaurant industry insight, news
and analysis. *Restaurant Finance Monitor. Retrieved from*
http://www.restfinance.com/Restaurant-Finance-Across-America/August-
2013/Colorado-Worlds-Fast casual-Capital/

6

**Begin the References or
Works Cited list on its own
page,** immediately after the
detailed discussion (body) of the
report.

**Include all secondary and
tertiary sources that are cited
in the report.** In MLA Works
Cited lists, also include entries
for interviews and personal
correspondence.

For a References list prepared in
APA style, follow these rules:

- List sources alphabetically
  by name (or title when there
  is no author).
- Place publication date
  immediately after the author
  (or title when there
  is no author).
- In source titles, capitalize
  only the first words and
  proper nouns.
- In journal titles, capitalize
  each word in the title.
- For web-based resources,
  include a "retrieved from"
  URL.
- For resources that are not
  web-based, end the entry
  with a period. Do not use
  periods at the end of webz
  addresses.

(continued)

FIGURE 10.10 *(Continued)*

O'Connor, C. (2015, March 5). Why Denver reigns as the capital of trendy fast-casual food. *The Denver Post*, p. C1.

Riffkin, R. (2014, August 7). Forty-five percent of Americans seek out organic foods. *Gallup*. Retrieved from http://www.gallup.com/poll/174524/forty-five-percent-americans-seek-organic-foods.aspx

Silver, M. (2014, October 14). 11 ways to eat seasonal and local in the winter. *Dining Out Denver and Boulder*. Retrieved from http://diningout.com/denverboulder/11-ways-to-eat-local-and-seasonal-in-the-winter/

6 strategies to integrate locally sourced food (n.d.). Retrieved from http://www.restaurant.org/Manage-My-Restaurant/Food-Nutrition/Trends/6-strategies-to-integrate-locally-sourced-food

Specter, M. (2015, November 11). Can fast food get healthy? *The New Yorker*. Retrieved from http://www.newyorker.com/magazine/2015/11/02/freedom-from-fries

Yelp Trends [Online data analysis tool]. (2017, July). Retrieved from https://www.yelp.com/trends

Yohn, D. L. (2014). *What great brands do: The seven brand-building principles that separate the best from the rest*. San Francisco, CA: Jossey-Bass.

When a reference list entry begins with a number, alphabetize the entry as you would if the number was spelled out.

For additional details about APA and MLA documentation, see Appendix B: Documentation and Reference Styles.

7

FIGURE 10.10 *(Continued)*

Appendix A: Evaluation of Key Competitors in the Fast Casual Market

These are the four fast casual style restaurants in the Denver area most likely to compete with Rosehip's new concept.

Honor Society Handcrafted Eatery (www.eatwithhonor.com)

Honor Society is most similar to the concept Rosehip is considering, with an emphasis on sustainable, local, and healthful food. Honor Society also leans heavily on seasonal dining, changing their menu according to the season. The menu is formed around several main "flavors" (roast vegetables, beef, chicken, and salmon), all of which can be combined in various sandwich, salad, or platter formats. Honor Society calls itself "fine casual" dining, aiming at a slightly higher price point (around $15 per dinner rather than the $10 per dinner typical for fast casual).

Larkburger (larkburger.com)

Larkburger takes the traditional burger concept and updates it to respond to consumer interest in natural and healthier ingredients. Larkburger sets itself apart by using natural ingredients (no preservatives or additives) and having a menu that is easily made gluten or dairy free. The company also uses biodegradable serving ware and containers. This commitment to health and environmental sustainability provides a good model for Rosehip to follow.

Mad Greens (www.madgreens.com)

Mad Greens is a salad and sandwich chain that makes healthy and tasty fast food. They work with suppliers throughout the Southwest to bring regionally sourced food to their cafes. Mad Greens was bought by Coors in 2013, which has allowed the company to expand and also to partner more effectively with farmers. While this expansion has given the company more reliable food sourcing, it has also diluted the company's local touch and Denver origins.

Modmarket (www.modernmarket.com)

Modmarket follows author Michael Pollan's food philosophy—"Eat food. Not too much. Mostly plants"—in crafting their menu. The restaurant aims to cater to a variety of dietary restrictions and choices, including vegan/vegetarian, gluten free, and paleo. While their mission includes a commitment to spreading farm-to-table eating to a wider population, ModMarket makes no explicit statements about how consistently local or sustainable their food sourcing is. A pledge for local and GMO-free food could be a useful way for Rosehip to set itself apart.

8

Use appendices for information that readers might find useful but that would clutter the report (for example, raw data, calculations, large tables, large graphics, and detailed descriptions) that do not need to be read within the flow of the report.

Begin each appendix on its own page, starting immediately after the reference list.

(continued)

FIGURE 10.10 *(Continued)*

Appendix B: Certified Organic Farms in the Metro Denver Area

The Metro Denver farms below are listed in the Colorado Farm Fresh Directory. The directory also lists additional certified organic farms throughout Colorado.

Farm	Certified Organic Products
Aspen Moon Farm Certified organic and biodynamic 7927 Hygiene Rd. Longmont www.aspenmoonfarm.com	fruits, vegetables
Berry Patch Farms 13785 Potomac St. Brighton www.berrypatchfarms.com	eggs, fruits
Cure Organic Farm 7416 Valmont Rd. Boulder cureorganicfarm@yahoo.com	beef, lamb, pork, poultry, sausage
Ela Family Farms/ Silver Spruce Orchards info@elafamilyfarms.com	fruits
Isabelle Farm 1640 W. Baseline Rd. Lafayette www.isabellefarm.com	fruits, vegetables, beef, chicken, pork, sausage,
KW Farms - Kretsinger Beef 7725 Road 1 South Alamosa www.kretsingerbeef.com	beef
Monroe Organic Farms, LLC. www.monroefarm.com	fruits, vegetables, beef, pork, lamb
Morton's Organic Orchards www.mortonsorchards.com	fruits
Rocky Mountain Pumpkin Ranch 9059 Ute Hwy. Longmont www.rockymtnpumpkinranch.com	fruits, vegetables

9

For multiple appendices, give each its own appendix heading, labeled sequentially with a letter (for example, Appendix A, Appendix B, etc.).

After each appendix heading, give the appendix a context-specific name.

Order the appendices in the same order that the report refers to them. The first appendix mention in the report is Appendix A, the second is Appendix B, and so forth.

External reports

Reports that are written for a broader external audience tend to use more design features to motivate the audience to read the report. For example, many organizations produce reports called **white papers**, which serve as marketing or sales tools. A white paper is a report intended to educate the audience—often potential customers—on a topic that is central to a company's business. Companies publish white papers to build credibility, to establish themselves as experts on a topic, and often to interest the audience in the company's products or services. Because no one is required to read a white paper, the document must entice the audience by the quality of both the content and the visual design. **Figure 10.11** (pages 373–374) and **Figure 10.12** (pages 375–376) are excerpts from two white papers. Figure 10.11 was written and published by Welch's Global Ingredients Group. Figure 10.12 is a white paper produced by The Lou Adler Group. The annotations in both of these figures identify some of the key design and formatting features.

white paper A report published by a company and intended to educate the audience—often potential customers—on a topic that is central to the company's business.

FIGURE 10.11 Example of a White Paper by Welch's Global Ingredients Group

The title page includes name of report, date, name of company publishing the report. It also includes a relevant graphic and introduces the reprort's color scheme.

The second page establishes a pattern that continues for several pages: key report findings are summarized in purple text at the top of the page.

MILLENNIALS: THE INFLUENTIAL SNACKERS

Consumer research by Mintel shows that **77% of Millennials believe they can't get through the day without eating a snack** – a significantly higher proportion than for any other demographic age group'. By contrast, just 49% of Baby Boomers say they can't get through the day without snacking, 58% of Generation Xers and 64% of people in the IGeneration.

It's clear, therefore, that **Millennial consumers are an important demographic group in the snacking category**, and that a good understanding of the preferences and habits of these influential consumers will be highly valuable for snack brands.

Against this backdrop, in January 2017, Welch's Global Ingredients Group commissioned independent market research in order to understand how American Millennials who snack regularly view the snacking category. Welch's Global Ingredients Group is the supplier of FruitWorx real fruit pieces – premium Concord and Niagara grape inclusions created for the snack and bakery category.

Carried out by Surveygoo, the **online survey questioned 300 male and female American snackers between the ages of 18 and 35 about their snacking habits and preferences.** The results provide insights into where and when Millennials snack, why they snack, and what they want from their snacks. These insights provide snack manufacturers with an insider's view of how Millennial snackers think.

Here, we outline the key findings of the consumer research and explain what they tell us about how these Millennials snack.

Snacking in Foodservice, US, Mintel 2016

The third page introduces a new element of the pattern: the page ends with insights and implications.

MILLENNIALS WHO SNACK, SNACK OFTEN

In the survey, the researchers **asked the respondents how often they ate a snack.** They found that over half of them do so **every day (53%)**, while **85% do so four days a week or more.** Furthermore, according to the survey, **62% of American Millennials who snack do so throughout the day.**

From our research we learned that the biggest single reason Millennial snackers eat snacks is because **they are hungry between meals (79%).** Other key drivers appear to be linked to Millennials' busy lives and include **tiredness (42%)** and being too busy to eat a sit-down **meal (39%).**

Millennial snackers are snacking at home and on the go, with **85%** of them consuming snacks at home, **48%** at work and **34%** in the car.

Q: **When do you usually snack?** (Pick as many answers as you like)

When I'm hungry between meals	79%
When I feel tired and need an energy boost	42%
When I'm too busy to eat a proper sit-down meal	39%
When I'm bored	38%
When I want to treat myself	36%
When I can't be bothered to cook a meal	17%
As part of my sports nutrition regime	6%

INSIGHTS & IMPLICATIONS

The survey findings highlight that American Millennial snackers are busy consumers for whom snacking is important. They do it often, and both at home and on the move. This means snacks need to be fit for purpose - easy to eat anywhere with minimal mess and fuss.

– Julie Cudmore, Senior Manager, Consumer Insights, Welch's

(continued)

FIGURE 10.11 *(Continued)*

The report continues to follow the pattern of presenting findings, insights, and implications.

The report ends with recommendations . . .

. . . and explains how the company's product can help other food businesses create appealing and healthy snacks. The bottom of the page provides contact information.

Screenshot from Welch's Global Ingredients Group. Printed with permission

FIGURE 10.12 Example of a White Paper by the Lou Adler Group

Whitepaper

The Job-Seeking Status of the Fully-Employed
December 2010
By Lou Adler

Executive Summary

This whitepaper summarizes the results of a survey conducted in September 2010 by the Adler Group and LinkedIn's Recruitment Insights team. The objective was to better understand the job-seeking behavior of professionals in the U.S., to determine how active they are in seeking new employment and what sources they use to find opportunities. Over 5,500 people responded, covering the gamut from individual contributors to senior executives. Of these, 4,543 categorized themselves as fully-employed, but not self-employed. Since this is the group most companies want to target for hiring purposes, we focused on these fully-employed respondents to understand their mood about the economy, their current level of job satisfaction, and the best means to source, recruit and hire them.

Our emphasis throughout is on the need for recruiting organizations to better understand when, why and how the best talent looks for new jobs, and the factors that most influence their final decision. This understanding will inform how companies go about hiring top talent on a more consistent basis.

Key Survey Findings

1. Only 18% of employed professionals are active candidates, but a further 60% are open to discussing opportunities

Only 18% of the fully-employed professional workforce are now actively looking and applying to a company's job postings. Another 44% are open to considering a new position, but need to be proactively contacted by a recruiter to discuss career opportunities. An additional 16% indicated that while they're not actively looking, they are reaching out to close associates to see if anything is available. Only 22% of respondents categorized themselves as Super Passive, i.e. not open to learning about new career opportunities.

2. The Early-Bird Sourcing Strategy wins

Finding candidates as soon as they enter the job market can improve overall candidate quality. This is referred to as an Early-Bird Sourcing Strategy and requires a combination of search engine optimization (SEO) and search engine marketing (SEM) techniques to be effective.

3. Traditional job postings only expose your opportunities to 23% of the viable candidate pool

Even with SEO and SEM techniques, 77% of fully-employed professionals who will consider opportunities – Tiptoers and Explorers – will not be found using the static job board-based sourcing programs still used by many companies today.

4. The active pool skews toward more junior, less tenured professionals

The 18% of fully-employed people who are either actively or semi-actively looking for a new job tend to be those with less tenure (2-3 years on the job) and at a more junior level (staff and managers) in the organization. This suggests that the active candidate pool is comprised of a higher proportion of less seasoned people who are not likely to stay and grow with the same organization.

5. Your next Director of Operations probably isn't actively looking

By contrast, only 13% of directors and executives indicated they are actively or semi-actively looking for a new position vs. 18% of managers and 20% of individual contributors. An active candidate sourcing program should therefore play a very minor role in recruiting senior management.

---

6. Those who aren't looking may not be as satisfied as you think

It's no surprise that there's a strong correlation between job satisfaction and job seeking. What is more interesting is the extent to which neutrality is the order of the day, even among those not actively looking for a job but open to the right opportunity. Tracking changes in employee satisfaction could represent a useful means to predict changes in voluntary turnover.

The Job-Seeking Status of the Fully-Employed

The following graph provides a high-level look at the job-seeking behavior of the 4,543 fully-employed people who participated in the survey. Some definitions are in order as we examine the data and the implications.

For the purposes of this survey, we wanted to effectively compare the differences between active and passive candidates, resulting in the following five categories featured in figure 1.

In addition, survey participants had to assign themselves to pre-defined levels of employment (fully-employed, self-employed, part-time, unemployed, etc.), as well as provide their titles, functions, and organizational level (from individual contributor to CEO). Much of the survey analysis is based on these more detailed categorizations.

By itself figure 1 is very revealing. It states that among the fully-employed (largely professional, exempt employees), only 18% are actively looking for a new job (the Very Active and Semi-Active categories). (Note: this 18% compares to 24% for all survey respondents, fully-employed or otherwise.) Another 16% are thinking about looking for other positions, but only reaching out to former close associates to do this. These are the Tiptoers. 66% of the fully-employed are not looking at all, but two-thirds of this passive group – called Explorers – would be open to talking with a recruiter about a potential career opportunity. The remaining third of those not looking are Super Passive and not interested in considering anything at this time.

Based on this, it's easy to conclude that with only 18% of the fully-employed professional workforce likely to find and apply to a company's job posting, sourcing programs should shift away from this active candidate pool, especially since many companies target the same group of people. While there might be a few top performers in this 18% Active candidate group, allocating major resources here is likely to be wasted effort. With 60% of the fully-employed professional workforce either Tiptoers or Explorers, most corporate recruiting departments need to focus on ways to proactively influence and convert these harder-to-reach candidates.

Reviewing the Survey from a Sourcing Strategy Perspective

For many organizations, this recommended focus on more 'passive' Tiptoers and Explorers will require a significant shift in sourcing approach. This is where the Early-Bird Sourcing Strategy comes into play. As you'll discover, tying this concept with the survey insights will allow you to quickly understand how changes in a company's sourcing strategy can impact quality of hire, cost per hire and time to fill.

Figure 2 provides an overview of the Early-Bird Sourcing concept. At its core, it's based on how top achievers change their job-hunting status as a function of job satisfaction. The rapid increase and plateauing, as shown by the "High Achiever Pattern" curve, reflects the traditional jump in job satisfaction when first starting a good job, and a flattening if the rate of growth and impact declines.

Figure 1
Job-Seeking Status of Fully-Employed
4,543 Respondents

Job-seeking Status Category Definitions

Very Active: actively looking for a new job and currently sharing their resume.

Semi-Active: casually looking for a new job 2-3 times per week and beginning to test the market.

Tiptoer: thinking about changing jobs and have reached out to close associates, but are not actively looking.

Explorer: not looking for a new job, but would discuss an opportunity with a recruiter if the job appeared meaningful.

Super Passive: completely happy in their current job and not interested in discussing new career opportunities.

2

This report does not have a separate title page. The top of the first page provides identifying information.

The report uses a two-column design. On the first page, the executive summary is in the narrower, left column. Key findings are on the right.

The report uses a simple color scheme, with headings and graphics in a contrasting color.

On this page, the narrow column is used for figures and definitions.

(continued)

FIGURE 10.12 *(Continued)*

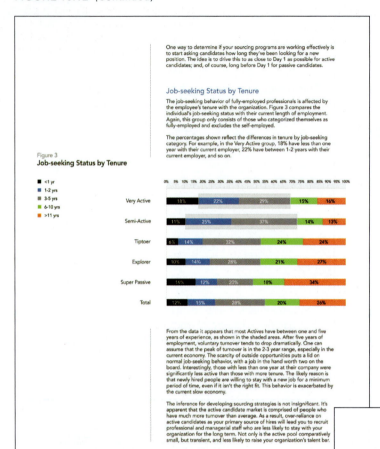

One way to determine if your sourcing programs are working effectively is to start asking candidates how long they've been looking for a new position. The idea is to drive this to as close to Day 1 as possible for active candidates; and, of course, long before Day 1 for passive candidates.

Job-seeking Status by Tenure

The job-seeking behavior of fully-employed professionals is affected by the employee's tenure with the organization. Figure 3 compares the individual's job-seeking status with their current length of employment. Again, this group only consists of those who categorized themselves as fully-employed and excludes the self-employed.

The percentages shown reflect the differences in tenure by job-seeking category. For example, in the Very Active group, 18% have less than one year with their current employer, 22% have between 1-2 years with their current employer, and so on.

Figure 3
Job-seeking Status by Tenure

- <1 yr
- 1-2 yrs
- 3-5 yrs
- 6-10 yrs
- >11 yrs

	<1 yr	1-2 yrs	3-5 yrs	6-10 yrs	>11 yrs
Very Active	18%	22%	29%	15%	16%
Semi-Active	11%	25%	37%	14%	13%
Tiptoer	6%	14%	32%	24%	24%
Explorer	10%	14%	28%	21%	27%
Super Passive	16%	12%	20%	18%	34%
Total	12%	15%	28%	20%	26%

From the data it appears that most Actives have between one and five years of experience, as shown in the shaded areas. After five years of employment, voluntary turnover tends to drop dramatically. One can assume that the peak of turnover is in the 2-3 year range, especially in the current economy. The scarcity of outside opportunities puts a lid on normal job-seeking behavior, with a job in the hand worth two on the board. Interestingly, those with less than one year at their company were significantly less active than those with more tenure. The likely reason is that newly hired people are willing to stay with a new job for a minimum period of time, even if it isn't the right fit. This behavior is exacerbated by the current slow economy.

The inference for developing sourcing strategies is not insignificant. It's apparent that the active candidate market is comprised of people who have much more turnover than average. As a result, over-reliance on active candidates as your primary source of hires will lead you to recruit professional and managerial staff who are less likely to stay with your organization for the long term. Not only is the active pool comparatively small, but transient, and less likely to raise your organization's talent bar.

A wide figure spans both columns.

Figures also appear in the wider column.

The last page provides supporting information: methodology, author biography, company description, and copyright information.

Figure 6
Change in Growth, Impact, and Satisfaction Over Time

The blue circles represent the percent of fully-employed people who categorized themselves into the job-seeking category shown. For purposes of this whitepaper, Networkers and Hunters and Posters were put into the Very Active Group. The green boxes represent the percent of people in each job-seeking group who categorized themselves as Quite Satisfied with their current positions. The data summarized in this report covers the responses of only those people who categorized themselves as fully-employed (4,543).

The overarching conclusion of this study is that only 18% of the fully-employed professional workforce in North America would categorize themselves as actively looking for a new position. While there are some top people in this active group, on a pure numbers basis there are far fewer of them than in the 60% (Tiptoers and Explorers) who said that would be open to explore a position if directly contacted by a recruiter or if a former associate led them to a potential opportunity.

The evidence also shows that those who have more tenure or play a more senior role at their company are even less likely to be actively looking. From a strategy standpoint, this suggests that companies need to do a better job of aligning resources by job seeker segment. This requires a significant shift in focus, primarily increasing emphasis on the Tiptoer and Explorer job-seeking categories. This is essential for any organization that needs to hire more talented people for professional and managerial positions.

Another major conclusion of this survey is that job satisfaction is worth exploring in conversations with candidates, as well as worth monitoring more proactively at your organization as a means to predict and stem voluntary turnover. It is quite evident that highly satisfied employees are far less likely to voluntarily leave their current positions even if directly contacted by an outside recruiter. Gallup and others have demonstrated this point in numerous studies, even demonstrating the financial impact of employee satisfaction on ROI. This suggests that in the current environment it's not job dissatisfaction that is driving the fully-employed professional worker to seek alternative employment.

The objective of this whitepaper was to provide recruiting leaders and company executives a better means to understand the market for top talent. It is clear that the fully-employed, professional worker has a different approach to looking for work and comparing job opportunities. This is ultimately driven by personal job satisfaction, the number of comparable opportunities available and overall business and economic conditions. All of this needs to be considered from a company perspective when developing sourcing and recruiting strategies, developing critical skill sets in your recruiting organization, implementing interviewing and screening tools, and even selecting the type of technology to use in managing your data.

Methodology

In September 2010 the Adler Group and LinkedIn conducted an online survey among members of the LinkedIn network to better understand their attitudes to job seeking and to their current employment situation. The survey attracted 5,525 respondents, of whom 4,543 categorized themselves as fully-employed (as opposed to self-employed, part-time or unemployed). The survey sample was balanced for active and less active LinkedIn members to be representative of LinkedIn's overall membership. Results were weighted to represent the actual mix of senior and junior professionals on LinkedIn.

About the author

Lou Adler is the CEO and founder of The Adler Group (www.adlerconcepts.com), a training, consulting and search firm helping companies implement Performance-based Hiring™. He is the Amazon best-seller author of *Hire With Your Head* (John Wiley & Sons, 3rd Edition, 2007) and the Nightingale-Conant audio program *Talent Rules! Using Performance-based Hiring to Hire Top Talent* (2007).

About LinkedIn

LinkedIn is an Internet platform company focused on connecting the world's professionals. The LinkedIn website launched in 2003 and is the world's largest professional network with more than 85 million members, representing every country and executives from every Fortune 500 company. Over two-thirds of the Fortune 100 now use LinkedIn Recruiting Solutions to find, contact and hire great talent for their organizations. For more information, go to http://talent.linkedin.com.

7

Organizations that want to make their reports even more visually appealing may choose to summarize and illustrate their data in the form of an **infographic**, a stand-alone visual display that typically combines multiple representations of data to provide a complete picture. **Figure 10.13** illustrates an infographic that summarizes the key findings in an industry report.[8]

infographic A representation of data or information in visual form. An infographic is a stand-alone visual display that typically combines multiple representations of data to provide a complete picture.

FIGURE 10.13 An Infographic Summarizing Key Report Findings

Choose the best electronic format for online distribution

Internal reports are typically emailed to recipients. You can distribute the report as a *native file*—a file in its original program, such as Word—or as a PDF (Portable Document Format). Deciding on the best electronic format for external reports is more complicated. The white papers in Figures 10.11 and 10.12 were both prepared as PDF files and distributed through the companies' websites. As an alternative, the companies could have published the reports as web pages. PDFs are by far the most common format for distributing reports electronically for three important reasons:

1. Documents are often easier to design than web pages.

2. Documents can be printed and stored on the audience's computer. They are durable and do not disappear when a web address changes.

3. Audiences can be required to submit contact information before downloading a PDF document, allowing the company to track people interested in the information and to market additional content and services to them.

In addition, if you have the right tools, such as Adobe Acrobat Pro or InDesign, you can even add a video to a PDF report.[9]

By contrast, web-based reports offer different advantages:

1. Readers can browse through sections of a report without taking time to download it.

2. Web-based reports can be more interactive, with links to multimedia content and animated data displays.

3. Reports can be updated frequently, without republishing the PDF.

Increasingly, companies are publishing their annual reports online in web formats as well as PDF. Web-based reports are effective at engaging investors' attention with interactivity, animation, videos, and multiple paths for reading. In addition, web-based reports can be optimized for easy reading on mobile devices. As **Figure 10.14** illustrates, a well-designed web-based report includes all its navigation features on the first screen so audiences will know the report's contents and will be able to go to any section within a few clicks. And within each section, it includes features designed to capture the audience's attention and keep them on the page longer.

TECHNOLOGY
HOW TO USE SOFTWARE FEATURES TO HELP FORMAT FORMAL REPORTS

Microsoft Word and other word processing programs offer powerful features that help you format formal reports. The following features will save you time and improve the professional look of your work. To learn about other features, use your program's help files.

- **Automated styles.** Word has a number of different text styles that control fonts, sizes, colors, and placement on the page. You can use one style for normal paragraphs, another for headings, a third for quotations, and a fourth for captions. Using styles rather than manually formatting paragraphs offers an important advantage: If you mark text as a specific style and then decide to change that style, the change occurs to all the marked text throughout the document.

- **Automated headings.** Word offers a set of styles called *Heading 1, Heading 2,* and *Heading 3.* You can customize those styles with any font and size. If you use these heading styles in your report, you can take advantage of Word's automated table of contents feature.

- **Automated table of contents.** Many word processing applications offer an easy process for designing and inserting a table of contents. When you select "Insert Table of Contents" in Word, the program finds all of the headings that you have created using the automated heading styles and copies them into a preformatted table of contents, along with their associated page numbers. As you modify your report, you can continue to update your table of contents to reflect changes in headings and page numbers.

- **Formatted tab styles, including dot leaders.** Many tables of contents include dots, called *dot leaders,* to connect the headings to their page numbers. Word allows you to insert those dot leaders automatically by formatting your tab style, regardless of whether you use an automated table of contents.

- **Automated page numbering, using both Roman and Arabic numerals.** You can control the placement of page numbers in your document by inserting headers or footers. You can further control page numbers by using Word's "Insert Section Break" feature and formatting the page numbers differently for each section. For example, you can create a title page with no page number. Then insert a section break and use small Roman numerals (i, ii, iii, and so on) for the page numbering on the table of contents page and executive summary. Insert another section break and begin the numbering again with Arabic numerals (1, 2, 3, and so on), with the introduction counting as page 1, even though sequentially it is not the first page of the file.

- **Automated footnotes, endnotes, citations, bibliographies.** Most word processing applications allow you to insert and number footnotes, endnotes, and citations automatically. As you add, remove, or cut and paste text in your draft, your note numbers automatically change to reflect their new position. Note, however, that some citation formats assign one style for the first use of a citation and a different style for all subsequent occurrences. So if you move text around, make sure to double-check your footnote styles in the final document.

- **Automated labeling of figures and tables.** You can automatically number and label figures and tables by using Word's "Insert Caption" command. As you move the figures and tables in your draft, you can instruct Word to update the figure and table numbers.

For a TECHNOLOGY exercise, go to Exercise 12 on page 404.

FIGURE 10.14 Pages from Home Depot Digital Annual Report

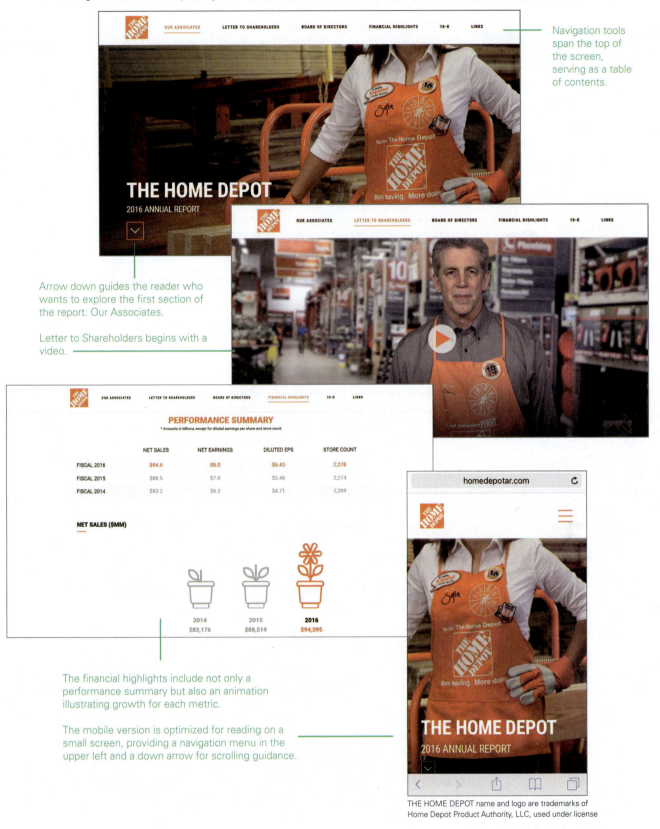

Navigation tools span the top of the screen, serving as a table of contents.

Arrow down guides the reader who wants to explore the first section of the report: Our Associates.

Letter to Shareholders begins with a video.

The financial highlights include not only a performance summary but also an animation illustrating growth for each metric.

The mobile version is optimized for reading on a small screen, providing a navigation menu in the upper left and a down arrow for scrolling guidance.

THE HOME DEPOT name and logo are trademarks of Home Depot Product Authority, LLC, used under license

SQ4 # What guidelines should you follow for writing report decks?

New Hires @ Work

Alicia Carroll

Northwestern University

Associate Director
@ Resolution Media

When a client requests information, we often provide it in a deck. A deck provides more room to be creative about how to present data—with images, tables, and charts—as opposed to a Word document that is mostly paragraphs and bullet points.

Photo courtesy of Alicia Carroll

When Josh Leibowitz, an executive with Carnival Cruise Corporation, first joined the company, he was surprised to find that PowerPoint is "the tool of choice for sharing management updates and plans."[10] In fact, many organizations use presentation software such as PowerPoint to write reports.[11] These PowerPoint-based reports, called *report decks*, differ from traditional slide presentations because decks are designed to be read as well as presented; therefore, they must be understandable without a presenter. Often, the writer sends the report deck as an email attachment, and the audience reads the report deck onscreen, one slide at a time. Sometimes, the writer prints the report deck as a handout for participants at a meeting. Meeting attendees go through the deck slide by slide to discuss the key points. The slides may or may not also be projected. The hybrid status of a report deck—partly report and partly presentation—explains why slides in report decks contain more detail than slides in traditional presentations.

Writing a report using presentation software requires a new way of thinking about how to structure a report and how to design individual slides. To be successful, use the following guidelines.

Understand why and when to use report decks

Organizations use report decks for three main reasons:

- When you need a written report and plan to present that report at a meeting, a report deck can serve both functions. Producing one document instead of two saves time and money.
- Producing the document in presentation software such as PowerPoint increases the chances that people will read the document, and it also facilitates discussion. As Eric Paley, the founder of a venture capital company, says, "Quick to read and easy to edit collaboratively, slide decks are the most concise way to express an idea for discussion and decision making. Prose is great for one-way conversations, but it falls short for any type of engagement in a group."[12]
- Compared to word processing software, presentation software gives writers a great deal of control in designing a page. It more easily allows you to place pictures, tables, and graphs in precise locations, page after page.

Report decks can be used for any type of report. Many consulting companies and business strategy organizations use decks to report the results of analyses to their clients. Other organizations prepare progress reports as decks that managers or team leaders present at monthly department meetings. Many science-based organizations use decks to report the results of technical investigations because presentation software easily allows them to include photographs and diagrams.

Design the deck effectively

Just like traditional word-processed reports, a report written in presentation software needs to be well designed. To ensure consistency among all the slides in your report deck, establish your design features on a master slide. Formats on the master slide will be applied to all the slides in your presentation, which will save you time and effort. **Figure 10.15** illustrates effective master slide design principles.

When choosing the design of your master slide, think inclusively to ensure that your slides are legible to anyone who might read them, including those with *visual disabilities*. For instance, use typefaces that are easily readable for people with dyslexia,[13] and test the color scheme of your slide to see how legible it is to people with various forms of color blindness.[14]

FIGURE 10.15 How to Format a Master Slide

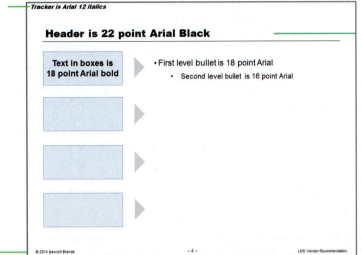

Leave space for a tracker on the upper-left or upper-right corner of your slides. Trackers, or road signs, indicate the section of the deck, like a header on a word-processed report.

Use a basic solid background. Background graphics or dramatic shading effects will compete with your text and graphics for the reader's attention.

Size your title box to accommodate two-line headlines, using a font that is approximately 22 to 24 points. This format will allow you to fit sentence-style headlines at the top of your slides.

Include a footer at the bottom of each slide. The footer contains the slide number, the name of the project, and a copyright marking.

Size your text to be read comfortably on a computer screen or projected in a small conference room.

Check to see how your master slide looks when printed in black and white. Make sure its content is still legible to those who do not read it onscreen.

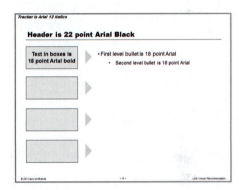

Design the deck content to be easy to follow

Because a reader should be able to follow the logic of a report deck without the benefit of a presenter's explanations, the deck needs to be easy to read. Like any other report, a good deck is divided into sections and begins with a preview. Some decks include executive summaries. All decks include an "agenda," or contents, slide that serves as a table of contents. This slide differs from a traditional table of contents in that it usually does not list the "page" numbers of sections of the report. However, if your deck is long, you may choose to help your reader by adding slide numbers. To remind your reader of the current section name while reading the report, place section titles in *trackers* (sometimes called *road signs*) at the upper-right or upper-left corner of the slide. And to help your audience quickly understand the content, use **message headlines** that concisely articulate the point of the slide.

message headlines Slide headlines that summarize the key point, or message, of each slide.

Individual slides also need to be easy to follow. **Figure 10.16** shows how to revise a traditional bulleted list into a more effective report deck slide. Although this slide uses more text than you would include in a traditional projected presentation, the text will be easy for someone to read on a computer screen or in a printout, which is how a report deck is typically distributed and read.

FIGURE 10.16 How to Design an Effective Report Slide

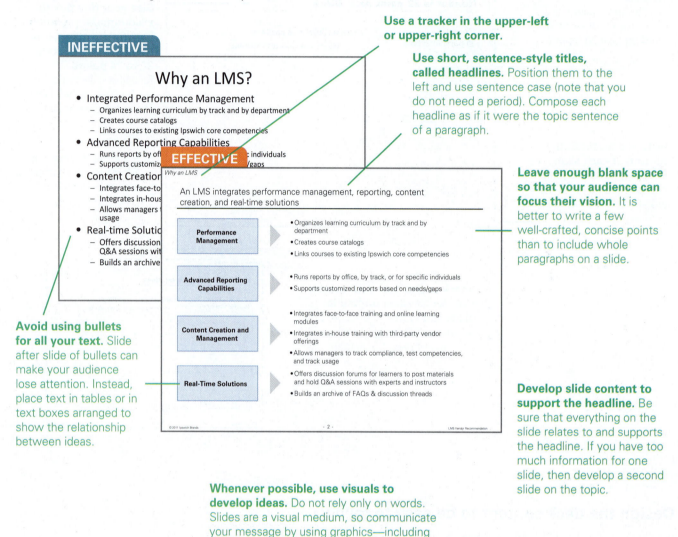

Producing a report deck requires creating many slides, with each designed to support a key point. **Figure 10.17** on pages 383–384 illustrates such a report deck. As you read through the report, pay attention to the annotations that identify its key features. Notice the message headlines and the different ways the slide content supports the headlines. Also note that this report does not include executive summary, although some report decks do. Finally, notice that this report uses an indirect organization, leading up to a recommendation of potential vendors at the end. This organization allows the author to explain the rationale and persuade readers with benefits before recommending specific vendors. More frequently, reports use a direct organization, introducing the recommendations toward the beginning of the report.

FIGURE 10.17 How to Design a PowerPoint Report Deck

This deck is an analytical report written for the chief learning officer of
Ipswich Brands, evaluating options for a new learning management system.

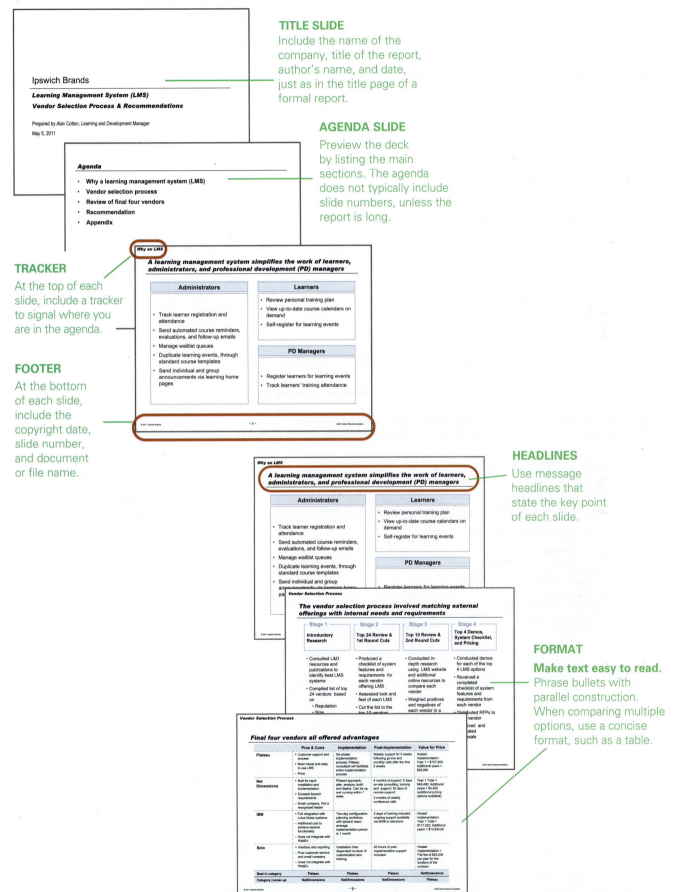

TITLE SLIDE
Include the name of the
company, title of the report,
author's name, and date,
just as in the title page of a
formal report.

AGENDA SLIDE
Preview the deck
by listing the main
sections. The agenda
does not typically include
slide numbers, unless the
report is long.

TRACKER
At the top of each
slide, include a tracker
to signal where you
are in the agenda.

FOOTER
At the bottom
of each slide,
include the
copyright date,
slide number,
and document
or file name.

HEADLINES
Use message
headlines that
state the key point
of each slide.

FORMAT
Make text easy to read.
Phrase bullets with
parallel construction.
When comparing multiple
options, use a concise
format, such as a table.

FIGURE 10.17 *(Continued)*

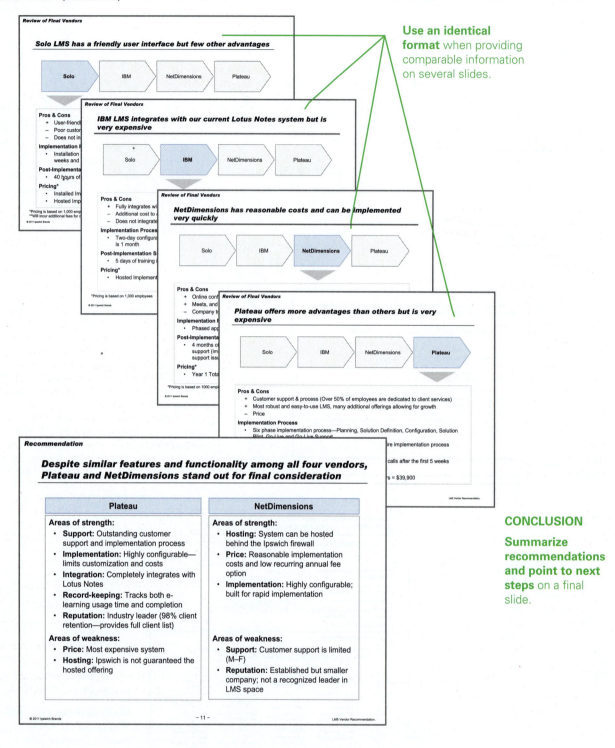

Use an identical format when providing comparable information on several slides.

CONCLUSION

Summarize recommendations and point to next steps on a final slide.

COLLABORATION
WRITING A REPORT AS A TEAM

In the course of your career, you might be tasked to write a report as part of a team, especially for long and comprehensive reports. There are many ways to write collaboratively, and what your team chooses to do will depend on factors such as the date the report is due, the size of the team, the location of team members, and the specific expertise of team members. Here are some things to keep in mind when approaching collaborative report writing at work. These same considerations can help you plan a better collaborative process in school also.

- **Team structure.** Before starting the writing process, it is helpful to establish the team's structure and assign members different responsibilities, according to their skills and expertise. Sometimes this might be decided for you from the outset; for instance, your manager might be part of your team and automatically take on the role of final reviewer before the report is submitted. Or some members may be on the team because they are subject matter experts who will provide data but do less actual writing. But in teams where hierarchy and job scope are less clear, it might take a preliminary discussion to go over everyone's skill sets and see how they can best serve the team.[15] At work, you do not need to assume that the team writing means that everyone should play an equal role on the team, which is what typically happens in school. Remember that in school, the goal is that all students learn from the report-writing process. At work, the goal is to ensure that the process leads to an excellent report.

- **Writing procedure.** Research in collaborative writing shows that writing teams approach their tasks in many different ways.[16] Sometimes they work in parallel, with the entire team planning the document and dividing the work into subtasks that different writers work on at the same time. Then the individual parts are compiled and reviewed. In other teams, one main writer composes the report and the team revises and edits. In other cases, writing, revising, and editing occur simultaneously. Writers use *groupware* such as Google Docs or Microsoft online or post their work to a shared site, where they can see each other's work and make suggestions and adjustments as the drafts develop. Choose a method that works well for your team. The method that you choose may depend on whether your team is **co-located**, with everyone in the same location, or **distributed**, with writers in different physical locations.

- **Communication protocol.** Writing can be a very solitary exercise, especially for writers who are not used to working on extensive projects in groups. But in group projects, it is unwise for writers to work without consulting each other. So, at the start of a project, it is important to discuss how team members will check in and communicate with each other, and what kind of discussion is appropriate for what stage of the writing process. For instance, a team on a months-long project might decide to meet in person or via conference call every two weeks to assess its progress and email each other between meetings. A small team on a tight deadline might prefer to meet every other day and use text messaging in addition to email. You might even consider discussing limits on informal communication to avoid disrupting each other's writing process.[17]

- **Feedback and editing.** In the process of collaborative report writing, you will likely receive feedback on your work or have your work edited by someone else in your team. You might also be expected to provide feedback on a team member's writing. Today, this back-and-forth is easier than ever before using groupware or platforms with commenting and change-tracking functions (for example, Microsoft Word and Google Docs). However, as information science professors Birnholtz and Ibara point out, these digital platforms are often "impoverished environments" for communication where "people [may] overinterpret certain cues," possibly leading to "exaggerated interpretations or impressions" and affecting "how credit and blame are attributed."[18] For instance, heavily editing someone else's work directly when that person expected a say in the changes could be construed as disrespectful. Equally problematic is the practice of suggesting changes only to grammar and style (as opposed to the content of the writing itself), which might suggest that you did not care to engage constructively with someone's work. As a result, it is important to be mindful of how your feedback and edits may be perceived when using these digital tools.

For COLLABORATION exercises, go to Exercises 13 and 31 on pages 404 and 409.

co-located team A team in which all members are in the same physical location.

distributed team A team in which members are in different physical locations.

SQ5 How do you integrate tables and graphs into reports?

New Hires @ Work

Darrell Coleman
Georgia Southern University

Data Analyst @ Georgia
Southern Career Services

To create effective graphs and
tables for my reports, I need
to simplify every-
thing and write
good data descrip-
tions so that the
graph catches the
audience's atten-
tion and speaks
for itself.

Photo courtesy of Darrell Coleman

Business reports often rely on numbers, and **data graphics**—tables and graphs—are the best tools for communicating these numbers. Have you ever read a complicated description of information and then looked at a table or graph and thought, "Now I understand"? Well-designed tables and graphs provide a picture of data and allow you to see relationships and trends much more clearly than with text alone. However, creating effective data graphics and integrating them into your text is not always easy. It involves a multistep process. This section provides a quick glimpse of that process so that you can begin using graphics effectively in your own documents.

Choose the best form of display: Table or graph

Tables and graphs represent data in different ways. **Tables** arrange data in columns and rows, allowing you to read down or across to see different relationships. **Graphs** illustrate the relationship among variables or sets of data as an image or shape drawn in relationship to two axes.

Because they represent data in different ways, tables and graphs have different uses. **Figure 10.18** illustrates the same data presented in text, graph, and table form. As you can see, it is difficult to understand the significance of numbers that are embedded in the paragraph. The table makes it very easy to find exact values. However, the table does not help you see specific patterns and trends. Although the graph does not provide exact values, it highlights trends and relationships by showing the data as a shape. You should choose the form of data graphic that helps your audience most clearly see the important points you want to make about the data.

FIGURE 10.18 Comparing Text, Tables, and Graphs

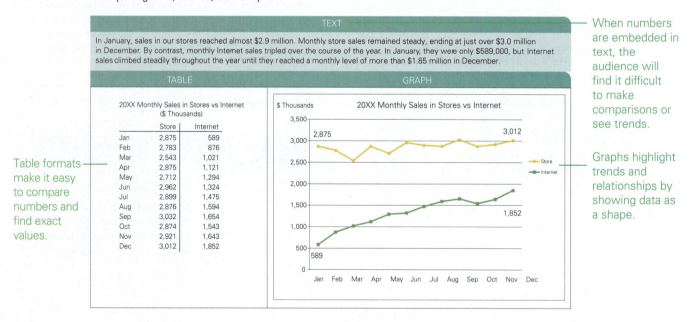

data graphics Visual representations of data, in tables and graphs, that allow you to see relationships and trends much more clearly than in text alone.

table A graphic that arranges content in columns and rows, allowing you to read down or across to see different relationships.

graph A visual representation of data that illustrates the relationship among variables, usually in relationship to *x*- and *y*-axes.

Choose the best type of graph

If using a graph is the best way to display your data, make sure to choose the type of graph that most effectively communicates your message. Although many graph types are available, most business documents rely on the core set of nine graph types illustrated in **Figure 10.19** on pages 387–388, along with some variations.[19] You can create all of these graphs with commonly available spreadsheet and graphing software. For each type of graph, Figure 10.19 provides a statement of the purpose, an illustration, and best practices for designing that type of graph. These best practices, which are explained in more detail in the next section, will help you communicate meaningful information about your data.

Design graphs and tables to communicate

Whether you are designing graphs or tables, follow the core principle of Edward Tufte, one of the most famous information designers in the world. Tufte recommends eliminating all distractions that do not help the audience understand the data.[20] For tables, this means

FIGURE 10.19 Guidelines for Selecting the Best Graph

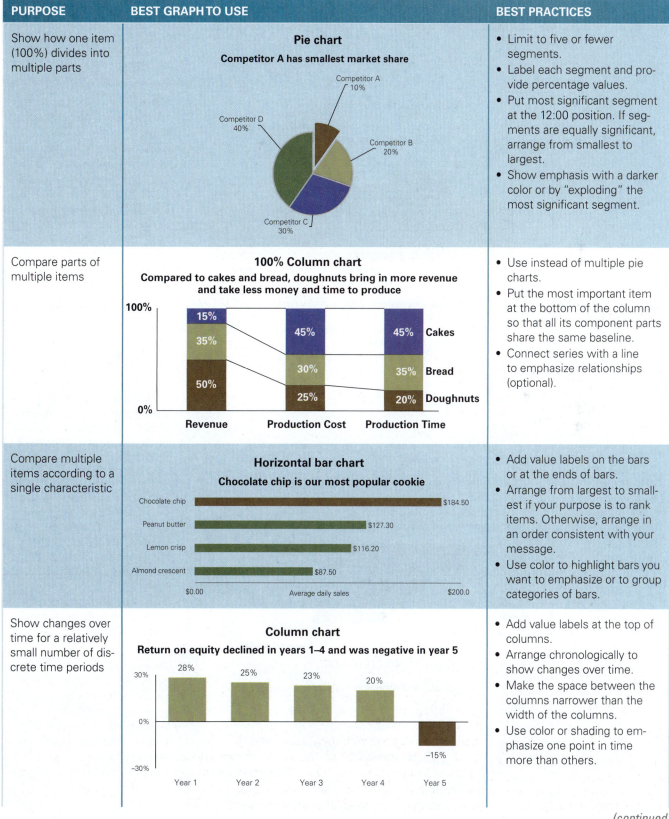

PURPOSE	BEST GRAPH TO USE	BEST PRACTICES
Show how one item (100%) divides into multiple parts	**Pie chart** **Competitor A has smallest market share** Competitor A 10% Competitor D 40% Competitor B 20% Competitor C 30%	• Limit to five or fewer segments. • Label each segment and provide percentage values. • Put most significant segment at the 12:00 position. If segments are equally significant, arrange from smallest to largest. • Show emphasis with a darker color or by "exploding" the most significant segment.
Compare parts of multiple items	**100% Column chart** **Compared to cakes and bread, doughnuts bring in more revenue and take less money and time to produce** Revenue: 15%, 35%, 50% Production Cost: 45%, 30%, 25% Production Time: 45%, 35%, 20% Cakes / Bread / Doughnuts	• Use instead of multiple pie charts. • Put the most important item at the bottom of the column so that all its component parts share the same baseline. • Connect series with a line to emphasize relationships (optional).
Compare multiple items according to a single characteristic	**Horizontal bar chart** **Chocolate chip is our most popular cookie** Chocolate chip $184.50 Peanut butter $127.30 Lemon crisp $116.20 Almond crescent $87.50 $0.00 — Average daily sales — $200.0	• Add value labels on the bars or at the ends of bars. • Arrange from largest to smallest if your purpose is to rank items. Otherwise, arrange in an order consistent with your message. • Use color to highlight bars you want to emphasize or to group categories of bars.
Show changes over time for a relatively small number of discrete time periods	**Column chart** **Return on equity declined in years 1–4 and was negative in year 5** Year 1: 28% Year 2: 25% Year 3: 23% Year 4: 20% Year 5: −15%	• Add value labels at the top of columns. • Arrange chronologically to show changes over time. • Make the space between the columns narrower than the width of the columns. • Use color or shading to emphasize one point in time more than others.

(continued)

FIGURE 10.19 *(Continued)*

PURPOSE	BEST GRAPH TO USE	BEST PRACTICES
Show changes over time to emphasize a trend	**Line chart** **Year to date, actual revenue is exceeding budgeted revenue** $175 $ million $0 Actual Revenue: 21, 32, 44, 65, 88, 92, 107 Budgeted Revenue: 12, 22, 30, 43, 55, 64, 73, 88, 101, 121, 135, 160 J F M A M J J A S O N D	• Limit the number of lines if the graph is difficult to read. • Provide value labels wherever possible. If too cluttered, label only select data points. • Label the lines instead of using a legend. • Use a bright or dark color to emphasize the most important line. • Use short labels on horizontal axis. Avoid diagonal labels.
Show how data are distributed in a series of ranges	**Histogram (step-column)** **Most stock trades last week were executed between $27.51 and $31.50 per share** # trades 350 0 215, 325, 275, 250, 205 <$27.50 $27.51–$29.50 $29.51–$31.50 $31.51–$33.50 >$33.51 Price per share	• Generally, use groups (buckets) of equal size, unless unequal groups make better sense. • Eliminate spaces between columns to emphasize that data are continuous. • Label the x-axis (horizontal axis) with range values. • Avoid overlapping range labels such as 0–5, 5–10, instead use 0–4.9, 5–9.9. • If you put value labels at the top of columns, eliminate gridlines.
Show the pattern of distribution for a continuous series of data	**HISTOGRAPH (FREQUENCY POLYGON)** **Most customer purchase orders are between $40K and $60K** # purchase orders 500 400 300 200 100 0 10 20 30 40 50 60 70 80 90 100 Size of purchase order ($000)	• Do not include range labels on the x-axis (horizontal axis). Instead, use discrete measurement points. • Use light gridlines to help a reader interpret the values on the y-axis (vertical axis). • Use light gray vertical reference lines to highlight a specific area of the distribution. Alternatively, shade the area under the relevant part of the curve.
Compare variables for a small data set	**Paired bar (tornado) chart** **No relationship exists between a salesperson's seniority and sales** Name Baker 29 $19.0 Gillman 21 $ 9.0 Carter 13 $ 6.5 Wallace 12 $ 4.8 Jones 8 $14.8 Samuels 4 $10.5 30 20 10 0 10 2 30 Years on job Annual sales ($000)	• Plot the independent variable on the left, in a low-to-high or high-to-low sequence. (If variables correlate according to the expected pattern, the paired bars will be mirror images.) • Place labels on the inside base of the bars, so that they line up vertically.
Compare variables for a large data set	**SCATTER PLOT** **Height and weight of high school senior class** Weight (lb) 350 300 250 200 150 100 50 50 55 60 65 70 75 80 85 Height (in.)	• Plot the independent variable on the x-axis (horizontal) and the dependent variable on the y-axis (vertical axis). • Add a trend line. If variables correlate, they will cluster around that line.

eliminating or minimizing all unnecessary gridlines and borders. For graphs, it means removing anything that exists only for decoration. All the graphs illustrated in Figure 10.19 follow current best practices in designing graphs.

Use **Figure 10.20** for advice about designing graphs. The numbered guidelines at the bottom of the figure correspond to the numbered elements on the graph. Like graphs, tables should

FIGURE 10.20 How to Design an Effective Graph

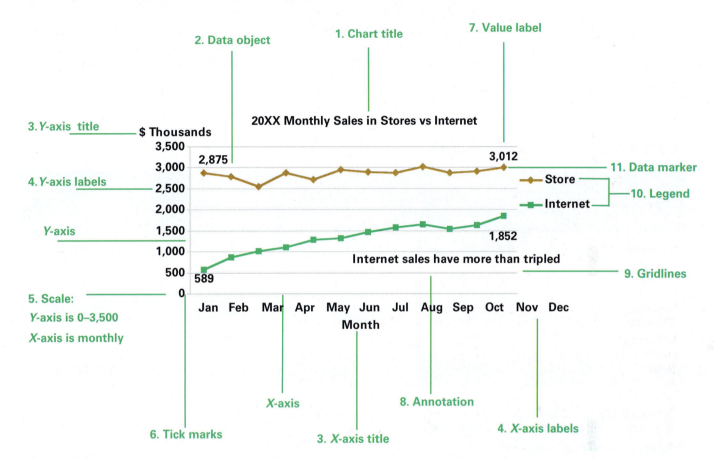

1. **Chart title:** Give every graph a title, or headline, that summarizes its data, purpose, and/or message. People who skim a document should know exactly what the graph is about—even without reading the surrounding text. Use the same headline style for all the graphs in a report. If the graph is plotting data from a specific time frame, it is good practice to indicate the time period in the title (or in a footnote).

2. **Data objects:** Design data objects such as lines, columns, bars, and points very simply. Keep lines thin. Avoid contrasting borders around data objects. Avoid three-dimensional effects, which make the data less precise and clutter the image.

3. **Axis titles:** Use descriptive axis titles, to indicate what is being measured and the units of measurement (for example, $ Thousands, Months, Widgets Sold). Be concise to avoid crowding. Position all titles horizontally, even on the y-axis.

4. **Axis labels:** Use axis labels to identify the data points you are measuring. Position labels horizontally, even on the x-axis.

5. **Scales:** Begin numerical scales at zero. Starting the scale at a higher number distorts the information.

6. **Tick marks:** Use tick marks only when helpful. These small dashes on the x- and y-axes are sometimes helpful to align the axis labels with data points.

7. **Value labels:** Place value labels on data points rather than relying only on the y-axis scale. Value labels communicate precise, not estimated, values. Use only enough labels to allow readers to interpret the data. If you use value labels on data points, you can also delete many of the numerical labels on the y-axis. Minimum and maximum values are often sufficient.

8. **Annotations:** Include descriptive annotations to highlight key data changes or to focus on specific data points.

9. **Gridlines:** Use minimal gridlines. If you must use gridlines, use light gray instead of black.

10. **Legends:** Avoid legends when possible. Consider using labels instead, placing them as closely as possible to the lines or bars. Legends require the audience to exert additional effort to match legend information to the data on the graph. If you do need to use a legend, be sure distinctions are visible when viewed both in color and in grayscale, and eliminate borders around legend boxes.

11. **Data markers:** Use small, subtle data markers to identify specific data points. In a line graph, data markers identify the specific data points you are connecting. For example, this graph covers one year but the lines are drawn from only 12 data points (one for each month).

be designed so the audience can easily see the data without any distracting content or format. Follow the guidelines illustrated in the table in **Figure 10.21** for best practices in designing tables.

Integrate data displays within the text

In a report, text and data displays need to work together to communicate the full message. The graph or table presents the data, and the text contextualizes and interprets the data. Do not simply repeat data that is in the graph itself. Instead, use text to explain what the audience is looking at and highlight the key point they should understand from the data. **Figure 10.22** illustrates how to integrate the verbal and visual elements of a document. Follow the guidelines in the figure when you are presenting graphs, tables, and other visual displays.

FIGURE 10.21 How to Design an Effective Table

FUNDS INVESTED IN CERTIFICATES OF DEPOSIT				
CD LENGTH	DATE OPENED	RENEWABLE	INTEREST RATE %	VALUE OF INVESTMENT
Six Month	06/01/20XX	Y	1.15	$ 870.27
One Year	08/13/20XX	Y	2.00	2,250.50
Three Year	11/01/20XX	N	3.25	10,311.73
Five Year	03/03/20XX	N	4.25	15,215.50
Total				**$ 28,648.00**

- **Title each table** concisely, describing the table's content and any key points you would like the audience to notice.
- **Arrange the columns and rows** in a meaningful order. This table is ordered from shortest CD length to longest.
- **Label columns and rows effectively** so that readers will know exactly what is in each cell.
- **Eliminate heavy gridlines**. You can separate columns and rows using light gray lines or white space.
- **Use shading strategically** to highlight data or distinguish alternate rows or columns. Notice how the last column here emphasizes the current value and total.
- **Align text to the left** to make it easy to read.
- **Align numbers to the right** to keep decimal points and digits aligned. Use a consistent number of decimal places in all values in a column.

- **Do not center content** unless every row in that column contains the same number of characters. In the "Date Opened," "Renewable," and "Interest Rate %" columns above, data is centered because the character lengths are identical. However, if one interest rate were 10 percent or larger, you would need to right align the numbers to make the decimal points line up.
- **Remove unnecessary repetition from cells**. You do not need to include a $ or % in all cells in a column. Put signs in the appropriate column or row header (as shown in the "Interest Rate" column here) or with the first value (as shown in the "Value of Investment" column).

FIGURE 10.22 How to Integrate Graphics Within Text

Label and number figures and tables sequentially throughout the report. You can either number figures and tables in their individual sequences (Figure 1, Figure 2, Table 1, Table 2), or you can combine tables and figures into one list, calling them Exhibit 1, Exhibit 2, Exhibit 3.

Refer the audience to the graphic within the text using the figure or table number.

Tell the audience what to notice in the graphic. In a data graphic, what are the important findings or trends? In a picture or illustration, where should the audience focus their attention? In a diagram, how should the audience read the illustrated relationships? Answer these questions in the text that accompanies the graphic.

Place the graphic as close as possible after the first reference. Do not place graphics before the text mentions them because this will confuse readers.

Design the graph to be self-explanatory, even though you have provided explanatory text. Provide enough labeling on the graphic and enough description in the figure name and caption so that readers can understand what they are seeing without reading the accompanying text. This allows readers to scan the document and derive a good deal of information by looking only at the graphics.

Provide source citations for your data directly under the graph or as part of the caption.

In the United States today, cigarette smoking is the greatest preventable cause of death. The Centers for Disease Control and Prevention estimates that each year 443,000 people die prematurely from smoking or exposure to second-hand smoke. In addition, more than 8 million people suffer from smoking-related illnesses.[1] To tackle this problem, it is crucial to prevent teenagers from beginning to smoke, since most current smokers began as teenagers.[2]

Attempts to decrease teenage smoking in the last decade have largely been successful. As Figure 1 shows, between 1999 and 2009, cigarette smoking decreased significantly among both male and female students, from 35 percent to 20 percent. However, most of that decline took place in the first five years of the decade. Since 2004, little progress has been made in lowering the percentage of students—or adults—that smoke. That is why it is critical to rethink our approach to preventing tobacco use.

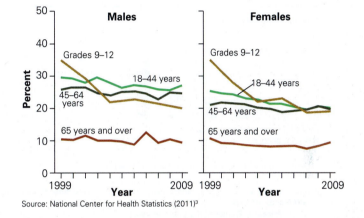

Source: National Center for Health Statistics (2011)[3]

Figure 1: Cigarette smoking among students in grades 9–12 and adults age 18 and older in the United States 1999–2009

---

[1] CDC, National Center for Chronic Disease Prevention and Health Promotion. (2010). *Tobacco use: Targeting the nation's leading killer—At a glance 2010*. Retrieved from http://www.cdc.gov/chronicdisease/resources/publications/aag/pdf/2010/tobacco_2010.pdf

[2] CDC. (2010). *Report of the Surgeon General: How tobacco smoke causes disease—What it means to you*. Retrieved from http://www.cdc.gov/tobacco/data_statistics/sgr/2010/consumer_booklet/pdfs/consumer.pdf

[3] National Center for Health Statistics. (2011). *Health, United States, 2010: With special feature on death and dying*. Retrieved from http://www.cdc.gov/nchs/data/hus/hus10.pdf

ETHICS
REPRESENTING DATA ETHICALLY

Businesses rely on data to make informed decisions. To support those decisions, graphs must display data ethically and not mislead the audience. Graphs can mislead in many ways. For example, they can manipulate the scale, distort perspective, and show data out of context. Even if graph designers do not intend to be dishonest, they may make design choices that result in bad graphs. As Naomi Robbins, an expert in data visualization, says, "The designers of many of the graphs we see daily pay more attention to grabbing the audience's attention than to communicating clearly and accurately. They choose design options that they think look better but are actually graphical mistakes, since they mislead or confuse their readers."[21]

Because ethical representation of data is so important, many organizations have developed guides to data ethics.[22] The following guidelines are among the most important to follow in business communication. The graphs on the left are potentially misleading. The versions on the right correct the errors.

For an ETHICS exercise, go to Exercise 21 on page 406.

1. Begin axis scales at zero.

Misleading graph: Because the y-axis (vertical) begins at $1.50, the distance between the Year 3 value and Year 4 value looks disproportionately large. At first glance, the audience may assume that earnings per share in Year 4 almost doubled compared to earnings per share in Year 3.

More accurate graph: By starting the y-axis at $0.00, the graph more accurately displays the actual difference between Year 3 and Year 4 earnings per share: 22%.

2. Avoid pictograms and 3D graphs, which distort size. Make differences in the size of data objects proportional to differences in the data.

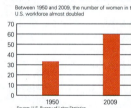

Misleading graph: The pictogram representing 2009 is twice as tall as the one representing 1950—and is also twice as wide. That means, in square inches, it is four times larger than the 1950 woman. The size difference between the two objects is not proportional to the difference in data. At first glance, the audience may assume the women in the workforce quadrupled.

More accurate graph: The 2009 bar is twice the height of the 1950 bar and is the same width. It is exactly twice the size of the 1950 bar. The size difference between the two bars is proportional to the difference in the data.

3. Show your data in context.

Misleading graph: Presenting just two years of data gives the impression that increasing the price of the product was a bad business decision.

More accurate graph: When the data is placed in a larger context, you can see that the drop in revenue was temporary.

4. Provide the absolute number ("n") when you graph percentages.

Misleading graph: The percentages give the impression that most employees prefer online training. However, the graph does not say how many employees responded to the survey, so it is unclear whether most employees prefer online or just a small subset.

More accurate graph: This graph puts the data in a larger context and it provides absolute numbers. It tells the reader that very few employees responded to the survey, but those who did respond favored online training.

How should you document your research?

Documenting—or citing your sources—is a key part of all writing in academia and most professional writing. Appropriate documentation serves many functions:

- **It adds credibility to your writing.** Many writers assume that they will seem smarter if they make their ideas appear original. In fact, the opposite is true. Your writing will be more impressive if it shows that you are well informed by having read relevant texts or talked to key people.
- **It strengthens your argument.** Most report writing relies on up-to-date and accurate data. By providing appropriate citations, you can give your audience confidence in the strength of your data.
- **It helps your audience locate information mentioned in your report.** Your audience may want to read more deeply into your topic. They will rely on your reference list to give them direction.
- **It helps demonstrate that you are ethical.** If you acknowledge all your sources, no one will accuse you of **plagiarism**, which is presenting others' ideas as your own.

To ensure good documentation, follow the advice below.

plagiarism Intentionally or unintentionally failing to acknowledge others' ideas in your work.

Determine what needs to be documented

Provide documentation for any information or opinion that you originally found in another source. Specifically, you need to document the following content:

- **Exact quotations. Quotations** are any phrases, sentences, paragraphs—even single, distinctive words—that you take from any of your sources. When you include a source's exact wording in your text, you need to enclose it in quotation marks. If it is a long quotation, indent and single space the block of text without quotation marks. With both formats, you need to document the original source. Depending on the documentation style you choose, you can use footnotes, endnotes, or *parenthetical citations*—inserting in parentheses the author's last name, year of publication (when using APA style), and the page number of the quotation in the original source.

  If you find that more than 10 percent of your content consists of quotations, then you are relying too heavily on your sources and not adding enough of your own analysis, critique, or explanation. Most business reports contain very few direct quotations. More often, writers choose to paraphrase or summarize the content. Reserve quotations for the following situations:
  - To present someone else's point of view in that person's own words
  - To cite an authority whose exact words are well phrased and powerful
  - To provide exact wording on which you plan to comment
  - To be very precise and the exact wording allows you to do so
- **Paraphrase.** A **paraphrase** is a version of someone else's original content but in your own words. A good paraphrase will have a completely different sentence structure than the original, not just a few replaced words. Cite paraphrased content with the author's name and, when using APA style, the year of publication. Including a page number is required in some documentation styles and just recommended in others.
- **Summary.** A **summary** is a very brief version of another person's point of view. When you summarize, you still need to acknowledge the source of those ideas by using a citation.
- **Specific facts and data.** You also need to cite every piece of information that is not common knowledge or the result of your own primary research. This includes opinions, arguments, and speculations as well as facts, details, figures, and statistics. Writers are often confused about what is common knowledge. Simply put, common knowledge includes things that most people know. For example, most people know that the capital of France is Paris. You would not need to cite a source for that. By contrast, most people do not know that the population of France is approximately 67 million people. For that data, you would need to cite the French National Institute of Statistics and Economic Studies.[23] This citation adds credibility to your statement and helps readers identify where to look for more information.
- **Tables, graphs, photographs, and other graphics.** If you copy a visual from another source and place it in your document, you need to cite the source for that visual. You do this by including the citation in your caption or directly under the visual, as illustrated in **Figure 10.23** on page 394, which uses the APA format for citing graphics.

quotations Any phrases, sentences, paragraphs—even single, distinctive words—that you take from any of your sources.

paraphrase A version of what someone else says, but in your own words and with your own emphasis.

summary A very brief version of someone else's text, using your own words.

FIGURE 10.23 Example of an APA Source Citation for a Graphic

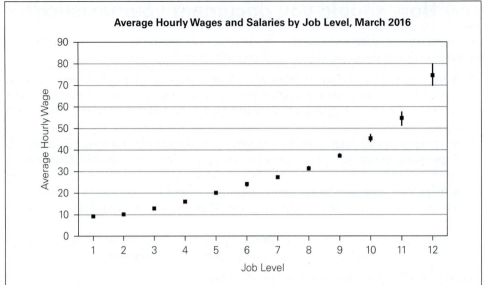

Source: Monaco, K. (2017, June). How pay and benefits change as job level rises: Data from the National Compensation Survey. *Beyond the Numbers: Pay & Benefits, 6* (8). Retrieved from U.S. Bureau of Labor Statistics website: https://www.bls.gov/opub/btn/volume-6/how-pay-and-benefits-change-as-job-level-rises-data-from-the-national-compensation-survey.htm

Prepare the documentation

In a formal report, you must acknowledge sources in three ways:

- **In-text citations.** Every time you use material from another source in your text, add a citation. Your citation may be in the form of a footnote, endnote, or parenthetical citation inserted directly after your reference. The form you use will depend on the requirements of your organization or school. The three most common formats or styles of documentation are:
  - APA (American Psychological Association), frequently used in social sciences and business
  - MLA (Modern Language Association), commonly used in the humanities
  - CMOS (Chicago Manual of Style), frequently used in business, history, and some social sciences.

    For details about these styles, see Appendix B: Documentation and Reference Styles.

- **Textual references.** Do not rely exclusively on citations to orient readers to your sources. Instead, introduce cited material by explicitly referring to the source within your text:

    According to the INSEE (2017), in 2014 the population of Paris was approximately 2.2 million.

  or

    The French National Institute of Statistics and Economic Studies reports that population of Paris in 2014 was approximately 2.2 million (INSEE, 2017).

- **Reference list or bibliography.** Provide a list of sources at the end of every research report. Each item in the list must include enough information for readers to find that document on their own. APA, MLA, and CMOS each have different names for this list:
  - APA titles the page *References.*
  - MLA titles the page *Works Cited.*
  - CMOS offers two options. If you are using footnotes or endnotes, title the page *Bibliography.* If you are using parenthetical citations, title the page *References.*

    In addition, each documentation style follows different rules about the kind of material to include in the list and how to format that material. For details and examples, see Appendix B: Documentation and Reference Styles.

    Write the citations, text references, and reference list entries as you work on your report. Do not wait to add them until after you've written your entire draft. Waiting to add citations and to document information leads to two problems. First, you may omit required information that will be hard to find later (and will waste time). Second, you may forget what you've quoted and unintentionally plagiarize material.

■ **In summary,** no matter where you work, you are likely to be asked to provide information or analysis that answers business questions. That means you will write reports, which may take the form of emails, memos, letters, formal manuscripts, online interactive documents, or report decks, or web pages. You can increase the effectiveness of your reports by using an objective style, formatting the information so it is easy to find, creating graphics that help the audience visualize the data and other complex material, and documenting your sources. The guidelines in this chapter help you manage all this material and present it in ways that will be clear to your audience, whether they read the report now or in the future.

REPORTS @ WORK   Center for Clear Communication, Inc.

As you have learned in this chapter, it can be challenging to design and write an effective report aimed at a relatively small audience—a manager, or a client, or a group of employees. But what if you are writing a report that will be delivered to more than 125 million people per year? And what if each reader needs to receive a personalized version of this report?

That was the challenge that the U.S. Social Security Administration (SSA) faced when Congress passed a bill requiring that all workers in the United States aged 25 and older receive a copy of a Social Security report that includes a personalized estimate of their benefits when they retire. The SSA had already created a benefits statement for workers near retirement (aged 60 and older). But the new mandate meant that the SAA needed a new report, one that would provide information useful to a much broader age group and that was easy for all working Americans to understand, no matter their level of education.

To address this challenge, the SSA partnered with Carolyn Boccella Bagin, president of the Center for Clear Communication, Inc., and an expert in plain English and document design. Bagin approached the challenge by working with key members of the SSA staff to implement a large-scale version of the ACE (analyze, compose, and evaluate) communication process. Here is a brief description of what she did—and the successful result.

Analyze

Bagin first analyzed the existing personal benefits statement. She looked at its strengths and weaknesses, identified what people had difficulty understanding, and pinpointed why they had difficulty.

Next, working with an SSA task force, Bagin created a visual map of the life cycle of the document and identified all the departments that work with the document—including customer service managers, legal staff, and production staff. She interviewed people from all those departments, asking what caused problems and what they would like to change: "Often internal people have the answers, but no one asks them or takes them seriously," says Bagin. "This

is especially true of frontline employees, who know how to explain things so that normal people can understand." In these interviews she learned about the constraints that influenced the report content and design; for example, she learned from production managers that equipment used to print the report is capable of including personalized information on only a few pages, leading to design challenges.

Compose and Evaluate

Based on what she learned in the analysis phase, Bagin revised the document several times. She consulted with internal stakeholders to be sure that the document contained the right information, phrased in a readable, conversational, plain English way. She created a sample document, which SSA researchers tested in focus groups to ensure that readers understood the document and could easily find important information, such as how much money they earned in a specific year. After analyzing focus group results, Bagin produced four distinct prototypes for further testing with audiences. In composing those designs, she considered such things as how the document folded, what readers saw on the first page when they opened the envelope, what information and headings fell at the top of a page, and where readers would find their personalized information. SSA researchers mailed the prototypes to 18,000 test readers. They found that all of the prototypes received good responses, so the SSA chose the design that was least expensive to produce.

The Result

The process of analyzing, composing, and evaluating a report of this magnitude took almost three years from start to finish. However, the investment of time paid off. A Gallup survey, taken the first year the report was launched, found that "the results to date are glowing. The new Social Security statements have played a significant role in increasing Americans' understanding of Social Security."[24] Just as importantly, the report has had staying power: The design, illustrated on the next page, has continued to be used without major revision for almost 20 years.[25]

(continued)

REPORTS @ WORK Center for Clear Communication, Inc. *(Continued)*

Source: Smith & Couch (2014).

Source: Interview with Carolyn Boccella Bagin, http://centerforclearcommunication.org.

Reporting Results to a Client

This case scenario will help you review the chapter material by applying it to a specific situation.

When Jeff Ellis graduated with a degree in civil engineering, he pictured himself designing buildings and bridges and managing construction teams. He never imagined himself behind a computer writing reports.

However, that is exactly where Jeff finds himself today. He has just finished his first major project at Schuyler Engineering, an environmental assessment of a plot of land on which a client wants to build an office park. Emily, the senior engineer on the project, has asked Jeff to write the client report. When Jeff asked Emily if she could give him a model to follow, Emily pointed to the file cabinet and said, "Sure, you'll find lots of reports in there."

Jeff did find a lot of reports: long ones, short ones, letter reports, and very formal reports. The diversity confused him and left him asking, "What is the best approach to take?" Jeff is glad he saved his business communication text from college. That may give him some better ideas for how to structure a professional report.

Writing a Report Introduction

Jeff begins writing his report with the first step of the ACE process: analyzing to determine the purpose, audience, and medium. His audience, the CEO of Halvorson Properties, wants to know whether it is safe to build an office park on the property he owns. Because this decision has significant financial and environmental effects, Jeff decides to write a formal letter report that clearly communicates the message that the property is safe. His research indicated that it has not been affected by hazardous waste or contaminated groundwater. He will provide enough details about his methodology and findings to give Mr. Halvorson confidence in this assessment.

With those decisions in mind, Jeff sits down to write the report's introduction. After writing his first paragraph, he emails it to Emily, who revises it.

Question 1: Compare Jeff's draft of the introduction with Emily's revision. What key differences do you notice between the two openings? Which opening would you choose?

Jeff's First Draft Introduction

Dear Mr. Halvorson:

At your request, we have conducted an investigation of the site defined by the attached survey map for the purposes of rendering an opinion as to whether the site contains hazardous waste or is being impacted by contaminated groundwater. Our investigations consisted of making soil borings and visual observations of the ground surface, vegetation, and drainage patterns and laboratory testing of soil samples. The testing included physical properties testing and chemical testing of the water extracted from the soil. In addition, we have examined various maps and aerial photos, contacted various government agencies, and contacted the power company in our efforts to determine whether hazardous waste is known to have impacted the site.

Our findings are as follows.

Emily's Revision

Dear Mr. Halvorson:

At your request, we have investigated the site defined by the attached survey map to determine (1) how the site was used, (2) whether the site contains hazardous waste, and (3) whether it is affected by contaminated groundwater. Our investigation is complete except for the results of governmental and power company records searches.

Assuming that these searches support our findings, it is our professional assessment that the site has not been impacted by hazardous waste or groundwater contamination that would render it unsuitable for development as an office park.

This letter describes our methodology and reports our findings.

Structuring the Report's Findings

As Jeff develops his investigation report, he decides that the detailed discussion of the report will include the specific findings of his investigation. Here is the first draft he produced.

Jeff's First Draft Findings

Our investigations indicate that nearly all of Parcel 1 has been idle for at least 10 to 15 years. An old house foundation exists near the south central portion of Parcel 1. Parcel 2 appears to have been idle for many years. However, recent dumping of construction debris and fill is apparent primarily along the eastern property line. Parcel 3 is vegetated with an old orchard near the center of the property, and remnants of abandoned residences are apparent. Parcel 3 also has been impacted with piles of construction debris dumped along its easternmost side. Parcel 4 is primarily a protected wetlands area identified by the U.S. Army Corps of Engineers. Some filling has occurred along the eastern and southern border of Parcel 4.

On the basis of soil borings, laboratory test results, and our observations of the previously referenced site, in our opinion it is unlikely that any storage, disposal, or release of oil, fuels, gases, chemicals, trash, garbage, or other solid or hazardous materials has taken place on this property. Only trace amounts of these materials are present, as associated with the residential occupancy and the relatively recent illegal dumping of debris. We have requested a letter from People's Electric certifying that the site is not presently served by transformers containing PCBs nor is the site known to have been impacted by spills of PCBs. Except for the possibility of old heating oil tanks or septic tanks associated with the previous homes, there are no buried tanks on the site. Considering the soil types encountered in the borings, it is extremely unlikely that fuel oils, even if they were present, could migrate more than a few inches. Therefore, we do not consider this site to have been affected by an oil spill or buried tanks or pesticides other than those associated with residential occupation and farming operations.

As Jeff reviews his draft, he realizes that the main ideas are not easy to find. This time, instead of giving his draft to Emily to review, he writes a new outline of the findings section on his own. His goal is to design the page so that the main ideas stand out, using both headings and good topic sentences for the paragraphs.

Here is his outline:

Findings about land use

1. Parcel 1:
2. Parcel 2:
3. Parcel 3:
4. Parcel 4:

Findings about contamination

1. Our investigations indicate it is unlikely that this property has been contaminated by any storage, disposal, or release of oil, fuels, gases, chemicals, trash, garbage, or other solid or hazardous materials.
2. It is also unlikely that the groundwater or soil on the site has been contaminated by activities on the adjacent sites.

Question 2: Using these headings, subheadings, and topic sentences, how would you complete the findings section of the report? Where would you place the supporting details from his draft?

Phrasing a Conclusion Accurately

As Jeff completes his report, he wonders how he should phrase the conclusions he reaches in his report. Here are two statements he is considering:

> **Option 1:** It is our professional opinion that the site has not been impacted by hazardous waste or groundwater contamination that would render it unsuitable for development as an office park.

> **Option 2:** It is our professional opinion that the site has not been impacted by hazardous waste or groundwater contamination and thus the site is safe for an office park.

Question 3: Which statement do you think is the better option, and why?

Study Questions in Review

 How can ACE help you write a business report? *(pages 348–353)*

- **Analyze to understand purpose and report type.** Some reports are informational; others are analytic.
- **Analyze to understand audience needs** and determine what content to include.
- **Analyze to choose the best medium.** Email, memo, and letter reports are usually short. Formal reports are often longer. Report decks are effective for any length.
- **Compose your report to meet audience expectations.** Include identifying information, a preview, detailed discussion, and supporting information. Most reports are organized directly.
- **Compose using an objective and easy-to-read style** by focusing on facts, analysis, and well-supported recommendations.
- **Evaluate by reviewing on your own and getting feedback from others** to ensure you are meeting audience and stakeholder needs. Use evaluation questions to review your report (see Figure 10.5 on page 353).

 What types of short, routine reports are typical in business? *(pages 354–359)*

- **Progress reports** provide information about the status of a long-term project.
- **Meeting minutes** document discussions and decisions at meetings.
- **Trip reports** document activities during business trips and outline accomplishments.
- **Feasibility reports** analyze whether a plan can be implemented as proposed.

SQ3 **How should you structure longer, formal reports for print and online distribution?** *(pages 360–379)*

- **Organize the report into useful sections.** Create a title page for identifying information, preview the report with preliminary sections, develop the details within body sections, and conclude the report with supporting information.
- **Design the report for your audience and purpose.** Use a manuscript style for most internal reports. If the audience is already interested in the content, no special design features are required. For reports distributed outside your organization or to a wide audience—such as white papers and annual reports—use design features to enhance the report's visual appeal.

- **Choose the best electronic format for online distribution.** For internal reports, native file formats or PDF files are typical. For external reports, use PDFs to simplify emailing, printing, and storing the report as well as downloading from a website. PDFs distributed through a website also allow a company to collect contact information from people who download the report. Use web-based reports to encourage browsing and interaction.

SQ4 **What guidelines should you follow for writing report decks?** *(pages 380–385)*

- **Understand why and when to use report decks.** They can double as both written reports and presentations, engage the audience, and allow more design flexibility.
- **Design the deck effectively** by using a solid background, appropriate font sizes, "road signs" to identify sections, and footers.
- **Design the deck content to be easy to follow** by using sentence-style headlines that summarize the main point of the slide and by designing the slide to support and explain the headline.

SQ5 **How do you integrate tables and graphs into reports?** *(pages 386–392)*

- **Choose the best form of display: Table or graph.** Tables arrange data in columns and rows, allowing you to read down or across to see different relationships. Graphs illustrate the relationship between data points or sets of data as a shape in relation to two axes.
- **Choose the best type of graph** by considering the purpose and relationship of the data.
- **Design graphs and tables to communicate.** Use titles, axes labels, thin lines, visible data markers, and annotations. Avoid 3-D, contrasting borders, gridlines, tick marks, and legends.
- **Integrate data displays within the text.** Help readers focus on the display and understanding its information.

 How should you document your research? *(pages 393–395)*

- **Determine what needs to be documented.** Document all content taken from other sources.
- **Prepare the documentation** by introducing sources in the narrative, providing citations in the text, and preparing a reference list as you compose.

Visual Summary

ANALYZE
- Understand purpose and report type
- Understand audience needs
- Choose the best medium

COMPOSE
- Meet reader expectations
- Use an objective, easy--to--read style

Detailed discussion
- Sections with clear headings
- Subsections as necessary
- Tables and graphs that communicate clearly

Supporting information
- References
- Appendices

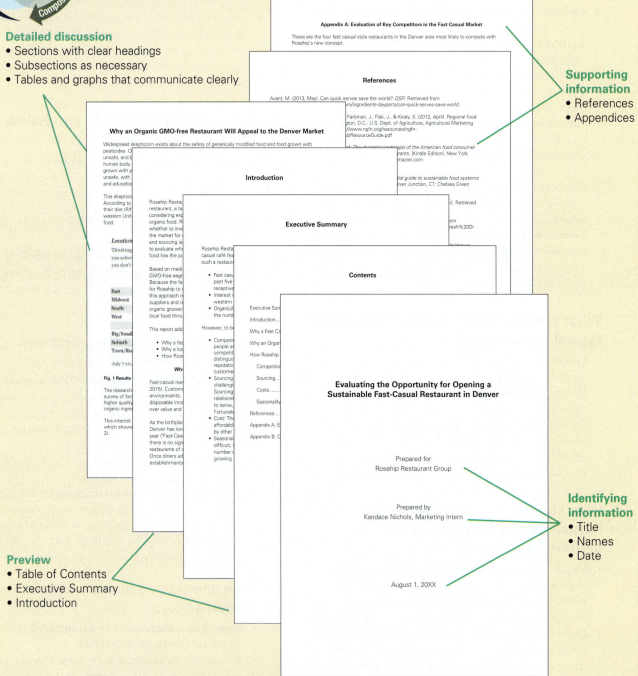

Preview
- Table of Contents
- Executive Summary
- Introduction

Identifying information
- Title
- Names
- Date

EVALUATE by reviewing on your own and getting feedback from others

Key Terms

Abstract p. 349
Analytical report p. 348
Appendix p. 351
Attachment p. 351
Co-located team p. 385
Data graphics p. 386
Distributed team p. 385

Evaluation report p. 360
Executive summary p. 349
Feasibility report p. 354
Graph p. 386
Infographic p. 377
Informational report p. 348
Minutes p. 354

Paraphrase p. 393
Plagiarism p. 393
Progress report p. 354
Quotations p. 393
Recommendation report
  p. 360
Reference list p. 351

Report deck p. 349
Summary p. 393
Table p. 386
Title page p. 360
Trip report p. 354
White paper p. 372

MyLab Business Communication

If your instructor is using MyLab Business Communication, go to **www.pearson.com/ mylab/business-communication** to complete the problems marked with this icon ⭐.

Review Questions

1 What is the difference between an informational report and an analytical report? Give an example of each kind.

2 What is the purpose of a report abstract? What kind of information does it include?

3 What is the purpose of an executive summary? What kind of information does it include?

4 What is the difference between an attachment and an appendix?

⭐ **5** Why is it important to use an objective, easy-to-read style in a report?

⭐ **6** What design features can you use in a report to enhance its visual appeal?

7 Name three reasons why businesses distribute electronic reports as PDFs.

8 What types of slide titles, or headlines, are typically used in report decks?

9 Where should you place figures and tables within a report?

10 What is the difference between a paraphrase and a summary?

Critical Thinking Questions

1 The Culture feature in this chapter offers three suggestions for writing reports for international audiences who will read the report in English. Imagine that your report will be translated into another language—for example, Spanish or Japanese. Would this same advice make the document easier to translate? In what ways? Based on your knowledge of other languages, what other advice would you give writers who are preparing reports that will be translated? **[Related to the Culture feature on page 353]**

⭐ **2** Formal reports contain a number of features that help readers navigate: a table of contents, lists of figures and tables, executive summaries, informative headings, and appendices for supplementary information. Why is it useful to include all rather than just some of these features?

3 A classmate or coworker suggests that it is redundant to include both an executive summary and an introduction in a report. How would you explain the different functions of an executive summary and introduction—and the reason for including both?

4 Figure 10.19 on pages 387–388 suggests using a horizontal bar chart to rank and compare items. Some writers also use column charts for that purpose. What are the pros and cons of using horizontal bars versus vertical columns for graphs that compare items?

⭐ **5** According to the old saying, "A picture is worth 1,000 words." If that is the case, then why is it important to explain all graphics within the text of your report rather than assume that the graphics will speak for themselves?

6 A letter report is a hybrid between a regular business letter and a formal report. What features does a letter report share with a business letter? What features does it share with a formal report?

7 Your manager asks you to write a type of report not illustrated in this chapter; for example, a compliance report. How would you go about learning the key features of a compliance report and the type of content that is required?

⭐ **8** Some organizations are asking employees to post information in wikis rather than write traditional reports. What would be the advantages and disadvantages of reporting information on an internal corporate wiki?

9 Assume that you have collected several secondary sources to support an informational report. However, when you prepare your reference list, you realize that you did not record the website address for a white paper you found online. It's been only a month since you found the source and printed it, but now that you search for the link online, you can no longer find it. Should you use the information if it is no longer available online? If you decide to use the information, how would it cite it?

10 You are writing an academic paper that relies on extensive secondary research. One of the sources (Source A) cites information from another source (Source B). You want to use a piece of information from B that is cited in A. If you haven't read B, should you cite B or A as the source of the information? If you want to use information from B, are you obligated to read B?

Key Concept Exercises

 How can ACE help you write a business report?
(pages 348–353)

1 Analyze to understand purpose and report type

For each of the following questions, identify the type of report you would write. Is it primarily informational or analytical? Refer to the report names in Figure 10.1 on page 348.

a. Has our new marketing plan met our sales objectives?

b. Why are so many of our widgets being returned as defective?

c. Are we on track with our project?

d. Can our client, Rose's Bakery, afford to open a new store next year?

e. Who is responsible for the property damage in our client's building? The construction crew? The painters? The tenants? The maintenance staff?

f. What new sales leads did you develop at the trade show?

2 Analyze to understand audience needs

For each of the questions listed in Exercise 1, determine what information the audience would need. Assume that your audience is a high-level manager or executive who has not been involved with your project.

3 Analyze to choose the best medium

For each of the questions listed in Exercise 1, decide what medium you would use to write the report. Pick a medium and explain why it is a good choice.

- Memo report
- Letter report
- Email report
- Formal report
- Report deck

4 Compose your report to meet audience expectations

Search the Internet for a report produced by a government agency. (One good example is the report *How Creativity Works in the Brain* by the National Endowment for the Arts, https://www.arts.gov/publications/how-creativity-works-brain). Quickly review that report and identify where and how it provides identifying information, a preview, detail discussion, and supporting information. Are the techniques that the report uses effective? Would you recommend any changes? Summarize your findings and conclusions in an email message to your instructor. Be sure to provide a complete citation for the report you are analyzing. For the information to include in a reference list entry, see Appendix B: Documentation and Reference Styles, in the back of the book.

5 Compose using an objective and easy-to-read style

Anya James works for AquaSafe Product Design, a company that designs and installs aquariums in homes and offices. Anya has been assigned to the new product development team. The team's job is to research and develop new product ideas. Currently, the team is exploring the idea of an interactive aquarium that allows users to engage more with the fish. At the end of the first three weeks on the project, Anya's manager asks for a progress report.

Review Anya's first draft on page 403. Evaluate this progress report:

- Is the style objective, focusing on the project? Or does it focus on the team's activities?
- Is the report sufficiently factual and detailed?
- Should the report contain any additional information?
- Based on your analysis, recommend at least two changes to the report.

6 Evaluate by reviewing on your own and getting feedback from others

Using the questions in Figure 10.5, evaluate the formal report in Figure 10.10. Write a memo to your instructor identifying what you believe is good about the report and what improvements, if any, you would recommend.

7 Making reports reader-friendly for international audiences [Related to the Culture feature on page 353]

The following well-written paragraphs come from the executive summary of a report titled *The State of the Paper Industry: Monitoring the Indicators of Environmental Performance*. Imagine that this report was being read by someone from another country who speaks English as a second or third language. What words, phrases, or sentences do you think would be challenging for that reader to understand? What revisions would you suggest?

> Despite predictions that the digital revolution would make paper as obsolete as the typewriter, paper remains central to our lives. Yet most of us, most of the time, give little thought to how much we depend on paper products. Think of the hundreds of times a day we touch paper—newspapers, cereal boxes, toilet paper, water bottle labels, parking tickets, streams of catalogs and junk mail, money, tissues, books, shopping bags, receipts, napkins, printer and copier paper at home and work, magazines, to-go food packaging. The list could fill a book.
>
> What's more, few people pay much heed to the ways in which our use of paper affects the environment. Yet the paper industry's activities—and our individual use and disposal of paper in our daily lives—have enormous impacts. These include loss and degradation of forests that moderate climate change, destruction of habitat for countless plant and animal species, pollution of air and water with toxic chemicals such as mercury and dioxin, and production of methane—a potent greenhouse gas—as paper decomposes in landfills, to name just a few.[26]

memo report

TO: Ryan Leffler, Project Manager

FROM: Anya James, New Product Development Team

DATE: March 16, 20XX

SUBJECT: Progress Report

For the past three weeks, we have been researching the interactive aquarium concept and have developed five concepts we plan to test. The Interactive Aquarium presents a unique problem to the design team. We began with a completely blank slate, since this project is based on an innovative idea and has very few comparable existing products. We had to consider a very delicate group of users (fish) when making decisions about the requirements of our design concepts. It was important for us to balance the goals of our company with the needs of the animals and the desires of the users.

Research

We began by researching fish behavior and learned interesting facts that will influence our design. We then had a productive brainstorm session in which we were able to generate design ideas. From there, we have identified five major design areas we would like to test.

Design Requirements

Based on our research and discussions with users, we developed a set of design requirements numbered and listed in Table 1. We rated these requirements by importance (5 is most important and 1 is least important).

Table 1: Design Requirements

REQUIREMENT #	REQUIREMENT	IMPORTANCE RATING
1	Child safe	5
2	Child friendly	3
3	Interesting	3
4	Animal safe	5
5	Animal friendly	5
6	Can be used in/around water	5
7	Environmentally sound	4
8	Durable	4
9	Easily cleaned	2
10	Easily accessible	3
11	Not too complicated to operate	1
12	Not too heavy	1
13	No complicated assembly	1

Plan

In the next two weeks, we plan to evaluate our five ideas according to these requirements.

Accompanies Exercise 5

 SQ2 **What types of short, routine reports are typical in business?** *(pages 354–359)*

8 Progress reports, meeting minutes, trip reports, and feasibility reports

Use a web search engine or business portal such as Biznar to find an example of one of the following types of reports:

- Progress report
- Meeting minutes
- Trip report
- Feasibility report

Evaluate the report in relation to the guidelines presented in this chapter. Write a memo to your instructor identifying what you believe is good about the report you found and what improvements you recommend.

 SQ3 **How should you structure longer, formal reports for print and online distribution?** *(pages 360–379)*

9 Organize the report into useful sections

The U.S. Government Accountability Office (GAO) prepares hundreds of reports each year, usually in response to requests from the Senate, Congress, or other government sources. You can find these reports on the GAO website if you browse by topic.

Select a report that interests you and download the full PDF file (not just the highlights). Review the report and answer the following questions in a memo to your instructor, or be prepared to discuss them in class:

a. What information is provided on the title page?

b. How is the executive summary (called "Highlights") structured? Where does it summarize the purpose of the report, the methodology, the findings, and recommendations?

c. After the table of contents, most GAO reports contain a list of abbreviations. Why do you think the reports provide a separate list rather than just define the terms the first time they appear in the report?

d. The first headline in most GAO reports is "Background." What kind of information is included in that section?

e. Most GAO reports contain many appendices. What kinds of information are in the appendices? Why do you think information about the report's scope and methodology is in an appendix rather than in the body of the report?

10 Design the report for your audience and purpose

Referring to the same GAO report you used in Exercise 9, answer the following questions in a memo to your instructor or be prepared to discuss them in class:

a. Many GAO reports are designed with the headlines in the left margin. Do you see benefits to that page design? Do you see disadvantages?

b. Most headlines are phrased as short, complete sentences that express a main point. Do those headlines help prepare you to read the details in the section?

11 Choose the best electronic format for online distribution

The Pew Research Center, which describes itself as a nonpartisan "fact tank," publishes up to 40 reports per month, providing unbiased information to policymakers, journalists, and academics. Pew distributes these reports in three electronic formats: standard web, mobile app, and PDF. Go to the Pew Research Center website, select a report to review, and compare the three versions of the report.

- Which do you find easiest to read?
- Which do you find easiest to navigate (that is, go to a specific section)?
- Which do you think will provide the easiest-to-read printout?

Based on your analysis, if you were to come back to the Pew website to read a different report, which format would you choose?

12 Using software features to help format formal reports [Related to the Technology feature on page 378]

Your instructor will provide you with a "sample report" file for this exercise. This file includes unformatted text for a formal report. The following elements are obvious based on their content: title page, location for the table of contents, executive summary, introduction, body of the report (including headings), conclusions, recommendations, references, and appendices. Use your word processor's features to make the following formatting changes:

- Apply appropriate heading styles to section titles and headings.
- Create section breaks so the title page is not numbered and the table of contents and executive summary are numbered with small Roman numerals (ii and iii). Starting with the introduction, page numbering should use Arabic numerals (1).
- Create a footer to add page numbers to the entire document, except the title page as previously noted.
- Generate an automated table of contents to appear after the title page.
- Add automated captions for figures and tables throughout the report.

Save the file, adding your name to the end of the filename. Submit the file electronically to your instructor.

13 Planning for a collaborative report writing project [Related to the Collaboration feature on page 385]

You and two other classmates, Carey and Shi Ping, have been given three weeks to research and produce a 20-page report on the state of social entrepreneurship in your city. You are a small but diverse group: you have experience reading financial reports and crunching numbers. Shi Ping is a journalism major who has written about social entrepreneurship in the past, while Carey enjoys data visualization and visual design. Compose a one-page plan for this collaborative report writing project that outlines your responsibilities, writing procedures, and communication methods.

 What guidelines should you follow for writing report decks? *(pages 380–385)*

14 Understand why and when to use report decks

Report decks are very different from traditional presentation files used to support oral presentations. Search for deck-style presentations at SlideShare or a similar website. You could also use the report deck included in the reference list at the end of this chapter (see note 15). Select a file that does not include an audio voice-over. Read the file. Who is the intended audience? Is the content organized logically? Is the content understandable without a presenter? Could the file double as a report *and* a presentation? Summarize your findings in a short email message to your instructor. Attach the report file to the email.

15 Design the deck effectively

Refer to the report deck you selected for Exercise 14. Evaluate the design of that deck. Is it on a plain and readable background? Does it include a table of contents or agenda? Does it use sentence-style headlines? Does it include a footer or header? How does the deck design help you read the deck effectively? Summarize your findings in a short email to your instructor. Attach the report file to the email.

16 Design the deck content to be easy to follow

You are creating a deck reporting on the state of corporate and business blogging. Refer to the following set of slide headlines for that report. On a piece of paper, write the headlines and then roughly sketch what you would put on each slide. It is not necessary to do any research for this exercise, but you may do research if you like.

a. An estimated 20,000 corporations now communicate to customers and stakeholders through blogging.

b. Not just Internet companies but traditional firms in manufacturing, retail, finance, and technology have business blogs.

c. Small-business blogs are most effective when they concentrate on the company's personality and expertise, not products.

d. Effective business blogging depends on a steady flow of new and updated information.

 How do you integrate tables and graphs into reports? *(pages 386–392)*

17 Choose the best form of display: table or graph

Create a table based on the following paragraph. Then create a graph. Explain the differences and justify which would better represent the data. Submit both visuals and your justification in a one-page memo report to your instructor.

Jamison Lumber Company has four regional branches: North, South, East, and West. Last year, the branch sales were as follows: North = $1.23 million, South = $1.57 million, East = $2.26 million, and West = $2.10 million. This year, the North and South branches recorded a 2.5 percent and 3.4 percent increase, respectively. However, the East and West branches experienced decreases of 1.3 percent and 0.7 percent, respectively.

18 Choose the best type of graph

For each of the following business messages, what type of graph will be most effective? Sketch a version of that graph and explain why your choice is the best option.

a. Gadget sales have tripled since 2005.

b. Of the four companies in the industry—Acme, Apex, Giant, and Excel—Acme has the smallest share of industry sales.

c. Sales of Product A exceed sales of Product B and Product C.

d. Earnings per share have decreased every year since 2010.

e. There is a strong relationship between the number of training courses a salesperson has completed and the amount of that person's annual sales.

19 Design graphs and tables to communicate

What changes would you make to the table below based on the table design guidelines presented in this chapter?

20 Integrate data displays within the text

As a member of the Acme Electric Safety Committee, you have been asked to write the committee report to the CEO answering the question, "Does our electrical equipment comply with safety standards?" You write the introduction to the report and decide to summarize the detailed findings in a table. However, you are unsure how to structure that table. Analyze the introduction in the memo to the right and the three options listed on the next page for structuring the table. Which data display integrates best with the text that introduces it? Explain why.

---

memo report

TO: George DiLeonardo, CEO
FROM: Acme Safety Review Committee
           (Devon Rasheed, Kevin Carroll, Risa Policaro, and Eric West)
DATE: February 12, 20XX
SUBJECT: Acme's Compliance with Safety Standards

Purpose of the Study

Over the past month, the Acme Safety Committee has conducted a thorough review of all the safety codes and standards that apply to Acme Electric's Belmont facility. These include two sets of mandatory standards that Acme must comply with and one set of voluntary standards.

Mandatory

- OSHA (Occupational Safety and Health Administration) standards
- NEC (National Electric Code) standards

Voluntary

- UL-1950 standards for information technology equipment, including electrical business equipment.

We have also reviewed all the wiring schematics and the equipment in the facility to identify all gaps in compliance.

Results of the Study

Although Acme's equipment is properly designed for electrical load/capacity, several design details do not comply with the codes and widely used standards. Some standards apply only to building wiring and other parts include equipment. These gaps compromise the safety of our employees and will put us at risk during regulatory inspections.

Table 1 summarizes the equipment and wiring that do not comply with applicable standards and offers recommendations for addressing the problems.

Accompanies Exercise 20

YTD International Revenue							
Product	Jan	Feb	Mar	Apr	May	Jun	Total
Disk Drives	$93,993.00	$84,773.00	$88,833.00	$95,838.00	$93,874.00	$83,994.00	$541,305.00
Monitors	$87,413.00	$78,838.00	$82,614.00	$89,129.00	$873,020.00	$78,114.00	$1,289,128.00
Printers	$90,035.00	$2,120,400.00	$85,093.00	$91,803.00	$899,210.00	$80,457.00	$3,366,998.00
Computers	$92,736.00	$83,640.00	$87,645.00	$94,557.00	$92,619.00	$82,871.00	$534,068.00
Memory Sticks	$3,624,500.00	$77,785.00	$81,510.00	$87,938.00	$86,136.00	$77,070.00	$4,034,939.00
Sound Cards	$88,832.00	$80,118.00	$83,956.00	$90,576.00	$88,720.00	$79,382.00	$511,584.00
Video Cards	$82,614.00	$74,510.00	$78,079.00	$84,236.00	$82,509.00	$73,825.00	$475,773.00
RAM	$85,092.00	$76,745.00	$80,421.00	$86,763.00	$84,985.00	$76,040.00	$490,046.00
Scanners	$87,645.00	$79,048.00	$82,834.00	$89,366.00	$87,534.00	$78,321.00	$504,748.00
Input Devices	$90,275.00	$81,419.00	$85,319.00	$920,470.00	$90,160.00	$80,671.00	$1,348,314.00
Total	$4,423,135.00	$2,837,276.00	$836,304.00	$1,730,676.00	$2,478,767.00	$790,745.00	$13,096,903.00

Accompanies Exercise 19

CHAPTER 10

Option 1

Regulator	Rule	Affected Area	Violation	Recommendation
OSHA	Rule A Rule B Rule C			
NEC	Rule 1 Rule 2 Rule 3			

Option 2

Equipment	Rule	Violation	Recommendation
Generator 1	OSHA Rule A NEC Rule 1 Local Rule A		
Junction Box 65	OSHA Rule B NEC Rule 2 Local Rule B		

Option 3

Priority	Affected Area	Violation	Rule	Recommendation
High	Generator 1 Junction Box 65 Conduit 64-65			
Medium	Main Bus B Riser Pipe 37 Conduit 33-34			

Accompanies Exercise 20

21 Represent data ethically [Related to the Ethics feature on page 392]

On April 20, 2010, a BP oil drilling platform in the Gulf of Mexico exploded, resulting in the world's largest accidental oil spill.[26] Nearly 5 million barrels of oil gushed from the wellhead into the Gulf before BP capped the well in July. During that time, BP worked diligently to contain the spill, capture oil, and develop a strategy to cap the wellhead. Approximately a month after the explosion, BP Senior Vice President Karl Wells gave a technical presentation to update the public on BP's containment efforts.[27] During this briefing, he presented a graph similar to Graph A and discussed the amount of oil collected from the wellhead in the seven days between May 16 and May 23.

Here is what he said:

> There's been a lot of questions around how much oil is being collected. What I am showing you here is a graph. We originally inserted the riser insertion tool into the riser on May 16. Since that period our operations and engineering group have been focused on how do we maximize the amount of oil we collect from the end of the riser. . . . Here you can see how we've continued to ramp up. [He points at increasingly long bars.] Today, we've collected a total of 13,500 barrels, which is averaging a little less than 2,000 barrels a day. The team is continuing to focus on what we can do to capture more of that oil.

At first glance, this graph certainly looks as if BP is ramping up its oil collection—that in fact it is collecting an increasing amount each day. However, this graph shows the cumulative amount of oil collected, with each day's oil collection added to the previous days'.

Graph B is a different, alternative graph, produced by data analyst Stephen Few, which graphs the oil collected each day:[28]

- Compare the two graphs and the two different representations of the data. Does the second graph support Wells's claim that oil collection has "continued to ramp up"?
- Which graph represents the data more ethically?

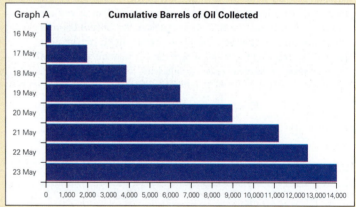

Accompanies Exercise 21

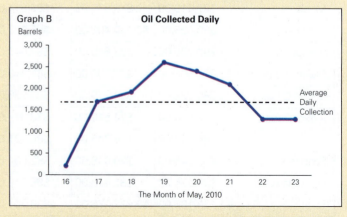

Accompanies Exercise 21

Graph B from "BP Oil Collection–Is the Effort Really Improving?" from Perceptual Edge website, May 26, 2010. Copyright © 2004–2014 by Perceptual Edge. Reprinted with permission.

SQ6 **How should you document your research?**
(pages 393–395)

22 Determine what needs to be documented

For each of the following situations, imagine that you are writing a report and need to decide whether you must provide documentation to give credit to a source. If you would document the source, how would you document it? Would you refer to the source in the text itself, use a parenthetical citation (or footnotes), use quotation marks, or include an entry in a reference list? Indicate as many options as apply. If you would not document the source, explain why not.

a. In your report, you are arguing against an opinion column in the local newspaper.

b. You are providing evidence from your own experience.

c. You are including a story that one of your coworkers told you.

d. In your research, you find a phrase that you really like and decide to use it.

e. You want to quote something from a source but the quotation is too long, so you change it a bit and leave out a few words.

f. You are writing a report analyzing the environmental issues relating to the U.S. newspaper industry, and in your research you come across some facts about how many trees are cut down each year for paper manufacture. You want to use these facts.

g. You mention that the majority of students on your campus did not vote in the last presidential election.

h. You want to prove that your company has been complying with a certain regulation, and your reader will need to know what the regulation says.

i. You are presenting the results of a survey you conducted.

j. You are summarizing information that you learned from an interview with an expert.

23 Using quotations, summaries, and paraphrases

Select an article that you are using in an ongoing project. If you are not currently working on a project, select a peer-reviewed journal article of interest to you. Select a passage from the article that contains a point that is vital to its argument. Write a paragraph explaining the point, including a paraphrase of the passage. Then rewrite the paragraph using a direct quotation instead of a paraphrase. Send your two versions and the original to your instructor with a cover message that states which of your two versions is more effective at explaining the article's point.

24 Prepare the documentation

For each of the following questions, find an appropriate source that you could use in a research report and prepare a reference list entry for that source. Use APA style, unless your instructor asks you to use a different style. (For a review of how to find good, credible sources, see Chapter 8: Finding and Evaluating Business Information.)

a. What is the current unemployment rate in the United States? How has the unemployment rate changed over the past 10 years?

b. What is the employment outlook for the career or profession you plan to enter?

c. What are some interesting facts about the history of your college or university?

d. What are some key facts about migrant farm workers in the United States?

e. How should a person calculate the amount of life insurance he or she needs?

Writing Exercises

25 Developing a mobile phone app

On-the-Go Software, a start-up company in your community, would like to develop a new mobile phone app that will be profitable. As part of the company's preliminary planning, the CEO, Etta Hawkins, has hired you to research the most popular apps for iPhones and other mobile devices and to analyze why you believe these apps are successful. As you research, identify who is buying these apps and hypothesize why. Also identify features that have received positive comments and hypothesize why these features are important.

Write a three- to five-page letter report to present the results of your research. In addition, include a list of references as an attachment. You may include other attachments if you believe they will be helpful.

Address your report to Etta Hawkins, On-the-Go Software, 1111 Main Street, MyTown, MyState, MyZip.

26 Recommending survey software

Your company (or your class) is planning to conduct survey research and needs to select an online survey tool to use. Your manager (or instructor) would like a program that meets these criteria:

- Allows an unlimited number of survey questions
- Allows an unlimited number of surveys
- Can be integrated into the company (or class) website
- Produces surveys that look professional rather than unformatted or poorly designed
- Is easy to use when writing questions

- Is easy to use when answering questions
- Gathers all the survey results into an easy-to-use database or spreadsheet
- Automatically produces graphs that can be used in research reports
- Is the most cost-effective option

Your job is to identify three programs that might be suitable, evaluate them, and write a recommendation report to justify a specific program. Write the report in memo form, and keep the body of the report to a maximum of three pages, though you may add attachments.

27 Evaluating and assessing the feasibility of sustainability initiatives

Your school is considering a number of sustainability initiatives that will make it a more "green" organization. Here are some of the initiatives the administration is considering:

- Installing compact fluorescent light bulbs in residences, classrooms, and offices
- Installing low-flush toilets throughout the building(s)
- Installing low-flow faucets and shower heads
- Purifying waste vegetable oil from the food service to fuel campus shuttles
- Installing a wind turbine on campus to generate electricity
- Implementing "trayless dining" in the dining halls (to reduce the amount of wasted food)

You receive one of the following assignments:

a. Research sustainability initiatives at five other campuses and write a report evaluating which initiatives have been most successful. You will need to identify—and justify—specific criteria for success. (As a starting place for your research, visit the website of the Association for the Advancement of Sustainability in Higher Education. You may also search the websites of various colleges and universities.)

b. Select one of the sustainability initiatives listed previously and assess the feasibility of implementing that initiative at your school. Consider the costs, the environmental benefits, and any financial benefits. Are there any obstacles that would make the chosen initiative particularly difficult? You do not need to recommend the option. You only need to report whether your research shows it would be feasible to implement the initiative at your school.

Depending on your instructor's requirements, you may prepare your report as either a formal report or as a report deck.

28 Evaluating SOS: An employee suggestion program

For the past two years, you have worked in the Human Resources Department of MetCo Manufacturing, a company that employs approximately 2,800 employees in the design and manufacture of small household products. MetCo's CEO believes that satisfied employees are crucial to the company's success and that the best solutions to problems often come from employees. You were hired to design and implement a program that encourages employees to make suggestions and register complaints, called SOS (Suggestions for Organizational Satisfaction).

SOS has been operating now for one year, and your CEO wants you to evaluate it. Specifically, she wants to know how extensively the program is being used, whether it is being used more for suggestions or complaints, what types of employees are using it and what types are not, and whether employees are satisfied with the program.

As a first step, you review data about the number of complaints and suggestions received each month for the past year. These data are presented in Table 1. Then you conduct a survey of all 2,800 employees. The results are in Tables 2 through 6.

Write a report in memo format analyzing the data and presenting results and conclusions. Be sure to:

- Write a clear introduction and specific subject line.

- Make your answers to the CEO's questions clear by providing informative headings, interpreting the data, and drawing conclusions supported by the data.

- Decide which tables you want to use in their current form, which you want to revise or turn into graphs, and which, if any, you want to eliminate.

TABLE 1 Monthly submissions to SOS

	Jan	Feb	Mar	Apr	May	June	July	Aug	Sept	Oct	Nov	Dec
Suggestions	57	61	157	102	107	94	98	82	90	72	66	62
Complaints	332	428	496	502	553	503	466	417	381	365	332	319

Note: In March, Human Resources sponsored a "Make a Suggestion" program, with a $100 cash prize for the best suggestion.

TABLE 2 Have you ever used the SOS program?

No	369
Once	601
More than Once	1,003

TABLE 3 Classifications of the 369 people who have not used the program

Classification	Total Number of Respondents in that Group	Number Not Using the Program
Age		
Under 25	458	127
25–40	731	51
41–55	542	87
Over 55	242	104
Gender		
Male	1,227	125
Female	746	244
Rank		
Nonmanagement	1,517	227
Management	456	142

TABLE 4 How satisfied were you with the response you received?

	Completely Satisfied	Partially Satisfied	Dissatisfied
Used SOS once	183	349	70
Used SOS more than once	692	272	39

TABLE 5 How confident are you that your question or complaint reached the right person?

	Confident	Not Confident
Used SOS once	196	405
Used SOS more than once	822	181

TABLE 6 Do you intend to use the SOS program again in the future?

Yes	1,331
No	82
Undecided	191

Collaboration Exercises

29 Reporting on consumer attitudes

Consumer Research, Inc., has hired your team to conduct a survey to learn how young adults respond to direct mail advertising sent by email. Research by the Direct Marketing Association indicates that, overall, advertising through postal mail results in more sales than advertising through email.[29] However, the research did not focus on specific age groups. Consumer Research, Inc., wants to know whether young adults (ages 18–25) purchase more as a result of email or postal mail advertising. Identify a group of people your team can survey and develop a set of questions to ask. For example, you could ask:

- How often do they open advertising they receive through email?
- What influences their decision to open the email? Is it the subject line, the sender, or something else?
- How often do they click through to a website?
- How often do they purchase something as a result of the email advertising?

Conduct your survey and then write a short report to Consumer Research, presenting your results. If possible, draw conclusions about the effectiveness of email marketing to young adults.

30 Evaluating fast-food restaurants

Your team works for a fast-food restaurant company that is planning to open a restaurant in your area. The district regional manager wants to know more about the competition. What are the strengths and weaknesses of the competitive restaurants? Is there opportunity for a new restaurant in the neighborhood?

As a team, choose three fast-food restaurants in the area and observe each restaurant for an hour at least three times within the next two weeks. Vary the day of the week and the time of day for each visit. During each visit, observe and collect data on the appearance of the restaurant, how many customers entered during that time period, the length of wait to place an order, the length of wait to receive an order, the quality of service, and the quality of food. During each visit, make a qualitative judgment about how happy the customers seem to be, and support your judgment with specific observations.

At the end of the two-week observation period, write a report to your district manager evaluating the competition and making recommendations about how your new restaurant can provide better service than the competitive restaurants you have studied.

31 Writing minutes for a team meeting [Related to the Collaboration feature on page 385]

If you have been working as a team on any project this term, submit to your instructor the minutes of any team meeting. Write the minutes so that they are a useful reference for team members and are informative for your instructor.

Social Media Exercises

32 Evaluating infographics on the web

Infographics are single-page reports that rely primarily on graphics to enhance the understanding and interpretation of data. Social media has fueled the growth of infographics on the web. Search the social media site Pinterest or another source of your choice to find an infographic that interests you. Evaluate that infographic as a brief report. Is it informative? Is it clear and easy to follow? Do you know the sources of the data? In your opinion, does the graphical representation of the data provide advantages over a purely written report? Be prepared to present your analysis in class or write a one-page evaluation report to your instructor.

33 Evaluating social media reports

With the growth of social media, the number of reports *about* social media has also grown. Using the search engine of your choice, conduct a search using the terms *report* and either *social media* or *LinkedIn, Facebook,* or *Twitter.* Select one report to evaluate. (Be sure to select an actual report, not a news story or article about a report.) Read the document and write a one-page evaluation report to your instructor, answering these questions:

- Who are the author and publisher of the report?
- What is the purpose of the report, and who is its intended audience?
- How was the information in the report researched or gathered?
- What are the report's key findings and recommendations, if any?
- What is your assessment of the report? Is it credible? Do you believe it offers valuable information or not? Would you recommend it?

Pick an appropriate format for your report: email, memo, letter, or report deck. Do not construct the report as a series of bullet points answering the listed questions. Instead, follow the advice in this chapter: Write an effective introduction that previews your main ideas, develop headings that help organize your material, and document your sources. Include a copy of the report you are evaluating as an attachment or appendix.

Speaking Exercises

34 Making informal/impromptu presentations

a. Randomly select one of the Critical Thinking Questions on page 401 and give a one-minute oral response. Provide a direct answer and give compelling support for your answer.

b. Give a brief report about your progress in your business communication course. What do you believe are your current communication strengths? What are your weaknesses, and how do you plan to address them?

c. Imagine you were assigned to write a feasibility report about a plan you are making for your life. (The research question would be: "Will it be feasible for me to . . ."?) What would you write about, and why?

d. Imagine you were asked to evaluate two fast-food restaurants in your area. What criteria would you use for evaluating them, and why?

e. How do you spend your time on a typical day or typical week? Quickly sketch a pie chart that divides your time into three or four major categories, with appropriate percentages for each. Present this pie chart and explain whether you are satisfied with this division of time or if you would like to make some changes.

35 Executive briefings

a. If you are working on a multiweek project in your class, prepare a written progress report for your instructor. Then plan a five-minute executive briefing to present this progress report to your instructor.

b. Prepare a five-minute executive briefing based on the feasibility report in Figure 10.9 on pages 358–359.

c. Search the Internet to find a report that you believe is well designed and easy to read. (Look for a report that you can download as a PDF or Word document, so that you can focus on the design.) Prepare a five-minute briefing on key features of the report design that you believe are effective. Conclude your briefing with a recommendation. Would you recommend that your class or your company adopt this report design for their work? Why or why not? Be sure to prepare at least one visual aid for your briefing.

d. Search the Internet, newspapers, or magazines to find one data display (table or graph) that you believe is effective. Create a visual aid of that data display and present it to the class. Explain the context in which you found it, the main point or purpose of the data display, and why you believe it communicates effectively.

e. Search the Internet, newspapers, or magazines to find one data display (table or graph) that you believe is *not* effective. Create a visual aid of that data display and present it to the class. Explain the context in which you found it, the main point or purpose of the data display, and why you believe it does not communicate effectively.

Grammar Exercises

36 Apostrophes (see Appendix C: Grammar, Punctuation, Mechanics, and Conventions—Section 2.6)

Type the following paragraph, correcting the 10 errors or omissions in the use of apostrophes. Underline all your corrections.

> Practicing for a telephone interview will give you confidence that you wont blow the real thing. Ask one of your parents' or a friend to conduct a mock interview with you. Have him or her phone you and ask an interviewers questions. Its also helpful to get a spouses' or father's-in-laws critique of your answers. Ask one of them to listen in, or, whats even more useful, tape record the mock interview for later analysis. Pay attention not only to the content of your answers, but also to the vocal quality; is your's clear, without too many "uhm's" "you knows," and "likes"? The practice sessions payoff is your improved interviewing skills.

37 Parentheses, dashes, brackets, and ellipses (see Appendix C: Grammar, Punctuation, Mechanics, and Conventions—Section 2.7)

Type the following paragraph, inserting parentheses, dashes, brackets, and ellipses where required. There are 10 omissions. Consider pairs of parentheses or brackets as a single omission. Underline all your corrections. In cases where there is more than one possibility, be ready to explain your choice.

> The time to research a potential employer is before not after the job interview. Interviewers expect job applicants to know something about a company's products goods or services its markets local, national, international and its operating locations. Job applicants can begin their research on an Internet search engine Google or Bing. Career advisor Martin Reis writes on his blog, "A company's URL Uniform Resource Locator is the gateway to a wealth of information new products, financial statements, press releases, the corporate mission statement . . . " There is something else a company's website may reveal its corporate culture. Web page photos can provide clues about dress standards casual or traditional, employee diversity ethnicity, gender, age, and community involvement.

MyLab Business Communication

Go to **www.pearson.com/mylab/business-communication** for Auto-graded writing questions as well as the following Assisted-graded writing questions:

1. What are the advantages of writing a report using a direct organization rather than an indirect organization? Are there any situations where an indirect report organization may be more effective?

2. Imagine that some of your coworkers complain that trip reports are just busy work and a way for management to make sure employees are conducting business and not just having a good time. How might you counter that argument? What are some of the real business purposes of a trip report?

References

1. Wolfe, J. (2010). *Team writing: A guide to writing in groups.* New York: Bedford/St. Martins.

2. Shin, J. K., & Crandall, J. A. (2014). Teaching English to young learners around the world: An Introduction. In *Teaching young learners English: From theory to practice* (pp. 1–22). Boston, MA: National Geographic Learning. Retrieved from http://ngl.cengage.com/assets/downloads/tyle_9781111771379/chapter_1_from_9781111771379_p02_lores.pdf

3. Gajšt, N. (2014). Business English as a lingua franca—A cross-cultural perspective of teaching English for business purposes. *ELOPE: English Language Overseas Perspectives and Enquiries, 11*(2), 77–87.

4. Crystal, D. (2013). Into the twenty-first century. In Lynda Mugglestone (Ed.), *The Oxford history of English* (Updated ed., pp. 488–513). New York, NY: Oxford University Press.

5. Kohn, J. R. (2008). *The global English style guide: Writing clear, translatable documentation for a global market.* Cary, NC: SAS Institute.

6. Michel, J. B., Shen, Y. K., Aiden, A. P., Veres, A., Gray, M. K., Pickett, J. P., . . . Aiden, E. L. (2011). Quantitative analysis of culture using millions of digitized books. *Science, 331*(6014), 176–182.

7. The Global Language Monitor. (2017). The number of words in the English language. Retrieved from http://www.languagemonitor.com/global-english/no-of-words/

8. Accenture. (2014, February 24). Mobility: Fueling the digital surge. *Accenture mobility insights report: 2014.* Retrieved from https://www.accenture.com/t20150527T211105__w__/fr-fr/_acnmedia/Accenture/Conversion-Assets/DotCom/Documents/Local/fr-fr/PDF_5/Accenture-Mobility-Research-Report-2014.pdf

9. Fridsma, L., & Gyncild, B. (2015, July 15). Adding multimedia files > Enhancing PDF documents. *Adobe Press.* Retrieved from http://www.adobepress.com/articles/article.asp?p=2415896&seqNum=9

10. Leibowitz, J. (2013, December 6). Four tips to put the "power" back in PowerPoint. Retrieved from https://www.linkedin.com/pulse/20131206050201-12921524-four-tips-to-put-the-power-back-in-powerpoint

11. For example, see McKinsey & Co. (2010, January). Electrical vehicles in cities: Shanghai charges up. Retrieved from http://online.wsj.com/public/resources/documents/mckinsey_electric_vehicle_0113.pdf

12. Paley, E. (2013, October). Advice to startups: Stack the deck. *Inc.* Retrieved from http://www.inc.com/magazine/201310/eric-paley/writing-advice-for-start-ups-and-entrepreneurs.html-

13. Typefaces for dyslexia. (n.d.). Retrieved from https://www.dyslexic.com/fonts/

14. Paradi, D. (2015, February 3). Testing how a slide looks to someone with color deficiency. Retrieved from http://www.thinkoutsidetheslide.com/issue-330-february-3-2015/

15. For a helpful assessment of tools for allocating responsibilities and a list of potential roles a team might require, see Hewett, B. L., & Robidoux, C. (2010). Optimizing team performance: Collaborative virtual writing. In *Virtual collaborative writing in the workplace: Computer-mediated communication technologies and processes* (pp. 174–189). Hershey, PA: IGI Global.

16. Schindler, K., & Wolfe, J. (2014). Beyond single authors: Organizational text production as collaborative writing. In E. Jakobs & D. Perrin (Eds). *Handbook of writing and text production* (pp. 159–173). Berlin: De Gruyter Mouton.

17. Hewett, B. L., & Robidoux, C. (2010). Engaging in virtual collaborative writing: Issues, obstacles and strategies. In *Virtual collaborative writing in the workplace: Computer-mediated communication technologies and processes* (pp. 65–87). Hershey, PA: IGI Global.

18. Birnholtz, J., & Ibara, S. (2012). Tracking changes in collaborative writing: Edits, visibility and group maintenance. *Proceedings of the ACM 2012 Conference on Computer Supported Cooperative Work, 809–818.*

19. Wong, D. (2013). The Wall Street Journal *guide to information graphics: The dos and don'ts of presenting data, facts, and figures.* New York: W. W. Norton.

20. Tufte, E. (2001). *The visual display of quantitative information* (2nd ed.). Cheshire, CT: Graphics Press.

21. Robbins, N. B. (2013, May–June). Avoiding common mistakes with graphs and tables: Information professionals should focus on communicating clearly and effectively rather than trying to use data to gain attention. *Information Outlook, 17*(3), 8+.

22. See, for example, National Forum on Education Statistics. (2010). *Forum guide to data ethics* (NFES 2010–801). U.S. Department of Education. Washington, DC: National Center for Education Statistics.

23. INSEE. (2017). National Institute of Statistics and Economic Studies. Retrieved from https://www.insee.fr/en/accueil

24. Lesser, J. (2004, January). You've got mail—Lots of mail. *Public Relations Tactics,* p. 4.

25. Smith, B. A., & Couch, K. A. (2014). The Social Security statement: Background, implementation, and recent developments. *Social Security Bulletin, 74*(2), 1–25.

26. Environmental Paper Network. (2007). The state of the paper industry: Monitoring the indicators of environmental performance. Retrieved from http://environmentalpaper.org/wp-content/uploads/2012/02/state-of-the-paper-industry-2007-full.pdf

27. Robertson, C., & Krauss, C. (2010, August 2). Gulf spill is the largest of its kind, scientists say. *The New York Times.* Retrieved from http://www.nytimes.com/2010/08/03/us/03spill.html

28. Wells, K. (2010, May 24). Technical briefing. [Video.] Retrieved from http://bp.concerts.com/gom/kentwells_update24052010.htm

29. Few, S. (2010, May 26). BP oil collection: Is the effort really improving? *Visual Business Intelligence.* [Blog entry.] Retrieved from http://www.perceptualedge.com/blog/?p=790

30. Haskel, D. (2017, January 20). Direct mail response rates are at their highest point in over a decade. Retrieved from https://www.iwco.com/blog/2017/01/20/direct-mail-response-rates-and-2016-dma-report/

11

Preparing and Delivering Business Presentations

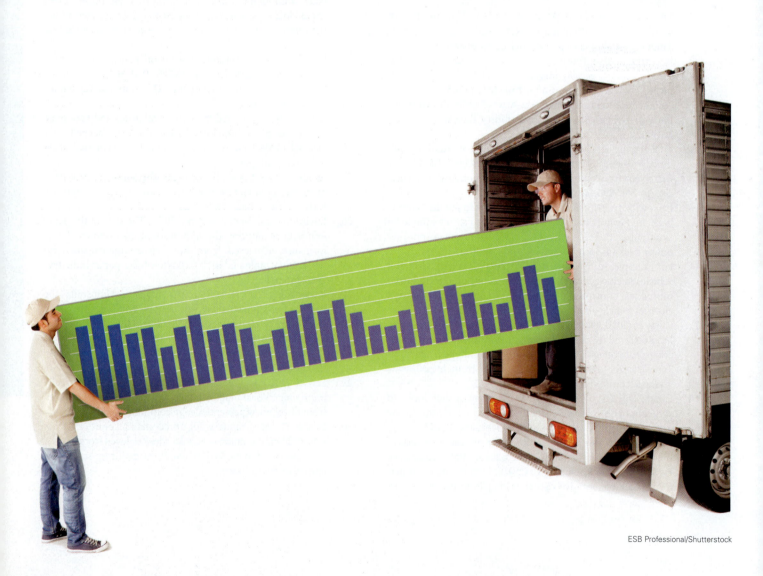

STUDY QUESTIONS

New Hires @ Work

Chris Harlow
Northwestern University

Consultant @ Capgemini Consulting

Creating a good presentation doesn't start with PowerPoint, it starts with a piece of paper and storyboarding. Make your presentation interesting without slides first by using a captivating storyline and narrative. I try to use slides with a minimalist design, bold statements, and one big idea per slide. It's often good to convey ideas through images instead of words. For example, one could depict an uphill battle with a photo of a person with climbing gear instead of a more cliché photo of a mountain. Likewise, instead of fireworks or dollar signs or smiley faces to convey "success," use a runner crossing a finish line or an iconic photo like NASA Mission Control cheering after the moon landing.

Courtesy of Chris Harlow

Chapter 11 | Introduction

You may think of a business presentation as a speech or as a set of slides that you deliver. But employers think of presentations differently. Employers value presentation skills because an employee's ability to present reflects a more fundamental ability to "frame ideas and share them."[1] In fact, presenting information and telling the company's story effectively is so critical that some companies, such as Cisco Systems, see presentation ability as a key indicator of leadership potential. Whenever a Cisco executive delivers a presentation internally or externally, members of the audience are asked to rate the presenter on both delivery and content on a five-point scale. Ron Ricci, Cisco's vice president of Customer Experience Services, explains that this rating method motivates executives to provide clear, concise, and relevant information in presentations. It also reinforces Cisco's commitment to be a customer-centric organization: "We care so much about how well we serve our customers that we're holding executives accountable for how well they perform in front of customers."[2]

You can prepare yourself for delivering presentations that will set you apart by practicing the systematic approach that you will learn in this chapter. The approach includes:

- Analyzing your purpose, audience, setting, and medium options
- Planning and organizing your key points
- Composing visual support materials, including slides and handouts
- Evaluating your presentation by practicing
- Delivering the presentation effectively
- Evaluating the audience's response

 What do you analyze when planning a business presentation?

Analyze

New Hires @ Work

Ray Holloman
Belmont University

Business Continuity Administrator @ HCA Healthcare

In school, a presentation may earn you extra credit, but in your career, a presentation is often a make-or-break situation.

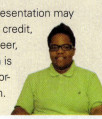

Assume that you work for the human resources department of Rowland-Grey, a large company that owns six department store brands throughout the United States. Your job is to study the work environment in individual stores and to recommend changes that will improve worker satisfaction and productivity. One day, your supervisor asks you to analyze the personnel problems in the company's computer call centers, which handle both online orders and customer feedback. The manager of the Midwest call center has been complaining that his unit is experiencing high rates of sales staff turnover and absenteeism as well as decreases in productivity. Your supervisor gave you exit interviews from 10 online sales clerks, all of whom quit due to headaches and eyestrain. Based on the exit interviews and additional research, you learn the following information:

- The annual turnover rate for employees who work in the call center is 55 percent, whereas the turnover rate for employees on the sales floor is 40 percent.
- The excess turnover in the call centers costs the company $660,000 a year in new employee training.
- Exit interviews show that people working in the call center routinely complain about headaches.
- The type of computer monitors combined with the lighting in the call centers lead to glare, which may be contributing to the headaches.

In a meeting with your supervisor, you report your findings and suggest that Rowland-Grey conduct a pilot program to determine if purchasing new computer monitors will reduce turnover and increase productivity. Your supervisor likes the idea and asks you to make a presentation to Carolyn Reese, senior vice president of planning

Photo courtesy of Ray Holloman

and development, to get funding for this pilot program. The business question you will address is this: What is the cause of high turnover and low productivity, and what can be done about it?

As you read the chapter, you will follow the ACE process to develop this presentation. Preparing the presentation begins long before the day you deliver it. In fact, it begins long before the day you start to write it. Using the ACE process, you can plan your presentation by analyzing the following areas:

- Purpose and desired outcome: Why are you presenting?
- Audience: Who will be listening, and what do they care about?
- Message: What will you say to achieve your desired outcome?
- Setting: Where will you present?
- Medium options: How will you deliver your message?

Analyze your purpose and desired outcome: Why are you presenting?

As leadership expert Stephen Covey suggests, "Begin with the end in mind."[3] Every good business presentation has both a purpose and a specific intended outcome. Ask yourself, "Why am I delivering this presentation, and what do I want to have happen as a result?" Visualize that outcome and then ensure that everything in the presentation contributes to achieving it.

Figure 11.1 illustrates how to determine your general purpose and specific outcome, along with examples of possible outcomes for the Rowland-Grey presentation. Although you may start with a general purpose like those in the left column, always move to a more specific outcome, like those in the right column. The more specific your outcome statement, the easier it is to create an effective presentation.

The Rowland-Grey presentation clearly needs to be persuasive. The objective is to convince Carolyn Reese, the senior VP, to approve the plan and fund a pilot program to purchase 100 new computer monitors that will reduce glare. With this specific outcome in mind, you can now analyze the audience: What will Ms. Reese need to know and believe to be convinced?

FIGURE 11.1 How to Determine Your General Purpose and Specific Outcome

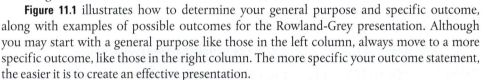

If I primarily want my audience to . . .	Then the general purpose of my presentation will be to . . .	For example, in the Rowland-Grey case, I might want this specific outcome:
Know something	Inform	The audience will know why the call center turnover is so high.
Believe something or do something	Persuade	The audience will approve a plan to fund a pilot program to purchase 100 new computer monitors that will reduce glare.
Know how to do something	Instruct	The audience will know how to install new monitors.
Work with me to reach an answer	Collaborate	The audience will discuss the pros and cons of purchasing new monitors and decide based on that discussion.

Analyze your audience: Who will be listening, and what do they care about?

Analyzing your audience helps you develop content. If you know the people in your audience, especially the decision makers, you can anticipate their needs, interests, attitudes, and possible biases. If you do not know your audience, imagine how they might respond.

Figure 11.2 lists questions that will help you understand your audience. Consider how you will answer the questions if you have a diverse audience, including people from different functional areas, with different interests, and with different knowledge about the topic. By answering these questions about each audience group, you'll be able to tailor the presentation to your audience, making it easier to achieve your goal.

In the Rowland-Grey scenario, the key decision maker is Carolyn Reese, who originally developed the call center eight years ago. She wants it to succeed. Ms. Reese is very interested in costs and cost savings and will not be motivated by arguments based solely on employee happiness or unhappiness. She is skeptical about big promises, and she values proposals that are supported by logic and research.

FIGURE 11.2 How to Analyze Your Audience

1. **Who are the key players?**

   Who are the key decision makers and important stakeholders whose response will affect your success?

2. **What do the key players care about?**

   What are their key questions and concerns? Attitudes and values? Personal agendas and hot buttons?

3. **How will the key players benefit?**

   How will the outcome or ideas you are presenting connect to what they care about? For example, will your ideas save money or time, resolve a pressing issue, or achieve a strategic objective?

4. **What does the audience already know about the situation or topic?**

   How much context do they need?

5. **How do they feel about you and your topic?**

   How much credibility do you have? What is their attitude toward your topic?

6. **What does the audience need or expect from you in this presentation?**

   Do their expectations match your intentions, or will you need to reset their expectations?

7. **How far do you need to move your audience before they act? Where do they fall on this continuum:**

Unaware of the issue? → Aware of the issue? → Understand the issue? → Believe it is worth addressing? → Care about addressing it? → Ready to act?

ACE
Analyze

Analyze your message: What will you say to achieve your desired outcome?

Imagine the audience of your presentation asking you, "What is the one thing you want me to remember from this presentation?" That one thing is your main message. The best messages answer a question for the audience. Sometimes an audience comes to a presentation with a question in mind. At other times, you need to raise the question for them in the first few minutes of your presentation.

For most business presentations, the main message should do all four of these things:

1. Take the audience's point of view (often using the words *you, we,* and *us*) and include other key players, such as the board of directors, employees, investors, customers, or partners, if they are involved.

2. Address a problem, concern, or need that your audience cares about—for example, growing the business, saving money, increasing return on investment, or enhancing employee satisfaction.

3. Present your solution and highlight what the audience will gain from that solution.
4. Explicitly or implicitly lead your audience to the outcome you intend.

In the Rowland-Grey scenario, the main message might be this: *Investing in new computer monitors may help solve our employee turnover problem and reduce the associated costs.*

Analyze your setting: Where and for how long will you present?

The setting of your presentation will affect the material you prepare and your presentation style. For some presentations, you may be standing in front of a screen with an audience arranged in rows or tables throughout the room. For other presentations, you may be sitting at a conference table with a few key decision makers. And in other situations, you may be delivering the presentation to a remote audience by video conference, web conference, or teleconference.

Before you prepare slides or select other visual aids to use, analyze your setting by answering these questions:

- **Will you be standing to present slides, or will you be sitting with others around a table or a computer, looking at small screens or printouts?** If the room is very big, you may need a microphone. Will you use a podium microphone, which will limit your movement? Or will you have a wireless microphone so you can move around the room more freely? If your audience will be looking at your slides from a distance, your fonts and images will need to be larger than if you are in a small room or are presenting around a table.
- **Will you be using your own computer to present slides and other visuals, or will you need to use equipment that is already in the room?** If you are using other equipment, be sure that it projects your material correctly and that all fonts, images, video, and audio work as planned.
- **Will your audience be looking at your presentation on a computer screen at a remote location and listening via computer or telephone?** If so, plan to design slides that are easy to follow and that do not require you to use your hands or a laser pointer to direct your audience's attention to key points. If you design your slides effectively, you will be able to direct the audience by *pointing with your voice*—for example, "the picture on the left illustrates" or "the numbers in red represent."

As you consider the setting, also consider the length of your presentation. In some instances, the length will be predetermined by the person convening the meeting. You will be given a certain amount of time on the agenda. In other instances, you will be asked to tell the meeting planner how long your presentation will be. As you plan, remember that shorter is better. Research indicates that the maximum length for a presentation should be 20 minutes.[4] The organizers of TED talks do not allow a presentation longer than 18 minutes.[5] Even 18 to 20 minutes is too long unless you reengage the audience at the 10-minute point. Biologist John Medina, who studies brain development and information processing, argues that even if an audience is interested in your presentation, boredom begins to set in at 10 minutes, so you need to work to recapture their interest before you reach that point.[6]

Analyze your medium options: How will you deliver your message?

As you plan your presentation, consider what tools you want to use and what materials you can provide to help your audience understand your message. Do not restrict yourself to using only slides. You can take advantage of a range of options and combine them in effective ways. For example, many people choose to project slides and also provide the audience with a hardcopy handout. You can embed video or audio files within your slides, or use a document camera to project a paper document while making notes about it on a flipchart. The best options depend on your purpose, audience, content, and setting. The criteria in **Figure 11.3** on page 418 can help you make good choices about your medium and presentation tools.

Figure 11.4 on page 418 summarizes the analysis for the Rowland-Grey presentation. This analysis can serve as a guide to focus the presentation in the composing stage.

FIGURE 11.3 How to Select a Medium

WHAT MEDIUM OPTIONS BEST FIT YOUR CRITERIA?	FLIPCHARTS, WHITEBOARDS	SLIDES	VIDEO, AUDIO, PODCASTS	DOCUMENT CAMERAS	PROPS	HANDOUTS
Purpose- and content-related criteria						
Encourage the audience to collaborate, interact, and create content	■				■	■
Encourage the audience to listen and look carefully		■	■	■		■
Communicate complex material that people need to look at carefully		■				■
Share content that is not in electronic form				■	■	■
Present lengthy content that could not easily be seen in slide form						■
Provide a demonstration				■	■	■
Have an electronic record of the material		■	■			■
Audience- and setting-related criteria						
Present to a large audience in a large room		■		■		■
Present to a small audience in a small room	■	■			■	■
Present to one or two people in an office or conference room	■	■			■	■
Present to a distant audience accessible by computer technology		■	■			■
Have the presentation available to people at a later time		■	■			■

FIGURE 11.4 Analysis for the Rowland-Grey Presentation

Purpose and Outcome: Why are you presenting?	*General purpose:* To persuade
	Specific outcome: The audience will approve the plan and fund a pilot program to purchase 100 new computer monitors that will reduce glare.
Audience: Who will be listening and what do they care about?	**Key player:** Carolyn Reese, Senior Vice President **What she cares about:** Costs and cost savings. **How she will benefit:** Reduced turnover costs. **Her attitude toward the topic:** Positive. Having established the call center eight years ago, she cares about it and wants it to succeed. **Her expectations:** A conservative proposal that is supported by logic and research. **How far she needs to be moved in the audience continuum:** She is almost ready to act; she cares about addressing the issue.
Message: What will you say to achieve the desired effect?	"Investing in new computer monitors may help solve our employee turnover problem and reduce the associated costs."
Setting: Where will you present?	A small conference room with a projector. We will be sitting down together at the table.
Medium: How will you deliver your message?	A slide presentation will help you walk Ms. Reese through the problem and solution. The paper copy of the slides will serve as a handout.

Compose

(SQ2) How do you compose the presentation?

What does it mean to *compose* a presentation? For some people, the first thing that comes to mind may be writing a speech. Other people may imagine writing a slide deck or putting together a set of visual aids. Still others may envision speaking extemporaneously, composing on the spot.

Whether you envision your presentation as a speech or as a conversation with the audience supported by slides, props, and flipcharts, you will need to develop content that engages the audience and meets their needs. If you are developing a slide presentation, you will need to design a slide deck that supports the presentation without boring, distracting, or confusing the audience. This section explains a seven-step process illustrated in **Figure 11.5** for developing effective slide presentations.

FIGURE 11.5 Process for Developing Slide Presentations

| Organize the content | Identify the role that slides will play | Create a storyboard | Develop a template | Design individual slides | Evaluate in a practice session | Create effective handouts |

Organize the content

Think of your presentation as a three-act play with an opening, a middle, and an end.

Compose an opening that engages the audience

Extensive research has shown that the common saying "You never get a second chance to make a first impression" is largely correct.[7] The *primacy effect*, or the fact that your audience is more likely to remember the first things they hear, makes it all the more important to plan carefully how you begin your presentation. The opening of a presentation has four main goals:

- Establish rapport with your audience
- Capture the audience's attention
- Motivate your audience to care about your presentation and your goal
- Provide a map or framework for the rest of the presentation

Establish rapport. At the beginning of a presentation, your audience wants to connect with you. They want to know who you are and feel confident that you have designed the presentation with their needs in mind. To make that connection, introduce yourself and identify common ground that you share with your audience. Have you had similar experiences, are you worried about the same problem, do you share the same goals? Start with something familiar that your audience already knows. This technique communicates to the audience that you can see things from their point of view. The goal is to capture their attention and build their interest before you introduce new ideas.

Capture attention. Research shows that information relevant to the audience's goals and intentions is especially attention-getting,[8] so get your audience involved right from the start of the presentation with information that is personally relevant to them. You can supplement this technique with other attention-getting devices. Take a look at the strategies and examples in **Figure 11.6** on page 420, which you could use in the opening of the Rowland-Grey presentation.

For example, the proposal to replace computer monitors at Rowland-Grey offers employees the benefit of a more comfortable working environment and better health, and it offers managers the benefit of improved employee productivity. However, neither of these benefits is of primary importance to your audience, Carolyn Reese. She is probably more concerned with cost savings. As a result, the opening that you choose needs to focus on that benefit.

Provide a framework or map. An audience easily gets lost and bored if they cannot anticipate the twists and turns the presentation may take. Providing specific directions about the content at the beginning of the presentation helps them stay on course and follow your logic. A visual map, such as the one in **Figure 11.7** on page 420, can also serve as an agenda. You can return to it throughout the presentation to make transitions between different sections.

Organize the middle of the presentation to be easy to understand

A presentation is easiest to follow when it has a clear and simple organization. Within that organization, you can provide as much data as you need to accomplish your goal, as long as you also do these three things:

FIGURE 11.6 Strategies for Capturing Attention

STRATEGY	ROWLAND-GREY EXAMPLE
Cite a surprising fact or statistic. A surprising fact can capture the audience's attention quickly. Even a mundane fact can be effective if it gets people to nod in agreement.	*Next to payroll, annual employee training represents the single largest cost in Rowland-Grey's computer call centers.*
Tell a relevant story or anecdote. An **anecdote** is a very short story, usually a true one, that can bring a subject to life. An anecdote is one of the most powerful ways to begin a presentation.	*A few weeks ago, I was driving from Albuquerque to Flagstaff and made the mistake of forgetting to bring sunglasses. Within 10 minutes, the glare on the windshield was blinding, my eyes were squinting, and I started to get a headache. Fortunately, I was able to get off the road and buy sunglasses at a service station. But the experience gave me a new perspective on the exit interviews I had been reading from employees who left our computer call center. Many said they left because the computer glare caused headaches. I can say, I know how they feel.*
Quote someone. You might quote an expert, someone well known, a familiar saying—or even someone from your audience. If you can find a quotation or saying that relates to your point, you can use it—or a variation of it—to get people to think.	*As the saying goes, you need to spend money to make money. It's also true that you sometimes need to spend money to save money. Today I'm presenting a proposal to spend money to update equipment, an expenditure that has the potential of saving us hundreds of thousands of dollars in costs related to employee turnover.*
Ask a question. Questions immediately involve your audience and get them thinking about your presentation. Your question can be a genuine one that you'd actually like members of your audience to answer, either in words or by a show of hands. Or your question can be a rhetorical one that you plan to answer yourself. The key is finding the right question to engage your audience and to set up the remainder of your introduction.	• *Would you be surprised to learn that employee turnover for online sales clerks costs Rowland-Grey $660,000 a year?* • *Why do Rowland-Grey online sales clerks leave their jobs more quickly than any other category of clerks in the company?*

anecdote A very short story, usually a true one, that is used to make a point and bring a subject to life.

FIGURE 11.7 Visual Map for Rowland-Grey Presentation

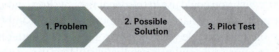

• Focus on points that are meaningful to the audience
• Limit the number of key points you include
• Make the relationship between points clear by using recognizable patterns

Focus on points that are meaningful to the audience. Presenters sometimes take the easy way out and let the information dictate the organization, for example two types of requirements, five training courses, three products, or six product features. For a more effective organization, think about what is meaningful to the audience. Instead of focusing on the features of a product, focus on how those features benefit the audience. Instead of explaining how a system works, highlight the problems the system solves. To identify the points most meaningful to the audience, return to the audience analysis questions you answered during the planning phase and identify what the audience wants to know during the presentation. Let that analysis be your guide.

Limit the number of key points. Your audience will remember your content better if you do not overload them with information. Presentation experts often recommend limiting the number of key points in a presentation (or bullet points on a slide) to a maximum of seven, based on influential research by George Miller.[9] However, more recent research has cut that estimate in half, and it is now generally accepted that people can keep four or five unrelated chunks of information in their short-term memory before forgetting important points.[10,11] This research suggests that if you keep your presentation to a small number of points, your audience will be able to remember it better when the presentation is over.

If you do have more than four or five points, group related items. For example, if you have seven recommendations to present, your audience will process the information and remember the recommendations better if you present them in two "chunks"—for example, three recommendations for saving costs and four recommendations for saving time.

Present your information using a recognizable pattern. Your audience will also find it easier to follow your information if they can recognize the pattern of your thinking. Consider the common patterns represented in **Figure 11.8**.

Which of these patterns will work best for the Rowland-Grey presentation? Although several approaches are feasible, perhaps the best one is the problem/solution, or motivated sequence, pattern because this pattern is likely to be effective in motivating the audience. Whether you choose one of these organizational patterns or a different one, be sure it fits your objective and the material you need to present. Remember to use keywords that make the pattern obvious to your audience, so that they understand your approach. In other words, if you are using a problem/solution pattern, use those words in your presentation.

Compose a memorable conclusion

The end of a presentation is as important as the beginning. Because the conclusion is the last thing the audience hears, it may be the first thing the audience remembers days or weeks after your presentation. This is called the *recency effect*.[12] Compose a powerful conclusion to your presentation by using at least one of the following strategies. The best endings typically use all four:

- **Summarize your main message.** All presentation guidelines recommend summarizing at the end. In other words, "Tell them what you told them." However, a good summary does more than just say "I've talked about our turnover problem and a proposed solution." Remind the audience why you talked about those topics. What makes the topics important to you and to the audience? What impact will the topics have? What are the benefits? How should the audience use the information or respond to it? Audiences need to hear again "What's in this for me?"
- **Ask for what you want.** What do you want the audience to do? Send you information? Schedule a meeting with a decision maker? Approve your proposal? Act on your recommendations? You'll need to create a call to action with specific, clear, and tangible tasks. As salespeople say, make the ask!
- **Visualize the outcome for the audience.** Paint a picture of the audience's world when your plans, product, or recommendations are in place. What will be more efficient, less costly, more comfortable, or more competitive? What kind of satisfaction will they experience?
- **Make next steps clear.** If your presentation leads to future action, outline the next steps and identify who is responsible for what. A simple checklist or timeline can effectively display the content and provide a visual reference.

For the Rowland-Grey presentation, you know that even if Ms. Reese believes the pilot is a good idea, she may not volunteer to pay for it. With this concern in mind, you decide that your conclusion needs to include an explicit request for funding along with the key reasons Ms. Reese should fund it.

Identify the role that slides will play

If you plan to use slides, now is the time to identify how you plan to use them. Typically, presenters choose between two different types of presentations that use slides in two different ways: stand-alone presentations and visual aid presentations.

FIGURE 11.8 Organizational Patterns for Presentations

ORGANIZATIONAL PATTERN	EXPLANATION
Categorization	Group the content under key categories, such as four reasons, five steps, or three options.
Component Parts	If you are discussing the problems in the company, you may divide the discussion into the component regions—for example, Northeast, Southeast, Midwest, and Southwest. Similarly, if you are talking about proposed changes to an automobile, you may present changes to the body, the engine and mechanical components, the chassis, and the interior.
Chronological Order	Chronology works well if you are presenting the timeline for a project or phases to implement a new computer system—any topic in which time is particularly important and meaningful.
Conceptual Order	For some presentations, you might find it useful to develop a model or diagram that illustrates the relationship between the ideas you plan to present, and then use that visual to organize your presentation. For example, if you were delivering an informative presentation about the ACE process, you might organize it by the three elements represented in the ACE diagram: Analyze, Compose, and Evaluate. In fact, you might even use this diagram as an agenda for the presentation.
Problem/Solution Or Monroe's Motivated Sequence	Because business presentations often aim to solve problems, organizing the content by problem/solution can be very useful. A similar pattern, the Motivated Sequence developed by Alan H. Monroe, is often taught in speech courses.[13] The five-step sequence is: 1. **Attention:** Use techniques for capturing the audience's attention. 2. **Need:** Show the audience how a problem negatively affects them. For example: *"Current call-center conditions cost us time and money."* 3. **Satisfaction:** Explain how your proposed action corrects or fulfills the identified need and will personally benefit the audience. For example, *"New computer monitors will halt rapid employee turnover, saving us training time and thousands of dollars."* 4. **Visualization:** Paint a vivid picture of the benefits that will come from your solution, or the negative consequences of not enacting it. For example, *"Once the program is fully implemented, imagine saving $441,000 a year."* 5. **Action:** Clearly identify what you want your audience to do. Provide short, concrete, easily accomplished action steps. For example, you might say, *"If you support this action, approve the pilot program."*
Opportunity/Action	Rather than focusing on the problem, emphasize an opportunity that will be valuable to your audience and then show how you can help them take advantage of this opportunity.
Questions/Answers	If you have done a good job of analyzing your audience, you may be able to imagine the questions that will be on their minds when they attend the presentation. These questions can help you organize the presentation. For example, if you are delivering an informational presentation about a new dental insurance option available to employees, you might organize the presentation around questions such as these: • Why did Acme add a new dental plan option? • What are the key features of each available option? • How can I choose between them? • How do I sign up for my preferred plan? • Can I change plans during the year? If you choose a question/answer structure, then the questions themselves become the agenda for your presentation.

FIGURE 11.9 A Stand-alone Slide with a Message Headline

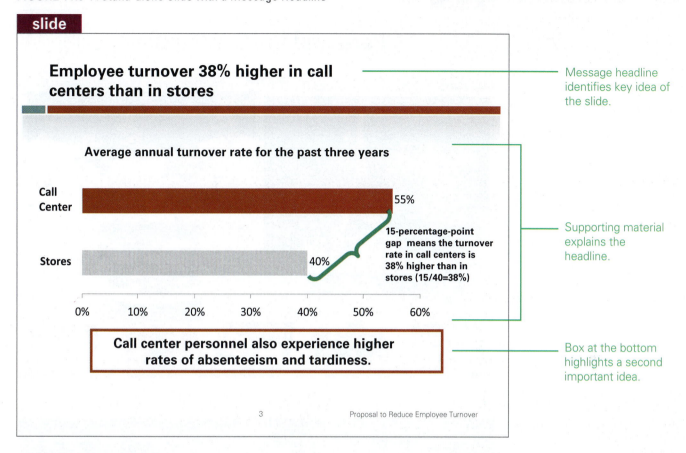

Stand-alone presentations

Many business presentations require that your **slide decks**—the set of slides you prepare for the presentation—serve as reference documents after the presentation and communicate the content effectively to people who didn't attend the presentation. These slide decks need to make "stand-alone sense,"[14] a term coined by managerial communication expert Mary Munter. Stand-alone sense does not mean that the deck will be comprehensive or include every word you plan to say. Instead, it means the presentation material will make sense to anyone who reads it without the benefit of the presenter to explain the information. In addition, each slide needs to make sense to someone who enters the room during the presentation, without hearing your introduction.

A **stand-alone presentation** is distinguished by three key features:

- An agenda slide that communicates the main ideas and logic of the presentation
- Sentence-style **message headlines** that summarize the key point, or message, of each slide
- Support material in the body of the slide that develops and explains the headline

Figure 11.9 illustrates a slide from a stand-alone presentation.

Visual aid presentations

In presentations where the speaker's words carry the main story of the presentation, the slides primarily provide illustration and backup. These **visual aid presentations** often have **topic headlines** at the top of the slide to announce what the slide is about—or they may have no headline at all. They also tend to devote more space to various forms of illustration that focus the discussion and demonstrate the points. The slide in **Figure 11.10** on page 424 is from a presentation promoting a culinary tour of France. The slide is visually appealing, but a presenter needs to explain the main point orally.

Even in a stand-alone presentation, you may decide to include some conceptual slides that are designed to pique the audience's interest and help them visualize a point. For example, you could use the image in **Figure 11.11** on page 424 as a transition to a call to action in a presentation, helping the audience visualize the point that you will say aloud: "We cannot do it alone."

slide deck A set of slides used for a presentation.

stand-alone presentation A slide deck that makes sense without the benefit of a presenter.

message headline Content at the top of the slide that summarizes the key point, or message, of each slide.

visual aid presentation A presentation in which the speaker's words carry the main story of the presentation, and the slides provide illustration and backup.

topic headline Content at the top of the slide that announces the topic of the slide.

FIGURE 11.10 A Visual Aid Slide That Requires a Presenter

FIGURE 11.11 Slide Visualizing the Concept "We Cannot Do It Alone"

Create a storyboard

Once you know the organization of your content and the type of slides you will develop, you can begin outlining the presentation by creating a storyboard. The concept of a storyboard comes from the film industry. Traditionally, a filmmaker plans a film, scene by scene, sketching the vision for each scene and including notes for direction and filming. Applied to a presentation, a **storyboard** is a slide-by-slide sketch that helps create a story flow based on the organization you developed. The storyboard also helps you see the big picture of the presentation before you get too involved in creating individual slides.

storyboard A slide-by-slide sketch of a presentation that is used as a tool for organizing the flow of the presentation.

To create a storyboard, sketch boxes for your slides (or use note cards or sticky notes) and write a headline in each box. Then sketch your vision for the body of each slide. How will you support that headline and illustrate that key idea? **Figure 11.12** illustrates a storyboard for the Rowland-Grey presentation. Notice that this presentation uses message headlines so that the presentation can stand alone.

FIGURE 11.12 Presentation Storyboard

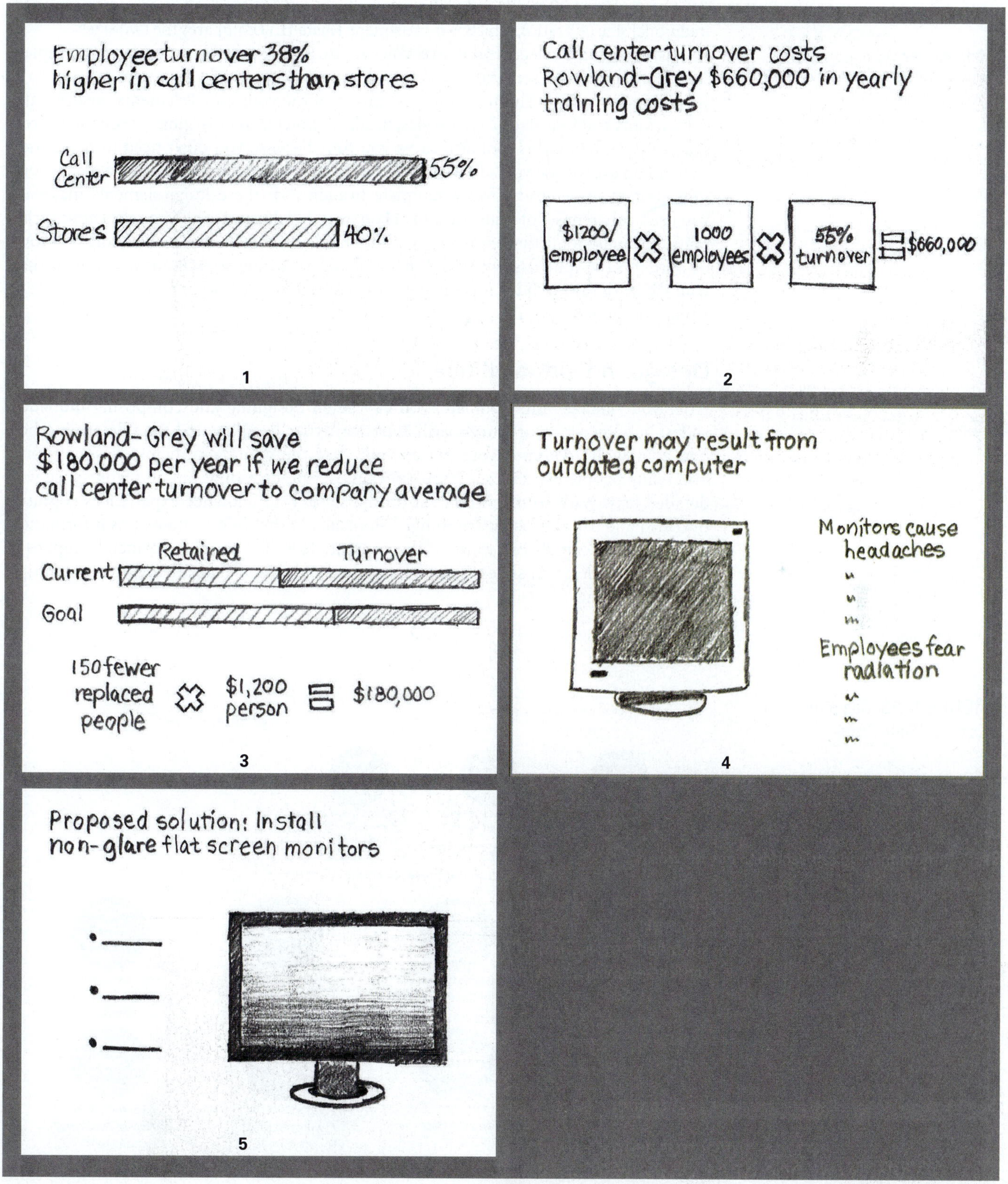

Develop a template

In business communication, a presentation's slide design should always be secondary to its message. You don't want your audience to focus more on the template's images, colors, and borders than on the message itself. The best approach is to keep your slide design simple so your audience can concentrate on the content. Fortunately, slide programs such as Power-Point and Keynote allow you to create your own slide templates. (PowerPoint templates are saved in the Microsoft template folder as .pot files.)

The first choice in designing a template is the size of the screen. You can choose a wide-screen template (16:9 width-to-height ratio), which is a modern look, or you can choose the traditional size (4:3 ratio), which is more square. **Figure 11.13** compares the two sizes.

After you have selected your size, you can use a **slide master** to design your template. A slide master is a presentation-editing tool that allows you to apply design features to all your slides in that file. This tool enforces consistency in your visual elements, ensuring that colors, fonts and font sizes, bullet styles, headers, footers, and margins are consistent from slide to slide. Using this tool also saves you time because you don't need to make these changes on every slide you add. **Figure 11.14** illustrates how you might set up elements on a slide master to develop an effective template. In addition to these design elements, make sure you use a coherent set of fonts. **Figure 11.15** on page 428 illustrates how to select appropriate fonts. If you use fonts that are not part of the standard set included in Microsoft Windows, be sure to save your file with the fonts embedded. Doing so will allow you to project your file with the intended fonts on any other Windows-based computer (though not on Apple computers).

slide master A tool in presentation software that allows you to select design features that apply to all slides.

Design individual slides

After you finalize your template, you can begin designing and composing individual slides, building on your storyboard. Start with your headline and then determine how best to visually communicate the content. Use the guiding principle "less is more." Too many people use slides as their speaking script, crowding out all blank space with detailed text. With so much content on the slide, your audience experiences cognitive overload and can't focus on anything.[15] Ironically, if the slide contains less information, your audience can absorb more of the content. This "less is more" principle applies to all types of slides: text slides, image slides, data slides, and slides that combine multiple types of content.

FIGURE 11.13 Comparison of Common Slide Sizes

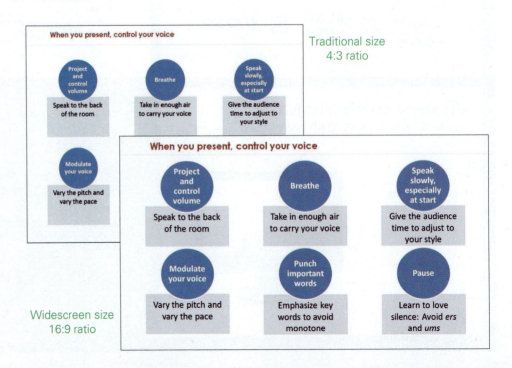

FIGURE 11.14 Guidelines for Designing a PowerPoint Template

Use a clean and simple look. Avoid templates with decorative, nonfunctional graphics. Avoid frequently used templates that immediately communicate a lack of originality. Use basic, solid backgrounds. Avoid backgrounds with dramatic color gradations that can conflict with the color of the font you choose. Use light backgrounds for presentations intended to be read on a computer, projected in a small or well-lit room, or printed for your audience. Use dark backgrounds to project in dark rooms.

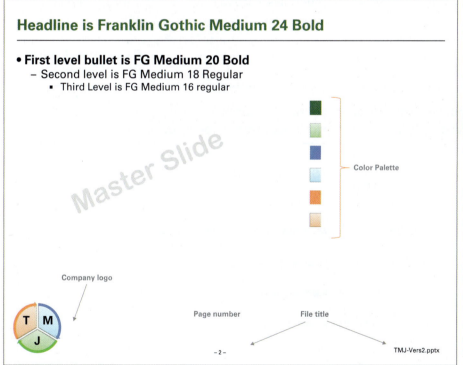

Position headlines appropriately. If you are using very short headlines, center them at the top of the slide. However, if you are using message headlines, begin them at the left margin.

Keep bullet style simple. Avoid ornate shapes that detract from your content and may not print correctly.

Use a consistent color palette. Choose an effective set of colors to use for graphs, tables, and emphasis in text. Color contrast is often sharper on your own computer screen than on a projected display. If you are planning to project slides, test your color combinations in the room where you will present to make sure that the headlines and text contrast sufficiently with the background.

Minimize the size of logos. If you would like a logo or other corporate identity item on each slide, reduce the size and put it in the footer or in a corner of the slide master where it will be visible but will not detract from the message.

Include a footer with slide numbers and other identifying information.

FIGURE 11.15 How to Select Fonts for Your Template

1. **Select a single font for your template.** It may either be a *serif* font (such as Times New Roman, which has extra "tails" at the end of each character) or a *sans serif* font such as Arial, which does not have tails.

2. **Identify the font variations you will use.** Variations can include styles of a single font and different members of the font family.

EXAMPLES OF SERIF FONTS	EXAMPLES OF SANS SERIF FONTS
Book Antiqua	Verdana
Times New Roman	Arial
Georgia	Franklin Gothic

EXAMPLE OF STYLES OF A SINGLE FONT	EXAMPLE OF A FONT FAMILY
Franklin Gothic	Franklin Gothic
Franklin Gothic italics	**Franklin Gothic Heavy**
Franklin Gothic bold	Franklin Gothic Medium
	Franklin Gothic Medium Condensed

3. **Select appropriate sizes and variations for the elements of your slides.** Keep your fonts and font sizes consistent throughout the slides.

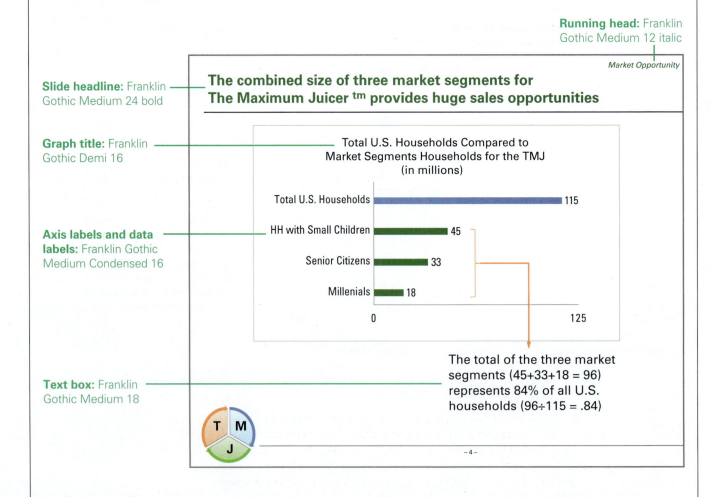

Running head: Franklin Gothic Medium 12 italic

Market Opportunity

Slide headline: Franklin Gothic Medium 24 bold

The combined size of three market segments for The Maximum Juicer ™ provides huge sales opportunities

Graph title: Franklin Gothic Demi 16

Total U.S. Households Compared to Market Segments Households for the TMJ (in millions)

Axis labels and data labels: Franklin Gothic Medium Condensed 16

Total U.S. Households — 115
HH with Small Children — 45
Senior Citizens — 33
Millenials — 18

0   125

The total of the three market segments (45+33+18 = 96) represents 84% of all U.S. households (96÷115 = .84)

Text box: Franklin Gothic Medium 18

– 4 –

Text slides

The bullet-point layout is the default layout for new slides in most presentation software, including PowerPoint. This default may be one reason writers overuse **bullet points** rather than use other means of formatting text. As **Figure 11.16** illustrates, bullets are certainly a better choice than dense paragraphs of text because bullets can help the audience more easily see the relationship among ideas. But bulleted or numbered lists work only if the relationship among ideas is clear.

As Figure 11.16 illustrates, bullet points work best for lists—items that can be labeled as members of one category, such as reasons, examples, results, solutions, steps, implications, or conclusions. To make the bullet points easy to read, be sure they are both logically and grammatically parallel. In other words, all the items should begin with the same part of speech (such as the verbs in Figure 11.16) and should be phrased with the same grammatical structure. As **Figure 11.17** on page 430 illustrates, if you want to include content that is not part of your list, you can position it as an introducer to the list, if appropriate. Alternatively, you can include it in a text box. Just be sure that the relationship between the bullet points and the other text is clear.

As a general guideline, limit the number of bullet points on a slide to three or four.[16] For visual aid presentations, also limit the number of words per line to six or seven. For stand-alone presentations, you may need more words.

bullet point One of a number of items printed in a vertical list, preceded by a symbol called a bullet.

FIGURE 11.16 How to Use Bullet Points to Eliminate Wordiness

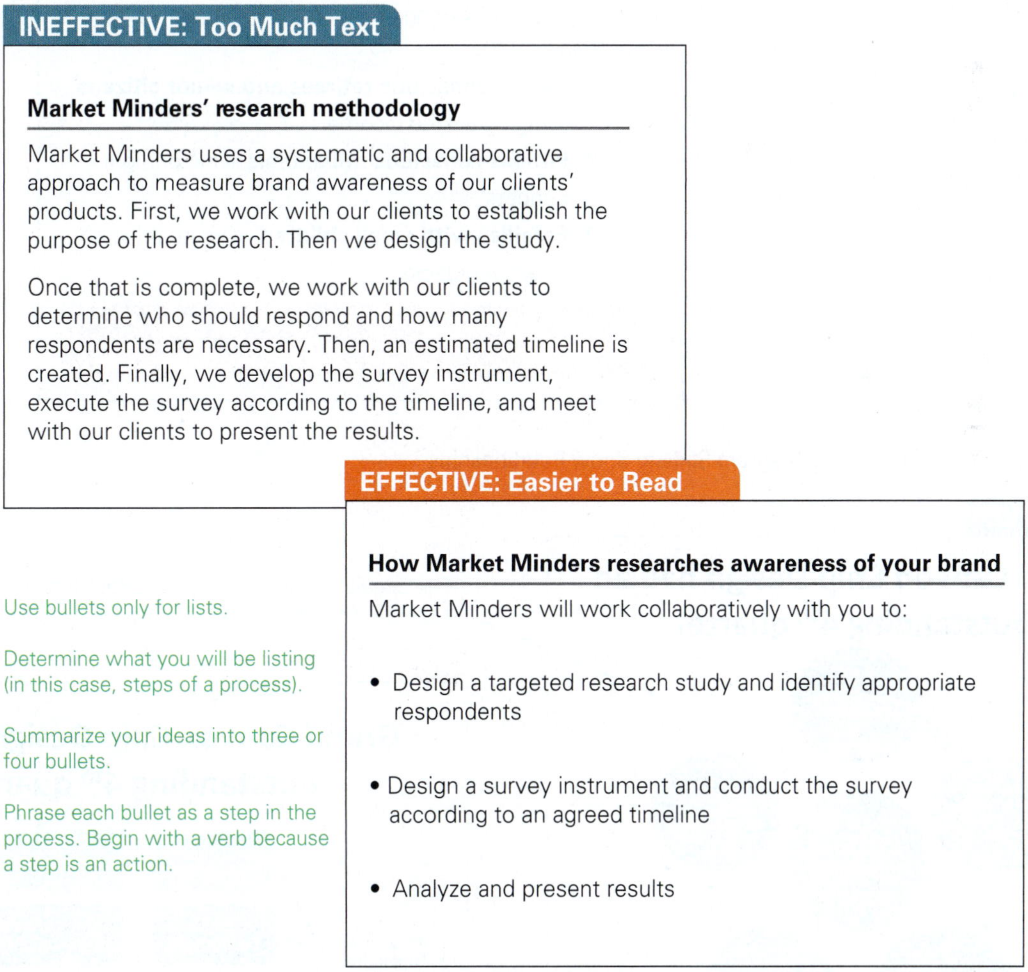

INEFFECTIVE: Too Much Text

Market Minders' research methodology

Market Minders uses a systematic and collaborative approach to measure brand awareness of our clients' products. First, we work with our clients to establish the purpose of the research. Then we design the study.

Once that is complete, we work with our clients to determine who should respond and how many respondents are necessary. Then, an estimated timeline is created. Finally, we develop the survey instrument, execute the survey according to the timeline, and meet with our clients to present the results.

EFFECTIVE: Easier to Read

How Market Minders researches awareness of your brand

Market Minders will work collaboratively with you to:

- Design a targeted research study and identify appropriate respondents
- Design a survey instrument and conduct the survey according to an agreed timeline
- Analyze and present results

Use bullets only for lists.

Determine what you will be listing (in this case, steps of a process).

Summarize your ideas into three or four bullets.

Phrase each bullet as a step in the process. Begin with a verb because a step is an action.

If your slide presents ideas that are not a logical list, eliminate the bullets and present the content in text boxes, shapes, or diagrams. If you choose to present text in the form of a diagram, be sure to choose a shape that reinforces the content. Avoid diagrams that are chosen only for visual appeal and that do not help your audience better understand the information. **Figure 11.18** on page 430 illustrates how to improve a diagram to help your audience quickly see the relationships among ideas.

FIGURE 11.17 How to Include Text That Does Not Belong in a Bullet-Point List

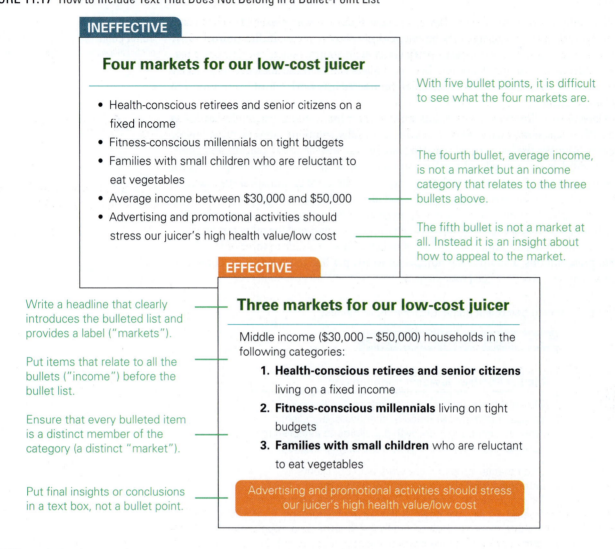

INEFFECTIVE

Four markets for our low-cost juicer

- Health-conscious retirees and senior citizens on a fixed income
- Fitness-conscious millennials on tight budgets
- Families with small children who are reluctant to eat vegetables
- Average income between $30,000 and $50,000
- Advertising and promotional activities should stress our juicer's high health value/low cost

With five bullet points, it is difficult to see what the four markets are.

The fourth bullet, average income, is not a market but an income category that relates to the three bullets above.

The fifth bullet is not a market at all. Instead it is an insight about how to appeal to the market.

EFFECTIVE

Three markets for our low-cost juicer

Middle income ($30,000 – $50,000) households in the following categories:

1. **Health-conscious retirees and senior citizens** living on a fixed income
2. **Fitness-conscious millennials** living on tight budgets
3. **Families with small children** who are reluctant to eat vegetables

Advertising and promotional activities should stress our juicer's high health value/low cost

Write a headline that clearly introduces the bulleted list and provides a label ("markets").

Put items that relate to all the bullets ("income") before the bullet list.

Ensure that every bulleted item is a distinct member of the category (a distinct "market").

Put final insights or conclusions in a text box, not a bullet point.

FIGURE 11.18 How to Compose a Diagram Slide to Show Relationships

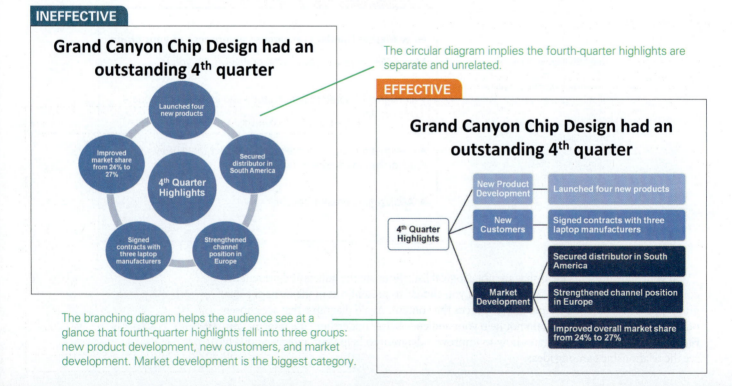

INEFFECTIVE

Grand Canyon Chip Design had an outstanding 4th quarter

Launched four new products

Improved market share from 24% to 27%

4th Quarter Highlights

Secured distributor in South America

Signed contracts with three laptop manufacturers

Strengthened channel position in Europe

The circular diagram implies the fourth-quarter highlights are separate and unrelated.

EFFECTIVE

Grand Canyon Chip Design had an outstanding 4th quarter

4th Quarter Highlights

New Product Development — Launched four new products

New Customers — Signed contracts with three laptop manufacturers

Market Development — Secured distributor in South America / Strengthened channel position in Europe / Improved overall market share from 24% to 27%

The branching diagram helps the audience see at a glance that fourth-quarter highlights fell into three groups: new product development, new customers, and market development. Market development is the biggest category.

Image slides

Image slides rely primarily on photos, drawings, and diagrams as the primary means of communication. The images may be literal. For example, if you want to present the features of a new product, then a photo or drawing of that product will help your audience visualize those features. Or the image may be conceptual, like the one in Figure 11.11: The silhouette of one mountain climber helping another communicates the concept of teamwork. You can also use icons, such as those available from The Noun Project (www.thenounproject.com), as a visual language. Because an **icon** is a graphic symbol whose form suggests its meaning, it communicates its meaning at a glance—and can even communicate across languages. **Figure 11.19** illustrates a slide that communicates the elements of a problem by using icons supplemented with a few words.

icon A graphical symbol whose form suggests its meaning.

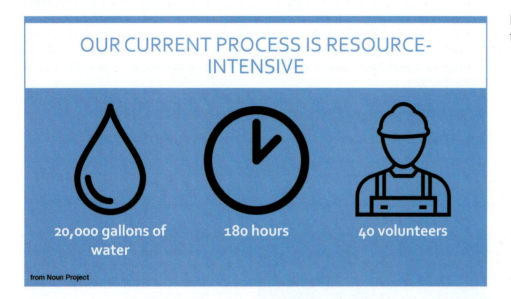

FIGURE 11.19 How to Use Icons to Communicate Key Ideas

Data slides

Business presentations often need to represent numerical data on slides. As **Figure 11.20** illustrates, graphs typically do a better job than tables of showing the relationships between numbers and the meaning of the data. For guidelines on designing effective graphs, see Chapter 10: Preparing Business Reports.

FIGURE 11.20 How to Represent Quantitative Data Effectively

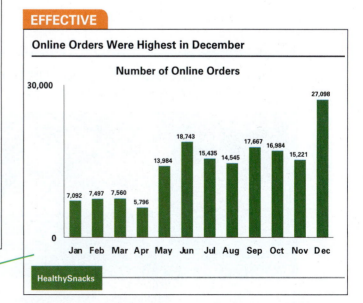

Combination slides

If your slides combine multiple elements—for example, multiple images with explanatory text—then follow the principles of visual design given the memorable acronym C.R.A.P. (*contrast*, *repetition*, *alignment*, and *proximity*) by designer Robin Williams:[17]

- **Contrast.** Ensure that your audience can see the difference between elements. Do not make different things too similar. For example, ensure that your headline text contrasts with the body text in size, weight, or color. If you choose to use a different font for your headlines and body text, make the fonts very different so that your audience can easily distinguish between them.
- **Repetition.** Repeat elements of design throughout the slide and throughout the deck so that the pattern is recognizable. For example, repeat the same type of headline on each slide. Repeat your pattern of where you place captions for images. Repetition teaches your readers how to read your slides.
- **Alignment.** Do not place elements randomly on the slide. Instead, align them with other elements on the slide. They may be aligned at the top, bottom, center, left, or right. The choice of where to align elements should be consistent throughout the slide and repeated throughout the slide deck.
- **Proximity.** Position related elements of the slide (for example, a photo and explanatory text) close enough together that your audience immediately sees the connection.

Figure 11.21 illustrates how to revise a slide using these elements of visual design.

FIGURE 11.21 How to Revise a Slide Using C.R.A.P. Principles

Ineffective

Our Goal: Reduce the Amount of Water Needed to Clean Crushed Coral

- Crushed coral needs to be rinsed prior to tank placement
- Current methods: 50-250 gallons of water per 50 lb. bag
- Large exhibits require 10,000-20,0000 lbs. of coral

Contrast: The headline does not sufficiently stand out from the body text. The headline uses a different but similar font, the same color, and a similar size.

Repetition: The bullets do not repeat the same parallel pattern. Unlike the first and third bullet points, the middle is not a complete sentence.

Alignment: The pictures do not align with each other or with the text above.

Proximity: It is hard to see how the three bullet points above relate to the two pictures below.

Effective

OUR GOAL: REDUCE THE AMOUNT OF WATER NEEDED TO CLEAN CRUSHED CORAL

Large aquarium exhibits require 10,000-20,000 lbs. of crushed coral

Coral needs to be rinsed before being placed in the exhibit tank

Process currently requires 50-250 gallons of water per 50 lb. bag of coral

Contrast: The headline contrasts with the body text in four ways: in color, in background, in size, and in case (upper versus lower).

Repetition: The placement of pictures and text repeats throughout the slide. The form of the text repeats also: all captions are complete sentences.

Alignment: The pictures and text boxes align at the top. Each picture left aligns with its corresponding text block.

Proximity: Text is immediately beneath the corresponding pictures.

Evaluate your slides in a practice session

As you design your slides, you may focus more on how a slide looks and what it says than on how you will present the slide. That is why it is important to practice presenting each slide and then to revise each slide to make it easier to present. As you evaluate your slides, consider both the arrangement of content and the animations.

Are the slides easy to present?

Consider the ineffective slide in **Figure 11.22**, which presents data about the potential number of total prescriptions for a medication (TRxs), organized by region. The slide is clean, clear, and easy to read. However, it would be difficult to present. What message do you see in the slide? What would you want to say about market potential? Because the regions are ordered geographically, from east to west, no clear message is obvious.

By contrast, the effective slide in Figure 11.22 is much easier to present. A presenter could look at the slide and say, "While there is substantial sales potential for our product throughout the country, that potential is not divided evenly across the sales districts. The graph on this slide is organized by size of potential. As you can see, the West district has over seven times more market potential than the New York Metro District."

FIGURE 11.22 How to Revise a Slide for Easier Presentation

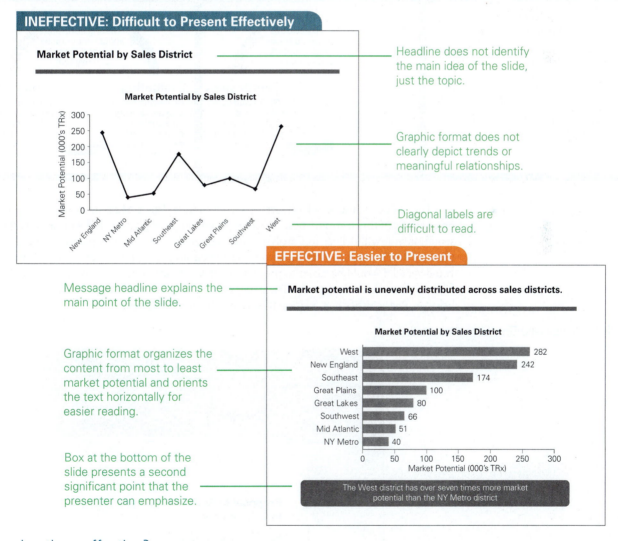

Are animations effective?

Practicing your presentation not only allows you to evaluate individual slides but also helps you make good decisions about whether to use slide **animations**—visual effects that control when and how elements appear on the slides while you present. As a general guideline, use animation only if it helps you present a slide effectively and if you believe it will help your audience better understand your points.

animations Visual effects that control when and how elements appear on your slides while you present.

For example, if you wanted to present the ACE process in a presentation, you might have the analyzing portion of a diagram appear first, then composing, then evaluating, discussing each part in turn, as shown in **Figure 11.23**. By the end, a complete circle would be visible, and you would discuss why ACE is a circular process. In this case, the animation would support your discussion.

If you choose to use animations in a presentation, follow these guidelines:

- **Be consistent within the presentation.** Use only one technique (for example, appear, dissolve, fade in) anywhere you use animations within the presentation.
- **Be conservative.** You might think it is entertaining to have images or words fly in from the left and right. However, this movement will not enhance your content. It will simply distract your audience and potentially interfere with their ability to retain the information.[18]
- **When possible, show the whole picture or list first.** Then fade that picture and begin the animation. Audiences often understand individual points better when they have first seen the big picture.
- **Practice.** Presenting an animated slide is more difficult than presenting one without animation. Practice delivering the slide so that you know how to take advantage of the animation. If you find the animation difficult to present, remove it from the slide.

FIGURE 11.23 Using Animation to Present Parts of a Diagram

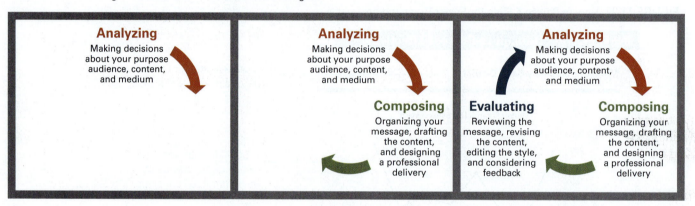

The slides for the Rowland-Grey presentation, in **Figure 11.24**, incorporate all the best practices from this section. These 13 slides presented through page 437 will support the presentation you will deliver to Carolyn Reese, senior vice president of planning and development at Rowland-Grey. Although you considered preparing just a handout with no slides, you decided it would be easier to present the problem and solution if you had a visual aid to focus your audience's attention. The paper copy of the slides will serve as a handout and will help Ms. Reese justify her decision to support the pilot program.

FIGURE 11.24 Rowland-Grey Slide Presentation

The title slide resembles the title page of a formal report.

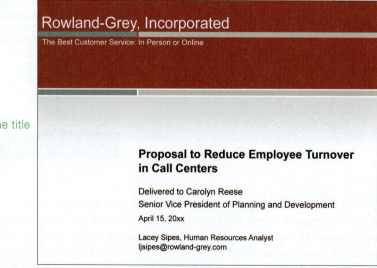

(continued)

FIGURE 11.24 *(Continued)*

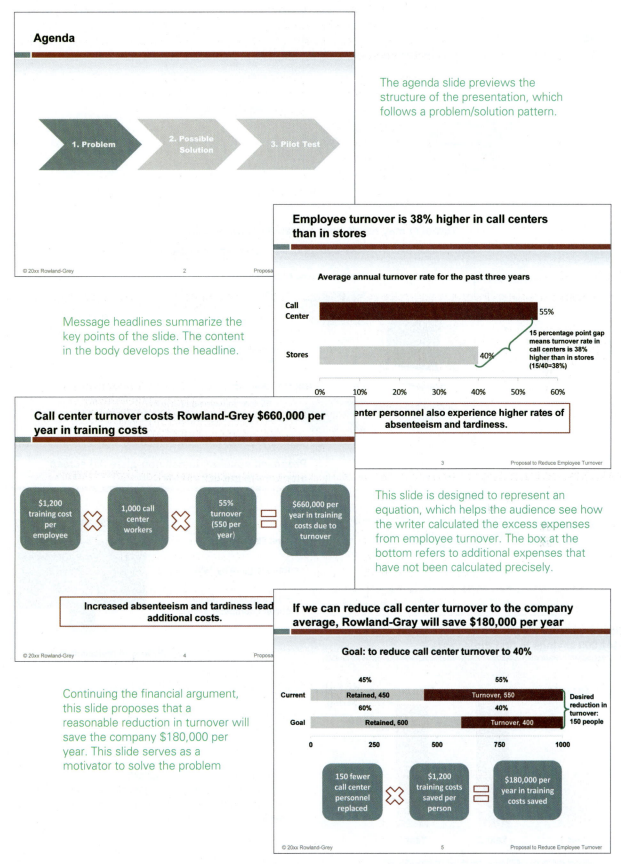

Agenda

1. Problem
2. Possible Solution
3. Pilot Test

© 20xx Rowland-Grey   2   Proposal

The agenda slide previews the structure of the presentation, which follows a problem/solution pattern.

Message headlines summarize the key points of the slide. The content in the body develops the headline.

Employee turnover is 38% higher in call centers than in stores

Average annual turnover rate for the past three years

Call Center — 55%

Stores — 40%

15 percentage point gap means turnover rate in call centers is 38% higher than in stores (15/40=38%)

0% 10% 20% 30% 40% 50% 60%

Call center personnel also experience higher rates of absenteeism and tardiness.

3   Proposal to Reduce Employee Turnover

Call center turnover costs Rowland-Grey $660,000 per year in training costs

$1,200 training cost per employee ⊗ 1,000 call center workers ⊗ 55% turnover (550 per year) = $660,000 per year in training costs due to turnover

Increased absenteeism and tardiness lead to additional costs.

© 20xx Rowland-Grey   4   Proposal

This slide is designed to represent an equation, which helps the audience see how the writer calculated the excess expenses from employee turnover. The box at the bottom refers to additional expenses that have not been calculated precisely.

Continuing the financial argument, this slide proposes that a reasonable reduction in turnover will save the company $180,000 per year. This slide serves as a motivator to solve the problem

If we can reduce call center turnover to the company average, Rowland-Gray will save $180,000 per year

Goal: to reduce call center turnover to 40%

	45%	55%
Current	Retained, 450	Turnover, 550
	60%	40%
Goal	Retained, 600	Turnover, 400

Desired reduction in turnover: 150 people

0   250   500   750   1000

150 fewer call center personnel replaced ⊗ $1,200 training costs saved per person = $180,000 per year in training costs saved

© 20xx Rowland-Grey   5   Proposal to Reduce Employee Turnover

(continued)

FIGURE 11.24 *(Continued)*

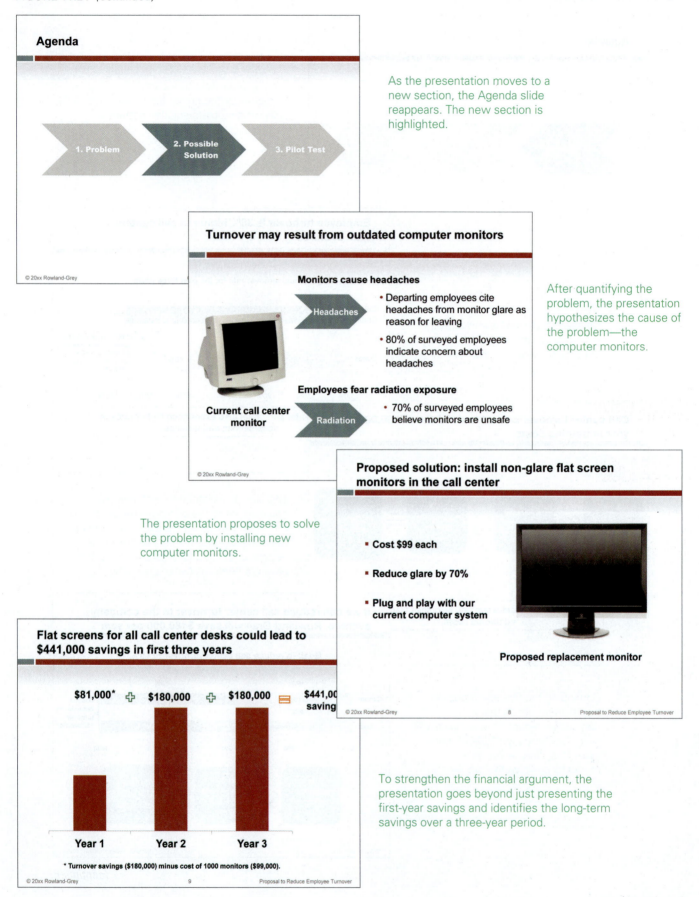

As the presentation moves to a new section, the Agenda slide reappears. The new section is highlighted.

After quantifying the problem, the presentation hypothesizes the cause of the problem—the computer monitors.

The presentation proposes to solve the problem by installing new computer monitors.

To strengthen the financial argument, the presentation goes beyond just presenting the first-year savings and identifies the long-term savings over a three-year period.

(continued)

FIGURE 11.24 *(Continued)*

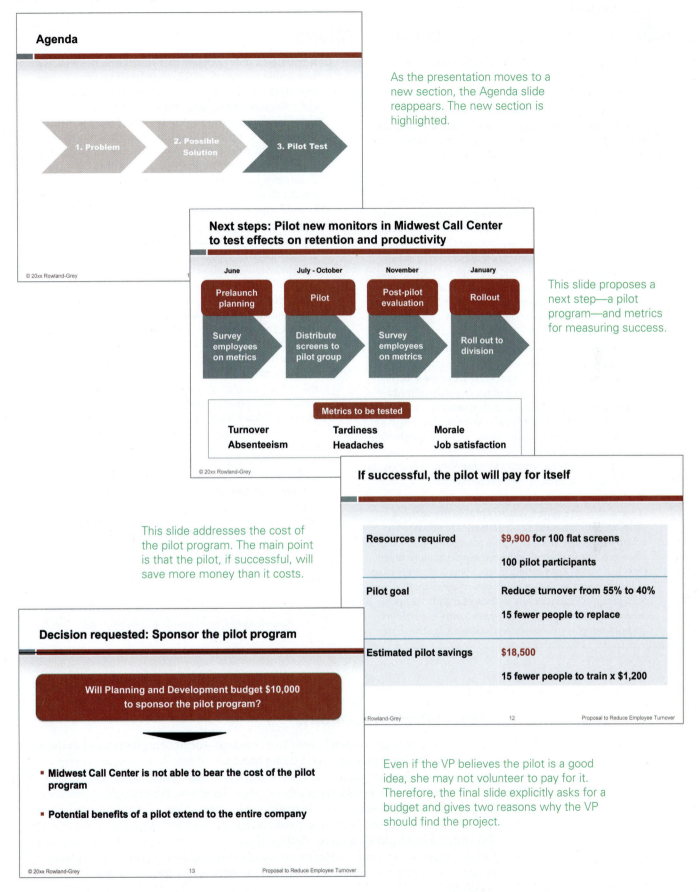

Agenda

1. Problem → 2. Possible Solution → 3. Pilot Test

© 20xx Rowland-Grey

As the presentation moves to a new section, the Agenda slide reappears. The new section is highlighted.

Next steps: Pilot new monitors in Midwest Call Center to test effects on retention and productivity

June	July - October	November	January
Prelaunch planning	Pilot	Post-pilot evaluation	Rollout
Survey employees on metrics	Distribute screens to pilot group	Survey employees on metrics	Roll out to division

Metrics to be tested

Turnover	Tardiness	Morale
Absenteeism	Headaches	Job satisfaction

© 20xx Rowland-Grey

This slide proposes a next step—a pilot program—and metrics for measuring success.

If successful, the pilot will pay for itself

Resources required	**$9,900** for 100 flat screens
	100 pilot participants
Pilot goal	**Reduce turnover from 55% to 40%**
	15 fewer people to replace
Estimated pilot savings	**$18,500**
	15 fewer people to train x $1,200

Rowland-Grey   12   Proposal to Reduce Employee Turnover

This slide addresses the cost of the pilot program. The main point is that the pilot, if successful, will save more money than it costs.

Decision requested: Sponsor the pilot program

Will Planning and Development budget $10,000 to sponsor the pilot program?

- **Midwest Call Center is not able to bear the cost of the pilot program**
- **Potential benefits of a pilot extend to the entire company**

© 20xx Rowland-Grey   13   Proposal to Reduce Employee Turnover

Even if the VP believes the pilot is a good idea, she may not volunteer to pay for it. Therefore, the final slide explicitly asks for a budget and gives two reasons why the VP should find the project.

ETHICS
AVOIDING PLAGIARISM IN PRESENTATIONS

Most people are aware of the rules for avoiding plagiarism in research reports. But what about in presentations? Do the same rules apply? Test your knowledge with the following questions.

1. **Is it acceptable to include in your presentation a photo found on the Internet? Do you need to acknowledge the source?** It is acceptable if you acknowledge the source in your presentation. You can include a source citation directly below the photo. However, if you are using your presentation for any commercial purposes—or if you are distributing it widely—for example, on SlideShare or in customer meetings—just acknowledging the source is not enough. You must get permission from the original owner of the photo to use it. For example, if you create a presentation to persuade firms to invest in India and want to use a photo of new skyscrapers in India to communicate economic growth, you must acquire the rights to use that photo by contacting the photographer or other copyright holder. As the U.S. Copyright office says: "Acknowledging the source of the copyrighted material does not substitute for obtaining permission."[19]

2. **If you purchase a license to use a presentation photo from a digital media source, such as Getty Images or Shutterstock, do you need to acknowledge the source?** Pay attention to what the license allows. Some digital media owners require that you provide an attribution if you are using the photo for "editorial" purposes but not if you are using it for "commercial" purposes. In other words, if you use the photo in a presentation, you must include credit adjacent to the photo—for example, "iStock.com/Artist's Member Name." If you use the same photo for advertising, no credit is required.[20]

3. **If other people in your company or organization have created effective slides, is it acceptable to use those slides in your business presentation? Do you need to acknowledge the source?** Within an organization, it is usually acceptable to share slides to use in presentations made on behalf of the organization. In fact, some companies create slide libraries to encourage employees to use slides that have been preapproved, especially for customer and other public presentations. Because your company "owns" the slide you are borrowing, you do not have to acknowledge the source.

4. **If you find a slide template that you like on the web, is it acceptable to copy that slide template if you don't copy any of the content?** It is not acceptable to copy someone else's slide template because graphic designs can be copyrighted in the same way content is copyrighted. If someone is selling a slide template design through the Internet, you may purchase and use it. Or if a company is explicitly giving away a free template, you may download and use that. However, if you simply download a presentation file from the Internet and decide to use that design for your presentation, you may be violating someone's copyright.

5. **If you include other people's work in your presentation—for example, data from another source—how do you acknowledge it?** Typically, you will acknowledge a data source under the graph or table that uses the data. Similarly, if you "borrow" concepts or ideas from another author, acknowledge it right on that slide. Many business presentations contain "footnotes" that acknowledge information sources. For examples of acknowledging sources on presentation slides, see Appendix B: Documentation and Reference Styles at the back of book.

While plagiarism has always been a risky practice, the risk of being caught has never been greater. In today's digital environment, where people are encouraged to share information with each other widely online, you should anticipate that a PowerPoint deck, Prezi, or video will travel beyond its intended audience. SlideShare.net is a highly popular website that showcases user-uploaded presentations, and all presentations made on Prezi's free service are available for public viewing. With more eyes on your work, it's all the more important that everything you incorporate into your presentation be ethically sourced and credited. Nothing sabotages a successful presentation more than your employer discovering that you used illegally downloaded software or material you were supposed to pay for but didn't—or that you used a colleague's research and didn't give credit.

For an ETHICS exercise, go to Exercise 13 on page 462.

Create effective handouts

Audiences and presenters often benefit from *handouts*—documents distributed to the audience during or after a presentation. Making handouts of presentation slides is very convenient. Standard formats include slide miniatures and slides with "notes" pages. However, your presentation may benefit from other types of handouts. For example, if you are making a detailed sales presentation or client proposal, your handout may include product specification sheets or spreadsheets that would be too detailed to read on a screen. Providing that material in a handout is more effective. If you have several resources to share—such as forms, sample designs, or documentation—you can use folders, report covers, or binders to organize your handout materials. **Figure 11.25** provides advice for choosing among types of handouts.

FIGURE 11.25 Choosing an Appropriate Handout Format

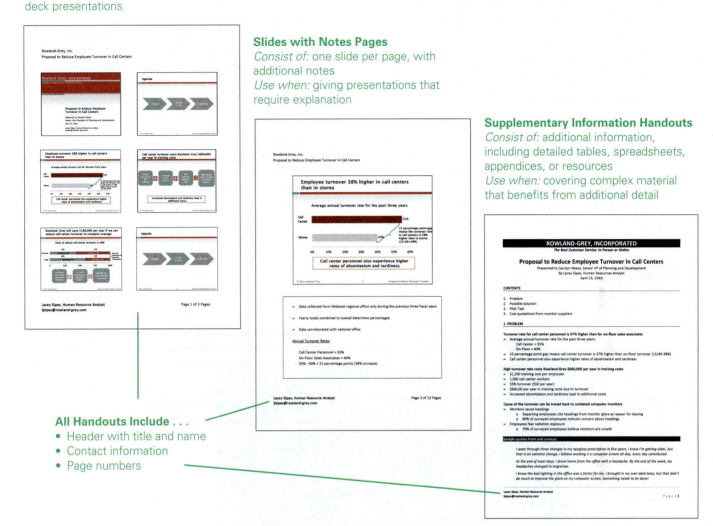

Slide Miniature Handouts
Consist of: slides that are reduced in size but still legible
Use when: giving stand-alone and report deck presentations

Slides with Notes Pages
Consist of: one slide per page, with additional notes
Use when: giving presentations that require explanation

Supplementary Information Handouts
Consist of: additional information, including detailed tables, spreadsheets, appendices, or resources
Use when: covering complex material that benefits from additional detail

All Handouts Include . . .
- Header with title and name
- Contact information
- Page numbers

When creating handouts, follow these guidelines:

- **Consider the needs of your audience.** Will they want to make notes on your handouts? If so, avoid slide miniatures that fill the entire page with no room for notes. Be sure to leave ample margins or provide other blank space.

- **Consider the impact of color.** Your audience may perceive handouts printed in color as having more impact than black-and-white documents. However, colorful handouts are more expensive to produce. Printing handouts in grayscale provides contrast without additional expense.

- **Proofread carefully before copying.** You can easily make changes to your electronic files before your presentation. However, if you find an error after you copy handouts, printing and recopying them will require extra time and money.

- **Make extra copies.** Even if you think you know how large your audience will be, make 10 percent more handouts in case extra people attend or someone wants to share copies with colleagues who cannot attend your presentation.

- **Decide when to distribute your handouts.** In some situations, you may want to distribute your handouts as your audience enters the room. They can preview the topic and begin to think about your information before the presentation begins. In other cases, you may want to distribute the handouts as you begin speaking. Having handouts during the presentation allows the audience to make notes and identify question areas as they follow along. If you do not want your audience to read a handout while you are presenting, you may decide to provide handouts only at the end of the presentation.

TECHNOLOGY
THE PROS AND CONS OF PREZI

Although PowerPoint is the most widely used presentation software in business, new competitors are emerging. The most intriguing alternative is Prezi, a cloud-based presentation program that requires a different approach to composing and delivering a presentation.

Prezi can help you do a number of unique things, including the following:

- **Identify a visual metaphor.** Like PowerPoint, Prezi provides an array of modifiable templates. However, Prezi's templates tend to feature visual metaphors, such as branching trees, networked webs, and forked roads, that can help you model connections between ideas. These metaphors can also help the audience grasp complex ideas in a glance.

- **Showcase the relationship between the whole and its parts.** Because you can easily zoom in and out of the Prezi canvas, it is easy to show the "big picture" and then focus on individual elements.

- **Toggle easily between elements.** While it's possible to skip past slides in linear presentation software, Prezi makes it easy to move freely from one point to the next. This flexibility is particularly helpful if you are paying close attention to the audience. If the audience seems confused or asks a question, you can quickly and easily return to the relevant point without clicking back through multiple slides.

- **Use analytics to evaluate the effectiveness of your presentation.** If your company subscribes to Prezi Business, you can use Prezi data to see who views your Prezi, which parts of it, and for how long.

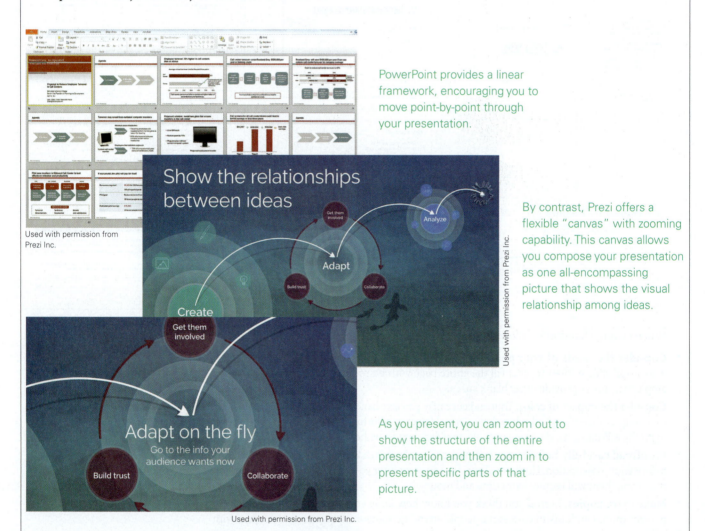

Used with permission from Prezi Inc.

PowerPoint provides a linear framework, encouraging you to move point-by-point through your presentation.

By contrast, Prezi offers a flexible "canvas" with zooming capability. This canvas allows you compose your presentation as one all-encompassing picture that shows the visual relationship among ideas.

Used with permission from Prezi Inc.

As you present, you can zoom out to show the structure of the entire presentation and then zoom in to present specific parts of that picture.

Used with permission from Prezi Inc.

(continued)

TECHNOLOGY
THE PROS AND CONS OF PREZI *(Continued)*

However, Prezi also has some limitations, such as these:

- **There can be a steep learning curve.** Prezi is not a great choice if you have to learn how to use the software and put together a presentation on a tight timeline.
- **Your audience is probably less familiar with it.** Novelty can be a pro or a con, depending on the context and presentation, but you don't want interest in your presentation style to distract from the content.

Entrepreneur and conservationist Mike Velings used Prezi to design and deliver a presentation making the case for aquaculture, or fish farming, as a way to solve a multifaceted problem that stretches from land to sea, across the globe—depletion of the fish population that billions of people rely on for food. To establish this point—and to keep the audience coming back to the big picture—Velings chose a globe, illustrated below, as the core image of his Prezi. The simple yet appealing graphics throughout keep the audience engaged, whereas bombarding the audience with text-filled slides might have alienated or bored them.

For more examples and tips, go to the blog section on the Prezi website.

Used with permission from Prezi Inc.

For a TECHNOLOGY exercise, go to Exercise 16 on page 462.

 SQ3 # How do you deliver and evaluate the presentation?

Many people get nervous when making presentations. Their minds go blank, their hands shake, or they talk too quickly or too softly. Even if you don't suffer from these problems, you can enhance your presentation skills—and your professional presence when presenting—so you can stand out among your peers. The only way to become a good presenter is to practice. This section offers you proven tips for presenting effectively. Pick one or two specific items to work on each time you practice your presentation. In time, you will incorporate all of them into your presenting style.

Set the stage

Use the following guidelines to ensure a professional presentation:

- **Practice (aloud).** It's easy to feel nervous when you are not well prepared. Presenting is similar to an athletic performance. A presenter needs to get ready—just as an athlete would practice regularly and then stretch to warm up. Practice means saying the words aloud, not merely going over them in your head, to create a "sound memory" to recall during your actual presentation.

- **Dress for the part.** For formal presentations, wear business-formal clothing, similar to what you would wear to a job interview. Even in less formal presentations, dress with care. Wear clothing that looks neat and allows you to move comfortably. You want people to pay attention to you, not your clothing. Empty your pockets of keys or loose change that can jingle when you move. Avoid distracting jewelry—and, of course, turn off cell phones.

- **Arrive early and warm up.** Warming up can take several forms. To feel comfortable with the audience, greet people individually, introduce yourself, get used to talking with them, and make a good first impression even before you begin to present. To focus your mind and relieve stress, use relaxation techniques. Breathe deeply from your diaphragm to control the adrenaline and relax the neck and jaw muscles. These techniques will also help you project your voice. To refresh your memory about your content, take a quick look at your notes, and review your opening and closing remarks. Finally, double-check handouts and equipment to ensure that everything is ready.

- **Set up all equipment and props.** If you plan to use presentation slides, turn on the projector or display monitor and have the title slide in place when the presentation begins. If you prefer to begin with a dark screen and display the title slide later, you can press the B key in PowerPoint to blacken the screen. Pressing B again makes your slide appear. If you're using flipcharts, a whiteboard, or props, make sure they are positioned to be easy to reach during your presentation. If you are using sound, adjust the volume before the presentation begins.

- **Decide where you will stand.** Whenever possible, avoid standing behind lecterns and large desks or tables because they create a barrier between you and the audience. If you are using a projector, position yourself on one side of the screen so that you do not have to walk between the screen and the projector's light. Clear space around the projector and other equipment so that you have plenty of room to move around comfortably and approach the audience. Using a remote control to change slides can help you navigate your presentation space.

- **Keep the lights up and attention on you.** If you choose a technology that requires low light, plan to begin speaking with the lights on. This guarantees that attention will be where you want it—on you and your message. It can be very effective to begin speaking before projecting any visuals. Connect with the audience and then move to the slides.

- **Have water available.** If you are speaking for a long time, you will need to drink water to prevent your mouth from drying out and your vocal cords from being constricted.

Control your body

Social psychologist Amy Cuddy recommends taking two minutes before a presentation or an important meeting and posing like a superhero.[21] Cuddy's research suggests that adopting a powerful posture affects your biochemistry and can, in fact, make you feel more powerful. Although the research surrounding "power posing" is controversial,[22] motivational speaker Tony Robbins says he's been using these power posing techniques to prepare for presentations for more than 30 years, and they help him command the room.[23]

Once you feel confident and powerful, get your body into position to present, just as you would get into position to swing a bat in baseball or make a jump shot in basketball. Try this stance:

- Hands loose at your side
- Knees and elbows relaxed
- Weight balanced on both feet
- Feet shoulder-width apart

If this position does not feel comfortable to you, find a position that does. Once you're in that comfortable and confident position, your gestures and movements will feel more natural.

Then use the techniques in **Figure 11.26** to help ensure that you look confident and professional during your presentation. Paying attention to body language is particularly important for a compelling presentation. Research conducted on viewer responses to TED talks found a correlation between positive nonverbal behavior, such as hand gestures and smiling, and the popularity of the video.[24]

Maintain good eye contact with your audience. If you are presenting with slides or a white board, you may be tempted to move away from the audience and turn toward your visual. Instead, hold eye contact with one person for two or three seconds, and then look at someone else. Engage everyone in your audience, not just the decision makers or those who are sitting front and center.

FIGURE 11.26 How to Look Confident and Professional While Presenting

Smile. A smile projects energy and makes you appear happy to be presenting. It also relaxes facial muscles to help you get the most from your speaking voice. Finally, it encourages your audience to smile in return, which will make them more receptive to your presentation.

Animate with body language. Rather than standing in one position, let your body move. Move away from the projector and screen, lean forward, and walk toward your audience. Use natural hand gestures to punctuate your points, just as you would in conversation. Do not think too much about gesturing. Take your hands out of your pockets and let them work naturally.

Andres Rodriguez/Fotolia

Use your voice effectively

Use the following techniques to improve your speaking skills:

- **Speak to the back of the room.** Speaking to the back of the room will help you adjust your volume so that you project your voice effectively. When you make eye contact with people in the front of the room, maintain the same level of volume so that people throughout the room can hear you. Too often, speakers lower their voices when they answer questions from people in the front of the room. Even in a small room, the person who cannot hear you will feel left out.

- **Speak slowly, especially at the beginning of the presentation.** Your audience may need a few minutes to get used to your style of speaking. You can help them by speaking slowly and enunciating clearly, especially at the beginning of your presentation.

- **Modulate your voice.** Nothing destroys audience attention more than a monotone presenter, and, according to that same study of TED talks, nothing does more to increase charisma than vocal variety.[25] One technique for animating your voice is to emphasize important words and phrases. If you are using slides, take your cue from the words you emphasized on the slides with color contrast or boldface.

- **Minimize verbal tics.** Many people unconsciously use certain words as fillers—for example, "like," "okay," and "you know." Be aware of your own speaking habits, and practice eliminating verbal tics in your speech.

- **Use pauses—a remedy for the "ers" and "ums."** Pausing intentionally is one of the best ways to prevent "ers" and "ums" because you give yourself permission to be silent. Silence can be a powerful tool. A quiet moment gives the audience time to process your information and indicates that something new is coming.

- **Do not apologize for nervousness or mistakes.** This takes attention away from your content. Just take a deep breath, regroup, and move ahead.

Present your visuals effectively

When presenting with visual aids, take cues from your visuals and avoid using note cards or a script. Reading from notes or a script does not build rapport with your audience. In addition, holding on to cards or paper prevents natural gestures and makes you look like a student in a speech class rather than a professional in a business setting. **Figure 11.27** on page 444 provides guidelines for how to present a visual effectively. If you need more memory cues than your visuals provide, try penciling notes on a flipchart or glancing discreetly at notes placed on a nearby table.

FIGURE 11.27 How to Present Your Visuals

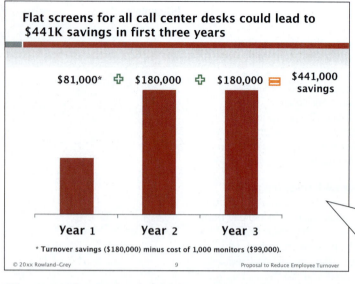

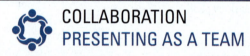

Introduce each visual by explaining your intended point as soon as the slide appears. For text slides, do not read the slide word for word. Instead, explain the purpose or main point of the slide, and then give the audience a few moments to look at the content before you launch into your discussion. For tables, identify how the information is organized and what appears in the columns and rows. For graphs, identify what the graph is depicting, what each axis is measuring, and the key point.

Sample Introduction

"If our pilot study shows that new monitors reduce turnover, we can save a substantial amount of money by implementing the screens throughout our call centers. Let's look at the anticipated savings over three years. As you can see from this graph, the screens will more than pay for themselves in the first year. Although we will spend $99,000 on the monitors, we anticipate saving $180,000 in turnover costs, leaving a benefit of $81,000 in the first year. In the following two years, we can save the full turnover cost, leading to a three-year savings of $441,000."

Direct attention to visuals with hand gestures and words. Visuals need your help to make a point. The best practice is to refer directly to material on a slide. You can move toward the side (but not turn your back on the audience), gesture to the screen, and direct your audience's attention with words: "As the left column shows…." If you place arrows and other highlighting marks directly on your slides, you can refer to those. Laser pointers help indicate a particular spot on the slide, but use them quickly to direct the audience's attention, and then turn them off.

COLLABORATION
PRESENTING AS A TEAM

Because a lot of work is team based, you can anticipate that many workplace presentations will be team based also. Presenting as a team is challenging, and the following guidelines will help:

- **Take advantage of everyone's strengths.** In a class, your instructor may require that everyone on your team participate equally in the presentation. However, in business, equal presenting time is not important. The only reason to plan a team presentation is to take advantage of each person's strengths and knowledge. Ensure that everyone who is presenting has a defined role in the presentation and that the team projects a unified and confident image. The whole should be greater than the sum of the parts.

- **Decide how you will handle introductions.** Will the first presenter introduce everyone at the beginning? Or will people introduce themselves? The difference may not seem to be significant, but unless you have planned introductions, team members may start talking over each other.

- **Practice transitions from person to person.** During team presentations, each speaker needs to make a connection between his or her content and the next speaker's. As you finish speaking, introduce the next speaker and topic, making that connection. For example, "Now that I've outlined the budget issues, Marla Whitt from IT will discuss implementation plans." These transitions help the audience follow the flow of your presentation.

- **Let your teammates speak.** If your teammate forgets to mention a point or presents material differently from the way you would explain it, do not interrupt to expand on the answer. Interrupting will damage the image of your team and undermine your teammate. Allow your teammate to finish. You can come back to the point later, if necessary.

- **Correct a teammate only when necessary.** If your teammate fumbles or says something wrong, do not immediately correct the error, especially if the point is not very important. If it is an important point that must be clarified, make the correction very politely and considerately.

- **Be prepared to present other teammates' slides.** Emergencies arise, and teammates may be late to a presentation or may not show up at all. Be sure that you are able to present every slide in the presentation in case you need to step in at the last moment.

For COLLABORATION exercises, go to Exercises 32, 33, and 34 on pages 464–465.

CULTURE
MEETING AUDIENCE EXPECTATIONS

If you have the opportunity to deliver a business presentation in a cross-cultural setting, you may need to adjust some of your presentation habits to meet audience expectations. The following examples illustrate some changes you may need to adopt:

FEATURE OF THE PRESENTATION	PRESENTING TO U.S. AUDIENCES	PRESENTING TO AUDIENCES FROM OTHER CULTURES
Introductions	After introducing themselves, presenters often go directly to the content of their presentation.	In more formal and more hierarchical cultures, politeness dictates that presenters acknowledge and thank the senior members of their audience for attending before beginning the presentation.
Speed	U.S. audiences often prefer a fast-paced presentation style that quickly gets to the point.	In Europe and Asia, audiences often prefer presentations that are slower and offer them an opportunity to think carefully and process information.
Body language	U.S. audiences appreciate lively presenters who use expressive body language.	In other cultures, presenters are more reserved and calm. To determine the appropriate use of hand gestures and expression, pay attention to other presenters from that culture. You can often find examples on YouTube and other media sites.
Eye contact	In the United States, presenters are trained to make eye contact with all members of the audience—and expect the audience to make eye contact in return.	In some Asian cultures, people are uncomfortable with direct eye contact and may look down or away rather than directly at the presenter. In these cultures, lack of eye contact may be a sign of respect.[26]
Vocabulary	When presenting to U.S. audiences, you can feel confident that people will understand your vocabulary if you use plain business language. Using synonyms for words will typically not confuse your audience.	Though many people in other cultures do speak English—or have learned English as a second or third language, you can help them understand you better by speaking slowly and clearly and by using relatively simple words—for example, avoid "ubiquitous" and instead say "widespread." Remember, too, that some words have different meanings in different cultures. For example, in the United States, if you talk about a "course" in school, you are referring to a specific class that you take for a semester or quarter. In the United Kingdom, a course refers to an entire program of study, similar to a major in the United States.
Humor	Making a joke is a common ice-breaking technique for Americans, especially at the beginning of a presentation, where humor can get the audience's attention and lift the mood.	Humor does not always translate well across cultural boundaries. For example, in China, while workplace humor is appropriate, language and cultural differences make it likely that American humor will not be understood.[27] In Japan, humor is rarely considered appropriate in the workplace.[28]
Reading the audience	In the United States, if audience members are nodding, that usually means they agree with the presenter. Presenters also look for smiles as signs of agreement.	In some cultures—for example, Japan—head nodding means only that the audience understands what the presenter is saying, not that they agree.[29] In some Eastern European cultures, such as the Russian culture, smiling is reserved for friends and relatives, people you know well.[30] Stony stares from an Eastern European audience may mean that they are paying attention, not that they are angry.

For CULTURE exercises, go to Critical Thinking Question 6 on page 459 and Exercise 24 on page 463.

Evaluate

Evaluate the audience's response

You'll have opportunities to evaluate audience response *before*, *during*, and *after* a presentation.

Before the presentation, practice in front of other people who will serve as a test audience. If you cannot assemble a practice audience, consider using a presentation feedback tool such as Podium (http://usepodium.com), which allows you to upload a video of yourself giving a presentation and invite specific people to leave time-stamped comments on the video with constructive feedback.

During the presentation, "listen" to the audience's feedback. Are they nodding in agreement with you or nodding off from boredom? Listening while you present can be challenging because you are also trying to think about what to say, navigate your slides, and maintain good eye contact. However, if you can gauge your audience's response as you are speaking, you have the opportunity to revise and adjust. One strategy you can use to "listen" while you present is to pause between sections. Scan the audience during transitions between slides or between major ideas. Do they seem attentive and interested? You can also ask questions. Ask only closed-ended questions that assess the audience's understanding unless you want to open the floor to a Q&A session during your presentation. For example, if you see someone looking confused, you could say, "I know this process is complicated. Would additional explanation help?"

After the presentation, reflect on your audience's overall response: Were there points in the presentation where the audience nodded in agreement? Did anything confuse or amuse the audience? Did you get the kinds of questions you expected? What surprised you? Could you have prevented any confusion or disagreement by presenting something differently? By answering these questions, you can evaluate your approach and your performance—and plan what to repeat or what to change the next time you present.

(SQ4) How do you handle questions and answers?

During a presentation, a question-and-answer (Q&A) session offers many benefits:

- Questions and answers increase audience engagement.
- As a presenter, you are likely to learn something important from questions, especially how well your audience understands your points.
- Questions give you a chance to emphasize and expand important points.
- An exchange with the audience helps build your credibility by demonstrating your expertise and openness.
- Skillful replies help you defuse criticism and objections.

impromptu speaking Speaking without advance knowledge of the topic or question.

Answering questions during a presentation is a form of **impromptu speaking**, speaking without advance knowledge of the topic or question. People often get nervous when they are required to speak spontaneously. This section offers advice about how to plan for a Q&A session and how to structure good answers to questions.

Plan for a question-and-answer (Q&A) session

Speakers often try to "wing" the Q&A portion of a presentation, but planning improves the chances that you will handle the Q&A well. During your planning process, decide how and when you will handle Q&A, anticipate questions and plan short answers, and make a plan for how your team will handle questions.

Decide how and when you will handle Q&A

Do you want to save questions until the end or invite the audience to ask questions as you go through the presentation? Whichever you choose, tell the audience what to expect in the introduction. When you're ready for questions, do not ask, "Are there any questions?" Instead, encourage participation by asking, "What questions do you have?"

Technology has also made it possible to collect questions throughout the course of the presentation to kick off the Q&A session at the end. For example, Google Slides allows viewers to submit questions via a link, where they can also vote for questions they'd like to see answered.[31] It is also be possible to use Twitter to create a **backchannel**—a networked

backchannel A networked conversation among audience members at a presentation.

conversation among audience members—that goes on simultaneously with your presentation.[32] By creating a hashtag for the presentation, then scrolling through the tweets with that hashtag afterward, you can see what questions have been asked. Of course, both these methods require that audience members use their phones or computers during the presentation. While some presenters may consider this form of engagement to be disrespectful, others recognize that these methods, when used well, can increase audience engagement.

Anticipate questions and plan short answers

Think in advance about questions your audience is likely to ask and draft a short answer in your head. When you anticipate questions and plan short answers, you avoid the temptation to ramble. Otherwise, you might talk aimlessly until you discover the point you want to make.

Decide how your team will handle questions

Without a plan, you run the risk of team members looking at each other blankly, waiting for someone else to answer. You also risk having multiple members trying to answer a question at the same time. Consider one of the following options for handling questions as a team. Both options depend on the team making a plan in advance about who will answer what kind of question:

- **Assign one team member to facilitate the Q&A session.** That team member will ask for questions and "assign" them to the team member designated to answer that kind of question. The facilitator may also answer questions but must be careful not to answer too many. Otherwise, he or she will seem to be claiming the spotlight.
- **Allow team members to decide whether a question falls under their designated area.** For this option to work well, the team member should not just launch into the answer. Instead, identify that you plan to answer it by saying, "I'll take that question." This signals to the rest of the team that the question is covered, and it prevents two people from beginning to answer at the same time.

Answer questions skillfully

It can be difficult to provide complete and relevant impromptu answers. The following advice will help you respond effectively.

Give a three-part answer

First, restate or summarize the question to be sure everyone heard it and that you understand it correctly. Repeating also gives you time to think of an answer. *Second,* begin your response with your main point. Otherwise, you may appear to be disorganized or evasive. *Finally,* follow up with details. As you answer, avoid looking only at the person who asked the question. Get the entire room involved in caring about—and understanding—your point. As you finish your answer, bring your eye contact back to the original questioner to signal that you have finished.

Break complex questions into parts

If you get a complex question that is difficult to answer, try breaking it into parts by listing the segments on a flipchart or whiteboard. Then answer each part separately, referring back to your list.

Be honest

If someone asks a question you cannot answer, don't be afraid to say "I don't know." Credibility disappears when a speaker gets caught making up an answer. Just admit that you need to find the answer and offer to follow up with the questioner after the presentation.

Avoid being defensive or dismissive

The following types of questions require especially skillful answers:

- **A hostile question.** If a questioner seems antagonistic, be careful not to become defensive. First, reframe the question, stating it in a way that seems less hostile and more objective. Then acknowledge the other person's position and try to identify the source of the objection. Work on creating a mutual understanding of the issue rather than trying to be right.

- **A question you plan to answer later.** If you plan to answer the question later, don't dismiss the question by saying "I'll get to that later." Instead, give the questioner a short answer immediately and then mention that more detail will follow. That should satisfy that person's need to know and keep him or her paying attention.

- **An idea that you've already rejected.** If someone raises an alternative you have already rejected, don't be too quick to dismiss the idea. The person could get defensive. Acknowledge the possible value of the alternative, and then explain objectively the reasoning that led you to reject it.

- **A question that takes the presentation off track.** If someone uses a question to try to take over the meeting, look for an opportunity to regain control of the discussion. Don't dismiss or insult the questioner by indicating that the question is irrelevant or off point. Instead, refer to the meeting agenda or the map of the presentation to get back on track.

How do you adapt your approach for online presentations?

Not all presentations are delivered face-to-face. In fact, with current advances in technology, you can take advantage of three different online modes to present to people who are not in the room with you:

- **Virtual presentation at an online meeting.** Given the expense of traveling and the ease of connecting with others through the Internet, you may be asked to present your material to distant audiences online using one of the many available online presentation tools, such as WebEx, Go To Meeting, Adobe Connect, or Skype for Business. Or you may choose to email a copy of your presentation deck to your audience or upload it to SlideShare so that your audience can access it during a telephone meeting.

- **Webinar, webcast, and other forms of live-streaming presentation.** A **webinar** is a web-based seminar that is broadcast over the Internet. Webinars have a live audience and are intended to be interactive. Like a webinar, a **webcast** is broadcast over the Internet to an audience who logs in or registers for that event, but a webcast is typically not interactive. It is a one-way communication. Although webinars and webcasts are originally delivered to a live audience over the Internet, they may be recorded and archived for future use. At that point, they resemble a podcast. Other forms of live-streaming presentations may be publicly available through Facebook, Periscope, and livestream.com. The advantage of these tools is that they allow for comments and can be interactive.

- **An audio or video podcast.** In contrast to a webcast, which has a live (although distant) audience, a **podcast** is recorded without an audience, posted on a website or a social media site such as YouTube or Vimeo, and distributed through website or social media links. Podcasts can be played online through streaming media or can be downloaded and played from your own computer or mobile device.

Delivering presentations in these three online modes presents a different set of challenges than presenting in person in a small meeting or larger group setting. You need to address each of these challenges to be a successful online presenter to a live audience or through a podcast.

In a live online presentation, manage the audience experience

When you present your material at an online meeting, you need to ensure that your audience is engaged and understands. You cannot rely on visual—or verbal—feedback, and you need to be proactive in managing the audience's needs. To run a successful webinar or online meeting, use the guidelines in **Figure 11.28**.

webinar An interactive web-based seminar that is broadcast over the Internet to a live audience.

webcast A web-based presentation or program that is broadcast over the Internet to a live audience but is not interactive.

podcast An audio or video presentation or program that is recorded without an audience, posted on a website or a social media site such as YouTube or Vimeo, and distributed through links.

FIGURE 11.28 How to Present Effectively Online

WHEN PRESENTING ONLINE	
DO:	**DON'T:**
Do ensure your audience has voice and visual connectivity. When you deliver a presentation online, you need to confirm with your audience that they are connected and can see the presentation. Did they get the link you sent them? Can they log on to any special software you are using? Wait for them to confirm they can see your presentation slides on their own screen before you begin. Whether you use a traditional land-line service or Internet-based telephony such as Skype or Google Talk, establish your voice connection before you have your audience look at the presentation slides.	**Don't struggle with faulty equipment or a bad connection.** Online presentations are like phone calls, so good phone etiquette applies. This means you need a good connection and good equipment so your audience can hear you. Speaker-phones can work if you want to be hands-free, but you may hear occasional static. Good headsets can also work, but test them first.
Do open the meeting early. An early start will allow those new to the technology to become familiar with the interface while they wait and will also give you time to provide a brief welcome. Include a welcome slide that confirms meeting details and displays your picture, and help establish rapport with the audience.	**Don't jump right into your planned content.** Audiences can easily get lost in online presentations if you do not give them time to settle themselves at their computers and get used to your voice.
Do control what your audience sees. Some online presentation software allows you to "share your screen," which means the audience sees on their screen exactly what's on your screen. As the presenter, you can control what they see and move forward from slide to slide at the pace you want. In this case, the online presentation resembles an in-person meeting, which is ideal, because it means your audience will focus on what you want them to see.	**Don't allow your audience to flip ahead.** If you are not sharing your screen but instead are relying on your audience to view a copy of your presentation on their own computers, provide direction about where you are in the presentation. For example, you can say, *"Here on slide 3, you can see . . . On the next slide, slide 4 . . . ."* For this reason, it is important to remember to number your slides. If you direct the audience to the specific slide number, they are less likely to click ahead (or lag behind) in the presentation.
Do engage the audience with your voice, pace, and screen motion. Although you cannot communicate with body language in an online presentation, you can engage the audience with excellent vocal delivery. To further engage the audience, plan for motion on the screen. Provide annotations on slides or use pointers to draw your audience's attention. And to facilitate a lively pace, divide your slide material into smaller chunks and change slides frequently.	**Don't dwell too long on one slide.** The medium changes the audience's expectation of the pace, so be sure to move quickly to keep the audience's attention. For example, if you want to discuss a long quotation, don't put the full quotation on one slide and expect your audience to read it. Instead, break it into several slides and read it to your audience, modulating your voice to emphasize important words and pausing before the final point.[33]
Do invite questions frequently. Ask for specific questions after each major point to ensure understanding. For webinars, build in additional opportunities for audience interaction, such as polls, if your software supports that function.	**Don't hold questions until the end.** When you make an online presentation, you can't get visual feedback from your audience. As a result, it's important to hear from them frequently. If the audience remains silent, you may not know if they are confused or if they have fallen asleep.

In a podcast, provide content that offers lasting value

If you develop good presenting skills, you may have the opportunity to create podcasts for your company. Both big and small organizations take advantage of podcasting as a way to make presentations available when the audience has time to pay attention. Listeners can download audio podcasts to MP3 players to enjoy while driving or exercising. Viewers can download video podcasts to watch on tablets or smartphones. Because podcasts are so versatile, the audience for them is growing.[34]

Some organizations use podcasts to substitute for newsletters or marketing materials for external audiences. Organizations also use podcasting for internal communication to update and engage employees on company or industry news.[35]

Podcasts can take many forms: Some are interviews, others are panel discussions, and many sound like radio shows. However, many podcasts resemble presentations, with one person offering engaging and relevant material for 10 to 20 minutes. If you become involved in podcasting, here are some guidelines to follow:

- **Choose the best medium for your audience, content, and purpose.** If you are podcasting about something with a strong visual component, choose a video podcast. Otherwise, an audio podcast may be more versatile and less expensive to produce.
- **Commit to a regular schedule so listeners will know when to expect your content.** Unlike a webinar or webcast, good podcasts are not one-time events. Gain a following by producing them weekly or monthly.
- **Choose content that will be relevant for a long time.** The audio and video files will be available on the web long after you first release them. Provide content that users will find useful in the future.
- **Make your podcasts easy to find.** Provide links to your podcasts through email, social media, and websites.
- **Write a script and practice.** A podcast is not an opportunity to improvise. It is an opportunity to compose content that will provide value to your audience and motivate them to return for more.

■ In summary,

business presentations offer you the opportunity to address a business issue and to impress your audience with your analytic, persuasive, and speaking skills. Using the ACE communication process helps you develop well-organized content that is targeted to your audience and appropriate for the medium you choose, whether it is presented in person or online. To communicate that content well, design effective slides and practice both your delivery skills and the specific presentation so that you know how to make each point and present each slide. Building a confident and professional presentation style offers benefits beyond just improving your business presentations. Being a confident presenter will also help you sell your strengths during job interviews and increase your chances for promotion to leadership positions.

elevator pitch A concise statement designed to communicate the value of an idea, a product, or a job candidate; intrigue the audience; and initiate a deeper conversation.

PRESENTATIONS @ WORK SwipeSense

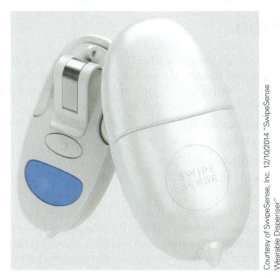

Courtesy of SwipeSense, Inc. 12/10/2014 "SwipeSense Wearable Dispenser"

Solid Model Drawing of SwipeSense

Muge Iseri, 12/6/2014 "Turkiye Inovasyon Haftasi: Turk Muctier"

Mert Iseri Delivering an Investor Presentation

Within the first five years after graduating college, Mert Iseri and Yuri Malina—the CEO and COO of SwipeSense—had achieved the kind of success that most young entrepreneurs only dream of. Their company was a finalist in the 2013 *Wall Street Journal* Startup of the Year competition. They had been featured in the *Harvard Business Review*, *Wall Street Journal*, and *Chicago Tribune*, and they had signed their first big customer, a major hospital network. They had also raised over $12 million in investor money. What accounts for their success?

First, they have an innovative product that meets a need. SwipeSense is "hand-washing 2.0"—a hand-sanitation device that medical professionals clip on their scrubs and swipe to dispense hand sanitizer. Combined with real-time data analytics, SwipeSense drastically increases hand hygiene in hospitals and reduces hospital-acquired infections.

But to achieve this success, they also had to spend a lot of time in front of people, delivering presentations. Iseri and Malina made investment pitches to potential funders, sales presentations to medical professionals and hospital executives, and conference presentations to other entrepreneurs and designers. They have even developed a 60-second **elevator pitch** that they can deliver to anyone at any time.

Based on their experience, they offer the following advice to all presenters.

- **Know your purpose.** Different presentations have different purposes. "In a sales presentation we're highlighting SwipeSense as a company and a product. In an investor presentation, the entrepreneur is the star of the show." These two purposes require different approaches.
- **Know your audience.** The presentation needs to resonate with the specific audience, so it's good to do a little homework in advance. Different people care about different things. "If there are a lot of chief financial officers in the room, then the presentation has to focus on the financial piece, including cost savings. If we are presenting to chief nursing officers, then it's important to discuss clinical acceptance and the implementation cycle."

- **Arrive early.** Iseri says he always arrives early to a presentation, shakes hands with as many people as he can, and gives them a summary of the presentation in advance. This tactic serves two purposes. First, he can see what people respond to and tailor his presentation to resonate with their concerns. Second, this initial conversation primes people to remember when they hear his message for a second time during the presentation.
- **Be adaptable.** Because you're never certain what will interest the audience, you need to be flexible and adaptable. Iseri says he may come into a presentation with six things he can talk about. But, as he talks about the first two points, he pays attention to the audience's body language and their eye contact. He says, "Those kinds of visual cues inform me which of the remaining four ideas I should share with the group."
- **Be confident but humble.** Especially in an investor pitch, "you need to convince the person sitting on the other side of the table that your team—and only your team—are the perfect people to execute this business idea." To get investors to believe in you, you need to be confident, look people in the eye, and be clear about how you will achieve your goals. But "you also need to be a bit humble. No one likes people who are full of themselves."
- **Be credible.** To be persuasive in a presentation, you need to convince your audience you know what you are talking about, and that means you need solid sources to back up your claims. Iseri says, "There needs to be some third-party validation of the claims you are making. People will call you out if they don't believe you, and it's tough to respond if you don't have evidence. In addition to citing studies in a footnote, sometimes we will actually have the scientific paper with us, with key evidence highlighted. In the presentation, I'll pull out the study, put it in front of the audience, and show them the highlighted paragraph. No one reads the study, but I've made a statement that I've done my homework. People get the message that I am credible, and at that point the conversation is easier."

Source: Based on an interview with Mert Iseri.

Culinary Adventure Tour Presentation

This case scenario will help you review the chapter material by applying it to a specific situation.

Planning a Presentation

Stephanie Lo graduated from college with a major in French and a minor in communication. She was very happy to get a job with JourneyFree, LLC, a company that specializes in organizing educational tours for students, professionals, and other groups. Ultimately, Stephanie would like to become a tour leader, but for now she is the assistant to the vice president of Tour Operations, Rachel Jones. Stephanie's role is to work on marketing communications.

Stephanie's first project required that she use all her strengths—developing communications to market JourneyFree's newest product, a culinary tour of France, specifically designed for culinary arts and nutrition teachers in high schools and trade schools. In addition to advertising online and sending brochures to high schools, Stephanie's supervisor, Rachel, plans to visit school districts in major cities and present the program to superintendents, principals, department chairs, and teachers. She will give a brief and colorful slide presentation and offer samplings of the French food that culinary arts teachers will experience on the tour.

Thirty culinary arts teachers have invited Rachel to give a presentation next week, so she needs a slide presentation fast. She asks Stephanie to design and develop a draft of the presentation. Together they work out the following outline:

- The Educational Experience
- Trip Overview
- Trip Logistics and Costs
- About JourneyFree, LLC
- Q&A

Rachel and Stephanie also discuss the audience and key selling points to make in the presentation. The next day, Stephanie puts together a draft of presentation slides. She is planning to meet Rachel to review the slides and to discuss the talking points that will go with the slides.

Stephanie would like your help in analyzing the audience, evaluating the presentation, and composing the content for the presentation. After the slides, you will find questions designed to help you think systematically about the presentation, using the ACE approach. Answer the questions to review the key concepts in the chapter.

Slide 3

Today's Itinerary

- The Educational Experience

- Trip Overview

- Trip Logistics and Costs

- About JourneyFree, LLC

- Q & A

Slide 4

The Educational Experience
Why do teachers need this trip?

- Expand teachers' cultural knowledge base

- Spark creativity

- Inspire new courses

- Refresh aging culinary school curriculum

Slide 5

The "Educational Vacation" Experience

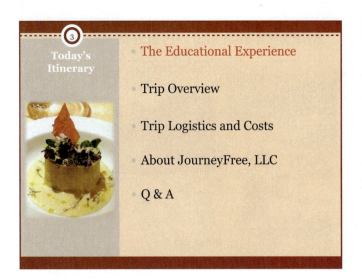

- Seminars

- Cooking sessions with professionals

- Restaurant visits and discussions with chefs

- Rich, insightful culinary experiences

Slide 6

Today's Itinerary

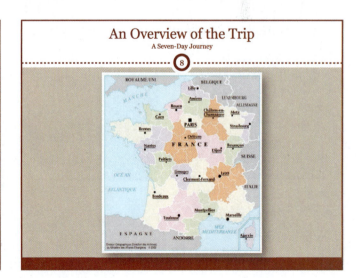

- The Educational Experience

- Trip Overview

- Trip Logistics and Costs

- About JourneyFree, LLC

- Q & A

Slide 7

Why France?

- The cooking capital of the world
- Each region offers new culinary wonders
- Less costly than one might think

"A journey through France is a journey of discovery. The French are passionate about food, and the cuisine of each province has its own distinctive style and its own unique pleasures."
-Laurent Duquette

Slide 8

An Overview of the Trip
A Seven-Day Journey

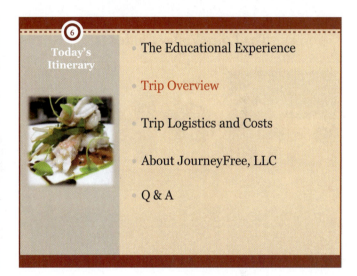

Paris and the Cordon Bleu
9

Brittany's Fish Markets and Pastry Shops
10

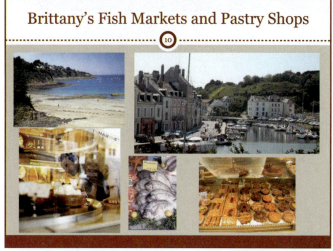

The Loire Valley Chateaus
11

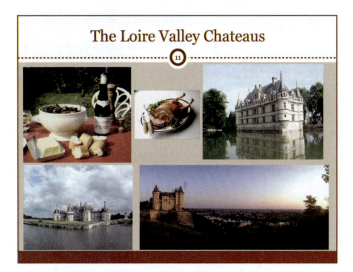

The Bordeaux Region and Its Vineyards
12

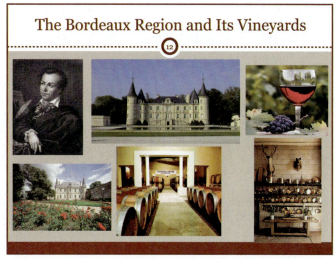

The Markets of Marseille and Gastronomy of Provence
13

14

Today's Itinerary

- The Educational Experience
- Trip Overview
- Trip Logistics and Costs
- About JourneyFree, LLC
- Q & A

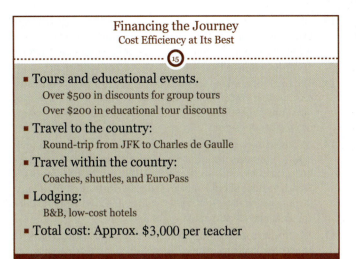

Financing the Journey
Cost Efficiency at Its Best
15

- **Tours and educational events.**
  - Over $500 in discounts for group tours
  - Over $200 in educational tour discounts
- **Travel to the country:**
  - Round-trip from JFK to Charles de Gaulle
- **Travel within the country:**
  - Coaches, shuttles, and EuroPass
- **Lodging:**
  - B&B, low-cost hotels
- **Total cost: Approx. $3,000 per teacher**

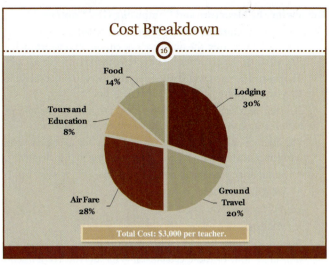

Cost Breakdown
16

Food 14%
Lodging 30%
Tours and Education 8%
Ground Travel 20%
Air Fare 28%

Total Cost: $3,000 per teacher.

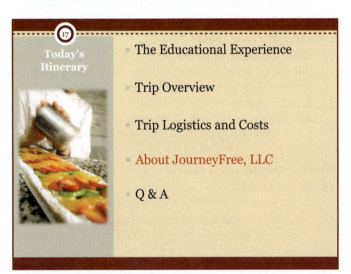

17

Today's Itinerary

- The Educational Experience
- Trip Overview
- Trip Logistics and Costs
- About JourneyFree, LLC
- Q & A

About JourneyFree
Why us?
18

- **Solid reputation, strong financials**
  - 24 years in the industry
  - $46 million in annual revenue last year
  - Publicly traded, privately run

- **A wide array of travel experiences**
  - Many destinations served
  - Partnerships with local touring agencies

- **A personal touch**
  - The Corporate Rewards program
  - Private agencies around the world

Questions?

Questions for Reviewing the Culinary Adventure Tour Presentation

Analyzing Purpose and Audience

1. What is the purpose of this presentation? Is it primarily informative or persuasive?

2. The ideal outcome of the presentation is that teachers sign up for the trip—or schools fund teachers for the trip. Should the slides end by asking for a "sale"? Or should the presenter do that orally? Or should the presenter leave the audience to think about the content and follow up later to sign up?

3. Imagine yourself as the target audience: high school teachers and administrators. What questions do you think they will have? Does this presentation leave any important questions unanswered?

Reviewing the Structure and Composing Oral Content

4. The slides themselves do not begin with a compelling opening designed to capture the audience's attention. Brainstorm what Rachel could say as she begins her presentation.

5. The presentation is divided into five parts. Do you think this is an effective structure? If so, why? If not, why not?

6. Between each section of the presentation, a transition slide appears to indicate the new section. Are the transition slides effective?

7. The end of the presentation simply asks for questions and answers. Consider the advice for endings given in this chapter:
   - Summarize your main message.
   - Visualize the outcome for the audience.
   - Ask for what you want.
   - Make next steps clear.

   Brainstorm what Rachel could say at the end of the presentation in all four of these categories. What do you recommend that she say?

Evaluating the Presentation Slides

8. This presentation is not designed to stand alone. It needs a presenter. In this case, would a stand-alone presentation be a good or bad idea? Explain your answer. Should Rachel bring handouts, brochures, or other written material to leave behind?

9. This presentation uses a consistent visual style and template. In your opinion, does it work well with this presentation? If so, why? If not, why not?

10. This presentation includes a number of bullet-point slides. Are the bullet points parallel? Are any slides too crowded? Are there any slides you would recommend revising?

11. This presentation includes only one data graphic: the pie chart on slide 16. Is that pie chart appropriate and easy to read? If so, what makes it effective? If not, how would you revise it?

12. Slides 9 through 13 present attractive pictures of the areas of France that the tour will visit. To be effective, the pictures should be similar. All the headlines mention some food- or beverage-related term—except for one headline. How could you revise that headline?

13. The final slide, asking for questions, features a picture of pastry. Assume that you'd like a picture that will help spark interesting questions. What picture(s) or text could the slide contain, instead of a picture of pastry?

14. As Stephanie evaluates whether the slides will be easy to present, she considers using animation on various slides. Perhaps the bullets should come up one by one. Perhaps the pictures of the French regions should appear gradually, instead of all at once. Identify which slides—if any—would be effective if they revealed content gradually rather than all at once.

15. As a final step in reviewing, Stephanie should proofread all slides for correctness and consistency. Consider typing errors, spelling, font size, consistent punctuation, consistent heading sizes, and consistent bullet points. Do you see anything that needs to be changed?

Delivering the Presentation

16. Slides 9 through 13 include no text. Rachel will need to talk through the key points on these slides. What kinds of information should she provide when she projects these slides?

17. Rachel intends to serve regional food at this presentation. Should she serve it at the beginning of the presentation? At the end? Or as she discusses each region? What is the rationale for your answer?

Handling Questions and Answers

18. Should Rachel plan to take questions throughout the presentation or just at the end? What is the rationale for your answer?

19. What questions should Rachel anticipate? Should she address any of those questions in the presentation itself?

Study Questions in Review

 SQ1 **What do you analyze when planning a business presentation?** *(pages 414–418)*

- **Analyze your purpose and desired outcome: Why are you presenting?** What do you want to have happen as the outcome of the presentation? Do you want your audience to know something (informational presentation), believe or do something (persuasive presentation), know how to do something (instructional presentation), or work with you during the presentation (collaborative presentation)?
- **Analyze your audience: Who will be listening, and what do they care about?** By understanding what motivates your audience, you can frame your presentation so that they will care.
- **Analyze your message: What will you say to achieve your desired outcome?** What is the main idea you would like your audience to remember from your presentation? That is your message. Be sure to phrase it in a way that will be meaningful to the audience.
- **Analyze your setting: Where and for how long will you present?** Plan to make your presentation short and concise. Consider any constraints or opportunities your setting offers.
- **Analyze your medium options: How will you deliver your message?** Identify the medium choices that best fit your needs (and your audience's). Possibilities include slides, handouts, video, audio, podcasts, flipcharts, posters, whiteboards, and props.

 SQ2 **How do you compose the presentation?** *(pages 419–441)*

- **Organize the content.** Think of the content as having three acts. Compose an opening that engages the audience, organize the middle of the presentation to be easy to understand, and compose a memorable conclusion.
- **Identify the role that slides will play.** Will your slides need to speak for themselves in a stand-alone presentation? Or will they serve only as visual aids that a speaker must explain? Stand-alone slides typically use message headlines and more complete content support than visual aid slides.
- **Create a storyboard** before writing detailed slides. A storyboard helps you take the organization you developed and create a story flow.
- **Develop a template.** Choose a simple slide design that will not compete with your content, and create a master slide that uses a consistent set of fonts and design features.
- **Design individual slides** to be easy to understand at a glance. Slides will be more effective if they are not crowded with content. Text can be presented in grammatically parallel bullet points, in text boxes, or in shapes. Diagrams should effectively show relationships. Data slides should make their point clearly. Animations should facilitate the presentation rather than make it more cumbersome.

- **Evaluate your slides in a practice session.** If a slide is not easy to present, redesign it. Determine whether animations will help or hinder your presentation.
- **Create effective handouts.** Select a format that best fits your purpose and your audience's needs.

 SQ3 **How do you deliver and evaluate the presentation?** *(pages 441–446)*

- **Set the stage** for a great presentation by warming up before the presentation and by dressing for the part. Arrive early to ensure that all equipment is functioning and to begin establishing rapport with your audience as they arrive.
- **Control your body.** Stand comfortably and confidently, use engaging body language, maintain eye contact with your audience, and smile.
- **Use your voice effectively.** Control your volume by speaking to the back of the room. Speak clearly, enunciate your words, use your voice to emphasize key ideas, and pause (or keep silent) as you are thinking rather than fill the air with "ers" and "ums."
- **Present your visuals effectively.** Introduce each visual by explaining your point, direct attention to visuals with gestures and words, and use visuals as cues rather than referring to note cards or scripts.
- **Evaluate the audience's response** by "listening" to the audience's nonverbal feedback.

 SQ4 **How do you handle questions and answers?** *(pages 446–448)*

- **Plan for a question-and-answer (Q&A) session.** Decide how and when you will handle Q&A, anticipate questions and plan short answers, and make a plan for how your team will handle questions.
- **Answer questions skillfully** using a three-part structure: repeat the question, give a short direct answer, and then provide details. Be prepared for challenging questions and plan strategies in advance.

SQ5 **How do you adapt your approach for online presentations?** *(pages 448–450)*

- **In a live online presentation, manage the audience experience.** Ensure that you and your audience have good Internet connectivity, control what the audience sees, open the meeting early, engage the audience, and invite questions frequently.
- **In a podcast, provide content that offers lasting value** and will keep the audience returning for more.

Visual Summary

ANALYZE	COMPOSE	DELIVER AND EVALUATE

ANALYZE

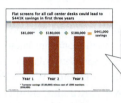

- What outcome do you want from this presentation?
- Who is your audience, and what do they need to know?
- What is your main message?
- How do you need to adapt to the setting?
- What medium options should you use: slides, a flipchart, whiteboard, video clips, handouts, props?

Radius Images/Getty Images

COMPOSE

- If you are composing slides, should they be able to stand alone, or are they visual aids?
- How should you organize the presentation—beginning, middle, and end?

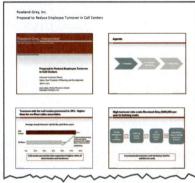

- How do you design individual slides to be clear and easy to understand?
- What handouts do you need?

DELIVER AND EVALUATE

Evaluate while you practice:

- Practice your opening: Is it smooth?
- Practice presenting each slide: If a slide is hard to present, revise it.

- Practice your delivery: Are you speaking loud enough for your audience to hear? Are you comfortable standing in the front of the room?
- Practice coordinating with your team: How will you transition from one person to the next?
- Practice questions and answers: Have you anticipated questions? Did you remember the guidelines for answering questions?

Evaluate while you deliver:

- During the presentation, "listen" to the audience's verbal and nonverbal feedback and adjust your presentation to meet their needs.
- After the presentation, reflect on your audience's overall response and plan what to repeat or change the next time you present.

Key Terms

Anecdote p. 420
Animations p. 433
Backchannel p. 446
Bullet point p. 429
Elevator pitch p. 451

Icon p. 431
Impromptu speaking
p. 446
Message headline p. 423
Podcast p. 448

Slide deck p. 423
Slide master p. 426
Stand-alone presentation
p. 423
Storyboard p. 424

Topic headline p. 423
Visual aid presentation
p. 423
Webcast p. 448
Webinar p. 448

MyLab Business Communication

If your instructor is using MyLab Business Communication, go to **www.pearson.com/ mylab/business-communication** to complete the problems marked with this icon ⭐.

Review Questions

1 Describe the difference between a persuasive presentation and a collaborative presentation.

⭐ **2** What are two elements of "setting" that affect how you plan to present?

⭐ **3** In addition to slides, what other communication tools can you use during a presentation?

4 What is the main difference between a visual aid presentation and a stand-alone presentation?

⭐ **5** What are the main goals of a presentation opening?

6 Name three recognizable patterns you can use to organize a presentation.

7 Name three guidelines to follow when choosing or designing a slide template.

8 What are verbal tics? Provide two examples.

9 What three things should you do when answering a question in a presentation?

10 What are the differences among a webinar, a webcast, and a podcast?

Critical Thinking Questions

⭐ **1** Research has shown that public speaking ability is a key predictor of career success. Why do you think this is the case?

2 Why is it important that you identify the outcome you want from a presentation before you begin composing it?

3 You are making a sales presentation and brought a few examples of the product you are selling to share with the audience. You wonder whether there is any advantage to having images of the product in a slideshow presentation as well. What would be the advantage of having projected images in addition to examples of the product to pass around?

4 You are giving a presentation proposing that your company *gamify* software training for all new employees in finance. Your audience consists of executives in both finance and informational technology. As you imagine your audience analysis, what relevant characteristics would the two groups of executives have in common? What are some key differences you would need to account for in your presentation?

5 During a presentation's question-and-answer session, it is a good practice to repeat a question to the entire audience before you

answer it. Name at least three advantages you gain by repeating a question.

6 If you are presenting to people in a different culture, how can you learn about that culture's preferences and expectations? **[Related to the Culture feature on page 445]**

⭐ **7** How would you describe the key differences between a business presentation and a speech? Why do you think presentations are more common than speeches in business?

8 You have a teammate who is a poor presenter. That person is required to participate in a class presentation. What are some options to ensure a valuable contribution from that presenter?

9 What are the advantages and disadvantages of animating bullet lists on slides?

10 You are presenting quarterly financial results at a meeting. You need to decide whether to present the key figures in a handout that the audience can look at as you present, to project the key figures on slides, or do both. What are the pros and cons of each option? What would you decide?

Key Concept Exercises

 What do you analyze when planning a business presentation? *(pages 414–418)*

1 Analyze your purpose and desired outcome: Why are you presenting?

For each of the following scenarios, determine the purpose and intended outcome of the presentation.

a. A presentation to a group of potential customers explaining various types of investment instruments

b. A presentation to a group of potential customers explaining why they should use your company as an investment firm

c. A presentation to your supervisor explaining how to implement a process you have developed

2 Analyze your audience: Who will be listening, and what do they care about?

Select one of the following scenarios and identify a real person who could be the audience. For your chosen scenario, answer the audience analysis questions as shown in Figure 11.2 for the specific audience you identified. Be sure the audience is someone you know.

a. A professor you know well is the executive director of your school's Young Entrepreneurs Club. You and a few of your classmates have an idea for an entrepreneurial business you would like the club to fund. Funding is competitive, and this professor makes the funding decisions. Identify your entrepreneurial idea, and analyze this professor as your audience.

b. Your family members or friends are debating where to go for a group vacation. The group decided that each person with a preferred location would develop a brief presentation to persuade the others. Identify your preferred location and specific audience members, and answer the audience analysis questions as shown in Figure 11.2 for the specific audience members you identified.

c. Your business communication class is planning a fundraiser and is in the process of planning where to donate the money. Your instructor invites members of the class to give a persuasive presentation, proposing a specific charitable organization. Using the questions in Figure 11.2, analyze your instructor and classmates as your audience.

3 Analyze your message: What will you say to achieve your desired outcome?

For each of the scenarios in Exercise 2, write a main message that meets the criteria for a main message listed on pages 416-417.

4 Analyze your setting: Where and for long will you present?

Prepare a written response for each of the following scenarios:

a. You are planning to give a presentation in the same setting where you hold your business communication class or some other specific classroom at your school. What key features of that setting should you keep in mind as you plan your presentation?

b. Now assume that you are planning to give the same presentation over the Internet (via WebEx or some other technology), with each person looking at your slides on his or her own computer and listening to you via telephone. What are some key differences between this setting and the classroom setting? What will you do differently as you prepare your presentation?

c. Imagine that instead of giving your presentation live, you will be video-recording it and posting it as a video podcast on YouTube,

Vimeo, or some other site for people to watch at their convenience. What will you do differently for that setting?

d. Now imagine that instead of video-recording your presentation, you will simply be posting your presentation slides for people to read. What will you do differently for that setting?

5 Analyze your medium options: How will you deliver your message?

For each of the scenarios in Exercise 2, explain which medium option(s) you would use and why. Also explain which medium options would not be appropriate and why.

 How do you compose the presentation? *(pages 419–441)*

6 Organize the content: Planning an opening

Select one of the scenarios in Exercise 2 and plan two different openings, using two of the following four techniques:

a. Cite a surprising fact or statistic.

b. Tell a relevant story or anecdote.

c. Quote an expert, someone well known, or a familiar saying.

d. Ask a question.

7 Organize the content: Planning your structure

For each of the options in Exercise 1 (repeated here), how would you organize the content of the presentation? What recognizable pattern would you use?

a. A presentation to a group of potential customers explaining various types of investment instruments

b. A presentation to a group of potential customers explaining why they should use your company as an investment firm

c. A presentation to your supervisor explaining how to implement a process you have developed

8 Organize the content: Planning your ending

For each of the options in Exercise 1 (Analyze your purpose and desired outcome: Why are you presenting?) and Exercise 2 (Analyze your audience: Who will be listening, and what do they care about?), choose one or more of the following options as an appropriate ending. How would you justify your decision?

- Summarize your main message.
- Visualize the outcome for the audience.
- Ask for what you want.
- Make the next steps clear.

9 Identify the role that slides will play

Conduct an Internet search with the advanced search function of Google, Bing, or some other search engine, looking specifically for PowerPoint files. Find a slide deck and identify whether the slides are easy to understand on their own or whether they require a presenter. Identify at least one slide from the deck to share with your class in order to support your evaluation.

10 Create a storyboard

A prospective employer has asked you to submit a slide deck along with your application. In five slides, you are to demonstrate why you are a good candidate for the job. Prepare a storyboard for this slide deck. The storyboard will consist of five rectangles, each representing a slide. For each "slide," write a clear headline and sketch the content of the slide body—or write notes about what you will include.

11 Develop a template

a. Many sites on the web offer downloadable PowerPoint templates. Conduct a search using the terms "PowerPoint templates," and find at least one template that you believe would be appropriate for a business presentation and one that you believe is not appropriate. Be prepared to share your findings with the class.

b. Select a template that you believe is acceptable and create an alternative version of that template by changing key features on the slide master. Change the size ratio of the slide, the font styles, the font sizes, the shape of bullets, and the colors. Compare the two versions and write a memo to your instructor explaining which version you like best and why.

12 Design individual slides

a. Select one slide from your storyboard in Exercise 10 and design two versions of the slide: one that uses bullets and one that does not.

b. The first slide below offers four communication recommendations. Write a message headline for this slide and then suggest changes to follow the visual design principles of consistency, repetition, alignment, and proximity.

c. The second slide below describes the target market of the grocery store chain Trader Joe's. What changes would you make in the design and wording of this slide? In addition, proofread the slide and fix any errors.

Accompanies Exercise 12b

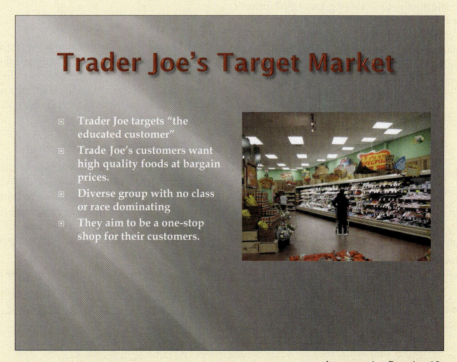

Accompanies Exercise 12c

13 Avoiding plagiarism in slide design [Related to the Ethics feature on page 438]

The following questions relate to the Trader Joe's slide in Exercise 12c.

a. The slide uses a picture of Trader Joe's found on the website Wikimedia Commons. The photographer and picture owner is Sage Ross. Under the picture, the website includes this licensing notice:

> I, the copyright holder of this work, hereby release it into the public domain. This applies worldwide. In case this is not legally possible, I grant anyone the right to use this work for any purpose, without any conditions, unless such conditions are required by law.

Is it legal and ethical to use this picture in a presentation? Is a citation required?

b. The first bullet in the slide includes a quotation that came from an article published in the *Seattle Times* on August 30, 2013: "Trader Joe's Targets 'Educated Buyers.'" The article was quoting the founder of Trader Joe's, Joe Coulombe. How would you cite this information in your presentation?

c. The template of this presentation is one of the many offered in PowerPoint. Would it be considered plagiarism to use this template?

Summarize your answers to these questions in a memo to your instructor.

14 Evaluate your slides in a practice session

a. Review the JourneyFree culinary tour presentation in the Case Scenario on pages 452–456. Imagine yourself presenting slides 7, 15, 16, and 18. Your job will be to present these slides without simply reading the bullet points. Select two of these slides and write a "script" of what you would say. Consider whether you would change these slides in any way to make them easier to present.

b. Publicly traded companies typically make their investor presentations available on their websites. These presentations are created as slides, which are often saved as PDF files. Go to the websites of the companies in the following list to find investor presentations, or search the Internet to find an investor presentation from any other company that interests you. (Hint: Use a search engine and type in "Investor presentations [company name].") You may have to explore the company websites to find these presentations.

- eBay
- General Electric
- Google
- IBM
- Johnson & Johnson
- JPMorgan Chase & Co.
- McDonald's
- Microsoft
- Verizon
- Walmart
- Wells Fargo

Select a brief presentation of 10 to 15 slides, or select a portion of a longer presentation. Review and analyze the selected slides, answering the following questions:

- Do the slides follow the principles of good slides presented in this chapter? Describe how the slides do or do not follow these principles.
- Can you read and understand the slides as an independent document without a speaker? Why or why not?

Make sure you attach the presentation to your answers.

15 Create effective handouts

Refer to Exercise 1 on page 460. For each of the scenarios, decide which handout format would best support the presentation. Identify the pros and cons for each of the following options: slide miniatures, slides with notes pages, or handouts with supplementary information. Summarize your explanation in a memo to your instructor.

16 Using Prezi for business presentations [Related to the Technology feature on pages 440–441]

You want to prepare either the Rowland-Grey presentation (Figure 11.20) or the JourneyFree presentation (pages 452–455) as a Prezi. Depending on what your instructor directs, either sketch the "zoomed out" canvas for the presentation or find an appropriate Prezi template online. Then write a one-page memo to your instructor to accompany the visual, discussing the pros and cons of using Prezi for this presentation versus PowerPoint.

 How do you deliver and evaluate the presentation? *(pages 441–446)*

17 Set the stage

Think about the last slide presentation you delivered, either in a class or at your job. Explain how you used the following presentation techniques to set the stage for your presentation: practice, dress for the part, arrive early and warm up, set up all equipment and props, decide where you will stand, keep the lights on so that attention is on you, and have water available. If you didn't use a technique, explain why not or whether it would have improved your presentation experience.

18 Control your body

Many people are not aware of the body movements they make during a presentation. Use a webcam or video camera to record yourself making one of the impromptu presentations in Exercise 34. Play the recording and evaluate your body language, eye contact, and facial expressions. Summarize your evaluation in a memo to your instructor.

19 Use your voice effectively

Refer to Exercise 17. Evaluate your presentation recording based on the techniques outlined in this section. Did you speak to the back of the room? Did you speak slowly, especially at the beginning of the presentation? Did you modulate your voice and minimize verbal tics? Did you use pauses instead of "ers" and "ums"? Summarize your evaluation in a memo to your instructor.

20 Present your visuals effectively

Watch a video of a business-related presentation you find online. You can find videos at Ted.com and on YouTube. Search for the name of a company that interests you or just browse to find one. Select a video in which the presenter uses projected visuals. In a memo to your instructor, identify the URL of the video and summarize your evaluation of the presentation based on following criteria:

Did the presenter:

- Introduce each visual by explaining the intended point?
- Direct attention to visuals with hand gestures and words?
- Take cues from the visual aids rather than using note cards or a script?
- Avoid apologies for nervousness or mistakes?

21 Evaluate the audience's response

Attend a presentation on campus or in your community, or watch a presentation on YouTube that frequently cuts to images of the audience. Pay attention to the audience and evaluate their responses. What signs do you see that the audience is engaged? What signs do you see that the audience is bored? Summarize your observations in an email to your instructor or be prepared to discuss them in class.

 How do you handle questions and answers?
(pages 446–448)

22 Plan for a question-and-answer (Q&A) session

a. Review the Rowland-Grey presentation in Figure 11.24. What questions should you anticipate from the audience?

b. Review the JourneyFree culinary tour presentation in the Case Scenario on pages 452–456. What questions should you anticipate from the audience?

c. For each of the presentations in a and b, would you recommend that the presenters invite questions at any time or ask the audience to hold questions until the end? Justify your answer.

23 Answer questions skillfully

Rachel Jones is giving the JourneyFree presentation (pages 452–455), and she receives the following questions. Plan answers to the questions.

a. **A hostile question:** "You say the tour is only $3,000, but that is a huge amount of money for underpaid teachers. How can we afford that?"

b. **Question to which you do not know the answer:** "Where can we apply for external funding for these kinds of educational experiences?"

c. **An idea you have already rejected:** "Wouldn't Japan or China be a better location, considering the importance of those cuisines for today's cooking?"

d. **A question that gets the presentation off track:** "I'm glad you're organizing this trip to France because France is my favorite country. I've been there five times, and each time I learn something new. In fact, the last time I was there. … "

24 Meeting audience expectations [Related to the Culture feature on page 445]

When you present to audiences in other cultures, it is important to follow that culture's rules of business etiquette. On YouTube (or another video-sharing site), find a video about business etiquette in a country other than the United States. Show the video to the class and then facilitate a class discussion about how you would apply those etiquette principles if you were delivering a business presentation in that culture. Your instructor may ask you to do this exercise individually or as a team.

 How do you adapt your approach for online presentations? *(pages 448–450)*

25 In a live online presentation, manage the audience experience

You are presenting the Rowland-Grey presentation (see Figure 11.24) online to Carolyn Reese, who is out of the office. Select one slide and plan how you would present that slide to her if she were viewing it on a computer in a different location.

26 In a podcast, provide content that offers lasting value

You work for JourneyFree (pages 452–456) and that Rachel Jones has asked you to propose ideas for a series of audio or video podcasts that the company can produce and distribute on its website, with links from JourneyFree's various social media outlets. The goal of the podcast is not to sell any products but to provide useful information that will keep people coming back to the JourneyFree sites. Develop ideas for three podcast episodes and present them persuasively in a three- to five-minute presentation with at least one visual aid.

Writing Exercises

27 Presentations recommending a purchase

You work for the information technology department at Reynolds Media and Marketing, a small public relations company with 30 employees. The company has budgeted $75,000 for this year to replace all desktop computers with laptop computers. For efficiency, the company would like everyone to have the same model of computer. However, employees can't agree on the best model. Some employees would like to switch to Macs. Others prefer PCs. The graphics staff wants big screens. Those who travel prefer lightweight computers, even if it means sacrificing some features.

Your manager asks you to select three good alternatives, evaluate them, and recommend one. Research computer alternatives and prepare a persuasive slide presentation, recommending one particular model. If your research leads you to believe the company should support two different models to meet the needs of different employees, recommend that in your presentation, supported by persuasive reasons. Include a hyperlink to the appropriate product page on each computer manufacturer's website.

If your instructor asks you to deliver this presentation in class, practice in advance, working on all the delivery skills you learned in Study Question 3 in this chapter. Your instructor may ask classmates to provide you with feedback on your presentation delivery.

28 Preparing a training presentation

Take any topic from this textbook and prepare a three- to five-minute presentation to teach the topic to students who are not enrolled in a business communication course. Begin with an opening designed to engage your audience and convince them of the importance of the topic (what's in it for them). Prepare a few slides to teach key points. Conclude with "next steps," providing advice about how your audience can continue learning about the topic.

If your instructor asks you to deliver this presentation in class, practice in advance, working on all the delivery skills you learned in Study Question 3 of this chapter. Your instructor may ask classmates to provide you with feedback on your presentation delivery.

29 Evaluating your presentation delivery skills

Prepare a three-minute "icebreaker" presentation about yourself to deliver to your classmates. Focus on your life, your hobbies and interests, your job, your family, your travel, your recent reading—or any combination of these topics. Here are four ideas for how you can organize this presentation:

a. **Chronological:** Present three or four events in your life that have been important to you and made you the person you are today.

b. **Topical:** Provide a sample of your life, telling your audience a little bit about different topics such as your family, your education, and your hobbies.

c. **Common thread:** Identify a common thread that runs through several events in your life, and provide examples.

d. **Key event:** Focus on one defining event that set your life on its current path.

If your instructor arranges for students' presentations to be video-recorded, watch the video and evaluate your presentation delivery skills, based on the advice in Study Question 3. Submit to your instructor a memo with your evaluation and a list of key presentation skills you will work on in the class.

30 Evaluating the presentation skills of others

Evaluate the presentation skills of a business presenter based on a presentation or speech you find on the Internet. Options include a speech by the head of a business such as Mark Zuckerberg (Facebook), Tim Cook (Apple), or Larry Page (Google); your state senator; or your favorite writer.

Where can you find such talks and presentations? In addition to YouTube, Vimeo, and Talks@Google, you can find presentations and speeches on the websites of the following organizations:

- American Enterprise Institute
- Brookings Institution
- Center for Strategic and International Studies
- Council on Foreign Relations
- C-SPAN
- FORA-TV
- Heritage Foundation

After you watch the presentation, write a memo to your instructor, answering the following questions:

- Did the presenter read a speech or talk extemporaneously?
- Did the presenter use visual aids? If so, were they effective?
- What was the presenter's main point? Summarize it in a few sentences.
- How was the presentation organized?
- What were the main claims of the presentation? Were the claims credible? Why or why not?
- Do you consider this presenter to be a good speaker? Provide evidence to support your point of view.
- Do you have any recommendations for the presenter? Explain them.

Collaboration Exercises

31 Developing presentation skills

a. Working with a team of classmates, develop a five-minute presentation-related activity for your class. It can be a brief ice-breaker for the beginning of a class session, an exercise to evaluate and revise a slide, an exercise to practice body-language and other presentation skills, or your own creative idea. Summarize your activity and provide directions on one or two well-designed slides for your instructor to evaluate.

b. As a team, prepare a five-minute presentation on some aspect of business communication that you find challenging (or that your instructor assigns). After the presentation, conduct a question-and-answer session with the class.

32 Delivering a slide presentation [Related to the Collaboration feature on page 444]

You and two teammates are presenting either the Rowland-Grey (Figure 11.24) or the JourneyFree presentation (pages 452–455). Your instructor will provide the presentation file. Practice the presentation, working on all the delivery skills you learned in Study Question 3 and in the collaboration feature of this chapter. Deliver this presentation in class. Your instructor may ask classmates to provide you with feedback on your presentation delivery.

33 Reporting on consumer attitudes [Related to the Collaboration feature on page 444]

Consumer Research, Inc., has hired your team to conduct a survey to learn how young adults respond to direct mail advertising sent by email. Research by the Direct Marketing Association indicates that, overall, advertising through postal mail results in more sales than advertising through email.[34] However, the research did not focus on specific age groups. Consumer Research, Inc., wants to know whether young adults (ages 18–25) purchase more as a result of email or postal mail advertising. Identify a group of people your

team can survey and develop a set of questions to ask. For example, you could ask:

- How often do they open advertising they receive through email?
- What influences their decision to open the email? Is it the subject line, the sender, or something else?
- How often do they click through to a website?
- How often do they purchase something as a result of the email advertising?

Conduct your survey and then prepare a presentation to Consumer Research, Inc., that outlines your results. If possible, draw conclusions about the effectiveness of email marketing to young adults.

If your instructor asks you to deliver this presentation in class, practice in advance, working on all the delivery skills you learned in Study Question 3 and the collaboration feature of this chapter. Your instructor may ask classmates to provide you with feedback on your presentation delivery.

34 Evaluating fast-food restaurants [Related to the Collaboration feature on page 444]

Your team works for a restaurant chain that is planning to open a restaurant in your area. The district regional manager wants to know more about the competition. Are the competitive restaurants excellent? Or is there room for a good new restaurant in the neighborhood?

As a team, choose three restaurants in the area and observe each restaurant at least three times within the next two weeks. Vary the day of the week and the time of day for each visit. During each visit, observe and collect data on the appearance of the restaurant, how many customers entered during that time period, the length of wait to place an order, the length of wait to receive an order, the quality of service, and the quality of food. During each visit, make a qualitative judgment about how happy the customers seem to be, and support your judgment with specific observations.

At the end of the two-week observation period, prepare a slide presentation to deliver to your district manager, evaluating the competition and making recommendations about how your new restaurant can provide better service than the competitive restaurants you have studied.

If your instructor asks you to make this presentation in class, practice in advance, working on all the delivery skills you learned in Study Question 3 and the Collaboration feature of this chapter. Your instructor may ask classmates to provide you with feedback on your presentation delivery.

Social Media Exercises

35 Distributing presentations through social media "channels"

Many businesses choose to consolidate their online presentations, slides, and podcasts on one or more dedicated social media "channels," such as a YouTube channel or a SlideShare Enterprise channel. On YouTube or SlideShare, find a social media channel of a company that interests you and review the archive of media on that channel. Choose one or two video presentations, slide decks, or podcasts, and prepare a five-minute presentation to your class. Explain how the company uses that social media channel, what kind of audio or video files are on that channel, and whether you believe the content is useful and provides a good image of the company. As part of your presentation, show a brief excerpt from one of the company's audio or video presentations.

36 Exploring the concept of curation

The concept of *curation* developed as a means of managing information overload on the Internet. A curator is someone who selectively organizes material on a specific topic, using a social media tool such as a blog, podcast, Pinterest, or Scoop.it, and then shares this collection of material with interested parties, using social media tools such as Twitter, Facebook, and Google+. Research the concept of curation and study at least two "curated" social media sites or collections. Then prepare a five-minute presentation to illustrate at least one way in which curation can benefit a business.

Speaking Exercises

37 Impromptu speaking

In a one- to two-minute presentation, answer one of the following questions. Be sure to begin your presentation with the short version of the answer and then elaborate.

a. What advice would you give students graduating from your high school this year and planning to attend your college?

b. What is your ideal job when you graduate?

c. If you could travel anywhere, where would it be?

d. What is the most valuable course you have taken thus far in college?

e. What one change would you recommend to the president of your college?

38 Executive briefings

a. If you are working on a long-term project, prepare an oral progress report for your instructor.

b. Assume that the business communication faculty at your school is trying to decide whether all students in business communication courses should be required to learn a presentation program, such as PowerPoint, Keynote, Impress, or Prezi. They have asked five current business communication students, including you, to present their views at a department meeting. You will have only three minutes to speak. Prepare a brief presentation to the faculty. Support your presentation with some form of visual aid.

Grammar Exercises

39 Capitalization (see Appendix C: Grammar, Punctuation, Mechanics, and Conventions—Section 3.1)

Type the following paragraph, correcting the 30 errors, which include both omissions and improper use of capital letters. Underline all of your corrections.

> Robin thompson, owner of etiquette network and Robin Thompson charm school, says, "personal phone calls are fine, so long as you limit them and choose the appropriate time." She also believes cell phones should be turned off at work; If you are at work, that means you have a desk phone and can be reached at that number most of the time. Cell phones and pagers don't belong in business meetings, either, she says. Would you interrupt your Vice President to answer your cell phone? (you wouldn't if you want to keep working for the Company.) Of course, when you are flying to Corporate Headquarters on the West Coast from the Regional Office in north Dakota, a cell phone can be a life saver. Because you had to take your daughter to her spanish lesson, you've missed your plane. The head of the division of specialty products wants that report by 5 P.M., president McMillan is expecting you for lunch, and your son forgot to order his date's corsage for the High School prom tonight. Note to self: text son about picking up tuxedo. Instead of a Master's Degree in business, you're thinking maybe you should have majored in Emergency Management. Thank heavens you have a blackberry.

40 Numbers (see Appendix C: Grammar, Punctuation, Mechanics, and Conventions—Section 3.2)

Type the following paragraph, correcting the 15 errors in the use of numbers. Underline all your corrections.

> 20 years ago mobile phones were novel and expensive. In the nineteen-eighties cellular telephones, luxury items used only

by top executives, cost almost $4000 and weighed more than 2 pounds. Today, of course, even ten-year-olds have them, and the lightest ones weigh two.65 ounces. Some people have more than one mobile phone; imagine carrying 2 2-pound phones in your purse. The International Telecommunications Union estimates that there are approximately 4,600,000,000 mobile telephones in use worldwide. That amounts to about sixty percent of the world's population. China ranks number 1 with a little over 57 percent of Chinese using cellular telephones. India ranks 2nd, adding more than six (6) million subscribers a month. According to *The Washington Post*, nearly 1/2 of the Indian population has wireless service—3 times the number of landlines in the country. The United States ranks third, with 91% of us using cell phones.

MyLab Business Communication

Go to **www.pearson.com/mylab/business-communication** for Auto-graded writing questions as well as the following Assisted-graded writing questions:

1. Why is it important to practice presenting a slide as part of the evaluating/revising process?

2. Teams often divide the work of creating presentation slides so that work is equally divided. What are the potential problems of this approach? How can you address or avoid those problems?

References

1. American Management Association. (2014, February 25). Communication skills most needed by individual contributors. Retrieved from http://www.amanet.org/news/9791.aspx

2. Gallo, C. (2014, August 13). Cisco's obsession with presentation skills makes managers better leaders. *Forbes*. Retrieved from https://www.forbes.com/sites/carminegallo/2014/08/13/ciscos-obsession-with-presentation-skills-makes-managers-better-leaders/

3. Covey, S. R. (n.d.). Habit 2: Begin with the end in mind. Retrieved from https://www.stephencovey.com/7habits/7habits-habit2.php

4. Murphy, M. (2007). *Improving learner reaction, learning score, and knowledge retention through the chunking process in corporate training.* (PhD dissertation). Retrieved from University of North Texas Digital Library. Retrieved from https://digital.library.unt.edu/ark:/67531/metadc5137/

5. Gallo, C. (2017, February 21). Neuroscience proves you should follow TED's 18-minute rule to win your pitch. Retrieved from https://www.inc.com/carmine-gallo/why-your-next-pitch-should-follow-teds-18-minute-rule.html

6. Medina, J. (2014). *Brain rules: 12 principles for surviving and thriving at work, home, and school* (2nd ed.). Seattle: Pear Press.

7. Sousa, D. (2011). *How the brain learns* (4th ed.). Thousand Oaks, CA: Corwin Press. For early research on the primacy effect in communication, see Gilkinson, H., Paulson, S. F., & Sikkink, D. E. (1954, April). Effects of order and authority in an argumentative speech. *Quarterly Journal of Speech, 40,* 183–192.

8. Young, R. O. (2011). *How audiences decide: A cognitive approach to business communication* (pp. 138–139). New York: Routledge.

9. Miller, G. (1956). The magical number seven plus or minus two: Some limits on our capacity for processing information. *Psychological Review, 63,* 81–97.

10. Cowan, N. (2001). The magical number 4 in short-term memory: A reconsideration of mental storage capacity. *Behavioral and Brain Sciences, 24*(1), 87–114.

11. Baddeley, A. (2010). Working memory. *Current Biology, 20*(4), R136–140.

12. Sousa, D. (2011). *How the brain learns* (4th ed.). Thousand Oaks, CA: Corwin Press.

13. Monroe, A. (1935). *Principles and types of speech.* New York: Scott Foresman.

14. Munter, M. (2013). *Guide to managerial communication* (10th ed., p. 54). Upper Saddle River, NJ: Prentice Hall.

15. Wecker, C. (2012). Slide presentations as speech suppressors: When and why learners miss oral information. *Computers & Education, 59*(2), 260–273.

16. Gallo, C. (2012, September 12). PowerPoint: The extreme makeover edition (before and after slides). *Forbes*. Retrieved from http://www.forbes.com/sites/carminegallo/2012/09/12/powerpoint-the-extreme-makeover-edition-before-and-after-slides/

17. Williams, R. (2014). *The non-designer's design book* (4th ed.). San Francisco, CA: Peachpit Press.

18. Mahar, S., Yaylacicegi, U., & Janicki, T. N. (2009, July 22). Less is more when developing PowerPoint animations. *Information Systems Education Journal, 7*(82), 1–11.

19. U.S. Copyright Office. (2017, April). U.S. Copyright Office Fair Use Index. Retrieved from http://www.copyright.gov/fls/fl102.html

20. iStock by Getty Images. (2017, June). iStock content license agreement. Retrieved from http://www.istockphoto.com/legal/license-agreement

21. Cuddy, A. (2012, June). Your body language shapes who you are. [Video]. Retrieved from https://www.ted.com/talks/amy_cuddy_your_body_language_shapes_who_you_are

22. Ranehill, E., Dreber, A., Johannesson, M., Leiberg, S., Sul, S., & Weber, R. A. (2015). Assessing the robustness of power posing: no effect on hormones and risk tolerance in a large sample of men and women. *Psychological Science, 26*(5), 653–656.

CHAPTER 11

23. Kaulbach, J., & Jean-Louis, J. (2017, January 17). Tony Robbins's favorite trick to immediately command the room. [Video.] *Inc.* Retrieved from https://www.inc.com/video/tony-robbins/no-1-posture-trick-to-immediately-decrease-your-stress-level.html

24. Van Edwards, V. (2015, March). 5 secrets of a successful TED talk. *Science of People.* Retrieved from https://www.scienceofpeople.com/2015/03/secrets-of-a-successful-ted-talk/

25. Van Edwards, V. (2015, March). 5 secrets of a successful TED talk. *Science of People.* Retrieved from https://www.scienceofpeople.com/2015/03/secrets-of-a-successful-ted-talk/

26. Zhou, H., & Zhang, T. (2008). Body language in business negotiation. *International Journal of Business and Management, 3*(2), 90–96. Retrieved from http://journal.ccsenet.org/index.php/ijbm/article/view/1680/1588

27. De Mente, B. L. (2016). *Etiquette guide to China: Know the rules that make the difference!* North Clarendon, VT: Tuttle Publishing.

28. McGraw, P., & Warner, J. (2014). *The humor code: A global search for what makes things funny.* New York, N.Y.: Simon & Schuster.

29. Huang, L. (2010). Cross-cultural communication in business negotiations. *International Journal of Economics and Finance, (2)*2, 196–199. Retrieved from http:ccsenet.org/journal/index.php/ijef/article/view/5907/4687

30. Krakovsky, M. (2009). National poker face. *Psychology Today, 42*(1), 20.

31. Google. (2017). Accept and present audience questions. Retrieved from https://support.google.com/docs/answer/6386827?co=GENIE.Platform%3DDesktop&hl=en

32. Atkinson, C. (2010). *The backchannel: How audiences are using twitter and social media and changing presentations forever.* San Francisco, CA: Peachpit Press.

33. Courville, R. (2009). *The virtual presenter's handbook.* Troutdale, OR:1080 Group LLC.

34. Edison Research. (2016). The infinite dial 2016. Retrieved from http://www.edisonresearch.com/the-infinite-dial-2016/

35. Baskin, E. C. (2015, October 26). Two great reasons to use podcasts for internal communication. [Blog post]. Retrieved from http://blog.tribeinc.com/2015/10/26/two-great-reasons-to-use-podcasts-for-internal-communications/

36. Haskel, D. (2017, January 20). IWCO direct. Direct mail response rates are at their highest point in over a decade. Retrieved from https://www.iwco.com/blog/2017/01/20/direct-mail-response-rates-and-2016-dma-report/

12

Communicating Your Professional Brand: Social Media, Résumés, Cover Letters, and Interviews

STUDY QUESTIONS

SQ1 How do you polish your professional presence for a job search? pages 470–477

> Analyze your career goals, strengths, and skills
> Compose your brand message and strategic social media content
> Evaluate your virtual professional image

SQ2 How do you compose an effective résumé? pages 477–486

> Analyze your options for organizing your résumé
> Compose effective résumé content
> Evaluate your content and design

SQ3 How do you find job opportunities and submit applications? pages 487–495

> Analyze your options for finding job opportunities
> Compose an effective elevator pitch
> Compose persuasive cover letters
> Select a medium for submission and follow up as necessary

SQ4 How do you prepare for a job interview? pages 495–501

> Analyze how to benefit from different types of interviews
> Compose good answers—and good questions
> Evaluate your professional appearance

SQ5 How can you make a positive impression during and after an interview? pages 502–510

> Project a professional presence
> Compose effective post-interview messages
> Evaluate your performance

MyLab Business Communication

⭐ Improve Your Grade!

If your instructor is using MyLab Business Communication, visit **www.pearson.com/mylab/business-communication** for videos, simulations, and writing exercises.

New Hires @ Work

Bianca Wallace

Eastern Kentucky University

Human Resources Representative @ Hendrickson Trailer Commercial Vehicle Systems

I have been an "interviewee" only twice in my life, but I have been an "interviewer" hundreds of times. We see a lot of the same mistakes. Here's my advice . . .

When you answer questions, be honest. Don't exaggerate your experience or abilities. Be prepared to provide an example that demonstrates your strengths and skills. Anyone can say he has good teamwork skills, but not everyone can back it up by explaining an actual situation. Also, give the interviewer enough information to show that you researched the job and the company, but don't bore them with a long-winded answer. Be energetic, look professional, and ask good questions-- you're interviewing the company as much as we're interviewing you!

Photo courtesy of Bianca Wallace

Chapter 12 | Introduction

Your professional presence is critical to your success during a job search. Employers will evaluate your skills and abilities, your character and fit with the job, and your growth potential. To pass that evaluation, you need to be confident that you are applying for the right job, and you need to communicate a strong **professional brand**—the image you present that makes you stand out compared with other applicants. This chapter helps you create a positive professional brand and communicate it through your social media presence, your résumé and cover letters, and your job interviews. Throughout the chapter, you will learn how to use the ACE process to:

- *Analyze* your career goals, strengths, and skills to determine how you can fit the needs of potential employers. This

analysis helps you identify industries and companies to target for your job search and how to sell yourself to those companies during the application and interview process.

- *Compose* your brand message, professional social media content, customized résumés and cover letters, effective interview questions and responses, and persuasive follow-up messages. You will use these methods of communication to emphasize your strengths and manage your employment search.

- *Evaluate* your virtual professional image, employment communication, and interview experiences. Through ongoing evaluation, you can continuously improve your skills not only during your employment search, but throughout your career as you continue to advance.

(SQ1) How do you polish your professional presence for a job search?

The first step in ensuring a professional presence is to develop confidence in your career goals and your suitability for the career you are planning. Confidence helps you target the right jobs and compose an effective brand message, social media content, and job search materials to persuasively market yourself for those jobs.

Analyze your career goals, strengths, and skills

Many college students choose a major based on their interests or academic strengths, such as English or math. Others choose a major based on specific career goals, such as accounting or law. Whichever approach you choose, you can do many things before you graduate to learn more about yourself and to analyze your goals, strengths, and skills. The more confidence you have in your career path and abilities, the more effectively you will be able to present yourself in a job search.

professional brand The image you present of yourself that makes you stand out compared to other applicants.

Analyzing career goals

The best way to analyze your career goals is to research your options, participate in career-oriented experiences such as professional clubs and internships, and continuously reflect on what you learn. Start these activities early in your education so you have time to consider all your options. **Figure 12.1** provides a suggested timeline of activities to help you plan and pace your analysis of your career goals throughout your degree. Many of these activities are ones you can return to multiple times in your life as you consider job or career changes.

FIGURE 12.1 How to Develop and Analyze Your Career Goals Throughout a Four-Year Degree

FRESHMAN YEAR: *Explore options and gain transferrable skills*	• Participate in clubs and organizations related to your major and volunteer for nonprofit organizations. • Research different positions using resources such as the *Occupational Outlook Handbook* published online by the U.S. Bureau of Labor Statistics. Learn about educational requirements, salary ranges, projected job growth, the nature of the work, and working conditions. • Experiment with a variety of internships, including virtual internships that could provide short-term contract work to help you "test the waters," gain skills, and build experience.[1] • Register with your school's career center and attend career fairs to learn about future opportunities (and then begin to prepare for them). • Focus on developing *transferrable skills* that relate to your career goals to help you demonstrate to employers that you can make an impact.

SOPHOMORE YEAR:
Focus your career options by targeting internships in a specific field or company
	Continue to explore options and gain transferrable skills but also begin to:
	• Reflect on the characteristics that will make you happy in a job:
	  – Do you prefer to work collaboratively with other people or on your own?
	  – Would you enjoy a creative position or a more procedural job?
	  – Do you see yourself working for a large or small company? In a large or small city?
	  – Would you enjoy a job that requires travel?
	  – Do you want to start your own business to promote a new product or service?
	• Start to build your professional brand by creating (or revising) social media content that projects the image you want employers see.
	• Target internship opportunities for a specific career path to enhance your résumé and develop field-specific skills. Interning early in your college career and experiencing a variety of internships will help you focus your career goals.[2]

JUNIOR YEAR: *Continue to narrow your focus and create a career plan*	***Continue the activities described above while you start to:*** • Think about what your career goals might be 5 or 10 years from now. What do you want to accomplish? • Create a career plan that navigates your path from school to work and into the future. • Focus on internships with companies that you want to work for after graduation. Research indicates that paid internships often lead to full-time job offers.[3]
SENIOR YEAR: *Put your plan into action, continuously analyze your options, and keep an open mind*	***Begin your professional job search:*** • Apply for a wide variety of positions within your career field. • Accept all interviews as opportunities to continue to analyze your options, build your knowledge about your career field, and create contacts. • Consider alternatives to working for a single employer, such as freelancing or entrepreneurship. • Stay flexible so you can find different ways to fulfill your career plan. • Be open to moving; you may find a perfect job in an unexpected location.

Analyzing strengths and skills

In addition to analyzing your goals, analyze your strengths and skills by creating a list like the one in **Figure 12.2** on page 472. Analyzing your strengths and skills helps you accomplish two goals. First, you can determine which jobs you are best qualified to pursue. Second, you can build evidence of your skills to use in your cover letters, résumés, and interviews to sell yourself to a potential employer. Remember to update your "skill inventory" frequently to keep the list current and to help tailor your résumé for different jobs.

FIGURE 12.2 How to Analyze Your Strengths and Skills

Outline all your work experiences and create three to five bullet points that identify the specific skills you developed on the job and the specific results you achieved.

Identify areas of expertise you developed outside of work—from coursework, extracurricular activities, and hobbies. Having a wide variety of talents will make you more marketable.

List your sellable qualities—abilities that make you an asset to a company. Identify how, where, and to what extent you developed them.

Identify weaknesses so you can work on improving them, especially if they are often required for jobs in your field. Avoid applying for positions that require skills you do not have.

Experience:

Internship with a financial management company

- Gained problem-solving and interpersonal skills while providing personal customer service to a diverse client base
- Improved data management by organizing client records, inputting data, and designing reports in the client database
- Analyzed spreadsheets to create effective charts and graphs to support persuasive client presentations
- Gathered information, evaluated content, and wrote articles for a monthly newsletter that provided financial management advice to clients

Areas of Expertise:

- Programming Java applets (learned from computer class)
- Designing web pages (self-taught)

Sellable Qualities:

- Enhanced interpersonal skills through co-writing and presenting role-playing scenarios for Students Against Drunk Driving (SADD) awareness events at local high schools
- Developed leadership skills as president of the campus Business Club; initiated two successful fundraising events, led meetings, and delegated duties
- Gained collaboration and negotiation skills working with parents and children as a youth soccer coach for four years

Weaknesses:

- Lack of experience preparing and delivering formal presentations
- Missing deadlines due to problems with time management

Compose

Compose your brand message and strategic social media content

By understanding your goals and skills, you can develop and market your professional brand—the image you present that makes you stand out compared to other applicants. You project your brand through your personal interactions, email messages, and social media content. When it comes to your brand, you are your own public relations (PR) manager. And if you don't take the time to manage your brand by design—the way *you want* to define it—you will likely end up not having a good one.[4]

Composing your brand message

brand message A statement that communicates the unique value you offer your employers.

At the core of a professional brand is a **brand message**—a statement that communicates the unique value you offer your employers. Begin to develop your brand message by synthesizing the core skills and talents you've already identified. What matters to you? What are you good at? What do you want to be known for? Consider your best characteristics and accomplishments. What does your track record prove? Note the example in **Figure 12.3**. Include your brand message in your social media profiles and consider adding a tag line to your email signature block and business cards. You might also include your brand message below your contact information on your résumé or create a fact sheet as a "leave behind" at the end of an interview.[5]

Composing strategic social media content

Social media is playing a larger and increasingly valuable role in the employment process.[6] Many job candidates are, in fact, *social job seekers*, using social media to find job opportunities, get job referrals, and learn employees' perspectives about a company.[7] At the same time, employers are using social media for their own purposes. The social recruiting company Jobvite surveys employers every year. Results consistently indicate that most employers use social media in their recruiting process.[8] The most popular social media site for employers is LinkedIn. Employers use LinkedIn more than twice as much as any other

FIGURE 12.3 How to Compose Your Brand Message

What should your brand message say?

"As a new marketing and international business professional, I am passionate about bridging culture gaps that stand in the way of effective marketing. I understand that not all cultures are alike. Products must be adapted to meet the needs of different cultures and marketed differently in different cultures.

I am a quick learner and an enthusiastic collaborator. I enjoy working in teams and with people from different cultures to understand their needs."

Explain who you are, what you do, what deeply interests you, and what value you offer a prospective employer.

Stress your **unique selling proposition**— the skills or qualities that set you apart from other applicants.

unique selling proposition The skills or qualities that set someone or something apart from the competition.

social media to search for potential candidates and to learn more about candidates who apply. However, they also use Facebook, Twitter, blogs, and Pinterest to get a feel for the personality of candidates.

As a result, to be competitive in today's job market, you need make yourself visible on social media by creating a professional social media presence and by engaging your **network**—the people you know who are aware of your career goals. You also need to make yourself valuable on social media. Provide employers with a reason to follow you and return to your sites. The following sections provide advice to ensure that your social media content is both visible and valuable.

network The circle of people who are aware of your career goals and can help you learn about career opportunities.

Making yourself visible

In addition to creating a professional presence on popular sites such as LinkedIn, Facebook, and Twitter, consider creating online content that anyone can access without having to link to you or "friend" you. Be visible and searchable: Create a blog, an online résumé, an e-portfolio, or a video résumé, and then link all your sites so employers can easily find your content.[9] Continuously update every site to ensure that your online content is current and effectively represents your professional brand.

Use the same photo of yourself on all your sites to create a consistent visible brand.[10] To ensure a professional image, avoid photos taken with cell phones or cropping yourself out of photos with other people. A plain background and diffused daylight often provides the best lighting.[11] Select a recent head shot and ensure that any visible clothing looks like interview attire or is at least appropriate to your career field. And, most importantly, smile. Research suggests that people's first impressions remain consistent over time—even after they have met you in person.[12] This means that your photo could play a significant role in your job search.[13] **Figure 12.4** on pages 474–475 outlines ways to use your Facebook, LinkedIn, and Twitter accounts during your job search. Each platform has unique benefits that you can leverage as part of your job search strategy.

Making yourself valuable

Even if you create a recognizable brand for yourself and put yourself "out there" in a variety of online locations, you will not be competitive if your content does not persuade the audience that you have something to offer. **Figure 12.5** on page 476 identifies ways to increase your perceived value to an employer through your social media content.

Evaluate your virtual professional image

As you develop a strategic social media presence, also consider the image you present across other communication mediums—including your business cards, your email messages, and your telephone conversations. Are you consistently communicating your brand message and your professionalism? Use **Figure 12.6** on pages 476–477 as a checklist to analyze and evaluate your virtual professional image to ensure that it is polished, relevant, and current.

New Hires @ Work

Christian Tucker
Georgia Southern University
Data Engineer at General Motors

I've found that recruiters want LinkedIn accounts. But selling your potential on LinkedIn requires more than posting résumé content. You have to update your status, comment on other people's status posts, participate in groups, and post links to industry information. You are what you post.

Photo courtesy of Christian Tucker

ACE

Evaluate

FIGURE 12.4 How to Target Specific Social Media Platforms During a Job Search

Facebook

Employers often use Facebook to review candidates and may assume that you have something to hide if they can't find you.[14] So rather than make your site completely private, ensure that your personal network is aware of your job search and revise your site to communicate your professional brand and present a positive image. Make full use Facebook's privacy settings to control what content is public and what can be seen only by friends. The example below provides more suggestions to enhance your professional Facebook presence.

Facebook page

- **Use a professional photo** of yourself as well as a cover photo that illustrates or helps define your brand.

- **Post recent activity updates** that highlight professional accomplishments. If you have attended conferences, read relevant books, or used your skills in volunteer work, make that information obvious.

- **"Like" companies that you want to work for** as well as professional groups and job sites. Interact with these sites by posting comments and asking questions.

- **Expand your connections** by sending friend requests to faculty, staff, and anyone you meet through professional contacts. Subscribe to sites of professionals who are in your desired job field.

- **Use job search applications** such as BranchOut, BeKnown, and Glassdoor that help connect you with recruiters and companies.

- **Use the Facebook timeline** to link all your social media activity, including your blog, tweets, and Pinterest posts, and then blog, tweet, and pin professional content that supports your brand.

Twitter

Use Twitter regularly to broadcast content related to your job search—both professional information about yourself and content about your field of study. Build your network by following companies and retweeting, commenting, or asking questions to connect with other people in your industry. These connections may become working relationships later in your career.[15] See the suggestions below to create a professional bio and further support your job search.

Create a compelling bio:

- **Keep it short.** A Twitter bio can be no more than 166 characters.

- **Use your real name** rather than a "Twitter handle" to increase your credibility.

- **Use keywords from your brand message** to compose your bio. Think of your bio as an elevator pitch—a concise statement designed to communicate your value and initiate a deeper conversation.

- **Include your college name, the year you will graduate, and any awards.** Twitter is less formal than other platforms, so it's possible to add some personality and still be professional.

Twitter bio

Shavon Alkins
@shavon-d-alkins
@CampusUniversity with honors. Marketing and International business major. Obsessed with bridging cultures. Focused on tailored marketing. Craves Sriracha.

Use Twitter as a job-search tool:

- **Subscribe to industry- or job-related lists** and participate in talks and discussions, and then tweet about the topics.

- **Follow important people in your field.** Research industry leaders and follow new people each month to continuously expand your network.

- **Post updates on your job search.**

- **Re-tweet interesting posts** from important people in your target industry, and tweet links to interesting industry-related articles.

(continued)

FIGURE 12.4 *(Continued)*

LinkedIn

Unlike Facebook, LinkedIn is primarily intended to be an interactive professional networking tool. During a job search, use LinkedIn to make yourself more visible to employers, to enlarge your network, and to complement your résumé. Your LinkedIn profile should not just copy your résumé content, but expand upon it with more detailed career summary information, recommendations, and links to relevant publications and videos.[16,17,18,19]

LinkedIn profile

Home   Profile   Contacts   Groups   Jobs   Inbox   Companies   More

Shavon Alkins

Seeking an opportunity to help a U.S. or global company expand international markets

Baltimore, Maryland   Marketing and Advertising

Current — Sales Associate at Target

Previous — Food Lion, Eastlawn Elementary, Campus University Language Lab

Education — Bachelor of Science (B.S.), Business Administration, Marketing, and International Business at Campus University

Improve your profile   Edit ▾   **151** connections

Summary

New marketing professional who is passionate about reaching international audiences and contributing to a creative marketing team.

I developed my interest in international work while studying abroad in the Philippines, Spain, and Italy. My passion for marketing stems from academic and work experiences—especially listening to the voice of the customer to improve marketing, sales, and customer service.

Key experiences and qualifications:

- Studied abroad in the Philippines, Spain, and Italy
- Led student team in succesful international marketing project in the Philippines
- Returned to Manila to present at the Philippine Business Conference & Expo
- Developed deep understanding of customer needs as a sales and customer service professional
- Achieved honors in marketing at Campus University
- Speak fluent Spanish

Eager to be employed by a U.S. or global company to help expand international markets.

Experience

Sales Associate, 2018–Present
Target Corporation, Robbins, MD
Use interpersonal skills to greet and assist customers courteously and efficiently. Assist with cashier functions and other duties as assigned.

Cashier/Sales Associate 2017–2018
Food Lion, LLC, Robbins, MD
Interacted with customers, facilitated transactions, and maintained cash drawer.

Blingual Classroom Assistant, 2015–2018
Eastlawn Elementary, Middletown MD
Worked with 5th grade children to develop their literacy skills and recognize word sets in Spanish and English.

Language Lab Assistant, 2014–2015
Campus University, Robbins, MD
Prepared lab coursework activities.

Cashier/ Sales Associate, 2013–2014
Family Dollar Inc., Pensacola, FL
Managed front-end sales and provided excellent customer service. Performed store setup tasks.

Skills & Expertise

Business Marketing   International Business   Accounting   Spanish
Leadership   Communication   Computer Skills

Education

Campus University, Robbins. MD
B.S., Business Administration, Marketing and International Business
2014–2018

Create a compelling profile:

- **Use a photo that presents you as a professional.** Research shows that professional recruiters who search LinkedIn spend the most time looking at a candidate's photo, education, and current job.

- **Write a persuasive headline**—the statement that appears below your name. Mention that you are looking for a new position and tailor your headline to sell your strengths. You goal is to persuade recruiters to continue to read your profile.

- **Create a summary that serves as an advertisement** for you and sells your professional brand. Highlight your strengths and abilities, and briefly mention what you achieved in the past year.

- **Provide compelling details.** Include your education, current and past employment, and other experiences that demonstrate your professional skills. Use keywords that recruiters might search.

- **Showcase visual and written work** with links to your personal website, your YouTube channel, eportfolios, and publications.

- **Create a unique, customized LinkedIn URL** that you can use on your résumé, business cards, email signature block.

Take advantage of LinkedIn as a job-search tool:

- **Use LinkedIn's built-in applications** to pull feeds from your Twitter account and blog postings, and then tweet and blog about your job search and industry-related content.

- **Use LinkedIn's "People You May Know" section** to increase your network. Use the "View All" feature, and check the list each week to search for new connection possibilities.

- **Ask for recommendations** from those in your network who can write about your strengths and skills. Recommendations enhance your credibility, especially when they come from industry professionals.

- **Link to companies that you want to work** for and read their updates to stay current with information that you can use during employment interviews.

- **Participate in discussion groups** that are related to jobs or fields that interest you.

- **Update your status** weekly so people in your network are reminded about you and your job search.

- **Download LinkedIn's Student App** to receive daily suggestions that will help you promote your job search, browse career options, learn more about employers in your field, and track the careers of other people who have taken the same education route.

FIGURE 12.5 How to Highlight Your Value to Employers in Your Social Media Content

Post positive status updates	• Post about things that sell your strengths, including everything from the professional events you attend to your volunteer work. • Avoid posting negative comments or "liking" questionable content (such as inappropriate photos or offensive jokes).[20]
Emphasize your accomplishments	• Post about your education, scholarships and awards, and your work experiences. • Include information about conferences or presentations you attend. • Comment about your volunteer work and other service-related activities.
Use *content marketing* techniques	• Provide valuable information without trying to "sell" anything. • Write about new trends in your industry to demonstrate your awareness. • Link to cutting-edge articles and comment about them. • Provide other examples that demonstrate your interest and knowledge.
Demonstrate positive work traits in your site profiles	• Demonstrate that you are organized and hardworking by organizing your site effectively and updating it with detailed posts. • Show that you are open to new ideas by posting comments about your travel, interesting articles and books, and new trends and concepts.

FIGURE 12.6 How to Evaluate Your Virtual Image

Review your telephone image

• **Create a professional greeting**—your recorded message that callers will hear when you are not able to answer your phone—that clearly states your name, requests callers to leave their name and number, and identifies that you will return the call as soon as possible.

• **Evaluate your greeting** to ensure it is clear, concise, and complete; and avoid distracting background music or cute sayings.

• **Smile when you talk;** it brightens the sound of your voice.

• **Check your voice mail messages every day** and respond within 24 hours, if not sooner.

Andres Rodriguez/Fotolia

Review your online image

• **Clean up your social media sites** before launching a job search, and then continuously monitor them.

• **Remove unprofessional content,** such as pictures, negative comments, and other information you do not want a potential employer to see.

• **Ask your friends to remove content** about you—or at least your identification—from their social media sites if that content may be perceived as unprofessional.

• **Google yourself** and also search within social media sites to see what others can find about you online.

Samuel Borges Photography/Shutterstock

(continued)

FIGURE 12.6 *(Continued)*

Review your email image

- **Use a professionally worded personal email address** rather than your school email account, which may be disabled a few months after you graduate. Consider the different images these email addresses communicate: "*2cool4school@gmail.com*" or "*jon.swartz@gmail.com.*"
- **Include a professional email signature block** to provide your contact information. Make sure the contact information you list in your email signature block is consistent with your business card.
- **Consider including a *tag line*** to help sell your professional brand.

email signature block

File   Message   Insert   Review

Send   To...
Subject:

Jana C. Smithers
Business Management Major
"Management and Communication Expertise"

NEW STATE UNIVERSITY
SCHOOL OF BUSINESS
BELVEDERE, MI 49720

http://www.nsu.edu/jcsmithers.htm
jcsmithers@gmail.com
204.555.4432

Review your business cards

- **Keep the design professional,** and list your contact information (phone number, email address, and your LinkedIn account).
- **Include URLs** if you have a web résumé, video résumé, or online portfolio to support your job search.
- **List your memberships,** especially those that relate to your degree, to enhance your professional networking possibilities.
- **Consider including bulleted skills,** highlights from your résumé, or a tag line on the back of your business card.

business card

JUAN VARGAS
Finance and Economics Major
President, Students in Free Enterprise
Member, Beta Gamma Sigma
www.LinkedIn.com/juan-vargas

City College at Pembroke
Mailbox #14223
Pembroke, Virginia 24136
(612) 555-8849
Jvargas@att.net

(SQ2) How do you compose an effective résumé?

Compose

Although social media is an important employment communication tool, a professional and targeted résumé remains an essential element of your job search. Most employers spend only six seconds in their initial review of a résumé, so yours needs to *quickly* communicate why you are qualified for the position.[21] To identify the most qualified candidates out of a pool of applicants, employers focus on a few critical data points: your job titles, employment history, start and end dates, and your education. Ensure that your résumé makes the first cut by eliminating red flags such as grammatical errors, unprofessional email addresses, vague wording, and bad formatting. The following guidelines will help you compose a highly effective résumé.

Analyze your options for organizing your résumé

Analyze

The three standard ways to organize your résumé content are chronological, functional, and combined. All of them include some key features that are listed in **Figure 12.7** on page 478. However, the three organizations differ in important ways. Use the one that best emphasizes your strengths and presents you as a desirable candidate for the job.

- **Use a chronological résumé to emphasize work experience.** The **chronological résumé** is a traditional format that organizes the content sequentially, starting with the most recent and working backward. It highlights education and work experience as the applicant's primary assets. This format is most appropriate for applicants who have work experience that explicitly qualifies them for the position. Figure 12.7 on page 478 illustrates the résumé of Brendan Neilly, who previously worked as a lifeguard for Oceanfront Properties. He recently saw that company's advertisement for a head lifeguard position and decided to apply. Figure 12.7 shows the job description and Brendan's résumé. He chose a chronological format to emphasize his work experience.

chronological résumé A traditional résumé style that lists content sequentially, starting with the most recent experience.

FIGURE 12.7 How to Create a Chronological Résumé to Focus on Experience

---

WANTED: Head Lifeguard. Supervise 15 guards, create schedules, oversee events, and maintain guard equipment inventory. Lifeguarding experience and certification required. Leadership and teamwork skills needed. We serve a diverse clientele including international tourists; global appreciation and cultural awareness a plus. Send your résumé to: Oceanfront Properties, One Oceanfront Blvd., Barnstable, MA 02630.

---

chronological résumé

Brendan G. Neilly
(508) 555-0210 | bgneilly@yahoo.com
www.linkedin.com/pub/brendan.neilly | Twitter@brendan.neilly

HOME ADDRESS	**CAMPUS ADDRESS**
188 Birch Road	8239 Riverside, Apt. 3B
Sidney, MA 02515	Piedmont Valley, MI 49494

OBJECTIVE
To provide effective leadership and model exceptional safety and customer service skills in the position of head lifeguard for Oceanfront Properties.

EDUCATION
Bachelor of Science in Business Administration, May 2021
Concentration in Finance, Minor in Economics, GPA: 3.6
Piedmont College, MI

EXPERIENCE
Lifeguard
Oceanfront Properties, Barnstable, MA, June–August 2018
- Fulfilled professional lifeguarding duties while maintaining an environment conducive to teamwork and safety
- Supervised weekly drills and assessments
- Communicated effectively with coworkers and diverse clientele

Sales Representative
Banana Republic, Natick, MA, May 2014–May 2017
- Offered exceptional customer service as a shoe and accessory salesperson
- Processed financial transactions including sales and returns

Shaw's Supermarket, Medfield, MA, November 2015–April 2016
- Greeted customers, bagged groceries, and maintained orderly working environment

SPECIAL RECOGNITIONS
- Acceptance into Piedmont Business Fellows Program, 2018
- Member of Piedmont Periclean Scholars, a competitive service learning program, 2016–Present

SKILLS, ABILITIES, & CERTIFICATIONS
- Lifeguard Management Certification, American Red Cross, January 2019
- Waterfront Lifeguard Certification, American Red Cross, May 2018
- Professional Rescuer CPR & First Aid Certification, YMCA (Piedmont Valley, MI), March 2018
- Leadership skills (cross country captain, religious education instructor)
- Teamwork skills (intramural sports, group projects, Habitat for Humanity)
- Microsoft Word, Excel, PowerPoint; Internet research skills

EXTRACURRICULAR CLUBS AND ACTIVITIES
- Delta, Delta, Delta Fraternity, 2018–Present
- Club Lacrosse, 2018–Present
- Habitat for Humanity, 2016–2018

SUMMER FOREIGN EXCHANGE PROGRAM
France, lived with an exchange family and was immersed into French culture, Summer 2017

For all résumés:

Select keywords from job advertisements you reply to, and use them to describe your skills or your job duties. If your résumé doesn't include the right keywords, it will likely be one of the many résumés that are thrown away.

Keep your résumé to one page if you are just starting your career.

Use contemporary fonts (Arial, Verdana, or Calibri) that are professional and easy to read. Align content with tabs, not spaces, to ensure neatness. Consider separating sections with lines or borders, but use them sparingly, especially if your sections are short.

List the one email address you are using for your job search and a phone number that has a professional voice mail greeting.

Include links to your professional social media sites, assuming they include professional content.

Compose a concise objective statement (if you choose to use one) that relates to the position you are applying for and outlines what you can do for the employer.

For chronological résumés:

List education near the top of your résumé, and include your GPA if you have less than five years of work experience. Never round up your GPA (a 2.95 is not the same as a 3.0).

List work experience in chronological order, beginning with the most recent position. Include internships even if they were volunteer jobs.

List honors, awards, or scholarships if you didn't list them with your education.

Identify your skills below your work experience, with the most relevant qualifications for the position at the top of the list. Include additional skills that relate to the job rather than repeating skills listed under work experience. Provide credibility by including supporting details. Place abilities that are not explicitly applicable at the end of the list. In this example, computer knowledge is not as relevant to a lifeguarding position as the related certifications.

Create a separate page of professional references that you can provide when it is requested, rather than including them on the résumé. Create the page with the same header as on your résumé. For each reference, list name, company, title, and complete contact information. Be sure to ask your references for permission to list them.

- **Use a functional résumé to emphasize skills.** The **functional résumé** emphasizes the skills that qualify you for the position. This format is appropriate for applicants who have limited work experience related to the position, such as students who are pursuing internships or professional positions immediately after graduation and who have no related work experience. **Figure 12.8** on page 480 illustrates the résumé that Brendan Neilly designed to apply for a different summer job, an internship in financial management. Because he has no related work experience, he reorganized the content to focus on skills before experience. Notice that he also includes different skills than he included in the lifeguarding résumé.

- **Use a combined résumé to balance experience and skills.** The **combined résumé** highlights the strengths of applicants who have both relevant experience and skills. This format is most appropriate for applicants who have worked in positions closely related to the one they are applying for and who also want to emphasize the advanced skill sets required for the new position. For example, assume that Shavon Alkins is applying for a senior sales associate position. Shavon's résumé, shown in **Figure 12.9** on page 481, demonstrates a balance of skills and experience by highlighting the required skills listed in the job posting (leadership, communication, and computer skills) and also documenting sales experience with several companies.

> **functional résumé** A contemporary résumé style that emphasizes categories of skills rather than job experience.

> **combined résumé** A résumé style that takes advantage of both the chronological and functional methods of organizing content by highlighting work experience by date and skill sets by category.

Although it's useful to follow one of these formats, avoid copying résumé templates (such as those available in Microsoft Word); you don't want your résumé to look like everyone else's. To differentiate yourself, use the best elements from several examples to design a résumé that is unique yet professional and persuasively sell your skills.[22] You might also experiment with graphic design software, such as Adobe Illustrator, Microsoft Publisher, or Canva. **Figure 12.10** on page 482, is an example of how a traditional résumé can be graphically enhanced in Canva. Regardless of which software you use, save your formatted file as a .doc or .pdf to ensure that the recipient will be able to open it.

It is also a wise idea to create a plain-text version of your résumé that you can use to cut and paste content into web-based databases, called *applicant tracking systems*, which companies often use to search and sort candidates' information. **Figure 12.11** on page 483 provides an example of how to create a plain-text version of your résumé.

ETHICS
EXAGGERATING RÉSUMÉ CONTENT IS LYING

In today's competitive job market, you may be tempted to help your résumé pass the automated screening process by listing job duties you did not perform, stretching your responsibilities to include qualifications you do not actually have, or inserting keywords from a job advertisement that do not apply to you.[23,24] Other common errors include changing dates of education or employment, increasing previous salary amounts, inflating titles and job responsibilities, and padding grade point averages.[25] Employers can easily check all these facts.

In a survey of hiring managers, CareerBuilder found that 77 percent of the hiring and human resources managers in the private sector reported having caught lies on résumés.[26] Although it may seem obvious not to lie on your résumé, potential employers can perceive even slight exaggerations of your accomplishments as lies—for example, rounding up your grade point average (GPA) or listing a "major" GPA without labeling it.

The following examples are based on actual—and unfortunate—student experiences:

- **Blatant exaggerations.** As an accounting major, Perry attended several of the Accounting Club's workshops and seminars on career development but never joined the club. When he updated his résumé his senior year, he decided to list membership in the club as an extracurricular activity. He listed his favorite professor (who also served as the club's advisor) as a reference. When employers called the professor to ask about Perry's qualifications, both the professor and the employer learned that Perry had misrepresented his membership.

- **Content copied from other people's résumés.** Sarah researched several different résumé templates, asked friends for copies of their résumés, and downloaded online résumé samples to help create a résumé that successfully communicated a professional brand and emphasized her strengths. She was particularly impressed with a friend's six-bullet item description of his skills and capabilities. Sarah cut and pasted the section from her friend's résumé to her own, not realizing that they might be applying for several of the same internships at their school. Later that semester, two employers complained to the school's career counseling center that students were submitting plagiarized résumés, and both Sarah and her friend were denied further access to the career center's services.

- **Unfulfilled intentions.** Jayne had every intention of filing the paperwork for her minor in psychology to complement her human resources major. Unfortunately, she missed the deadline to file the paperwork before graduation. Although her transcript would list the classes, they would not be documented as an official minor. Because she fulfilled the requirements, she decided to list the minor on her résumé anyway. Six months later and after applying for dozens of jobs without getting any interviews, she learned that potential employees discarded her résumé when they couldn't verify her "minor" on her transcript.

> For an ETHICS exercise, go to Exercise 11 on page 518.

FIGURE 12.8   How to Create a Functional Résumé to Focus on Skills

Financial Management Internships

Local financial management company seeks summer interns for 10-week, full-time, paid position. Rising junior and senior finance and financial management majors only. Analytical and communication skills required. Computer skills expected. Submit your résumé and letter of interest to Daniel Shaw, Career Services, Piedmont College, by February 1. Three letters of reference required.

functional résumé

Brendan G. Neilly

(508) 555-0210 | bgneilly@yahoo.com
www.linkedin.com/pub/brendan.neilly | Twitter@brendan.neilly

HOME ADDRESS	**CAMPUS ADDRESS**
188 Birch Road	8239 Riverside, Apt. 3B
Sidney, MA 02515	Piedmont Valley, MI 49494

OBJECTIVE
To obtain a summer internship with a financial firm that requires analytical detail and excellent communication skills.

EDUCATION
Bachelor of Science in Business Administration, May 2021
Concentration in Finance, Minor in Economics, GPA: 3.6
Piedmont College, MI

SKILLS AND ABILITIES
- Financial: created a business plan for a nonprofit company as a fraternity service project, 2019
- Analytical: prepared expenses and income (fundraising) statements for lacrosse team, 2019
- Communication: effectively met needs of a diverse clientele (Banana Republic), 2016–2017
- Desktop Publishing: created professional flyers and brochures (Habitat for Humanity), 2017
- Computer: effectively use Microsoft Word, Excel, PowerPoint; and Internet research skills

SPECIAL RECOGNITIONS
- Acceptance into Piedmont Business Fellows Program, 2018
- Member of Piedmont Periclean Scholars, a competitive service learning program, 2018–Present

EXPERIENCE
Lifeguard
Oceanfront Properties, Barnstable, MA, June–August 2018
Performed professional lifeguard duties and supervised weekly drills and assessments

Sales Representative
Banana Republic, Natick, MA, May 2016–May 2017
Processed financial transactions including sales and returns

Shaw's Supermarket, Medfield, MA, November 2015–April 2016
Greeted customers, bagged groceries, and maintained orderly working environment

EXTRACURRICULAR CLUBS AND ACTIVITIES
- Delta, Delta, Delta Fraternity, 2018–Present
- Club Lacrosse, 2018–Present
- Habitat for Humanity, 2016–2018

STUDY ABROAD EXPERIENCE
France, lived with an exchange family and was immersed into French culture, Summer 2017

To create a skills-focused functional résumé:

Compose an objective (if you choose to use one) that targets the position and highlights your applicable skills.

List your education first when it specifically qualifies you for the position.

Emphasize related skills when your work experience does not specifically qualify you for the position. In this case, note that Brendan's lifeguarding and CPR certifications are not included since they are not relevant to the internship.

Document work experience but do not include descriptions of duties when they do not support your objective. In this case, Brendan's prior work experience is not specifically related to the financial management internship.

FIGURE 12.9 How to Create a Combined Format to Balance Skills and Experience

Senior Sales Associate. Minimum three years of sales experience required. Leadership, communication, and computer skills a must. Preference given to candidates with demonstrated interpersonal skills, appreciation for a diverse clientele, and fluency in Spanish. Submit your résumé online at www.osasco.com.

MyLab Business Communication
Apply Figure 12.9's key concepts by going to **www.pearson.com/mylab/business-communication**

combined format résumé

Shavon D. Alkins
Box 3106, Robbins, MD 21214
sdalkins@gmail.com | (338) 555-7959
www.linkedin.com/pub/shavon-d-alkins | Twitter@shavon-d-alkins

EDUCATION

Bachelor of Science in Business Administration, 3.87 GPA · · · · · · · · · · · · · May 2018
Concentration in Marketing and International Business
Minors in Accounting and Spanish
Campus University, Robbins, MD

Study Abroad Experiences
- Philippines · January 2017
- Italy, Spain · Summer 2015

Honors
- Dean's List, School of Business & Economics · · · · · · · · · · · · · · 2016–2018
- Phillips-Perry Academic Excellence Award · · · · · · · · · · · · · · · · May 2017
  (presented to the study abroad student with the highest GPA every year)

RELEVANT SKILLS

Leadership
- As treasurer of the Spanish Club, managed budgets and funds while providing effective customer service to a diverse membership

Communication
- Communicate daily with customers while performing sales associate duties
- Read, write, and speak Spanish fluently

Computer Skills
- Skilled in Microsoft Office (Word, Excel, PowerPoint, and Outlook)
- Proficient in Microsoft Access and Adobe Dreamweaver

WORK EXPERIENCE

Sales Associate · October 2018–Present
Target Corporation, Robbins, MD
- Use interpersonal skills to greet and assist customers courteously and efficiently
- Assist with cashier functions and other duties as assigned

Cashier/Sales Associate · · · · · · · · · · · · · · · · · August 2017–October 2018
Food Lion, LLC, Robbins, MD
- Interacted with customers, facilitated transactions, and maintained cash drawer

Bilingual Classroom Assistant · · · · · · · · · · · · · · · August 2015–May 2018
Eastlawn Elementary, Middletown, MD
- Worked with 5th grade children to develop their literacy skills and recognize word sets in Spanish and English

Language Lab Assistant · August 2014–May 2015
Campus University, Robbins, MD
- Prepared lab coursework activities

Cashier/Sales Associate · · · · · · · · · · · · · · · · September 2013–July 2014
Family Dollar Inc., Pensacola, FL
- Managed front-end sales and provided excellent customer service
- Performed store setup tasks

To create a combined-format résumé:

Include all education-related content in the same section, such as study abroad experiences, honors/awards, and extracurricular activities.

Organize relevant skills by keywords listed in the job advertisement.

Document work experience and include descriptions of job duties when they support your application.

Include dates to document that you have the required experience for the position.

FIGURE 12.10 How to Transform a Traditional Résumé into a Graphically Enhanced Résumé

traditional résumé

Shavon D. Alkins
Box 3106, Robbins, MD 21214
sdalkins@gmail.com | (338) 555-7959
www.linkedin.com/pub/shavon-d-alkins | Twitter@shavon-d-alkins

EDUCATION

Bachelor of Science in Business Administration, 3.87 GPA   May 2018
Concentration in Marketing and International Business
Minors in Accounting and Spanish
Campus University, Robbins, MD

Study Abroad Experiences:
- Philippines
- Italy, Spain   January 2017

Honors:
- Dean's List, School of Busines
- Phillips-Perry Academic Excelle
  (presented each year to the st

RELEVANT SKILLS

Leadership
- As treasurer of the Spanish Clu
  providing effective customer s
Communication
- Communicate daily with custo
- Read, write, and speak Spanis
Computer Skills
- Skilled in Microsoft Office (Wo
- Proficient in Microsoft Access

WORK EXPERIENCE

Sales Associate
Target Corporation, Robbins, MD
- Use interpersonal skills to gre
  and efficiently
- Assist with cashier functions a

Cashier/Sales Associate
Food Lion, LLC, Robbins, MD
- Interacted with customers, fac
  cash drawer

Bilingual Classroom Assistant
Eastlawn Elementary, Middletown, M
- Worked with 5th grade childre
  and recognize word sets in Spa

Language Lab Assistant
Campus University, Robbins, MD
- Prepared lab coursework activi

Cashier/Sales Associate
Family Dollar, Inc., Pensacola, FL
- Managed front-end sales and p
- Performed store setup tasks

---

graphically enhanced resume

SHAVON D. ALKINS
MARKETING & INTERNATIONAL BUSINESS

CONTACT

Box 3016, Robbins, MD 21214
sdalkins@gmail.com
(338) 555-7959

www.linkedin.com/pub/
shavon-d-alkins

Twitter@shavon-d-alkins

STUDY ABROAD

Philippines - January 2017
Italy, Spain - Summer 2015

HONORS

Dean's List, School of Business &
Economics, 2016 - 2018

Phillips-Perry Academic
Excellence Award, May 2014
(presented to the study abroad
student with the highest GPA
every year)

RELEVANT SKILLS

LEADERSHIP
As the treasurer of the Spanish
Club, managed budgets and
funds while providing effective
customer service.

COMMUNICATION
Communicate daily with
customers while providing sales
associate duties. Read, write, and
speak Spanish fluently.

COMPUTER SKILLS
Skilled in Microsoft Office (Word,
Excel PowerPoint, and Outlook).
Proficient in Microsoft Access and
Adobe Dreamweaver.

PROFILE

New marketing professional who is passionate about reaching
international audiences and contributing to a creative marketing
team.

EDUCATION

BACHELOR OF SCIENCE IN BUSINESS ADMINISTRATION, 3.87 GPA
Concentration in Marketing and International Business
Minors in Accounting and Spanish

Campus University | May 2018

WORK EXPERIENCE

SALES ASSOCIATE
Target Corporation, Robbins, MD | October 2018 - Present
Use interpersonal skills to greet and assist customers.
Assist with cashier functions and other duties as assigned.

CASHIER/SALES ASSOCIATE
Food Lion, LLC, Robbins, MD | August 2017 - October 2018
Interacted with customers, facilitated transactions, and
maintained cash drawer.

BILINGUAL CLASSROOM ASSISTANT
Eastlawn Elementary, Middletown, MD | August 2015 - May 2108
Worked with 5th grade children to develop their literacy skills and
recognize word sets in Spanish and English.

LANGUAGE LAB ASSISTANT
Campus University, Robbins, MD | August 2014 - May 2015
Prepared lab coursework activities.

CASHIER/SALES ASSOCIATE
Family Dollar, Inc., Pensacola, FL | September 2013 - July 2014
Managed front-end sales and provided excellent customer service.
Performed store set up tasks.

FIGURE 12.11 How to Generate a Plain-Text Version of Your Résumé

formatted résumé

Shavon D. Alkins
Box 3106, Robbins, MD 21214
sdalkins@gmail.com | (338) 555-7959
www.linkedin.com/pub/shavon-d-alkins | Twitter@shavon-d-alkins

EDUCATION

Bachelor of Science in Business Administration, 3.87 GPA   May 2018
Concentration in Marketing and International Business
Minors in Accounting and Spanish
Campus University, Robbins, MD

Study Abroad Experiences:
- Philippines
- Italy, Spain

Honors:
- Dean's List, School of Busines
- Phillips-Perry Academic Excelle
  (presented each year to the st

RELEVANT SKILLS

Leadership
- As treasurer of the Spanish Clu
  providing effective customer s
Communication
- Communicate daily with custo
- Read, write, and speak Spanisl
Computer Skills
- Skilled in Microsoft Office (Wo
- Proficient in Microsoft Access

WORK EXPERIENCE

Sales Associate
Target Corporation, Robbins, MD
- Use interpersonal skills to gree
  and efficiently
- Assist with cashier functions a

Cashier/Sales Associate
Food Lion, LLC, Robbins, MD
- Interacted with customers, fac
  cash drawer

Bilingual Classroom Assistant
Eastlawn Elementary, Middletown, M
- Worked with 5th grade childre
  and recognize word sets in Spa

Language Lab Assistant
Campus University, Robbins, MD
- Prepared lab coursework activi

Cashier/Sales Associate
Family Dollar, Inc., Pensacola, FL
- Managed front-end sales and p
- Performed store setup tasks

plain-text résumé

Shavon D. Alkins
Box 3106, Robbins, MD 21214
sdalkins@gmail.com / (338) 555-7959
www.linkedin.com/pub/shavon-d-alkins | Twitter@shavon-d-alkins

EDUCATION

Bachelor of Science in Business Administration, May 2018
Concentration in Marketing and International Business
Minors in Accounting and Spanish
Campus University, Robbins, MD

Study Abroad Experiences:
Philippines, January 2017
Italy, Spain, Summer 2015
Honors:
Dean's List, 2016-2018
Phillips-Perry Academic Excellence Award, May 2015

RELEVANT SKILLS

Leadership - As treasurer of the Spanish Club, managed budgets and funds while providing
effective customer service to a diverse membership
Communication - Communicate daily with customers while performing sales associate duties
Read, write, and speak Spanish fluently
Computer Skills - Skilled in Microsoft Office (Word, Excel, PowerPoint, Outlook); Proficient in
Access, FrontPage

WORK EXPERIENCE

Sales Associate, October 2018–Present
Target Corporation, Robbins, MD
Use interpersonal skills to greet and assist guests effectively and efficiently
Assist with cashier functions and other duties as assigned

Cashier/Sales Associate, August 2015 - October 2016
Food Lion, LLC, Robbins, MD
Interact with customers, facilitate transactions, and maintain cash drawer

Bilingual Grade Classroom Assistant, August 2011 - May 2014
Eastlawn Elementary, Middletown, MD
Worked with 5th grade children to develop their literacy skills and recognize word sets

Language Lab Assistant, August 2012 - May 2013
Campus University, Robbins, MD
Prepared lab coursework activities

Cashier/Sales Associate, September 2011 - July 2012
Family Dollar Inc., Pensacola, FL
Managed front-end sales and provided excellent customer service
Performed store setup tasks

Create a plain-text version of your résumé content for web-based résumé databases. Follow these directions:

1. Open your formatted résumé in your word processing application and select "Save As" to rename your document as a "Plain Text" file (.txt). This option is available in most word processing programs.

2. Reformat your .txt document to ensure legibility in plain text.
   - Change the line spacing to single (with no extra spacing programmed to automatically be added before or after paragraphs).
   - Add line spaces where necessary to separate categories.
   - Remove any borders, lines, symbols, and tabs.
   - Use ALL CAPS to indicate headings.

Compose effective résumé content

When composing your résumé, tailor the content for the specific job you are seeking. Many job applicants incorrectly assume that an all-inclusive list of skills and experience on a résumé helps them be everything to every employer. However, résumés with long lists require prospective employers to hunt to find the relevant qualifications. To make the information easy to find, organize your content as illustrated in the sample résumés.

The chronological résumé illustrated in Figure 12.7 on page 478 identifies design and content guidelines that apply to all résumés. Content guidelines for functional and combination résumés are provided in Figures 12.8 and 12.9 on pages 480 and 481. A few specific sections of résumés are particularly challenging to compose. These include objective statements, work experience, and relevant skills. For advice about how to write these sections, look at the targeted recommendations in **Figure 12.12** on page 484.

ACE

Compose

FIGURE 12.12 How to Compose Effective Résumé Components: Summary Statements, Work Experience, and Skills

Summary Statement

Use an objective statement to show how your goals can help an employer.

Use a qualifications summary if you have strengths and skills that qualify you for the job but little, if any, related work experience.

Traditional Objective:	Qualifications Summary:
To secure a challenging financial management position that requires strong analytical, interpersonal, and communication skills to help investors achieve their financial goals.	Financial management major with experience: • Analyzing detailed income and profit/loss statements • Explaining complicated tax requirements to clients • Managing Microsoft Dynamics, Quicken, and ERP application systems

Professional Profile:

Professional financial manager with 12 years of experience in asset management and risk analysis. Proven leadership in directing a $28 million business (110 employees) where responsibilities included controlling costs and growing profits by developing strategic financial plans, inventory control systems, and profit/loss management procedures. Implemented and evaluated ongoing assessment strategies to enhance short- and long-term budgeting goals. Seasoned know-how in interpersonal communication and collaboration. Recent industry certifications demonstrate advanced skills in financial management (CFM), analysis (CFA), and planning (CFP).

Use a professional profile if you have a well-established work history and more professional experience to offer. A professional profile includes specifics about achievements that make you stand out as a candidate.

Work Experience

INEFFECTIVE	EFFECTIVE	
• Responsible for the night crew at Arby's	• Supervised an eight-person night crew • Handled all customer and worker complaints	**Be specific about capabilities.** Avoid vague, generic phrases.
• Experience with general office duties	• Typed and filed confidential correspondence • Formatted fliers, brochures, and newsletters	**Quantify your accomplishments** by using numbers and metrics to demonstrate your impact.
• Worked as a packager on an assembly line	• Learned the value of precision and teamwork while working as a packager on a fast-paced assembly line • Received Employee-of-the-Month Award during first year	**Don't exaggerate your capabilities;** as discussed in the Ethics feature on page 479, this misleading information may cause problems.
• Developed excellent communication skills	• Wrote a comprehensive policy and procedures manual for new interns	**Begin each item with an action verb,** never with the personal pronoun "I," which would be repetitive.
• Effective team player	• Collaborated on a successful client proposal, working with personnel from product design, marketing, and manufacturing	**Be consistent with verb tenses within each job you list.** Use present-tense verbs for current jobs and past-tense verbs for previous jobs.
• Detail oriented	• Developed monthly and yearly sales and budget forecasts	

FIGURE 12.12 *(Continued)*

Skills

Manager Needed

Sparrow Associates, a leading management consulting company in the Baltimore area, seeks an enthusiastic and professional office manager to join our team. Effective collaboration is a must. Technical competencies in Microsoft Office software required. Analytical skills—especially as related to budget data—are highly valued. Online applications accepted through June 15 only at www.Sparrow.Associates.com.

Relevant Skills

Collaboration
- Participated in several committees and fund-raising initiatives as an active member and treasurer of Spanish Club—a campus-based student organization

Technical Competence
- Skilled in Microsoft Office (Word, Excel, PowerPoint, and Outlook)
- Proficient in Microsoft Access and Adobe Dreamweaver

Analytical Skills
- Analyzed operating budget of a local not-for-profit organization and made recommendations for achieving cost savings and modifying a store's product line as part of a 60-hour service-learning requirement for a managerial accounting course

Use keywords from the job advertisement to describe your skills. If your résumé doesn't have the right keywords, it might be rejected by an *applicant tracking system*.

Provide credibility by including supporting details or evidence. Include volunteer and extracurricular activities that helped develop relevant skills.

Be prepared to provide additional details during a job interview.

CULTURE
REVISING YOUR RÉSUMÉ FOR INTERNATIONAL OPPORTUNITIES

You can broaden your employment options by applying for internships and positions in other countries, either with foreign companies or with U.S.-based companies that have international branches. Although most international employers will accept a U.S.-style résumé, revising your résumé for an international audience will help convince the employer that you are knowledgeable about international differences and will be effective in a cross-cultural work environment. Here are three ways to revise your résumé:

- **Adapt the résumé for the country where you are applying.** The differences in expectations might surprise you.[27] For example, although U.S. employers prefer one-page résumés for entry-level applicants, two- to four-page résumés are standard internationally. In addition, photos are expected on résumés submitted in most Asian and European countries (other than the United Kingdom). These countries also expect more personal information, such as nationality, gender, age, and marital status—information that is discouraged in the United States and United Kingdom because of discrimination laws.

- **Add a section that sells your cross-cultural experience and skills.** Include all cross-cultural and international experiences gained from jobs, internships, or volunteer experiences. If you don't have any yet, capitalize on any study-abroad opportunities your school offers. Also include any relevant academic courses, multicultural academic experiences, language abilities, and personal international travel. Grouping this material in one section increases its impact and decreases the chance that employers will miss it when reading your résumé.

- **In your skills and abilities section, stress the skills required to succeed when working in another culture.** For example, include bullet points such as these:

  - Relate well to people with different personalities and backgrounds
  - Able to adapt to change and new environments
  - Adept at learning languages quickly
  - Appreciate different work styles
  - Collaborate effectively on multicultural teams

Including this kind of content will demonstrate that you are aware that working in a cross-cultural environment requires a special set of skills.

For a CULTURE exercise, go to Exercise 17 on page 519.

Evaluate

Evaluate your content and design

As part of the ACE process, use the checklist in **Figure 12.13** to evaluate your résumé and ensure that it communicates a professional image.

FIGURE 12.13 Checklist for Evaluating the Content and Design of Your Résumé

Is the content clear, complete, and concise?	☐ Ask someone who is not familiar with your school or work experience to review your content to ensure that the wording is clear. ☐ Reword or explain any vague information. ☐ Carefully review your content to ensure you aren't forgetting relevant experiences. ☐ Remove any irrelevant content or redundancies, such as listing the same job duties for different jobs.
Does the content specifically use keywords from the job you are applying for?	☐ Ensure that your objective statement or qualifications summary relates to the job description and that you use keywords from the job advertisement.
Is the most important information emphasized?	☐ Organize the content directly by placing the most important information—what qualifies you for the job—at the beginning of your résumé. ☐ Grab the attention of prospective employers who often quickly scan résumés to find the content they need to make interview decisions.
Is the résumé designed well and spaced to fit the page?	☐ If your résumé is shorter than one page, use extra spaces between sections or increase the line spacing throughout the page to fill a single standard 8½″ × 11″ page with balanced margins. ☐ If your résumé is longer than one page, evaluate the content. Do not compress it by minimizing side margins. If you have enough relevant and concisely worded content to require a longer résumé, make sure you have balanced amounts of text on all pages.
Are alignment and style consistent?	☐ Use the same format for content in all sections. If you used bold and italics for a job title in one of your work experiences, make sure you used the same format for the rest of your job titles. If you right-aligned your dates in your work experience, be consistent with all dates throughout your résumé.
Is the résumé carefully proof-read for spelling and typos?	☐ Check names, locations, and employment dates of companies. ☐ Check the spellings of any names (such as awards and scholarships) to ensure they are correct.
Have you obtained sufficient feedback?	☐ Ask people in your network to evaluate your résumé. Provide them with a copy of the job advertisement so they can assess whether you have met the needs of the employer. ☐ Get feedback from a variety of different perspectives, such as instructors, career counselors, and previous employers or supervisors. ☐ Consider getting feedback from résumé review websites such as vMock and Naukri FastForward that use algorithms to analyze content and suggest improvements. ☐ If you receive conflicting advice, consider the suggestions from the potential employer's perspective.

How do you find job opportunities and submit applications?

With one or more résumés drafted and ready to be customized, how do you find appropriate job opportunities and apply for them? This section helps you use the ACE process to analyze your options for finding job opportunities, compose effective cover letters that persuade employers to interview you, and submit and track your application.

Analyze your options for finding job opportunities

Analyze

You may already be familiar with the services and opportunities provided by your school's career center as well as online job banks such as Monster, Glassdoor, SimplyHired, or Career Builder. Many job banks provide access to company profiles and other resources to help with your job search. To take advantage of these resources, use these tips:

- Create an account with job banks so you can make connections with employers
- Search for jobs by keyword, title, company, or location
- Access career resources such as video interview practice, résumé builders, and electronic portfolio systems
- Post your résumé to get free résumé critiques, to be searchable by employers, and to apply for jobs
- Research company profiles and read reviews from employees

Sources of job opportunities are more diverse than you might think. Traditional options, such as job banks and your personal and professional networks, are still important. But also be aware of the growing number of job-related features available through social media. For example, Facebook supports a job search tool that lets employers post want ads (see the "Jobs" link in the "Explore" section).[28] By default, the postings are from employers in your local area, but you can change the location and filter for both industry type and job type (such as full-time, part-time, internship, volunteer, and contract work). In addition, connecting with Facebook groups can extend your network and provide opportunities to gain experience.[29] And you can use Twitter's advanced search feature to find jobs in specific areas or industries.[30] Keep an open mind about opportunities that do not match your ideal job or ideal location; you never know what opportunity might lead to another option.

To find unadvertised job opportunities, draw on your network for referrals, including using word-of-mouth strategies through social media. Referrals can provide you with a substantial advantage in the job market. A LinkedIn survey reported that 85 percent of people surveyed found their last job through networking.[31] Other research suggests that 71 percent of human resource professionals believe employee referrals provide the best job applicants.[32] To support referrals, some companies offer referral bonuses to current and former employees.[33] **Figure 12.14** on page 488 outlines activities that will increase the number of job openings you identify.

Compose an effective elevator pitch

Compose

You never know when you might be in position to start a conversation with someone who can help connect you with a job opportunity. You might be introduced to a friend of a friend at a party who happens to an HR manager, or you could find yourself in an elevator with a CEO. That's where the term **elevator pitch** comes from: In informal situations like these, you need a concise statement that is designed to communicate *quickly* (within the time of an elevator ride) who you are, what you do, and how you offer value as a potential employee. Think of it as a commercial about yourself.[34]

Your elevator pitch should be related to your brand message and unique selling proposition (see pages 472–473), but because your elevator pitch is delivered in person, it also needs to include a hook to intrigue the audience and initiate a deeper conversation. Here are some tips to do that:[35,36]

- **Start with a rhetorical question** that sets the stage for your pitch. The question should put your unique selling proposition in context and gain the audience's attention so they want to hear more.

elevator pitch A concise statement designed to communicate the value of an idea, a product, or a job candidate; intrigue the audience; and initiate a deeper conversation.

FIGURE 12.14 How to Analyze Your Options for Finding Job Opportunities

Register with career centers	• Take advantage of career-counseling services, résumé assistance, mock interviews, and workshops that focus on employability skills. • Use these services to obtain internships or service-learning opportunities, such as volunteering to do office work for a charity organization. • Identify other resources, such as employment agencies or head-hunting firms that specialize in matching employers with qualified job applicants.
Search employment advertisements and job banks	• Check print sources, such as newspapers and trade journals, as well as online resources, such as CareerBuilder, ZipRecruiter, and Monster. • Use online job banks to set up email alerts based on your search parameters to review postings that match your interests.
Join professional organizations	• Determine which student clubs at your school relate to your career goals. • Identify both social and academic clubs that focus on specific disciplines, such as the Society for Human Resource Management (SHRM), or opportunities to enhance your professional development, such as Toastmasters.
Develop professional and personal networks	• Share your career goals with your *network*—the people you know, including fellow students, friends, coworkers, faculty, staff, business contacts, and family members. • Tell everyone in your network that you are looking for a job. Word of mouth is one of the most effective ways to learn about employment opportunities, many of which are not posted in job advertisements or company websites. • Expand your network by exploring alumni databases, attending career fairs, joining professional associations, volunteering in your community, and participating in campus workshops or presentations sponsored by companies in your area.
Use social networking outlets and mobile apps	• Use professional sites, such as LinkedIn, to analyze companies you want to work for and the kinds of job opportunities they provide. • Download apps such as "LinkedIn Students" to explore jobs and access resources to support your search. Other mobile apps are available from Indeed, Good.Co, Switch, Glassdoor, SnagAJob, and Simply Hired.[37] • "Like" and follow companies on social sites—such as Facebook and Twitter—to learn more about the company and job opportunities • Expand your word-of-mouth network by actively using these sites to let your friends know you are looking for a job.
Target specific employers	• Research the company to familiarize yourself with its mission, products or services, corporate culture, and financial health. • Examine its current challenges and reputation with Google News, study its stock history with Yahoo! Finance, read past articles about its performance in *Fortune* magazine or *Forbes*, gain insight about workplace culture with Glassdoor, and talk to current or former employees. • Use professional and social networking sites such as LinkedIn, Facebook, and YouTube to find additional information about the company.

- **Highlight skills** that complement your experience and relate to the position you want.
- **Tell a short but memorable story** to demonstrate your skills in action.
- **Avoid technical terms** to ensure that any audience will understand your pitch.
- **End with what you want** by specifically asking for it, but keep in mind that this will change depending on your audience. You might be requesting an interview, an opportunity to follow up, or a referral to someone else who can help you with your next steps.
- **Time yourself** to ensure that your pitch is less than one minute long.
- **Memorize it** but don't talk to fast when you repeat it. You need to sound conversational.

Practice your pitch with others and use their feedback to evaluate and continually improve your content. Your pitch will change throughout your professional career as you work toward promotions and other opportunities.

Compose persuasive cover letters

When you find a job opportunity, revise your standard résumé to ensure that it's targeted for this specific job. Then compose a customized **cover letter**—a persuasive message that highlights your relevant skills and persuades an employer to spend time reviewing your résumé. A cover letter can take the form of a formal business letter, or it can be an email if you are submitting your résumé electronically. Recruiters suggest that, even in a changing hiring environment where applications are often read by digital tracking systems, a cover letter is still important for several reasons.[38] It allows you to:

- Highlight the knowledge and experiences that are most important to this position
- Direct the employer to pay attention to the key elements of your résumé
- Speak directly to an employer about your fit with the company
- Set yourself apart from the competition by conveying your professional personality and demonstrating your writing skills

The following advice will help you write an effective cover letter.

Compose

cover letter A persuasive letter or email sent to a prospective employer along with a résumé that "sells" your résumé to the employer.

Analyze the position requirements

A cover letter typically includes a standard set of information. It introduces you and your résumé, specifies the position you are applying for, highlights your qualifications for that position, and requests an interview. Although all cover letters contain this basic information, an effective cover letter will be tailored to meet the employer's needs by describing how you are qualified for the specific position. To determine how to customize your cover letter, use all the information available to identify which keywords to stress. Look for words that describe job duties, job requirements, and the desired characteristics of a job candidate. For example, if you were applying for the position described in **Figure 12.15**, you might include the following keywords in your cover letter and résumé: *management, leadership, collaborative, communication skills, computer skills, business experience, project management, interpersonal skills, written communications, presentation skills, diversity, teamwork,* and *travel.* However, you must go beyond simply listing these keywords. Indicate how you exemplify these traits or characteristics by describing how you gained the experience or mastered the skills.

Analyze

To customize your message even more, analyze the company's website to learn about its mission, goals, and past performance. Search for news items about the company and its industry to become familiar with current events and trends. The more you know about the company, its products or services, and the specific job you want, the better you can portray

FIGURE 12.15 How to Analyze Position Requirements

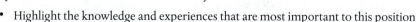

Assistant Sales Manager–Dover Industries, Plymouth, Michigan
This position is responsible for assisting the sales manager of a regional chain of department stores. The role requires leadership skills to manage collaborative processes, effective communication skills to ensure deadlines are met, and efficient computer skills to coordinate and manage large volumes of data. The assistant sales manager develops and maintains positive working relationships with store managers, develops promotional strategies, executes promotional activities, reviews market strategies to identify potential customers and new business opportunities, conducts competitive research, prepares sales analysis reports, and helps store managers achieve sales and profit goals.

Job Requirements:
- Undergraduate degree in business administration or related field
- Minimum two to five years of general business experience; project management experience preferred
- Outstanding interpersonal, written communications, and presentation skills
- Effective collaboration in diverse team environments to achieve business results
- Travel requirement of 10 to 15 percent

To analyze job requirements, highlight key terms in job advertisements and in the employment section of a company's website.

yourself as a viable candidate in your cover letter. Bookmark the website or print the documentation so you can easily reference this material later to prepare for an interview.

Compose

Compose persuasive content

You may be tempted to begin drafting your cover letter by using a sample that you find online or in a book. Instead of copying from a sample, create your own personal template that persuasively sells your strengths to a potential employer. Business communicators who compose persuasive messages to sell products and services often use the **AIDA** pattern—**A**ttention, **I**nterest, **D**esire, and **A**ction—to create or increase sales. You can use AIDA in your cover letter as well to sell yourself to an employer. The following guidelines will help you compose persuasive cover letters:

AIDA An acronym used in marketing to suggest the organization of sales communication: Attention, Interest, Desire, Action.

- **Gain attention at the beginning of the message.** Gaining attention is relatively easy when you write a *solicited cover letter*—your reply to an employment advertisement or job posting that requests applications. The audience is actively looking for someone to fill the job; to catch their attention, all you need to do is name the position you are applying for. To motivate the audience to read further, you can explain why you believe you are a good fit for the job, or you can demonstrate relevant knowledge about the company. If during your research about the company you find interesting information, you may be able to include something similar to this example: "I'm targeting companies that know how to take good care of their clients, and the recent article in the *Chicago Tribune* spotlighting your efforts to reward your most customer-focused employees grabbed my attention."

- In an *unsolicited cover letter*, gaining attention is more challenging. Because the company did not request applications, you need to persuade the audience to read your message rather than ignore or discard it. One approach is to send the message to someone in the company with whom you have a connection through your professional network. That person is likely to read the message and perhaps pass it on to the human resources department or a hiring manager. In that case, you need to convince your audience that you have enough interest or knowledge to be worth considering the next time an opening occurs.

- **Build interest/desire with keywords.** The middle paragraph(s) of your cover letter should outline your skills that specifically qualify you for the position. Use the keywords outlined during your analysis of the job position to identify how your skills fit the employer's needs. Rather than simply restating the content of your résumé, demonstrate your knowledge of the company by showing how your abilities match the mission or goals of the potential employer. If you do not have a skill or qualification listed in the job advertisement, do not exaggerate your abilities. Be honest but de-emphasize that qualification—for example, "Although my full-time work experience is less than five years, my three internships in banks and brokerage firms have provided me a diverse understanding of the financial services industry."

- **Motivate action in the closing.** End your cover letter by requesting an interview. Avoid weak wording, such as "I hope you will contact me." Be confident but not presumptuous. A statement such as "I know you will want to interview me for this position" does not motivate action. The sample cover letters in **Figure 12.16** on page 491 and **Figure 12.17** on page 492 illustrate different ways to motivate action: requesting an interview, requesting more information, and expressing enthusiasm for the job. Providing your contact information at the end of the message, even if it also appears in your letterhead or email signature block, can also help motivate the employer to contact you because the contact information is so easy to find. Figure 12.16 is an example of a solicited cover letter sent as an email in response to an advertisement, and Figure 12.17 is an example of an unsolicited cover letter to a company not currently requesting applications.

Evaluate

Evaluate content and format

Like all other correspondence, cover letters benefit from critical evaluation and revision. Use the checklist in **Figure 12.18** on page 493 to evaluate the content and format of your cover letters to ensure they are targeted and persuasive.

FIGURE 12.16 How to Write a Solicited Cover Letter

email

File	Message	Insert	Options	Format Text	Review		

Send

To... jw.herrick@dover.com

Cc...

Subject: Application for Assistant Sales Manager Position

Attachment: Shavon_Alkins_Resume.pdf

Dear Mr. Herrick:

Thank you for the opportunity to apply for the Assistant Sales Manager position at Dover Industries. I was very pleased to learn from Monster.com that you are currently hiring. I first became interested in working for Dover when we studied the company's Quality Care program in my marketing class last year. Since then, I've been following Dover Industries and have been particularly impressed by the company's ability to promote its mission to "be the preferred shopping experience for a diverse clientele by providing quality products and services."

As my attached résumé indicates, I can bring to Dover over three years of sales associate and customer service experience, most of which I gained while a full-time student. This experience, along with academic work in marketing and other business concentrations, has helped me develop the leadership, communication, and collaboration skills required to be a valuable member of your management team. I had an opportunity to develop those skills further during my junior year study-abroad term in the Philippines, where I played a leadership role on an international and interdisciplinary team of students working on an intense, month-long market research project about reaching underserved populations. I was also one of the team members chosen to return to the Philippines to present our results at the Philippine Business Conference and Expo in Manila. More recently, I had the opportunity to demonstrate my abilities as one of the team leaders in our local Target's Customer Comes First Campaign, which significantly increased our customer satisfaction ratings.

I am enthusiastic about working at Dover and would appreciate the opportunity to meet with you to discuss how I can use my experience to exceed your customer care goals. Please contact me by phone (338-555-7959) or email (sdalkins@gmail.com) at your earliest convenience to arrange an interview.

Thank you for your time and consideration.

Sincerely,

Shavon Alkins

Shavon D. Alkins
Box 3106
Robbins, MD 21214
sdalkins@gmail.com
(338) 555-7959
www.linkedin.com/pub/shavon-d-alkins
Twitter@shavon-d-alkins

To take advantage of the AIDA pattern, follow these steps for a solicited cover letter:

Gain **attention** in the first paragraph by expressing a long-term interest in and knowledge about the company that goes beyond the information in the job advertisement.

Build **interest/desire** by relating education and experience to the job requirements using keywords, but don't exaggerate your abilities. Provide examples that demonstrate skills.

Motivate **action** by expressing enthusiasm, requesting an interview, including contact information, and mentioning a benefit to the employer.

FIGURE 12.17 How to Write an Unsolicited Cover Letter

letter

Shavon D. Alkins
Box 3106, Robbins, MD 21214
sdalkins@gmail.com | (338) 555-7959
www.linkedin.com/pub/shavon-d-alkins | Twitter@shavon-d-alkins

October 15, 20XX

Ms. Margaret Beckstein
Director of Sales
Baylin Technologies, Inc.
526 Industrial Parkway
Hanover, MD 21182

Dear Ms. Beckstein:

Your assistant director, Robert Taylor, suggested I contact you about any management positions that may become available soon. I met Mr. Taylor at a Campus University alumni event and was very excited when I learned he was with Baylin Technologies. I am particularly interested in becoming a member of your international mobile technology team, and am enclosing my résumé for your consideration.

I first began following Baylin Technologies during my junior-year study abroad experience in the Philippines. During that term, I worked with an international and interdisciplinary team of students on a research project to provide wireless technologies to underserved populations. In that project, which we presented at the Philippine Business Conference and Expo in Manila, we researched Baylin's Southeast Asia initiative. I was impressed with the company's leadership in providing both technology and customer service in rural areas around the world. I would like to contribute to that mission.

As a recent business administration graduate with concentrations in both marketing and international business and a minor in Spanish, I believe I have the knowledge, skills, and interest to make a valuable contribution to your team. I am also well equipped to work with a diverse clientele based on more than three years of sales associate and customer service experience.

Even if you have no specific job openings at this time, I would value the opportunity to meet with you and discuss how I can best prepare myself for a future opening at Baylin. Please contact me by phone (338-555-7959) or email (sdalkins@gmail.com) to schedule an interview.

Sincerely,

Shavon Alkins

Shavon Alkins

Enclosure

To take advantage of the AIDA pattern, follow these steps for an unsolicited cover letter:

Gain **attention** by including any or all of the following content: addressing the letter to a specific person, stating the purpose of the message, mentioning a mutual contact, and indicating a specific reason for interest in this company.

Build **interest/desire** by demonstrating knowledge about the company and highlighting experience that relates to the company's focus.

Also build **interest/desire** by highlighting your education and relating your coursework to skills and company needs.

Motivate **action** by asking the recipient to contact you, even if no job openings exist. Express an interest in future job openings.

The enclosure notation tells the audience to look for additional pages in the envelope.

FIGURE 12.18 Checklist for Evaluating Cover Letter Content and Format

Is the message complete and targeted to the employer?	☐ Review the job advertisement to ensure you know what information is being requested and what keywords belong in your letter. ☐ Review your letter to ensure you have included the requested information and keywords. ☐ Read your message from the employer's perspective to determine if you are meeting the company's needs.
Is the message clear and concise?	☐ Read the message aloud to ensure that the sentences are clear and make sense. ☐ Check to be sure that you have used paragraphs effectively to group similar content. ☐ Ensure that you haven't overused the pronoun "I," which leads to a monotonous writing style. ☐ Cut material, if necessary, to keep your letter to one page.
Did you include your résumé?	☐ Ensure you have explicitly said you are enclosing or attaching your résumé. ☐ If writing a letter, include an enclosure notation after the complimentary closing. ☐ If attaching your résumé to an email message, use a meaningful filename. For example, do not save your résumé file with a name like *"resume.pdf"* or *"Shavon'sRez.doc."* Instead, include your full name in the filename: *"Shavon_Alkins_Resume.pdf."* ☐ Check to ensure your résumé is actually attached or enclosed.
Is the message formatted professionally?	☐ Use a standard letter or email format. ☐ For a letter format, use the same heading at the top of your cover letter that you use on your résumé to help your documents look consistent. ☐ For an email format, use an appropriate subject line that identifies the job title. Rather than vague subject lines, such as *"Job Application,"* be specific, such as *"Application for Assistant Sales Manager Position."* In some cases, the job listing will indicate specific content for the subject line, such as a job code.
Are there typos or misspellings?	☐ Proofread your message several times, but pay additional attention to the spelling of names and double check the accuracy of numbers.
Have you obtained sufficient feedback?	☐ Ask your instructors, advisors, and career counselors to help you evaluate your cover letters. Provide them with a copy of the job advertisement and your résumé. ☐ Get input from professionals in the field, if possible. Take advantage of guest speakers in your classes, alumni of your school, colleagues of your parents, or your friends' parents.

Select a medium for submission and follow up as necessary

With all your employment materials completed, you have a few remaining decisions to make. How do you submit your application? And how do you follow up when necessary?

Evaluate your application submission options

Over the past decade, methods of delivering job applications have evolved as technology has improved. Very few employers currently request résumés and cover letters on paper. Instead, they prefer email applications[39,40] and online submissions through tools such as LinkedIn or their own web-based or mobile applications. However, unsolicited letters may get more attention if sent by postal mail because unsolicited email often goes unread. **Figures 12.19** and **12.20** on page 494 offer checklists for submitting job applications by email and postal mail.

On rare occasions, you may have the option of providing your application materials in person. Don't assume you will simply drop off your documents with a receptionist and leave unnoticed. Dress professionally and be polite. The employer could consider the receptionist's impression of you. In addition, even if you have not made an appointment, you may have the opportunity to meet with someone to discuss the position. Be prepared to make a good impression.

Follow up as necessary

Keep records of all your employment communication by using an individual tracking sheet for each company you apply to. This sheet should include company contact information, the title and description of the position applied for, materials you submitted, and the dates

FIGURE 12.19 Checklist for Submitting Your Job Application by Email

Decide whether to attach the cover letter as a separate file or include it within the body of the email message	*If you attach both your cover letter and résumé:* ☐ Include a short but formatted email message indicating which position you are applying for and what application documents are attached. ☐ Be aware that although attached letters are more formal, they may be inadvertently overlooked. *If you decide to include your cover letter content in the body of the email message:* ☐ Use a standard email format rather than a formal letter style. ☐ Be aware that cover letters included in the body of an email message may be problematic for recipients who read email on mobile devices.
Use portable document file attachments and appropriate filenames	☐ Use PDF (Portable Document Format) attachments unless the job advertisement requests a specific file type, such as Word files or .rtf formats. ☐ Be consistent with your résumé and cover letter filenames, for example, *"Shavon_Alkins_Resume.pdf"* and *"Shavon_Alkins_Cover_Letter.pdf."*
Confirm your message was received	☐ Use a return-receipt feature with an email submission, which offers two benefits: It communicates to the recipient that the message is important, and it provides you documentation that your message was received. ☐ Send a follow-up email requesting confirmation if your email system does not support return receipts or if you do not receive a response.
Follow up	☐ If after two weeks you have not yet heard from the employer, follow up with an email indicating your interest in the position. This additional effort can make a positive impression and increase your chances of being considered for an interview. (See Figure 12.21 for an example of a follow-up email message.)

FIGURE 12.20 Checklist for Submitting Your Job Application by Postal Mail

Ensure consistent font/style among all documents, including the envelope	☐ Ensure your cover letter, résumé, and envelope complement each other by using the same paper quality, font, and formatting features. ☐ Create business cards with the same format as well. Your business card stock should match the paper color and style of your cover letter and résumé.
Print your cover letter and résumé on quality paper	☐ Use high-quality bond paper in a professional color, such as white or buff. ☐ Avoid gray or patterned paper that does not photocopy well. ☐ Look for paper that has a *watermark*—a barely visible logo that can be seen only when the paper is held to light. ☐ Print your documents on a laser-quality printer and load the paper tray so the watermark is right side up.
Project a professional image	☐ Use a handwritten signature to send a nonverbal message about your personality and professionalism. ☐ Use a readable cursive writing style and stay within the boundaries of the signature block. Sloppy or wildly artistic signatures can be perceived as flamboyant and inappropriate for business correspondence. ☐ Mail your documents in a large mailing envelope rather than folding them into a standard envelope. ☐ Print a label or feed the envelope through the printer rather than hand printing the recipient's address and your return address on the envelope.
Follow up	☐ Just as with emailed applications, follow up with the employer if you have not yet heard from the employer within two weeks. (See Figure 12.21 for an example.)

when you made contact.[41] Review your tracking information regularly so you can follow up with employers. If you have not heard from an employer a week or 10 days after the application submission deadline, you can contact the employer to inquire about the status of your application. Research indicates that HR mangers prefer to receive follow-ups from applicants by email (87 percent) and phone calls (81 percent) over handwritten notes (38 percent) or social media (27 percent) or text messages (10 percent).[42] If you choose to call, be prepared by outlining what you plan to say and calling from a private location free from noise or possible interruptions. Whether you call or email, use the opportunity to further sell your fit for the job. See **Figure 12.21** for suggestions on how to compose a follow-up message.

FIGURE 12.21 How to Write a Job Application Follow-up Message

Address the hiring manager or contact person by name.

Indicate the position you applied for and when you sent your résumé.

Briefly identify your knowledge of the company and your interest in a long-term career with the company.

Ask if additional information is required.

Request an interview and provide your contact information.

Close on a positive, forward-looking note.

career fair A gathering of representatives or recruiters from many companies seeking to fill open positions.

virtual interview An interview conducted by telephone, Skype, or teleconference call, often used to narrow the candidate pool before scheduling an onsite visit.

panel interview An interview format that involves several people, such as a search committee, who gather in a conference or seminar room with a job applicant to discuss the position.

group interview An interview format in which an employer meets with several applicants at the same time to assess their approach to working collaboratively with others.

Analyze

action interview An interview format that requires applicants to make a presentation or perform under work-based conditions, which could be simulated or real.

(SQ4) How do you prepare for a job interview?

If your cover letters and résumés present you as someone who meets an employer's needs, you may receive an invitation to interview. A job interview is a mutual learning experience. The employer will learn more about you to determine whether you are a good fit for the job, and you will learn more about the company and the position to determine whether the job is a good fit for you. Because you may get only one opportunity to persuade an employer that you are the best applicant, it is important to develop professional interview skills.

Analyze how to benefit from different types of interviews

Although traditional one-on-one interviews are still common, you may participate in several different kinds of interviews. For example, your first contact with a company may be a mini-interview at a **career fair**. Later, the company may ask you to participate in a campus interview or **virtual interview** before inviting you to visit the company. Once there, you may be involved in **panel interviews**, **group interviews**, or **action interviews** before meeting with a hiring manager. Each of these interview formats has a different goal, and **Figure 12.22** on page 496 outlines ways to maximize your benefit from each one.

FIGURE 12.22 How to Get the Most Benefit from Different Types of Interviews

For all interview formats	• Review the websites of the companies you want to meet with ahead of time so you are knowledgeable about their products or services, mission statements, and open positions. • Dress like a businessperson rather than a college student. • Adopt a confident and professional attitude. Be slightly more formal than you normally are. • Make a strong professional first impression by using a firm handshake, make eye contact, and smile (practice greeting people ahead of time to feel confident about your body language). • Demonstrate your knowledge and interest in the company. • Project a professional voice by speaking clearly and at a normal pace. • Pause before speaking to gather your thoughts, then breathe deeply, articulate your words, and smile—even if you are on the telephone. • Ask good questions about the company's current projects or news items you have read to indicate your interest in the company. Ask the recruiter what he/she likes about the company. • Ask for a business card and make notes on the back of the card to help you remember the interviewer who gave it to you. • Thank interviewers for taking the time to speak with you.
Career fairs— *gathering of representatives from many companies seeking to fill open positions*	• Study the floor plan map to find out which employers will participate and where their booths will be located. • Plan a strategy for the recruiters you want to talk to first, second, and third. • Arrive early to avoid long lines and to maximize your time with recruiters. • Approach recruiters and make the first move to start the conversation with your elevator pitch. Have two or three questions ready. The quality of the conversations you have far outweigh the number of résumés you hand out.[43] • Take notes to demonstrate your interest in the company and to prepare for onsite interviews. • Follow up after the fair with a short email message thanking recruiters for their time. Reiterating your interest in a particular position says a lot about your professionalism and attention to detail. You might also want to attach a PDF copy of your résumé so they have an electronic version to share with others at their company.
Virtual interviews— *conducted by telephone or webcam to filter candidates before scheduling onsite interviews*	• Plan to be in a quiet location where you feel comfortable and will not be disturbed. Ask anyone near the room not to come in or make any noise or distractions. • Use a landline rather than a cell phone or wired connection to minimize the possibility of a dropped call or bad connection. • If you are calling in, begin professionally by identifying yourself before you ask for the person you're calling. • Write down the interviewers' names and job titles as they introduce themselves. If they don't provide their job titles, ask for them so you can ask specific questions that relate to people's positions. • Feel free to ask people to repeat or reword a question if you did not hear them clearly or are not sure what they are asking you. • Smile to brighten the tone of your voice. • Let the interviewer end the call first, both as a professional courtesy and to ensure that the interviewer has no final questions. • Be prepared to be asked to pre-record a one-way video interview that you will submit on the employer's website or through commercial software such as Spark Hire. See the Technology feature for more details on this interview format.
On campus and onsite company interviews— *vary greatly from simple one-on-one interviews that may last only a half hour, to detailed agendas that span two days and involve many people in several interviews, presentations, and meals*	**One-on-one Interviews** • Establish that you have a natural fit with the organization and this person. • Ask questions about the supervisor's expectations, the challenges of the position, and daily activities. **Panel Interviews—several interviewers talking with one applicant** • Take the initiative to approach each person and introduce yourself as you extend your arm to shake hands. • Begin your responses by first looking at the person who asked the question, make eye contact with the rest of the panel during your response, and conclude your answer by returning your eyes to the questioner. • When the interview concludes, thank each person for taking his or her time to meet with you. **Group Interviews—several job applicants being interviewed at the same time** • Take advantage of interviewing with several job candidates simultaneously by demonstrating your collaborative skills, knowledge, and abilities. • Listen intently, ask questions, and offer advice, but do not lead the discussion unless someone from the company's search committee asks you to do so. **Action Interviews—applicants performing tasks under work-based conditions** • Leverage these work-based interviews by using your common sense, time management skills, and ability to think logically under pressure. • Practice ahead of time by researching "case interview" resources. You will find many examples of case scenarios and questions that you can use to help you practice.

Compose good answers—and good questions

Compose

Regardless of the interview's format, interviewers often use standard questions to help them learn about a candidate and assess that person's suitability for a job. As part of your interview preparation, develop clear, concise answers to these questions, along with details that allow you to elaborate about your strengths and sell your professional brand. Rather than bringing scripted responses with you, practice beforehand (and aloud) so your answers sound natural. The advice in **Figure 12.23** will help you respond to several of these questions—ones that people often have trouble answering.

FIGURE 12.23 How to Answer Typical Interview Questions

Tell me about yourself.	• Prepare a 30- to 60-second summary of information that is relevant to the job. • Focus on your professional brand, why you chose your major, and the strengths or accomplishments that uniquely qualify you for this position.
What do you know about our company? What interests you the most?	• Use the research you conduct about the company ahead of time to demonstrate your knowledge. • Explain what you find interesting about the company and the possibility of working there. • Be prepared to talk intelligently about the company's business and how you can contribute.
Why should we hire you?	• Evaluate your qualifications to determine how you fit the job and the company. • Provide clear, specific evidence of your strengths and skills. • Bring a copy of your cover letter to the interview to refer to, if necessary.
Describe your ideal job.	• Identify attributes in the job that appeal to you and that demonstrate your work ethic and abilities; for example, "My ideal job is a position that does not feel like work. I want a job that allows me to solve problems, help people, and contribute to the organization every day." • Describe the future job that this entry-level position will prepare you to do. • Do not share information that would make you a less desirable candidate, such as wanting to start your own business in five years. You want a potential employer to see you as a long-term human resource investment, not as a future competitor.
What are your greatest strengths and weaknesses?	• Describe how your greatest strength directly relates to the job. • Mention a real weakness to show you are aware of your shortcomings (we all have them). • Identify constructive criticism you have received from previous employers or instructors, outline the steps you are taking to improve, note any progress, and predict your future success in this area.
Why are you leaving your current position?	• Do not speak negatively about your current job, or a former employer or company. Complaining about an employer is one of the most common and most detrimental mistakes candidates make at interviews. • Focus on the job you are applying for as a way to advance your career—what you're moving toward more than what you're getting away from. • Emphasize positive qualities, such as your desire for a greater challenge or more responsibility.
What are your career plans (short and long range)?	• Identify that your goal is to get the job you're applying for in the interview and prove to the company that you are a valuable member of their team. • Mention your continued growth and level of responsibility at the company as your long-range plan. • Use your research about the company to cite specific job titles or projects that you are interested in pursuing. • Demonstrate that you are invested in a long-term relationship with the company.
What are your salary expectations?	• Suggest that you are flexible and willing to negotiate your salary based on industry averages and the current market conditions. • Avoid stating a minimum amount, which might result in a lower salary than they had planned to offer you. • Avoid indicating a salary much higher than they budgeted, which could cause them to stop considering you as a candidate.

COLLABORATION
DEMONSTRATING TEAMWORK IN GROUP INTERVIEWS

As described in Figure 12.22, the group interview format brings together several job candidates simultaneously. Sometimes the group members take turns answering questions; other times they are asked to work together to solve a problem or complete a simulation.[44] Either way, hiring managers use this format to assess your collaborative nature and how well you might fit into the company's culture.[45] It's one thing to *say* that you are a team player, but it's entirely different to be under pressure to demonstrate it, especially in an interview. Whether you are competing for one position or a few selected spots, one thing is consistent—you will be compared to the rest of the people in the room based on what you say and how you act. Don't let your competitive nature single you out as aggressive. Take advantage of the opportunity to demonstrate your collaborative skills. Here are some suggestions:[46]

- **Be confident.** Employers seldom inform job candidates in advance that they will be participating in a group interview. Don't let the surprise show. If you have time as people are settling into their seats, greet the other candidates around you by smiling, shaking hands, and introducing yourself. If you're waiting in a reception area ahead of time, facilitate interaction among the group. In some cases, the reception area is monitored to assess applicants' interpersonal skills.

- **Show respect for the other candidates** during the interview providing good eye contact and positive body language. Nod in agreement to good answers, but do not interrupt. Lean forward to show interest in what others say.

- **Demonstrate leadership** without taking over. You can do this by referring to other applicants by name and positively building on their comments. In addition, when appropriate, answer questions by using examples of your past leadership experiences.

- **Be yourself.** Interviews give employers an opportunity to get to know who you are. Let your personality show, for better or worse. You need to know if the position will be a good fit for you, too.

For a COLLABORATION exercise, go to Critical Thinking Question 5 on page 516.

---

behavioral questions A type of interview question designed to determine how you would make decisions, solve problems, or respond to stressful situations.

STAR method A method of answering a behavioral interview question by explaining a situation, a task, and an action that led to a positive result.

In addition to these standard questions, you should be prepared to address **behavioral questions**, which are designed to determine how you would make decisions, solve problems, or respond to stressful situations.[47] Some of these questions are also designed to elicit specific behavior in the interview. Your answers to these questions should demonstrate your collaborative skills, innovative thinking, and leadership abilities. One well-established method of responding to behavioral questions is to use the **STAR method**, which stands for Situation, Task, Action, and Result.[48] Using this framework, you develop a story that identifies a *situation* in which you completed a *task* (such as solving a problem or making a decision) by implementing a specific *action* that ended in a positive *result*. Research suggests that problem-solving stories are a powerful way to communicate competence.[49] **Figure 12.24** shows how to use the STAR method to answer a typical behavioral question. However, it is important that your answers not be overly scripted. Research shows that two of the most important characteristics interviewers look for are self-awareness and honesty.[50] These characteristics are hard to demonstrate if your answer seems pre-packaged.

In addition to asking you questions, an interviewer is likely to ask you if you have any questions. Not having good questions to ask is a common and detrimental interview mistake; it suggests to the interviewer that you are not interested in the position.[51] Always prepare a list of at least 8 to 10 questions ahead of time. Some of your questions may be answered during the interview, so having a long list gives you a better chance of having something to ask at the end. Avoid asking questions that your research would have answered. For example, asking where the company's headquarters is located or how many employees they have tells the interviewer that you did not do your research. Also avoid asking questions that are more relevant once you have been offered a position, such as questions about health benefits and retirement plans. If you have done your research, you should be able to ask several meaningful and appropriate questions about the company and the position.

Figure 12.25 provides some general questions that may be helpful to ask of all potential employers. But in addition to these scripted questions, be prepared to "listen and learn" during the interview so you can ask questions that build on the conversation.[52] For example, if the interviewer mentioned a new sales promotion, you could ask about the process that went into developing the promotion, how the goals were set, or how the effort will be evaluated. Make the interview a conversation about the position and the company to demonstrate your

FIGURE 12.24 Example of the STAR Method to Answer a Behavioral Question

**STAR
Method**

Situation   **Result**

Task   **Action**

QUESTION:
Tell me about a time when you worked successfully under pressure.

ANSWER:

Last semester, I worked on a market research project for a small business near the university. Our team had difficulty collecting data. By the time we had collected it all, we had only one week left to complete the project. } **Situation**

In that one week, we needed to analyze all the data, develop a justified set of recommendations, and write a complete report for the client. } **Task**

To get that work done under pressure, we really needed to take advantage of teamwork. I took the initiative to develop a work plan that delegated the work and set deadlines. We all worked in pairs to ensure that all the analysis was double checked by another member of the team. Then we held a team meeting where we developed recommendations and thoroughly planned the report so that we could distribute the work and write efficiently. } **Action**

As a result of this approach, we not only completed our report on time, but our client agreed with our analysis and decided to implement three of our four recommendations. It was a stressful but, ultimately, a good learning experience. } **Result**

FIGURE 12.25 Sample Questions to Ask During the Interview

Questions you can ask about the company:

1. The mission statement indicates that your goal is to. . . . How does the company fulfill this goal at an operational level on a day-to-day basis?
2. How would you describe the company's culture?
3. What does communication look like in this company? Is there a strong meeting culture or email culture?
4. What are the company's plans for long-term growth?
5. Can you tell me about the typical career paths for people in the position for which I'm interviewing?
6. Does the company offer or support professional development? What are typical opportunities?
7. What advice do you wish you'd received when you were starting here?

Questions you can ask about the position:

1. What is a typical day like in this job?
2. What are the greatest challenges of this position?
3. Who last had this position, and is he or she available if I have questions once I start the job?
4. How large is the department or team that I would be working with? How does the team interact?
5. Who would I be working most closely with on a daily basis?
6. What do you consider the next year's highest priority for someone in this position?
7. How would I be evaluated in this position, and by whom?
8. When do you expect to make a hiring decision?

interest. Toward the end of the interview, be sure to ask about the next steps.[53] You can ask when the company expects to make a decision or even if there's any reason you might not be considered for the job. The answers to these questions will tell you how seriously you are being considered as a candidate.

Evaluate your professional appearance

Evaluate

As part of your planning for an interview, evaluate your appearance and consider how best to project professionalism. You do not need to spend a fortune on new clothing, but you do need at least one good interview outfit and appropriate accessories.

You may have heard the saying "Clothes don't make the man (or woman)," but what you wear certainly communicates a message about you. Employers cite dressing inappropriately as one of the biggest mistakes job applicants make in interviews.[54] These unsuccessful applicants dress much too casually, wearing street clothes such as jeans, low-slung pants, short skirts, gym shoes, or sandals. Or they may wear tight clothing that is too revealing. When dressing for interviews, follow one key rule: Even if you are interviewing in a more casual workplace, wear business formal attire to the interview.

Historically, business attire was always formal. Men wore three-piece suits, and women wore suits or dresses. Some businesses still adhere to a formal dress code. For example, in financial management and legal environments, attire is neutral and conservative. In many companies, however, the dress code is business casual, a professional but more relaxed way of dressing. In fact, according to a Gallup Poll, business casual is the most common form of dress in business today.[55] For men, business casual means an ironed button-down or polo shirt, slacks or khakis with a belt, and dark socks and shoes. Women have many casual attire options—slacks, skirts, dresses, blouses, sweaters. **Figure 12.26** provides examples of both business formal and business casual options.

FIGURE 12.26 How to Dress: Business Formal Versus Business Casual

BUSINESS FORMAL

- Matching jackets and slacks or skirts
- Dark colors with light shirts
- Coordinating tie for men (no loud colors or patterns)
- Neutral or dark hose and dark shoes for women
- Dark socks and dark shoes for men
- Polished, unscuffed shoes
- Conservative jewelry

BUSINESS CASUAL

- Clothes that are pressed and clean
- Well-maintained shoes (no sneakers)
- Coordinating colors and accessories
- Good grooming

Although business casual may be the dress code in the company where you are interviewing, unless you are explicitly told otherwise, wear business formal clothing to job interviews. Wear a well-pressed professional business suit (jacket with matching slacks or skirt) in a conservative color. Your interview attire should fit you well and conform to the one hanger rule; it should look like it was purchased on one hanger. In other words, the jacket and slacks (or skirt) are a set rather than mix-and-match tops and bottoms that you piece together. To complete your professional look, be conservative in your grooming and makeup, bring a portfolio or business case and a good pen, wear a watch, and turn off your cell phone. Your goal at an interview is not to express your personality through clothing and accessories but to dress in a way that allows people to focus on what you say.

TECHNOLOGY
PREPARING FOR VIDEO INTERVIEWS

Employers are increasingly taking advantage of interviewing job candidates by video instead of in person. Video interviews are less expensive than onsite interviews for non-local applicants, and they help employers get a better sense of the candidate than do telephone interviews. Employers may use web-based conferencing technology such as Skype or Zoom, or they may invest in commercial software that is specifically designed as a recruitment and evaluation tool, such as Spark Hire or VidCruiter. The format may take one of two forms: (1) a traditional live interview that is scheduled at a specific time or (2) an asynchronous interview that you pre-record and submit to the employer.

To ensure that you present a professional image in a video interview, regardless of the format, follow the advice for all virtual interviews listed in Figure 12.22 as well as these additional video-specific guidelines.[56,57,58]

- **Ensure a good connection and equipment.** If possible, use a wired Internet connection on a computer that is fully charged or plugged into an electrical source. The combination of voice and video transmissions can significantly reduce your computer's resources. You don't want to lose your connection partway through your interview. Also use a good camera and microphone and make sure the connections are secure so you won't inadvertently unplug something as you gesture during the interview. If a technical problem occurs, stay calm, gracious, and courteous. Your reaction could be used to assess how well you work under pressure.

- **Select a professional background.** What the interviewer sees behind you can be as important as what you are wearing. If possible, use a business office or a conference room. If you don't have access to a professional environment, position yourself in front of a neatly organized bookshelf or desk. Blank walls provide no visual interest, and busy backgrounds may be too distracting. Regardless of the background, select a quiet area where you will not be interrupted.

- **Use good lighting.** Choose natural light rather than fluorescent or other lights that cast shadows or over-illuminate your face. Your computer should be between you and a sunny window or table lamp so the interviewer can see you without shadows or glare. Consider using lights on both sides of the camera for a natural-looking effect.

- **Wear interview attire.** Your appearance should be as professional as if you were interviewing in person. You might

need to stand up to adjust the camera or lighting, so be well-dressed from head to toe. Dark solid colors are better on video than bright hues or patterns.

- **Look at the camera, not the computer.** In a face-to-face interview, eye contact is important to make a positive impression. Eye contact is equally important in a Skype interview that includes video. Although looking at the interviewer's face on your computer monitor may seem like you're making good eye contact, you actually need to look at your camera lens in order to appear to be looking directly at the interviewer.

- **Use good body language.** In addition to making eye contact, as previously mentioned, sit up straight, smile, and lean in toward the computer to look engaged. Sit at a comfortable distance so the interviewer can see more than your head, and use normal gestures.

- **Use notes and take notes.** Create a cheat sheet ahead of time with important points to remember or questions to ask, but do read directly from your notes or refer to them too frequently.

- **In a live interview, take notes and use active listening cues.** If you are participating in a live interview, ask questions and take notes to show that you are interested in the answers. To demonstrate your connection to the speaker, make "listening" noises such as "hmm" and "right," and nod in agreement now and then.

- **In a recorded one-way interview, pay attention to whether a question allows you "think time" before the recording starts.** Use that time to organize your answer in your head. Also notice whether the software allows you multiple "takes" for any questions. If it does, feel free to re-record your answer if you think you can do it better the second time. Remember that your responses should sound conversational, and you should have good eye contact with the camera.

- **Practice.** Test your background, lighting, eye contact, and connection quality with friends and family to ensure you are presenting a professional image. Ask for feedback about your interview attire, the tone and volume of your voice, and any distracting background sights or sounds.

For a TECHNOLOGY exercise, go to Exercise 19 on page 519.

SQ5 How can you make a positive impression during and after an interview?

When you have confidence in your preparation and your appearance, you are ready to go to your interview. Your goal during the interview is to be your best self and make a strong, positive impression. To achieve this goal, you need to act like a professional from the moment you arrive until the end of the interview, including during meals.

Project a professional presence

You get just one shot at a first impression, and research suggests that employers may form their opinion of you within the first few seconds of meeting you.[59] Body language and eye contact are strong influencers,[60] but it is equally important to act like you are ready to be in the workplace. Starting from when you walk in the door, your professional presence can make a strong, positive, and lasting impression. The guidelines in **Figure 12.27** provide a good starting place for managing first impressions during an interview.

FIGURE 12.27 How to Manage First Impressions

Arrive early	• Know how long it will take you to get to the interview location, where you will be able to park, and, if possible, how to get from the parking area to the interviewer's office or reception area. • Plan to enter the reception area about 10 minutes before the interview time and, if time permits, use the restroom before the interview begins.
Look ready to work	• Carry a pad of paper and a nice pen. • Bring copies of your résumé, printed on good paper. • Have business cards handy with your name, email address, and phone number. • Bring several copies of your list of references with complete contact information. • Include personal notes or website printouts about the company and the job. • Bring a list of questions you plan to ask the interviewer. • Ensure you have necessary personal items, such as mints and tissues.
Greet people professionally	• Use people's names when you meet them. • Use people's last names until they ask you to use their first names. • Shake hands with everyone you meet, and practice your handshake ahead of time to ensure a firm, solid grip.
Treat support staff with courtesy and respect	• Be polite and respectful to everyone you meet during your interview experience, including the receptionist who asks you to wait in an outer office and the assistant who offers you a cup of coffee.
Be prepared for meals and social gatherings	• Plan for conversation by familiarizing yourself with current events in the news and business world so you can contribute to conversation or raise related topics. • Listen more than you talk but make a point to talk with as many people as you can. • Follow the host in ordering food; do not order steak and lobster if everyone else is ordering soup and salad.

Compose

Compose effective post-interview messages

Following an interview, you have many opportunities to reinforce the positive impression you have made and keep the lines of communication open. You can continue to impress prospective employers by sending thank-you messages and checking on the status of your application in a professional manner. If you are offered a position, how you respond is particularly important. Whether you choose to accept, negotiate, or refuse the job offer, your response needs to strengthen the company's confidence that they made a good decision. Even if you are not offered a position, you have the option of responding to communicate your interest in future opportunities. You may also be able to gather some information about the results of any background checks that the company conducted.

Compose thank-you messages

Within 24 hours after an interview, send a thank-you message to offer your sincere gratitude for the time people took out of their busy schedules to meet with you. If you collected business cards during your interview or made good notes, you will have all the contact information you need to thank each person who met with you.

Before writing each message, review your interview notes so that you can personalize the content. For example, you may have learned about a particular company project from one person and enjoyed a lunch conversation about a professional development opportunity with another person. Your thank-you messages should reflect your conversations with the person to whom you are writing and stress one or two key points, such as things you forgot to mention during the interview or responses to any potential concerns that may have been discussed during the interview.[61]

Your thank-you note may take the form of an email or a handwritten note. From both professional and personal perspectives, people view a handwritten message as a sincere gesture that speaks volumes about your character and indicates a personal interest in the company or relationship. However, a mailed thank-you note will take time to reach your audience—time you may not have before the job is offered to someone else. Also, handwritten thank-you notes should be short. If you need to explain objections or reiterate expertise, an email message would be a better option. Follow the guidelines in **Figure 12.28** to compose your message.

FIGURE 12.28 How to Write a Thank-you Message

handwritten note

Dear Mr. Jacobson,

Thank you for the opportunity on March 15 to discuss my qualifications for the open training manager's position. I enjoyed our conversation, and after learning more about the organization, I am eager to become a part of the Higgins Consulting management team.

The company's current objective to expand training services to the IT market is an exciting, yet challenging, goal. I believe my minor in MIS combined with my marketing major can provide a perspective that will benefit the company in this effort.

I look forward to hearing from you by email (ematthews@gmail.com) or telephone (218.555.2552).

Sincerely,
Ellyn Matthews

Keep the message short– just one or two paragraphs. Begin with a thank you followed immediately by the date of the interview and position.

Personalize the message by mentioning something learned during the interview, and emphasize a strength that contributes to the company.

Conclude with a positive, forward-looking statement that encourages a response and includes contact information.

Compose follow-up messages

Following an interview, an employer may need several weeks to interview other applicants, contact references, and process background checks. Therefore, unless an employer indicated that you would be contacted by a certain date, don't be concerned if it takes a while to receive a response. Analyze the situation to determine when you should follow up and with whom. Typically, after two weeks, you can inquire about the status of the position and communicate your continued interest. Consider the guidelines in **Figure 12.29** on page 504.

Compose

FIGURE 12.29 How to Compose a Follow-up Message

Contact only one person.
- Follow up with only your primary contact person rather than emailing everyone you met during the interview.

Choose an appropriate medium.
- Use a communication medium that best suits the employer's preferences based on your initial communications. Email is the least invasive medium and most convenient to answer. By contrast, a telephone call indicates a more assertive attempt to contact the employer.

Don't go overboard:
- Evaluate your message to ensure that you don't seem overly anxious about the position.
- Do not use multiple methods of contacting an employer. Sending several emails and leaving multiple telephone messages could be interpreted as unprofessional and overzealous.

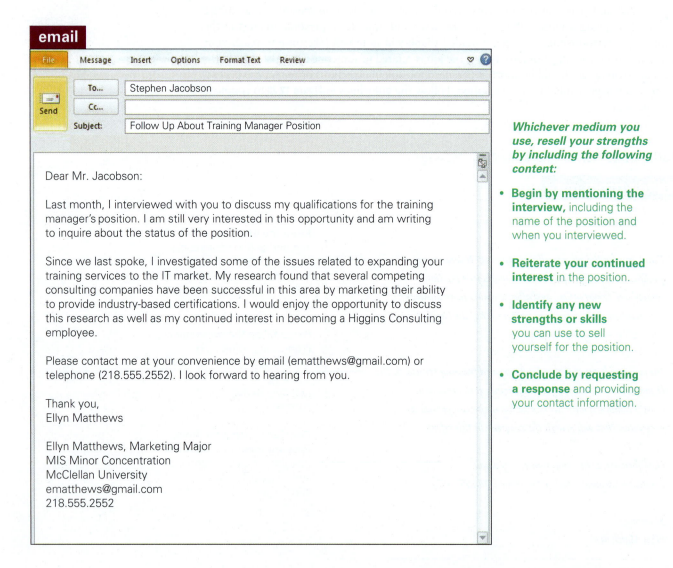

email

| File | Message | Insert | Options | Format Text | Review |

To... Stephen Jacobson
Cc...
Subject: Follow Up About Training Manager Position

Dear Mr. Jacobson:

Last month, I interviewed with you to discuss my qualifications for the training manager's position. I am still very interested in this opportunity and am writing to inquire about the status of the position.

Since we last spoke, I investigated some of the issues related to expanding your training services to the IT market. My research found that several competing consulting companies have been successful in this area by marketing their ability to provide industry-based certifications. I would enjoy the opportunity to discuss this research as well as my continued interest in becoming a Higgins Consulting employee.

Please contact me at your convenience by email (ematthews@gmail.com) or telephone (218.555.2552). I look forward to hearing from you.

Thank you,
Ellyn Matthews

Ellyn Matthews, Marketing Major
MIS Minor Concentration
McClellan University
ematthews@gmail.com
218.555.2552

Whichever medium you use, resell your strengths by including the following content:

- **Begin by mentioning the interview,** including the name of the position and when you interviewed.

- **Reiterate your continued interest** in the position.

- **Identify any new strengths or skills** you can use to sell yourself for the position.

- **Conclude by requesting a response** and providing your contact information.

At this stage of the job-search process, you may need to compose other follow-up messages as well. These could include messages negotiating a job offer, accepting a job offer, rejecting a job offer, withdrawing your job application, or responding to a job rejection:

- **Negotiating the details of a job offer.** When making a job offer, employers usually outline the salary and related benefits. If the employer calls you with this information, ask for details in an email so you have the offer in writing.[62] If you have researched the company, the job, and the industry in general, you will know if the offer is competitive. However, before responding to either accept or reject the offer, do some additional research so that you can make well-informed decisions and reasonable requests about salary, benefits, and other details of the job offer. Although you may feel uncomfortable negotiating, it is often a good idea. People who negotiate are often able to increase their salary offers by 5 to 10 percent,[63] which significantly increases their earnings throughout their career.[64] But if the offer indicates that the salary is set, negotiate for other resources, such as professional development support.[65]

Negotiations are usually best conducted in person or by telephone. In those cases, it's a good idea to practice what you will say ahead of time.[66] However, you may decide to begin the negotiation with an email or letter. For an example of a letter that negotiates the details of a job offer, see **Figure 12.30**.

FIGURE 12.30 How to Initiate a Job Offer Negotiation

letter

Ellyn Matthews
1651 Randolph Avenue, Apt. 3G, McClellan, MI 49449
ematthews@gmail.com | 218.555.2552

April 23, 20XX

Mr. Stephen Jacobson
Higgins Consulting
8153 Higgins Road
Chicago, IL 60632

Dear Mr. Jacobson:

Thank you for your offer to join Higgins Consulting as your newest training manager. I am very interested in the position and pleased with the salary you quoted. However, before I feel comfortable accepting the job, I have two requests:

- Your offer included reimbursement for moving expenses up to $500. However, the three estimates I received all exceeded $1,000. Are you able to increase my reimbursement allocation?

- The benefits packet you sent mentions that Higgins Consulting reimburses MBA and other relevant graduate education after the employee's second year on the job. As you know, I have already begun my Master of Education degree in Global Training and Development in the online program at State University. I would like to keep my momentum going with this program. Will you be willing to start reimbursing these courses right away? What I learn from my coursework will be immediately useful on the job at Higgins, and I understand that Higgins will require repayment if I do not stay at the company for the required period of time.

I look forward to discussing these issues with you in more detail and appreciate the opportunity to begin my career as a Higgins employee. Please call (218.555.2552) or email (ematthews@gmail.com) at your convenience.

Sincerely,

Ellyn Matthews

Ellyn Matthews, Marketing Major
MIS Minor Concentration
McClellan University

Begin with gratitude for the offer.

Mention the positive aspects of the offer before indicating points of concern.

Provide reasons for each of your requests. Bullet or number multiple issues for discussion to make them easier to refer to in future communication.

Conclude positively.

Motivate action by requesting response.

- **Accepting or refusing job offers.** When you decide to accept a job offer, analyze your medium options. Even if you plan to accept the position by telephone, following up in writing provides documentation for both you and the employer. Because you are communicating good news, organize the content directly, indicating at the beginning of your message that you are accepting the position. If you receive a job offer for a position you are not interested in, you need to communicate to the company that you are not accepting the offer. Even though you will not be working for this company, maintain professionalism and courtesy in your message and buffer your "bad news." To learn how to compose both job acceptance and refusal letters, see **Figure 12.31** and **Figure 12.32**.

FIGURE 12.31 How to Accept a Job Offer

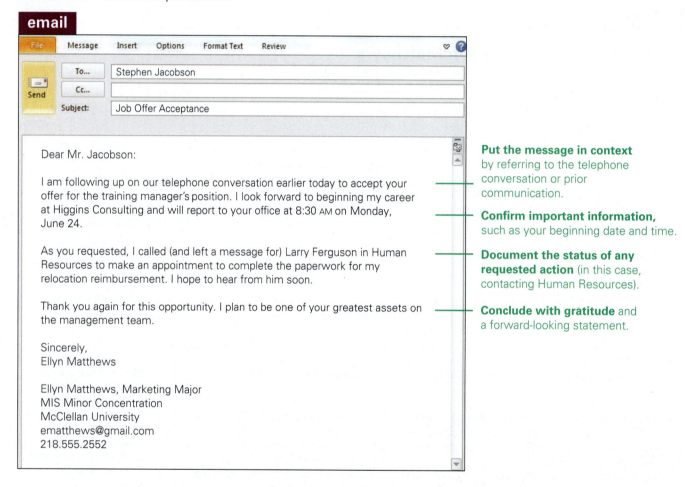

email	

File Message Insert Options Format Text Review

Send

To... Stephen Jacobson
Cc...
Subject: Job Offer Acceptance

Dear Mr. Jacobson:

I am following up on our telephone conversation earlier today to accept your offer for the training manager's position. I look forward to beginning my career at Higgins Consulting and will report to your office at 8:30 AM on Monday, June 24.

As you requested, I called (and left a message for) Larry Ferguson in Human Resources to make an appointment to complete the paperwork for my relocation reimbursement. I hope to hear from him soon.

Thank you again for this opportunity. I plan to be one of your greatest assets on the management team.

Sincerely,
Ellyn Matthews

Ellyn Matthews, Marketing Major
MIS Minor Concentration
McClellan University
ematthews@gmail.com
218.555.2552

Put the message in context by referring to the telephone conversation or prior communication.

Confirm important information, such as your beginning date and time.

Document the status of any requested action (in this case, contacting Human Resources).

Conclude with gratitude and a forward-looking statement.

FIGURE 12.32 How to Turn Down a Job Offer

letter

Ellyn Matthews
1651 Randolph Avenue, Apt. 3G, McClellan, MI 49449
ematthews@gmail.com | 218.555.2552

April 30, 20XX

Ms. Charlene Chyung
Td3 Management Solutions
300 S. Grand Avenue
Los Angeles, CA 90071

Dear Ms. Chyung:

Thank you for the offer to join the Td3 Management Solutions. I enjoyed meeting you and your staff and appreciated the opportunity to learn about your company.

Your collaborative work environment was energizing, and I could see myself fitting in well with your team. Although your offer is tempting, I have decided to accept a position in a city closer to my family. If in the future my circumstances change and I am more able to relocate, I would be very interested in working on your team.

Best wishes,

Ellyn Matthews

Ellyn Matthews, Marketing Major
MIS Minor Concentration
McClellan University

Begin with appreciation for the opportunity to interview for the position.

Buffer the bad news (the refusal) with gratitude.

Decline the offer and identify reasons for the decision.

Conclude with a positive, friendly statement.

- **Withdrawing from a job search after accepting another offer.** When you accept a job offer, you may have applications under consideration with other employers. If your application has advanced as far as the interview process, courtesy requires that you contact those employers immediately and withdraw your name from consideration. If you do not withdraw, you are essentially being dishonest, as you are implying that you are still an active candidate. By contrast, if you do formally withdraw, you have an excellent opportunity to make a good impression with the employer, which can be an asset later in your career. Employment experts suggest that telephone is the best medium to use if you have established a connection with the hiring manager or a human resources representative. Otherwise, email is an acceptable medium.[67] You may also follow up more formally with a letter, such as the one illustrated in **Figure 12.33**.

FIGURE 12.33 How to Withdraw a Job Application

letter

Ellyn Matthews

1651 Randolph Avenue, Apt. 3G, McClellan, MI 49449
ematthews@gmail.com | 218.555.2552

May 2, 20XX

Mr. Arvind Balaji
The Marius-Richmond Group
50 West Washington Street
Chicago, IL 60602

Dear Mr. Balaji:

Thank you for including me in the interview process for the marketing consultant position at The Marius-Richmond Group. I enjoyed meeting with the interview team and especially enjoyed the case-based interview exercises, which were interesting and intellectually challenging. I know that a job at Marius-Richmond would be equally satisfying.

That is why I regret having to withdraw from consideration for the position. As I explained on the telephone earlier today, I have accepted an employment offer for a managerial position in training and development, which is an area I am interested in exploring.

Thank you again for giving me the opportunity to learn about The Marius-Richmond Group.

Best wishes,

Ellyn Matthews

Ellyn Matthews, Marketing Major
MIS Minor Concentration
McClellan University

Annotations:

Begin by expressing appreciation for the opportunity to interview for the position.

Indicate positive feelings about the company to promote goodwill.

Formally withdraw your application and include a brief explanation.

Conclude with a positive, friendly statement.

- **Responding to job rejections.** When you don't receive a job offer, you may feel hurt or angry. Rather than taking the rejection personally, use it as one last opportunity to make a good impression by writing a final message to your interviewer, such as the letter in **Figure 12.34**.

FIGURE 12.34 How to Respond to a Job Rejection

letter

92 Allerton Street
Plymouth, MA 02360

April 23, 20XX

Mr. Stephen Jacobson
Higgins Consulting
8153 Higgins Road
Chicago, IL 60632

Dear Mr. Jacobson:

I just received your letter today, indicating that you have selected another candidate for the training manager position. Although I am disappointed, I appreciate you letting me know your decision in such a timely manner. I also appreciate the courtesy and professionalism you have shown during the entire interview process.

I want to reiterate my strong interest in working for Higgins Consulting. Please keep me in mind when you have another opening in the near future.

Again, thank you for the opportunity to interview, and best wishes to your company.

Sincerely,

Roderick Brown

Roderick Brown
Learning and Organizational Communication
Middleboro University

Begin by graciously by accepting the rejection.

Express gratitude for being considered.

Emphasize continuing interest in the company.

Conclude positively.

If you suspect that your job rejection was influenced by negative results from a background check (for which the employer must receive your permission), you are entitled to receive a free copy of the background report from the employer or the company that prepared it. According to a study by the National Consumer Law Center, 93 percent of employers perform background checks on potential employees and new hires.[68] Sixty percent of private employers use credit checks to screen applicants.[69] Others verify claims made on your résumé and in the job interview as well as look at news reports and criminal records. Because many applicants are damaged by incorrect information in their background checks, you should request the results to verify that the reports are correct and to prepare explanations that you can use in future interviews.

Evaluate

Evaluate your performance

Each interview you have helps you refine your communication skills and prepare for your next opportunity. Immediately after an interview, evaluate your performance and identify your strengths as well as your weaknesses to increase your chances for success the next time. The questions in **Figure 12.35** can guide your evaluation.

FIGURE 12.35 How to Evaluate Your Performance

Did you make a good impression?	• Recall the interviewers' subtle nonverbal messages. Did they take a quick glance at your clothing and nod approvingly or raise an eyebrow in surprise? Did they introduce you to other people or offer to take you on a quick tour of the office? They wouldn't show you around if they weren't impressed.
Did you bring everything you needed?	• Consider whether you had everything you needed, such as pen and paper, and extra copies of your résumé. Make a checklist of things to remember next time.
Did you stumble with any answers?	• Think about any questions you found difficult to answer. Write them down and work on answers that you will remember next time. Create a list of bullet points you can recall to jog your memory. Chances are good you will face similar questions again.
What went well?	• Evaluate the positive aspects of your interview. When did you feel most comfortable? How can you duplicate that experience next time?

■ **In summary,** the job search can be a long process, involving many different kinds of communication: social media content, résumés, cover letters, interviews, and follow-up messages. As you move through the process, you can expect to become increasingly skilled at projecting your professional presence and matching your messages with employers' needs, especially if you evaluate your performance after each interview and make adjustments. At every step along the way, the ACE communication process is a useful tool to help you be more strategic and take better advantage of communication opportunities.

SOCIAL RECRUITING @ WORK EY

Photo courtesy of Ken Bouyer

EY (Ernst & Young) is a multinational accounting firm and one of the four largest professional services networks worldwide, known as the "Big Four." With more than 231,000 employees in more than 700 offices in 150 countries, EY is ranked by *Fortune* magazine as 29th on its list "The 100 Best Companies to Work For."[70] Ken Bouyer is EY Americas Director of Inclusiveness Recruiting and has plenty of advice for job seekers, especially when it comes to social media:

- **Go beyond your keyboard!** Bouyer says, "Try to connect with people through social media who already work for the company. Introduce yourself. You can learn so much about the culture, benefits, and other positive opportunities by speaking with people who are already employees." Bouyer also recommends adding a little personality to your LinkedIn profile. "Don't just fill out your job title and invite everyone you come across [to link to you]. Making thoughtful connections and actively participating in discussions and groups can take your career to a whole new level."

- **Sell your experience.** "We believe all experience is good experience," Bouyer says. He recommends that applicants highlight their internships and other experiences where they have demonstrated a good work ethic and the ability to work well on a team. "Authenticity and the ability to relate are key. It's also important for candidates to have a global mindset." If you have not yet traveled abroad, Bouyer suggests emphasizing experiences where you have collaborated on diverse teams or studied other cultures.

- **Demonstrate critical thinking and problem solving.** "We are always going to probe into what we don't see on a résumé, so individuals should always be prepared to share their personal story and provide examples where they used critical thinking and problem solving." These examples can be integrated into your LinkedIn content, Facebook posts, and tweets.

- **Avoid social media mistakes.** Bouyer stresses the importance of having an active online presence but cautions job seekers to avoid the common mistakes he sees when reviewing applicants. "Don't display unprofessional photos, don't bash a potential or current employer, and don't allow friends to post unprofessional comments." Those are easy ways to eliminate yourself from the short list.

- **Research companies' core values.** "At EY," Bouyer says, "we hire for potential. In addition to strong academics, we look for well-rounded individuals. If their core values align with ours, we believe they can make smart decisions for our company as well." Most companies post their mission, vision, and/or core value statements on their websites. Before an interview, research this information and the organizations' social media content so you understand what they stand for and how their core values guide what they do, how they do it, and whether you are a good fit to help the company meet its vision.

Source: Based on an interview with Ken Bouyer.

Starting an Employment Search

This case scenario will help you review the chapter material by applying it to a specific situation.

Raymond Varga has a problem. For the first time in his life, he has to organize a job search, and he doesn't know what to do.

Two years ago, after his junior year at Middleton College, Raymond completed a summer internship at Metrix Manufacturing and was happy to receive a job offer from the company. Raymond had a sense of security as he started his senior year knowing that he had a job when he graduated. The job proved to be all that Raymond expected. During his first year, he worked on several challenging projects that offered him the opportunity to expand his skills and apply the strategic management concepts he had learned during his last year of college. He liked his coworkers and was happy in his position.

Therefore, he was surprised today when his manager, Marilyn, explained to him that due to Metrix's pending merger with its leading competitor, the company would be eliminating redundant positions based on a LIFO (last in, first out) plan. As a recent hire, Raymond would certainly be let go within the next month. Marilyn wanted to warn him so he could start his career search while he was still employed with Metrix.

Now, as Raymond thinks about starting a new job search, he feels overwhelmed. He never searched for a job during college because he learned about the Metrix internship at a career fair. He never wrote a cover letter because Metrix required him to apply online and did not offer the option of uploading a cover letter along with his résumé. And he never updated his résumé after his junior year. Metrix offered him a job as soon as he completed his internship. Raymond isn't sure where to begin.

Expanding the Possibilities

Raymond considers his employment options. He would like to find a job in the same city so he doesn't have to move. He also hopes to find a similar position where he can manage manufacturing projects for large customer orders.

He knows he has excellent experience that he can offer. Over the past two years, he has assisted the regional manager in developing contracts with clients and coordinating their projects. In the process, he has learned about many of the larger manufacturing companies in the Midwest. In addition to managing projects, he also created an orientation workshop for new interns and coordinated a new database that tracked customers by demographics and sales volume. The database project required a significant amount of detailed research into past purchase orders as well as follow-up calls with purchasing agents. Raymond is also confident that his communication skills have significantly improved while at Metrix and that he will be able to apply these strengths to a new job.

Now he has to research career options and chart a path to his next position. He would like to build on what he has learned on the job. However, he knows that limiting himself to his comfort zone will also limit his opportunities.

Question 1: How can Raymond expand his possibilities?
a. Given his skills and work experience, what industries besides manufacturing can Raymond explore?
b. How should Raymond let his personal and professional network know he's looking for a new job? Whom should he contact? What should he say?
c. How can Raymond use social networking sites such as LinkedIn, Twitter, and Facebook to communicate that he is looking for a job? Is this a good idea in Raymond's case?
d. How can he expand his current professional network?
e. While networking, Raymond will need to explain in a positive way why he is looking for a job. Suggest some phrasing options he can use.

Updating a Résumé

After contacting people in his professional network and creating a profile with the career center at his college, Raymond spends the next evening composing the content for his résumé, shown on page 513.

Question 2: Carefully evaluate the content, keeping in mind that Raymond has not yet formatted his résumé or targeted a specific position. What does Raymond need to change, add, or remove? Itemize your suggestions, providing a rationale for each, or create a formatted version of Raymond's content using your suggestions.

Drafting a Cover Letter

Assume that Raymond wants to apply for the job advertised in Figure 12.15 on page 489.

Question 3: Refer to his résumé on page 513 and draft a cover letter using the AIDA approach. Evaluate your draft using the guidelines described in this section.

Composing Answers to Standard Interview Questions

At a coffee shop on a Saturday afternoon, Raymond meets with a friend who is also looking for a job. They decide to help each other prepare for interviews. They review the standard interview questions and help each other brainstorm responses to the question "Why should we hire you?"

Question 4: Compose a list of five bullet points Raymond could use during his interview to highlight his qualifications and strengths.

rough draft résumé

Raymond Ramón Varga
1484 Vista Ridge, Apt. 2B, Middleton, OH 43433
Phone: 419-555-4250 / Cell: 419-555-5503 / email: rvarga@metrix.com

EDUCATION

Business Administration Degree, Middleton College, OH, May 2018

WORK EXPERIENCE

May 2018–Present
Asst. Regional Sales Manager, Development Office, Metrix Manufacturing, Middleton, OH
Currently serve in an entry-level managerial position where I provide assistance to the regional manager as he develops and coordinates projects for our Midwest clients.

Summer, 2017
Internship, Development Office, Metrix Manufacturing, Middleton, OH
Provided general office duties, temped for the receptionist, routed correspondence, made photocopies

CAPABILITIES AND SKILLS

- Professional communication skills and dedicated work ethic
- Attention to detail and extremely organized
- Work well with others and possess exceptional interpersonal skills

PROFESSIONAL ORGANIZATIONS & VOLUNTEER ACTIVITIES

- Toastmasters International, 2017–Present
- Big Brothers, 2018–Present
- Habitat for Humanity, 2016–2018

End of Chapter

Study Questions in Review

SQ1 How do you polish your professional presence for a job search? *(pages 470–477)*

- **Analyze your career goals, strengths, and skills.** Gain experience with internships and summer jobs, and gain transferrable skills by volunteering. Outline your experiences and identify areas of expertise and sellable qualities. Recognize your weaknesses.
- **Compose your brand message and strategic social media content.** Create a brand message that communicates your value to an employer and make that content visible in your email, business cards, and online content. Take advantage of social media to project your professional presence. Target specific social media communication outlets, such as Facebook, LinkedIn, and Twitter. Post positive status updates, emphasize your accomplishments, and highlight your value to employers.
- **Evaluate your virtual professional image** by reviewing your email image, your business cards, your telephone image, and your online image.

SQ2 How do you compose an effective résumé? *(pages 477–486)*

- **Analyze your options for organizing your résumé.** Choose a format that allows you to highlight your strengths—either the chronological, functional, or combined format. Use templates as guides, not absolutes, to enhance your image with professional page layout and design techniques.
- **Compose effective résumé content** beginning with your name and contact information. If you include an objective, focus on what you can do for the employer. Sections on education and work experience are standard; these can include or can be followed by a separate section on capabilities and skills targeted to the employer's needs. Also include activities and accomplishments that highlight your strengths. Develop multiple résumés, if necessary, for different types of jobs. Ensure that your content is honest. Blatant exaggerations and content copied from résumé samples can quickly lead to rejection.
- **Evaluate your content and design.** Is it clear, complete, and concise? Does it use keywords from the job listing and emphasize information important to the job? Is it well designed? Is it proofread? Ask others to read your résumé and provide feedback.

SQ3 How do you find job opportunities and submit applications? *(pages 487–495)*

- **Analyze your options for finding job opportunities** by registering with career centers and job banks. Join professional organizations, and target specific employers. Develop a professional network and use social networking outlets.
- **Compose an effective elevator pitch** to ensure that you are well prepared to persuasively sell yourself. Start with a rhetorical question, highlight your skills with a short story, avoid technical terms, and end with a direct request. Time yourself to ensure that it's less than a minute long, and memorize your pitch, but sound conversational when you deliver it.
- **Compose persuasive cover letters,** using AIDA to gain *attention* in the first paragraph, build the employer's *interest* and *desire* in the middle paragraph(s), and motivate *action* in the last paragraph. Letters for unsolicited applications—and letters for jobs where you are not a perfect fit—require more persuasion than solicited responses for jobs that are a perfect match for your qualifications.
- **Select a medium for submission and follow up as necessary.** Many employers require online submissions, though emailed applications also are often accepted. Unsolicited applications may be best

through regular postal mail. If you do not hear from an employer within a reasonable amount of time, follow up by email or telephone.

SQ4 How do you prepare for a job interview? *(pages 495–501)*

- **Analyze how to benefit from different types of interviews.** Capture interest in preliminary interviews, which often begin at career fairs. Because you will have only a few minutes with a recruiter, be assertive, demonstrate your knowledge, and ask good questions. Some companies also send recruiters to campus for preliminary, first-round interviews, which offer you a little more time to impress the recruiter with your knowledge and questions. If you live far from the company, you may also be interviewed virtually, either by telephone, live video, or a recorded interview. If you are invited to interview onsite at the company, prepare for several formats, including traditional one-on-one interviews, panel and group interviews, and action interviews. Whatever type of interview you have, be sure to sell your strengths.
- **Compose good answers—and good questions.** Compose effective answers to typical questions. Typical questions focus on you, your past employment, your job search, and your suitability for the job. For each question, plan a 30- to 60-second summary of your strengths, focusing on skills and qualities required for the job. Provide evidence that convinces the employer to hire you. Use the STAR method to respond to behavioral questions to demonstrate how you handled past challenges. Also, compose questions to ask about the company and the position to demonstrate your interest. Do not ask questions you could have easily found answered online.
- **Evaluate your professional appearance.** Wear business formal attire to an interview, even if the company culture is casual. Your goal is not to express your personality through your clothing but to allow people to focus on what you say. Look professional by ensuring your clothes fit properly, being conservative in your grooming and makeup, bringing a portfolio or business case, wearing a watch, and turning off your cell phone.

SQ5 How can you make a positive impression during and after an interview? *(pages 502–510)*

- **Project a professional presence.** Manage first impressions by arriving a few minutes early and looking ready to work. Greet people professionally, and treat support staff with courtesy and respect. Be prepared for meals and social gatherings. Learn proper dining etiquette, plan for conversation and small talk, and be sure to talk to everyone at the table.
- **Compose effective post-interview messages,** such as thank-you messages that show gratitude, demonstrate what you learned, sell your strengths, and focus on audience benefits. If you have not heard anything after two weeks, compose a follow-up message to inquire about the status of an open position When you get a job offer, follow up by accepting, rejecting, or negotiating the offer. When you accept an offer, withdraw yourself from consideration for other jobs. When you receive job rejections, follow up politely to leave a good impression.
- **Evaluate your performance** by asking yourself several questions: Did you make a good impression? Did you bring everything you needed? Did you stumble with any answers? What went well? Identify your strengths and weaknesses to evaluate your performance and increase your interview success.

Visual Summary

Communicating Your Professional Brand:
Social Media, Résumés, Cover Letters, and Interviews
To support your employment success, build your professional presence on a comprehensive and well-prepared collection of content—not only during your job search, but throughout your professional career.

Begin analyzing your career goals early and prepare yourself continuously throughout your degree.

ATTEND JOB FAIRS

JOIN PROFESSIONAL ORGANIZATIONS

CREATE A UNIQUE SELLING PROPOSITION

DEVELOP A BRAND MESSAGE

APPLY FOR INTERNSHIPS

GAIN TRANSFERABLE SKILLS

Analyze your professional strengths and skills and emphasize them in your social media content.

Create résumé content and formats that are targeted to each job application.

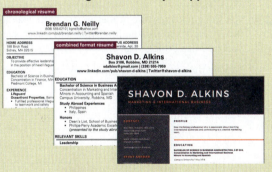

Continually evaluate the virtual image you project through telephone, email, social media, and business cards.

Analyze your options to find job opportunities

SEARCH JOB ADS

TARGET SPECIFIC EMPLOYERS

REGISTER WITH CAREER CENTERS

DEVELOP PROFESSIONAL NETWORKS

USE SOCIAL NETWORKING OUTLETS

Write persuasive cover letters, elevator pitches, and follow-up messages.

Continually evaluate your performance and continuously improve.

Prepare for job interviews by drafting answers to questions as well as questions to ask.

STAR Method

Situation   Result

Task   Action

Key Terms

Action interview p. 495
AIDA p. 490
Behavioral questions p. 498
Brand message p. 472
Career fair p. 495

Chronological résumé p. 477
Combined résumé p. 479
Cover letter p. 489
Elevator pitch p. 487
Functional résumé p. 479

Group interview p. 495
Network p. 473
Panel interview p. 495
Professional brand
  p. 470

STAR method p. 498
Unique selling proposition
  p. 473
Virtual interview p. 495

MyLab Business Communication

If your instructor is using MyLab Business Communication, go to **www.pearson.com/ mylab/business-communication** to complete the problems marked with this icon ⭐.

Review Questions

⭐ **1** What can you do to analyze your strengths and skills?

2 What questions should you ask yourself to analyze your professional image?

⭐ **3** How can you maintain a professional social media presence?

4 What guidelines should you follow to select an effective résumé design and format?

5 What questions should you ask yourself when you evaluate the content and format of your cover letters?

6 How would you sell your strengths during onsite company interviews?

7 Select a company you would like to work for, and list specific print, online, and social media resources you would use to analyze the company.

⭐ **8** How can you ensure a positive first impression during an interview?

⭐ **9** List the guidelines to consider before participating in an interview meal or social gathering. Explain why each suggestion helps you present a professional image.

10 Explain the questions you should ask yourself after an interview to evaluate your performance.

Critical Thinking Questions

⭐ **1** Having a career plan is important, though experts suggest keeping an open mind about what you might want to do and where you might want to work. Describe your "perfect" job after graduation. Then identify jobs that may lead to that "perfect" job in a few years.

2 Creating a professional brand is critical to your job search. If you were to begin a job search today, what would your brand message be? What changes to your email address, signature block, voice mail greeting, social media content, and communication habits would you need to make to ensure that you appear professional? Provide specific examples.

3 Many employers list effective communication, collaboration, and interpersonal skills as job requirements. How can you demonstrate these qualities in your social media content? Identify examples of posts, tweets, pins, and other content or interaction that would provide specific evidence of your skills.

⭐ **4** Job candidates sometimes produce video résumés in order to stand out from competitors. What are the pros and cons of sending a video résumé to a potential employer?

5 Assume that you will be participating in a group interview in which several applicants for an internship program will meet with the company's recruiting team. You don't know what questions will be asked, but you do know that of the eight applicants in the room, only five will be selected for the program. What strengths do you currently have that will help you do well in this situation? What weaknesses could you improve to help your chances? [**Related to the Collaboration feature on page 498.**]

6 When applicants do not adequately prepare for standard interview questions, they often provide ineffective answers to inquiries about their weaknesses. Why is it a bad idea simply to admit a weakness such as being late on deadlines, procrastinating, or disliking group work? Why does giving yourself a backhanded compliment (for example, "I'm so focused on the details that I often don't see the big picture") come across as an insincere weakness? Why is it important always to include a description of how you are addressing the weakness?

7 Employers' expectations about appropriate business attire may vary based on the industry. Why do you think people in financial management and legal professions often dress more formally than people who work in computer and service-based industries?

8 Two weeks after her interview with a small company in town, Cara has not heard from the employer. She sends a follow-up email message, but a week later she still has not heard anything. She calls and leaves a message, and a week later has still not received a reply. She's very interested in the position, and the interviewer indicated it might take a couple of weeks to make a decision. However, after a month, Cara would at least like to know the status of her application. What advice would you give Cara? Explain.

9 Assume that you spent the last four months of your senior year looking for the perfect job. You interviewed with dozens of companies; however, given the competitive job market, you haven't received any offers. Today, suddenly, you receive two very good offers from two very good companies. The salary and compensation packages are nearly identical, and the opportunities for advancement are similar. Both jobs are in the same town where you currently live. How would you decide which job to take? Make a list of at least five criteria you would use to help you make a decision.

10 During March, Raúl interviewed for five internships for the upcoming summer before his senior year. Of the five, he was most interested in Baylor Industries. By April 10, he had received offers from every company except Baylor, which indicated it would make a decision by April 30 at the latest. Unfortunately, the other four companies needed his response before then. Raúl concluded that because he had received offers from the rest of the companies, his odds were fairly good to receive an offer from Baylor, too. But he wondered if he shouldn't take one of the four offers while he still had them rather than turn down a sure thing. What would you do? Explain why.

Key Concept Exercises

(SQ1) How do you polish your professional presence for a job search? *(pages 470–477)*

1 Analyze your career goals, strengths, and skills: Career goals

Even if you think you know what you want to do with your career, identifying your strengths and preferences can help you narrow your focus. Answer the following questions and support your responses with examples, evidence, or explanation:

- Do you prefer to work collaboratively with other people or on your own?
- Would you enjoy a creative position or a more procedural job?
- Do you see yourself working for a large or small company? In a large or small city?
- Would you enjoy a job that requires travel?

Based on your strengths and preferences, what kind of jobs related to your major would you be interested in pursuing after graduation? Provide your responses in a one-page summary.

2 Analyze your career goals, strengths, and skills: Strengths and skills

Even if you do not have any full-time work experience, you most likely have strengths and skills that can translate into assets for a potential employer. Create a one-page summary based on the following four-part analysis. Be as specific as possible about your skills and word them to relate to your chosen career path.

- Outline your experiences.
- Identify areas of expertise.
- List your sellable qualities.
- Identify your weaknesses.

3 Compose your brand message and strategic social media content: Brand message

Compose a brand message that stresses your value as a prospective employee. Then create a tag line that you can add to your email signature block and business cards. Provide this information to your instructor in a one-page summary.

4 Compose your brand message and strategic social media content: Strategic social media content

Review your current social media sites and make a list of content that you would want to remove before you conduct a job search. Categorize your list by images, posts you've made, comments others have posted to your site, and content you've "liked," shared, or pinned. Then make a list of strategies you would use to make yourself visible and valuable to potential employers. Finally, make a list of content you might include in a blog, e-portfolio, or video résumé. Summarize this information in a message to your instructor.

5 Evaluate your virtual professional image

Use the criteria in Figure 12.6 on pages 476 to evaluate the image of you that your email messages, business cards, and telephone conversations portray. Write a one-page report to your instructor outlining how your current image conforms to the advice in Figure 12.6 and what you can do to improve your image. Be specific and include examples. For instance, if you don't have business cards, compose content and design a sample to include with your report.

(SQ2) How do you compose an effective résumé? *(pages 477–486)*

6 Analyze your options for organizing your résumé

Which résumé format—chronological, functional, or combined—would you recommend for the following scenarios? Explain your choice for each scenario and explain how the applicants should highlight their strengths on their résumés.

a. Sally is a junior, applying for an internship with a company that is looking for business students with proven analytical skills and attention to detail. Sally hasn't had any related work experience, but she has completed two service learning volunteer projects: one in a nursing home, where she helped plan activities, and the other for the local public television station, where she prepared financials for grant applications.

b. George is applying for an entry-level managerial position with a manufacturing company. George spent five years working full time as a loader in the warehouse of a large manufacturing company while he put himself through college. However, he does not have any managerial experience.

c. Tamara has 10 years of clerical experience working as an administrative assistant in one of the academic offices on her campus. While working, she has taken classes part-time and is finally ready to graduate with a degree in business administration. She is applying for a position as an office manager for a Fortune 500 company.

7 Compose effective résumé content: Objective

Assume that you are applying for an internship to gain experience related to your major. The internship advertisement indicates the company prefers students with effective oral and written communication skills who are able to work efficiently in both individual and team environments. Based on your experience, draft an objective statement, qualifications summary, or professional profile for this position. Submit your information to your instructor for evaluation.

CHAPTER 12

8 Compose effective résumé content: Extracurricular activities

Riko is a friend you've known for several years. You are both first-semester juniors with the same major. Although you have been very involved in clubs and organizations on campus, Riko has not yet participated in any extracurricular activities. After reading this chapter, you know how important educational experiences and activities can be when applying for jobs. To help Riko prepare for his employment search, suggest at least three clubs, activities, or related opportunities on your campus that he could pursue that would help him prepare for his profession and would enhance his résumé. For each opportunity, list the requirements and costs to join, when and how often they meet, and the benefits of membership. Submit the information to your instructor for evaluation.

9 Compose effective résumé content: Work history

Although your résumé should highlight your experience that specifically qualifies you for a position, maintaining a comprehensive work history provides you with a database of your experiences for future reference. Create a document titled "Complete Work History" or something similar. List in chronological order (beginning with your most recent job) every position you have held, including both paid and volunteer jobs. Use a professional format that highlights job titles, company names, locations, supervisors' names and contact information, dates of employment, beginning and ending salary information, specific job duties, and reasons for leaving. For example, a job may have been seasonal work or you may have relocated for school or family reasons. Proofread the document carefully and submit it to your instructor for evaluation.

10 Compose effective résumé content

Assume that your friend Estelle asked you to help her with her résumé. She wants to apply for the Undergraduate Internship Program at the Central Intelligence Agency (CIA). Estelle is majoring in general business, but is in the process of changing her major to economics. When you ask why she's interested in the internship, she says she reads a lot of spy novels and thinks the CIA is her "dream job." She would enjoy being a CIA operative because she is good with people and fits in easily in new situations. In her study abroad, she got along well with her host family and participated in a volunteer program at a local hospital. She would enjoy being a CIA analyst because she has a lot of computer experience. Even though she's not majoring in a computer technology program, she has almost enough courses for a minor. Read the information about the CIA's Undergraduate Internship Program at https://www.cia.gov/careers/student-opportunities and then determine if the preliminary content Estelle has gathered is effective (her draft is below). Is it tailored to this position? Does it focus on the employer's needs? Does it reflect her skills and abilities? Estelle knows she needs to expand her résumé and asks for your input. Use the information presented in the résumé guidelines section of this chapter to provide a comprehensive list of suggested improvements and additional content for Estelle's résumé.

11 Exaggerating your résumé content is lying [Related to the Ethics feature on page 479]

Assume that you are applying for an internship that requires a minimum of two years of full-time undergraduate work and at least a 3.00 GPA. After high school, you earned a year's worth of community college credits part-time while you were working full-time to save enough money to start taking classes at your university. You have enough credits to be classified as a junior, but you are finishing your first year as a full-time student. In addition, although you earned a 3.5 GPA at your community college and all your credits transferred, the grades did not transfer to your university GPA. You struggled with a statistics course last semester, and your current university GPA is 2.95. How could you ethically represent your experience and academic ability on your résumé and still have a chance at being considered for this internship?

---

résumé draft

ESTELLE GANT
526 Maple Leaf Way, Rockville, MD 20851, 240.555.7837, e.gant@yahoo.com

CAREER OBJECTIVE
Part-time intern for the CIA

EDUCATION

Bachelor of Science, Morgan State University, GPA: 3.01	In Progress
Study Abroad Experience: Ghana: Social Transformation and	
Cultural Expression program	Fall 2017

WORK EXPERIENCE

Teller, Bank of America, Rockville, MD	2018–Current

- Greet customers and process banking transactions
- Analyze daily drawer reports and troubleshoot discrepancies

EXTRACURRICULAR ACTIVITIES

• Volunteer, Rockville Memorial Hospital	2017–Current
• Member, Technocrats	2018–Current

REFERENCES
Available Upon Request

Accompanies Exercise 10

12 Evaluate your content and design

If you have not updated it recently, evaluate your résumé based on the guidelines outlined in this chapter. Is your content clear, complete, and concise? Does it emphasize the most important information? Is it well-designed to fit the page? Does it look professional? Are alignment and style consistent? Critically evaluate your résumé and make a list of changes you will incorporate to improve the overall content and format. Submit your list of changes to your instructor. Your instructor may also ask you to provide before and after versions of your résumé based on your evaluation.

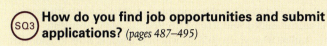

How do you find job opportunities and submit applications? *(pages 487–495)*

13 Analyze your options for finding job opportunities

Use at least three different websites that list job advertisements to search for your "dream job" after graduation. You can search Monster, CareerBuilder, US.jobs, websites of a specific company, or websites tailored specifically to your field. Using the same search criteria, select a job advertisement that interests you from each site. Choose positions you will be eligible to apply for immediately after graduation rather than 5 or 10 years later. What skills are listed in all three postings? Are any skills required for one position, but not the rest? Are there any other differences among the positions? Will you be qualified for these positions after graduation? If so, list the strengths you would emphasize in a cover letter or résumé to persuade the employers to schedule an interview with you. If not, describe how you will equip yourself with the skills you will need. Summarize your findings in a one-page message to your instructor.

14 Compose an effective elevator pitch

Draft an elevator pitch for the next job position you plan to seek—perhaps it's a part-time summer job, an internship, your first career-related position after graduation, or a promotion with your current employer. Using a word processing application, create a two-column format. On the left, double space your elevator pitch. On the right, single space annotations that explain how your pitch follows the recommendations on pages 487–488.

15 Compose persuasive cover letters

Find a job advertisement or posting for a position you are qualified for. Print the advertisement and circle the keywords. Write a persuasive cover letter based on the guidelines presented in this chapter. Evaluate the effectiveness of your letter and proofread carefully before submitting it and the advertisement to your instructor. If you have previously designed a résumé, ensure that the cover letter coordinates well with the résumé in content and visual style.

16 Select a medium for submission and follow up as necessary

Refer to Exercises 10 and 11. Assume that your friend Estelle applied to the CIA but did not receive a response. Help Estelle compose a follow-up email, following the model in Figure 12.21.

17 Revising your résumé for international opportunities [Related to the Culture feature on page 485]

Find an advertisement for an internship or full-time position located in a European or Asian country. Create an international version of your résumé based on the information provided in the Culture feature. Write a message to your instructor explaining what changes you made, and submit it to your instructor along with the position advertisement and your international résumé.

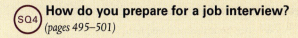

How do you prepare for a job interview? *(pages 495–501)*

18 Analyze how to benefit from different types of interviews

Attend a local career fair to observe the format and layout of the event. Note both the employers and the job seekers. Were there obvious differences in attire, professionalism, or image? Talk to students who spoke with recruiters. What kinds of questions did they ask? What was the experience like? What advice do the students recommend? Summarize your findings and highlight those that specifically relate to your career goals. Be prepared to present this information in class or in a message to your instructor.

19 Preparing for video interviews [Related to the Technology feature on page 501]

Find an advertisement for an internship or full-time position in your career field that interests you. Assume that the employer has asked you to submit a pre-recoded interview based on the eight questions in Figure 12.23 on page 497. Prepare talking notes and plan your answers to be no more than one to two minutes per question. Consider all the guidelines provided in this chapter about virtual interviews, including interview location and your attire. Prepare talking notes that you can refer to during your interview. Record the interview on your phone or laptop. Then watch the video and evaluate yourself. What did you do well? What could you improve? Summarize your evaluation in a one-page message to your instructor.

20 Compose good answers—and good questions

The STAR method is an effective format to use when responding to behavioral questions. Outline a scenario, task, action, and result you could use to respond to the following interview prompts:

a. Describe a time when you worked well under pressure or organized a major project.

b. Describe something you have done that shows you have initiative and creativity.

c. Describe a time when you faced frustration. How did you deal with it?

Be prepared to share your responses in class or in a message to your instructor. Evaluate your response based on feedback you receive.

21 Evaluate your professional appearance

Pat is a senior marketing major who spent college working two jobs: as a short-order cook at a local diner on weeknights and as a coach for a large K–12 indoor soccer league on the weekends. Pat is also on the school's soccer team and typically wears gym clothes to classes to be ready to go to soccer practice. Pat's wardrobe does not include any businesslike clothing, not even business casual options. In preparation to begin interviewing for jobs, Pat knows investing in a business wardrobe is important. However, Pat does not have a lot of money to spend. Help Pat determine what to buy and where to buy it to stay within a reasonable budget (assume that Pat's gender is the same as yours). Provide Pat with two interview options, complete with accessories and portfolio, as well as three business casual outfits that can be mixed and matched to extend the wardrobe. Research every detail: stores, labels, styles, shoes, and so forth. Be prepared to share your findings in class or summarize them in a message to your instructor.

How can you make a positive impression during and after an interview? *(pages 502–510)*

22 Project a professional presence

Several business etiquette quizzes are available online. Search for the following titles or other interactive business etiquette sites:

- USA Today—Miss Business Manner's Etiquette Quiz
- GradView—Test Your Business Etiquette
- International Social and Business Savvy Quotient

Take one quiz and score your responses. What percentage of questions did you answer correctly? Summarize the questions you answered incorrectly, and be prepared to share what you learned in class or in writing to your instructor.

23 Compose effective post-interview messages

Assume you responded to an advertisement for a summer internship with a local business, Metrix Marketing Consultants. After submitting your cover letter and résumé, the assistant to the human resources director (you forgot to record her name) called to invite you to participate in a panel interview. At the beginning of the interview, you wrote down the names and positions of the five panel members, none of whom was the person who called you or the human resources director. Each panel member asked questions and responded to your questions. Philip Peterson, a marketing research analyst, appeared to be the most senior member of the panel, but he didn't lead the interview. In fact, none of the panel members *led* the interview. Phyllis McEwen started the interview with an overview of the process, and Rayna

Hampton concluded the interview, asking if you had any questions and finally indicating that they would follow up in two weeks with a decision. At the end of the interview, you asked for business cards, but no one had one. Before you left, you thanked and shook hands with each person. It was a good interview. When you get home, you remember that you should write a thank-you note. Do you send a note to one person or to each of the five panel members? If you send five notes, do you say the same thing in each one, or do you customize? In addition, you're not sure if you have the correct spellings of their names: Phillip or Philip, Peterson or Petersen, McEwen or Macuen, Rayna or Reyna? Whom do you contact for this information, and how? You don't have a phone number or email address for anyone, and you submitted your résumé electronically on the company's website. Outline what you would do, whom you would write to, and what you would say.

24 Evaluate your performance

Register with your school's career services office, if you have not already done so, and schedule a mock interview with one of the career counselors. Ask for feedback from the counselor, and then evaluate your performance based on the criteria outlined in the chapter. Summarize your evaluation in a one-page message to your instructor.

Writing Exercises

25 Writing a professional résumé

Select a job advertisement or internship listing that interests you and create (or modify) your résumé to apply for that job using the guidelines presented in this chapter. Use the résumé format—chronological, functional, or combined—that bests suits your experience. Submit the advertisement and your résumé to your instructor for evaluation, either in hard copy or PDF form.

26 Creating a plain-text résumé

Transform the résumé that you created in Exercise 24 into a plain-text version that you can easily cut and paste into a web-based form or the body of an email message. Submit your résumé by email to your instructor for evaluation.

27 Writing a persuasive cover letter

Find a job advertisement or posting for a position you are qualified for. Print the advertisement and circle the keywords. Write a persuasive cover letter based on the guidelines presented in this chapter. Evaluate the effectiveness of your letter and proofread carefully before submitting it and the advertisement to your instructor. If you have previously designed a résumé, ensure that the cover letter coordinates well with the résumé in content and visual style.

28 Compiling effective references

Brainstorm the people you know who can be part of your professional network. Make a comprehensive list noting your relationship with the people, their contact information, and their professional affiliations, if applicable. From that list, select three to five professional people who can serve as professional references for you. Format a reference sheet with a heading similar to your résumé heading, and add an appropriate title, such as "References," before listing their names and contact information.

29 Designing business cards

Design a business card that complements the format or style of your cover letter and résumé. Include your name and contact information. Consider including your major and institutional affiliation as well.

30 Writing your own recommendation letter

Find a job posting for an internship or job you would be interested in pursuing after graduation. Assume that you have applied for the position and scheduled an interview. The employer is requesting a letter of recommendation from your faculty advisor. When you ask your advisor for the letter, she indicates that she is really very busy and won't be able to provide a letter by the time you need it unless you draft it for her. She assures you that she'll edit it as necessary to make it sound like her, but she needs you to put the content on the page and in an appropriate format. Research content for professional recommendation letters and then draft your own letter, being sure to integrate evidence that supports your qualifications for this specific job. Evaluate your letter and submit it and your job advertisement to your instructor for evaluation.

31 Preparing responses to interview questions

Find a reputable resource that lists interview questions specific to your discipline. (Tip: You can search the web using the name of your field and the phrase "interview questions," for example "accounting interview questions.") Select five questions and draft your responses in a one-page report. Be prepared to share your questions and answers in class or submit your report to your instructor for evaluation.

32 Composing targeted thank-you messages

Assume that earlier today you interviewed for a competitive summer internship with McMillen-Scott, Inc., a local company. Your contact person, Carla Ruiz, an assistant manager and director of the internship program, was in the reception area when you arrived. Carla greeted you and led you to a conference room where you met Andre Moore and Toby Smith, who were also assistant managers. During the next hour, you learned that the internship would give you a wide breadth of experience at the company by helping with several projects in three different departments while regular employees are on vacation. Your interview concluded just before lunch, and although it wasn't planned as part of your interview experience, Andre and Toby invited you to have lunch with them. Carla had a lunch meeting with a client. During lunch, Andre and Toby shared their insights about the company and, in response to your request for career advice, talked at length about graduate school and professional development options. You thanked Toby when he paid for your lunch.

As you reflect on the interview and lunch, you realize the internship will require good time management and prioritization skills to balance the many projects and needs of different departments. Your skills in these areas are very strong, and you regret that you forgot to emphasize that during your interview. However, you decide you can work them into your thank-you messages to Carla, Andre, and Toby. Compose unique thank-you messages to each person, carefully evaluate your messages, and submit your documents to your instructor.

Collaboration Exercises

33 Comparing companies' résumé submission requirements

As part of a team, brainstorm a list of companies within a specific industry; for example, sports-related (Nike, Reebok, Adidas), technology-related (Microsoft, Intel, Google), or financial services (Citibank, Bank of America, Wells Fargo) companies. The number of companies you list should equal the number of people in your team. Assign one company to each team member. Visit the companies' websites to determine the employment opportunities they provide. How do they prefer applicants to submit employment information (for example, web-based submissions, emailed résumés, or hardcopy mailings)? Discuss the similarities and differences among the companies and collaboratively write a one-page message that summarizes your findings.

34 Role-playing interview skills

In small groups of three or four, assign the role of interviewer to one student and the role of interviewee to another student. The remaining student(s) will serve as an observer and recorder. The interviewee describes an entry-level job related to his or her career goal, and the interviewer selects three to five questions from the list of standard interview questions presented in Figure 12.23 (page 497). For five minutes, role-play an interview. The observer/recorder makes notes about the interviewee's responses, and, at the conclusion of the interview, provides both positive and constructive feedback. Rotate roles and repeat the process, ensuring that different interview questions are selected with each round. If time permits, ensure everyone in the group has had an opportunity to serve as the interviewee. Review the strengths and weaknesses of the group's collective interview responses. What similarities exist? What differences? Be prepared to present a summary of your findings in class or in a message to your instructor.

Social Media Exercises

35 Connecting with companies

Make a list of the companies where you might want to intern next summer or work after graduation. Connect with those companies through Facebook, LinkedIn, and/or Twitter and look for ways to interact with the company. Make a list of important people in your industry to "friend" and follow. Share your lists and connections in a message to your instructor, or be prepared to present your information in a short presentation to the class.

36 Videotape yourself during a mock interview

Ask a friend to interview you, or schedule a mock interview with your school's career center if you can record it. Post the interview to your Facebook page or YouTube channel. Ask your professional network to provide constructive feedback. Summarize the responses you receive and your own conclusions in a short report to your instructor.

Speaking Exercises

37 Making informal/impromptu presentations

a. What are your career goals? What is your "dream job"? In a one- to two-minute presentation, identify the kind of job you hope to obtain immediately after graduation and the job you hope to achieve 10 or 15 years later. Explain what you will do to prepare yourself for your dream job.

b. What skill or strength do you currently possess that will help you secure a job related to your major after graduation? In a one- to two-minute presentation, describe the skill, when you obtained it, and how it will benefit your career.

c. What skill do you need to develop or enhance before you begin your job search? In a one- to two-minute presentation, describe the skill, when and how you plan to develop it, and how it will benefit your career.

d. Imagine you could write the job description for your "perfect job." Identify the job title and summarize the specific duties in a one- to two-minute presentation.

e. Identify five capabilities and skills you currently possess that you could highlight on your résumé. Describe specific evidence to support each ability. For example, you could support your ability to work well with others by citing your leadership during a two-day car wash fundraiser last semester when you successfully organized 25 volunteers.

38 Briefing your class about job-search resources

a. Research the student organizations your school supports. How many are there? How many of the organizations focus on students' academic or professional development? Which ones would help prepare you for your career goals? Identify three organizations and describe their goals, benefits, and (if applicable) any membership requirements. Prepare a visual aid that outlines this information, and describe your findings to your audience in a three- to five-minute presentation.

b. Research three different websites that provide résumé-writing tips. Compare their suggestions for creating professional résumés and identify what you perceive to be the three most important tips that all three recommend, as they will relate to your job search. Prepare a visual aid, such as a slide or handout, that outlines these three tips, and describe your findings to your audience in a three- to five-minute presentation.

c. Use the *Occupational Outlook Handbook* from the U.S. Bureau of Labor Statistics to learn about a specific job related to your major. List up to five things you read that you already knew about this position and identify where you learned about them. Then list up to five things you read that you did not know about this position. Prepare a visual aid to support a three- to five-minute presentation that describes your findings.

d. Select a specific company for which you would like to work. Research its website to familiarize yourself with its mission, products or services, corporate culture, and financial outlook. Summarize your findings in a three- to five-minute presentation during which you display either selected pages from the company's website or other visual aids you have prepared. Throughout your presentation, indicate why the information persuades you to want to work for this company.

e. Research international internship opportunities. In a three- to five-minute presentation, outline where students can find international internship opportunities and what skills are required to be a competitive candidate. Prepare a one-page handout summarizing this information to support your presentation.

39 Presenting research

Research one of the following topics and prepare a visual aid to support a three- to five-minute presentation:

a. Visit your school's career center, either in person or online. Research the career fair opportunities it provides or recommends in your area. Determine whether career-specific fairs, such as for business, the health industry, or education occupations, are available. Also, research the companies that recruit on campus outside of career fairs. Summarize your findings and highlight those that specifically relate to your career goals.

b. Select a company that you would be interested in working for after graduation. Research the company's website to become familiar with its history, mission and/or vision statement, financial health, and recent developments or projects. Brainstorm five questions specific to this company that you could ask during an interview. In your presentation, display the website highlighting the information upon which your questions are based. Then present your questions and explain how you would use the employer's answers to determine if the job is a good fit for you.

c. Interviews can be nerve-wracking experiences for even the most prepared applicants. Find at least two sources that provide stress-relieving suggestions you can use to reduce your anxiety before and during interviews. Explain the suggestions and, if possible, demonstrate them during your presentation.

d. Find online images or take photos of friends (or yourself) in "street clothes," business casual outfits, and business formal attire. Display the photos in a PowerPoint presentation that includes annotated descriptions of how or why the outfits fit into each category. Explain the outfits and their accessories during the presentation, moving from most casual to most formal.

e. What are your salary expectations? Research salaries for jobs you are interested in pursuing after graduation. What is the range? What are the differences among various geographic regions? What differences in an applicant's qualifications would justify a salary at the upper end of the range? In addition to salary, what other benefits are included in typical compensation packages?

Grammar Exercise

40 Spelling (see Appendix C: Grammar, Punctuation, Mechanics, and Conventions—Section 4)

Type the following paragraph, correcting the 10 incorrect homonyms or near homonyms, which a spell checker may not catch. Underline all of your corrections.

Businesses rely on text messaging for many things besides advertising. Texting can compliment other forms of communication and surpass some for speed and affectiveness. To site one example, let's consider instant communication between a stockbroker and investor. The broker can council the investor about the movement of a stock price and get a "buy" or "sell" decision quickly. Vendors can confirm deliveries, customers can track shipments, and contractors can tell there on-sight crews to precede with construction. Another principle advantage of text messages is the ability to communicate silently. In situations where speaking may be awkward or impossible but immediate communication is important, texting makes more sense then a phone call. Instead of searching in vain for a place to take a call, a person can simply tap out a reply, waving the need for privacy.

MyLab Business Communication

Go to **www.pearson.com/mylab/business-communication** for Auto-graded writing questions as well as the following Assisted-graded writing questions:

1. Creating a unique but consistent format for your résumé and cover letter is one method of demonstrating your skills with word processing and page design applications. How else might you demonstrate specific skills through your employment communication, including your social media communication?

2. Although telephone interviews may cause less stress than face-to-face interaction, they do not provide you with visual cues that help you interpret people's feelings and attitudes. Identify the kinds of information that you might perceive from visual cues in an interview. What strategies could you use in a telephone interview to elicit this kind of information?

References

1. Sabitano, C. (2017). Should I intern as a college freshman? Retrieved from http://www.internships.com/student/resources/prep/should-i-intern-as-a-college-freshman

2. Sanchez, K. (2016, September 20). 5 reasons to get an internship ASAP. Retrieved from https://studybreaks.com/2016/09/20/5-reasons-obtain-internship-asap/

3. Loretto, P. (2016, July 7). Survey results—Paid internships lead to full-time job offers. Retrieved from https://www.thebalance.com/paid-internship-full-time-1987131

4. Florentine, S. (2016, August 31). 4 tips to help build your professional brand. Retrieved from http://www.cio.com/article/3114235/it-skills-training/4-tips-to-help-build-your-professional-brand.html

5. Kennedy, J. L. (2014). How to create a personal brand for your job search. Retrieved from http://www.dummies.com/careers/find-a-job/how-to-create-a-personal-brand-for-your-job-search/

6. Smith, P. (2017). How social media helps your job search [Infographic]. Retrieved from http://www.careerglider.com/blog/infographic-social-media-help-job-search/

7. Gausepohl, S. (2016, June 17). Social media success: A guide for job seekers. *Business News Daily*. Retrieved from http://www.businessnewsdaily.com/7728-social-media-job-seeker-guide.html

8. Jobvite. (2016). Jobvite recruiter nation report 2016. Retrieved from https://www.jobvite.com/wp-content/uploads/2016/09/RecruiterNation2016.pdf

9. Augustine, A. (2014, March 4). How to tap into the hidden job market. Retrieved from https://www.theladders.com/p/1253/hidden-job-market

10. Doyle, A. (2016, August 13). How to create a professional brand: Best tips for creating a professional brand. Retrieved from https://www.thebalance.com/how-to-create-a-professional-brand-2059761

11. Hur, J. (2017). Best LinkedIn profile picture tips. Retrieved from http://bebusinessed.com/linkedin/best-linkedin-profile-picture-tips/

12. Gunaydin, G., Selcuk, E., & Zayas, V. (2016, August 25). Impressions based on a portrait predict, 1-month later, impressions following a live interaction. *Social Psychological and Personality Science, 18*(1), 36–44.

13. Morin, A. (2016, December 3). Why your LinkedIn picture plays the biggest role in determining whether you land a job. *Forbes*. Retrieved from https://www.forbes.com/sites/amymorin/2016/12/03/why-your-linkedin-picture-plays-the-biggest-role-in-determining-whether-you-land-a-job/

14. Bellis, R. (2016, May 12). Here's how to use social media at each stage of your career. *Fast Company*. Retrieved from https://www.fastcompany.com/3059718/your-most-productive-self/hereshow-to-use-social-media-at-each-stage-of-your-career

15. Bellis, R. (2016, May 12). Here's how to use social media at each stage of your career. *Fast Company*. Retrieved from https://www.fastcompany.com/3059718/your-most-productive-self/hereshow-to-use-social-media-at-each-stage-of-your-career

16. Ryan, L. (2016, December 10). How to update your LinkedIn profile for 2017. *Forbes*. Retrieved from https://www.forbes.com/sites/lizryan/2016/12/10/how-to-update-your-linkedin-profile-for-2017/

17. Fleming, J. (2017, February 13). 17 steps to a better LinkedIn profile in 2017. Retrieved from https://business.linkedin.com/en-uk/marketing-solutions/blog/posts/content-marketing/2017/17-steps-to-a-better-LinkedIn-profile-in-2017

18. Converge Interns. (2016, July 11). 5 student perspectives on the LinkedIn students app. Retrieved from http://convergeconsulting.org/2016/07/11/5-student-perspectives-on-the-linkedin-students-app/

19. Chaykowski, K. (2016, April 18). LinkedIn has a new app for job-hunting college students. *Forbes*. Retrieved from https://www.forbes.com/sites/kathleenchaykowski/2016/04/18/linkedin-has-a-new-app-for-job-hunting-college-students/#6cb26f6d3de4

20. Symonds, M. (2014, March 14). 5 social media tips to protect your future from your online past. *Forbes*. Retrieved from http://www.forbes.com/sites/mattsymonds/2014/03/14/5-social-media-tips-to-protect-your-future-from-your-online-past/

21. Smooke, D. (2017, January 9). What makes a recruiter stop reading your résumé? [Infographic]. *Recruiter.com*. Retrieved from https://www.recruiter.com/i/what-makes-a-recruiter-stop-reading-your-resume-infographic/

22. Sundberg, J. (2017, February 5). Don't use a résumé template if you want to land a new job. *The Undercover Recruiter*. Retrieved from http://theundercoverrecruiter.com/dont-use-resume-template-if-want-land-new-job/

23. Amare, N., & Manning, A. (2009, March). Writing for the robot: How employer search tools have influenced résumé rhetoric and ethics. *Business Communication Quarterly, 72*(1), 35–60.

24. Hu, J. (2016, August 11). 8 things you need to know about applicant tracking systems [Blog post]. Retrieved from https://www.jobscan.co/blog/8-things-you-need-to-know-about-applicant-tracking-systems/

25. Dishman, L. (2016, April 15). The most common résumé lies (and who is most likely to tell them). *Fast Company*. Retrieved from https://www.fastcompany.com/3058918/the-most-common-resume-lies-and-who-is-most-likely-to-tell-them

26. CareerBuilder. (2016, September 22). Retrieved from http://www.careerbuilder.com/share/aboutus/pressreleasesdetail.aspx?sd=9%2F22%2F2016&id=pr967&ed=12%2F31%2F2016

27. Giolando, E. (2015, September 10). How to write a résumé for anywhere in the world. Retrieved from https://www.gooverseas.com/blog/how-to-write-a-resume-for-anywhere-in-the-world

28. Bahler, K. (2017, February 17). How to use Facebook's new job search feature. *Money*. Retrieved from http://time.com/money/4674436/facebook-new-jobs/

29. Lastoe, S. (2017). Facebook groups: The best-kept secret for boosting your career. Retrieved from https://www.themuse.com/advice/facebook-groups-the-bestkept-secret-for-boosting-your-career

30. Whitcomb, S. (2017). Getting started on Twitter: 25 tips for job-seekers to take advantage of the web's best-kept job search secret. Retrieved from https://www.livecareer.com/quintessential/job-seeeker-twitter-tips

31. Adler, L. (2016, February 29). New survey reveals 85% of all jobs are filled via networking. Retrieved from https://www.linkedin.com/pulse/new-survey-reveals-85-all-jobs-filled-via-networking-lou-adler

32. Matta, V. (2016, July 25). This is how you get an employee referral. Retrieved from https://careershift.com/blog/2016/07/get-employee-referral/

33. Salemi, V. (2016, February 18). 5 hiring trends to watch in 2016. *Forbes*. Retrieved from https://www.forbes.com/sites/vickisalemi/2016/02/18/5-hiring-trends-to-watch-in-2016-2/

34. Simpson, M. (2017). How to write a killer elevator pitch (examples included). Retrieved from https://theinterviewguys.com/write-elevator-pitch/

35. Homayun, O. (2016, April 10). 5 tips to nail your elevator pitch. *Forbes*. Retrieved from https://www.forbes.com/sites/omaidhomayun/2016/04/10/5-tips-to-nail-your-elevator-pitch/

36. Power, R. (2017, March 16). A 3-step formula for a great elevator pitch. Retrieved from http://www.cnbc.com/2017/03/16/a-3-step-formula-for-a-great-elevator-pitch.html

37. Doyle, A. (2017, March 22). Top 7 best free job search apps. Retrieved from https://www.thebalance.com/best-free-apps-job-searching-2061001

38. O'Brien, P., & Davis-Ali, S. (2013, November 8). Do cover letters still matter? *USAToday*. Retrieved from http://www.usatoday.com/story/money/2013/11/07/cover-letters-still-make-a-difference/3465629/

39. Balachandran, M., & Blair, R. B. (2007). Résumé preferences of U.S. businesses. *Business Education Digest, XVI*, 60–69.

40. Schullery, N. M., Ickes, L., & Schullery, S. E. (2009). Employer preferences for résumés and cover letters. *Business Communication Quarterly, 72*(2), 163–176.

41. Isaacs, K. (2017). Six tips to get the interview. Retrieved from https://www.monster.com/career-advice/article/get-the-interview

42. Doyle. A. (2016, October 14). Tips for making a follow-up call after a job interview. What to say when you call to say thank you for an interview. Retrieved from https://www.thebalance.com/job-interview-follow-up-phone-call-do-s-and-don-ts-2061305

43. Thompson, K. (2016, August 4). Know the benefits of attending a job fair [Blog post]. Retrieved from http://blog.chron.com/careerrescue/2016/08/know-the-benefits-of-attending-a-job-fair/

44. Cobert, A. (2017). Standing out from the crowd: How to nail a group interview. Retrieved from https://www.themuse.com/advice/standing-out-from-the-crowd-how-to-nail-a-group-interview

45. Doyle. A. (2017, January 6). Group interview questions and interviewing tips. Retrieved from https://www.thebalance.com/group-interview-questions-and-interviewing-tips-2061157

46. Simpson, M. (2016). How to ace a group interview (questions included). Retrieved from https://theinterviewguys.com/group-interview-questions-included/

47. Doyle. A. (2017, February 4). Top 10 behavioral interview questions and answers. How to use the STAR technique when interviewing. Retrieved from https://www.thebalance.com/top-behavioral-interview-questions-2059618

48. Llarena, M. (2012, April 12). R.A.T.S. is how employers prioritize the S.T.A.R. method. Retrieved from https://melissallarena.com/rats-how-employers-prioritize-star-method/

49. Blazkova, H. (2011). Telling tales of professional competence: Narrative in 60-second business networking speeches. *Journal of Business Communication, 48*(4), 446–463.

50. Shwom, B., Eisenstein, A., & Broderick, M. (2016, October). What do they really want to know? Preparing students to answer job interview questions. Presentation at the meeting of the Association for Business Communication, Albuquerque, NM.

51. Augustine, A. (2014, May 27). 9 signs you didn't land the job. Retrieved from https://www.theladders.com/p/2433/job-interviews-gone-wrong

52. Ryan, L. (2017, January 3). 20 interview questions to ask your next boss. *Forbes*. Retrieved from https://www.forbes.com/sites/lizryan/2017/01/03/20-interview-questions-for-your-next-boss/

53. Green, A. (2012, April 18). The 10 best interview questions to ask. *U.S. News & World Report*. Retrieved from http://money.usnews.com/money/blogs/outside-voices-careers/2012/04/18/the-10-best-interview-questions-to-ask

54. Smith, J. (2013, February 21). The 13 most outrageous job interview mistakes. *Forbes*. Retrieved from http://www.forbes.com/sites/jacquelynsmith/2013/02/21/the-13-most-outrageous-job-interview-mistakes/

55. Caroll, J. (2007, October 4). "Business casual" most common work attire. Gallup.com. Retrieved from http://www.gallup.com/poll/101707/Business-Casual-Most-Common-Work-Attire.aspx

56. Steed, A. (2016, May 13). Job interview via Skype? Here's how to nail it, not fail it. *The Telegraph*. Retrieved from http://www.telegraph.co.uk/expat/before-you-go/job-interview-via-skype-heres-how-to-nail-it-not-fail-it/

57. Grove, J. (2017, April 6). Career advice: How to do a Skype job interview. Retrieved from https://www.timeshighereducation.com/unijobs/article/career-advice-how-to-do-a-skype-job-interview

58. Doyle, A. (2016, September 5). Tips on using Skype for video job interviews. Retrieved from https://www.thebalance.com/video-interviewing-with-skype-2061627

59. Ward, M. (2017, January 9). Why the first second of a job interview can make or break you. Retrieved from https://www.cnbc.com/2017/01/09/why-the-first-second-of-a-job-interview-can-make-or-break-you.html

60. Goman, C. K. (2012, May 7). 10 body language tips to help you land that first job. *Forbes*. Retrieved from http://www.forbes.com/sites/carolkinseygoman/2012/05/07/10-tips-to-help-you-land-that-first-job/

61. Enelow, W. S. (2017). Write winning thank-you letters. Retrieved from https://www.monster.com/career-advice/article/write-winning-thank-you-letters

62. Alderton, M. (2016, November 15). How to accept a job offer the right way. Retrieved from http://www.successfulmeetings.com/Strategy/SM-How-To/How-to-Accept-a-Job-Offer-the-Right-Way/

63. Lockert, M. (2015, June 23). Increase your salary by 5-10% (or more) with these negotiation strategies. Retrieved from https://studentloanhero.com/featured/negotiate-your-salary-earn-more-with-these-strategies/

64. Bosch, J. (2016, October 3). 5 salary negotiation tips to get the sales compensation you deserve. Retrieved from http://www.peaksalesrecruiting.com/salary-negotiation-sales-compensation/

65. Harvard University. Program on Negotiation (2015). *Salary negotiations: How to negotiate salary: Learn the best techniques to help you manage the most difficult salary negotiations and what you need to know when asking for a raise*. Retrieved from https://www.pon.harvard.edu/freemium/salary-negotiations/

66. Ryan, L. (2016, December 13). Script: How to negotiate a job offer. *Forbes*. Retrieved from https://www.forbes.com/sites/lizryan/2016/12/13/script-how-to-negotiate-a-job-offer/

67. Doyle, A. (2013, June 22). How to withdraw from consideration for a job. Retrieved from http://jobsearch.about.com/od/job-offers/a/withdraw-from-a-job.htm

68. National Consumer Law Center. (2012, April). Broken records: How errors by criminal background checking companies harm workers and businesses. Retrieved from http://www.nclc.org/issues/broken-records.html

69. Hannon, K. (2012, January 31). Bad credit can cost you a job. *Forbes*. Retrieved from http://www.forbes.com/sites/kerryhannon/2012/01/31/bad-credit-can-cost-you-a-job/

70. *Fortune Magazine*. (2017). Fortune 100 best companies to work for. Retrieved from http://beta.fortune.com/best-companies

Appendix A

Formats for Business Documents

Using standard formatting guidelines for basic business documents will help you ensure your written communication looks professional. This appendix provides advice and annotated examples you can use to help you format your emails, memos, letters, and reports. If your instructor or employer requests formats that are different from the samples provided, keep in mind that your goal should always be to ensure a professional-looking document that effectively communicates your purpose.

Email

Follow email formatting guidelines to ensure you include all the elements needed in business emails and to ensure that your content is easy to read on a computer or mobile device.

Email formatting guidelines

A professional business email message includes the following elements:

- **Email addresses.** When composing an email message, put the recipient's email address on the "To" line. If you want to send the same message to several recipients, separate their email addresses with commas. If you want to send a courtesy copy ("cc") to a secondary audience, add their email addresses on the "cc" line. The "bcc" line is for a "blind courtesy copy" and is used to send a copy of the message to people without communicating that fact to the "To" and "cc" recipients.
- **Subject line.** Always include a short and meaningful subject line. The best subject lines clearly communicate the purpose of your message. For example, *"Sales Meeting"* is not a meaningful subject line. The recipients would have to open your message to know whether you are trying to schedule a sales meeting or following up after a meeting. If you are sending meeting minutes requiring no response, your subject line might be *"Sales Meeting Minutes,"* which would indicate that the message is not urgent and recipients can read it when they have time. However, if you are trying to schedule a meeting and need their quick response, your subject line might be *"Need Input for Meeting Date Before 5 PM,"* which would prompt recipients to read the message right away.
- **Salutation.** The salutation or greeting addresses the message to the primary audience. How the salutation is worded sets the tone for the rest of the document. Formal business emails frequently use "Dear" in the salutation, such as *"Dear Mr. Smith."* However, contemporary business writers are moving away from the traditional use of "Dear," especially in informal emails, often choosing instead to use a salutation such as *"Hi, John"* or *"Hello, Mr. Smith."* In some cases, you might simply use the person's name without any salutation, although some audiences may consider it rude to omit a salutation.

  Different salutations require different punctuation. In a formal email, a salutation like *"Dear Mr. Smith"* ends with a colon. There is no other punctuation. In the less formal salutation, *"Hello, John,"* a comma separates the greeting from the name, and the salutation ends with a colon or comma, depending on the level of formality you want to convey. In rare cases, you may see salutations formatted with *open punctuation,* which means neither the salutation nor the complimentary closing includes punctuation.

- **Name.** Whether you use a person's first or last name in the salutation depends on how you address the individual in face-to-face settings. If your boss has asked you to call him "John," address your email to him as "John" rather than "Mr. Smith." However, when emailing new clients or customers for the first time, do not assume they want you to use their first names. Practice professional business etiquette by erring on the side of formality. Similarly, do not assume that a woman is a "Mrs." unless you know your recipient prefers "Mrs." It is better to use "Ms." or a professional title such as "Dr." or "Rev." when applicable.

- **Paragraphs.** Short email messages may include just a few lines of text. Longer messages should use the following paragraphing techniques to organize the content effectively:

  - Keep the first paragraph short (50 words or less) and quickly get to the point of the message. Imagine that your audience is reading the message on a smartphone or other mobile device. Make sure the main idea is visible on the first screen so the audience doesn't have to scroll to find it. Also, do not begin with *"This email is about…."* Your subject line tells the recipient the topic of the email.

  - Begin the middle paragraph(s) with a topic sentence that identifies the main point of the paragraph. Keep the middle paragraphs relatively short; average paragraphs are roughly 100 words in length.

  - End the message with a short paragraph requesting any action, indicating any deadlines, and maintaining goodwill with the audience.

- **Complimentary closing.** In formal situations, use a closing such as *"Sincerely."* In less formal messages, you might use *"Thanks"* or *"Regards."* The closing is followed by a comma and then your name on the next line. Using just your first name is fine for informal messages to people who will immediately recognize your email address. However, if you are writing to someone who does not know you, use your first name and last name. Do not use a personal title such as "Mr." or "Ms." with your name unless the recipient cannot identify your gender from your first name (such as Pat, Chris, or Rathi). In these cases, use your personal title so the recipient knows to address you as either Mr. or Ms. in a response to your message.

- **Signature block.** In formal emails, always include an electronic signature block that displays all relevant contact information, including your name, position title, department, company, email address, phone number, and fax number. Even in informal emails within your own organization, using a signature block is a good practice. If someone wants to respond to your message by telephone, your telephone number will be immediately available. Further, if the recipient forwards your email or prints it, your contact information will remain with the message.

- **Attachments.** If you include attachments with an email, always identify the attachments within the body of the message to ensure that the recipient is aware of the attached files and knows what they include.

Refer to the annotated examples on the next page when formatting informal and formal email messages. **Figure A.1** provides an example of an informal email message, and **Figure A.2** is an example of a formal email.

FIGURE A.1 Informal Email Message Format

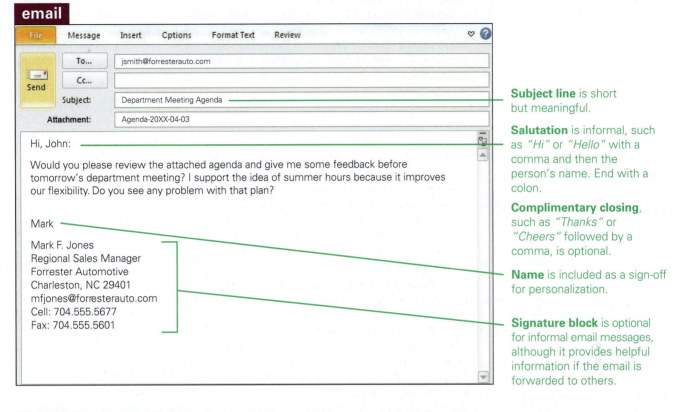

Subject line is short but meaningful.

Salutation is informal, such as *"Hi"* or *"Hello"* with a comma and then the person's name. End with a colon.

Complimentary closing, such as *"Thanks"* or *"Cheers"* followed by a comma, is optional.

Name is included as a sign-off for personalization.

Signature block is optional for informal email messages, although it provides helpful information if the email is forwarded to others.

FIGURE A.2 Formal Email Message Format

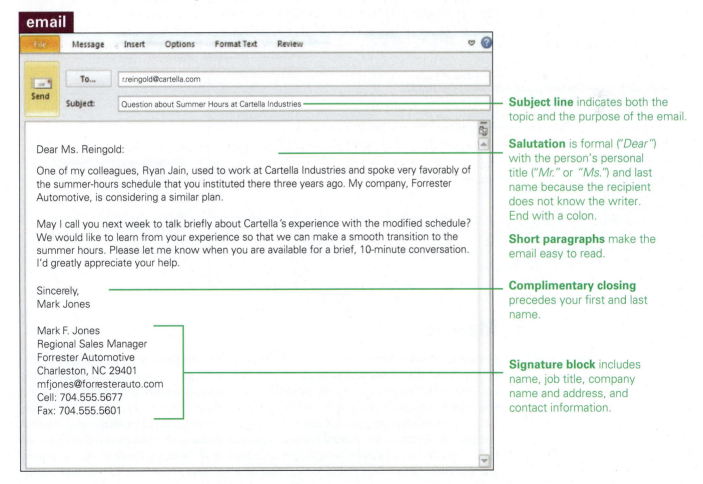

Subject line indicates both the topic and the purpose of the email.

Salutation is formal (*"Dear"*) with the person's personal title (*"Mr."* or *"Ms."*) and last name because the recipient does not know the writer. End with a colon.

Short paragraphs make the email easy to read.

Complimentary closing precedes your first and last name.

Signature block includes name, job title, company name and address, and contact information.

Email report format

You can compose informal email reports to share information with people within your organization. Email reports may also be appropriate for external audiences if the context is informal and you know the audience prefers email over other medium options. **Figure A.3** provides an example of an email report format. Notice that the salutation and complimentary closing are optional.

FIGURE A.3 Email Report Format

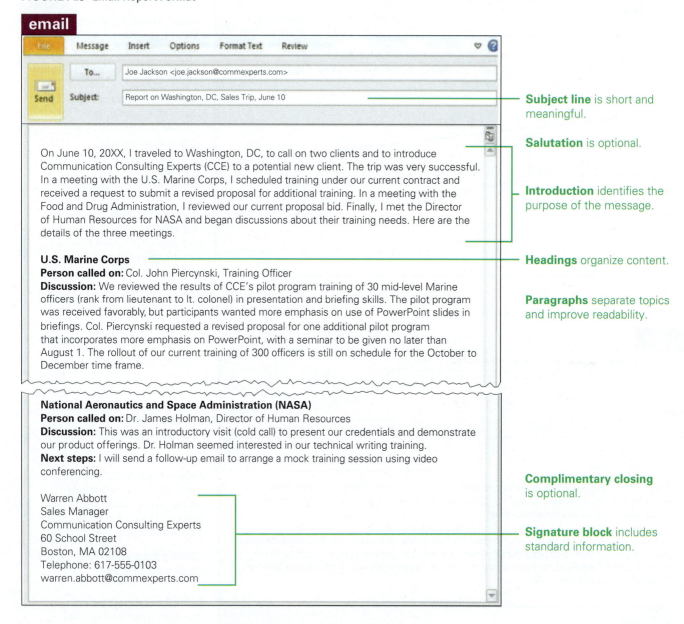

Subject line is short and meaningful.

Salutation is optional.

Introduction identifies the purpose of the message.

Headings organize content.

Paragraphs separate topics and improve readability.

Complimentary closing is optional.

Signature block includes standard information.

Memos

Memos are similar to email messages with the exception that they are either printed and distributed as hard copies or sent as email attachments. When printed, memos often accompany documents that cannot be sent electronically, such as forms requiring signatures or carbon documents completed in triplicate. When sent as email attachments, memos provide the formality of an official company document as compared to an informal email message. Memos are generally intended for internal audiences (people within an organization rather than customers or clients) and can be designed on letterhead or plain paper. Quite often, a company will determine a standard memo format that all employees should use to promote consistency in style throughout the organization.

Memo formatting guidelines

Use standard memo headings and organize the content by placing the main idea or reason for writing in the first line or paragraph. Short memos, such as the example in **Figure A.4**, may require only one paragraph. In longer memos, as shown in **Figure A.5**, organize the content by paragraph, using headings to separate topics as you would in a report.

FIGURE A.4 Short Memo Format

memo

TO: Cherilyn Martins, Vice President, Sales
FROM: Tonya Wyoll, Assistant Manager, Sales
DATE: March 15, 20XX
SUBJECT: Resources for Summer-Hours Schedule

As you requested, attached are printouts of the three web resources I found that support our decision to implement a summer-hours work schedule between Memorial Day and Labor Day this year. Let me know if you need additional information.

Attachments (3)

TO, FROM, DATE, SUBJECT (or RE) headings are standard and can be single or double spaced. Use the tab key after the colons to align the text. Be consistent with the use of personal titles and/or job titles. Create a short but specific subject line.

No salutation is used. Two blank lines separates the headings from the first paragraph.

Single space paragraphs.

Attachment notation indicates the number of items attached.

No complimentary closing or signature block is used.

FIGURE A.5 Long Memo Format

memo

TO: Ms. Cherilyn Martins, Vice President, Sales
FROM: Ms. Tonya Wyoll, Assistant Manager, Sales
DATE: February 12, 20XX
SUBJECT: Proposal for Summer-Hours Work Schedule

At our last department meeting, we briefly discussed how a summer-hours work schedule might improve employee morale. I'd like to propose that we try a summer schedule this year. I believe this change will be easy to implement and will benefit our company. This memo summarizes the detailed content in my attached proposal.

How the Schedule Will Work
The summer schedule will begin on June 1 and end on August 31. During that period, employees can choose to work normal hours of 9 AM to 5 PM each day or come in and leave an hour earlier (8 AM to 4 PM). All employees will be present during our busiest hours between 9 AM to 4 PM. We will not need to adjust lunch hours or breaks because the proposed hours are very similar to our current working hours.

Ms. Cherilyn Martins, Page 2
February 12, 20XX

Next Steps
Please let me know if you need additional information or if you would like me to draft a formal proposal to present at next week's upper-management meeting. I look forward to your response.

Attachments:
• Summer-Hours Work Schedule Report
• Web Resources

Standard headings with aligned content, consistent use of titles, and a short but specific subject line.

No salutation is used. Two blank lines separate the headings from the first paragraph.

First paragraph presents the main idea and mentions the attached proposal.

Specific headings let the audience know how the message is organized.

Paragraphs are single spaced; one blank line separates paragraphs.

Second page heading includes recipient's name, page number, and date.

Attachment notation lists the documents attached.

No complimentary closing or signature block is used.

Use the following guidelines to ensure your memos project a positive professional image (keeping in mind that your instructor or company may provide specific design criteria):

- **Top margin.** Begin at the top margin setting or a few lines below the company logo if using letterhead.

- **Memo headings.** The page title "Memorandum" is optional. However, four memo headings are required: TO:, FROM:, DATE:, and SUBJECT: (or RE:). Use colons to separate the heading labels from the text that follows the labels, and use the Tab key to move from the colon (:) to the text in order to ensure the text is aligned.

- **TO/FROM content.** Be consistent with the use of personal titles (Mr., Ms., Dr.) and employment positions (such as Director of Sales). For example, if you are writing to "*Mr. John Smith,*" include Mr. or Ms. with your name on the FROM line. However, if you are writing to "*John Smith*" (without a title), do not include a personal title with your name. When including employment positions after a name, separate them from the name with a comma and use initial caps (such as "*Mr. John Smith, Director of Sales*"). In a printed memo, sign the hard copy by writing your initials next to your name. If you are sending the memo as an email attachment, no signature is needed.

- **Date.** Write out the date's month (for example, "*January 10, 20XX*") on the date line.

- **Subject line.** Use a short (three- to five-word) subject line to indicate the topic of your message. Use two blank lines after the SUBJECT line to separate the memo headings from the message.

- **Salutation.** Memos do not use salutations because the recipient's name is prominently displayed on the TO line.

- **Body.** If the content of a memo is very short, such as in the memo in Figure A.4, write the message in a single paragraph. If the content is lengthy, divide the content into multiple paragraphs. Make the first paragraph short (two or three lines) and get to the point (do not begin with "*This memo is about …*"). In a lengthy memo, also keep the middle paragraphs short, roughly 100 words each. Be sure each paragraph has a purpose and begins with a topic sentence. Single space the paragraphs. Use one blank line between paragraphs. Use paragraph headings to separate major topics.

- **Second page heading.** For long memos that extend beyond one page, format the second and subsequent page headings as shown in Figure A.5. Include the recipient's name, the page number, and the date.

- **Closing.** Do not use a complimentary closing or a signature block in a memo. Your name is displayed on the FROM line. However, if your message requests a reply, be sure to indicate your telephone number and/or email address in the last paragraph (for example, "*Please call me at 555-1522 by Friday with your response.*").

- **Attachment notation.** If you are attaching additional documents to your memo, describe them in the message (for example, "*Attached is a list of resources you may find useful.*"). Then, remind the audience of the attachments by placing an "*Attachment*" notation at the end of your memo. Leave one blank line between the last paragraph and the attachment notation. You can include the number of attachments in parentheses (as shown in Figure A.4) or name the attachment(s) (as shown in Figure A.5).

Letters

Letters are generally intended for external audiences—people outside an organization, such as customers or clients. They may also be used for formal correspondence within a company, such as letters of resignation or letters offering a promotion. Letters are printed on letterhead and mailed, or they are written on electronic letterhead, saved as PDFs, and sent as email attachments.

Just as with memo formats, companies often promote consistency in style throughout an organization by identifying a standard letter format that all employees use. Two main letter formatting styles exist—block and modified block.

- **Block style.** Align all parts of the letter at the left margin and do not indent paragraphs. Block style is the most efficient letter style because you do not have to indent or align any of the letter elements. See **Figure A.6** for an example of a block-style letter.

FIGURE A.6 Block-Style Letter

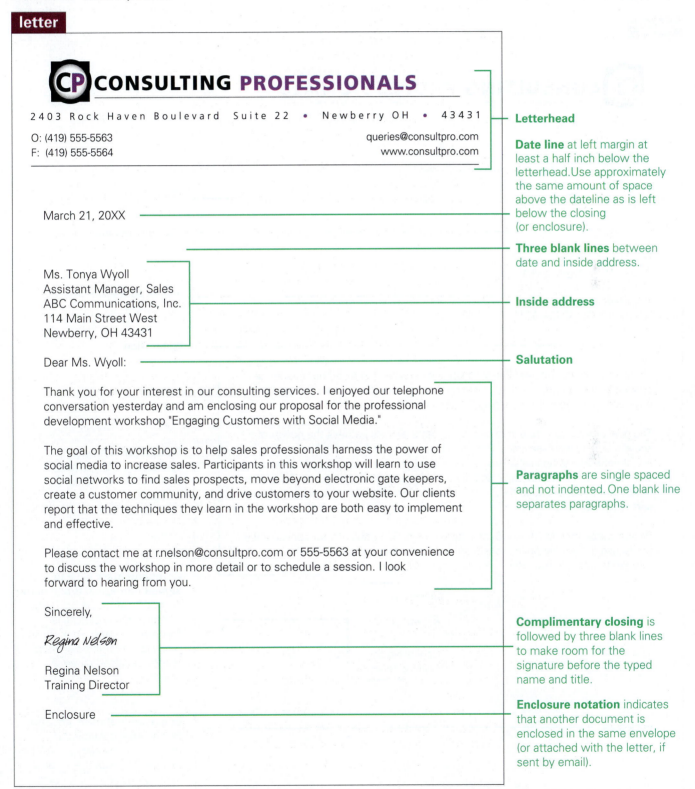

- **Modified block style.** This style positions the return address (if no letterhead is used), date, complimentary closing, and signature block at the center of the page. Paragraphs are typically not indented. A blank line separates paragraphs. See **Figure A.7** for an example of a modified-block-style letter.

FIGURE A.7 Modified-Block-Style Letter

letter

CP CONSULTING PROFESSIONALS

2403 Rock Haven Boulevard Suite 22 • Newberry OH • 43431

O: (419) 555-5563 queries@consultpro.com
F: (419) 555-5564 www.consultpro.com

March 21, 20XX — **Date line** begins at the center point.

Three blank lines between date and inside address.

Ms. Tonya Wyoll
Assistant Manager, Sales
ABC Communications, Inc. **Inside address** begins at the
114 Main Street West left margin.
Newberry, OH 43431-9271

Dear Ms. Wyoll: — **Salutation**

Thank you for your interest in our consulting services. I enjoyed our telephone conversation yesterday and am enclosing our proposal for the professional development workshop "Engaging Customers with Social Media."

The goal of this workshop is to help sales professionals harness the power of social media to increase sales. Participants in this workshop will learn to use social networks to find sales prospects, move beyond electronic gate keepers, create a customer community, and drive customers to your website. Our clients report that the techniques they learn in the workshop are both easy to implement and effective.

Paragraphs are single spaced and not indented. A blank line separates paragraphs.

Please contact me at r.nelson@consultpro.com or 555-5563 at your convenience to discuss the workshop in more detail or to schedule a session. I look forward to hearing from you.

Sincerely,

Regina Nelson

Regina Nelson
Training Director

Complimentary closing, signed name, and **typed name** also begin at the center point. Complimentary closing is followed by three blank lines to make room for the signature before the typed name and title.

Enclosure — **Enclosure notation** indicates that another document is enclosed in the same envelope (or attached with the letter, if sent by email).

Letter formatting guidelines

When designing a letter, use the following guidelines to ensure that the letter projects a positive, professional image.

- **Letterhead or return address.** Most companies create custom-designed letterhead with their logo and/or company name and address at the top (or sometimes at the bottom or side) of the page. When sending letters for personal business, you might create your own letterhead to enhance the professionalism of your message. At a minimum, your personal letterhead should include your name and mailing address. You might also include your phone number, email address, and LinkedIn account.

- If you are not using letterhead, provide your return address at the top of the page, starting either at the left margin (block style) or in the center of the page (modified block style). The return address includes your street address on the first line and your city, state, and zip code on the next line. See **Figure A.8** and **Figure A.9** for examples.

- **Date.** Write out the month and separate the day from the year with a comma (for example, *"January 10, 20XX"*). At a minimum, place the date a half inch (usually three lines, depending on the font size) below the letterhead or two lines below the return address. Typically, letters should be centered vertically on the page. If your letter is short, position the date several lines lower to balance the amount of blank space on the top and bottom of the page. If using a

FIGURE A.8 Return Address Date, and Inside Address

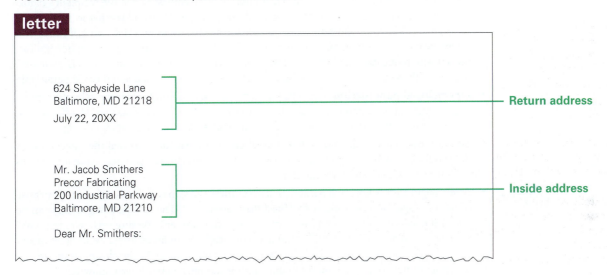

FIGURE A.9 Personalized Letterhead

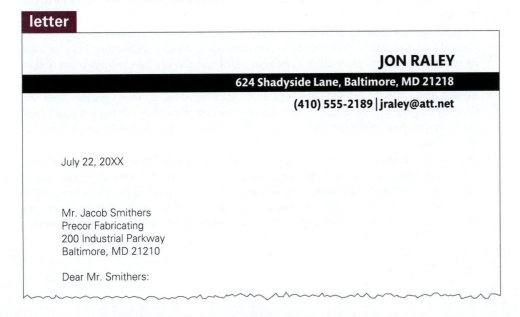

personal return address (with no letterhead), place the date on the line below your city, state, and zip code. Following the date, leave three blank lines (pressing the Enter key four times) between the date and inside address. If you are including a special notation, leave two blank lines between the date and the special notation.

- **Special notations.** If you are sending a letter by special delivery or certified mail, add these notations in ALL CAPS. If you are sending a letter to someone in a company but want to mark it as personal or confidential, add one of the following notations in ALL CAPS: *personal, confidential, private and confidential,* or *strictly confidential.* Align a special notation at the left margin placing it two lines below the date and two lines above the inside address.

- **Inside address.** The inside address includes the name and address of the person to whom the letter will be sent. Follow these guidelines:
  - First line: Use *"Mr."* or *"Ms."* or some other courtesy title such as *"Dr."* or *"Professor"* in front of the person's name. If you include an employment title such as *"Director of Marketing"* after the name, capitalize it and separate it from the name with a comma.
  - Second line: Type the person's company name, if applicable.
  - Third line: Type the street address.
  - Fourth line: Type the city, state, and zip code. Use the two-letter state abbreviation (see the list of states, territories, and provinces on page 518) and one space between all elements. Use a comma only between the city and state.
  - Leave one blank line between the inside address and the salutation.

- **Salutation.** The use of *"Dear"* in the salutation is traditional. However, it is not required in letters to people whom you know well. The salutation may consist of just the recipient's name. For formal letters, use the recipient's personal title (*"Mr."* or *"Ms."*) and last name. In informal situations and when you know the person well, use just the recipient's first name. If you do not know the name of the person who should receive your letter, create an attention line indicating a position title (such as *"Attention: Human Resources Director"* or *"Attention: Sales Department"*) in place of the salutation. Leave one blank line between the salutation and the first paragraph.

- **Open/closed punctuation.** *Closed punctuation style* uses a colon (:) after the salutation and a comma after the complimentary closing. *Open punctuation style,* which is used less frequently, uses no punctuation at the end of the salutation or after the complimentary closing.

- **Subject line.** Subject lines are optional in letters. If you use them, format the subject line as you would in a memo. Depending on your company's preference, you may place it two lines above or two lines below the salutation.

- **Body.** Begin with a short first paragraph (two or three lines) that quickly explains the purpose of the message. Do not begin with *"This letter is about. . . ."*. The middle paragraph(s) can be longer if necessary, up to 8 or 10 lines of text in each paragraph. Be sure each paragraph has a purpose and begins with a topic sentence. Use headings, bulleted lists, or enumerations as needed. The last paragraph should be short (two or three lines). In the closing, indicate any deadlines or next steps, include your contact information, and reinforce goodwill.

- **Second (and subsequent) page headings.** Use the same format for second page headings in letters as described for memos: include the recipient's name, page number, and date of the message.

- **Complimentary closing.** Start the signature block with a complimentary closing, such as *"Sincerely"* or *"Best regards,"* followed by a comma (if using closed punctuation). Leave at least three blank lines between the closing and your typed name so you have enough room to sign your name.

- **Signed name.** On the printed copy, sign above your typed name. Your signature does not have to be legible, but it should fit neatly between the complimentary closing and your typed name. Flamboyant "celebrity-style" signatures do not project a professional image in business documents.

- **Typed name.** Position your typed name (as the author of the letter) three lines below the complimentary closing. Do not use a personal title such as *"Mr."* or *"Ms."* with your name unless the recipient cannot identify your gender from your first name (such as Pat, Chris, or Rathi). If you include your job title on the same line as your name, separate it with a comma. If your job title is long, place it on the line below your typed name (without a comma after your name).

- **Enclosure notation.** If you are including additional documentation with the letter, indicate that by typing *"Enclosure"* below your typed name. Leave one blank line between your typed name and the enclosure notation.
- **Copy notation.** If you are sending a copy of the letter to someone else, indicate that by adding a *"cc"* notation below your typed name (or enclosure/attachment notation). The "cc" used to mean "carbon copy," but today it is commonly referred to as a "courtesy copy." Include the name and job title of the person receiving a copy. If you are sending copies to many people, list each one on a separate line (but use "cc" only on the first line). Align each person's name vertically (use a tab setting).
- **Postscript.** Commonly prefaced with *"PS,"* postscripts are additional short content placed as an afterthought at the end of the message. They may be used in informal letters and sales letters (to retain the audience's attention), but should be avoided in most formal contexts. If the content is important, move it into the body of the message.
- **Vertical placement.** If the letter does not fill an entire page, center the content vertically (top to bottom) on the page. You can do this manually by positioning the cursor at the date, zooming out to a full page view, and then pressing the "Enter" key until approximately the same amount of space appears at the top (between the letterhead and the date line) and the bottom (between the last typed line and the bottom of the page). Alternatively, you can use your word processor's page setup feature to change the page's vertical alignment to center.

Envelope format

Most word processing programs include a mailing feature that helps you format envelopes. Use a format similar to that shown in **Figure A.10**. Place your return address on the front of the envelope in the upper left corner. If the company uses envelopes with a preprinted return address, you may add your name above the preprinted text. Begin the recipient's mailing address approximately in the center of the envelope. The U.S. Postal Service suggests typing the address in ALL CAPS with no punctuation, although some companies use initial caps for easier reading. The postal service also recommends using the recipient's ZIP+4 code. When addressing letters to international recipients, use the format shown in Figure A.10 and replace the state with the province or other principal subdivision. Add the country name in ALL CAPS in English on a line by itself at the end of the address block.[1]

FIGURE A.10 Envelope Format

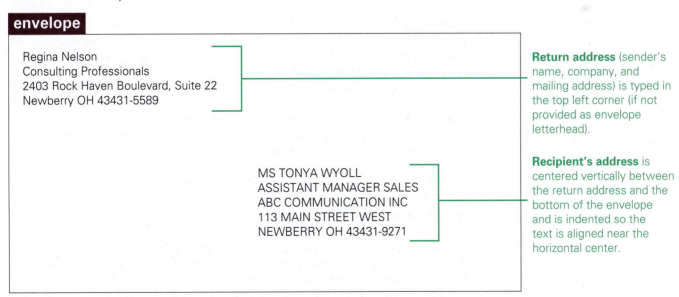

envelope

Regina Nelson
Consulting Professionals
2403 Rock Haven Boulevard, Suite 22
Newberry OH 43431-5589

MS TONYA WYOLL
ASSISTANT MANAGER SALES
ABC COMMUNICATION INC
113 MAIN STREET WEST
NEWBERRY OH 43431-9271

Return address (sender's name, company, and mailing address) is typed in the top left corner (if not provided as envelope letterhead).

Recipient's address is centered vertically between the return address and the bottom of the envelope and is indented so the text is aligned near the horizontal center.

Abbreviations of states, territories, and provinces

Refer to the following list of abbreviations for addresses in letters and on envelopes.

State	Abbr.	State	Abbr.	State	Abbr.
Alabama	AL	Louisiana	LA	Ohio	OH
Alaska	AK	Maine	ME	Oklahoma	OK
Arizona	AZ	Maryland	MD	Oregon	OR
Arkansas	AR	Massachusetts	MA	Pennsylvania	PA
California	CA	Michigan	MI	Rhode Island	RI
Colorado	CO	Minnesota	MN	South Carolina	SC
Connecticut	CT	Mississippi	MS	South Dakota	SD
Delaware	DE	Missouri	MO	Tennessee	TN
Florida	FL	Montana	MT	Texas	TX
Georgia	GA	Nebraska	NE	Utah	UT
Hawaii	HI	Nevada	NV	Vermont	VT
Idaho	ID	New Hampshire	NH	Virginia	VA
Illinois	IL	New Jersey	NJ	Washington	WA
Indiana	IN	New Mexico	NM	West Virginia	WV
Iowa	IA	New York	NY	Wisconsin	WI
Kansas	KS	North Carolina	NC	Wyoming	WY
Kentucky	KY	North Dakota	ND		

Abbreviations of commonwealths/territories

Name	Abbr.	Name	Abbr.
American Samoa	AS	Northern Mariana Islands	MP
District of Columbia	DC	Palau	PW
Federated States of Micronesia	FM	Puerto Rico	PR
Guam	GU	Virgin Islands	VI
Marshall Islands	MH		

Abbreviations of military "states"

Name	Abbr.	Name	Abbr.
Armed Forces Africa	AE	Armed Forces Europe	AE
Armed Forces Americas	AA	Armed Forces Middle East	AE
Armed Forces Canada	AE	Armed Forces Pacific	AP

Reports

Chapter 10 provides a complete discussion of report formats. Refer to **Figure A.11** on pages 537–539 for basic guidelines.

FIGURE A.11 Report Format

report

**Evaluating the Opportunity for Opening a
Sustainable Fast-Casual Restaurant in Denver**

Prepared for
Rosehip Restaurant Group

Prepared by
Kandace Nichols, Marketing Intern

August 1, 20XX

Contents

ii

Executive Summary

Rosehip Restaurant Group is considering expanding in Denver by opening a sustainable fast-casual café featuring local, GMO-free organic food. Industry and media research suggests that such a restaurant can be successful for Rosehip for several reasons:

- Fast casual has been the fastest and most consistently growing dining category over the past five years. Denver was an early adopter of fast casual dining, making the area highly receptive to a new fast casual restaurant concept from Rosehip.

- Interest in local and organic foods is growing, especially in urban areas and in the western United States where Denver is located.

- Organic/GMO-free food appeals to younger, more affluent diners, which could increase the number of new customers with ample disposable income.

However, to be successful, Rosehip must address four challenges:

- **Competition:** Because Denver has twice as many fast-casual restaurants per 100,000 people as the national average, Rosehip will face substantial competition. However, no competitors have settled into the sustainable fast casual niche, so Rosehip can distinguish itself from others. In addition, Rosehip restaurants have an excellent reputation and loyal following in Denver, giving this new restaurant an initial base of customers.

- **Sourcing:** Finding a consistent and reliable source of local, organic foods can be challenging. Rosehip can source this food through food hubs or directly from farmers. Sourcing directly from farmers offers several benefits: it allows Rosehip to foster good relationships with farmers, request that the farmers plant the food that Rosehip wants to serve, and get information from farmers that will help the restaurant plan menus. Fortunately, the Denver area has many organic farms.

- **Cost:** The cost of organic food is higher than conventional food. To make prices affordable, Rosehip can follow best practices in sustainability that have been developed by other restaurants.

- **Seasonality:** Maintaining a supply of local, organic food during the Colorado winter is difficult, but not impossible. Restaurants committed to local foods have developed a number of successful strategies, including using root cellars, preserving food during the growing season, and growing some foods indoors.

iii

Introduction

Rosehip Restaurant Group operates four traditional sit-down restaurants in Denver: a fine dining restaurant, a tapas restaurant, a brew pub, and a contemporary French bistro. The group is considering expanding by opening a sustainable fast-casual café featuring local, GMO-free organic food. Rosehip is new to the fast-casual format and to sustainable dining. Before deciding whether to invest in a financial analysis and business plan, Rosehip wants to learn more about the market for organic fast-casual foods in Denver, the competition in the area, and the costs and sourcing issues associated with sustainable dining. Rosehip requested this preliminary study to evaluate whether opening a new fast-casual café that supports organic and locally sourced food has the potential to be successful in the Denver area.

Based on media and industry research, this study found that both the fast casual and the organic GMO-free segments of the market are growing (Bryant, 2016; Maze, 2015; O'Connor, 2013). Because the fast casual market is so crowded in Denver, this research suggests that the best way for Rosehip to distinguish itself from competitors is to be local, organic, and GMO-free. Taking this approach requires that Rosehip address two challenges: finding reliable and cost-effective suppliers and remaining seasonal and local in the winter. Fortunately, the Denver area has many organic growers, and the culinary community in Colorado has developed strategies for serving local food throughout the year.

This report addresses the following topics:

- Why a fast casual restaurant will appeal to the Denver market

- Why a local, organic, GMO-free restaurant will appeal to the Denver market

- How Rosehip can meet the challenges of implementing this restaurant concept

Why a Fast Casual Restaurant Will Appeal to the Denver Market

Fast-casual restaurants are the fastest-growing category of restaurants in the U.S. (Specter, 2015). Customers are increasingly looking for quick, high-quality food in well-designed environments. Fast-casual restaurants appeal in particular to younger diners who have disposable income and who have grown up in foodie cultures that prize ingredients and variety over value and predictability (Barron, 2015; Hennessy, 2015).

As the birthplace of Chipotle, the restaurant chain credited for starting the fast-casual trend, Denver has long been an incubator of fast-casual dining, with more restaurants opening each year ("Fast-Casual Dining in Denver," n.d.; O'Connor, 2015). Although the market is crowded, there is no sign that it is saturated. In fact, some restaurant experts suggest that having multiple restaurants of similar styles in one area actually improves business for all those restaurants. Once diners adopt a new restaurant style—like fast casual—they are eager to visit similar establishments (Fields, 2007).

1

The **title page** typically includes the following information:
- title of the report (in bolded and larger font)
- name of the company or person for whom the report is prepared
- name and job title of the author (include your company name if different from the recipient's)
- date

Balance spacing between major elements. Do not number the title page.

Preliminary pages, such as the table of contents and executive summary, use lower-case Roman numbers at the bottom of the page (left, center, or right aligned). Use a consistent location for all page numbers throughout the manuscript.

The **table of contents** lists the section titles and headings with their corresponding page numbers. Use dot leaders with a right-aligned margin tab to align numbers.

An **executive summary** is optional, depending on the formality and length of the report. An executive summary should summarize the purpose, main idea or conclusion, and key sections of the report.

Headings can be boldfaced for emphasis. Use consistent styles for similar heading levels throughout the manuscript.

The **introduction** may be a separate section in formal reports, or it could be a paragraph or two at the beginning of the body of the report.

(continued)

FIGURE A.11 Report Format *(Continued)*

Why an Organic GMO-free Restaurant Will Appeal to the Denver Market

Widespread skepticism exists about the safety of genetically modified food and food grown with pesticides. Of the adults surveyed by Pew Research, 57% think that genetically modified food is unsafe, and 67% doubt that scientists fully understand how genetically modified food affects the human body (Funk & Rainie, 2015). Likewise, Americans overwhelmingly believe that foods grown with pesticides are unsafe to eat. Of those surveyed by Pew, 69% think pesticides are unsafe, with the majority of Americans agreeing across racial, economic, political, gender, and educational demographics (Funk & Rainie, 2015).

This skepticism about food safety is accompanied by an increasing interest in organic foods. According to a 2014 Gallup poll, 45% of Americans are interested in including organic food in their diet (Riffkin, 2014). As Figure 1 shows, this interest is even higher in urban areas and in the western United States, suggesting that residents of Denver are particularly interested in organic food.

Location and Eating Organic Foods

Thinking about the food you eat, for each of following please say if it is something you actively try to include in your diet, something you actively try to avoid, or something you don't think about either way. How about organic foods?

	%Actively try to include	%Actively try to avoid	%Don't think about either way
East	39	18	41
Midwest	47	17	34
South	43	13	41
West	54	12	34
Big/Small city	50	16	32
Suburb	46	8	44
Town/Rural	37	19	41

July 7-10, 2014

Fig. 1 Results of Gallup poll comparing interest in organic food, by location. Source: Riffkin, 2014.

The research also suggests that restaurants can benefit from offering healthy, organic foods. In a survey of fast casual restaurant visitors, 38% said they were "motivated to visit more often" by higher quality, fresh ingredients; 36% found healthier options attractive, and 20% wanted more organic ingredients (Bryant, 2016).

This interest in local, organic fast food is supported by an analysis of Yelp searches in Denver, which shows persistent occurrence of the search terms "organic," "local," and "fast" (see Figure 2).

2

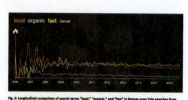

Fig. 2: Longitudinal comparison of search terms "local," "organic," and "fast" in Denver-area Yelp searches from 2007 to 2016. "Local" rendered in orange, "organic" rendered in blue, and "fast" rendered in yellow. Source: Yelp Trends, 2017.

How Rosehip Can Meet the Challenges of Implementing This Restaurant Concept

Although the Denver market is strong for a sustainable fast-casual restaurant, Rosehip will need to overcome several challenges. The discussion below identifies the challenges and offers some suggestions for addressing them.

Competition

The Denver market is already crowded with fast casual restaurants. In 2013, the metro area boasted 12.76 fast casual restaurant locations per 100,000 people, over twice the national average (Maze, 2013). Rosehip already has one advantage in this competitive landscape: an excellent reputation and a loyal following among its four other Denver restaurants. However, to succeed in the fast-casual market, Rosehip must distinguish itself from other competitors.

Marketing this new restaurant as organic and GMO-free will give Rosehip a way to set itself apart from the competition. As the evaluation discussion in Appendix A shows, none of the competitors have settled into the sustainable fast-casual niche. If Rosehip can work with local farmers, then the locally sourced food will solve potential supply chain issues and be an additional selling point for consumers.

Sourcing

To meet customer expectations, Rosehip must be able to consistently and reliably source local organic food. Broadly speaking, restaurants have two choices for sourcing local foods.

- **Food hubs:** They can source local food from regional food hubs, which sell food from a variety of local sellers. As defined by the U.S. Department of Agriculture, a regional food

3

---

hub is "business or organization that actively manages the aggregation, distribution, and marketing of source-identified food products primarily from local and regional producers to strengthen their ability to satisfy wholesale, retail, and institutional demand" (Barham et al., p. 4).

- **Farmers:** Alternatively, restaurants can work with farmers directly—a trend that has been called the Farm-to-Table movement (Benjamin & Virkler, 2016). Food hubs may offer lower prices, but working with a farmer directly provides the opportunity to negotiate good prices in exchange of guaranteed business. Working with local sellers also allows information sharing: restaurants let farmers know what food is in high demand and farmers can plan their planting accordingly (Avant, 2013). Fostering close relationships with growers also gives restaurants fast access to information on peak-season produce and fluctuations in supply, allowing them ample time to adjust their menus for seasonal produce.

The only way to ensure that food is GMO-free is to source food that is certified as organic. The Colorado Farm Fresh Directory lists dozens of organic farms in Colorado (Colorado Department of Agriculture, 2016). Appendix B includes the names and products of the farms located in the Metro Denver area. Another strategy for identifying sources is to scout for growers at farmers' markets in the Denver area ("6 Strategies to Integrate," n.d.).

Costs

Organic, GMO-free products can be expensive. Even Chipotle, which can use economies of scale to take advantage of a massive supply chain, spends more on food than on staffing (Yohn, 2014). However, researchers, restaurants, and other food service providers have developed a set of best practices to make local, organic, and GMO-free food affordable. These include reducing food waste, rethinking portion size, using the whole animal, and marketing effectively to draw in new customers (Flaccavento & Harvey, 2014).

The fast casual chain Sweetgreen, for example, features a popular "wastED" salad made of typically discarded food, such as carrot tops and broccoli stems (Specter, 2015). And SCALE, an advocacy group promoting sustainable food, finds that reducing portion sizes by small amounts can make a big impact on costs. SCALE reports that this practice

most commonly relates to meat items, where portions of locally sourced items might be reduced by 1 – 2 oz., depending upon the dish and the cost. Because portion sizes have grown so much in recent years, this "reduction" in portion size is in most respects a return to the more reasonable size portions that were once the norm. According to the chefs and dining service leaders surveyed, most patrons did not notice these reductions, and in some cases were pleased not to have to waste excess food. (Flaccavento & Harvey, 2014, p. 7)

By developing good supplier relationships and thinking creatively about how to eliminate waste, Rosehip can effectively manage costs.

4

Seasonality

Sourcing local foods in Colorado during the winter can be challenging because the growing season ends in November. However, restaurants can take advantage of year-round farmers' markets, such as the Four Seasons Farmers' and Artisan's Market in Wheat Ridge, that sell local cheese, meat, and grain products.

In addition, chefs in the Denver and Boulder area recommend the following strategies for remaining local and seasonal in the winter (Silver, 2014):

- Develop seasonal menus and a repertoire of seasonal foods.
- Create a root cellar to store root vegetables—or ask the local farmers that you buy from to store the vegetables in their root cellars.
- Preserve food during the growing season. Methods include curing, pickling, freezing, canning, dehydrating, and fermenting.
- Grow your own sprouted beans, lentils, and grains indoors to add fresh tastes to meals.

Finally, when a restaurant does need to use foods that are not local, organic, or GMO-free, the restaurant must be honest with customers and explain clearly what foods do not meet those standards—and why the restaurant is using them. This strategy will help manage customer expectations.

5

The **body** of the report can be single or double spaced. If double spaced, indent the first line of paragraphs without adding extra space between the paragraphs.

Figures and **tables** appear after they are first introduced in the narrative. Use consistent styles for figure and table headings or captions.

Page numbers throughout the body of the report are formatted as Arabic numerals that are positioned in the same location as the page numbers in the preliminary pages.

Bullets and/or **enumerations** help the reader recognize lists and understand the content more easily.

FIGURE A.11 Report Format *(Continued)*

References

Avant, M. (2013, May). Can quick serves save the world? *QSR*. Retrieved from https://www.qsrmagazine.com/ingredients-dayparts/can-quick-serves-save-world

Barham, J., Tropp, D., Enterline, K., Farbman, J., Fisk, J., & Kiraly, S. (2012, April). Regional food hub resource guide. Washington, D.C.: U.S. Dept. of Agriculture, Agricultural Marketing Service. Retrieved from http://www.ngfn.org/resources/ngfn-database/knowledge/FoodHubResourceGuide.pdf

Barron, P. (2015). *The Chipotle effect: The changing landscape of the American food consumer and how fast casual is impacting the future of restaurants.* [Kindle Edition]. New York City, NY: Transmedia. Retrieved from https://www.amazon.com

Benjamin, D., & Virkler, L. (2016). *Farm to table: The essential guide to sustainable food systems for students, professionals, and consumers.* White River Junction, CT: Chelsea Green Publishing.

Bryant, C. (2016). Fast casual restaurants - US - February 2016. Mintel. [White paper]. Retrieved from http://store.mintel.com/fast-casual-restaurants-us-february-2016

Colorado Department of Agriculture. (2016). 2016 Colorado farm fresh. Retrieved from https://www.colorado.gov/pacific/sites/default/files/Colorado%20Farm%20Fresh%20Directory_1.pdf

Fast-casual dining in Denver (n.d.). Retrieved from http://www.denver.org/restaurants/denver-dining/fast-casual/

Fields, R. (2007). Restaurant success by the numbers. Berkeley, CA: Ten Speed Press.

Flaccavento, A., & Harvey, L. (2014, August 10). Putting local on the menu: Tools and strategies for increasing the utilization of locally raised food in restaurants and food service. [White paper]. *Sequestering Carbon, Accelerating Local Economies.* Retrieved from http://www.ruralscale.com/resources/downloads/PuttingLocalOnTheMenu.pdf

Funk, C., & Rainie, L. (2015, July 1). Public opinion about food. *Pew Research Center: Internet, Science & Tech.* Retrieved from http://www.pewinternet.org/2015/07/01/chapter-6-public-opinion-about-food/

Hennessy, M. (2016, 22 July). Fine dining restaurants turning fast casual: Food trends in Chicago, IL. [Blog post]. *Thrillist.* Retrieved from https://www.thrillist.com/eat/chicago/fine-dining-restaurants-turning-fast-casual-food-trends-in-chicago-il

Maze, J. (2013, August). Colorado: World's fast casual capital: Restaurant industry insight, news and analysis. *Restaurant Finance Monitor.* Retrieved from http://www.restfinance.com/Restaurant-Finance-Across-America/August-2013/Colorado-Worlds-Fast-casual-Capital/

6

O'Connor, C. (2015, March 5). Why Denver reigns as the capital of trendy fast-casual food. *The Denver Post,* p. C1.

Riffkin, R. (2014, August 7). Forty-five percent of Americans seek out organic foods. *Gallup.* Retrieved from http://www.gallup.com/poll/174524/forty-five-percent-americans-seek-organic-foods.aspx

Silver, M. (2014, October 14). 11 ways to eat seasonal and local in the winter. *Dining Out Denver and Boulder.* Retrieved from http://diningout.com/denverboulder/11-ways-to-eat-local-and-seasonal-in-the-winter/

6 strategies to integrate locally sourced food (n.d.). National Restaurant Association. Retrieved from http://www.restaurant.org/Manage-My-Restaurant/Food-Nutrition/Trends/6-strategies-to-integrate-locally-sourced-food

Specter, M. (2015, November 11). Can fast food get healthy? *The New Yorker.* Retrieved from http://www.newyorker.com/magazine/2015/11/02/freedom-from-fries

Yelp Trends [Online data analysis tool]. (2017, July). Retrieved from https://www.yelp.com/trends

Yohn, D. L. (2014). *What great brands do: The seven brand-building principles that separate the best from the rest.* San Francisco, CA: Jossey-Bass.

7

*The **references** section lists all sources alphabetically. Use a standard reference style, such as APA or MLA, and provide complete documentation.*

Appendix A: Evaluation of Key Competitors in the Fast Casual Market

These are the four fast casual style restaurants in the Denver area most likely to compete with Rosehip's new concept.

Honor Society Handcrafted Eatery (www.eatwithhonor.com)

Honor Society is most similar to the concept Rosehip is considering, with an emphasis on sustainable, local, and healthful food. Honor Society also leans heavily on seasonal dining, changing their menu according to the season. The menu is formed around several main "flavors" (roast vegetables, beef, chicken, and salmon), all of which can be combined in various sandwich, salad, or platter formats. Honor Society calls itself "fine casual" dining, aiming at a slightly higher price point (around $15 per dinner rather than the $10 per dinner typical for fast casual).

Larkburger (larkburger.com)

Larkburger takes the traditional burger concept and updates it to respond to consumer interest in natural and healthier ingredients. Larkburger sets itself apart by using natural ingredients (no preservatives or additives) and having a menu that is easily made gluten or dairy free. The company also uses biodegradable serving ware and containers. This commitment to health and environmental sustainability provides a good model for Rosehip to follow.

Mad Greens (www.madgreens.com)

Mad Greens is a salad and sandwich chain that makes healthy and tasty fast food. They work with suppliers throughout the Southwest to bring regionally sourced food to their cafes. Mad Greens was bought by Coors in 2013, which has allowed the company to expand and also to partner more effectively with farmers. While this expansion has given the company more reliable food sourcing, it has also diluted the company's local touch and Denver origins.

Modmarket (www.modernmarket.com)

Modmarket follows author Michael Pollan's food philosophy—"Eat food. Not too much. Mostly plants"—in crafting their menu. The restaurant aims to cater to a variety of dietary restrictions and choices, including vegan/vegetarian, gluten free, and paleo. While their mission includes a commitment to spreading farm-to-table eating to a wider population, ModMarket makes no explicit statements about how consistently local or sustainable their food sourcing is. A pledge for local and GMO-free food could be a useful way for Rosehip to set itself apart.

8

Appendix B: Certified Organic Farms in the Metro Denver Area

The Metro Denver farms below are listed in the Colorado Farm Fresh Directory. The directory also lists additional certified organic farms throughout Colorado.

Farm	Certified Organic Products
Aspen Moon Farm Certified organic and biodynamic 7927 Hygiene Rd. Longmont www.aspenmoonfarm.com	fruits, vegetables
Berry Patch Farms 13785 Potomac St. Brighton www.berrypatchfarms.com	eggs, fruits
Cure Organic Farm 7416 Valmont Rd. Boulder cureorganicfarm@yahoo.com	beef, lamb, pork, poultry, sausage
Ela Family Farms/ Silver Spruce Orchards info@elafamilyfarms.com	fruits
Isabelle Farm 1640 W. Baseline Rd. Lafayette www.isabellefarm.com	fruits, vegetables, beef, chicken, pork, sausage,
KW Farms - Kretsinger Beef 7725 Road 1 South Alamosa www.kretsingerbeef.com	beef
Monroe Organic Farms, LLC. www.monroefarm.com	fruits, vegetables, beef, pork, lamb
Morton's Organic Orchards www.mortonsorchards.com	fruits
Rocky Mountain Pumpkin Ranch 9059 Ute Hwy. Longmont www.rockymtnpumpkinranch.com	fruits, vegetables

9

***Appendices** contain supplementary material at the end of the report. If the report includes only one appendix, label it as shown here (Appendix). If the report includes multiple appendices, label them as Appendix A, Appendix B, and so forth. Page numbers continue from the body of the report.*

Reference

1. U.S. Postal Service. (2017). Destination Address. Retrieved from http://pe.usps.com/text/imm/immc1_008.htm

Documentation and Reference Styles

Whenever you quote, paraphrase, or use material from a source, you need to identify the source and provide enough information so your readers can find the sources you reference. You do this by providing citations within the body of the text and a complete, alphabetized reference (or works cited) list at the end of the document. This is true whether you are writing a report, presentation, web page, or blog.

Different fields of study use different reference styles, and your instructor, employer, or publisher will usually identify the style you are expected to use. Three styles are typical in academia:

1. APA style, found in the *Publication Manual of the American Psychological Association*
2. Chicago style (sometimes referred to as CMOS), found in *The Chicago Manual of Style*
3. MLA style from the Modern Language Association

This appendix outlines the most common rules you will need to follow in two of these styles: APA, which is commonly used in business departments, and MLA, which is commonly used in English departments. The APA guidelines are based on the 6th edition of the *Publication Manual* and the *APA Style Guide to Electronic References*. The MLA guidelines are based on the *MLA Handbook*, 8th edition, as well as updates on the MLA website. For the rules of the Chicago style, see the online or print version of *The Chicago Manual of Style*.

APA in-text citations

Within your text, indicate the source of a citation by inserting authors' last names, the year of publication, and in some cases the page on which the material can be found (or the paragraph in an online source). Where you place this information in the citation depends on whether you paraphrase the original source or quote the source word for word.

Paraphrased content

Paraphrased content consists of information from a source presented in your own words. When paraphrasing, or referring to another work, the citation can be part of the narrative or placed at the end of the sentence (inside the ending punctuation). Citations for paraphrases must include the author and date of the publication. In addition, APA guidelines encourage—but do not require—writers to include page or paragraph numbers to help readers find the paraphrased material in the original source.

For example, here is a quotation from a *New Yorker* article about changes in the fast food market:

> Speed and convenience matter as much as ever to American diners. But increasingly people also demand the information that places like Sweetgreen offer. They want to know what they are eating and how it was made; they prefer to watch as their food is prepared, see the ingredients, and have a sense of where it all came from. And they are willing to pay more for what they perceive to be healthier fare. (Specter, 2015, par. 5).

You can paraphrase this quotation in one of the following three ways:

Single-author paraphrased source

In a 2015 *New Yorker* article, Michael Specter explained how new trends in healthy eating are challenging the fast food industry.

Or

New Yorker staff writer Michael Specter (2015) explained how new trends in healthy eating are challenging the fast food industry.

Or

Although Americans still want the convenience of fast food, they seem to value healthy food even more. (Specter, 2015).

The following examples provide additional information about how to cite sources with multiple authors, sources with no identified author, and multiple sources.

Multiple-author paraphrased source

Anthony Flaccavento and LeAnne Harvey (2014) of SCALE, an advocacy group promoting sustainable food, suggest reducing portion sizes by small amounts in order to reduce costs.

Or

SCALE, an advocacy group promoting sustainable food, finds that reducing portion sizes by small amounts can make a big impact on costs (Flaccavento & Harvey, 2014).

Works with no identified author

Another strategy for identifying local food sources is to scout for growers at farmers' markets in the Denver area ("6 Strategies to Integrate," n.d.).

Multiple sources used to support one statement

As the birthplace of Chipotle, the restaurant chain credited for starting the fast-casual trend, Denver has long been an incubator of fast-casual dining, with more restaurants opening each year ("Fast-Casual Dining in Denver," n.d.; Yohn, 2016).

Multiple sources by the same author to support one statement

Fast-casual restaurants are evolving—for instance, many fast-casual pizza restaurants are arriving on the scene (Bryant, A., 2015; Bryant, C., 2015).

Multiple sources by the same author published in the same year#

Restaurants let farmers know what food is in high demand, and farmers can plan their planting accordingly, although farmers cannot account for unpredictable elements like severe weather (Avant, 2013a; Avant, 2013b).

Personal communication

Michelle Carson, who studies North American dining trends, thinks fast-casual dining will diversify into even more cuisines and food types in future (personal communication, July 1, 20XX).

Experts predict that fast-casual dining will diversify into even more cuisines and food types in future (Carson, M., personal communication, July 1, 20XX).

The author's name and the publication date can be integrated into the text itself.

The author's name can be integrated into the text with the date in parentheses immediately following the name. If the source has no date, use n.d. in the parentheses.

If the author's name is not integrated into the text, then the author's last name and the date—separated by a comma—appear in parentheses at the end of the sentence.

If the author's name is not integrated into the text, then the author's last name and the date—separated by a comma—appear in parentheses at the end of the sentence.

When the authors' names are not integrated into the text, use only their last names in the parentheses and use "&" to separate the last author's name from the previous name.

When a cited work has no author, use the first few words of the reference list entry and the year, if available. The first few words are usually the title. Note that the title is written differently than in the reference list: All words in the title (except short prepositions and conjunctions) are capitalized, and the title of an article is enclosed in quotation marks.

List sources alphabetically. When the last names of authors are the same, use first initials to determine the order of the sources. Separate sources with a semicolon.

When the last names of authors are the same, use first initials to determine the order of the sources

When sources are written by the same author and published in the same year, order the sources as they are ordered in the reference list, which assigns a letter after the date to differentiate the sources. Use that letter in the citation.

Identify personal communications with in-text citations only; APA style does not list personal communications on the reference page.

Quoted content

Quoted—word for word—content from a source uses a citation style similar to that for paraphrases. However, the quoted text must also be surrounded by quotation marks or set off as a *block quotation* if it is more than 40 words long. In addition, the page or paragraph number for quotations must always be included. Just as with paraphrased content, the exact placement of these elements varies. Note the following examples.

Single-author quoted source

As *Denver Post* writer Colleen O'Connor (2015) explains, "the Denver, an incubator of this national trend, has the right demographics for fast-casual dining" (p. C1).

Or

"The Denver area, an incubator of this national trend, has the right demographics for fast-casual dining" (O'Connor, 2015, p. C1).

Multiple-author quoted source

According to Flaccavento and Harvey (2014) of sustainable food advocacy group SCALE, this practice

> most commonly relates to meat items, where portions of locally sourced items might be reduced by 1–2 oz, depending upon the dish and the cost. Because portion sizes have grown so much in recent years, this "reduction" in portion size is in most respects a return to the more reasonable size portions that were once the norm. According to the chefs and dining service leaders surveyed, most patrons did not notice these reductions, and in some cases were pleased not to have to waste excess food. (p. 7)

Marques et al. (2014) wrote: "Ultimately, the success of GM foods will depend upon government approval and market uptake, as well as the extent to which the public accepts or rejects either side of the debate" (p. 602).

Quotations with words omitted

According to the SCALE report, "because portion sizes have grown so much in recent years, this 'reduction' in portion size is in most respects a return to the more reasonable size portions that were once the norm. . . . [M]ost patrons did not notice these reductions, and in some cases were pleased not to have to waste excess food" (Flaccavento & Harvey, 2014, p. 7).

APA reference list

At the end of your paper, include a page titled "References" that presents an alphabetical list of all the sources you cited in your text. Reference list entries for most sources include four major elements in the following order: the author(s), year of publication, name of work, and publication information. The entire reference list is organized alphabetically according to the first word in the entry, usually the author's last name. If more than one source begins with the same word, then the order is determined by a different element—the date of publication or name of the work—as described in the following sections.

Surround the quoted content with quotation marks. Put the date in parentheses after the author's name. Always place the page number after the quotation. Use a lowercase "p" followed by a period to abbreviate "page." If the quotation spans more than one page, use "pp." Place the parentheses between the ending quotation mark and final period.

If all the citation elements appear in the parentheses, use commas to separate author, year, and page number.

The first time a source is used, list all authors' names (up to five).

When a quotation is longer than 40 words, do not enclose it in quotation marks. Instead, indent the content as a block quotation and place the page number in parentheses after the final punctuation mark.

The second and all subsequent times you refer to a source with three or more authors, list only the first author with "et al." to represent "and others." (Note: Two-author sources should always list both authors, such as Flaccavento & Harvey.)

Use ellipses (three spaced periods) to indicate you have omitted words from quoted text. If you have omitted words between two sentences, end the first sentence with a period and then provide the ellipsis (for a total of four spaced periods). If you need to change capitalization or grammar to make the quotation make sense, enclose any changes in square brackets.

Authors

RULES	EXAMPLES
• List authors' last names first, use initials only for authors' first and middle names, and use one space between initials. • Separate authors' names with commas, even when only two authors are listed. Use an ampersand (&) before the name of the final author.	Flaccavento, A., & Harvey, L.
• If an author has a hyphenated first name, include the hyphen and a period after each initial.	Marques, M. D., Critchley, C.-A., & Walshe, J.
• List all authors in the order in which they appear on the publication. (Do not alphabetize them.) • If the source lists more than seven authors, list the first six followed by an ellipsis (. . .) to indicate a break in the list and then the final author's name. In this instance, do not use an ampersand (&) before the final name.	van Kleef, E., Frewer, L. J., Chryssochoidis, G. M., Houghton, J. R., Korzen-Bohr, S., Krystallis, T., . . . Rowe, G.
• If the author is an organization, use a period at the end of the name to separate the author content from the next element of the reference.	National Restaurant Association.
• If a work has no author, begin the entry with the title of the work. • If an entry begins with a numeral, alphabetize it as if the number was spelled out. In this instance, alphabetize the entry as if the first word was "Six."	6 strategies to integrate locally sourced food.

Publication date

RULES	EXAMPLES
• For books and journal articles, put the year of publication in parentheses immediately after the author information. If a work has no author, put the year after the name of the work. End with a period after the final parenthesis.	Barron, P. **(2015).**
• For newspaper, magazine, and online articles (including blog posts and social media updates), include the month and day of publication *after* the year. End with a period after the final parenthesis.	O'Connor, C. **(2015, March 5).**
• If no date is available, put "n.d." in the parentheses. End with a period after the final parenthesis.	Fast-casual dining in Denver. **(n.d.).**
• If a reference list contains multiple sources for the same author, order the sources from oldest to newest.	Avant, M. **(2013, April).** Avant, M. **(2013, May).**
• If a reference list contains multiple sources written by the same author and published the same year, use the titles to determine alphabetic sequence and differentiate the sources with lowercase letters added to the dates.	Bryant, C. **(2016a).** Family midscale dining. Bryant, C. **(2016b).** Fast-casual restaurants.

Titles

The format you use depends on the type of work. Complete works, such as books and websites, have just one title. By contrast, journal, newspaper, and magazine articles have article titles as well as publication titles.

RULES	EXAMPLES
Articles and Blog Posts • Use plain text. Do not italicize, underline, or use quotation marks around the title. • Use sentence case, capitalizing only the first word of the title, the first word of a subtitle, and all proper nouns such as company names. • End with a period. • If your audience will need additional information to identify the type of publication, place that descriptive information in brackets immediately after the title.	Hennessy, M. (2016, 22 July). **Fine dining restaurants turning fast casual: Food trends in Chicago, IL. [Blog post].** *Thrillist.* Retrieved from https://www.thrillist.com/eat/chicago/fine-dining-restaurants-turning-fast-casual-food-trends-in-chicago-il
Books, videos, podcasts, etc. • Italicize the title. Do not underline. • Use sentence case, capitalizing only the first word of the title, the first word of a subtitle, and all proper nouns such as company names. • End with a period. • If your audience will need additional information to identify the type of publication, place that descriptive information in brackets immediately after the title.	Benjamin, D. & Virkler, L. (2016). ***Farm to table: The essential guide to sustainable food systems for students, professionals, and consumers.*** White River Junction, CT: Chelsea Green Publishing.
Journals and other periodicals • Italicize the title. Do not underline. • Use title case, beginning the first word and each word of four letters or more with a capital letter. Also capitalize any major words that are shorter than four letters as well as the first word after a colon, semicolon, dash, or period. • Conclude with a comma.	O'Connor, C. (2015, March 5). Why Denver reigns as the capital of trendy fast-casual food. ***The Denver Post,*** p. C1.

Publication information

How you list the publication information depends on the kind of source you reference. For example, journal articles usually require volume, issue, and page numbers. However, books list only the publishing company's location and name, and websites usually require only a "Retrieved from" web address.

RULES	EXAMPLES
Journal and other periodical articles • Following the title of the periodical itself, provide the volume number in italics immediately followed by the issue number in plain text and in parentheses. No space separates the volume number from the issue number. • Follow the issue number with a comma and page numbers. Page numbers do not use a page abbreviation ("p." or "pp."), as is used for in-text citations. Indicate the range of page numbers with an en dash. • End with a period.	Author, A. A., Author, B. B., & Author, C. C. (Year). Title of article. *Title of Periodical,* **volume(issue), pages.** Marques, M., Critchley, C., & Walshe, J. (2015). Attitudes to genetically modified food over time: How trust in organizations and the media cycle predict support. ***Public Understanding of Science, 24(5),*** 601–618.

RULES	EXAMPLES
Books and e-books • List the city and name of publisher, separated by a colon. • For an e-book, include the e-book version you read in brackets. Also provide the URL from which you downloaded the book. • End with a period.	Author, A. A., & Author, B. B. (Year). *Title of publication.* **City, ST: Publisher's Name.** Benjamin, D., & Virkler, L. (2016). *Farm to table: The essential guide to sustainable food systems for students, professionals, and consumers.* **White River Junction, CT: Chelsea Green Publishing.** Barron, P. (2015). *The Chipotle effect: The changing landscape of the American food consumer and how fast casual is impacting the future of restaurants.* **[Kindle Edition]. New York City, NY: Transmedia. Retrieved from https://www.amazon.com**
Websites • If the name of the website is included in the URL or is obvious from the author's name, use "Retrieved from" followed by the URL. • If the name of the website is not included in the URL or not obvious from the author's name, then include it as part of the retrieval statement. • Remove the hyperlink (blue font color and underlines) format from web addresses. • When necessary, insert a space to allow long addresses to wrap effectively to the right margin. • Do not use a period at the end of a web address.	Author, A. A., & Author, B. B. (Year). Title of article. **Retrieved from http://xxxx** 6 strategies to integrate locally sourced food. (n.d.). **Retrieved from National Restaurant Association website: http://www.restaurant.org/Manage-My-Restaurant/Food-Nutrition/Trends/6-strategies-to-integrate-locally-sourced-food**

Other types of sources

Adapt the four-part citation elements to other types of reference sources. Here are some examples that may not fit the "normal" format. If it is not clear from the name what type of source it is, then provide descriptive information in brackets immediately after the title.

TYPE OF SOURCE	EXAMPLES
Annual report	World Bank. (2016). *The World Bank annual report 2016.* Retrieved from https://openknowledge.worldbank.org/handle/10986/24985
Brochure	University of Cincinnati Undergraduate Admissions. (2016). *International admissions* [Brochure]. Retrieved from https://admissions.uc.edu/international/brochure.html
Government publication	U.S. Bureau of Labor Statistics, U.S. Department of Labor. (2017). *Occupational outlook handbook.* Washington, DC: U.S. Government Printing Office. Retrieved from http://www.bls.gov/ooh
Online encyclopedia or dictionary	Diaz, J. M., & Fridovich-Keil, J. L. (2016, Nov. 28). Genetically modified organism (GMO). In *Encyclopaedia Britannica.* Retrieved from https://www.britannica.com/science/genetically-modified-organism

(continued)

(continued)

TYPE OF SOURCE	EXAMPLES
Podcast • For audiovisual material, list the main contributors in the author position, followed by their contribution in parentheses	Smith, R. (Host), Jiang, J., Bennin, P., & Kulas, E. (Producers). (2017, March 8). *Episode 596: Hacking the iPhone for fun, profit, and maybe espionage* [Audio podcast]. Retrieved from http://www.npr.org/sections/money/2017/03/08/519298871/episode-596-hacking-the-iphone-for-fun-profit-and-maybe-espionage
Slide presentation found online	Samuel, L. (2017, February 16). *How to become a thought leader in your niche* [Online presentation]. Retrieved from https://www.slideshare.net/LeslieSamuel/how-to-become-a-thought-leader-in-your-niche
Online video (such as on YouTube)	Taraboulsy, G. (Director/Producer), & Verdi-Rose, C. (Producer). (2015). *Farm to table in Rockland, Maine with chef Melissa Kelly of Primo* [Video file]. Retrieved from https://www.youtube.com/watch?v=vlMDhgvjtOE
Tweet or twitter update • Use the writer's real name, followed by the screen name in brackets. If you know only the screen name, provide it without brackets. • Include the entire text of the Tweet in the citation.	FoodTank. (2017, March 16). We are building a global community for safe, healthy, nourished eaters. We educate, inspire, and create change. #GoodFoodMedia @FoodTank [Tweet]. Retrieved from https://twitter.com/foodtank/status/842390996218400768
Facebook page • Put the author's first name in parentheses, to make the page easier to retrieve. • Spell out the full name of organizations. • Include a retrieval date when the publication date is unknown.	Vargas, J. A. (Jose). (n.d.). Timeline [Facebook page]. Retrieved March 14, 2017, from https://www.facebook.com/jav AACSB International. (n.d.). BizSchoolJobs [Facebook page]. Retrieved March 14, 2017, from http://www.facebook.com/AACSB/app_106877302704651
Facebook update • No retrieval date is necessary because all updates have publication dates.	APA Style. (2017, March 9). Include commas in numbers with four or more digits to ease readability: 1,000 ms, not 1000 ms #APA-Style [Facebook status update]. Retrieved from https://www.facebook.com/APAStyle/posts/1795546843804061

Sample APA reference page

Double space the text throughout the References page. To indent second and subsequent lines of a reference citation, use your word processor's "hanging indent" paragraph format feature rather than manually tabbing or spacing the text.

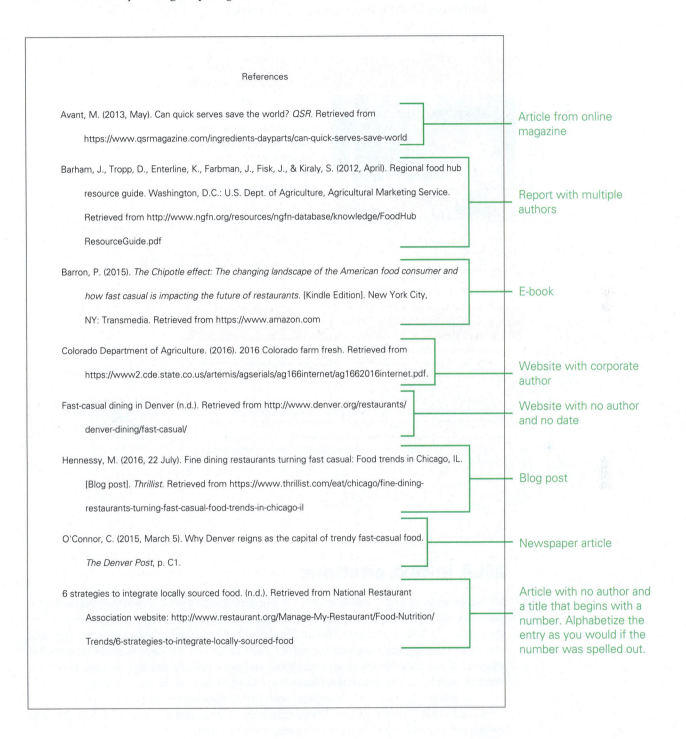

References

Avant, M. (2013, May). Can quick serves save the world? *QSR*. Retrieved from
    https://www.qsrmagazine.com/ingredients-dayparts/can-quick-serves-save-world

Article from online magazine

Barham, J., Tropp, D., Enterline, K., Farbman, J., Fisk, J., & Kiraly, S. (2012, April). Regional food hub
    resource guide. Washington, D.C.: U.S. Dept. of Agriculture, Agricultural Marketing Service.
    Retrieved from http://www.ngfn.org/resources/ngfn-database/knowledge/FoodHub
    ResourceGuide.pdf

Report with multiple authors

Barron, P. (2015). *The Chipotle effect: The changing landscape of the American food consumer and
    how fast casual is impacting the future of restaurants.* [Kindle Edition]. New York City,
    NY: Transmedia. Retrieved from https://www.amazon.com

E-book

Colorado Department of Agriculture. (2016). 2016 Colorado farm fresh. Retrieved from
    https://www2.cde.state.co.us/artemis/agserials/ag166internet/ag1662016internet.pdf.

Website with corporate author

Fast-casual dining in Denver (n.d.). Retrieved from http://www.denver.org/restaurants/
    denver-dining/fast-casual/

Website with no author and no date

Hennessy, M. (2016, 22 July). Fine dining restaurants turning fast casual: Food trends in Chicago, IL.
    [Blog post]. *Thrillist*. Retrieved from https://www.thrillist.com/eat/chicago/fine-dining-
    restaurants-turning-fast-casual-food-trends-in-chicago-il

Blog post

O'Connor, C. (2015, March 5). Why Denver reigns as the capital of trendy fast-casual food.
    The Denver Post, p. C1.

Newspaper article

6 strategies to integrate locally sourced food. (n.d.). Retrieved from National Restaurant
    Association website: http://www.restaurant.org/Manage-My-Restaurant/Food-Nutrition/
    Trends/6-strategies-to-integrate-locally-sourced-food

Article with no author and a title that begins with a number. Alphabetize the entry as you would if the number was spelled out.

Sample APA documentation in presentation files

Whether you're creating a traditional presentation file or a report deck, cite your in-text sources on the slides, either immediately after the content or in the corner of the slide as shown. Add a reference page to the end of report deck files or presentation handouts so your audience can refer to the original sources, if necessary.

MARKET DEMAND FOR LOCAL FOOD

"A much higher proportion of people eat locally grown foods than organic foods. When they think local, they think fresh and want to support local growers/packers."

Source: National Grocers Association. (2015).

Wavebreak Media Ltd/123RF

Source is added to the slide where content appears. Use standard in-text citation formats.

REFERENCES

Colorado Department of Agriculture. (2016). *2016 Colorado farm fresh.* Retrieved from https://www2.cde.state.co.us/artemis/agserials/ag166internet/ag1662016internet.pdf.

National Grocers Association. (2015). *2015 National Grocers Association/SupermarketGuru consumer survey report.* Retrieved from http://www.nationalgfocers.org/docs/default-source/Surveys-Reports-(2015-2016)/consumersurveyreport2015_pdf

6 strategies to integrate locally sourced food. (n.d.). Retrieved from National Restaurant Association website: http://www.restaurant.org/Manage-My-Restaurant/Food-Nutrition/Trends/6-strategies-to-integrate-locally-sourced-food

The complete reference citation is included in a references slide at the end of the report deck (or presentation handout).

MLA in-text citations

MLA uses a simple and consistent style for all references to a source, whether the content is paraphrased or quoted. Provide enough information in the citation to help your audience find the correct work on the reference list and find the cited material in the source itself. Typically, this means that citations include the author's last name and the page number for the cited material. If you are referring to an entire work and not a specific passage, no page number is needed. MLA in-text citations never include publication dates in the parentheses.

The following examples correspond with the APA examples on pages 541–542 but are formatted as MLA-style citations. Fewer examples are provided because MLA uses the same format for quoted content as it does for paraphrased content.

Paraphrased content

When paraphrasing content—using source information in your own words—or even just referring to a source, cite the original work by including the author's name within the narrative or in an in-text citation at the end of the sentence (before the ending punctuation).

For example, if the original source states "the Denver area, an incubator of this national trend, has the right demographics for fast-casual dining" (O'Connor C1), paraphrased content could be worded in either of the following ways:

Single-author source

In 2015, *Denver Post* writer Colleen O'Connor noted the demographics of the Denver area make it suited to fast-casual dining, a national trend it has helped grow (C1).

Or

The demographics of the Denver area make it suited to fast-casual dining, a national trend it has helped grow (O'Connor C1).

If the author's name is used in the narrative, include only the page number in the parenthetical citation. Place the parentheses at the first natural pause, usually at the end of the relevant passage.

If the author's name is not used in the narrative, both the author and page number(s) appear in parentheses (with no comma separating them).

Works with no identified author

Rosehip can start by scouting for growers at farmers' markets in the Denver area ("6 Strategies to Integrate").

When a cited work has no author, use the first few words of the Works Cited list entry. Works Cited list usually begins with the title.

Multiple-author source

Restaurants can source local food from food hubs, which sell food from a variety of local sellers, or work with farmers directly—a trend that, as Darryl Benjamin and Lyndon Virkler explained in *Farm to Table*, has been called the Farm-to-Table movement.

Or

Restaurants can source local food from food hubs, which sell food from a variety of local sellers, or work with farmers directly—a trend that has been called the Farm-to-Table movement (Benjamin and Virkler).

Or

Many factors can influence the public's attitudes towards genetically modified food, including media coverage and levels of trust in scientists and watchdogs (Marques et al.).

If the authors' names are used in the narrative and you are referring to an entire work, rather than content from a specific page of the source, no parenthetical reference is necessary.

When including multiple authors' names in the parenthetical reference, separate the last name with "and."

Whether in the narrative or in parentheses, sources with three or more authors can be cited with the name of the first author, followed by "et al."

Multiple sources used to support one statement

As the birthplace of Chipotle, the restaurant chain credited for starting the fast-casual trend, Denver has long been an incubator of fast-casual dining (O'Connor C1; Yohn).

When citing multiple sources in one reference citation, list sources alphabetically and separate with semicolons. When citing websites without page numbers or books in their entirety, no page numbers are needed.

Multiple sources by the same author to support one statement

Restaurants let farmers know what food is in high demand and famers can plan their planting accordingly, although farmers cannot account for unpredictable elements like severe weather (Avant, "Quick Serves" 1; Avant, "Tricks" 2).

To differentiate between two works by the same author, include the first word or an abbreviated form of the title after the author's name (with comma) and before the corresponding page number (no comma).

Personal communication

In contrast to APA style, in MLA, personal communications such as interviews, letters, and emails are listed in the reference list, so the in-text citation does not need to indicate that the source is a personal communication.

Michelle Carson, who studies North American dining trends, thinks fast-casual dining will diversify into even more cuisines and food types in future.

Or

Experts predict that fast-casual dining will diversify into even more cuisines and food types in future (Carson).

A personal communication is treated in the same way as a written source.

Quoted content

Quoted—word-for-word—content from a source uses a citation style similar to that for paraphrases. However, the quoted text must also be surrounded by quotation marks or set off as a block of text if it is more than four lines long. In addition, the page or paragraph number for quotations must always be included. Note the following examples.

Single-author quoted source

In 2015, *Denver Post* writer Colleen O'Connor wrote, "the Denver area, an incubator of this national trend, has the right demographics for fast-casual dining" (C1).

Or

"The Denver area, an incubator of this national trend, has the right demographics for fast-casual dining" (O'Connor C1).

Multiple-author quoted source

According to Anthony Flaccavento and LeAnne Harvey of sustainable food advocacy group SCALE, this practice

> most commonly relates to meat items, where portions of locally sourced items might be reduced by 1–2 oz, depending upon the dish and the cost. Because portion sizes have grown so much in recent years, this "reduction" in portion size is in most respects a return to the more reasonable size portions that were once the norm. According to the chefs and dining service leaders surveyed, most patrons did not notice these reductions, and in some cases were pleased not to have to waste excess food. (7)

Or

Barham et al. define a food hub as ""business or organization that actively manages the aggregation, distribution, and marketing of source-identified food products primarily from local and regional producers to strengthen their ability to satisfy wholesale, retail, and institutional demand" (4).

Quotations with words omitted

According to the SCALE report, "because portion sizes have grown so much in recent years, this 'reduction' in portion size is in most respects a return to the more reasonable size portions that were once the norm. . . . [M]ost patrons did not notice these reductions, and in some cases were pleased not to have to waste excess food" (Flaccavento and Harvey 7).

MLA works cited list

At the end of your paper, include a "Works Cited" list: a double-spaced alphabetical list of all the sources you cited in your text.

Entries for most sources include three major elements in the following order: the author(s), the title, and publication information (which includes the name of the publisher, the publication date, etc.). In addition, some sources require supplemental information to help a reader find the material. These major elements are separated by periods. The entire reference list is organized alphabetically according to the first word in the entry, usually the author's last name. If more than one source begins with the same word, then the order is determined by a different element—author's first name or title—as described in the following sections.

Surround the quoted content with quotation marks. Always place the page number after the quotation. The number is not preceded by the word "page" or abbreviation "p." Place the parentheses between the ending quotation mark and final period.

If the author's name is not used in the narrative, both the author and page number(s) appear in parentheses (with no comma separating them).

When a source has two authors, list all their names in the text or the citation.

When a quotation is longer than four lines, do not enclose it in quotation marks. Instead, format the content as a block quotation. Start the quotation on a new line, indent it one inch from the left margin, and place the page number after the final punctuation mark.

When a source has three or more authors, list the name of the first author, followed by "et al" ("and others") in plain text, not italics.

Use ellipses (three spaced periods) to indicate you have omitted words from quoted text. If you have omitted words between two sentences, end the first sentence with a period and then provide the ellipsis (for a total of four spaced periods). If you need to change capitalization or grammar to make the quotation make sense, enclose any changes in square brackets.

Authors

RULES	EXAMPLES
• For an entry with one author, list the first author's last name first, followed by a comma and his or her full first name (and middle initial or name if available). • End with a period.	Flaccavento, Anthony.
• For entries with two or three authors, list all the authors in the order they appear on the publication. • List the first author's last name first, followed by a comma and his or her full first name (and middle initial or name if available). • List the remaining authors with their first names before their last names. • Use a comma to separate names (even when only two authors are listed). • Use "and" before the last author's name. • End with a period.	Flaccavento, Anthony, and LeAnne Harvey. Barham, James, Debra Tropp, and Stacia Kiraly.
• For entries with more than three authors, reverse the name of the first author, followed by a comma and "et al." ("and others") in plain text, not italics.	Barham, et al.
• If the author is an organization, use a period at the end of the name to separate the author name from the next element of the reference. • If the organization is both author and publisher, list the organization only as the publisher and begin the entry with the title of the work.	National Restaurant Association. *Occupational Outlook Handbook.* U.S. Bureau of Labor Statistics, U.S. Department of Labor, 2017.
• If the author of a work held a role that was something other than creating the source, follow the name of the author with a short description of his or her role.	Taraboulsy, Gab, director, and Clenet Verdi-Rose, producer.
• If you have cited more than one work by a specific author, order the entries alphabetically by title. For every entry after the first, use three hyphens in place of the author's name.	Bryant, Caleb. "Family Midscale Dining." ---. "Fast Casual Restaurants."
• If a work has no author, begin the entry with the title of the work. • If an entry begins with a numeral, alphabetize it as if the number was spelled out. In this instance, alphabetize the entry as if the first word was "Six."	"6 Strategies to Integrate Locally Sourced Food."

Titles

RULES	EXAMPLES
All titles • Use title case: the first letter of every word is capitalized, except for *a, an, the,* and short prepositions.	Barron, Paul. ***The Chipotle Effect: The Changing Landscape of the American Food Consumer and How Fast Casual Is Impacting the Future of Restaurants.*** Transmedia, 2015. Kindle file.
Short works, such as articles in periodicals, book chapters, blog posts, and specific pages on a website • Put quotation marks around the title. • Follow the title with a period inside the closing quotation mark. • If the title itself concludes with different punctuation, such as a question mark, that punctuation serves as the final punctuation mark.	Avant, Mary. **"Can Quick Serves Save the World?"** *QSR,* May 2013, www.qsrmagazine.com/ingredients-dayparts/can-quick-serves-save-world. Accessed 9 July, 20XX.
Long works, such as books, plays, encyclopedias, videos, entire websites • Use italics for titles • Follow the title with a period or other ending punctuation if the title itself includes it.	Barron, Paul. ***The Chipotle Effect: The Changing Landscape of the American Food Consumer and How Fast Casual Is Impacting the Future of Restaurants.*** Transmedia, 2015. Kindle file.

Publication information

After the title, include additional publication information about the source. Include all the elements below that apply. Omit elements that are not relevant. Separate each of the elements with a comma, and a period after the last item of publication information.

RULES	EXAMPLES
Title of the "container": the larger whole that the work is part of—such as a journal, newspaper, a video series, website, or electronic database. • Use italics for title • Follow the title with a comma, because the information that comes next will describe the container. • If a source is nested in multiple containers, list them all. For example, an article is contained in a journal which may be contained in a database.	Avant, Mary. "Can Quick Serves Save the World?" ***QSR,*** May 2013, www.qsrmagazine.com/ingredients-dayparts/can-quick-serves-save-world. Accessed 9 July, 20XX. "6 Strategies to Integrate Locally Sourced Food." ***National Restaurant Association,*** www.restaurant.org/Manage-My-Restaurant/Food-Nutrition/Trends/6-strategies-to-integrate-locally-sourced-food. Accessed 8 July. 20XX. Marques, Mathew D., Christine R Critchley, and Jarrod Walshe. "Attitudes to Genetically Modified Food over Time: How Trust in Organizations and the Media Cycle Predict Support." ***Public Understanding of Science,*** vol. 24, no. 5, 2015, pp. 601-18. ***SAGE Journals,*** doi: 10.1177/0963662514542372.
Other contributors If other people contributed to the work—for example, as an editor, translator, adapter, director, producer, etc.—name these contributors, preceded by a description of their role. Contributors who play a role in the creation of the source cited, but not the larger container, should be listed after the title of the source rather than the title of the container.	Malthus, Thomas Robert. *An Essay on the Principle of Population.* **Edited by Joyce E. Chaplin,** Norton Critical Edition, W. W. Norton, 2017. Ferrante, Elena. *Those Who Leave and Those Who Stay.* **Translated by Ann Goldstein.** The *Neapolitan Novels,* vol. 3, Europa Editions, 2014.

(continued)

(continued)

RULES	EXAMPLES
Versions If the source cited is a version of the work, • Identify which version or edition you are citing. • Use numerals and abbreviations ("rev." for "revised" and "ed." for "edition"). • Do not abbreviate version names that are also proper nouns (for example, "Authorized King James Version" and "Norton Critical Edition").	Ross, David Frederick. Distribution Planning and Control: Managing in the Era of Supply Chain Management. **3rd ed.,** Springer, 2015. Malthus, Thomas Robert. An Essay on the Principle of Population. Edited by Joyce E. Chaplin, **Norton Critical Edition,** W. W. Norton, 2017.
Numbers Sometimes sources are part of a numbered series. For instance, the volume and issue numbers of a journal article should be listed, using the abbreviations "vol." and "no." • If the volume number is the first piece of publication information, begin "Vol" with a capital V. • If the volume number is not the first piece of publication information, begin "vol" with a small v.	Nelson, William D., editor. *Advances in Business and Management.* **Vol. 10**, Nova Science Publishers, 2016. Marques, Mathew D, Christine R Critchley, and Jarrod Walshe. "Attitudes to Genetically Modified Food over Time: How Trust in Organizations and the Media Cycle Predict Support." *Public Understanding of Science*, **vol. 24, no. 5,** 2015, pp. 601-18. SAGE Journals, doi: 10.1177/0963662514542372.
Publisher The publisher is the organization or institution chiefly responsible for producing or publicizing the source. If a source has two or more publishers who seem equally responsible for the work, list both, separating the names with a forward slash. • Abbreviate long publisher names. • Omit publisher names for the following: ▪ Periodicals (journals, magazines, newspapers) ▪ A self-published or self-released work ▪ A website whose title is essentially the same as the name of its publisher ▪ A web platform that is not involved in creating the works hosted on it (for example, YouTube or SlideShare)	**Examples:** Rogers, David L. *The Digital Transformation Playbook: Rethink Your Business for the Digital Age.* **Columbia UP**, 2016. Fares, Robert. "The U.S. Electric Grid's Cost in 2 Charts." *Plugged In,* **Scientific American Blogs,** 5 Apr. 2017, blogs. scientificamerican.com/plugged-in/ the-u-s-electric-grids-cost-in-2-charts/.
Date • Include the date as you find it in the source. • Format the date by listing the day first, then the month followed by the year (for example, 4 Sept. 2017). Months except May, June and July may be abbreviated. • If a source has been republished, consider giving the date of original publication if this information is relevant. List it immediately after the source's title.	Malthus, Thomas Robert. *An Essay on the Principle of Population.* Edited by Joyce E. Chaplin, Norton Critical Edition, W. W. Norton, **2017.** Specter, Michael. "Can Fast Food Get Healthy?" The *New Yorker,* **11 Nov. 2015,** www.newyorker.com/magazine/2015/11/02/ freedom-from-fries. Seligman, Martin E. P. "Phobias and Preparedness." **1971.** *Behavior Therapy,* vol. 47 no. 5, **Sept. 2016,** pp. 577-84. ScienceDirect.

(continued)

(continued)

RULES	EXAMPLES
Location within container • **For print sources,** a source's location list page number(s). Use hyphens to indicate a range of page numbers and commas for page breaks (for example, pp.12-16, 20). Precede a single page number by the letter p and a period (for example, p. 5). For a range of pages, use pp and a period (for example, pp. 168-89). • **For web sources,** list the URL. Do not include "http." If a digital online identifier (or DOI) is available, use that instead of the URL.	Marques, Mathew D, Christine R Critchley, and Jarrod Walshe. "Attitudes to Genetically Modified Food Over Time: How Trust in Organizations and the Media Cycle Predict Support." *Public Understanding of Science,* vol. 24, no. 5, 2015, **pp. 601-18**. O'Connor, Colleen. "Why Denver Reigns as the Capital of Trendy Fast-Casual Food." *The Denver Post,* 4 Mar. 2015, **p. C1**. Specter, Michael. "Can Fast Food Get Healthy?" *The New Yorker,* 11 Nov. 2015, www.newyorker.com/**magazine/2015/11/02/ freedom-from-fries**. Ross, David Frederick. *Distribution Planning and Control: Managing in the Era of Supply Chain Management.* 3rd ed., Springer, 2015. Springer eBooks, **doi: 10.1007/978-1-4899-7578-2**

Supplemental information

This content can include additional information that will help the audience identify the source used. MLA does not require city of publication, unless it is useful to identify a source.

TYPES OF INFORMATION	EXAMPLES
Date accessed • Identify the date you accessed a web source, especially for sources that have no date available. • Precede the date with the word "Accessed."	"6 Strategies to Integrate Locally Sourced Food." National Restaurant Association, www. restaurant.org/Manage-My-Restaurant/Food-Nutrition/Trends/6-strategies-to-integrate-locally-sourced-food. **Accessed 8 March 2017.** "Fast-Casual Dining in Denver." Visit Denver, www.denver.org/restaurants/denver-dining/fast-casual. **Accessed 8 March 2017.**
Other facts At the end of the entry, you may provide other facts that will help someone better locate the source, for example: • Total number of volumes for a book that is part of a multivolume publication or long series • Format for a source that is in an unexpected format, such as an e-book	Nelson, William D., editor. *Advances in Business and Management.* Vol. 10, Nova Science Publishers, 2016. **11 vols.** Barron, Paul. *The Chipotle Effect: The Changing Landscape of the American Food Consumer and How Fast Casual Is Impacting the Future of Restaurants.* Transmedia, 2015. **Kindle file.**

Other types of sources

Adapt the four-part citation formula (author, title, publication information, supplemental information) to other types of reference sources. Here are some examples that may not fit the "normal" format. If it is not clear from the name what type of source it is, then provide descriptive information at the end of the entry.

TYPE OF SOURCE	EXAMPLES
Annual report Note: When an organizational author is also the publisher, the organization is listed only as the publisher. The entry begins with the title of the work.	*The World Bank Annual Report 2016.* The World Bank, 2016, openknowledge.worldbank.org/handle/10986/24985. Accessed 20 Mar. 2017.
Brochure	*International Admissions.* University of Cincinnati Undergraduate Admissions, 2016, admissions.uc.edu/international/brochure.html. Accessed 20 Mar. 2017. Brochure.
Government publication	*Occupational Outlook Handbook.* U.S. Bureau of Labor Statistics, U.S. Department of Labor, 2017, www.bls.gov/ooh. Accessed 20 Mar. 2017.
Online encyclopedia or dictionary	Diaz, Julia M., and Judith L. Fridovich-Keil, "Genetically Modified Organism (GMO)." *Encyclopaedia Britannica,* 28 Nov. 2016, www.britannica.com/science/genetically-modified-organism. Accessed 20 Mar. 2017.
Podcast Note: In a podcast, the producer is another contributor.	Smith, Robert, host. "Episode 596: Hacking the iPhone For Fun, Profit, and Maybe Espionage." Produced by Elizabeth Kulas. *NPR Planet Money,* 8 Mar. 2017, www.npr.org/sections/money/2017/03/08/519298871/episode-596-hacking-the-iphone-for-fun-profit-and-maybe-espionage. Podcast.
Slide presentation found online Note: If the slideshow is independent, the title is italicized. SlideShare is not considered a publisher because it had no role in making the slideshow.	Samuel, Leslie. *How to Become a Thought Leader in Your Niche.* 16 Feb. 2017, www.slideshare.net/LeslieSamuel/how-to-become-a-thought-leader-in-your-niche. Slideshow.
Online video (such as on YouTube) Note: If the director and producer are equally important, they may both be listed in the author position.	Taraboulsy, Gab, director, and Clenet Verdi-Rose, producer. "Farm to Table in Rockland, Maine with Chef Melissa Kelly of Primo." *Tastemade,* 30 Dec. 2015, www.youtube.com/watch?v=vlMDhgvjtOE. Video.
Tweet or twitter update • Use the writer's real name, followed by the screen name in parentheses. If you know only the screen name, provide it without parentheses. • Include the entire text of the Tweet in the citation, using the same capitalization as in the original tweet. • Include the date and time of the tweet.	FoodTank. "We are building a global community for safe, healthy, nourished eaters. We educate, inspire, and create change. #GoodFoodMedia @FoodTank" 16 Mar. 2017, 9.03 a.m, twitter.com/foodtank/status/842390996218400768. Tweet.
Facebook page • Include author's full name. • Include an access date when the publication date is unknown.	Vargas, Jose Antonio. "Timeline." *Facebook,* www.facebook.com/jav. Accessed 20 Mar. 2017. AACSB International. "BizSchoolJobs." *Facebook,* www.facebook.com/AACSB/app_106877302704651. Accessed 20 Mar. 2017.
Facebook update • If the Facebook update is brief, reproduce the full text without changes, in place of a title. • If the update is longer, reproduce the first few words of the text. • Do not include an access date. Instead, include the publication date.	APA Style. "Include commas in numbers with four or more digits to ease readability: 1,000 ms, not 1000 ms #APAStyle." *Facebook,* 9 Mar. 2017, www.facebook.com/APAStyle/posts/1795546843804061.
Interview	Carson, Michelle. Personal interview. 1 July 2017. Carson, Michelle. Telephone interview. 1 July 2017.
Email	Carson, Michelle. "Re: Follow-up Questions to Interview." Received by Kandace Nichols, 5 July 2017. E-mail.

Sample MLA works cited page

Double space the text throughout the Works Cited page. To indent lines following the first line, use your word processor's hanging indent paragraph format feature rather than manually tabbing or spacing the text.

Works Cited

Avant, Mary. "Can Quick Serves Save the World?" *QSR*, May 2013, ——— **Article from online magazine**

    www.qsrmagazine.com/ingredients-dayparts/can-quick-serves-save-world. Accessed

    9 July 2017.

Barham, James, et al. *Regional Food Hub Resource Guide*. U.S. Dept. of Agriculture, Agricultural ——— **Report with multiple authors**

    Marketing Service, 2012.

Barron, Paul. *The Chipotle Effect: The Changing Landscape of the American Food Consumer and how* ——— **E-book**

    Fast Casual is Impacting the Future of Restaurants. Transmedia, 2015. Kindle file.

Carson, Michelle. Personal interview. 1 July 2017. ——— **Personal interview**

"Fast-Casual Dining in Denver." *Visit Denver,* www.denver.org/restaurants/denver-dining/fast-casual. ——— **Website with no author and no date**

    Accessed 8 July 2017.

Hennessy, Maggie. "Fine Dining Restaurants Turning Fast Casual: Food Trends in Chicago, IL." ——— **Blog post**

    Thrillist, 22 July 2016, www.thrillist.com/eat/chicago/fine-dining-restaurants-turning-fast-casual-

    food-trends-in-chicago-il. Accessed 9, July 2017.

O'Connor, Colleen. "Why Denver Reigns as the Capital of Trendy Fast-Casual Food." *The Denver Post,* ——— **Newspaper article**

    4 Mar. 2015, p. C1.

"6 Strategies to Integrate Locally Sourced Food." National Restaurant Association, ——— **Article with no author and a title that begins with a number. Alphabetize the entry as you would if the number was spelled out.**

    www.restaurant.org/Manage-My-Restaurant/Food-Nutrition/Trends/6-strategies-to-integratelocally-

    sourced-food. Accessed 8 July 2017.

2016 Colorado Farm Fresh. Colorado Department of Agriculture, 2016, April, ——— **Website with corporate author that is also the publisher. Begin with the title and include the corporate entity in the publisher position. Alphabetize the title as you would if the number was spelled out.**

    www2.cde.state.co.us/artemis/agserials/ag166internet/ag1662016internet.pdf.

    Accessed 8 July 2017.

Sample MLA documentation in presentation files

When citing sources in presentation files or report decks, use an in-text citation on the slide where the content is presented and add a "Works Cited" page at the conclusion of the file.

Wavebreak Media Ltd/123RF

MARKET DEMAND FOR LOCAL FOOD

"A much higher proportion of people eat locally grown foods than organic foods. When they think local, they think fresh and want to support local growers/packers."

Source: 2015 National Grocers Association

Source is added to the slide where content appears. Use standard in-text citation formats.

WORKS CITED

"6 Strategies to Integrate Locally Sourced Food." National Restaurant Association, /www.restaurant.org/Manage-My-Restaurant/Food-Nutrition/Trends/6-strategies-to-integrate-locally-sourced-food. Accessed 8 July. 2017.

2015 National Grocers Association/SupermarketGuru Consumer Survey Report. National Grocers Association, 2015, www.nationalgrocers.org/docs/default-source/ Surveys-Reports-(2015-2016)/consumersurveyreport2015.pdf. Accessed 8 July 2017.

2016 Colorado Farm Fresh. Colorado Department of Agriculture, 2016, April, www2.cde.state.co.us/artemis/agserials/ag166internet/ag1662016internet.pdf. Accessed 8 July 2017.

The complete reference citation is included in a references slide at the end of the report deck (or presentation handout).

Grammar, Punctuation, Mechanics, and Conventions

This appendix covers the basics of grammar, punctuation, mechanics, and conventions in written business communication.

The appendix begins with a diagnostic test to help you identify strengths and weaknesses in your sentence-level writing skills. Identify the areas that you need to improve, and then use the numbered sections to refresh your understanding of the rules, check your writing, and correct any mistakes. Headings such as GRAMMAR ALERT! and PUNCTUATION ALERT! draw attention to especially common writing errors.

Sentence-level skills diagnostic test

The following test covers common sentence-level errors. After you have completed the test, ask your instructor for the answer sheet to score your answers. Use the **Skills Assessment Table** following the test to record your scores in each category. The assessment will identify the skill areas you need to strengthen and where to find their associated rules in this appendix.

Use and Formation of Nouns and Pronouns

Each of the following sentences is either correct or contains an error. If the sentence is correct, write "C" in the blank. If the sentence contains an error, underline the error and write the correct form in the blank.

1. _____ Our supervisor wanted George and I to come in early on Tuesday.
2. _____ If your sure that everyone has left, turn out the lights.
3. _____ I will speak with whoever is in the office this morning.
4. _____ For three months in a row this Dealership had the highest sales.
5. _____ There are fewer jobs and less employments during a recession.

Use and Formation of Adjectives and Adverbs

Each of the following sentences is either correct or contains an error. If the sentence is correct, write "C" in the blank. If the sentence contains an error, underline the error and write the correct form in the blank.

6. _____ Most consumers prefer the least costly of the two service plans.
7. _____ He sees badly in the dark because of his cataracts.
8. _____ Remember to drive slow in a school zone.
9. _____ Wasn't it snowing real hard last evening?
10. _____ The timing of the winter sale was absolutely perfect.

Sentence Fragments, Run-On (Fused) Sentences, and Comma Splices

Each of the following sentences is either correct or incorrect. If the sentence is correct, write "C" in the blank. If it is incorrect, insert the punctuation and/or wording that would make the sentence correct. Adjust capitalization as necessary.

11. _____ When people enjoy their jobs. They usually perform better.
12. _____ Many younger employees rate job satisfaction over high salary, they want meaningful work.
13. _____ Baby boomers, on the other hand, have spent their lives working to get ahead their goal has been to reach the top.
14. _____ Finding the right balance between work, family, and leisure that fits a person's personal and professional goals.

15. _____ Women usually have a more difficult time than men, however, achieving this balance.

Subject–Verb Agreement and Pronoun–Antecedent Agreement

Each of the following sentences is either correct or contains an error. If the sentence is correct, write "C" in the blank. If the sentence contains an error, write the correction in the blank.

16. _____ Each generation defines their relationship to work.
17. _____ There is sometimes considerable differences in attitudes.
18. _____ Members of one generation believes in "living to work."
19. _____ Conversely, the goals and philosophy of the next generation is "working to live."
20. _____ To be satisfied, everybody has to find what works best for them.

Commas

Each of the following sentences is either correct or incorrect in its use of commas. If the sentence is correct, write "C" next to it. If it is incorrect, insert or delete punctuation to make it correct.

21. _____ Many cultures value recreation, and family time highly and business practices reflect these norms.
22. _____ In Europe for example workers get at least a month of vacation in the summer.
23. _____ Although some businesses stay open many are closed for most of August.
24. _____ Posting an "On Vacation" sign in the window collecting the family and gassing up the car business owners across the continent head for the beach or the mountains.
25. _____ This practice of closing up shop and going on vacation for a month which annoys Americans traveling abroad in August is considered "therapeutic and necessary for good physical and mental health" says Doris Pernegger an Austrian travel agent.

Commas and Semicolons

Each of the following sentences is either correct or incorrect in its use of commas and semicolons. If the sentence is correct, write "C" next to it. If it is incorrect, insert or delete punctuation to make it correct.

26. _____ In France the workweek is 35 hours; but most Americans still work a 40-hour week.
27. _____ The number of hours one can work is set by national law in many countries, however U.S. labor laws allow for variations among employee categories.
28. _____ Many U.S. companies classify workers as "exempt" employees, who may work extra hours without extra pay, "non-exempt" employees, who must be paid a minimum wage and receive higher overtime pay for extra hours, and part-time employees, who may be covered by minimum-wage laws but who are not necessarily being paid a higher wage for overtime.

29. _____ The average worker in Germany spends about 1,500 hours on the job per year; the average worker in India annually spends about twice that number on the job.

30. _____ The most leisure time contrary to popular belief was enjoyed by prehistoric hunter-gatherers, not modern humans.

Other Punctuation Marks

In each of the following sentences, insert or delete colons, end punctuation, apostrophes, parentheses, quotation marks, dashes, and hyphens as needed. If a sentence is correct, write "C" next to it.

31. _____ Some of the benefits of a four day workweek may be: improved levels of education (extra time for classes), improved health less stress, and money saved on transportation.

32. _____ If we dont have to drive to work as often, we reduce carbon related automobile emissions.

33. _____ Some economists argue that unemployment will decrease if the workweek is shortened a big if.

34. _____ This is the theory: People working fewer hours will create a demand for additional workers in order to produce the same amount of goods and services.

35. _____ The old expression work smarter, not harder describes my philosophy.

Capitalization

In each of the following sentences, insert or delete capital letters as needed. If a sentence is correct, write "C" next to it.

36. _____ In the Western world the workweek for many employees is Monday through friday.

37. _____ Of course, doctors and nurses, people with md or rn after their name, as well as public safety and hospitality employees often work weekend shifts.

38. _____ the workweek in a number of muslim countries is Sunday through Thursday or Saturday through Wednesday, because Friday is a Holy Day.

39. _____ My Mother says Washington's and lincoln's birthdays used to be celebrated separately, but they have been lumped together to create presidents' day, giving many employees a three-day weekend in mid-february.

40. _____ We say "tgif," meaning "Thank Goodness It's Friday," to salute the end of the workweek.

Numbers

Each of the following sentences is either correct or incorrect in the way numbers are expressed. If the sentence is correct, write "C" next to it. If it is incorrect, insert the necessary changes.

41. _____ South Koreans average thirty-four percent more work hours per year than U.S. workers.

42. _____ Most South Koreans start work at eight a.m., take a break for dinner, and don't leave work until after 10 o'clock at night.

43. _____ 2004 marked the end of the 6-day workweek in South Korea; before then, everyone worked Saturdays.

44. _____ A South Korean accountant averaged about twenty-seven hundred dollars a month in 2005; the average annual income was 22,928 dollars, or 18,544,199 Korean wons.

45. _____ Since Korean employees are expected to stay at their desks until their superiors leave, we really shouldn't complain about our measly 5 8-hour days.

Spelling

In each of the following sentences, correct spelling as needed. If a sentence is correct, write "C" next to it.

46. _____ Before making a judgement about excepting a job offer, you might want to explore what "work" means in that companies' culture.

47. _____ Some people find it inconcievable that they are expected to wear a suit and tie to work; its tee shirts and flip-flops for them.

48. _____ Does the employer have a flextime policy, leting you come and go as you please as long as you meet your deadlines and attend meetings?

49. _____ What seems like a miner inconvienence when your first hired may be a major hurdle after you have been on the job awhile.

50. _____ Ask yourself weather you can acommodate the company policies and expectations or if you would be happyer and more productive in a different inviroment.

Sentence-level skills assessment

In **Table C.1**, on page 562, record the number of questions you answered **incorrectly** in each category. If you got more than two answers wrong in any category, it is likely that you are making similar errors in your writing. Review the relevant sections of the appendix. If you are still having trouble with sentence-level errors in any category, you may want to seek additional help at your school's writing center or writing lab.

1. Sentences

A sentence is often described as a group of words that expresses a complete thought. However, a sentence does more than that. Sentences convey information and establish relationships between ideas. Your ability to communicate well—effectively manage sentences and their parts—will contribute to your success in the workplace.

1.1. Parts of Speech

Words in sentences belong to categories that describe their function within the sentence. Just as particular departments within a business have particular functions—accounting, sales, shipping and receiving—words are categorized according

TABLE C.1 Skills Assessment Table

QUESTIONS	SKILL AREA	NUMBER OF INCORRECT ANSWERS	SECTION(S)
1–5	Nouns and Pronouns		1.1.1., 3.1.2.
6–10	Adjectives and Adverbs		1.1.3.
11–15	Fragments, Run-on (Fused) Sentences, Comma Splices		1.2.2., 1.3.1., 1.3.2.
16–20	Subject–Verb Agreement, Pronoun–Antecedent Agreement		1.1.2., 1.3.3., 1.3.4.
21–25	Commas		2.2.–2.2.4.
26–30	Commas and Semicolons		2.3.
31–35	Other Punctuation Marks		2.4.–2.7.
36–40	Capitalization		3.1.–3.1.2.
41–45	Numbers		3.2.–3.2.11.
46–50	Spelling		4.

to the functions they serve in sentences. These categories are commonly called the **parts of speech**. Knowing the names and functions of the parts of speech enables people to talk about how sentences work—or don't work when there are errors.

As you can see from the examples in **Table C.2**, the same word (e.g., *email*) may serve different functions, depending on its use in a sentence.

1.1.1. Naming Words: Nouns and Pronouns

a. **Nouns** name persons, places, things, and concepts. They can be classified as indicated in **Table C.3**.

Many nouns form the plural **regularly** by adding *-s* or *-es* at the end: *report, reports; expense, expenses*. Some nouns have an **irregular** plural form, often formed by a change in vowel: *man, men; mouse, mice; goose, geese*.

b. **Pronouns** replace or refer to nouns. The word that a pronoun replaces or refers to is called its **antecedent** (meaning "to go before"): *Shanice* said *she* received the memo. *She* is the pronoun; *Shanice* is the antecedent. Like nouns, pronouns can be classified, as described in **Table C.4**.

c. **Pronoun case.** As **Table C.5**, on page 564, illustrates, pronouns show their function in a sentence by means of **case: subjective, objective**, or **possessive**.

TABLE C.2 Functions of Parts of Speech

FUNCTION	PART OF SPEECH	EXAMPLES
Naming	Nouns Pronouns	computer, IBM, email you, itself, hers, everyone
Showing action or being	Verbs	email, was, will hire, has run
Modifying	Adjectives Adverbs	expensive, clear, legal quickly, really, well
Connecting	Prepositions Conjunctions	in, under, after, of, to, on and, but, although, since
Exclaiming	Interjections	oh, well, hey, indeed Ouch! Help! Stop! Wow!

TABLE C.3 Types of Nouns

TYPE OF NOUN	FUNCTION	EXAMPLES
Common nouns	Refer to general groups, people, places, things, and ideas. They are not capitalized.	intern, street, company, soda, capitalism
Proper nouns	Refer to particular people, places, things, and ideas. They are capitalized.	Monica, Wall Street, Progressive Insurance Company, Coca-Cola, Marxism
Count nouns	Refer to people, places, and things that can be counted individually. Count nouns have singular and plural forms.	two interns, 15 insurance companies, one customer, $3 million, raindrops, job
Mass nouns (noncount nouns)	Refer to things that cannot be counted individually but that exist in a mass or aggregate. Mass nouns do not usually have plural forms, and they take singular verbs.	rain, milk, steel, money, overstock The *milk is* cold.
Collective nouns	Refer to groups that are singular in form but, depending on context, may be singular or plural in meaning.	committee, team, sales force, board of directors, faculty, staff, herd, flock The *staff* [collectively] *is* meeting this afternoon. The *staff* [individually] *are* registering for the conference.
Abstract nouns	Refer to intangible conditions, qualities, or ideas.	wealth, illness, technology, sound, capitalism
Concrete nouns	Refer to things perceived by the five senses.	euros, diabetes, sonogram, applause, stockholder

TABLE C.4 Types of Pronouns

TYPE OF PRONOUN	FUNCTION	EXAMPLES
Personal pronouns	Refer to specific persons, places, or things.	I, me you, she, her, he, him, it, they, their, them
Indefinite pronouns	Do not refer to specific persons, places, or things; do not require antecedents. Pronouns indicating individuals are singular: any, each, every, -body, -one, -thing, no. Pronouns indicating several are plural: all, many, most, some.	all, any, anyone, anybody, both, each, everyone, everybody, everything, many, most, none, no one, nobody, nothing, some, somebody, something *Everybody hopes* for a raise. *Some are* counting on it.
Relative pronouns	Introduce subordinate clauses that refer to a noun or pronoun the clause modifies.	that, who, whom, whose, which The vice president *who gave the presentation* used to be my boss.
Interrogative pronouns	Introduce questions.	what, who, whom, whose, which *What* happened next?
Demonstrative pronouns	Identify particular people or things.	this, that, these, those *Those* are the most recent sales figures available.
Intensive pronouns Reflexive pronouns	Emphasize the antecedent. Refer to the receiver of an action who is the same as the performer of the action.	Same form for both types: myself, yourself, himself, herself, itself, ourselves, yourselves, themselves a. The *President himself* will attend the conference. b. *We* congratulated *ourselves* on a job well done.
Reciprocal pronouns	Refer to separate parts of a plural antecedent.	each other, one another The new *employees* introduced themselves to *each other*.

TABLE C.5   Pronoun Cases

PERSONAL PRONOUNS: SINGULAR	FUNCTIONING AS A SUBJECT: SUBJECTIVE CASE	FUNCTIONING AS AN OBJECT: OBJECTIVE CASE	FUNCTIONING TO SHOW POSSESSION: POSSESSIVE CASE
First person (denotes person speaking)	I *I* sent an email.	me Rob sent an email to *me*.	my, mine *My* mailbox was full.
Second person (denotes person or thing spoken to)	you Were *you* the recipient?	you Mae saw *you* in the lobby.	your, yours Did you find *your* ticket?
Third person (denotes person or thing spoken of)	he, she, it *It* came in the mail.	him, her, it Alyse found *it* on the desk.	his, her, hers, its The storm ruined *his* travel plans.
PERSONAL PRONOUNS: PLURAL	**SUBJECTIVE CASE**	**OBJECTIVE CASE**	**POSSESSIVE CASE**
First person (persons speaking)	we When *we* arrived, the meeting had already started.	us Let *us* know the date.	our, ours *Our* flight was canceled.
Second person (persons or things spoken to)	you As new employees, *you* have temporary security clearances.	you I wish *you* the best of luck.	your, yours *Your* supervisors will distribute the new software.
Third person (persons or things spoken of)	they *They* completed the project.	them The department head recommended *them* for a raise.	their, theirs They earned *their* reward.
RELATIVE OR INTERROGATIVE PRONOUNS	**SUBJECTIVE CASE**	**OBJECTIVE CASE**	**POSSESSIVE CASE**
Singular and plural forms are the same	who Lee was the person *who* phoned.	whom To *whom* am I speaking?	whose Please tell me *whose* turn is next.

GRAMMAR ALERT! MISUSE OF PRONOUN CASE

If a pronoun is in the wrong **case**, the sentence will be grammatically incorrect.

Use the objective case for the object of a transitive verb (a verb that passes the action to a recipient—or object—of that action).

Incorrect   The division manager asked him and *I* to report our findings.
(Incorrect use of subjective case: *I* is not the subject of the sentence.)

Correct   The division manager asked him and *me* to report our findings.
(Correct use of objective case: The pronoun *me* is the object of the verb *asked*.)

Use the subjective case with intransitive verbs such as linking or being verbs.

Incorrect   The principal researchers on the project were *him* and *me*.
(Incorrect use of objective case: The subject antecedent, *researchers*, and pronouns referring to it are linked by a "be" verb—*were*—so both are subjective case.)

Correct   The principal researchers on the project were *he* and *I*.

Use the subjective case when answering a caller's question, "Is [your name] there?"

Incorrect   This is *her*. (Incorrect use of objective case; *me* renames the subject *this, which refers to the antecedent subject [your name] in the question,* so use subjective case.)

Correct   This is *she*.

Sometimes you can hear the correct case if you modify the wording of the sentence and start with the pronoun(s) in the subject spot: *He and I* were the principal researchers on the project. Another test is to switch to the plural: The division manager asked *us* to report our findings. *Us* sounds (and is) correct, so the corresponding singular objective form, *him and me*, will be correct.

Do not confuse *their/they're*, *your/you're*, or *its/it's*. Possessive pronouns are never formed with an apostrophe, but contractions ending in *-s* always are.

They're the lawyers who handle corporate mergers in *their* law firm. (contraction of *they are*; possessive pronoun)

Your application is due if *you're* interested in being considered for the job. (possessive pronoun; contraction of *you are*)

You can't tell a book by *its* cover, although *it's* tempting to try. (possessive pronoun; contraction of *it is*)

1.1.2. Action and Being Words: Verbs

Verbs	express action, occurrence, or state of being.
Action	Stock prices *rose* in late December.
Occurrence	That often *happens* at the end of the year.
State of Being	The phenomenon *is known* as the "year-end bump."

a. **Verb forms.** Verbs change form to show **time (tense), person, number, voice, and mood,** as illustrated in **Table C.6**.

b. **Expletives** are introductory words such as *there* or *it* followed by a linking verb (*is, are, was, were*).

It is probable that Jean won't attend.

There were six people on the conference call.

Expletives function more as signal expressions used for emphasis than as true conveyers of content. For example, *There were six people on the conference call* could as easily be expressed as *Six people were on the conference call*. Examine your writing to eliminate expletives, when possible. Although they can be used effectively to manage the pace and emphasis in a sentence, expletives can also add words that may not be necessary.

Verbs must agree with their subjects in person and number. The subject cannot be in a prepositional phrase. Find the true subject and make the verb agree.

Incorrect	The members of the Federal Reserve Board *sets* interest rates. (Verb *sets* is incorrect because subject *members* is plural.)
Correct	The *members* of the Federal Reserve Board *set* interest rates.

Contractions should be separated and matched with the correct person.

Incorrect	He *don't* want to be late, and I don't either. (Verb form *don't* or *do not* disagrees with third-person singular subject *he*.)
Correct	He *doesn't* want to be late, and I don't either. OR He *does not* want to be late, and I *do not* either.

Also see "Subject–Verb Agreement" in *Common Sentence Errors*.

Wordy	It is probable that Jean won't attend.
Revised	Jean probably won't attend.

When a sentence begins with the expletive *there*, the verb is singular or plural depending on the number of the noun or pronoun that follows it. In other words, the verb must agree with the true grammatical subject of the sentence; *there* and *here* are adverbial modifiers and cannot be grammatical subjects.

Incorrect	There was two possible solutions.
Correct	There *were* two possible *solutions*.

To check for correct agreement between subject and verb, try putting the sentence in subject–verb word order: Two possible *solutions were* there.

TABLE C.6 Features of Verbs

FEATURE	VARIATIONS	EXAMPLE
Time (tense)	present, past, future	The stock market *rose* 58 points. Prices *will increase*.
Person	first, second, third	*You and I think* it is a bull market. *He thinks* it is a bear market.
Number	singular, plural	A rising *tide raises* all boats, but ill financial *winds raise* many fears.
Voice	Active voice: Subject performs action of verb. Passive voice: Subject receives action of verb.	Corporate losses *caused* a market decline. The market decline *was caused* by corporate losses.
Mood	Indicates whether action expresses a fact or question (indicative), gives a command (imperative), or expresses a condition contrary to fact (subjunctive).	Indicative: She *saves* part of every paycheck. *Does* she *save* part of every paycheck? Imperative: *Save* part of every paycheck. Subjunctive: If she *were saving* part of every paycheck, she would be financially secure. [But the fact is she is not saving, so she is not secure.]

1.1.3. Modifying Words: Adjectives and Adverbs

a. **Adjectives** modify nouns and pronouns: Put the expense report in the *tall, gray filing* cabinet. Adjectives answer the questions *which one? what kind of?* or *how many?*

   "Modify" means to identify, describe, limit, or qualify in some way. For example, the *tall, gray filing* cabinet describes the height, color, and type of cabinet, differentiating it from the *low, white* equipment cabinet next to it.

b. **Adverbs** modify verbs, adjectives, other adverbs, and occasionally prepositions, conjunctions, or even whole sentences: I *quickly* located the cabinet but *unfortunately* could *not* pull *open* the *very firmly stuck* drawer. Adverbs answer the questions *how? when? where? why? to what extent?* or *to what degree?*

c. **Degree of comparison.** Many adjectives and adverbs change form to indicate three degrees of **comparison:**
   - **positive** (nothing being compared)
   - **comparative** (higher or lower degree when comparing two)
   - **superlative** (highest or lowest degree when comparing three or more)

The changes in form are indicated in three ways.

1. By adding *-er* or *-est* to the positive form of a one-syllable adjective or adverb or an adjective that ends in *-ly: tall, taller, tallest; few, fewer, fewest; fast, faster, fastest; friendly, friendlier, friendliest.*

2. By adding the prefix words *more* and *most* or *less* and *least* to the positive form of adjectives with three or more syllables or adverbs with two or more syllables: *expensive, less expensive, least* expensive; *simply, more* simply, *most* simply.

3. By using an irregular form: *good, better, best; bad, worse, worst.*

Some adjectives are considered **absolute**, not comparable. Absolute adjectives include *perfect, unique, square, straight, endless,* and *dead.* Something cannot be *more dead* than something else; it can, however, be *almost* or *nearly dead.*

GRAMMAR ALERT! MISUSE OF *BAD* AND *GOOD*

Use adjectives, not adverbs, with linking verbs (*be, become, is, are, was, were*) and verbs of the senses (*feel, smell, taste, look, appear, seem*). One of the most common adjective/adverb errors is confusion of *good* and *well, bad* and *badly.*

Incorrect	He *looks well* in that suit. (An adjective should be used instead of the adverb *well*, because it describes the subject, *he*.)
Correct	He *looks good* in that suit.
Incorrect	She *felt badly* about missing the appointment. (The "sensing" verb *felt* requires an adjective, not an adverb, because it describes the subject, *she*.)
Correct	She *felt bad* about missing the appointment.
But	Because her fingers were numb with cold, she *felt badly* and couldn't tell her car key from her house key. (The adverb form *badly* is correct because it describes the verb, her ability to feel or touch.)

1.1.4. Connecting Words: Prepositions and Conjunctions

a. **Prepositions** connect a noun or pronoun (called the "object" of the preposition) to some other word in a sentence. These prepositional "phrases" usually function as modifiers, describing the words to which they are connected: The office *on the left* belongs to the corporate lawyer. Common prepositions include *in, out, up, down, before, behind, over, under, to, from, above, below, on, off, by, through,* and *around.* Although we sometimes end sentences with prepositions in conversation ("Where are you from?"), try to avoid these "danglers" in writing. Follow the preposition with a noun or a pronoun as the object, unless doing so makes the sentence unusually awkward.

b. **Conjunctions** connect words, phrases, or clauses to show relationships between them: **coordination, correlation,** or **subordination.** The difference between them is described in **Table C.7.**

TABLE C.7 Types of Conjunctions

TYPE	FUNCTION	EXAMPLES
Coordinating conjunctions	Join words, phrases, or clauses of equal grammatical rank.	and, but, or, nor, for, so, yet
Correlative conjunctions	Work in pairs to join words, phrases, or clauses of equal grammatical rank.	both/and, either/or, neither/nor, not/but, not only/but also
Subordinating conjunctions	Join clauses that are not of equal rank. The clause beginning with the subordinating conjunction cannot stand by itself as a sentence.	after, although, as, because, before, if, since, rather than, that, unless, when, where, whether, while
Conjunctive adverbs	Join independent clauses only, clauses that can stand by themselves as sentences. These are adverbs, not true conjunctions, so they need to be preceded by a semicolon.	however, therefore, nevertheless, furthermore, instead, besides, consequently, then, meanwhile, thus

Note that some conjunctions also function as other parts of speech. For example, *after* can be a preposition or a conjunction, depending on whether it is followed by a noun or pronoun as an object or begins a phrase or clause containing a verb form.

GRAMMAR ALERT! AGREEMENT ERROR WITH PREPOSITIONAL OBJECT

The object of a preposition cannot be the subject of a sentence. Consequently, the verb should not be made to agree with it but rather with the true subject of the sentence.

Incorrect The box of name badges are on your desk. (The subject is not *badges*; *badges* is the object of the preposition *of*.)

Correct The *box* of name badges *is* on your desk. (The subject is *box*; the verb *is* agrees with the subject.)

Prepositional Phrase	Jason returned to the office *after* lunch.
	(*Lunch* is a noun.)
Conjunction Joining Independent Clauses	Jason returned to the office *after* he finished lunch.
	(*He finished lunch* is a clause.)

1.1.5. Exclaiming Words: Interjections

Interjections are considered a part of speech, but their only function is to express strong feeling. Although a few interjections can be interpreted as single-word commands with understood subjects or objects (*Help! Stop!*), most are grammatically unconnected to the rest of the sentence. An interjection may be accompanied by an explanation mark if the emotion is to be interpreted as particularly strong: "*Ouch!* I just got a paper cut from that file folder."

Interjections are common in speech, so they may be appropriate (if used with discretion) in written business messages that are more informal and conversational. Conversely, they are seldom appropriate in formal business writing, unless used for instructions that must grab the reader's attention.

Spoken Conversation	*Hey,* Lynn, do you have a minute?
Informal Email	*Wow!* I was impressed by her accomplishments.
Written Instructions	*Attention!* Set the brake before starting the engine.

Be aware that interjections that might be appropriate for texting friends will create an unprofessional, immature tone in business correspondence.

1.2. Sentence Parts and Patterns

As the old song says, "The knee bone is connected to the thigh bone," not to the heel bone or the toe bone. Understanding the components that make up a sentence and how they work together can help writers and speakers eliminate errors and use language more effectively.

1.2.1. Subjects and Predicates

The largest structural parts of sentences are their subjects and predicates. The **subject** explains who or what the sentence is about, who is performing or receiving the action described in the sentence. The **predicate** states the action or state of existence.

a. **Simple subject and predicate.** A sentence can be as short as two words—one word for the subject, and one word for the predicate: *Prices rose*. If the sentence is a command with an understood subject, it can even be just one word: *Run!* Usually sentences are longer, with their subjects and predicates composed of more words, conveying more information: *The prices for new homes rose in the third quarter*. However, every sentence can be pared down to its essential elements, the **simple subject** (noun, pronoun, or noun equivalent) and **simple predicate** (verb): *Prices rose*.

b. **Complete subject and predicate.** The simple subject along with all its modifiers is called the **complete subject**.

> *The prices for new homes* rose in the third quarter.

Similarly, the simple predicate along with all its modifiers, objects, and complements is the **complete predicate**.

> The prices for new homes *rose in the third quarter*.

In the previous sentence, the complete predicate includes only the verb and its modifiers: rose in the third quarter. That is because the verb *rose* is an intransitive verb, a verb that does not take an object.

If the verb is a transitive verb—one that takes an object—the complete predicate will include a **direct object** that receives the action of the verb: We bought *a house*. It may also include an **indirect object**, telling to or for whom or what the action occurred: The real estate agent sent *us the contract*.

If the predicate has a linking verb, it may include a **complement**—a noun, pronoun, or adjective that "completes" the verb, renaming or describing the subject: The house *is a two-story colonial*. The price *was reasonable*.

c. **Inverted word order** can sometimes make locating the subject and predicate difficult. For example, questions have inverted word order, in which the verb (or part of a verb phrase) precedes the subject. In the following questions, the simple predicates are *did rise* and *are*. The simple subjects are *prices* and *they*: **Did** home prices **rise** last month? **Are** they still reasonable?

1.2.2. Phrases and Clauses

a. **Phrases** are word groups that may contain a subject or a predicate, but not both. They function as a single part of speech, as described in **Table C.8**.

b. **Clauses** are word groups that have both a subject and a predicate. The subject and predicate may contain no modifiers or many; they may contain no phrases or many.

Prices rose. (no modifiers)

Prices *for new homes* rose *in the third quarter*. (two modifying phrases)

An **independent clause** (main clause) can stand by itself as a complete sentence, but a **dependent clause** cannot stand alone.

Dependent clauses (also called subordinate clauses) add information to the main idea, but they are incomplete without the main clause to which they are attached. You can identify an adverbial dependent clause by the subordinating conjunction

TABLE C.8 Functions of Phrases

FUNCTION OF PHRASE	EXAMPLE	EXPLANATION
Functions as noun	*Remembering all my computer passwords* is difficult.	Noun phrase takes subject position in sentence.
Functions as verb	I *have been writing* them on sticky notes.	Verb phrase takes verb position in sentence.
Functions as adjective	Dozens *of these notes* are stuck to my computer. *Looking at all these notes stuck on my computer,* I wish I did not need this memory aid.	Adjectival prepositional phrase modifies noun *dozens*, telling what kind. Present participial phrase *looking at all these notes* modifies the pronoun *I*. Past participial phrase *stuck on my computer* modifies the noun *notes*, telling which ones.
Functions as adverb	However, I can't seem to remember my passwords *from one day to the next.*	Adverbial prepositional phrase modifies verb *seem to remember*, telling when.

that connects it to the main clause (see "Connecting Words"). You can identify an adjectival subordinate clause (also called a relative clause) by the relative pronoun (*who, whom, whose, that,* or *which*) or the relative adverb (*when, where,* or *why*) that connects it to the main clause. **Table C.9** illustrates the differences between independent and dependent clauses.

simple to complex, sentence structure can help create and rein-force meaning. **Table C.10** illustrates the four sentence types.

Subjects and predicates may have compound elements, but those compound elements do not necessarily make the sentence itself compound. For example, a simple sentence with a compound verb is still a simple sentence: People live longer *but* save less.

PUNCTUATION ALERT! SENTENCE FRAGMENT

Do not punctuate a **dependent clause** as if it were a sentence. Doing so creates a sentence fragment (see "Common Sentence Errors: Sentence Fragments").

Incorrect	My computer doesn't work. Although the technician checked it. (*Although the technician checked it* is a dependent clause—a sentence fragment—not a complete sentence.)
Correct	My computer doesn't work although the technician checked it.

1.2.3. Sentence Types: Simple, Compound, Complex, Compound-Complex

Sentences can be classified according to the number and types of clauses they contain. Good communicators take advantage of these sentence types to express their ideas most effectively. From

---

PUNCTUATION ALERT! MISUSE OF COMMA

Do not punctuate a simple sentence with a compound subject or compound predicate as if it were a compound sentence. Before putting a comma in front of *and* or *but*, check to make sure the conjunction connects two independent clauses.

Incorrect	I turned off my computer, and then went to get the mail. (This is a single independent clause with a compound predicate.)
Correct	I turned off my computer and then went to get the mail.
Correct	I turned off my computer, and then I went to get the mail. (Each clause is independent, so the comma is required.)

TABLE C.9 Independent versus Dependent Clauses

TYPE OF CLAUSE	EXAMPLE
Independent Dependent	**I can't remember my passwords** because I have too many of them. (Boldface words can stand alone.) I can't remember my passwords **because I have too many of them**. (Boldface words cannot stand alone.)
Independent Dependent	**I can't even remember the password** that I selected yesterday. (Boldface words can stand alone.) I can't even remember the password **that I selected yesterday**. (Boldface words cannot stand alone.)
Independent Dependent	**Now I just need to find the sticky notes** where I wrote down my passwords. (Boldface words can stand alone.) Now I just need to find the sticky notes **where I wrote down my passwords**. (Boldface words cannot stand alone.)

TABLE C.10 Sentence Types

SENTENCE TYPE	STRUCTURE	EXAMPLES
Simple	One **independent** clause; no *dependent* clauses	**People want to save for retirement.**
Compound	Two or more **independent** clauses; no *dependent* clauses	**People want to save for retirement,** but they seldom do it.
Complex	One **independent** clause; one or more *dependent* clauses	*Although people want to save for retirement,* **they seldom do it voluntarily.**
Compound-Complex	Two or more **independent** clauses; one or more *dependent* clauses	**People say** *that they want to save for retirement,* but **they seldom do it** *while they are young.*

1.3. Common Sentence Errors

The most frequent sentence errors are **fragments**, **run-ons** or **fused sentences**, **comma splices**, and **agreement errors**. The first three errors occur because the writer has incorrectly indicated where one sentence stops and another begins. These errors can prevent readers from understanding the meaning the writer intended. Although our daily speech is full of these "not sentence" constructions, listeners have many more cues to help determine meaning—including the opportunity to ask questions. Business writers need to get it right the first time, or they may cause serious miscommunication.

1.3.1. Sentence Fragments

A sentence contains at least one independent clause, having a subject and a verb, and can stand alone as a complete thought. When a word group (phrase or dependent clause) lacking these characteristics is punctuated as if it were a sentence, a **fragment** results. A fragment can be corrected by rewriting it as a complete sentence. Join the fragment to the sentence before or after it, or supply the missing subject or verb to make the fragment an independent clause.

Incorrect	People would rather have rewards now. Than wait patiently for rewards in the future. (phrases punctuated as a sentence)
Correct	People would rather have rewards now than wait patiently for rewards in the future.
Incorrect	Behavioral economists say people choose immediate rewards. Because they overly discount the future. (dependent clause punctuated as a sentence)
Correct	Behavioral economists say people choose immediate rewards because they overly discount the future.
Incorrect	People buying things on credit that they can't afford. (phrases and dependent clause punctuated as a sentence)
Correct	People buy things on credit that they can't afford.

Compound predicates (joined by *and, but, or, yet,* and so on) are sometimes punctuated as complete sentences, especially when the sentence is long. However, if the clause beginning with "but" is short, combine it with the first sentence.

Incorrect	Sometimes people have to run up their credit card bills. But they shouldn't make a habit of it.
Correct	Sometimes people have to run up their credit card bills, but they shouldn't make a habit of it.

A polite request or command may appear to be missing a subject, and therefore be a sentence fragment; however, the sentence is complete because the subject is the understood pronoun *you*.

Correct	Please send your response as soon as possible.
	(The understood subject is *you*.)

1.3.2. Run-on (Fused) Sentences and Comma Splices

Run-on or **fused sentences** are independent clauses joined together without a connecting conjunction.

Classical economists believe humans rationally weigh costs and benefits **conversely, behavioral economists point out humans' irrational decision making.**

Comma splices are independent clauses joined together by a comma.

Rational humans are marvelous in theory, **in reality they do not exist.**

Run-ons and comma splices are both incorrect, and both can be fixed in one of five ways:

1. **Connect the independent clauses with a comma and a coordinating conjunction.**

   Classical economists believe humans rationally weigh costs and benefits, *but* behavioral economists point out humans' irrational decision making.

2. **Connect the independent clauses with a semicolon.**

   Rational humans are marvelous in theory; in reality they do not exist.

3. **Make a separate sentence of each independent clause.**

   Classical economists believe humans rationally weigh costs and benefits. Conversely, behavioral economists point out humans' irrational decision making.

4. **Change one independent clause to a dependent clause.**

   Although rational humans are marvelous in theory, in reality they do not exist.

5. **Change one independent clause to a phrase.**

   Marvelous in theory, rational humans do not exist in reality.

1.3.3. Subject–Verb Agreement

Subjects and verbs need to agree in number and person. If the subject of a clause is singular, the verb must be singular as well; if plural, it must be plural. If the subject is in third person, the verb must reflect that. (Also see 1.1.2 "Action and Being Words: Verbs.") Agreement errors are most common in the following instances.

- **Words and phrases between subject and verb.** Locate the subject and verb and make them agree, ignoring everything in between.

  The *aroma* of baking cupcakes *convinces* me to start my diet tomorrow. (The verb *convinces* should agree in number with the subject *aroma*, not with *cupcakes*, the object of the preposition *of*.)

  Even though words such as *with, together with,* and *as well as* suggest plural meaning, they are not part of the subject. When they follow singular subjects, use singular verbs.

  Temptation, as well as immediate sweet rewards, *undermines* my willpower.

- **Indefinite pronouns as subjects.** Use singular verbs with indefinite pronouns indicating one: *another, each, either, much, neither, one,* and all pronouns ending in *-one, -body,* and *-thing.*

  Everybody believes in doing what is best for the future; nevertheless, *each* of us occasionally *gives* in to immediate gratification.

  Use plural verbs with indefinite pronouns indicating more than one: *both, few, many, others,* and *several.*

  Many behave irrationally, but *few view* their choices as irrational.

  The indefinite pronouns *all, any, most, more, none,* and *some* take either a singular or a plural verb, depending on whether the noun to which they refer is singular or plural.

  Some people are good at delaying gratification, but *none find* it very easy. (*None* refers to *people* and so requires the plural verb *find.*)

  Most of the cake is gone, but some is still on the plate. (*Most* and *some* refer to one item—most of it and some of it.)

- **Collective nouns as subjects.** Collective nouns are singular in form but name a group of persons or things: *committee, crowd, jury, team, task force.* Use a singular verb when the group is considered as a unit acting collectively as one. Use a plural verb when the members of the group are acting separately as individuals.

  The task force has reported its findings to the director. (Task force is considered a unit acting collectively.)

The *task force have* agreed to conduct follow-up studies in their own departments. (Individuals on the task force are acting separately.)

OR

The task force *members have* agreed to conduct follow-up studies in their own departments.

- **Plural forms that have singular meanings.** Some nouns are plural in form but singular in meaning: *economics, mathematics, news, measles.* Use a singular verb with these.

  Behavioral *economics explains* why consumers can't resist a sale.

  However, some nouns in plural form, such as *athletics, politics, statistics,* and *acoustics,* may be singular or plural, depending on whether they refer to a singular or plural idea.

  The Republican Party's *politics is* generally conservative, although members' *politics reflect* a wide spectrum of views.

> **GRAMMAR ALERT!** DATA
>
> A singular verb is often used with the word *data*: *The data appears in the appendix.* However, people in technical and scientific fields typically think of data as plural, as compilations of separate pieces of numerical information. Therefore, they usually prefer plural verbs: *The data appear in the appendix.* Follow the practice of the business, industry, or field for which you are writing. If the word *data* is considered plural in meaning, use a plural verb: *The data are reliable.* *Her data show* that more testing should be done. The singular form is *datum,* or you can write about an individual *data point.*

- **Subjects joined by coordinating conjunctions *and, or,* or *nor.*** Use a plural verb when two or more subjects are joined by *and,* unless the parts of the compound subject refer to the same thing.

  Our *wants and* our *needs are* often not the same thing.

  Robert's *son and executor* of his estate *has signed* the documents.

  When *each* or *every* precedes a compound singular subject joined by *and,* the subject is considered singular and takes a singular verb.

  Every employee and his or her guest *has been issued* an identification badge.

  When subjects are joined by *or, nor,* or *not only/but also,* the verb should agree in number with the subject that is nearer.

  Neither the employee nor her *guests have been issued* badges, so either the receptionist or the *department head has to call* Security for clearance.

  Neither the guests *nor* the *employee has been issued* badges.

- **Relative pronouns *who, which,* and *that* as subjects.** When the relative pronoun *who, which,* or *that* is the subject of a dependent clause, make the verb agree with the pronoun's antecedent.

  Please give me a list of the *guests who need* badges. (*Who* refers to the antecedent *guests,* so the verb must be plural.)

- **Inverted word order.** Be sure to check agreement when the verb comes before the subject. Test for correctness by putting the subject first. (Also see 1.1.2.b. "Expletives.")

    After a vacation *comes* the *reality* of an overflowing in-box. (The *reality* of an overflowing in-box *comes* after a vacation.)

    There *appears* to be no *excuse* for his behavior. (No *excuse* for his behavior *appears* to be there.)

- **Quantities.** Total amounts are usually considered a single unit and take singular verbs.

    Two weeks is not enough vacation, according to Europeans.

    I think *$100 is* outrageous for weekly parking.

    If the individual parts of a unit are being emphasized, choose a plural verb.

    Twenty-four grams of fat *have* to be spread over three meals, not eaten in a single sitting.

    If a percentage refers to things that are plural and countable, the verb should be plural.

    Thirty percent of the engine parts *do* not pass quality standards.

    If a percentage refers to something that is singular, the verb is singular.

    Ten percent of his income *goes* to charity.

    The number takes a singular verb, but *a number* takes a plural verb.

    A number of faulty parts *were found*, although *the number* of returns *was* low.

- **Business names, products, titles, and words used as words.** Even if the form of a business name or product or the title of a work is plural, it takes a singular verb because it is a single thing. The same is true for words discussed as words.

    I think *Twinings makes* the best cup of Earl Grey tea.

    Hot, Flat, and Crowded by Thomas Friedman *has* sold millions of copies.

    Geese is the plural of *goose*.

1.3.4. Pronoun–Antecedent Agreement

Pronouns must agree in number with their antecedents, the words to which they refer. Most agreement situations are obvious: The *interns* received *their* orientation yesterday. However, the following situations can be tricky.

- **Indefinite pronouns.** As the word "indefinite" suggests, these pronouns do not refer to specific persons, places, or things: for example, *some, all, many,* and *anyone* are indefinite pronouns. Although people tend to use plural pronouns when speaking, in writing use singular pronouns to refer to indefinite pronoun antecedents such as *person, one, any, each, either,* and *neither* and indefinite pronouns ending in -one, -body, and -thing, such as *anybody, someone,* or *everything*.

Incorrect	*Everybody* knows *they* should dress appropriately for a job interview.
Correct	*Everybody* knows *he or she* should dress appropriately for a job interview.

- **Collective nouns.** Use a singular pronoun if the antecedent is a group being considered as a unit. Use a plural pronoun if the members of the group are being considered individually.

    The review *panel* started *its* tour of the laboratory at 9:30 AM. (The panel toured as a group.)

    The review *panel* asked many questions when *they* met with the research director. (Individual members of the group asked questions.)

- **Compound antecedents.** Antecedents connected by *and* take plural pronouns. Pronouns referring to compound antecedents connected by *or* or *nor* should agree with the antecedent closer to it. If that choice is awkward or ambiguous, do not use a pronoun.

Incorrect	If you ask either Jenny or Paul, they will help you.
Incorrect	If you ask either the supervisors or Jenny, they will help you.
Correct	If you ask *Jenny and Paul, they* will help you.
Correct	If you ask either *Jenny or Paul, one of them* will help you.
Correct	If you ask either Jenny *or the supervisors, they* will help you.
Correct	If you ask either the supervisors *or Jenny, someone* will help you. (Avoid using the grammatically correct pronoun, *she,* because the resulting sentence implies that the supervisors will not help: If you ask either the supervisors *or Jenny, she* will help you.)

When a compound antecedent is introduced by *each* or *every,* or when it refers to a single person or thing, use a singular pronoun.

Each hospital and clinic has *its* own evacuation plan.

The president and CEO delivered *his* annual state-of-the-company speech.

1.3.5. Vague Pronoun Reference

The antecedent to which a pronoun refers should be clear. Pronouns should refer to

- only one antecedent. It may be plural or compound, but it should be only one.

- an antecedent that is nearby. Readers generally assume the antecedent is the closest previous noun or noun substitute.

- a specific antecedent, not an implied person or thing or the general idea of a preceding clause or sentence. A pronoun should refer to a noun or noun substitute that exists in a previous phrase or clause. Revise if *this, that,* or *which* refers to the general idea of a preceding clause or sentence.

Vague	We need to survey more customers. *This* will give us better data, so we can develop better products. *They* will benefit in the long run. (*This* vaguely refers to the whole idea in the previous sentence. *They* could refer to customers, data, or products; the closest noun, *products*, doesn't make sense.)
Clear	We need to survey more customers. A bigger sampling will give us better data, so we can develop better products. Customers will benefit in the long run.

2. Punctuation

Punctuation marks fall into four basic categories: (1) end punctuation that marks the endings of sentences and indicates how the sentence is to be read; (2) internal punctuation that shows the relationship of individual words or sentence parts to the rest of a sentence; (3) direct-quotation punctuation that indicates speakers and changes of speaker as well as where words have been added or omitted from the original text; and (4) word punctuation that indicates words or letters having a special use. These functions are illustrated in the sections that follow.

2.1. End Punctuation

The punctuation at the ends of sentences signals where ideas stop and marks the end of complete grammatical units that can stand alone. End punctuation also indicates whether the sentence is to be understood as a question (**question mark**), statement, command, indirect question, or polite request (**period**), or strong expression of emotion (**exclamation point**).

> **Examples:**
> I will now ask your name.
> Tell me your name.
> Will you please state your name?
> What is your name?
> What a wonderful name!

2.1.1. Question Marks

Direct questions are punctuated with a question mark: *What time is the meeting? She asked me, "What time is the meeting?"*

2.1.2. Periods

Periods mark the ends of statements and commands as well as indirect questions and polite requests. An **indirect question** implies a question but does not actually ask one: *I want to know what time the meeting is.* One clue that the previous sentence is not a direct question is the word order: The subject and verb are not inverted in indirect questions, as they are in a direct question (what time *is the meeting?*). A **polite request** may be phrased like a question, but it is really a command stated nicely. Therefore, it is often punctuated with a period rather than a question mark:

When you have scheduled the meeting, please let me know. Deciding whether a sentence is a polite request or a question may also have to do with who is making the request. A polite request that is a command from a supervisor would require a period: *"Will you please attend the meeting for me."* A polite request for a favor from a coworker would require a question mark: *"Will you please attend the meeting for me?"*

Periods also are normally used with initials and with abbreviations ending with lowercase letters.

Dr. Janice Brown   Sen. Ben Cardin   St. Jerome   Mr. Kim

Academic degrees and professional certifications in some fields omit the period from abbreviations; for example, PhD, RN, or MD may appear without periods. Consult the style manual of the profession if in doubt. Your company may also have a style manual that specifies how abbreviations are to be handled in company correspondence and publications.

2.1.3. Exclamation Points

Interjections and sentences that require strong emphasis or express extreme emotion are often punctuated with exclamation points: *Attention! Fire on the third floor! Evacuate the building using the stairs!*

Unfortunately, many people have adopted the habit of sprinkling their writing liberally with exclamations, particularly in text messages and emails: *OMG!! Guess who showed up at the company party?!* More formal business communication should contain few if any exclamation points. Overusing exclamations either diminishes their effect or makes the writing sound hysterical and immature. In some fields, such as court reporting, exclamation points are never used.

2.2. Commas

Commas separate parts of a sentence, guiding readers through complex constructions, indicating modifiers, separating series, and generally ordering things into understandable units of meaning. Think of commas as markers that signal changes in the road. Although there are many rules for using commas, most business writing relies on a fairly limited number.

2.2.1. Between Clauses

- **Independent clauses joined by coordinating conjunctions *and, but, or, nor, for, so, yet.*** The comma before the coordinating conjunction linking the clauses signals that one complete thought is finished and another is about to begin:

  > I prepared the slides, *and* Mavis printed the handouts.

  The comma can be omitted between very short clauses if there is no possibility of confusion:

  > You drive *and* I'll navigate.

  Do not use a comma with a coordinating conjunction linking compound predicates (verbs plus objects or complements plus modifiers). Check to be sure the conjunction links independent clauses.

Incorrect	I prepared the slides for the meeting, and then printed the handouts.
Correct	I prepared the slides for the meeting, and then I printed the handouts
Or	I prepared the slides for the meeting and then printed the handouts.

Also see 1.2.3. "Sentence Types: Simple, Compound, Complex, Compound-Complex."

- **Dependent clauses and phrases preceding the independent clause.** The comma following an introductory dependent clause or phrase signals that the main clause containing the main idea is about to begin. It helps the reader differentiate modifying information from the meat of the sentence, announcing "OK, now pay attention. Here comes the most important stuff."

  When the presentation was finished, the speaker answered questions.

  Having missed the first 15 minutes, I was a bit confused.

  If it will not cause misreading, the comma can be omitted after very short introductory clauses or phrases.

Clear	After lunch we returned to the office.
Confusing	Before long smears appeared on the glass.
Clear	Before long, smears appeared on the glass.
Confusing	After she ate lunch was served to the rest of us.
Clear	After she ate, lunch was served to the rest of us.

2.2.2. Between Adjectives

- **Coordinate and cumulative adjectives.** If each adjective in a series modifies the noun separately, they are **coordinate** and need commas between them.

  The *personable, youthful, but knowledgeable* guide led the way.

- If any adjective in a series forms a total concept along with the noun, they are cumulative and do not need commas.

  International currency exchange rates are posted on the Internet. (*Currency exchange rates* is a total concept.)

To test for coordinate adjectives, see if the adjectives can be rearranged and if *and* can be inserted between them without altering the basic meaning: *knowledgeable and youthful and personable* guide. If the result is nonsense, the adjectives are cumulative, interdependent, and should not be separated from each other by commas: *international currency exchange rates* must appear in that order, or the statement makes no sense.

2.2.3. Between Items in a Series

Three or more words, phrases, or clauses in a series are said to be **serial** or **coordinate**. Their equal importance is indicated by their equal grammatical rank and parallel grammatical form.

- **Serial words, phrases, or clauses.** Serial items are differentiated from one another by the commas between them.

Many U.S. companies have found that outsourcing call-center jobs *cuts costs, increases productivity, and allows 24-hour global service.*

Although writing in newspapers, magazines, and websites often omits the comma before the conjunction, use it in business writing to prevent misreading—which could be not only confusing but also costly.

Confusing	Charge the plane tickets for the vice president, board chairwoman and president and CEO to the corporate account. (Three tickets or four?)
Clear	Charge the plane tickets for the vice president, board chairwoman, and president and CEO to the corporate account. (Three tickets, because the president and the CEO are the same person.)

2.2.4. Around Clauses, Phrases, or Words

a. **Nonrestrictive clauses and phrases.** If the information in a modifying clause or phrase can be omitted without changing the basic meaning of a sentence, it is **nonrestrictive** and is set off by commas. If readers would be unable to understand the sentence's core meaning without the modifying information, it is **restrictive** and is not set off by commas. Restrictive modifiers limit meaning to a particular set within a category and are crucial to the sentence.

Nonrestrictive	The sales award went to McKenzie, *who landed six new accounts.* (The clause provides additional information about McKenzie, but without it we would still know who got the award.)
Restrictive	Everyone *who has been with the company for three years* is eligible for profit sharing. (The clause restricts who qualifies; otherwise, the company would have to include all employees in profit sharing.)

GRAMMAR ALERT! *THAT* AND *WHICH*

That and *which* are not interchangeable. Use *that* to introduce restrictive clauses and *which* to introduce nonrestrictive clauses:

The retirement plan *that I chose* is split between annuities and stock funds. The stock funds, *which are invested in Fortune 500 companies,* showed a good return last year.

Remember that nonrestrictive clauses, *which are set off by commas,* can be removed without destroying the basic meaning of the sentence. Most of the time, if you use *that,* you will be making the correct choice.

Use *who,* not *which* or *that,* when referring to people; use *which* or *that* when referring to things or ideas:

Incorrect	Dr. Phillips is the only veterinarian *that* keeps Sunday hours.
Correct	Dr. Phillips is the only veterinarian *who* keeps Sunday hours.

b. **Appositives.** An appositive is a noun, with or without modifiers, that identifies the noun immediately preceding it. Appositives can be nonrestrictive or restrictive, accordingly written with or without commas.

> Mnemonics, *memory aids,* can help you learn things. (nonrestrictive)

> The mnemonic *"every good boy does fine"* refers to the musical notes E, G, B, D, and F. (restrictive)

> I learned that mnemonic from Mr. Glonner, *my third-grade music teacher.* (nonrestrictive)

c. **Direct address and other parenthetical elements.** If you insert the name of the person to whom you are speaking or writing into a sentence, you are using **direct address**. Set these names off with commas: Thank you, *Leela,* for closing the door. *Committee members,* are we ready to vote?

> **Parenthetical elements** such as interjections, transition words, words expressing contrast, and other interrupting words that are unrelated to the grammatical structure of a sentence should also be set off with commas.

> *Yes,* everyone is present and ready to vote. We shall, *therefore,* proceed. *Oh,* before we do, someone needs to second the motion. Parliamentary procedure, *unlike the consensus method,* requires a second.

d. **Dates and places.** Dates and places in sentences are treated similarly to parenthetical elements. In general, place a comma after each element. Exceptions: Do not put a comma between the state and zip code. If there is no day, do not put a comma between the month and year. If the date is written with the day before the month and year, use no commas.

> *October 29, 1929,* is known as Black Tuesday, the day the New York stock market crashed.

> No American will forget *11 September 2001.*

> Isn't NBC's headquarters at *30 Rockefeller Plaza, New York, NY 10112,* in mid-town Manhattan?

> The annual convention will be held in *Boise, Idaho,* next year and *Toronto, Canada,* the year after that.

e. **Direct quotations.** Direct quotations are set off with commas. Any comma at the end of a quotation **always** goes inside the quotation marks. Also see 2.5, "Quotation Marks and Italics."

> The manager told the sales associates, "We need better customer service."

> "I'm hearing too many complaints," she explained, "and we're losing business."

Use a question mark at the end of the quotation if it is a question.

> "Does anyone have a suggestion?" she asked.

f. **Salutations.** In formal business correspondence, punctuate the salutation or greeting with a colon, not with a comma. Commas should be reserved for personal, social correspondence written on personal stationery. Follow this convention even if you know the recipient and use his or her first name in the salutation.

Not	Dear Dr. Spaulding,	or	Dear Jerry,
But	Dear Dr. Spaulding:	or	Dear Jerry:

The colon announces that the subject of the correspondence is business—but conventions are somewhat more flexible for business email. See Appendix B for formatting examples.

2.3. Semicolons

In a sentence, semicolons have two distinctly different uses.

2.3.1. Joining Independent Clauses

Use a semicolon between grammatically independent clauses that are closely related in thought. In these instances, the semicolon is the equivalent of a period. It signals the end of one complete thought and the beginning of another. Reserve semicolons for sentences in which the thoughts in the independent clauses are closely related. If the thoughts are not closely related, use a period. When the second clause is introduced by a conjunctive adverb (*however, moreover, therefore, consequently*), place a comma after the conjunctive adverb. Do not use a semicolon between independent clauses joined by coordinating conjunctions (*and, but, so, for*), unless the clauses are quite long or internally punctuated.

Incorrect	Pollution threatens air quality; and everything that breathes is at risk.
Correct	Pollution threatens air quality; everything that breathes is at risk.
Correct	Pollution threatens air quality; consequently, everything that breathes is at risk.

2.3.2. Between Items in a Series

Use semicolons between serial items if any parts of the series have internal commas. The semicolons help readers sort things into the appropriate subsets and prevent misreading.

> Over the last 20 years, international negotiators have tried to reach agreement about global emission standards several times, including the Montreal Protocol of 1989; the Kyoto Protocol adopted on December 11, 1997; and the largely unsuccessful Copenhagen Climate Conference held December 7–18, 2009.

2.4. Colons

A colon signals that what follows will explain, clarify, or illustrate preceding information.

2.4.1. Preceding a List

Use a colon after phrases such as *the following* or *as follows* to signal the beginning of a list or series.

> Businesses can be "greener" and also save money by taking the following steps: insulate the building well, switch to fluorescent lighting, and recycle disposable items.

2.4.2. Preceding an Explanation or Illustration

Use a colon between explanatory material and the independent clause that introduces it.

> Polluting industries that balk at stricter standards usually offer one reason: the expense of compliance.

2.4.3. Preceding a Rule, Formal Quotation, or Subtitle

> Carpenters follow this advice: cut once, measure twice. (rule)

> The Declaration of Independence assumes inherent human rights: "We hold these truths to be self evident." (formal quotation)

> *The World Is Flat: A Brief History of the Twenty-First Century* (subtitle)

PUNCTUATION ALERT! MISUSE OF COLONS

Be sure that a complete sentence, not a partial statement, precedes the colon—even if the clause ends with *including* or *such as*. Do not put a colon between a verb and its object or complement or between a preposition and its object.

Incorrect	Our office has adopted "green" initiatives including: recycling soda cans and installing energy-efficient light bulbs.
Correct	Our office has adopted "green" initiatives, including recycling soda cans and installing energy-efficient light bulbs.
Correct	Our office has initiated two successful green initiatives: recycling soda cans and installing energy-efficient light bulbs.
Incorrect	I try to cut down carbon emissions by: biking to work, combining errands, and driving a hybrid car.
Correct	I try to cut down on carbon emissions by biking to work, combining errands, and driving a hybrid car
Correct	I try to cut down on carbon emissions in the following ways: biking to work, combining errands, and driving a hybrid car.

However, if the items following a verb or preposition are presented as a vertical list, use a colon.

Correct	Signs that the planet is warming include:

- melting glaciers
- invasive tropical species in temperate zones
- more frequent violent weather systems

2.5. Quotation Marks and Italics

Quotation marks and italics indicate that words are being used in a distinct way, most commonly to identify direct address, titles, and special meaning or emphasis.

2.5.1. Quotation Marks

Use quotation marks to signal direct quotations, titles of shorter works, and words that are being used in a special sense.

a. **Direct quotation.** Use double quotation marks for language that has been reproduced exactly as someone spoke or wrote it. Use single quotation marks to indicate a quotation within a quotation.

> According to this morning's news, "The President reminded his audience that economic recessions can be partly psychological. President Roosevelt said, 'We have nothing to fear but fear itself.' You know, he was right."

According to American punctuation usage, periods and commas always go inside single and double quotation marks. Colons and semicolons always go outside quotation marks. Question marks and exclamation points go either inside or outside the quotation marks, depending on whether the punctuation is part of the quotation or part of the sentence in which the quotation appears.

> "Shouldn't we recycle these computer printouts?" Marge asked.

> Did Marge say, "We should recycle these computer printouts"?

> I am sick of hearing the expression "waste not, want not"!

> Did Marge ask, "Shouldn't we recycle these computer printouts?" (This sentence requires only one question mark—inside the quotation marks—to signal that both the main sentence and the quoted sentence are questions.)

b. **Titles that are part of longer works.** Use quotation marks around titles of short stories, poems, chapters, articles, sections, songs, or episodes that are part of whole works. The title of the complete work in which a shorter work appears is italicized. Also see 2.5.2, "Italics."

> The article "Putting Green Technology into Bricks" in *The Wall Street Journal* makes the point that venture capital investment in the "green" building sector has nearly doubled in the past year.

c. **Words used as words or in a special sense.** Quotation marks signal that a word is being used in a special way. In the previous example, the quotation marks around "green" in *"green" building sector* alert the reader that "green" doesn't mean buildings painted green but green in the sense of "ecologically friendly."

2.5.2. Italics

Italics are used to distinguish titles of whole works from parts of works, to indicate some special uses of words, and to provide emphasis.

a. **Titles.** Place titles of works in italics; place title of parts of works in quotation marks:

> One of my favorite features in *The New York Times Magazine* is William Safire's "On Language" column.

If the word *The* is part of the title, be sure to capitalize and italicize it.

Some well-known titles of works are not italicized: religious works such as the Bible (and books of the Bible), the Koran, and the Talmud, and founding governmental documents such as the Declaration of Independence, the Bill of Rights, the Magna Carta, and the U.S. Constitution.

b. **Letters, numbers, words used as words, foreign words, names of ships and aircraft.** Italics are used to signal that a letter, number, or word is being identified as such.

> To an American, a *7* written by a German looks more like the number *1*.

Italics are also used to identify foreign words that have not been accepted into English.

> One of my favorite William Safire columns is a discussion of the Yiddish word *schlep*.

Words that have become part of the English language need not be italicized: bourgeois, milieu, zeitgeist, fiesta. Names of ships and aircraft are italicized but not the abbreviations that precede them: U.S.S. *Saratoga*, H.M.S. *Bounty*, the space shuttle *Atlantis*.

c. **Emphasis.** Italics can also be used for special emphasis.

> This is absolutely the *last* time we can accept a late shipment.

However, as with exclamation points, in business writing emphasizing too many words soon becomes tiresome to readers. It is like crying wolf; soon no one is paying attention, even when the wolf really is at the door. Use italicized emphasis sparingly.

2.6. Apostrophes

Apostrophes have two main functions in business writing: to show possession and to indicate the omission of a letter.

2.6.1. Possessive Case

a. **Singular nouns, plural nouns not ending in -s, and indefinite pronouns.** Add *'s*. Also see 1.1.1.c. "Pronoun Case." **Table C.11** provides examples of how to form the possessive. In compounds, make only the last word possessive.

> his brother-in-law's mortgage (singular possessive)
>
> mothers-in-law's Christmas gifts (plural possessive)
>
> somebody else's parking space
>
> the writer-in-residence's latest one-act play

b. **Plural nouns ending in -s.** Add the apostrophe after the -s.

> the presidents' terms in office
>
> the stocks' dramatic rebound after the sell-off
>
> the pharmaceutical companies' profits
>
> the auto workers' union

c. **Joint possession.** Make the last noun possessive. In cases of individual possession, make both nouns possessive.

> Beth and Earl's project is due tomorrow. (joint possession)
> Beth's and Earl's offices are on different floors. (individual possession)

d. **Personal pronouns.** Do not use an apostrophe to form the possessive of personal pronouns. The pronouns *his*, *hers*, *its*, *ours*, *yours*, *theirs*, and *whose* are possessive as they stand.

> Ours is the second house on the right.
> Its expiration date is past.

Be especially careful not to confuse its (possessive form of it) and it's (the contraction for it is) or whose (possessive form of who) and who's (contraction for who is).

2.6.2. Contractions

Apostrophes in contractions show where letters or numbers have been omitted.

can't = cannot	they're = they are	o'clock = of the clock
it's = it is	won't = will not	the crash of '29 = the crash of 1929

2.7. Other Punctuation Marks

In business writing, the following internal punctuation marks are used less frequently than commas, semicolons, and colons. However, when they are called for, it is important to use them correctly.

2.7.1. Parentheses, Dashes, Brackets, and Ellipses

Parentheses, dashes, brackets, and ellipses signal that words are being inserted or being left out.

a. **Parentheses.** Use parentheses to set off incidental or nonessential information.

> Mortgages that are "underwater" (meaning the property is worth less than the amount owed on it) have resulted in numerous foreclosures.
>
> The findings of the study (pp. 12–14) are quite surprising.

b. **Dashes.** If you want more emphasis for inserted incidental information, surround it with a pair of **dashes** instead of parentheses. You may also use dashes to emphasize important information. If the emphasized word or phrase comes at the

TABLE C.11 Examples of Forming the Possessive with *'s*

ADD *'s* TO SHOW POSSESSION	SINGULAR NOUNS	PLURAL NOUNS NOT ENDING IN *-s*	INDEFINITE PRONOUNS
Examples	my child's education, the boss's office, an individual's rights, a person's income, Dow Jones's sales, James's paycheck	his children's education, the mass media's influence, the people's choice, the mice's mutations	another's misfortune, someone's benefit, nobody's fault

end or beginning of the sentence, separate it from the rest of the sentence with only one dash.

> Wilkins missed the start of the meeting—again—and so didn't hear about the new deadline.

> The two problems we discussed at the meeting—absenteeism and tardiness—cost us thousands of dollars each month.

> Absenteeism and tardiness—these problems cost us thousands of dollars each month.

> Wilkens will never get promoted—unless he changes his behavior.

Be careful not to overuse dashes in formal business documents, especially for incidental information. They can give writing a breezy, chatty tone that is better reserved for email and notes to close associates.

c. **Brackets.** If you insert information, explanation, or comment into quoted material, use **brackets** to indicate that the words are not those of the quoted speaker or writer. To make a quotation grammatical when you insert it into your writing, you may sometimes have to add or change a word. These additions or changes should also be bracketed.

> "Innovation is not necessarily discovering new things, but discovering how to use old things [in a new way]," he said.

d. **Ellipses.** When quoting an author or speaker, you may choose to use only part of the material. You need to be honest with your readers and let them know that you have omitted some words or sentences. Use **ellipses**, spaced periods, to show the omission. If you are leaving out words within a sentence, use three ellipsis marks. If the omission comes at the end of a sentence, use three ellipses followed by whatever is the punctuation mark at the end of the quoted sentence.

> "While the rest of the industry has retreated, . . . green construction has actually grown," says Paul Holland, a partner at venture firm Foundation Capital. He continues, "Why wouldn't smart contractors promote green construction for schools, shopping centers, [and] office buildings . . . ?"

e. If the omission comes between two sentences, end the first quoted sentence with the appropriate punctuation mark. Then indicate the omission with the ellipses.

> Holland is not surprised by the trend toward green construction: "While the rest of the industry has retreated, it makes sense that green construction has actually grown. . . . Why wouldn't smart contractors promote green construction for schools, shopping centers, office buildings and other major construction projects?"

If you find that the quotation is lengthy and you are removing words at more than one or two spots, it is better to summarize or paraphrase the ideas rather than butchering the original passage. Remember that you need to cite the source of paraphrases and summaries, just as you do for quotations.

2.7.2. Hyphens

Hyphens are used to form compound words, to write some numbers expressed as words, and to attach some prefixes and suffixes. A hyphen may also be used when it is necessary to divide a word at the end of a line. In this case, divide the word between syllables as shown in a dictionary. Most word processing programs take care of this issue by "wrapping" the word to the next line.

a. **Compound words.** Hyphens are used to join words into a single concept: *second-string* quarterback. Most hyphenated compounds are adjectives: *well-known* company, *back-ordered* items. Omit the hyphen when the first word is an adverb ending in *-ly*: *slowly rising* temperature, *previously paid* bill.

PUNCTUATION ALERT! MISUSE OF HYPHENS

When a compound modifier follows the word it modifies, the hyphen is omitted:

> The company is *well known* for its progressive policies. Your items have been *back ordered*.

Compound nouns used as adjectives before another noun are not hyphenated either: *data processing* software; *high school* reunion; *income tax* return; *life insurance* policy.

---

b. **Numbers as words.** Use a hyphen to form fractions and compound numbers twenty-one through ninety-nine when they are spelled out as words: *two-fifths, one-third, twenty-six.*

c. **Prefixes and suffixes.** Use a hyphen with the prefixes *all-, self-, ex-,* and the suffix *-elect: all-important, self-evident, ex-mayor, president-elect.* Do not capitalize *ex-* or *-elect,* even when it is part of a title that precedes a name: *ex-President* George Bush, *Councilwoman-elect* Betsy M. Clark. Do not use hyphens with prefixes such as *anti, extra, inter, non, pre, pro, re,* and *un: interoffice* memorandum, *pretrial* motion. The exception is if the prefix occurs before a proper noun or the first letter of the root word is the same as the last letter of the prefix: *anti-American* demonstration, *non-negotiable* demands.

Some words have changed over time from a hyphenated form to a single word. For example, *co-worker* has lost its hyphen and is now commonly written as *coworker.* When in doubt about whether a prefix is hyphenated, consult an up-to-date dictionary.

3. Mechanics and Business Conventions

Written English has many conventions, standard ways of doing things that developed over time: "It's just the way things are." Business writing has some of its own conventions that differ from standard written English and from writing in the sciences or the humanities. Where these differences are important, they will be noted in the following sections.

3.1. Capitalization

Text messaging and social media have spawned writing that features little or no capitalization. In these cases, the technology drives the behavior: It is difficult to capitalize on a small keypad where each key functions for several letters. However, the correct use of capital letters is still important for clarity in emails, business letters, memos, reports, and presentation decks. Capital letters signal beginnings as well as differentiate between the particular and the general.

3.1.1. First Words

Capitalize the first word of a sentence, a direct quotation, a complete sentence enclosed within parentheses or brackets, and a complete sentence following a colon.

> *Job* interviews can be nerve wracking. (sentence)
>
> He said, "*Please* have a seat." (direct quotation)
>
> Sales for the last three quarters have been flat. (*See* Table 2 for specific figures.) (sentence in parentheses)
>
> There are two alternatives: *We* can raise prices, or we can cut costs. (complete sentence following colon)

3.1.2. Proper Nouns vs. Common Nouns

Proper nouns name particular persons, places, and things: Mark Zuckerberg, Grand Hyatt, Honda Accord. Common nouns name general categories of persons, places, and things: investor, hotel, automobile.

a. **Proper nouns and adjectives formed from them.** The names of particular persons, places, and things are capitalized, as are nicknames, adjectives, and abbreviations formed from them. Foreign countries and languages are always capitalized. The words Internet and World Wide Web are always capitalized (as in "search the Internet" and "surf the World Wide Web"), but do not capitalize intranet, web, or website.

> *William Jefferson Clinton* prefers to be called *Bill.*
>
> How many people know that *IBM* is the abbreviation for the *International Business Machine Corporation?*
>
> The *National Cathedral* stands on the highest point in *Washington, D.C.*
>
> Claire took a job with a *French* pharmaceutical company.
>
> I did most of the research on the *Internet.*
>
> Post your résumé on your website.

b. **Places and directions.** Follow the conventions of standard American English. Capitalize place names following the examples in **Table C.12**.

- Official place names are capitalized.
- Common nouns that are part of official place names are also capitalized.
- Place names that simply refer to a general category are not capitalized.

Directions are capitalized if they serve as recognized names of regions or are part of an official name: the *South* of France, *Northwest* Airlines. They are not capitalized when they refer to points of the compass: the *east* side of town, a *westerly* breeze. Some directional nouns and adjectives may appear either way: the southern hemisphere, the Southern Hemisphere. When in doubt, check a dictionary.

c. **Brand and product names, organizations and institutions.** The brand names of products and the names of organizations and institutions are proper nouns and, therefore, are capitalized: Jell-O, Citibank, General Electric Company, Chicago Cubs, Google, the National Science Foundation, the Mayo Clinic, the United States Senate.

   Take care to capitalize and spell brand names correctly. Most of them are registered trademarks, even though they may be widely used as generic terms. A generic term following a brand name is not capitalized.

Incorrect	post-it notes, jello, realtor, xerox, kleenex, ipod
Correct	Post-it notes, Jell-O, Realtor, Xerox, Kleenex tissues, iPod
Correct	sticky notes, gelatin, real estate agent, photocopy, tissues, portable media player

d. **Titles, offices, positions, and abbreviations.** Capitalize titles, offices, and positions when they precede a proper name. Capitalize abbreviations of professional certificates and degrees when they follow a proper name.

Secretary of State Clinton	Dr. Snow	Professor Okpala
Bridget Brennan, CPA	Ty Ray, RN	Chairman Bill Gates

   Do not capitalize a title, office, or position that follows a name unless the office is one of high distinction. Do not

TABLE C.12 Capitalizing Place Names

OFFICIAL PLACE NAME: CAPITALIZE	GENERAL CATEGORY: DON'T CAPITALIZE
West Virginia	the western Virginia plateau
Woodrow Wilson High School graduate	high school graduate
Miami International Airport	the Miami airport
Seattle is in the Pacific Northwest.	Is Seattle northwest of Tacoma?
The Office of the Vice President is on the third floor of the Arnold Administration Building.	The vice president's office is on the third floor of the administration building.

capitalize a title, office, or position that follows a name if the title is preceded by "the."

Incorrect	Bill Gates, Chairman of Microsoft Corporation.
Correct	Bill Gates, chairman of Microsoft Corporation
Incorrect	John Roberts, the Chief Justice of the United States
Correct	John Roberts, Chief Justice of the United States or John Roberts, the chief justice of the United States

e. **Organizations and parts of organizations.** Names of specific organizations are capitalized, as are the official names of parts of organizations: *Clark Equipment Company, Off-Road Vehicles Division, Department of Internal Affairs.* When the organization or a part is being referred to in a general way, do not capitalize: the *dealership,* the *internal affairs department.*

Department names deserve special mention because the conventions governing their capitalization can be confusing. Should it be Accounting Department or accounting department? If it is the actual name of the department in your organization or you know it is the actual name of the department in another organization, then it is capitalized. Otherwise, don't capitalize department names: *Send your résumé to our Human Resources Department. He sent his résumé to their personnel department.*

When writing about your own company or organization, observe its capitalization conventions. Many organizations capitalize words that would not be capitalized in standard usage. Consider, for example, this sentence from a Ford Motor Company annual report: *"We believe we are on track for the total Company and North American Automotive pre-tax results."* Although contrary to standard convention, Ford's documents always capitalize *Company,* even when the word stands alone. The words *North American Automotive* refer to the official title of a Ford business unit and therefore conform to standard capitalization conventions.

f. **Courses, academic subjects, majors, and degrees.** Capitalize specific course titles but not majors or general areas of study. Capitalize the abbreviation of a degree, but not a generic degree name.

Patrick needs business law, *Intermediate Chinese,* and *Economics 315* to complete his bachelor's degree. He hopes his B.S. in international business will help him land a job with a global company.

g. **Days of the week; months; holidays; holy days and names; historical events, periods, and documents; and seasons.**

Tuesday	Easter	Labor Day	The Great Depression
November	Ramadan	Yom Kippur	the Fourth of July
Black Friday	Allah	Treaty of Versailles	the Middle Ages

Do not capitalize seasons: *summer* vacation, last *spring, midwinter* doldrums, *fall* foliage.

h. **Titles of works.** Capitalize the first word of a title and all other words except articles (*a, an, the*) and prepositions (for example, *for, to, in, from*). Some styles recommend capitalizing prepositions longer than five or more letters, such as *before, after,* and *inside.* The first word following the colon in a subtitle is always capitalized, even if it is a preposition or article.

The Wealth of Nations, The Wall Street Journal

Businessweek, "Why China Is No Match for the Internet"

Predictably Irrational: The Hidden Forces That Shape Our Decisions

From Here to Eternity

3.2. Numbers

The conventions for expressing numbers vary from field to field. Historians spell out numbers up through 100; psychologists spell out only those less than 10. Lawyers may follow a number expressed as a word with the figure (numerals) in parentheses; business people do not. Chemists use decimals instead of fractions to indicate parts of a whole. As a general rule, the more numbers are used in a field, the more likely they are to be expressed as figures rather than words. Business is such a field.

3.2.1. Words vs. Figures

Amounts expressed as figures in a sentence are usually easier to read than amounts expressed as words. Consequently, business writers generally express only numbers from one through nine as words and use figures for 10 and greater: *four* customers, *24* orders.

Use commas in numbers of four figures or more: *2,400; 76,000,000.* Numbers of one million or more can be expressed in a combination of figures and words: *12 billion* light years, *6.2 million* people.

> **NUMBER ALERT!** FIGURES IN PARENTHESES
>
> Do not follow a number expressed as a word with a parenthetical figure for the same number.
>
> **Incorrect** We are shipping three (3) printers by UPS.
> **Revised** We are shipping three printers by UPS.
>
> Although technical and legal writing sometimes follow this practice, business writing does not. The repetition is unnecessary.

3.2.2. Consecutive Numbers

Unrelated numbers that appear next to each other should be separated by a comma to avoid confusion. If the sentence remains potentially confusing, reorder the words.

Correct	Of the three, two shipments were damaged.
Confusing	The report stated that in 2010, 468 orders were delayed.
Revised	The report stated that 468 orders were delayed in 2010.

3.2.3. Related Numbers

Related numbers appearing in the same sentence or same paragraph should be expressed in the same way. Opinions differ regarding whether to use figures or words. However, readers appreciate simplicity; if any of the numbers is 10 or greater, use figures.

> Members of Congress against the law outnumber those in favor by 10 to 1.

> While most auto enthusiasts own 3 or 4 cars, John owns more than 20.

3.2.4. Indefinite or Approximate Numbers

Spell out numbers that express approximate quantities: *hundreds* of tickets, *tens* of *thousands* of gallons, *millions* of dollars.

3.2.5. Numbers at the Beginning of Sentences

Always spell out a number that begins a sentence, even if it would ordinarily be written as a figure.

> Fifty thousand students from India are studying in the United States today.

If spelling out the number makes the sentence awkward, rewrite it so that another word comes first.

Awkward	Two-thousand seven was the beginning of a severe economic recession.
Revised	In 2007, a severe economic recession began.

3.2.6. Fractions and Ordinals

Express fractions as words, unless the fraction is a mixed number (a whole number and a fraction).

> Only one-third of the members were present, so we did not have a quorum.
> The administrative staff is 1 1/2 times larger than it was 10 years ago.

Express ordinals (*first, second, tenth*, and so on) as words, unless they are longer than one word.

> The board always meets on the fourth Tuesday, which is the 25th of this month.

3.2.7. Decimals and Percentages

Express decimals as figures. To avoid misreading, place a zero before the decimal if there is no whole number.

> We drove 388.4 miles on one tank of gas, but ran out of fuel 0.6 miles from home.

> More than 2.8 million bachelor's degrees in science and engineering were awarded worldwide in 2003; Asian students earned 1.2 million of them.

Express percentages as figures, followed by the word *percent*. Use the % symbol only in tables, charts, and graphs.

> Science and engineering jobs are increasing 5 percent per year.

3.2.8. Money

Express precise amounts of money in figures, but do not use decimals and zeros with whole amounts: *$14.25*; a *$50* check (not a $50.00 check); *$5* worth of quarters (not $5.00 worth); a condominium priced at *$389,000*.

Express indefinite or approximate amounts of money in words: *almost thirty* pesos; a *few hundred* euros; *over a trillion* dollars.

Express amounts of money of one million or more by combining figures and words: *$2.5 million*; *€ 30 billion*.

3.2.9. Dates and Times

In U.S. business documents, dates are usually written month, day, year. Place a comma between the day and the year. When the date occurs in a sentence, place a comma after the year also. Incomplete dates have no commas. Many other countries use international style: day, month, and year, with no commas. In either case, express dates in figures, spelling out the month.

> June 14, 2010   June 2010   June 14   14 June 2010

> The contract was signed on June 14, 2010, after all parties had agreed to terms.

Express hours and minutes as figures when using am and pm in small caps (also spelled a.m. and p.m.). Use words with fractional times and with *o'clock*. Times on the hour do not require zeros unless the sentence contains another time in hours and minutes.

> 10:45 AM   eleven o'clock   half past eight
> from 4:00 PM to 5:30 PM   from 4 PM to 5 PM

3.2.10. Measurements and Compound-Number Adjectives

Express precise units of measurement in figures, even if the number is less than 10. Within a sentence, spell out the unit name, rather than abbreviating it: The room measured *9 feet* by *12 feet*. In the case of compound-number adjectives, when quantities and units are next to each other, write one number as a word and the other as a figure to avoid confusion. Spell out the first of the two or the shorter of the two.

> six 10-foot poles   24 two-liter bottles   8 two-ton trucks

3.2.11. Addresses and Telephone Numbers

If you have direct information about how to write a specific address—for example, from letterhead stationery, the return address on an envelope, the signature block with address from an email, or an example from a website—use the same format. Lacking direct information, use the following guidelines.

Express street numbers from one through nine in words; use figures for those 10 and higher. Express building numbers as figures, except for the number one. Ordinarily in formal business correspondence, words that are part of the address, such as *street, avenue, boulevard, place, way, terrace*, and compass points (*north, west*, and so on), are not abbreviated.

> 305 Fourth Avenue   One West 16th Street
> 1437 Wooten Parkway

Use figures for highway numbers: I-80, U.S. 17, A-5.

Telephone numbers are always expressed as figures. Although the U.S. style is to place a hyphen between the parts of a telephone number, with the globalization of business the trend is to adopt international style, which places one space between the international code, country code, city code, and number.

U.S. Style   1-505-555-4523

International Style   001 505 555 4523

3.3. Abbreviations, Acronyms, and Initialisms

Abbreviations, acronyms, and initialisms are a kind of shorthand, allowing writers to avoid awkward, laborious repetition of lengthy names and terminology. They work fine when everyone knows what they mean, when they do not create confusion, and when writers follow generally accepted guidelines.

3.3.1. Definitions, Forms, and Functions

a. **Abbreviations.** An **abbreviation** is a shortened version of a word or series of words, usually formed by cropping or contracting the word or by combining the first letter of each word: *Dr.* (doctor), *Mr.* (mister), *Pres.* (president), *etc.* (et cetera).

b. **Acronyms.** An **acronym** is an abbreviation formed from the first letters of a series of words, with the combination pronounced as a word: scuba (self-contained underwater breathing apparatus), OSHA (Occupational Safety and Health Administration), UNICEF (United Nations Children's Emergency Fund).

c. **Initialisms.** An **initialism** is an abbreviation formed from the first letters of a series of words, but the letters are pronounced separately: CIA (Central Intelligence Agency), MIT (Massachusetts Institute of Technology), PM (post meridian), UPS (United Parcel Service), CEO (chief executive officer), ROI (return on investment), mph (miles per hour).

3.3.2. When to Use Abbreviations—or Not

Within the text of business documents, generally do not use abbreviations unless they are well known to your readers. Remember that abbreviations common to a particular business or subject may be unfamiliar to readers outside that field. In general, save abbreviations for tables, charts, graphs, and other places where space is limited.

When you feel an abbreviation is appropriate (to avoid repetition of a lengthy name or term, for instance), always spell out the term in its first use and write the abbreviation in parentheses, unless it is commonly understood and cannot be confused with some other term. For example, AMA can stand for either the American Management Association or the American Medical Association, so it needs to be spelled out at the first use: *He is a member of the American Management Association (AMA). He became president of the AMA last year.* In some cases, an abbreviation may be more widely recognized than the name for which

it stands and therefore does not require being spelled out at the first use: for example, FBI (Federal Bureau of Investigation). Assess your audience, and act accordingly. When in doubt, provide the parenthetical information.

The following guidelines will help you decide how and when to abbreviate.

a. **Titles before names.** Except for *Mr., Mrs., Ms.,* and *Dr.,* courtesy and professional titles are generally spelled out in formal business writing.

Ms. Eames	Dr. Sanchez	Senator Lewkowski
President Lee	Lieutenant Wells	Professor Jones

b. **Titles appearing independently or following names.** Academic, religious, military, and civilian titles that follow a proper name or stand alone should not be abbreviated: John Wells, the *lieutenant* who handled the arrest, appeared as a witness for the prosecution.

c. **Academic degrees and professional certifications.** Degrees and certifications are abbreviated when they follow a proper name. These abbreviations can also stand by themselves. However, do not use both a professional title before a name and the equivalent degree after it.

Incorrect   Dr. Lenora Sanchez, MD, also holds a PhD from Stanford.

Correct   Lenora Sanchez, MD, also holds a PhD from Stanford.

d. **Company names.** Use abbreviations for only those words that the company itself abbreviates: Eli Lilly and *Company*, but Barnes & Noble, *Inc.*, *IBM*, *AT&T*.

e. **Names of people; countries, states, and place names; days, months, and holidays; organizational units; and academic subjects.** Ordinarily, spell out first names. Use initials if that is what the individual uses professionally or prefers: *I. F. Stone, Dr. H. C. Brown.* Countries and states may be abbreviated when part of mailing addresses, but should be spelled out in the text of documents. Days and months are often abbreviated in informal notes and emails but should be spelled out in more formal documents. Similarly, organizational units (such as departments and divisions) as well as academic subjects should be spelled out.

Incorrect   Chas. was transferred to our biochem div. in the UK during Mar. but he emailed his report last Tues. in time for the BOT meeting.

Correct   Charles was transferred to our biochemistry division in the United Kingdom during March, but he emailed his report last Tuesday in time for the board of trustees meeting.

f. **Units of measurement, times, and dates.** Use abbreviations for units of measurement when they are expressed as figures—*13 oz, 28 mpg, 6 ft 2 in.*—unless they are in full sentences. Then spell them out (see 3.2.10). Note that "in." is the only abbreviation for measurement that ends with a period, to avoid confusion with "in" the preposition. Use abbreviations for exact times and dates: 9:30 AM, 4:00 PM, 800 BC, AD 1603.

3.3.3. Spacing and Punctuation of Abbreviations

For most **lowercase abbreviations** that stand for multiple words, put a period after each letter of the abbreviation with no spaces between them: *i.e., e.g., c.o.d.*

Exceptions are lowercase abbreviations for precise units of measurement following figures. These are abbreviated without periods with one space between the figure and the abbreviation: for example, *23 mpg, 65 mph, 90 wpm, 10 ft, 7 in, 3 yd, 5 gal, 40 km, 3 1/2 tsp, 2 mg.* Note that the singular and plural forms are the same when used with figures: *3 yd,* not *3 yds.*

Most **capitalized abbreviations** do not use periods or internal spaces: *MD, RN, CPA, ACLU, IRS, SEC.* Opinions differ on whether abbreviations for academic degrees such as Ph.D., M.S., and B.A. should contain periods; however, the trend is toward omitting them: *PhD, MS, BA.*

4. Spelling

Use your computer's spell checker to help you edit your work. However, it is important to proofread documents carefully and more than once. Spell checkers will not catch homonyms (words that are similar in sound but different in meaning: *council, counsel; to, two*), misspelled proper names, dropped endings, and other errors. The following "rules of thumb" can help you deal with some of the spelling questions that occur most often.

4.1. Four Rules of Thumb for Adding Endings

a. **Suffix added to one-syllable word.** Double the final consonant before the suffix if a vowel precedes the consonant and the suffix begins with a vowel. Do not double the final consonant if the suffix begins with a consonant. **Table C.13** illustrates this rule.

b. **Stress on final syllable.** Double the final consonant before a suffix if the last syllable is accented: *submit, submitted; occur, occurrence; regret, regretted; propel, propeller.* Note that for suffixes added to *program,* the *-m* may or may not be doubled. Both are considered correct: *programmed, programed; programming, programing.* Just make the spelling consistent throughout the document.

c. **Final *-e* dropped.** For words ending in *-e,* drop the *-e* before the suffix if the suffix begins with a vowel but not if the suffix begins with a consonant. **Table C.14** illustrates this rule.

The *-e* is retained after a soft *c* or *g* before *a* or *o: noticeable, changeable.* It is dropped in some words taking the suffix *-ful, -ly,* or *-ment: awe, awful; due, duly; true, truly; judge, judgment; acknowledge, acknowledgment.*

d. **Final *-y* changed to *i.*** For words ending in *-y,* change the *y* to *i* unless the suffix begins with *i.* **Table C.15** illustrates this rule.

TABLE C.13 Adding a Suffix to a One-Syllable Word

VOWEL PRECEDES CONSONANT	SUFFIX BEGINS WITH VOWEL: DOUBLE FINAL CONSONANT	VOWEL PRECEDES CONSONANT	SUFFIX BEGINS WITH CONSONANT: DO NOT DOUBLE FINAL CONSONANT
stop	stopping	live	lively
drop	dropped	fit	fitness
put	putting	ship	shipment

TABLE C.14 Adding a Suffix to a Word Ending with *-e*

ROOT FORM	SUFFIX BEGINS WITH VOWEL: DROP FINAL *-e*	ROOT FORM	SUFFIX BEGINS WITH CONSONANT: RETAIN FINAL *-e*
locate	loca*tion*	manage	manag*ement*
use	us*able*	use	us*eful*
come	com*ing*	sure	sur*ely*

TABLE C.15 Adding a Suffix to a Word Ending with -y

ROOT FORM	SUFFIX BEGINS WITH LETTER OTHER THAN "i": CHANGE "-y" TO "i"	ROOT FORM	SUFFIX BEGINS WITH "i": RETAIN FINAL "y"
mercy	merc*iful*	comply	compl*ying*
ninety	ninet*ieth*	rectify	rectif*ying*
company	compan*ies*	thirty	thirt*yish*
deny	den*ial*	deny	den*ying*

4.2. Memory Aids for *ie* and *ei*

The rhyming jingle heading in **Table C.16** will help you remember whether to choose *ie* or *ei*. Common exceptions to this rule include *either, neither, leisure, foreigners, height, seize, being,* and *weird.*

TABLE C.16 Choosing *ie* or *ei*

WRITE "i" BEFORE "e"	EXCEPT AFTER "c"	OR WHEN SOUNDED LIKE "a" AS IN *neighbor* AND *weigh*
relief	conceive	eight
believe	ceiling	freight
yield	deceive	reign
wield	receive	vein

4.3. Commonly Misspelled Words

Spelling a word correctly from memory is still faster than using a spell checker. All of us have personal spelling challenges that we simply have to keep working on throughout our lives. The following list contains words that are frequently misspelled in business writing. Renew your efforts to master the ones that are problems for you.

absence	benefited	debt	exaggerate
accessible	bulletin	deceive	existence
accommodate	bureau	definitely	extraordinary
achieve	calendar	description	familiar
acknowledgment	campaign	desirable	fascinate
advisable	canceled	develop	feasible
advantageous	catalog	dilemma	flexible
aggressive	ceiling	disappoint	foreign
alignment	changeable	disbursement	forty
all right	collateral	discrepancy	fourth
amateur	column	dissatisfied	freight
among	committee	efficient	government
analyze	competitor	eighth	grateful
annually	concede	eligible	guarantee
apparent	conceive	embarrassment	harass
argument	congratulations	emphasis	hors d' oeuvre
assistant	consensus	entrepreneur	illegible
attendance	convenient	environment	immediate
bankruptcy	courteous	emphasize	incidentally
believable	criticism	especially	independent

indispensable	negotiable	privilege	sergeant
irresistible	ninety	procedure	sincerely
itinerary	noticeable	proceed	succeed
jewelry	occasional	profited	suddenness
judgment	occurrence	pursue	surprise
knowledgeable	omission	questionnaire	tenant
labeling	omitted	receipt	thorough
legitimate	opportunity	receive	truly
leisure	paid	recommend	unanimous
license	parallel	remittance	until
maintenance	pastime	repetition	usable
manageable	perceive	restaurant	usage
mileage	permanent	rhythm	vacuum
misspell	personnel	ridiculous	volume
mortgage	persuade	secretary	weird
necessary	precede	seize	yield
negligence	prerogative	separate	

4.4.   Commonly Confused Words

The following words are homonyms, or near homonyms—words that sound the same but have different spellings and meanings. Spell checkers won't catch these confusions. Check your writing to be sure you have chosen the correct word and spelling for the meaning you intend.

accede	to agree to		choose	(present-tense verb) to select
exceed	to go beyond		chose	past tense of *choose*
accept	to receive		cite	to quote or refer to
except	to exclude		sight	to see, the ability to see
access	to gain admittance		site	location
excess	too much, more than enough		coarse	rough in texture, not delicate
advice	(noun) a suggestion		course	route taken, movement in a direction, duration
advise	(verb) to suggest		complement	to add to or complete
affect	to influence		compliment	to flatter
effect	(verb) to bring about; (noun) result		conscience	sense of right and wrong
aid	(verb) to help		conscious	aware, alert
aide	(noun) an assistant		council	governing body or advisory group
allowed	permitted		counsel	(verb) to advise; (noun) advice, a lawyer
aloud	audible, out loud		defer	to put off until later
all ready	prepared		differ	to be different from; to disagree
already	previously, by now		desert	to abandon; arid wasteland
ascent	act of rising		dessert	last course of a meal, usually sweet
assent	agreement		device	a mechanism or instrument
assure	to inform confidently		devise	to plan, create, arrange
ensure	to make certain		disburse	to pay out
insure	to protect from financial loss		disperse	to scatter
biannual	occurring twice a year		discreet	careful, circumspect
biennial	occurring every two years		discrete	separate, individual
capital	money or wealth; seat of government		do	to perform, fulfill, complete
capitol	building housing state or national governing body		due	payable, debt owed

elicit	to draw out
illicit	illegal, unlawful
eligible	qualified, worthy
illegible	not legible, impossible to read
envelop	to surround
envelope	container for a letter
everyday	ordinary
every day	each day
farther	a greater distance
further	additional
forth	forward
fourth	ordinal form of the number four
holey	full of holes
holy	sacred
wholly	entirely, completely
hear	(verb) to perceive by ear
here	at or in this place
human	characteristic of humans
humane	kind
incidence	frequency
incidents	events, occurrences
imply	to express indirectly, to suggest
infer	to conclude from evidence, deduce
instance	example, case
instants	brief moments, seconds
interstate	between states
intrastate	within a state
its	possessive form of *it*
it's	contraction for *it is*
later	afterward
latter	the second or last of two
lay	to place, put down
lie	to recline
lead	chemical element, metal; (verb) to guide
led	(verb) past tense of lead, guided
lean	to rest at an angle
lien	a claim against property for debt
loose	not tight; (verb) to free
lose	to misplace, to be deprived of
miner	a person who works in a mine
minor	a person who is not of legal age; something comparatively less
moral	virtuous, good character; lesson of a story or tale
morale	state of mind, sense of well-being
overdo	to act in excess
overdue	past the due date, unpaid
passed	(verb) to move, go around, hand out
past	(noun, adjective) time before the present

patience	willingness to wait, perseverance
patients	recipients of medical treatment
peace	absence of conflict
piece	a portion, fragment
pedal	a foot lever
peddle	to sell
persecute	to torment
prosecute	to bring legal action
personal	individual, private
personnel	employees
populace	the population, the people
populous	densely populated
precede	(verb) to come before
proceed	(verb) to move ahead, advance
principal	chief or main; leader or head; sum of money
principle	basic law or general rule
right	correct
rite	ceremony
write	to form words on a surface
role	a part that one plays
roll	(noun) a list; (verb) to tumble
stationary	fixed, not moving
stationery	writing paper
than	as compared with
then	at that time
their	(pronoun) possessive form of *they*, belonging to them
there	(adverb) in that place
they're	contraction for *they are*
to	(preposition) suggesting "toward"
too	(adverb) also, an excessive degree
two	the number
vain	futile, useless; excessive pride in appearance or achievements
vein	tubular, branching vessel; bed of minerals; line of thought or action
waist	area between rib cage and pelvis
waste	(verb) to use carelessly (noun) undesirable by-product
waive, waiver	to set aside; intentional relinquishment of right or claim
wave	a swell of water; a sweeping gesture
weather	atmospheric conditions
whether	if
who's	contraction for *who is*
whose	possessive form of *who*
your	possessive form of *you*
you're	contraction for *you are*

Appendix D

Answer Key to Grammar Exercises

CHAPTER 1 Nouns and Pronouns

(See Appendix C, Section 1.1.1.)

Type the following two paragraphs, correcting the errors in use or formation of nouns and pronouns. Underline all your corrections.

> Whomever answers the phone may be the only contact a caller has with a business. Everyone has their own personal preferences. However, find out how your employer wants the telephone answered, what your expected to say. When you pick up the phone, its important to speak politely and provide identifying information. Clearly state the company's name and you're name. Should you identify the Department, too?

> These are the kinds of question's to settle before the phone rings. If the caller asks for you by name, say, "This is me." Don't leave the caller wondering who he or she has reached. Remember that when on the telephone at work, you are the Company.

Answers:

The 10 corrected answers are highlighted in color and listed in the order they appear in the paragraph.

1. Whoever answers
2. Everyone has his or her own
3. what you're expected
4. the phone, it's important
5. and your name.
6. identify the department
7. kinds of questions to settle
8. "This is I."
9. wondering whom he
10. you are the company.

CHAPTER 2 Verbs

(See Appendix C, Section 1.1.2.)

Type the following paragraph, correcting the errors in use or formation of verbs. Underline all your corrections.

> If my first boss had ran his businesses the way he answered the phone, he would have went broke long ago. Usually he grabbed the receiver and growls, "Barker." The person at the other end probably thought, "That don't sound like a human, more like a rottweiler." If George Barker was a dog, he would probably be more courteous on the phone. No doubt there was lots of offended customers. The other day he asked my coworker, Jess, and me to stop by his office. He still answered the phone the same way. George's phone offenses amounts to quite a long list. Instead of "barking," there is several other things he could say. "Hello, Barker Contracting" or "This is George Barker" make a better impression.

Answers:

The 10 corrected answers are highlighted in color and listed in the order they appear in the paragraph.

1. If my first boss had run
2. have gone broke
3. he grabs the receiver
4. "That doesn't sound
5. Barker were a dog,
6. there were lots
7. still answers the phone
8. offenses amount to
9. there are several
10. George Barker" makes a better impression.

CHAPTER 3 Adjectives and Adverbs

(See Appendix C, Section 1.1.3.)

Type the following paragraphs, correcting the errors in use or formation of adjectives and adverbs. Underline all your corrections.

> Does your telephone etiquette speak good of you? Because most people answer their own phones at work, poor phone manners make both you and your company look badly. Which greeting will make the best impression: "How may I help you?" or "What do you want?" It is important to sound cheerfully on the phone.

> Even if you don't feel well, try to respond positively. A more simple way to sound positive is to smile when

speaking. Smiling actually does make a person seem more friendlier over the phone. Some people like to have the most unique telephone greeting in the office: "Yo, super service representative Skip speaking!" A greeting like that just makes "Skip" seem real unprofessional. Instead of being named "Best Employee of the Month," he is likely to be awarded "Worse Phone Manners of the Year."

Answers:

The 10 corrected answers are highlighted in color and listed in the order they appear in the paragraph.

1. speak well
2. look bad.
3. make the better impression
4. sound cheerful
5. feel good,
6. A simpler way
7. more friendly
8. have a unique telephone greeting [eliminate "in the office"]
9. seem really unprofessional.
10. "Worst Phone Manners

CHAPTER 4   Prepositions and Conjunctions

(See Appendix C, Section 1.1.4.)

In the following paragraph, identify the prepositions (P), coordinating conjunctions (CC), correlative conjunctions (CorC), subordinating conjunctions (SC), and conjunctive adverbs (CA). There are a total of 10 prepositions and conjunctions. Count correlative conjunction pairs as one.

The way you begin a business call is very important; however, the conclusion is equally important. Have you ever been caught in an awkward spot, wondering who should end the call? If you initiated the call, the convention is for you to conclude it. After you have obtained the information you need, thank the person you called and then say good-bye. The person at the other end either can just say good-bye or can end with a pleasantry: for example, "I'm glad I could help."

Answers:

The 10 prepositions and conjunctions are highlighted in color and listed in the order they appear in the paragraph. Correlative conjunction pairs are counted as one.

1. important; however (CA),
2. caught in (P) an awkward spot
3. If (SC) you
4. is for (P) you
5. After (SC) you
6. called and (CC) then
7. person at (P) the other
8. either (CorC) can . . . or (CorC) can
9. with (P) a pleasantry
10. for (P) example

CHAPTER 5   Phrases and Clauses

(See Appendix C, Section 1.2.2.)

It is easier to write grammatical sentences when you understand the difference between phrases and clauses. In the following paragraph, circle or highlight each phrase. Underline each dependent clause once and each independent clause twice. There are a total of 10 dependent and independent clauses and a total of 15 phrases.

In the list of tech-etiquette offenders, the "misguided multitasker" may be the worst, although the "broadcaster" is a close second. Holding their iPhones under the table, multitaskers send email or text messages during meetings. The nonverbal message that they are sending to everyone else is that the meeting is not important to them. Broadcasters use their cell phones anytime, anywhere, and they apparently don't mind being overheard by others. On a crowded elevator, they will discuss the intimate details of a medical procedure or they will talk loudly about confidential business matters.

Answers:

The phrases are highlighted in color, with the type of phrase indicated in parentheses: noun (N), verb (V), preposition (Pr), or participial (Pa). The independent clauses are boldfaced and underlined. The dependent clauses are in plain text and underlined. There are a total of 10 clauses and a total of 15 phrases.

In the list (P) of tech-etiquette offenders (P), **the "misguided multitasker" may be (V) the worst,** although the "broadcaster" is a close second. Holding their iPhones (Pa) under the table (P), **multitaskers send email or text messages** during meetings (P). **The nonverbal message** that they are sending (V) to everyone else (P) **is** that the meeting is not important to them (P). **Broadcasters use their cell phones** anytime, anywhere, and **they apparently don't mind** being overheard (V) by others (P). On a crowded elevator (P), **they will discuss (V) the intimate details** of a medical procedure (P) or **they will talk loudly** about confidential business matters (P).

CHAPTER 6   Common Sentence Errors: Run-on (Fused) Sentences and Comma Splices

(See Appendix C, Section 1.3.2.)

Type the following paragraph, correcting the 10 run-on or fused sentences and comma splices (see Sections 1.3.1 and 1.3.2). Underline all your corrections.

One business etiquette consultant believes that good telephone manners begin in childhood, children should be taught how to answer the phone courteously and take messages. Diane Eaves says, "I work with a lot of people who are technically ready for work however, they apparently missed a lot of the teaching of manners." For instance, asking who is calling can be taught in childhood then it will be a habit. Parents know how annoying it is to have a child report that "somebody called and wants you to call back"

Sonny doesn't remember who it was and didn't write down the number. Thank goodness for caller ID it can be a big help, nevertheless, children should be taught to ask for and write down names and numbers. It's surprising how many people don't identify themselves when they make business calls, they expect listeners to recognize their voice. That may be OK if you speak frequently with the caller on the other hand it's mystifying when a voice you don't recognize launches right into a subject. It is the caller's responsibility to identify himself or herself, if he or she doesn't you can politely say, "Excuse me, I didn't catch your name."

Answers:

The 10 run-on (RO) sentences and commas splices (CS) are identified in the first paragraph. They are corrected in the second paragraph.

Run-on Sentences (RO) and Comma Splices (CS) Identified

One business etiquette consultant believes that good telephone manners begin in childhood, (CS) children should be taught how to answer the phone courteously and take messages. Diane Eaves says, "I work with a lot of people who are technically ready for work (RO) however, they apparently missed a lot of the teaching of manners." For instance, asking who is calling can be taught in childhood (RO) then it will be a habit. Parents know how annoying it is to have a child report that "somebody called and wants you to call back" (RO) Sonny doesn't remember who it was and didn't write down the number. Thank goodness for caller ID (RO) it can be a big help, (CS) nevertheless, children should be taught to ask for and write down names and numbers. It's surprising how many people don't identify themselves when they make business calls, (CS) they expect listeners to recognize their voice. That may be OK if you speak frequently with the caller (RO) on the other hand it's mystifying when a voice you don't recognize launches right into a subject. It is the caller's responsibility to identify himself or herself, (CS) if he or she doesn't you can politely say, "Excuse me, (CS) I didn't catch your name."

Run-on Sentences and Comma Splices Corrected (answers will vary)

One business etiquette consultant believes that good telephone manners begin in childhood. Children should be taught how to answer the phone courteously and take messages. Diane Eaves says, "I work with a lot of people who are technically ready for work; however, they apparently missed a lot of the teaching of manners." For instance, asking who is calling can be taught in childhood; then it will be a habit. Parents know how annoying it is to have a child report that "somebody called and wants you to call back." Sonny doesn't remember who it was and didn't write down the number. Thank goodness for caller ID. It can be a big help. Nevertheless, children should be taught to ask for and write down names and numbers. It's surprising how many people don't identify themselves when they make business calls. They expect listeners to recognize their voice. That may be OK if you speak frequently with the caller. On the other hand it's mystifying when a voice you don't recognize launches right into a subject. It is the caller's responsibility to identify himself or herself. If he or she doesn't, you can politely say, "Excuse me. I didn't catch your name."

CHAPTER 7 Common Sentence Errors: Subject–Verb Agreement

(See Appendix C—Section 1.3.3.)

Type the following paragraph and edit it, correcting the 10 errors in subject–verb agreement. Underline all your corrections.

When making a business call, being put on hold for countless minutes fray even patient people's nerves. Having to wait, as well as not knowing for how long, are upsetting. Each of us have our own way of coping with this irritant. *The Sounds of Silence* apply not only to the Simon and Garfunkel song but also to endless minutes on hold. Three minutes feel like forever to the person waiting. If you must put someone on hold, there is several things you should do. First, ask, "May I put you on hold?" and then give the caller an estimate of the probable waiting time. The person on the other end might be one of those callers who really need to know how long the wait might be. The unknown number of minutes are what drive people crazy. Data collected by Hold On America, Inc. shows that callers become frustrated after 20 seconds. After 90 seconds, 50 percent of callers hangs up.

Answers:

The 10 subject–verb agreement errors are highlighted in color in the first paragraph. They are corrected in the second paragraph.

Agreement Errors Identified

When making a business call, being put on hold for countless minutes fray even patient people's nerves. Having to wait, as well as not knowing for how long, are upsetting. Each of us have our own way of coping with this irritant. The *Sounds of Silence* apply not only to the Simon and Garfunkel song but also to endless minutes on hold. Three minutes feel like forever to the person waiting. If you must put someone on hold, there is several things you should do. First, ask, "May I put you on hold?" and then give the caller an estimate of the probable waiting time. The person on the other end might be one of those callers who really need to know how long the wait might be. The unknown number of minutes are what drive people crazy. Data collected by Hold On America, Inc. shows that callers become frustrated after 20 seconds. After 90 seconds, 50 percent of callers hangs up.

Verbs Corrected

When making a business call, being put on hold for countless minutes frays even patient people's nerves. Having to wait, as well as not knowing for how long, is upsetting. Each of us has our own way of coping with this irritant. *The Sounds of Silence* applies not only to the Simon and Garfunkel song but also to endless minutes on hold. Three minutes feels like forever to the person waiting. If you must put someone on hold, there are several things you should do. First, ask, "May I put you on hold?" and then give the caller an estimate of the probable waiting time. The person on the other end might be one of those callers who really needs to know how long the wait might be. The unknown number of minutes **is** what **drives** people crazy. Data collected by Hold On America, Inc. **show** that callers become frustrated after 20 seconds. After 90 seconds, 50 percent of callers **hang** up.

Common Sentence Errors: Pronoun–Antecedent Agreement

(See Appendix C—Section 1.3.4.)

Type the following paragraph and edit it, correcting the 10 errors in pronoun–antecedent agreement. Underline all your corrections.

> Everybody has preferences about their communication tools. A person may prefer email rather than telephone, so they might respond to a voice mail message by sending an email instead of returning the call. If you ask either of my managers, Jenny or Kurt, they will tell you that I would rather email them. Business professionals will often choose the one with which he or she is most at ease. Considering its total number of calls versus emails per month, the sales team obviously would rather talk than write. Each of these communication media has their advantages and disadvantages. Text messages and email may be best because it will be delivered whether the recipient is there or not. On the other hand, someone who leaves a voice mail message probably assumes you will call them back, not send a text. Otherwise, they would have texted you instead of calling.

Answers:

The 10 pronoun–antecedent agreement errors are highlighted in color in the first paragraph. The antecedent is in blue and the pronoun is in red. They are corrected in the second paragraph. (The corrections are in red and alternative options are in parentheses in blue.)

Agreement Errors Identified

Everybody has preferences about their communication tools. A person may prefer email rather than telephone, so they might respond to a voice mail message by sending an email instead of returning the call. If you ask either of my managers, Jenny or Kurt, they will tell you that I would rather email them. Business professionals will often choose the one with which he or she is most at ease. Considering its total number of calls versus emails per month, the sales team obviously would rather talk than write. Each of these communication media has their advantages and disadvantages. Text messages and email may be best because it will be delivered whether the recipient is there or not. On the other hand, someone who leaves a voice mail message probably assumes you will call them back, not send a text. Otherwise, they would have texted you instead of calling.

Agreement Errors Corrected

Everybody has preferences about his or her communication tools. A person (people) may prefer email rather than telephone, so he or she (they) might respond to a voice mail

message by sending an email instead of returning the call. If you ask either of my managers, Jenny or Kurt, she or he will tell you that I would rather email her or him. Business professionals will often choose the one with which they are most at ease. Considering their total number of calls versus emails per month, the sales team obviously would rather talk than write. Each of these communication media has its advantages and disadvantages. Text messages and email may be best because they will be delivered whether the recipient is there or not. On the other hand, someone (people) who leaves (leave) a voice mail message probably assumes you will call him or her (them) back, not send a text. Otherwise, he or she (they) would have texted you instead of calling.

CHAPTER 8   Commas: Clauses and Phrases

(See Appendix C—Section 2.2.)

Type the following paragraph, correcting the 10 errors in the use of commas with independent clauses, dependent clauses, and phrases (see Section 2.2.1). Underline all of your corrections.

> Although most final job interviews are face to face telephone interviews have become common for screening interviews. Employers find that phone interviews are not only economical but they are also an effective way to determine which candidates merit a closer look. While you are on the job market a potential employer or networking contact might call, and ask, "Do you have a few minutes to talk?" Being interviewed over the phone isn't easy so you need to be prepared. What initially seems like an informal conversation about a job might actually be the first round of screening, or the first test of your communication skills. After the initial introductions and pleasantries let the caller take the lead, and guide the conversation. When you answer questions keep your responses short and to the point. The caller will ask follow-up questions if necessary, and will bring the interview to a close.

Answers:

The 10 corrected uses of commas are highlighted in color and listed in the order they appear in the paragraph. The reason for each is given in parentheses.

1. Although . . . face to face, telephone (introductory dependent clause)
2. economical, but they are (independent clauses joined by coordinating conjunction)
3. While . . . job market, a potential employer (introductory dependent clause)
4. might call (delete comma) and (compound predicate requires no comma)
5. isn't easy, so you (independent clauses joined by coordinating conjunction)
6. screening (delete comma) or the first test (compound predicate requires no comma)
7. pleasantries, let the caller (long introductory phrase)
8. take the lead (delete comma) and guide (compound predicate requires no comma)

9. When you answer questions, keep (introductory dependent clause)

10. if necessary (delete comma) and will bring (compound predicate requires no comma; "if necessary" requires no special emphasis)

Commas: Coordinates, Cumulatives, and Series

(See Appendix C—Section 2.2.)

Type the following paragraph, correcting the 10 errors in the use of commas with coordinate and cumulative adjectives and with serial words, phrases, and clauses, Each missing or unnecessary comma counts as one error (see Sections 2.2.2 and 2.2.3). Underline all of your corrections.

> After you have sent out résumés and applied for jobs, be ready willing and able to handle a telephone interview. Keep your résumé a pad and pen and a bottle of water near the phone. You will need your résumé for reference the pad and pen to take notes and the water in case your throat gets dry. Is your cell phone, service, provider reliable, or do you have to worry about dropped calls? If so, consider using a landline. Send roommates, friends, spouses, children and pets from the room when a potential employer calls. You want to be completely calmly focused and undistracted during a telephone interview.

Answers:

The 10 corrected uses of commas are highlighted in color and listed in the order they appear in the paragraph. The reason for each is given in parentheses.

1,2. ready, willing, and able (coordinate adjectives)

3,4. your résumé, a pad and pen, and a bottle (serial elements)

5,6. your résumé for reference, the pad and pen to take notes, and the water (serial elements)

7,8. cell phone (delete comma) service (delete comma) provider (cumulative adjectives: no commas)

9. spouses, children, and pets (serial nouns)

10. completely, calmly focused (coordinate adverbs)

Commas: Restrictive and Nonrestrictive Elements

(See Appendix C—Section 2.2.)

Type the following paragraph, correcting the 13 errors in the use of commas with restrictive, nonrestrictive, or parenthetical words, phrases, or clauses. Each missing or unnecessary comma counts as one error. There are also two mistakes in the use of *that, which*, or *who* (see Sections 2.2.2 and 2.2.3). Underline all your corrections.

> Anyone, who has been through an employment interview, knows it is nerve-wracking. A telephone interview which provides none of the nonverbal cues available in a face-to-face situation can be even trickier. The interviewer's word choice, tone of voice, and level of enthusiasm may therefore be important indicators. The interviewee the person that is being interviewed must listen carefully. The

> advice, "sit up and pay attention," certainly applies in this situation. Companies, who use telephone interviews for employment screening, have heard it all everything from bad grammar to burping.

Answers:

The 13 errors in the use of commas with restrictive, nonrestrictive, or parenthetical words, phrases, or clauses and the two mistakes in the use of *that, which*, or *who* are highlighted in color. The reason for each is given in parentheses. Each missing or unnecessary comma counts as one error.

1,2. Anyone (delete comma) who has . . . interview (delete comma) (restrictive clause identifies who and requires no commas)

3,4. interview, which provides . . . situation, can (nonrestrictive clauses require commas)

5,6. may, therefore, be (parenthetical element)

7,8. interviewee, the person who is being interviewed, must (nonrestrictive appositive requires commas; *who* is the correct pronoun for referring to a person, *interviewee*)

9,10. advice (delete comma) "sit up and pay attention" (delete comma) (restrictive appositive requires no commas)

11,12. Companies (delete comma) that use telephone interviews for employment screening (delete comma) (restrictive clause requires no commas; *that* is the correct pronoun for referring to a thing, *companies*)

13. have heard it all, everything (nonrestrictive appositive explaining *all* requires comma)

CHAPTER 9 Semicolons and Colons

(See Appendix C—Sections 2.3. and 2.4.)

Type the following paragraph, correcting the 10 errors or omissions in the use of semicolons and colons (see Sections 2.3 and 2.4). Underline all your corrections.

> In the online article "How to Give a Professional Voicemail Greeting The Business Etiquette of Voicemail Greetings," author James Bucki asks, "What would I want to know from the voicemail greeting?" The greeting may be perfectly clear to you however, the caller may be mystified. His advice create the greeting as if you were the listener at the other end. As a general rule, the length of a voicemail greeting should be: no longer than 20–25 seconds. Some of the most annoying greetings are: long introductions, greetings that are too casual or personal, and background music of any kind (especially music that drowns out the message). Avoid endings that are not business related (such as "have a blessed day"); because they may strike customers and clients as presumptuous. Here is an example of a bad voicemail greeting; "Hi. This is Accounting. Leave me a message." Callers have no idea whether they have reached the right person; nor do they know if they even have the right company. Too little information is bad, conversely, so is too much information. Business callers don't want personal details, including: the fun spot where you are vacationing; or that you are out sick with the flu.

Answers:

The 10 corrected uses of semicolons and colons are highlighted in color and listed in the order they appear in the paragraph. The reason for each is given in parentheses.

1. "How to . . . Voicemail Greeting: The Business . . . Greetings" (preceding subtitle)
2. clear to you; however, (independent clause introduced by conjunctive adverb)
3. His advice: create the greeting (preceding an explanation or rule)
4. greeting should be (delete colon) no longer (no colon between verb and complement)
5. greetings are (delete colon) long introductions (no colon between verb and complement)
6. blessed day") (delete semicolon) because they ("because" clause is dependent)
7. voicemail greeting: (colon preceding an illustration)
8. is bad; conversely, so (independent clause introduced by conjunctive adverb)
9. details, including (delete colon) (not preceded by a complete statement)
10. vacationing (delete semicolon) or (not followed by an independent clause)

Quotation Marks and Italics

(See Appendix C—Section 2.5.)

Type the following paragraph, correcting the 10 errors or omissions in the use of quotation marks and italics. Count pairs of quotation marks as one (see Sections 2.5.1 and 2.5.2). Underline all your corrections.

> It's a *good* idea to review the voicemail greeting on your personal phone, especially if potential employers might call. As part of his greeting, my friend Joe recorded John Cleese speaking lines from the *Dead Parrot Sketch* from the British television comedy "Monty Python's Flying Circus." His friends all thought it was really funny, using the words hilarious and clever to describe the greeting. One afternoon he retrieved a phone message that said, You really should use a more professional greeting. The voice continued, I called to offer you a job interview, but I've changed my mind. Joe thought, 'I wouldn't want to work for someone who didn't understand the humor in the "Dead Parrot Sketch," anyway. Sounds like this guy just doesn't get it.' Maybe not, but Joe's chances with that company are kaput.

Answers:

The 10 corrected uses of quotation marks and italics are highlighted in color and listed in the order they appear in the paragraph. The reason for each is given in parentheses. Pairs of quotation marks count as one error

1. It's a good idea (the word needs no special emphasis)
2. "Dead Parrot Sketch" (title of a segment, part of a longer work)
3. *Monty Python's Flying Circus* (title of television program, complete work)

4. using the words "hilarious" (direct quotation)
5. and "clever" (direct quotation)
6. "You really . . . greeting." (direct quotation)
7. "I called . . . my mind." (direct quotation)
8,9. "I wouldn't . . . in the 'Dead Parrot Sketch,' anyway . . . doesn't get it." (quotation and quotation within a quotation)
10. are *kaput*. (2.5.2. foreign word)

CHAPTER 10   Apostrophes

(See Appendix C—Section 2.6.)

Type the following paragraph, correcting the 10 errors or omissions in the use of apostrophes. Underline all your corrections.

> Practicing for a telephone interview will give you confidence that you wont blow the real thing. Ask one of your parents' or a friend to conduct a mock interview with you. Have him or her phone you and ask an interviewers questions. Its also helpful to get a spouses' or father's-in-laws critique of your answers. Ask one of them to listen in, or, whats even more useful, tape record the mock interview for later analysis. Pay attention not only to the content of your answers, but also to the vocal quality; is your's clear, without too many "uhm's," "you knows," and "likes"? The practice sessions payoff is your improved interviewing skills.

Answers:

The 10 corrected uses of apostrophes are highlighted in color and listed in the order they appear in the paragraph. The reason for each is given in parentheses.

1. you won't (contraction of *will not*)
2. parents (delete apostrophe) (plural but not possessive)
3. an interviewer's (singular possessive)
4. It's also (contraction of *it is*)
5. spouse's (singular possessive)
6. father-in-law's (singular possessive)
7. what's (contraction of *what is*)
8. Is yours (delete apostrophe) (possessive form of *you*)
9. uhms (delete apostrophe) (not possessive)
10. practice session's (singular possessive)

Parentheses, Dashes, Brackets, and Ellipses

(See Appendix C—Section 2.7.)

Type the following paragraph, inserting parentheses, dashes, brackets, and ellipses where required. There are 10 omissions. Consider pairs of parentheses or brackets as a single omission. Underline all your corrections. In cases where there is more than one possibility, be ready to explain your choice.

> The time to research a potential employer is before not after the job interview. Interviewers expect job applicants to know something about a company's products goods or services its markets local, national, international

and its operating locations. Job applicants can begin their research on an Internet search engine Google or Bing. Career advisor Martin Reis writes on his blog, "A company's URL Uniform Resource Locator is the gateway to a wealth of information new products, financial statements, press releases, the corporate mission statement. . ." There is something else a company's website may reveal its corporate culture. Web page photos can provide clues about dress standards casual or traditional, employee diversity ethnicity, gender, age, and community involvement.

Answers:

The 10 corrected insertions of parentheses, dashes, brackets, and ellipses are highlighted in color and listed in the order they appear in the paragraph. The reason for each is given in parentheses. Pairs of dashes, parentheses, and brackets are considered single insertions. Answers may vary.

1. before—not after—the job interview. (emphasis)
2. a company's products (goods or services), (incidental information)
3. its markets (local, national, international), (incidental information)
4. search engine—Google or Bing. (emphasis on inserted information)
5. company's URL [Uniform Resource Locator] (editorial information inserted into direct quotation)
6. information—new products (emphasis on inserted information)
7. mission statement . . . . "(words omitted from end of direct quotation; requires ellipses and period)
8. may reveal—its corporate culture. (emphasis)
9. dress standards (casual or traditional), (incidental information)
10. employee diversity (ethnicity, gender, age), (incidental information)

CHAPTER 11 Capitalization

(See Appendix C—Section 3.1.)

Type the following paragraph, correcting the 30 errors, which include both omissions and improper use of capital letters. Underline all of your corrections.

Robin thompson, owner of etiquette network and Robin Thompson charm school, says, "personal phone calls are fine, so long as you limit them and choose the appropriate time." She also believes cell phones should be turned off at work; If you are at work, that means you have a desk phone and can be reached at that number most of the time. Cell phones and pagers don't belong in business meetings, either, she says. Would you interrupt your Vice President to answer your cell phone? (you wouldn't if you want to keep working for the Company.) Of course, when you are flying to Corporate Headquarters on the West Coast from the Regional Office in north Dakota, a cell phone can be a life saver. Because you had to take your

daughter to her spanish lesson, you've missed your plane. The head of the division of specialty products wants that report by 5 PM, president McMillan is expecting you for lunch, and your son forgot to order his date's corsage for the High School prom tonight. Note to self: text son about picking up tuxedo. Instead of a Master's Degree in business, you're thinking maybe you should have majored in Emergency Management. Thank heavens you have a blackberry.

Answers:

The 30 corrected uses of capital letters are highlighted in color and listed in the order they appear in the paragraph. For many items, the reason for the capitalization choice is given in parentheses.

1. Robin Thompson,
2. owner of Etiquette
3. Network and
4. Robin Thompson Charm
5. School (proper nouns: name of person; name of companies)
6. "Personal (first word of sentence)
7. work; if you (sentence following a semicolon requires no capital)
8. your vice
9. president (common noun)
10. (You wouldn't (first word of complete sentence in parentheses)
11. the company.) (common noun)
12. corporate (common noun)
13. headquarters (common noun)
14. regional
15. office
16. North Dakota (proper noun: state)
17. Spanish lesson (adjective formed from proper noun: language)
18. Division of
19. Specialty
20. Products (proper noun: official name of part of organization)
21. President McMillan (proper noun: official title or position)
22. high
23. school (common noun)
24. Note to self: Text son (first word of complete sentence following a colon)
25. master's
26. degree (common nouns: generic degree name)
27. emergency
28. management (common noun: academic major)
29. Black
30. Berry (proper noun: brand/product name. This product name illustrates "camel case" or "medial capitals": compound words in which the first letters of the parts are capitalized. Names using camel case should always be capitalized as branded or trademarked—for example, PowerPoint.)

Numbers

(See Appendix C—Section 3.2.)

Type the following paragraph, correcting the 15 errors in the use of numbers. Underline all your corrections.

> 20 years ago mobile phones were novel and expensive. In the nineteen-eighties cellular telephones, luxury items used only by top executives, cost almost $4000 and weighed more than 2 pounds. Today, of course, even 10-year-olds have them, and the lightest ones weigh two. 65 ounces. Some people have more than one mobile phone; imagine carrying 2 2-pound phones in your purse. The International Telecommunications Union estimates that there are approximately 4,600,000 mobile telephones in use worldwide. That amounts to about sixty percent of the world's population. China ranks number 1 with a little over 57 percent of Chinese using cellular telephones. India ranks 2nd, adding more than six (6) million subscribers a month. According to *The Washington Post*, nearly 1/2 of the Indian population has wireless service—3 times the number of landlines in the country. The United States ranks third, with 91% of us using cell phones.

Answers:

The 15 corrected uses of numbers are highlighted in color and listed in the order they appear in the paragraph. The reason for each is given in parentheses.

1. Twenty years (word, not figure, at beginning of sentence)
2. In the 1980s (year date)
3. almost four thousand dollars (approximate amounts of money)
4. weighed more than two pounds. (approximate measurement)
5. 10-year-olds (number 10 or greater)
6. 2.65 ounces. (precise measurement, decimal)
7. two 2-pound phones (measurements, compound-number adjectives)
8. approximately 4.6 million (decimals)
9. about 60 percent (percentage)
10. number one (number less than 10)
11. ranks second (one-word ordinal number)
12. more than six million (approximate number; do not use parenthetical figure)
13. one-half of (fraction that is not a mixed number)
14. three times (number less than 10)
15. with 91 percent (*percent* as word when part of paragraph, not table or graph)

CHAPTER 12 Spelling

(See Appendix C—Section 4.)

Type the following paragraph, correcting the 10 incorrect homonyms or near homonyms, which a spell checker may not catch. Underline all of your corrections.

> Businesses rely on text messaging for many things besides advertising. Texting can compliment other forms of communication and surpass some for speed and affectiveness. To site one example, let's consider instant communication between a stockbroker and investor. The broker can council the investor about the movement of a stock price and get a "buy" or "sell" decision quickly. Vendors can confirm deliveries, customers can track shipments, and contractors can tell there on-sight crews to precede with construction. Another principle advantage of text messages is the ability to communicate silently. In situations where speaking may be awkward or impossible but immediate communication is important, texting makes more sense then a phone call. Instead of searching in vain for a place to take a call, a person can simply tap out a reply, waving the need for privacy.

Answers:

The 10 corrected homonyms are highlighted in color and listed in the order they appear in the paragraph. See Section 4.4 of Appendix C for an extended list of commonly confused words and their meanings.

1. can complement
2. and effectiveness
3. To cite
4. can counsel
5. tell their
6. on-site
7. to proceed
8. Another principal
9. sense than
10. reply, waiving

Proofreader's Marks

The third component of the ACE communication process is evaluating, which includes revising, editing, proofreading, and reviewing feedback. This appendix will help you proofread your own writing as well as provide feedback to colleagues who ask you to proofread their work. See Chapter 3 for more detailed advice about proofreading.

Proofreading tips

- **Separate proofreading from composing.** If you stop at the end of each sentence to proofread before composing the next sentence, you may lose the flow of your content.
- **Proofread in a comfortable environment.** You will catch more errors if you are not distracted or interrupted. Proofread in a quiet location with good lighting.
- **Proofread for different kinds of errors separately.** If you try to proofread from the top of a document to the bottom in one pass, you are not likely to find all of the errors. Instead, look for specific kinds of errors by proofreading separately for each of the following problems:
  - **Content errors.** Examples include missing information, poor organization, and incorrect numbers. Proofing for content errors requires you to focus on the meaning of the words.
  - **Spelling errors.** Do not rely solely on your word processor's spell checking program to catch all your spelling errors. Double check the names of people, places, and organizations.
  - **Typographical errors.** Examples include words you left out when composing and errors caused from editing too quickly, such as correcting the last half of a sentence without re-reading the entire sentence to check for problems with the flow of the words. Transpositions in wording and spelling (such as "was" and "saw") are also examples of typographical errors.
  - **Usage errors.** These errors occur when you use a word incorrectly, such as "accumulative GPA" instead of "cumulative GPA."
  - **Grammatical errors.** Although some word processors include grammar checkers that will find grammatical errors (such as sentence fragments and dangling modifiers), you should always double check to be sure your writing is correct.
  - **Format errors.** Inconsistencies in format vary from missing dates, inconsistent headings, and differences in fonts, just to name a few. When proofing the format, look at the page as a whole rather than at the words, and compare your document to a formatting guide for reference. (See Appendix A: Formatting Business Documents.)
  - **Your typical errors.** People tend to make the same kinds of errors when they write. Make a list of the errors you often make, and carefully proof your writing specifically for those problems.
- **Proofread aloud.** Reading your writing aloud slows the speed of your proofreading and allows you to hear your words, which increases your chances of finding errors.
- **Proofread backwards.** Reading from the bottom to the top of the page also slows your proofreading process and helps you concentrate on each word individually.
- **Ask a colleague to proofread your work.** Most people find it difficult to be objective about their own work. Additionally, it is easy for your brain to fill in missing words. You know what you meant to write. Asking someone else to help you proofread will improve your chances of finding all your errors as well as getting feedback about your writing.

Correction symbols

Some people choose to use word processing features, such as Track Changes, when correcting written drafts. However, other people find it easier to proofread from a printed document rather than from a computer screen. Many editors use the following symbols to mark corrections. You may find them useful when you review your own writing.

DELETE OR REMOVE			
SYMBOL	**MEANING**	**EXAMPLE**	**CORRECTION**
l	**Delete**	On my ~~the~~ recent trip	On my recent trip
⌒	**Close space**	I met with George Bonet	I met with George Bonet
l	**Delete and close space**	I recommend that	I recommend that
No ¶	**Delete paragraph break; no new paragraph**	Enclosed is an example for your review. *No ¶* Let me know what you think.	Enclosed is an example for your review. Let me know what you think.

MODIFY TEXT FORMATTING / TYPOGRAPHICAL SIGNS			
SYMBOL	**MEANING**	**EXAMPLE**	**CORRECTION**
Bf	**Boldface**	This should be <u>bold.</u> *(Bf)*	This should be **bold.**
Ital	**Italics**	This should be <u>italicized.</u> *(ital)*	This should be *italicized.*
⸺	**Underline**	This should be <u>underlined.</u>	This should be <u>underlined.</u>
rom	**Roman type (not italics)**	This should not be in *<u>italics.</u>* *(rom)*	This should not be in italics.
≡	**Capitalize**	This should be capitalized.	This should be Capitalized.
≣	**ALL CAPS**	This should be all caps.	This should be ALL CAPS.
lc	**Lowercase**	This should be LOWERCASE. *(lc)*	This should be lowercase.
wf	**Wrong font**	Change the font <u>to be consistent.</u> *(wf)*	Change the font to be consistent.

INSERT WORDS AND PUNCTUATION MARKS

SYMBOL	MEANING	EXAMPLE	CORRECTION
1 or V — Inserted term may be placed above or below the caret.	Insert (caret)	I will call you next week.	I will call you next week.
	Insert comma	If the meeting goes well we will approve the plan.	If the meeting goes well, we will approve the plan.
	Insert period	Thank you I appreciate your time.	Thank you. I appreciate your time.
	Insert question mark	Who will attend the fundraiser I have a conflict.	Who will attend the fundraiser? I have a conflict.
	Insert exclamation mark	Thank you I appreciate your time and effort.	Thank you! I appreciate your time and effort.
	Insert colon	Please provide the following items signed contracts, budget revisions, and project report updates.	Please provide the following items: signed contracts, budget revisions, and project report updates.
	Insert semicolon	He needs to sign the contract it won't be processed without a signature.	He needs to sign the contract; it won't be processed without a signature.
	Insert hyphen	Attached is the third quarter summary.	Attached is the third-quarter summary.
	Insert apostrophe	The managers decision will be final.	The manager's decision will be final.
	Insert ellipses	He stated, "The negotiations will take several days of hard work."	He stated, "The negotiations will take several days...."
	Insert en dash (often used to separate number ranges)	See pages 24 to 26 for details.	See pages 24–26 for details.
	Insert em dash (often used to offset phrases)	The results were misleading which could be not only confusing but also costly.	The results were misleading—which could be not only confusing but also costly.
	Insert double quotation marks	The word responsible was used frequently in the press release.	The word "responsible" was used frequently in the press release.
(/)	Insert parentheses	The rates will reflect the same percentage increase see Figure 12.	The rates will reflect the same percentage increase (see Figure 12).
[/]	Insert brackets	She suggested that "the change is required for everyone in the IT department."	She suggested that "the change is required for everyone [in the IT department]."
#	Insert space	Thetiming is right for this new procedure.	The timing is right for this new procedure.
	Insert new line or move text	1421 Milrose Avenue NW 3rd Floor, Suite 10	1421 Milrose Avenue NW 3rd Floor, Suite 10
	Insert paragraph break	We ask for your help in funding these grants I will contact you next Tuesday after you've had an opportunity to review this proposal.	We ask for your help in funding these grants. I will contact you next Tuesday after you've had an opportunity to review this proposal.

MODIFY CONTENT FORMATTING

SYMBOL	MEANING	EXAMPLE	CORRECTION
∥	**Align vertically**	Budget Reports Fiscal Statements Forecast Documents	Budget Reports Fiscal Statements Forecast Documents
][	**Center**	Title Goes Here	Title Goes Here
] SS	**Single space**	The recommendation is to allocate more resources to the project.	The recommendation is to allocate more resources to the project.
] DS	**Double space**	The recommendation is to allocate more resources to the project.	The recommendation is to allocate more resources to the project.
⌊ ⌋	**Move down**	Pharmaceutical sales increased.	Pharmaceutical sales increased.
[	**Move left**	Pharmaceutical sales increased.	Pharmaceutical sales increased.
]	**Move right**	Pharmaceutical sales increased.	Pharmaceutical sales increased.
⌐	**Move up**	Pharmaceutical sales increased.	Pharmaceutical sales increased.
⌐	**Flush left**	Budget Reports Fiscal Statements Forecast Documents	Budget Reports Fiscal Statements Forecast Documents
⌐	**Flush right**	Budget Reports Fiscal Statements Forecast Documents	Budget Reports Fiscal Statements Forecast Documents
⌒	**Keep text together / Close up space**	Our profits are with in the forecasted range.	Our profits are within the forecasted range.
∨	**Superscript**	… as was indicated in the study.1	… as was indicated in the study.[1]
∧	**Subscript**	H2O	H_2O

MODIFY WORDING

SYMBOL	MEANING	EXAMPLE	CORRECTION
agr	**Agreement problem**	The box of name badges are on your desk. *agr*	The box of name badges is on your desk.
AWK	**Awkward wording**	The focus group participants were *Awk* predominantly woman employees.	The focus group included mostly female employees.
CS	**Comma splice**	Rational humans are marvelous in theory, in reality, they do not exist. *CS*	Rational humans are marvelous in theory; in reality, they do not exist.
dgl	**Dangling construction**	To increase sales, more telephone calls were made. *dgl*	To increase sales, sales reps made more telephone calls.
frag	**Fragment**	My computer doesn't work. Although the technician checked it. *frag*	My computer doesn't work although the technician checked it.
STET	**Let stand (restore)**	This is okay as ~~originally~~ worded. *STET*	This is okay as originally worded.
//	**Problem with parallel construction**	We will present the findings, recommendations, and make // conclusions.	We will present the findings, recommendations, and conclusions.
pron	**Problem with pronoun**	*pron* Was it him who went to the conference?	Was it he who went to the conference?
ref	**Reference unclear (ambiguous)**	I called the purchasing managers about the new vendors. They are too busy to meet with us today. *ref*	I called the purchasing managers about the new vendors. The managers are too busy to meet with us today.
rep	**Repetition/redundancy**	Please refer back to the minutes from our last meeting. *rep*	Please refer to the minutes from our last meeting.
R-O	**Run-on sentence**	It was a great meeting everyone *R-O* participated.	It was a great meeting. Everyone participated.
sp	**Spell out**	We need 5 more days to complete *sp* the project.	We need five more days to complete the project.
sp	**Spelling error**	She made an *sp* impresive presentation.	She made an impressive presentation.
‿	**Transpose**	Thank you for your effort and time on this project.	Thank you for your time and effort on this project.
WC	**Word choice**	*WC* Please affix a first-class stamp.	Please use a first-class stamp.
wdy	**Wordy**	As your assistant manager, I am suggesting that we review our *wdy* departmental procedures.	I suggest we review our departmental procedures.
ww	**Wrong word**	Do you know which one is there car? *ww*	Do you know which one is their car?

Glossary

A

Abstract One or two paragraphs—often included at the beginning of a formal informational report—that either (a) describe the content of the report so that a reader can decide whether to read the report or (b) briefly summarize the report, including the main points, conclusions, and recommendations. *p. 349*

Abstract language Language that refers to broad concepts that an audience can interpret in multiple ways. *p. 98*

Action interview An interview format that requires applicants to make a presentation or perform under work-based conditions, which could be simulated or real. *p. 494*

Active listening A learned skill that requires you to attentively focus on the speaker's communication, interpret the meaning of the content, and respond with feedback to ensure understanding. *p. 11, 37*

Active voice A sentence structure in which the subject performs the action of the verb. *p. 99*

Advance organizer Information that precedes details and provides a framework for understanding details. *p. 88*

Affective conflict A conflict that results from differences in personalities and relationships. If affective conflicts remain unstated and unaddressed, they can lead to tension, stress, and dysfunctional work processes. *p. 45*

Agenda A detailed plan or outline of the items to be discussed at a meeting. *p. 61*

AIDA An acronym used in marketing to suggest the organization of sales communication: Attention, Interest, Desire, Action. *p. 175, 480*

Analytical report A report that analyzes information to solve a problem or support a business decision. *p. 348*

Analyzing The process of looking critically at four elements of your message: purpose and outcome, audience, content, and medium. *p. 81*

Anecdotal evidence Information you can get from a subjective report that may not be scientifically valid or representative but that may provide insight on your topic. *p. 295*

Anecdote A very short story, usually a true one, that is used to make a point and bring a subject to life. *p. 420*

Animations Visual effects that control when and how elements appear on your slides while you present. *p. 433*

Announcement A message that publicly notifies people of information they need or want to know. *p. 134*

Appendix A section (or multiple sections, called appendices) included at the end of a formal report or proposal that provides supplementary information. *p. 351*

Argumentation A persuasive appeal that supports a position with reasons and evidence. *p. 163*

Attachment A document that is included with a memo, an email, or a letter report to provide supplementary information. *p. 351*

Audience The intended recipients of your communication. *p. 10, 81*

Audience benefits The positive outcomes your audience will experience by agreeing with or acting on your message. *p. 83, 127*

B

Backchannel A networked conversation among audience members at a presentation. *p. 446*

Barrier An obstacle that gets in the way of effective communication. *p. 5*

Behavioral questions A type of interview question designed to determine how you would make decisions, solve problems, or respond to stressful situations. *p. 498*

Brand message A statement that communicates the unique value you offer your employers. *p. 472*

Buffer An introductory sentence or paragraph that leads up to and softens a bad-news message. *p. 198*

Bullet point One of a number of items printed in a vertical list, preceded by a symbol called a bullet. *p. 429*

Bullet point lists Vertically formatted lists, with each item preceded by a dot or another simple shape. *p. 93*

Business case A justification for a proposal showing that the recommended course of action is good for an organization and makes business sense. *p. 320*

C

Career fair A gathering of representatives or recruiters from many companies seeking to fill open positions. *p. 495*

Chronological résumé A traditional résumé style that lists content sequentially, starting with the most recent experience. *p. 477*

Clarity The quality of being unambiguous and easy to understand. *p. 15, 98*

Clichés Commonplace and often overused phrases that have lost their force and meaning. *p. 99*

Cloud computing Software applications that run on the Internet and are accessed through the web or that allow you to store files remotely to access through the web. *p. 297*

Cognitive conflict A conflict that results from differences in understanding content or tasks. Working through a cognitive conflict often leads to better decisions and work products. *p. 45*

Coherence The connection of ideas at the level of the entire text. *p. 101*

Cohesion The connection of ideas at the sentence level. *p. 101*

Collaboration The process of working with others to achieve a common goal. *p. 21*

Collectivist culture A culture that puts the good of the group or organization before people's individual interests. *p. 54*

Co-located team A team in which all members are in the same physical location. *p. 385*

Combined résumé A résumé style that takes advantage of both the chronological and functional methods of organizing content by highlighting work experience by date and skill sets by category. *p. 479*

Communication The process by which participants not only exchange messages (information, ideas, and feelings) but also co-create and share meaning. *p. 5*

Communication strategy A plan for what and how you are going to communicate to ensure that your message achieves your purpose. *p. 10*

Composing The multistep process of producing content, organizing it so that it is understandable from the audience's perspective, putting it into coherent sentences and logical paragraphs, and designing a format or delivery approach that is professional and makes the communication easy to follow. *p. 87*

Comprehension How well you understand what you hear or read. *p. 38*

Concession An admission that the opposing point of view has merit but does not invalidate your argument. *p. 157*

Conciseness Using no more words than necessary for a message to accomplish its purpose. *p. 15, 100*

Concrete language Language that is specific, making it likely that everyone will interpret it the same way. *p. 98*

Confirmation message An acknowledgment that you have received information or understood a message correctly. *p. 132*

Congratulatory message Communication sent to recognize someone's achievements or important events. *p. 139*

Content The substance of your message. *p. 84*

Content marketing A technique for persuading customers by providing them valuable information without trying to sell them anything. *p. 249*

Context The external circumstances and forces that influence communication. *p. 6*

Context (relating to culture) A term that describes how people in a culture deliver, receive, and interpret messages. Low-context cultures rely on explicit language to communicate. High-context cultures derive meaning not just from words but from everything surrounding the words. *p. 53*

Convenience sample A survey population selected because you have easy access to that group. *p. 288*

Cover letter A persuasive letter or email sent to a prospective employer along with a résumé that "sells" your résumé to the employer. *p. 489*

Cover message A letter, a memo, or an email accompanying a formal report or proposal, designed to explain the document and persuade the audience to read it. *p. 333*

Credibility An audience's belief that you have expertise and are trustworthy based on your knowledge, character, reputation, and behavior. *p. 5, 162*

Critical thinking A disciplined approach to analyzing, synthesizing, and evaluating information to guide actions and decisions. *p. 5*

Culture The learned and shared attitudes, values, and behaviors that characterize a group of people. *p. 20, 52*

Customer claim A request from a customer to a store or vendor to accept a return, exchange an item, refund money, or perform a repair. *p. 172, 207*

D

Dashboard A single-screen display of data aggregated from different sources. *p. 246*

Data graphics Visual representations of data, in tables and graphs, that allow you to see relationships and trends much more clearly than in text alone. *p. 386*

Data literacy The ability to access, assess, interpret, manipulate, summarize, and communicate data. *p. 22*

Decode To interpret the words, images, and actions of a message and attach meaning to them. *p. 5*

Deliverables The items or services you agree to deliver to your audience. *p. 316*

Desktop search tool A search engine designed to search for files on your computer or file server that contain specific words or that were produced within a specific time period. *p. 280*

Direct organization The method of arranging content in a message to present the main idea of the message before the supporting details. *p. 88*

Distributed team A team in which members are in different physical locations. *p. 385*

Drafting A creative process that involves getting information on the paper or computer screen before revising and editing it. *p. 91*

E

Elevator pitch A concise statement designed to communicate the value of an idea, a product, or a job candidate; intrigue the audience; and initiate a deeper conversation. *p. 450, 487*

Emotional intelligence The ability to perceive and understand emotions and to use that knowledge to guide your own behavior and respond to others. *p. 36*

Encode To translate the meaning of a message into words, images, or actions. *p. 5*

Ethics The principles used to guide decision making and lead a person to do the right thing. *p. 16*

Ethnocentrism An inappropriate belief that your own culture is superior to all others. *p. 53*

Evaluating The process of critically reviewing a communication to ensure that it is complete, clear, concise, easy to understand, and error free. *p. 41, 97*

Evaluation report A report that assesses the success of a project. *p. 360*

Executive summary A separate, stand-alone mini-document, included at the beginning of a longer document, that completely summarizes the document's main ideas. *p. 332, 349*

External audiences People with whom you communicate outside your organization. *p. 94*

External benefits Advantages that someone else—a third party that your audience cares about—gains when your audience complies with a request. *p. 127*

External proposal A proposal addressed to people outside your organization. *p. 315*

F

Face In Chinese, Indian, and other collectivist cultures, the position or standing that a person has in the eyes of others. *p. 54*

Fallacy A violation of logical reasoning that leads to a flawed argument. *p. 166*

Feasibility report A report that analyzes whether a plan can be implemented as proposed. It may also consider how to change the plan to make it feasible. *p. 354*

Feedback Any form of verbal or nonverbal response to a message. *p. 5*

Forming A stage of team development in which members get to know each other. *p. 58*

For-your-information (FYI) message A message written as an act of kindness to pass along information you think someone might appreciate knowing. *p. 140*

Functional résumé A contemporary résumé style that emphasizes categories of skills rather than job experience. *p. 479*

G

Globalization (or internationalization) The process of preparing a document to be localized. *p. 105*

Goodwill A positive relationship between you (or your company) and your audience. *p. 20, 81, 194*

Goodwill message Any message that gives you the opportunity to establish and sustain a positive relationship with your audience. *p. 125*

Grant proposal A proposal requesting funding, typically from government agencies or charitable foundations. *p. 327*

Graph A visual representation of data that illustrates the relationship among variables, usually in relationship to x- and y-axes. *p. 386*

Group interview An interview format in which an employer meets with several applicants at the same time to assess their approach to working collaboratively with others. *p. 494*

Groupthink A process by which a group reaches a decision by eliminating all critical thinking that threatens consensus. *p. 60*

Guanxi In China, a network of long-term mutually beneficial relationships built on trust. *p. 55*

I

Icon A graphical symbol whose form suggests its meaning. *p. 431*

Idiom An expression that means something other than the literal meaning of its words. *p. 20, 56*

Implicit request A request that hints at what you want rather than stating it directly. *p. 125*

Impromptu speaking Speaking without advance knowledge of the topic or question. *p. 446*

Indirect organization The method of arranging content in a message to present the supporting details before the main idea. *p. 88*

Individualistic culture A culture that values an individual's achievements, satisfaction, and independent thinking. *p. 54*

Infographic A representation of data or information in visual form. An infographic is a stand-alone visual display that typically combines multiple representations of data to provide a complete picture. *p. 377*

Informational report A report that provides readers with facts that they can easily understand and refer to when necessary. Meeting minutes, trip reports, and progress reports are types of informational reports. *p. 348*

Interactive communication Multi-directional exchange of information. *p. 86*

Internal audiences People with whom you communicate inside your organization. *p. 93*

Internal benefits Advantages that your audience will directly receive from complying with your request. Examples include a reduced workload, increased professional recognition, and financial gains. *p. 127*

Internal proposal A proposal addressed to people within your organization. *p. 315*

Interpersonal communication The ongoing process of interacting with others and exchanging information and meaning to achieve understanding. *p. 36*

Interpretation Analyzing the meaning of what you hear, read, or see to determine its intention. *p. 38*

Interview A research method involving a structured discussion between two or more people, usually in a question-and-answer format. *p. 286*

J

Jargon The specialized language of a specific field. *p. 38*

L

Letters Formal correspondence, generally intended for external audiences. Letters can be sent through postal mail or by email attachment for quicker delivery. *p. 94*

Limitations The characteristics of your specific research that prevent you from generalizing your findings more broadly. *p. 277*

Localization The process of adapting text to local languages, cultures, and countries. *p. 105*

M

Mean The average derived by adding all responses and dividing the sum by the number of responses. *p. 289*

Median The number that represents the middle number in a distribution or the most central number. *p. 289*

Medium The method you use to deliver a message (for example, telephone, face-to-face meeting, email, text message, or website). *p. 5, 84*

Meeting minutes Notes that describe what was discussed at a meeting, what was decided, and what actions will follow. *p. 62*

Memos Hardcopy documents that follow a set format and are typically sent to internal audiences. *p. 93*

Message headline Content at the top of the slide that summarizes the key point, or message, of each slide. *p. 381, 423*

Minutes A written report of a meeting that identifies who was present, summarizes the discussion, and records specific decisions and action items. *p. 354*

Mode The number that most frequently appears in a distribution. *p. 289*

Monochronic culture A culture that values punctuality and efficiency. *p. 55*

N

Network The group of people who are aware of your career goals and can help you learn about career opportunities. *p. 473*

Nominalization A noun formed from a verb or an adjective. *p. 99*

Noncompetitive proposal A proposal that has no competition because your audience will not be considering any offers other than yours. *p. 316*

Nonverbal communication Messages conveyed through means other than words, such as tone of voice, facial expressions, gestures, and body language. *p. 38*

O

Observational research A research method that involves watching people perform relevant activities and recording details about what you observe. *p. 286*

Outcome The result of your communication; what you want the recipients of your message to know, do, or feel about the subject of your message. *p. 10, 81*

Outline An organizational plan that identifies key topics in the order they will be presented. *p. 88*

P

Panel interview An interview format that involves several people, such as a search committee, who gather in a conference or seminar room with a job applicant to discuss the position. *p. 494*

Parallel phrasing Using the same grammatical form for each item in a list. *p. 100, 134*

Paraphrase A version of what someone else says, but in your own words and with your own emphasis. *p. 393*

Paraphrasing Restating someone's point in different words to ensure that you completely understand. *p. 40*

Passive listening Hearing what someone says without actively paying attention to ensure understanding. *p. 37*

Passive voice A sentence structure in which the subject is passive and receives the action expressed by the verb. *p. 99*

Persuasion The process of influencing an audience to agree with your point of view, accept your recommendation, grant your request, or change their beliefs or actions in a way that facilitates a desired outcome. *p. 13, 81, 156*

Persuasive request A request that persuades the audience to do you a favor by making the audience feel good about doing the favor and, if possible, by stressing audience benefits. *p. 171*

Plagiarism Intentionally or unintentionally failing to acknowledge others' ideas in your work. *p. 393*

Podcast An audio or video presentation or program that is recorded without an audience, posted on a website or a social media site such as YouTube or Vimeo, and distributed through links. *p. 448*

Polychronic culture A culture that has a relaxed attitude toward time and punctuality. *p. 55*

Power distance A characteristic of cultures that describes how the culture perceives inequality and authority. *p. 54*

Pre-suasion The process of influencing an audience's state of mind before delivering a persuasive message. *p. 167*

Primary audience The person or people to whom your message is addressed. *p. 83, 157*

Primary research The process of collecting your own data from original sources. *p. 84*

Primary sources Sources from which you collect your own raw data. *p. 277*

Professional brand The image you present of yourself that makes you stand out compared to other applicants. *p. 470*

Professionalism The qualities that make you appear businesslike in the workplace. *p. 13*

Professional presence Your ability to project competence, credibility, and confidence in your communication. *p. 5*

Progress report A report that updates supervisors or clients on the status of a long-term project. *p. 354*

Proofread A systematic process of reviewing writing for errors. *p. 103*

Proposal A communication designed to persuade a business decision maker to adopt a plan, approve a project, choose a product or service, or supply funding. *p. 314*

Pull communication Information stored in a convenient location so that recipients can access, or "pull," it when needed. *p. 86*

Purpose The reason you are communicating. *p. 10, 81*

Push communication One-way communication, often "pushed out" to multiple people. *p. 86*

Q

Qualitative research Research that provides insight into the attitudes, values, and concerns of research subjects through interviews and observation. *p. 278*

Quantitative research Research that relies on numerical data, such as that gathered from structured survey responses to which you can assign numbers. *p. 278*

Quotations Any phrases, sentences, paragraphs—even single, distinctive words—that you take from any of your sources. *p. 393*

R

Random sample A population sample selected broadly from all available members of the population you want to study. *p. 288*

Range The span between the highest and lowest values. *p. 289*

Recommendation A business message that suggests a solution to a business problem. *p. 170*

Recommendation report A report that analyzes options and recommends a course of action. *p. 360*

Redundancy Unnecessary repetition of an idea. *p. 101*

Reference list A list of secondary research sources used in a research report. *p. 351*

Refutation A response intended to prove that an objection is wrong. *p. 157*

Report deck A report document written in PowerPoint or other presentation software. *p. 349*

Repurposing content Reusing content you have already created. *p. 325*

Request for proposal (RFP) An invitation for suppliers to competitively submit proposals to provide a product or service. *p. 315*

Revising A logical process that involves evaluating the effectiveness of a message in relation to your audience and purpose and then making changes in content, organization, or wording, as necessary. *p. 91*

Routine business message A short, nonsensitive, straightforward communication that asks questions, answers questions, provides information, or confirms agreements. *p. 125*

RSS (really simple syndication or rich site summary) A format for delivering frequently changing web content to subscribers; referred to as an RSS feed or news aggregator. *p. 234*

S

Sample A representative portion of your survey population. *p. 288*

Scope The range of your research; a broad scope includes a wide range of content, whereas a narrow scope focuses on specific aspects of the topic. *p. 277*

Secondary audience People other than the primary audience who may read or hear your message. *p. 83, 157*

Secondary research The process of searching published reports, articles, and books for information other people have collected. *p. 84*

Secondary sources The results of other people's research that you consult as part of your research. *p. 278*

Slang Nonstandard, informal language that may communicate well within a certain group but often excludes people from different countries, cultures, and social groups. *p. 99*

Slide deck A set of slides used for a presentation. *p. 423*

Slide master A tool in presentation software that allows you to select design features that apply to all slides. *p. 426*

Social media Web-based applications, such as blogs, Facebook, and Twitter, designed to promote social interaction. *p. 9*

Software as a Service (SaaS) Software that is hosted by the software provider and available on the Internet. *p. 325*

Solicited proposal A proposal that your audience has requested. *p. 315*

Solicited sales communication A response to a request for sales information. *p. 175*

Stakeholders People who will be affected by the outcome of your message. *p. 157*

Stand-alone presentation A slide deck that makes sense without the benefit of a presenter. *p. 423*

STAR method A method of answering a behavioral interview question by explaining a situation, a task, and an action that led to a positive result. *p. 498*

Statement of work (SOW) A proposal or section of a proposal that identifies exactly what you will deliver, at what cost, in what time frame, and under what circumstances. *p. 321*

Stereotypes Oversimplified images or generalizations of a group. *p. 53*

Storming A stage of team development in which teams experience conflict and begin to confront differences. *p. 58*

Storyboard A slide-by-slide sketch of a presentation that is used as a tool for organizing the flow of the presentation. *p. 424*

Style How you express yourself as distinct from what you express. *p. 98*

Subject line The line in the header of an email that communicates what the message is about and influences whether the audience will read the message. *p. 88*

Summary A very brief version of someone else's text, using your own words. *p. 393*

Survey A predetermined list of questions used to collect a structured set of information from a selected audience. *p. 286*

Survey population The audience from whom you want to collect survey responses. *p. 288*

Sympathy message A message that expresses compassion and understanding when someone experiences a loss. *p. 140*

Synchronous communication Communication in which all communicators are present at the same time; face-to-face conversations, telephone conversations, and meetings are examples of synchronous communication. *p. 36*

T

Table A graphic that arranges content in columns and rows, allowing you to read down or across to see different relationships. *p. 386*

Targeted sample A population sample that consists of only specific people from the group you are studying. *p. 288*

Team Two or more people who recognize and share a commitment to a specific, common goal and who collaborate in their efforts to achieve that goal. *p. 56*

Teaming The process of bringing people together for a short period of time to solve a specific problem or complete a specific project. *p. 59*

Template A model or file that contains key features of a document and serves as a starting point for creating a new document. *p. 194*

Tertiary sources Books and articles that synthesize material from secondary sources. *p. 278*

Thank-you message An expression of appreciation when someone has done something for you. *p. 136*

Title page The first page of a formal report, which includes identifying information, such as the report's title; the name of the person or organization for whom the report was written; the author's name, position, and organization; and the date of submission. *p. 360*

Tone The attitude your language conveys toward your topic and your audience. *p. 102*

Topic headline Content at the top of the slide that announces the topic of the slide. *p. 423*

Topic sentence A sentence that identifies the main point or overall idea of the paragraph. Most frequently, it is the first sentence in a paragraph. *p. 92*

Topic-specific headings Section or paragraph titles that are short but include key ideas. They are often in the form of a short sentence and include a verb. *p. 93*

Transition words and phrases Language that signals the relationship between sentences and between paragraphs. *p. 101*

Trip report A report that documents activities on a business trip and presents accomplishments and issues. *p. 354*

U

Uncertainty avoidance A measure of how comfortable a culture is with ambiguity, risk, and change. *p. 55*

Unique selling proposition The skills or qualities that set someone or something apart from the competition. *p. 473*

Unsolicited proposal A proposal that your audience did not request. *p. 315*

Unsolicited sales communication Sales messages you send to audiences who did not request the information, also called "cold-call sales messages." *p. 175*

V

Virtual interview An interview conducted by telephone, Skype, or teleconference call, often used to narrow the candidate pool before scheduling an onsite visit. *p. 495*

Visual aid presentation A presentation in which the speaker's words carry the main story of the presentation, and the slides provide illustration and backup. *p. 423*

Vlogger Video blogger, a blogger who provides content primarily through video rather than text or images. *p. 251*

W

Webcast A web-based presentation or program that is broadcast over the Internet to a live audience but is not interactive. *p. 448*

Webinar An interactive web-based seminar that is broadcast over the Internet to a live audience. *p. 448*

White paper A report published by a company and intended to educate the audience—often potential customers—on a topic that is central to the company's business. *p. 372*

Writer's block An inability to begin or continue writing. *p. 91*

Y

"You" perspective An approach to communication that presents the information from the audience's point of view. The "you" perspective focuses on what the audience needs and wants. It also considers how the audience benefits from the message. *p. 126*

Index

Page numbers in *italic* indicate figures. Key terms and the page number on which they are defined appear in **boldface**.